# Sources for the History of Western Civilization
# of Western Civilization
# Volume I

# Sources for the History of Western Civilization
## Volume I

edited by Michael Burger

Copyright © 2003  Michael Burger
First published by Broadview Press 2003
Reprinted 2009 by University of Toronto Press

www.utphighereducation.com

LIBRARY AND ARCHIVES CANADA CATALOGUING IN PUBLICATION

Sources for the history of western civilization / edited by Michael Burger.
Includes index.
ISBN 978-1-55111-326-5
1. Civilization, Western—History—Sources.        I. Burger, Michael, 1962–
D5.S68 2002        909'.09821        C2002–904203–8

We welcome comments and suggestions regarding any aspect of our publications — please feel free to
contact us at news@utphighereducation.com or visit our internet site at www.utphighereducation.com.

**North America**
5201 Dufferin Street
Toronto, Ontario, Canada, M3H 5T8

2250 Military Road
Tonawanda, New York, USA, 14150

ORDERS PHONE: 1-800-565-9523

ORDERS FAX: 1-800-221-9985

ORDERS EMAIL: utpbooks@utpress.utoronto.ca

**UK, Ireland, and Continental Europe**
NBN International
Estover Road, Plymouth, PL6 7PY, UK
TEL: 44 (0) 1752 202301
FAX ORDER LINE: 44 (0) 1752 202333
orders@nbninternational.com

University of Toronto Press acknowledges the financial support for its publishing activities of the
Government of Canada through the Book Publishing Industry Development Program (BPIDP).

Typesetting and assembly: True to Type Inc., Mississauga, Canada

Printed in Canada

*To Emily Zack Tabuteau,*
*with much gratitude and affection*

# CONTENTS

Preface   11

Introduction for Students   15

1   *The Descent of Ishtar*   17
2   *The Code of Hammurabi*   20
3   The *Enuma Elish*   32
4   Inscription of Uni   38
5   Stele of Neferhotep   41
6   *Hymn to Aton*   43
7   *First Book of Kings*, 15-19   46
8   *Book of Job* 1-14, 21-24, 38-42   52
9   Homer, The *Iliad*   69
10   Plutarch, *Life of Solon*   108
11   Aristophanes, *Lysistrata*   124
12   Plato, *The Symposium*   146
13   Plutarch, *Life of Alexander the Great*   174
14   Material Evidence Concerning the Greek World   197
       14.1   Vase (detail) (Sixth Century BC)   197
       14.2   The "Priam Painter," Hydria (*c.* 520-510 BC)   198
       14.3   Kylix (detail) (*c.* 520-510 BC)   199
       14.4   Kylix (detail), Attica (*c.* 490-480 BC)   200
       14.5   Column Krater, Attica (*c.* 460 BC)   201
       14.6.1   Funerary Vase (*c.* 440 BC): Right side of front   202
       14.6.2   Funerary Vase (*c.* 440 BC): Left side of front   203
       14.7   Harmodius and Aristogeiton, Athens (Fifth Century BC)   204
       14.8.1   House on Slope of the Areopagus (Fifth Century BC): Probable Functions
               of Rooms   205
       14.8.2   House on Slope of the Areopagus (Fifth Century BC): Areas Used by
               Women and by Men   205
       14.9   Polycleitus, Doryphorus (*c.* 440-435 BC)   206
       14.10   Caryatid from the Erectheum, Athens (Roman Copy; Original Late Fifth Century BC)   207
       14.11   Praxiteles, Aphrodite of Cnidos (*c.* 350 BC)   208
       14.12   Praxiteles, Hermes (*c.* 325 BC)   209
       14.13   Crouching Aphrodite (Hellenistic)   210
       14.14   Gaul (with his Wife) Killing Himself (*c.* 230-220 BC)   211
       14.15   The Pharaoh Sesostris I (?) (Egypt, Second Millennium BC)   212
       14.16   Queen Arsinoë II (Egypt, *c.* 210 BC)   213
       14.17   Queen Cleopatra (II?) (Egypt, *c.* 170 BC)   214
       14.18   Agesander, Athenodorus, and Polydorus of Rhodes, Lacoön and His Sons (*c.* 125 BC)   215
       14.19   Market Woman (First Century BC)   216

15    Marcus Tullius Cicero, *Letters*   217
    15.1    To Julius Caesar   217
    15.2    To C. Trebatius Testa   218
    15.3    To Gaius Claudius Marcellus, Consul Elect   218
    15.4    To Gaius Claudius Marcellus, the Augur   219
    15.5    To Terentia and Tullia   219
    15.6    To Terentia and Tullia   219
    15.7    To Terentia   220
    15.8    To L. Munatius Plancus   220
16    Quintus Cicero, *Letter to His Brother*   222
17    Vergil, The *Aeneid*   232
18    Augustus, *The Deeds of the Divine Augustus*   270
19    Pliny the Younger, *Letters*   277
    19.1    To Junius Mauricus   277
    19.2    To Priscus   278
    19.3    To Acilius   279
    19.4    To Trajan   280
    19.5    Trajan's Reply   280
    19.6    To Trajan   280
    19.7    To Trajan   280
    19.8    Trajan's Reply   281
    19.9    To Trajan   281
    19.10   Trajan's Reply   282
20    Papyri from Oxyrhynchus   283
    20.1    Petition of Syra, daughter of Theon for the Return of her Dowry   283
    20.2    Notice to Chaereas the Strategus of a Transfer of Cattle   283
    20.3    Petition of Tryphon, Son of Dionysius, Against his Wife Demetrous   284
    20.4    Report of a Lawsuit Concerning the Identity of a Child   284
    20.5    Petition to the Praefect from the Husband of Saraeus   284
    20.6    Record of the Sale of a House by Pnepheros, Son of Papontos, to Tryphon, Son of Dionysius   285
    20.7    Declaration of Bacche Regarding her Sale of Sarapous   285
    20.8    Report of a Purchase of Land by Marcus Porcius   285
    20.9    Agreement between Agathodaemon and Gaius Julius Germanus Concerning the Sale of Dioscorous   286
    20.10   Lease of Land by Dionysia, Daughter of Chaeremon, to Psenamounis, Son of Thonis   286
    20.11   Receipt from Chosion, Son of Sarapion, Concerning Wages of Tanenteris, Daughter of Thonis   287
    20.12   Petition of Tabesammon, Daughter of Ammonius, Regarding Appointment of a Guardian   287
    20.13   Two Petitions to Clodius Culcianus, Praefect   287
    20.14   Declaration of Aurelius Pambechis to the Chief of the Treasury of Oxyrhynchus   288
21    Inscription from Mactar   290
22    *Book of Matthew* 3–9.32   291
23    John, *Book of Revelation* 15–20   298

24  Perpetua and Others, *The Martyrdom of Saint Perpetua*  303
25  Augustine, *Confessions*  310
26  Tacitus, *De Germania*  335
27  Sidonius Apollinaris, *Letters*  349
    27.1  To Donidius  349
    27.2  To Bishop Lupus  351
    27.3  To Magnus Felix  351
    27.4  To Ecdicius  351
28  Benedict of Nursia, *The Rule*  354
29  *Life of Balthild*  385
30  Einhard, *Life of Charlemagne*  391
31  The *Dooms of King Alfred*  406
32  Gregory VII, Henry IV, and the German Bishops, *Documents*  414
    32.1  Gregory VII, The *Dictatus Papae*  414
    32.2  Letter of Gregory VII to Henry IV, Holy Roman Emperor  415
    32.3  Letter of Henry IV to Gregory VII  417
    32.4  Letter of Bishops in Germany to Gregory VII  418
    32.5  First Deposition and Banning of the Emperor Henry IV by Gregory VII  420
33  *Speech of Urban II at the Council of Clermont*: Two Accounts  421
    33.1  Account of Fulcher of Chartres  421
    33.2  Account of Robert the Monk  423
34  Two Letters from Crusaders  426
    34.1  Letter of Anselm of Ribemont to Manasses II, Archbishop of Reims  426
    34.2  Letter from Stephen, Count of Blois to Adele, his Wife  428
35  Marie de France, *Eliduc*  430
36  *Magna Carta*  439
37  Canons of the Fourth Lateran Council  447
38  Court Rolls of the Abbots of Ramsey and Battle  475
    38.1  Court Roll of the Abbot of Ramsey for Elton  475
    38.2  Court Roll of the Abbot of Battle for Brightwaltham  478
39  Thomas Aquinas, *Summa Contra Gentiles*  482
40  Ralph of Shrewsbury, *Letter*  503
41  City Officials of Cologne, *Letter*  505
42  The Statute of Laborers  507
43  English Statute of 1363 on Food and Clothing  509
44  Catherine of Siena, *Dialogue*  513
45  Barduccio di Piero Canigiani, *Letter*  531
46  Petrarch, *Letters of Familiar Intercourse*  535
    46.1  To Socrates  535
    46.2  To Tomasso da Messina  542
    46.3  To Marcus Tullius Cicero  544
47  Niccolò Machiavelli, *The Prince*  546
48  Desiderius Erasmus, *Letters*  575
    48.1  To Anne of Borselle  575
    48.2  To Jacobus Battus  577
    48.3  To Pope Leo X  578

48.4    To Lambertus Grunnius   580

48.5    Lambertus Grunnius's Reply   593

48.6    To Cardinal Wolsey   593

49   Martin Luther, *Letters*   598

49.1    To George Spalatin   598

49.2    To Paul Speratus   600

49.3    To George Spalatin   602

49.4    To Wolfgang Reissenbusch   602

49.5    To George Spalatin   604

50   John Calvin, *Letters*   606

50.1    To the Duchess of Ferrara   606

50.2    To the Priest of Cernex   611

50.3    To an Unknown Person   616

50.4    To Melancthon   618

50.5    To Monsieur de Falais   619

50.6    To Viret   620

50.7    To Viret   621

50.8    To the Faithful of France   621

50.9    To the Protector Somerset   623

50.10   To Henry Bullinger   631

50.11   To Melancthon   633

51   *Articles of the Catholic League*   636

52   Michel de Montaigne, *Essays*   638

52.1    *On Cannibals*   638

52.2    *That It is Folly to Measure Truth and Error by Our Own Capacity*   646

53   Marie de l'Incarnation, *Letters*   649

53.1    Letter to a lady of rank (Quebec, September 3, 1640)   649

53.2    Letter to her son (Quebec, September 4, 1641)   650

53.3    Letter to her son (Quebec, 1647)   651

53.4    Letter to her son (Quebec, September 24, 1654)   652

53.5    Letter to her son (Quebec, September, 1661)   653

53.6    Letter to her son (Quebec, August 10, 1662)   655

53.7    Letter to her son (Quebec, August 9, 1668)   655

53.8    Letter to her son (Quebec, September 1, 1668)   656

54   The Grand Remonstrance and Petition from Parliament to King Charles I (December 1, 1641) and Charles's Reply (December 23, 1641)   658

54.1    The Grand Remonstrance and Parliament's Petition   658

54.2    Charles I's Reply   675

55   John Locke, *Second Treatise of Government*   677

56   Isaac Newton, The *Principia*   721

Credits   725

Index of Topics   728

# PREFACE

It seems presumptuous to present a collection of sources with which students are to study the sweep of Western civilization. Yet editors continue to do so – a necessity if beginning history students are to have in their hands a variety of sources and, at the same time, have the guidance which an editor can provide both by making selections and by annotating them, and to have these things at a reasonable cost. Nonetheless, in producing this reader I have become painfully aware of inadequacies; no sources are essential, and yet most have some claim to be included. Moreover, editing a reader of this sort inevitably takes one far beyond the specialization which is common to modern academic historians, and so far from comfort; the giddy feeling is like that which one experiences teaching the course, only worse. I hope that other merits will compensate for the greater assurance which a team of specialists can muster. I will certainly be happy to receive notices of deficiencies of all kinds.

In selecting sources, I have sought to include a variety of subject matter. Students will find evidence that pertains to cultural, intellectual, social, gender, and political history. Indeed, particular sources address all these and other concerns at once. I have also taken some account of contemporary worries over cultural literacy, and so have sometimes chosen canonical sources over others which might serve similar purposes. Thus, for example, Locke appears rather than Hooker. I have, however, avoided letting such concerns become a straightjacket. In order to facilitate comparative discussion, I have stressed certain genres—hence the special prominence of letters, biographical sources (to which students are often drawn), and legislative documents from different periods. This feature especially marks the first volume, as it covers such a long time. Although Western civilization readers generally center on Europe, in the second volume I have gone beyond the usual readings on nineteenth- and twentieth-century imperialism to include sources from the new world to remind North American students that Western civilization is not to be found simply overseas. The first volume appropriately begins in Mesopotamia and Egypt.

In editing sources I have followed two principles. In the first place, students can get a better sense of how rich a single document can be as historical evidence if they read sources either in their entirety or at least in substantial excerpts. I have thus avoided short snippets; many sources appear here complete, and few excerpts constitute less than 20 per cent of the original. (I have counted readings such as individual letters or books of the Bible as single sources. The inclusion of some very short sources, such as letters, can help instructors who would like students to read a source on the spot.) Secondly, editors of books for teaching should know their place; students must have the opportunity to draw conclusions for themselves, and instructors, rather than editors, know how much their students need to be led through a document. For these reasons, in introducing the sources I have tried not to usurp the student's or instructor's rightful roles by telling students what the source shows or directing them toward the issues for which I think the source is important. I have for the same reasons worked to restrict the notes to matters of fact rather than interpretation, although the line between the two has sometimes proved very fine. It is true, of course, that instructors themselves often do want some guidance for sources with which they are unfamiliar. Instructors in this position may wish to consult *Commentaries on Sources for the History of Western Civilization With Questions for Students*, also available from Broadview Press. In editing the readings,

I have also tried to give students some sense of the challenge posed historians by the physical condition of some of the sources.

It is important to keep the cost of these volumes within reason. This goal demanded that I select most of the sources from the public domain, which means that many of the translations date to the early part of the twentieth century, or even earlier. I have, however, worked to avoid a danger this poses; hence, nearly all the translations which appear here have been silently revised. Sometimes I have made revisions in order to bring the reading closer to modern English idiom; sometimes for greater clarity; sometimes simply for accuracy. Where possible, readings have been made to conform to modern American conventions in spelling and punctuation. The concern for clarity led me, with some reluctance, to prefer prose translations of ancient verse. Biblical citations in the notes are to the Bible as ordered by Protestants. Biblical citations by authors themselves are in the form adopted by the writer.

I have incurred so many debts in developing this collection that I am afraid I will fail to acknowledge them all. But I would very much like to do so, and to state emphatically that I alone am responsible for all the shortcomings of these volumes.

First of all, I am grateful to a number of colleagues and friends who very generously volunteered to read transcribed selections for errors: John Alford, Brian Anderson, Linda Cox, Thomas Easterling, Beverly Hammond, Ginger Hitt, Ralph Hitt, Nora Howell, Susan Lack, Carol Mead, Rick Millikin, Deborah Miranda, Mildred Moore, Amy Pardo, Reba Porter, Barry Posin, Héloïse Séailles, Gail Smith, Judy Turnage, Tom Velek, and Nancy Wheeley. I have also profited from comments from the readers of the initial proposal for these volumes, and so am much indebted to Steven Beaudoin, M.A. Claussen, Robin Fleming, Timothy Haggerty, Cassandra Potts, Marylou Ruud, and Lisa Sigel. At an even earlier stage William Glass made very useful suggestions. I would like to thank Kendall Dunkelberg as well for occasionally suggesting that I look for a publisher, and heroically providing help and instruction regarding the computer equipment now so important in producing this sort of book. I am also grateful to the anonymous readers for Broadview Press. I owe some fine work of scanning and initial proofreading to Jill Belarmino and Vassil Nedkov, two enthusiastic student assistants. Carol Moore generously got me out of a pickle by typing up one of the sources. Curt Lamar kindly helped me negotiate Spanish, as did Héloïse Séailles French and Italian. Tom Velek advised me on Latin American matters. Gail Gunter, who handles interlibrary loans at Mississippi University for Women, fulfilled my many and often difficult requests with unfailing determination and good humor. Lloyd Bush generously helped me find information about Marx's and Engels's translator. Bridget Pieschel, head of Humanities at Mississippi University for Women, has given her very helpful encouragement to the project.

The scholarly apparatus of the editions used in this collection often eased the work of annotating the texts, and so I gratefully acknowledge here the unwitting help of those, mostly long dead, editors. For the sake of simplicity I have not distinguished between my notes and those of earlier editors, although I have inserted notices to indicate which notes come from the original author of a source. In addition, I am grateful to Stephanie Gustafson, who kindly read the *Grand Remonstrance* and improved its introduction and notes, and to John Burbidge who much improved the Biblical citations. I should also thank Lorne Macdonald for answering questions about de Gouges's *Declaration of the Rights of Woman and of the Female Citizen* and thank Kathleen Renne for answering questions about Canadian history. In revising translations I have had occasional recourse to translations by others for confirmation, inspiration or guidance. More specifically, I am especially grateful to Rita Hinton and Héloïse

Séailles for essential guidance on Greek; they are in fact the co-revisors of some of the translations which appear here—Rita Hinton of Plato, Héloïse Séailles of Plutarch and Homer. In translating the English Statute of 1363 on Diet and Clothing I received helpful prompts from the translation which appears in *Statutes of the Realm*. Karen Bell graciously answered my questions about German and German sources and provided an elegant English version of the verse which appears in the selection by Karl Pearson. I would also like to thank M.A. Claussen for translating the inscription from Mactar for this reader. Various holders of copyright gave me permission to include work in this book, for which I am very grateful, as I am to the collections and individuals who supplied photographs and permissions for their reproduction. I am further indebted to the estate of Paulette Goddard Remarque for allowing me to make certain revisions in the translation of *All Quiet on the Western Front*. (All permissions for readings are specified in the list of credits; credits for visual material are listed with the pictures.)

In working on this project, I have come to appreciate having what one of Broadview Press's authors calls a "civilized publisher." Don Le Pan, Barbara Conolly, Mical Moser and Carol Richardson earn the Press that description.

All these are recent debts. Teachers, however, are in many ways creatures of their predecessors and so, often, are their choices of sources with which to teach. I am happy to acknowledge such benefits here, and in particular to thank Hal Drake, Sharon Farmer, Robin Fleming, the late Warren Hollister, Sears McGee, and Paul Sonnino. Instructors also often say they learn from their students. I have done so, and am grateful to the students who, over the years, have helped me see the sources in new ways. My gratitude to Miriam Davis is of a different order. My debts to her go incalculably beyond years of discussing the history of Western civilization course and her criticisms of aspects of this reader, but those are the contributions which will be most evident here.

Finally, it seems right to dedicate volumes of this kind to the two teachers who did the most to teach me that historians use evidence. It is small compensation.

# INTRODUCTION FOR STUDENTS

The past influences the present; that is one reason many people study history. Yet, in an important sense, the past is dead. One cannot go back in time, and so one can never inspect the past "as it happened."

So how do historians come to conclusions about what happened in the past? They rely on clues to reconstruct the past in the same way that detectives use clues to reconstruct the events and conditions that led to a crime. Historians find their clues, or evidence, in "primary sources"—that is, writings, art, buildings, and other material produced by people in the past which survive in the present.

This book is a collection of primary sources produced over the course of Western civilization. You might find that your use of these sources is rather like a history lab. In a chemistry course your instructor lays out a series of generalizations about, say, chemical reactions. In the lab, your job is to test those generalizations, to see whether the chemical reactions which you actually observe match what your instructor would have predicted. Primary sources offer history students a similar experience. A consideration of certain matters can help you take that opportunity. The first thing to do is to grapple with the source itself. Here are some questions which might be useful:

—Who produced the source? When was it produced? Where was it produced?
—What kind of source is it? (E.g., a personal letter? A law?)
—Is the source trying to say or show something? If so, in your own words, explain what. In doing so, it is best to set aside the matter of whether the person is right or wrong in what she or he is saying.
—What unspoken assumptions does the source make?
—Who seems to have been the expected audience?

Ultimately, however, your answers to such questions are only a step toward a larger goal of most historians, who are generally concerned not only with the source, but with the world which lies behind the source:

—What conclusions can you draw from the source about the time that produced it? Do your answers to the above set of questions in any way influence or limit what conclusions you can draw from the source? Does whoever produced the source have any reason to mislead?

There are also narrower questions which might be of use in trying to draw historical conclusions from the source. Here is a (far from exhaustive) list:

—What or whom does the source seem to view as authoritative?
—Does the source divide people into groups in any way? If so, what are those groups? Does the source make assumptions about how those groups do or should relate to one another? About how individuals relate to one another?
—Does the source make moral distinctions? If so, what is viewed as good? As bad? What values does the source seem to assume?

—If the source makes an argument, what is the argument about? What issues seem to be debated in this society? In what terms?

—Does the source attempt to explain anything? If so, how does it go about doing so?

—Does the source provide evidence of actions taken by people in the past? If so, what conclusions can you draw from those actions? How well informed can you suppose the writer to have been about the events recounted? How reliable a reporter?

Finally, there is the matter of the significance of the conclusions you draw:

—Do your conclusions have implications for your understanding of larger questions historians have about the period you are studying?

—Do your conclusions help you identify causes or effects of events or developments you have studied?

—Do your conclusions imply change or continuity between the time that produced the source on the one hand, and earlier or later history on the other?

—Do your conclusions imply change or continuity between past and present?

Why is all this important? There are at least a couple of reasons. In the first place, since you are taking a history course, it makes sense that you should come to understand what historians do, and so get an understanding of the grounds on which a knowledge of the past, such as it is, rests. But there is another reason. By using historical evidence, you will be sharpening your skills at reasoned argument from any kind of evidence. Most people encounter arguments which purport to be based on evidence. Journalists, business people, lawyers, politicians, and many other people try to persuade one that evidence—"the facts"—shows this or that. By learning how to handle historical evidence well, you learn how better to come to reasoned acceptance or rejection of what you hear or read in, and out of, the classroom. In other words, the historian's skills, which this reader aims to help you develop, are not just for history. They are for life.

# THE DESCENT OF ISHTAR

*The Descent of Ishtar* recounts a visit of Ishtar, a Mesopotamian goddess of fertility, to the land of the dead. Dating to sometime in the second millennium BC, the poem was recited annually in the city of Ninevah at a ceremony in which the statue of Tammuz, Ishtar's lover, was bathed.

To the land of no return, the land of [darkness?]
Ishtar, the daughter of Sin[1] directed her thought,
Directed her thought, Ishtar, the daughter of Sin,
To the house of shadows, the dwelling of Irkalla,[2]
To the house without exit for him who enters therein,
To the road whence there is no turning,
To the house without light for him who enters therein,
The place where dust is their nourishment, clay their food.
They have no light, in darkness they dwell.
Clothed like birds, with wings as garments,
Over door and bolt, dust has gathered.
Ishtar on arriving at the gate of the land of no return,
To the gate-keeper thus addressed herself:
"Gate-keeper, ho, open your gate!
Open your gate that I may enter!
If you do not open the gate to let me enter,
I will break the door, I will wrench the lock,
I will smash the door-posts, I will force the door
I will bring up the dead to eat the living.   *zombie*
And the dead will outnumber the living."
The gate-keeper opened his mouth and spoke,

Spoke to the lady Ishtar:
"Desist, O lady, do not destroy it.
I will go and announce your name to my queen Ereshkigal."
The gate-keeper entered and spoke to Ereshkigal:
"Ho! Here is your sister, Ishtar,
Who holds the keppu-toy."[3]
When Ereshkigal heard this,
As when one hews down a tamarisk [she trembled?]
As when one cuts a reed, [she shook?]:
"What has moved her heart, what has stirred her liver?
Ho there, does this one [wish to dwell?] with me?
To eat clay as food, to drink [dust?] as wine?
I weep for the men who have left their wives.
I weep for the wives torn from the embrace of their husbands;
For the little ones cut off before their time.
Go, gate-keeper, open your gate for her,
Deal with her according to the ancient decree."
The gate-keeper went and opened his gate to her:
"Enter, O lady, let Cuthah[4] greet you.

---

1 The moon god; the name did not have negative moral connotations.
2 I.e., the land of the dead.
3 A kind of top?
4 A city whose patron was Nergal, the god of pestilence.

Let the palace of the land of no return rejoice at your
   presence!"
He bade her enter the first gate which he opened
   wide, and took the large crown off her head:
"Why, O gate-keeper, do you remove the large crown
   off my head?"
"Enter, O lady, such are the decrees of Ereshkigal."
The second gate he bade her enter, opening it wide
   and removed her earrings:
"Why, O gate-keeper, do you remove my earrings?"
"Enter, O lady, for such are the decrees of Ereshkigal."
The third gate he bade her enter, opened it wide and
   removed her necklace:
"Why, O gate-keeper, do you remove my necklace?"
"Enter, O lady, for such are the decrees of Ereshkigal."
The fourth gate he bade her enter, opened it wide
   and removed the ornaments of her breast:
"Why, O gate-keeper, do you remove the ornaments
   of my breast?"
"Enter, O lady, for such are the decrees of Ereshkigal."
The fifth gate he bade her enter, opened it wide and
   removed the girdle of her body studded with
   birth-stones.
"Why, O gate-keeper, do you remove the girdle of
   my body, studded with birth-stones?"
"Enter, O lady, for such are the decrees of Ereshkigal."
The sixth gate, he bade her enter, opened it wide and
   removed the spangles off her hands and feet.
"Why, O gate-keeper, do you remove the spangles off
   my hands and feet?"
"Enter, O lady, for such are the decrees of Ereshkigal."
The seventh gate he bade her enter, opened it wide
   and removed her loin-cloth.
"Why, O gate-keeper, do you remove my loin-cloth?"
"Enter, O lady, for such are the decrees of Ereshkigal."
Now when Ishtar had gone down into the land of no
   return,
Ereshkigal saw her and was angered at her
   presence.
Ishtar without reflection threw herself at her.
Ereshkigal opened her mouth and spoke,
To Namtar, her messenger, she addressed herself:

"Go Namtar, imprison her in my palace.
Send against her 60 diseases, [to punish?] Ishtar.
Eye disease against her eyes,
Disease of the side against her side,
Foot disease against her foot,
Heart disease against her heart,
Head disease against her head,
Against her whole being, against [her entire body?]."
After the lady Ishtar had gone down into the land of
   no return,
The bull did not mount the cow, the ass did not
   approach the she-ass,
To the maid in the street, no man drew near,
The man slept in his apartment,
The maid slept by herself.
The countenance of Papsukal, the messenger of the
   great gods fell, his face was troubled.
In mourning garbs he was clothed, in soiled gar-
   ments clad.
Shamash[5] went to Sin, his father, weeping,
In the presence of Ea,[6] the king, he went with flow-
   ing tears.
"Ishtar has descended into the earth and has not
   come up.
The bull does not mount the cow, the ass does not
   approach the she-ass.
The man does not approach the maid in the street,
The man sleeps in his apartment,
The maid sleeps by herself."
Ea in the wisdom of his heart formed a being,
He formed Asu-shu-namir, the eunuch.
"Go, Asu-shu-namir, to the land of no return direct
   your face!
The seven gates of the land without return be opened
   before you,
May Ereshkigal at sight of you rejoice!
After her heart has been assuaged, her liver quieted,
Invoke against her the name of the great gods,
Raise your head, direct your attention to the *khalziku*
   skin."
"Come, lady, let them give me the *khalziku* skin, that I
   may drink water out of it"

5  God of the sun, and also of justice.
6  God of the waters.

When Ereshkigal heard this, she struck her side, bit
  her finger,
"You have expressed a wish that cannot be granted.
Go, Asu-shu-namir, I curse you with a great curse,
The sweepings of the gutters of the city be your food,
The drains of the city be your drink,
The shadow of the wall be your abode,
The thresholds be your dwelling-place;
Drunkard and sot strike your cheek!"
Ereshkigal opened her mouth and spoke,
To Namtar, her messenger, she addressed herself.
"Go, Namtar, knock at the strong palace,
Strike the threshold of precious stones,
Bring out the Anunnaki,[7] seat them on golden thrones.
Sprinkle Ishtar with the waters of life and take her
  out of my presence."
Namtar went, knocked at the strong palace,
Tapped on the threshold of precious stones.
He brought out the Anunnaki and placed them on
  golden thrones,
He sprinkled Ishtar with the waters of life and took
  hold of her.
Through the first gate he led her out and returned to
  her her loin cloth.
Through the second gate he led her out and returned
  to her the spangles of her hands and feet.
Through the third gate he led her out and returned to
her the girdle of her body, studded with birth-
  stones.
Through the fourth gate he led her out and returned
  to her the ornaments of her breast.
Through the fifth gate he led her out and returned to
  her her necklace.
Through the sixth gate he led her out and returned to
  her her earrings.
Through the seventh gate he led her out and
  returned to her the large crown for her head.
"If Ishtar will not grant you her ransom,
To Tammuz, the lover of Ishtar's youth,
Pour out pure waters, pour out fine oil;
Deck him with a festival garment that he may play
  on the flute of *lapis lazuli*,
That the votaries[8] may lament."
Belili[9] had gathered the treasure,
With precious stones had filled her bosom.
When Belili heard the lament of her brother, she
  dropped her treasure,
She scattered the precious stones before her.
"O do not let my only brother perish!
On the day when Tammuz returns with the flute of
  lapis lazuli, and the porphyry ring,
Together with him, play for me, you weepers and
  lamenting women!
That the dead may arise and inhale the incense."[10]

---

7  A group of minor gods.
8  I.e., prostitutes associated with a temple.
9  Sister of Tammuz.
10  In another, longer version, Belili asks for Tammuz's repeated release from the land of the dead, thus explaining fertility.

# 2

# *THE CODE OF HAMMURABI*

Hammurabi, king of the city of Babylon (1792-1750 BC) united Mesopotamia under his rule, thus creating the Babylonian empire. Although his law code was not the first one produced in Mesopotamia—fragments of earlier ones have been discovered— Hammurabi's is the oldest law code to survive in extensive (though not complete) sections. It was found on a *stele*, or large inscribed stone, which had been put up in a public place. Above the text are carved the figures of Shamash (the god of justice), seated on a throne, and Hammurabi standing before him. Some of the earlier laws also appear in Hammurabi's code, most of which is reproduced below.

When Anu,[1] the majestic, king of the Anunnaki,[2] and Bel,[3] the lord of heaven and earth, who established the fate of the land, had given to Marduk,[4] the ruling son of Ea,[5] dominion over mankind, magnified him among the Igigi,[6] and called Babylon by his great name; when they made it great upon the earth by founding therein an eternal kingdom, whose foundations are as firmly grounded as are those of heaven and earth—it was then that Anu and Bel called me, Hammurabi, the exalted prince, a god-fearing man, by name, to cause justice to be practiced in the land, to destroy the wicked and the evil alike, to prevent the strong from oppressing the weak, so that I might go forth like Shamash[7] to rule over the black-haired people,[8] to give light to the land, and, like Anu and Bel, promote the welfare of mankind.

I am Hammurabi, the prince called by Bel to pour out riches and abundance, procuring everything possible for Nippur and Durilu,[9] the majestic patron of E-kur,[10] the brave king, who restored Eridu,[11] and purified the cult of E-apsu,[12] who subjected the four quarters of the world, and made great the name of

---

1 God of the heavens.
2 A group of lesser gods.
3 A god worshipped at the city of Nippur.
4 The patron god of Babylon.
5 The god of the waters, worshipped chiefly at the city of Eridu.
6 I.e., kind spirits.
7 The sun god, and god of justice.
8 A Sumerian expression for humanity.
9 Two cities in Mesopotamia.
10 I.e., Bel's temple at Nippur.
11 The city was the chief site of the worship of Ea.
12 A temple of Ea at Eridu.

_irrigation_

Babylon, and made glad the heart of Marduk, his lord, and who daily worships in Esagila,[13] the royal scion, begotten by Sin,[14] who enriched Ur;[15] the pious, the submissive one, who brings riches to Gish-shir-gal;[16] the wise king favored by Shamash; the powerful one, who laid again the foundations of Sippar;[17] who clothed with green the tomb [or shrines] of Malkat;[18] who beautified E- bab-bar,[19] which is built like a heavenly place; the warrior, who protected Larsa,[20] and rebuilt E-bab-bar for Shamash, his helper; the lord, who gave life to the city of Uruk and brought abundance of waters to its inhabitants; who built up the towers of E-anna,[21] who brought riches to Anu and Nana;[22] the shield of the land; who again reassembled the scattered inhabitants of Isin,[23] who enriched E-gal-mah;[24] the patron king of the city, the brother of Zama-ma;[25] who firmly established the settlements of Kish;[26] who surrounded E-me-te-ur-sag[27] with glory; who increased the sacred treasures of Nana, the patron of the temple of Harsag-Kalama,[28] the grave of the ene-mies; whose help brings victory; who enriched the places of Cutha;[29] who made everything glorious in E-shid-lam;[30] the mighty bull[31] which trampled down his foes, the favorite of the god Tu-tu; who made the city of Borsippa fruitful; the majestic, who is untiring in his efforts for E-zida;[32] the divine king of the city, the wise, the clever one, who extended the cultivation of the ground at Dilbat;[33] who gave abundant grain for Urash;[34] the lord, to whom belongs scepter and crown; whom the wise Ma-ma[35] created, who determined the boundaries of the temple of Kish; who provided abundantly for the sacred feasts of Nin-tu;[36] the cautious, the careful, who provided food and drink for Lagash and Girsu;[37] who furnished the temple of Nin-girsu with abundance of sacrificial offerings; who arrested the enemies; the elect of the oracle, which fulfilled the word of Hallab;[38] who rejoiced the heart of Anunit;[39] the pure prince, whose prayers are heard by Adad;[40] who pacifies the heart of Adad, the warrior in Karkar;[41] who restored the sacred vessels in E-ud-gal-

---

13  Marduk's temple at Babylon.
14  The moon god, especially worshipped at Ur; the name did not have negative ethical connotations.
15  A Mesopotamian city.
16  The temple of Sin at Ur.
17  A Mesopotamian city.
18  The wife of Shamash; or inanimate nature.
19  The temple of Shamash at Sippar and the city of Larsa.
20  A Mesopotamian city.
21  The temple of Ishtar, goddess of fertility, at Uruk.
22  This is the same as Ishtar, goddess of fertility.
23  A Mesopotamian city.
24  A temple at Isin.
25  A goddess of Kish.
26  A Mesopotamian city.
27  A city near Kish or a temple of that place.
28  A temple in Kish.
29  A city or region of Babylonia.
30  A temple of Nergal.
31  A term used for Marduk.
32  A temple in Borsippa.
33  A Mesopotamian city.
34  A sun god.
35  Consort of Urash.
36  A goddess worshipped at Kish.
37  Two Mesopotamian cities.
38  A Mesopotamian city.
39  I.e., the goddess Ishtar.
40  God of the storm.
41  A Mesopotamian city.

*expounding*

gal;[42] the king who gave life to the city of Adab;[43] the leader of Emach;[44] the princely king of the city; the irresistible warrior who gave life to the inhabitants of Mashkan shabri,[45] and superabundance to the temple of Shidlam; the wise, the active, who penetrated the hiding-place of the bandits; who gave a hiding-place to the people of Malka[46] in their misfortune, and established their habitation in riches; who endowed Ea[47] and Dam-gal-nun-na;[48] who had made the kingdom great and lasting, with abundance of sacrificial gifts; the princely king of the city, who subjected the districts on the Ud-kib-nun-na[49] Canal to the dominion of Dagon,[50] his creator; who spared the inhabitants of Mera and Tutul;[51] the majestic prince, who caused the face of Ninni[52] to shine; who gave sacred meals to the goddess Ni-na-zu; who took care of the inhabitants in their need, and provided in peace their portion in Babylon; the shepherd of his subjects, whose deeds are well-pleasing to Anunit; who made provision for Anunit in the temple of Dumash,[53] in the suburb of Agade; who proclaims the right; who brings in law; who restored to Ashur[54] its benevolent, protecting god; who permitted the name of Ishtar of Nineveh to dwell in E-mish-mish;[55] the majestic, who humbles himself to the great gods; the successor of Sumula-il;[56] the mighty son of Sin-muballit;[57] the royal scion of Eternity; the mighty king; the sun of Babylon, who shed its bright rays over the land of Sumer and Akkad; the king obeyed by the four quarters of the world, the favorite of Ninni am I.

When Marduk sent me to rule over men, to grant protection to the land, then I put law and righteousness in the mouth of the people, and brought well-being to my subjects.

1   If a man makes a false accusation of manslaughter against a man, and cannot prove it, then the accuser shall be put to death.

2   If a man charges a man with being a sorcerer, and is unable to sustain such a charge, the one who is accused shall go to the river, he shall plunge himself into the river, and if he sinks into the river, his accuser shall take his house. If, however, the river shows forth the innocence of this man, and he escapes unhurt, then he who accused him of sorcery shall be put to death, while he who plunged into the river shall appropriate the house of his accuser.

3   If a man (in a case pending judgment) threatens the witnesses, or does not establish that which he has testified, if that case is a case involving life, that man shall be put to death.

4   If a man offers grain or money as a bribe to witnesses, he himself shall bear the sentence of the court in that case.

5   If a judge passes judgment, renders a decision, delivers a verdict, signed and sealed, and afterwards alters the judgment which he has rendered, he shall be called to account for the alteration of the judgment, and he shall pay twelve-fold the penalty which was in the said judgment, and in the assembly[58] they shall

---

42   A temple in Karkar.
43   A Mesopotamian city.
44   A section of Marduk's temple.
45   A Mesopotamian city.
46   A Mesopotamian city.
47   A god worshipped at Eridu.
48   A Bablyonian goddess.
49   I.e., along the Euphrates river.
50   A Canaanite god.
51   Two Mesopotamian cities.
52   The same goddess as Ishtar, goddess of fertility.
53   A temple of Anunit in the city of Agade.
54   A city which would become the capital of the Assyrian empire.
55   A temple of Ishtar in Ninevah.
56   An earlier Babylonian king.
57   King of Babylon and Hammurabi's father.
58   The nature of this assembly is unclear.

expel him from his judgment seat, and he shall not return, and he shall no more take his seat with the judges in a case.

6   If a man steals the property of a god, or [royal] palace, that man shall be put to death, and so, too, he who may receive from his hand stolen goods shall be put to death.

7   If a man buys silver, gold, slaves (male or female), an ox, sheep, ass, or anything whatsoever from the son or slave of any person, without witness or contract, or receives the same on deposit, he is regarded as a thief, and shall be put to death.

8   If a man steals an ox, or sheep, or ass, or pig, or boat, from a god or palace, he shall pay thirty-fold; if from a freeman, he shall pay ten-fold. If the thief has nothing with which to pay, he shall be put to death.

14   If a man steals the minor son of a freeman, he shall be put to death.

15   If any man takes a male or female slave of the [royal] palace, or the male or female slave of a freeman, outside the gates of the city, he shall be put to death.

16   If a man conceals in his house a male or female slave, a fugitive from the palace, or from a freeman, and does not produce the same at the order of the officer, the master of that house shall be put to death.

17   If a man finds a fugitive slave, male or female, in the open country, and brings the same to the owner, the owner of the said slave shall pay that man two shekels of silver.

18   If that slave refuses to give the name of his master, he shall be brought to the palace; an inquiry shall be made into his past, and he shall be restored to his owner.

19   If he forcibly detains that slave in his house, and that slave is later caught in his house, then that man shall be put to death.

21   If a man makes a breach into a house, one shall kill him in front of the breach, and bury him in it.

22   If a man carries on highway robbery, and is captured, he shall be put to death.

23 If the highwayman is not captured, he who has been robbed shall declare before the god under oath in open court the amount lost; then the city and official in whose territory and district the robbery took place shall compensate him for that which he lost.

24   If a life was lost, the city and official shall pay one mina of silver to his heirs.

26   If an officer or man [common soldier] who has been ordered to proceed on the king's business does not go, but hires a substitute whom he sends in his place, that officer or man shall be put to death; his substitute shall take possession of his house.

27   If an officer or a man is captured in the garrison of the king, and subsequently his field and garden have been given to another, and this one takes possession, and if he [the former owner] returns and reaches his place, his field and garden shall be restored to him, and he shall take it again.

28   If an officer or a man is captured in the garrison of the king, and if his son is able to take charge of his business, the field and the garden shall be given to him, and he shall take his father's field.

29   If his son is a minor, and is not able to take charge of the business, a third of the field and garden shall be given to his mother, who shall bring him up.

45   If a man lets his field to another for a fixed rent, and has received the rent for the field, but Adad[59] comes and destroys the crops, the loss falls upon the renter.

46   But if he has not received a fixed rent for his field, but let it out for one-half or one- third [of the crop], the grain on the field shall be divided proportionately between the renter and the owner of the field.

47   If the renter, because in the first year he did not gain sustenance, has given the field into the charge of another, the owner shall not object; the field has been cultivated, and he shall take his share of the grain according to the contract.

48   If anyone owes a debt on which he pays interest, and Adad devastates his field and destroys the grain or, owing to a scarcity of water, grain has not grown in the field, in that year he need not give any grain to the creditor. He shall moisten his contract tablet in water, and need pay no interest that year.

53   If any one neglects to keep his dyke in proper con-

---

59   The storm god.

dition and does not strengthen his dyke, and if a breach takes place, and the farmland is inundated by the water, the man in whose dyke the breach has taken place shall pay back for the grain which was thereby destroyed.

54  If he is unable to replace the grain, he shall be sold, and also his property for money, and the farmers whose grain the waters destroyed shall share the proceeds.

55  If a man has opened his trenches for irrigation in such a careless way as to overflow his neighbor's field, he shall pay his neighbor in grain [the amount being based on the adjoining fields].

56  If a man lets in the water and the water carries off the crop of the adjoining field, he shall measure 10 *gur* of grain for every 10 *gan* of grain.

57  If a shepherd, without the consent or permission of the owner of a field, has pastured his sheep upon the growing grain, the owner shall reap his field, and the shepherd, who without his permission has pastured his flock in the field, shall pay in addition 20 *gur* of grain for every 10 *gan*.

103  If, while on a journey, an enemy robs an agent of anything which he may have, the agent shall take an oath in the name of the god, and shall be acquitted.

104  If a merchant has given an agent grain, wool, oil, or any other goods for trading purposes, the agent shall give in writing a receipt for the amount and give it to the merchant. Then he shall receive a receipt from the merchant for the money paid the merchant.

106  If an agent obtains money from a merchant and disputes it with the merchant, the latter shall charge the agent before the god and witnesses[60] with having the money. Then in [case of conviction] the agent shall pay three times the amount given him.

107  If a merchant has cheated the agent, and the agent has returned already all which the merchant had given him, but the merchant denies having received what was returned to him, then the agent shall accuse the merchant before the god and witnesses. The mer-

chant, because he denied having received all that he had received, shall pay the agent six times the amount.

108  If a female tavern-keeper does not accept grain according to gross weight as pay for drinks, but takes silver, and the price of the drink as compared with that of the grain is less, she shall be convicted and thrown into the water.

109  If conspirators assemble in the house of a tavern-keeper, who are not captured and delivered to the court, that tavern-keeper shall be put to death.

110  If a priestess or a woman dedicated to a god opens a tavern, or enters a tavern for the purpose of drinking, that woman shall be burned to death.

117  If a man incurs a debt and sells his wife, son, or daughter for money, or binds them over to forced labor, three years shall they work in the house of their taskmaster; in the fourth year they shall be set free.

118  If he binds a male or female slave to forced labor, and the merchant lets them out to another for pay, no objections can be made.

119  If a man incurs a debt, and sells for money a female slave who has borne him children, the money which the merchant has paid shall be returned by the owner of the slave, and he shall ransom his female slave.

126  If a man, who has not lost anything, says that he has lost something, and puts forth false claims, he shall make known his (pretended) loss in the presence of the god,[61] then he shall pay double the amount of his alleged loss.

127  If a man points his finger at a woman dedicated to a god or at a man's wife, but cannot prove his charge, he shall be taken before the judge, and shall be branded on his forehead.

128  If a man marries a wife, but has made no contract with her, this woman is not a wife.

129  If a man's wife is caught lying with another man, both shall be bound and thrown into the water, unless the husband of that woman desires to pardon his wife, or the king shall spare the life of his servant.

130  If anyone violates the betrothed wife of a man

---

60  I.e., in open court.
61  I.e., before a court of law.

THE CODE OF HAMMURABI

who has not known a man[62] and is caught, he shall be put to death, but the woman shall go free.

131　If a man has accused his own wife, but she has not been caught lying with another man, she shall swear by the name of the god, and then may return to her house.[63]

132　If the finger has been pointed against a man's wife, but she has not been caught lying with another man, she shall plunge into the river for her husband's sake.

133　If a man is taken captive in war, and there is sustenance in his house, and his wife has left his house and has entered the house of another, because that woman has not guarded her body, but entered another's house, she shall be condemned according to law and thrown into the waters.

134　If a man has been taken captive in war, and there is no sustenance in his house, when the wife of this man enters another's house, this woman incurs no penalty.

135　If a man has been taken captive in war, and there is no sustenance in his house, when his wife has entered into the house of another, and has borne children, and if the first husband returns later and comes to his home, that woman shall return to her first husband, but the children shall follow their father.

136　If a man leaves his native city and runs away, and his wife subsequently enters into another's house, but if the man returns and desires to retake his wife, this wife shall not return to him because he left his native place and ran away.

137　If a man has made up his mind to separate from a concubine who has borne him children, or from his wife who has borne him children, then he shall give back to that woman her dowry, and the usufruct[64] of the field, garden, and property, so that she may bring up her children; when she shall have brought up the children she shall have a share equal to that of a son of

all that has been given to her children. She may marry the man of her choice.

138　If a man puts away his wife who has not borne him children, he must give her the amount of the marriage settlement and the dowry which she brought from the house of her father; then he may put her away.

139　If there was no marriage settlement, he shall give her one mina of silver for a divorce.

140　If he is a freedman,[65] he shall give her one-third of a mina of silver.

141　If a man's wife, living in his house, has made up her mind to leave that house, and through extravagance runs into debt, has wasted her house, and neglected her husband, one may proceed judicially against her; if her husband consents to her divorce, then he may let her go her way. He shall not give her anything for her divorce. If her husband does not consent to her divorce and takes another wife, the former wife shall remain in the house as a servant.

142　If a wife quarrels with her husband, and says, "You shall not possess me," then the reasons for her prejudices must be examined. If she is without blame, and there is no fault on her part, but her husband has been tramping around, belittling her very much, then this woman shall be blameless; she shall take her dowry and return to the house of her father.

143　If she is not frugal, if she has been going out, ruining her house and belittling her husband, they shall throw that woman into the water.

144　If anyone marries a priestess,[66] and this wife gives a woman slave to her husband, and the latter bears children, but this man makes up his mind to take a lay sister,[67] one shall not countenance him. He may not take a concubine.

145　If a man marries a priestess, and she bears him no children, and he makes up his mind to take a lay sister, if he takes the lay sister and brings her to his

---

62　I.e., had sexual relations with a man.
63　This may be her father's house.
64　I.e., the value of the produce.
65　"Freedman" in this source may not in fact refer to a former slave, but a person of dependent status, though not a slave.
66　Married priestesses were not permitted to bear children.
67　A sort of lesser priestess, who could bear children.

house, this lay sister shall not stand in equality with his wife.

146   If a man marries a priestess and she gives her husband a woman slave for a wife, and this one bears him children, and then this woman slave tries to make herself equal to her mistress because she has borne him children, her mistress may not sell her for money, but may mark her as a slave, and count her as one of her slaves.

147   If she has not borne sons, then the mistress may sell her for money.

148   If a man takes a wife, and sickness attacks her, and if he then sets his face to take a second one, he may; but he shall not put away his wife, whom disease has attacked. On the other hand, she shall dwell in the house he has built, and he shall support her as long as she lives.

149   If this woman is unwilling to dwell in her husband's house, then he must give back to her the dowry which she brought from her father's house, and she may go.

150   If a man gives his wife a field, garden, house, or goods, and gives her a sealed deed for the same, after the death of her husband her sons cannot present claims. The mother may will what she leaves to that one of her sons whom she may prefer, but need not give anything to the other brothers.

151   If a woman dwelling in the house of a man has contracted with her husband that no creditor of his can arrest her for his obligations, and has forced from him a contract to this effect, so, if that man had a debt before he had taken this wife, the creditor cannot hold the wife for it, and if this woman had a debt before she entered her husband's house, the creditor may not hold the husband responsible.

152   If a debt has been contracted after the woman entered the house of a man, both of them are responsible to the merchant.

153   If a man's wife, on account of another, causes the death of her husband, she shall be impaled.

154   If a man has known his daughter, he shall be driven from his city.

155   If a man has betrothed a girl to his son, and his son has known her, but the father afterwards lies with her, and is caught with her, they shall bind him and throw him into the water.

156   If a man has betrothed a bride to his son, and his son has not known her, but the father afterwards lies with her, he shall pay one-half mina of silver, and return all she brought from her father's house. She may marry the man of her choice.

157   If a man after his father is dead lies with his mother, one shall burn them both.

158   If a man, after his father is dead, is surprised lying with a wife of his father, who has borne children, he shall be driven out of the house of his father.

159   If a man who has brought a present into his father-in-law's house and, given the dowry, looks upon another woman, and says to his father-in-law, "I will not take your daughter as wife," the woman's father will keep all that he brought him.

160   If a man brings presents into the house of his father-in-law, and gives a dowry, and if then the girl's father says, "I will not give my daughter to you," then he shall give back fully all that was given him.

161   If a man brings a present into the house of his father-in-law, and gives a dowry, and a friend slanders him, and his father-in-law says to the young suitor, "You shall not have my daughter," then he shall give back fully all that was brought to him, double the amount, but the friend may not marry his wife.

162   If a man takes a wife and she bears him children, and if that woman dies, her father may have no claim in her dowry. It belongs to her children.

163   If a man takes a wife, and she bears him no children, and if that woman dies, if the father-in-law returns the dowry which that man brought to his house, the husband has no claim upon the marriage portion of that woman. It belongs to the house of her father.

167   If a man takes a wife, who bears him children, and that woman dies, and he takes a second wife, who bears him children, and then the father dies, the children shall not partition the estate according to the mothers; they shall take only the marriage portion of their mothers, but in the goods of their father all share equally.

168   If a man decides to thrust out[68] his son, and says

---

68   I.e., disinherit.

to the judge, "I will thrust out my son," then the judge shall inquire into his reasons, and if the son has no grievous fault which justifies his being thrust out, the son may not be cut off from sonship.

169　If he has committed a grave fault, which may justify the father cutting him off from sonship, he shall pardon the first offense. But if he has committed a grave fault the second time, the father may deprive him of sonship.

170　If a man's wife bears him children, or his woman slave bears him children, and the father during his lifetime says to the children whom his woman slave has borne him, "My children," and counts them with the children of his wife, after the death of the father, the children of his wife and those of his woman slave shall share equally in the goods of the father's house. The children of the wife have to divide and to choose.

171　If the father during his lifetime has not said to the children, whom the woman slave has borne him, "My children," after the father dies, the children of the woman slave shall not share with those of the wife. The woman slave and her children shall be given their freedom; the children of the wife may have no claim for servitude upon the children of the woman slave. The wife shall receive her dowry and the marriage portion which her husband gave and deeded her, and she shall remain in the house of her husband as long as she lives, and shall enjoy the property left to her. She cannot sell it for money. What she leaves belongs to her sons.

175　If a slave of the palace, or a slave of a freedman, takes as a wife the daughter of a freeman and begets children, the master of the slave shall have no claim for service upon the children of this free woman.

178　If a woman dedicated to a god, a priestess or a sacred prostitute[69] to whom her father has given a dowry and a deed for the same, but has not stated in the deed, which he has drawn up for her, that she may bequeath her estate to whomsoever she pleases, and has not explicitly granted her full power for disposing of it, if her father dies, her brothers shall take her field and her garden, and they shall give her grain, oil, and wool according to the value of her portion, and they

shall satisfy her. If her brothers do not give her grain, oil, and wool according to the value of her portion, and do not satisfy her, she may give her field and garden to a renter, whom she may select, and this renter shall support her. Field and garden, and all which her father gave her, she shall enjoy as long as she lives. She may not sell or transfer it to any other. What she has inherited belongs to her brothers.

179　If a woman consecrated to a god or a sacred prostitute, to whom her father has given a dowry for the same, and has stated in the deed that she may bequeath her estate to whomsoever she pleases, and has granted her full powers to dispose of it, after her father dies, she may bequeath her estate to whomsoever she pleases. Her brothers have no claim on it.

188　If an artisan adopts a child and teaches him his trade, no one can demand him back.

189　If he has not taught him a trade, the adopted child may return to his father's house.

190　If a man does not treat as one of his own sons the child whom he has adopted as a son and reared, that adopted son may return to his father's house.

191　If a man, who has adopted a son and brought him up, founds his own house, and has children after the adoption of the former, and sets his face to thrust out the adopted son, that son shall not simply go his way; his foster-father shall give him one-third the share of a son; then he may go. He shall not give him of the field, garden, or house.

194　If a man gives his child to a wet nurse, and that child dies while on her hands, and the wet nurse, without the knowledge of the father and the mother, substitutes another child, one shall charge her with having nursed another child, and because she procured another child without the knowledge of the father or mother, one shall cut off her breast.

195　If a son strikes his father, one shall cut off his hand.

196　If a man destroys the eye of another man, one shall destroy his eye.

197　If anyone breaks a man's bone, one shall break his bone.

198　If he destroys the eye of a freedman, or break the

69　I.e., a prostitute associated with a temple.

bones of a freedman, he shall pay one mina of silver.

199　If he destroys the eye of a man's slave, or breaks the bone of a man's slave, he shall pay one-half his value.

200　If a man knocks out the teeth of a man who is his equal in rank, one shall knock out his teeth.

201　If he knocks out the teeth of a freedman, he shall pay one-third mina of silver.

202　If a man strikes a man of higher rank than himself, one shall give him 60 strokes with a cowhide whip in public.

203　If a free-born man strikes a man of his own rank, he shall pay one mina of silver.

204　If a freeman strikes a freeman, he shall pay 10 shekels of silver.

205　If the slave of a freeman strikes a freeman, one shall cut off his ear.

206　If one man strikes another in a quarrel and wounds him, he shall swear, "I did not strike him intentionally," and he shall pay the physician.

207　If the man dies of his wounds, he shall swear likewise, and if the victim is a free-born man, he shall pay one-half mina of silver.

208　If he is a freedman, he shall pay one mina of silver.

209　If a man strikes the daughter of a man, and produces a miscarriage, he shall pay 10 shekels of silver for the loss.

210　If that woman dies, one shall put his daughter to death.

211　If the daughter of a common man suffers miscarriage on account of having been struck by a man, he shall pay five shekels of silver.

212　If that woman dies, he shall pay one-half mina of silver.

213　If a man strikes the slave of a freeman, and thus produces a miscarriage, he shall pay two shekels of silver.

214　If that woman slave dies, he shall pay one-third mina of silver.

215　If a physician treats a man for a severe wound with a bronze knife and heals the man, or if he opens an abscess near the eye with a bronze knife, and saves the eye, he shall receive 10 shekels of silver.

216　If the patient is a freedman, he shall receive five shekels.

217　If it is a man's slave, his owner shall pay the physician two shekels of silver.

218　If a physician treats a man for a severe wound with a bronze knife and kills him, or if he opens an abscess near the eye and destroys the eye, one shall cut off his hand.

219　If a physician treats the slave of a freeman for a severe wound with a bronze knife, and kills him, he must replace the slave with another of equal value.

220　If he opens an abscess near the eye with a bronze knife, and destroys the eye, he shall pay one half what the slave was worth.

221　If a physician heals the broken limb of a man, or cures his diseased bowels, the patient shall pay five shekels of silver.

222　If he is a freedman, he shall pay three shekels of silver.

223　If he is a slave, his owner shall pay the physician two shekels of silver.

224　If a cow doctor or an ass doctor treats a cow or an ass for a severe wound, and cures the animal, the owner shall pay the doctor one-sixth of a shekel of silver as the fee.

225　If he treats a cow or ass for a severe wound, and kills it, he shall pay the owner one-fourth its value.

226　If a brander, without the knowledge of the owner of a slave, brands a slave with the mark of a slave, who cannot be sold, the hand of that brander shall be cut off.[70]

228　If a builder builds a house for anyone and finishes it, he shall be paid two shekels of silver for each sar[71] of surface.

229　If a builder builds a house for anyone and does not build it solid, and the house which he has built falls down and kills the owner, one shall put that builder to death.

230　If it kills a son of the owner of the house, one shall put to death the son of the builder.

---

70　This can be translated as a barber cutting off the forelock of the slave, which may also have marked out the slave as a slave.

71　A unit of measure, perhaps equalling about 18 square yards.

231   If it kills a slave of the owner of the house, he shall give the owner of that house another slave.

232   If it destroys any property, he shall compensate for all that it destroyed, and because he did not build the house solid, and because it fell down, he shall rebuild the house from his own goods.

233   If a builder builds a house for anyone, and has not entirely completed the work, and if the wall becomes rickety, the builder shall strengthen that wall at his own expense.

240   If a boat runs against another boat at anchor and sinks it, the owner of the sunken boat shall declare before the god[72] the extent of his loss; the owner of the boat which ran down the one at anchor shall make reparation for the boat and all that was lost.

245   If a man hires an ox and by neglect or bad treatment kills it, he shall give its owner another ox of like value in its place.

247   If a man hires an ox and destroys its eye, he shall pay its owner one-half of its value.

249   If a man hires an ox, and a god strikes it, and it dies, the man who hired it shall swear before the god and he shall be acquitted.

250   If an ox, while passing through the streets, gores and kills a man, this case is not subject to litigation.

251   If a man's ox is known to gore, and he has been notified that it was a gorer, and he has not bound up its horns, and has not shut it up, and the ox gores a free-born man, and kill him, he shall pay one-half mina of silver.

253   If a man hires a man to tend his field, furnishes him seed, entrusts him with oxen, and engages him to cultivate the field, if the man so engaged steals grain or plants, and they are found in his hands, one shall cut off his hand.

254   If he takes the seed-grain, and does not work the oxen, he shall replace the quantity of grain received for sowing [two-fold?].

265   If a shepherd to whom cows and sheep have been given to pasture acts fraudulently, or makes false returns regarding the increase, or sells them for money, he shall be indicted, and shall render to their owner oxen and sheep ten-fold for what he has stolen.

266   If a stroke of god happens in a stable, or a lion kills any beast, the shepherd shall declare his innocence before the god, and the owner of the stable shall suffer the loss.

280   If a man buys in a foreign country a male slave or a female slave, and he returns to his own land, and the former owner of this male slave or female slave recognizes the same, if the male slave or female slave is a native of the country, he shall grant their freedom without money.

281   If they are natives of another country, the buyer shall declare before the god the sum of money he paid for them, and the former owner of the male slave or female slave shall give to the merchant the money paid for them, and the former owner shall recover his male or his female slave.

282   If a slave says to his master, "You are not my master," if his master shall prove him to be his slave, he may cut off his ear.

These are the just laws, which Hammurabi, the wise king, established, by which he taught the land a just law and a pious statute. I am Hammurabi, the protecting king. I have not withdrawn myself. I have not been neglectful of the black-haired people which Bel presented me, whose rule Marduk gave me. I procured for them a peaceful habitation. I opened up steep passes. I made the light to shine upon them. With the mighty weapons which Zamama and Ishtar delivered to me, with the keenness of vision with which Ea endowed me, with the wisdom which Marduk bestowed upon me, I have exterminated the enemy above and below,[73] subdued the earth, brought well-being to the land, caused the inhabitants to dwell securely, and I tolerated no disturber of their rest.

The great gods called me, and I am the salvation-bringing shepherd, whose scepter is straight, and whose good protection extends over my city. In my breast I cherish the inhabitants of Sumer and Akkad; in my protection have I caused them to rest in peace;

72   I.e., in open court.
73   I.e., north and south.

in my wisdom have I hidden them. That the strong might not injure the weak, and that the widow and the orphan might be safe, I have in Babylon, the city of Anu and Bel, who raised her high head[74] in Esagila, the temple whose foundations are firm as the heavens and the earth, in order to administer justice in the land, to decide disputes, to heal injuries, my precious words written upon my monument, before my image as king of righteousness have I set up.

I am the king, who towers up among city-kings. My words have been well considered, my wisdom is beyond compare. By the command of Shamash, the great judge of heaven and earth, may righteousness arise over the land. By the order of Marduk, my lord, let no damage be done to my monument. In Esagila, which I love, let my name be remembered forever. Let the oppressed, who has a lawsuit, come before my image as king of righteousness. Let him read the inscription on my monument, and understand my precious words. Let my inscription throw light upon his case, and may he discover his rights, and let his heart be made glad, so that he may say: "Hammurabi is a lord who is a father to his subject; he has obtained reverence for the words of Marduk; he has achieved victory for Marduk above and below. He rejoices the heart of Marduk, his lord; he has brought happiness to his subjects forever, and has given order to the land." When he reads the document, let him pray out of a full heart, before Marduk, my lord, and Zarpanit,[75] my lady. Then shall the tutelary deities and the gods who enter Esagila graciously recommend his thoughts every day to Marduk, my lord, and to Zarpanit, my lady.

For the future, always and forevermore: may the king who is in the land observe the words of righteousness which I have inscribed upon my monument; let him not alter the law of the land, which I have given, or the decisions which I have rendered, and let him not injure my monument. If such a prince has wisdom and is able to maintain order in his land, let him observe the words which I have inscribed on this monument, for this inscription will show him the rule of conduct, the statutes, the laws of the land which I have given, and the decisions which I have rendered. He shall rule his subjects according to them; he shall administer law to them, render decisions, and he shall exterminate the wicked and criminals from his land, and grant prosperity to his subjects.

I am Hammurabi, the king of righteousness, to whom Shamash has granted righteousness. My words are well considered; my deeds are beyond compare: to bring low the high, to humble the proud, and to drive out insolence.

If that prince heeds my words which I have written upon my monument, does not injure my law, does not change my words, nor alters my inscription, then may Shamash prolong his rule as he has mine, who am the king of righteousness, that he may rule his subjects in righteousness. If that prince pays no attention to my words, which I have written in my inscription, if he despises my curses, and does not fear the curse of the god, as well as the law I have given, changes my words, and alters my inscription, effaces my name from the monument, and writes his own name there-on—or, fearing the curses, commissions another to do so—that man, be he king or lord, *patesi*[76] or common-er, or whatsoever he may be, may the great god,[77] the father of the gods, who has decreed my reign, with-draw from him the glory of his kingdom, break in pieces his scepter, and curse his destiny.

May Bel, the lord who decides destiny, whose com-mand is immutable, who has made my kingdom great, order against him a rebellion which his hand cannot control. May he cause the wind [?] of his destruction to blow against his habitation; may he ordain, as his destiny, years of groaning in his king-dom, shortness of life, years of famine, darkness with-out light, a death visible to his eyes. May he decree by his omnipotent command the destruction of his city, the dispersion of his subjects, the cutting off of his dominion, and the obliteration of his name and mem-ory from the land.

---

74   I.e., towers.
75   Marduk's wife.
76   I.e., ruler of the priestly class.
77   I.e., Anu.

May Belit,[78] the great mother, whose command is powerful in Ekur,[79] the lady who hearkens graciously to my wishes, frustrate his plans before Bel at the place of judgment and of decision. May she put in the mouth of Bel, the king, the devastation of his land, the annihilation of his subjects, and the pouring out of his life as water.

May Ea, the great prince, whose decrees govern destiny, have precedence; may Ea, the leader of the gods, who is omniscient, who prolongs the days of my life, deprive him of understanding and wisdom, lead him into forgetfulness, dam up his streams at their sources, and not allow grain, the life of man, to grow in his land.

May Shamash, the great judge of heaven and earth, the supporter of every living thing, the lord of living courage, shatter his kingdom; may he not execute his laws, destroy his path, undo the march of his troops; may he give him, in his visions, evil premonitions, foreboding the extirpation of the very foundations of his kingdom and the destruction of his land. May the judgments of Shamash overtake him quickly above[80] among the living, and may he deprive his spirit of water down below the earth.

May Sin, the lord of heaven, the great father, whose sickle shines among the gods, deprive him of his crown and royal throne, impose upon him grievous guilt, the great transgression which will not leave him; may he finish the days, months, years of his reign in sighs and tears; may he increase the burdens of his dominion; may he inflict upon him life that is like death.

May Adad, the god of storms, the lord of fertility, the prince of heaven and earth, my helper, withhold from him rain from the sky, the floods of water in their springs; may he destroy his land by famine and want, rage furiously over his city, and make his land a heap.

May Zamama, the great warrior, the first-born son of Ekur, who marches at my right hand, break in pieces his armor on the battlefield, turn his day into night, and give his enemy victory over him.

May Ishtar, the lady of battle and combat, who loosens my weapons, my gracious protecting deity, who loves my reign, in her angry heart, in her great wrath, curse his kingdom, turn his good into evil, and shatter his weapons on the field of battle and combat; may she create disorder and uproar for him, strike down his warriors, that the ground may drink their blood; may she throw down in large numbers the bodies of his warriors on the battlefield; may she not grant him a life of mercy, but deliver him into the hands of his enemies, and bring him captive into the land of his enemies.

May Nergal, the mighty one among the gods, who is irresistible in battle, who grants me victory, in his great power burn up his subjects like a slender reed-stock, cut off his limb with a mighty weapon, and shatter him like an earthen image.

May Nintu, the daughter of Anu, the exalted mistress of countries, the child-bearing mother, deny him a son; may she not grant him a name; may she give him no progeny upon the earth.

May Nin-karak, the daughter of Anu, who promises me mercy in Ekur, cause to come upon his members grievous diseases, violent fevers, bad wounds which cannot be healed, the natures of which are not known to the physicians, which he cannot treat with bandages, which, like the bite of death, cannot be removed until they destroy his life; may he lament the loss of his vital powers.

May the great gods of heaven and earth, all the Anunnaki, bring a curse and an evil upon the outskirts of the temple, the walls of this E-barra, and upon his reign, his land, his warriors, his subjects, and his troops.

May Bel curse him with a powerful curse from his mouth, which is irrevocable, and may it overtake him speedily.

---

78 Consort of Bel.
79 Bel's temple at Nippur.
80 I.e., on earth.

# 3

# THE *ENUMA ELISH*

The *Enuma Elish* gets its title from its first two words, which mean "When on high." The poem is thought to have originated in Mesopotamia sometime in the sixteenth through thirteenth centuries BC. The text has been pieced together from several tablets. Every year on the fourth day of the New Year's festival the poem was recited before the statue of Marduk in his temple at Babylon, the dominant state in Mesopotamia.

TABLET 1

When on high, heaven was not named,[1]
Below, dry land was not named.
Apsu, their first begetter,
Mummu and Tiamat, the mother of all of them,
Their waters combined together.
Field was not marked off, sprout had not come forth.
When none of the gods had yet come forth,
Had not borne a name,
No destinies had been fixed;
The gods were created in the midst of heaven.
Lakhmu and Lakhamu came forth....
Then Apsu, the begetter of the great gods,
Cried out, to Mummu, to his messenger, he spoke:
"O Mummu, joy of my liver,
Come, unto Tiamat let us go."
They went, and before Tiamat they crouched,
Hatching a plan with regard to the gods
Apsu opened his mouth and spoke,
Unto Tiamat, the splendid one addressed a word:
[defective line] "... their course against me
By day I have no rest, at night I cannot lie down, I
    wish to destroy their course,

So that the clamor will cease and we may again lie
    down to sleep."
When Tiamat heard this,
She raged and shrieked for revenge [?],
She herself became furiously enraged.
Evil she conceived in her heart.
"All that we have made let us destroy,
That their course may be full of misery so that we
    may have release."
Mummu answered and counseled Apsu,
Hostile was the counsel of Mummu.
"Come, their course is strong, destroy it!
Then by day you will have rest,
At night you will lie down."
Apsu hearkened, and his face shone;
He planned evil against the gods, his sons....
[Mummu and Apsu are defeated and captured
    by the gods. Tiamat gathers an army of
    monsters.]
They [creatures recruited by Tiamat] uttered curses
    and at the side of Tiamat advanced.
In fury and rage they devised plans ceaselessly night
    and day.
They rushed to the conflict, raging and furious.

---

1    To have a name meant to exist.

They grouped themselves and ranged the battle
     array.
Ummu-Khubur,[2] creator of all things,
Gathering invincible weapons, she brought forth
     huge monsters,
Sharp of tooth and merciless of fang.
With poison instead of blood she filled their bodies.
She clothed with terror the terrible dragons,
Decking them with brilliancy, giving them a lofty
     stature,
So that whoever beheld them would be overcome
     with terror.
With their bodies reared up, none could withstand
     their attack.
She brought forth great serpents, dragons and the
     Lakhami,[3]
Hurricanes, raging dogs and scorpion men,
Mighty tempests, fish men, and rams,
Bearing cruel weapons, fearless in combat,
Mighty in command, irresistible.
In all eleven monsters of this kind she made.
Among the gods, the first born who formed the
     assembly,
She exalted Kingu, giving him high rank in their
     midst;
To march in advance and to direct the host;
To be foremost in arming for the attack,
To direct the fight in supreme control,
To his hand she confided. She decked him out in
     costly garments:
"I have uttered your magic formula, in the assembly
     of the gods I have exalted you."
The dominion over all the gods was entrusted into
     his hands:
"Be you exalted, my one and only husband;
May the Anunnaki[4] exalt your name above all the
     gods!"
She gave him the tablets of fate, to his breast she
     attached them,
"O, your command will be irresistible!
Firmly established will be the utterance of your
     mouth!

Now Kingu is exalted, endowed with the power of
     Anu;
Among the gods, his children, he fixes destinies.
By the word of your mouth fire will be quenched;
The strong in battle will be increased in strength."

TABLET 2

Tiamat finished her work.
The evil that she contrived against the gods her off-
     spring,
To avenge Apsu, Tiamat planned evil.
When she had equipped her army, it was revealed to
     Ea;
Ea heard the words,
And was grievously afflicted, and overwhelmed with
     grief.
Days passed by and his anger was appeased.
To Anshar, his father, he took the way.
To Father Anshar who begot him he went.
All that Tiamat had planned he repeated to him.
"Tiamat our mother has taken a dislike to us,
She has assembled a host, she rages furiously.
All the gods are gathered to her,
Indeed, even those whom you have created, march at
     her side."
... [Anshar calls upon Ea and Anu to fight against
     Tiamat. Neither Ea nor Anu seems able or willing
     to do so, and so Anshar addresses his son Mar-
     duk.]
"You are my son of strong courage, draw nigh to the
     battle!
... [defective line] at sight of you there shall be
     peace."
The lord rejoiced at the word of his father.
He drew nigh and stood in front of Anshar;
Anshar saw him and his heart was full of joy.
He kissed him on the mouth, and fear departed from
     him.
"O my father, may the words of your lips not be
     taken back,
May I go and accomplish the desire of your heart!"

---

2   A title of Tiamat, perhaps meaning "mother of totality."
3   A collective name for a group of monsters.
4   A group of minor gods.

... [Anshar repeats his lines to Marduk, and then says
to him:]
"O my son, full of all knowledge,
Quiet Tiamat with your supreme incantation;
Quickly proceed on your way!
Your blood will not be poured out, you shall surely
    return."
The lord rejoiced at the word of his father,
His heart exulted and he spoke to his father.
"O Lord of the gods, who fixes the fate of the great
    gods,
If I become your avenger,
Conquering Tiamat, and giving life to you,
Call an assembly and proclaim the preeminence of
    my lot!
That when in Upshukkinaku[5] you joyfully seat
    yourself,
My command in place of yours should fix fates.
What I do should be unaltered,
The word of my lips shall never be changed or
    annulled."

### TABLET 3

[*The third tablet opens with an address of Anshar to
Gaga his messenger, asking the latter to go to the gods
and tell them to gather together for a banquet and listen
to the message which Anshar sends them. The message
itself recounts the rebellious purpose of Tiamat and her
monsters, repeats the detailed description of the vipers,
dragons, hurricanes, raging hounds, fish-men and the
strange host with Kingu at the head, already encountered
in the epic.*]

... Then they gathered and went,
The great gods, all of them, who fix fates,
Came into the presence of Anshar, they filled the
    assembly hall
Embracing one another in the assembly hall,
They prepared themselves to feast at the banquet.
They ate bread, they mixed the wine,
The sweet mead confused their senses.
Drunk, their bodies filled with drink,
They shouted aloud, with their livers exalted,

For Marduk, their avenger, they fixed the
    destiny.

### TABLET 4

They prepared for him a royal chamber,
In the presence of his fathers as ruler he stood.
"You are the weightiest among the great gods.
Your power of decreeing fate is unrivalled, your com-
    mand is like that of Anu.
Oh Marduk, you are mightiest among the great gods!
Your power of decreeing fate unrivaled, your word is
    like that of Anu!
From now on your decree will not be altered,
Your power it shall be to raise up and to bring low,
Your utterance be established, against your com-
    mand, no rebellion!
None among the gods will transgress the limit set by
    you.
Abundance is pleasing to the shrines of the gods,
The place of their worship will be established as your
    place.
Oh Marduk, you are our avenger!
We give you kingship over the entire universe,
Take your seat in the assembly, your word be exalted;
Your weapon be not overcome, may it crush your
    enemies.
O lord, the life of him who trusts in you will be
    spared,
But pour out the life of the god who has planned evil."
Then they placed in their midst a garment
To Marduk, their first born, they spoke:
"Your fate, O lord, be supreme among the gods!
For destruction and creation speak, and it shall be
    done;
Declare that the garment vanish,
And speak the word again that the garment be
    intact."
Then he gave the command, and the garment van-
    ished;
He commanded again, and the garment appeared.
When the gods his fathers, thus beheld the power of
    his utterance
They rejoiced and paid homage to Marduk, King;

---

5   The residence of the gods.

They bestowed on him scepter, throne and palu;[6]
They gave him an invincible weapon, *Overcoming the Enemy*.
"Go and cut off the life of Tiamat,
That the wind may carry her blood to hidden spots."
When the gods, his fathers, had decreed the fate of the lord,
They brought him on the road leading to peace and success.
He made a bow and took it as his weapon,
He took a spear and fastened it with a cord,
He raised the club, taking hold of it with his right hand,
The bow and quiver he hung at his side,
Placed the lightning on his face,
With a burning flame he filled his body,
He made a net to enclose Tiamat therein.
The four winds he took hold of, that nothing whatsoever should escape.
The South Wind, North Wind, East Wind, West Wind,
He brought to the side of the net, the gift of his father Anu.
He created the hostile wind, the tempest and the hurricane,
The four-day wind and the seven-day wind, the whirlwind, and the wind without rival.
He sent forth the winds which he had created, the seven of them;
To trouble the spirit of Tiamat, they followed behind him.
Then the lord raised on high the Deluge, his mighty weapon.
He mounted the storm chariot, unequalled in power,
He harnessed and attached to it four horses,
Merciless, overwhelming, swiftly flying.
Sharp of teeth, bearing poison....
Then the lord drew nigh, piercing Tiamat with his glance;
He saw the purpose of Kingu, her spouse,
As he[7] gazed, he[8] tottered in his gait.
His mind was destroyed, his action upset,
And the gods, his helpers, marching at his side,

Saw the terror of the hero and leader.
But Tiamat uttered a cry and did not turn her back,
From her lips there gushed forth rebellious words
"[defective line] ... coming to you as lord of the gods ...
[defective lines]
As in their own sanctuaries they are gathered in your sanctuary."
Then the lord raised on high the Deluge, the great weapon,
And against Tiamat, who was foaming with wrath, thus sent forth his answer.
"You are great! You have exalted yourself greatly.
Your heart has prompted you to arrange for battle,
You have exalted Kingu to be your husband,
You have given him power to issue the decrees of Anu.
Against the gods, my fathers, you have planned evil,
Against the gods, my fathers, you have planned evil.
Let your army be equipped, your weapons be girded on;
Stand; I and you, let us join in battle."
When Tiamat heard this,
She was beside herself, she lost her reason.
Tiamat shouted in a paroxysm of fury,
Trembling to the root, shaking in her foundations.
She uttered an incantation, she pronounced a magic formula.
The gods of battle appeal to their weapons.
Then stepped forth Tiamat and the leader of the gods, Marduk.
To the fight they advanced, to the battle they drew nigh.
The lord spread his net and encompassed her,
The evil wind stationed behind him he drove into her face.
Tiamat opened her mouth to its full extent.
He drove in the evil wind before she could close her lips.
The terrible winds filled her belly,
Her heart was seized, and she held her mouth wide open.

---

6   Some symbol of royal power—perhaps a crown?
7   I.e., Marduk.
8   I.e., Kingu.

He drove in the spear and burst open her belly,
Cutting into her entrails, he slit her heart.
He overcame her and destroyed her life;
He cast down her carcass and stood upon it.
When he had thus subjected Tiamat, the leader,
Her host was scattered, her assembly was dissolved;
And the gods, her helpers, who marched beside her,
In fear and trembling turned about,
Taking to flight to save their lives.
But they were surrounded and could not escape.
He captured them and smashed their weapons,
They were cast into the net, and brought into the
 snare;
After he had bound and cast down his enemies,
Had battered down the arrogant foe,
Had completely gained the victory of Anshar over
 the enemy,
The hero Marduk had attained the aim of Nudim-
 mud,
He strengthened his hold over the captive gods.
To Tiamat, whom he had bound, he came back,
And the lord trampled under foot the foundation of
 Tiamat.
With his merciless weapon he smashed her skull,
He cut the channels of her blood,
And made the north wind carry them to secret
 places.
His fathers beheld and rejoiced exceeding glad,
Presents and gifts they brought to him.
Then the lord rested and looked at the carcass.
He divided the flesh of the monster, and created mar-
 velous things.
He split her like a fish flattened into two halves;
One half he took and made it a covering for
 heaven.
He drew a bolt, he stationed a watchman,
Enjoining that the waters be not permitted to flow
 out.
He passed over the heavens, inspecting the regions
 thereof,

And over against the Apsu,[9] he set the dwelling of
 Nudimmud.
The lord measured the structure of the Deep.
He established E-sharra as a palace corresponding to
 it.
The palace E-sharra which he created as heaven,
He caused Anu, Enlil and Ea to inhabit their districts.

### TABLET 5

He made stations for the great gods,
The stars, their counterparts, the twin stars he fixed.
He fixed the year and divided it into divisions.
For the twelve months he fixed three stars
Also for the days of the year he had fashioned pic-
 tures.[10]
He founded the station of Nibir[11] to regulate their
 limits,
That none might err or go astray.
He placed the station of Enlil and Ea with him.
He opened great gates to both sides,
He supplied a strong bolt to the left and the right.
In the midst of the heavens he fixed the zenith,
He caused Sin[12] to shine forth, entrusting to him the
 night;
He assigned to him the control of the night for count-
 ing the days;
Each month without interruption he covered him
 with a crown.[13]
[Marduk said to Sin,] "At the beginning of the month
 in rising over the land
You will show a horn for a period of six days.
On the seventh day the crown will be divided.
On the fourteenth day you will stand opposite, it
 being the half of the month,
When the sun god in the foundation of heaven is
 opposite you."

[*The tablet becomes very defective at this point. Most of
the rest of its text is lost or illegible.*]

---

9   I.e., "the Deep."
10   I.e., constellations.
11   I.e., Jupiter, the brightest of the planets.
12   The moon god; this god has nothing to do with moral crimes.
13   I.e., the crescent of the new moon.

## TABLET 6

Upon Marduk's hearing the word of the gods,
His heart led him to create marvellous things.
He opened his mouth and spoke to Ea
What he had conceived in his heart he imparted to
   him:
"My blood I will take and bone I will form.
I will set up man that man [defective line]
I will create man to inhabit the earth,
That the worship of the gods be fixed, that they may
   have shrines....

## TABLET 7

[*Marduk names the other gods*]

Asari, the source of planting, the founder of
   sowing,
Creator of grain and flour, causing the verdure to
   spring forth.
Asaru-alim, honored in the house of counsel abound-
   ing in counsel.
To him the gods pay homage, and of him they stand
   in dread.
Asaru-alim-nunna, the mighty, the light of his father
   who begat him,
Who prescribes the laws for Anu, Enlil and Ea,
Who provides for them, who fixes their bounds,
Who provides abundance, brings out [defective
   line] ...
Tutu, "the creator who renews them,"
May their sanctuaries be purified, may they be paci-
   fied.
May he bring about an incantation, that the gods
   may be calmed.

When they attack in fury may he repulse their
   advance!
Be he exalted even in the assembly of the gods.
None among the gods is like to him....
Nibiru[14] be his name, the one who seized the inside;
May he maintain the stars of heaven in their path,
Shepherding all the gods like sheep!
May he keep Tiamat enchained,
Crushing and putting an end to her life.
In the future of mankind, when the days grow old,
May one hear this without ceasing, may it survive
   forever!
Since he created the region of heaven, and formed
   the earth,
Lord of the worlds, father Enlil called him,
The name which all the Igigi[15] proclaimed.
Ea heard and his liver rejoiced,
"He whose name his fathers have made glorious,
Be he like I am, Ea be his name!
All my commands be in his control,
All my decrees let him pronounce!"
By the name "fifty" did the great gods
Confer upon him fifty names to make his path
   supreme.
Let them be remembered, let the older speak of them!
Let the wise and the intelligent reflect on them
   together,
Let father repeat and teach them to his son!
Let pastor and shepherd open their ears,
To rejoice in Marduk, the lord of the gods,
That his land may be fertile and prosper.
His word[16] is firm, his command unchangeable.
What he utters no god annuls,
He casts a glance and turns not his neck.
In his wrath no god can withstand him,
But wide is his heart, broad is his mind....

---

14  I.e., "inside of Tiamat."
15  A group of minor gods.
16  I.e., Marduk's.

# 4

# INSCRIPTION OF UNI

Uni, who lived in the Old Kingdom about 2650 BC, became a high governmental official under one Egyptian pharaoh, or king, and served under two more. This inscription was carved on his tomb at Abydos, in Egypt.

Under this king[1] Uni passed his childhood and entered upon his official career at the bottom of the ladder as an under-custodian of a royal domain.

[Count, governor of the South], chamber-attendant, attached to Nekhen, lord of Nekheb, sole companion, revered before Osiris,[2] First of the Westerners, Uni. He says: [I was a child] who fastened on the girdle under the majesty of Teti; my office was that of supervisor of [uncertain word] and I filled the office of inferior custodian of the domain of Pharaoh.

[Four missing words] [I was] eldest of the [uncertain word] chamber under the majesty of Pepi. His majesty appointed me to the rank of companion and inferior prophet of his pyramid-city. While my office was [missing word] his [majesty made me] judge attached to Nekhen. He loved me more than any servant of his. I heard cases in court, being alone with only the chief judge and vizier, in every private matter in the name of the king, of the royal harem and of the six courts of justice because the king loved me more than any official of his, more than any noble of his, more than any servant of his.

Then I besought [word missing] the majesty of the king that there be brought for me a limestone sarcophagus from Troja.[3] The king had the treasurer of the god ferry over, together with a troop of sailors under his hand, in order to bring for me this sarcophagus from Troja; and he arrived with it, in a large ship belonging to the court, together with [its] lid, the false door; the [setting?], two [uncertain word], and one offering-tablet. Never was the like done for any servant, for I was excellent to the heart of his majesty, for I was pleasant to the heart of his majesty, for his majesty loved me.

While I was judge, attached to Nekhen, his majesty appointed me as sole companion and superior custodian of the domain of Pharaoh, and [uncertain word] of the four superior custodians of the domain of Pharaoh, who were there. I did so that his majesty praised me, when preparing court, when preparing the king's journey or when making stations. I did throughout so that his majesty praised me for it above everything.

When legal procedure was instituted in private in the harem against the queen, Imtes, his majesty caused me to enter, in order to hear the case alone. No chief

---

1  I.e., the pharaoh Teti.
2  Osiris was the god of the afterlife and of vegetation.
3  These were quarries five or six miles from modern Cairo.

judge and vizier at all, no prince at all was there, but only I alone, because I was excellent, because I was pleasant to the heart of his majesty, because his majesty loved me. I alone was the one who put it in writing, together with a single judge attached to Nekhen, while my office was only that of superior custodian of the domain of Pharaoh. Never before had one like me heard the secret of the royal harem, except that the king caused me to hear it, because I was more excellent to the heart of his majesty than any official of his, than any noble of his, than any servant of his.

His majesty made war on the Asiatic Sand-dwellers[4] and his majesty made an army of many ten thousands: in the entire South, southward to Elephantine, and northward to Aphroditopolis; in the Northland on both sides entire in the [stronghold?], and in the midst of the [strongholds?], among the Irthet blacks, the Mazoi blacks, the Yam blacks, among the Wawat blacks, among the Kau blacks, and in the land of Temeh.[5]

His majesty sent me at the head of this army while the counts, while the wearers of the royal seal, while the sole companions of the palace, while the nomarchs[6] and commanders of strongholds belonging to the South and the Northland, the companions, the caravan-conductors, the superior prophets belonging to the South and the Northland, the overseers of the crown-possessions, were each at the head of a troop of the South or the Northland, of the strongholds and cities which they commanded, and of the blacks of these countries. I was the one who made for them the plan while my office was only that of superior custodian of the domain of Pharaoh of [three uncertain words]. Not one thereof [uncertain verb] with his neighbor; not one thereof plundered [dough] or sandals from the wayfarer; not one thereof took bread from any city; not one thereof took any goat from any people. I dispatched them from the Northern Isle, the Gate of Ihotep, the bend of Horus, Nibmat. While I was of this rank [three missing words] everything, I

[inspected?] the number of these troops, although never had any servant inspected.

This army returned in safety, after it had hacked up the land of the Sand-dwellers; this army returned in safety, after it had destroyed the land of the Sand-dwellers; this army returned in safety, after it had overturned its strongholds; this army returned in safety, after it had cut down its figs and its vines; this army returned in safety, after it had thrown fire in all its [troops?]; this army returned in safety, after it had slain troops therein, in many ten thousands; this army returned in safety after [it had carried away?] therefrom a great multitude as living captives. His majesty praised me on account of it above everything.

His majesty sent me to dispatch [this army] five times, in order to traverse the land of the Sand-dwellers at each of their rebellions, with these troops. I did so that [his] majesty praised me [on account of it].

When it was said there were revolters because of a matter among these barbarians in the land of Gazelle-nose,[7] I crossed over in troop-ships with these troops, and I voyaged to the back of the height of the ridge on the north of the Sand-dwellers. When this army had been [brought] in the highway, I came and smote them all and every revolter among them was slain.

[A line on the stone separates the above text from what follows.]

When I was [master of the footstool?] of the palace and sandal-bearer, the king of Upper and Lower Egypt, Mernere, my lord, who lives forever, made me count, and governor of the South, southward to Elephantine, and northward to Aphroditopolis; for I was excellent to the heart of his majesty, for I was pleasant to the heart of his majesty, for his majesty loved me.

When I was [master of the footstool?] and sandal-bearer, his majesty praised me for the watchfulness and vigilance which I showed in the place of audience, above his every official, above [his every] noble, above

---

4   I.e., against the Bedouin.
5   These are all Nubian areas.
6   Governors of the nomes, or administrative districts, into which Egypt was divided.
7   I.e., southern Palestine.

his every servant. Never before was this office conferred upon any servant. I acted as governor of the South to his satisfaction. Not one therein [same uncertain verb as above] with [his] neighbor. I accomplished all tasks; I numbered everything that is counted to the credit of the court in this South twice; all the drafted labor that is counted to the credit of the court in this South twice. I performed the [four missing words] in this South; never before was the like done in this South. I did throughout so that his majesty praised me for it.

His majesty sent me to Ibhet,[8] to bring the sarcophagus named "Chest-of-the-Living," together with its lid and the costly, splendid pyramidion[9] for the pyramid called "Mernere-Shines-and-is-Beautiful," of the queen.

His majesty sent me to Elephantine to bring a false door of granite, together with its offering-tablet, doors and [settings?] of granite; to bring doorways and offering-tablets of granite, belonging to the upper chamber of the pyramid called "Mernere-Shines-and-is-Beautiful," of the queen. Then I sailed down-stream to the pyramid called: "Mernere-Shines-and-is-Beautiful," with six cargo-boats, three [tow]-boats and three [missing word] boats to only one warship. Never had Ibhet and Elephantine been visited in the time of any kings with only one warship. Whatsoever his majesty commanded me I carried out completely according to all that his majesty commanded me.

His majesty sent me to Hatnub to bring a huge offering-table of hard stone of Hatnub. I brought down this offering-table for him in only 17 days, it having been quarried in Hatnub, and I had it proceed down-stream in this cargo-boat. I hewed for him a cargo-boat of acacia wood of 60 cubits in its length, and 30 cubits in its breadth, built in only 17 days, in the third month of the third season (eleventh month). Although there was no water on the [flats?], I landed in safety at the pyramid called "Mernere-Shines-and-is-Beautiful"; and the whole was carried out by my hand, according to the mandate which the majesty of my lord had commanded me.

His majesty sent [me] to dig five canals in the South and to make three cargo-boats and four [tow?]-boats of acacia wood of Wawat. Then the black chiefs of Irthet, Wawat, Yam and Mazoi drew timber therefore, and I did the whole in only one year. They were launched and laden with very large granite blocks for the pyramid called "Mernere-Shines-and-is-Beautiful." I then [uncertain word] for the palace in all these five canals, because I honored, because I [uncertain word], because I praised the fame of the king of Upper and Lower Egypt, Mernere, who lives forever, more than all gods, and because I carried out everything according to the mandate which his ka[10] commanded me.

I was one beloved of his father, and praised of his mother; first-born [missing word] pleasant to his brothers, the count, the real governor, of the South, revered by Osiris, Uni.

---

8  A quarry.
9  The top of an obelisk or tall stone spire; the pyramidion was itself pyramid shaped.
10  Egyptian belief held that each person had three aspects—body, mind, and the "ka," a kind of spiritual double. The pharaoh's ka was divine, helping to account for his divine status.

# 5

# STELE OF NEFERHOTEP

The Pharaoh Neferhotep, a member of Egypt's thirteenth dynasty, was the son of a priest, and so had not been in line to become pharaoh from birth. His *stele*, or large upright stone carved with an inscription, is roughly six feet tall and three feet wide. It was originally on a wall leading to a temple of Osiris, the god of the afterlife and of vegetation, in Abydos, in Egypt, and dates to, very roughly, *c.* 1700 BC, during Egypt's Second Intermediate Period.

---

Year 2, under the majesty of King Neferhotep, born of the royal mother, Kemi,[1] who is given life, stability, satisfaction, like Re,[2] forever. His majesty appeared upon the throne of Horus[3] in the palace, "[Structure?]-of-Beauty." His majesty spoke to the nobles and companions, who were in his suite, the real scribes of the hieroglyphs, the masters of all secrets: "My heart has desired to see the ancient writings of Atum; open for me for a great investigation; let the god know concerning his creation, and the gods concerning their fashioning, their offerings and [their] oblations [many words missing] let me know the god in his form, that I may fashion him as he was formerly, when they made the [statues?] in their council, in order to establish their monuments upon earth.[4] They have given to me the inheritance [of Re as far as?] the circuit of the sun [many words missing] I will increase that which I shall have discovered what I owe, and they shall [increase] love for me [missing word] to do according to that which they command."

These companions said, "That which your ka[5] has [commanded?] is that which happens, O sovereign and lord. Let your majesty proceed to the libraries, and let your majesty see every hieroglyph."

His majesty proceeded to the library. His majesty opened the rolls together with these companions. Lo, his majesty found the rolls of the House of Osiris, First of the Westerners, lord of Abydos.

His majesty said to these companions, "My majesty hails my father Osiris, First of the Westerners, lord of Abydos. I will fashion [him, his limbs (missing word) his face, his fingers?] according to that which my majesty has seen in the rolls [two uncertain words] his [form?] as King of Upper and Lower Egypt, at his coming forth from the body of Nut."[6]

---

1  Although the inscription describes his mother as having been of royal blood, this description might have been invented after Neferhotep became pharaoh—perhaps by conspiracy or force.
2  The sun god.
3  Horus was the son of Osiris, god of the afterlife and vegetation. The pharaoh was Horus.
4  Apparently the gods once held a council in which they decided the form of Osiris's statue for all time. This decision is to be found in the writings at Atum.
5  Egyptian belief held that each person had three aspects—body, mind, and the "ka," a kind of spiritual double. The pharaoh's ka was divine, helping to account for his divine status.
6  Nut was an Egyptian goddess who embodied the heavens.

His majesty had the king's confidant, who was in his majesty's suite, called to him; his majesty said to him: "Go southward [two missing words] [together with?] troops and marines. Do not sleep, night or day, until you arrive at Abydos; cause the First of the Westerners to proceed forth. May I make his monuments as they were specified at the beginning."

These companions said, "That which you command [is that which happens, O sovereign?] and lord; you do all [missing word] in Abydos for your father, First of the Westerners."

This official betook himself southward [to do] that which his majesty commanded him. He arrived at [Abydos] [uncertain word] [two missing words]. The majesty of this god came to the sacred barge of the lord of eternity [two missing words] the banks of the river were flooded [with his fragrance and with?] the odors of Punt.[7] [The majesty of this god] arrived in the midst [three missing words]. One came to inform his majesty, saying, "This god has proceeded in peace."

His majesty proceeded [in?] the sacred ship [many missing words] together with this god, causing that sacred offerings be presented to his father, the First of the Westerners: myrrh [missing word] and sacred things for Osiris, First of the Westerners, in all his names [many missing words] those hostile to the sacred barge were overthrown. Lo, the majesty of this god appeared in procession, his ennead united [with him?]. Upwawet[8] was before him, he opened the ways [many missing words].

Lo, [his majesty caused that this god should proceed to?] [word missing] that he should rest [on] his throne in the house of gold; in order to fashion the beauty of his majesty[9] and his ennead, his oblation-tables [three missing words] of every splendid, costly stone of god's-Land. Behold, [the king] himself led the work on them [missing word] gold, for his majesty was pure with the purity of a god [many missing or uncertain words].

[Neferhotep is speaking.] "Be vigilant for the temple, look to the monuments which I have made. I put the eternal plan before me, I sought that which was useful for the future by putting this example in your hearts, which is about to occur in this place, which the god made, because of my desire to establish my monuments in his temple, to perpetuate my contracts[10] in his house. His majesty[11] loves that which I have done for him, he rejoices over that which I have decreed to do, [for?] triumph [has been given?] to him. I am his son, his protector, he gives to me the inheritance of the earth. [I] am the king, great in strength, excellent in commandment. He shall not live who is hostile to me; he shall not breathe the air who revolts against me; his name shall not be among the living; his ka shall be seized before the officials; he shall be cast out for this god, [together with?] him who shall disregard the command of my majesty and those who shall not do according to this command of my majesty, who shall not exalt me to this august god, who shall not honor that which I have done concerning his offerings [who shall not] give to me praise at every feast of this temple, of the entire [lay priesthood] of the sanctuary of this temple, and every office of Abydos. Behold, my majesty has made these monuments, for my father, Osiris, First of the Westerners, Lord of Abydos, because I so much loved him, more than all gods; that he might give to me a reward for this [which I have done], [three missing words] consisting of millions of years [many missing words].

---

7   A land near present-day Somalia, and the original home of the Egyptian gods.

8   A god whose name means "opener of the ways."

9   I.e., the god.

10   These are contracts with the priests at Abydos for offerings after the pharaoh's death.

11   I.e., the god.

# 6

# *Hymn to Aton*

The Egyptian Pharaoh Amenhotep IV (1369-1353 BC) established the worship of the god Aton, identified as the disk of the sun, as the focus of Egyptian religion. Amenhotep changed his own name, which meant "Amon is satisfied" (Amon being the traditional chief god of the Egyptians) to "Akhenaton" ("It pleases Aton"). He also declared himself to be "the son of Aton," moving his capital from Thebes to a new city dedicated to Aton (Akhetaton, "the horizon of Aton," modern Tell el-Amarna). Within a generation after Amenhotep's death, his religious policy was reversed and the capital was restored to Thebes. Italics indicate an uncertain translation.

---

Praise of Reharakhti,[1] Rejoicing on the Horizon, in His Name as Shu Who Is in the Aton-disc,[2] living forever and ever; the living great Aton who is in jubilee, lord of all that the Aton encircles, lord of heaven, lord of earth, lord of the House of Aton in Akhetaton; [and praise of] the King of Upper and Lower Egypt, who lives on truth, the Lord of the Two Lands:[3] Neferkheperure Waenre;[4] the Son of Re, who lives on truth, the Lord of Diadems: Akhenaton, long in his lifetime; [and praise of] the Chief Wife of the King, his beloved, the Lady of the Two Lands: Neferneferuaton[5] Nefertiti, living, healthy, and youthful forever and ever; [by] the Fan-Bearer on the Right Hand of the King ... Eye. He[6] says:

Thou appearest beautifully on the horizon of heaven,
Thou living Aton, the beginning of life!

When thou art risen on the eastern horizon,
Thou hast filled every land with thy beauty.
Thou art gracious, great, glistening, and high over
    every land;
Thy rays encompass the lands to the limit of all that
    thou hast made:
As thou art Re, thou reachest to the end of them;
[Thou] subduest them [for] thy beloved son.
Though thou art far away, thy rays are on earth;
Though thou art in *their* faces, *no one knows thy*
    *going.*

When thou settest in the western horizon,
The land is in darkness, in the manner of death.
They sleep in a room, with heads wrapped up,
Nor sees one eye the other.

---

1    I.e., a synthesis of the gods Re and a lesser solar god of the horizon, Harakhti.
2    The Aton had a dogmatic name written within a royal cartouche and including the three old solar deities. Re, Harakhti, and Shu. The cartouche was revised in Akhenaton's ninth year to include only Re.
3    Upper and Lower Egypt.
4    I.e., Amenhotep IV. "Neferkheperu" means "Beautiful are the Manifestations of Re." On Re, see above, n 1.
5    "Neferneferuaton": "Perfect is the goodness of Aton."
6    I.e., Eye, the Fan-Bearer.

All their goods which are under their heads might be
    stolen,
[But] they would not perceive [it].
Every lion is come forth from his den;
All creeping things, they sing.
Darkness *is a shroud*, and the earth is in stillness.
For he who made them rests in his horizon.

At daybreak, when thou arisest on the horizon,
When thou shinest as the Aton by day,
Thou drivest away the darkness and givest thy rays.
The Two Lands are in festivity *every day*,
Awake and standing upon [their] feet,
For thou hast raised them up.
Washing their bodies, taking (their) clothing,
Their arms are [raised] in praise at thy appearance.
All the world, they do their work.

All beasts are content with their pasturage;
Trees and plants are flourishing.
The birds which fly from their nests,
Their wings are [stretched out] in praise to thy *ka*.[7]
All beasts spring upon [their] feet.
Whatever flies and alights,
They live when thou hast risen [for] them.
The ships are sailing north and south as well,
For every way is open at thy appearance.
The fish in the river dart before thy face;
Thy rays are in the midst of the great green sea.

Creator of seed in women,
Thou who makest fluid into man,
Who maintainest the son in the womb of his mother,
Who soothest him with that which stills his weeping,
Thou nurse [even] in the womb,
Who givest breath to sustain all that he has made!
When he descends from the womb to *breathe*
On the day when he is born,
Thou openest his mouth completely,
Thou suppliest his necessities.
When the chick in the egg speaks within the shell,
Thou givest him breath within it to maintain him.

When thou hast made him his fulfillment within the
    egg, to break it,
He comes forth from the egg to speak at his complet-
    ed [time];
He walks upon his legs when he comes forth from it.

How manifold it is, what thou hast made!
They are hidden from the face [of man].
O sole god, like whom there is no other!
Thou didst create the world according to thy desire,
Whilst thou wert alone;
All men, cattle, and wild beasts,
Whatever is on earth, going upon [its] feet,
And what is on high, flying with its wings.

The countries of Syria and Nubia, the *land* of Egypt,
Thou settest every man in his place,
Thou suppliest their necessities:
Everyone has his food, and his time of life is
    reckoned.
Their tongues are separate in speech,
And their natures as well;
Their skins are distinguished,
As thou distinguishest the foreign peoples.
Thou makest a Nile in the underworld,
Thou bringest it forth as thou desirest
To maintain the people [of Egypt]
According as thou madest them for thyself,
The lord of all of them, wearying [himself] with
    them,
The lord of every land, rising for them,
The Aton of the day, great of majesty.

All distant foreign countries, thou makest their life
    [also],
For thou hast set a Nile in heaven,
That it may descend for them and make waves upon
    the mountains,
Like the great green sea,
To water their fields in their towns.
How effective they are, thy plans, O lord of
    eternity!

---

7  Egyptian belief held that each person, including the gods, had three aspects: body, mind, and the "ka," a kind of spiritual
    double.

The Nile in heaven, it is for the foreign peoples
And for the beasts of every desert that go upon
[their] feet;
[While the true] Nile comes from the underworld for
Egypt.

Thy rays suckle every meadow.
When thou risest, they live, they grow for thee.
Thou makest the seasons in order to rear all that thou
has made,
The winter to cool them,
And the heat that *they* may taste thee.
Thou hast made the distant sky in order to rise
therein,
In order to see all that thou dost make.
Whilst thou wert alone,
Rising in thy form as the living Aton,
Appearing, shining, *withdrawing or approaching,*
Thou madest millions of forms of thyself alone.
Cities, towns, fields, road, and river–
Every eye beholds thee over against them,
For thou art the Aton of the day over *the earth*....

Thou art in my heart,
And there is no other that knows thee
Save thy son Neferkheperure Waenre,
For thou hast made him well-versed in thy plans and
in thy strength.

The world came into being by thy hand,
According as thou hast made them.
When thou hast risen they live,
When thou settest they die.
Thou art lifetime thy own self,
For one lives [only] through thee.
Eyes are [fixed] on beauty until thou settest.
All work is laid aside when thou settest in the west.
[But] when [thou] risest [again],
[*Everything is*] made to flourish for the king, ...
Since thou didst found the earth
And raise them up for thy son,
Who came forth from thy body:
the King of Upper and Lower Egypt, ... Akhenaton, ...
and the Chief Wife of the King ...
Nefertiti, living and youthful forever and ever.

# 7

## FIRST BOOK OF KINGS, 15–19

The books of Kings make up part of the Hebrew sacred texts known to Christians as the Old Testament and to Jews and others as the Hebrew Bible. The events recounted in the portion of 1 Kings which appears here occurred in the late tenth through mid-ninth century BC, a period in which there were two Hebrew kingdoms, the northern kingdom of Israel and the southern kingdom of Judah.

Like other books of the Bible, 1 Kings has a complicated origin. It was originally part of a longer continuous narrative of the Hebrew people, represented in the modern Bible by the two books of Samuel, 1 Kings and 2 Kings. Modern scholars conclude that much of 1 Kings was written by some person in the late seventh century BC. For the portion of 1 Kings reproduced here, that writer drew on earlier written accounts of the eighth and seventh centuries, now lost, and on oral tradition. This material continued to be revised in succeeding centuries, perhaps as late as the second century BC.

---

15 Now in the eighteenth year of King Jeroboam[1] the son of Nebat, Abijam began to reign over Judah. He reigned three years in Jerusalem, and his mother's name was Maacah the daughter of Abishalom. And he walked in all the sins of his father,[2] which he had done before him, and his heart was not perfect with the Lord his God, as the heart of David[3] his father. Nevertheless for David's sake did the Lord his God give him a lamp in Jerusalem, not set up his son after him, and to establish Jerusalem because David did that which was right in the eyes of the Lord, and turned not aside from anything that he commanded him all the days of his life, save only in the matter of Uriah the Hittite.[4] Now there was war between Rehoboam[5] and Jeroboam all the days of his life. And the rest of the acts of Abijam, and all that he did, are they not written in the book of the chronicles of the kings of Judah?[6] And there was war between Abijam and Jeroboam. And Abijam slept with his fathers; and they buried him in the city of David, and Asa his son reigned in his stead.

And in the twentieth year of Jeroboam, king of

---

1  King of Israel. He transgressed against the Hebrew God, Yaweh, by setting up golden calves for worship, among other acts.
2  Abijam's father, King Rehoboam, had committed various transgressions against Yaweh, the Hebrew god.
3  This is King David (early tenth century BC), perhaps the best known of the Hebrew kings, and ancestor of Abijam.
4  David had sent Uriah the Hittite to his death so he could have Uriah's wife, Bathsheba. This had led to a rebuke from Yaweh delivered by the prophet Nathan.
5  Abijam's predecessor.
6  This source is now lost.

Israel, Asa began to reign over Judah. And he reigned forty and one years in Jerusalem, and his mother's name was Maacah the daughter of Abishalom. And Asa did that which was right in the eyes of the Lord, as did David his father. And he put away the sodomites out of the land, and removed all the idols that his fathers had made. And also Maacah his mother he removed from being queen because she had made an abominable image for Asherah;[7] and Asa cut down her image, and burned it at the brook Kidron. But the high places[8] were not taken away. Nevertheless the heart of Asa was perfect with the Lord all his days. And he brought into the house of the Lord the things that his father had dedicated, and the things that he himself had dedicated, silver, and gold, and vessels. And there was war between Asa and Baasha, king of Israel, all their days. And Baasha, king of Israel, went up against Judah, and built Ramah, that he might not suffer any to go out or come in to Asa, king of Judah. Then Asa took all the silver and the gold that were left in the treasures of the house of the Lord, and the treasures of the king's house, and delivered them into the hand of his servants. And King Asa sent them to Ben-hadad, the son of Tabrimmon, the son of Hezion, king of Syria, that dwelt at Damascus, saying, "There is a league between me and you, between my father and your father; behold, I have sent to you a present of silver and gold; go, break your league with Baasha, king of Israel, that he may depart from me." And Ben-hadad hearkened to King Asa, and sent the captains of his armies against the cities of Israel, and smote Ijon, and Dan, and Abel-bethmaacah, and all Chinneroth, with all the land of Naphtali. And it came to pass, when Baasha heard thereof, that he left off the building of Ramah, and dwelt in Tirzah. Then King Asa made a proclamation to all Judah; none was exempted; and they carried away the stones of Ramah, and the timber thereof, wherewith Baasha had built, and King Asa built therewith Geba of Benjamin, and Mizpah. Now the rest of all the acts of Asa, and all his might, and all that he did, and the cities which he built, are they not written in the book of the chronicles of the kings of Judah? But in the time of his old age he was diseased in his feet. And Asa slept with his fathers, and was buried with his fathers in the city of David his father, and Jehoshaphat his son reigned in his stead.

And Nadab the son of Jeroboam began to reign over Israel in the second year of Asa, king of Judah, and he reigned over Israel two years. And he did that which was evil in the sight of the Lord, and walked in the way of his father, and in his sin wherewith he made Israel to sin. And Baasha the son of Ahijah, of the house of Issachar, conspired against him; and Baasha smote Nadab at Gibbethon, which belonged to the Philistines, for Nadab and all Israel were laying siege to Gibbethon. Even in the third year of Asa, king of Judah, did Baasha slay him, and reigned in his stead. And it came to pass that, as soon as he was king, he smote all the house of Jeroboam; he left not to Jeroboam any that breathed, until he had destroyed him, according to the saying of the Lord, which he spoke by the hand of his servant Ahijah the Shilonite: for the sins of Jeroboam which he sinned, and wherewith he made Israel to sin because of his provocation wherewith he provoked the Lord, the God of Israel, to anger. Now the rest of the acts of Nadab, and all that he did, are they not written in the book of the chronicles of the kings of Israel?[9] And there was war between Asa and Baasha, king of Israel, all their days.

In the third year of Asa, king of Judah, Baasha the son of Ahijah began to reign over all Israel in Tirzah, and reigned twenty and four years. And he did that which was evil in the sight of the Lord, and walked in the way of Jeroboam, and in his sin wherewith he made Israel to sin.

16    And the word of the Lord came to Jehu the son of Hanani against Baasha, saying, "Forasmuch as I exalted you out of the dust, and made you prince over my people Israel, and you have walked in the way of Jeroboam, and have made my people Israel to sin, to provoke me to anger with their sins, behold, I will utterly sweep away Baasha and his house; and I will make

---

7    A Canaanite goddess.
8    Shrines on hills to other gods.
9    A source now lost.

your house like the house of Jeroboam the son of Nebat. Whoever belongs to Baasha that dies in the city shall the dogs eat; and whoever belongs to him that dies in the field shall the fowls of the air eat." Now the rest of the acts of Baasha, and what he did, and his might, are they not written in the book of the chronicles of the kings of Israel? And Baasha slept with his fathers, and was buried in Tirzah; and Elah his son reigned in his stead. And moreover by the hand of the prophet Jehu the son of Hanani came the word of the Lord against Baasha, and against his house, both because of all the evil that he did in the sight of the Lord, to provoke him to anger with the work of his hands, in being like the house of Jeroboam, and because he smote him.

In the twenty and sixth year of Asa, king of Judah, Elah the son of Baasha began to reign over Israel in Tirzah, and reigned two years. And his servant Zimri, captain of half his chariots, conspired against him; now he was in Tirzah, drinking himself drunk in the house of Arza, which was over the household in Tirzah, and Zimri went in and smote him, and killed him, in the twenty and seventh year of Asa, of Judah, and reigned in his stead. And it came to pass, when he began to reign, as soon as he sat on his throne, that he smote all the house of Baasha; he left him not a single man child, neither of his kinsfolk, nor of his friends. Thus did Zimri destroy all the house of Baasha, according to the word of the Lord, which he spoke against Baasha by Jehu the prophet, for all the sins of Baasha, and the sins of Elah his son, which they sinned, and wherewith they made Israel to sin, to provoke the Lord, the God of Israel, to anger with their vanities. Now the rest of the acts of Elah, and all that he did, are they not written in the book of the chronicles of the kings of Israel?

In the twenty and seventh year of Asa, king of Judah, did Zimri reign seven days in Tirzah. Now the people were encamped against Gibbethon, which belonged to the Philistines. And the people that were encamped heard say, "Zimri has conspired, and has also smited the king," wherefore all Israel made Omri, the captain of the host, king over Israel that day in the camp. And Omri went up from Gibbethon, and all Israel with him, and they besieged Tirzah. And it came to pass, when Zimri saw that the city was taken that

he went into the castle of the king's house, and burned the king's house over him with fire, and died, for his sins which he sinned in doing that which was evil in the sight of the Lord, in walking in the way of Jeroboam, and in his sin which he did, to make Israel to sin. Now the rest of the acts of Zimri, and his treason that he wrought, are they not written in the book of the chronicles of the kings of Israel?

Then were the people of Israel divided into two parts: half of the people followed Tibni the son of Ginath, to make him king, and half followed Omri. But the people that followed Omri prevailed against the people that followed Tibni the son of Ginath. So Tibni died, and Omri reigned. In the thirty and first year of Asa, king of Judah, Omri began to reign over Israel, and reigned twelve years: he reigned six years in Tirzah. And he bought the hill Samaria of Shemer for two talents of silver, and he built on the hill, and called the name of the city which he built, after the name of Shemer, the owner of the hill, Samaria. And Omri did that which was evil in the sight of the Lord, and dealt wickedly more than all that were before him. For he walked in all the way of Jeroboam the son of Nebat, and in his sins wherewith he made Israel to sin, to provoke the Lord, the God of Israel, to anger with their vanities. Now the rest of the acts of Omri which he did, and his might that he showed, are they not written in the book of the chronicles of the kings of Israel? So Omri slept with his fathers, and was buried in Samaria, and Ahab his son reigned in his stead.

And in the thirty and eighth year of Asa, king of Judah, Ahab the son of Omri began to reign over Israel, and Ahab the son of Omri reigned over Israel in Samaria twenty and two years. And Ahab the son of Omri did that which was evil in the sight of the Lord more than all that were before him. And it came to pass, as if it had been a light thing for him to walk in the sins of Jeroboam the son of Nebat, that he took to wife Jezebel the daughter of Ethbaal, king of the Zidonians, and went and served Baal, and worshipped him. And he reared up an altar for Baal in the house of Baal, which he had built in Samaria. And Ahab made an image; and Ahab did yet more to provoke the Lord, the God of Israel, to anger than all the kings of Israel that were before him.

In his days did Hiel the Bethelite build Jericho; he

laid the foundation thereof with the loss of Abiram his firstborn, and set up the gates thereof with the loss of his youngest son Segub, according to the word of the Lord, which he spake by the hand of Joshua the son of Nun.

17 And Elijah the Tishbite, who was of the sojourners of Gilead, said to Ahab, "As the Lord, the God of Israel, lives, before whom I stand, there shall not be dew or rain these years, but according to my word." And the word of the Lord came to him,[10] saying, "Go hence, and turn eastward, and hide yourself by the brook Cherith, that is before Jordan. And it shall be that you shall drink of the brook; and I have commanded the ravens to feed you there." So he went and did according to the word of the Lord, for he went and dwelt by the brook Cherith, that is before Jordan. And the ravens brought him bread and flesh in the morning, and bread and flesh in the evening; and he drank of the brook. And it came to pass after a while that the brook dried up, because there was no rain in the land.

And the word of the Lord came to him, saying, "Arise, go to Zarephath, which belongs to Zidon, and dwell there; behold, I have commanded a widow woman there to sustain you." So he arose and went to Zarephath; and when he came to the gate of the city, behold, a widow woman was there gathering sticks; and he called to her, and said, "Fetch me, I pray you, a little water in a vessel, that I may drink." And as she was going to fetch it, he called to her, and said, "Bring me, I pray you, a morsel of bread in your hand." And she said, "As the Lord your God lives, I do not have bread, but a handful of meal in a barrel, and a little oil in a jar; and, behold, I am gathering two sticks, that I may go in and prepare it for me and my son, that we may eat it, and die." And Elijah said to her, "Fear not; go and do as you have said, but make me thereof a little bread first, and bring it forth to me, and afterward make for you and for your son. For thus says the Lord, the God of Israel, 'The barrel of meal shall not waste, neither shall the jar of oil fail, until the day that the Lord sends rain upon the earth.'" And she went and did according to the saying of Elijah; and she, and he, and her house, did eat many days. The barrel of meal did not waste, neither did the jar of oil fail, according to the word of the Lord, which he spoke by Elijah. And it came to pass after these things that the son of the woman, the mistress of the house, fell sick; and his sickness was so sore that there was no breath left in him. And she said to Elijah, "What have I to do with you, you man of God? You have come to me to bring my sin to remembrance, and to slay my son!" And he said to her, "Give me your son." And he took him out of her bosom, and carried him up into the chamber, where he abode, and laid him upon his own bed. And he cried to the Lord, and said, "O Lord my God, have you also brought evil upon the widow with whom I sojourn, by slaying her son?" And he stretched himself upon the child three times, and cried to the Lord, and said, "O Lord my God, I pray you, let this child's soul come into him again. And the Lord hearkened to the voice of Elijah, and the soul of the child came into him again, and he revived. And Elijah took the child, and brought him down out of the chamber into the house, and delivered him to his mother, and Elijah said, "See, your son lives." And the woman said to Elijah, "Now I know that you are a man of God, and that the word of the Lord in your mouth is truth."

18 And it came to pass after many days that the word of the Lord came to Elijah in the third year, saying, "Go, show yourself to Ahab, and I will send rain upon the earth." And Elijah went to show himself to Ahab. And the famine was sore in Samaria. And Ahab called Obadiah, who was over the household. (Now Obadiah feared the Lord greatly, for it was so, when Jezebel cut off the prophets of the Lord, that Obadiah took a hundred prophets, and hid them by fifty in a cave, and fed them with bread and water.) And Ahab said to Obadiah, "Go through the land, to all the fountains of water, and to all the brooks, peradventure we may find grass and save the horses and mules alive, that we lose not all the beasts." So they divided the land between them to pass throughout it; Ahab went one way by himself, and Obadiah went another way by himself. And as Obadiah was on his way, behold, Elijah met him, and he knew him, and fell on his face, and said, "Is it you, my lord Elijah?" And he answered

---

10  I.e., to Elijah.

him, "It is I; go, tell your lord: Behold, Elijah is here.'"
And he said, "Wherein have I sinned, that you would
deliver your servant into the hand of Ahab, to slay
me? As the Lord your God lives, there is no nation or
kingdom where my lord has not sent to seek you; and
when they said, 'He is not here,' he took an oath of the
kingdom and nation, that they found you not. And
now you say, 'Go, tell your lord: Behold, Elijah is here.'
And it shall come to pass, as soon as I am gone from
you, that the spirit of the Lord shall carry you whither
I do not know; and so when I come and tell Ahab, and
he cannot find you, he shall slay me; but I your servant
fear the Lord from my youth. Was it not told my lord
what I did when Jezebel slew the prophets of the Lord,
how I hid a hundred men of the Lord's prophets by
fifty in a cave, and fed them with bread and water?
And now you say, 'Go, tell your lord: Behold. Elijah is
here,' and he shall slay me." And Elijah said, "As the
Lord of hosts lives, before whom I stand, I will surely
show myself to him today." So Obadiah went to meet
Ahab, and told him; and Ahab went to meet Elijah.
And it came to pass, when Ahab saw Elijah, that Ahab
said to him, "Is it you, you troubler of Israel?" And he
answered, "I have not troubled Israel; but you, and
your father's house, in that you have forsaken the
commandments of the Lord, and you have followed
the Baals. Now therefore send for, and gather to me,
all Israel on mount Carmel, and the prophets of Baal
four hundred and fifty, and the prophets of the Asherah four hundred, which eat at Jezebel's table."

So Ahab sent to all the children of Israel, and gathered the prophets together on mount Carmel. And
Elijah came near to all the people, and said, "How
long do you halt between two opinions? If the
Lord be God, follow him: but if Baal, then follow
him." And the people answered him not a word. Then
said Elijah to the people, "I, even I alone, am left a
prophet of the Lord, but Baal's prophets are four hundred and fifty men. Let them therefore give us two
bulls; and let them choose one bull for themselves,
and cut it in pieces, and lay it on the wood, and put no
fire under. And I will prepare the other bull, and lay it
on the wood, and put no fire under. And you call on
the name of your god, and I will call on the name of
the Lord. And the God that answers by fire, let him be
God." And all the people answered and said, "It is

well spoken." And Elijah said to the prophets of Baal,
"Choose one bull for yourselves, and prepare it first,
for you are many; and call on the name of your god,
but put no fire under." And they took the bull which
was given them, and they prepared it, and called on
the name of Baal from morning even until noon, saying, "O Baal, hear us." But there was no voice, nor any
that answered. And they leaped about the altar which
was made. And it came to pass at noon, that Elijah
mocked them, and said, "Cry aloud, for he is a god;
either he is musing, or he is gone aside, or he is on a
journey, or peradventure he sleeps, and must be awakened." And they cried aloud, and cut themselves after
their manner with knives and lances, until the blood
gushed out upon them. And it was so, when midday
was past, that they prophesied until the time of the
offering of the evening offering; but there was neither
voice, nor any to answer, nor any that regarded. And
Elijah said to all the people, "Come near me; and all
the people came near him. And he repaired the altar of
the Lord that was thrown down. And Elijah took
twelve stones according to the number of the tribes of
the sons of Jacob, to whom the word of the Lord came,
saying, "Israel shall be your name." And with the
stones he built an altar in the name of the Lord; and he
made a trench about the altar, as great as would contain two measures of seed. And he put the wood in
order, and cut the bull in pieces, and laid it on the
wood. And he said, "Fill four barrels with water, and
pour it on the burned offering, and on the wood." And
he said, "Do it a second time," and they did it the second time. And he said, "Do it a third time," and they
did it the third time. And the water ran around the
altar; and he filled the trench also with water. And it
came to pass at the time of the offering of the evening
offering, that Elijah the prophet came near, and said,
"O Lord, the God of Abraham, of Isaac, and of Israel,
let it be known this day that you are God in Israel, and
that I am your servant, and that I have done all these
things at your word. Hear me, O Lord, hear me, that
this people may know that you, Lord, are God, and
that you have turned their heart back again." Then the
fire of the Lord fell, and consumed the burned offering, and the wood, and the stones, and the dust, and
licked up the water that was in the trench. And when
all the people saw it, they fell on their faces, and they

said, "The Lord, he is God; the Lord, he is God." And Elijah said to them, "Take the prophets of Baal; let not one of them escape." And they took them, and Elijah brought them down to the brook Kishon, and slew them there. And Elijah said to Ahab, "Get up, eat and drink, for there is the sound of abundance of rain." So Ahab went up to eat and to drink. And Elijah went up to the top of Carmel, and he bowed himself down upon the earth, and put his face between his knees. And he said to his servant, "Go up now, look toward the sea." And he went up, and looked, and said, "There is nothing." And he said, "Go again seven times." And it came to pass at the seventh time, that he said, "Behold, there arises a cloud out of the sea, as small as a man's hand." And he said, "Go up, say to Ahab, 'Make ready your chariot, and go down so that the rain does not stop you.'" And it came to pass in a little while, that the heavens grew black with clouds and wind, and there was a great rain. And Ahab rode, and went to Jezreel. And the hand of the Lord was on Elijah; and he girded up his loins, and ran before Ahab to the entrance of Jezreel.

19 And Ahab told Jezebel all that Elijah had done, and withal how he had slain all the prophets with the sword. Then Jezebel sent a messenger to Elijah, saying, "So let the gods do to me, and more also, if I do not make your life as the life of one of them by tomorrow about this time." And when he saw that, he arose, and went for his life, and came to Beersheba, which belongs to Judah, and left his servant there. But he himself went a day's journey into the wilderness, and came and sat down under a juniper tree; and he requested for himself that he might die, and said, "It is enough; now, O Lord, take away my life, for I am not better than my fathers." And he lay down and slept under a juniper tree; and, behold, an angel touched him and said to him, "Arise and eat." And he looked, and, behold, there was at his head a cake baked on the coals, and a jar of water. And he did eat and drink, and laid him down again. And the angel of the Lord came again the second time and touched him, and said, "Arise and eat, because the journey is too great for you." And he arose, and did eat and drink, and went in the strength of that meat forty days and forty nights to Horeb the mountain of God. And he came thither to a cave, and lodged there; and, behold, the word of the Lord came to him,

and he said to him, "What are you doing here, Elijah?" And he said, "I have been very jealous for the Lord, the God of hosts; for the children of Israel have forsaken your covenant, thrown down your altars, and slain your prophets with the sword; and I, even I alone, am left; and they seek my life, to take it away." And he said, "Go forth, and stand upon the mountain before the Lord." And, behold, the Lord passed by, and a great and strong wind rent the mountains, and broke in pieces the rocks before the Lord, but the Lord was not in the wind; and after the wind an earthquake, but the Lord was not in the earthquake; and after the earthquake a fire, but the Lord was not in the fire; and after the fire a still small voice. And it was so, when Elijah heard it, that he wrapped his face in his mantle, and went out, and stood in the entrance of the cave. And, behold, there came a voice to him, and said, "What are you doing here, Elijah?" And he said, "I have been very jealous for the Lord, the God of hosts; for the children of Israel have forsaken your covenant, thrown down your altars, and slain your prophets with the sword; and I, even I alone, am left; and they seek my life, to take it away." And the Lord said to him, "Go, return on your way to the wilderness of Damascus; and when you arrive, you shall anoint Hazael to be king over Syria; and you shall anoint Jehu the son of Nimshi to be king over Israel; and you shall anoint Elisha the son of Shaphat of Abel-meholah to be prophet in your place. And it shall come to pass, that him that escapes from the sword of Hazael shall slay Jehu, and him that escapes from the sword of Jehu shall slay Elisha. Yet will I leave me seven thousand in Israel, all the knees which have not bowed to Baal, and every mouth which has not kissed him. So he departed thence, and found Elisha the son of Shaphat, who was plowing, with twelve yoke of oxen before him, and he with the twelfth; and Elijah passed over to him, and cast his mantle upon him. And he left the oxen, and ran after Elijah, and said, "Let me, I pray you, kiss my father and my mother, and then I will follow you." And he said to him, "Go back again; for what have I done to you?" And he returned from following him, and took the yoke of oxen, and slew them, and boiled their flesh with the instruments of the oxen, and gave to the people, and they did eat. Then he arose, and went after Elijah, and ministered to him.

# 8

## BOOK OF JOB
### 1–14, 21–24, 38–42

The book of Job makes up part of the Hebrew sacred text, known to Christians as the Old Testament and to Jews and others as the Hebrew Bible. A prologue and an epilogue, both written in prose, are marked here in *italics*. These portions are believed to be the oldest elements of the work. The bulk, written in verse, is held to have been composed some time *c.* 580-400 BC. (Two other sections, chapters 28 and 32-37, which do not appear here, are thought to be even later additions.)

---

1   *There was a man in the land of Uz[1] whose name was Job; and that man was perfect and upright, and one that feared God, and eschewed evil. And there were born to him seven sons and three daughters. His substance also was 7,000 sheep, and 3,000 camels, and 500 yoke of oxen, and 500 she-asses, and a very great household, so that this man was the greatest of all the children of the East. And his sons went and held a feast in the house of each one upon his day to do so, and they sent and called for their three sisters to eat and to drink with them. And it was so, when the days of their feasting were gone about, that Job sent and sanctified them, and rose up early in the morning, and offered burned offerings according to the number of them all; for Job said, "It may be that my sons have sinned, and renounced God in their hearts." Thus did Job continually.*

*Now there was a day when the sons of God came to present themselves before the Lord, and the Adversary[2] came also among them.*

*And the Lord said to the Adversary, "Where are you coming from?"*

*Then the Adversary answered the Lord, and said, "From going to and fro on the earth, and from walking up and down on it."*

*And the Lord said to the Adversary, "Have you considered my servant Job? For there is none like him on the earth, a perfect and an upright man, one that fears God, and eschews evil."*

*Then the Adversary answered the Lord, and said, "Does Job fear God for nought? Have you not made a hedge about him, and about his house, and about all that he has, on every side? You have blessed the work of his hands, and his substance is increased in the land. But put forth your hand now, and touch all that he has, and he will renounce you to your face."*

*And the Lord said to the Adversary, "Behold, all that he has is in your power; only do not put forth your hand on himself."*

*So the Adversary went forth from the presence of the Lord. And it fell on a day when his sons and his daughters were eating and drinking wine in their eldest brother's*

---

1   A place of uncertain location, perhaps northern Arabia.
2   The translation of the term "Satan."

*house, that there came a messenger to Job, and said, "The oxen were plowing, and the asses feeding beside them; and the Sabeans fell upon them, and took them away; yea, they have slain the servants with the edge of the sword; and I alone have escaped to tell you!"*

*While he was yet speaking, there came also another, and said, "The fire of God has fallen from heaven, and has burned up the sheep, and the servants, and consumed them; and I alone have escaped to tell you!"*

*While he was yet speaking, there came also another, and said, "The Chaldeans made three bands, and fell upon the camels, and have taken them away, yea, and slain the servants with the edge of the sword; and I alone have escaped to tell you!"*

*While he was yet speaking, there came also another, and said, "Your sons and your daughters were eating and drinking wine in their eldest brother's house, and, behold, there came a great wind from the wilderness, and smote the four corners of the house, and it fell upon the young men, and they are dead; and I alone have escaped to tell you!"*

*Then Job arose, and rent his mantle, and shaved his head, and fell down upon the ground, and worshipped; and he said, "Naked I came out of my mother's womb, And naked shall I return there! The Lord gave, and the Lord has taken away!*

*Blessed be the Name of the Lord!"*

*In all this Job did not sin, nor charged God with wrongfulness.*

2 *Again there was a day when the sons of God came to present themselves before the Lord, and the Adversary came also among them to present himself before the Lord.*

*And the Lord said to the Adversary, "Where are you coming from?"*

*And the Adversary answered the Lord, and said, "From going to and fro on the earth, and from walking up and down on it."*

*And the Lord said to the Adversary, "Have you considered my servant Job? For there is none like him on the earth, a perfect and an upright man, one that fears God, and eschews evil; and he still holds fast his integrity, although you moved me against him, to destroy him without cause."*

*And the Adversary answered the Lord, and said, "Skin for skin, yea, all that a man has will he give for his life. But put forth your hand now, and touch his bone and his flesh, and he will renounce you to your face."*

*And the Lord said to the Adversary, "Behold, he is in your hand; only spare his life."*

*So the Adversary went forth from the presence of the Lord, and smote Job with sore boils from the sole of his foot to his crown. And he took him a potsherd to scrape himself withal; and he sat among the ashes.*

*Then his wife said to him, "Do you still hold fast your integrity? Renounce God, and die."*

*But he said to her, "You speak as one of the foolish women speaks. What? shall we receive good at the hand of God, and shall we not receive evil?"*

*In all this Job did not sin with his lips.*

*Now when Job's three friends heard of all this evil that was come upon him, they came every one from his own place: Eliphaz the Temanite, and Bildad the Shuhite, and Zophar the Naamathite; and they made an appointment together to come to bemoan him and to comfort him. And when they lifted up their eyes far off, and did not know him, they lifted up their voice, and wept; and every one rent his mantle, and sprinkled dust upon their heads toward heaven. So they sat down with him upon the ground for seven days and seven nights, and none spoke a word to him; for they saw that his grief was very great.*

3   After this Job opened his mouth, and cursed the
     day of his birth,
"Let the day perish wherein I was born
And the night which said, 'There is a male child
     conceived!'
Let that day be darkness;
Let God not regard it from above,
Neither let the light shine upon it!
Let darkness and the shadow of death claim it for
     their own;
Let a cloud dwell upon it;
Let all that makes black the day terrify it.
As for that night, let thick darkness seize upon it,
Let it not rejoice among the days of the year;
Let it not come into the number of the months!
Lo, let that night be barren;
Let no joyful voice come therein!
Let them curse it that curse the day,
Who are ready to rouse up Leviathan![3]

---

3   A giant sea creature.

Let the stars of the twilight thereof be dark!
Let it look for light, but have none;
Neither let it behold the eyelids of the morning,
Because it did not shut up the doors of my mother's
    womb,
Nor hid trouble from my eyes!
Why did I not die from the womb?
Why did I not give up the ghost when I came out of
    the belly?
Why did the knees receive me?
Or why the breasts, that I should suck?
For now I would have lain down and been quiet;
I would have slept; then I would have been at rest,
With kings and counsellors of the earth,
Which built solitary piles for themselves;
Or with princes that had gold,
Who filled their houses with silver;
Or as a hidden untimely birth I had not been,
As infants which never saw light.
There the wicked cease from troubling;
And there the weary are at rest.
There the prisoners are at ease together;
They do not hear the voice of the taskmaster.
The small and great are there;
And the servant is free from his master.
Wherefore is light given to him that is in misery,
And life to the bitter in soul,
Which long for death, but it does not come,
And dig for it more than for hidden treasures;
Which rejoice exceedingly,
And are glad when they can find the grave?
Why is light given to a man whose way is hidden,
And whom God has hedged in?
For my sighing comes before I eat,
And my roarings are poured out like water.
For the thing which I fear comes upon me,
And that which I am afraid of comes to me.
I am not at ease, neither am I quiet,
Neither have I rest, but trouble comes!"
4   Then Eliphaz the Temanite answered,
"If one tries to commune with you, will you be
    grieved?
But who can withhold himself from speaking?
Behold, you have instructed many,
And you have strengthened weak hands.
Your words have upheld him that was falling,

And you have confirmed feeble knees.
But now it comes to you, and you faint;
It touches you, and you are troubled.
Is not your fear of God your confidence,
And your hope the integrity of your ways?
Remember, I pray you, whoever perished, being
    innocent?
Or where were the upright cut off?
According as I have seen, they that plow iniquity,
And sow trouble, reap the same.
By the breath of God they perish,
And by the blast of his anger they are consumed.
The roaring of the lion, and the voice of the fierce
    lion,
And the teeth of the young lions are broken.
The old lion perishes for lack of prey,
And the whelps of the lioness are scattered abroad.
Now a thing was secretly brought to me,
And my ear received a whisper thereof.
In thoughts from the visions of the night,
When deep sleep falls on men,
Fear came upon me, and trembling,
Which made all my bones shake.
Then a spirit passed before my face;
The hair of my flesh stood up.
It stood still, but I could not discern the appearance
    thereof;
A form was before my eyes:
There was silence, and I heard a voice, saying,
'Shall mortal man be just before God?
Shall a man be pure before his Maker?
Behold, he puts no trust in his servants;
And he charges his angels with folly;
How much more them that dwell in houses of clay,
Whose foundation is in the dust,
Which are crushed before the moth!
Between morning and evening they are destroyed;
They perish forever without any regarding it.
Is not their tent-cord plucked up within them?
They die, without wisdom.'
5   Call out now; is there any that will answer you?
And to which of the holy ones will you turn?
For vexation kills the foolish man,
And jealousy slays the simple one.
I have seen the foolish taking root,
But suddenly I cursed his habitation.

His children are far from safety,
And they are crushed in the gate,
Neither is there any to deliver them.
Whose harvest the hungry eat up,
And take it even out of the thorns,
And the snare gapes for their substance.
For affliction does not come forth of the dust,
Neither does trouble spring out of the ground;
But man is born to trouble,
As the sparks fly upward.
But as for me, I would seek God,
And to God would I commit my cause,
Who does great and unsearchable things,
Marvellous things without number;
Who gives rain upon the earth,
And sends waters upon the fields;
So that he sets up on high those that are low,
And those which mourn are exalted to safety.
He frustrates the devices of the crafty,
So that their hands cannot perform their enterprise.
He takes the wise in their own craftiness,
And the counsel of the forward is carried headlong.
They meet with darkness in the daytime,
And grope at noonday as in the night.
But he saves from the sword of their mouth,
Even the needy from the hand of the mighty.
So the poor have hope,
And iniquity stops up her mouth.
Behold, happy is the man whom God corrects;
Therefore do not despise the chastening of the
    Almighty.
For he makes sore, and binds up;
He wounds, and his hands make whole.
He shall deliver you in six troubles;
Yea, in seven there shall no evil touch you.
In famine he shall redeem you from death;
And in war from the power of the sword.
You shall be hidden from the scourge of the tongue;
Neither shall you be afraid of destruction when it
    comes.
At destruction and dearth you shall laugh;
Neither shall you be afraid of the beasts of the earth.
For you shall be in league with the stones of the field,
And the beasts of the field shall be at peace with you.
And you shall know that your tent is in peace,
And you shall visit your fold and shall miss nothing.

You shall know also that your seed shall be great,
And your offspring be as the grass of the earth.
You shall come to your grave in a full age,
Like a sheaf of grain comes in its season.
Lo this, we have searched it out, so it is;
Hear it, and know it for your good."
6   Then Job answered,
"Oh that my vexation were but weighed,
And my calamity laid in the balances together with
    it!
For now it would be heavier than the sand of the
    seas,
Therefore my words have been rash.
For the arrows of the Almighty are within me,
The poison of which my spirit drinks up;
The terrors of God set themselves in array against
    me.
Does the wild ass bray when he has grass?
Or does the ox low over his fodder?
Can that which has no savor be eaten without salt?
Or is there any taste in the white of an egg?
These things my soul refused to touch,
They are as my loathsome food.
Oh that I might have my request,
And that God would grant me the thing that I long
    for!
Even that it would please God to crush me;
That he would let loose his hand and cut me off!
Then should I yet have comfort;
Yea, I would exult in pain that does not spare,
For I have not denied the words of the Holy One.
What is my strength, that I should hope?
And what is my end, that I should be patient?
Is my strength the strength of stones?
Or is my flesh of brass?
Is it not that I have no help in me,
And that sound wisdom is driven quite from me?
To him that is ready to faint, kindness should be
    shown by his friend;
Even to him that forsakes the fear of the Almighty.
My brethren have dealt deceitfully as a brook,
Like the channel of brooks that pass away,
Which are black by reason of the ice,
And wherein the snow hides itself;
When they wax warm, they vanish;
When it is hot, they are consumed out of their place.

The paths of their way are turned aside,
They go up into the waste and perish.
The caravans of Tema looked for the waters,
The travelling merchants of Sheba waited for them;
They were ashamed because they had hoped;
They came thither and were confounded.
For now you are nothing;
You see a terror, and are afraid.
Did I say, 'Give to me'?
Or, 'Offer a present to me of your substance'?
Or, 'Deliver me from the adversary's hand'?
Or, 'Redeem me from the hand of the oppressors'?
Teach me, and I will hold my peace,
And cause me to understand wherein I have erred.
How forcible are words of uprightness!
But what does your arguing reprove?
Do you imagine to reprove words?
Seeing that the speeches of one that is desperate are
    as wind.
Yea, you would cast lots upon the fatherless,
And make merchandise of your friend.
Now therefore be pleased to look upon me,
For surely I shall not lie to your face.
Return, I pray you, let there be no injustice;
Yea, return again, my cause is still righteous.
Is there injustice on my tongue?
Cannot my taste discern mischievous things?
Is there not a time of service to man upon earth?
And are not his days like the days of a hireling?
As a servant that earnestly desires the shade,
And as a hireling that looks for his wages,
So am I made to possess months of vanity,
And wearisome nights are appointed to me.
When I lie down, I say, 'When shall I arise?'
But the night is long,
And I am full of tossings to and fro,
Until the dawning of the day.
My flesh is clothed with worms and clods of dust;
My skin closes up and breaks out afresh.
My days are swifter than a weaver's shuttle,
And are spent without hope.
Oh remember that my life is wind;

My eye shall see good no more.
The eye of him that sees me shall behold me no
    more:
Your eyes shall be upon me, but I shall not be.
As the cloud is consumed and vanishes away,
So he that goes down to Sheol[4] shall come up no
    more.
He shall return no more to his house,
Neither shall his place know him any more.
Therefore I will not restrain my mouth;
I will speak in the anguish of my spirit;
I will complain in the bitterness of my soul.
Am I a sea, or a sea monster,
That you[5] set a watch over me?
When I say, 'My bed shall comfort me,
My couch shall ease my complaint,'
Then you scare me with dreams,
And terrify me through visions,
So that my soul chooses strangling,
And death rather than these my bones.
I loathe my life;
I would not live always;
Let me alone,
For my days are vanity.
What is man, that you should magnify him,
And that you should set your heart upon him,
And that you should visit him every morning,
And try him every moment?
How long will you not look away from me,
Nor let me alone until I swallow down my spittle?
If I have sinned, what can I do to you, O you watcher
    of men?
Why have you set me as a mark for you,
So that I am a burden to myself?
And why do you not pardon my transgression,
And take away my iniquity?
For now shall I lie down in the dust;
And you shall seek me diligently, but I shall not be!"
8    Bildad the Shuhite answered,
"How long will you speak these things?
And how long shall the words of your mouth be like
    a mighty wind?

---

4   The place where the dead go.
5   Addressing God at this point. Job continues, switching back and forth between referring to God in the second and third
    person.

Does God pervert judgment?
Or does the Almighty pervert justice?
If your children have sinned against him,
He has delivered them into the hand of their trans-
    gression.
If you would diligently seek God,
And make your supplication to the Almighty,
If you were pure and upright, surely now he would
    awake for you,
And make the habitation of your righteousness pros-
    perous.
And though your beginning was small,
Yet your latter end would greatly increase.
For inquire, I pray you, of the former age,
And apply yourself to that which their fathers have
    searched out—
For we are but of yesterday, and know nothing,
Because our days upon earth are a shadow—
Shall not they teach you and tell you,
And utter words out of their heart?
Can the rush grow up without mire?
Can the reed grow without water?
While it is yet in its greenness, and not cut down,
It withers before any other herb.
Thus are the paths of all that forget God;
And the hope of the godless man shall perish,
Whose confidence shall break off,
And whose trust is a spider's web.
He shall lean upon his house, but it shall not stand;
He shall hold fast thereby, but it shall not endure.
He is green before the sun, and his shoots go forth
    over his garden;
His roots are wrapped about the heap, he beholds the
    place of stones.
If he is destroyed from his place,
Then it shall deny him, saying, 'I have not seen you.'
Behold, this is the joy of his way,
And out of the earth shall others spring.
Behold, God will not cast away a perfect man,
Neither will he uphold evil-doers.
He will yet fill your mouth with laughter,
And your lips with shouting.

They that hate you shall be clothed with shame,
And the tent of the wicked shall be no more."
9   Then Job answered,
"Truly, I know that it is so:
But how can man be just before God?
If he is pleased to contend with him,[6]
He cannot answer him once in a thousand.
He is wise in heart, and mighty in strength;
Who has hardened himself against him, and pros-
    pered?
He removes the mountains and they do not know it,
When he overturns them in his anger.
He shakes the earth out of her place,
And the pillars thereof tremble.
He commands the sun and it does not rise,
And he seals up the stars.
He alone stretches out the heavens,
And treads upon the waves of the sea.
He makes the Bear, Orion, and the Pleiades,[7]
And the circle of the southern stars.
He does great things past finding out;
Yea, marvelous things without number.
Lo, he goes by me, and I do not see him;
He passes on also, but I do not perceive him.
Behold, he seizes the prey, who can hinder him?
Who will say to him, 'What are you doing?'
God will not withdraw his anger;
The allies of the proud are prostrate under him.
How much less can I answer him,
And choose out my words to reason with him!
He, whom, though I were righteous,
Yet I could not answer;
I would make supplication to my adversary.
If I had called,
And he had answered me;
Yet would I not believe that he hearkened to my
    voice.
For he breaks me with a tempest,
And multiplies my wounds without cause.
He will not suffer me to take my breath,
But fills me with bitterness.
If we speak of the strength of the mighty,

6   I.e., with God.
7   Various constellations.

Lo, he is there!
And if of judgment,
Who will appoint me a time in court?
Though I be righteous, my own mouth shall con-
    demn me;
Though I be perfect, it shall prove me perverse.
Though I be perfect, I will not regard myself;
I despise my life.
It is all one; therefore I say,
'He destroys the perfect and the wicked.'
If the scourge slays suddenly,
He mocks at the trials of the innocent.
The earth is given into the hand of the wicked;
He covers the faces of the judges thereof.
If it is not *he*,
*Who* then is it?
Now my days are swifter than a runner;
They flee away, they see no good;
They pass away like swift ships,
As the eagle that swoops on the prey.
If I say,
'I will forget my complaint,
I will put off my sad countenance,
And be of good cheer,'
I am afraid of all my sorrows,
I know that you will not hold me innocent;
I shall be condemned;
Why then do I labor in vain?
If I wash myself with snow water,
And make my hands ever so clean,
You will still plunge me in the ditch,
And my own clothes shall abhor me.
For he is not a man as I am, that I can answer him,
That we can go together in court;
There is no mediator between us,
That might lay his hand upon us both;
Let him take his rod away from me,
And do not let his terror make me afraid,
Then would I speak and not fear him;
But I am not so.
10  My soul is weary of my life;
I will give free course to my complaint;
I will speak in the bitterness of my soul.
I will say to God, Do not condemn me;
Show me wherefore you contend with me.
Is it good to you that you should oppress,

That you should despise the work of your hands,
And shine upon the counsel of the wicked?
Do you have eyes of flesh,
Or do you see as man sees?
Are your days as the days of man,
Or your years as man's days,
That you inquire after my iniquity,
And search after my sin,
Although you know that I am not wicked,
And there is none that can deliver out of your hand?
Your hands have made me
And fashioned me together round about;
Yet you destroy me.
Remember, I beseech you, that you have fashioned
    me as clay;
And will you bring me into dust again?
Have you not poured me out like milk,
And curdled me like cheese?
You have clothed me with skin and flesh,
And knit me together with bones and sinews.
You have granted me life and favor,
And your care has preserved my spirit.
Yet these things you have hidden in your heart;
I know that this is with you;
If I sin,
Then you mark me,
And you will not acquit me of my iniquity.
If I am wicked,
Woe to me;
And if I am righteous,
Yet I shall not lift up my head,
Being filled with ignominy,
And looking upon my affliction.
And if my head exalts itself,
You hunt me as a lion,
And again you show yourself marvelous against me.
You renew your witnesses against me,
And increase your indignation against me;
Host after host is against me.
Why then have you brought me forth out of the
    womb?
I had rather given up the ghost, and no eye had seen
    me.
I would have been as though I had not been;
I would have been carried from the womb to the
    grave.

Are not my days few?
Cease then, and let me alone,
That I may take comfort a little,
Before I go whence I shall not return;
Even to the land of darkness and of the shadow of
    death,
A land of thick darkness, as darkness itself;
A land of the shadow of death, without any order;
And where the light is as darkness."
11   Then Zophar the Naamathite answered,
"Should not the multitude of words be answered?
And should a man full of talk be justified?
Should your boastings make men hold their peace?
And when you mock, shall no man make you
    ashamed?
For you say, 'My doctrine is pure,
And I am clean in your eyes.'
But Oh that God would speak,
And open his lips against you;
And that he would show you the secrets of wisdom;
For sound wisdom is manifold.
Know therefore that God exacts from you
Less than your iniquity deserves.
Can you by searching find out God?
Can you find out the Almighty to perfection?
It[8] is high as heaven;
What can you do?
It is deeper than Sheol;
What can you know?
The measure thereof is longer than the earth,
And broader than the sea.
If he pass through, and imprisons,
And calls to judgment, then who can hinder him?
For he knows vain men;
He sees iniquity also, and considers it.
But vain man is void of understanding,
Yea, man is born as a wild ass' colt.
If you set your heart aright,
And stretched out your hands toward him,
If iniquity were in your hand, and you put it far
    away,
And did not let unrighteousness dwell in your tents,
Surely then could you lift up your face without a
    spot;

Yea, you could be steadfast, and not fear,
For you would forget your misery;
You would remember it as waters that are passed
    away,
And your life would be clearer than the noonday;
Though there would be darkness, it would be as the
    morning.
And you would be secure,
Because there is hope;
Yea, you would search about you,
And take your rest in safety.
Also you would lie down,
And no one would make you afraid;
Yea, many would make suit to you.
But the eyes of the wicked shall fail,
And they shall have no way to flee,
And their hope shall be the giving up of the ghost."
12   Job answered,
"No doubt you are the people,        ] Job's
And wisdom shall die with you.       ] sarcasm
But I have understanding as well as you;
I am not inferior to you;
Yea, who does not know such things as these?
I am as one that is a laughingstock to his neighbor,
A man that called upon God, and God answered
    him;
The just, the perfect man is a laughingstock.
In the thought of him that is at ease there is contempt
    for misfortune,
It is ready for them whose foot slips.
The tents of robbers prosper,
And they that provoke God are secure,
In what God's hand provides.
But ask now the beasts, and they shall teach you;
And the fowls of the air, and they shall tell you;
Or, speak to the earth, and it shall teach you;
And the fishes of the sea shall declare to you:
Who does not know in all these that the hand of the
    Lord has wrought this?
In whose hand is the soul of every living thing,
And the breath of all mankind?
Does not the ear try words
Even as the palate tastes its food?
Wisdom is with aged men,

---

8   I.e., God in his perfection.

And understanding is in length of days.
Wisdom and might are with him;
He has counsel and understanding.
Behold, he breaks down,
And it cannot be built again;
He imprisons a man,
And there can be no liberation.
Behold, he withholds the waters,
And they dry up.
He sends them out again,
And they overturn the earth.
Strength and sound wisdom are with him;
The deceived and the deceiver are his to use.
He leads counsellors away despoiled,
And he makes fools of judges.
He looses the bonds put on by kings,
And binds their loins with a belt.
He leads priests away despoiled,
And overthrows the mighty.
He removes the speech of the trusty,
And takes away the understanding of the elders.
He pours contempt upon princes,
And looses the belt of the strong.
He discovers deep things out of darkness,
And brings the shadow of death into the light.
He increases the nations,
And destroys them;
He spreads the nations abroad,
And brings them in.
He takes away the heart of the chiefs of the people of
    the earth,
And causes them to wander in a wilderness where
    there is no way.
They grope in the dark without light,
And he makes them stagger like a drunken man.
13   Lo, my eye has seen all this,
My ear has heard and understood it.
What you know, the same I know also;
I am not inferior to you.
Surely I would speak to the Almighty,
And I desire to reason with God.
But you are forgers of lies,
You are all physicians of no value.
Oh that you would altogether hold your peace!
And it should be your wisdom.
Hear now my reasoning,

And hearken to the pleadings of my lips.
Will you speak unrighteously for God,
And talk deceitfully for him?
Will you be partial to him?
Will you contend for God?
Will it be good when he should search you out?
Or as one deceives a man, will you deceive him?
He will surely reprove you,
If you are secretly partial.
Shall not his excellence make you afraid,
And dread of him fall upon you?
Your memorable sayings are proverbs of ashes,
Your defenses are defenses of clay.
Hold your peace, let me alone, that I may speak,
And let come on me what will.
At all events I will take my flesh in my teeth,
And put my life in my hand.
Though he slays me, yet will I trust him.
Nevertheless, I will defend my ways before him.
He also shall be my salvation;
For a godless man shall not come before him.
Hear diligently my speech,
And let my declaration be in your ears.
Behold now, I have ordered my case;
I know that I shall be justified.
Who is he that will contend with me?
For now if I hold my peace I shall give up the ghost.
Only do not do two things to me,
Then will I not hide myself from your face:
Withdraw your hand far from me,
And let not your terror make me afraid;
Then call, and I will answer;
Or let me speak, and you answer me.
How many are my iniquities and sins?
Make me know my transgression and my sin.
Wherefore do you hide your face,
And hold me as your enemy?
Will you harass a driven leaf?
And will you pursue dry stubble?
For you write bitter things against me,
And make me inherit the iniquities of my youth.
You also put my feet in the stocks,
And mark all my paths.
You draw a line about the soles of my feet,
Though I am like a rotten thing that decays,
Like a garment that is moth-eaten.

14 Man that is born of a woman
Is of few days, and full of trouble;
He comes forth like a flower, and is cut down,
He flees also like a shadow and does not continue.
And do you open your eyes on such a one,
And bring me into judgment with you?
Who can bring a clean thing out of an unclean one?
    No one!
Seeing his days are determined,
The number of his months is with you,
And you have appointed his bounds that he cannot
    pass;
Look away from him, that he may rest,
Until, like a hireling, he shall complete his day.
For there is hope for a tree, if it is cut down,
That it will sprout again,
And that the tender branch thereof will not cease;
Though the root thereof waxes old in the earth,
And the stock thereof dies in the ground,
Yet through the scent of water it will bud,
And put forth boughs like a plant.
But man dies, and wastes away;
Yea, man gives up the ghost, and where is he?
As the waters fail from the sea,
And the river decays and dries up,
So man lies down and does not rise;
Until the heavens be no more they shall not awake,
Nor be roused out of their sleep.
Oh that you would hide me in Sheol,
That you would hide me until your wrath is over,
That you would appoint me a set time and remember
    me.
If a man dies, shall he live again?
All the days of my warfare would I wait, until my
    release should come;
You would call, and I would answer you;
You would have a desire for the work of your hands.
But now you number my steps.
Do you not watch over my sin?
My transgression is sealed up in a bag,
And you heap up my iniquity.
And surely the mountain falling comes to nought,
And the rock is removed out of its place,
The waters wear the stones,
The overflowings thereof wash away the dust of the
    earth.

And thus you destroy the hope of man:
You prevail forever against him, and he passes;
You change his countenance, and send him away;
His sons come to honor, and he does not know it,
And they are brought low, but he does not perceive
    it.
Only for himself his flesh has pain,
And for himself his soul mourns."

*[The discussion among Job and his companions, and Job's
    addresses to God, continue.]*

21 Job answered,
"Hear my speech diligently,
And let this be your consolation.
Suffer me, and I will also speak:
And after I have spoken, mock on.
As for me, is my complaint against man?
And why should I not be impatient?
Mark me, and be astonished,
And lay your hand upon your mouth.
Even when I remember I am troubled,
And horror takes hold of my flesh.
Wherefore do the wicked live,
Become old, yea, wax mighty in power?
Their seed is established with them in their sight,
And their offspring before their eyes.
Their houses are safe from fear,
Neither is the rod of God upon them.
Their bull breeds, and does not fail;
Their cow calves, and does not cast off her calf.
They send forth their little ones like a flock,
And their children dance.
They sing to the timbrel and harp,
And rejoice at the sound of the pipe.
They spend their days in prosperity,
And in a moment they go down to Sheol.
Yet they said to God, 'Depart from us,
For we do not desire the knowledge of your ways.
What is the Almighty that we should serve him?
And what profit would we have if we pray to him?'
Lo, their prosperity is not in their hand,
The counsel of the wicked is far from me.
How often is it that the lamp of the wicked is put
    out?
That their calamity comes upon them?

That God distributes sorrows in his anger?
That they are as stubble before the wind,
And as chaff that the storm carries away?
One says, 'God lays up his iniquity for his children.'
Let him recompense it to him, that he may know it.
Let his own eyes see his destruction,
And let him drink of the wrath of the Almighty.
For what pleasure does he have in his house after
    him,
When the number of his months is cut off in the
    midst?
Shall any teach God knowledge,
Seeing he judges those that are high?
One dies in his full strength,
Being wholly at ease and quiet;
His buckets are full of milk,
And the marrow of his bones is moistened.
And another dies in bitterness of soul,
And never tastes of good.
They lie down alike in the dust,
And the worm covers them."

[*Job's companions offer to interrupt?*]

"Behold, I know your thoughts,
And the devices which you wrongfully imagine
    against me.
For you say, 'Where is the house of the prince?
And where is the tent wherein the wicked dwelled?'
Have you not asked them that go by the road?
And do you not know their tokens?
That the evil man is spared in the day of calamity?
That they are led away in the day of wrath?
Who shall declare his way to his face?
And who shall repay him what he has done?
Moreover he is borne to the grave,
And they shall keep watch over his tomb;
The clods of the valley are sweet to him,
And all men follow him,
As there were innumerable before him.
How then comfort me with vain words,
Seeing that in your answers there remains only false-
    hood?"
22   Eliphaz the Temanite answered,
"Can a man be profitable to God?
Surely he that is wise is profitable to himself.

Is it any pleasure to the Almighty that you are
    righteous?
Or is it gain to him that you make your ways perfect?
Is it for your fear of him that he reproves you,
That he enters with you into judgment?
Is not your wickedness great?
Neither is there any end to your iniquities.
For you have taken pledges of your brother for
    nought,
And stripped the naked of their clothing.
You have not given water to the weary to drink,
And you have withheld bread from the hungry.
But as for the mighty man, he had the land,
And the honorable man, he dwelled in it.
You have sent widows away empty,
And the arms of the fatherless have been broken.
Therefore snares are round about you,
And sudden fear troubles you,
Or darkness, so that you cannot not see,
And abundance of waters covers you.
Is not God in the height of heaven?
And behold the height of the stars, how high they
    are!
And you say, 'What does God know?
Can he judge through the thick darkness?
Thick clouds are a covering to him, so that he does
    not see;
And he walks in the circuit of heaven.'
Will you keep the old way
Which wicked men have trodden?
Who were snatched away before their time,
Whose foundation was destroyed by a flood,
Who said to God, 'Depart from us';
And, 'What can the Almighty do to us?'
Yet he filled their houses with good things:
But the counsel of the wicked is far from me.
The righteous see it, and are glad;
And the innocent laugh them to scorn,
Saying, 'Surely they that did rise up against us are
    cut off,
And the remnant of them the fire has consumed.'
Acquaint now yourself with him and be at peace;
Good shall thereby come to you.
Receive, I pray you, the law from his mouth,
And lay up his words in your heart.
If you return to the Almighty,

You shall be built up;
If you put away unrighteousness far from your tents.
And lay your treasure in the dust,
And the gold of Ophir among the stones of the
    brooks.
And the Almighty shall be your treasure,
And precious silver to you.
For then shall you delight yourself in the Almighty,
And shall lift up your face to God.
You shall make your prayer to him,
And he shall hear you;
And you shall pay your vows.
You shall also decree a thing,
And it shall be established for you;
And light shall shine upon your ways.
When they cast you down,
You shall say, 'There is lifting up';
And he shall save the humble person.
He shall deliver even him that is not innocent;
Yea, he shall be delivered through the cleanness of
    your hands."
23   Then Job answered,
"Even today my complaint is rebellious:
My stroke is weaker than my groaning.
Oh that I knew where I might find him,
That I might come even to his seat!
I would order my case before him,
And fill my mouth with arguments.
I would know the words which he would answer
    me,
And understand what he would say to me.
Would he contend with me in the greatness of his
    power?
Nay, but he would heed me;
There the upright might reason with him;
So should I be delivered forever from my judge.
Behold, I go forward,
But he is not there;
And backward,
But I cannot perceive him;
On the left hand, when he does work,
I cannot behold him;
He hides himself on the right hand,
So that I cannot see him.
But he knows the way that I take;
When he has tried me, I shall come forth as gold.

*[handwritten margin note: Job wants to take God to court]*

My foot has held fast to his steps;
I have kept his way, and not turned aside.
I have not gone back from the commandment of his
    lips;
I have treasured up the words of his mouth more
    than my necessary food.
But he is singular,
And who can change him?
And what his soul desires,
Even that he does.
For he performs that which is appointed for me;
And many such things are with him.
Therefore I am troubled at his presence;
When I consider, I am afraid of him.
For God has made my heart faint,
And the Almighty has troubled me;
Because I was not cut off from the darkness,
Neither did he cover the thick darkness from my
    face.
24   Why are times not hidden from the Almighty?
And why do not they who know him see his days?
There are those that remove boundary markers;
They violently take away flocks, and feed them.
They drive away the ass of the fatherless,
They take the widow's ox for a pledge.
They turn the needy off the way,
So the poor of the earth hide themselves together.
Behold, as wild asses in the desert they go forth to
    their work,
Seeking diligently for food;
The wilderness yields them food for their children.
They cut his provender in the field;
And they glean in the vineyard of the wicked.
They lie all night naked without clothing,
And have no covering in the cold.
They are wet with the showers of the mountains,
And embrace the rock for want of a shelter.
There those are that pluck the fatherless from the
    breast,
And take in pledge from the poor,
So that the poor go about naked without clothing.
And hungry, they carry the sheaves;
They make oil within the walls of these men;
They tread their winepresses, and suffer thirst.
From out of the populous city men groan,
And the soul of the wounded cries out,

Yet God ignores their prayer.
These are of them that rebel against the light;
They do not know the ways thereof,
Nor abide in the paths thereof.
The murderer rises with the light,
He kills the poor and needy,
And in the night he is as a thief.
The eye also of the adulterer waits for the twilight,
Saying, 'No eye shall see me,'
And he puts a covering on his face.
In the dark they dig through houses;
They shut themselves up in the daytime,
They do not know the light.
For the morning is to all of them
As the shadow of death;
For they know the terrors of the shadow of death.
They are scum upon the face of the waters;
Their portion is cursed in the earth;
The laborer does not turn by the way of their vine-
    yards;
As drought and heat consume the snow waters,
So does Sheol those which have sinned;
The womb shall forget him, the worm shall feed
    sweetly on him;
He shall be no more remembered,
And unrighteousness shall be broken like a tree;
Even he that devours the barren woman that bears
    not,
And does not do good to the widow.
Yet God by his power makes the mighty to
    continue;
They rise up, when they did not believe that they
    should live.
God gives them to be in security,
And they rest therein;
And his eyes are upon their ways.
They are exalted for a little while, and they are
    gone:
Yea, they are brought low, they are gathered in, as all
    others;
And are cut off as the tops of the ears of corn.
And if it is not so now, who will prove me a liar;
And make my speech worth nothing?"

*[Job continues to defend his innocence and his companions
proclaim God's goodness.]*

38   Then the Lord answered Job out of the whirl-
    wind, and said,
"Who is this that darkens counsel by words without
    knowledge?
Gird up now your loins like a man,
For I will demand of you, and you declare to me.
Where were you when I laid the foundations of the
    earth?
—Declare, if you have understanding—
Who determined the measures thereof, if you know?
Or who stretched the line upon it?
Whereupon were the foundations thereof fastened?
Or who laid the cornerstone thereof,
When the morning stars sang together,
And all the sons of God shouted for joy?
Or who shut up the sea with doors,
When it broke forth, and issued out of the womb,
When I made the cloud the garment thereof,
And thick darkness a swaddling band for it,
And prescribed for it my decree,
And set bars and doors,
And said, 'Hitherto shall you come, but no further;
And here shall your proud waves be stayed'?
Have you commanded the morning since your days
    began,
And caused the dayspring to know its place
That it might take hold of the ends of the earth,
And the wicked be shaken out of it?
It is changed as clay under a seal;
And all things stand forth as a garment,
And from the wicked their light is withheld,
And the raised arm is broken.
Have you entered into the springs of the sea?
Or have you walked in the recesses of the deep?
Have the gates of death been revealed to you?
Or have you seen the gates of the shadow of death?
Have you comprehended the breadth of the earth?
—Declare, if you know it all—
Where is the way to the dwelling of light,
And as for darkness, where is the place thereof,
That you should take it to the bound thereof,
And that you should discern the paths to the house
    thereof?
—Doubtless, you know, for you were born then,
And the number of your days is great!—
Have you entered the treasuries of the snow,

Or have you seen the treasuries of the hail,
Which I have reserved against the time of trouble,
Against the day of battle and war?
By what way is light parted,
Or the east wind scattered upon the earth?
Who has cleft a channel for the waterflood,
Or a path for the lightning of the thunder;
To cause it to rain on a land where no man is;
On the wilderness, wherein there is no man;
To satisfy the waste and desolate ground;
And to cause the tender grass to spring forth?
Has the rain a father?
Or who has begotten the drops of dew?
Out of whose womb came the ice?
And the hoary frost of heaven, who has gendered it?
The waters harden like stone,
And the face of the deep is frozen.
Can you bind the cluster of the Pleiades,
Or loose the bands of Orion?
Can you lead forth the signs of the Zodiac in their
    season?
Or can you guide the Bear with her train?
Do you know the ordinances of the heavens?
Can you establish the dominion thereof in the
    earth?
Can you lift up your voice to the clouds,
That abundance of waters may cover you?
Can you send forth bolts of lightning, that they may
    go,
And say to you, 'Here we are'?
Who has put wisdom in the inward parts?
Or who has given understanding to the mind?
Who can number the clouds by wisdom?
Or who can pour out the bottles of heaven,
When the dust runs into a mass,
And the clods cleave fast together?
Will you hunt the prey for the lioness?
Or satisfy the appetite of the young lions,
When they crouch in their dens,
And abide in the cover to lie in wait?
Who provides for the raven his food,
When his young ones cry to God,
And wander for lack of meat?

39   Do you know the time when the wild goats of
        the rock bear young?
Or can you mark when the hinds give birth?
Can you number the months that they fulfill?
Or do you know the time when they bear young?
They bow themselves, they bring forth their young,
They cast out their sorrows.
Their young ones are in good liking,
They grow up in the open field;
They go forth, and do not return again.
Who has sent out the wild ass free?
Or who has loosed the bonds of the wild ass,
Whose house I have made the wilderness,
And the salt[9] land his dwelling place?
He scorns the tumult of the city,
Neither does he hear the shoutings of the driver.
The range of the mountains is his pasture,
And he searches after every green thing.
Will the wild ox be content to serve you?
Or will he abide by your manger?
Can you bind the wild ox with his bond in the furrow?
Or will he harrow the valleys after you?
Will you trust him, because his strength is great?
Or will you leave to him your labor?
Will you confide in him, that he will bring home
        your seed,
And gather the corn of your threshing-floor?
The wing of the ostrich rejoices,
But are her pinions and feathers kindly?
For she leaves her eggs on the earth,
And warms them in the dust,
And forgets that the foot may crush them,
Or that the wild beast may trample them.
She is hardened against her young ones, as if they
        were not hers;
Though her labor be in vain, she is without fear,
Because God has deprived her of wisdom,
Neither has he imparted to her understanding.
At the time she lifts up herself on high,
She scorns the horse and his rider.
Have you given the horse his might?
Have you clothed his neck with the quivering mane?
Have you made him to leap as a locust?

9   I.e., barren.

The glory of his snorting is terrible.
He paws in the valley, and rejoices in his strength;
He goes out to meet the armed men.
He mocks at fear and is not dismayed;
Neither does he turn back from the sword.
The quiver rattles against him,
The flashing spear and the javelin.
He swallows the ground with fierceness and rage;
Neither does he stand still at the voice of the trum-
    pet.
As often as the trumpet sounds, he says, 'Aha!'
And he smells the battle far off,
The thunder of the captains, and the shouting.
Does the hawk soar by your wisdom,
And stretch her wings toward the south?
Does the eagle mount up at your command,
And make her nest on high?
She dwells on the rock, and has her lodging there,
Upon the crag of the rock and the stronghold.
From there she spies out the prey;
Her eyes behold it afar off.
Her young ones also suck up blood,
And where the slain are, there is she.
40   Shall he that cavils contend with the Almighty?
He that argues with God, let him answer it."
Then Job answered the Lord,
"Behold, I am of small account; what shall I answer
    you?
I lay my hand upon my mouth.
Once have I spoken, and I will not answer;
Yea twice, but I will proceed no further."
The Lord answered out of the whirlwind,
"Gird up your loins now like a man;
I will demand of you, and you declare to me.
Will you even annul my judgment?
Will you condemn me, that you may be justified?
Or have you an arm like God?
And can you thunder with a voice like him?
Deck yourself now with excellence and dignity,
And array yourself with honor and majesty.
Pour forth the overflowings of your anger,
And look upon every one that is proud, and abase
    him.

Look on everyone that is proud, and bring him low,
And tread down the wicked where they stand.
Hide them in the dust together;
Bind their faces in the hidden place.
Then will I also confess to you
That your own right hand can save you.
Behold now the behemoth,[10] which I made with
    you;
He eats grass like an ox.
Lo now, his strength is in his loins,
And his force is in the muscles of his belly.
He moves his tail like a cedar;
The sinews of his thighs are knit together.
His bones are like tubes of brass;
His limbs are like bars of iron.
He is the first of the ways of God;
Only he that made him can make his sword
    approach him,
Surely the mountains bring him forth food,
Where all the beasts of the field do play.
He lies under the lotus trees,
In the cover of the reed, and the fen.
The lotus trees cover him with their shadow;
The willows of the brook surround him.
Behold, if a river overflows, he does not tremble;
He is confident, though the Jordan river swells even
    to his mouth.
Shall any take him when he is on the watch,
Or pierce through his nose with a snare?
41   Can you draw out leviathan with a fish hook?
Or press down his tongue with a cord?
Can you put a rope into his nose?
Or pierce his jaw through with a hook?
Will he make many supplications to you?
Or will he speak soft words to you?
Will he make a covenant with you,
That you should take him as a servant forever?
Will you play with him as with a bird?
Or will you bind him for your maidens?
Shall the bands of fishermen make a meal of him?
Shall they divide him among the merchants?
Can you fill his skin with barbed irons,
Or his head with fish spears?

---

10   A kind of large animal.

Lay your hand upon him;
Remember the battle,
And do so no more.
Behold, the hope of him is in vain;
Shall one not be cast down even at the sight of him?
None is so fierce that he dares stir him up.
Who then is he that can stand before me?
Who has first given to me, that I should repay him?
Everything that is under the whole heaven is mine.
I will not keep silence concerning his limbs,
Nor his mighty strength, nor his comely
    proportion.
Who can strip off his outer garment?
Who shall come within his double bridle?
Who can open the doors of his face?
Round about his teeth is terror.
His strong scales are his pride,
Shut up together as with a close seal.
One is so near to another,
That no air can come between them.
They are joined one to another;
They stick together, that they cannot be sundered.
His sneezes flash forth light,
And his eyes are like the eyelids of the morning.
Out of his mouth go burning torches,
And sparks of fire leap forth.
Out of his nostrils a smoke goes,
As of a seething pot and burning rushes.
His breath kindles coals,
And a flame goes forth from his mouth.
In his neck abides strength,
And terror dances before him.
The flakes of his flesh are joined together;
They are firm upon him, they cannot be moved.
His heart is as firm as a stone;
Yea, firm as the nether millstone.
When he raises himself up, the mighty are afraid;
By reason of consternation they are beside them-
    selves.
If one lays at him with the sword, it cannot avail;
Nor can the spear, the dart, nor the pointed shaft.
He accounts iron as straw,
And brass as rotten wood.
The arrow cannot make him flee;
Slingstones are turned with him into stubble.
Clubs are counted as stubble;

He laughs at the rushing of the javelin.
His underparts are like sharp potsherds;
He spreads as it were a threshing wain upon the
    mire.
He makes the deep to boil like a pot;
He makes the sea like ointment.
He makes a path to shine after him;
One would think the deep to be hoary.
Upon earth there is not his like,
That is made without fear.
He beholds everything that is high;
He is king over all the sons of pride."
42   Then Job answered,
"I know that you can do all things,
And that no purpose of yours can be restrained.
You asked, 'Who is this that hides counsel without
    knowledge?'
Therefore have I uttered that which I did not under-
    stand,
Things too wonderful for me, which I did not
    know.
Hear, I beseech you, and I will speak.
You said, 'I will demand of you, and you declare to
    me.'
I had heard of you by the hearing of the ear;
But now my eye sees you;
Wherefore I abhor myself, and repent
In dust and ashes."
*And it was so, that after the Lord had spoken these words to Job, the Lord said to Eliphaz the Temanite, "My wrath is kindled against you, and against your two friends, for you have not spoken of me the thing that is right, as my servant Job has. Now therefore, take to you seven bulls and seven rams, and go to my servant Job, and offer up for yourselves a burned offering; and my servant Job shall pray for you; for him will I accept, that I deal not with you after your folly; for you have not spoken of me the thing that is right, as my servant Job has."*

*So Eliphaz the Temanite and Bildad the Shuhite and Zophar the Naamathite went, and did as the Lord commanded them; and the Lord accepted Job.*

*And the Lord turned the captivity of Job, when he prayed for his friends; and the Lord gave Job twice as much as he had before. Then came there to him all his brethren, and all his sisters, and all they that had been of his acquaintance before, and ate bread with him in his house; and they bemoaned him, and comforted him concerning all the evil that the Lord had brought upon him; every man also gave him a piece of money, and every one a ring of gold.*

*So the Lord blessed the latter end of Job more than his beginning; and he had 1,400 sheep, and 6,000 camels, and 1,000 yoke of oxen, and 1,000 she-asses. He had also seven sons and three daughters. And he called the name of the first Jemimah; and the name of the second, Keziah; and the name of the third, Keren-happuch. And in all the land were no women found so fair as the daughters of Job, and their father gave them inheritance among their brethren.*

*And after this Job lived 140 years, and saw his sons, and his sons' sons, even four generations. So Job died, being old and full of days.*

# 9

# HOMER, THE *ILIAD*

The Greeks believed that a blind poet named Homer composed the *Iliad* and the *Odyssey*, the best known works among the ancient Greeks. Most modern scholars, however, doubt whether the same person composed the two poems, and whether either can be attributed to a person called "Homer," who may not even have existed. Both works are thought to have been created over the generations out of stories handed down by word of mouth, although the degree to which either lacks the stamp of a single poet is disputed. The *Iliad* probably reached its present form in roughly the eighth century BC. It concerns events which, if they took place, occurred several hundred years earlier. When the poem opens, the Greeks have for years beseiged the city of Troy. They have come to take back Helen, wife of the Greek Menelaus, king of Sparta. She had been brought to Troy by Paris, son of Troy's king, Priam. The Greeks are led by King Agamemnon of Mycenae, Menelaus's brother, but their greatest warrior is another Greek king, Achilles.

---

1 Sing, O goddess, the anger of Achilles, son of Peleus, that brought countless ills upon the Achaeans.[1] Many a brave soul did it send hurrying down to Hades,[2] and many a hero did it yield a prey to dogs and vultures, for so were the counsels of Zeus fulfilled from the day on which the son of Atreus,[3] king of men, and great Achilles, first fell out with one another.

And which of the gods was it that set them on to quarrel? It was the son of Zeus and Leto;[4] for he was angry with the king and sent a pestilence upon the host to plague the people, because the son of Atreus[5] had dishonored Chryses his priest. Now Chryses had come to the ships of the Achaeans to free his daughter, and had brought with him a great ransom; moreover he bore in his hand the scepter of Apollo wreathed with a suppliant's wreath, and he besought the Achaeans, but most of all the two sons of Atreus, who were their chiefs.

"Sons of Atreus," he cried, "and all other Achaeans, may the gods who dwell in Olympus grant you to sack the city of Priam, and to reach your homes in safety; but free my daughter, and accept a ransom for her, in reverence to Apollo, son of Zeus."

On this the rest of the Achaeans with one voice were for respecting the priest and taking the ransom

---

1  I.e., the Greeks.
2  The god of the dead, often used to refer to the land of the dead.
3  Son of Atreus: i.e., Agamemnon. Menelaus was also a son of Atreus.
4  I.e., Apollo, god of prophecy.
5  I.e., Agamemnon.

that he offered; but not so Agamemnon, who spoke fiercely to him and sent him roughly away. "Old man," he said, "let me not find you tarrying about our ships, nor yet coming hereafter. Your scepter of the god and your wreath shall profit you nothing. I will not free her. She shall grow old in my house at Argos far from her own home, busying herself with her loom and visiting my bed; so go, and do not provoke me or it shall be the worse for you."

The old man feared him and obeyed. Not a word he spoke, but went by the shore of the sounding sea and prayed apart to King Apollo whom lovely Leto had borne. "Hear me," he cried, "O god of the silver bow, that protects Chryses and holy Cilla and rules Tenedos with your might, hear me, O you Smintheus.[6] If I have ever decked your temple with garlands, or burned your thighbones in fat of bulls or goats, grant my prayer, and let your arrows avenge my tears upon the Danaans."[7]

Thus did he pray, and Apollo heard his prayer. He came down furious from the summits of Olympus, with his bow and his quiver upon his shoulder, and the arrows rattled on his back with the rage that trembled within him. He sat himself down away from the ships with a face as dark as night, and his silver bow rang death as he shot his arrow in the midst of them. First he struck their mules and their hounds, but presently he aimed his shafts at the people themselves, and all day long the pyres of the dead were burning.

For nine whole days he shot his arrows among the people, but upon the tenth day Achilles called them in assembly, moved thereto by Hera, who saw the Achaeans in their death-throes and had compassion upon them. Then, when they were gotten together, he rose and spoke among them.

"Son of Atreus," he said, "I deem that we should now turn roving home if we would escape destruction, for we are being cut down by war and pestilence at the same time. Let us ask some priest or prophet, or some reader of dreams (for dreams, too, are from Zeus) who can tell us why Phoebus[8] Apollo is so angry, and say whether it is for some vow that we have broken, or hecatomb[9] that we have not offered, and whether he will accept the savor of lambs and goats without blemish, so as to take the plague away from us."

With these words he sat down, and Calchas son of Thesto, wisest of augurs, who knew things past, present, and to come, rose to speak. It was he who had guided the Achaeans with their fleet to Ilium[10] through the prophecies with which Phoebus Apollo had inspired him. With all sincerity and goodwill he addressed them thus: "Achilles, loved of heaven, you bid me tell you about the anger of Lord Apollo. I will therefore do so, but consider first and swear that you will stand by me heartily in word and deed, for I know that I shall offend one who rules the Argives[11] with might and to whom all the Achaeans are in subjection. A plain man cannot stand against the anger of a king, who if he swallows his displeasure now, will yet nurse revenge until he has wreaked it. Consider, therefore, whether or not you will protect me."

And Achilles answered, "Do not fear, but speak as it is borne in upon you from heaven, for by Apollo, Calchas, to whom you pray, and whose oracles you reveal to us, not a Danaan at our ships shall lay his hand upon you, while I yet live to look upon the face of the earth—no, not even if you name Agamemnon himself, who is by far the foremost of the Achaeans."

Thereon the seer spoke boldly. "The god," he said, "is angry neither about some vow nor hecatomb, but for the sake of his priest, whom Agamemnon has dishonored, in that he would not free his daughter or take a ransom for her. Therefore has he sent these evils upon us, and will send yet others. He will not deliver the Danaans from this pestilence until Agamemnon has restored the girl without fee or ransom to her

6   Another term for Apollo.
7   I.e., Greeks.
8   Another name for Apollo, referring to him as god of the sun.
9   A large sacrifice to the gods, especially of a hundred oxen.
10  I.e., Troy.
11  A term often used in the Iliad simply to refer to the Greeks. It could also refer to the people of Argos, a city in Greece.

father and has sent a holy hecatomb to Chryse.[12] In this way we may perhaps appease him."

With these words he sat down, and Agamemnon rose in anger. His heart was black with rage, and his eyes flashed fire as he scowled at Calchas and said, "Seer of evil, you never yet prophesied smooth things concerning me, but have always loved to foretell that which was evil. You have brought me neither comfort nor performance; and now you come divining among the Danaans, and saying that Apollo has plagued us because I would not take a ransom for this girl, the daughter of Chryses. I have set my heart on keeping her in my own house, for I love her better even than my own wife, Clytemnestra, whose peer she is both in form and feature, in understanding and accomplishments. Still, I will give her up if I must, for I would have the people live, not die. But you must find me a prize instead, or I alone among the Argives shall be without one. This is not well, for you behold, all of you, that my prize is to go elsewhere."

And Achilles answered, "Most noble son of Atreus, covetous beyond all mankind, how shall the Achaeans find you another prize? We have no common store from which to take one. Those we took from the cities[13] have been awarded. We cannot disallow the awards that have been made already. Give this girl, therefore, to the god, and if ever Zeus grants us to sack the city of Troy we will recompense you three and fourfold."

Then Agamemnon said, "Achilles, valiant though you are, you shall not thus outwit me. You shall not overreach and you shall not persuade me. Are you to keep your own prize, while I sit tamely under my loss and give up the girl at your bidding! Let the Achaeans find me a prize in fair exchange to my liking, or I will come and take your own, or that of Ajax[14] or of Odysseus; and he to whomsoever I may come shall rue my coming. But of this we will take thought later; for the present, let us draw a ship into the sea, and find a crew expressly for her; let us put a hecatomb on board, and let us send Chryseis also; further, let some chief man among us be in command, either Ajax, or Idomeneus, or yourself, son of Peleus, mighty warrior that you are, that we may offer sacrifice and appease the anger of the god."

Achilles scowled at him and answered, "You are steeped in insolence and lust for gain. With what heart can any of the Achaeans do your bidding, either on a foray or in open fighting! I did not come warring here for any ill the Trojans have done me. I have no quarrel with them. They have not raided my cattle or my horses, or cut down my harvests on the rich plains of Phthia, for between me and them there is a great space, both mountain and sounding sea. We have followed you, Sir Insolence, for your pleasure, not ours—to gain satisfaction from the Trojans for you, dog face, and for Menelaus. You forget this, and threaten to rob me of the prize for which I have toiled, and which the sons of the Achaeans have given me. Never when the Achaeans sack any rich city of the Trojans do I receive so good a prize as you do, although it is my hands that do the better part of the fighting. When the sharing comes, your share is far the largest and I must go back to my ships, take what I can get and be thankful, when my labor of fighting is done. Now, therefore, I shall go back to Phthia; it will be much better for me to return home with my ships, for I will not stay here, dishonored, to gather gold and substance for you."

And Agamemnon answered, "Flee if you wish, I shall make you no prayers to stop you. I have others here who will do me honor, and above all Zeus, the lord of counsel. There is no king here so hateful to me as you are, for you are ever quarrelsome and ill affected. What if you are brave? Was it not heaven that made you so? Go home, then, with your ships and comrades to lord it over the Myrmidons.[15] I care neither for you nor for your anger; and I will do this: since Phoebus Apollo is taking Chryseis from me, I shall send her with my ship and my followers, but I shall come to your tent and take your own prize Briseis, that you may learn how much stronger I am than you are, and that another may fear to set himself up as comparable with me."

---

12  The town of Chryses, Apollo's priest, near Troy. His daughter is Chryseis.
13  I.e., the cities under Trojan influence which the Greeks have already taken.
14  Often spelled "Aias."
15  Achilles's own people.

wants his prize

equality, fairness

The son of Peleus was furious, and his heart within his shaggy breast divided whether to draw his sword, push the others aside, and kill the son of Atreus, or to restrain himself and check his anger. While he was thus in two minds, and was drawing his mighty sword from its scabbard, Athena[16] came down from heaven (for Hera had sent her in the love she bore to them both), and seized the son of Peleus by his yellow hair, visible to him alone, for of the others no man could see her. Achilles turned in amazement and by the fire that flashed from her eyes at once knew that she was Athena. "Why are you here," he said, "daughter of aegis-bearing Zeus! To see the pride of Agamemnon, son of Atreus? Let me tell you—and it shall surely be—he shall pay for this insolence with his life."

And Athena said, "I come from heaven, if you will hear me, to bid you stay your anger. Hera has sent me, who cares for both of you alike. Cease, then, this brawling, and do not draw your sword. Rail at him if you will, and your railing will not be vain, for I tell you—and it shall surely be—that you shall hereafter receive gifts three times as splendid by reason of this present insult. Hold back, therefore, and obey."

"Goddess," answered Achilles, "however angry a man may be, he must do as you two command him. This will be best, for the gods always hear the prayers of him who has obeyed them."

He stayed his hand on the silver hilt of his sword, and thrust it back into the scabbard as Athena bade him. Then she went back to Olympus among the other gods, and to the house of aegis-bearing Zeus.

But the son of Peleus again began railing at the son of Atreus, for he was still in a rage. "Wine-bibber," he cried, "with the face of a dog and the heart of a hind, you never dare to go out with the host in battle, nor yet with our chosen men in ambush. You shun this as you do death itself. You would rather go around and rob his prizes from any man who contradicts you. You devour your people, for you are king over a feeble folk; otherwise, son of Atreus, henceforward you would insult no man. Therefore I say, and swear it

with a great oath—no, by this scepter of mine which shall sprout neither leaf nor shoot, nor bud anew from the day on which it left its parent stem upon the mountains, for the ax stripped it of leaf and bark, and now the sons of the Achaeans bear it as judges and guardians of the decrees of heaven—so surely and solemnly do I swear that hereafter they shall look longingly for Achilles and shall not find him. In the day of your distress, when your men fall dying by the murderous hand of Hector,[17] you shall not know how to help them, and shall rend your heart with rage for the hour when you offered insult to the bravest of the Achaeans."

With this the son of Peleus dashed his gold-bestudded scepter on the ground and took his seat, while the son of Atreus was starting fiercely from his place upon the other side. Then rose smooth-tongued Nestor, the facile speaker of the Pylians, and the words fell from his lips sweeter than honey. Two generations of men born and bred in Pylos had passed away under his rule, and he was now reigning over the third. With all sincerity and good will, therefore, he addressed them thus: "Of a truth," he said, "a great sorrow has befallen the Achaean land. Surely Priam with his sons would rejoice, and the Trojans be glad at heart if they could hear this quarrel between you two, who are so excellent in battle and counsel. I am older than either of you; therefore be guided by me. Moreover I have been the familiar friend of men even greater than you are, and they did not disregard my counsels. Never again can I behold such men as Pirithous and Dryas, shepherd of his people, or as Caeneus, Exadius, godlike; Polyphemus and Theseus, son Aegeus, peer of the immortals. These were the mightiest men ever born upon this earth; mightiest were they, and when they fought the fiercest tribes of mountain savages they utterly overthrew them. I came from distant Pylos, and went about among them, for they would have me come, and I fought as it was in me to do. Not a man now living could withstand them, but they heard my words, and were persuaded by them. So be it also with yourselves, for this is the better way.

---

16   Goddess of wisdom.

17   Hector, one of Priam's 50 sons, and the leading Trojan warrior.

✻ obedience to the gods

*they both should calm down*

Therefore, Agamemnon, though you are strong, do not take this girl away, for the sons of the Achaeans have already given her to Achilles. And you, Achilles, do not strive further with the king, for no man who by the grace of Zeus wields a scepter has like honor with Agamemnon. You are strong, and have a goddess for your mother, but Agamemnon is stronger than you, for he has more people under him. Son of Atreus, check your anger, I implore you. End this quarrel with Achilles, who in the day of battle is a tower of strength to the Achaeans."

And Agamemnon answered, "Sir, all that you have said is true, but this fellow must become our lord and master; he must be lord of all, king of all, and captain of all, and this shall hardly be. Granted that the gods have made him a great warrior, have they also given him the right to speak with railing?"

Achilles interrupted him. "I should be a mean coward," he cried, "if I were to give in to you in all things. Order other people around, not me, for I shall obey no longer. Furthermore, I say—and lay my saying to your heart—I shall fight neither you nor any man about this girl, for those that take were those also that gave. But of all else that is at my ship you shall carry away nothing by force. Try, so others may see; if you do, my spear shall be reddened with your blood."

When they had quarrelled thus angrily, they rose, and broke up the assembly at the ships of the Achaeans. The son of Peleus went back to his tents and ships with the son of Menoetius[18] and his company, while Agamemnon drew a vessel into the water and chose a crew of 20 oarmen. He escorted Chryseis on board and sent moreover a hecatomb for the god. And Odysseus went as captain.

These, then, went on board and sailed their ways over the sea. But the son of Atreus bade the people purify themselves. So they purified themselves and cast their filth into the sea. Then they offered hecatombs of bulls and goats without blemish on the seashore, and the smoke with the savor of their sacrifice rose curling up towards heaven.

Thus did they busy themselves throughout the host. But Agamemnon did not forget the threat that he had made against Achilles, and called his trusty messengers and henchmen, Talthybius and Eurybates. "Go," he said, "to the tent of Achilles, son of Peleus; take Briseis by the hand and bring her here; if he will not give her, I shall come with others and take her—which will press him harder."

He charged them strictly further and dismissed them, whereon they went their way sorrowfully by the seaside, until they came to the tents and ships of the Myrmidons. They found Achilles sitting by his tent and his ships, and ill-pleased he was when he beheld them. They stood fearfully and reverently before him, and never spoke a word, but he knew them and said, "Welcome, heralds, messengers of gods and men; draw near. My quarrel is not with you, but with Agamemnon who has sent you for the girl Briseis. Therefore, Patroclus, bring her and give her to them, but let them be witnesses by the blessed gods, by mortal men, and by the fierceness of Agamemnon's anger, that if ever again there is need of me to save the people from ruin, they shall seek and they shall not find. Agamemnon is mad with rage and does not know how to look before and after so that the Achaeans may fight by their ships in safety."

Patroclus did as his dear comrade had bidden him. He brought Briseis from the tent and gave her over to the heralds, who took her with them to the ships of the Achaeans—and the woman was reluctant to go. Then Achilles went all alone by the side of the hoarse sea, weeping and looking out upon the boundless waste of waters. He raised his hands in prayer to his immortal mother, "Mother," he cried, "you bore me to live but for a little season. Surely Zeus, who thunders from Olympus, might have made that a little glorious. It is not so. Agamemnon, son of Atreus, has done me dishonor, and has robbed me of my prize by force."

As he spoke, he wept aloud, and his mother heard him where she was sitting in the depths of the sea, hard by the old man her father. Forthwith she rose as it were a gray mist out of the waves, sat down before him as he stood weeping, caressed him with her hand, and said, "My son, why are you weeping? What is it

---

18   Son of Menoetius: i.e., Patroclus, Achilles's companion.

that grieves you? Do not keep it from me, but tell me, so we may know it together."

Achilles drew a deep sigh and said, "You know; why tell you what you know well already? We went to Thebe, the strong city of Eetion, sacked it and brought the spoils here. The sons of the Achaeans shared it duly among themselves, and chose lovely Chryseis as the reward of Agamemnon. But Chryses, priest of Apollo, came to the ships of the Achaeans to free his daughter, and brought with him a great ransom. Moreover, he bore in his hand the scepter of Apollo, wreathed with a suppliant's wreath, and he sought the Achaeans, but most of all the two sons of Atreus who were their chiefs.

"On this, the rest of the Achaeans with one voice were for respecting the priest and taking the ransom that he offered; but not so Agamemnon, who spoke fiercely to him and sent him roughly away. So he went back in anger, and Apollo, who loved him dearly, heard his prayer. Then the god sent a deadly dart upon the Argives, and the people died thick on one another, for the arrows went everywhere among the wide host of the Achaeans. At last a seer in the fullness of his knowledge declared to us the oracles of Apollo, and I was myself first to say that we should appease him. Whereon the son of Atreus rose in anger, and threatened that which he has since done. The Achaeans are now taking the girl in a ship to Chryse, and sending gifts of sacrifice to the god; but the heralds have just taken from my tent the daughter of Briseus, whom the Achaeans had awarded to me.

"Help your brave son, therefore, if you are able. Go to Olympus, and if you have ever done him service in word or deed, implore the aid of Zeus. Often in my father's house I have heard you glory in that you alone of the immortals saved the son of Cronus[19] from ruin, when the others, with Hera, Poseidon, and Pallas[20] Athena would have put him in bonds. It was you, goddess, who delivered him by calling to Olympus the hundred-handed monster whom gods call Briareus, but men Aegaeon, for he is stronger even than his father. When therefore he took his seat, all-glorious

beside the son of Cronus, the other gods were afraid, and did not bind him. Go, then, to him, remind him of all this, clasp his knees, and bid him give help to the Trojans. Let the Achaeans be hemmed in at the sterns of their ships and perish on the seashore, so that they may reap what joy they may of their king, and that Agamemnon may rue his blindness in offering insult to the foremost of the Achaeans."

Thetis wept and answered, "My son, woe is me that I should have borne or suckled you. Would indeed that you had lived your span free from all sorrow at your ships, for it is all too brief. Alas, that you should be at once short of life and long of sorrow above your peers. Woe, therefore, was the hour in which I bore you. Nevertheless, I will go to the snowy heights of Olympus, and tell this tale to Zeus, if he will hear our prayer. Meanwhile, stay where you are with your ships, nurse your anger against the Achaeans, and hold aloof from battle. For Zeus went yesterday to Oceanus to a feast among the noble Ethiopians, and the other gods went with him. He will return to Olympus 12 days hence; I will then go to his mansions paved with bronze and will beseech him; nor do I doubt that I shall be able to persuade him."

On this she left him, still furious at the loss of her that had been taken from him. Meanwhile Odysseus reached Chryse with the hecatomb. When they had come inside the harbor, they furled the sails and laid them in the ship's hold; they slackened the forestays, lowered the mast into its place, and rowed the ship to the place where they would have her lie; there they cast out their mooring stones and made fast the hawsers. They then got out upon the seashore and landed the hecatomb for Apollo. Chryseis also left the ship, and Odysseus led her to the altar to deliver her into the hands of her father. "Chryses," he said, "King Agamemnon has sent me to bring you back your child, and to offer sacrifice to Apollo on behalf of the Danaans, that we way propitiate the god who has now brought much sorrow upon the Argives."

So saying he gave the girl over to her father, who received her gladly, and they ranged the holy

---

19   Son of Cronus: i.e., Zeus.
20   A name of uncertain significance often applied to Athena.

hecatomb, all orderly around the altar of the god. They washed their hands and took up the barley meal to sprinkle over the victims, while Chryses lifted up his hands and prayed aloud on their behalf. "Hear me," he cried, "O god of the silver bow, that protects Chryse and holy Cilla, and rules Tenedos with your might. Just as you heard me when I prayed before, and pressed hard upon the Achaeans, so hear me yet again, and stay this fearful pestilence from the Danaans."

Thus did he pray, and Apollo heard his prayer. When they had finished praying and sprinkling the barley meal, they drew back the heads of the victims and killed and flayed them. They cut out the thigh-bones, wrapped them in two layers of fat, set some pieces of raw meat on top of them, and then Chryses laid them on the wood fire and poured wine over them, while the young men stood near him with five pronged spits in their hands. When the thighbones were burned and they had tasted the inward meats, they cut the rest up small, put the pieces upon the spits, roasted them until they were done, and drew them off. Then, when they had finished their work and the feast was ready, they ate it, and every man had his full share, so that all were satisfied. As soon as they had had enough to eat and drink, young men filled the mixing-bowl with wine and water and handed it around, after giving every man his drink offering.

Thus all day long the young men worshipped the god with song, hymning him and chanting the joyous paean, and the god took pleasure in their voices. But when the sun went down, and it came on dark, they laid themselves down to sleep by the stern cables of the ship, and when the child of morning, rosy-fingered Dawn, appeared, they again set sail for the host of the Achaeans. Apollo sent them a fair wind, so they raised their mast and hoisted their white sails aloft. As the sail bellied with the wind, the ship flew through the deep blue water, and the foam hissed against her bows as she sped onward. When they reached the wide stretching host of the Achaeans, they drew the vessel ashore, high and dry upon the sands, set her strong props beneath her, and went their ways to their own tents and ships.

But Achilles camped at his ships and nursed his rage. He did not go to the honorable assembly, and did not sally forth to fight, but gnawed at his own heart, pining for battle and the war cry.

Now after 12 days the immortal gods came back in a body to Olympus, and Zeus led the way. Thetis was not unmindful of the charge her son had laid upon her, so she rose from under the sea and went through great heaven with early morning to Olympus, where she found the mighty son of Cronus sitting all alone upon its topmost ridges. She sat herself down before him, and with her left hand seized his knees, while with her right she caught him under the chin and besought him, saying, "Father Zeus, if I ever did you service in word or deed among the immortals, hear my prayer, and do honor to my son, whose life is to be cut short so early. King Agamemnon has dishonored him by taking his prize and keeping her. Honor him then yourself, Olympian lord of counsel, and grant victory to the Trojans until the Achaeans give my son his due and load him with riches in requital."

Zeus sat silent for a while, and without a word, but Thetis still kept firm hold of his knees, and besought him a second time. "Incline your head," she said, "and promise me surely or else deny me—for you have nothing to fear—so I may learn how greatly you disdain me."

At this Zeus was much troubled and answered, "I shall have trouble if you set me quarrelling with Hera, for she will provoke me with her taunting speeches; even now she is always railing at me before the other gods and accusing me of giving aid to the Trojans. Go back now, lest she should find out. I will consider the matter, and will bring it about as you wish. See, I incline my head that you may believe me. This is the most solemn token that I can give to any god. I never revoke my word, or deceive, or fail to do what I say, when I have nodded my head."

As he spoke the son of Cronus bowed his dark brows, and the ambrosial locks swayed on his immortal head, until vast Olympus reeled.

When the pair had thus laid their plans, they parted—Zeus to his own house, while the goddess left the splendor of Olympus, and plunged into the depths of the sea. The gods rose from their seats, before the coming of their father. Not one of them dared to remain sitting, but all stood up as he came among them. There, then, he took his seat. But Hera, when she saw him, knew that he and the old merman's daughter, silver-footed Thetis, had been hatching mischief, so she at once began to upbraid him. "Trickster," she cried, "which of the gods have you been taking into your counsels now? You are always settling matters in secret behind my back, and have never yet told me, if you could help it, one word of your intentions."

"Hera," replied the father of gods and men, "you must not expect to be informed of all my counsels. You are my wife, but you would find it hard to understand them. When it is proper for you to hear, there is no one, god or man, who will be told sooner, but when I mean to keep a matter to myself, you must not pry or ask questions."

"Dread son of Cronus," answered Hera, "what are you talking about? I? Pry and ask questions? Never. I let you have your own way in everything. Still, I have a strong misgiving that the old merman's daughter Thetis has been talking you over, for she was with you and had hold of your knees this selfsame morning. I believe, therefore, that you have been promising her to give glory to Achilles, and to kill many people at the ships of the Achaeans."

"Wife," said Zeus, "I can do nothing but you suspect me and find it out. You will take nothing by it, for I shall only dislike you the more, and it will go harder with you. Granted that it is as you say; I mean to have it so; sit down and hold your tongue as I bid you for if I once begin to lay my hands on you, though all heaven were on your side, it would profit you nothing."

On this Hera was frightened, so she curbed her stubborn will and sat down in silence. But the heavenly beings were disquieted throughout the house of Zeus, till the cunning workman Hephaestus[21] began to try and pacify his mother Hera. "It will be intolerable," he said, "if you two fall to wrangling and setting heaven in an uproar about a pack of mortals. If such ill counsels are to prevail, we shall have no pleasure at our banquet. Let me then advise my mother—and she must herself know that it will be better—to make friends with my dear father Zeus, lest he again scold her and disturb our feast. If the Olympian Thunderer wants to hurl us all from our seats, he can do so, for he is far the strongest, so give him fair words, and he will then soon be in a good humor with us."

As he spoke, he took a double cup of nectar, and placed it in his mother's hand. "Cheer up, my dear mother," he said, "and make the best of it. I love you dearly, and would be very sorry to see you get a thrashing; however grieved I might be, I could not help you, for there is no standing against Zeus. Once before when I was trying to help you, he caught me by the foot and flung me from the heavenly threshold. All day long, from morning till evening, was I falling, till at sunset I came to ground in the island of Lemnos, and there I lay, with very little life left in me, till the Sintians came and tended me."

Hera smiled at this, and as she smiled she took the cup from her son's hands. Then Hephaestus drew sweet nectar from the mixing bowl, and served it around among the gods, going from left to right; and the blessed gods laughed out loud applause as they saw him bustling about the heavenly mansion.[22]

Thus through the livelong day to the going down of the sun they feasted, and everyone had his full share, so that all were satisfied. Apollo struck his lyre, and the Muses lifted up their sweet voices, calling and answering one another. But when the sun's glorious light had faded, they went home to be each in his own abode, which lame Hephaestus with his consummate skill had fashioned for them. So Zeus, the Olympian Lord of Thunder, went to the bed in which he always slept; and when he had gotten on it he went to sleep, with Hera of the golden throne by his side.

[*Zeus has lived up to his word to Thetis.*]

9   Thus did the Trojans watch. But Panic, comrade of bloodstained Rout, had taken fast hold of the Achaeans, and their princes were all of them in despair. As when the two winds that blow from Thrace—the north and the northwest—spring up of a sudden and rouse the fury of the main—in a moment the dark waves uprear their heads and scatter their sea-wrack in all directions—even thus troubled were the hearts of the Achaeans.

---

21   God of the forge.
22   Hephaestus's fall left him permanently lame.

The son of Atreus in dismay bade the heralds call the people to a council man by man, but not to cry the matter aloud; he made haste also himself to call them, and they sat sorry at heart in their assembly. Agamemnon shed tears like a running stream or cataract on the side of some sheer cliff; and thus, with many a heavy sigh he spoke to the Achaeans. "My friends," he said, "princes and councillors of the Argives, the hand of heaven has been laid heavily upon me. Cruel Zeus gave me his solemn promise that I should sack the city of Troy before returning, but he has played me false, and is now bidding me go ingloriously back to Argos with the loss of many people. Such is the will of Zeus, who has laid many a proud city in the dust as he will yet lay others, for his power is above all. Now, therefore, let us all do as I say and sail back to our own country, for we shall not take Troy."

Thus he spoke, and the sons of the Achaeans for a long while sat sorrowful there, but they all held their peace, till at last Diomedes of the loud battle-cry made answer, saying, "Son of Atreus, I will chide your folly, as is my right in council. Do not then be aggrieved that I should do so. In the first place you attacked me before all the Danaans and said that I was a coward and no soldier. The Argives young and old know that you did so. But the son of scheming Cronus endowed you by halves only. He gave you honor as the chief ruler over us, but valor, which is the highest both right and might, he did not give you. Sir, do you think that the sons of the Achaeans are indeed as unwarlike and cowardly as you say they are? If your own mind is set upon going home—go—the way is open to you; the many ships that followed you from Mycenae stand ranged upon the seashore; but the rest of us will stay here till we have sacked Troy. No, though these too should turn homeward with their ships, Sthenelus and myself will still fight on till we reach the goal of Ilium, for heaven was with us when we came."

The sons of the Achaeans shouted applause at the words of Diomedes, and presently Nestor rose to speak. "Son of Tydeus," he said, "in war your prowess is beyond question, and in council you excel all who are of your own years; no one of the Achaeans can make light of what you say or gainsay it, but you have not yet come to the end of the whole matter. You are still young—you might be the youngest of my own children—still you have spoken wisely and have counselled the chief of the Achaeans not without discretion; nevertheless I am older than you and I will tell you everything; therefore let no man, not even King Agamemnon, disregard my words, for he that foments civil discord is a clanless, heartless outlaw.

"Now, however, let us obey the behests of night and get our suppers, but let the sentinels, every man of them, camp by the trench that is outside the wall. I am giving these instructions to the young men; when they have been attended to, you, son of Atreus, give your orders, for you are the most royal among us all. Prepare a feast for your councillors; it is right and reasonable that you should do so; there is abundance of wine in your tents, which the ships of the Achaeans bring from Thrace daily. You have everything at your disposal wherewith to entertain guests, and you have many subjects. When many have been gotten together, you can be guided by him whose counsel is wisest— and sorely do we need shrewd and prudent counsel, for the foe has lit his watchfires hard by our ships. Who can be other than dismayed? This night will either be the ruin of our host, or save it."

Thus did he speak, and they did even as he had said. The sentinels went out in their armor under command of Nestor's son, Thrasymedes, a captain of the host, and of the bold warriors Ascalaphus and Ialmenus; there were also Meriones, Aphareus and Deipyrus, and the son of Creon, noble Lycomedes. There were seven captains of the sentinels, and with each there went a hundred youths armed with long spears; they took their places midway between the trench and the wall, and when they had done so they lit their fires and got every man his supper.

The son of Atreus then bade many councillors of the Achaeans to his quarters and prepared a great feast in their honor. They laid their hands on the good things that were before them, and as soon as they had had enough to eat and drink, old Nestor, whose counsel was ever truest, was the first to lay his mind before them. He, therefore, with all sincerity and goodwill addressed them thus.

"With yourself, most noble son of Atreus, king of men, Agamemnon, will I both begin my speech and end it, for you are king over many people. Zeus, moreover, has vouchsafed you to wield the scepter and to uphold righteousness, that you may take thought for your people under you; therefore it behooves you above all others both to speak and to give ear, and to carry out the counsel of another who shall have been minded to speak wisely. All turns on you and on your commands, therefore I will say what I think will be best. No man will be of a truer mind than that which has been mine from the hour when you, sir, angered Achilles by taking the girl Briseis from his tent against my judgment. I urged you not to do so, but you yielded to your own pride, and dishonored a hero whom heaven itself had honored—for you still hold the prize that had been awarded to him. Now, however, let us think how we may appease him, both with presents and fair speeches that may conciliate him."

And King Agamemnon answered, "Sir, you have reproved my folly justly. I was wrong. I own it. One whom heaven befriends is in himself a host, and Zeus has shown that he befriends this man by destroying many people of the Achaeans. I was blinded with passion and yielded to my worse mind; therefore I will make amends, and will give him great gifts by way of atonement. I will tell them in the presence of you all. I will give him 7 tripods[23] that have never yet been on the fire, and 10 talents of gold. I will give him 20 iron cauldrons and 12 strong horses that have won races and carried off prizes. Rich, indeed, both in land and gold is he that has as many prizes as my horses have won me. I will give him 7 excellent workwomen, from Lesbos, whom I chose for myself when he took Lesbos[24]—all of surpassing beauty. I will give him these, and with them her whom I before took from him, the daughter of Briseus; and I swear a great oath that I never went up into her bed, nor have been with her after the manner of men and women.

"All these things will I give him now down, and if hereafter the gods vouchsafe me to sack the city of Priam, let him come when we Achaeans are dividing the spoil, and load his ship with gold and bronze to his liking; furthermore let him take 20 Trojan women, the loveliest after Helen herself. Then, when we reach Achaean Argos, wealthiest of all lands, he shall be my son-in-law and I will show him like honor with my own dear son Orestes, who is being nurtured in all abundance. I have three daughters, Chrysothemis, Laodice, and Iphianassa; let him take the one of his choice, freely and without gifts of wooing, to the house of Peleus; I will add such dower to boot as no man ever yet gave his daughter, and will give him seven well-established cities, Cardamyle, Enope, and Hire, where there is grass, holy Pherae and the rich meadows of Anthea, Aepea also, and the vine-clad slopes of Pedasus, all near the sea, and on the borders of sandy Pylos. The men that dwell there are rich in cattle and sheep; they will honor him with gifts as though he were a god, and be obedient to his comfortable ordinances. All this will I do if he will now forgo his anger. Let him then yield—it is only Hades who is utterly ruthless and unyielding—and hence he is of all gods the one most hateful to mankind. Moreover I am older and more royal than himself. Therefore, let him now obey me."

Then Nestor answered, "Most noble son of Atreus, king of men, Agamemnon: the gifts you offer are no small ones; let us then send chosen messengers, who may go to the tent of Achilles son of Peleus without delay. Let those go whom I shall name. Let Phoenix, dear to Zeus, lead the way; let Ajax and Odysseus follow, and let the heralds Odius and Eurybates go with them. Now bring water for our hands, and bid all keep silence while we pray to Zeus the son of Cronus, if so be that he may have mercy upon us."

Thus did he speak, and his saying pleased them well. Men-servants poured water over the hands of the guests, while pages filled the mixing-bowls with wine and water, and handed it around after giving every man his drink offering; then, when they had made their offerings, and each had drunk as much as he wished, the envoys set out from the tent of Agamemnon, son of Atreus; and Nestor, looking first to one and then to another, but most especially to Odysseus, was instant with them that they should prevail with the noble son of Peleus.

---

23  A kind of three-legged cauldron, thought originally to have been for use in religious ceremonies, but which at some point also came to be given as gifts.

24  The island was near the supposed site of Troy.

They went their way by the shore of the sounding sea, and prayed earnestly to earth-encircling Poseidon that the high spirit of the son of Aeacus[25] might incline favorably towards them. When they reached the ships and tents of the Myrmidons, they found Achilles playing on a lyre, fair, of cunning workmanship, and its cross-bar was of silver. It was part of the spoils which he had taken when he sacked the city of Eetion, and he was now diverting himself with it and singing the feats of heroes. He was alone with Patroclus, who sat opposite to him and said nothing, waiting till he should cease singing. Odysseus and Ajax now came in—Odysseus leading the way—and stood before him. Achilles sprang from his seat with the lyre still in his hand, and Patroclus, when he saw the strangers, rose also. Achilles then greeted them, saying, "All hail and welcome—you must come upon some great matter, you, who for all my anger are still dearest to me of the Achaeans."

With this he led them forward, and bade them sit on seats covered with purple rugs; then he said to Patroclus who was close by him, "Son of Menoetius, set a larger bowl upon the table, mix less water with the wine, and give every man his cup, for these are very dear friends, who are now under my roof."

Patroclus did as his comrade bade him; he set the chopping-block in front of the fire, and on it he laid the loin of a sheep, the loin also of a goat, and the chine of a fat hog. Automedon held the meat while Achilles chopped it; he then sliced the pieces and put them on spits while the son of Menoetius made the fire burn high. When the flame had died down, he spread the embers, laid the spits on top of them, lifting them up and setting them upon the spit-racks, and he sprinkled them with salt. When the meat was roasted, he set it on platters, and handed bread around the table in fair baskets, while Achilles dealt them their portions. Then Achilles took his seat facing Odysseus against the opposite wall, and bade his comrade Patroclus offer sacrifice to the gods; so he cast the offerings into the fire, and they laid their hands upon the good things that were before them. As soon as they had had enough to eat and drink,

Ajax made a sign to Phoenix, and when he saw this, Odysseus filled his cup with wine and pledged Achilles.

"Hail," he said, "Achilles, we have had no lack of good cheer, neither in the tent of Agamemnon, nor yet here; there has been plenty to eat and drink, but our thought turns upon no such matter. Sir, we are in the face of great disaster, and without your help do not know whether we shall save our fleet or lose it. The Trojans and their allies have camped hard by our ships and by the wall; they have lit watch-fires throughout their host and deem that nothing can now prevent them from falling on our fleet. Zeus, moreover, has sent his lightning on their right; Hector, in all his glory, rages like a maniac; confident that Zeus is with him he fears neither god nor man, but has gone raving mad, and prays for the approach of day. He vows that he will hew the high sterns of our ships in pieces, set fire to their hulls, and make havoc of the Achaeans while they are dazed and smothered in smoke; I much fear that heaven will make good his boasting, and it will prove our lot to perish at Troy far from our home in Argos. Up, then, and late though it is, save the sons of the Achaeans who faint before the fury of the Trojans. You will repent bitterly hereafter if you do not, for when the harm is done there will be no curing it; consider before it is too late, and save the Danaans from destruction.

"My good friend, when your father Peleus sent you from Phthia to Agamemnon, did he not charge you saying, 'Son, Athena and Hera will make you strong if they choose, but check your high temper, for the better part is in goodwill. Eschew vain quarrelling, and the Achaeans old and young will respect you more for doing so.' These were his words, but you have forgotten them. Even now, however, be appeased, and put your anger away from you. Agamemnon will make you great amends if you will forgive him; listen, and I will tell you what he has said in his tent that he will give you. He will give you 7 tripods that have never yet been on the fire, and 10 talents of gold; 20 iron cauldrons, and 12 strong horses that have won races and carried off prizes. Rich indeed both in land and

---

25   Father of Peleus, and so grandfather of Achilles. Achilles is at times referred to as the son of Aeacus.

gold is he who has as many prizes as these horses have won for Agamemnon. Moreover he will give you 7 excellent workwomen, from Lesbos, whom he chose for himself when you took Lesbos—all of surpassing beauty. He will give you these, and with them her whom he before took from you, the daughter of Briseus, and he will swear a great oath that he has never gone up into her bed nor been with her after the manner of men and women. All these things will he give you now down, and if hereafter the gods vouch-safe him to sack the city of Priam, you can come when we Achaeans are dividing the spoil, and load your ship with gold and bronze to your liking. You can take 20 Trojan women, the loveliest after Helen herself. Then, when we reach Achaean Argos, wealthiest of all lands, you shall be his son-in-law, and he will show you like honor with his own dear son Orestes, who is being nurtured in all abundance. Agamemnon has three daughters, Chrysothemis, Laodice, and Iphi-anassa; you may take the one of your choice, freely and without gifts of wooing, to the house of Peleus; he will add such dower to boot as no man ever yet gave his daughter, and will give you seven well-established cities, Cardamyle, Enope, and Hire where there is grass, holy Pherae and the rich meadows of Anthea, Aepea also, and the vine-clad slopes of Pedasus, all near the sea, and on the borders of sandy Pylos. The men that dwell there are rich in cattle and sheep; they will honor you with gifts as though you were a god, and be obedient to your comfortable ordinances. All this will he do if you will now forgo your anger. More-over, though you hate both him and his gifts with all your heart, yet pity the rest of the Achaeans who are being harassed in all their host; they will honor you as a god, and you will earn great glory at their hands. You might even kill Hector; he will come within your reach, for he is infatuated, and declares that not a Danaan whom the ships have brought can hold his own against him."

Achilles answered, "Odysseus, noble son of Laertes, I should give you formal notice plainly and in all fixity of purpose that there be no more of this cajol-ing, from whatsoever quarter it may come. Him do I

hate even as the gates of Hades who says one thing while he hides another in his heart; therefore I will say what I mean. I will be appeased neither by Agamem-non son of Atreus nor by any other of the Danaans, for I see that I have no thanks for all my fighting. He that fights fares no better than he that does not; coward and hero are held in equal honor, and death deals like measure to him who works and him who is idle. I have taken nothing by all my hardships—with my life ever in my hand; as a bird when she has found a morsel takes it to her nestlings, and herself fares hard-ly, even so many a long night have I been wakeful, and many a bloody battle have I waged by day against those who were fighting for their women. With my ships I have taken 12 cities, and 11 around about Troy have I stormed with my men by land; I took great store of wealth from every one of them, but I gave all up to Agamemnon son of Atreus. He stayed where he was by his ships, yet of what came to him he gave lit-tle, and kept much himself.

"Nevertheless he did distribute some prizes of honor among the chieftains and kings, and these have them still; from me alone of the Achaeans did he take the woman in whom I delighted—let him keep her and sleep with her. Why, pray, must the Argives fight the Trojans? What made the son of Atreus gather the host and bring them? Was it not for the sake of Helen? Are the sons of Atreus the only men in the world who love their wives? Any man of common right feeling will love and cherish her who is his own, as I this woman, with my whole heart, though she was but a fruitling of my spear. Agamemnon has taken her from me; he has played me false; I know him; let him tempt me no further, for he shall not move me. Let him look to you, Odysseus, and to the other princes to save his ships from burning. He has done much without me already. He has built a wall; he has dug a trench deep and wide all around it, and he has planted it within with stakes; but even so he does not stay the murder-ous might of Hector. So long as I fought among the Achaeans Hector did not suffer the battle to range far from the city walls; he would come to the Scaean gates[26] and to the oak tree, but no further. Once he

---

26    The great gates of Troy.

stayed to meet me—and hardly did he escape my onset. Now, however, since I am in no mood to fight him, I will tomorrow offer sacrifice to Zeus and to all the gods; I will draw my ships into the water and then duly victual them; tomorrow morning, if you care to look, you will see my ships on the Hellespont,[27] and my men rowing out to sea with might and main. If great Poseidon vouchsafes me a fair passage, in three days I shall be in Phthia. I have much there that I left behind me when I came here to my sorrow, and I shall bring back still further store of gold, of red copper, of fair women, and of iron, my share of the spoils that we have taken; but one prize he who gave has insolently taken away. Tell him all as I now bid you, and tell him in public that the Achaeans may hate him and beware of him should he think that he can yet dupe others—for his effrontery never fails him.

"As for me, hound that he is, he dares not look me in the face. I will take no counsel with him, and will undertake nothing in common with him. He has wronged me and deceived me enough, he shall not cozen me further; let him go his own way, for Zeus has robbed him of his reason. I loathe his presents, and for himself care not one straw. He may offer me 10 or even 20 times what he has now done, no—not though it be all that he has in the world, both now or ever shall have; he may promise me the wealth of Orchomenus or of Egyptian Thebes, which is the richest city in the whole world, for it has a hundred gates through each of which 200 men may drive at once with their chariots and horses; he may offer me gifts like the sands of the sea or the dust of the plain in multitude, but even so he shall not move me till I have been revenged in full for the bitter wrong he has done me. I will not marry his daughter; she may be fair as Aphrodite,[28] and skillful as Athena, but I will have none of her—let another take her, who may be a good match for her and who rules a larger kingdom. If the gods spare me to return home, Peleus will find me a wife; there are Achaean women in Hellas[29] and Phthia, daughters of kings that have cities under them; of these I can take whom I will and marry her. Many a time was I mind-ed when at home in Phthia to woo and wed a woman who would make me a suitable wife, and to enjoy the riches of my old father Peleus. My life is more to me than all the wealth of Ilium while it was yet at peace before the Achaeans went there, or than all the treasure that lies on the stone floor of Apollo's temple beneath the cliffs of Pytho. Cattle and sheep are to be had for carrying off, and a man may buy both tripods and horses if he wants them, but when his life has once left him it can neither be bought nor won back again by force.

"My mother Thetis tells me that there are two ways in which I may meet my end. If I stay here and fight, I shall not return alive but my name will live forever, whereas if I go home my name will die, but it will be long before death shall take me. To the rest of you, then, I say, 'Go home, for you will not take Ilium.' Zeus has held his hand over her to protect her, and her people have taken heart. Go, therefore, as in duty bound, and tell the princes of the Achaeans the message that I have sent them; tell them to find some other plan for the saving of their ships and people, for so long as my displeasure lasts the one that they have now hit upon will not be. As for Phoenix, let him sleep here that he may sail with me in the morning if he so wishes. But I will not take him by force...."

[*Achilles remains adamant, and eventually the envoys return to the Greek camp. Before they go, Achilles states that he will take no part in the fighting unless the Trojans attack his ships. When Book 16 opens, the Trojans are attacking the Greek ships, though have not attacked Achilles's.*]

16   Thus did they fight around the ship of Protesilaus. Then Patroclus drew near to Achilles with tears welling from his eyes, as from some spring whose crystal stream falls over the ledges of a high precipice. When Achilles saw him thus weeping he was sorry for him and said, "Why, Patroclus, do you stand there weeping like some silly child that comes running to her mother, and begs to be taken up and carried—she

---

27   The narrow waters between Europe and Asia.
28   Goddess of (sexual) love and beauty.
29   I.e., Greece.

catches hold of her mother's dress to stay her though she is in a hurry, and looks tearfully up until her mother carries her—even such tears, Patroclus, are you now shedding. Have you anything to say to the Myrmidons or to myself? Or have you had news from Phthia which you alone know? They tell me Menoetius, son of Actor, is still alive, as also Peleus son of Aeacus, among the Myrmidons men whose loss we two would bitterly deplore; or are you grieving about the Argives and the way in which they are being killed at the ships, through their own high-handed doings? Do not keep it from me, but tell me, so we may know it together."

Then, O Patroclus the rider, with a deep sigh you answered, "Achilles, son of Peleus, foremost champion of the Achaeans, do not be angry, but I weep for the disaster that has now befallen the Argives. All those who have been their champions so far are lying at the ships, wounded by sword or spear. Brave Diomedes son of Tydeus has been hit with a spear, while famed Odysseus and Agamemnon have received sword-wounds; Eurypylus again has been struck with an arrow in the thigh; skilled apothecaries are attending to these heroes, and healing them of their wounds; are you still, O Achilles, so inexorable? May it never be my lot to nurse such a passion as you have done, to the baning of your own good name. Who in future story will speak well of you unless you now save the Argives from ruin? You know no pity; Peleus the rider was not your father or Thetis your mother, but the gray sea bore you and the sheer cliffs begot you, so cruel and remorseless are you. If, however, you are kept back through knowledge of some oracle, or if your mother Thetis has told you something from the mouth of Zeus, at least send me and the Myrmidons with me, if I may bring deliverance to the Danaans. Let me, moreover, wear your armor; the Trojans may thus mistake me for you and leave the field, so that the hard-pressed sons of the Achaeans may have breathing time—which while they are fighting may hardly be. We who are fresh might soon drive tired men back from our ships and tents to their own city."

He did not know what he was asking or that he was suing for his own destruction. Achilles was deeply moved and answered, "What, noble Patroclus, are you saying? I know no prophecies which I am

heeding, nor has my mother told me anything from the mouth of Zeus, but I am cut to the very heart that one of my own rank should dare to rob me because he is more powerful than I am. This, after all that I have gone through, is more than I can endure. The girl whom the sons of the Achaeans chose for me, whom I won as the fruit of my spear on having sacked a city— her has King Agamemnon taken from me as though I were some common vagrant. Still, let bygones be bygones—no man may keep his anger forever; I said I would not relent till battle and the cry of war had reached my own ships; nevertheless, now gird my armor about your shoulders, and lead the Myrmidons to battle, for the dark cloud of Trojans has burst furiously over our fleet; the Argives are driven back on to the beach, cooped up within a narrow space, and the whole people of Troy have taken heart to sally out against them, because they do not see the visor of my helmet gleaming near them. Had they seen this, there would not have been a creek or watercourse that would not have been filled with their dead as they fled back again. And so it would have been, if only King Agamemnon had dealt fairly by me. As it is the Trojans have beset our host. Diomedes, son of Tydeus, no longer wields his spear to defend the Danaans, neither have I heard the voice of the son of Atreus coming from his hated head, whereas that of murderous Hector rings in my ears as he gives orders to the Trojans, who triumph over the Achaeans and fill the whole plain with their cry of battle. But even so, Patroclus, fall upon them and save the fleet, lest the Trojans fire it and prevent us from being able to return. Do, however, as I now bid you, that you may win me great honor from all the Danaans, and that they may restore the girl to me again and give me rich gifts into the bargain. When you have driven the Trojans from the ships, come back again. Though Hera's thundering husband should put triumph within your reach, do not fight the Trojans further in my absence, or you will rob me of glory that should be mine. And do not for lust for battle go killing the Trojans or lead the Achaeans on to Ilium, lest one of the ever-living gods from Olympus attack you—for Phoebus Apollo loves them well; return when you have freed the ships from peril, and let others wage war upon the plain. Would, by father Zeus, Athena, and Apollo, that not a single man of all the Trojans might be left alive, or yet of the Argives, but that we two might be alone left to tear aside the mantle that veils the brow of Troy."

Thus did they converse. But Ajax could no longer hold his ground for the shower of darts that rained upon him; the will of Zeus and the javelins of the Trojans were too much for him; the helmet that gleamed about his temples rang with the continuous clatter of the missiles that kept pouring on to it and on to the cheek-pieces that protected his face. Moreover his left shoulder was tired from having held his shield so long, yet for all this, let fly at him as they would, they could not make him give ground. He could hardly draw his breath, the sweat rained from every pore of his body, he had not a moment's respite, and on all sides he was beset by danger upon danger.

And now, tell me, O Muses that hold your mansions on Olympus, how fire was thrown on the ships of the Achaeans. Hector came close up and let drive with his great sword at the ashen spear of Ajax. He cut it clean in two just behind where the point was fastened onto the shaft of the spear. Ajax, therefore, had now nothing but a headless spear, while the bronze point flew some way off and came ringing down on to the ground. Ajax knew the hand of heaven in this, and was dismayed at seeing that Zeus had now left him utterly defenseless and was willing victory for the Trojans. Therefore he drew back, and the Trojans flung fire upon the ship which was at once wrapped in flame.

The fire was now flaring about the ship's stern, whereon Achilles struck his two thighs and said to Patroclus, "Up, noble rider, for I see the glare of hostile fire at our fleet; up, lest they destroy our ships, and there be no way by which we may retreat. Gird on your armor at once while I call our people together."

As he spoke Patroclus put on his armor. First he greaved his legs with greaves of good make, and fitted with ankle clasps of silver; after this he donned the breastplate of the son of Aeacus, richly inlaid and studded. He hung his silver-studded sword of bronze about his shoulders, and then his mighty shield. On his comely head he set his helmet, well wrought, with a nest of horse-hair that nodded menacingly on above it. He grasped two redoubtable spears that suited his hands, but he did not take the spear of noble Achilles, so stout and strong, for none other of the Achaeans could wield it though Achilles could do so easily. This was the ashen spear from Mount Pelion, which Chiron had cut upon a mountain top and had given to Peleus, wherewith to deal out death among heroes. He bade Automedon yoke his horses with all speed, for he was the man whom he held in honor next after Achilles, and on whose support in battle he could rely most firmly. Automedon therefore yoked the fleet horses Xanthus and Balius, steeds that could fly like the wind; these were they whom the harpy Podarge bore to the west wind, as she was grazing in a meadow by the waters of the river Oceanus. In the side traces he set the noble horse Pedasus, whom Achilles had brought away with him when he sacked the city of Eetion, and who, mortal steed though he was, could take his place along with those that were immortal.

Meanwhile Achilles went about everywhere among the tents, and bade his Myrmidons put on their armor. Even as fierce ravening wolves that are feasting upon a horned stag which they have killed upon the mountains, and their jaws are red with blood—they go in a pack to lap water from the clear spring with their long thin tongues; and they reek of blood and slaughter; they do not know what fear is, for it is hunger that drives them—even so did the leaders and counsellors of the Myrmidons gather around the good guardian of the fleet descendant of Aeacus, and among them stood Achilles himself cheering on both men and horses.

Fifty ships had noble Achilles brought to Troy, and in each there was a crew of fifty oarsmen. Over these he set five captains whom he could trust, while he was himself commander over them all. Menesthius of the gleaming corslet, son to the river Spercheus that streams from heaven, was captain of the first company. Fair Polydora, daughter of Peleus, bore him to everflowing Spercheus—a woman mated with a god—but he was called son of Borus son of Perieres, with whom his mother was living as his wedded wife, and who gave great wealth to gain her. The second company was led by noble Eudorus, son to an unwedded woman. Polymela, daughter of Phylas the graceful dancer, bore him; the mighty slayer of Argus[30] was enamored of her as he saw her among the singing women at a dance held in honor of Artemis, the rushing huntress of the golden arrows; therefore he—Hermes,[31] giver of all good—went with her into an upper chamber, and lay with her in secret, whereon she bore him a noble son, Eudorus, singularly fleet of foot and valiant in fight. When Ilithuia, goddess of the pains of childbirth, brought him to the light of day, and he saw the face of the sun, mighty Echecles, son of Actor, took the mother to wife, and gave great wealth to gain her, but her father Phylas brought the child up, and took care of him, doting as fondly upon him as though he were his own son. The third company was led by Pisander, son of Maemalus, the finest spearman among all the Myrmidons next to Achilles's own comrade Patroclus. The old horseman Phoenix was captain of the fourth company, and Alcimedon, noble son of Laerces of the fifth.

When Achilles had chosen his men and had stationed them all with their captains, he charged them strictly, saying, "Myrmidons, remember your threats against the Trojans while you were at the ships in the time of my anger, and you were all complaining of me. 'Cruel son of Peleus,' you would say, 'your mother must have suckled you on gall, so ruthless are you. You keep us here at the ships against our will; if you are so relentless it would be better if we went home over the sea.' Often have you gathered and thus chided me. The hour has now come for those high feats of arms that you have so long been pining for; therefore keep high hearts each one of you to do battle with the Trojans."

With these words he put heart and soul into them all, and they serried their companies yet more closely when they heard the words of their king. As the stones which a builder sets in the wall of some high house which is to give shelter from the winds—even so closely were the helmets and bossed shields set against one another. Shield pressed on shield, helm on helm, and man on man; so close were they that the horse-hair plumes on the gleaming ridges of their helmets touched each other as they bent their heads.

In front of them all two men put on their armor—Patroclus and Automedon—two men, with but one mind to lead the Myrmidons. Then Achilles went inside his tent and opened the lid of the strong chest which silver-footed Thetis had given him to take on board ship, and which she had filled with shirts, cloaks to keep out the cold, and good thick rugs. In this chest he had a cup of rare workmanship, from which no man but himself might drink, nor would he make offering from it to any other god save only to father Zeus. He took the cup from the chest and cleansed it with sulphur; this done he rinsed it in clean water, and after he had washed his hands he drew wine. Then he stood in the middle of the court and prayed, looking towards heaven, and making his drink-offering of wine; nor was he unseen by Zeus whose joy is in thunder. "King Zeus," he cried, "lord of Dodona, god of the Pelasgi, who dwells afar, you who hold wintry Dodona in your sway, where your prophets the Selli dwell around you with their feet unwashed and their beds made upon the ground—if you heard me when I prayed to you before, and did me honor while you sent disaster on the Achaeans, vouchsafe me now the fulfillment of yet this further prayer. I shall stay here where my ships are lying, but I shall send my comrade into battle at the head of many Myrmidons. Grant, O all-seeing Zeus, that victory may go with him; put your courage into his heart that Hector may learn whether my attendant is man enough to fight alone, or whether his might is only then so indomitable when I myself enter the turmoil of war. Afterwards when he has chased the fight and the cry of battle from the ships, grant that he may return unharmed, with his armor and his comrades, fighters in close combat."

Thus did he pray, and all-counselling Zeus heard his prayer. Part of it he did indeed vouchsafe him—but not the whole. He granted that Patroclus should thrust back war and battle from the ships, but refused to let him come safely out of the fight.

When he had made his drink-offering and had thus

30  I.e., Hermes, the god of trade and luck, often also the herald of the gods. Argus was a creature with a hundred eyes.
31  See previous note.

prayed, Achilles went inside his tent and put the cup back into his chest.

Then he again came out, for he still loved to look upon the fierce fight that raged between the Trojans and Achaeans.

Meanwhile the armed band that was about Patroclus marched on till they sprang high in hope upon the Trojans. They came swarming out like wasps whose nests are by the roadside, and whom silly children love to tease, whereon anyone who happens to be passing may get stung—or again, if a wayfarer going along the road vexes them by accident, every wasp will come flying out in a fury to defend his little ones—even with such rage and courage did the Myrmidons swarm from their ships, and their cry of battle rose heavenwards. Patroclus called out to his men at the top of his voice, "Myrmidons, followers of Achilles, son of Peleus, be men my friends, fight with might and with main, that we may win glory for the son of Peleus, who is by far the foremost man at the ships of the Argives—he, and his close fighting followers. The son of Atreus, King Agamemnon, will thus learn his folly in showing no respect to the bravest of the Achaeans."

With these words he put heart and soul into them all, and they fell in a body upon the Trojans. The ships rang again with the cry which the Achaeans raised, and when the Trojans saw the brave son of Menoetius and his attendant all gleaming in their armor, they were daunted and their battalions were thrown into confusion, for they thought the fleet son of Peleus must now have put aside his anger, and have been reconciled with Agamemnon; every one, therefore, looked around to see where he might flee for safety.

Patroclus first aimed a spear into the middle of the press where men were packed most closely, by the stem of the ship of Protesilaus. He hit Pyraechmes who had led his Paeonian horsemen from the Amydon and the broad waters of the river Axius; the spear struck him on the right shoulder, and with a groan he fell backwards in the dust; on this his men were thrown into confusion, for by killing their leader, who was the finest soldier among them, Patroclus struck panic into them all. He thus drove them from the ship and quenched the fire that was then blazing—leaving the half-burned ship to lie where it was. The Trojans were now driven back with a shout that rent the skies, while the Danaans poured after them from their ships, shouting also without ceasing. As when Zeus, gatherer of the thunder-cloud, spreads a dense canopy on the top of some lofty mountain, and all the peaks, the jutting headlands, and forest glades show out in the great light that flashes from the bursting heavens, even so when the Danaans had now driven back the fire from their ships, they took breath for a little while; but the fury of the fight was not yet over, for the Trojans were not driven back in utter rout, but still gave battle, and were ousted from their ground only by sheer fighting.

The fight then became more scattered, and the chieftains killed one another when and how they could. The valiant son of Menoetius first drove his spear into the thigh of Areilycus just as he was turning around; the point went clean through, and broke the bone so that he fell forward. Meanwhile Menelaus struck Thoas in the chest, where it was exposed near the rim of his shield, and he fell dead. The son of Phyleus[32] saw Amphiclus about to attack him, and before he could do so took aim at the upper part of his thigh, where the muscles are thicker than in any other part; the spear tore through all the sinews of the leg, and his eyes were closed in darkness. Of the sons of Nestor, one, Antilochus, speared Atymnius, driving the point of the spear through his throat, and down he fell. Maris then sprang on Antilochus in hand-to-hand fight to avenge his brother, and bestrode the body spear in hand; but valiant Thrasymedes was too quick for him, and in a moment had struck him in the shoulder before he could deal his blow; his aim was true, and the spear severed all the muscles at the root of his arm, and tore them right down to the bone, so he fell heavily to the ground and his eyes were closed in darkness. Thus did these two noble comrades of Sarpedon[33] go down to Erebus[34] slain by the two

32  I.e., Meges, a Greek.
33  One of the chief Trojan warriors, and beloved son of Zeus.
34  A resident of the land of Hades used to refer to the underworld itself.

sons of Nestor; they were the warrior sons of Amiso-
darus, who had reared the invincible Chimaera,[35] to
the bane of many. Ajax,[36] son of Oileus, sprang on
Cleobulus and took him alive as he was entangled in
the crush; but he killed him then and there by a sword-
blow on the neck. The sword reeked with his blood,
while dark death and the strong hand of fate gripped
him and closed his eyes.

Peneleos[37] and Lycon now met in close fight, for
they had missed each other with their spears. They
had both thrown without effect, so now they drew
their swords. Lycon struck the plumed crest of
Peneleos's helmet but his sword broke at the hilt,
while Peneleos struck Lycon on the neck under the ear.
The blade sank so deep that the head was held on by
nothing but the skin, and there was no more life left in
him. Meriones[38] gave chase to Acamas on foot and
caught him up just as he was about to mount his chariot; he drove a spear through his right shoulder so that
he fell headlong from the car, and his eyes were closed
in darkness. Idomeneus speared Erymas in the mouth;
the bronze point of the spear went clean through it
beneath the brain, crashing in among the white bones
and smashing them up. His teeth were all of them
knocked out and the blood came gushing in a stream
from both his eyes; it also came gurgling up from his
mouth and nostrils, and the darkness of death enfolded him around.

Thus did these chieftains of the Danaans each of
them kill his man. As ravening wolves seize on kids or
lambs, fastening on them when they are alone on the
hillsides and have strayed from the main flock
through the carelessness of the shepherd—and when
the wolves see this they pounce upon them at once
because they cannot defend themselves— even so did
the Danaans now fall on the Trojans, who fled with ill-
omened cries in their panic and had no more fight left
in them.

Meanwhile great Ajax kept on trying to drive a
spear into Hector, but Hector was so skillful that he
held his broad shoulders well under cover of his ox-
hide shield, ever on the lookout for the whizzing of
the arrows and the heavy thud of the spears. He well
knew that the fortunes of the day had changed, but
still stood his ground and tried to protect his comrades.

As when a cloud goes up into heaven from Olympus, rising out of a clear sky when Zeus is brewing a
gale—even with such panic-stricken rout did the Trojans now flee, and there was no order in their going.
Hector's fleet horses bore him and his armor out of the
fight, and he left the Trojan host penned in by the deep
trench against their will. Many a yoke of horses
snapped the pole of their chariots in the trench and left
their master's car behind them. Patroclus gave chase,
calling impetuously on the Danaans and full of fury
against the Trojans, who, being now no longer in a
body, filled all the ways with their cries of panic and
rout; the air was darkened with the clouds of dust
they raised, and the horses strained every nerve in
their flight from the tents and ships towards the city.

Patroclus kept on heading his horses wherever he
saw the most men fleeing in confusion, cheering on
his men the while. Chariots were being smashed in all
directions, and many a man came tumbling down
from his own car to fall beneath the wheels of that of
Patroclus, whose immortal steeds, given by the gods
to Peleus, sprang over the trench at a bound as they
sped onward. He was intent on trying to get near Hector, for he had set his heart on spearing him, but Hector's horses were now hurrying him away. As the
whole dark earth bows before some tempest on an
autumn day when Zeus rains his hardest to punish
men for giving crooked judgment in their courts, and
driving justice therefrom without heed to the decrees
of heaven—all the rivers run full and the torrents tear
many a new channel as they roar headlong from the
mountains to the dark sea, and it fares ill with the
works of men—even such was the stress and strain of
the Trojan horses in their flight.

Patroclus now cut off the battalions that were nearest to him and drove them back to the ships. They

35   A terrible monster with the head of a lion, the body of a goat, and the tail of a snake.
36   Also known as "little Ajax," and not to be confused with the other Ajax ("great Ajax"), son of Telemon.
37   A Greek.
38   A Greek.

were doing their best to reach the city, but he would not let them, and bore down on them between the river and the ships and wall. Many a fallen comrade did he then avenge. First he hit Pronous with a spear on the chest where it was exposed near the rim of his shield, and he fell heavily to the ground. Next he sprang on Thestor, son of Enops, who was sitting all huddled up in his chariot, for he had lost his head and the reins had been torn out of his hands. Patroclus went up to him and drove a spear into his right jaw; he thus hooked him by the teeth and the spear pulled him over the rim of his car, as one who sits at the end of some jutting rock and draws a strong fish out of the sea with a hook and a line—even so with his spear did he pull Thestor all gaping from his chariot; he then threw him down on his face and he died while falling. On this, as Erylaus was coming on to attack him, he struck him full on the head with a stone, and his brains were all battered inside his helmet, whereon he fell headlong to the ground and the pangs of death took hold upon him. Then he laid low, one after the other, Erymas, Amphoterus, Epaltes, Tlepolemus, Echius, son of Damastor, Pyris, Ipheus, Euippus, and Polymelus, son of Argeas....

[*Patroclus continues to slay Trojans, including Sarpedon. Zeus then has Sarpedon's body removed from the battle and cared for.*]

Meanwhile Patroclus, with many a shout to his horses and to Automedon, pursued the Trojans and Lycians in the pride and foolishness of his heart. Had he but obeyed the bidding of the son of Peleus, he would have escaped death and have been scatheless; but the counsels of Zeus pass man's understanding; he will put even a brave man to flight and snatch victory from his grasp, or again he will set him on to fight, as he now did when he put a high spirit into the heart of Patroclus.

Who then first, and who last, was slain by you, O Patroclus, when the gods had now called you to meet your doom? First Adrestus, Autonous, Echeclus, Perimus, the son of Megas, Epistor, and Melanippus; after

these he killed Elasus, Mulius, and Pylartes. These he slew, but the rest saved themselves by flight.

The sons of the Achaeans would now have taken Troy by the hands of Patroclus, for his spear flew in all directions, had not Phoebus Apollo taken his stand upon the wall to defeat his purpose and to aid the Trojans. Three times did Patroclus charge at an angle of the high wall, and three times did Apollo beat him back, striking his shield with his own immortal hands. When Patroclus was coming on like a god for yet a fourth time, Apollo shouted to him with an awful voice and said, "Draw back, noble Patroclus, it is not your lot to sack the city of the Trojan chieftains, nor yet will it be that of Achilles who is a far better man than you are." On hearing this, Patroclus withdrew to some distance and avoided the anger of Apollo.

Meanwhile Hector was waiting with his horses inside the Scaean gates, in doubt whether to drive out again and go on fighting, or to call the army inside the gates. As he was thus doubting Phoebus Apollo drew near him in the likeness of a young and lusty warrior Asius, who was Hector's uncle, being own brother to Hecuba,[39] and son of Dymas who lived in Phrygia by the waters of the river Sangarius; in his likeness Zeus's son Apollo now spoke to Hector saying, "Hector, why have you left off fighting? It is ill done of you. If I were as much better a man than you, as I am worse, you would soon rue your slackness. Drive straight towards Patroclus, if it so be that Apollo may grant you a triumph over him, and you may kill him."

With this the god went back into the hurly-burly, and Hector bade Cebriones drive again into the fight. Apollo passed in among them, and struck panic into the Argives, while he gave triumph to Hector and the Trojans. Hector let the other Danaans alone and killed no man, but drove straight at Patroclus. Patroclus then sprang from his chariot to the ground, with a spear in his left hand, and in his right a jagged stone as large as his hand could hold. He stood still and threw it, nor did it go far without hitting someone; the cast was not in vain, for the stone struck Cebriones, Hector's charioteer, a bastard son of Priam, as he held the reins in his hands. The stone hit him on the forehead and

39 Hector's mother.

drove his brows into his head, for the bone was smashed, and his eyes fell to the ground at his feet. He dropped dead from his chariot as though he were diving, and there was no more life left in him. Over him did you then mock, O rider Patroclus, saying, "Bless my heart, how active he is, and how well he dives. If we had been at sea this fellow would have dived from the ship's side and brought up as many oysters as the whole crew could stomach, even in rough water, for he has dived beautifully off his chariot onto the ground. It seems, then, that there are divers also among the Trojans."

As he spoke he flung himself on Cebriones with the spring, as it were, of a lion that while attacking a stockyard is himself struck in the chest, and his courage is his own bane—even so furiously, O Patroclus, did you then spring upon Cebriones. Hector sprang also from his chariot to the ground. The pair then fought over the body of Cebriones. As two famished lions fight fiercely on some high mountain over the body of a stag that they have killed, even so did these two mighty warriors, Patroclus, son of Menoetius, and brave Hector, hack and hew at one another over the corpse of Cebriones. Hector would not let him go when he had once got him by the head, while Patroclus kept fast hold of his feet, and a fierce fight raged between the other Danaans and Trojans. As the east and south wind buffet one another when they beat upon some dense forest on the mountains— there is beech and ash and spreading cornel trees; the tops of the trees roar as they beat on one another, and one can hear the boughs cracking and breaking—even so did the Trojans and Achaeans spring upon one another and lay about each other, and neither side would give way. Many a pointed spear fell to ground and many a winged arrow sped from its bow-string around the body of Cebriones; many a great stone, moreover, beat on many a shield as they fought around his body, but there he lay in the whirling clouds of dust, all huge and hugely, heedless of his driving now.

So long as the sun was still high in mid-heaven the weapons of either side were alike deadly, and the people fell; but when he went down towards the time when men loose their oxen, the Achaeans proved to be beyond all forecast stronger, so that they drew Cebriones out of range of the darts and tumult of the Trojans, and stripped the armor from his shoulders. Then Patroclus sprang like Ares[40] with fierce intent and a terrific shout upon the Trojans, and three times did he kill nine men; but as he was coming on like a god for a fourth time, then, O Patroclus, was the hour of your end approaching, for Phoebus fought you in deadly earnest. Patroclus did not see him as he moved about in the crush, for he was enshrouded in thick darkness, and the god struck him from behind on his back and his broad shoulders with the flat of his hand, so that his eyes turned dizzy. Phoebus Apollo beat the helmet from off his head, and it rolled rattling off under the horses' feet, where its horse-hair plumes were all begrimed with dust and blood. Never indeed had that helmet fared so before, for it had served to protect the head and comely forehead of the godlike hero Achilles. Now, however, Zeus delivered it over to be worn by Hector. Nevertheless the end of Hector also was near. The bronze-shod spear, so great and so strong, was broken in the hand of Patroclus, while his shield that covered him from head to foot fell to the ground as did also the hand that held it, and Apollo undid the fastenings of his corslet.

On this his mind became clouded; his limbs failed him, and he stood as one dazed; whereon Euphorbus, son of Panthous, a Dardanian, the best spearman of his time, as also the finest horseman and fleetest runner, came behind him and struck him in the back with a spear, midway between the shoulders. This man as soon as ever he had come up with his chariot had dismounted 20 men, so proficient was he in all the arts of war—he it was, O rider Patroclus, that first drove a weapon into you, but he did not quite overpower you. Euphorbus then ran back into the crowd, after drawing his ashen spear out of the wound; he would not stand firm and wait for Patroclus, unarmed though he now was, to attack him; but Patroclus, unnerved alike by the blow the god had given him and by the spear-wound, drew back under cover of his men in fear for

---

40  God of war.

his life. On this, Hector, seeing him to be wounded and giving ground, forced his way through the ranks, and when close up with him struck him in the lower part of the belly with a spear, driving the bronze point right through it, so that he fell heavily to the ground to the great grief of the Achaeans. As when a lion has fought some fierce wild-boar and worsted him—the two fight furiously upon the mountains over some little fountain at which they would both drink, and the lion has beaten the boar till he can hardly breathe—even so did Hector, son of Priam, take the life of the brave son of Menoetius who had killed so many, striking him from close at hand, and vaunting over him the while. "Patroclus," he said, "you deemed that you should sack our city, rob our Trojan women of their freedom, and carry them off in your ships to your own country. Fool, Hector and his fleet horses were ever straining their utmost to defend them. I am foremost of all the Trojan warriors to stave the day of bondage from them; as for you, vultures shall devour you here. Poor wretch, Achilles with all his bravery availed you nothing; and yet I think when you left him he charged you strictly, saying, 'Do not come back to the ships, rider Patroclus, till you have rent the bloodstained shirt of murderous Hector about his body.' Thus I think did he charge you, and your fool's heart answered him 'yes' within you."

Then, as the life ebbed out of you, you answered, O rider Patroclus, "Hector, glory as you will, for Zeus the son of Cronus and Apollo have vouchsafed you victory; it is they who have vanquished me so easily, and they who have stripped the armor from my shoulders; had 20 such men as you attacked me, all of them would have fallen before my spear. Fate and the son of Leto have overpowered me, and among mortal men Euphorbus; you are yourself third only in the killing of me. I say further, and lay my saying to your heart, you too shall live but for a little season; death and the day of your doom are close upon you, and they will lay you low by the hand of Achilles, son of Aeacus."

When he had thus spoken his eyes were closed in death, his soul left his body and flitted down to the house of Hades, mourning its sad fate and bidding farewell to the youth and vigor of its manhood. Dead though he was, Hector still spoke to him, saying,

"Patroclus, why should you thus foretell my doom? Who knows but Achilles, son of lovely Thetis, may be smitten by my spear and die before me?"

As he spoke he drew the bronze spear from the wound, planting his foot upon the body, which he thrust off and let lie on its back. He then went spear in hand after Automedon, comrade in arms of the fleet descendant of Aeacus, for he longed to lay him low, but the immortal steeds which the gods had given as a rich gift to Peleus bore him swiftly from the field.

[*The battle continues. Hector strips the armor worn by Patroclus and puts it on. The Greeks and Trojans, however, fight over Patroclus's body.*]

18   Thus then did they fight as it were a flaming fire. Meanwhile the fleet runner Antilochus, who had been sent as messenger, reached Achilles, and found him sitting by his tall ships and boding that which was indeed too surely true. "Alas," he said to himself in the heaviness of his heart, "why are the Achaeans again scouring the plain and flocking towards the ships? Heaven grant the gods are not now bringing that sorrow upon me of which my mother Thetis spoke, saying that while I was yet alive the bravest of the Myrmidons should fall before the Trojans, and see the light of the sun no longer. I fear the brave son of Menoetius has fallen through his own daring—and yet I bade him return to the ships as soon as he had driven back those that were bringing fire against them, and not join battle with Hector."

As he was thus pondering, the son of Nestor came up to him and told his sad tale, weeping bitterly the while. "Alas," he cried, "son of noble Peleus, I bring you bad tidings, would indeed that they were untrue. Patroclus has fallen, and a fight is raging about his naked body—for Hector holds his armor."

A dark cloud of grief fell upon Achilles as he listened. He filled both hands with dust from off the ground, and poured it over his head, disfiguring his comely face, and letting the refuse settle over his shirt so fair and new. He flung himself down all huge and hugely at full length, and tore his hair with his hands. The women slaves whom Achilles and Patroclus had taken captive screamed aloud for grief, beating their breasts, and with their limbs failing them for sorrow.

Antilochus bent over him the while, weeping and holding both his hands as he lay groaning, for he feared that Achilles might plunge a knife into his own throat. Then Achilles gave a loud cry and his mother heard him as she was sitting in the depths of the sea by the old man her father, whereon she screamed, and all the goddesses daughters of Nereus that dwelled at the bottom of the sea came gathering around her. There were Glauce, Thalia and Cymodoce, Nesaia, Speo, Thoe, and dark-eyed Halie, Cymothoe, Actaea and Limnorea, Melite, Iaera, Amphithoe and Agave, Doto and Proto, Pherusa and Dynamene, Dexamene, Amphinome and Callianeira, Doris, Panope, and the famous sea nymph Galatea, Nemertes, Apseudes and Callianassa. There were also Clymene, Ianeira and Ianassa, Maera, Oreithuia and Amatheia of the lovely locks, with other Nereids[41] who dwell in the depths of the sea. The crystal cave was filled with their multitude and they all beat their breasts while Thetis led them in their lament.

"Listen," she cried, "sisters, daughters of Nereus, that you may hear the burden of my sorrows. Alas, woe is me, woe in that I have borne the most glorious of offspring. I bore him fair and strong, hero among heroes, and he shot up as a sapling; I tended him as a plant in a goodly garden, and sent him with his ships to Ilium to fight the Trojans, but never shall I welcome him back to the house of Peleus. So long as he lives to look upon the light of the sun he is in heaviness, and though I go to him I cannot help him. Nevertheless I will go, that I may see my dear son and learn what sorrow has befallen him though he is still holding aloof from battle."

She left the cave as she spoke, while the others followed after, weeping, and the waves opened a path before them. When they reached the rich plain of Troy, they came up out of the sea in a long line on to the sands, at the place where the ships of the Myrmidons were drawn up in close order around the tents of Achilles. His mother went up to him as he lay groaning; she laid her hand upon his head and spoke piteously, saying, "My son, why are you thus weeping? What sorrow has now befallen you? Tell me; do not hide it from me. Surely Zeus has granted you the prayer you made him, when you lifted up your hands and besought him that the Achaeans might all of them be pent up at their ships, and rue it bitterly in that you were no longer with them."

Achilles groaned and answered, "Mother, Olympian Zeus has indeed vouchsafed me the fulfillment of my prayer, but what does it profit me, seeing that my dear comrade Patroclus has fallen—he whom I valued more than all others, and loved as dearly as my own life? I have lost him; yes, and Hector when he had killed him stripped him of the wondrous armor, so glorious to behold, which the gods gave to Peleus when they laid you in the bed of a mortal man. Would that you were still dwelling among the immortal sea nymphs, and that Peleus had taken to himself some mortal bride. For now you shall have infinite grief by reason of the death of that son whom you can never welcome home—no, I will neither live nor go about among mankind unless Hector falls by my spear, and thus pays me for having slain Patroclus, son of Menoetius."

Thetis wept and answered, "Then, my son, your end is near at hand—for your own death awaits you swiftly after that of Hector."

Then said Achilles in his great grief, "I would die here and now, in that I could not save my comrade. He has fallen far from home, and in his hour of need my hand was not there to help him. What is there for me? Return to my own land I shall not, and I have brought no saving either to Patroclus or to my other comrades of whom so many have been slain by mighty Hector; I stay here by my ships, a useless burden upon the earth, I, who in fight have no peer among the Achaeans, though in council there are better than I. Therefore, perish strife both from among gods and men, and anger, wherein even a righteous man will harden his heart—which rises up in the soul of a man like smoke, and the taste thereof is sweeter than drops of honey. Even so has Agamemnon angered me. And yet—so be it, for it is over; I will force my soul into subjection as I must; I will go; I will pursue Hector who has slain him whom I loved so dearly, and will

_J_

---

41   I.e., goddess daughters of Nereus.

then abide my doom when it may please Zeus and the other gods to send it. Even Hercules, the best beloved of Zeus—even he could not escape the hand of death, but fate and Hera's fierce anger laid him low, as I too shall lie when I am dead if a like doom awaits me. Till then I will win fame, and will bid Trojan and Dardanian women wring tears from their tender cheeks with both their hands in the grievousness of their great sorrow; thus shall they know that he who has held aloof so long will hold aloof no longer. Do not hold me back, therefore, in the love you bear me, for you shall not move me."

Then silver-footed Thetis answered, "My son, what you have said is true. It is well to save your comrades from destruction, but your armor is in the hands of the Trojans; Hector bears it in triumph upon his own shoulders. Full well I know that his glory shall not be lasting, for his end is close at hand; do not go, however, into the press of battle till you see me return here; tomorrow at break of day I shall be here, and will bring you goodly armor from King Hephaestus."

On this she left her brave son, and as she turned away she said to the sea nymphs her sisters, "Dive into the bosom of the sea and go to the house of the old sea god my father. Tell him everything; as for me, I will go to the cunning workman Hephaestus on high Olympus, and ask him to provide my son with a suit of splendid armor."

When she had so spoken, they dived forthwith beneath the waves, while silverfooted Thetis went her way that she might bring the armor for her son....

[*Thetis succeeds in procuring armor for Achilles from Hephaestus, and Achilles goes into battle and kills many Trojan warriors. Achilles's entry into battle also allows the Greeks to bring Patroclus's body out of the reach of the Trojans. Apollo has taken on the guise of Agenor, a Trojan warrior, in order to lead Achilles away from Troy. This ruse has allowed the Trojans, with the exception of Hector, to retreat within the city walls.*]

22 Thus the Trojans in the city, scared like fawns, wiped the sweat from off themselves and drank to quench their thirst, leaning against the goodly battlements, while the Achaeans with their shields laid upon their shoulders drew close up to the walls. But stern fate bid Hector stay where he was before Ilium and the Scaean gates. Then Phoebus Apollo spoke to the son of Peleus, saying "Why, son of Peleus, do you, who are but a man, give chase to me who am immortal? Have you not yet found out that it is a god whom you chase so furiously? You did not harass the Trojans whom you had routed, while you have been decoyed here away from them. Me you cannot kill, for death can take no hold on me."

Achilles was greatly angered and said, "You have baulked me, Far-Darter, most malicious of all gods, and have drawn me away from the wall, where many another man would have bitten the dust before he got within Ilium; you have robbed me of great glory and have saved the Trojans at no risk to yourself, for you have nothing to fear, but I would indeed have my revenge if it were in my power to do so."

On this, with deadly intent he made towards the city, and as the winning horse in a chariot race strains every nerve when he is flying over the plain, even so fast and furiously did the limbs of Achilles bear him onwards. King Priam was the first to note him as he scoured the plain, all radiant as the star which men call Orion's Hound, and whose beams blaze forth in time of harvest more brilliantly than those of any other that shines by night; brightest of them all though he is, he yet bodes ill for mortals, for he brings fire and fever in his train—so did Achilles's armor gleam on his breast as he sped onwards. Priam raised a cry and beat his head with his hands as he lifted them up and shouted out to his dear son, imploring him to return; but Hector stayed before the gates, for his heart was set upon doing battle with Achilles. The old man reached out his arms towards him and bade him for pity's sake to come within the walls. "Hector," he cried, "my son, do not stay to face this man alone and unsupported, or you will meet death at the hands of the son of Peleus, for he is mightier than you. Monster that he is; would indeed that the gods loved him no better than I do, for so dogs and vultures would soon devour him as he lay stretched out on the earth, and a load of grief would be lifted from my heart, for many a brave son has he seized from me, either by killing them or selling them in the islands that are beyond the sea; even now I miss two sons among the Trojans who have crowded within the city, Lycaon and Polydorus, whom Laothoe, peeress among women, bore me. Should they still be alive and in the hands of the Achaeans, we will ransom them with gold and bronze, of which we have store, for the old man Altes[42] endowed his daughter richly; but if they are already dead and within the house of Hades, sorrow will it be to us who were their parents; albeit the grief of others will be more short-lived unless you too perish at the hand of Achilles. Come, then, my son, within the city, be the guardian of Trojan men and Trojan women, or you will both lose your own life and afford a mighty triumph to the son of Peleus. Have pity also on your unhappy father while life yet remains to him—on me, whom the son of Cronus will destroy by a terrible doom on the threshold of old age, after I have seen my sons slain and my daughters haled away as captives, my bridal chambers pillaged, little children dashed to earth amid the rage of battle, and my sons' wives dragged away by the cruel hands of the Achaeans; in the end fierce hounds will tear me in pieces at my own gates after someone has beaten the life out of my body with sword or spear—hounds that I myself reared and fed at my own table to guard my gates, who will yet lap up my blood and then lie all distraught at my doors. When a young man falls by the sword in battle, he may lie where he is and there is nothing unseemly; let what will be seen, all is honorable in death, but when an old man is slain there is nothing in the world more pitiable than that dogs should defile his gray hair and beard and that all men hide for shame."

The old man tore his gray hair as he spoke, but he did not move the heart of Hector. His mother hard by wept and moaned aloud as she bared her bosom and pointed to the breast which had suckled him. "Hector," she cried, weeping bitterly the while, "Hector, my son, do not spurn this breast, but have pity upon me too if I have ever given you comfort from my own bosom; think on it now, dear son, and come within the wall to protect us from this man; do not stand outside to meet him. Should the wretch kill you, neither I nor your richly dowered wife shall ever weep, dear offshoot of myself, over the bed on which you lie, for dogs will devour you at the ships of the Achaeans."

Thus did the two with many tears implore their son, but they did not move the heart of Hector, and he stood his ground awaiting huge Achilles as he drew nearer towards him. As a serpent in its den upon the mountains, full fed with deadly poisons, waits for the approach of man—he is filled with fury and his eyes glare terribly as he goes writhing around his den—even so Hector leaned his shield against a tower that jutted out from the wall and stood where he was, undaunted.

"Alas," he said to himself in the heaviness of his heart, "if I go within the gates, Polydamas[43] will be the first to heap reproach upon me, for it was he that urged me to lead the Trojans back to the city on that awful night when Achilles again came forth against us. I would not listen, but it would have been indeed better if I had done so. Now that my folly has destroyed the host, I dare not look Trojan men and Trojan women in the face, lest a worse man should say, 'Hector has ruined us by his self-confidence.' Surely it would be better for me to return after having fought Achilles and slain him or to die gloriously here before the city. What, again, if I were to lay down my shield and helmet, lean my spear against the wall and go straight up to noble Achilles? What if I were to promise to give up Helen, who was the fountainhead of all this war, and all the treasure that Alexander[44] brought with him in his ships to Troy, yes, and to let the Achaeans divide half of everything that the city contains among themselves? I might make the Trojans, by the mouths of their princes, take a solemn oath that they would hide nothing, but would divide into two shares all that is within the city—but why argue with myself in this way? Were I to go up to him he would show me no kind of mercy; he would kill me then and there as easily as though I were a woman, when I had put off my armor. There is no parleying with him from some rock or oak tree as young men and maidens prattle with one another. Better to fight him at once, and learn to which of us Zeus will vouchsafe victory."

---

42  Father of Laothoe.
43  A Trojan commander.
44  Another name for Paris.

Thus did he stand and ponder, but Achilles came up to him like Ares himself, plumed lord of battle. From his right shoulder he brandished his terrible spear of Pelian ash, and the bronze gleamed around him like flashing fire or the rays of the rising sun. Fear fell upon Hector as he beheld him, and he dared not stay longer where he was, but fled in dismay from before the gates, while Achilles darted after him at his utmost speed. As a mountain falcon, swiftest of all birds, swoops down upon some cowering dove—the dove flies before him but the falcon with a shrill scream follows close after, resolved to have her—even so did Achilles make straight for Hector with all his might, while Hector fled under the Trojan wall as fast as his limbs could take him.

On they flew along the wagon road that ran hard by under the wall, past the lookout station, and past the weather-beaten wild fig tree, till they came to two fair springs which feed the river Scamander. One of these two springs is warm, and steam rises from it as smoke from a burning fire, but the other even in summer is as cold as hail or snow, or the ice that forms on water. Here, hard by the springs, are the goodly washing troughs of stone, where in the time of peace before the coming of the Achaeans the wives and fair daughters of the Trojans used to wash their clothes. Past these did they fly, the one in front and the other giving chase behind him; good was the man that fled, but better far was he that followed after, and swiftly indeed did they run, for the prize was no mere beast for sacrifice or bullock's hide, as it might be for a common foot race, but they ran for the life of Hector. As horses in a chariot race speed around the turning posts when they are running for some great prize—a tripod or woman—at the games in honor of some dead hero, so did these two run full speed three times around the city of Priam. All the gods watched them, and the father of gods and men was the first to speak.

"Alas," he said, "my eyes behold a man who is dear to me being pursued around the walls of Troy; my heart is full of pity for Hector, who burned the thighbones of many a heifer in my honor while on the crests of many-valleyed Ida, and again on the citadel of Troy; now I see noble Achilles in full pursuit of him around the city of Priam. What say you? Consider among yourselves and decide whether we shall now save him or let him fall, valiant though he is, before Achilles, son of Peleus."

Then Athena said, "Father, wielder of the lightning, lord of cloud and storm, what do you mean? Would you pluck this mortal, whose doom has long been decreed, out of the jaws of death? Do as you will, but we others shall not be of a mind with you."

And Zeus answered, "My child, third born, take heart. I did not speak in full earnest, and I will let you have your way. Do without let or hindrance as you are minded."

Thus did he urge Athena who was already eager, and down she darted from the topmost summits of Olympus.

Achilles was still in full pursuit of Hector, as a hound chasing a fawn which he has started from its cover on the mountains, and hunts through glade and thicket. The fawn may try to elude him by crouching under cover of a bush, but he will scent her out and follow her up until he gets her—even so there was no escape for Hector from the fleet son of Peleus. Whenever he made set to get near the Dardanian gates and under the walls, that his people might help him by showering down weapons from above, Achilles would gain on him and head him back towards the plain, keeping himself always on the city side. As a man in a dream who fails to lay hands upon another whom he is pursuing—the one cannot escape or the other overtake—even so neither could Achilles come up with Hector, nor Hector break away from Achilles; nevertheless he might even yet have escaped death had not the time come when Apollo, who thus far had sustained his strength and nerved his running, was now no longer to stay by him. Achilles made signs to the Achaean host, and shook his head to show that no man was to aim a dart at Hector, lest another might win the glory of having hit him and he might himself come in second. Then, at last, as they were nearing the springs for the fourth time, the father of all balanced his golden scales and placed a doom in each of them, one for Achilles and the other for Hector. As he held the scales by the middle, the doom of Hector fell down deep into the house of Hades—and then Phoebus Apollo left him. Thereon Athena went close up to the son of Peleas and said, "Noble Achilles, favored of heaven, we two shall surely take back to the ships a triumph for the Achaeans by slaying Hector, for all his lust for battle. Do what Apollo may as he lies grovelling before his father, aegis-bearing Zeus, Hector cannot escape us any longer. Stay here and take breath, while I go up to him and persuade him to make a stand and fight you."

Thus spoke Athena. Achilles obeyed her gladly, and stood still, leaning on his bronze-pointed ashen spear, while Athena left him and went after Hector in the form and with the voice of Deiphobus.[45] She came close up to him and said, "Dear brother, I see you are hard pressed by Achilles who is chasing you at full speed around the city of Priam; let us await his onset and stand on our defense."

And Hector answered, "Deiphobus, you have always been dearest to me of all my brothers, children of Hecuba and Priam, but henceforth I shall rate you yet more highly, inasmuch as you have ventured outside the wall for my sake when all the others remain inside."

Then Athena said, "Dear brother, my father and mother went down on their knees and implored me, as did all my comrades, to remain inside, so great a fear has fallen upon them all; but I was in an agony of grief when I beheld you; now, therefore, let us two make a stand and fight, and let there be no keeping our spears in reserve, that we may learn whether Achilles shall kill us and bear off our spoils to the ships, or whether he shall fall before you."

Thus did Athena inveigle him by her cunning, and when the two were now close to one another great Hector was first to speak. "I will no longer flee from you, son of Peleus," he said, "as I have been doing hitherto. Three times have I fled around the mighty city of Priam, without daring to withstand you, but now, let me either slay or be slain, for I am in the mind to face you. Let us, then, give pledges to one another by our gods, who are the fittest witnesses and guardians of all covenants; let it be agreed between us that if Zeus vouchsafes me the longer stay and I take your life, I am not to treat your dead body in any unseemly fashion, but when I have stripped you of your armor, I am to give up your body to the Achaeans. And you do likewise."

Achilles glared at him and answered, "Fool, do not prate to me about covenants. There can be no covenants between men and lions; wolves and lambs can never be of one mind, but hate each other out and out all through. Therefore there can be no understanding between you and me, nor may there be any covenants between us, till one or other shall fall and glut grim Ares with his life's blood. Put forth all your strength; you have need now to prove yourself indeed a bold soldier and man of war. You have no more chance, and Pallas Athena will forthwith vanquish you by my spear; you shall now pay me in full for the grief you have caused me on account of my comrades whom you have killed in battle."

He poised his spear as he spoke and hurled it. Hector saw it coming and avoided it; he watched it and crouched down so that it flew over his head and stuck in the ground beyond; Athena then snatched it up and gave it back to Achilles without Hector's seeing her; Hector thereupon said to the son of Peleus, "You have missed your aim, Achilles, peer of the gods, and Zeus has not yet revealed to you the hour of my doom, though you made sure that he had done so. You were a false-tongued liar when you deemed that I should forget my valor and quail before you. You shall not drive your spear into the back of a runaway—drive it, should heaven so grant you power, drive it into me as I make straight towards you; and now for your own part avoid my spear if you can—would that you might receive the whole of it into your body; if you were once dead the Trojans would find the war an easier matter, for it is you who have harmed them most."

He poised his spear as he spoke and hurled it. His aim was true for he hit the middle of Achilles's shield, but the spear rebounded from it, and did not pierce it. Hector was angry when he saw that the weapon had sped from his hand in vain, and stood there in dismay, for he had no second spear. With a loud cry he called Deiphobus and asked him for one, but there was no man; then he saw the truth and said to himself, "Alas! the gods have lured me on to my destruction. I deemed that the hero Deiphobus was by my side, but he is within the wall, and Athena has inveigled me;

---

45   A son of Priam.

death is now indeed exceedingly near at hand and there is no way out of it—for so Zeus and his son Apollo the far-darter have willed it, though heretofore they have been ever ready to protect me. My doom has come upon me; let me not then die ingloriously and without a struggle, but let me first do some great thing that shall be told among men hereafter."

As he spoke he drew the keen blade that hung so great and strong by his side, and gathering himself together he sprang on Achilles like a soaring eagle which swoops down from the clouds on to some lamb or timid hare—even so did Hector brandish his sword and spring upon Achilles. Achilles mad with rage darted towards him, with his wondrous shield before his breast, and his gleaming helmet, made with four layers of metal, nodding fiercely forward. The thick tresses of gold with which Hephaestus had crested the helmet floated around it, and as the evening star that shines brighter than all others through the stillness of night, even such was the gleam of the spear which Achilles poised in his right hand, fraught with the death of noble Hector. He eyed his fair flesh over and over to see where he could best wound it, but all was protected by the goodly armor of which Hector had despoiled Patroclus after he had slain him, save only the throat where the collarbones divide the neck from the shoulders, and this is a most deadly place; here then did Achilles strike him as he was coming on towards him, and the point of his spear went right through the fleshy part of the neck, but it did not sever his windpipe so that he could still speak. Hector fell headlong, and Achilles exulted over him saying, "Hector, you deemed that you should come off scatheless when you were despoiling Patroclus, and did not reckon on myself who was not with him. Fool that you were, for I, his comrade, mightier by far than he, was still left behind him at the ships, and now I have laid you low. The Achaeans shall give him all due funeral rites, while dogs and vultures shall work their will upon yourself."

Then Hector said, as the life ebbed out of him, "I pray you by your life and knees, and by your parents, do not let dogs devour me at the ships of the Achaeans, but accept the rich treasure of gold and bronze which my father and mother will offer you, and send my body home, that the Trojans and their wives may give me my dues of fire when I am dead."

Achilles glared at him and answered, "Dog, do not talk to me either of knees or parents; would that I could be as sure of being able to cut your flesh into pieces and eat it raw for the ill you have done me, as I am nothing shall save you from the dogs—it shall not be, though they bring ten or twentyfold ransom and weigh it out for me on the spot, with promise of yet more hereafter. Though Priam, son of Dardanus, should bid them offer me your weight in gold, even so your mother shall never lay you out and make lament over the son she bore, but dogs and vultures shall eat you utterly up."

Hector with his dying breath then said, "I know you, what you are, and was sure that I would not move you, for your heart is hard as iron; look to it that I do not bring heaven's anger upon you on the day when Paris and Phoebus Apollo, valiant though you are, shall slay you at the Scaean gates."

When he had thus spoken, the shrouds of death enfolded him, whereupon his soul went out of him and flew down to the house of Hades, lamenting its sad fate that it should enjoy youth and strength no longer. But Achilles said, speaking to the dead body, "Die; for my part I will accept my fate whensoever Zeus and the other gods see fit to send it."

As he spoke he drew his spear from the body and set it on one side; then he stripped the blood-stained armor from Hector's shoulders while the other Achaeans came running up to view his wondrous strength and beauty; and no one came near him without giving him a fresh wound. Then would one turn to his neighbor and say, "It is easier to handle Hector now than when he was flinging fire onto our ships"— and as he spoke he would thrust his spear into him anew.

When Achilles had finished despoiling Hector of his armor, he stood among the Argives and said, "My friends, princes and counsellors of the Argives, now that heaven has vouchsafed us to overcome this man, who has done us more harm than all the others together, consider whether we should not attack the city in force, and discover in what mind the Trojans may be. We should thus learn whether they will desert their city now that Hector has fallen, or will still hold out even though he is no longer living. But why argue with myself in this way, while Patroclus is still lying at the ships unburied, and unmourned—he whom I can never forget so long as I am alive and my strength does not fail? Though men forget their dead when once they are within the house of Hades, yet not even there will I forget the comrade whom I have lost. Now, therefore, Achaean youths, let us raise the song of victory and go back to the ships taking this man along with us; for we have achieved a mighty triumph and have slain noble Hector to whom the Trojans prayed throughout their city as though he were a god."

On this he treated the body of Hector with contempt; he pierced the sinews at the back of both his feet from heel to ankle and passed thongs of ox-hide through the slits he had made; thus he made the body fast to his chariot, letting the head trail upon the ground. Then when he had put the goodly armor on the chariot and had himself mounted, he lashed his horses on and they flew forward nothing loth. The dust rose from Hector as he was being dragged along, his dark hair flew all about, and his head once so comely was laid low on earth, for Zeus had now delivered him into the hands of his foes to do him outrage in his own land.

Thus was the head of Hector being dishonored in the dust. His mother tore her hair, and flung her veil from her with a loud cry as she looked upon her son. His father moaned piteously, and throughout the city the people fell to weeping and wailing. It was as though the whole of frowning Ilium was being besmirched with fire. Hardly could the people hold Priam back in his hot haste to rush outside the gates of the city. He grovelled in the mire and besought them, calling each one of them by his name. "Let be, my friends," he cried, "and for all your sorrow, suffer me to go single-handed to the ships of the Achaeans. Let me beseech this cruel and terrible man, if perhaps he will respect the feeling of his fellow men, and have compassion on my old age. His own father is even such another as myself—Peleus, who bred him and reared him to be the bane of us Trojans, and of myself more than of all others. Many a son of mine has he slain in the flower of his youth, and yet, grieve for these as I may, I do so for one—Hector—more than for them all, and the bitterness of my sorrow will bring me down to the house of Hades. Would that he had

died in my arms, for so both his ill-starred mother who bore him, and myself, should have had the comfort of weeping and mourning over him."

Thus did he speak with many tears, and all the people of the city joined in his lament. Hecuba then raised the cry of wailing among the Trojans. "Alas, my son," she cried, "what have I left to live for now that you are no more? Night and day did I glory in you throughout the city, for you were a tower of strength to all in Troy, and both men and women alike hailed you as a god. So long as you lived you were their pride, but now death and destruction have fallen upon you."

Hector's wife had as yet heard nothing, for no one had come to tell her that her husband had remained outside the gates. She was at her loom in an inner part of the house, weaving a double purple web, and embroidering it with many flowers. She told her maids to set a large tripod on the fire, so as to have a warm bath ready for Hector when he came out of battle; poor woman, she did not know that he was now beyond the reach of baths, and that Athena had laid him low by the hands of Achilles. She heard the cry coming as from the wall, and trembled in every limb; the shuttle fell from her hands, and again she spoke to her waiting-women. "Two of you," she said, "come with me that I may learn what it is that has befallen; I heard the voice of my husband's honored mother; my own heart beats as though it would come into my mouth and my limbs refuse to carry me; some great misfortune for Priam's children must be at hand. May I never live to hear it, but I greatly fear that Achilles has cut off the retreat of brave Hector and has chased him on to the plain where he was singlehanded; I fear he may have put an end to the reckless daring which possessed my husband, who would never remain with the body of his men, but would dash on far in front, foremost of them all in valor."

Her heart beat fast, and as she spoke she flew from the house like a maniac, with her waiting-women following after. When she reached the battlements and the crowd of people, she stood looking out upon the wall, and saw Hector being borne away in front of the city—the horses dragging him without heed or care over the ground towards the ships of the Achaeans. Her eyes were then shrouded as with the darkness of night and she fell fainting backwards. She tore the ornaments from her head and flung them from her, the frontlet and net with its plaited band, and the veil which golden Aphrodite had given her on the day when Hector took her with him from the house of Eetion, after having given countless gifts of wooing for her sake. Her husband's sisters and the wives of his brothers crowded around her and supported her, for she wished to die in her distraction; when she again presently breathed and came to herself, she sobbed and made lament among the Trojans saying, "Woe is me, O Hector; woe, indeed, that to share a common lot we were born, you at Troy in the house of Priam, and I at Thebe under the wooded mountain of Placos in the house of Eetion who brought me up when I was a child—ill-starred father of an ill-starred daughter—would that he had never begotten me. You are now going into the house of Hades under the secret places of the earth, and you leave me a sorrowing widow in your house. The child, of whom you and I are the unhappy parents, is as yet a mere infant. Now that you are gone, O Hector, you can do nothing for him nor he for you. Even if he escapes the horrors of this woeful war with the Achaeans, yet shall his life henceforth be one of labor and sorrow, for others will seize his lands. The day that robs a child of his parents severs him from his own kind; his head is bowed, his cheeks are wet with tears, and he will go about destitute among the friends of his father, plucking one by the cloak and another by the shirt. Some one or other of these may so far pity him as to hold the cup for a moment towards him and let him moisten his lips, but he must not drink enough to wet the roof of his mouth; then one whose parents are alive will drive him from the table with blows and angry words. 'Out with you,' he will say, 'you have no father here,' and the child will go crying back to his widowed mother— he, Astyanax, who before would sit upon his father's knees, and have none but the daintiest and choicest morsels set before him. When he had played till he was tired and went to sleep, he would lie in a bed, in the arms of his nurse, on a soft couch, knowing neither want nor care, whereas now that he has lost his father

his lot will be full of hardship—he, whom the Trojans name Astyanax,[46] because you, O Hector, were the only defense of their gates and battlements. The wriggling, writhing worms will now eat you at the ships, far from your parents, when the dogs have glutted themselves upon you. You will lie naked, although in your house you have fine and goodly raiment made by the hands of women. This will I now burn; it is of no use to you, for you can never again wear it, and thus you will have respect shown you by the Trojans, both men and women."

In this way did she cry aloud amid her tears, and the women joined in her lament.

24 [*In honor of Patroclus, Achilles has held a series of athletic games among the Greek camped by Troy.*]

The assembly now broke up and the people went their ways, each to his own ship. There they made ready their supper, and then bethought them of the blessed boon of sleep; but Achilles still wept for thinking of his dear comrade, and sleep, before whom all things bow, could take no hold upon him. This way and that did he turn as he yearned after the might and manfulness of Patroclus; he thought of all they had done together, and all they had gone through both on the field of battle and on the waves of the weary sea. As he dwelled on these things he wept bitterly and lay now on his side, now on his back, and now face downwards, till at last he rose and went out as one distraught to wander upon the seashore. Then, when he saw dawn breaking over beach and sea, he yoked his horses to his chariot, and bound the body of Hector behind it that he might drag it about. Three times did he drag it around the tomb of the son of Menoetius, and then went back into his tent, leaving the body on the ground at full length and with its face downwards. But Apollo would not suffer it to be disfigured, for he pitied the man, dead though he now was; therefore he shielded him with his golden aegis continually, that he might take no harm while Achilles was dragging him.

Thus shamefully did Achilles in his fury dishonor  Hector; but the blessed gods looked down in pity from

---

heaven, and urged Hermes, slayer of Argus, to steal the body. All were of this mind save only Hera, Poseidon, and Zeus's gray-eyed daughter,[47] who persisted in the hate which they had ever borne towards Ilium with Priam and his people; for they did not forgive the wrong done them by Alexander in disdaining the goddesses who came to him when he was in his sheepyards, and preferring her who had offered him a wanton to his ruin.[48]

When, therefore, the morning of the twelfth day had now come, Phoebus Apollo spoke among the immortals saying, "You gods ought to be ashamed of yourselves; you are cruel and hard-hearted. Did not Hector burn you thighbones of heifers and of unblemished goats? And now do you not dare rescue even his dead body, for his wife to look upon, with his mother and child, his father Priam, and his people, who would forthwith commit him to the flames, and give him his due funeral rites? So, then, you would all be on the side of mad Achilles, who knows neither right nor how to bend? He is like some savage lion that in the pride of his great strength and daring springs upon men's flocks and gorges on them. Even so has Achilles flung aside all pity, and all that conscience which at once so greatly banes yet greatly boons him that will heed it. A man may lose one far dearer than Achilles has lost—a son, it may be, or a brother born from his own mother's womb—yet when he has mourned him and wept over him he will let him abide, for it takes much sorrow to kill a man; whereas Achilles, now that he has slain noble Hector, drags him behind his chariot around the tomb of his comrade. It would be better of him, and for him, that he should not do so, for brave though he is, we gods may take it ill that he should vent his fury upon dead clay."

Hera spoke up in a rage. "This would be well," she cried, "O lord of the silver bow, if you would give like honor to Hector and to Achilles; but Hector was mortal and suckled at a woman's breast, whereas Achilles is the offspring of a goddess whom I myself reared and brought up. I married her to Peleus, who is above

measure dear to the immortals; you gods came all of you to her wedding; you feasted along with them yourself and brought your lyre—false, and fond of low company, that you have ever been."

Then Zeus said, "Hera, do not be so bitter. Their honor shall not be equal, but of all that dwell in Ilium, Hector was dearest to the gods, as also to myself, for his offerings never failed me. Never was my altar stinted of its dues, nor of the drink-offerings and savor of sacrifice which we claim by right. I shall therefore permit the body of mighty Hector to be stolen; and yet this may hardly be without Achilles coming to know it, for his mother stays night and day beside him. Let some one of you, therefore, send Thetis to me; and I will impart my counsel to her, namely that Achilles is to accept a ransom from Priam, and give up the body."

On this Iris fleet as the wind went forth to carry his message. Down she plunged into the dark sea midway between Samos and rocky Imbrus; the waters hissed as they closed over her, and she sank into the bottom as the lead at the end of an ox-horn that is sped to carry death to fishes. She found Thetis sitting in a great cave with the other sea goddesses gathered around her; there she sat in the midst of them weeping for her noble son who was to fall far from his own land, on the rich plains of Troy. Iris went up to her and said, "Rise Thetis; Zeus, whose counsels do not fail, bids you come to him." And Thetis answered, "Why does the mighty god so bid me? I am in great grief, and shrink from going in and out among the immortals. Still, I will go, and the word that he may speak shall not be spoken in vain."

The goddess took her dark veil—no robe more somber—and went forth with fleet Iris leading the way before her. The waves of the sea opened them a path, and when they reached the shore they flew up into the heavens, where they found the all-seeing son of Cronus with the blessed gods that live forever assembled near him. Athena gave up her seat to her, and she sat down by the side of father Zeus. Hera then placed a fair golden cup in her hand, and spoke to her

---

47  I.e., Athena.

48  Paris, while looking after sheep, was asked to judge whether Hera, Athena, or Aphrodite was the most beautiful. Aphrodite promised him the most beautiful woman in the world if he would choose her. Paris chose Aphrodite, and the goddess rewarded him with Helen.

in words of comfort, whereon Thetis drank and gave her back the cup; and the father of gods and men was the first to speak.

"So, goddess," he said, "for all your sorrow, and the grief that I well know reigns ever in your heart, you have come here to Olympus, and I will tell you why I have sent for you. This nine days past the immortals have been quarrelling about Achilles sacker of cities and the body of Hector. The gods would have Hermes slayer of Argus steal the body, but in furtherance of our peace and amity henceforward, I will concede such honor to your son as I will now tell you. Go, then, to the host and lay these commands upon him; say that the gods are angry with him, and that I am myself more angry than them all, in that he keeps Hector at the ships and will not give him up. He may thus fear me and let the body go. At the same time I will send Iris to great Priam to bid him go to the ships of the Achaeans, and ransom his son, taking with him such gifts for Achilles as may give him satisfaction."

Silver-footed Thetis did as the god had told her, and forthwith down she darted from the topmost summits of Olympus. She went to her son's tents where she found him grieving bitterly, while his trusty comrades around him were busy preparing their morning meal, for which they had killed a great woolly sheep. His mother sat down beside him and caressed him with her hand saying, "My son, how long will you keep on thus grieving and moaning? You are gnawing at your own heart, and think neither of food nor of woman's embraces; and yet these too were well, for you have no long time to live, and death with the strong hand of fate are already close beside you. Now, therefore, heed what I say, for I come as a messenger from Zeus; he says that the gods are angry with you, and himself more angry than them all, in that you keep Hector at the ships and will not give him up. Therefore let him go, and accept a ransom for his body."

And Achilles answered, "So be it. If Olympian Zeus of his own motion thus commands me, let him that brings the ransom bear the body away."

Thus did mother and son talk together at the ships in long discourse with one another. Meanwhile the son of Cronus sent Iris to the strong city of Ilium. "Go," he said, "fleet Iris, from the mansions of Olym-

pus, and tell King Priam in Ilium that he is to go to the ships of the Achaeans and free the body of his dear son. He is to take such gifts with him as shall give satisfaction to Achilles, and he is to go alone, with no other Trojan, save only some honored servant who may drive his mules and wagon, and bring back the body of him whom noble Achilles has slain. Let him have no thought or fear of death in his heart, for we will send the slayer of Argus to escort him, and bring him within the tent of Achilles. Achilles will not kill him or let another do so, for he will take heed to his ways and not be imprudent, and he will treat a suppliant with all honorable courtesy."

On this, Iris, fleet as the wind, sped forth to deliver her message. She went to Priam's house, and found weeping and lamentation therein. His sons were seated around their father in the outer courtyard, and their raiment was wet with tears; the old man sat in the midst of them with his mantle wrapped close about his body, and his head and neck all covered with the filth which he had clutched as he lay grovelling in the mire. His daughters and his sons' wives went wailing about the house, as they thought of the many and brave men who lay dead, slain by the Argives. The messenger of Zeus stood by Priam and spoke softly to him, but fear fell upon him as she did so. "Take heart," she said, "Priam, offspring of Dardanus, take heart and do not fear. I bring no evil tidings, but am minded well towards you. I come as a messenger from Zeus, who though he is not near, takes thought for you and pities you. The lord of Olympus bids you go and ransom noble Hector, and take with you such gifts as shall give satisfaction to Achilles. You are to go alone, with no other Trojan, save only some honored servant who may drive your mules and wagon, and bring back to the city the body of him whom noble Achilles has slain. You are to have no thought or fear of death, for Zeus will send the slayer of Argus to escort you. When he has brought you within Achilles's tent, Achilles will not kill you or let another do so, for he will take heed to his ways and not be imprudent, and he will treat a suppliant with all honorable courtesy."

Iris went her way when she had thus spoken, and Priam told his sons to get a mule-wagon ready, and to make the body of the wagon fast upon the top of its bed. Then he went down into his fragrant store-room, high vaulted, and made of cedar-wood, where his many treasures were kept, and he called Hecuba his wife. "Wife," he said, "a messenger has come to me from Olympus, and has told me to go to the ships of the Achaeans to ransom my dear son, taking with me such gifts as shall give satisfaction to Achilles. What do you think of this matter? For my own part I am greatly moved to pass through the host of the Achaeans and go to their ships."

His wife cried aloud as she heard him, and said, "Alas, what has become of that judgment for which you have been ever famous both among strangers and your own people? How can you venture alone to the ships of the Achaeans, and look into the face of him who has slain so many of your brave sons? You must have iron courage, for if the cruel savage sees you and lays hold of you, he will know neither respect nor pity. Let us then weep for Hector from afar, here in our own house, for when I gave him birth the threads of over-ruling fate were spun for him that dogs should eat his flesh far from his parents, in the house of that terrible man on whose liver I would fasten and devour. Thus would I avenge my son, who showed no cowardice when Achilles slew him, and thought neither of flight nor of avoiding battle as he stood in defense of Trojan men and Trojan women."

Then Priam said, "I would go; do not therefore stay me or be as a bird of ill omen in my house, for you will not move me. Had it been some mortal man who had sent me—some prophet or priest who divines from sacrifice—I should have deemed him false and have given him no heed; but now I have heard the goddess and seen her face to face, therefore I will go and her speaking shall not be in vain. If it is my fate to die at the ships of the Achaeans even so would I have it; let Achilles slay me, if I may but first have taken my son in my arms and mourned him to my heart's comforting."

So saying he lifted the lids of his chests, and took out 12 goodly vestments. He took also 12 cloaks of single fold, 12 rugs, 12 fair mantles, and an equal number of shirts. He weighed out 10 talents of gold, and brought moreover 2 burnished tripods, 4 cauldrons, and a very beautiful cup which the Thracians had given him when he had gone to them on an embassy; it was very precious, but he did not grudge even this,

so eager was he to ransom the body of his son. Then he chased all the Trojans from the court and rebuked them with words of anger. "Out," he cried, "shame and disgrace to me that you are. Have you no grief in your own homes that you have come to plague me here? Do you think it is a small thing that the son of Cronus has sent this sorrow upon me, to lose the bravest of my sons? No, you shall prove it in person, for now he is gone the Achaeans will have easier work in killing you. As for me, let me go down within the house of Hades before my eyes behold the sacking and wasting of the city."

He drove the men away with his staff, and they went forth as the old man sped them. Then he called to his sons, upbraiding Helenus, Paris, noble Agathon, Pammon, Antiphonus, Polites of the loud battle-cry, Deiphobus, Hippothous, and Dius. These nine did the old man call near him. "Come to me at once," he cried, "worthless sons who do me shame; would that you had all been killed at the ships rather than Hector. Miserable man that I am, I have had the bravest sons in all Troy—noble Nestor, Troilus the dauntless chari-oteer, and Hector who was a god among men, so that one would have thought he was son to an immortal—yet there is not one of them left. Ares has slain them and those of whom I am ashamed are alone left me. Liars, and light of foot, heroes of the dance, robbers of lambs and kids from your own people, why do you not get a wagon ready for me at once, and put all these things upon it that I may set out on my way?"

Thus did he speak, and they feared the rebuke of their father. They brought out a strong mule-wagon, newly made, and set the body of the wagon fast on its bed. They took the mule-yoke from the peg on which it hung, a yoke of boxwood with a knob on the top of it and rings for the reins to go through. Then they brought a yoke-band 11 cubits long, to bind the yoke to the pole; they bound it on at the far end of the pole, and put the ring over the upright pin making it fast with three turns of the band on either side the knob, and bending the thong of the yoke beneath it. This done, they brought from the store chamber the rich ransom that was to purchase the body of Hector, and they set it all orderly on the wagon; then they yoked the strong harness-mules which the Mysians had once given as a goodly present to Priam; but for Priam himself they yoked horses which the old king had bred, and kept for his own use.

Thus heedfully did Priam and his servant see to the yoking of their cars at the palace. Then Hecuba came to them all sorrowful, with a golden goblet of wine in her right hand, that they might make a drink-offering before they set out. She stood in front of the horses and said, "Take this, make a drink-offering to father Zeus, and since you are minded to go to the ships in spite of me, pray that you may come safely back from the hands of your enemies. Pray to the son of Cronus lord of the whirlwind, who sits on Ida and looks down over all Troy, pray him to send his swift messenger on your right hand, the bird of omen which is strongest and most dear to him of all birds, that you may see it with your own eyes and trust it as you go forth to the ships of the Danaans. If all seeing Zeus will not send you this messenger, however set upon it you may be, I would not have you go to the ships of the Argives."

And Priam answered, "Wife, I will do as you desire me; it is well to lift hands in prayer to Zeus, if so he may have mercy upon me."

With this the old man bade the serving-woman pour pure water over his hands, and the woman came, bearing the water in a bowl. He washed his hands and took the cup from his wife; then he made the drink-offering and prayed, standing in the middle of the courtyard and turning his eyes to heaven. "Father Zeus," he said, "that rules from Ida, most glorious and most great, grant that I may be received kindly and compassionately in the tents of Achilles, and send your swift messenger upon my right hand, the bird of omen which is strongest and most dear to you of all birds, that I may see it with my own eyes and trust it as I go forth to the ships of the Danaans."

So did he pray, and Zeus the lord of counsel heard his prayer. Forthwith he sent an eagle, the most unerring portent of all birds that fly, the dusky hunter that men also call the Black Eagle. His wings were spread abroad on either side as wide as the well-made and well-bolted door of a rich man's chamber. He came to them flying over the city upon their right hands, and when they saw him they were glad and their hearts took comfort within them. The old man made haste to mount his chariot, and drove out through the inner gateway and under the echoing gatehouse of the outer court. Before him went the mules drawing the four-wheeled wagon, and driven by wise Idaeus; behind these were the horses, which the old man lashed with his whip and drove swiftly through the city, while his friends followed after, wailing and lamenting for him as though he were on his road to death. As soon as they had come down from the city and had reached the plain, his sons and sons-in-law who had followed him went back to Ilium.

But Priam and Idaeus as they showed out upon the plain did not escape the notice of all-seeing Zeus, who looked down upon the old man and pitied him; then he spoke to his son Hermes and said, "Hermes, for it is you who are the most disposed to escort men on their way, and to hear those whom you will hear, go, and so conduct Priam to the ships of the Achaeans that no other of the Danaans shall see him or take note of him until he reaches the son of Peleus."

Thus he spoke, and Hermes, guide and guardian, slayer of Argus, did as he was told. Forthwith he bound on his glittering golden sandals with which he could fly like the wind over land and sea; he took the wand with which he seals men's eyes in sleep, or wakes them just as he pleases, and flew holding it in his hand till he came to Troy and to the Hellespont. To look at, he was like a young man of noble birth in the hey-day of his youth and beauty with the down just coming upon his face.

Now when Priam and Idaeus had driven past the great tomb of Ilus,[49] they stayed their mules and horses that they might drink in the river, for the shades of night were falling; when, therefore, Idaeus saw Hermes standing near them he said to Priam, "Take heed, descendant of Dardanus; here is matter which demands consideration. I see a man who I think will presently fall upon us; let us fly with our horses, or at least embrace his knees and implore him to take compassion upon us."

When he heard this the old man's heart failed him, and he was in great fear; he stayed where he was as

---

49  Grandfather of Priam.

one dazed, and the hair stood on end over his whole body; but the bringer of good luck came up to him and took him by the hand, saying, "Where, father, are you thus driving your mules and horses in the dead of night when other men are asleep? Are you not afraid of the fierce Achaeans who are hard by you, so cruel and relentless? Should some one of them see you bearing so much treasure through the darkness of the fleeting night, what would not your state then be? You are no longer young, and he who is with you is too old to protect you from those who would attack you. For myself, I will do you no harm, and I will defend you from anyone else, for you remind me of my own father."

And Priam answered, "It is indeed as you say, my dear son; nevertheless some god has held his hand over me, in that he has sent such a wayfarer as yourself to meet me so opportunely; you are so comely in face and figure, and your judgment is so excellent that you must come of blessed parents."

Then said the slayer of Argus, guide and guardian, "Sir, all that you have said is right; but tell me and tell me true, are you taking this rich treasure to send it to a foreign people where it may be safe, or are you all leaving strong Ilium in dismay now that your son has fallen who was the bravest man among you and was never lacking in battle with the Achaeans?"

And Priam said, "Who are you, my friend, and who are your parents, that you speak so truly about the fate of my unhappy son?"

The slayer of Argus, guide and guardian, answered him, "Sir, you would test me, that you question me about noble Hector. Many a time have I set eyes upon him in battle when he was driving the Argives to their ships and putting them to the sword. We stood still and marvelled, for Achilles in his anger with the son of Atreus did not suffer us to fight. I am his attendant, and came with him in the same ship. I am a Myrmidon, and my father's name is Polyctor; he is a rich man and about as old as you are; he has six sons besides myself, and I am the seventh. We cast lots, and it fell upon me to sail here with Achilles. I have now come from the ships on to the plain, for with daybreak the Achaeans will set battle in array about the city. They chafe at doing nothing, and are so eager that their princes cannot hold them back."

Then Priam answered, "If you are indeed the attendant of Achilles, son of Peleus, tell me now the whole truth. Is my son still at the ships, or has Achilles hewn him limb from limb, and given him to his hounds?"

"Sir," replied the slayer of Argus, guide and guardian, "neither hounds nor vultures have yet devoured him; he is still just lying at the tents by the ship of Achilles, and though it is now 12 days that he has lain there, his flesh is not wasted nor have the worms eaten him although they feed on warriors. At daybreak Achilles drags him cruelly around the sepulcher of his dear comrade, but it does him no harm. You should come yourself and see how he lies fresh as dew, with the blood all washed away, and his wounds every one of them closed though many pierced him with their spears. Such care have the blessed gods taken of your brave son, for he was dear to them beyond all measure."

The old man was comforted as he heard him and said, "My son, see what a good thing it is to have made due offerings to the immortals; for as sure as that he was born, my son never forgot the gods that hold Olympus, and now they requite it to him even in death. Accept therefore at my hands this goodly chalice; guard me and with heaven's help guide me till I come to the tent of the son of Peleus."

Then answered the slayer of Argus, guide and guardian, "Sir, you are tempting me and playing upon my youth, but you shall not move me, for you are offering me presents without the knowledge of Achilles whom I fear and hold it great guiltiness to defraud, lest some evil presently befall me; but as your guide I would go with you even to Argos itself, and would guard you so carefully whether by sea or land that no one should attack you through making light of him who was with you."

The bringer of good luck then sprang onto the chariot, and seizing the whip and reins he breathed fresh spirit into the mules and horses. When they reached the trench and the wall that was before the ships, those who were on guard had just been getting their suppers, and the slayer of Argus threw them all into a deep sleep. Then he drew back the bolts to open the gates, and took Priam inside with the treasure he had upon his wagon. Before long they came to the lofty dwelling of the son of Peleus for which the

Myrmidons had cut pine and which they had built for their king; when they had built it they thatched it with coarse sedge grass which they had mown out on the plain, and all around it they made a large courtyard, which was fenced with stakes set close together. The gate was barred with a single bolt of pine which it took three men to force into its place, and three to draw back so as to open the gate, but Achilles could draw it by himself. Hermes opened the gate for the old man, and brought in the treasure that he was taking with him for the son of Peleus. Then he sprang from the chariot onto the ground and said, "Sir, it is I, immortal Hermes, that have come with you, for my father sent me to escort you. I will now leave you, and will not enter into the presence of Achilles, for it might anger him that a god should befriend mortal men thus openly. Go within, and embrace the knees of the son of Peleus; beseech him by his father, his lovely mother, and his son; thus you may move him."

With these words Hermes went back to high Olympus. Priam sprang from his chariot to the ground, leaving Idaeus where he was, in charge of the mules and horses. The old man went straight into the house where Achilles, loved of the gods, was sitting. There he found him with his men seated at a distance from him; only two, the hero Automedon, and Alcimus of the race of Ares, were busy in attendance about his person, for he had but just finished eating and drinking, and the table was still there. King Priam entered without their seeing him, and going right up to Achilles he clasped his knees and kissed the dread murderous hands that had slain so many of his sons.

As when some cruel spite has befallen a man that he should have killed someone in his own country, and must flee to a great man's protection in a land of strangers, and all marvel who see him, even so did Achilles marvel as he beheld Priam. The others looked one to another and marvelled also, but Priam besought Achilles saying, "Think of your father, O Achilles like the gods, who is such even as I am, on the sad threshold of old age. It may be that those who dwell near him harass him, and there is none to keep war and ruin from him. Yet when he hears of you as being still alive, he is glad, and his days are full of hope that he shall see his dear son come home to him from Troy; but I, wretched man that I am, had the bravest in all Troy for

my sons, and there is not one of them left. I had 50 sons when the Achaeans came here; 19 of them were from a single womb, and the others were borne to me by the women of my household. The greater part of them has fierce Ares laid low, and Hector, him who was alone left, him who was the guardian of our city and ourselves, him have you lately slain; therefore I have now come to the ships of the Achaeans to ransom his body from you with a great ransom. Fear, O Achilles, the wrath of heaven; think on your own father and have compassion upon me, who am the more pitiable, for I have steeled myself as no man has ever yet steeled himself before me, and have raised to my lips the hand of him who slew my son."

Thus spoke Priam, and the heart of Achilles yearned as he thought of his father. He took the old man's hand and moved him gently away. The two wept bitterly—Priam, as he lay at Achilles's feet, weeping for Hector, and Achilles now for his father and now for Patroclus, till the house was filled with their lamentation. But when Achilles was now sated with grief and had unburdened the bitterness of his sorrow, he left his seat and raised the old man by the hand, in pity for his white hair and beard; then he said, "Unhappy man, you have indeed dared greatly; how could you venture to come alone to the ships of the Achaeans, and enter the presence of him who has slain so many of your brave sons? You must have iron courage; sit now upon this seat, and for all our grief we will hide our sorrows in our hearts, for weeping will not avail us. The immortals know no care, yet the lot they spin for man is full of sorrow; on the floor of Zeus's palace there stand two urns, the one filled with evil gifts, and the other with good ones. He for whom Zeus the lord of thunder mixes the gifts he sends, will meet now with good and now with evil fortune; but he to whom Zeus sends none but evil gifts will be pointed at by the finger of scorn, the hand of famine will pursue him to the ends of the world, and he will go up and down the face of the earth, respected neither by gods nor men. Even so did it befall Peleus; the gods endowed him with all good things from his birth upwards, for he reigned over the Myrmidons excelling all men in prosperity and wealth, and mortal though he was they gave him a goddess for his bride. But even on him too did heaven send misfortune, for there is no race of royal children born to him in his house, save one son who is doomed to die all untimely; nor may I take care of him now that he is growing old, for I must stay here at Troy to be the bane of you and of your children. And you too, O Priam, I have heard that you were happy in earlier times. They say that in wealth and plenitude of offspring you surpassed all that is in Lesbos, the realm of Makar to the northward, Phrygia that is more inland, and those that dwell upon the great Hellespont; but from the day when the dwellers in heaven sent this evil upon you, war and slaughter have been about your city continually. Bear up against it, and let there be some intervals in your sorrow. Mourn as you may for your brave son, you will take nothing by it. You cannot raise him from the dead, before you do so yet another sorrow shall befall you."

And Priam answered, "O king, do not bid me be seated, while Hector is still lying uncared for in your tents, but accept the great ransom which I have brought you, and give him to me at once that I may look upon him. May you prosper with the ransom and reach your own land in safety, seeing that you have suffered me to live and to look upon the light of the sun."

Achilles looked at him sternly and said, "Vex me no longer, old man; I am of myself minded to give up the body of Hector. My mother, daughter of the old man of the sea, came to me from Zeus to bid me deliver it to you. Moreover I know well, O Priam, and you cannot hide it, that some god has brought you to the ships of the Achaeans; otherwise no man however strong and in his prime would dare to come to our host; he could neither pass our guard unseen, nor draw the bolt of my gates thus easily; therefore, provoke me no further, lest I offend against the word of Zeus, and do not suffer you, suppliant though you are, within my tents."

The old man feared him and obeyed. Then the son of Peleus sprang like a lion through the door of his house, not alone, but with him went his two attendants Automedon and Alcimus who were closer to him than any others of his comrades now that Patroclus was no more. These unyoked the horses and mules, and bade Priam's herald and attendant be seated within the house. They lifted the ransom for Hector's body from the wagon, but they left two mantles and a goodly shirt, that Achilles might wrap the body in them when he gave it to be taken home. Then he called to his servants and ordered them to wash the body and anoint it, but he first took it to a place where Priam would not see it, lest if he did so, he should break out in the bitterness of his grief, and enrage Achilles, who might then kill him and offend against the word of Zeus. When the servants had washed the body and anointed it, and had wrapped it in a fair shirt and mantle, Achilles himself lifted it onto a bier, and he and his men then laid it on the wagon. He cried aloud as he did so and called on the name of his dear comrade, "Do not be angry with me, Patroclus," he said, "if you hear even in the house of Hades that I have given Hector to his father for a ransom. It has been no unworthy one, and I will share it equitably with you."

Achilles then went back into the tent and took his place on the richly inlaid seat from which he had risen, by the wall that was at right angles to the one against which Priam was sitting. "Sir," he said, "your son is now laid upon his bier and is ransomed according to your desire; you shall look upon him when you take him away at daybreak; for the present let us prepare our supper. Even lovely Niobe had to think about eating, though her 12 children—6 daughters and 6 lusty sons—had been all slain in her house. Apollo killed the sons with arrows from his silver bow in order to punish Niobe, and Artemis slew the daughters, because Niobe had likened herself to the beautiful-cheeked Leto; she said Leto had borne 2 children only, whereas she had herself borne many—whereon the 2 killed the many. Nine days did they lie weltering, and there was no one to bury them, for the son of Cronus turned the people into stone; but on the tenth day the gods in heaven themselves buried them, and Niobe then took food, being worn out with weeping. They say that somewhere among the rocks on the mountain pastures of Sipylus, where the nymphs live that haunt the river Achelous, there, they say, she lives in stone and still nurses the sorrows sent upon her by the hand of heaven. Therefore, noble sir, let us two now take food; you can weep for your dear son hereafter as you are bearing him back to Ilium—and many a tear will he cost you."

With this Achilles sprang from his seat and killed a sheep of silvery whiteness, which his followers skinned and made ready all in due order. They cut the meat carefully up into smaller pieces, spitted them, and drew them off again when they were well roasted. Automedon brought bread in fair baskets and served it around the table, while Achilles dealt out the meat, and they laid their hands on the good things that were before them. As soon as they had had enough to eat and drink, Priam, descendant of Dardanus, marveled at the strength and beauty of Achilles, for he was like a god to see, and Achilles marveled at Priam as he listened to him and looked upon his noble presence. When they had gazed their fill Priam spoke first. "And now, O king," he said, "take me to my bed that we may lie down and enjoy the blessed boon of sleep. Never once have my eyes been closed from the day your hands took the life of my son; I have grovelled without ceasing in the mire of my stableyard, moaning and brooding over my countless sorrows. Now, moreover, I have eaten bread and drunk wine; hitherto I have tasted nothing."

As he spoke Achilles told his men and the women-servants to set beds in the room that was in the gatehouse, and make them with good red rugs, and spread coverlets on the top of them with woollen cloaks for Priam and Idaeus to wear. So the maids went out carrying a torch and got the two beds ready in all haste. Then Achilles said jeeringly to Priam, "Dear sir, you shall lie outside, lest some counsellor of those who in due course keep coming to advise with me should see you here in the darkness of the fleeting night, and tell it to Agamemnon. This might cause delay in the delivery of the body. And now tell me and tell me true, for how many days would you celebrate the funeral rites of noble Hector? Tell me, that I may hold aloof from war and restrain the host."

And Priam answered, "Since, then, you suffer me to bury my noble son with all due rites, do thus, Achilles, and I shall be grateful. You know how we are pent up within our city; it is far for us to fetch wood from the mountain, and the people live in fear. Nine days, therefore, will we mourn Hector in my house; on the tenth day we will bury him and there shall be a public feast in his honor; on the eleventh we will build

a mound over his ashes, and on the twelfth, if there be need, we will fight."

And Achilles answered, "All, King Priam, shall be as you have said. I will stay our fighting for as long a time as you have named."

As he spoke he laid his hand on the old man's right wrist, in token that he should have no fear; thus then did Priam and his attendant sleep there in the forecourt, full of thought, while Achilles lay in an inner room of the house, with fair Briseis by his side.

And now both gods and mortals were fast asleep through the livelong night, but upon Hermes alone, the bringer of good luck, sleep could take no hold, for he was thinking all the time how to get King Priam away from the ships without his being seen by the strong force of sentinels. He hovered therefore over Priam's head and said, "Sir, now that Achilles has spared your life, you seem to have no fear about sleeping in the thick of your foes. You have paid a great ransom, and have received the body of your son; were you still alive and a prisoner the sons whom you have left at home would have to give three times as much to free you; and so it would be if Agamemnon and the other Achaeans were to know of your being here."

When he heard this the old man was afraid and roused his servant. Hermes then yoked their horses and mules, and drove them quickly through the host so that no man perceived them. When they came to the ford of eddying Xanthus, begotten of immortal Zeus, Hermes went back to high Olympus, and dawn in a robe of saffron began to break over all the land. Priam and Idaeus then drove on towards the city lamenting and moaning, and the mules drew the body of Hector. No one, neither man nor woman, saw them, till Cassandra, fair as golden Aphrodite standing on Pergamus, caught sight of her dear father in his chariot, and his servant that was the city's herald with him. Then she saw him that was lying upon the bier, drawn by the mules, and with a loud cry she went about the city saying, "Come here Trojans, men and women, and look on Hector; if ever you rejoiced to see him coming from battle when he was alive, look now on him that was the glory of our city and all our people."

At this there was neither man nor woman left in the city, so great a sorrow had possessed them. Hard by the gates they met Priam as he was bringing in the body. Hector's wife and his mother were the first to mourn him: they flew towards the wagon and laid their hands upon his head, while the crowd stood weeping around them. They would have stayed before the gates, weeping and lamenting the livelong day to the going down of the sun, had not Priam spoken to them from the chariot and said, "Make way for the mules to pass you. Afterwards when I have taken the body home you shall have your fill of weeping."

On this the people stood apart, and made a way for the wagon. When they had borne the body within the house they laid it upon a bed and seated minstrels around it to lead the dirge, whereon the women joined in the sad music of their lament. Foremost among them all Andromache led their wailing as she clasped the head of mighty Hector in her embrace. "Husband," she cried, "you have died young, and leave me in your house a widow; he of whom we are the ill-starred parents is still a mere child, and I fear he may not reach manhood. Before he can do so our city will be razed and overthrown, for you who watched over it are no more—you who were its savior, the guardian of our wives and children. Our women will be carried away captives to the ships, and I among them; while you, my child, who will be with me will be put to some unseemly tasks, working for a cruel master. Or, it may be some Achaean will hurl you (O miserable death) from our walls, to avenge some brother, son, or father whom Hector slew; many of them have indeed bitten the dust at his hands, for your father's hand in battle was no light one. Therefore do the people mourn him. You have left, O Hector, sorrow unutterable to your parents, and my own grief is greatest of all, for you did not stretch forth your arms and embrace me as you lay dying, or say to me any words that might have lived with me in my tears night and day forevermore."

Bitterly did she weep the while, and the women joined in her lament. Hecuba in her turn took up the strains of woe. "Hector," she cried, "dearest to me of all my children. So long as you were alive the gods loved you well, and even in death they have not been utterly unmindful of you; for when Achilles took any

other of my sons, he would sell him beyond the seas, to Samos, Imbrus or rugged Lemnos; and when he had slain you too with his sword, many a time did he drag you around the sepulcher of his comrade—though this could not give him life—yet here you lie all fresh as dew, and comely as one whom Apollo has slain with his painless shafts."

Thus did she too speak through her tears with bitter moaning, and then Helen for a third time took up the strain of lamentation. "Hector," she said, "dearest of all my brothers-in-law—for I am wife to Alexander who brought me here to Troy—would that I had died before he did so—20 years have come and gone since I left my home and came from over the sea, but I never heard one word of insult or unkindness from you. When another would chide me, as it might be one of your brothers or sisters or of your brothers' wives, or my mother-in-law—for Priam was as kind to me as though he were my own father—you would rebuke and check them with words of gentleness and good will. Therefore my tears flow both for you and for my unhappy self, for there is no one else in Troy who is kind to me, but all shrink and shudder as they go by me."

She wept as she spoke and the vast crowd that was gathered around her joined in her lament. Then King Priam spoke to them saying, "Bring wood, O Trojans, to the city, and fear no cunning ambush of the Argives, for Achilles when he dismissed me from the ships gave me his word that they would not attack us until the morning of the twelfth day."

Forthwith they yoked their oxen and mules and gathered together before the city. Nine days long did they bring in great heaps of wood, and on the morning of the tenth day with many tears they took brave Hector forth, laid his dead body upon the summit of the pile, and set fire thereto. Then when the child of morning rosy-fingered Dawn appeared on the eleventh day, the people again assembled around the pyre of mighty Hector. When they were gotten together, they first quenched the fire with wine wherever it was burning, and then his brothers and comrades with many a bitter tear gathered his white bones, wrapped them in soft robes of purple, and laid them in a golden urn, which they placed in a grave and covered over with large stones set close together. Then they built a barrow hurriedly over it keeping guard on every side lest the Achaeans should attack them before they had finished. When they had heaped up the barrow they went back again into the city, and being well assembled they held high feast in the house of Priam their king.

Thus, then, did they celebrate the funeral of Hector tamer of horses.

# 10

# PLUTARCH, *LIFE OF SOLON*

Plutarch (*c.* 46-120), a Greek writer living under Roman rule in the city of Chaeronea, is best known for writing a series of *Lives of the Greeks and Romans*. The work is made up of paired biographies of Greeks and Romans, each pair designed to highlight the moral value and danger of some character trait or activity. The life of the Athenian statesman Solon (*c.* 638-559 BC) which appears below is taken from this larger work. Except where indicated, all the verses quoted by Plutarch are those of Solon. Solon's poetry survives only in the form of quotation by later writers, such as Plutarch.

---

Didymus,[1] the grammarian, in his answer to Asclepiades concerning Solon's Tables of Law, mentions a passage of one Philocles, who states that Solon's father's name was Euphorion, contrary to the opinion of all others who have written concerning him; for they generally agree that he was the son of Execestides, a man of moderate wealth and power in the city, but of a most noble stock, being descended from Codrus. Solon's mother, as Heraclides Ponticus affirms,[2] was cousin to Pisistratus's mother,[3] and the two at first were great friends, partly because they were akin, and partly because of Pisistratus's noble qualities and beauty. And they say Solon loved him; that is the reason, I suppose, that when afterwards they differed about the citizenship, their enmity never produced any hot and violent passion; they remembered their old kindnesses, and retained

Still in its embers living the strong fire

of their love and dear affection. For that Solon was not proof against beauty, nor of courage to stand up to passion and meet it

hand to hand as in the ring[4]

we may conjecture by his poems, and one of his laws, in which there are practices forbidden to slaves, which he would appear, therefore, to recommend to free men. Pisistratus, it is stated, was similarly attached to one Charmus; it was he who dedicated the figure of Love in the Academy, where the runners in the sacred torch race light their torches. Solon, as Hermippus[5] writes, when his father had ruined his estate in doing benefits and kindnesses to other men, though he had

---

1  First century BC.
2  A philosopher of the later fourth century BC.
3  Pisistratus was tyrant of Athens in 560 BC and, after being driven from the city, returned and kept a firm grip on power from 554 until his death in 527.
4  I.e., as one wrestler meets another.
5  Athenian comic playwright of the later fifth century BC.

friends enough that were willing to contribute to his relief, yet was ashamed to be beholden to others, since he was descended from a family who were accustomed to do kindnesses rather than receive them; and therefore Solon applied himself to merchandise in his youth, though others assure us that he travelled rather to get learning and experience than to make money. It is certain that he was a lover of knowledge, for when he was old he would say, that he

Each day grew older, and learned something new,

and yet he was no admirer of riches, esteeming as equally wealthy the man

Who has both gold and silver in his hand,
Horses and mules, and acres of wheatland,
And him whose all is decent food to eat,
Clothes to his back and shoes upon his feet,
And a young wife and child, since so it will be,
And no more years than will with that agree;

and in another place

Wealth I would have, but wealth by wrong procure
I would not; justice, even if slow, is sure.

And it is perfectly possible for a good man and a statesman, without being solicitous for superfluities, to show some concern for sufficient necessities. In his time, as Hesiod[6] says,

Work was a shame to none,

nor was distinction made with respect to trade, but merchandise was a noble calling, which brought home the good things which the barbarous nations enjoyed, was the occasion of friendship with their kings, and a great source of experience. Some merchants have built great cities, as Protis, the founder of Massilia,[7] to whom the Gauls, near the Rhone, were much

attached. Some report also that Thales[8] and Hippocrates the mathematician traded, and that Plato defrayed the charges of his travels by selling oil in Egypt. Solon's softness and profuseness, his popular rather than philosophical tone about pleasure in his poems, have been ascribed to his trading life; for, having suffered a thousand dangers, it was natural they should be recompensed with some gratifications and enjoyments; but that he accounted himself poor rather than rich is evident from the lines

Some wicked men are rich, some good are poor,
We will not change our virtue for their store:
Virtue's a thing that none can take away;
But money changes owners all the day.

At first he used his poetry only in trifles, not for any serious purpose, but simply to pass away his idle hours; but afterwards he introduced moral sentences and public matters, which he did, not to record them merely as an historian, but to justify his own actions, and sometimes to correct, chastise, and stir up the Athenians to noble acts. Some report that he tried to put his laws into heroic verse, and that they began thus:

We humbly beg a blessing on our laws
From mighty Zeus, and honor, and applause.

In philosophy, as did most of the wise men then, he chiefly esteemed the political part of morals; in physics, he was very plain and antiquated as appears by this:

It is the clouds that make the snow and hail,
And thunder comes from lightning without fail;
The sea is stormy when the winds have blown,
But it deals fairly when it's left alone.

And, indeed, it is probable that at that time Thales alone had raised philosophy above mere practice into speculation, and the rest of the wise men[9] were so

---

6   Hesiod (eighth century BC) was the author of the first surviving major Greek poems after Homer.
7   A Greek colony which became modern Marseilles.
8   Greek philosopher (sixth century BC), who believed that the basic substance of all that exists is water.
9   I.e., the men known in classical antiquity as the "seven wise men of Greece"; Solon was counted among their number.

called from prudence in political concerns. It is said that they had an interview at Delphi, and another at Corinth, by the procurement of Periander,[10] who arranged a meeting for them, and a supper. But their reputation was chiefly raised by sending a tripod[11] to them all, and by their modest refusal of it, and complaisant yielding of it to one another. For, as the story goes, when some of the Coans were fishing with a net, and some strangers, Milesians, bought the catch on speculation, the net brought up a golden tripod, which, they say, Helen, at her return from Troy, upon the remembrance of an old prophecy, threw in there. Now, the strangers at first contesting with the fishers about the tripod, and the cities espousing the quarrel so far as to engage themselves in a war, Apollo decided the controversy by commanding that it be presented to the wisest man. First it was sent to Thales at Miletus, the Coans freely presenting him with that for which they fought against the whole body of the Milesians; but Thales declaring Bias[12] the wiser person, it was sent to him; from him to another; and so, going around to them all, it came to Thales a second time; and, at last, being carried from Miletus to Thebes, was there dedicated to Apollo Ismenius. Theophrastus[13] writes that it was first presented to Bias at Priene, and next to Thales at Miletus, and so through all it returned to Bias, and was afterwards sent to Delphi. This is the general report, only some, instead of a tripod, say this present was a cup sent by Croesus;[14] others, a piece of plate that one Bathycles had left. It is stated that Anacharsis and Solon, and Solon and Thales, were familiarly acquainted and some have delivered parts of their discourse; for, they say, Anacharsis, coming to Athens, knocked at Solon's door, and told him that he, being a stranger, had come to be his guest, and contract a friendship with him; and Solon replying, "It is better to make friends at home," Anacharsis replied, "Then you that are at home make friends with me." Solon, somewhat surprised at the readiness of the repartee, received him

kindly, and kept him some time with him, being already engaged in public business and the compilation of his laws which, when Anacharsis understood, he laughed at Solon for imagining the dishonesty and covetousness of his countrymen could be restrained by written laws, which were like spiders' webs, and would catch, it is true, the weak and poor, but easily be broken by the mighty and rich. To this Solon answered that men keep their promises when neither side can get anything by breaking them, and he would so fit his laws to the citizens that all should understand it was more advantageous to be just than to break the laws. But the event rather agreed with the conjecture of Anacharsis than Solon's hope. Anacharsis, being once at the Assembly, expressed his wonder at the fact that in Greece wise men spoke and fools decided.

Solon went, they say, to Thales, at Miletus, and wondered that Thales took no care to get himself a wife and children. To this, Thales made no answer for the present, but a few days after procured a stranger to pretend that he had left Athens ten days ago; and Solon inquiring what news there was there, the man, according to his instructions, replied, "None but a young man's funeral, which the whole city attended; for he was the son, they said, of an honorable man, the most virtuous of the citizens, who was not then at home, but had been travelling a long time." Solon replied, "What a miserable man is he! But what was his name?" "I have heard it," says the man, "but have now forgotten it, only there was a great talk of his wisdom and his justice." Thus Solon was drawn on by every answer, and his fears heightened, till at last, being extremely concerned, he mentioned his own name, and asked the stranger if that young man was called Solon's son; and the stranger assenting, he began to beat his head, and to do and say all that is usual with men in transports of grief. But Thales took his hand and, with a smile, said, "These things, Solon, keep me from marriage and rearing children, which

---

10 Tyrant of Corinth (625-585 BC) and one of the "seven wise men of Greece."
11 A three-legged cauldron, apparently first used in religious ceremonies, and often given as a gift.
12 Known for his maxims (sixth century BC).
13 Philosopher (third century BC) and student of Aristotle.
14 A famously wealthy king (c. 560-546) of the Medes, in Asia Minor.

are too great for even your constancy to support; however, do not be concerned at the report, for it is a fiction." Hermippus relates this from Pataecus, who boasted that he had inherited Aesop's soul.

However, it is irrational and poor-spirited not to seek conveniences for fear of losing them, for upon the same account we should not allow ourselves to like wealth, glory, or wisdom, since we may fear to be deprived of all these; nay, even virtue itself, than which there is no greater or more desirable possession, is often suspended by sickness or drugs. Now Thales, though unmarried, could not be free from solicitude unless he likewise felt to care for his friends, his kinsman, or his country; yet we are told he adopted Cybisthus, his sister's son. For the soul, having a principle of kindness in itself, and being born to love, as well as perceive, think, or remember, inclines and fixes upon some stranger, when a man has none of his own to embrace. And alien or illegitimate objects insinuate themselves into his affections, as into some estate that lacks lawful heirs; and with affection come anxiety and care, insomuch that you may see men that use the strongest language against the marriage-bed and the fruit of it almost killed with grief, and abjectly lamenting, when some servant's or concubine's child is sick or dies. Some have given way to shameful and desperate sorrow at the loss of a dog or horse; others have borne the death of virtuous children without any extravagant or unbecoming grief, have passed the rest of their lives like men, and according to the principles of reason. It is not affection, it is weakness that brings men, unarmed against fortune by reason, into these endless pains and terrors; and they indeed do not have even the present enjoyment of what they dote upon, the possibility of the future loss causing them continual pangs, tremors, and distresses. We must not provide against the loss of wealth by poverty, or of friends by refusing all acquaintance, or of children by having none, but by morality and reason. But of this too much.

Now, when the Athenians were tired with a tedious and difficult war that they conducted against the Megarians[15] for the island Salamis, and made a law that it should be death for any man, by writing or speaking, to assert that the city ought to endeavor to recover it, Solon, vexed at the disgrace, and perceiving thousands of the youth wished for somebody to begin, but did not dare to stir first for fear of the law, counterfeited a distraction, and by his own family it was spread about the city that he was mad. He then secretly composed some elegiac verses, and learning them by heart, that it might seem spontaneously, ran out into the marketplace with a cap upon his head, and, the people gathering about him, got upon the herald's stand, and sang that elegy which begins thus:

I am a herald come from Salamis the fair,
My news from there my verses shall declare.

The poem is called *Salamis*; it contains a hundred verses very elegantly written; when it had been sung, his friends commended it, and especially Pisistratus exhorted the citizens to obey his directions, insomuch that they revoked the law, and renewed the war under Solon's conduct. The popular tale is that he sailed with Pisistratus to Colias[16] and, finding the women, according to the custom of the country there, sacrificing to Demeter,[17] he sent a trusty friend to Salamis, who would pretend to be a renegade, and advise them that if they desired to seize the chief Athenian women, they should come with him at once to Colias. The Megarians presently sent off men in the vessel with him and Solon, seeing it set off from the island, commanded the women to be gone, and some beardless youths, dressed in their clothes, their shoes and caps, and secretly armed with daggers, to dance and play near the shore till the enemies had landed and the vessel was in their power. Things being thus ordered, the Megarians were lured with the appearance, and, coming to the shore, jumped out, eager to be the first to seize a prize, so that not one of them escaped; and the Athenians set sail for the island and took it.

Others say that it was not taken this way, but that he first received this oracle from Delphi:

---

15  Megara was a Greek city near Athens.
16  A community in Athens's territory of Attica.
17  Goddess of the harvest.

Those heroes that in fair Asopia rest,
All buried with their faces to the west,
Go and appease with offerings of the best,

and that Solon, sailing by night to the island, sacrificed to the heroes Periphemus and Cychreus, and then taking 500 Athenian volunteers (a law having passed that those that took the island should be highest in the governing of it), with a number of fishing boats and one thirty-oared ship anchored in a bay of Salamis that looks towards Nisaea; and the Megarians that were then in the island, hearing only an uncertain report, hurried to their arms, and sent a ship to reconnoiter the enemies. This ship Solon took and, securing the Megarians, manned it with Athenians, and gave them orders to sail to the island with as much secrecy as possible. Meanwhile, he, with the other soldiers, marched against the Megarians by land, and while they were fighting, those from the ship took the city. And this narrative is confirmed by the following ceremony observed afterwards: an Athenian ship used to sail silently at first to the island, then, with noise and a great shout, one armed man leaped out, and with a loud cry ran to the promontory Sciradium to meet those that approached upon the land. And just by there stands a temple which Solon dedicated to Ares.[18] For he beat the Megarians, and as many as were not killed in the battle he sent away upon conditions.

The Megarians, however, still contending, and both sides having received considerable losses, they chose the Spartans for arbitrators. Now many affirm that Homer's authority did Solon a considerable kindness, and that, introducing a line into the Catalog of Ships,[19] when the matter was to be determined, he read the passage as follows:

Twelve ships from Salamis stout Ajax[20] brought,
And ranked his men where the Athenians fought.

The Athenians, however, call this but an idle story, and report that Solon made it appear to the judges that Philaeus and Eurysaces, the sons of Ajax, being made citizens of Athens, gave them the island, and that one of them dwelled at Brauron in Attica, the other at Melite; and they have a township of Philaidae, to which Pisistratus belonged, deriving its name from this Philaeus. Solon took a further argument against the Megarians from the dead bodies, which, he said, were not buried after their fashion, but according to the Athenian; for the Megarians turn the corpse to the east, the Athenians to the west. But Hereas the Megarian denies this, and affirms that they likewise turn the body to the west, and also that the Athenians have a separate tomb for everybody, but the Megarians put two or three into one. However, some of Apollo's oracles,[21] where he calls Salamis Ionian,[22] made much for Solon. This matter was determined by five Spartans: Critolaidas, Amompharetus, Hypsechidas, Anaxilas, and Cleomenes.

For this, Solon grew famous and powerful; but his advice in favor of defending the oracle at Delphi, to give aid, and not to suffer the Cirrhaeans to profane it, but to maintain the honor of the god, got him the most repute among the Greeks; for upon his persuasion the Amphictyons[23] undertook the war, as amongst others, Aristotle[24] affirms, in his enumeration of the victors at the Pythian games, where he makes Solon the author of this counsel. Solon, however, was not general in that expedition, as Hermippus states, relying on Evanthes the Samian, for Aeschines the orator[25] says no such thing, and, in the Delphian records, Alcmaeon, not Solon, is named as commander of the Athenians.

---

18  The Greek god of war.
19  A section of the *Iliad* listing how many ships various Greek cities purportedly sent to the Trojan war.
20  A leading Greek warrior in the *Iliad*.
21  I.e., the prophecies of Apollo, god of prophecy.
22  The Athenians were part of that larger Greek linguistic group, the Ionian Greeks.
23  I.e., the Amphictyonic council, which represented various Greek poleis which held Apollo's temple at Delphi sacred.
24  Fourth century BC.
25  Fourth century BC.

Now the Cylonian pollution[26] had a long while disturbed the city, ever since the time when Megacles the archon[27] persuaded the conspirators with Cylon that took sanctuary in Athena's temple to come down and stand to a fair trial. And they, tying a thread to Athena's image, and holding one end of it, went down to the tribunal; but when they came to the temple of the Furies, the thread broke of its own accord, upon which, as if the goddess had refused them protection, they were seized by Megacles and the other magistrates; as many as were outside the temples were stoned, those that fled for sanctuary were butchered at the altar, and only those escaped who made supplication to the wives of the magistrates. But they from that time were considered under pollution, and regarded with hatred. The remainder of the faction of Cylon grew strong again, and had continual quarrels with the family of Megacles; and now the quarrel being at its height, and the people divided, Solon, being high in reputation, interposed along with the most eminent of the Athenians, and by entreaty and admonition persuaded the polluted to submit to a trial and the decision of 300 noble citizens. And Myron of Phlya being their accuser, they were found guilty, and as many as were then alive were banished, and the bodies of the dead were dug up, and scattered beyond the confines of the country. In the midst of these distractions, the Megarians falling upon them, they lost Nisaea and Salamis again; besides, the city was disturbed with superstitious fears and strange appearances, and the priests declared that the sacrifices indicated some villainies and pollutions that were to be expiated. Upon this, they sent for Epimenides the Phaestian from Crete, who is counted the seventh wise man by those that will not admit Periander into the number. He seems to have been thought a favorite of heaven, possessed of knowledge in all the supernatural and ritual parts of religion and, therefore, the men of his age

called him a new Curies,[28] and son of a nymph named Balte. When he came to Athens, and grew acquainted with Solon, he served him in many instances, and prepared the way for his legislation. He made them moderate in their forms of worship, and abated their mourning by ordering some sacrifices presently after the funeral, and taking off those severe and barbarous ceremonies which the women usually practiced;[29] but the greatest benefit was his purifying and sanctifying the city, by certain propitiatory and expiatory ceremonies, and foundations of sacred buildings, by that means making them more submissive to justice, and more inclined to harmony. It is reported that, looking upon Munychia,[30] and considering a long while, he said to those that stood by, "How blind is man in future things! for had the Athenians foreseen what mischief this would do their city, they would even eat it with their own teeth to be rid of it." A similar anticipation is ascribed to Thales; they say he commanded his friends to bury him in an obscure and condemned quarter of the territory of Miletus, saying that it would someday be the marketplace of the Milesians. Epimenides, being much honored, and receiving from the city rich offers of large gifts and privileges, requested but one branch of the sacred olive, and, on that being granted, returned.

The Athenians, now that the Cylonian sedition was over and the polluted had gone into banishment, fell into their old quarrels about civil policy, there being as many different parties as there were different areas in the country. The Hill quarter favored democracy, the Plain, oligarchy, and those that lived by the Seaside stood for a mixed sort of government, and so hindered either of the other parties from prevailing. And the disparity of fortune between the rich and the poor, at that time, also reached its height, so that the city seemed to be in a truly dangerous condition, and no other means for freeing it from disturbances and set-

---

26 In about 632 BC, Cylon attempted to seize power at Athens. He and his followers failed, and took refuge and met their death as described below.

27 The archons were Athens's governing officials.

28 I.e., a priest of Zeus on the island of Crete, who was particularly celebrated because the young Zeus had been raised by the Cretans.

29 Women traditionally played the major, and public, role in mourning the dead.

30 A fortified portion of Athens's port, the Piraeus, which would later be occupied by Athens's conquerors.

tling it to be possible but a tyranny. All the people were indebted to the rich; and either they tilled their land for their creditors, paying them a sixth part of the increase, and were, therefore, called *hectemorioi*[31] and *thetes*,[32] or else they engaged their bodies for the debt, and might be seized, and either sent into slavery at home, or sold to strangers; some (for no law forbade it) were forced to sell their children, or flee their country to avoid the cruelty of their creditors; but the most part and the bravest of them began to combine together and encourage one another to stand firm, to choose a leader, to liberate the condemned debtors, divide the land, and change the government.

Then the wisest of the Athenians, perceiving Solon was of all men the only one not implicated in the troubles—that he had not joined in the exactions of the rich, and was not involved in the necessities of the poor—pressed him to succor the commonwealth and compose the differences. Though Phanias of Lesbos affirms that Solon, to save his country, played a trick upon both parties, and privately promised the poor a division of the land, and the rich security for their debts, Solon, however, himself says that it was reluctantly at first that he engaged in state affairs, being afraid of the pride of one party and the greediness of the other; he was chosen archon, however, after Philombrotus, and em-powered to be an arbitrator and lawgiver, the rich consenting because he was wealthy, the poor because he was honest. There was a saying of his current before the election, that when things are "even" there never can be war, and this pleased both parties, the wealthy and the poor; the one conceived him to mean that when all have their fair proportion, the others that when all are absolutely equal. Thus, there being great hopes on both sides, the chief men pressed Solon to take the government into his own hands, and, when he was once settled, manage the business freely and according to his pleasure; and many of the commons, perceiving it would be a difficult change to be effected by law and reason, were

willing to have one wise and just man set over affairs; and some say that Solon had this oracle from Apollo:

> Take the mid-seat, and be the vessel's guide;
> Many in Athens are upon your side.

But chiefly his familiar friends chided him for disaffecting monarchy only because of the name, as if the virtue of the ruler could not make it a lawful form; Euboea had made this experiment when it chose Tynnondas, and Mitylene, which had made Pittacus its tyrant; yet this could not shake Solon's resolution but, as they say, he replied to his friends that a true tyranny was a very fair spot, but it had no way down from it; and in a copy of verses to Phocus he writes

> that I spared my land,
> And withheld from usurpation and from violence
>    my hand,
> And forbore to fix a stain and a disgrace on my
>    good name,
> I regret not; I believe that it will be my chief fame.

From which it is manifest that he was a man of great reputation before he gave his laws. The several jibes that were put upon him for refusing power, he records in these words:

> Solon surely was a dreamer, and a man of simple
>    mind;
> When the gods would give him fortune, he of his
>    own will declined;
> When the net was full of fishes, over-heavy think-
>    ing it,
> He declined to haul it up, through want of heart
>    and want of wit.
> Had but I that chance of riches and of kingship, for
>    one day
> I would give my skin for flaying, and my house to
>    die away.

---

31  I.e., the "sixth parters."
32  An old term for free persons who were so poor they had to work for others.

Thus he makes the many and the low people speak of him. Yet though he refused the government, he was not too mild in the affair; he did not show himself mean and submissive to the powerful or make his laws to please those that chose him. For where it was well before, he applied no remedy, nor altered anything, for fear lest

Overthrowing altogether and disordering the state,

he should be too weak to new-model and recompose it to a tolerable condition; but what he thought he could effect by persuasion upon the pliable, and by force upon the stubborn, this he did, as he himself says

With force and justice working both in one.

And, therefore, when he was afterwards asked if he had left the Athenians the best laws that could be given, he replied, "The best they could receive." The way which, the moderns say, the Athenians have of softening the badness of a thing, by ingeniously giving it some pretty and innocent name, calling harlots, for example, mistresses, tributes customs, a garrison a guard, and the jail the chamber, seems originally to have been Solon's contrivance, who called cancelling debts *seisacthea*, a relief, or disencumbrance. For the first thing which he settled was that what debts remained should be forgiven, and no man, for the future, should engage the body of his debtor for security. Though some, such as Androtion, affirm that the debts were not cancelled, but the interest only lessened, which sufficiently pleased the people, so that they named this benefit the *seisacthea*, together with the enlarging of their measures, and raising the value of their money; for he made a pound, which before passed for 73 drachmas, go for 100, so that, though the number of pieces in the payment was equal, the value was less, which proved a considerable benefit to those that were to discharge great debts, and no loss to the creditors. But most agree that it was the taking away of the debts that was called *seisacthea*, which is con-

firmed by some places in his poem, where he takes honor to himself, that

The mortgage stones that covered her, by me
Removed—the land that was a slave is free,

that some who had been seized for their debts he had brought back from other countries, where

so far their lot to roam,
They had forgot the language of their home,

and some he had set at liberty

Who here in shameful servitude were held.

While he was designing this, a most vexatious thing happened; for when he had resolved to undo the debts, and was considering the proper form and fit beginning for it, he told some of his friends, Conon, Clinias, and Hipponicus, in whom he had a great deal of confidence, that he would not meddle with the land, but only free the people from their debts. Upon learning this, they, using their advantage, made haste and borrowed some considerable sums of money, and purchased some large farms. When the law was enacted, they kept the possessions, and would not return the money, which brought Solon into great suspicion and dislike, as if he himself had not been abused, but was concerned in the contrivance. But he presently stopped this suspicion by releasing his debtors of 5 talents (for he had lent so much), according to the law; others, such as Polyzelus the Rhodian, say 15; his friends, however, were ever afterward called *chreocopidie*, repudiators.

In this he pleased neither party, for the rich were angry about their money, and the poor that the land was not divided among them and, as Lycurgus[33] ordered in his commonwealth, all men[34] reduced to equality. He, it is true, being the eleventh descendent from Hercules, and having reigned many years in Lacedaemon,[35] had got a great reputation and friends

---

33  The figure who, according to tradition, gave the Spartans their laws.
34  I.e., citizens.
35  I.e., Sparta.

and power, which he could use in modelling his state; and applying force more than persuasion, insomuch that he lost his eye in the scuffle, was able to employ the most effectual means for the safety and harmony of a state, by not permitting any to be poor or rich in his commonwealth. Solon could not rise to that in his polity, being but a citizen of the middle classes; yet he acted fully up to the height of his power, having nothing but the good will and good opinion of his citizens to rely on; and that he offended the majority, who looked for another result, he declares in the words

> Formerly they boasted of me vainly; with averted
>     eyes
> Now they look askance upon me; friends no more,
>     but enemies.

And yet had any other man, he says, received the same power

> He would not have forborne, nor let alone,
> But made the fattest of the milk his own.

Soon, however, realizing the good that was done, they laid aside their grudges, made a public sacrifice, calling it *seisacthea*, and chose Solon to new-model and make laws for the commonwealth, giving him the entire power over everything—their magistracies, their assemblies, courts, and councils—so that he would decide the number, times of meeting, and what estate they must have to qualify for these, and dissolve or continue any of the present customs, according to his pleasure.

First, then, he repealed all Draco's laws,[36] except those concerning homicide, because they were too severe, and the punishment too great; for death was designated for almost all offenses, insomuch that those that were convicted of idleness were to die, and those that stole a cabbage or an apple to suffer even as villains that committed sacrilege or murder. For this reason Demades, in later times, was thought to have

said very happily that Draco's laws were written not with ink but blood. Draco himself, being once asked why he made death the punishment for most offenses, replied, "Small ones deserve that, and I have none higher for the greater crimes."

Next, Solon, being willing to continue the magistracies in the hands of the rich men, and yet receive the people into the other part of the government, took an account of the citizens' estates, and those that were worth 500 measures of fruit, dry and liquid, he placed in the first rank, calling them *pentacosiomedimnoi*;[37] those that could keep a horse, or were worth 300 measures, were named Hippeis *teluntes*,[38] and made the second class; the Zeugitia,[39] that had 200 measures, were in the third; and all the others were called *thetes*, who were not admitted to any office, but could come to the assembly, and act as jurors; which at first seemed nothing, but afterwards was found an enormous privilege, as almost every matter of dispute came before them in this latter capacity. Even in the cases which he assigned to the archon's cognizance, he allowed an appeal to the courts. Besides, it is said that he was obscure and ambiguous in the wording of his laws in order to increase the honor of his courts; for since their disputes could not be adjusted by the letter of the law, they would have to bring all their causes to the judges, who thus were in a manner masters of the laws. Of this equalization he himself makes mention in this manner:

> Such power I gave the people as might do,
> Abridged not what they had, nor lavished new,
> Those that were great in wealth and high in place
> My counsel likewise kept from all disgrace.
> Before them both I held my shield of might,
> And let not either touch the other's right.

And for the greater security of the weak commons, he gave general liberty of indicting for an act of injury; if anyone was beaten, maimed, or suffered any violence,

---

36  Draco, an archon of the Athenians (late seventh century BC).
37  I.e., 500 bushellers.
38  I.e., "Horsemen."
39  I.e., "those yoked together," i.e., of wealth sufficient to support a hoplite, a kind of heavily armored soldier.

any man that would and was able might prosecute the wrong-doer. He intended by this to accustom the citizens, like members of the same body, to resent and be sensible of one another's injuries. And there is a saying of his agreeable to his law, for, being asked what city was best modelled, he said, "That where those that are not injured try and punish the unjust as much as those that are."

When he had constituted the Areopagus[40] of those who had been yearly archons, of which he himself was a member therefore, observing that the people, now free from their debts, were unsettled and imperious, he formed another council of 400, 100 out of each of the four tribes,[41] which was to inspect all matters before they were put before the people, and to take care that nothing but what had been first examined would be brought before the general assembly. The upper council, or Areopagus, he made inspectors and keepers of the laws, conceiving that the city, held by these two councils, like anchors, would be less liable to be tossed by tumults, and the people be more quiet. Such is the general statement that Solon instituted the Areopagus, which seems to be confirmed because Draco makes no mention of the Areopagites, but in all cases of homicide refers to the Ephetai;[42] yet Solon's thirteenth table contains the eighth law set down in these very words: "Whoever before Solon's archonship were disenfranchised, let them be restored, except those that, being condemned by the Areopagus, Ephetai, or in the Prytanis[43] by the king archons,[44] for homicide, murder or attempting a tyranny, were in banishment when this law was made"; and these words seem to show that the Areopagus existed before Solon's laws, for who could be condemned by that council before his time, if he was the first that instituted the court? unless, which is probable, there is some ellipsis, or want of precision in the language, and it should run thus: "Those that are convicted of such offenses as belong to the cognizance of the Areopagites, Ephetai, or the Prytanis, when this law was made" shall remain still in disgrace, while others are restored; of this the reader must judge.

Among his other laws, one is very peculiar and surprising, which disenfranchises all who stand neutral in a sedition; for it seems he would not have anyone remain insensible and regardless of the public good, and securing his private affairs, glory that he has no feeling of the distempers of his country, but at once join with the good party and those that have the right upon their side, assist and venture with them rather than keep out of harm's way and watch who would get the better. It seems an absurd and foolish law which permits an heiress, if her lawful husband is impotent, to marry his nearest kinsman; yet some say this law was well contrived against those who, conscious of their own unfitness, yet, for the sake of the marriage portion, would marry heiresses, and make use of law to put violence upon nature; for now, since she can leave him for whom she pleases, they would either abstain from such marriages, or continue them with disgrace, and suffer for their covetousness and deliberate affront; it is well done, moreover, to confine her to her husband's nearest kinsman so that the children may be of the same family. Agreeable to this is the law that the bride and bridegroom shall be shut into a chamber, and eat a quince together; and that the husband of an heiress shall have intercourse with her three times a month; for though there may be no children, yet it is an honor and due affection which a husband ought to pay to a virtuous chaste wife; it removes all petty differences, and will not permit their little quarrels to proceed to a rupture.

In all other marriages he forbade dowries to be given; the wife was to have three suits of clothes, a little inconsiderable household stuff, and that was all; for he would not have marriages contracted for gain or an estate but for pure love, kind affection, and birth

---

40  Membership in this body had previously been restricted to aristocratic families, as had the archonships.

41  In Athenian legend, the four tribes were each descended from one of the sons of Ion, for whom the Ionian Greeks were also named. Each tribe had aristocratic branches.

42  A kind of jury selected by lot.

43  A supervisory council.

44  Certain select archons with religious duties.

of children. When Dionysius[45] was desired by his mother to marry her to one of his citizens, he said "Indeed, by my tyranny I have broken my country's laws, but cannot put violence upon those of nature by an unseasonable marriage." Such disorder is never to be suffered in a city, nor such unseasonable and unloving and unperforming marriages, which attain no due end or fruit; any provident governor or lawgiver might say to an old man that takes a young wife what is said to Philoctetes in the tragedy,

Truly, in a fit state you to marry !46

and if he finds a young man, with a rich and elderly wife, growing fat in his place, like the partridges, removes him to a young woman of proper age. And of this enough.

Another commendable law of Solon is that which forbids men to speak evil of the dead; for it is pious to think the deceased sacred, and just, not to meddle with those that are gone, and politic to prevent the perpetuity of discord. He likewise forbade them to speak evil of the living in the temples, the courts of justice, the public offices or at the games, or else to pay three drachmas to the person, and two to the public. For never to be able to control passion shows a weak nature and ill breeding; and always to moderate it is very hard, and to some impossible. And laws must look to possibilities, if the maker designs to punish few in order to obtain their amendment, and not many to no purpose.

He is likewise much commended for his law concerning wills; for before him none could be made, but all the wealth and estates of the deceased belonged to his family; but he, by permitting them, if they had no children, to bestow it on whom they pleased, showed that he esteemed friendship a stronger tie than kindred, and affection than necessity, and made every man's estate truly his own. Yet he did not allow all

sorts of legacies, but those only which were not extorted by the frenzy of disease, charms, imprisonment, force, or the persuasions of a wife, with good reason thinking that being seduced into wrong was as bad as being forced, and that between deceit and necessity, flattery and compulsion, there was little difference, since both may equally suspend the exercise of reason.

He regulated the public appearance of women, their festivals and mourning, and took away everything that was either unbecoming or immodest; when they walked outside, no more than three articles of dress were allowed them; an obol's worth of meat and drink; and no basket above a cubit high; and at night they were not to go about unless in a chariot with a torch before them. Mourners tearing themselves to raise pity, and set wailings, and at one man's funeral to lament for another, he forbade. To offer an ox at the grave was not permitted, nor to bury above three pieces of dress with the body, or visit the tombs of any besides their own family, unless at the actual funeral; most of which are likewise forbidden by our laws,[47] but this is further added in ours, that those that are convicted of extravagance in their mournings are to be punished as soft and effeminate by the censors[48] of women.

Observing the city to be filled with persons that flocked from all parts into Attica for security of living, and that most of the country was barren and unfruitful, and that traders at sea import nothing to those that could give them nothing in exchange, he turned his citizens to trade, and made a law that no son be obliged to relieve a father who had not bred him up to any calling. It is true, Lycurgus, having a city free from all strangers, and land, according to Euripides,[49]

Large for large hosts, for twice their number much,

and, above all, an abundance of helots[50] around Sparta, who should not be left idle, but be kept down with

---

45  Tyrant of the Greek city of Syracuse in Sicily.
46  This play does not survive.
47  I.e., of Plutarch's city of Chaeronea.
48  Officers charged with monitoring moral behavior, rather than with controlling written or verbal expresssion.
49  Playwright (fifth century BC).
50  A term for a neighboring people, the Messenians, enslaved by the Spartans.

continual toil and work, did well to release his citizens from laborious and mechanical occupations, and keep them to their arms, and teach them only the art of war. But Solon, fitting his laws to the state of things, and not making things to suit his laws, and finding the ground scarcely rich enough to maintain the farmers, and altogether incapable of feeding an unoccupied and leisured multitude, brought trades into credit, and ordered the Areopagites to examine how every man got his living, and chastise the idle. But that law was yet more rigid which, as Heraclides Ponticus delivers, declared the sons of unmarried mothers not obliged to relieve their fathers; for he that avoids the honorable form of union shows that he does not take a woman for children, but for pleasure, and thus gets his just reward and has taken away from himself every title to upbraid his children, to whom he has made their very birth a scandal and reproach.

Solon's laws in general about women are his strangest, for he permitted anyone to kill an adulterer that found him in the act, but if anyone forced a free woman, 100 drachmas was the fine; if he enticed her, 20, except those that sell themselves openly, that is, harlots, who go openly to those that hire them. He made it unlawful to sell a daughter or a sister, unless, being yet unmarried, she was found wanton. Now it is irrational to punish the same crime sometimes very severely and without remorse, and sometimes very lightly, and as it were in sport, with a trivial fine; unless there being little money then in Athens, scarcity made those fines the more grievous punishment. In the valuation for sacrifices, a sheep and a bushel were both estimated at a drachma; the victor in the Isthmian games was to have for reward 100 drachmas as the conqueror, in the Olympian, 500; he that brought a wolf 5 drachmas; for a whelp, 1; the former sum, as Demetrius the Phalerian asserts, was the value of an ox, the latter, of a sheep. The prices which Solon, in his sixteenth table, sets on choice victims, were naturally far greater; yet they, too, are very low in comparison with the present. The Athenians were, from the beginning, great enemies to wolves, their fields being better for pasture than for grain. Some affirm their tribes did not take their names from the sons of Ion, but from the different sorts of occupation that they followed; the soldiers were called *hoplitai*, the craftsmen *ergadeis*

and, of the remaining two, the farmers *geleontes*, and the shepherds and graziers *aegicores*.

Since the country has but few rivers, lakes, or large springs, and many used wells which they had dug, there was a law made that, where there was a public well within a hippicon, that is, four furlongs, all should draw at that; but when it was farther off, they should try and procure a well of their own; and if they had dug ten fathoms deep and could find no water, they had liberty to fetch a pitcherful of four gallons and a half in a day from their neighbors', for he thought it prudent to make provision against want, but not to supply laziness. He showed skill in his orders about planting, for anyone that would plant another tree was not to set it within five feet of his neighbor's field; but if a fig or an olive, not within nine, for their roots spread farther, nor can they be planted near all sorts of trees without damage, for they draw away the nourishment, and in some cases are noxious by their effluvia. He that would dig a pit or a ditch was to dig it at the distance of its own depth from his neighbor's ground, and he that would raise stocks of bees was not to place them within 300 feet of those which another had already raised.

He permitted only oil to be exported, and those that exported any other fruit, the archon was solemnly to curse, or else pay 100 drachmas himself; and this law was written in his first table, and, therefore, let none think it unbelievable, as some affirm, that the exportation of figs was once unlawful and the informer against the delinquents called a sycophant. He also made a law concerning hurts and injuries from beasts, in which he commands the master of any dog that bit a man to deliver him up with a pole four and a half feet long fastened around its neck, a happy device for men's security. The law concerning naturalizing strangers is of doubtful character; he permitted only those to be made citizens of Athens who were in perpetual exile from their own country, or came with their whole family to trade there; this he did, not to discourage strangers, but rather to invite them to a permanent participation in the privileges of citizenship; and, besides, he thought those would prove the more faithful citizens who had been forced from their own country, or voluntarily forsook it. The law of public feasting (*parasitein* is his name for it) is also peculiarly Solon's; for if any man came often, or if he that was invited refused, they were punished, for he concluded that one was greedy, the other contemptuous of the public authority.

All his laws he established for a hundred years, and wrote them on wooden tables or rollers, named *axones*, which might be turned around in oblong cases; some of their remains were in my time still to be seen in the *Prytaneum*, or common hall at Athens. These, as Aristotle states, were called *cyrbes*, and there is a passage of Cratinus the comedian,

> By Solon, and by Draco, if you please,
> Whose Cyrbes make the fires that parch our peas.

But some say those are properly cyrbes which contain laws concerning sacrifices and the rites of religion, and all the others are axones. The council all jointly swore to confirm the laws, and every one of the Thesmothetai[51] vowed for himself at the stone in the marketplace, that if he broke any of the statutes, he would dedicate a golden statue, as big as himself, at Delphi.

Observing the irregularity of the months, and that the moon does not always rise and set with the sun, but often in the same day overtakes and gets before him, he ordered the day should be named the Old and New, attributing that part of it which was before the conjunction to the old moon, and the rest to the new, he being the first, it seems, that understood that verse of Homer,

> The end and the beginning of the month,

and the following day he called the new moon. After the twentieth he did not count by addition, but, like the moon itself in its wane, by subtraction; thus up to the thirtieth.

Now when these laws were enacted, and some came to Solon every day to commend or criticize them, and to advise, if possible, to leave out or put in something, and many criticized and desired him to explain, and tell the meaning of such and such a passage, he, knowing that to do so was useless, and not to

do it would get him ill will, and desiring to bring himself out of all difficulties, and to escape all displeasure and exceptions, it being a hard thing, as he himself says,

> In great affairs to satisfy all sides,

as an excuse for travelling, bought a trading vessel, and, having leave for ten years' absence, departed, hoping that by that time his laws would have become familiar.

His first voyage was for Egypt, and he lived, as he himself says,

> Near Nile's mouth, by fair Canopus's shore,

and spent some time in study with Psenophis of Heliopolis, and Sonchis the Saite, the most learned of all the priests, from whom, as Plato says, getting knowledge of the story of Atlantis,[52] he put it into a poem, and proposed to bring it to the knowledge of the Greeks. From there he sailed to Cyprus, where he was made much of by Philocyprus, one of the kings there, who had a small city built by Demophon, Theseus's son, near the river Clarius, in a strong situation, but incommodious and not of easy access. Solon persuaded him, since there lay a fair plain below, to remove and build there a pleasanter and more spacious city. And he stayed himself, and assisted in gathering inhabitants and in fitting it both for defense and convenience of living, so much so that many flocked to Philocyprus, and the other kings imitated the design, and therefore to honor Solon, he called the city Soli, which was formerly named Aepea. Solon himself, in his *Elegies*, addressing Philocyprus, mentions this foundation in these words,

> Long may you live, and fill the Solian throne,
> Succeeded still by children of your own;
> And from your happy island while I sail,
> Let Cyprus send for me a favoring gale;
> May she advance, and bless your new command,
> Prosper your town, and send me safe to land.

---

51  I.e., "layers down of the rules."
52  A fabled lost island or continent.

That Solon should converse with Croesus, some do not think agreeable with chronology, but I cannot reject so famous and well attested a narrative and, what is more, one so agreeable to Solon's temper, and so worthy of his wisdom and greatness of mind, because it does not agree with some supposed chronological canons, which thousands have endeavored to regulate, and yet, to this day, can never bring their differing opinions to any agreement. They say, therefore, that Solon, coming to Croesus at his request, was in the same condition as an inland man when first he goes to see the sea; for as he fancies every river he meets with to be the ocean, so Solon, as he passed through the court, and saw a great many nobles richly dressed, and proudly attended by a multitude of guards and footboys, thought every one was the king, until he was brought to Croesus, who was decked with every possible rarity and curiosity of ornaments of jewels, purple, and gold that could make him a grand and gorgeous spectacle. Now when Solon came before him, and seemed not at all surprised nor gave Croesus those compliments he expected, but showed himself to all discerning eyes to be a man that despised the gaudiness and petty ostentation of it, he commanded them to open all his treasure houses, and carry him to see his sumptuous furniture and luxuries, though he did not wish it; Solon could judge of him well enough by the first sight of him. When Solon returned from viewing everything, Croesus asked him if ever he had known a happier man than he. And when Solon answered that he had known one Tellus, a fellow-citizen of his own, and told him that this Tellus had been an honest man, had had good children, a competent estate, and died bravely in battle for his country, Croesus took him for an ill-bred fellow and a fool for not measuring happiness by the abundance of gold and silver, and preferring the life and death of a private and mean man before so much power and rule. He asked him, however, again, if, besides Tellus, he knew any other man more happy. And Solon replying, yes, Cleobis and Biton, who were loving brothers, and extremely dutiful sons to their mother, and, when the oxen delayed her, harnessed themselves to a wagon, and drew her to Hera's temple, her neighbors all calling her happy, and she herself rejoicing; then, after sacrificing and feasting, they went to rest, and never rose again, but died in the midst of their honor a painless and tranquil death. "What," said Croesus, angrily, "and do you not reckon me amongst the happy men at all?" Solon, unwilling either to flatter or exasperate him more, replied, "The gods, O king, have given the Greeks all other gifts in moderate degree; and so our wisdom, too, is a cheerful and a homely, not a noble and kingly wisdom; and this, observing the numerous misfortunes that attend all conditions, forbids us to grow insolent in our present enjoyment, or to admire any man's happiness that may yet, in course of time, suffer change. For the uncertain future has yet to come, with every possible variety of fortune; and him only to whom the divinity has continued happiness to the end we call happy; to salute as happy one that is still in the midst of life and hazard, we think as little safe and conclusive as to crown and proclaim as victorious the wrestler that is yet in the ring." After this he was dismissed, having given Croesus some pain, but no instruction.

Aesop, who wrote the fables, being then at Sardis upon Croesus's invitation, and very much esteemed, was concerned that Solon was so ill received, and gave him this advice: "Solon, let your conversation with kings be either short or seasonable." "Nay, rather," replied Solon, "either short or reasonable." So at this time Croesus despised Solon; but when he was overcome by Cyrus,[53] had lost his city, was condemned to be burned, and laid bound upon the pyre before all the Persians and Cyrus himself, he cried out as loud as he possibly could three times, "O Solon!" and Cyrus being surprised, and sending some to inquire what man or god this Solon was, who alone he invoked in this extremity, Croesus told him the whole story, saying, "He was one of the wise men of Greece, whom I sent for, not to be instructed, or to learn anything that I wanted, but that he should see and be a witness of my happiness, the loss of which was, it seems, to be a greater evil than the enjoyment was a good; for when I had them they were goods only in opinion, but now

---

53  King of Persia.

the loss of them has brought upon me intolerable and real evils. And he, conjecturing from what then was, this that now is, bade me look to the end of my life, and not rely and grow proud upon uncertainties." When this was said to Cyrus, who was a wiser man than Croesus, and saw in the present example Solon's maxim confirmed, he not only freed Croesus from punishment, but honored him as long as he lived; and Solon had the glory, by the same saying, to save one king and instruct another.

When Solon was gone, the citizens began to quarrel. Lycurgus led the Plain; Megacles, the son of Alcmaeon, the Coast; and Pisistratus the Hill-party, in which were the poorest people, the *thetes*, and greatest enemies to the rich. Though the city still used the new laws, yet all looked for and desired a change of government, hoping that the change would be better for them, and put them above the opposing faction. Affairs standing thus, Solon returned, and was revered by all, and honored; but his old age would not permit him to be as active, and to speak in public, as formerly. Yet, by privately conferring with the heads of the factions, he endeavored to resolve the conflicts, Pisistratus appearing the most tractable, for he was extremely smooth and engaging in his language, a great friend to the poor, and moderate in his resentments; and what nature had not given him, he had the skill to imitate, so that he was trusted more than the others, being accounted a prudent and orderly man, one that loved equality, and would be an enemy to any that moved against the present settlement. Thus he deceived the majority of people; but Solon quickly discovered his character, and found out his design before anyone else. Yet Solon did not hate him, but endeavored to humble him, and bring him off from his ambition, and often told him and others that if anyone could banish the passion for preeminence from his mind, and cure him of his desire for absolute power, none would make a more virtuous man or a more excellent citizen. Thespis, at this time, beginning to act tragedies, and the thing, because it was new, attracting the multitude, though it was not yet made a matter of competition,[54] Solon, being by nature fond of hearing and learning some-

thing new, and now, in his old age, living idly, and enjoying himself, indeed, with music and with wine, went to see Thespis himself, as the ancient custom was, act. After the play was done, he addressed him, and asked him if he was not ashamed to tell so many lies before such a number of people; and Thespis replying that it was no harm to say or do so in play, Solon vehemently struck his staff against the ground: "Ah," he said, "if we honor and commend such play as this, we shall find it some day in our business."

Now when Pisistratus, having wounded himself, was brought into the marketplace in a chariot, and stirred up the people, as if he had been thus treated by his opponents because of his political conduct, and a great many were enraged and cried out, Solon, coming close to him, said, "This, O son of Hippocrates, is a bad copy of Homer's Odysseus; you do, to trick your countrymen, what he did to deceive his enemies." After this, the people were eager to protect Pisistratus, and met in an assembly, where one Ariston making a motion that they should allow Pisistratus 50 men armed with clubs as a guard for his person, Solon opposed it, and said much to the same purport as what he has left us in his poems,

You dote upon his words and taking phrase

and again

True, you are singly each a crafty soul,
But all together make one empty fool.

But observing that the poor men were tumultuous and bent on gratifying Pisistratus, and the rich fearful and getting out of harm's way, he departed, saying he was wiser than some and stouter than others; wiser than those that did not understand the design, stouter than those that, though they understood it, were afraid to oppose the tyranny. Now, the people, having passed the law, were not nice with Pisistratus about the number of his clubmen, but he took no notice of it, though he enlisted and kept as many as he would until he seized the Acropolis.[55] When that was done, and the

---

54  In the course of the fifth century, the Athenians began to give prizes to the author of the year's best plays.
55  The highest point of the city, and a fortified place.

city in an uproar, Megacles, with all his family, at once fled; but Solon, though he was now very old, and had no one to back him, yet came into the marketplace and made a speech to the citizens, partly blaming their inadvertency and meanness of spirit, and in part urging and exhorting them not thus tamely to lose their liberty; and likewise then spoke that memorable saying, that, before, it was an easier task to stop the rising tyranny, but now the great and more glorious action was to destroy it, when it had already begun, and had gathered strength. But all being afraid to side with him, he returned home, and, taking his arms, he brought them out and laid them in the porch before his door, with these words: "I have done my part to maintain my country and my laws," and then he busied himself no more. His friends advising him to flee, he refused, but wrote poems, and reproached the Athenians in them thus:

If now you suffer, do not blame the Powers,
For they are good, and all the fault was ours,
All the strongholds you put into his hands,
And now his slaves must do what he commands.

And many telling him that the tyrant would take his life for this, and asking what he trusted to, that he ventured to speak so boldly, he replied, "To my old age." But Pisistratus, having got the command, so extremely courted Solon, so honored him, obliged him, and sent to see him, that Solon gave him his advice, and approved many of his actions; for he retained most of Solon's laws, observed them himself, and compelled his friends to obey. And he himself, though already absolute ruler, being accused of murder before the Areopagus, came quietly to clear himself, but his accuser did not appear. And he added other laws, one of which is that the maimed in war should be maintained at the public charge. Heraclides Ponticus records this, and that Pisistratus followed Solon's example in this, who had decreed it in the case of one Thersippus, that was maimed; and Theophrastus

asserts that it was Pisistratus, not Solon, that made that law against laziness, which was the reason that the country was more productive, and the city more tranquil.

Now Solon, having begun the great work in verse, the history or fable of the Atlantis, which he had learned from the wise men in Sais, and thought convenient for the Athenians to know, abandoned it—not, as Plato says, by reason of want of time, but because of his age, and being discouraged at the greatness of the task; for that he had leisure enough such verses testify as

Each day grow older, and learn something new

and again

But now the Powers, of Beauty, Song, and Wine,
Which are most men's delights, are also mine.

Plato, willing to improve the story of Atlantis, as if it were a fair estate that wanted an heir and came with some title to him, formed, indeed, stately entrances, noble enclosures, large courtyards, such as never yet introduced any story, fable, or poetic fiction; but, beginning it late, ended his life before his work; and the reader's regret for the unfinished part is the greater, as the satisfaction he takes in that which is complete is extraordinary. For as the city of Athens left only the temple of Zeus Olympius unfinished, so Plato, amongst all his excellent works, left only this piece about Atlantis imperfect. Solon lived after Pisistratus seized the government, as Heraclides Ponticus asserts, a long time; but Phanias the Eresian says not two full years; for Pisistratus began his tyranny when Comias was archon, and Phanias says Solon died under Hegestratus, who succeeded Comias. The story that his ashes were scattered about the island of Salamis is too strange to be easily believed, or be thought anything but a mere fable; and yet it is given, amongst other good authors, by Aristotle, the philosopher.

# 11

# ARISTOPHANES, *LYSISTRATA*

Aristophanes (*c*. 450-385 BC) was one of the leading comic playwrights of classical Athens. His *Lysistrata* was performed there in 411 BC, during the Peloponnesian War (431-404 BC), fought between the Peloponnesian League, an alliance of Greek city states dominated by Sparta, and Athens, which headed what was in theory a voluntary alliance called the "Delian League," but which in fact was so dominated by the Athenians that its members were generally involuntary allies. The year of *Lysistrata*'s first production also saw Athens's democracy overthrown and replaced by an oligarchy. (The democracy would be restored in 410.) In this play, the Spartan characters all speak in an unsophisticated dialect; no attempt to reproduce this is made here.

---

Scene: In a square at Athens

LYSISTRATA: Ah! if only they had been invited to a Dionysian reveling, or a feast of Pan or Aphrodite or Genetyllis,[1] why! the streets would have been impassable for the thronging tambourines! Now there's never a woman here—ah! except my neighbor Calonice, whom I see approaching yonder.... Good day, Calonice.

CALONICE: Good day, Lysistrata; but pray, why this dark, forbidding face, my dear? Believe me, you don't look at all pretty with those black, lowering brows.

LYSISTRATA: Oh! Calonice, my heart is on fire; I blush for our sex. Men will have it we are tricky and sly.

CALONICE: And they are quite right, upon my word.

LYSISTRATA: Yet, look: when the women are summoned to meet for a matter of the last importance, they lie in bed instead of coming.

CALONICE: Oh! they will come, my dear; but it's not easy, you know, for women to leave the house. One is busy pottering about her husband; another is getting up the slave; a third is putting her child asleep, or washing the brat or feeding it.

LYSISTRATA: But I tell you, the business that calls them here is far and away more urgent.

CALONICE: And why do you summon us, dear Lysistrata? What is this all about?

LYSISTRATA: About a big affair.

CALONICE: And is it thick too?

LYSISTRATA: Yes indeed; both big and great.

CALONICE: And we are not all on the spot!

LYSISTRATA: Oh! if it were what you suppose, there would never be an absentee. No, no, it concerns a

---

1   These religious celebrations all involved a great relaxation of controls on women. The festival of Dionysius was also imagined as involving women wandering the countryside in a mad frenzy, although the strength of the evidence that this was actually the case in the fifth century BC is unclear. "Genetyllis" was another name for Aphrodite, the goddess of love.

thing I have turned about and about this way and that for many sleepless nights.

CALONICE: It must be something mighty fine and subtle for you to have turned it about so!

LYSISTRATA: So fine, it means just this: Greece saved by the women!

CALONICE: By women! Why, its salvation hangs on a poor thread then!

LYSISTRATA: Our country's fortunes depend on us—it is for us to undo utterly the Peloponnesians.[2]

CALONICE: That would be truly a noble deed!

LYSISTRATA: To exterminate the Boeotians[3] to a man!

CALONICE: But surely you would spare the eels.[4]

LYSISTRATA: For Athens's sake I will never threaten so fatal a doom; trust me for that. However, if the Boeotian and Peloponnesian women join us, Greece is saved.

CALONICE: But how should women perform so wise and glorious an achievement, we women who dwell in the retirement of the household, clad in diaphanous garments of yellow silk and long flowing gowns, decked out with flowers and shod with dainty little slippers?

LYSISTRATA: Indeed, but those are the very sheet-anchors of our salvation—those yellow tunics, those scents and slippers, those cosmetics and transparent robes.

CALONICE: How so, pray?

LYSISTRATA: There is not a man will wield a lance[5] against another—

CALONICE: Quick, I will get me a yellow tunic from the dyer's.

LYSISTRATA: —or want a shield—

CALONICE: I'll run and put on a flowing gown.

LYSISTRATA: —or draw a sword.

CALONICE: I'll rush and buy a pair of slippers this instant.

LYSISTRATA: Now tell me, would not the women have done best to come?

CALONICE: Why, they should have flown here!

LYSISTRATA: Ah! my dear, you'll see that like true Athenians, they will do everything too late. Why, there's not a woman come from the shoreward parts, not one from Salamis.[6]

CALONICE: But I know for certain they embarked at daybreak.

LYSISTRATA: And the dames from Acharnae![7] why, I thought they would have been the very first to arrive.

CALONICE: Theagenes's wife at any rate is sure to come; she has actually been to consult Hecate[8].... But look! here are some arrivals—and there are more behind. Ah! ha! now what countrywomen may they be?

LYSISTRATA: They are from Anagyrae.[9]

CALONICE: Yes! upon my word, it's a levy *en masse* of the whole female population of Anagyra!

MYRRHINE: Are we late, Lysistrata? Tell us, pray; what, not a word?

LYSISTRATA: I cannot say much for you, Myrrhine! You have not bestirred yourself overmuch for an affair of such urgency.

MYRRHINE: I could not find my belt in the dark. However, if the matter is so pressing, here we are; so speak.

LYSISTRATA: No, but let us wait a moment more, until the women of Boeotia arrive and those from the Peloponnese.

MYRRHINE: Yes, that is best.... Ah! here comes Lampito.

LYSISTRATA: Good day, Lampito, dear friend from

---

2  I.e., the Spartans and their allies.

3  Other opponents of Athens in the war.

4  Boeotia was known for its eels (which were eaten).

5  The hoplite, or heavy-armed infantryman, held a thrusting spear or lance.

6  The island, now subject to Athens, where the Athenians defeated the Persian forces during the Persian Wars of the fifth century BC.

7  A town in Attica, and so Athenian territory. Citizens of this region were especially in favor of the war.

8  A goddess.

9  A small and unimportant section of Athens.

Lacedaemon.[10] How well and handsome you look! What a rosy complexion! And how strong you seem; why, you could strangle a bull surely!

LAMPITO: Yes, indeed, I really think I could. It's because I do gymnastics and practice the kick dance.

LYSISTRATA: And what superb bosoms!

LAMPITO: La! You are feeling me as if I were a beast for sacrifice.

LYSISTRATA: And this young woman, what country-woman is she?

LAMPITO: She is a noble lady from Boeotia.

LYSISTRATA: Ah! my pretty Boeotian friend, you are as blooming as a garden.

CALONICE: Yes, on my word! and the garden is so prettily weeded too!

LYSISTRATA: And who is this ?

LAMPITO: It's an honest woman, by my faith; she comes from Corinth.

LYSISTRATA: Oh! honest, no doubt then—as honesty goes at Corinth.[11]

LAMPITO: But who has called together this council of women, pray?

LYSISTRATA: I have.

LAMPITO: Well then, tell us what you want of us.

LYSISTRATA: With pleasure, my dear.

MYRRHINE: What is the most important business you wish to inform us about?

LYSISTRATA: I will tell you: But first answer me one question.

MYRRHINE: What is that?

LYSISTRATA: Don't you feel sad and sorry because the fathers of your children are far away from you with the army? For I'll undertake to say that there is not one of you whose husband is not abroad at this moment.

CALONICE: Mine has been the last five months in Thrace—looking after Eucrates.[12]

LYSISTRATA: It's seven long months since mine left me for Pylos.[13]

LAMPITO: As for mine, if he ever does return from service, he's no sooner back than he takes down his shield again and flies back to the wars.

LYSISTRATA: And not so much as the shadow of a lover! Since the day the Milesians betrayed us, I have never once seen an eight-inch-long dildo even, to be a leather[14] consolation to us poor widows.... Now tell me, if I have discovered a means of ending the war, will you all second me?

MYRRHINE: Yes truly, by all the goddesses, I swear I will, even if I have to put my gown in pawn, and drink the money the same day.

CALONICE: And so will I, though I must be split in two like a flat fish, and have half myself removed.

LAMPITO: And I too; why, to secure Peace, I would climb to the top of Mount Taygetus.[15]

LYSISTRATA: Then I will come out with it at last, my mighty secret! Oh! sister women, if we would compel our husbands to make peace, we must refrain—

MYRRHINE: Refrain from what? tell us, tell us!

LYSISTRATA: But will you do it ?

MYRRHINE: We will, we will, though we should die of it.

LYSISTRATA: We must refrain from sex altogether. No, why do you turn your backs on me? Where are you going? So, you bite your lips, and shake your heads, eh? Why these pale, sad looks? Why these tears? Come, will you do it—yes or no? Do you hesitate?

MYRRHINE: No, I will not do it; let the War go on.

LYSISTRATA: And you, my pretty flat fish, who declared just now they might split you in two?

CALONICE: Anything, anything but that! Bid me go through the fire, if you will; but to rob us of the sweetest thing in all the world? My dear, dear Lysistrata!

LYSISTRATA: And you?

---

10   I.e., Sparta.

11   Corinth had a reputation for prostitution.

12   An Athenian general suspected of treachery.

13   A town on the coast in Spartan territory which had been seized from the sea by the Athenians.

14   Dildos were made of leather.

15   In Spartan territory; Spartan women celebrated rites of Dionysius there.

MYRRHINE: Yes, I, agree with the others; I too would sooner go through the fire.

LYSISTRATA: Oh, wanton, vicious sex! the poets have done well to make tragedies about us; we are good for nothing then but love and lewdness! But you, my dear, you from hardy Sparta, if you join me, all may yet be well; help me, second me, I conjure you.

LAMPITO: It's a hard thing, by the two goddesses[16] it is! for a woman to sleep alone without ever a standing weapon in her bed. But there, Peace must come first.

LYSISTRATA: Oh, my dear, my dearest, best friend, you are the only one deserving the name of woman!

CALONICE: But if—which the gods forbid—we do refrain altogether from what you say, would we get peace any sooner?

LYSISTRATA: By the two goddeses, of course we would! We need only sit indoors with painted cheeks, and meet our mates lightly clad in transparent gowns of Amorgos silk, and with our mounds nicely plucked smooth; then their tools will stand like mad and they will be wild to lie with us. That will be the time to refuse, and they will hasten to make peace, I am convinced of that!

LAMPITO: Yes, just as Menelaus, when he saw Helen's naked bosom,[17] threw away his sword, they say.

CALONICE: But, poor devils, suppose our husbands go away and leave us.

LYSISTRATA: Then, as Pherecrates says, we must "flay a skinned dog,"[18] that's all.

CALONICE: Bah! these proverbs are all idle talk.... But if our husbands drag us by main force into the bedchamber?

LYSISTRATA: Hold on to the door posts.

CALONICE: But if they beat us?

LYSISTRATA: Then yield to their wishes, but with a bad grace; there is no pleasure for them when they do it by force. Besides, there are a thousand ways of tormenting them. Never fear, they'll soon tire of the game; there's no satisfaction for a man, unless the woman shares it.

CALONICE: Very well, if you *will* have it so, we agree.

LAMPITO: For ourselves, no doubt we shall persuade our husbands to conclude a fair and honest peace; but there is the Athenian populace, how are we to cure these folk of their warlike frenzy?

LYSISTRATA: Have no fear; we undertake to make our own people hear reason.

LAMPITO: No, impossible, so long as they have their trusty ships and the vast treasures stored in the temple of Athena.[19]

LYSISTRATA: Ah! but we have seen to that; this very day the Acropolis[20] will be in our hands. That is the task assigned to the older women; while we are here in council, they are going, under pretense of offering sacrifice, to seize the citadel.

LAMPITO: Well said indeed! so everything is going for the best.

LYSISTRATA: Come, quick, Lampito, and let us bind ourselves by an inviolable oath.

LAMPITO: Recite the terms; we will swear to them.

LYSISTRATA: With pleasure. Where is our Scythian woman?[21] Now, what on the earth are you staring at, pray? Lay this shield before us, its hollow upwards, and someone bring me the victim's entrails.

CALONICE: Lysistrata, say, what oath are we to swear?

LYSISTRATA: What oath? Why, in Aeschylus,[22] they sacrifice a sheep, and swear over a shield; we will do the same.

---

16 Demeter and Proserpina.

17 From Greek mythology. Menelaus, husband of Helen, was ready to slay her after the Trojan war in revenge for abandoning him for Paris.

18 Pherecrates was a comic playwright of Aristophanes's time. The proverb means it is useless to do what it is already too late to do—such as flogging a dead horse. Flaying a dog can also be a way of procuring leather to make a dildo.

19 The treasury of the Delian League, now functioning as an Athenian empire, was kept in the temple of Athena in Athens, and so under Athenian control. It was used to support Athens's navy.

20 The highest section of the city, a fortified area, where Athena's temple stood.

21 At Athens the police and ushers in court and at the assembly of citizens were (male) Scythian slaves.

22 A reference to Aeschylus's play *The Seven Against Thebes* (fifth century BC).

CALONICE: No, Lysistrata, one cannot swear peace over a shield, surely.

LYSISTRATA: What other oath do you prefer?

CALONICE: Let's take a white horse, and sacrifice its entrails.

LYSISTRATA: But where to get a white horse from?

CALONICE: Well, what oath shall we take then?

LYSISTRATA: Listen to me. Let's set a great black bowl on the ground; let's sacrifice a wine-skin of Thasian wine into it, and take an oath not to add one single drop of water.

LAMPITO: Ah! that's an oath that pleases me more than I can say.

LYSISTRATA: Let them bring me a bowl and a skin of wine.

CALONICE: Ah! my dears, what a noble, big bowl! what a delight it will be to empty it!

LYSISTRATA: Set the bowl down on the ground, and lay your hands on the victim.... Almighty goddess, Persuasion, and you, bowl, boon comrade of joy and merriment, receive this our sacrifice, and be propitious to us poor women!

CALONICE: Oh! the fine red blood! how well it flows!

LAMPITO: And what a delicious savor, by the two goddesses!

LYSISTRATA: Now, my dears, let me swear first, if you please.

CALONICE: No, by the goddess of love, let us decide that by lot.

LYSISTRATA: Come then, Lampito, and all of you, put your hands to the bowl; and you, Calonice, repeat in the name of all the solemn terms I am going to recite. Then you must all swear, and pledge yourselves by the same promises: "I will have nothing to do whether with lover or husband ...

CALONICE: I will have nothing to do whether with lover or husband ...

LYSISTRATA: Albeit he comes to me with a stiff and standing tool ...

CALONICE: Albeit he comes to me with a stiff and standing tool ... Oh ! Lysistrata, I cannot bear it!

LYSISTRATA: I will live at home in perfect chastity ...

CALONICE: I will live at home in perfect chastity ...

LYSISTRATA: Beautifully dressed and wearing a saffron-colored gown ...

CALONICE: Beautifully dressed and wearing a saffron-colored gown ...

LYSISTRATA: To the end I may inspire my husband with the most ardent longings ...

CALONICE: To the end I may inspire my husband with the most ardent longings ...

LYSISTRATA: Never will I give myself voluntarily ...

CALONICE: Never will I give myself voluntarily ...

LYSISTRATA: And if he has me by force ...

CALONICE: And if he has me by force ...

LYSISTRATA: I will be cold as ice, and never stir a limb ...

CALONICE: I will be cold as ice, and never stir a limb ...

LYSISTRATA: I will not lift my legs in the air ...

CALONICE: I will not lift my legs in the air ...

LYSISTRATA: Nor will I crouch with bottom upraised, like carved lions on a knife handle.

CALONICE: Nor will I crouch with bottom upraised, like carved lions on a knife handle.

LYSISTRATA: And if I keep my oath, may I be allowed to drink of this wine.

CALONICE: And if I keep my oath, may I be allowed to drink of this wine.

LYSISTRATA: But if I break it, let my bowl be filled with water.

CALONICE: But if I break it, let my bowl be filled with water.

LYSISTRATA: Will you all take this oath?

MYRRHINE: Yes, yes!

LYSISTRATA: Then lo! I immolate the victim.[23] [She drinks.]

CALONICE: Enough, enough, my dear; now let us all drink in turn to cement our friendship.

LAMPITO: Listen! what do those cries mean?

LYSISTRATA: It's what I was telling you; the women have just occupied the Acropolis. So now, Lampito, return to Sparta to organize the plot, while your comrades here remain as hostages.[24] For our-

---

23  Sacrificed animals were burned or cooked after being slaughtered. The gods fed off the smell.

24  In 425 the Athenians had captured 120 Spartan soldiers, and held them as hostages in order to prevent Sparta from invading Athenian territory.

selves, let us go join the rest in the citadel, and let us push the bolts well home.

CALONICE: But don't you think the men will march up against us?

LYSISTRATA: I laugh at them. Neither threats nor flames shall force open our doors; they shall open only on the conditions I have named.

CALONICE: Yes, yes, by the goddess of love! let us keep up our old-time reputation for obstinacy and spite.

CHORUS OF OLD MEN: Go easy, Draces, go easy; why, your shoulder is all chafed by these plaguey heavy olive sticks. But forward still, forward, man, as must be. What unlooked-for things do happen, to be sure, in a long life! Ah! Strymodorus, who would ever have thought it? Here we have the women, who used, for our misfortune, to eat our bread and live in our houses, daring nowadays to lay hands on the holy image of the goddess, to seize the Acropolis and draw bars and bolts to keep any from entering! Come, Philurgus man, let's hurry there; let's lay our faggots all around the citadel, and on the blazing pile burn with our hands these vile conspiratresses, one and all—and Lycon's wife, Lysistrata, first and foremost! No, by Demeter, I will never let 'em laugh at me, whiles I have a breath left in my body. Cleomenes himself, the first who ever seized our citadel,[25] had to leave it to his sore dishonor; spite his Lacedaemonian pride, he had to deliver me up his arms and slink off with a single garment to his back. My word! but he was filthy and ragged! and what an unkempt beard, to be sure! He had not had a bath for six long years! Oh! but that was a mighty siege! Our men were ranged seventeen deep before the gate, and never left their posts, even to sleep. These women, these enemies of Euripides[26] and all the gods—shall I do nothing to hinder their inordinate inso-

lence? else let them tear down my trophies of Marathon.[27] But look, to finish our toilsome climb, we have only this last steep bit left to mount. Truly it's no easy job without beasts of burden, and how these logs bruise my shoulder! Still let us go on, and blow on our fire and see it does not go out just as we reach our destination. Phew! phew! [blows on the fire]. Oh! dear! what a dreadful smoke! It bites my eyes like a mad dog. It is Lemnos[28] fire for sure, or it would never devour my eyelids like this. Come on, Laches, let's hurry, let's bring help to the goddess; it's now or never! Phew! phew! [blows on the fire]. Oh! dear! what confounded smoke! There now, there's our fire all bright and burning, thank the gods! Now, why not first put down our loads here, then take a vine-branch, light it at the brazier and hurl it at the gate like a battering-ram? If they don't answer our summons by pulling back the bolts, then we set fire to the woodwork, and the smoke will choke 'em. Ye gods! what smoke! Pfaugh! Is there never a Samos general[29] who will help me unload my burden? Ah! it shall not gall my shoulder any more. [Tosses down his wood.] Come, brazier, do your duty, make the embers flare so I may kindle a brand; I want to be the first to hurl one. Help me, heavenly Victory; let us punish for their insolent audacity the women who have seized our citadel, and may we raise a trophy[30] of triumph for success!

CHORUS OF WOMEN: Oh! my dears, I think I see fire and smoke; can it be a conflagration? Let us hurry all we can. Fly, fly, Nicodice, before Calyce and Critylle perish in the fire, or are stifled in the smoke raised by these accursed old men and their pitiless laws. But, great gods, can it be I come too late? Rising at dawn, I had the utmost trouble to fill this vessel at the fountain.[31] Oh! what a crowd there was, and what a din! What a rattling of water pots!

---

25  Much earlier in the fifth century.
26  A contemporary of Aristophanes and one of the leading playwrights of Athens, Euripides had a reputation for misogyny.
27  The great Athenian victory over the Persians during the Persian wars.
28  Lemnos was associated with frequent disaster.
29  Samos had just established a democracy and sided with Athens before Lysistrata was produced.
30  Traditionally, the victor of a battle set up a "trophy," made up of the arms of the defeated dead, on the field of battle.
31  This would be a public water source.

Servants and slave-girls pushed and thronged me! However, here I have it full at last; and I am running to carry the water to my fellow townswomen, whom our foes are plotting to burn alive. News has been brought us that a company of old, doddering graybeards, loaded with enormous faggots, as if they wanted to heat a furnace, have taken the field, vomiting dreadful threats, crying that they must reduce these horrible women to ashes. Do not allow them, oh! goddess, but of your grace may I see Athens and Greece cured of their warlike folly. It's to this end, oh! guardian deity of our city, goddess of the golden helmet,[32] they have seized your sanctuary. Be their friend and ally, Athena, and if any man hurls against them lighted firebrands, help us carry water to extinguish them.

STRATYLLIS: Let me be, I say. Oh! oh! [She calls for help.]

CHORUS OF WOMEN: What is this I see, you wretched old men? Honest and pious folk you cannot be who act so vilely.

CHORUS OF OLD MEN: Ah, ha! here's something new! a swarm of women stand posted outside to defend the gates!

CHORUS OF WOMEN: Ah! ah! we frighten you, do we? we seem a mighty host, yet you do not see the ten-thousandth part of our sex.

CHORUS OF OLD MEN: Ho, Phaedrias! shall we stop their cackle? Suppose one of us were to break a stick across their backs, eh?

CHORUS OF WOMEN: Let us set down our water pots on the ground, to be out of the way, in case they dare offer us violence.

CHORUS OF OLD MEN: Let someone knock out two or three teeth for them, as they did to Bupalus;[33] they won't talk so loud then.

CHORUS OF WOMEN: Come on then; I wait for you with an unflinching foot, and I will snap off your testicles like a bitch.

CHORUS OF OLD MEN: Silence! before my stick cuts short your days.

CHORUS OF WOMEN: Now, just you dare to touch Stratyllis with the tip of your finger!

CHORUS OF OLD MEN: And if I batter you to pieces with my fists, what will you do?

CHORUS OF WOMEN: I will tear out your lungs and entrails with my teeth.

CHORUS OF OLD MEN: Oh! what a clever poet is Euripides! how well he says that woman is the most shameless of animals.

CHORUS OF WOMEN: Let's pick up our water jars again, Rhodippe.

CHORUS OF OLD MEN: Ah! accursed whore, what do you mean to do here with your water?

CHORUS OF WOMEN: And you, old death-in-life, with your fire? Is it to cremate yourself?

CHORUS OF OLD MEN: I am going to build you a pyre to roast your female friends upon.

CHORUS OF WOMEN: And I—I am going to put out your fire.

CHORUS OF OLD MEN: You put out my fire—you!

CHORUS OF WOMEN: Yes, you shall soon see.

CHORUS OF OLD MEN: I don't know what prevents me from roasting you with this torch.

CHORUS OF WOMEN: I am getting you a bath ready to clean off the filth.

CHORUS OF OLD MEN: A bath for me, you dirty slut, you!

CHORUS OF WOMEN: Yes, indeed, a nuptial bath—he, he!

CHORUS OF OLD MEN: Do you hear that? What insolence!

CHORUS OF WOMEN: I am a free woman, I tell you.

CHORUS OF OLD MEN: I will make you hold your tongue, never fear!

CHORUS OF WOMEN: Ah, ha! you shall never sit more amongst the heliasts.[34]

CHORUS OF OLD MEN: Burn off her hair for her!

CHORUS OF WOMEN: Water; do your office! [The Women pitch the water in their water pots over the old men.]

CHORUS OF OLD MEN: Oh, dear! oh, dear! oh, dear!

---

32  Athena, who wore a helmet and armor.
33  A sculptor who was so harshly attacked in verse by a poet whose image he had sculpted in an ugly fashion that he killed himself.
34  The panels of judges/jurors who heard legal cases at Athens.

CHORUS OF WOMEN: Was it hot?

CHORUS OF OLD MEN: Hot, great gods! Enough, enough!

CHORUS OF WOMEN: I'm watering you, to make you bloom afresh.

CHORUS OF OLD MEN: Alas! I am too dry! Ah, me! how I am trembling with cold!

MAGISTRATE: These women, have they made din enough, I wonder, with their tambourines? Bewept Adonis enough upon their terraces?[35] I was listening to the speeches last assembly day, and Demostratus,[36] whom heaven confound! was saying we must all go over to Sicily—and lo! his wife was dancing round repeating: Alas! alas! Adonis, woe is me for Adonis!

Demostratus was saying we must levy hoplites[37] at Zacynthus[38]—and lo! his wife, more than half drunk, was screaming on the house-roof: "Weep, weep for Adonis!" while that infamous Mad Ox[39] was bellowing away on his side. Do you not blush, you women, for your wild and uproarious doings?

CHORUS OF OLD MEN: But you don't know all their effrontery yet! They abused and insulted us, and then soused us with the water in their water pots, and have set us wringing out our clothes, for all the world as if we had bepissed ourselves.

MAGISTRATE: And it's well done too, by Poseidon![40] We men must share the blame for their ill conduct; it is we who teach them to love riot and dissoluteness and sow the seeds of wickedness in their hearts. You see a husband go into a shop: "Look, jeweler," he says, "you remember the necklace you made for my wife. Well, the other evening, when she was dancing, the catch came open. Now, I am bound to start for Salamis; will you make it convenient to go over tonight to make her fastening secure?" Another will go to a cobbler, a great, strong fellow, with a great, long tool, and tell him: "The strap of one of my wife's sandals presses her little toe, which is extremely sensitive; come in about midday to soften the thing and stretch it." Now see the results. Take my own case—as a Magistrate I have enlisted rowers;[41] I want money to pay 'em, and lo! the women slam the door in my face. But why do we stand here with arms crossed? Bring me a crowbar; I'll chastise their insolence!—Ho! there, my fine fellow! [addressing one of his attendant officers] what are you gaping at the crows for? looking for a tavern, I suppose, eh? Come, crowbars here, and force open the gates. I will put a hand to the work myself.

LYSISTRATA: No need to force the gates; I am coming out—here I am. And why bolts and bars? What we want here is not bolts and bars and locks, but common sense.

MAGISTRATE: Really, my fine lady! Where is my officer? I want him to tie that woman's hands behind her back.

LYSISTRATA: By Artemis, the virgin goddess! if he touches me with the tip of his finger, officer of the public peace though he might be, let him look out for himself!

MAGISTRATE [to the officer]: How now, are you afraid? Seize her, I tell you, around the middle. Two of you at her, and have done with it!

FIRST WOMAN: By Pandrosos![42] if you lay a hand on her, I'll stomp you underfoot till you shit your guts!

---

35 A reference to the festival which commemorated the death of the mythical figure Adonis, a very handsome male, beloved of Aphrodite. The festival was celebrated by women with great weeping on the terraces and rooftops of Athens, and with tambourines.

36 Demostratus was in fact a politician who proposed an Athenian military expedition to Sicily (415-413) on the first day of the festival of Adonis. The expedition not only helped bring on a resumption of hostilities in the Peloponnesian War, but also was in itself a military disaster.

37 A kind of heavily armed infantryman.

38 An ally of Athens.

39 A nickname of Demostratus.

40 God of the sea.

41 For warships.

42 Goddess of the dew.

MAGISTRATE: Oh, there! my guts! Where is my other officer? Bind that minx first, who speaks so prettily!

SECOND WOMAN: By Phoebe,[43] if you touch her with one finger, you'd better call quick for a surgeon!

MAGISTRATE: What do you mean? Officer, where have you got to? Lay hold of her. Oh! but I'm going to stop your foolishness for you all!

THIRD WOMAN: By the Tauric Artemis, if you go near her, I'll pull out your hair, scream as you like.

MAGISTRATE: Ah! miserable man that I am! My own officers desert me. What ho! are we to let ourselves be bested by a mob of women? Ho! my Scythians,[44] close up your ranks, and forward!

LYSISTRATA: By the holy goddesses! you'll have to make acquaintance with four companies of women, ready for the fray and well armed to boot.

MAGISTRATE: Forward, Scythians, and bind them!

LYSISTRATA: Forward, my gallant companions; march forth, you vendors of grain and eggs, garlic and vegetables, keepers of taverns and bakeries, wrench and strike and tear; come, a torrent of invective and insult! [They beat the officers.] Enough, enough! now retire, never rob the vanquished!

MAGISTRATE: Here's a fine exploit for my officers!

LYSISTRATA: Ah, ha! so you thought you had only to do with a set of slave-women! You did not know the ardor that fills the bosom of free-born women.

MAGISTRATE: Ardor! yes, by Apollo,[45] ardor enough—especially for the wine cup!

CHORUS OF OLD MEN: Sir, sir! Why waste words? They are of no avail with wild beasts of this sort. Don't you know how they have just washed us down—and with no very fragrant soap!

CHORUS OF WOMEN: What would you have? You should never have laid rash hands on us. If you start afresh, I'll knock your eyes out. My delight is to stay at home as coy as a young maid, without hurting anybody or moving any more than a milestone; but beware the wasps, if you go stirring up the wasps' nest!

CHORUS OF OLD MEN: Ah! great gods! how to get the better of these ferocious creatures? It's past all bearing! But come, let us try to find out the reason for the dreadful scourge. With what end in view have they seized the citadel of Cranaus,[46] the sacred shrine that is raised upon the inaccessible rock of the Acropolis? Question them; be cautious and not too credulous. It'd be culpable negligence not to pierce the mystery, if we may.

MAGISTRATE [addressing the women]: I would ask you first why you have barred our gates.

LYSISTRATA: To seize the treasury; no more money, no more war.

MAGISTRATE: Then money is the cause of the War?

LYSISTRATA: And of all our troubles. It was to find occasion to steal that Peisander[47] and all the other agitators were forever raising revolutions. Well and good! but they'll never get another drachma[48] here.

MAGISTRATE: What do you propose to do then, pray?

LYSISTRATA: You ask me that! Why, we propose to administer the treasury ourselves.

MAGISTRATE: You do?

LYSISTRATA: What is there in that to surprise you? Do we not administer the budget of household expenses?

MAGISTRATE: But that is not the same thing.

LYSISTRATA: How so—not the same thing?

MAGISTRATE: It is the treasury that supplies the expenses of the War.

LYSISTRATA: That's our first principle—no War!

MAGISTRATE: What! And the safety of the city?

LYSISTRATA: We will provide for that.

MAGISTRATE: You?

---

43  Another name for Artemis, goddess of the moon and of the hunt.
44  See above, n 21.
45  The god of prophecy, music, and other arts.
46  In myth, the second king of Athens.
47  A politician who carried out the oligarchic coup at Athens in 411.
48  Unit of currency.

LYSISTRATA: Yes, just we.

MAGISTRATE: What a sorry business!

LYSISTRATA: Yes, we're going to save you, whether you wish it or no.

MAGISTRATE: Oh! the impudence of the creatures!

LYSISTRATA: You seem annoyed! but there, you've got to come to it.

MAGISTRATE: But it's the very height of iniquity!

LYSISTRATA: We're going to save you, my man.

MAGISTRATE: But if I don't want to be saved?

LYSISTRATA: Why, all the more reason!

MAGISTRATE: But what a notion, to concern yourselves with questions of Peace and War!

LYSISTRATA: We will explain our idea.

MAGISTRATE: Out with it then; quick, or ... [threatening her].

LYSISTRATA: Listen, and never a movement, please!

MAGISTRATE: Oh! it is too much for me! I cannot keep my temper!

A WOMAN: Then look out for yourself; you have more to fear than we have.

MAGISTRATE: Stop your croaking, old crow, you! [To Lysistrata] Now you, say your say.

LYSISTRATA: Willingly. All the long time the War has lasted, we have endured in modest silence all you men did; we never allowed ourselves to open our lips. We were far from satisfied, for we knew how things were going; often in our homes we would hear you discussing, upside down and inside out, some important turn of affairs. Then with sad hearts, but smiling lips, we would ask you: "Well, in today's Assembly did they vote Peace?" But the husband would growl, "Mind your own business! Hold your tongue!" And I would say no more.

A WOMAN: I would not have held my tongue though, not I!

MAGISTRATE: You would have been reduced to silence by blows then.

LYSISTRATA: Well, for my part, I would say no more. But presently I would come to know you had arrived at some fresh decision more fatally foolish than ever. "Ah! my dear man," I would say, "what madness next!" But he would only look at me askance and say: "Just weave your web, or else your cheeks will smart for hours. War is men's business!

MAGISTRATE: Bravo! well said indeed!

LYSISTRATA: How now, wretched man? not to let us contend against your follies was bad enough! But presently we heard you asking out loud in the open street: "Is there never a man left in Athens?" and, "No, not one, not one," you were assured in reply. Then, then we made up our minds without more delay to make common cause to save Greece. Open your ears to our wise counsels and hold your tongues, and we may yet put things on a better footing.

MAGISTRATE: *You* put things indeed! Oh! it's too much! The insolence of the creatures! Silence, I say.

LYSISTRATA: Silence yourself!

MAGISTRATE: May I die a thousand deaths before I obey one who wears a veil!

LYSISTRATA: If that's all that troubles you, here, take my veil, wrap it around your head, and hold your tongue. Then take this basket; put on a girdle, card wool,[49] munch beans. The War shall be women's business.

CHORUS OF WOMEN: Lay aside your water pots, we will guard them, we will help our friends and companions. For myself, I will never weary of the dance; my knees will never grow stiff with fatigue. I will brave everything with my dear allies, on whom nature has lavished virtue, grace, boldness, cleverness, and whose wisely directed energy is going to save the State. Oh! my good, gallant Lysistrata, and all my friends, be ever like a bundle of nettles; never let your anger slacken; the winds of fortune blow our way.

LYSISTRATA: May gentle Love[50] and the sweet Cyprian Queen[51] shower seductive charms on our bosoms and all our person. If only we can stir so amorous a lust among the men that their tools stand stiff as sticks, we shall indeed deserve the name of peacemakers among the Greeks.

---

49  I.e., comb wool in order to straighten its fibers, prior to spinning.

50  That is Eros (Cupid), the son of Aphrodite.

51  I.e., Aphrodite.

MAGISTRATE: How will that be, pray?

LYSISTRATA: To begin with, we shall not see you any more running like mad fellows to the Market holding lance in fist.

A WOMAN: That will be something gained, anyway, by the Paphian goddess,[52] it will!

LYSISTRATA: Now we see 'em, mixed up with saucepans and kitchen stuff, armed to the teeth, looking like wild Corybantes![53]

MAGISTRATE: Why, of course; that's how brave men should do.

LYSISTRATA: Oh! but what a funny sight, to behold a man wearing a Gorgon's-head shield coming along to buy fish!

A WOMAN: The other day in the Market I saw a phylarch[54] with flowing ringlets; he was on horseback, and was pouring into his helmet the broth he had just bought at an old dame's stall. There was a Thracian warrior too, who was brandishing his lance like Tereus in the play;[55] he had scared a good woman selling figs into a perfect panic, and was gobbling up all her ripest fruit.

MAGISTRATE: And how, pray, would you propose to restore peace and order in all the states of Greece?

LYSISTRATA: It's the easiest thing in the world!

MAGISTRATE: Come, tell us how; I am curious to know.

LYSISTRATA: When we are winding thread, and it is tangled, we pass the spool across and through the skein, now this way, now that way; even so, to finish off the War, we shall send embassies hither and thither and everywhere, to disentangle matters.

MAGISTRATE: And it's with your yarn, and your skeins, and your spools, you think to appease so many bitter enmities, you silly women?

LYSISTRATA: If only you had common sense, you would always do in politics the same as we do with our yarn.

MAGISTRATE: Come, how is that, eh?

LYSISTRATA: First we wash the yarn to separate the grease and filth; do the same with all bad citizens, sort them out and drive them forth with rods—it's the refuse of the city. Then for all such as come crowding up in search of employments and offices, we must card them thoroughly; then, to bring them all to the same standard, pitch them pell-mell into the same basket, resident aliens or no, allies, debtors to the State, all mixed up together. Then as for our colonies, you must think of them as so many isolated wool coils; find the ends of the separate threads, draw them to a center here, wind them into one, make one great coil of the lot, out of which the public can weave itself a good, stout tunic.

MAGISTRATE: Is it not a sin and a shame to see them carding and winding the State, these women who have neither skill nor part in the burdens of the War?

LYSISTRATA: What! wretched man! why, it's a far heavier burden to us than to you. In the first place, we bear sons who go off to fight far away from Athens.

MAGISTRATE: Enough said! do not recall sad and sorry memories!

LYSISTRATA: Then secondly, instead of enjoying the pleasures of love and making the best of our youth and beauty, we are left to languish far from our husbands, who are all with the army. But say no more of ourselves; what afflicts me is to see our girls growing old in lonely grief.

MAGISTRATE: Don't the men grow old too?

LYSISTRATA: That is not the same thing. When the soldier returns from the wars, even though he has white hair, he very soon finds a young wife. But a woman has only one summer; if she does not make hay while the sun shines, no one will afterwards have anything to say to her, and she spends her days consulting oracles that never send her a husband.

MAGISTRATE: But the old man who can still erect his organ ...

LYSISTRATA: But you, why don't you get done with it

---

52  I.e., Aphrodite.
53  Priests of the goddess Cybele who engaged in wild dances while beating cymbals in worship of the goddess.
54  A captain of the cavalry.
55  A lost play of Euripides is about Tereus, son of the war god, Ares, and king of the Thracians.

and die? You are rich; go buy yourself a bier, and I will knead you a honey cake for Cerberus.[56] Here, take this garland.[57] [Drenching him with water.]

FIRST WOMAN: And this one too. [Drenching him with water.]

SECOND WOMAN: And these headbands. [Drenching him with water.]

LYSISTRATA: What more do you lack? Step aboard the boat; Charon[58] is waiting for you, you're keeping him from pushing off.

MAGISTRATE: To treat me so scurvily! What an insult! I will go show myself to my fellow magistrates just as I am.

LYSISTRATA: What! are you blaming us for not having exposed you according to custom?[59] No, console yourself; we will not fail to offer up the third-day sacrifice for you, first thing in the morning.

CHORUS OF OLD MEN: Awake, friends of freedom; let us hold ourselves ready to act. I suspect a mighty peril; I foresee another tyranny like Hippias's.[60] I am sore afraid the Laconians may have assembled here with Cleisthenes[61] to, by a stratagem of war, stir up these women, enemies of the gods, and seize our treasury and the funds whereby I lived.[62] Is it not a sin and a shame for them to interfere in advising the citizens, to prate of shields and lances, and to ally themselves with Laconians,[63] fellows I trust no more than I would so many famished wolves? The whole thing, my friends, is nothing else but an attempt to re-establish tyranny. But I will never submit; I will be on my guard for the future; I will always carry a blade hidden under myrtle boughs;[64] I will post myself in the Public Square under arms, shoulder to shoulder with Aristogeiton.[65] And now, to make a start, I must just break a few of that cursed old jade's teeth yonder.

CHORUS OF WOMEN: No, never play the brave man, else when you go back home, your own mother won't know you. But, dear friends and allies, first let us lay our burdens down; then, citizens all, hear what I have to say. I have useful counsel to give our city, which deserves it well at my hands for the brilliant distinctions it has lavished on my girlhood. At seven years of age, I was bearer of the sacred vessels;[66] at ten, I pounded barley for the altar of Athena;[67] next, clad in a robe of yellow silk, I was a little bear to Artemis at the Brauronia;[68] presently, grown a tall, handsome maiden, they put a necklace of dried figs about my neck, and I was Basket-Bearer.[69] So surely I am bound to give my best advice to Athens. What matters that I was born a woman, if I can cure your misfortunes? I pay my share of tolls and taxes by giving men to the State. But you, you miserable graybeards, you contribute nothing to the public charges; on the

---

56    The dead were interred with a honey cake with which to occupy the fierce three-headed dog, Cerberus, who guarded the entrance to the land of the dead.

57    Of wool, presumably.

58    Charon ferried the dead over the river Styx to Hades, the land of the dead.

59    The dead were laid out by women for viewing.

60    Hippias the tyrant was the son of Pisistratus, tyrant of Athens. Hippias was driven out of Athens in 510 BC, bringing an end to the tyranny. These events followed the assassination of Hippias's brother, Hipparchus, by the lovers Harmodius and Aristogeiton, who were remembered by the Athenians as heroic opponents of tyranny.

61    Not to be confused with the more famous Cleisthenes of the later sixth century BC.

62    Athenian citizens were paid for attending the Assembly and serving as judges/jurors. They were also paid for serving in the navy.

63    I.e., the Spartans.

64    A reference to a popular drinking song about the assassination of Hipparchus (for which see above n 60).

65    See above n 60.

66    Four girls carried objects sacred to Athena in a semiannual festival.

67    Another ritual; the flour was used to make cakes offered to Athena.

68    An annual Athenian festival for Artemis at which girls dressed as bears and performed a "bear dance." Their participation in certain aspects of the festival may have signalled their eligibility for marriage.

69    A woman who carried cake and led processions at important Athenian festivals.

contrary, you have wasted the treasure of our fore-fathers, as it was called, the treasure amassed in the days of the Persian Wars. You pay nothing at all in return; and into the bargain you endanger our lives and liberties by your mistakes. Have you one word to say for yourselves? ... Ah! don't irritate me, you there, or I'll lay my slipper across your jaws, and it's pretty heavy.

CHORUS OF OLD MEN: Outrage upon outrage! things are going from bad to worse. Let us punish the minxes, every one of us that has a man's appendages to boast of. Come, off with our tunics, for a man must savor of manhood; come, my friends, let us strip naked from head to foot.[70] Courage, I say, we who in our day garrisoned Lipsydrion;[71] let us be young again, and shake off old age. If we give them the least hold over us, it's all up! Their audacity will know no bounds! We shall see them building ships, and fighting sea-fights, like Artemisia;[72] nay, if they want to mount and ride as cavalry, we had best cashier the cavalry, for indeed women excel in riding, and have a fine, firm seat for the gallop.[73] Just think of all those squadrons of Amazons Micon[74] has painted for us engaged in hand-to-hand combat with men. Come then, we must even fit collars to all these necks to put them in the stocks.

CHORUS OF WOMEN: By the blessed goddesses, if you anger me, I will let loose the beast of my evil passions, and a very hailstorm of blows will send you yelling for help. Come, dames, off with the tunics, and quick's the word; women must scent the savor of women in the throes of passion.... Now just you dare to measure strength with me, old graybeard, and I warrant you you'll never more eat garlic or black beans. No, not a word! My anger is at boiling point, and I'll do with you what the beetle did with the eagle's eggs.[75] I laugh at your

threats, so long as I have on my side Lampito here, and the noble Theban, my dear Ismenia.... Pass decree on decree, you can do us no hurt, you wretch abhorred of all your fellows. Why, only yesterday, on occasion of the feast of Hecate, I asked my neighbors of Boeotia for one of their daughters for whom my girls have a lively liking—a fine, fat eel to wit. And if they did not refuse, all along of your silly decrees! We shall never cease to suffer the like, till someone gives you a neat trip-up and breaks your neck for you!

CHORUS OF WOMEN: [addressing Lysistrata] You, Lysistrata, you who are leader of our glorious enterprise, why do I see you coming towards me with so gloomy an air?

LYSISTRATA: It's the behavior of these naughty women, it's the female heart and female weakness that so discourages me.

CHORUS OF WOMEN: Tell us, tell us, what is it?

LYSISTRATA: I only tell the simple truth.

CHORUS OF WOMEN: What has happened that is so disconcerting; come, tell your friends.

LYSISTRATA: Oh! the thing is so hard to tell—yet so impossible to conceal.

CHORUS OF WOMEN: No, never seek to hide any ill that has befallen our cause.

LYSISTRATA: To blurt it out in a word—we are in heat!

CHORUS OF WOMEN: Oh! Zeus, oh! Zeus!

LYSISTRATA: What use calling upon Zeus? The thing is even as I say. I cannot stop them any longer from lusting after the men. They are all for deserting. The first I caught was slipping out by the postern gate near the cave of Pan; another was letting herself down by a rope and pulley; a third was busy preparing her escape; while a fourth, perched on a bird's back, was just taking wing for Orsilochus's house, when I seized her by the hair. One and all,

---

70  Greek athletes competed in the nude. Heroic male figures were also portrayed nude.

71  A town in Athenian territory which was taken from Athens but returned to it with the fall of the tyranny there.

72  Queen of Halicarnassus and an ally of the king of Persia in the Persian war. She sailed with her battleships in the naval battle of Salamis.

73  "The horse" was a sexual position in which the woman mounts the man.

74  Micon, a famous painter, had painted frescoes at Athens depicting battles between the Athenians and the Amazons, a mythical clan of woman warriors.

75  In a fable of Aesop, the beetle throws the eagle's eggs out of the nest, breaking them.

they are inventing excuses to be off home. Look! there goes one, trying to get out! Halloa there! where are you going so fast?

FIRST WOMAN: I want to go home; I have in the house some Miletus wool which is getting all eaten up by the worms.

LYSISTRATA: Bah! you and your worms! go back, I say!

FIRST WOMAN: I will return immediately, I swear I will by the two goddesses! I only have just to spread it out on the bed,

LYSISTRATA: You shall not do anything of the kind! I say, you shall not go.

FIRST WOMAN: Must I leave my wool to spoil then?

LYSISTRATA: Yes, if need be.

SECOND WOMAN: Unhappy woman that I am! Alas for my flax! I've left it at home unstripped!

LYSISTRATA: So, here's another trying to escape to go home and strip her flax forsooth!

SECOND WOMAN: Oh! I swear by the goddess of light, the instant I have put it in condition I will come straight back.

LYSISTRATA: You shall do nothing of the kind! If once you began, others would want to follow suit.

THIRD WOMAN: Oh! goddess divine, Ilithyia, patroness of women in labor, stay, stay the birth, till I have reached a spot less hallowed than Athena's Mount!

LYSISTRATA: What mean you by these silly tales?

THIRD WOMAN: I am going to have a child—now, this minute.

LYSISTRATA: But you were not pregnant yesterday!

THIRD WOMAN: Well, I am today. Oh! let me go in search of the midwife, Lysistrata, quick, quick!

LYSISTRATA: What is this fable you are telling me? Ah! what have you got there so hard?

THIRD WOMAN: A male child.

LYSISTRATA: No, no, by Aphrodite! nothing of the sort! Why, it feels like something hollow—a pot or a kettle. Oh! you baggage, if you have not got the sacred helmet of Pallas[76]—and you said you were with child!

THIRD WOMAN: And so I am, by Zeus, I am!

LYSISTRATA: Then why this helmet, pray?

THIRD WOMAN: For fear my pains should seize me in the Acropolis; I mean to lay my eggs in this helmet, as the doves do.

LYSISTRATA: Excuses and pretenses every word! The thing's as clear as daylight. Anyway, you must stay here now until the fifth day, your day of purification.

THIRD WOMAN: I cannot sleep any more in the Acropolis, now I have seen the snake that guards the Temple.[77]

FOURTH WOMAN: Ah! and those confounded owls[78] with their dismal hooting! I cannot get a wink of rest, and I'm just dying of fatigue.

LYSISTRATA: You wicked women, have done with your falsehoods! You want your husbands, that's plain enough. But don't you think they want you just as badly? They are spending dreadful nights, oh! I know that well enough. But hold out, my dears, hold out! A little more patience, and the victory will be ours. An oracle promises us success, if only we remain united. Shall I repeat the words?

FIRST WOMAN: Yes, tell us what the oracle declares.

LYSISTRATA: Silence then! Now, "When the swallows, fleeing before the hoopoes,[79] shall have all flocked together in one place, and shall refrain them from all amorous commerce, then will be the end of all the ills of life; yes, and Zeus, which thunders in the skies, shall set above what was before below—"

CHORUS OF WOMEN: What! shall the men be underneath?

LYSISTRATA: "But if dissension arises among the swallows, and they take wing from the holy Temple, it will be said there is never a more wanton bird in all the world."

CHORUS OF WOMEN: Ye gods! the prophecy is clear. No, never let us be cast down by calamity! Let us

---

76  I.e., Athena, who wore armor.

77  A mythical snake.

78  The owl was the symbol of Athena (and so of Athens).

79  A kind of crested bird.

be brave, and go back to our posts. It would be shameful indeed not to trust the promises of the Oracle.

CHORUS OF OLD MEN: I want to tell you a fable they used to relate to me when I was a little boy. This is it: Once upon a time there was a young man called Melanion, who hated the thought of marriage so sorely that he fled away to the wilds. So he lived in the mountains, wove himself nets, kept a dog and caught hares. He never, never came back, he had such a horror of women. As chaste as Melanion, we loathe the jades just as much as he did.

AN OLD MAN: You dear old woman, I would kiss you.

A WOMAN: I will set you crying without onions.

OLD MAN: And give you a sound kicking.

OLD WOMAN: Ah, ha! what a dense forest you have there! [Pointing.]

OLD MAN: So was Myronides one of the best-bearded of men of this side; his backside was all black, and he terrified his enemies as much as Phormio.[80]

CHORUS OF WOMEN: I want to tell you a fable too, to match yours about Melanion. Once there was a certain man called Timon,[81] a tough customer, and a whimsical, a true son of the Furies, with a face that seemed to glare out of a thorn bush. He withdrew from the world because he couldn't abide bad men, after vomiting a thousand curses at 'em. He had a holy horror of ill-conditioned fellows, but he was mighty tender towards women.

A WOMAN: Suppose I up and broke your jaw for you!

AN OLD MAN: I am not a bit afraid of you.

A WOMAN: Suppose I let fly a good kick at you?

OLD MAN: I should see your backside then.

WOMAN: You would see that, for all my age, it is very well attended to, and all fresh singed smooth.

LYSISTRATA: Ho there! come quick, come quick!

FIRST WOMAN: What is it? Why these cries?

LYSISTRATA: A man! a man! I see him approaching all afire with the flames of love. Oh! divine Queen of Cyprus, Paphos and Cythera, I pray you still be propitious to our enterprise.

FIRST WOMAN: Where is he, this unknown foe?

LYSISTRATA: Yonder—beside the Temple of Demeter.[82]

FIRST WOMAN: Yes, indeed, I see him; but who is it?

LYSISTRATA: Look, look! does any of you recognize him?

FIRST WOMAN: I do, I do! it's my husband Cinesias.

LYSISTRATA: To work then! Let your task be to inflame and torture and torment him. Seductions, caresses, provocations, refusals, try every means! Grant every favor—always excepting what is forbidden by our oath on the wine bowl.

MYRRHINE: Have no fear, I undertake the work.

LYSISTRATA: Well, I will stay here to help you cajole the man and set his passions aflame. The rest of you, withdraw.

CINESIAS: Alas! alas! how I am tortured by spasm and rigid convulsion! Oh! I am racked on the wheel!

LYSISTRATA: Who is this that dares to pass our lines?

CINESIAS: It is I.

LYSISTRATA: What, a man?

CINESIAS: Yes, no doubt about it, a man!

LYSISTRATA: Begone!

CINESIAS: But who are you that thus repulses me?

LYSISTRATA: The sentinel of the day.

CINESIAS: By all the gods, call Myrrhine hither.

LYSISTRATA: Call Myrrhine here. And pray, who are you?

CINESIAS: I am her husband, Cinesias, son of Peon.

LYSISTRATA: Ah! good day, my dear friend. Your name is not unknown amongst us. Your wife has it for ever on her lips; and she never touches an egg or an apple without saying: "This is for Cinesias."

CINESIAS: Really and truly?

LYSISTRATA: Yes, indeed, by Aphrodite! And if we fall to talking of men, your wife quickly declares: "Oh! all the rest, they're good for nothing compared with Cinesias."

CINESIAS: Oh! I beseech you, go and call her to me.

---

80  Both men mentioned were well-known Athenian military commanders.
81  An actual contemporary of Aristophanes.
82  The goddess of the harvest.

LYSISTRATA: And what will you give me for my trouble?

CINESIAS: All this, if you like. I will give you what I have here!

LYSISTRATA: Well, well, I will tell her to come.

CINESIAS: Quick, oh! be quick! Life has no more charms for me since she left my house. I am sad, sad, when I go indoors; it all seems so empty; my victuals have lost their savor. Desire is eating out my heart!

MYRRHINE: I love him, oh! I love him; but he won't let himself be loved. No! I shall not come.

CINESIAS: Myrrhine, my little darling Myrrhine, what are you saying? Come down to me quick.

MYRRHINE: No indeed, not I.

CINESIAS: I call you, Myrrhine, Myrrhine; will you not come?

MYRRHINE: Why should you call me? You do not want me.

CINESIAS: Not want you! Why, my weapon stands stiff with desire!

MYRRHINE: Good-bye.

CINESIAS: Oh! Myrrhine, Myrrhine, in our child's name, hear me; at any rate hear the child! Little lad, call your mother.

CHILD: Mommy, mommy, mommy!

CINESIAS: There, listen! Don't you pity the poor child? It's six days now you've not washed and not fed the child.

MYRRHINE: Poor darling, your father takes mighty little care of you!

CINESIAS: Come down, dearest, come down for the child's sake.

MYRRHINE: Ah! what a thing it is to be a mother! Well, well, we must come down, I suppose.

CINESIAS: Why, how much younger and prettier she looks! And how she looks at me so lovingly! Her cruelty and scorn only redouble my passion.

MYRRHINE: You are as sweet as your father is provoking! Let me kiss you, my treasure, mother's darling!

CINESIAS: Ah! what a bad thing it is to let yourself be led away by other women! Why give me such pain and suffering, and yourself into the bargain?

MYRRHINE: Hands off, sir!

CINESIAS: Everything is going to rack and ruin in the house.

MYRRHINE: I don't care.

CINESIAS: But your web[83] that's all being pecked to pieces by the cocks and hens, don't you care for that?

MYRRHINE: Precious little.

CINESIAS: And Aphrodite, whose mysteries you have not celebrated for so long? Oh! won't you come back home?

MYRRHINE: No, at least, not until a sound Treaty puts an end to the War.

CINESIAS: Well, if you wish it so much, why, we'll make it, your Treaty.

MYRRHINE: Well and good! When that's done, I will come home. Until then, I am bound by an oath.

CINESIAS: At any rate, let's have a short time together.

MYRRHINE: No, no, no! ... all the same I cannot say I don't love you.

CINESIAS: You love me? Then why refuse what I ask, my little girl, my sweet Myrrhine.

MYRRHINE: You must be joking! What, before the child!

CINESIAS: Manes, carry the lad home. There, you see, the child is gone; there's nothing to hinder us; let us get to work!

MYRRHINE: But, miserable man, where, where are we to do it?

CINESIAS: In the cave of Pan;[84] nothing could be better.

MYRRHINE: But how to purify myself, before going back into the citadel?

CINESIAS: Nothing easier! you can wash at the Clepsydra.[85]

MYRRHINE: But my oath? Do you want me to perjure myself?

---

83  I.e., the cloth Myrrhine has been weaving.

84  A god with a reputation for lechery.

85  A spring on the acropolis.

CINESIAS: I take all responsibility; never make yourself anxious.

MYRRHINE: Well, I'll be off, then, and find a bed for us.

CINESIAS: Oh! it's not worthwhile; we can lie on the ground surely.

MYRRHINE: No, no! bad man as you are, I don't like your lying on the bare earth.

CINESIAS: Ah! how the dear girl loves me!

MYRRHINE: [coming back with a bed] Come, get to bed quick; I am going to undress. But, plague take it, we must get a mattress.

CINESIAS: A mattress! Oh! no, never mind!

MYRRHINE: No, by Artemis![86] lie on the bare sacking, never! That would be too squalid.

CINESIAS: A kiss!

MYRRHINE: Wait a minute!

CINESIAS: Oh! by the great gods, be back quick!

MYRRHINE: [coming back with a mattress] Here is a mattress. Lie down, I am just going to undress. But, but you've got no pillow.

CINESIAS: I don't want one, no, no.

MYRRHINE: But I do.

CINESIAS: Oh! dear, oh, dear! they treat my poor penis for all the world like Heracles.[87]

MYRRHINE: [coming back with a pillow] There, lift your head, dear!

CINESIAS: That's really everything.

MYRRHINE: Is it everything, I wonder.

CINESIAS: Come, my treasure.

MYRRHINE: I am just unfastening my belt. But remember what you promised me about making Peace; mind you keep your word.

CINESIAS: Yes, yes, upon my life I will.

MYRRHINE: Why, you have no blanket.

CINESIAS: Great Zeus! Does that matter? It's you I want to fuck.

MYRRHINE: Never fear—directly, directly! I'll be back in no time.

CINESIAS: The woman will kill me with her blankets!

MYRRHINE: [coming back with a blanket] Now, get up for one moment.

CINESIAS: But I tell you, our friend here is up—all stiff and ready!

MYRRHINE: Would you like me to perfume you?

CINESIAS: No, by Apollo, no, please!

MYRRHINE: Yes, by Aphrodite, but I will, whether you wish it or not.

CINESIAS: Ah! great Zeus, may she soon be done!

MYRRHINE: [coming back with a flask of perfume] Hold out your hand; now rub it in.

CINESIAS: Oh! in Apollo's name, I don't much like the smell of it; but perhaps it'll improve when it's well rubbed in. Somehow it does not smack of the marriage bed!

MYRRHINE: There, what a scatterbrain I am: if I have not brought Rhodian perfumes!

CINESIAS: Never mind, dearest, let it be now.

MYRRHINE: You are joking!

CENESIAS: Deuce take the man who first invented perfumes, say I!

MYRRHINE: [coming back with another flask] Here, take this bottle.

CINESIAS: I have a better all ready for your service, darling. Come, you provoking creature, to bed with you, and don't bring another thing.

MYRRHINE: Coming, coming; I'm just slipping off my shoes. Dear boy, will you vote for peace?

CINESIAS: I'll think about it. [Myrrhine runs away.] I'm a dead man, she is killing me! She has gone, and left me in torment! I must have someone to fuck, I must! Ah me! the loveliest of women has swindled and cheated me. Poor little lad [addressing his penis], how am I to give you what you want so badly? Where is Dog-fox?[88] quick, man, get him a nurse!

CHORUS OF OLD MEN: Poor, miserable wretch, balked in your amorousness! what tortures are yours! Ah! you fill me with pity. Could any man's back and loins stand such a strain? His organ

---

86  Goddess of the moon and the hunt.
87  The Greek name of the heroically strong Hercules. In comedies he was often depicted as a glutton who waits indefinitely for appetizing dishes.
88  Nickname of Philostratus, a brothel-keeper at Athens.

stands stiff and rigid, and there's never a wench to help him!

CINESIAS: You gods in heaven, what pains I suffer!

CHORUS OF OLD MEN: Well, there it is; it's her doing, that abandoned hussy!

CINESIAS: Nay, nay! rather say that sweetest, dearest darling.

CHORUS OF OLD MEN: That dearest darling? no, no, that hussy, I say! Zeus, god of the skies, can you not let loose a hurricane, to sweep them all up into the air, and whirl 'em round, then drop 'em down, crash! and impale them on the point of his weapon!

A HERALD: Say, where shall I find the Elders and the Prytanes?[89] I am bearer of dispatches.

MAGISTRATE: But are you a man or a Priapus,[90] pray?

HERALD: Oh! but he's mighty simple. I am a herald, of course, I swear I am, and I come from Sparta about making peace.

MAGISTRATE: But look, you are hiding a lance under your clothes, surely.

HERALD: No, nothing of the sort.

MAGISTRATE: Then why do you turn away like that, and hold your cloak out from your body? Have you gotten swellings in the groin from your journey?

HERALD: By the twin brethren! the man's an old maniac.

MAGISTRATE: Ah, ha! my fine lad, why I can see it standing, oh fie!

HERALD: I tell you no! but enough of this foolery.

MAGISTRATE: Well, what is it you have there then?

HERALD: A Lacedaemonian skytale.[91]

MAGISTRATE: Oh, indeed, a skytale, is it? Well, well, speak out frankly; I know all about these matters. How are things going at Sparta now?

HERALD: Why, everything is turned upside down at Sparta, and all the allies are half dead with lusting. We simply must have Pellene.[92]

MAGISTRATE: What is the reason of it all? Is it the god Pan's doing?

HERALD: No, but Lampito's and the Spartan women's, acting at her instigation; they have denied the men all access to their cunts.

MAGISTRATE: But whatever do you do?

HERALD: We are at our wits' end; we walk bent double, just as if we were carrying lanterns in a wind. The jades have sworn we shall not so much as touch their cunts until we have all agreed to conclude peace.

MAGISTRATE: Ha, ha! So I see now, it's a general conspiracy embracing all Greece. You go back to Sparta and bid them send envoys with plenary powers to treat for peace. I will urge our Elders myself to name ambassadors with full power from us, and to persuade them, why, I will show them *this*.

HERALD: What could be better? I fly at your command.

CHORUS OF OLD MEN: No wild beast is there, no flame of fire, more fierce and untamable than woman; the panther is less savage and shameless.

CHORUS OF WOMEN: And yet you dare to make war upon me, wretch, when you might have me for your most faithful friend and ally.

CHORUS OF OLD MEN: Never, never can my hatred towards women cease.

CHORUS OF WOMEN: Well, please yourself. Still I cannot bear to leave you all naked as you are; folks would laugh at me. Come, I am going to put this tunic on you.

CHORUS OF OLD MEN: You are right, upon my word it was only in my confounded fit of rage I took it off.

CHORUS OF WOMEN: Now at any rate you look like a man, and they won't make fun of you. Ah! if you

---

89 An executive council.

90 The god of gardens, son of Aphrodite and, according to some, Dionysus. A lascivious figure, he was depicted with an enormous erect penis.

91 A device for sending secret messages. A strip of leather was wrapped around a staff and a message was written along the length. The leather was then removed, and the message could be read only by wrapping the leather around a staff of the same thickness.

92 A city which had long been the aim of the Spartans to seize. It may be that Pellene was also the name of some well-known woman (a prostitute?) of the time.

had not offended me so badly, I would take out that nasty insect you have in your eye for you.

CHORUS OF OLD MEN: Ah! so that's what was annoying me so! Look, here's a ring, just remove the insect, and show it to me. By Zeus! it has been hurting my eye for so very long.

CHORUS OF WOMEN: Well, I agree, though your manners are not over and above pleasant. Oh! what a huge great gnat! just look! It's from Tricorysus,[93] for sure.

CHORUS OF OLD MEN: A thousand thanks! the creature was digging a regular well in my eye; now it's gone, my tears flow freely.

CHORUS OF WOMEN: I will wipe them for you— bad, naughty man though you are. Now, just one kiss.

CHORUS OF OLD MEN: No—a kiss, certainly not!

CHORUS OF WOMEN: Just one, whether you like it or not.

CHORUS OF OLD MEN: Oh! those confounded women! how they cajole us! How true the saying: "It's impossible to live with the baggages, impossible to live without 'em"! Come, let us agree for the future not to regard each other any more as enemies; to clinch the bargain, let us sing a choral song.

CHORUS OF WOMEN: We desire, Athenians, to speak ill of no one, but on the contrary, to say much good of everyone, and to do the like. We have had enough of misfortunes and calamities. Is there anyone, man or woman, who wants a bit of money, two or three minas or so? Well, our purse is full. If only peace is concluded, the borrower will not have to pay back. Also I'm inviting to supper a few Carystian friends,[94] who are excellently well qualified. I have still a drop of good soup left, and a young porker I'm going to kill, and the flesh will be sweet and tender. I shall expect you at my house today; but first away to the baths with you, you and your children; then come all of you, ask no

one's leave, but walk straight up, as if you were at home; never fear, the door will be ... shut in your faces!

CHORUS OF OLD MEN: Ah! here come the envoys from Sparta with their long flowing beards; why, you would think they wore a cage between their thighs. [The Lacedaemonian envoys enter.] Hail to you, first of all, Laconians;[95] then tell us how you fare.

A LACONIAN: No need for many words; you see what a state we are in.

CHORUS OF OLD MEN: Alas! the situation grows more and more strained! the intensity of the thing is just frightful.

LACONIAN: It's beyond belief. But to work! summon your commissioners, and let us patch up the best peace we can.

CHORUS OF OLD MEN: Ah! our men too, like wrestlers in the arena, cannot endure a rag over their bellies; it's an athlete's malady, which only exercise can remedy.

AN ATHENIAN: Can anybody tell us where Lysistrata is? Surely she will have some compassion on our condition.

CHORUS OF OLD MEN: Look! It's the very same complaint. [Addressing the Athenian.] Don't you feel a strong nervous tension in the mornings?

ATHENIAN: Yes, and a dreadful, dreadful torture it is! Unless peace is made very soon, we shall find no resource but to fuck Cleisthenes.

CHORUS OF OLD MEN: Take my advice, and put on your clothes again; one of the fellows who mutilated the Hermae[96] might see you.

ATHENIAN: You are right.

LACONIAN: Quite right. There, I will slip on my tunic.

ATHENIAN: Oh! what a terrible state we are in! Greetings to you, Laconian fellow-sufferers.

LACONIAN: [addressing one of his countrymen] Ah! my boy, what a thing it would have been if these

---

93  A marshy, wooded, and buggy district of Attica.

94  Carystus was a city notorious for loose-living.

95  I.e., Spartans.

96  The Hermae were sacred statues with enormous erect penises. They stood before doorways and other public spaces in Athens. During the Peloponnesian War they were desecrated.

fellows had seen us just now when our tools were on full stand!

ATHENIAN: Speak out, Laconians, what is it that brings you here?

LACONIAN: We have come to treat for peace.

ATHENIAN: Well, said; we are of the same mind. Better call Lysistrata then; she is the only person who will bring us to terms.

LACONIAN: Yes, yes—and Lysistratus[97] into the bargain, if you will.

CHORUS OF OLD MEN: Needless to call her; she has heard your voices, and here she comes.

ATHENIAN: Hail, boldest and bravest of womankind! The time has come to show yourself in turn uncompromising and conciliatory, exacting and yielding, haughty and condescending. Call up all your skill and artfulness. Lo! the foremost men in Greece, seduced by your fascinations, are agreed to entrust the task of ending their quarrels to you.

LYSISTRATA: It'll be an easy task—if only they refrain from mutual indulgence in masculine love; if they do, I shall know the fact at once. Now, where is the gentle goddess, Peace? Lead here the Laconian envoys. But, look, no roughness or violence; our husbands always behaved so boorishly. Bring them to me with smiles, as women should. If any refuse to give you his hand, then catch him by the penis and draw him politely forward. Bring up the Athenians too; you may take them just how you will. Laconians, approach; and you, Athenians, on my other side. Now hearken all! I am but a woman, but I have good common sense; Nature has dowered me with discriminating judgment, which I have yet further developed, thanks to the wise teachings of my father and the elders of the city. First I must bring a reproach against you that applies equally to both sides. At Olympia, and Thermopylae, and Delphi, and a score of other places too numerous to mention, you celebrate before the same altars ceremonies common to all Greeks; yet you go cutting each other's throats and sacking Greek cities, when all the while the Barbarian[98] is yonder threatening you! That is my first point.

ATHENIAN: Ah, ah! lust is killing me!

LYSISTRATA: Now it's to you I address myself, Laconians. Have you forgotten how Periclides,[99] your own countryman, sat as a suppliant before our altars? How pale he was in his purple robes! He had come to crave an army of us; 'twas the time when Messenia was pressing you sore, and the Seagod was shaking the earth. Cimon marched to your aid at the head of four thousand hoplites, and saved Lacedaemon.[100] And, after such a service as that, you ravage the soil of your benefactors!

ATHENIAN: They do wrong, very wrong, Lysistrata.

LACONIAN: We do wrong, very wrong. Ah! great gods! what lovely thighs she has!

LYSISTRATA: And now a word to the Athenians. Have you no memory left of how, in the days when you wore the tunic of slaves, the Laconians came, spear in hand, and slew a host of Thessalians and partisans of Hippias the Tyrant?[101] They, and they only, fought on your side on that eventful day; they delivered you from despotism, and thanks to them our people could change the short tunic of the slave for the long cloak of the free man.

LACONIAN: I have never seen a woman with more gracious dignity.

ATHENIAN: I have never seen a woman with a finer cunt!

LYSISTRATA: Bound by such ties of mutual kindness, how can you bear to be at war? Stop, stay the hateful strife, be reconciled; what hinders you?

LACONIAN: We are quite ready, if they will give us back our rampart.

LYSISTRATA: What rampart, my dear man?

LACONIAN: Pylos, which we have been asking for and craving for ever so long.

---

97 The masculine of Lysistrata.

98 I.e., the Persians in this case. The Greek by this time referred to all non-Greeks as "barbarians."

99 In 464 BC an earthquake nearly ended Sparta's control over the enslaved Messenians (known as helots). Sparta sent Periclides to ask Athens for help.

100 Actually, the Spartans, nervous about an Athenian army in Spartan territory, sent the Athenians home.

101 See above, n 60.

ATHENIAN: In the Sea-god's name, you shall never have it!

LYSISTRATA: Agree, my friends, agree.

ATHENIAN: But then what city shall we be able to stir up trouble in?

LYSISTRATA: Ask for another place in exchange.

ATHENIAN: Ah! that's the ticket! Well, to begin with, give us Echinus, the Maliac gulf adjoining, and the two legs of Megara.[102]

LACONIAN: Oh! surely, surely not all that, my dear sir.

LYSISTRATA: Come to terms; never make a difficulty of two legs more or less!

ATHENIAN: Well, I'm ready now to off my coat and plough my land.

LACONIAN: And I too, to fertilize it to start with.

LYSISTRATA: That's just what you shall do, once peace is signed. So, if you really want to make it, go consult your allies about the matter.

ATHENIAN: What allies, I should like to know? Why, we are all on the stand; not one but is mad to be fucking. What we all want is to be in bed with our wives; how could our allies fail to second our project?

LACONIAN: And ours the same, for certain sure!

ATHENIANS: The Carystians first and foremost, by the gods!

LYSISTRATA: Well said, indeed! Now be off to purify yourselves for entering the Acropolis, where the women invite you to supper; we will empty our provision baskets to do you honor. At table, you will exchange oaths and pledges; then each man will go home with his wife.

ATHENIAN: Come along then, and as quick as may be.

LACONIAN: Lead on; I'm your man.

ATHENIAN: Quick, quick's the word, say I.

CHORUS OF WOMEN: Embroidered stuffs, and dainty tunics, and flowing gowns, and golden ornaments, everything I have, I offer them to you with all my heart; take them all for your children, for your girls, against the time they are chosen to be "basket-bearers" to the goddess. I invite you every one to enter, come in and choose whatever you will; there is nothing so well fastened, you cannot break the seals, and carry away the contents. Look about you everywhere ... you won't find a blessed thing, unless you have sharper eyes than mine. And if any of you lacks grain to feed his slaves and his young and numerous family, why, I have a few grains of wheat at home; let him take what I have to give, a big 12-pound loaf included. So let my poorer neighbors all come with bags and wallets; my man, Manes, shall give them grain; but I warn them not to come near my door, or—beware the dog!

A MARKET-LOUNGER: I say, you, open the door!

A SLAVE: Go your way, I tell you. Why, bless me, they're sitting down now; I shall have to singe 'em with my torch to make 'em stir! What an impudent lot of fellows!

MARKET-LOUNGER: I don't mean to budge.

SLAVE: Well, as you must stop, and I don't want to offend you—but you'll see some queer sights.

MARKET-LOUNGER: Well and good, I've no objection.

SLAVE: No, no, you must be off—or I'll tear your hair out, I will; be off, I say, and don't annoy the Laconian envoys; they're just coming out from the banquet hall.

AN ATHENIAN: Such a merry banquet I've never seen before! The Laconians were simply charming. After the drink is in, why, we're all wise men, all. It's only natural, to be sure, for sober, we're all fools. Take my advice, my fellow-countrymen, our envoys should always be drunk. We go to Sparta; we enter the city sober; why, we must be picking a quarrel immediately. We don't understand what they say to us, we imagine a lot they don't say at all, and we report home all wrong, all topsy-turvy. But, look: today it's quite different; we're enchanted whatever happens; instead of Clitagoras,[103] they might sing us Telamon,[104] and we would clap our hands just the same. A perjury or two into the bar-

---

102 The legs of Megara are the long walls which joined the city of Megara to the sea.

103 A composer of drinking songs.

104 A composer of war songs.

gain, la! what does that matter to merry companions in their cups?

SLAVE: But here they are back again! Will you begone, you loafing scoundrels.

MARKET-LOUNGER: Ah ha! here's the company coming out already.

A LACONIAN: My dear, sweet friend, come, take your flute in hand; I would dance and sing my best in honor of the Athenians and our noble selves.

AN ATHENIAN: Yes, take your flute, in the god's name. What a delight to see him dance.

CHORUS OF LACONIANS: Oh Mnemosyne![105] inspire these men, inspire my muse who knows our exploits and those of the Athenians. With what a godlike ardor did they swoop down at Artemisium on the ships of the Medes![106] What a glorious victory was that! For the soldiers of Leonidas,[107] they were like fierce wild boars whetting their tushes. The sweat ran down their faces, and drenched all their limbs, for truly the Persians were as many as the sands of the seashore. Oh! Artemis, huntress queen whose arrows pierce the denizens of the woods, virgin goddess, be favorable to the Peace we conclude; through you may our hearts be long united! May this treaty draw close forever the bonds of a happy friendship! No more wiles and stratagems! Help us, oh! help us maiden huntress!

LYSISTRATA: All is for the best; and now, Laconians, take your wives away home with you, and you, Athenians, yours. May husband live happily with wife, and wife with husband. Dance, dance, to celebrate our bliss, and let us be heedful to avoid like mistakes for the future.

CHORUS OF ATHENIANS: Appear, appear, dancers, and the Graces with you! Let us invoke, one and all, Artemis and her heavenly brother, gracious Apollo, patron of the dance, and Dionysus, whose eye darts flame, as he steps forward surrounded by the Maenads,[108] and Zeus, who wields the flashing lightning, and his august, thrice-blessed spouse, the Queen of Heaven! Let us invoke these and all the other gods, calling all the inhabitants of the skies to witness the noble peace now concluded under the fond auspices of Aphrodite. Io Paean! Io Paean![109] Dance, leap, as in honor of a victory won. Evoe! Evoe![110] And you, our Laconian guests, sing us a new and inspiring strain!

CHORUS OF LACONIANS: Leave once more, oh! leave once more the noble height of Taygetus, oh! Muse of Lacedaemon, and join us in singing the praises of Apollo of Amyclae,[111] and Athena of the Bronze House,[112] and the gallant twin sons of Tyndarus,[113] who practice arms on the banks of Eurotas river.[114] Haste, hasten hither with nimble-footed pace, let us sing Sparta, the city that delights in choruses divinely sweet and graceful dances, when our maidens bound lightly by the river side, like frolicsome fillies, beating the ground with rapid steps and shaking their long locks in the wind, as Maenads wave their wands in the wild revels of the Wine-god. At their head, oh! chaste and beauteous goddess, daughter of Latona, Artemis, lead the song and dance. A hair band binding your waving tresses, appear in your loveliness; leap like a fawn; strike your divine hands together to animate the dance, and help us to honor the valiant goddess of battles, great Athena of the Bronze House!

---

105 I.e., Memory, the mother of the muses.

106 The Greeks defeated the Persian navy at Artemisium in the Persian War.

107 Leonidas was the Spartan commander at the battle of Thermopylae, where a few hundred Greeks held up many more Persians—a near-legendary event of the Persian War.

108 Women who, in their worship of Dionysius, were held to go about as though mad. See above, n 1.

109 An invocation of the gods and an expression of joy.

110 An expression denoting Dionysian frenzy (see n 1).

111 A town near Sparta, where a temple of Apollo stood.

112 Athena had a temple with bronze-covered walls at Chalcis.

113 Castor and Pollux, twin heroes who were especially revered at Sparta.

114 The river which ran by Sparta.

# 12

## PLATO, *THE SYMPOSIUM*

Most of what is known of the thought of Socrates (*c.* 479-399 BC) comes from the works of his student and admirer, Plato (*c.* 427-347 BC), who, it should be noted, often represented his own ideas as Socrates's. Plato's *Symposium* recounts events at a drinking party which, if it happened, occurred at Athens in 416 BC. The work was, however, written sometime after 385 BC and is generally treated as Plato's invention. The guests at the gathering were real people, as was Apollodorus. The social setting is aristocratic. The work opens with Apollodorus answering a question put to him by a companion.

---

I believe that I am not ill-prepared with an answer concerning the things about which you ask to be informed. For the day before yesterday I was coming from my own home at Phalerum to the city, and an acquaintance, who had caught a sight of me from behind, calling out playfully in the distance, said, "Apollodorus, O you Phalerian man,[1] halt!" So I did as I was asked, and then he said, "I was looking for you, Apollodorus, only just now, that I might ask you about the speeches in praise of love, which were delivered by Socrates, Alcibiades, and others, at Agathon's drinking party. Phoenix, the son of Philip, told another person who told me of them; his narrative was very indistinct, but he said that you knew, and I wish that you would give me an account of them. Who, if not you, should be the reporter of the words of your friend? And first tell me, he said, were you present at this meeting?"

"Your informant, Glaucon," I said, "must have been very indistinct indeed, if you imagine that the occasion was recent, or that I could have been of the party."

"Why, yes," he replied, "I thought so."

"Impossible." I said. "Are you ignorant that for many years Agathon has not resided at Athens; and not three have elapsed since I became acquainted with Socrates, and have made it my daily business to know all that he says and does? There was a time when I was running about the world, fancying myself to be well employed, but I was really a most wretched being, no better than you are now. I thought that I ought to do anything rather than be a philosopher."

"Well," he said, "jesting apart, tell me when the meeting occurred."

"In our boyhood," I replied, "when Agathon won the prize with his first tragedy,[2] on the day after that on which he and his chorus offered the sacrifice of victory."

---

1 Apollodorus is being addressed formally, using the name of his *deme*, or district in Athens. This may be a mock formality in this case.

2 Theater at Athens was performed as part of a religious festival, which included a competition, with prizes, for the best tragedy.

"Then it must have been a long while ago," he said. "And who told you—did Socrates?"

"No indeed," I replied, "but the same person who told Phoenix; he was a little fellow, who never wore any shoes, Aristodemus, of the *deme* of Cydathenaeum. He had been at Agathon's feast; and I think that in those days there was no one who was a more devoted admirer of Socrates. Moreover, I have asked Socrates about the truth of some parts of his narrative, and he confirmed them."

"Then," said Glaucon, "let us have the tale over again; is not the road to Athens just made for conversation?"

And so we walked, and talked of the discourses on love; and therefore, as I said at first, I am not ill-prepared to comply with your request, and will have another rehearsal of them if you like. For to speak or to hear others speak of philosophy always gives me the greatest pleasure, to say nothing of the profit. But when I hear another kind of strain, especially that of you rich men and traders, such conversation displeases me; and I pity you who are my companions, because you think that you are doing something when in reality you are doing nothing. And I dare say that you pity me in return, whom you regard as an unhappy creature, and very probably you are right. But I certainly know of you what you only think of me—there is the difference.

Apollodorus's companion: I see, Apollodorus, that you are just the same—always speaking evil of yourself, and of others. I do believe that you pity all mankind, with the exception of Socrates, yourself first of all, true in this to your old name, which, however deserved, I do not know how you acquired, of Apollodorus the madman; for you are always raging against yourself and everybody but Socrates.

Apollodorus: Yes, friend, and the reason why I am said to be mad, and out of my wits, is just because I have these notions of myself and you; no other evidence is required.

Companion: No more of that, Apollodorus; but let me renew my request that you would repeat the conversation.

Apollodorus: Well, the tale of love went this way— but perhaps I had better begin at the beginning, and endeavor to give you the exact words of Aristodemus.

He said that he met Socrates fresh from the bath and sandalled; and as the sight of the sandals was unusual, he asked him where he was going that he had been converted into such a *beau.*

*"To a banquet at Agathon's," he replied, "whose invitation to his sacrifice of victory I refused yesterday, fearing a crowd, but promising that I would come today instead; and so I have put on my finery, because he is such a fine man. What say you to going with me unasked?"*

*"I will do as you ask me," I replied.*

*"Follow then," he said, "and let us demolish the proverb 'To the feasts of inferior men the good unbidden go,' instead of which our proverb will run 'To the feasts of the good the good unbidden go,' and this alteration may be supported by the authority of Homer himself, who not only demolishes but literally outrages the proverb. For, after picturing Agamemnon as the most valiant of men, he makes Menelaus, who is but a faint-hearted warrior, come unbidden to the banquet of Agamemnon, who is feasting and offering sacrifices, not the better to the worse, but the worse to the better."*

*"I rather fear, Socrates," said Aristodemus, "lest this may still be my case and that, like Menelaus in Homer, I shall be the inferior person, who 'To the feasts of the wise unbidden goes.' But I shall say that I was bidden by you, and then you will have to make an excuse."*

*"'Two going together,'" he replied, in Homeric fashion, "one or other of them may invent an excuse by the way."*

*This was the style of their conversation as they went along. Socrates dropped behind in a fit of abstraction, and desired Aristodemus, who was waiting, to go on before him. When he reached the house of Agathon he found the doors wide open, and a comical thing happened. A servant coming out met him, and led him at once into the banqueting-hall in which the guests were reclining, for the banquet was about to begin.*

*"Welcome, Aristodemus," said Agathon, as soon as he appeared, "you are just in time to dine with us; if you come on any other matter, put it off, and make one of us, as I was looking for you yesterday and meant to have asked you, if I could have found you. But what have you done with Socrates?"*

*I turned around, but Socrates was nowhere to be seen. I had to explain that he had been with me a moment before, and that I came by his invitation to the drinking.*

*"You were quite right in coming," said Agathon, "but where is he himself?"*

"He was behind me just now, as I entered," he said, "and I cannot think what has become of him."

"Go and look for him, servant,"[3] said Agathon, "and bring him in. And you, Aristodemus, meanwhile take the place by Eryximachus."

The servant then assisted him to wash, and he lay down, and presently another servant came in and reported that our friend Socrates had retired into the portico of the neighboring house. "There he is fixed," he said, "and when I call to him he will not stir."

"How strange," said Agathon, "then you must call him again, and keep calling him."

"Let him alone," said my informant. "He has a way of stopping anywhere and losing himself without any reason. I believe that he will soon appear; do not therefore disturb him."

"Well, if you think so, I will leave him," said Agathon. And then, turning to the servants, he added, "Let us have supper without waiting for him. Serve up whatever you please, for there is no one to give you orders; hitherto I have never left you to yourselves. But on this occasion imagine that you are our hosts, and that I and the company are your guests; treat us well, and then we shall commend you." After this, dinner was served, but still no Socrates; and during the meal Agathon several times expressed a wish to send for him, but Aristodemus objected. At last when the feast was about half over—for the fit, as usual, was not of long duration—Socrates entered. Agathon, who was reclining alone at the end of the table, begged that he would take the place next to him; that "I may touch you," he said, "and have the benefit of that wise thought which came into your mind in the portico, and is now in your possession. For I am certain that you would not have come away until you had found what you sought."

"How I wish," said Socrates, taking his place as desired, "that wisdom could be infused by touch, out of the fuller into the emptier man, as water runs through wool out of a fuller cup into an emptier one. If that were so, how greatly would I value the privilege of reclining at your side! For you would have filled me full with a plenteous and fair stream of wisdom, whereas my own is of a very mean and questionable sort, no better than a dream. But yours is bright and full of promise, and was manifested forth in all the splendor of youth the day before yesterday, in the presence of more than 30,000 Greeks."

"Socrates, you are mocking," said Agathon, "and before long you and I will have to determine who bears off the palm of wisdom—of this Dionysus shall be the judge; but at present you are better occupied with dinner."

Socrates took his place on the couch, and ate with the rest; and then libations were offered, and after a hymn had been sung to the god, and there had been the usual ceremonies, they were about to start drinking, when Pausanias said, "And now, my friends, how can we drink with least injury to ourselves? I can assure you that I feel severely the effect of yesterday's potations, and must have time to recover. I suspect that most of you are in the same predicament, for you were of the party yesterday. Consider then: How can the drinking be made easiest?"

"I entirely agree," said Aristophanes,[4] "that we should, by all means, avoid hard drinking, for I was myself one of those who were yesterday drowned in drink."

"I think that you are right," said Eryximachus, the son of Acumenus. "But I would still like to hear one other person speak: Is Agathon able to drink hard?"

"I am not equal to it," said Agathon.

"Then," said Eryximachus, "the weak heads like myself, Aristodemus, Phaedrus, and others who never can drink, are fortunate in finding that the stronger ones are not in a drinking mood. (I do not include Socrates, who is able either to drink or to abstain, and will not mind, whichever we do.) Well, as none of the company seems disposed to drink much, I may be forgiven for saying, as a physician, that drinking deep is a bad practice, which I never follow, if I can help it, and certainly do not recommend to someone else, least of all to anyone who still feels the effects of yesterday's carouse."

"I always do what you advise, and especially what you prescribe as a physician," rejoined Phaedrus the Myrrhinusian, "and the rest of the company, if they are wise, will do the same."

It was agreed that drinking was not to be the order of the day, but that they were all to drink only so much as they pleased.

"Then," said Eryximachus, "as you are all agreed that

---

3   Here and below Plato uses the term *pais*, which could be rendered as "servant" or as "child." The term was also used to designate a slave.

4   Aristophanes was a leading comic playwright in Athens. He satirized Socrates in *The Clouds*.

*drinking is to be voluntary, and that there is to be no com-pulsion, I move, in the next place, that the flute-girl, who has just made her appearance, be told to go away and play to herself, or, if she likes, to the women who are within. Today let us have conversation instead; and, if you will allow me, I will tell you what sort of conversation."*

*This proposal having been accepted, Eryximachus pro-ceeded as follows:*

*"I will begin, he said, after the manner of Melanippe in Euripides,[5] 'Not mine the word' which I am about to speak, but that of Phaedrus. For often he says to me in an indig-nant tone, 'What a strange thing it is, Eryximachus, that, whereas other gods have poems and hymns made in their honor, the great and glorious god, Love, has no encomiast among all the poets who are so many. There are the worthy sophists too—the excellent Prodicus for example, who have discoursed in prose on the virtues of Heracles and other heroes. What is still more extraordinary, I have met with a philosophical work in which the utility of salt has been made the theme of an eloquent discourse; many other like things have had a like honor bestowed upon them. And only to think that there should have been an eager interest created about them, and yet that to this day no one has ever dared worthily to sing Love's praises! So entirely has this great deity been neglected.' Now in this Phaedrus seems to me to be quite right, and therefore I want to offer him a contribu-tion; also I think that at the present moment we who are here assembled cannot do better than honor the god Love. If you agree with me, there will be no lack of conversation; for I mean to propose that each of us in turn, going from left to right, shall make a speech in honor of Love. Let him give us the best which he can. Phaedrus, because he is sitting first on the left hand, and because he is the father of the idea, shall begin."*

*"No one will vote against you, Eryximachus," said Socrates. "How can I oppose your motion, who profess to understand nothing but matters of love; nor, I presume, will Agathon and Pausanias, and there can be no doubt of Aristophanes, whose whole concern is with Dionysus and Aphrodite;[6] nor will anyone disagree of those whom I see around me. The proposal, as I am aware, may seem rather hard upon us whose place is last, but we shall be contented*

*if we hear some good speeches first. Let Phaedrus begin the praise of Love, and good luck to him." All the company expressed their assent, and desired him to do as Socrates asked him.*

*Aristodemus did not recollect all that was said, nor do I recollect all that he related to me; but I will tell you what I thought most worthy of remembrance, and what the chief speakers said.*

[Phaedrus's speech]

Love is a mighty god, and wonderful among gods and men, but especially wonderful in his birth. For he is the eldest of the gods, which is an honor to him. A proof of his claim to this honor is that there is no mem-ory of his parents; neither poet nor prose-writer has ever affirmed that he had any. As Hesiod[7] says,

First Chaos came, and then broad-bosomed Earth,
The everlasting seat of all that is,
And Love.

In other words, after Chaos, the Earth and Love came into being. Also Parmenides sings of Generation, 'First in the train of gods, he fashioned Love.' And Acusi-laus agrees with Hesiod. Thus numerous are the wit-nesses who acknowledge Love to be the eldest of the gods. And not only is he the eldest, he is also the source of the greatest benefits to us. For I do not know any greater blessing to a young man who is beginning life than a youthful lover, or to the lover than a beloved youth. For the principle which ought to be the guide of men who would live nobly—that principle, I say, neither kindred, nor honor, nor wealth, nor any other motive is able to implant so well as love. Of what am I speaking? Of the sense of honor and dis-honor, without which neither states nor individuals ever do any good or great work. And I say that a lover who is detected in doing any dishonorable act, or sub-mitting through cowardice when any dishonor is done to him by another, will be more pained at being detected by his beloved than at being seen by his father, or by his companions, or by anyone else. The beloved too, when he is found in any disgraceful

---

5  Playwright (fifth century BC).
6  The gods, respectively, of wine and of (sexual) love.
7  The poet (eighth century BC). The quotation is from his *Theogony*.

situation, has the same feeling about his lover. And if there were only some way of contriving that a state or an army should be made up of lovers and their loves, they would be the very best governors of their own city, abstaining from all dishonor, and emulating one another in honor, and when fighting at each other's side, although a mere handful, they would overcome the world. For what lover would not choose rather to be seen by all mankind than by his beloved, either when abandoning his post or throwing away his arms? He would be ready to die a thousand deaths rather than endure this. Or who would desert his beloved or fail him in the hour of danger? The basest coward would become an inspired hero, equal to the bravest, at such a time. Love would inspire him. That courage which, as Homer says, the god breathes into the souls of some heroes, Love of his own nature infuses into the lover.

Love will make men dare to die for their beloved—love alone, and women as well as men. Of this, Alcestis,[8] the daughter of Pelias, is a monument to all Greece; for she was willing to lay down her life on behalf of her husband, when no one else would, although he had a father and mother; but the tenderness of her love so far exceeded theirs, that she made them seem to be strangers in blood to their own son, and in name only related to him. So noble did this action of hers appear to the gods, as well as to men, that among the many who have acted virtuously she is one of the very few to whom, in admiration of her noble action, they have granted the privilege of returning alive to earth. Such exceeding honor is paid by the gods to the devotion and virtue of love. But Orpheus,[9] the son of Oeagrus, the harper, they sent empty away, and presented to him an apparition only of her whom he sought, but herself they would not give up, because he showed no spirit. He was only a harp player, and did not dare like Alcestis to die for love, but was contriving how he might enter Hades alive. Moreover, they afterwards caused him to suffer death at the hands of women, as the punishment of his cowardliness. Very different was the reward of the true love of Achilles towards his lover Patroclus[10]—his lover and not his love (the notion that Patroclus was the beloved one is a foolish error into which Aeschylus[11] has fallen, for Achilles was surely the fairer of the two, fairer also than all the other heroes, and, as Homer informs us, he was still beardless, and younger by far. And greatly as the gods honor the virtue of love, still the return of love on the part of the beloved to the lover is more admired and valued and rewarded by them, for the lover is more divine because he is inspired by a god. Now Achilles was quite aware, for he had been told by his mother, that he might avoid death and return home, and live to a good old age, if he abstained from slaying Hector.[12] Nevertheless he gave his life to revenge his friend, and dared to die, not only in his defense, but after he was dead. Wherefore the gods honored him even above Alcestis, and sent him to the Islands of the Blessed. These are my reasons for affirming that Love is the eldest and noblest and mightiest of the gods, and the chief author and giver of virtue in life, and of happiness after death.

*This, or something like this, was the speech of Phaedrus; and some other speeches followed which Aristodemus did not remember; the next which he repeated was that of Pausanias.*

[Pausanias's speech]

Phaedrus, the argument has not been set before us, I think, quite in the right form. We should not be called upon to praise Love in such an indiscriminate manner. If there were only one Love, then what you said would be well enough; but since there are more Loves than

---

8   According to legend, Apollo told Admetus, king of Pherae, that he would die unless he could find someone willing to take his place in Hades, the land of the dead. After Admetus's parents refused to this, his wife, Alcestis, volunteered to do so. The gods later removed her from Hades.

9   Orpheus went to Hades to retrieve his wife Eurydice, whose shade remained in the underworld when, against instructions, he looked back to confirm she was following him to the land of the living. Orpheus was later torn apart by women driven mad by Dionysius.

10  In the *Iliad*, Achilles is driven to return to the Trojan war when Hector, a Trojan, kills Patroclus.

11  The playwright (fifth century BC).

12  Phaedrus refers to Homer's account here.

one, you should have begun by determining which of them was to be the theme of our praises. I will amend this defect and first of all I will tell you which Love is deserving of praise, and then try to praise the worthy one in a manner fit for him. For we all know that Love is inseparable from Aphrodite, and if there were only one Aphrodite there would be only one Love; but as there are two goddesses there must be two Loves. And am I not right in asserting that there are two goddesses? The elder one, having no mother, who is called the heavenly Aphrodite—she is the daughter of Uranus; the younger, who is the daughter of Zeus and Dione—her we call common; and the Love who is her fellow-worker is rightly named common, as the other love is called heavenly. All the gods ought to have praise given to them, but not without distinction of their natures. Therefore, I must try to distinguish the characters of the two Loves. Now actions vary according to the manner of their performance. Take, for example, that which we are now doing: drinking, singing and talking. These actions are not in themselves either good or evil, but they turn out in this or that way according to the mode of performing them; and when well done they are good, and when wrongly done they are evil; and in like manner not every love, but only that which has a noble purpose, is noble and worthy of praise.

The Love who is the offspring of the common Aphrodite is essentially common, and has no discrimination, being such as the meaner sort of men feel, and is apt to be of women as well as of youths, and is of the body rather than of the soul. The most foolish beings are the objects of this love which desires only to gain its end,[13] but never thinks of accomplishing the end nobly, and therefore does good and evil quite indiscriminately. The goddess who is his mother is far younger than the other, and she was born of the union of the male and female, and partakes of both.

But the offspring of the heavenly Aphrodite is derived from a mother in whose birth the female has no part. She is from the male only; this is that love which is of youths, and the goddess being older, there is nothing of wantonness in her. Those who are inspired by this love turn to the male, and delight in him who is the more valiant and intelligent nature. Anyone may recognize the pure enthusiasts in the very character of their attachments. For they do not love boys, but intelligent beings whose reason is beginning to be developed, much about the time at which their beards begin to grow. And in choosing young men to be their companions, they mean to be faithful to them, and pass their whole life in company with them, not to take them in their inexperience, and deceive them, and play the fool with them, or run away from one to another of them.

But the love of young boys should be forbidden by law, because their future is uncertain; they may turn out good or bad, either in body or soul, and much noble enthusiasm may be thrown away upon them. In this matter the good are a law to themselves, and the coarser sort of lovers ought to be restrained by force, as we restrain or attempt to restrain them from fixing their affections on women of free birth. These are the persons who bring a reproach on love. Some have been led to deny the lawfulness of such attachments because they see the impropriety and evil of them; for surely nothing that is decorously and lawfully done can justly be censured.

Now here and in Lacedaemon[14] the rules about love are perplexing, but in most cities they are simple and easily intelligible. In Elis and Boeotia, and in countries having no gifts of eloquence, they are very straightforward. The law is simply in favor of these connections, and no one, whether young or old, has anything to say to their discredit, the reason being, as I suppose, that they are men of few words in those parts, and therefore the lovers do not like the trouble of pleading their suit.

In Ionia and other places, and generally in countries which are subject to the barbarians,[15] the custom is held to be dishonorable. Love of youths shares the evil repute in which philosophy and gymnastics are held—because it undermines tyranny. For the interests of rulers require that their subjects should be poor

---

13   The end here is sexual gratification.
14   I.e., Sparta.
15   I.e., the Persians.

in spirit, and that there should be no strong bond of friendship or society among them, which love, above all other motives, is likely to inspire, as our Athenian tyrants learned by experience, for the love of Aristogeiton and the constancy of Harmodius had a strength which undid their power.[16] And, therefore, the ill-repute into which these attachments have fallen is to be ascribed to the evil condition of those who make them to be ill-reputed, that is to say, to the self-seeking of the governors and the cowardice of the governed. On the other hand, the indiscriminate honor which is given to them in some countries is attributable to the laziness of those who hold this opinion of them.

In our own country a far better principle prevails, but, as I was saying, the explanation of it is rather perplexing. For, observe that open loves are held to be more honorable than secret ones, and that the love of the noblest and highest, even if their persons are less beautiful than others, is especially honorable. Consider, too, how great is the encouragement which all the world gives to the lover; neither is he supposed to be doing anything dishonorable; but if he succeeds he is praised, and if he fails he is blamed. And in the pursuit of his love custom allows him to do many strange things, which philosophy would bitterly censure if they were done from any motive of self-interest, or wish for office or power. He may pray, and entreat, and supplicate, and swear, and lie on a mat at the door, and endure a slavery worse than that of any slave—in any other case friends and enemies would be equally ready to prevent him, but now there is no friend who will be ashamed of him and admonish him, and no enemy will charge him with meanness or flattery. The actions of a lover have a grace which ennobles them, and custom has decided that they are highly commendable and that there is no loss of character in them. What is strangest of all, he only may swear and forswear himself (so men say), and the gods will forgive his transgression, for there is no such thing as a lover's oath. Such is the complete liberty which gods and men have allowed the lover, according to the custom which prevails in our part of the world.

From this point of view a man fairly argues that in Athens to love and to be loved is held to be a very honorable thing. But when parents forbid their sons to talk with their lovers, and place them under a tutor's care, who is appointed to see to these things, and their companions and equals cast in their teeth anything of the sort which they may observe, and their elders refuse to silence the reprovers and do not rebuke them—anyone who reflects on all this will, on the contrary, think that we hold these practices to be most disgraceful.

But, as I was saying at first, the truth, as I imagine it, is that whether such practices are honorable or whether they are dishonorable is not a simple question. They are honorable to him who follows them honorably, dishonorable to him who follows them dishonorably. There is dishonor in yielding to the evil, or in an evil manner, but there is honor in yielding to the good, or in an honorable manner. Evil is the vulgar lover who loves the body rather than the soul, inasmuch as he is not even stable, because he loves a thing which is in itself unstable, and therefore when the bloom of youth which he was desiring is over, he takes wing and flies away, in spite of all his words and promises, whereas the love of a noble disposition is lifelong, for it becomes one with the everlasting.

The custom of our country would have both of them proven well and truly, and would have us yield to the one sort of lover and avoid the other, and therefore encourages some to pursue, and others to fly, testing both the lover and beloved in contests and trials, until they show to which of the two classes they respectively belong. And this is the reason why, in the first place, a hasty attachment is held to be dishonorable, because time is the true test of this as of most other things. Secondly, there is a dishonor in being overcome by the love of money, or of wealth, or of political power, whether a man is frightened into surrender by the loss of them or, having experienced the benefits of money and political corruption, is unable to rise above the seductions of them. For none of these things is of a permanent or lasting nature, not to mention that no generous friendship ever sprang from

---

16   This pair of lovers tried to overthrow the Athenian tyrant Hippias in 514 BC. They died in the attempt, and were later celebrated as heroes by the Athenians.

them. There remains, then, only one way of honorable attachment which custom allows in the beloved, and this is the way of virtue. For as we admitted that any service which the lover does to him is not to be accounted flattery or a dishonor to himself, so the beloved has one way only of voluntary service which is not dishonorable, and this is virtuous service.

For we have a custom, and according to our custom anyone who does service to another under the idea that he will be improved by him either in wisdom, or in some other particular of virtue—such a voluntary service, I say, is not to be regarded as a dishonor, and is not open to the charge of flattery. And these two customs, one the love of youth, and the other the practice of philosophy and virtue in general, ought to meet in one, and then the beloved may honorably indulge the lover. For when the lover and beloved come together, having each of them a law, and the lover thinks that he is right in doing any service which he can to his gracious loving one; and the other that he is right in showing any kindness which he can to him who is making him wise and good; the one capable of communicating wisdom and virtue, the other seeking to acquire them with a view to education and wisdom; when the two laws of love are fulfilled and meet in one, then, and then only, may the beloved yield with honor to the lover. Nor when love is of this disinterested sort is there any disgrace in being deceived, but in every other case there is equal disgrace in being or not being deceived. For he who is gracious to his lover under the impression that he is rich, and is disappointed of his gains because he turns out to be poor, is disgraced all the same: for he has done his best to show that he would give himself up to anyone's base uses for the sake of money, which is not honorable. And on the same principle he who gives himself to a lover because he is a good man, and in the hope that he will be improved by his company, shows himself to be virtuous, even though the object of his affection turns out to be a villain, and to have no virtue, and if he is deceived he has committed a noble error. For he has proved that for his part he will do anything for anybody with a view to virtue and improvement, than which there can be nothing nobler. Thus noble in every case is the acceptance of another for the sake of virtue. This is that love which is the love of the heav-enly goddess, and is heavenly, and of great price to individuals and cities, making the lover and the beloved alike eager in the work of their own improvement. But all other loves are the offspring of the other, who is the common goddess. To you, Phaedrus, I offer this my contribution in praise of love, which is as good as I could make spontaneously.

*Pausanias came to a pause—this is the balanced way in which I have been taught by the wise to speak. Aristodemus said that Aristophanes's was next, but Aristophanes either had eaten too much, or for some other reason had the hiccups, and was obliged to change turns with Eryximachus the physician, who was reclining on the couch below him. "Eryximachus," he said, "you ought either to stop my hiccups or to speak in my turn."*

*"I will do both," said Eryximachus. "I will speak in your turn, and you will speak in mine, and while I am speaking let me recommend that you hold your breath, and if after you have done so for some time the hiccups are no better, then gargle with a little water. If they still continue, tickle your nose with something and sneeze. If you sneeze once or twice, even the most violent hiccups are sure to go."*

*"I will do as you prescribe," said Aristophanes. "So now start."*

[Eryximachus's speech]

Seeing that Pausanias made a fair beginning, and but a lame ending, I must endeavor to supply his deficiency. I think that he has rightly distinguished two kinds of love. But my art further informs me that the double love is not merely an affection of the soul of man towards the fair, or towards anything, but is to be found in the bodies of all animals and in productions of the earth and, I may say, in all that exists; such is the conclusion which I seem to have gathered from my own art of medicine, from which I learn how great and wonderful and universal is the deity of love, whose empire extends over all things, divine as well as human.

And from medicine I will begin in order to do honor to my art. There are in the human body these two kinds of love, which are confessedly different and unlike, and being unlike, they have loves and desires which are unlike. The desire of the healthy is one, and the desire of the diseased is another, and as Pausanias was just now saying that to indulge good men is honorable, and bad men dishonorable, so too, in the body, the good and healthy elements are to be indulged, and the bad elements and the elements of disease are not to be indulged, but discouraged. And this is what the physician has to do, and in this the art of medicine consists, for medicine may be regarded generally as the knowledge of the loves and desires of the body, and how to satisfy them or not. The best physician is he who is able to separate fair love from foul, or to convert one into the other; and he who knows how to eradicate and how to implant love, whichever is required, and can reconcile the most hostile elements in the constitution and make them loving friends, is a skilful practitioner. Now the most hostile are the most opposite, such as hot and cold, bitter and sweet, moist and dry, and the like. And our ancestor, Asclepius, knowing how to implant friendship and accord in these elements, was the creator of our art, as our friends the poets here tell us, and I believe them. Not only medicine in every branch, but the arts of gymnastics and husbandry are under his dominion.

Anyone who pays the least attention to the subject will also perceive that in music there is the same reconciliation of opposites, and I suppose that this must have been the meaning of Heracleitus,[17] although his words are not accurate; for he says that the One "is united by disunion like the harmony of the bow and the lyre." Now there is an absurdity in saying that harmony is discord or is composed of elements which are still in a state of discord. But he probably meant that harmony is composed of differing notes of higher or lower pitch which disagreed once, but are now reconciled by the art of music. For if the higher and lower notes still disagreed, there could be no harmony—clearly not. For harmony is a symphony, and symphony is an agreement, but there cannot be an agreement of disagreements while they disagree; you cannot harmonize that which disagrees. In like manner rhythm is composed of fast and slow elements, once differing and now brought into accord, which accord, as in the former instance, medicine, so in all these other cases, music implants, making love and unison to grow up among them. Thus music, too, is concerned with the principles of love in their application to harmony and

rhythm. Again, in the essential nature of harmony and rhythm there is no difficulty in discerning love; love has not yet become double. But when you want to use them in actual life, either in the composition of songs or in the correct performance of airs or meters composed already, which latter is called education, then the difficulty begins, and the good artist is needed. Then the old tale has to be repeated of fair and heavenly love—the love of Urania the fair and heavenly muse, and of the duty of accepting the temperate, and those who are as yet intemperate only that they may become temperate, and of preserving their love; and again, of the vulgar Polyhymnia, who must be used with circumspection so that the pleasure may be enjoyed, but may not generate licentiousness. Just as in my own art it is a great matter so to regulate the desires of the epicure that he may gratify his tastes without the attendant evil of disease. Whence I infer that in music, in medicine, in all other things human as well as divine, both loves ought to be vigilantly attended to, for they are both present in all things.

The course of the seasons is also full of both these principles. When, as I was saying, the elements of hot and cold, moist and dry, attain the harmonious love of one another and blend in temperance and harmony, they bring to men, animals, and plants health and plenty, and do them no harm. Whereas the wanton love, getting the upper hand and affecting the seasons of the year, is very destructive and injurious, being the source of pestilence, and bringing many other kinds of diseases on animals and plants; for hoar-frost and hail and blight spring from the excesses and disorders of these elements of love. To study these effects in relation to the revolutions of the heavenly bodies and the seasons of the year is termed astronomy.

Furthermore, all sacrifices and the whole province of divination, which is the art of communion between gods and men—these, I say, are concerned only with the preservation of the good love and the cure of the evil love. For all manner of impiety is likely to ensue if, instead of accepting and honoring and revering the harmonious love in all his actions, a man honors the other love, whether in his feelings towards gods or

---

17   Greek philosopher (active *c.* 500 BC).

parents, towards the living or the dead. Wherefore, the business of divination is to see to these loves and to heal them, and divination is the peacemaker of gods and men, working by a knowledge of the religious or irreligious tendencies which exist in human loves.

Such is the great and mighty, or rather omnipotent force of love in general. And the love, more especially, which is concerned with the good, and which is perfected in company with temperance and justice, whether among gods or men, has the greatest power, and is the source of all our happiness and harmony, and makes us friends with the gods who are above us, and with one another. I dare say that I too have omitted several things which might be said in praise of Love, but this was not intentional, and you, Aristophanes, may now supply the omission or take some other line of argument, for I perceive that you are cured of the hiccups.

*"Yes," said Aristophanes, who followed, "the hiccups are gone—not, however, until I tried sneezing. I wonder whether the harmony of the body has a love of such noises and ticklings, for I no sooner sneezed than I was cured."*

*Eryximachus said "Beware, friend Aristophanes, although you are going to speak, you are making fun of me, and I shall have to watch and see whether I cannot have a laugh at your expense, when you might speak in peace."*

*"You are quite right," said Aristophanes, laughing. "I will unsay my words. But please do not watch me, as I fear that in the speech which I am about to make, instead of others laughing with me, which is to the manner born of our muse and would be all the better, I shall only be laughed at by them."*

*"Do you expect to shoot your bolt and escape, Aristophanes? Well, perhaps if you are very careful and bear in mind that you will be called to account, I may be induced to let you off."*

*Aristophanes professed to open another vein of discourse; he had a mind to praise Love in another way, unlike that either of Pausanias or Eryximachus.*

[Aristophanes's speech]

Mankind, judging by their neglect of him, have never, as I think, at all understood the power of Love. For if they had understood him they would surely have built noble temples and altars, and offered solemn sacrifices in his honor. But this is not done, and most certainly ought to be done: since of all the gods

he is the best friend of men, the helper and the healer of the ills which are the great impediment to the happiness of the race. I will try to describe his power to you, and you shall teach the rest of the world what I am teaching you. In the first place, let me treat of the nature of man and what has happened to it, for the original human nature was not like the present, but different. The sexes were not two as they are now, but originally three in number. There was man, woman, and the union of the two, having a name corresponding to this double nature, which had once a real existence, but is now lost, and the word "androgynous" is only preserved as a term of reproach. In the second place, the original human beings were round, with back and sides forming a circle, and had four hands and four feet, one head with two faces, looking opposite ways, set on a round neck and precisely alike, and also four ears, two sets of sexual organs, and the remainder as you would imagine. They could walk upright as today, backwards or forwards as they pleased, and they could also roll over and over at a great pace, turning on four hands and four feet, eight in all, like tumblers going over and over with their legs in the air; this was when they wanted to run fast. Now the sexes were three, and such as I have described them because the sun, moon, and earth are three. The man was originally the child of the sun, the woman of the earth, and the man-woman of the moon, which is made up of sun and earth, and they were all round and moved around and around like their parents. Their might and strength were terrible, and the thoughts of their hearts were great, and they made an attack upon the gods. The tale of Otys and Ephialtes who, as Homer says, dared to scale heaven, and would have laid hands upon the gods is told of them. Doubt reigned in the celestial councils. Should the gods kill them and annihilate the race with thunderbolts, as they had done the giants? Then there would be an end of the sacrifices and worship which men offered to them. On the other hand, the gods could not suffer their insolence to be unrestrained. At last, after a good deal of reflection, Zeus discovered a way. He said, "I think I have a plan which will humble their pride and improve their manners. Human beings shall continue to exist, but I will cut them in two and then they will be diminished in strength and increased in numbers. This will have the advantage of making them more profitable to us. They shall walk upright on two legs, and if they continue to be insolent and will not be quiet, I will split them again and they shall hop about on a single leg. He spoke and cut men in two, like a sorb-apple which is halved for pickling, or as you might divide an egg with a hair; and as he cut them one after another, he ordered Apollo to give the face and the half of the neck a turn in order that human beings might contemplate their own division and thus learn a lesson of humility. Apollo was also ordered to heal their wounds and compose their forms. So he gave a turn to the face and pulled the skin from the sides all over that which in our language is called the belly, like the purses which draw in, and he made one mouth at the center, which he fastened in a knot (the same which is called the navel); he also molded the breast and took out most of the wrinkles, much as a shoemaker might smooth leather upon a last. He left a few, however, in the region of the belly and navel, as a memorial of the primeval state.

After the division the two parts of a human being, each desiring its other half, came together, and throwing their arms about one another, entwined in mutual embraces, longing to grow into one; they were on the point of dying from hunger and self-neglect, because they did not like to do anything apart; and when one of the halves died and the other survived, the survivor sought another mate, man or woman as we call them—being the halves of entire men or women—and clung to that. They were being destroyed, when Zeus in pity for them invented a new plan: he turned the sexual organs around to the front, for this had not been always their position, and they sowed the seed no longer as hitherto like grasshoppers in the ground, but in one another. After the transposition the male generated in the female in order that by the mutual embraces of man and woman they might breed, and the race might continue. Or if man came to man, they might be satisfied, and rest, and go their ways to the business of life. So ancient is the desire of one another which is implanted in us, reuniting our original nature, making one out of two, and healing the state of humanity.

Each of us when separated, having one side only, like a flat fish, is but the one half of a human being, and is always looking for the other half. Men who are a section of that double nature which was once called androgynous are lovers of women. Adulterers are generally of this breed, and also adulterous women who lust after men. The women who are a half of the woman do not care for men, but have female attachments; the female companions are of this sort. But they who are a section of the male follow the male, and while they are young, being slices of the original man, they hang about men and embrace them, and they are themselves the best of boys and youths, because they have the most manly nature. Some indeed assert that they are shameless, but this is not true, for they do not act thus from any want of shame, but because they are valiant and manly, and have a manly countenance, and they embrace that which is like them. When they grow up, they and they only become our statesmen, which is a great proof of the truth of what I am saying. When they reach manhood they are lovers of youth, and are not naturally inclined to marry or beget children—if at all, they do so only in obedience to the law. But they are satisfied if they are allowed to live with one another unwedded. Such a nature is prone to love and ready to return love, always embracing that which is akin to him. And when one of them meets with his other half, the actual half of himself, whether he is a lover of youth or a lover of another sort, the pair are lost in an amazement of love and friendship and intimacy, and one will not be out of the other's sight, as I may say, even for a moment. These are the people who pass their whole lives together, yet they could not explain what they desire of one another. For the intense yearning which each of them has towards the other does not appear to be the desire of lover's intercourse, but of something else which the soul of either evidently desires and cannot tell, and of which she has only a dark and doubtful presentiment. Suppose Hephaestus,[18] with his instruments, to come to the pair who are lying side by side and to say to them, "What do you people want of one another?" they would be unable to explain. And suppose further, that

---

18   The Greek god of the forge.

when he saw their perplexity he said, "Do you desire to be wholly one, always day and night to be in one another's company? For if this is what you desire, I am ready to melt you into one and let you grow together, so that being two you shall become one, and while you live live a common life as if you were a single man, and after your death in the world below still be one departed soul instead of two. I ask whether this is what you lovingly desire, and whether you are satisfied to attain this?" There is not a man among them who, when he heard the proposal, would deny or would not acknowledge that this meeting and melting into one another, this becoming one instead of two, was the very expression of his ancient need. And the reason is that human nature was originally one and we were a whole, and the desire and pursuit of the whole is called love.

There was a time, I say, when we were one, but now because of the wickedness of mankind the god has dispersed us, as the Arcadians were dispersed into villages by the Lacedaemonians.[19] And if we are not obedient to the gods, there is a danger that we shall be split up again and go about in bas-relief, like the profile figures having only half a nose which are sculptured on monuments, and that we shall be like tallies. Wherefore let us exhort all men to piety, that we may avoid evil, and obtain the good, of which Love is to us the lord and minister. And let no one oppose him—he who opposes him is the enemy of the gods. For if we are friends of the god and at peace with him we shall find our own true loves, which rarely happens in this world at present.

I am serious, and therefore I must beg Eryximachus not to make fun or to find any allusion in what I am saying to Pausanias and Agathon, who, as I suspect, are both of the manly nature, and belong to the class which I have been describing. But my words have a wider application—they include men and women everywhere. I believe that if our loves were perfectly accomplished, and each one returning to his primeval nature had his original true love, then our race would be happy. And if this would be best of all, the best in the next degree and under present circumstances must

be the nearest approach to such a union, and that will be the attainment of a congenial love. Wherefore, if we would praise him who has given to us the benefit, we must praise the god Love, who is our greatest benefactor, both leading us in this life back to our own nature, and giving us high hopes for the future, for he promises that if we are pious, he will restore us to our original state, and heal us and make us happy and blessed. This, Eryximachus, is my discourse of love, which, although different from yours, I must beg you to leave unassailed by the shafts of your ridicule, in order that each may have his turn each, or rather either, for Agathon and Socrates are the only ones left.

*"Indeed, I am not going to attack you," said Eryximachus, "for I thought your speech charming, and did I not know that Agathon and Socrates are masters in the art of love. I should be really afraid that they would have nothing to say, after the world of things which have been said already. But, for all that, I am not without hopes."*

*Socrates said, "You played your part well, Eryximachus but if you were as I am now, or rather as I shall be when Agathon has spoken, you would, indeed, be in a great strait."*

*"You want to cast a spell over me, Socrates," said Agathon, "in the hope that I may be disconcerted at the expectation raised among the audience that I shall speak well."*

*"I would be strangely forgetful, Agathon," replied Socrates, "of the courage and magnanimity which you showed when your own compositions were about to be exhibited, and you came upon the stage with the actors and faced the vast theater altogether undismayed, if I thought that your nerves could be fluttered at a small party of friends."*

*"Do you think, Socrates," said Agathon, "that my head is so full of the theater as not to know how much more formidable to a man of sense a few good judges are than many fools?"*

*"No," replied Socrates, "I would be very wrong in attributing to you, Agathon, that or any other lack of refinement. And I am quite aware that if you happened to meet with any whom you thought wise, you would care for their opinion much more than for that of the many. But then we,*

---

19   In 385 BC one of the cities in Arcadia was defeated by Sparta, and its population dispersed.

*having been a part of the foolish many in the theater, cannot be regarded as the select wise; though I know that if you happened to be in the presence, not of one of ourselves, but of some really wise man, you would be ashamed of disgracing yourself before him—would you not?"*

*"Yes," said Agathon.*

*"But before the many you would not be ashamed, if you thought that you were doing something disgraceful in their presence?"*

*Here Phaedrus interrupted them, saying, "Do not answer him, my dear Agathon, for if he can only get a partner with whom he can talk, especially a good-looking one, he will no longer care about the completion of our plan. Now I love to hear him talk, but just at present I must not forget the encomium on Love which I ought to receive from him and from everyone. When you and he have paid your tribute to the god, then you may talk."*

*"Very good, Phaedrus," said Agathon. "I see no reason why I should not proceed with my speech, as I shall have many other opportunities of conversing with Socrates."*

[Agathon's speech]

Let me say first how I ought to speak, and then speak. The previous speakers, instead of praising the god Love, or unfolding his nature, appear to have congratulated mankind on the benefits which he confers upon them. But I would rather praise the god first, and then speak of his gifts; this is always the right way of praising everything. May I say without impiety or offense, that of all the blessed gods he is the most blessed because he is the fairest and best? And he is the fairest for, in the first place, he is the youngest, and of his youth he is himself the witness, fleeing out of the way of age, who is swift enough, swifter truly than most of us like. Love hates age and will not come near him, but youth and love live and move together—like to like, as the proverb says. Many things were said by Phaedrus about Love in which I agree with him; but I cannot agree that he is older than Iapetus and Cronus[20]—not so; I maintain him to be the youngest of the gods, and ever youthful. The ancient doings among the gods of which Hesiod and Parmenides

spoke,[21] if the tradition of them is true, were done of Necessity and not of Love. Had Love lived in those days, there would have been no chaining or mutilation of the gods, or other violence, but peace and sweetness, as there is now in heaven, since the rule of Love began. Love is young and also tender. He ought to have a poet like Homer to describe his tenderness, as Homer says of Ate,[22] that she is a goddess, and a tender one:

Her feet are tender, for she sets her steps,
Not on the ground but on the heads of men.

Herein is an excellent proof of her tenderness: that she walks not upon the hard but upon the soft. Let us adduce a similar proof of the tenderness of Love: for he does not walk upon the earth, nor yet upon the skulls of men, which are not so very soft, but in the hearts and souls of both gods and men, which are of all things the softest; in them he walks and dwells and makes his home. He does not do so in every soul without exception, for where there is hardness he departs, where there is softness—there he dwells, and nestling always with his feet and in all manner of ways in the softest of soft places, how can he be other than the softest of all things?

Truly, he is the tenderest as well as the youngest, and also he is of fluid form, for if he were hard and without suppleness he could not enfold all things, or wind his way into and out of every soul of man undiscovered. A proof of his flexibility and symmetry of form is his grace, which is universally admitted to be in a particular manner the attribute of Love. Ungainliness and love are always at war with one another.

The fairness of his complexion is revealed by his habitation among the flowers, for he dwells not amid bloomless or fading beauties, whether of body or soul or anything else, but in the place of flowers and scents—there he sits and abides. Concerning the beauty of the god I have said enough. Yet there remains much more which I might say. Of his virtue I have

---

20  Iapetus was in Greek myth the father of all humanity and Cronus the father of the Olympian gods.

21  Hesiod's *Theogony* discusses various acts of violence by the gods. None of the surviving fragments from the philosopher Parmenides (active in the earlier fifth century BC) discusses such incidents.

22  I.e., "Mischief."

now to speak. His greatest glory is that he can neither do nor suffer wrong to or from any god or any man, for he suffers not by force if he suffers. Force does not come near him, neither when he acts does he act by force. For all men in all things serve him of their own free will, and where there is voluntary agreement, there, as the laws which are the lords of the city say, is justice.

Not only is he just, but he is exceedingly temperate, for Temperance is the acknowledged ruler of the pleasures and desires, and no pleasure ever masters Love; he is their master and they are his servants. If he conquers them he must be temperate indeed. As to courage, even the god of War is no match for him. War is the captive and Love is the lord, for love, the love of Aphrodite, masters him, as the story goes,[23] and the master is stronger than the servant. And if he conquers the bravest of all others, he must be himself the bravest.

I have spoken of his courage and justice and temperance, but I have yet to speak of his wisdom. According to the measure of my ability, I must try to do my best. In the first place he is a poet (and here, like Eryximachus, I honor my art), and he is also the source of poesy in others, which he could not be if he were not himself a poet. And at the touch of him everyone becomes a poet, even though he had no music in him before. This also is a proof that Love is a good poet and accomplished in all the fine arts, for no one can give to another that which he has not himself, or teach that of which he has no knowledge. Who will deny that the creation of the animals is his doing? Are they not all the works of his wisdom, born and begotten of him? And as to the artists, do we not know that he only of them whom love inspires has the light of fame? He whom Love does not touch walks in darkness. The arts of medicine and archery and divination were discovered by Apollo, under the guidance of love and desire, so that he, too, is a disciple of Love. Also the melody of the Muses, the metallurgy of Hephaestus, the weaving of Athena, the rule of Zeus over gods and men, are all due to Love, who was the inventor of them. And so Love set in order the rule of the gods—the love of beauty, as is evident, for with deformity Love has no concern. In the days of old, as I began by saying, dreadful deeds were done among the gods, for they were ruled by Necessity. But now since the birth of Love, and from the Love of the beautiful, has sprung every good in heaven and earth. Therefore, Phaedrus, I say of Love that he is the fairest and best in himself, and the cause of what is fairest and best in all other things. And there comes into my mind a line of poetry in which he is said to be the god who

Gives peace on earth and calms the stormy deep,
Who stills the winds and bids the sufferer sleep.

Love is he who empties men of disaffection and fills them with affection, who makes them meet together at banquets such as sacrifices, feasts, dances. In these, is our lord, who sends courtesy and sends away discourtesy, who always gives kindness and never gives unkindness; the friend of the good, the wonder of the wise, the amazement of the gods; desired by those who have no part in him, and precious to those who have the better part in him; parent of delicacy, luxury, desire, fondness, softness, grace; regardful of the good, regardless of the evil; savior, pilot, comrade, helper in every word, work, wish, fear; glory of gods and men, leader best and brightest, in whose footsteps let every man follow, sweetly singing in his honor and joining in that sweet strain with which love charms the souls of gods and men. Such is the speech, Phaedrus, half-playful, yet having a certain measure of seriousness, which, according to my ability, I dedicate to the god.

*When Agathon had finished speaking, Aristodemus said that there was a general cheer. The young man was thought to have spoken in a manner worthy of himself, and of the god. And Socrates, looking at Eryximachus, said, "Tell me, son of Acumenus, was there not reason in my fears? Was I not a true prophet when I said that Agathon would make a wonderful oration, and that I would be in a quandary?"*

*"The part of the prophecy which concerns Agathon,"* replied Eryximachus, *"appears to me to be true; but not the other part—that you will be in a quandary."*

---

23 Ares, the god of war, was trapped in bed with the goddess Aphrodite by her husband, Hephaestus.

*"Why, my dear friend," said Socrates, "must not I or anyone be in a quandary who has to speak after he has heard such a rich and varied discourse? I am especially struck with the beauty of the concluding words—who could listen to them without amazement? When I reflected on the immeasurable inferiority of my own powers, I was ready to run away for shame, if there had been a possibility of escape. For I was reminded of Gorgias, and at the end of his speech I fancied that Agathon was shaking at me the Gorginian or Gorgonian head[24] of the great master of rhetoric, which was simply to turn me and my speech into stone, as Homer says, and strike me dumb. And then I perceived how foolish I had been in consenting to take my turn with you in praising love, and saying that I too was a master of the art, when I really had no conception how anything ought to be praised. For in my simplicity I imagined that the topics of praise should be true, and that this being presupposed, out of the true the speaker was to choose the best and set them forth in the best manner. And I felt quite proud, thinking that I knew the nature of true praise, and would speak well. Whereas I now see that the intention was to attribute to Love every species of greatness and glory, whether really belonging to him or not, without regard to truth or falsehood—that was no matter, for the original proposal seems to have been not that each of you should really praise Love, but only that you should appear to praise him. And so you attribute to Love every imaginable form of praise which can be gathered anywhere; and you say that 'he is all this,' and 'the cause of all that,' making him appear the fairest and best of all to those who do not know him, for you cannot impose upon those who know him. You have rehearsed a noble and solemn hymn of praise. But as I misunderstood the nature of the praise when I said that I would take my turn, I must beg to be absolved from the promise which I made in ignorance, and which (as Euripides would say) was a promise of the lips and not of the mind. Farewell then to such a strain: for I do not praise in that way. No, indeed, I cannot. But if you like to hear the truth about love, I am ready to speak in my own manner, though I will not make myself ridiculous by entering into any rivalry with you. Say then, Phaedrus, whether you would like to have the truth about love, spoken in any words and in any order which may happen to come into my mind at the time. Will that be agreeable to you?"*

*Aristodemus said that Phaedrus and the company asked him to speak in any manner which he thought best. "Then," he added, "let me have your permission first to ask Agathon a few more questions, in order that I may take his admissions as the premises of my discourse."*

*"I grant the permission," said Phaedrus. "Ask your questions." Socrates then proceeded.*

*"In the magnificent oration which you have just uttered, I think that you were right, my dear Agathon, in proposing to speak of the nature of Love first and afterwards of his works—that is a way of beginning which I very much approve. And as you have spoken so eloquently of his nature, may I ask you further, Whether love is the love of something or of nothing? And here I must explain myself: I do not want you to say that love is the love of a father or the love of a mother (that would be ridiculous), but to answer as you would, if I asked is a father a father of something? to which you would find no difficulty in replying, of a son or daughter, and the answer would be right."*

*"Very true," said Agathon.*

*"And you would say the same of a mother?" He assented.*

*"Yet let me ask you one more question in order to illustrate my meaning: Is not a brother to be regarded essentially as a brother of something?"*

*"Certainly," he replied.*

*"That is, of a brother or sister?"*

*"Yes," he said.*

*"And now." said Socrates, "I will ask about Love: Is Love of something or of nothing?"*

*"Of something, surely," he replied.*

*"Keep in mind what this is, and tell me what I want to know—whether Love desires that of which love is."*

*"Yes, surely."*

*"And does he possess, or does he not possess, that which he loves and desires?"*

*"Probably not, I should say."*

*"No," replied Socrates, "I would have you consider whether 'necessarily' is not rather the word. The inference that he who desires something is in want of something, and that he who desires nothing is in want of nothing, is in my judgment, Agathon, absolutely and necessarily true. What do you think?"*

*"I agree with you," said Agathon.*

---

24   Gorgias was a contemporary sophist. The head of the Gorgon, a monster, was said to turn anyone who saw it into stone.

"Very good. Would he who is big, desire to be big, or he who is strong, desire to be strong?"

"That would be inconsistent with our previous admissions."

"True. For he who is anything cannot want to be that which he is?"

"Very true."

"And yet," added Socrates, "if a man being strong desired to be strong, or being swift desired to be swift, or being healthy desired to be healthy, in that case he might be thought to desire something which he already has or is. I give the example in order that we may avoid misconception. For the possessors of these qualities, Agathon, must be supposed to have their respective advantages at the time, whether they choose or not; and who can desire that which he has? Therefore, when a person says, 'I am well and wish to be well, or I am rich and wish to be rich, and I desire simply to have what I have'—to him we shall reply, 'You, my friend, having wealth and health and strength, want to have the continuance of them, for at this moment, whether you choose or no, you have them. And when you say, I desire that which I have and nothing else, is not your meaning that you want to have what you now have in the future?' He must agree with us, must he not?"

"He must," replied Agathon.

"Then," said Socrates, "he desires that what he has at present may be preserved to him in the future, which is equivalent to saying that he desires something which is non-existent to him, and which as yet he has not got."

"Very true," he said.

"Then he and everyone who desires, desires that which he has not already, and which is future and not present, and which he has not, and is not, and of which he is in want—these are the sort of things which love and desire seek?"

"Very true," he said.

"Then now," said Socrates, "let us recapitulate the argument. First, is not love love of something, and also of something which is wanting to a man?"

"Yes," he replied.

"Remember further what you said in your speech, or if you do not remember I will remind you: you said that the love of the beautiful set in order the rule of the gods, for that of deformed things there is no love—did you not say something of that kind?"

"Yes," said Agathon.

"Yes, my friend, and the remark was a just one. And if this is true, Love is the love of beauty and not of deformity?"

He assented.

"And the admission has been already made that Love is of something which a man wants and does not have?"

"True," he said.

"Then Love wants and does not have beauty?"

"Certainly," he replied.

"And would you call that beautiful which wants and does not possess beauty?"

"Certainly not."

"Then would you still say that love is beautiful?"

Agathon replied, "I fear that I did not understand what I was saying."

"You made a very good speech, Agathon," replied Socrates, "but there is yet one small question which I would ask: Is not the good also the beautiful?"

"Yes."

"Then in wanting the beautiful, love wants also the good?"

"I cannot refute you, Socrates," said Agathon. "Let us assume that what you say is true."

"Say rather, beloved Agathon, that you cannot refute the truth, for Socrates is easily refuted."

[Socrates recounts his discussion with Diotima of Mantinea.]

And now, taking my leave of you, I will rehearse a tale of love which I heard from Diotima of Mantinea, a woman wise in this and in many other kinds of knowledge, who in the days of old, when the Athenians offered sacrifice before the coming of the plague, delayed the disease ten years.

She was my instructor in the art of love, and I shall repeat to you what she said to me, beginning with the admissions made by Agathon, which are nearly if not quite the same which I made to the wise woman when she questioned me. I think that this will be the easiest way, and I shall recount both sides of the discussion, as well as I am able. As you, Agathon, suggested, I must speak first of the being and nature of Love, and then of his works. First I said to her in nearly the same words which he used to me that Love was a mighty god, and likewise fair; and she proved to me as I proved to him that, by my own showing, Love was neither fair nor good.

"What do you mean, Diotima," I said, "is love then evil and foul?"

"Hush," she said. "Must that be foul which is not fair?"

"Certainly," I said.

"And is that which is not wise, ignorant? Do you not see that there is a mean between wisdom and ignorance?"

"And what may that be?" I said.

"Right opinion," she replied, "which, as you know, being incapable of giving a reason, is not knowledge (for how can knowledge be devoid of reason? nor again, ignorance, for neither can ignorance attain the truth), but is clearly something which is a mean between ignorance and wisdom."

"Quite true," I replied.

"Do not then insist," she said, "that what is not fair is of necessity foul, or what is not good evil, or infer that because love is not fair and good he is therefore foul and evil, for he is in a mean between them."

"Well," I said, "Love is surely admitted by all to be a great god."

"By those who know or by those who do not know?"

"By all."

"And how, Socrates," she said with a smile, "can Love be acknowledged to be a great god by those who say that he is not a god at all?"

"And who are they?" I said.

"You and I are two of them," she replied.

"How can that be?" I said.

"It is quite intelligible," she replied; "for you yourself would acknowledge that the gods are happy and fair—of course you would—would you dare to say that any god was not?"

"Certainly not," I replied.

"And you mean by the happy, those who are the possessors of things good or fair?"

"Yes."

"And you admitted that Love, because he was in want, desires those good and fair things of which he is in want?"

"Yes, I did."

"But how can he be a god who has no portion in what is either good or fair?"

"Impossible."

"Then you see that you also deny the divinity of Love."

"Then what is Love?" I asked. "Is he mortal?"

"No."

"What then?"

"As in the former instance, he is neither mortal nor immortal, but in a mean between the two."

"What is he, Diotima?"

"He is a great spirit, and like all spirits he is intermediate between the divine and the mortal."

"And what," I said, "is his power?"

"He interprets," she replied, "between gods and men, conveying and taking across to the gods the prayers and sacrifices of men, and to men the commands and replies of the gods; he is the mediator who spans the chasm which divides them, and therefore in him all is bound together, and through him the arts of the prophet and the priest, their sacrifices and mysteries and charms, and all prophecy and incantation, find their way. For gods do not mingle with humanity, but through Love all the intercourse and discourse between the gods and humanity, whether awake or asleep, is carried on. The wisdom which understands this is spiritual. All other wisdom, such as that of arts and handicrafts, is mean and vulgar. Now these spirits or intermediate powers are many and diverse, and one of them is Love."

"And who," I said, "was his father, and who his mother?"

"The tale," she said, "will take time. Nevertheless, I will tell you. On the birthday of Aphrodite there was a feast of the gods, at which the god Poros or Plenty, who is the son of Metis, or Discretion, was one of the guests. When the feast was over, Penia, or Poverty, as the manner is on such occasions, lingered at the doors to beg. Now Plenty, who was the worse for nectar (there was no wine in those days), went into the garden of Zeus and fell into a heavy sleep; and Poverty considering her own straitened circumstances, plotted to have a child by him, and accordingly she lay down at his side and conceived Love, who partly because he is naturally a lover of the beautiful, and because Aphrodite is herself beautiful, and also because he was born on her birthday, is her follower and attendant. And as his parentage is, so also are his fortunes. In the first place he is always poor, and anything but tender and fair, as the many imagine him. He is rough and squalid, and has no shoes, nor a house in which to dwell. Exposed on the bare earth, he lies under the open heaven, in the streets, or at the doors of houses, taking his rest and, like his mother, he is always in distress. Like his father too, whom he also partly resembles, he is always plotting against the fair and good. He is bold, enterprising, strong, a mighty hunter, always weaving some intrigue or other, keen in the pursuit of wisdom, fertile in resources, a philosopher at all times, terrible as an enchanter, sorcerer, sophist. He is by nature neither mortal nor immortal, but alive and flourishing at one moment when he is in plenty, and dead at another moment, and again alive by reason of his father's nature. But that which is always flowing in is always flowing out, and so he is never in want and never in wealth. Further, he is in a mean between ignorance and knowledge. The truth of the matter is this: no god is a philosopher or seeker after wisdom, for he is wise already, nor does any man who is wise seek after wisdom. Neither do the ignorant seek after wisdom. For herein is the evil of ignorance, that he who is neither good nor wise is nevertheless satisfied with himself: he has no desire for that of which he feels no want."

"But who then, Diotima," I said, "are the lovers of wisdom, if they are neither the wise nor the foolish?"

"A child may answer that question," she replied. "They are those who are in a mean between the two; Love is one of them. For wisdom is a most beautiful thing, and Love is of the beautiful and therefore Love is also a philosopher or lover of wisdom, and being a lover of wisdom is in a mean between the wise and the ignorant. And of this too his birth is the cause, for his father is wealthy and wise, and his mother poor and foolish. Such, my dear Socrates, is the nature of the spirit Love. The error in your conception of him was very natural, and as I imagine from what you say, has arisen out of a confusion of love and the beloved, which made you think that love was all beautiful. For the beloved is the truly beautiful, and delicate, and perfect, and blessed; but the principle of love is of another nature, and is such as I have described."

I said, "Madam,[25] you are right. But, assuming Love to be such as you say, what is the use of him to humanity?"

"That, Socrates," she replied, "I will attempt to unfold. I have already spoken of his nature and birth. You acknowledge that love is of the beautiful. But someone will say, 'Of the beautiful in what, Socrates and Diotima?' Or rather let me put the question more clearly, and ask: When a man loves the beautiful, what does he desire?"

I answered her, "That the beautiful may be his."

"Still," she said, "the answer suggests a further question: What is given by the possession of beauty?"

"To what you have asked," I replied, "I have no answer ready."

"Then," she said, "let me put the word 'good' in the place of the beautiful, and repeat the question once more: If he who loves loves the good, what is it then that he loves?"

"The possession of the good," I said.

"And what does he gain who possesses the good?"

"Happiness," I replied. "There is less difficulty in answering that question."

"Yes," she said, "the happy are made happy by the acquisition of good things. Nor is there any need to ask why a man desires happiness; the answer is already final."

"You are right," I said.

"And is this wish and this desire common to all? And do all people always desire their own good, or only some? What do you say?"

"All men," I replied. "The desire is common to all."

"Why, then," she rejoined, "are not all people, Socrates, said to love, but only some of them? Whereas you say that all people are always loving the same things."

"I myself wonder," I said, "why this is."

"There is nothing to wonder at," she replied. "The reason is that one part of love is separated off and receives the name of the whole, but the other parts have other names."

"Give an illustration," I said.

She answered me as follows: "There is poetry, which, as you know, is complex and manifold. All cre-

---

25  Socrates uses a term which indicates that Mantinea is a stranger or foreigner.

ation or passage of non-being into being is poetry or making, and the processes of all art are creative; and the masters of arts are all poets or makers."

"Very true."

"Still," she said, "you know that they are not called poets, but have other names; only that portion of the art which is separated off from the rest, and is concerned with music and meter, is termed poetry, and they who possess poetry in this sense of the word are called poets."

"Very true," I said.

"And the same holds of love. For you may say generally that all desire of good and happiness is only the great and subtle power of love; but they who are drawn towards him by any other path, whether the path of money-making or gymnastics or philosophy, are not called lovers. The name of the whole is appropriated to those whose affection takes one form only; they alone are said to love, or to be lovers."

"I dare say," I replied, "that you are right."

"Yes," she added, "and you hear people say that lovers are seeking for their other half. But I say that they are seeking neither for the half of themselves, nor for the whole, unless the half or the whole be also a good. And they will cut off their own hands and feet and cast them away, if they are evil, for they do not love what is their own, unless perchance there be someone who calls what belongs to him the good, and what belongs to another the evil. For there is nothing which people love but the good. Is this not correct?"

"Certainly."

"Then," she said, "the simple truth is, that people love the good."

"Yes," I said.

"To which must be added that they love the possession of the good?"

"Yes, that must be added."

"And not only the possession, but the everlasting possession of the good?"

"That must be added too."

"Then love," she said, "may be described generally as the love of the everlasting possession of the good?"

"That is most true."

"Then if this be the nature of love, can you tell me further," she said, "what is the manner of the pursuit? What are they doing who show all this eagerness and heat which is called power of love? And what is the object which they have in view? Answer me."

"No, Diotima," I replied, "if I had known, I would not have wondered at your wisdom, neither would I have come to learn from you about this very matter."

"Well," she said, "I will teach you. The object which they have in view is birth in beauty, whether of body or soul."

"I do not understand you," I said. "The oracle requires an explanation."[26]

"I will make my meaning clearer," she replied. "I mean to say that all people are pregnant in their bodies and in their souls. There is a certain age at which human nature desires procreation, which must be in beauty and not in deformity, and this procreation is the union of man and woman, and is a divine thing, for conception and generation are an immortal principle in the mortal creature, and in the inharmonious they can never be. But the deformed is always inharmonious with the divine, and the beautiful harmonious. Beauty, then, is the destiny or goddess of parturition who presides at birth, and therefore, when approaching beauty, the conceiving power is propitious, and diffusive, and benign, and begets and bears fruit. At the sight of ugliness she frowns and contracts and has a sense of pain, and turns away, and shrivels up, and not without a pang refrains from conception. And this is the reason why, when the hour of conception arrives, and the teeming nature is full, there is such a flutter and ecstasy about beauty whose approach is the alleviation of the pain of childbirth. For love, Socrates, is not, as you imagine, the love of the beautiful only."

"What then?"

"The love of generation and of birth in beauty."

"Yes," I said.

"Yes, indeed," she replied.

"But why of generation?"

"Because to the mortal creature, generation is a sort of eternity and immortality," she replied. "And if, as

---

26  The prophecies of Greek oracles were notoriously cryptic.

has been already admitted, love is of the everlasting possession of the good, all men will necessarily desire immortality together with good. Wherefore, love is of immortality."

All this she taught me at various times when she spoke of love. And I remember her once saying to me, "What is the cause, Socrates, of love, and the attendant desire? Do you not see how all animals, birds, as well as beasts, in their desire of procreation, are in agony when they are infected by love, which begins with the desire of union? To which is added the care of offspring, on whose behalf the weakest are ready to battle against the strongest even to the uttermost, and to die for them, and will let themselves be tormented with hunger or suffer anything in order to maintain their young. Humanity may be supposed to act thus from reason, but why should animals have these passionate feelings? Can you tell me why?" Again, I replied that I did not know.

She said to me, "And do you expect ever to become a master in the art of love, if you do not know this?"

"But I have told you already, Diotima, that my ignorance is the reason why I come to you; for I am conscious that I need a teacher. Tell me then the cause of this and of the other mysteries of love."

"Do not marvel," she said, "if you believe that love is of the immortal, as we have several times acknowledged, for here again, and on the same principle too, the mortal nature is seeking as far as is possible to be everlasting and immortal. This is only to be attained by generation, because generation always leaves behind a new existence in the place of the old. Nay, even in the life of the same individual there is succession and not absolute unity: a man is called the same, and yet in the short interval which elapses between youth and age, and in which every animal is said to have life and identity, he is undergoing a perpetual process of loss and repair—hair, flesh, bones, blood, and the whole body are always changing. This is true not only of the body, but also of the soul, whose habits, tempers, opinions, desires, pleasures, pains, fears, never remain the same in any one of us, but are always

coming and going. This is equally true of knowledge, and what is still more surprising to us mortals, not only do the sciences in general spring up and decay, so that in respect of them we are never the same, but each of them individually experiences a like change. For what is implied in the word 'recollection,' but the departure of knowledge, which is ever being forgotten, and is renewed and preserved by recollection, and appears to be the same although in reality new, according to that law of succession by which all mortal things are preserved, not absolutely the same, but by substitution, the old worn-out mortality leaving another new and similar existence behind, unlike the divine, which is always the same and not another? And in this way, Socrates, the mortal body, or mortal anything, partakes of immortality, but the immortal in another way. Do not marvel, then, at the love which all men have of their offspring, for that universal love and interest is for the sake of immortality."

I was astonished at her words, and said, "Is this really true, O wise Diotima?"

And she answered with all the authority of an accomplished sophist, "Of that, Socrates, you may be assured. Think only of the ambition of human beings, and you will wonder at the senselessness of their ways, unless you consider how they are stirred by the love of an immortal fame. They are ready to run all risks greater by far than they would have run for their children, and to spend money and undergo any sort of toil, and even to die, for the sake of leaving behind them a name which shall be eternal. Do you imagine that Alcestis would have died to save Admetus, or Achilles to avenge Patroclus, or your own Codrus[27] in order to preserve the kingdom for his sons, if they had not imagined that the memory of their virtues, which still survives among us, would be immortal?"

"No," she said, "I am persuaded that all people do all things, and the better they are the more they do them, in hope of the glorious fame of immortal virtue, for they desire the immortal."

"Those who are pregnant in the body only, betake themselves to women and beget children—this is the

---

27  Codrus was a legendary king of Athens. When Athens was under attack, an oracle predicted that the side whose king died in battle would win. In an effort to make Athens's victory certain, Codrus went into battle in disguise in order to meet his death, which he did.

character of their love. Their offspring, as they hope, will preserve their memory and give them the blessedness and immortality which they desire in the future. But souls which are pregnant—for there certainly are those who are more creative in their souls than in their bodies—conceive that which is proper for the soul to conceive or contain. And what are these conceptions? Wisdom and virtue in general. And such creators are poets and all artists who deserve the name inventor. But the greatest and fairest sort of wisdom by far is that which is concerned with the ordering of states and families, and which is called temperance and justice. And whoever in youth has the seed of these implanted in oneself and is inspired, when that one comes to maturity desires to beget and generate. That one wanders about seeking beauty in order beget offspring—for in deformity one will beget nothing—and naturally embraces the beautiful rather than the deformed body. Above all, when such a one finds a fair and noble and well-nurtured soul, that one embraces the two in one person, and to such a one he is full of speech about virtue and the nature and pursuits of a good man, and he tries to educate him, and at the touch of the beautiful which is ever present to his memory, even when absent, he brings forth what he had conceived long before, and in company with him tends what he brings forth. They are married by a far nearer tie and have a closer friendship than those who beget mortal children, for the children who are their common offspring are fairer and more immortal. Who, thinking of Homer and Hesiod and other great poets, would not rather have their children than ordinary human ones? Who would not emulate them in the creation of children such as theirs, which have preserved their memory and given them everlasting glory? Or who would not have such children as Lycurgus[28] left behind him to be the saviors, not only of Lacedaemon, but of Greece, as one may say? There is Solon,[29] too, who is the revered father of Athenian laws, and many others there are in many other places, both among Greeks and barbarians, who have given to the world many noble works, and have been the parents of virtue of every kind. Many temples have been raised in their honor for the sake of children such as theirs, which were never raised in honor of anyone for the sake of his mortal children.

"These are the lesser mysteries of love, into which even you, Socrates, may enter. I do not know whether you will be able to attain to the greater and more hidden ones which are the crown of these, and to which, if you pursue them in a right spirit, they will lead. But I will do my utmost to inform you, and you follow if you can. For he who would proceed aright in this matter should begin in youth to visit beautiful bodies. And first, if he is correctly guided by his instructor, to love one such body only—out of that he should create fair thoughts. Soon he will of himself perceive that the beauty of one body is akin to the beauty of another. Then if beauty of body in general is his pursuit, how foolish would he be not to recognize that the beauty in every body is one and the same! And when he perceives this he will abate his violent love of the one, which he will despise and deem a small thing, and will become a lover of all beautiful bodies. In the next stage he will consider that the beauty of the mind is more honorable than the beauty of the outward body. So that if a virtuous soul has but a little comeliness, he will be content to love and tend him, and will search out and bring to the birth thoughts which may improve the young, until he is compelled to contemplate and see the beauty of institutions and laws, and to understand that the beauty of them all is of one family, and that personal beauty is a trifle. After laws and institutions he will go on to the sciences, that he may see their beauty, being not like a servant in love with the beauty of one youth or man or institution, himself a mean and narrow-minded slave, but drawing towards and contemplating the vast sea of beauty, he will create many fair and noble thoughts and notions in boundless love of wisdom, until on that shore he grows and waxes strong, and at last the vision is revealed to him of a single science, which is the science of beauty everywhere. To this I will proceed. Please give me your very best attention.

---

28  Lycurgus, held to have been the founder of the constitution of Sparta, or Lacedaemon.
29  Solon (c. 638-559 BC) reshaped Athens's constitution.

"He who has been instructed thus far in the things of love, and who has learned to see the beautiful in due order and succession, when he comes toward the end will suddenly perceive a nature of wondrous beauty (and this, Socrates, is the final cause of all our former labors)—a nature which in the first place is everlasting, not growing and decaying, or waxing and waning; secondly, not fair in one way and foul in another, or at one time or in one relation to one thing or at one place fair, at another time or in relation to another thing or at another place foul, as if fair to some and foul to others, or in the likeness of a face or hands or any other part of the bodily frame, or in any form of speech or knowledge, or existing in any other being, as for example, in an animal; or in heaven, or in earth, or in any other place; but beauty absolute, separate, simple, and everlasting, which without diminution and without increase, or any change, is imparted to the ever- growing and perishing beauties of all other things. He who from these beautiful boys ascending under the influence of true love, begins to perceive that beauty, is not far from the end. And the true order of going, or being led by another, to the things of love, is to begin from the beauties of earth and mount upwards for the sake of that other beauty, using these as steps only, and going from one on to two, and from two to all fair bodies, and from fair bodies to fair practices, and from fair practices to fair notions, until from fair notions he arrives at the notion of absolute beauty, and at last knows what the essence of beauty is. This, my dear Socrates," said the stranger from Mantinea, "is that life above all others which people should live, in the contemplation of absolute beauty, a beauty which if you once beheld it, you would not think to be after the measure of gold, and garments, and fair boys and youths, whose presence now entrances you. You and many a one would be content to live seeing them only and conversing with them without meat or drink, if that were possible—you only want to look at them and to be with them. But what if man had eyes to see the true beauty—the divine beauty, I mean, pure and clear and unalloyed, not clogged with the pollutions of mortality and all the colors and vanities of human life, looking at that, and holding converse with the true beauty, simple and divine? Remember how in that communion only, beholding beauty with the eye of the mind, he will be enabled to bring forth, not images of beauty, but realities (for he does not grasp an image but a reality), and bringing forth and nourishing true virtue to become dear to the gods and be immortal, if mortal man may. Would that be an ignoble life?"

Such, Phaedrus—and I speak not only to you, but to all of you—were the words of Diotima, and I am persuaded of their truth. And being persuaded of them, I try to persuade others that, in the attainment of this end, human nature will not easily find a helper better than love. And therefore, also, I say that every man ought to honor him as I myself honor him, and walk in his ways, and exhort others to do the same, and praise the power and spirit of love according to the measure of my ability now and ever. The words which I have spoken, you, Phaedrus, may call an encomium of love, or anything else which you please.

*When Socrates had finished speaking, the company applauded, and Aristophanes was beginning to say something in answer to the allusion which Socrates had made to his own speech, when suddenly there was a great knocking at the door of the house, as of revelers, and the sound of a flute-girl was heard. Agathon told the attendants to go and see who the intruders were. "If they are friends of ours," he said, "invite them in, but if not, say that the drinking is over."*

*A little while afterwards they heard the voice of Alcibiades[30] resounding in the court. He was in a great state of intoxication, and kept roaring and shouting, "Where is Agathon? Lead me to Agathon," and at length, supported by the flute-girl and some of his attendants, he found his way to them. "Hail, friends," he said, appearing at the door crowned with a massive garland of ivy and violets, his head flowing with ribbons. "Will you have a very drunken man as a companion of your revels? Or shall I crown Agathon, which was my intention in coming, and go away? For I was unable to come yesterday, and therefore I am here today,*

---

30  A leading Athenian politician, Alcibiades was known for his good looks and high living. He eventually betrayed Athens to Sparta in the Peloponnesian War.

*wearing these ribbons, that taking them from my own head, I may crown the head of this fairest and wisest of men, as I may be allowed to call him. Will you laugh at me because I am drunk? Yet I know very well that I am speaking the truth, although you may laugh. But first tell me: if I come in shall we have the understanding of which I spoke? Will you drink with me or not?"*

*The company was vociferous in begging that he would take his place among them, and Agathon specially invited him. Thereupon he was led in by the people who were with him. As he was being led, intending to crown Agathon, he took the ribbons from his own head and held them in front of his eyes. He was thus prevented from seeing Socrates, who made way for him, and Alcibiades took the vacant place between Agathon and Socrates, and in taking the vacant place he embraced Agathon and crowned him.*

*"Take off his sandals," said Agathon, "and let him make a third on the same couch."*

*"By all means; but who makes the third partner in our revels?" said Alcibiades, turning around and starting up as he caught sight of Socrates. "By Heracles," he said, "what is this? Here is Socrates always lying in wait for me, and always, as his way is, coming out at all sorts of unsuspected places. Now, what have you to say for yourself, and why are you lying here, where I perceive that you have contrived to find a place, not by a joker or lover of jokes, like Aristophanes, but by the fairest of the company?"*

*Socrates turned to Agathon and said, "I must ask you to protect me, Agathon, for the passion of this man has grown quite a serious matter to me. Since I became his admirer I have never been allowed to speak to any other fair one, or so much as to look at one. If I do, he goes wild with envy and jealousy, and not only abuses me but can hardly keep his hands off me, and at this moment he may do me some harm. Please either reconcile me to him, or, if he attempts violence, protect me, as I am in bodily fear of his mad and passionate attempts."*

*"There can never be reconciliation between you and me," said Alcibiades, "but for the present I will defer your chastisement. And I must beg you, Agathon, to give me back some of the ribbons that I may crown the marvelous head of this universal despot—I would not have him complain about me for crowning you, and neglecting him, who*

*in conversation is the conqueror of all mankind, and this not only once, as you were the day before yesterday, but always." Whereupon, taking some of the ribbons, he crowned Socrates, and again reclined.*

*Then Alcibiades said, "You seem, my friends, to be sober, which is a thing not to be endured. You must drink—for that was the agreement under which I was admitted—and I elect myself master of the feast until you are well drunk. Let us have a large goblet, Agathon, or rather," he said, addressing the attendant, "bring me that wine-cooler." The wine-cooler which had caught his eye was a vessel holding more than two quarts—this he filled and emptied, and ordered the servant to fill it again for Socrates. "Observe, my friends," said Alcibiades, "that this ingenious trick of mine will have no effect on Socrates, for he can drink any quantity of wine and not be at all nearer being drunk." Socrates drank the cup which the attendant filled for him.*

*Eryximachus said, "What is this, Alcibiades? Are we to have neither conversation nor singing over our cups, but simply drink as if we were thirsty?"*

*Alcibiades replied, "Hail, worthy son of a most wise and worthy sire!"*

*"The same to you," said Eryximachus, "but what shall we do?"*

*"That I leave to you," said Alcibiades. "'The wise physician skilled our wounds to heal'[31] shall prescribe and we will obey. What do you want?"*

*"Well," said Eryximachus, "before you appeared we had passed a resolution that each one of us in turn would make a speech in praise of love, and as good a one as he could. The turn was passed around from left to right; and as all of us have spoken, and you have not spoken, and although you have drunk a lot, you ought to speak, and then impose upon Socrates any task which you please, and he on his right-hand neighbor, and so on."*

*"That is good, Eryximachus," said Alcibiades. "Yet the comparison of a drunken man's speech with those of sober men is hardly fair, and I would like to know, sweet friend, whether you really believe what Socrates was just now saying. For I can assure you that the very reverse is the fact, and that if I praise anyone but himself in his presence, whether god or man, he will hardly keep his hands off me."*

*"For shame," said Socrates.*

---

31  Quoting Homer, the *Iliad*.

*"Hold your tongue," said Alcibiades, "for by Poseidon, there is no one else whom I will praise when you are of the company."*

*"Well then," said Eryximachus, "if you like, praise Socrates."*

*"What do you think, Eryximachus?" said Alcibiades. "Shall I attack him and inflict the punishment before you all?"*

*"What are you about?" said Socrates. "Are you going to raise a laugh at my expense? Is that the meaning of your praise?"*

*"I am going to speak the truth, if you will permit me."*

*"I not only permit, but exhort you to speak the truth."*

[Alcibiades's speech]

Then I will begin at once, and if I say anything which is not true, you may interrupt me if you will, and say "that is a lie," though my intention is to speak the truth. But you must not wonder if I speak any how as things come into my mind. For the fluent and orderly enumeration of all your singularities is not a task which is easy to a man in my condition.

And now, men, I shall praise Socrates in a figure which will appear to him to be a caricature, and yet I speak, not to make fun of him, but only for the truth's sake. I say that he is exactly like the busts of Silenus, which are set up in the statuaries' shops, holding pipes and flutes in their mouths. They are made to open in the middle, and have images of gods inside them, I say also that he is like Marsyas the satyr.[32] You yourself will not deny, Socrates, that your face is like that of a satyr. Yes, and there is a resemblance in other ways too. For example, you are a bully, as I can prove by witnesses, if you will not confess. And are you not a flute player? That you are, and a performer far more wonderful than Marsyas. He indeed with instruments used to charm the souls of men by the power of his breath, and the players of his music do so still, for the melodies of Olympus[33] are derived from Marsyas who taught them, and these, whether they are played by a great master or by a miserable flute-girl, have a power which no others have. They alone possess the soul and reveal the wants of those who have need of gods and mysteries, because they are divine. But you produce the same effect with your words only, and do not require the flute: that is the difference between you and him. When we hear any other speaker, even a very good one, he produces absolutely no effect upon us, or not much, whereas the mere fragments of you and your words, even at second-hand, and however imperfectly repeated, amaze and possess the souls of every man, woman, and child who comes within hearing of them. And if I were not afraid that you would think me hopelessly drunk, I would have sworn as well as spoken to the influence which they have always had and still have over me. For my heart leaps within me more than that of any Corybantian reveler,[34] and my eyes rain tears when I hear them. And I observe that many others are affected in the same manner. I have heard Pericles[35] and other great orators, and I thought that they spoke well, but I never had any similar feeling. My soul was not stirred by them, nor was I angry at the thought of my own slavish state. But this Marsyas has often brought me to such a pass that I have felt as if I could hardly endure the life which I am leading (this, Socrates, you will admit); and I am conscious that if I did not shut my ears against him, and fly as from the voice of the siren, my fate would be like that of others—he would transfix me, and I would grow old sitting at his feet. For he makes me confess that I ought not to live as I do, neglecting the wants of my own soul, and busying myself with the concerns of the Athenians. Therefore I hold my ears and tear myself away from him.

He is the only person who ever made me ashamed, which you might think not to be in my nature, and there is no one else who does the same. For I know that I cannot answer him or say that I ought not to do as he bids, but when I leave his presence, the love of popularity gets the better of me. And therefore I run away and fly from him, and when I see him I am

---

32 Satyrs were mythical creatures, part goat, part human being, driven by animal desires, especially sexual ones. Marsyas competed with Apollo in music.

33 A mythical musician loved by Marsyas.

34 The Corybants were mythical worshippers of Cybele; they went wild through music.

35 A leading Athenian politician (fifth century BC).

ashamed of what I have confessed to him. Many a time have I wished that he were dead, and yet I know that I would be much more sorry than glad if he were to die, so that I am at my wit's end. And this is what I and many others have suffered from the flute playing of this satyr. Yet hear me once more while I show you how exact the image is, and how marvelous is his power. For let me tell you: none of you knows him, but I will reveal him to you. Having begun, I must go on. See how he is amorously affected by the beautiful? He is always with them and is always being smitten by them, and then again he knows nothing and is ignorant of all things—such is the appearance which he puts on. Is he not like a Silenus in this? To be sure he is. His outer mask is the carved head of the Silenus. But, O my companions in drink, when he is opened, what temperance there is residing within! You should know that beauty and wealth and honor, at which the many wonder, are of no account with him, and are utterly despised by him. He does not at all regard the persons who are gifted with them; mankind is nothing to him; all his life is spent in mocking and flouting at them. But when I opened him, and looked within at his serious purpose, I saw in him divine and golden images of such fascinating beauty that I was ready to do in a moment whatever Socrates commanded; they may have escaped the observation of others, but I saw them. Now I fancied that he was seriously enamored of my beauty, and I thought that I would therefore have a grand opportunity of hearing him tell what he knew, for I had a wonderful opinion of the attractions of my youth. In execution of this design, when I next went to him, I sent away the attendant who usually accompanied me (I will confess the whole truth, and beg you to listen; and if I speak falsely, you, Socrates, expose the falsehood). Well, he and I were alone together, and I thought that when there was nobody with us, I would hear him speak the language which lovers use to their loves when they are by themselves, and I was delighted. Nothing of the sort. He conversed as usual, and spent the day with me and then went away.

Afterwards I challenged him to the *palaestra*,[36] and he wrestled and closed with me several times when there was no one present. I fancied that I might succeed in this manner. Not a bit. I got nowhere with him. Lastly, as I had failed hitherto, I thought that I must take stronger measures and attack him boldly, and, as I had begun, not give him up, but see how matters stood between him and me. So I invited him to dine with me, just as if he were a fair youth, and I a designing lover. He was not easily persuaded to come. He did, however, after a while accept the invitation, and when he came the first time, he wanted to go away at once as soon as dinner was over, and I did not have the courage to detain him. The second time, still in pursuance of my design, after we had eaten, I went on conversing far into the night, and when he wanted to go away, I pretended that the hour was late and that he had much better remain. So he lay down on the couch next to me, the same on which he had eaten, and there was no one but ourselves there.

All this may be told without shame to anyone. But what follows I could hardly tell you if I were sober. Yet, as the proverb says, "There's truth in wine," whether with boys or without them, and therefore I must speak. Nor, again, would I be justified in concealing the lofty actions of Socrates when I come to praise him. Moreover I have felt the serpent's sting. He who has suffered, as they say, is willing to tell his fellow-sufferers only, as they alone will be likely to understand him, and will not be extreme in judging of the sayings or doings which have been wrung from his agony. For I have been bitten by a more than viper's tooth; I have known in my soul, or in my heart, or in some other part, that worst of pangs, more violent in ingenuous youth than any serpent's tooth, the pang of philosophy, which will make a man say or do anything. And you whom I see around me, Phaedrus and Agathon and Eryximachus and Pausanias and Aristodemus and Aristophanes, all of you, and I need not say Socrates himself, have had experience of the same madness and passion in your longing after wisdom. Therefore listen and excuse my doings then and my sayings now. But let the house slaves and other profane and unmannered persons close up the doors of their ears.

36   I.e., gymnasium.

When the lamp was put out and the servants had gone away, I thought that I must be plain with him and have no more ambiguity. So I gave him a shake, and I said, "Socrates, are you asleep?"

"No," he said.

"Do you know what I have been thinking?"

"What have you been thinking?" he said.

"I think," I replied, "that of all the lovers whom I have ever had you are the only one who is worthy of me, and you appear to be too modest to speak. Now I feel that I would be a fool to refuse you this or any other favor and therefore I come to lay at your feet all that I have and all that my friends have, in the hope that you will assist me in the way of virtue, which I desire above all things, and in which I believe that you can help me better than anyone else. And I would certainly have more reason to be ashamed of what wise men would say if I were to refuse a favor to such as you, than of what the world, who are mostly fools, would say of me if I granted it."

To these words he replied in the ironic manner which is so characteristic of him, "Alcibiades, my friend, you have indeed an elevated aim if what you say is true, and if there really is in me any power by which you may become better. Truly you must see in me some rare beauty of a kind infinitely higher than any which I see in you. And therefore, if you mean to share with me and to exchange beauty for beauty, you will have greatly the advantage of me. You will gain true beauty in return for appearance—like 'gold in exchange for bronze.'[37] But look again, sweet friend, and see whether you are not deceived in me. The mind begins to grow critical when the bodily eye fails, and it will be a long time before you get old."

Hearing this, I said, "I have told you my purpose, which is quite serious. Consider what you think best for you and me."

"That is good," he said. "At some other time then we will consider and act as seems best about this and about other matters."

Whereupon, I fancied that he was smitten, and that the words which I had uttered had, like arrows, wounded him, and so without waiting to hear more I got up, and throwing my mantle about him, crept under his threadbare cloak, as the time of year was winter, and there I lay during the whole night having this wonderful monster in my arms. This again, Socrates, will not be denied by you. And yet, notwithstanding all, he was so superior to my solicitations, so contemptuous and derisive and disdainful of my beauty, which really, as I fancied, had some attractions—hear, O judges, for judges you shall be of the haughty virtue of Socrates—nothing more happened, but in the morning when I awoke (let all the gods and goddesses be my witnesses) I arose as from the couch of a father or an elder brother.

What do you suppose must have been my feelings, after this rejection, at the thought of my own dishonor? And yet I could not help wondering at his natural temperance and self-restraint and manliness. I never imagined that I could have met with a man such as he is in wisdom and endurance. And therefore I could not be angry with him or renounce his company, any more than I could hope to win him. For I well knew that if Ajax could not be wounded by steel,[38] much less he by money, and my only chance of captivating him by my personal attractions had failed. So I was at my wit's end. No one was ever more hopelessly enslaved by another.

All this happened before he and I went on the expedition to Potidaea.[39] There we messed together, and I had the opportunity of observing his extraordinary power of sustaining fatigue. His endurance was simply marvelous when, being cut off from our supplies, we were compelled to go without food. On such occasions, which often happen in time of war, he was superior not only to me but to everybody. There was no one to be compared to him. Yet at a festival he was the only person who had any real powers of enjoyment. Though not willing to drink, he could, if compelled, beat us all at that. Wonderful to tell, no human being has ever seen Socrates drunk. His powers, if I am not mistaken, will be tested before long. His fortitude in enduring cold was also surprising. There was

---

37  A reference to an episode in the *Iliad* in which, unthinkingly, a warrior exchanges gold armor for bronze.

38  Ajax, one of the finest Greek warriors of the *Iliad*, had a shield which protected him from the enemy's weapons.

39  To put down a rebellion against Athenian control in 432 BC.

a severe frost, for the winter in that region is really tremendous, and everybody else either remained indoors, or if they went out had on an amazing quantity of clothes, and were well shod, and had their feet swathed in felt and fleeces. In the midst of this, Socrates with his bare feet on the ice and in his ordinary dress marched better than the other soldiers who had shoes, and they looked daggers at him because he seemed to despise them.

I have told you one tale, and now I must tell you another, which is worth hearing, "Of the doings and sufferings of the enduring man,"[40] while he was on the expedition. One morning he was thinking about something which he could not resolve. He would not give it up, but continued thinking from early dawn until noon. There he stood fixed in thought, and at noon attention was drawn to him, and the rumor ran through the wondering crowd that Socrates had been standing and thinking about something ever since the break of day. At last, in the evening after supper, some Ionians out of curiosity (I should explain that this was not in winter but in summer), brought out their mats and slept in the open air so they might watch him and see whether he would stand all night. There he stood until the following morning. With the return of light he offered up a prayer to the sun, and went his way. I will also tell, if you please—and indeed I am bound to tell—of his courage in battle, for who but he saved my life? Now this was the engagement in which I received the prize of valor, for I was wounded and he would not leave me, but he rescued me and my arms. He ought to have received the prize of valor which the generals wanted to confer on me partly on account of my rank, and I told them so (this, again, Socrates will not impeach or deny), but he was more eager than the generals that I and not he should have the prize. There was another occasion on which his behavior was very remarkable—in the flight of the army after the battle of Delium,[41] where he served among the heavy-armed. I had a better opportunity of seeing him than at Potidaea, for I was myself on horseback, and there-

fore comparatively out of danger. He and Laches were retreating, for the troops were in flight, and I met them and told them not to be discouraged, and promised to remain with them. There you might see him, Aristophanes, as you describe, just as he is in the streets of Athens, stalking like a pelican, and rolling his eyes, calmly contemplating enemies as well as friends, and making very intelligible to anybody, even from a distance, that whoever attacked him would be likely to meet with a stout resistance and in this way he and his companion escaped, for this is the sort of man who is never touched in war. Only those who are running away headlong are pursued. I particularly observed how superior he was to Laches in presence of mind. Many are the marvels which I might narrate in praise of Socrates. Most of his ways might perhaps be paralleled in another man, but his absolute unlikeness to any human being that is or ever has been is perfectly astonishing. You may imagine Brasidas[42] and others to have been like Achilles; or you may imagine Nestor and Antenor[43] to have been like Pericles. The same may be said of other famous men, but of this strange being you will never be able to find any likeness, however remote, either among men who now are or who ever have been, other than that which I have already suggested of Silenus and the satyrs; and they represent in a figure not only himself, but his words. For, although I forgot to mention this to you before, his words are like the images of Silenus which open. They are ridiculous when you first hear them. He clothes himself in language that is like the skin of the wanton satyr—for his talk is of pack-asses and smiths and cobblers and tanners, and he is always repeating the same things in the same words, so that any ignorant or inexperienced person might feel disposed to laugh at him. But he who opens the bust and sees what is within will find that they are the only words which have a meaning in them, and also the most divine, abounding in fair images of virtue, and of the widest comprehension, or rather extending to the whole duty of a good and honorable man.

---

40   A line from Homer's *Odyssey* referring to Odysseus.
41   In 424 BC.
42   A Spartan commander in the Peloponnesian War.
43   Wise advisors in war who appear in the *Iliad*.

This, friends, is my praise of Socrates. I have added my blame of him for his ill-treatment of me, and he has ill-treated not only me, but Charmides the son of Glaucon, and Euthydemus the son of Diocles, and many others in the same way. Beginning as their lover, he has ended by making them pay their addresses to him. Wherefore I say to you, Agathon, do not be deceived by him. Learn from me and take warning, and do not be a fool and 'learn by experience,' as the proverb says."

*When Alcibiades had finished, there was a laugh at his outspokenness, for he seemed to be still in love with Socrates.* "You are sober, Alcibiades," said Socrates, "or you would never have done so much to hide the purpose of your satyr's praises, for this whole long story is only an ingenious circumlocution, of which the point comes in by the way at the end. You want to start a quarrel between me and Agathon, and your notion is that I ought to love you and nobody else, and that you and you only ought to love Agathon. But the plot of this Satyric or Silenic drama has been detected, and you must not allow him, Agathon, to set us at variance."

"I believe you are right," said Agathon, "and I am disposed to think that his intention in placing himself between you and me was only to divide us. But he shall gain nothing by that move, for I will go and lie on the couch next to you."

"Yes, yes," replied Socrates, "by all means come here and lie on the couch below me."

"Alas," said Alcibiades, "how I am fooled by this man. He is determined to get the better of me at every turn. I do beseech you, allow Agathon to lie between us."

"Certainly not," said Socrates. "As you praised me, and I in turn ought to praise my neighbor on the right, he will be out of order in praising me again when he ought rather to be praised by me, and I must entreat you to consent to this, and not be jealous, for I have a great desire to praise the youth."

"Hurrah!" cried Agathon, "I will rise instantly, that I may be praised by Socrates."

"The usual way," said Alcibiades. "Where Socrates is, no one else has any chance with the handsome. Now how readily has he invented a specious reason for attracting Agathon to himself."

*Agathon arose in order that he might take his place on the couch by Socrates, when suddenly a band of revelers entered, and spoiled the order of the banquet. Someone who was going out having left the door open, they had found their way in, and made themselves at home. Great confusion ensued, and everyone was compelled to drink large quantities of wine. Aristodemus said that Eryximachus, Phaedrus, and others went away. He himself fell asleep, and as the nights were long took a good rest. He was awakened towards daybreak by a crowing of cocks, and when he awoke, the others were either asleep, or had gone away. There remained only Socrates, Aristophanes, and Agathon, who were drinking out of a large goblet which they passed around, and Socrates was discoursing to them. Aristodemus was only half awake, and he did not hear the beginning of the discourse. The chief thing which he remembered was Socrates compelling the other two to acknowledge that a genius for comedy was the same as that for tragedy, and that the true artist in tragedy was an artist in comedy also. To this they were constrained to assent, being drowsy, and not quite following the argument. And first of all Aristophanes dropped off. Then, when the day was already dawning, Agathon. Socrates, having laid them to sleep, rose to depart. Aristodemus, as his manner was, followed him. At the Lyceum he took a bath, and passed the day as usual. In the evening he retired to rest at his own home.*

# 13

# PLUTARCH,
## *LIFE OF ALEXANDER THE GREAT*

Plutarch (*c.* 46-120), a Greek writer living under Roman rule in the city of Chaeronea, is best known for writing a series of *Lives of the Greeks and Romans*. The work is made up of paired biographies of Greeks and Romans, each pair designed to highlight the moral value and danger of some character trait or activity. The biography of Alexander the Great (336-323 BC) which appears below is taken from this larger work. Alexander's father, King Philip II of Macedon (359-336 BC), a kingdom to the north of Greece, had brought the city states of the Greek mainland under his rule before his death, when he had laid plans for an attack on the enormous Persian empire to the east. Aside from the occasional inscription, nothing in the way of written evidence for Alexander's career survives from Alexander's own time.

It being my purpose to write the lives of Alexander the king and of Caesar,[1] by whom Pompey was destroyed, the multitude of their great actions affords so large a field that I would be to blame if I should not by way of apology forewarn my reader that I have chosen rather to epitomize the most celebrated parts of their story than to insist at large on every particular circumstance of it. It must be borne in mind that my design is not to write histories, but lives. And the most glorious exploits do not always furnish us with the clearest discoveries of virtue or vice in men; sometimes a matter of less importance, an expression or a jest, informs us better of their characters and inclinations than do the most famous sieges, the greatest armaments, or the bloodiest battles whatsoever. Therefore, just as portrait painters are more exact in

the lines and features of the face, in which the character is seen, than in the other parts of the body, so I must be allowed to give my more particular attention to the marks and indications of the souls of men, and while I endeavor by these to portray their lives, may I be free to leave more weighty matters and great battles to be treated of by others.

It is agreed on by all hands that, on his father's side, Alexander descended from Hercules by Caranus, and from Aeacus[2] by Neoptolemus[3] on his mother's side. His father Philip, being in Samothrace, when he was quite young, fell in love there with Olympias, in company with whom he was initiated in the religious ceremonies of the country, and her father and mother being both dead, soon after, with the consent of her brother, Arymbas, he married her. The night before the

---

1  Julius Caesar (first century BC), with whom Plutarch paired his life of Alexander.
2  Son of Zeus.
3  Son of Achilles.

consummation of their marriage, she dreamed that a thunderbolt fell upon her body, which kindled a great fire, whose divided flames dispersed themselves all around, and then were extinguished. And Philip, some time after he was married, dreamed that he sealed up his wife's body with a seal, whose impression, as he fancied, was the figure of a lion. Some of the diviners interpreted this as a warning to Philip to watch his wife closely; but Aristander of Telmessus, considering how unusual it was to seal up anything that was empty, assured him the meaning of his dream was that the queen was with a boy child, who would one day prove as stout and courageous as a lion. Once, moreover, a serpent was found lying by Olympias as she slept, which more than anything else, it is said, abated Philip's passion for her. Whether he feared her as an enchantress, or thought she was the partner of some god, and so looked on himself as excluded, he was ever after less fond of sleeping with her. Others say that the women of this country having always been extremely addicted to the enthusiastic Orphic rites, and the wild worship of Dionysius[4] (upon which account they were called Clodones, and Mimallones[5]), imitated in many things the practices of the Edonian and Thracian women about Mount Haemus, from whom the word *threskeuein* seems to have been derived, as a special term for superfluous and superstitious ceremonies; and that Olympias, zealously affecting these fanatical and enthusiastic inspirations, to perform them with more barbaric dread, was accustomed in the dances proper to these ceremonies to have great tame serpents about her, which sometimes creeping out of the ivy in the mystic winnowing baskets, sometimes winding themselves around the women's wands and garlands, made a spectacle which men could not look upon without terror.

Philip, after this vision, sent Chaeron of Megalopolis to consult the oracle of Apollo at Delphi, by which he was commanded to perform sacrifice, and henceforth pay particular honor, above all other gods, to Ammon,[6] and was told he would one day lose that eye with which he presumed to peep through that chink of the door, when he saw the god, in the form of a serpent, in the company of his wife. Eratosthenes[7] says that Olympias, when she attended Alexander on his way to the army in his first expedition, told him the secret of his birth, and bade him behave himself with courage suitable to his divine extraction. Others again affirm that she wholly disclaimed any pretensions of the kind, and was accustomed to say, "When will Alexander leave off slandering me to Hera?"[8]

Alexander was born the sixth of Hecatombaeon,[9] which month the Macedonians call Lous, the same day that the temple of Artemis at Ephesus was burned, which Hegesias of Magnesia[10] makes the occasion of a conceit frigid enough to have stopped the conflagration. The temple, he says, caught fire and was burned while its mistress was absent, assisting at the birth of Alexander. And all the Eastern soothsayers who happened to be then at Ephesus, looking upon the ruin of this temple to be the forerunner of some other calamity, ran around the town, beating their faces, and crying that this day had brought forth something that would prove fatal and destructive to all Asia.

Just after Philip had taken Potidaea,[11] he received these three messages at one time: that Parmenio[12] had overthrown the Illyrians in a great battle, that his race-horse had won the course at the Olympic games, and that his wife had given birth to Alexander; with which being naturally well pleased, as an addition to his satisfaction, he was assured by the diviners that a

---

4   Both of which involved women having wild revels; Dionysius was the god of wine.
5   Macedonian names for ecstatic worshippers of Dionysius.
6   I.e., Zeus, identified with the chief Egyptian god, Ammon.
7   A scholar at Alexandria (second century BC).
8   Wife of Zeus.
9   A festival in honor of Hera.
10  A Greek historian (fourth century BC).
11  In 356 BC. The city had been in Athens's sphere of influence.
12  A general of Philip, and later of Alexander.

son whose birth was accompanied with three such successes could not fail to be invincible.

The statues that gave the best representation of Alexander's person were those of Lysippus (by whom alone he would suffer his image to be made), those peculiarities which many of his successors afterwards and his friends used to affect to imitate, the inclination of his head a little on one side towards his left shoulder, and his melting gaze, having been expressed by this artist with great exactness. But Apelles, who drew him with thunderbolts in his hand, made his complexion browner and darker than it was naturally, for he was fair and of a light color, passing into ruddiness in his face and upon his breast. Aristoxenus[13] in his *Memoirs* tells us that a most agreeable odor exhaled from his skin, and that his breath and body all over was so fragrant as to perfume the clothes which he wore next to him, the cause of which might probably be the hot and dry temperament of his body. For sweet smells, Theophrastus[14] believes, are produced by the concoction of moist humors by heat, which is the reason that those parts of the world which are driest and most burned up afford spices of the best kind and in the greatest quantity; for the heat of the sun exhausts all the superfluous moisture which lies on the surface of bodies ready to generate putrefaction. It may be that this hot constitution rendered Alexander so addicted to drinking and so choleric. His temperance as to the pleasures of the body was apparent in him in his very childhood, as he was with much difficulty incited to them, and always used them with great moderation; though in other things he was extremely eager and vehement, and in his love of glory, and the pursuit of it, he showed a solidity of high spirit and magnanimity far above his age. For he neither sought nor valued it upon every occasion, as his father Philip did (who affected to show his eloquence almost to a degree of pedantry, and took care to have the victories of his racing chariots at the Olympic games engraved on his coins), but when he was asked by some around him whether he would run a race in the Olympic

games, as he was very swift-footed, he answered, he would, if he might have kings to run with him. Indeed, he seems in general to have looked with indifference, if not with dislike, upon the whole race of athletes. He often appointed prizes, for which not only tragedians and musicians, pipers and harpers, but rhapsodists[15] also, strove to outvie one another; and delighted in all manner of hunting and in fighting with staves, but never gave any encouragement to contests either of boxing or of the pancration.[16]

While he was yet very young, he entertained ambassadors from the king of Persia, in the absence of his father, and entering into much conversation with them, gained so much upon them by his affability, and the questions he asked them, which were far from being childish or trifling (for he inquired of them the length of the ways, the nature of the road into inner Asia, the character of their king, how he carried himself to his enemies, and what forces he was able to bring into the field), that they were struck with admiration of him, and looked upon the ability so much famed of Philip to be nothing in comparison with the forwardness and high purpose that appeared thus early in his son. Whenever he heard Philip had taken any town of importance, or won any signal victory, instead of rejoicing at it altogether, he would tell his companions that his father would anticipate everything, and leave him and them no opportunities of performing great and illustrious actions. For being more bent upon action and glory than upon either pleasure or riches, he esteemed all that he would receive from his father as a diminution and prevention of his own future achievements. He would have chosen to succeed to a kingdom involved in troubles and wars, which would have afforded him frequent exercise of his courage, and a large field of honor, rather than to one already flourishing and settled, where his inheritance would be an inactive life, and the mere enjoyment of wealth and luxury.

The care of his education, as it might be presumed, was committed to a great many attendants, precep-

---

13  A Student of Aristotle.
14  Student of Plato and Aristotle.
15  Professional reciters of poetry.
16  A sporting contest in which two men fought without weapons, and without rules, except for a ban on bites and gouges.

tors, and teachers, over the whole of whom Leonidas, a near kinsman of Olympias, a man of an austere temper, presided; he did not indeed himself decline the name of what in reality is a noble and honorable office, but in general his dignity, and his near relationship, obtained for him from other people the title of Alexander's foster father and governor. But he who took upon himself the actual place and title of his tutor was Lysimachus the Acarnanian, who, though he had nothing specially to recommend him but his lucky fancy of calling himself Phoenix,[17] Alexander Achilles, and Philip Peleus,[18] was therefore well enough esteemed, and ranked in the next degree after Leonidas.

Philonicus the Thessalian brought the horse Bucephalus to Philip, offering to sell him for 13 talents; but when they went into the field to try him, they found him so very vicious and unmanageable that he reared up when they endeavored to mount him, and would not endure so much as the voice of any of Philip's attendants. Upon which, as they were leading him away as wholly useless and untractable, Alexander, who stood by, said, "What an excellent horse do they lose for want of skill and boldness to manage him!" Philip at first took no notice of what he said; but when he heard him repeat the same thing several times, and saw he was much vexed to see the horse sent away, he said, "Do you reproach those who are older than yourself, as if you knew more, and were better able to manage him than they?" "I could manage this horse," Alexander replied, "better than others do." "And if you do not," Philip said, "what will you forfeit for your rashness?" "I will pay," answered Alexander, "the whole price of the horse." At this the whole company broke out laughing. As soon as the wager was settled amongst them, he immediately ran to the horse, and taking hold of the bridle, turned him directly towards the, sun, having, it seems, observed that he was disturbed at and afraid of the motion of his own shadow; then letting him go forward a little, still keeping the reins in his hands, and stroking him gently when he found him beginning to grow eager

and fiery, he let fall his upper garment softly, and with one nimble leap securely mounted him, and when he was seated, little by little drew in the bridle, and curbed him without either striking or spurring him. Presently, when he found him free from all rebelliousness, and impatient only for the course, he let him go at full speed, inciting him now with a commanding voice, and urging him also with his heel. Philip and his friends looked on at first in silence and anxiety for the result, till seeing him make his turn in proper fashion, and come back rejoicing and in triumph about what he had performed, they all burst out into acclamations of applause. His father shedding tears, it is said, for joy, kissed him as he came down from his horse, and said, "O my son, look for a kingdom equal to and worthy of yourself, for Macedonia is too little for you."

After this, considering him to be of a temper easy to be led to his duty by reason, but by no means to be compelled, he always endeavored to persuade rather than to command or force him to anything; and now looking upon the instruction and education of his youth to be of greater difficulty and importance than to be wholly trusted to the ordinary masters in music and poetry, and the common school subjects, and to require, as Sophocles[19] says,

The bridle and the rudder too,

he sent for Aristotle, the most learned and most celebrated philosopher of his time, and rewarded him with a munificence proportionate to and becoming the care he took to instruct his son. For he repeopled Aristotle's native city Stagira, which he had caused to be demolished a little before, and restored all the citizens, who were in exile or slavery, to their habitations. As a place for the pursuit of their studies and exercise, he assigned the temple of the Nymphs, near Mieza, where, to this very day, they show you Aristotle's stone seats, and the shady walks which he was accustomed to frequent. It would appear that Alexander received from him not only his doctrines of morals

---

17　Teacher of Achilles.
18　Father of Achilles.
19　Playwright (fifth century BC).

and of politics, but also something of those more abstruse and profound theories which these philosophers, by the very names they gave them, professed to reserve for oral communication to the initiated, and did not allow many to become acquainted with. For when he was in Asia, and heard Aristotle had published some treatises of that kind, he wrote to him, using very plain language to him in behalf of philosophy, the following letter. "Alexander to Aristotle, greeting. You have not done well to publish your books of oral doctrine; for what is there now that we excel others in, if those things which we have been particularly instructed in be laid open to all? For my part, I assure you, I would rather excel others in the knowledge of what is excellent, than in the extent of my power and dominion. Farewell." And Aristotle, soothing this passion for preeminence, speaks, in his excuse for himself, of these doctrines as in fact both published and not published: as indeed, to say the truth, his books on metaphysics are written in a style which makes them useless for ordinary teaching, and instructive only in the way of aids to the memory for those who are already conversant in that sort of learning.

Doubtless also it was to Aristotle that he owed the inclination he had, not to the theory only, but likewise to the practice of the art of medicine. For when any of his friends were sick, he would often prescribe them their course of diet, and medicines proper to their disease, as we may find in his epistles. He was naturally a great lover of all kinds of learning and reading, and Onesicritus[20] informs us that he constantly laid Homer's *Iliad*, according to the copy corrected by Aristotle, called the casket copy, with his dagger under his pillow, declaring that he esteemed it a perfect portable treasure of all military virtue and knowledge. When he was in upper Asia, being destitute of other books,

he ordered Harpalus to send some, who furnished him with Philistus's *History*,[21] a great many of the plays of Euripides, Sophocles, and Aeschylus,[22] and some dithyrambic odes, composed by Telestes and Philoxenus. For a while he loved and cherished Aristotle no less, as he was wont to say himself, than if he had been his father, giving this reason for it: that as he had received life from the one, so the other had taught him to live well. But afterwards, upon some mistrust of him, yet not so great as to make him do him any harm, his familiarity and friendly kindness to him lost so much of its former force and affection as to make it evident he was alienated from him. However, his violent thirst and passion for learning, once implanted, still grew up with him, and never decayed, as appears by his veneration of Anaxarchus,[23] by the present of 50 talents which he sent to Xenocrates,[24] and his particular care and esteem of Dandamis and Calanus.

While Philip went on his expedition against the Byzantines, he left Alexander, then 16 years old, his lieutenant in Macedonia, committing the charge of his seal to him. Alexander, so as not to sit idle, reduced the rebellious Maedi, and having taken their chief town by storm, drove out the barbarous inhabitants, and planting a colony of several nations in their place, called the place after his own name, Alexandropolis.[25] At the battle of Chaeronea, which his father fought against the Greeks,[26] he is said to have been the first man that charged the Thebans' sacred band. And even in my remembrance there stood an old oak near the river Cephisus, which people called Alexander's oak because his tent was pitched under it. And not far off are to be seen the graves of the Macedonians who fell in that battle. This early bravery made Philip so fond of him that nothing pleased him more than to hear his subjects call himself their general and Alexander their king.

---

20  A contemporary of Alexander, who knew him and wrote his biography which, however, had a reputation in the ancient world for romantic exaggeration.
21  A history of Sicily (fourth century BC).
22  Three leading writers of tragedy in fifth-century BC Athens.
23  A philosopher and companion of Alexander.
24  Master of Plato's school, the Academy, in Alexander's time.
25  I.e., "Alexander city."
26  And which sealed Philip's dominance over the Greek mainland.

But the disorders of his family, chiefly caused by his new marriages and attachments (the troubles that began in the women's chambers spreading, so to speak, to the whole kingdom), raised various complaints and differences between them, which the violence of Olympias, a woman of a jealous and implacable temper, made wider by exasperating Alexander against his father. Among the rest, this accident contributed most to their falling out. At the wedding of Cleopatra, whom Philip fell in love with and married, she being much too young for him, her uncle Attalus in his cups desired that the Macedonians would implore the gods to give them a lawful successor to the kingdom by his niece. This so irritated Alexander that, throwing one of the cups at his head, he said, "You villain, what am I then, a bastard?" Then Philip, taking Attalus's part, rose up and would have run his son through; but by good fortune for them both, either his over hasty rage, or the wine he had drunk, made his foot slip, so that he fell down on the floor. At this Alexander reproachfully insulted him: "See there," he said, "the man who makes preparations to pass out of Europe into Asia, overturned in passing from one seat to another." After this debauch, he and his mother Olympias withdrew from Philip's company, and when he had placed her in Epirus, he himself retired into Illyria.

At about this time, Demaratus the Corinthian, an old friend of the family, who had the freedom to say anything among them without offense, coming to visit Philip, after the first compliments and embraces were over, Philip asked him whether the Greeks were in agreement with one another. "It ill becomes you," replied Demaratus, "to be so solicitous about Greece, when you have involved your own house in so many dissensions and calamities." He was so convinced by this seasonable reproach that he immediately recalled his son home, and by Demaratus's mediation prevailed with him to return. But this reconciliation did not last not long....

Not long after this, Pausanias,[27] having had an outrage done to him at the instance of Attalus and Cleopatra, when he found he could get no reparation at Philip's hands for his disgrace, murdered him. The guilt of which fact was laid for the most part upon Olympias, who was said to have encouraged and exasperated the enraged youth to revenge. Some sort of suspicion attached even to Alexander himself, who, it was said, when Pausanias came and complained to him of the injury he had received, repeated the verse from Euripides's *Medea*,

On husband, and on father, and on bride.[28]

However, he took care to find out and punish the accomplices of the conspiracy severely, and was very angry with Olympias for treating Cleopatra inhumanly in his absence.

Alexander was but 20 years old when his father was murdered, and succeeded to a kingdom beset on all sides with great dangers and rancorous enemies. For not only the barbarous nations that bordered on Macedonia were impatient of being governed by any but their own native princes, but Philip likewise, though he had been victorious over the Greeks, yet, as the time had not been sufficient for him to complete his conquest and accustom them to his sway, had simply left all things in a general disorder and confusion. It seemed to the Macedonians a very critical time; and some would have persuaded Alexander to give up all thought of keeping the Greeks in subjection by force of arms, and rather to apply himself to win back by gentle means the allegiance of the tribes who were planning revolt, and try the effect of indulgence in arresting the first motions towards revolution. But he rejected this counsel as weak and timorous, and looked upon it to be more prudent to secure himself by resolution and magnanimity than, by seeming to cater to anyone, to encourage all to trample over him. In pursuit of this opinion, he reduced the barbarians to tranquillity, and put an end to all fear of war from them by a rapid expedition into their country as far as the river Danube, where he defeated Syrmus, king of the Triballians, in a great battle. And hearing the Thebans[29] were in revolt,

---

27  A companion of Philip.
28  In the play Medea exacts her vengeance on her husband, the new bride for whom he left her, and on the bride's father.
29  Thebes was one of the chief cities of the Greek mainland.

and the Athenians in correspondence with them, he immediately marched through the pass of Thermopylae, saying that to Demosthenes,[30] who had called him a child while he was in lllyria and in the country of the Triballians, and a youth when he was in Thessaly, he would appear a man before the walls of Athens.

When he came to Thebes, to show how willing he was to accept their repentance for what was past, he demanded of them only Phoenix and Prothytes, the authors of the rebellion, and proclaimed a general pardon to those who would come over to him. But when the Thebans merely retorted by demanding Philotas and Antipater to be delivered into their hands, and by a proclamation on their part invited all who would assert the liberty of Greece to come over to them, he presently applied himself to make them feel the last extremities of war. The Thebans indeed defended themselves with a zeal and courage beyond their strength, being much outnumbered by their enemies. But when the Macedonian garrison sallied out upon them from the citadel, they were so hemmed in on all sides that the greater part of them fell in the battle; the city, itself being taken by storm, was sacked and razed. Alexander's hope was that so severe an example might terrify the rest of Greece into obedience and did this also in order to gratify the hostility of his confederates, the Phocians and Plataeans.[31] So that, except the priests, and some few who had heretofore been the friends and connections of the Macedonians, the family of the poet Pindar, and those who were known to have opposed the public vote for the war, all the rest, to the number of 30,000, were publicly sold as slaves; it is computed that upwards of 6,000 were put to the sword.

Among the other calamities that befell the city, it happened that some Thracian soldiers, having broken into the house of a matron of high character and repute, named Timoclea, their captain, after he had raped her, to satisfy his avarice as well as lust, asked her if she knew of any money concealed there, to which she readily answered she did and bade him follow her into a garden, where she showed him a well into which, she told him, upon the taking of the city,

she had thrown what she had of most value. The greedy Thracian presently stooping down to view the place where he thought the treasure lay, she came behind him and pushed him into the well, and then flung great stones in upon him, till she had killed him. Afterward, when the soldiers led her away bound to Alexander, her very manner and gait showed her to be a woman of dignity, and of a mind no less elevated, not betraying the least sign of fear or astonishment. And when the king asked her who she was, she said "I am the sister of Theagenes, who fought the battle of Chaeronea against your father Philip, and fell there in command for the liberty of Greece." Alexander was so surprised, both at what she had done and what she said, that he could not choose but give her and her children their freedom to go where they pleased.

After this he received the Athenians into favor, although they had shown themselves so much concerned at the calamity of Thebes that out of sorrow they omitted the celebration of the Mysteries,[32] and entertained those who escaped with all possible humanity. Whether because, like the lion, his passion was now satisfied, or, after an example of extreme cruelty, he had a mind to appear merciful, it happened well for the Athenians; for he not only forgave them all past offenses, but bade them look to their affairs with vigilance, remembering that if he should miscarry, they were likely to be the arbiters of Greece. Certain it is, too, that in later times he often repented of his severity to the Thebans, and his remorse had such influence on his temper as to make him ever after less rigorous to all others. He imputed also the murder of Cleitus, which he committed in his cups, and the unwillingness of the Macedonians to follow him against the Indians, by which his enterprise and glory were left imperfect, to the wrath and vengeance of Dionysius, the protector of Thebes. And it was observed that whatsoever any Theban, who had the good fortune to survive this victory, asked of him, he was sure to grant without the least difficulty.

Soon after, the Greeks, being assembled at the Isthmus, declared their resolution of joining with Alexan-

---

30  An Athenian orator and politician who had tried to rally the Athenians to resist Macedonian influence in the Greek world.
31  Phocis and Plataea were two Greek cities.
32  I.e., the annual religious rites at Eleusis in Attica.

der in the war against the Persians, and proclaimed him their general. While he stayed here, many public ministers and philosophers came from all parts to visit him and congratulated him, but contrary to his expectations, Diogenes of Sinope,[33] who then was living at Corinth, thought so little of him that instead of coming to compliment him, he never so much as stirred out of the suburb called the Craneion, where Alexander found him lying in the sun. When he saw so much company near him, he raised himself a little, and vouchsafed to look upon Alexander. When Alexander kindly asked him whether he wanted anything, "Yes," he said, "I would have you not stand between me and the sun." Alexander was so struck at this answer, and surprised at the greatness of the man, who had taken so little notice of him, that as he went away he told his followers, who were laughing at the moroseness of the philosopher, that if he were not Alexander, he would choose to be Diogenes.

Then he went to Delphi in order to consult Apollo concerning the success of the war he had undertaken, and happening to come on one of the forbidden days, when it was esteemed improper to give any answer from the oracle, he sent messengers to desire the priestess to do her office. When she refused, on the plea of a law to the contrary, he went up himself, and began to draw her by force into the temple, until tired and overcome with his importunity, she said, "My son, you are invincible." Alexander, taking hold of what she said, declared he had received such an answer as he wished for, and that it was needless to consult the god any further. Among other prodigies that attended the departure of his army, the image of Orpheus[34] at Libethra, made of cypress wood, was seen to sweat in great abundance, to the discouragement of many. But Aristander told him that, far from presaging any ill to him, it signified he would perform acts so important and glorious as would make the poets and musicians of future ages labor and sweat to describe and celebrate them.

His army, by the computation who think it the smallest, consisted of 30,000 foot and 4,000 horse; and those who make the most of it, speak but of 43,000 foot and 3,000 horse. Aristobulus[35] says he did not have a fund of above 70 talents for their pay, nor had he more than 30 days' provision, if we may believe Duris;[36] Onesicritus tells us he was 200 talents in debt. However narrow and disproportionate the beginnings of so vast an undertaking might seem to be, yet he would not embark his army until he had informed himself particularly what means his friends had to enable them to follow him, and supplied what they wanted by giving good farms to some, a village to one, and the revenue of some hamlet or harbor town to another. So that at last he had portioned out or engaged almost all the royal property. When this gave Perdiccas an occasion to ask him what he would leave himself, he replied, his hopes. "Your soldiers," replied Perdiccas, "will be your partners in those," and refused to accept any of the estate he had assigned him. Some others of his friends did the like, but to those who willingly received or desired assistance from him, he liberally granted it, as far as his patrimony in Macedonia would reach, the most part of which was spent in these donations.

With such vigorous resolutions, and his mind thus disposed, he passed the Hellespont,[37] and at Troy sacrificed to Athena, and honored the memory of the heroes who were buried there with solemn libations, especially Achilles, whose gravestone he anointed, and with his friends, as the ancient custom is, ran naked about Achilles's sepulcher, and crowned it with garlands, declaring how happy he esteemed him, in having while he lived so faithful a friend, and when he was dead, so famous a poet to proclaim his actions. While he was viewing the rest of the antiquities and curiosities of the place, being told he might see Paris's[38] harp, if he pleased, he said he thought it not worth looking on, but he would be glad to see that of Achilles, with which he used to sing the glories and great actions of brave men....

---

33  A philosopher of the Cynic school.
34  A celebrated musician in myth; there was an ancient tradition that he became a god after his death.
35  A follower of Alexander who later wrote about him, and one known for his exaggeration.
36  An historian (mid-third century BC).
37  Which separates Europe from Asia Minor.
38  Paris brought Helen to Troy. Like other characters in Homer's *Iliad*, he was also known by another name: Alexander.

[In a series of encounters Alexander defeats Darius, king of Persia, and conquers most of Darius's empire, and more.]

From hence[39] he marched into Parthia[40] where, not having much to do, he first put on barbarian dress, perhaps with the view of making it easier to soften men's hearts, as nothing gains more upon men than a conformity to their fashions and customs. Or it may have been as a first trial whether the Macedonians might be brought to adore him as the Persians did their kings,[41] by accustoming them little by little to bear with the alteration of his rule and course of life in other things. However, he did not follow the Median fashion, which was altogether foreign and uncouth, and adopted neither the trousers nor the sleeved vest, nor the tiara for the head, but taking a middle way between the Persian mode and the Macedonian, so contrived his clothing that it was not so flaunting as the one, and yet more full of pomp and magnificent than the other. At first he wore this habit only when he conversed with the barbarians, or indoors, among his intimate friends and companions, but afterwards he appeared in it in public, when he rode out, and at public audiences, a sight which the Macedonians beheld with grief; but they so respected his other virtues and good qualities that they felt it reasonable in some things to gratify his fancies and his passion of glory, in pursuit of which he hazarded himself so far that, besides his other adventures, he had but lately been wounded in the leg by an arrow, which had so shattered the shank-bone that splinters were taken out. And on another occasion he received a violent blow with a stone on the nape of the neck, which dimmed his sight for a good while afterwards. And yet all this could not hinder him from exposing himself freely to any dangers, insomuch that he passed the river Orexartes, which he took to be the Tanais,[42] and putting the Scythians[43] to flight, followed them for

more than a hundred furlongs, though suffering all the time from diarrhoea.

Here many affirm that the queen of the Amazons[44] came to give him a visit. So Cleitarchus, Polycleitus, Onesicritus, Antigenes, and Ister tell us. But Aristobulus and Chares, who held the office of reporter of requests, Ptolemy and Antidides, Philon the Theban, Philip of Theangela, Hecatieus the Eretrian, Philip the Chalcidian, and Duris the Samian say it is wholly a fiction. And truly Alexander himself seems to confirm the latter statement, for in a letter in which he gives Antipater an account of all that happened, he tells him that the king of Scythia offered him his daughter in marriage, but makes no mention at all of the Amazon. And many years after, when Onesicritus read this story in his fourth book to Lysimachus, who then reigned, the king laughed quietly and asked, "Where could I have been at that time?"

But it signifies little to Alexander whether this be credited or no. It is certain that, apprehending the Macedonians would be weary of pursuing the war, he left the greater part of them in their quarters; and having with him in Hyrcania[45] the choice of his men only, amounting to 20,000 foot and 3,000 horse, he spoke to them to this effect: that hitherto the barbarians had seen them no otherwise than as it were in a dream, and if they should think of returning when they had only alarmed Asia, and not conquered it, their enemies would set upon them as upon so many women. However, he told them he would keep none of them with him against his will; they might go if they pleased; he would merely enter his protest, that when on his way to make the Macedonians the masters of the world, he was left alone with a few friends and volunteers. This is almost word for word, as he wrote in a letter to Antipater, where he adds that when he had thus spoken to them, they all cried out, they would go along with him wherever it was his pleasure

---

39  Hyrcania, in modern northern Iran, on the northeast coast of the Caspian sea.
40  In modern northern Iran.
41  Like most rulers in the ancient Near East, the kings of Persia ruled as theocrats, and their nearly divine status was marked by their magnificent clothing and the reverence with which they were to be treated by those around them.
42  I.e., the modern river Don.
43  The inhabitants of a region northeast of the Black Sea.
44  An ancient people whose warriors were women, considered by modern scholarship to have been mythical.
45  See above n 39.

to lead them. After succeeding with these, it was no hard matter for him to bring over the multitude, which easily followed the example of their betters. Now, also, he more and more accommodated himself in his way of living to that of the natives, and tried to bring them also as near as he could to Macedonian customs, wisely considering that while he was engaged in an expedition which would carry him far from there, it would be wiser to depend upon the good will which might arise from intermixture and association as a means of maintaining tranquillity, than upon force and compulsion. In order to this, he chose out 30,000 boys, whom he put under masters to teach them the Greek tongue, and to train them up to arms in the Macedonian discipline. As for his marriage with Roxana,[46] whose youthfulness and beauty had charmed him at a drinking entertainment, where he first happened to see her taking part in a dance, it was, indeed, a love affair, yet it seemed at the same time to be conducive to the object he had in hand. For it gratified the conquered people to see him choose a wife from among themselves, and it made them feel the most lively affection for him, to find that in the only passion which he, the most temperate of men, was overcome by, he yet forbore till he could obtain her in a lawful and honorable way.

Noticing also that among his chief friends and favorites, Hephaestion most approved all that he did, and complied with and imitated him in his change of habits, while Craterus continued to be strict in the observation of the customs and fashions of his own country, he made it his practice to employ the first in all transactions with the Persians, and the latter when he had to do with the Greeks or Macedonians. And in general he showed more affection for Hephaestion, and more respect for Craterus. Hephaestion, as he used to say, being Alexander's, and Craterus the king's, friend. And so these two friends always bore in secret a grudge against each other, and at times quarrelled openly, so much so that once in India they drew their swords on one another, and were proceeding in good earnest, with their friends on each side to second them, when Alexander rode up and publicly reproved

Hephaestion, calling him a fool and a madman not to be aware that without his favor he was nothing. He rebuked Craterus also in private, severely, and then causing them both to come into his presence, he reconciled them, at the same time swearing by Ammon and the rest of the gods that he loved those two above all other men, but if ever he perceived them fall out again, he would be sure to put both of them to death, or at least the aggressor. After which they neither ever did nor said anything, so much as in jest, to offend one another.

There was scarcely anyone who had greater repute among the Macedonians than Philotas, the son of Parmenio. For besides that he was valiant and able to endure any fatigue of war, he was also next to Alexander himself the most munificent, and the greatest lover of his friends, one of whom asking him for some money, he commanded his steward to give it to him; when the steward told him he did not have the wherewithal, he said, "Do you not have any plate, then, or any clothes of mine to sell?" But he carried his arrogance and his pride of wealth and his habits of display and luxury to a degree of offensiveness unbecoming a private man; and affecting all the loftiness without succeeding in showing any of the grace or gentleness of true greatness, by this mistaken and spurious majesty he gained so much envy and ill will that Parmenio would sometimes tell him, "My son, to be not quite so great would be better." For he had long before been complained of and accused to Alexander. Particularly when Darius was defeated in Cilicia, and immense booty was taken at Damascus, among the rest of the prisoners who were brought into the camp, there was one Antigone of Pydna, a very handsome woman, who fell to Philotas's share. The young man one day in his cups, in the vaunting, outspoken, soldier's manner, declared to his mistress that all the great actions were performed by him and his father, the glory and benefit of which, he said, together with the title of king, the boy Alexander reaped and enjoyed by their means. She informed someone of her acquaintance of what he had said and he, as is usual in such cases, told another, till at last the story came to

---

46   A woman of royal rank in the Persian empire taken prisoner by Alexander.

the ears of Craterus, who brought the woman secretly to the king. When Alexander had heard what she had to say, he commanded her to continue her intrigue with Philotas, and give him an account from time to time of all that should fall from him to this purpose. He, thus unwittingly caught in a snare, to gratify sometimes a fit of anger, sometimes a love of vainglory, let himself utter numerous foolish, indiscreet speeches against the king in Antigone's hearing, of which, though Alexander was informed and convinced by strong evidence, yet he would take no notice at present, whether it was that he confided in Parmenio's affection and loyalty, or that he apprehended their power and reputation. But about this time, one Limnus, a Macedonian of Chalastra, conspired against Alexander's life, and communicated his design to a youth whom he was fond of, named Nicomachus, inviting him to be of the party. But he, not relishing the thing, revealed it to his brother Balinus, who immediately addressed himself to Philotas, requiring him to introduce them both to Alexander, to whom they had something of great moment to impart which very closely concerned him. But he, for what reason is uncertain, did not bring them in, professing that the king was engaged with affairs of more importance. And when they had urged him a second time, and were still slighted by him, they applied themselves to another, by whose means being admitted into Alexander's presence, they first told about Limnus's conspiracy, and by the way let appear the negligence of Philotas, who had twice disregarded their application to him. Alexander was greatly incensed, and on finding that Limnus had defended himself, and had been killed by the soldier who was sent to seize him, he was still more discomposed, thinking he had thus lost the means of detecting the plot. As soon as his displeasure against Philotas began to appear, presently all his old enemies showed themselves, and said openly that the king was too easily imposed on to imagine that one so inconsiderable as Limnus, a Chalastrian, would undertake such an enterprise on his own, and that in all likelihood he was but subservient to a design, an instrument that was moved by some greater power, and that those ought to be more strictly examined about the matter whose interest it was so much to conceal it. When they had once gained the

king's ear for insinuations of this sort, they went on to show a thousand grounds of suspicion against Philotas, till at last they prevailed to have him seized and put to torture, which was done in the presence of the principal officers, Alexander himself being placed behind some tapestry to understand what passed. Where, when he heard in what a miserable tone, and with what abject submissions, Philotas applied himself to Hephaestion, he broke out, it is said, in this manner: "Are you so mean spirited and effeminate, Philotas, and yet can engage in so desperate a design?" After his death, he presently sent into Media, and put also Parmenio, his father, to death, who had done brave service under Philip, and was the only man of his older friends and counsellors who had encouraged Alexander to invade Asia. Of three sons whom he had had in the army, he had already lost two, and now was himself put to death with the third. These actions rendered Alexander an object of terror to many of his friends, and chiefly to Antipater, who, to strengthen himself, sent messengers privately to treat for an alliance with the Aetolians, who stood in fear of Alexander because they had destroyed the town of the Oeniadae; on being informed of which, Alexander had said the children of the Oeniadae need not revenge their father's quarrel, for he would himself take care to punish the Aetolians.

Not long after this happened came the deplorable end of Cleitus, which, to those who barely hear the matter, may seem more inhuman than that of Philotas; but if we consider the story with its circumstance of time, and weigh the cause, we shall find it to have occurred rather through a sort of mischance of the king's, whose anger and heavy drinking offered an occasion to the evil genius of Cleitus. The king had a present of Greek fruit brought him from the sea coast, which was so fresh and beautiful that he was surprised at it, and called Cleitus to him to see it, and to give him a share of it. Cleitus was then sacrificing, but he immediately left off and came, followed by three sheep, on whom the drink-offering had been already poured preparatory to sacrificing them. Alexander, being informed of this, told his diviners, Aristander and Cleomantis the Lacedaemonian, and asked them what it meant; on whose assuring him it was an ill omen, he commanded them in all haste to offer sacrifices for Cleitus's safety, forasmuch as three days before he himself had seen a strange vision in his sleep, of Cleitus all in mourning, sitting by Parmenio's sons who were dead. Cleitus, however, did not stay to finish his devotions, but came straight to supper with the king, who had sacrificed to Castor and Pollux. And when they had drunk pretty hard, some of the company fell to singing the verses of one Pranichus, or as others say of Pierion, which were made upon those captains who had been lately worsted by the barbarians, on purpose to disgrace and turn them to ridicule. This gave offense to the older men who were there, and they upbraided both the author and the singer of the verses, though Alexander and the younger men about him were much amused to hear them, and encouraged them to go on, till at last Cleitus, who had drunk too much, and was besides of a forward and willful temper, was so nettled that he could hold back no longer, saying it was not well done to expose the Macedonians before the barbarians and their enemies, since though it was their unhappiness to be overcome, yet they were much better men than those who laughed at them. And when Alexander remarked that Cleitus was pleading his own cause, giving cowardice the name of misfortune, Cleitus started up: "This cowardice, as you are pleased to term it," he said to him, "saved the life of a son of the gods, when in flight from Spithridates's sword;[47] it is by the expense of Macedonian blood, and by these wounds, that you are now raised to such a height as to be able to disown your father Philip, and call yourself the son of Ammon." "You base fellow," said Alexander, who was now thoroughly exasperated, "do you think to say these things about me everywhere, and stir up the Macedonians to sedition, and not be punished for it?" "We are sufficiently punished already," answered Cleitus, "if this is the recompense of our toils, and we must esteem theirs a happy lot who have not lived to see their countrymen scourged with Median rods and forced to sue to the Persians to have access to their king." While he talked thus at random, and those near Alexander got up from their seats and began to revile him in turn, the elder men did what they could to compose the dis-

order. Alexander, in the meantime, turning about to Xenodochus, the Pardian, and Artemius, the Colophonian, asked if they were not of the opinion that the Greeks, in comparison with the Macedonians, behaved themselves like so many demigods among wild beasts. But Cleitus for all this would not yield, desiring Alexander to speak out if he had anything more to say, or else why did he invite men who were freeborn and accustomed to speak their minds openly without restraint to sup with him. He would rather live and converse with barbarians and slaves who would not scruple to bow the knee to his Persian belt and his white tunic. These words so provoked Alexander that, not able to suppress his anger any longer, he threw one of the apples that lay upon the table at him, and hit him, and then looked about for his sword. But Aristophanes, one of his life-guard, had hidden that out of the way, and others came around him and besought him, but in vain; for, breaking from them, he called out aloud to his guards in the Macedonian language, which was a certain sign of some great disturbance in him, and commanded a trumpeter to sound, giving him a blow with his clenched fist for not instantly obeying him, though afterwards the same man was commended for disobeying an order which would have put the whole army into tumult and confusion. Cleitus, still refusing to yield, was with much trouble forced by his friends out of the room. But he came in again immediately at another door, very irreverently and confidently singing the verses of Euripides's *Andromache*,

In Greece, alas! how ill things ordered are!

Upon this, at last, Alexander, snatching a spear from one of the soldiers, met Cleitus as he was coming forward and was putting by the curtain that hung before the door, and ran him through the body. He fell at once with a cry and a groan. Upon this, the king's anger immediately vanishing, he came perfectly to himself, and when he saw his friends about him all in a profound silence, he pulled the spear out of the dead body, and would have thrust it into his own throat if

---

47  Alexander had earlier nearly been killed in battle by the Persian Spithridates, but had been saved by Cleitus.

the guards had not held his hands, and by main force carried him away into his chamber, where all that night and the next day he wept bitterly, till being quite spent with lamenting and exclaiming, he lay as it were speechless, fetching only deep sighs. His friends apprehending some harm from his silence, broke into the room, but he took no notice of what any of them said, till Aristander, putting him in mind of the vision he had seen concerning Cleitus, and the prodigy that followed, as if all had come to pass by an unavoidable fatality, he then seemed to moderate his grief. They now brought Callisthenes, the philosopher, who was the near friend of Aristotle, and Anaxarchus of Abdera, to him. Callisthenes used moral language, and gentle and soothing means, hoping to find access for words of reason, and get a hold upon the passion. But Anaxarchus, who had always taken a course of his own in philosophy, and had a reputation for despising and slighting his contemporaries, as soon as he came in, cried aloud, "Is this the Alexander whom the whole world looks to, lying here weeping like a slave for fear of the censure and reproach of men, to whom he himself ought to be a law and measure of equity, if he would use the right his conquests have given him as supreme lord and governor of all, and not be the victim of a vain and idle opinion? Do you not know," he said, "that Zeus is represented as having Justice and Law on each side of him, to signify that all the actions of a conqueror are lawful and just?" With these and like speeches, Anaxarchus indeed allayed the king's grief, but rendered him more audacious and lawless than he had been. Nor did he fail with these means to insinuate himself into his favor, and to make Callisthenes's company, which at all times, because of his austerity, was not very acceptable, more uneasy and disagreeable to him....

Alexander, now intent upon his expedition into India, took notice that his soldiers were so loaded with booty that it hindered their marching. Therefore, at break of day, as soon as the baggage wagons were laden, first he set fire to his own, and to those of his friends, and then commanded those which belonged to the rest of the army to be burned. This was an act which in its deliberation had seemed more dangerous and difficult than it proved in the execution, and one with which few were dissatisfied; for most of the sol-

diers, as if they had been inspired, uttering loud cries and warlike shoutings, supplied one another with what was absolutely necessary, and burned and destroyed all that was superfluous, the sight of which redoubled Alexander's zeal and eagerness for his design. And, indeed, he had now grown very severe and inexorable in punishing those who committed any fault. For he put Menander, one of his friends, to death for deserting a fortress where he had placed him in garrison, and shot down Orsodates, one of the barbarians who revolted against him, with his own hand.

At this time a sheep happened to bring forth a lamb with the perfect shape and color of a tiara upon its head, and testicles on each side. Alexander regarded this portent with such dislike that he immediately caused his Babylonian priests, whom he usually carried about with him for such purposes, to purify him, and told his friends that he was not so much concerned for his own sake as for theirs, out of an apprehension that after his death the divine power might suffer his empire to fall into the hands of some degenerate, impotent person. But this fear was soon removed by a wonderful thing that happened not long after, and was thought to presage better. For Proxenus, a Macedonian, who was the chief of those who looked after the king's furniture, as he was breaking up the ground near the river Oxus to set up the royal pavilion, discovered a spring of a fat, oily liquid, which, after the top was taken off, ran with pure, clear oil, without any difference either of taste or smell, having exactly the same smoothness and brightness, and that, too, in a country where no olives grew. Indeed, the water of the river Oxus is said to be the smoothest to the feeling of all waters, and to leave a gloss on the skins of those who bathe themselves in it. Whatever might be the cause, it is certain that Alexander was wonderfully pleased with it, as appears by his letters to Antipater, where he speaks of it as one of the most remarkable presages with which heaven had ever favored him. The diviners told him it signified his expedition would be glorious in the event, but very painful and attended with many difficulties; for oil, they said, was bestowed on mankind by heaven as a refreshment of their labors.

Nor did they judge amiss, for he exposed himself to many hazards in the battles which he fought, and received very severe wounds, but the greatest loss in his army was occasioned through the unwholesomeness of the air and the want of necessary provisions. But he still applied himself to overcome fortune and whatever opposed him by resolution and virtue, and thought nothing impossible to true intrepidity, and on the other hand nothing secure or strong for cowardice. It is told of him that when he besieged Sisimithres, who held an inaccessible, impregnable rock against him, and his soldiers began to despair of taking it, he asked Oxyartes whether Sisimithres was a man of courage, who assuring Alexander he was the greatest coward alive, "Then you tell me," he said, "that the place may easily be taken, since what is in command of it is weak." And in a little time he so terrified Sisimithres that he took it without any difficulty. At an attack which he made upon another such precipitous place with some of his Macedonian soldiers, he called to one whose name was Alexander and told him he at any rate must fight bravely if it were but for his name's sake. The youth fought gallantly and was killed in the action, at which Alexander was sensibly afflicted. Another time, seeing his men march slowly and unwillingly to the siege of the place called Nysa, because of a deep river between them and the town, he advanced before them and standing upon the bank, said "What a miserable man am I, that I have not learned to swim!" and then was hardly dissuaded from endeavoring to pass over it on his shield. Here, after the assault was over, the ambassadors from several towns which he had blocked up came to submit to him and make their peace were surprised to find him still in his armor, without anyone in waiting or attendance upon him, and when at last someone brought him a cushion, he made the oldest of them, named Acuphis, take it and sit down upon it. The old man, marveling at his magnanimity and courtesy, asked him what his countrymen should do to merit his friendship. "I would have them," said Alexander, "choose you to govern them, and send 100 of the most worthy men among them to remain with me as hostages." Acuphis laughed and answered, "I shall govern them with more ease, sir, if I send you so many of the worst, rather than the best of my subjects."

The extent of King Taxiles's dominions in India was thought to be as large as Egypt, abounding in good pastures, and producing beautiful fruits. The king himself had the reputation of a wise man, and at his first interview with Alexander he spoke to him in these terms: "To what purpose," he said, "should we make war upon one another if the plan of your coming into these parts is not to rob us of our water or our necessary food, which are the only things that wise men are indispensably obliged to fight for? As for other riches and possessions, as they are accounted in the eye of the world, if I am better provided with them than you, I am ready to let you share with me; but if fortune has been more liberal to you than me, I have no objection to be obliged to you." This discourse pleased Alexander so much that, embracing him, Alexander said to him, "Do you think your kind words and courteous behaviour will bring you off in this interview without a contest? No, you shall not escape so. I shall contend and do battle with you so far, that however obliging you are, you shall not have the better of me." Then, receiving some presents from him, Alexander returned him others of greater value, and to complete his bounty gave him in money ready coined 1,000 talents. His old friends were much displeased at this, but it gained him the hearts of many of the barbarians. But the best soldiers of the Indians, now entering into the pay of several of the cities, undertook to defend them, and did it so bravely that they put Alexander to a great deal of trouble, till at last, after a capitulation, upon the surrender of the place, he fell upon them as they were marching away, and put them all to the sword. This one breach of his word remains as a blemish upon his achievements in war, which he otherwise had performed throughout with that justice and honor that became a king. Nor was he less troubled by the Indian philosophers, who inveighed against those princes who joined his party, and solicited the free nations to oppose him. He took several of these also and caused them to be hanged.

Alexander, in his own letters, has given us an account of his war with Porus.[48] He says the two

---

48  Ruler beyond the Hydaspes river, in modern northeastern Pakistan.

armies were separated by the river Hydaspes, on whose opposite bank Porus continually kept his elephants in order of battle, with their heads towards their enemies, to guard the passage; that he, on the other hand, made every day a great noise and clamor in his camp in order to dissipate the apprehensions of the barbarians; that one stormy dark night he passed the river, at a distance from the place where the enemy lay, into a little island, with part of his foot and the best of his horse. Here there fell a most violent storm of rain, accompanied with lightning and whirlwinds, and seeing some of his men burned and dying with the lightning, he nevertheless left the island and went over to the other side. The Hydaspes, he says, after the storm, was now so swollen and had grown so rapid as to have made a breach in the bank, and a part of the river was now pouring in, so that when he came across it was with difficulty that he got a footing on the land, which was slippery and unsteady, and exposed to the force of the currents on both sides. This is the occasion when he is related to have said, "O you Athenians, will you believe what dangers I incur to merit your praise?" This, however, is Onesicritus's story. Alexander says that here the men left their boats, and passed the breach in their armor, up to the breast in water, and that then he advanced with his horse about 20 furlongs before his foot, concluding that if the enemy charged him with their cavalry he would be too strong for them; if with their foot, his own would come up in enough time to assist him. Nor did he judge amiss; for being charged by a thousand horse and 60 armed chariots, which advanced before their main body, he took all the chariots, and killed 400 horse upon the place. Porus, by this time, guessing that Alexander himself had crossed over, came on with his whole army, except a party which he left behind, to hold the rest of the Macedonians in play if they should attempt to pass the river. But he, apprehending the multitude of the enemy, and to avoid the shock of their elephants, dividing his forces, attacked their left wing himself, and commanded Coenus to fall

upon the right, which was performed with good success. For by this means both wings being broken, the enemies fell back in their retreat upon the center, and crowded in upon their elephants. Rallying there, they fought a hand-to-hand battle, and it was the eighth hour of the day before they were entirely defeated. This description the conqueror himself has left us in his own epistles.

Almost all the historians agree in relating that Porus was four cubits and a span[49] tall, and that when he was upon his elephant, which was of the largest size, his stature and bulk were such that he appeared to be mounted in proportion to a horseman on his horse. This elephant, during the whole battle, gave many singular proofs of sagacity and of particular care for the king, whom as long as he was strong and in a condition to fight, he defended with great courage, repelling those who set upon him; and as soon as he perceived him overpowered with his numerous wounds and the multitude of darts that were thrown at him, to prevent his falling off, he softly knelt down and began to draw out the darts with his trunk. When Porus was taken prisoner, and Alexander asked him how he expected to be treated, he answered, "Like a king." For that expression he said, when the same question was put to him a second time, comprehended everything. And Alexander, accordingly, not only suffered him to govern his own kingdom as a satrap[50] under himself, but gave him also the additional territory of various independent tribes whom he subdued, a district which, it is said, contained 15 different nations, and 5,000 significant towns, besides an abundance of villages. To another government three times as large as this, he appointed Philip, one of his friends.

Some little time after the battle with Porus, Bucephalus died as most of the authorities state, under cure of his wounds, or as Onesicritus says, of fatigue and age, Bucephalus being 30 years old. Alexander was no less concerned at his death than if he had lost an old companion or an intimate friend,

---

49   I.e., six feet three inches.

50   In the Persian empire, a satrap was the Persian king's governor of a territory, who was largely autonomous of the king, and
     was responsible for supplying the king tribute and soldiers.

and built a city, which he named Bucephalia, in memory of him, on the bank of the river Hydaspes. He also, we are told, built another city and called it after the name of a favorite dog, Peritas, which he had brought up himself. So Sotion assures us he was informed by Potamon of Lesbos.[51]

But this last combat with Porus took off the edge of the Macedonians' courage, and stayed their further progress into India. For having found it hard enough to defeat an enemy who brought but 20,000 foot and 2,000 horse into the field, they thought they had reason to oppose Alexander's plan to lead them on to pass the Ganges too, which they were told was 32 furlongs broad and 100 fathoms deep, and the banks on the further side covered with multitudes of enemies. For they were told the kings of the Gandaritans and Praesians expected them there with 80,000 horse, 200,000 foot, 8,000 armed chariots, and 6,000 fighting elephants. Nor was this a mere vain report, spread to discourage them. For Sandrocottus,[52] who not long after reigned in those parts made a present of 500 elephants at one time to Seleucus,[53] and with an army of 600,000 men subdued all India. Alexander at first was so grieved and enraged at his men's reluctance that he shut himself up in his tent and threw himself upon the ground, declaring, if they would not pass the Ganges, he owed them no thanks for anything they had hitherto done and that to retreat now was plainly to confess himself vanquished. But at last the reasonable persuasion of his friends and the cries and lamentations of his soldiers, who in a suppliant manner crowded about the entrance of his tent, prevailed with him to think of returning. Yet he could not refrain from leaving behind him various deceptive memorials of his expedition to impose upon later times and to exaggerate his glory for posterity, such as arms larger than were really worn, and mangers for horses with bits and bridles greater the usual size, which he set up and distributed in several places. He erected altars, also, to the gods, which the kings of the Praesians even in our time do honor to when they pass the river, and offer sacrifice upon them after the Greek manner. Androcottus, then a boy, saw Alexander there, and is said often afterwards to have been heard to say that he missed but little of making himself master of those countries, their king, who then reigned, was so hated and despised for the viciousness of his life and the meanness of his extraction.

Alexander was now eager to see the ocean.[54] To this purpose he caused a great many towboats and rafts to be built, in which he went gently down the rivers at his leisure, yet so that his navigation was neither unprofitable nor inactive. For by several descents upon the bank, he made himself master of the fortified towns, and consequently of the country on both sides. But at a siege of a town of the Mallians, who have the reputation of being the bravest people of India, he ran in great danger of his life. For having beaten off the defenders with showers of arrows, he was the first man that mounted the wall by a scaling ladder, which, as soon as he was up, broke and left him almost alone, exposed to the darts which the barbarians threw at him in great numbers from below. In this distress, turning himself as well as he could, he leaped down in the midst of his enemies, and had the good fortune to land upon his feet. The brightness and clattering of his armor when he came to the ground made the barbarians think they saw rays of light, or some bright phantom playing before his body, which frightened them so much at first that they ran away and dispersed. Seeing him seconded by only two of his guards, they fell upon him hand to hand, and some, while he bravely defended himself, tried to wound him through his armor with their swords and spears. And one who stood further off drew a bow with such strength that the arrow, finding its way through his breastplate, stuck in his ribs under the breast. This stroke was so violent that it made him step back, and set one knee to

---

51  Early second century.

52  The Greek version of Chandragupta of the Mauryan dynasty; he established his rule over northern India as well as modern Pakistan and Afghanistan. He also eliminated Alexander's garrisons.

53  Alexander's general, who after his death seized many of Alexander's most eastern conquests, thus creating one of the successor states to Alexander's empire.

54  I.e., the body of water which the Greeks believed surrounded the single land mass on earth—Asia, Africa, and Europe.

the ground, upon which the man ran up with his drawn scimitar, thinking to despatch him, and would have done it, if Peucestes and Limnaeus had not interposed, who were both wounded, Limnaeus mortally, but Peucestes stood his ground, while Alexander killed the barbarians. But this did not free him from danger, for, besides many other wounds, at last he received so weighty a stroke of a club upon his neck that he was forced to lean his body against the wall, still, however, facing the enemy. At this extremity, the Macedonians made their way in and gathered around him. They took him up, just as he was fainting away, having lost all sense of what was done near him, and conveyed him to his tent, upon which it was presently reported all over the camp that he was dead. But when they had with great difficulty and pains sawed off the shaft of the arrow, which was of wood, and so with much trouble gotten off his breastplate, they came to cut the head of it, which was three fingers broad and four long, and stuck fast in the bone. During the operation he was taken with almost mortal swoonings, but when it was out he came to himself again. Yet, though all danger was past, he continued to be very weak, and confined himself a great while to a regular diet and the method of his cure, till one day hearing the Macedonians clamoring outside in their eagerness to see him, he took his cloak and went out. And having sacrificed to the gods, without more delay he went on board again, and as he coasted along subdued a great deal of the country and several considerable cities on both sides.

On this voyage he took prisoner ten of the Indian philosophers prisoners who had been most active in persuading Sabbas to revolt, and had caused the Macedonians a great deal of trouble. These men, called gymnosophists, were reputed to be extremely ready and succinct in their answers, which he made trial of by putting difficult questions to them, letting them know that those whose answers were not pertinent would be put to death, of which he made the eldest of them judge. The first being asked which he thought the most numerous, the dead or the living, answered, "The living because those who are dead are not at all." The second, of whom Alexander desired to know whether the earth or the sea produced the largest beasts, told him, "The earth, for the sea is but a part of it." Alexander's question to the third was, which is the most cunning of beasts? "That," he said, "which men have not yet found out." Alexander bade the fourth tell him what argument he used to Sabbas to persuade him to revolt. "None other," he said, "than that he should either live or die nobly." Of the fifth Alexander asked, which was the eldest, night or day? The philosopher replied, "Day was eldest, by one day at least." But perceiving Alexander not well satisfied with that account, he added that he ought not to wonder if strange questions had as strange answers made to them. Then he went on and inquired of the next what a man should do to be exceedingly beloved. "He must be very powerful," he said, "without making himself too much feared." The answer of the seventh to his question, how a man might become a god, was, "By doing that which was impossible for men to do." The eighth told him, "Life is stronger than death, because it supports so many miseries." And the last being asked, how long he thought it decent for a man to live, said "Till death appeared more desirable than life." Then Alexander turned to him whom he had made judge, and commanded him to give sentence: "All that I can determine," he said, "is that they have every one answered worse than another." "Nay," said the king, "then you shall die first for giving such a sentence." "Not so, O king," replied the gymnosophist, "unless you said falsely that he would die first who made the worst answer." In conclusion he gave them presents and dismissed them.

But to those who were in greatest reputation among them and lived a private, quiet life, he sent Onesicritus, one of Diogenes the Cynic's disciples, desiring them to come to him. Calanus, it is said, very arrogantly and roughly commanded him to strip himself and hear what he said naked; otherwise he would not speak a word to him, though he came from Zeus himself. But Dandamis received him with more civility, and hearing him discourse of Socrates, Pythagoras, and Diogenes, told him he thought them men of great parts and to have erred in nothing so much as in having too great respect for the laws and customs of their country. Others say Dandamis only asked him the reason why Alexander undertook so long a journey to come into those parts. Taxiles, however, persuaded Calanus to wait upon Alexander. His proper name

All of the voyages & marches

was Sphines, but because he was wont to say *Cale*, which in the Indian tongue is a form of salutation, to those he met with anywhere, the Greeks called him Calanus. He is said to have shown Alexander an instructive emblem of government, which was this. He threw a dry, shrivelled hide upon the ground, and trod upon the edges of it. The skin when it was pressed in one place still rose up in another wherever he trod about it, till he set his foot in the middle, which made all the parts lie even and quiet. The meaning of this similitude was that he ought to reside most in the middle of his empire, and not spend too much time on the borders of it.

His voyage down the rivers took up seven months' time, and when he came to the sea, he sailed to an island which he himself called Scillustis, others Psiltucis, where, going ashore, he sacrificed, and made what observations he could as to the nature of the sea and the seacoast. Then having asked the gods that no other man might ever go beyond the bounds of this expedition, he ordered his fleet, of which he made Nearchus admiral and Onesicritus pilot, to sail about, keeping the Indian shore on the right hand, and returned himself by land through the country of the Orites, where he was reduced to great difficulties for want of provisions, and lost a vast number of his men, so that of an army of 120,000 foot and 15,000 horse, he scarcely brought back above a fourth part out of India, they were so diminished by disease, ill diet, and the scorching heat, but most by famine. For their march was through an uncultivated country whose inhabitants fared miserably, possessing only a few sheep, and those of a wretched kind, whose flesh was rank and unsavory because of their continual feeding upon sea fish.

After 60 days' march he came into Gedrosia, where he found a great plenty of all things, which the neighboring kings and governors of provinces, hearing of his approach, had taken care to provide. When he had here refreshed his army, he continued his march through Carmania, feasting all the way for seven days together. He with his most intimate friends banqueted

and revelled night and day upon a platform erected on a lofty, conspicuous scaffold, which was slowly drawn by eight horses. This was followed by a great many chariots, some covered with purple and embroidered canopies, and some with green boughs, which were continually supplied afresh, and in them the rest of his friends and commanders drinking, and crowned with garlands of flowers. Here was now no target or helmet or spear to be seen; instead of armor, the soldiers handled nothing but cups and goblets and Thericlean[55] drinking vessels, which, along the whole way, they dipped into large bowls and jars, and drank one another's health, some seating themselves to it, others as they went along. All places resounded with music of pipes and flutes, with harping and singing, and women dancing as in the rites of Dionysius. For this disorderly, wandering march, besides the drinking part of it, was accompanied with all the sportiveness and insolence of bacchanals, as much as if the god himself had been there to countenance and lead the procession. As soon as he came to the royal palace of Gedrosia, he again refreshed and feasted his army; and one day after he had drunk pretty hard, it is said he went to see a prize of dancing contended for, in which his favorite Bagoas having gained the victory, crossed the theater in his dancing clothes and sat down close by him, which so pleased the Macedonians that they made loud acclamations for him to kiss Bagoas, and never stopped clapping their hands and shouting till Alexander put his arms around him and kissed him.

Here his admiral, Nearchus, came to him, and delighted him so much with the narrative of his voyage that he resolved himself to sail out of the mouth of the Euphrates with a great fleet, with which he planned to go around by Arabia and Africa, and so by Hercules's Pillars[56] into the Mediterranean, in order for which he directed all sorts of vessels to be built at Thapsacus and made great provisions everywhere of seamen and pilots. But the tidings of the difficulties he had gone through in his Indian expedition, the danger to his person among the Mallians, the reported loss of

---

55  Thericles (fifth century BC) had been an eminent potter at Corinth.
56  I.e., the Straits of Gibraltar.

a considerable part of his forces, and a general doubt as to his own safety, had begun to give occasion for revolt among many of the conquered nations, and for acts of great injustice, avarice, and insolence on the part of the satraps and commanders in the provinces, so that there seemed to be a universal fluctuation and disposition to change. Even at home, Olympias and Cleopatra had raised a faction against Antipater,[57] and divided his government between them, Olympias seizing Epirus and Cleopatra Macedonia. When Alexander was told of it, he said his mother had made the best choice, for the Macedonians would never endure to be ruled by a woman. Upon this he despatched Nearchus again to his fleet to carry the war into the maritime provinces, and as he marched that way himself he punished those commanders who had behaved ill, particularly Oxyartes, one of the sons of Abuletes, whom he killed with his own hand, thrusting him through the body with his spear. And when Abuletes brought him 3,000 talents in coined money instead of the necessary provisions which he ought to have furnished, Alexander ordered it to be thrown to his horses, and when they would not touch it, he said "What good will this provision do us?" and sent him away to prison.

When he came into Persia, he distributed money among the women, as their own kings had been accustomed to do, who as often as they came there, gave every one of them a piece of gold. On account of this custom, some of them, it is said, had come rarely, and Ochus was so sordidly covetous that, to avoid this expense, he never visited his native country once in all his reign. Then finding Cyrus's[58] sepulcher opened and rifled, Alexander put Polymachus, who did it, to death, though he was a man of some distinction, a born Macedonian of Pella. And after he had read the inscription, he caused it to be cut again below the old one in Greek characters, the words being these: "O man, whoever you are, and from wherever you come (for I know you will come), I am Cyrus, the founder of the Persian empire; do not

grudge me this little earth which covers my body." The reading of this deeply touched Alexander, filling him with the thought of the uncertainty and mutability of human affairs. At the same time Calanus, having been a little while troubled with a disease of the bowels, requested that he might have a funeral pyre erected, to which he came on horseback, and, after he had said some prayers and sprinkled himself and cut off some of his hair to throw into the fire, before he ascended it, he embraced and took leave of the Macedonians who stood by, desiring them to pass that day in mirth and good-fellowship with their king, whom in a little time, he said, he did not doubt he would see again at Babylon. Having said this, he lay down, and covering up his face, he did not stir when the fire came near him, but continued still in the same posture as at first, and so sacrificed himself, as it was the ancient custom of the philosophers in those countries to do. The same thing was done long after by another Indian who came with Caesar[59] to Athens, where they still show you "the Indian's monument." At his return from the funeral pyre, Alexander invited a great many of his friends and principal officers to supper, and proposed a drinking match, in which the victor would receive a crown. Promachus drank 12 quarts[60] of wine, and won the prize, which was a talent from them all; but he survived his victory but three days, and was followed, as Chares says, by 41 more, who died of the same debauch, some extremely cold weather having set in shortly after.

At Susa, he married Darius's daughter Statira, and celebrated also the nuptials of his friends, bestowing the noblest of the Persian women upon the worthiest of them, at the same time making it an entertainment in honor of the other Macedonians whose marriages had already taken place. At this magnificent festival, it is reported, there were no less than 9,000 guests, to each of whom he gave a golden cup for the libations. Not to mention other instances of his wonderful magnificence, he paid the debts of his army, which amounted to 9,870 talents. But Antigenes, who had

---

57   A general whom Alexander had left in charge of Macedonia and Greece.
58   Cyrus (sixth century BC), the ruler who had founded the Persian empire through many conquests.
59   I.e., Augustus Caesar (32 BC - AD 14).
60   It should be noted that the ancients generally mixed their wine with water.

lost one of his eyes, though he owed nothing, got his name set down in the list of those who were in debt, and bringing one who pretended to be his creditor, and to have supplied him from the bank, received the money. But when the cheat was found out, the king was so incensed that he banished him from court and took away his command, though he was an excellent soldier and a man of great courage. For when he was but a youth, and served under Philip at the siege of Perinthus, where he was wounded in the eye by an arrow shot out of an engine, he would neither let the arrow be taken out nor be persuaded to leave the field till he had bravely repulsed the enemy and forced them to retire into the town. Accordingly he was not able to support such a disgrace with any patience, and it was plain that grief and despair would have made him kill himself, but the king fearing it, not only pardoned him, but let him also enjoy the benefit of his deceit.

The 30,000 boys whom he left behind him to be taught and disciplined were so improved at his return, both in strength and beauty, and performed their exercises with such dexterity and wonderful agility, that he was extremely pleased with them, which grieved the Macedonians, and made them fear he would have the less value for them. And when he proceeded to send down the infirm and maimed soldiers to the sea, they said they were unjustly and infamously dealt with, after they were worn out in his service upon all occasions, now to be turned away with disgrace and sent home into their country among their friends and relations in a worse condition than when they came out; therefore they desired him to dismiss them one and all, and to account his Macedonians useless now that he was so well furnished with a set of dancing boys, with whom, if he pleased, he might go on and conquer the world. These speeches so incensed Alexaider that, after he had given them a great deal of reproachful language in his passion, he drove them away, and committed the watch to Persians, out of whom he chose his guards and attendants. When the Macedonians saw him escorted by these men, and themselves excluded and shamefully disgraced, their high spirits fell, and conferring with one another, they found that jealousy and rage had almost distracted them. But at last com-

ing to themselves again, they went without their arms, with only their under garments on, crying and weeping to offer themselves at his tent, and desired him to deal with them as their baseness and ingratitude deserved. However, this would not prevail; for though his anger was already something mollified, yet he would not admit them into his presence, nor would they stir from there, but continued two days and nights before his tent, bewailing themselves and imploring him as their lord to have compassion on them. But the third day he came out to them, and seeing them very humble and penitent, he wept himself a great while, and after a gentle reproof spoke kindly to them, and dismissed those who were unserviceable with magnificent rewards, and with his recommendation to Antipater that when they came home they, crowned with garlands of flowers, should sit on the best and foremost seat at all public shows and in the theaters. He ordered, also, that the children of those who had lost their lives in his service should have their father's pay continued to them.

When he came to Ecbatana in Media, and had attended to his most urgent affairs, he began to divert himself again with spectacles and public entertainments, to carry on which he had a supply of 3,000 actors and artists, newly arrived out of Greece. But they were soon interrupted by Hephaestion's falling sick of a fever, in which, being a young man and soldier too, he could not confine himself to so exact a diet as was necessary; for while his physician, Glaucus, was gone to the theater, he ate a fowl for his dinner, and drank a large drink of wine, upon which he became very ill, and shortly after died. At this misfortune, Alexander was so transported beyond all reason that, to express his sorrow, he immediately ordered the manes and tails of all his horses and mules to be cut, and threw down the battlements of the neighboring cities. He crucified the poor physician, and forbade playing on the flute or any other musical instrument in the camp a great while, till directions came from the oracle of Ammon, and enjoined him to honor Hephaestion, and sacrifice to him as a hero. Then seeking to alleviate his grief in war, he set out, as it were, to a hunt and chase of men, for he fell upon the Cossaeans, and put the whole nation to the sword. This was

called a sacrifice to Hephaestion's ghost. On his sepulcher and monument and the adorning of them he
intended to bestow 10,000 talents; and designing
that the excellence of the workmanship and the sin-
gularity of the design might outdo the expense, his
wishes turned, above all other artists, to Stasicrates,
because he always promised something very bold,
unusual, and magnificent in his projects. Once when
they had met before, he had told him that, of all the
mountains he knew, that of Athos in Thrace was the
most capable of being adapted to represent the
shape and lineaments of a man. If Alexander pleased
to command him, he would make it the noblest and
most durable statue in the world, which in its left
hand would hold a city of 10,000 inhabitants, and
out of its right would pour a copious river into the
sea. Though Alexander declined this proposal, yet
now he spent a great deal of time with workmen to
invent and contrive others even more extravagant
and sumptuous.

As he was upon his way to Babylon, Nearchus,
who had sailed back out of the ocean up the mouth
of the river Euphrates, came to tell him he had met
with some Chaldaean diviners, who had warned
him against Alexander's going there. Alexander,
however, took no thought of it, and went on, and
when he came near the walls of the place, he saw a
great many crows fighting with one another, some of
whom fell down just by him. After this, being privately informed that Apollodorus, the governor of
Babylon, had sacrificed to know what would
become of him, he sent for Pythagoras, the sooth-
sayer, and on his admitting the thing, asked him in
what condition he found the victim;[61] and when he
told him the liver was defective in its lobe, "A great
presage indeed!" said Alexander. However, he
offered Pythagoras no injury, but was sorry that he
had neglected Nearchus's advice, and stayed for the
most part outside the town, removing his tent from
place to place, and sailing up and down the
Euphrates. Besides this, he was disturbed by many
other prodigies. A tame ass fell upon the biggest and

handsomest lion that he kept, and killed him by a
kick. And one day after he had undressed himself to
be anointed, and was playing at ball, just as they
were going to bring his clothes again, the young men
who played with him perceived a man clad in the
king's robes with a diadem upon his head, sitting
silently upon his throne. They asked him who he
was, to which he gave no answer for a good while,
till at last, coming to himself, he told them his name
was Dionysius, that he was of Messenia, that for
some crime of which he was accused he was brought
there from the seaside, and had been kept long in
prison, that Serapis[62] appeared to him, had freed
him from his chains, conducted him to that place,
and commanded him to put on the king's robe and
diadem, and to sit where they found him, and to say
nothing. Alexander, when he heard this, by the
direction of his soothsayers, put the fellow to death,
but he lost his spirits, and grew diffident concerning
the protection and assistance of the gods, and suspicious of his friends. His greatest apprehension was
of Antipater and his sons, one of whom, Iolaus, was
his chief cupbearer, and Cassander, who had lately
arrived, and had been bred up in Greek manners, the
first time he saw some of the barbarians adore the
king, could not forbear laughing at it aloud, which
so incensed Alexander that he took him by the hair
with both hands and dashed his head against the
wall. Another time Cassander would have said
something in defense of Antipater to those who
accused him, but Alexander interrupting him said,
"What is it you say? Do you think people, if they had
received no injury, would come such a journey only
to charge your father falsely?" To which when Cassander replied that their coming so far from the evidence was a great proof of the falseness of their
charges. Alexander smiled and said those were some
of Aristotle's sophisms, which would serve equally
on both sides, and added that both he and his father
would be severely punished if they were found
guilty of the least injustice towards those who complained. All this made such a deep impression of ter-

---

61  I.e., the animal which had been sacrificed.
62  This god was a synthesis of aspects of Greek and Egyptian gods created under the sponsorship of Egypt's ruler following
    Alexander's death, Ptolemy I (323-285 BC), in order to serve as the patron god of the city of Alexandria.

ror in Cassander's mind that, long after, when he was king of Macedonia and master of Greece, as he was walking up and down at Delphi, and looking at the statues, at the sight of that of Alexander he was suddenly struck with alarm, and shook all over, his eyes rolled, his head grew dizzy, and it was a long time before he recovered himself.

When once Alexander had given way to fears of supernatural influence, his mind grew so disturbed and so easily alarmed that, if the least unusual or extraordinary thing happened, he thought it a prodigy or a presage, and his court was thronged with diviners and priests whose business was to sacrifice and purify and foretell the future. So miserable a thing is incredulity and contempt of divine power on the one hand, and so miserable, also, superstition on the other, which like water, where the level has been lowered, flowing in and never stopping, fills the mind with slavish fears and follies, as now in Alexander's case. But upon some answers which were brought him from the oracle concerning Hephaestion, he laid aside his sorrow, and fell again to sacrificing and drinking, and having given Nearchus a splendid entertainment, after he had bathed as was his custom, just as he was going to bed, at Medius's request he went to supper with him. Here he drank all the next day, and was attacked with a fever which seized him, not as some write, after he had drunk from the bowl of Hercules,[63] nor was he taken with any sudden pain in his back, as if he had been struck with a lance, for these are the inventions of some authors who thought it their duty to make the last scene of so great an action as dramatic and moving as they could. Aristobulus[64] tells us that, in the rage of his fever and a violent thirst, he took a drink of wine, upon which he fell into a delirium, and died on the thirtieth day of the month Daesius.

But the journals give the following record. On the eighteenth day of the month he slept in the bathing-room on account of his fever. The next day he bathed and removed to his chamber, and spent his time in playing at dice with Medius. In the evening he bathed and sacrificed and ate freely, and had fever through the night. On the twentieth, after the usual sacrifices and bathing, he lay in the bathing-room and heard Nearchus's narrative of his voyage, and the observations he had made in the great sea. The twenty-first he passed in the same manner, his fever still increasing, and suffered much during the night. The next day the fever was very violent and he had himself removed and his bed set by the great bath, and discoursed with his principal officers about finding fit men to fill up the vacant places in the army. On the twenty-fourth he was much worse, and was carried out of his bed to assist at the sacrifices, and gave order that the general officers should wait within the court, while the inferior officers kept watch outside. On the twenty-fifth he was removed to his palace on the other side the river, where he slept a little, but his fever did not abate, and when the generals came into his chamber, he was speechless and continued to be so the following day. The Macedonians, therefore, supposing he was dead, came with great clamors to the gates, and menaced his friends so that they were forced to admit them, and let them all pass through unarmed by his bedside. The same day Python and Seleucus were despatched to the temple of Serapis to inquire if they should bring Alexander there, and were answered by the god that they should not remove him. On the twenty-eighth, in the evening, he died. This account is most of it word for word as it is written in the journals.

At the time, nobody had any suspicion of his being poisoned, but upon some information given six years after, they say Olympias put many to death, and scattered the ashes of Iolaus, then dead, as if he had given it to him. But those who affirm that Aristotle counselled Antipater to do it, and that by his means the poison was brought, adduced one Hagnothemis as their authority, who, they say, heard King Antigonus[65] speak of it, and tell us that the poison was water, deadly cold as ice, distilled from a rock in the district of Nonacris, which they gathered like a

---

63  A kind of large, two-handled cup.
64  An historian who served on several of Alexander's campaigns.
65  A general of Alexander who would eventually displace Cassander as ruler of Macedonia and Greece, founding one of the successor kingdoms to Alexander's empire.

thin dew, and kept in an ass' hoof, for it was so very cold and penetrating that no other vessel would hold it. However, most are of opinion that all this is a mere made-up story, no slight evidence of which is that during the dissensions among the commanders, which lasted several days, the body continued clear and fresh, without any sign of such taint or corruption, though it lay neglected in a close and sultry place.

Roxana, who was now with child, and upon that account much honored by the Macedonians, being jealous of Statira, sent for her by a counterfeit letter, as if Alexander had been still alive; and when she had her in her power, killed her and her sister, and threw their bodies into a well, which they filled up with earth, not without the knowledge and assistance of Perdiccas, who in the time immediately following the king's death, under cover of the name of Arrhidaeus, whom he carried about him as a sort of guard to his person, exercised the chief authority. Arrhidaeus,[66] who was Philip's son by an obscure woman of the name of Philinna, was himself of weak intellect, not that he had been originally deficient either in body or mind, on the contrary, in his childhood he had shown a happy and promising character enough. But a diseased habit of body, caused by drugs which Olympias gave him, had ruined not only his health, but his understanding.

---

66   Also known as Philip III, he never held real power, and was eventually executed.

# 14

# MATERIAL EVIDENCE CONCERNING THE GREEK WORLD

14.1   Vase (detail) (Sixth Century BC)
Staatliche Antikensammlungen und Glyptothek, Munich (AS 1468)
Reproduced by permission.

14.2    The "Priam Painter," Hydria (*c.* 520-510 BC)
Photo: Tim Thayer, Toledo Museum of Art, Toledo, Ohio (1961.23)
Reproduced by permission.
A hydria was used to hold water. The figures pictured are at a well.

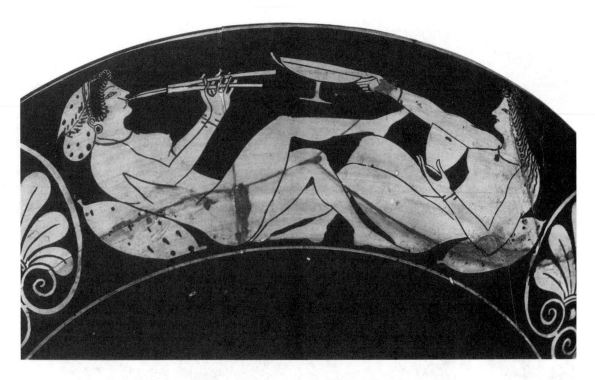

14.3   Kylix (detail) (*c.* 520-510 BC)
Archivo Fotográfico, Museo Arqueológico Nacional, Madrid (6508/1)
Reproduced by permission.
A kylix was used to drink wine. The woman on the right is holding a typical kylix.

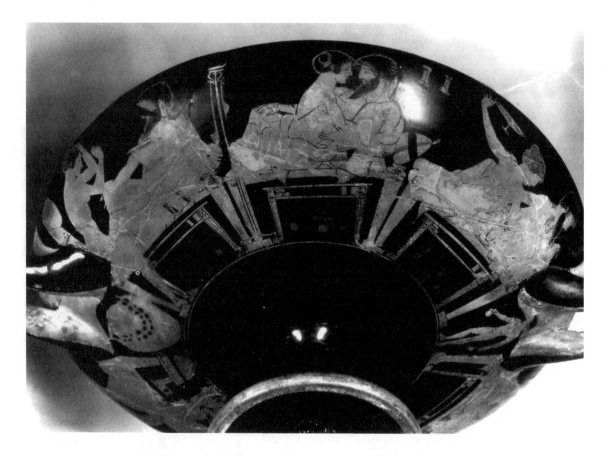

14.4    Kylix (detail), Attica (*c.* 490-480 BC), signed by the potter Hieron
The Metropolitan Museum of Art, New York, Rogers Fund, 1920 (20.246)

14.5   Column Krater, Attica (*c.* 460 BC)
The Metropolitan Museum of Art, Rogers Fund, New York, 1907 (07.286.74)
Reproduced by permission. All rights reserved, The Metropolitan Museum of Art.

14.6.1   Funerary Vase (*c.* 440 BC): Right side of front
National Archaeological Museum, Athens
Reproduced by permission.

14.6.2    Funerary Vase (*c.* 440 BC): Left side of front
National Archaeological Museum, Athens
Reproduced by permission.
A monument to the deceased stands between the two figures.

14.7   Harmodius and Aristogeiton, Athens (Fifth Century BC)
Museo Archeologico Nazionale, Naples
Reproduced by permission.

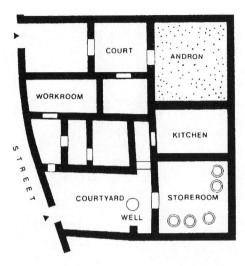

14.8.1    House on Slope of the Areopagus (Fifth Century BC): Probable Functions of Rooms
(from Susan Walker, "Women and Housing in Classical Greece: The Archaeological Evidence,"
in *Images of Women in Antiquity*, ed. Averil Cameron and Amélie Kuhrt [Routledge, 1983] p. 87)
Reproduced by permission of International Thomson Publishing Services Ltd. on behalf of Routledge.

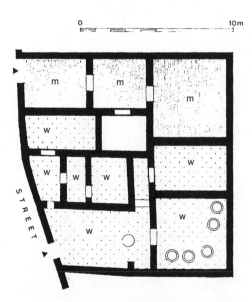

14.8.2    House on Slope of the Areopagus (Fifth Century BC): Areas Used by Women and by Men
(Ibid.)
Reproduced by permission of International Thomson Publishing Services Ltd. on behalf of Routledge.
Areas used by women marked by "w."
Areas used by men marked by "m."
Entrances from the street marked by arrows.

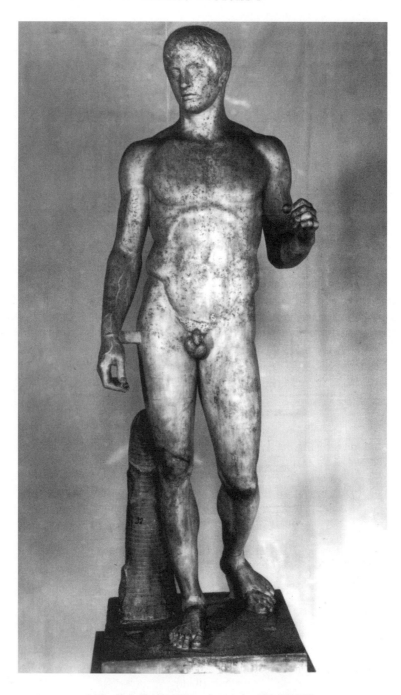

14.9   Polycleitus, Doryphorus (*c.* 440-435 BC)
Museo Archeologico Nazionale, Naples
Reproduced by permission.

14.10  Caryatid from the Erectheum, Athens (Roman Copy; Original Late Fifth Century BC)
Museo Vaticano, Rome
Reproduced by permission.
A caryatid was a sculpture of a human form used as a column to support a roof.

14.11   Praxiteles, Aphrodite of Cnidos (*c.* 350 BC)
Musei Vaticani, Rome
Reproduced by permission.

14.12   Praxiteles, Hermes (*c.* 325 BC)
Olympia Museum, Greece
Reproduced by permission.

14.13   Crouching Aphrodite (Hellenistic)
Museo Nazionale Romano, Rome (108.597)
Reproduced by permission.

14.14   Gaul (with his Wife) Killing Himself (*c.* 230-220 BC)
Museo Nazionale Romano, Rome (8608)
Reproduced by permission.

14.15   The Pharaoh Sesostris I (?), Egypt, (Second millennium BC)
The Metropolitan Museum of Art, New York, Museum Excavations, 1913-14; Rogers Fund supplemented by
contribution of Edward S. Karkness (14.13.17).

14.16   Queen Arsinoë II (Egypt, *c.* 210 BC)
The Metropolitan Museum of Art, New York, Rogers Fund, 1920 (20.2.21)

14.17   Queen Cleopatra (II?) (Egypt, *c.* 170 BC)
The Metropolitan Museum of Art, New York, Gift of Joseph W. Drexel, 1889 (89.2.660)
Reproduced by permission. All rights reserved, The Metropolitan Museum of Art.

14.18   Agesander, Athenodorus, and Polydorus of Rhodes, Lacoön and His Sons (*c.* 125 BC)
Musei Vaticani, Rome
Reproduced by permission.

14.19    Market Woman (First Century BC)
The Metropolitan Museum of Art, New York, Rogers Fund, 1909 (09.39)

# 15

# MARCUS TULLIUS CICERO, *LETTERS*

Marcus Tullius Cicero (106-43 BC) was regarded as the leading Roman orator and literary figure of his time. His prose style was the model for as long as Latin remained a living language. He was also an active politician, being elected consul in 63 BC. After Julius Caesar's assassination in 44 BC, he vigorously attacked Marc Antony as a threat to the Roman Republic, and the triumphant Antony had him executed the following year. Hundreds of Cicero's letters survive, as well as many letters written to him.

---

### 15.1

#### LETTER OF CICERO (IN ROME) TO JULIUS CAESAR (IN GAUL), ABOUT APRIL, 54 BC

*At this point Caesar was a member of the first triumvirate, an unofficial, and by now shaky, alliance among Caesar, Pompey, and Crassus which dominated Roman politics. When Cicero wrote this letter, Caesar was in Gaul, which he had conquered for Rome, and was preparing to invade Britain.*

Cicero greets Caesar, *imperator*.[1] Observe how far I have convinced myself that you are my second self, not only in matters which concern me personally, but even in those which concern my friends. It had been my intention to take Gaius Trebatius with me for whatever destination I should be leaving town, in order to bring him home again honored as much as my zeal and favor could make him. But when Pompey remained at home longer than I expected, and a certain hesitation on my part (with which you are not unacquainted) appeared to hinder, or at any rate to retard, my departure, I presumed upon what I will now explain to you. I begin to wish that Trebatius should look to you for what he had hoped from me, and, in fact, I have been no more sparing of my promises of goodwill on your part than I had been accustomed to be of my own. Moreover, an extraordinary coincidence has occurred which seems to support my opinion and to guarantee your kindness. For just as I was speaking to our friend Balbus[2] about this very Trebatius at my house, with more than usual earnestness, a letter from you was handed to me, at the end of which you say, "M. Rufus, whom you recommend to me, I will make king of Gaul or put him under the care of Lepta.[3] Send me someone else to promote." I and Balbus both lifted our hands in surprise: it came so exactly in the nick of time, that it

---

1 An honorary title for a successful general.
2 L. Cornelius Balbus, an agent of Caesar, whom Cicero had represented in court.
3 An assistant to Caesar.

appeared to be less the result of mere chance than something providential. I therefore send you Trebatius, and on two grounds: first that it was my spontaneous idea to send him, and secondly because you have invited me to do so.

I would beg you, my dear Caesar, to receive him with such a display of kindness as to concentrate on his single person all that you can be possibly induced to bestow for my sake upon my friends. As for him, I guarantee—not in the sense of that hackneyed expression of mine, at which, when I used it in writing to you about Milo, you very properly jested, but in good Roman language such as sober men use—that no more honest, better, or more modest a man exists. Added to this, he is at the top of his profession in civil law, possesses an unequalled memory, and the most profound learning. For such a man I ask neither a tribuneship, prefecture, nor any definite office, I ask only your good will and liberality: and yet I do not wish to prevent your complimenting him, if it so pleases you, with even these marks of distinction. In fact, I transfer him entirely from my hand, so to speak, to yours,[4] one as distinguished for good faith as for victory. Excuse my being somewhat importunate, though with a man like you there can hardly be any pretext for it—however, I feel that it will be allowed to pass. Be careful of your health and continue to love me as ever.

### 15.2
#### LETTER OF CICERO (AT CUMAE) TO C. TREBATIUS TESTA (IN GAUL), APRIL, 54 BC

In all my letters to Caesar or Balbus there is a sort of statutory appendix containing a recommendation of you, and not one of the ordinary kind, but accompanied by some special mark of my warm feeling towards you. See only that you get rid of that feeble regret of yours for the city and city ways, and carry out with persistence and courage what you had in your mind when you set out. We, your friends, shall

pardon your going away for that purpose as much as "The wealthy noble dames who held the Corinthian peak"[5] pardoned Medea, whom, with hands whitened to the utmost with chalk, she persuaded not to think ill of her for being absent from her fatherland, for "Many have served themselves abroad and served the state as well; many have spent their lives at home to be but counted fools." You would have certainly been in the latter category, had I not forced you abroad. But I will write more another time. You who learned to look out for others, look out, while in Britain, that you are not yourself taken in by the war charioteers, and, since I have begun quoting *Medea*, remember this line: "The sage who cannot serve himself is vainly wise I know."

Take care of your health.

### 15.3
#### LETTER OF CICERO (AT LYCAONIA) TO GAIUS CLAUDIUS MARCELLUS, CONSUL ELECT, SEPTEMBER, 51 BC

*Cicero had by this point gone to Cilicia, in the eastern empire, as* proconsul, *or governor.*

I rejoiced exceedingly to hear of your election as consul, and pray that the gods may bless your office, and that it may be administered by you in a manner worthy of your own and your father's position. For I have always loved and regarded you, as well as having had reason to know your exceeding affection for myself in all the course of my varied fortunes. Moreover, having been both defended in times of adversity and honored in times of prosperity by numerous acts of kindness from your father, I not only am, but am bound to be, devoted to your family, especially as from your most revered and excellent mother I have been fully aware of having received greater services in support of my safety and position than were to be expected from a woman. Wherefore I beg you with more than common earnestness to continue to regard and support me in my absence.

---

4   The expression comes from Roman law.
5   The quotations in this letter are from the play *Medea* by the Roman writer Ennius (third century BC), a translation or adaptation of the *Medea* of Euripides, the classical Athenian playwright. Only fragments of Ennius's work survive.

## 15.4
### CICERO (AT LYCAONIA) TO GAIUS CLAUDIUS MARCELLUS THE AUGUR,[6] SEPTEMBER, 51 BC

That your son Marcellus has been elected consul, and that you have experienced the joy which you above all things desired, give me extraordinary pleasure, and that both for his own sake, and because in my opinion you richly deserve every success of the best sort. For I have had reason to know your unexampled goodness to me both in troubled and triumphant times; in fact, I have experienced the greatest kindness and the most eager support from your whole family, whether it were a question of my civil existence or official advancement. Wherefore I shall be much obliged if you will congratulate for me that most revered and excellent woman, your wife Junia. From you I ask your habitual regard and support in my absence.

## 15.5
### LETTER OF CICERO (AT FORMIAE) TO HIS WIFE TERENTIA AND HIS DAUGHTER TULLIA (AT ROME), JANUARY 22, 49 BC

*By this time the first triumvirate had fallen apart and civil war had broken out between Caesar and Pompey. Caesar had earlier that month crossed the Rubicon river with his army, and was heading toward Rome, while Pompey was in retreat. Cicero, along with most of the Senate, was a supporter of Pompey.*

Tullius to his wife, and her father to his dearest daughter, and Cicero to his mother and sister, sends warm greetings. I think, my darlings, you should carefully consider and reconsider what to do, whether to stay at Rome, or to join me, or seek some place of safety. This is not a point for my consideration alone, but for yours also. What occurs to me is this: you may be safe at Rome under Dolabella's[7] protection, and that circumstance may prove serviceable to us in case of any violence or plunder commencing. But, on the other hand, I am shaken in this idea by seeing that all the loyalists

have left Rome and have the women of their families with them. Again, the district in which I now am consists of towns and estates also which are in my power, so you could be a good deal with me, and, if you left me, could very conveniently stay in domains belonging to us. I cannot as yet quite make up my mind which of the two is the better course for you to take. Please observe for yourselves what other women of your rank are doing, and be careful not to be cut off from the power of leaving town when you do wish to do so. I would have you carefully consider it again and again with each other and with your friends. Tell Philotimus[8] to secure the house with barricades and a watch. Also please organize a regular service of letter-carriers, so that I may hear something from you every day. Above all attend to your health, if you wish me to maintain mine.

## 15.6
### LETTER OF CICERO (AT MINTURNAE) TO HIS WIFE TERENTIA AND HIS DAUGHTER TULLIA (AT ROME), JANUARY 23, 49 BC

Tullius to Terentia, her father to Tullia, his two sweethearts, and Cicero to his excellent mother and darling sister, sends warm greetings. If you are well, we are so too. It is now for you to consider, and not for me only, what you must do. If Caesar means to come to Rome in a peaceable manner, you can stay at home with safety for the present. But if in his madness he is going to give up the city to plunder, I fear Dolabella himself may not be able to protect us sufficiently. Besides, I am alarmed lest we should be cut off from you, so that when you do wish to leave town you may be prevented. There is one other thing, which you are in the best position to observe yourselves—are other ladies of your rank remaining in Rome? If not, it deserves consideration whether you can do so with propriety. As things stand at present, indeed, always provided that I am allowed to hold this district, you will be able to stay with me or on one of our estates with the greatest comfort. There is another thing I am afraid of—a want

---

6  I.e., a member of the board of priests responsible for reading omens regarding the future.

7  Dolabella, Tullia's husband, was a supporter of Caesar.

8  A freedman of Cicero.

of provisions in the city before long. On these points pray consult with Pomponius, with Camillus, with anybody you think right; above all do not be frightened. Labienus has made things better for us. Piso, too, is helpful in leaving the city and declaring his own son-in-law guilty of treason. Dear hearts, write to me as often as possible, and tell me how you are and what is going on around you. Quintus and his son and Rufus send their love. Good-bye.

### 15.7
#### LETTER OF CICERO (AT FORMIAE) TO TERENTIA (AT CUMAE), JUNE 7, 49 BC

*In March Caesar had defeated Pompey in battle, but the conflict continued. Cicero writes from the camp of Pompey, who is about to leave for the eastern Mediterranean for support.*

All those uneasy feelings and melancholy thoughts, by which I kept you in such extreme distress, which makes me more uneasy than anything—as well as Tulliola,[9] who is dearer to me than life itself—I have got rid of and ejected. I discovered the reason for it all the day after I left you. I threw up sheer bile during the night. I was at once so much relieved that I really think some god worked the cure. Pray make full and pious acknowledgment to the god (Apollo or Aesculapius), according to your wont. I hope I have a very good ship. I write this at the moment of embarkation. Presently I will compose a large number of letters to our friends, to whose protection I will commend you and our dear Tulliola with the greatest earnestness. I would have added exhortations to you with a view to raising your courage, had I not known that you were more courageous than any man. And, after all, I hope affairs are of such a nature that I may venture to expect you to be as comfortable as possible there, and myself to be at last likely, in company with men like-minded with myself, to be acting in defense of our country. Let your first care be your health; next, if it seems to you possible, make use of the villas farthest removed from the soldiers. If the price of food goes up, you can with advantage use the place at Arpinum with your town establishment. Our charming young Cicero[10] sends his warmest love. Good-bye, good-bye.

### 15.8
#### CICERO (AT ROME) TO L. MUNATIUS PLANCUS (IN GAUL), APRIL 11, 43 BC

*Caesar, after defeating Pompey and becoming master of the Roman world, was assassinated in 44 BC. Caesar's assistant Marc Antony and his heir Octavian have become dominant at Rome, a development which Cicero hoped to stop in favor of a resumption of leadership by the Senate. In this situation, Plancus, who was in command of an army in Gaul, has sent a letter to the Senate promising to defend the Republic. (In the end, however, Plancus was to support Marc Antony.)*

Although on public grounds I ought to be extremely rejoiced that you have given the state so much protection and so much aid in what is almost a desperate crisis, yet while I shall embrace you with my whole heart as a conqueror if the constitution is restored, still what causes me a great part of my joy is the position you occupy, which I perceive is and will be of the most splendid kind. For do not imagine that any dispatch was ever read in the Senate which gave greater satisfaction than yours. And that was the result not only of what I may call the brilliance of your services to the Republic, but also of the loftiness of your language and sentiments. To me, indeed, it was nothing new, for I knew you, remembered the promises contained in your private letter to myself, and had a thorough acquaintance with your views from our friend Furnius. But to the Senate your words seemed beyond what they had expected, not because it had ever doubted your good intentions, but because it had not thoroughly realized how much you could do nor how far you were willing to go. Accordingly, when Marcus Varisidius handed me your letter early in the morning of the 7th of April, and I had read it, I felt an amazing thrill of joy. As a great crowd of the most distinguished men and citizens were escorting me from my house, I

9   The diminutive of Tullia.
10   Their son.

at once made them all sharers in my pleasure. Meanwhile our friend Munatius came as usual to see me. Well, I handed him your letter, for as yet he knew nothing about you, Varisidius having come to me before anyone else, saying that such were your orders. A little later Munatius also allowed me to read the letter you had sent him, as well as your public dispatch. We decided to transmit the dispatch at once to the city praetor Cornutus, who, in the absence of the consuls, was, according to traditional custom, performing the consular functions. A meeting of the Senate was at once summoned, and there was a large attendance, owing to the rumor and general anticipation in regard to your dispatch. After your dispatch had been read a religious difficulty was suggested to Cornutus, because the *pullarii*[11] informed him that he had not taken the auspices with the proper formalities, and that was confirmed by our board of augurs. Accordingly, business was postponed to the next day. Well, on that day I had a warm debate with Servilius in defense of your position.[12] He had exercised his influence to get his motion put first, but a large majority of senators left him and voted directly against it. But when my motion, which was put second, was being largely supported, at the request of Servilius it was vetoed by P. Titius.[13] The business was deferred till the next day. Servilius came prepared "to fight Jupiter[14] himself," in whose temple the debate was to be held. How I crushed him, and with what fiery eloquence I brought the vetoing Titius upon his knees, I would rather you learned from the letters of others. Take this one fact from mine. The Senate could not have been more resolute and firm or better disposed to your glory than it was on this occasion. Not that the Senate is a bit more friendly to you than the whole body of citizens. For there is a surprising unanimity of feeling among the entire Roman people, with the united aspiration of all conditions and classes, in favor of recovering the public liberty. Go on, then, as you have begun, to make your name immortal! And as for all those empty shows of glory, founded on the most unsubstantial badges of external splendor, despise them, and regard them as short-lived, counterfeit, and perishable. True glory rests on virtue, which is shown to the highest advantage by services done to the state. You have the most excellent opportunity for performing these. Since you have embraced it and still possess it, see that the state owes you as much as you owe the state. You will find in me not only a supporter of your high position, but a promoter of its increase. That much I think I owe both to the Republic, which is dearer to me than life itself, and to our friendship. And in these exertions, which I have consecrated to the support of your position, I have found a great pleasure in the still clearer view I have gained of the wisdom and loyalty of Titus Munatius—though I knew these before—as displayed in his extraordinary devotion and activity in your service.

---

11   These were officials in charge of sacred chickens who foretold omens based on how the chickens ate. Such omens were consulted when deciding whether to undertake official business.
12   Cicero was advocating a vote of thanks to Plancus by the Senate.
13   A tribune, who had the right to veto.
14   The chief Roman god.

# 16

## QUINTUS CICERO, LETTER TO HIS BROTHER

This short treatise takes the form of a letter from Quintus Cicero to his brother, the better known Roman politician and writer, Marcus Tullius Cicero, and so presumably dates to about 65 BC, when Cicero was preparing to run for consul, the highest office under the Roman Republic. (Quintus's authorship has, however, been challenged, and it has been argued that the work was really written even a century later.)

---

Quintus Cicero to his brother at Rome:

Although you have all the accomplishments within the reach of human genius, experience, or acuteness, yet I thought it only consistent with my affection to set down in writing what occurred to my mind while thinking, as I do, day and night about your campaign, not with the expectation that you would learn anything new from it, but that the considerations on a subject, which appeared to be disconnected and without system, might be brought under one view by a logical arrangement.

Consider what the state is; what it is you seek; who you are that seek it. Almost every day as you go down to the forum you should say to yourself, "I am new";[1] "I am a candidate for the consulship"; "This is Rome."

You will best compensate for the newness of your name by the brilliance of your oratory. That has always carried with it very great political distinction. A man who is held worthy of defending consulars[2] in court cannot be thought unworthy of the consulship. For this reason, since your reputation in this is your starting point, since whatever you are, you are from this, approach each individual case with the persuasion that your entire reputation depends on it as a whole. See that those aids to natural ability, which I know are your special gifts, are ready for use and always available; remember what Demetrius[3] wrote about the hard work and practice of Demosthenes;[4] finally, take care that both the number and rank of your friends are unmistakable. For you have such as few *novi homines*[5] have had—all the *publicani*,[6] nearly

---

1  Or in other words, a "novus homo," that is, a "new man." The term was used for consuls (or in this case, one who seeks that office) who did not have ancestors who had held the consulate.
2  That is, people who have been consuls or are so now.
3  A Greek scholar of the early third century BC.
4  One of the leading orators of Athens in the fourth century BC. He is said to have practiced giving speeches with pebbles in his mouth in order to learn to enunciate more clearly, as well as undertaking other strenuous measures to improve his public speaking.
5  Plural of *novus homo*, for which, see above n 1.
6  I.e., public contractors, especially used of those collecting state revenue.

the whole equestrian order,[7] many municipalities[8] specially devoted to you, many persons who have been defended in court by you, men of every rank, many *collegia*,[9] and, besides these, a large number of the rising generation who have become attached to you in their enthusiasm for rhetoric, and, finally, your friends who visit you daily in large numbers and with such constant regularity. See that you retain these advantages by reminding these persons, by appealing to them, and by using every means to make them understand that this, and this only, is the time for those who are in your debt to show their gratitude and for those who wish for your services in the future to place you under an obligation. It also seems possible that a *novus homo* may be much assisted by the fact that he has the good wishes of *nobiles*,[10] and especially of consulars. It is a point in your favor that you should be thought worthy of this position and rank by the very men to whose position and rank you wish to attain. All these men must be canvassed with care, agents must be sent to them, and they must be convinced that we have always been at one with the *optimates*[11] concerning the Republic, that we have never been demagogues in any way, that if we seem ever to have said anything in the spirit of that party, we did so with the view of attracting Pompey[12] so that we might have the man of the greatest influence either actively on our side in our campaign, or at least not opposed to us. Furthermore, take pains to get on your side the young men of high rank, or retain the affection of those you already have. They will contribute much to your political position. You have very many; make them feel how much you think depends on them: if

you induce those to be positively eager who are merely not disinclined, they will be of very great advantage to you.

It is also a great set off to your newness that the *nobiles* who are your competitors are of such a kind that no one can venture to say that their nobility ought to stand them in greater stead than your high character. For instance, who could think of P. Galba and L. Cassius, though by birth of the highest rank, as candidates for the consulship? You see, therefore, that there are men of the greatest families, who from defect of ability are not your equals. But, you will say, Catiline[13] and Antonius are formidable. Rather I should say that a man of energy, industry, unimpeachable character, great eloquence and high popularity with those who are the ultimate judges should wish for such rivals— both from their boyhood stained with blood and lust, both of ruined fortunes. Of one of them[14] we have seen the property put up for sale, and actually heard him declare on oath that at Rome he could not contend in court with even a Greek or obtain an impartial tribunal. We know that he was ejected from the Senate by the judgment of genuine censors; in our praetorship we had him as a competitor, with such men as Sabidius and Panthera to back him, because he had no one else to appear for him at the scrutiny of votes. Yet in this office he bought a mistress from the slave market whom he kept openly at his house. Moreover, in his campaign for the consulship, he has preferred to be robbing all the innkeepers, under the disgraceful pretext of being a legate,[15] rather than to be in town and supplicate the Roman people. But the other! Good heavens what is his distinction? Is he of equally noble

---

7   The social rank below senator.

8   I.e., towns with Roman citizenship rights.

9   I.e., a group with a common purpose, including what today might be called a club. The term could also refer to a board of priests or government officials.

10  Plural of *nobilis*. Sometimes translated as "noble," *nobilis* referred to someone whose ancestor had served as consul.

11  From the late second century BC, two loosely used political designations became current at Rome: the *optimates*, who publicly supported continued dominance of Roman politics by the Senatorial aristocracy, and the *populares*, who advocated more popular measures such as those of the Gracchi. Neither of these groups was so formally organized as to constitute what today would be called a political party, and the leading *populares* were as aristocratic in their backgrounds as the *optimates*.

12  I.e., Pompey the Great.

13  Whose conspiracy against the state Marcus Tullius Cicero would quash once he became consul.

14  I.e., Antonius.

15  A lieutenant of a Roman governor or general, or a person sent on a diplomatic mission.

birth? No. Is he richer? No. In manliness, then? How do you make that out? Why, because while Antonius fears his own shadow, this man does not even fear the laws! A man born in the house of a bankrupt father, nurtured in the society of a disgraced sister, grown to manhood amidst the massacre of fellow citizens, whose first entrance to public life was made by the slaughter of Roman equestrians! For Sulla[16] had specially selected Catiline to command that band of Gauls which we remember, who cut off the heads of the Titinii and Nannii and Tanusi, and with them he killed with his own hands the best man of the day, his own sister's husband, Quintus Caecilius, who was a Roman equestrian, a man belonging to no party, always quiet by inclination, and then so from age also.

Why should I speak of him as a candidate for the consulship, who caused Marcus Marius,[17] a man most beloved by the Roman people, to be beaten with vinerods in the sight of that Roman people from one end of the city to the other, forced him up to the *bustum*,[18] lacerated him with every kind of torture, and while he was still alive and breathing, cut off his head with his sword in his right hand, while he held the hairs on the crown of his head with his left, and carried off his head in his own hand with streams of blood flowing through his fingers? A man who afterwards lived with actors and gladiators on such terms that the former ministered to his lust, the latter to his crimes—who never approached a place so sacred or holy as not to leave there, even if no actual crime were committed, some suspicion of dishonor founded on his wickedness; a man whose closest friends in the senate were the Curii and the Annii, in the auction rooms the Sapalae and Carrilii, in the equestrian order the Pompilii and Vettii; a man of such consummate impudence, such abandoned profligacy, in sum, such cunning and success in lasciviousness, that he corrupted youths[19] when almost in the bosoms of their parents? Why should I after this mention Africa[20] to you, or the

depositions of the witnesses? They are well known—read them again and again yourself. Nevertheless, I think that I should not omit to mention that he left that court in the first place as poor as some of the jurors were before the trial, and in the second place the object of such hatred that another prosecution against him is called for every day. His position is such that he is more likely to be nervous even if you do nothing than contemptuous if you start any proceedings.

What much better fortune in your campaign is yours than that which not long ago fell to the lot of another *novus homo*, Gaius Caelius! He had two men of the highest rank as competitors, but they were of such a character that their rank was the least of their recommendations—genius of the highest order, supreme modesty, very numerous public services, excellent methods of conducting a campaign, and diligence in carrying them out. And yet Caelius, though much inferior in birth, and superior in hardly anything, beat one of them. Wherefore, if you do what your natural ability and studies, which you have always pursued, enable you to do, what the necessities of your present position require, what you are capable of doing and are bound to do, you will not have a difficult struggle with competitors who are by no means so conspicuous for their birth as notorious for their vices. For what citizen can there be found so ill-affected as to wish by one vote to draw two daggers against the Republic?

Having thus set forth what advantages you have and might have to set against your newness, I think I ought now to say a word on the importance of what you are trying for. You are seeking the consulship, an office of which no one thinks you unworthy, but of which there are many who will be jealous. For, while by birth of equestrian rank, you are seeking the highest rank in the state, and yet one which, though the highest, reflects much greater splendor on a man of courage, eloquence, and pure life than on others. Do

---

16   The Roman military commander who took control of the city by force and had himself named dictator and his political enemies slaughtered (82-79 BC).
17   A relative of the more famous politician C. Marius, Sulla's opponent.
18   The place where bodies were burned and buried.
19   I.e., *praetextati liberi*: males under 17 years of age.
20   Catiline was charged with committing extortion in this Roman province while its governor.

not suppose that those who have already held that office are blind to the political position you will occupy, when once you have obtained it. I suspect, however, that those who, though born of consular families, have not attained the position of their ancestors, will, unless they happen to be strongly attached to you, feel some jealousy. Even new men who have been praetors I think, unless under great obligations to you, will not like to be surpassed by you in official rank. Lastly, in the populace itself, I am sure it will occur to you how many are envious, how many, from the precedents of recent years, are averse to *novi homines*. It must also be that some are angry with you in consequence of the cases which you have pleaded. Indeed, carefully consider this also, whether, seeing that you have devoted yourself with such fervor to the promotion of Pompey's glory, you can suppose certain men to be your friends on that account. Wherefore, seeing that you are seeking the highest place in the state, and at the same time that there do exist sentiments opposed to you, you must positively employ every method, and all your vigilance, labor, and attention to business.

Again, the campaign for office resolves itself into an activity of two kinds, of which one is concerned with the loyalty of friends, the other with the feelings of the people. The loyalty of friends must be secured by acts of kindness and attention, by length of time, and by an easy and agreeable temper. But this word "friends" has a wider application during a campaign than in other times of our life. For whosoever gives any sign of an inclination to you, or habitually visits at your house, must be put down in the category of friends. But yet the most advantageous thing is to be beloved and pleasant in the eyes of those who are friends on the more regular grounds of relationship by blood or marriage, of membership in the same club, or of some close tie or other. Farther, you must take great pains that, in proportion as a man is most intimate and most closely connected with your household, he should love you and desire your highest honor—as, for instance, your tribesmen,[21] neighbors, clients, and finally your freedmen and even your slaves, for nearly all the talk which forms one's public reputation emanates from domestic sources. In a word, you must secure friends of every class—for show: men conspicuous for their office or name, who, even if they do not give any actual assistance in campaign, yet add some dignity to the candidate; to maintain your just rights: magistrates, consuls first and then tribunes; to secure the votes of the centuries[22]—men of eminent popularity. Take all pains to collect and secure those who either have gained or hope to gain the vote of a tribe or century, or any other advantage, through your influence. For during recent years men of ambition have exerted themselves with all their might and main to become sure of getting from their tribesmen what they sought. Also do your very best, by every means in your power, to make such men attached to you from the bottom of their hearts and with the most complete devotion. If, indeed, men were as grateful as they ought to be, all this should be ready to your hand, as I trust in fact that it is. For within the last two years you have put under an obligation to you four clubs of men who have the very greatest influence in promoting an election, those of C. Fundanius, Q. Gallius, C. Cornelius, C. Orchivius. I am acquainted with what their clubsmen undertook and promised you to do when they committed the defense of these men to you, for I was present at the interview. For this reason you must insist at the present juncture on exacting from them your due by reminding them, appealing to them, solemnly assuring them, and taking care that they thoroughly understand that they will never have any other opportunity of showing their gratitude. I cannot doubt that these men, from hope of your services in the future as well as from the benefits recently received, will be roused to active exertions. And speaking generally, since your candidature is most

---

21 The body of Roman citizens was divided into territorial designations called "tribes." In some Roman elections, but not all, citizens were assembled at the city in the *comitia tributa* (tribal assembly), where each tribe cast one vote. Voting could take place only in Rome, and there was no absentee ballot.

22 For purposes of voting in some situations, but not all, the body of Roman citizens met in the *comitia centuriata* (centuriate assembly). In such a meeting, they were divided into a number of income categories, called "centuries." Different centuries had different numbers of votes, and votes were made by the century. Consuls were elected in the *comitia centuriata*.

strongly supported by that class of friendships which you have gained as a counsel for the defense, take care that to all those, whom you have placed under this obligation to you, their duty should in every case be clearly defined and set forth. And as you have never been in any matter importunate with them, so be careful that they understand that you have reserved for this occasion all that you consider them to owe you.

But since men are principally induced to show goodwill and zeal at the polls by three considerations—kindness received, hope of more, and personal affection and good feeling—we must take notice how best to take advantage of each of these. Men are induced by very small favors to think that they have sufficient reason for giving support at the polls, and surely those you have saved (and their number is very large) cannot fail to understand that, if at this supreme crisis they fail to do what you wish, they will never have anyone's confidence.[23] And although this is so, nevertheless they must be appealed to, and must even be led to think it possible that they, who have hitherto been under an obligation to us, may now put us under an obligation to them. Those, again, who are influenced by hope (a class of people much more apt to be scrupulously attentive) you must take care to convince that your assistance is at their service at any moment, and to make them understand that you are carefully watching the manner in which they perform the duties they owe you, and to allow no mistake to exist as to your clearly perceiving and taking note of the amount of support coming from each one of them. The third class which I mentioned is that of spontaneous and sincere friends, and this class you will have to make more secure by expressions of your gratitude; by making your words tally with the motives which it shall appear to you influenced them in taking up your cause; by showing that the affection is mutual; and by suggesting that your friendship with them may ripen into intimacy and familiar intercourse. In all these classes alike consider and weigh carefully the amount of influence each possesses, in order to know both the kind of attention to pay to each and what you are to expect and demand from each. For certain men are

popular in their own neighborhoods and towns; others have energy and wealth, who, even, if they have not heretofore sought such popularity, can yet easily obtain it at the moment for the sake of one to whom they owe or wish to do a favor. Your attention to such classes of people must be such as to show them that you clearly understand what is to be expected from each, that you appreciate what you are receiving, and remember what you have received. There are, again, others who either have no influence or are positively disliked by their tribesmen, and have neither the spirit nor the ability to exert themselves on the spur of the moment; be sure you distinguish between such men, that you may not be disappointed in your expectation of support by placing too much hope on some particular person.

But although you ought to rely on, and be fortified by, friendships already gained and firmly secured, yet very numerous and useful friendships are acquired in the course of the campaign itself. For among its annoyances a candidature has this advantage: you can without loss of dignity, as you cannot in other affairs of life, admit whomsoever you choose to your friendship, to whom if you were at any other time to offer your society, you would be thought guilty of an eccentricity; whereas during a campaign, if you do not do so with many, and take pains about it besides, you would be thought to be no use as a candidate at all. Moreover, I can assure you of this, that there is no one, unless he happens to be bound by some special tie to some one of your rivals, whom you could not induce, if you took pains, to earn your affection by his good services, and to seize the opportunity of putting you under an obligation; let him but fully understand that you value him highly, that you really mean what you say, that he is making a good investment, and that there will accrue from it not only a brief and electioneering friendship, but a firm and lasting one. There will be no one, believe me, if he has anything in him at all, who will let slip this opportunity offered of establishing a friendship with you, especially when by good luck you have competitors whose friendship is one to be neglected or avoided, and who not only are unable to

---

23  It should be noted that there was no secret ballot.

secure what I am urging you to secure, but cannot even make the first step towards it. For how should Antonius make the first step towards attaching people to himself, when he cannot even call them, unaided, by their proper names? I, for one, think that there can be no greater folly than to imagine a man solicitous to serve you whom you do not know by sight. Extraordinary indeed must be the fame, the political position, and extent of the public services of that man whom complete strangers, without supporters to back him, would elect to office. That a man without principle or energy, without doing any good service, and without ability, lying under a cloud of discredit, and without friends, should beat a man fortified with the devotion of a numerous circle and by the good opinion of all, cannot possibly occur except from gross negligence.

Wherefore see that you have the votes of all the centuries secured to you by the number and variety of your friends. The first and most obvious thing is that you should embrace the Roman senators and equestrians, and the active and popular men of all the other orders. There are many city men of good business habits; there are many freedmen engaged in the forum who are popular and energetic: try to make these men eager on your behalf with all your might, both personally and by common friends—send agents to them, show them that they are putting you under the greatest obligation. After that, review the entire city, all colleges, districts, neighborhoods. If you attach the leading men of these to yourself, you will by their means easily keep a hold upon the multitude. When you have done that, take care to have in your mind a chart of all Italy laid out according to the tribe of each town, and learn it by heart, so that you may not allow any municipality, colony, prefecture, or, in a word, any spot in Italy to exist in which you have not a sufficient foothold. Inquire also for and trace out individuals in every region, inform yourself about them, seek them out, strengthen their resolution, secure that in their own neighborhoods they shall canvass for you, and be as it were candidates in your interest. They will wish for you as a friend, if they once see that their friendship is your object. Make sure that they understand

this by directing your speech especially to this point. Men of municipalities or from the country think themselves in the position of friends if we of the city know them by name. If, however, they think that they are also securing some protection for themselves, they do not let slip the opportunity of being obliging. Of such people others in town, and above all your rivals, do not so much as know the existence; you know about them and will easily recognize them, without which friendship is impossible. Nor is such recognition enough (though it is a great thing) unless some hope of material advantage and active friendship follows; for your object is not to be looked upon as a mere *nomenclator*[24] but as a sincere friend also. So when you have both got the favor of these same men in the centuries, who from the means they have taken to secure their personal objects enjoy most popularity among their fellow tribesmen; and have made those entirely desirous of your success who have influence in any section of their tribe, owing to considerations attaching to their municipality or neighborhood or college, then you may allow yourself to entertain the highest hopes.

Again, the centuries of the equestrians appear to me capable of being won over, if you are careful, with considerably more ease. Let your first care be to acquaint yourself with the equestrians, for they are comparatively few. Then make advances to them, for they are mostly young, and it is much easier to gain the friendship of young men at their time of life. Then again, you have on your side the best of the rising generation, and the most devoted to learning. Moreover, as the equestrian order is yours, they will follow the example of that order, if only you take the trouble to confirm the support of those centuries, not only by the general good affection of the order, but also by the friendship of individuals. Finally, the hearty zeal of the young in canvassing for votes, appearing at various places, bringing intelligence, and being in attendance on you in public are surprisingly important as well as creditable.

And since I have mentioned "attendance," I may add that you should be careful to see large groups of

---

24 A slave who accompanied a candidate to remind him of the names of people he met.

every class and order every day, for from the mere number of these a guess may well be made as to the amount of support you are likely to have in the election itself. Such visitors are of three kinds: one consists of morning callers who come to your house; a second of those who escort you to the forum; a third of those who attend you on your campaign. In the case of the morning callers, who are less select and, according to the prevailing fashion, come in greater numbers, you must contrive to make them think that you value even this slight attention very highly. Let those who come to your house see that you notice it; show your gratification to such of their friends as will repeat it to them; frequently mention it to the persons themselves. It often happens that people, when they visit a number of candidates, and observe that there is one who above the rest notices these attentions, devote themselves to him; leave off visiting the others; little by little become devoted to one instead of being neutral, and from sham turn out real supporters. Furthermore, carefully remember this: if you have been told or have discovered that a man who has given you his promise is "dressing for the occasion," as the phrase goes, act as though you had neither heard it nor knew it; if any offers to clear himself to you because he thinks himself suspected, assert roundly that you have never doubted his sincerity and have no right to doubt it. For the man who thinks that he is not giving satisfaction can never be a friend. You ought, however, to know each man's real feeling, in order to settle how much confidence to place in him.

Secondly, of those who escort you to the forum: since this is a greater attention than a morning call, indicate and make clear that it is still more gratifying to you, and as far as it shall lie in your power go down to the forum at fixed times. The daily escort by its numbers produces a great impression and confers great personal distinction. The third class is that of numbers perpetually attending you on your canvass. See that those who do so spontaneously understand that you regard yourself as forever obliged by their extreme kindness. From those, on the other hand, who owe you this attention, frankly demand that, as far as

their age and business allow, they should constantly be in personal attendance, and that those who are unable to accompany you in person should find relations to take their place in performing this duty. I am very anxious, and think it extremely important, that you should always be surrounded by large numbers. Besides, it confers a great reputation and great distinction to be accompanied by those who by your exertions have been defended, preserved, and acquitted in the law courts. Put this demand fairly before them, that, since by your means and without any payment some have retained their property, others their honor, others their civil existence and entire fortunes, and since there will never be any other time at which they can show their gratitude, they should remunerate you by this service.

And since the point now in discussion is entirely a question of the loyalty of friends, I must not, I think, pass over one caution. Deception, intrigue, and treachery are everywhere. This is not the time for a formal discussion of the indications by which a true friend may be distinguished from a false; all that remains now is to give you a hint. Your exalted character has compelled many to pretend to be your friends while really jealous of you. For this reason, remember the saying of Epicharmus,[25] "the muscle and bone of wisdom is to believe nothing rashly." Again, when you have got the feelings of your friends in a sound state, you must then acquaint yourself with the attitude and varieties of your detractors and opponents. There are three: first, those whom you have attacked; second, those who dislike you without definite reason; third, those who are warm friends of your competitors. As to those attacked by you while pleading a friend's lawsuit against them, frankly excuse yourself; remind them of the ties constraining you; give them reason to hope that you will act with equal zeal and loyalty in their cases, if they become your friends. As for those who dislike you without reason, do your best to remove that prejudice either by some actual service, or by holding out hopes of it, or by indicating your kindly feeling towards them. As for those whose wishes are against you owing to friendship for your competi-

---

25   A Greek poet and philosopher from Sicily (fifth century BC).

tors, gratify them also by the same means as the former, and, if you can get them to believe it, show that you are kindly disposed to the very men who are standing against you.

Having said enough about securing friendships, I must now speak on another department of a candidate's task, which is concerned with the conciliation of the people. This demands a knack of remembering names, insinuating manners, constant attendance, liberality, the power of setting a report afloat and creating a hopeful feeling in the Republic. First of all, make the faculty you possess of recognizing people conspicuous, and go on increasing and improving it every day. I do not think there is anything so popular or so conciliatory. Next, if nature has denied you some quality, resolve to assume it, so as to appear to be acting naturally. Although nature has great force, yet in a business lasting only a few months it seems probable that the artificial may be the more effective. For although you are not lacking in the courtesy which good and polite men should have, yet there is great need of a flattering manner which, however faulty and discreditable in other transactions of life, is yet necessary during a candidacy. For when it makes a man worse by constantly agreeing, it is wrong; but when only more friendly, it does not deserve so harsh a term, while it is absolutely necessary to a candidate, whose face, expression, and style of conversation have to be varied and accommodated to the feelings and tastes of everyone he meets. As for "constant attendance," there is no need of laying down any rule—the phrase speaks for itself. It is, of course, of very great consequence not to go away anywhere, but the real advantage of such constant attendance is not only being at Rome and in the forum, but the pushing of one's campaign assiduously, the addressing oneself again and again to the same persons, the making it impossible (as far as your power goes) for anyone to say that he has not been asked by you, and earnestly and carefully asked. Liberality is, again, of wide application; it is shown in regard to the management of your private property, which, even if it does not actually reach the multitude, yet, if spoken of with praise by friends, earns the favor of the multitude. It may also be displayed in banquets, which you must take care to attend yourself and to cause your friends to attend, whether open ones or those confined to particular tribes. It may, again, be displayed in giving practical assistance, which I would have you render available far and wide—and be careful therein to be accessible to all by day and night, and not only by the doors of your house, but by your face and countenance, which is the door of the mind; for, if that shows your feelings to be those of reserve and concealment, it is of little good to have your house doors open. For men desire not only to have promises made to them, especially in their applications to a candidate, but to have them made in a liberal and complimentary manner. Accordingly, it is an easy rule to make that you should indicate that whatever you are going to do you will do with heartiness and pleasure; it is somewhat more difficult, and rather a concession to the necessities of the moment than to your inclination, that when you cannot do a thing you should either promise or put your refusal pleasantly: the latter is the conduct of a good man, the former of a good candidate. For when a request is made which we cannot grant with honor or without loss to ourselves, for instance, if a man were to ask us to appear in a suit against a friend, a refusal must be given in a gentlemanly way: you must point out to him that your hands are tied, must show that you are exceedingly sorry, must convince him that you will make up for it in other ways.

I have heard a man say about certain orators, to whom he had offered his lawsuit, "that he had been better pleased with the words of the one who declined, than of the one who accepted." So true it is that men are more taken by look and words than by actual services. This latter course, however, you will readily approve; the former it is somewhat difficult to recommend to a Platonist like you, but yet I will have regard for your present circumstances. For even those to whom you are forced by any other tie to refuse your advocacy may yet leave you mollified and with friendly feelings. But those to whom you only excuse a refusal by saying that you are hindered by the affairs of closer friends, or by cases more important or previously undertaken, leave you with hostile feelings, and are one and all disposed to prefer an insincere promise to a direct negative from you. Gaius Cotta, a master in the art of electioneering, used to say that, so long as the request was not directly contrary to moral duty, he used to promise his assistance to all, to bestow it on those with whom he thought it would be most advantageously invested. He refused no one, because something often turned up to prevent the person whom he promised from availing himself of that promise, and it often also occurred that he himself was less engaged than he had thought at the time. Nor could anyone's house be full of suitors who undertook only what he saw his way to perform; by some accident or other the unexpected often happens, while business, which he believed to be actually in hand, for some reason or other does not come off. Moreover, the worst that can happen is that the man to whom he made a false promise is angry. This last risk, supposing you to make the promise, is uncertain, is prospective, and only affects a few; but, if you refuse, the offense given is certain, immediate, and more widely diffused. For many more ask to be allowed to avail themselves of the help of another than actually do so. Wherefore it is better that some of them should at times be angry with you in the forum, than all of them perpetually at your own house, especially as they are more inclined to be angry with those who refuse than with a man whom they perceive to be prevented by so grave a cause as to be compatible with the desire to fulfill his promise if he possibly could. But that I may not appear to have abandoned my own classification, since the department of a candidate's work which I am now discussing is that which refers to the populace, I insist on this: that all these observations have reference not so much to the feelings of friends as to popular rumor. Though there is something in what I say which comes under the former head—such as answering with kindness, and giving zealous assistance in the business and the dangers of friends—yet in this part of my argument I am speaking of the things which enable you to win over the populace: for instance, the having your house full of visitors before daybreak, the securing the affection of many by giving them hope of your support, the contriving that men should leave you with more friendly feelings than they came, the filling the ears of as many as possible with the most telling words.

For my next theme must be popular report, to which very great attention must be paid. But what I have said throughout the foregoing discussion applies also to the diffusion of a favorable report: the reputation for eloquence; the favor of the *publicani* and equestrian order; the goodwill of men of rank; the crowd of young men; the constant attendance of those whom you have defended; the number of those from municipalities who have notoriously come to Rome on your account; the observations which men make in your favor—that you recognize them, address them politely, are assiduous and earnest in campaigning, that they speak and think of you as kind and liberal; the having your house full of callers long before daybreak; the presence of large numbers of every class; that your look and speech give satisfaction to all, your acts and deeds to many; that everything is done which can be done by hard work, skill, and attention, not to cause the fame arising from all these displays of feeling to reach the people, but to bring the people itself to share them. You have already won the city populace and the affections of those who control the public meetings by your panegyric[26] of Pompey, by undertaking the suit of Manilius, by your defense of Cornelius. We must not let those advantages be forgotten, which hitherto no one has had without possessing at the same time the favor of the great. We must also take care that everyone knows that Pompey is strongly in your favor, and that it emphatically suits his purpose that you should win your election. Lastly, take care that your whole candidacy is vigorous, brilliant, splendid, suited to the popular taste, presenting a spectacle of the utmost dignity and magnificence. See also, if possible, that some new scandal is started against your competitors for crime or loose living or corruption, such as is in harmony with their characters.

Above all, in this election you must see that the Republic entertains a good hope and an honorable opinion of you. And yet you must not enter upon political measures in the Senate house and public meetings while a candidate; you must hold such things in abeyance, in order that from your lifelong

___
26  A long public speech of praise.

conduct the Senate may judge you likely to be the supporter of their authority; the Roman equestrians, along with the loyalists and wealthy, judge you from your past to be eager for peace and quiet times; and the people think of you as not likely to be hostile to their interests from the fact that in your style of speaking in public meetings, and in your declared convictions, you have been on the popular side.

This is what occurred to me to say on the subject of these two morning reflections, which I said you ought to turn over in your mind every day as you went down to the forum: "I am new"; "I am a candidate for the consulship." There remains the third, "This is Rome," a city made up of a combination of nations, in which many snares, much deception, many vices enter into every department of life; in which you have to put up with the arrogant pretensions, the wrong-headedness, the ill-will, the pride, the disagreeable temper and offensive manners of many. I well understand that it requires great prudence and skill for a man, living among social vices of every sort, so many and so serious, to avoid giving offense, causing scandal, or falling into traps, and in his single person to adapt himself to such a vast variety of character, speech, and feeling. Wherefore, I say again and again, go on persistently in the path you have begun. Put yourself above rivalry in eloquence; it is by this that people at Rome are charmed and attracted, as well as deterred from obstructing a man's career or inflicting an injury upon him. And since the chief plague of our state is that it allows the prospect of a bribe to blind it to virtue and worth, be sure that you are fully aware of your own strength, that is, understand that you are the man capable of producing in the minds of your rivals the strongest fear of legal proceeding and legal peril. Let them know that they are watched and scrutinized by you; they will be in terror of your energy, as well as of your influence and power of speech, and above all of the affection of the equestrian order towards you. But although I wish you to hold this out before them, I do not wish you to make it appear that you are already meditating an action, but to use this terror so as to facilitate the gaining of your object. In a word, in this contest strain every nerve and use every faculty in such a way as to secure what we seek. I notice that there are no elections so deeply tainted with corruption, but that some centuries return men closely connected with them without receiving money. Therefore, if we are as vigilant as the greatness of our object demands, and rouse our well-wishers to put forth all their energies; and if we allot to men of influence and zeal in our service their several tasks; if we put before our rivals the threat of legal proceedings; if we inspire their agents with fear, and by some means check the distributors, it is possible to secure either that there shall be no bribery or that it shall be ineffectual.

These are the points that I thought, not that I knew better than you, but that I could more easily than you—in the pressing state of your present engagements—collect together and send you written out. And although they are written in such terms as not to apply to all candidates for office, but to your special case and to your particular election, yet I would be glad if you would tell me of anything that should be corrected or entirely struck out, or that has been omitted. For I wish this little essay "on the duties of a candidate" to be regarded as complete in every respect.

# 17

## VERGIL, THE *AENEID*

Vergil was born in Italy, near Mantua, in 70 BC. He was regarded as the greatest of Roman poets in his own time, and this reputation has lasted for centuries. During the rule of Augustus, whose crony Maecenas provided Vergil material support, Vergil undertook the *Aeneid* which, even before it was completed, was expected to be an epic with the same standing among the Romans that Homer's *Iliad* and *Odyssey* had among the Greeks. The *Aeneid* indeed gained that status—every educated Roman of later generations read it. Vergil worked on this, his longest poem, for 11 years. On his death in 19 BC, a few verses were still incomplete, and Vergil left instructions that the work was to be destroyed. On the direction of Augustus, this wish was not followed.

---

4 [*The Trojans have lost the Trojan war. One of the Trojan nobles, Aeneas, has fled with his elderly father Anchises, his young son Ascanius, and a number of followers. They are pursuing a prophecy which says that they are to found a new city in Italy, from which long ago the Trojan people had originated. Jupiter (also known as "Jove" and the Roman equivalent of the Greek god Zeus) has decreed that the people of this new Troy (the Romans) will come to rule the world. However, the goddess Juno (the Roman equivalent of the Greek goddess Hera), an enemy of Troy, has in a rage sent a storm to destroy Aeneas and his ships. That storm has blown the ships off course, and they have landed on the Libyan coast of North Africa, near the city of Carthage, ruled by Queen Dido. In order to prevent a hostile attack and gain help for the Trojans, Aeneas's mother, Venus (the Roman equivalent of Aphrodite, the Greek goddess of love), has increased Aeneas's physical attractions so Dido will fall in love with him. Moreover, Venus has sent her son Cupid disguised as Ascanius, who,*

*to use Vergil's language, poisons Dido with a mad love for Aeneas as she dandles Ascanius in her lap. As Book 4 opens, Aeneas has told Dido the hair-raising story of how the Greeks violently and treacherously entered Troy and burned it to the ground, and how Aeneas and his followers, though not his wife, escaped death and fled. He then recounted their subsequent adventures, including the death of Anchises.*]

But the queen, long since smitten with a grievous love-pang, feeds the wound with her life-blood, and is wasted with an unseen fire. The chief's valor and his glorious stock often rush to her heart. His looks and words cling fast within her bosom, and the pang keeps calm rest from her limbs.

The next day's dawn was lighting the earth with the lamp of Phoebus[1] and had scattered from the sky the dewy shades, when, much distraught, she speaks to her sister, sharer of her heart:

---

1  I.e., Apollo, god of the sun.

"Anna, my sister, what dreams thrill me with fears? Who is this foreign guest that has entered our home? How noble his appearance! How brave in heart and feats of arms! I well believe (nor is assurance vain) that he is sprung from gods. It is fear that proves souls base-born. Alas! by what fates is he vexed! What wars, long endured, did he recount! If the purpose were not planted in my mind, fixed and immovable, to ally myself with no one in the bond of wedlock, since my first love, turning traitor, cheated me by death—if I were not utterly weary of the bridal bed and torch, I might have yielded to this one weakness! Anna (for I will admit it) since the death of my poor husband Sychaeus, and the shattering of our home by a brother's murder,[2] he alone has swayed my will and overthrown my tottering soul. I recognize the traces of the old flame. But I would pray that the earth yawn for me to its depths, or the Almighty Father hurl me with his bolt to the shades—the pale shades and abysmal night of Erebus[3]—before, O Shame, I violate you or break your laws! He who first linked me to himself has taken away my heart; may he keep it with him, and guard it in the grave!" So saying, she filled her bosom with welling tears.

Anna replies: "O dearer to your sister than the light, will you pine away all your youth long, lonely and sad, and not know sweet children or love's rewards? Do you think that dust or buried shades give heed to that? Grant that before now no wooers moved your sorrow, not in Libya, not before then in Tyre. Grant that Iarbas[4] was slighted, and other lords too, whom the African land, rich in triumphs, rears. Will you also resist a love that pleases? And do you not call to mind in whose lands you are settled? On this side Gaetulian cities, a nation invincible in war, unbridled Numidians, and the unfriendly Syrtis hem you in. On the other side lie a tract barren with drought and the Barcaeans, raging far and near. Why speak of the wars rising from Tyre, and your brother's threats? With favoring gods, I think indeed, and with Juno's aid, the Ilian[5] ships have held their course hither with the wind. What a city you will see rise here, my sister, what a realm, by reason of such wedlock! With Teucrian[6] arms beside us, to what heights will Punic[7] glory soar? Only ask favor of the gods and, with sacrifice duly offered, be lavish with your welcome, and weave pleas for delay, while at sea winter rages fiercely and Orion is stormy, while the ships are shattered, and the skies intractable!"

With these words she fanned into flame the queen's love-enkindled heart, put hope in her wavering mind, and loosed the bonds of shame. First they visit the shrines and sue for peace at every altar. Duly they slay chosen sheep to Ceres the lawgiver, to Phoebus and father Lyaeus, above all to Juno, guardian of wedlock bonds. Dido herself, matchless in beauty, with cup in hand, pours libation midway between the horns of a white heifer, or in presence of the gods moves slowly to the rich altars, and solemnizes the day with gifts, then, gazing into the opened breasts of victims, consults the quivering entrails. Ah, blind souls of seers! Of what avail are vows or shrines to one wild with love? All the while the flame devours her tender heartstrings, and deep in her breast lives the silent wound. Unhappy Dido burns, and through the city wanders in frenzy—even as a hind, smitten by an arrow, which, all unwary, amid the Cretan woods, a shepherd hunting with darts has pierced from afar, leaving in her the winged steel, unknowing. She ranges the Dictaean woods and glades in flight, but the deadly shaft clings fast to her side. Now through the city's midst she leads with her Aeneas, and displays her Sidonian wealth and the built city. She tries to speak and stops with the word half-spoken. Now, as day wanes, she seeks that same banquet, again madly craves to hear the sorrows of Ilium and again hangs on the speaker's

---

2   Dido's husband, Sychaeus, had been murdered by Dido's brother, Pygmalion, king of Tyre in Phoenicia, in the Middle East. As a result, Dido fled from Tyre with Pygmalion's treasury and founded Carthage.
3   Erebus was a god of the underworld, or land of the dead, often used to signify the land of the dead itself.
4   A son of Jupiter and king of Gaetulia in north Africa, from whom Dido bought the land on which to found Carthage. Iarbas had also tried to marry her.
5   Troy was sometimes called "Ilium."
6   Teucer was an early ancestor of the kings of Troy. "Teucrian" thus means "Trojan."
7   I.e., "Carthaginian."

lips. Then when all have gone their ways, and in turn
the dim moon sinks her light, and the setting stars
invite sleep, alone she mourns in the empty hall, and
falls on the couch he has left. Though absent, each
from each, she hears him, she sees him or, captivated
by his father's look, she holds Ascanius on her lap, if
so she may beguile a passion beyond all utterance. No
longer do the towers rise which were begun, no longer
do the youth exercise in arms, or toil at building
havens or bulwarks for safety in war. The works are
broken off and idle—huge threatening walls and the
construction engine towering up to heaven.

As soon as the beloved wife of Jove saw that Dido
was held in a passion so fatal, and that her good
name was now no bar to her frenzy, the daughter of
Saturn[8] accosts Venus thus: "Splendid indeed is the
praise and rich the spoils you win, you and your boy.
Divine power is mighty and glorious if one woman is
subdued by the guile of two gods! It does not escape
me how, in fear of our city, you have held in suspicion the homes of high Carthage. But what shall be
the end? Or how far goes all this contest now? Why
do we not instead make an enduring peace and a
plighted wedlock? You have what you sought with
all your heart; Dido is on fire with love and has
drawn the madness through her veins. Let us then
rule this people jointly with equal sovereignty; let
her serve a Phrygian[9] husband and yield her Tyrians
to your hand as dowry!"

To her—for she knew that Juno had spoken with
feigned purpose, to turn the empire from Italy to
Libya's coasts—Venus thus began in reply: "Who
would be so mad as to refuse such terms, or choose
rather to strive with you in war, if only Fortune favors
the fulfillment of your word? But the Fates send me
adrift, uncertain whether Jupiter wills that there be
one city for the Tyrians and the wanderers from Troy
and approves the blending of peoples and the league
of union. You are his wife. You may probe his heart
with begging. Go on; I will follow!"

Then queenly Juno thus replied: "That task shall
rest with me. Listen and I will explain in brief in what
way the present purpose can be achieved. Aeneas and
unhappy Dido plan to go hunting together in the forest, as soon as tomorrow's sun shows his rising and
unveils the world with his rays. On them, while the
hunters run to and fro and cover the glades with nets,
I will pour down from above a black rain mingled
with hail, and wake the whole sky with thunder. The
company will scatter and be veiled in gloom of night,
and Dido and the Trojan chief will come to the same
cave. I will be there and, if certain of your goodwill,
will link them in sure wedlock, sealing her for his
own; this shall be their bridal!" Yielding, the Cythere-
an[10] gave assent and smiled at the evident guile.

Meanwhile, Dawn rose and left the ocean. When
sunlight has burst forth, there issues from the gates a
chosen band of youths. Massylian[11] horsemen and
their strong, keen-scented hounds stream forth with
meshed nets, traps, broad-pointed hunting spears. As
the queen lingers in her bower, the Punic princes
await her at the doorway. Her prancing steed stands
brilliant in purple and gold, and fiercely champs the
foaming bit. At last she comes forth, attended by a
mighty throng, and clad in a Sidonian robe with
embroidered border. Her quiver is of gold, her tresses
are knotted into gold, golden is the buckle to clasp her
purple cloak. With her pace a Phrygian train and joyous Iulus.[12] Aeneas himself, more handsome than all
the rest, advances to join her and unites his band with
hers. Just as when Apollo leaves Lycia, his winter
home, and the streams of Xanthus, to visit his mother's Delos, and renews the dance, while mingling
about his altars Cretans and Dryopes and painted
Agathyrsians raise their voices—he himself treads the
Cynthian ridges, and with soft leafage shapes and
binds his flowing locks, braiding it with a golden
crown; the shafts rattle on his shoulders: so, no less
lightly than he, went Aeneas; such beauty shines forth
from his noble face! When they came to the mountain

---

8   I.e., Juno.
9   Phrygia was the country of Troy.
10  I.e., Venus.
11  The Massylians were a people of north Africa.
12  Another name of Aeneas's son, Ascanius.

heights and pathless lairs, lo! wild goats dislodged from the rocky peaks ran down the ridges; in another part stags scurry across the open moors and amid clouds of dust mass their bands in flight as they leave the hills behind. But in the midst of the valleys the young Ascanius glories in his fiery steed, galloping past now these, now those, and prays that amid the fearful herds a foaming boar may be granted to his vows or a tawny lion come down from the mountain.

Meanwhile, in the sky begins the turmoil of a wild uproar; rain follows, mingled with hail. The scattered Tyrian following and the Trojan youths with the Dardan[13] grandson of Venus in their fear seek shelter here and there over the fields; torrents rush down from the heights. Dido and the Trojan chief come to the same cave. Primal Earth and nuptial Juno give the sign; fires flashed in Heaven the witness to their bridal, and on the mountaintop the Nymphs screamed. That day was the first day of death, the first cause of evils, for no longer is Dido swayed by appearances or reputation, no more does she dream of a secret love; she calls it marriage and with that name veils her fault!

Immediately, Rumor runs through Libya's great cities—Rumor, of all evils the most swift. Speed lends her strength, and she wins vigor as she goes; at first small through fear, soon she mounts up to heaven, and walks the ground with head hidden in the clouds. It is said that Mother Earth, provoked to anger against the gods, brought her forth last as a sister to Coeus and Enceladus, swift of foot and fleet of wing, a monster awful and huge, who for the many feathers in her body has as many watchful eyes below (wondrous to tell) as many tongues, as many sounding mouths, as many pricked-up ears. By night, midway between heaven and earth, she flies through the gloom, screeching, nor droops her eyes in sweet sleep. By day she sits on guard on high rooftops or lofty turrets and terrifies great cities, clinging to the false and wrong, yet heralding truth. At this time, exulting with mani-fold gossip, she filled the nations and sang alike of fact and falsehood, how Aeneas, born of Trojan blood, to whom in marriage fair Dido deigns to join herself, has come. Now they spend the winter, all its length, in wanton ease together, heedless of their realms and enthralled by shameless passion. These tales the foul goddess spreads here and there upon the lips of men. She immediately bends her course to King Iarbas, and with her words fires his spirit and heaps high his wrath.

He, son of Jupiter-Ammon by a ravished Garamantian Nymph, set up to Jupiter in his broad realms a hundred vast temples, a hundred altars, and had hallowed the wakeful fire, the eternal sentry of the gods. The ground was fat with the blood of beasts and the portals bloomed with varied garlands. Distraught in mind and fired with the bitter tale, they say that before the altars and amid the divine presences he often sought Jove in prayer with upturned hands: "Almighty Jupiter, to whom now the Moorish nation, feasting on embroidered couches, pours a Lenaean[14] offering, do you see these things? Is it in vain, O father, that we shudder at you when you hurl your thunderbolts? And do aimless fires amid the clouds terrify our souls and stir murmurs without purpose? This woman who, straying within our boundaries, set up a tiny city at a price, to whom we gave coastland to plough and terms of tenure, has spurned my offers of marriage and welcomed Aeneas into her realm as lord. And now that Paris with his train of half-men,[15] a Maeonian[16] band propping his chin and perfumed locks, grasps the spoil, while we bring offerings to your temples, yours forsooth, and cherish an idle story."

As he pleaded with such words, clasping the altars, the Almighty gave ear and turned his eyes on the royal city and the lovers forgetful of their nobler fame. Then he speaks to Mercury and gives this charge: "Go forth my son, call the Zephyr,[17] glide on your wings,

---

13 Dardanus was the founder of Troy.

14 "Lenaeus" was another name for Bacchus, the god of wine and sometimes insane revelry.

15 Paris was the Trojan who carried off Helen, thus beginning the Trojan war. In Homer's *Iliad* he is very good-looking and also less masculine than Troy's best warrior, Hector.

16 Maeonia was in Asia Minor, as was Troy.

17 The West wind.

and speak to the Dardan chief, who now dallies in Tyrian Carthage and does not heed the cities granted by the Fates; so carry down my words through the swift winds. His lovely mother did not promise to us that he would be this kind of man, nor for this did she twice rescue him from Greek arms. He was to rule over Italy, a land teeming with empire and clamorous with war, to hand on a race from Teucer's noble blood, and bring all the world beneath his laws. If the glory of such a fortune does not fire him and he does not shoulder the burden for his own fame's sake, does he, a father, grudge Ascanius the towers of Rome? What is he planning? In what hope does he linger among a hostile people and not regard Ausonia's[18] nation and the Lavinian[19] fields? Let him set sail. That is all; let that be the message from me."

He ceased. The god made ready to obey his mighty father's bidding, and first binds on his feet the golden shoes which carry him up, borne on wings over sea or land, swift as the gale. Then he takes his wand, with which he calls pale ghosts from Orcus and sends others down to gloomy Tartarus, gives or takes away sleep and unseals eyes in death.[20] Relying on this, he drives the winds and skims the stormy clouds. And now in flight he spies the peak and steep sides of toiling Atlas, who props heaven on his head—Atlas, whose pine-wreathed head is ever girt with black clouds, and beaten with wind and rain; fallen snow mantles his shoulders, while rivers plunge down the aged chin and his rough beard is stiff with ice. Here, poised on even wings, the Cyllenian[21] first halted; hence with his whole frame he sped sheer down to the waves like a bird, which around the shores, around the fish-haunted cliffs, flies low near to the waters. Even thus between earth and sky flew Cyllene's nursling to Libya's sandy shore, and cut the winds, coming from his mother's sire.

As soon as he reached the huts on winged feet, he sees Aeneas founding towers and building new houses. And lo! his sword was starred with yellow jasper, and a cloak hung from his shoulders ablaze with Tyrian purple—a gift that wealthy Dido had made, interweaving the web with thread of gold. At once he assails Aeneas: "Are you now laying the foundations of lofty Carthage, and building up a fair city, a wife's minion? Alas, forgetful of your own kingdom and fortunes! He, the Sovereign of the gods, who sways heaven and earth with his power, sends me down to you from bright Olympus. He himself bids me bring this charge through the swift breezes: What are you planning? In what hope do you waste idle hours in Libyan lands? If the glory of such a fortune does not stir you, and for your own fame's sake you do not shoulder the burden, have regard for growing Ascanius and the promise of Iulus your heir, to whom the kingdom of Italy and the Roman land are due." Such words the Cyllenian spoke, and while yet speaking left the sight of men and far away from their eyes vanished into thin air.

But in truth, Aeneas, aghast at the sight, was struck dumb; his hair stood up in terror and the voice stuck in his throat. He burns to fly away and leave that pleasant land, awed by that warning and divine commandment. Ah, what to do? With what speech does he now dare approach the frenzied queen? What opening words to choose first? Now here, now there he swiftly throws his mind, casting it in various ways, and turns to every possibility. As he wavered, this seemed the better counsel: he calls Mnestheus and Sergestus and brave Serestus, bidding them make ready the fleet in silence, gather the crews to the shore, and order the armament, but to hide the cause of his altered plans. He, meanwhile, since gracious Dido knows nothing, nor expects the breaking of so strong a love, will try an approach and seek the plan auspicious for his purpose, the best time speak. At once all gladly obey his command and do his bidding.

But the queen (who may deceive a lover?) divined

---

18  For Vergil, "Ausonia" means "Italy."

19  After the events of the *Aeneid*, Aeneas will marry Lavinia, and found a city which will be called "Lavinium." Rome will derive from that city.

20  Orcus is another name for Pluto, god of the dead, and Tartarus was that part of the underworld where the shades of the wicked were punished. Mercury conducted the shades of the dead to their destination. He was also the god of dreams.

21  Mercury was born on the mountain of Cyllene.

his guile, and fearful even when all was safe, early caught news of the coming stir. The same heartless Rumor brought her the maddening news that they arm the fleet and make ready for voyaging. Helpless in mind, she rages, and all aflame raves through the city, like some Thyiad startled by the shaken emblems of Bacchus, when, hearing the Bacchic cry, the biennial revels fire her and at night Cithaeron summons her with its din.[22] At length, she accosts Aeneas first:

"False one! Did you hope also to cloak so foul a crime, and to pass from my land in silence? Can neither our love keep you, nor the pledge once given, nor the doom of a cruel death for Dido? Even in the winter season do you labor at your fleet and in the midst of northern gales hasten to pass overseas, heartless one? What! If you were not in quest of alien lands and unknown homes, if ancient Troy still stood, would Troy be sought by your ships over stormy seas? Do you flee from me? By these tears and your right hand, I pray you, since nothing else, alas! have I left myself, by our marriage, by the wedlock begun, if ever I deserved well of you, or if anything of mine has been sweet in your sight, pity a falling house, and if there is yet any room for prayers, put away this purpose of yours. Because of you the Libyan tribes and Numidian chiefs hate me, the Tyrians are my foes. Because of you, too, have I lost my honor and that former reputation by which alone I was winning a title to the stars. To whom do you leave me, a dying woman, O guest, since that alone is left from the name of husband? Why do I linger? Is it until Pygmalion, my brother, overthrows this city, or the Gaetulian Iarbas leads me into captivity? At least, if before your flight a child had been born to me by you, if in my hall a tiny Aeneas were playing, whose face, in spite of all, would bring back yours, I should not think myself utterly vanquished and forlorn."

She ceased. He, by Jove's command, held his eyes steadfast and with a struggle smothered the pain deep within his heart. At last he briefly replies: "I will never deny, O Queen, that you have deserved of me the utmost you can set forth in speech, nor shall my memory of Elissa be bitter while I have memory of myself and while breath still sways these limbs. I will say little concerning this matter. I did not hope—do not think so—to veil my flight in stealth. I never held out the bridegroom's torch nor entered such a contract. If the Fates would allow me to shape my life after my own pleasure and order my sorrows at my own will, my first care would be the city of Troy and the sweet relics of my kin. Priam's[23] high house would still abide and my own hand should have set up a revived Pergamus[24] for the vanquished. But now Grynean Apollo,[25] divining in Lycia by lots, has ordered me to lay hold of great Italy. There is my love, there my country! If the towers of Carthage and the sight of the Libyan city charm you, a Phoenician, why in the world grudge the Trojans their settling on Ausonian land? We, too, may well seek a foreign realm. To me as often as night with dewy shades veils the earth, as often as the starry fires arise, in my dreams my father Anchises's troubled ghost brings warning and terror. To me comes the thought of young Ascanius and the wrong done to one so dear, whom I am cheating of an Hesperian[26] kingdom and predestined lands. Now, too, the messenger of the gods sent from Jove himself—by your head and mine, I swear—has carried his command down through the swift breezes. My own eyes saw the god in the clear light of day come within our walls and these ears drank in his words. Cease to fire yourself and me with your complaints. I do not go after Italy of my own free will!"

As he spoke, she gazes on him askance all the while, turning her eyes to and fro, and with silent glances scans the whole man. Then thus inflamed, she cries out:

"False one! no goddess was your mother, nor was Dardanus founder of your line, but rugged Cauca-

---

22 The Thyiads were female worshippers of Bacchus at Elis who went mad at the Thyia, a festival held there in honor of Bacchus. Cithaeron was a mountain where such worship took place.
23 Priam: the king of Troy when it fell.
24 Another term for Troy.
25 I.e., Apollo's oracle in Grynium, in Asia Minor.
26 Hesperia: "land of the evening," a Greek term for Italy and Sicily.

sus[27] on his flinty rocks begat you, and Hyrcanian[28] tigresses gave you suck. For why hide my feelings? For what greater wrongs do I hold myself back? Did he sigh while I wept? Did he give me a glance? Did he yield and shed tears or pity her who loved him? What shall I say first? What next? Now, now neither mighty Juno nor the Saturnian sire[29] looks on these things with righteous eyes! Nowhere is faith secure. I welcomed him, a castaway on the shore, a beggar, and madly gave him a share in my throne. I rescued his lost fleet, I saved his crews from death. Alas! I am whirled on the fires of frenzy. Now prophetic Apollo, now the Lycian oracles, now the messenger of the gods, sent from Jove himself brings through the air this dread command. Truly, this is work for gods, this is care to vex their peace! I do not keep you; I do not refute your words. Go, follow Italy with the winds; seek your kingdom over the waves. Yet I trust, if the righteous gods can avail anything, that on the rocks midway you will drain the cup of vengeance and often call on Dido's name. Though far away, I will chase you with dark flames and, when chill death has severed soul and body, everywhere my shade shall haunt you. Shameless one, you will pay! I shall hear, and the tale will reach me in the depths of the world below!"

So saying, she breaks off her speech midway and flees in anguish from the light, turning away, tearing herself from his sight, and leaving him in fear and much hesitance, though wanting to say much. Her maids support her, carry her swooning form to her marble bower, and lay her on her bed.

But pious[30] Aeneas, though longing to soothe and assuage her grief and by his words turn aside her sorrow, with many a sigh, his soul shaken by his mighty love, still follows Heaven's command and returns to the fleet. Then, indeed, the Teucrians fall to and all along the shore launch their tall ships. The keels, well-pitched, are set afloat; the sailors, eager for flight,

bring from the woods leafy boughs for oars and unhewn logs. One could see them moving away and streaming forth from each part of the city—just as when ants, mindful of winter, plunder a huge heap of wheat and store it in their home; over the plain moves a black column, and through the grass they carry the spoil on a narrow path; some strain with their shoulders and heave on the huge grains, some close up the ranks and rebuke delay; all the path is aglow with work. What feelings then were yours, Dido, at such a sight! Or what sighs did you utter, viewing from the top of the fortress the beach aglow far and near, and seeing before your eyes the whole sea astir with loud cries! O tyrant Love, to what do you not drive mortal hearts! Once more she must break into tears, once more assail him with prayer, and humbly bow down her pride to love, lest she leave anything untried and go to death in vain.

"Anna, you see the bustle all along the shore; they have gathered from all sides. Already the canvas courts the breeze, and the joyous sailors have crowned the sterns with garlands. If I have had strength to foresee this great sorrow, I shall also, sister, have strength to endure it. Yet this one service, Anna, do for me—for that traitor has made you alone his friend; to you he confided even his secret thoughts; you alone know the hour for easy access to him—go, sister, and humbly address our haughty foe. I never conspired with the Danaans at Aulis[31] to root out the Trojan race. I never sent a fleet to Pergamus or tore up the ashes and spirit of his father Anchises. Why does he refuse to admit my words to his stubborn ears? Where does he hasten? Let him grant his poor lover this last favor: let him wait for an easy flight and favoring winds. I plead no longer for the old marriage-tie which he forswore, nor that he give up fair Latium and resign his realm. I ask for empty time, for peace and reprieve for my frenzy, until fortune may teach my vanquished soul to grieve. This last grace I crave—pity your sister—and

 does what he's told

---

27  A mountain chain.
28  Hyrcania was in northeast Persia.
29  I.e., Jupiter, whose father was Saturn.
30  Wherever the word "pious" is used in this translation, the Latin is *pius*, a term for someone who lives up to obligations. This can refer to obligations to the gods or to others.
31  Danaans: another term for Greeks; Aulis: the place from which the Greeks set sail for Troy.

when he has granted it, I will repay with full interest in my death."

Such was her prayer and such the tearful pleas the unhappy sister delivers again and again. But by no tearful pleas is he moved, nor in yielding mood does he pay heed to any words. Fate obstructed them, and a god seals his kindly, mortal ears. Just as when northern Alpine winds, blowing now here, now there, competitively strive to uproot an oak strong with the strength of years, and there comes a roar, the stem quivers and the high leafage thickly strews the ground, but the oak clings to the crag, and as far as it lifts its top to the airs of heaven, so far it strikes its roots down towards Tartarus—just so, with ceaseless appeals, from this side and from that, the hero is buffeted, and in his mighty heart feels grief deeply, and his will stands steadfast. The tears fall in vain.

Then, indeed, awed by her doom, luckless Dido prays for death; she is weary of gazing on the arch of heaven. And to make her more surely fulfill her purpose and leave the light, she saw, as she laid her gifts on the altars ablaze with incense—fearful to tell— the holy water darken and the poured out wine change into loathsome gore. Of this sight she spoke to no one—no, not to her sister. Moreover, there was in the palace a marble chapel dedicated to her former husband, which she cherished in wondrous honor, wreathing it with snowy fleeces and festal foliage. She heard from there, it seemed, sounds and speech like those of her husband calling, whenever dark night held the world. And alone on the housetops with ill-boding song the owl would often complain, drawing out its lingering notes into a wail, and likewise many a saying of the seers of old terrifies her with fearful boding. In her sleep, fierce Aeneas himself hounds her in her frenzy, and she always seems to be left lonely, always travelling, companionless, on an endless way, seeking her Tyrians in a forlorn land—just as raving Pentheus[32] sees the Furies' band, a double sun and two-fold Thebes rise to view or as when Agamemnon's son, Orestes,[33] driven over the stage, flees from his mother, who is armed with brands and black serpents, while at the doorway crouch the avenging Furies.

So when, worn out with anguish, she caught the madness and resolved to die, in her own heart she determines the time and manner, and accosts her sorrowful sister with a manner that veils her plan and the calm of hope on her brow.

"My sister, I have found a way—wish your sister joy—to return him to me or release me from my love for him. Near Ocean's end and the setting sun lies Ethiopia, farthest of lands, where mightiest Atlas turns the sphere, inset with gleaming stars, on his shoulders. I have been told of a priestess from there, of the Massylian nation. She is the guardian of the temple of the Hesperides, who gave dainties to the dragon and guarded the sacred boughs on the tree, sprinkling dewy honey and slumberous poppies. With her spells she professes to set free the hearts of whom she wills, but on others to bring cruel love-pains, to stay the flow of rivers and turn back the stars. She awakes the ghosts of night and, as you will see, makes the earth rumble under your feet and ash-trees come down from mountains. I call heaven to witness and you, my dear sister, and your dear life, that against my will I arm myself with magic arts! Secretly raise up a pyre in the inner court under the sky, and heap on it the arms that heartless one left hanging in my bower, and all his attire and the bridal bed that was my undoing. I would destroy all remembrance of the abhorred wretch, and the priestess so directs." Thus she speaks and is silent, while pallor spreads over her face. Yet Anna does not think that her sister veils her death under these strange rites. Her mind does not dream of such frenzy, nor does she fear anything worse than when Sychaeus died. So she makes ready as ordered.

But the queen, when in her innermost dwelling the pyre rose heavenward, piled high with pine-fagots and hewn ilex,[34] hangs the place with garlands and festoons it with funeral boughs. On top, upon the couch, she lays his garments, the sword he left, and his

---

32   A mythical king of Thebes who was driven mad by Bacchus.
33   In Greek myth and in Aeschylus's trilogy of plays, the *Oresteia*, Orestes, to avenge his murdered father, killed his mother, whose shade invokes the Furies to chase him across the earth in revenge.
34   A kind of evergreen.

image, knowing well the end. Round about stand altars, while with streaming hair the priestess calls in thunder tones on thrice a hundred gods, Erebus[35] and Chaos, and threefold Hecate, triple-faced maiden Diana.[36] Waters, too, she had sprinkled, feigned to be from the spring Avernus,[37] and herbs were sought, cut by moonlight with brazen sickles, and juicy with milk of black venom. The love-charm, torn from the brow of a colt at birth before the mother snatched it, was also sought. She herself, with holy meal and holy hands, beside the altars, with one foot unsandalled and belt loosened, calls on the gods and on the stars, witnesses of her doom, before she dies. Then she prays to whatever power, righteous and mindful, watches over lovers unequally allied.

It was night, and over the earth weary creatures were tasting peaceful slumber. The woods and wild seas had sunk to rest—the hour when stars roll midway in their gliding course, when all the land is still, and beasts and gay birds, both they that far and near haunt the limpid lakes, and they that dwell in fields of tangled thickets, are couched in sleep beneath the silent night. But not so the soul-racked Phoenician queen. She never sinks to sleep, nor draws the night into eyes or heart. Her pangs redouble, and her love, swelling up, surges afresh, as she heaves with a mighty tide of passion. Thus then she begins, and thus discusses her thoughts with her heart alone: "Lo, what am I to do? Shall I once more make trial of my old wooers, only to be mocked, and shall I humbly sue for marriage with Numidians, whom I have scorned so often as husbands? Shall I then follow the Ilian ships and the Trojan's uttermost commands? Is it because they are grateful for aid once given, and thankfulness for past kindness stands firm in mindful hearts? But who—suppose that I do wish it—will suffer me, or take one so hateful on those haughty ships? Ah! lost one, do you not yet understand or perceive the treason of Laomedon's[38] race? What then? Shall I alone accompany the exultant sailors in their flight? Or shall I do so surrounded by all my Tyrian band, and so

again drive seaward the men whom I could barely tear from their city, Sidon, and bid them unfurl their sails to the winds? No. Die as you deserve, and end your sorrow with steel. Won over by my tears, you, my sister, you were first to load my frenzied soul with these ills, and drive me on the foe. Ah, that I could not spend my life apart from wedlock, a blameless life, even as some wild creature, not knowing such cares! I have not kept the faith vowed to the ashes of Sychaeus!" Such were the wails that kept bursting from her heart.

But now that all was duly ordered, and now that he was resolved on going, Aeneas was snatching sleep on his vessel's high stern. In his sleep there appeared to him a vision of the god, as he came again with the same aspect, in all details like Mercury, in voice and hue, in golden hair and the graceful limbs of youth, and once more seemed to warn him thus: "Goddess-born, when such hazard threatens, can you still slumber, and do you not see the perils that henceforth hem you in, madman! Do you not hear the kindly breezes blowing? She, resolved on death, revolves in her heart deadly craft and crime, and is tossed on the changing surge of passion. Will you not flee from here in haste, while hasty flight is possible? Soon you will see the waters swarming with ships, see fierce brands ablaze, and soon the shore flashing with flames, if the dawn finds you lingering in these lands. Ho! Break off delay! Woman is ever a fickle and changeful thing." So he spoke and melted into the black night.

Then indeed Aeneas, scared by the sudden vision, tears himself from sleep and bestirs his comrades. "Make haste, my men, awake and man the benches! Unfurl the sails with speed! A god sent from high heaven, lo again spurs us to hasten our flight and cut the twisted cables. We follow you, holy among gods, whoever you are, and again joyfully obey your command. Oh, be with us, give your gracious aid, and bring kindly stars in heaven!" He spoke, and snatches his flashing sword from its sheath and strikes the hawser with the drawn blade. The same zeal catches

---

35  A god of the underworld.
36  Hecate was a goddess of the underworld. She was called "Luna" when in heaven and "Diana" when on earth.
37  Avernus was a putrid lake, thought to be at the entrance to the underworld.
38  Laomedon was the father of Priam, Troy's last king.

all at once. Hurrying and scurrying, they left the shore. The sea is hidden under their fleets. They lustily churn the foam and sweep the blue waters.

And now early Dawn, leaving the saffron bed of Tithonus, was sprinkling her fresh rays upon the earth. As soon as the queen from her watch-tower saw the light whiten and the fleet move on with even sails, and knew the shores and harbors were void of oarsmen, she struck her comely breast with her hand three and four times, and tearing her golden hair, cries "O Jupiter, shall he go? Shall the intruder have made of our realm a laughing-stock? Will my people not bring arms with speed, and pursue from all the city, and some tear the ships from the docks? Go, fetch fire in haste, serve weapons, ply the oars! What do I say? Or where am I? What madness sways my brain? Unhappy Dido! Now your impious deeds come home to you! The right time was *then*, when you offered the crown. Lo! this is the pledge and faith of him who, they say, carries about with him his country's home-gods! Who bore on his shoulders a father worn out with age![39] Could I not have seized him, torn him limb from limb and scattered him on the waves? Could I not have slain his comrades with the sword—indeed, Ascanius himself, and served him in the feast at his father's table? But the issue of battle had been doubtful! Be it so; doomed to death, whom had I to fear? I should have fired his camp, filled his decks with flames, blotted out father and son with the whole race, and flung myself on top of all. O Sun, who with your beams surveys all the works of earth, and you, Juno, mediatress and witness of these my sorrows, and Hecate, whose name is shrieked by night at the crossroads of cities, you avenging Furies, and you gods of dying Elissa, hear this, and, as is merited, let your power stoop to my ills and hear my prayers! If that accursed wretch must touch his haven and float to shore—if Jove's fate demands it, and there his goal stands fixed—yet, beset in war by the arms of a gallant race, driven from his borders, and torn from Iulus's embrace, let him beg for help and see the cruel slaughter of his friends! Then, when he has yielded to the terms of an unjust peace,

may he not enjoy his kingdom or the pleasant light, but let him fall before his time and lie unburied in the sand! This is my prayer; this last utterance I pour out with my blood. Then, O Tyrians,[40] pursue his whole stock and the nation to come with hate, and offer this tribute to my dust! Let there be no love nor league between the nations. Arise from my ashes, unknown avenger!, to chase with fire and sword the Dardan settlers, today, hereafter, whenever strength be given! May shore clash with shore, I pray, waters with waters, arms with arms. May they have war, they and their children's children!"

So she spoke, and turned her mind on all sides, seeking how to cut short the hateful life with all speed. Then briefly she spoke to Barce, nurse of Sychaeus, for the pyre's black ashes held her own nurse in her former homeland: "Dear nurse, bring Anna my sister here to me. Tell her to hasten to sprinkle her body with river water, and bring with her the victims and offerings ordained for atonement. So let her come, and you, too, veil your brows with a pure chaplet. I am minded to fulfill the rites of Stygian[41] Jove that I have duly ordered and begun, to put an end to my woes, and give over to the flames the pyre of that Dardan wretch."

So she spoke. The nurse hastened her steps with an old woman's zeal. But Dido, trembling and frenzied with her awful purpose, rolling her bloodshot eyes, her quivering cheeks flecked with burning spots, and pale at the coming of death, bursts into the inner courts of the house, mounts in madness the high pyre and unsheathes the Dardan sword, a gift besought for no such end. Then, as she saw the Trojan garb and the familiar bed, pausing a while in tearful thought, she threw herself on the bed and spoke her last words:

"O relics once dear, while the god and fate allowed! Take my spirit, and release me from my woes! I have lived, I have finished the course that Fortune gave, and now in majesty my shade shall pass beneath the earth. I have built a noble city. I have seen my own walls. Avenging my husband, I have exacted punishment from my brother and foe—happy, ah! too happy,

---

39  Aeneas carried his father, Anchises, out of burning Troy on his back. He also carried Troy's gods.
40  I.e., Carthaginians.
41  I.e., of the underworld or, more precisely, having to do with the Styx, the marshy river of the underworld.

had but the Dardan keels never touched our shores!" She spoke, and burying her face in the bed, she cries: "I shall die unavenged, but let me die! Thus, thus I go gladly into the dark! Let the cruel Dardan's eyes drink in this fire from the deep, and carry with him the omen of my death!"

She ceased. Even as she spoke her handmaids see her fallen on the sword, the blade reeking with blood and her hands bespattered with it. A scream rises to the lofty roof; Rumor riots through the startled city. The palace rings with lamentation, with sobbing and women's shrieks, and heaven echoes with loud wails—just as though all Carthage or ancient Tyre were falling before the inrushing foe, and fierce fires were rolling on over the roofs of men, over the roofs of gods. Swooning, her sister heard, and in dismay rushed through the throng, tearing her face with her nails, and beating her breast with her fists, as she called on the dying woman by name: "Was this it, sister? Did you aim your fraud at me? Was this for me the meaning of your pyre, of your altar and fires? Forlorn, what first shall I lament? Did you scorn your sister's company in your death? You should have called me to share your fate. The same sword-pain might have taken us both at the same hour! Did these hands indeed build the pyre, and did my voice call on our father's gods in order that, when you were lying thus, I, the cruel one, should be far away? You have destroyed yourself and me, O sister, the Sidonian senate and people, and your city. Let me bathe her wounds with water, and catch with my lips whatever last breath flutters over hers!" Thus speaking, she had climbed the high steps and, throwing her arms round her dying sister, sobbed and clasped her to her bosom, stanching with her robe the dark streams of blood. Dido, trying to lift her heavy eyes, swoons again, and the deep-set wound gurgles in her breast. Thrice rising, she struggled to lift herself upon her elbow; thrice she rolled back on the couch, and with wandering eyes sought the light in high heaven and, as she found it, moaned.

Then almighty Juno, pitying her long pain and hard departure, sent Iris down from Olympus to release her struggling soul from the imprisoning limbs. For since she perished neither in the course of fate, nor by a death she had earned, but, miserable, before her day, and fired by sudden madness, Proserpina had not yet taken from her head the golden lock and consigned her to Stygian Orcus.[42] So Iris, all dewy on saffron wings, flits down through the sky, trailing over the sun a thousand shifting tints, and halted above her head. "This offering, sacred to Pluto, I take as ordered, and from your body set you free"; so she speaks, and with her hand shears the lock. Therewith all the warmth ebbed away, and the life passed away into the winds.

6   [*Sailing to his destination in Italy, Aeneas has discovered that his friend Palinurus has been lost overboard in the night, and has been lamenting him.*]

Thus he cries weeping, and gives his fleet the reins, and at last glides up to the shores of Euboean Cumae.[43] They turn the prows seaward, then with the grip of anchors' teeth the ships made fast, and the round keels fringe the beach. In hot haste the youthful band leaps forth onto the Hesperian shore. Some seek the seeds of flame hidden in veins of flint, some pillage the woods, the thick coverts of game, and point to new-found streams. But pious Aeneas seeks the heights, where Apollo sits enthroned, and a vast cavern close by, the hidden haunt of the dread Sibyl, into whom the Delian seer[44] breathes a mighty mind and soul, revealing the future. Now they pass under the grove of Trivia[45] and the roof of gold.

Daedalus,[46] it is said, when fleeing from Minos's

---

42   Before animals were sacrificed, a few hairs were plucked from their foreheads. Hairs were similarly plucked from the foreheads of people as they died to signify their sacrifice to the gods. Proserpina, queen of the underworld, is visualized as doing the plucking here.

43   Near Naples, in Italy.

44   I.e., Apollo.

45   Another name for Hecate.

46   Daedalus, a prisoner of King Minos of the island of Crete, escaped by making himself and his son Icarus wings made of feathers and wax. Icarus disobeyed his father's instructions and, flying too near the sun, fell into the sea to his death when the wax melted.

realm, dared on swift wings to trust himself to the sky. On his unwonted way he floated forth towards the cold North, and at last stood lightly poised above the Chalcidian hill. Here first restored to earth, he dedicated to you, O Phoebus, the oarage of his wings and built a vast temple. On the doors is the death of Androgeos,[47] then the children of Cecrops,[48] bidden, alas! to pay as yearly tribute seven living sons. There stands the urn, the lots now drawn.[49] Opposite, rising from the sea, the Gnosian[50] land faces this; here is the cruel love of the bull with which Pasiphae craftily mated, and the mongrel breed of the Minotaur, a two-formed offspring, record of a monstrous love; there is that house of toil, an inextricable maze. But lo! Daedalus, pitying the princess's great love, himself unwound the deceptive tangle of the palace, guiding blind feet with thread.[51] You, too, O Icarus, would have had a large share in such a work, if grief permitted: twice had Daedalus tried to fashion your fall in gold; twice the father's hands sank. Yes, and the Trojans' eyes would have scanned throughout the whole story, but now Achates, who had been sent ahead, came back, and with him the priestess of Phoebus and Trivia, Deiphobe, daughter of Glaucus, who speaks to the king thus: "Not sights like these does this hour demand! Now it would be better to sacrifice seven bullocks from the unbroken herd, and as many ewes fitly chosen." Having thus addressed Aeneas—and they are not slow to do her sacred bidding—the priestess calls the Teucrians into the lofty temple.

The huge side of the Euboean rock is hewn into a cavern, to which lead a hundred wide mouths, a hundred gateways, from which rush as many voices, the answers of the Sibyl. They had come to the threshold, when the maiden cries: "It is time to ask the oracles; the god, lo! the god!" As she spoke before the doors, suddenly neither her countenance nor color was the same, nor did her tresses stay braided. But her bosom heaves, her heart swells with wild frenzy, and she is taller to behold, nor has her voice a mortal ring, since now she feels the nearer breath of deity. "Are you slow to vow and to pray?" she cries. "Are you slow, Trojan Aeneas? For until then the mighty mouths of the awestruck house will not gape open." So she spoke and was mute. A chill shudder ran through the Teucrians' sturdy frames, and their king pours forth prayers from his inmost heart:

"O Phoebus, who has always pitied the heavy woes of Troy, who guided the Dardan shaft and hand of Paris against the body of Aeacus's son,[52] under your guidance did I enter so many seas, skirting mighty lands, the far remote Massylian tribes and the fields which the Syrtes[53] fringe. Now at last we grasp the shores of elusive Italy—thus far only may Troy's fortune have followed us! You, too, may now fitly spare the nation of Pergamus, all you gods and goddesses, whom Troy and Dardania's great glory offended. And you, most holy prophetess, who foreknows the future, grant—I ask no realm unpledged by my fate—that the Teucrians may rest in Latium[54] with the wandering gods and storm-tossed powers of Troy. Then I will set up a temple of solid marble, and festal days in Phoebus's name to Phoebus and Trivia. A stately shrine also awaits you in our realm, for there will I place your oracles and mystic utterances, told to my people, and ordain chosen men, O gracious one. Only do not trust your verses to leaves, lest they fly in disorder, the sport of rushing winds; chant them yourself, I pray." His lips ceased speaking.

But the prophetess, not yet accepting the sway of Phoebus, storms wildly in the cavern, as if she might shake the mighty god from off her breast. So much the more he tires her raving mouth, tames her wild heart, and molds her by constraint. And now the hundred

---

47   Androgeos, the son of King Minos, was killed by the Athenians.
48   In Greek legend, an Egyptian who founded Athens.
49   Greek myth holds that Minos demanded an annual tribute of seven Athenian youths as a sacrifice.
50   Gnossos (also spelled "Cnossos" or "Knossos") was Minos's capital.
51   The Minotaur was half human, half bull. Minos hid it away in a labyrinth. Daedalus helped Princess Ariadne make her way out of the labyrinth by giving her some thread to use to retrace her steps to the entrance.
52   Aeacus was an ancestor of Achilles.
53   Two bays in north Africa.
54   I.e., central Italy.

mighty mouths of the house have opened of their own will, and bring through the air the seer's reply:

"O you that at last have fulfilled the great perils of the sea—yet by land more grievous woes await you—into the realm of Lavinium the sons of Dardanus shall come. Relieve your heart of this care, yet they shall not also have joy in their coming. I see wars, grim wars, and Tiber[55] foaming with streams of blood. You shall not lack a Simois, nor a Xanthus,[56] nor a Greek camp. Even now another Achilles[57] is raised up in Latium, he, too, goddess-born. Nor shall Juno anywhere fail to dog the Trojans, while you, a suppliant in your need, what nations, what cities of Italy shall you not implore! The cause of all this Trojan woe is again an alien bride, again a foreign marriage![58] Do not yield to ills, but go forth to face them more boldly than your Fortune shall allow you! Your path of safety shall first, little as you expect it, be opened from a Greek city."

In such words the Cumaean Sibyl chants from the shrine her dread enigmas and echoes from the cavern, wrapping truth in darkness—so does Apollo shake the reins as she rages, and ply the spur beneath her breast. As soon as the frenzy ceased and the raving lips were hushed, Aeneas the hero begins: "No strange or unlooked for form of toils arises, O maiden. All this I forecast and inwardly traversed in thought before now. One thing I pray: since the famed gate of the nether king, and the gloomy marsh from Acheron's overflow are here, may it be granted to me to pass into my dear father's sight and presence. Teach me the way and open the hallowed portals! I rescued him on these shoulders amid flames and a thousand pursuing spears, and brought him safe from the enemy's midst. He, the partner of my way, endured with me all the seas and all the menace of ocean and sky, weak as he was, beyond the strength and portion of age. Indeed, he, too, prayed and charged me humbly to seek you and draw near to your threshold. Pity both son and father, I beseech you, gracious one, for you are all-powerful, and Hecate has not made you mistress in the groves of Avernus in vain. If Orpheus was able to summon his wife's shade, strong in his Thracian lyre and tuneful strings,[59] if Pollux, dying in turn, ransomed his brother and so often comes and goes his way[60]—why speak of great Theseus, why of Alcides?—I, too, have descent from Jove most high!"

With such words he prayed and clasped the altar, when the prophetess began to speak thus: "Sprung from blood of gods, son of Trojan Anchises, the descent to Avernus is easy: night and day the door of gloomy Dis stands open. But to recall your steps and pass out to the upper air, this is the task, this the toil! Some few, whom kindly Jupiter has loved, or whom shining worth lifted up to heaven, sons of the gods, have been able to do it. In all the mid-space lie woods, and river the Cocytus girds it, gliding with murky folds. But if such love is in your heart—if such a yearning, twice to swim the Stygian lake, twice to see black Tartarus—and if you are pleased to give rein to the mad endeavor, hear what must first be done. There lurks in a shady tree a bough with golden leaves and pliant stem held sacred to nether Juno.[61] The whole grove hides this, and shadows veil in the dim valleys. But it is not given to pass beneath earth's hidden places, except to him who has plucked from the tree the golden-tressed produce. Beautiful Proserpina has ordained this to be brought to her as her own gift. When the first is torn away, a second appears, golden too, and the spray bears leaf of the selfsame ore. Search then with eyes aloft and, when found, duly

---

55  The river on which Rome sits.
56  The Simois and Xanthus were rivers by Troy.
57  The chief warrior of the Greeks at the Trojan war, and hero of Homer's *Iliad*, Achilles killed Hector, the chief warrior of the Trojans.
58  The Trojan war began when Paris ran off with Helen, wife of the Greek King Menelaus, and married her.
59  In Greek myth, Orpheus, the finest singer in the world, was allowed to visit his wife Eurydice in the underworld. He played so beautifully that the gods of the underworld allowed him to try to bring Eurydice back to the living.
60  In Greek legend, Castor and Pollux were brothers. Pollux, however, was immortal. On Castor's death, Pollux bargained with Zeus to allow Castor to return to life. Whenever Castor was to enjoy life on earth, Pollux would have to stay in the land of the dead.
61  I.e., Proserpina.

pluck it with your hand. For if fate calls you, it will beak off for you freely and with ease. Otherwise, with no amount of force will you be able to win it or cut it with hard steel. Moreover, there lies the dead body of your friend—ah! you do not know—and it defiles all the fleet with death, while you seek counsel and hover on our threshold. Carry him first to his own place and hide him in the tomb. Lead black cattle; may these be your first peace-offerings. Only so shall you survey the Stygian groves and the realms the living may not tread." She spoke, and with closed lips was silent.

With sad countenance and downcast eyes, Aeneas wends his way, leaving the cavern, and ponders his dark fortune in his mind. At his side goes loyal Achates, and plants his steps under a like load of care. They talk about varied things, each with each—of what dead comrade spoke the soothsayer, of what body for burial? And lo! as they came, they see on the dry beach Misenus, cut off by untimely death—Misenus, son of Aeolus, surpassed by none in stirring men with his bugle's blare, and in kindling with his clang the god of war. He had been great Hector's comrade, at Hector's side he braved the fray, glorious for clarion and spear alike. But when Achilles, victorious, stripped his chief of life, the valiant hero came into the fellowship of Dardan Aeneas, following no meaner standard. Yet on that day, while he stoutly makes the seas ring with his hollow shell (madman!) and with his blare calls the gods to compete, jealous Triton—if the tale can win belief—caught and plunged him in the foaming waves amid the rocks. So all were mourning with loud lament, pious Aeneas above all. Then, weeping, they quickly carry out the Sibyl's commands, and toil in piling trees for the altar of his tomb and in rearing it to the sky. They pass into the primeval forest, the deep lairs of beasts. The pitchy pines drop, and the ilex rings with the stroke of the axe. Ashen logs and splintering oak are cleft with wedges, and from the mountains they roll in huge rowan-trees.

Aeneas, first amid such toils, cheers his comrades and girds like weapons. And alone he ponders with his own sad heart, gazing on the boundless forest and, as it happened, prays: "O if that golden bough would now show itself to us on the tree in the deep wood! For all things truly—ah! too truly—the seer spoke of you, Misenus." Scarcely had he said this when under his very eyes twin doves, as it happened, came flying from the sky and lit on the green grass. Then the great hero knew them for his mother's birds, and prays with joy: "O be my guides, if there is any way, and steer a course through the air into the grove, where the rich bough overshades the fruitful ground! And you, O goddess-mother, do not fail my dark hour!" So speaking, he checked his steps, marking what signs they bring, to where they direct their course. They, as they fed, advanced in flight just so far as a pursuer's eyes could keep them within sight. Then, when they came to the jaws of noisome Avernus, they swiftly rise and, dropping through the pure air, settle on the longed-for site, the twofold tree, from which, with diverse hue, the gleam of gold shone out amid the branches. As in winter's cold, amid the woods, the mistletoe, sown of an alien tree, is accustomed to bloom with strange leafage, and with yellow fruit embrace the shapely stems, such was the vision of the leafy gold on the shadowy ilex, so rustled the foil in the gentle breeze. Forthwith Aeneas plucks it and greedily breaks off the clinging bough, and carries it beneath the roof of the prophetic Sibyl.

Meanwhile on the beach the Teucrians were weeping for Misenus and paying the last dues to the thankless dust. And first they raise a huge pyre, rich with pitchy pine and oak logs. They entwine its sides with somber foliage, set funereal cypresses in front, and adorn it above with gleaming arms. Some heat water, setting cauldrons bubbling on the flames, and wash and anoint the cold body. The wailing is loud. Then, their weeping done, they lay his limbs upon the couch, and over them cast purple robes, his familiar dress. Some shouldered the heavy bier—sad service!—and in ancestral fashion, with averted eyes, held the torch below. The gifts are piled up in the blaze: frankincense, flesh, viands, and bowls of flowing oil. After the ashes fell in and the flame died away, they washed the remnant of thirsty dust with wine, and Corynaeus, gathering the bones, hid them in a bronze urn. He, too, with pure water thrice encircled his comrades and cleansed them, sprinkling light dew from a fruitful olive bough, and spoke the words of farewell. And pious Aeneas heaps over him a massive tomb, with the soldier's own arms, his oar and trumpet, beneath a lofty mount, which now is called Misenus after him,[62] and keeps from age to age an ever-living

    name.

This done, he fulfills the Sibyl's orders with haste. There was a deep cave, yawning wide and vast, rugged, and sheltered by a dark lake and woodland gloom, over which no flying creatures could safely wing their way—a vapor poured from those black jaws into the overarching heaven, which is why the Greeks spoke of "Avernus," the birdless place. Here first the priestess set in line four dark-backed heifers, and pours wine upon their brows. Then, plucking the topmost bristles from between the horns, she lays them on the sacred fire for the first offering, calling aloud on Hecate, powerful both in heaven and in Erebus. Others set knives to the throat and catch the warm blood in bowls. Aeneas himself slays with the sword a black-fleeced lamb to the mother of the Eumenides and her great sister, and to you, O Proserpina, a barren heifer. Then for the Stygian king he inaugurates an altar by night, and lays upon the flames whole carcasses of bulls, pouring fat oil over the blazing entrails. But lo! just after the dawning light of the early sun, the ground rumbled underfoot, the wooded ridges began to quiver, and through the gloom dogs seemed to howl as the goddess drew near. "Away! away! unhallowed ones!" shrieks the seer, "withdraw from all of the grove! And you, Aeneas, rush on the road and unsheathe your sword! Now you need your courage, now your stout heart!" So much she said, and plunged madly into the opened cave. He, with fearless steps, keeps pace with his advancing guide.

You gods, who hold the domain of spirits! You voiceless shades! You, Chaos, and you, Phlegethon,[63] you broad, silent tracts of night! Suffer me to tell what I have heard, suffer me of your grace to unfold secrets buried in the depths and darkness of the earth!

They went on dimly, beneath the lonely night amid the gloom, through the empty halls of Dis and his phantom realm, just as a path in the forest lies under the grudging light of an inconstant moon, when Jupiter has buried the sky in shade, and black Night has stolen from the world her hues. Just before the entrance, even within the very jaws of Orcus, Grief and avenging Cares have made their bed. Pale Diseases dwell there, and sad Age, and Fear, and ill-counseling Famine, and loathsome Poverty, shapes terrible to view; and Death and Distress; next, Death's own brother Sleep, and the soul's Guilty Joys, and, on the threshold opposite, the death-bearer War, and the Furies' iron cells, and savage Strife, her snaky locks entwined with bloody headbands.

In the midst an elm, shadowy and vast, spreads her boughs and aged arms, the home which, it is said, false Dreams hold in throngs, clinging under every leaf. And many monstrous forms besides of various beasts are stabled at the doors: Centaurs and double-shaped Scyllas, and the hundredfold Briareus, and the beast of Lerna, hissing horribly, and the Chimaera armed with flame, Gorgons and Harpies, and the shape of the three-bodied shade. Here in a sudden, trembling dread, Aeneas grasps his sword, and turns the naked edge against their coming. If his wise companion had not warned him that these were but faint, bodiless lives, flitting under a hollow semblance of form, he would have rushed upon them and vainly cut shadows with the steel.

From there a road leads to the waters of Tartarean Acheron. Here, thick with mire and of fathomless flood, a whirlpool seethes and belches all its sand into Cocytus. A grim warden guards these waters and streams, terrible in his squalor: Charon, on whose chin lies a mass of unkempt, hoary hair. His eyes are staring orbs of flame. His squalid garb hangs by a knot from his shoulders. Unaided, he poles the boat, tends the sails, and in his murky craft convoys the dead. He is aged, but a god's old age is hardy and green. There rushed all the throng, streaming to the banks: mothers and men and bodies of high souled heroes, their life now done, boys and unwedded girls, and sons placed on the pyre before their fathers' eyes, thick as the leaves of the forest that at autumn's first frost fall dropping, and thick as the birds that from the seething

---

62   In Vergil's time Cape Misenus was the name for a point near Naples.

63   A river of the underworld whose waters burn.

deep flock shoreward when the chill of the year drives them overseas and sends them into sunny lands. They stood, pleading to be the first ferried across, and stretched out hands in yearning for the farther shore. But the surly boatman takes now these, now those, while he thrusts others apart, back from the brink. Then aroused and amazed by the disorder, Aeneas cries: "Tell me, O maiden, what does the crowding to the river mean? What do the spirits seek? By what rule do some retreat from the banks, and others sweep the lurid stream with oars?" To him the aged priestess spoke briefly: "Son of Anchises, true offspring of gods, you see the deep pools of Cocytus and the Stygian marsh, by whose power the gods fear to swear falsely. All this crowd you see is helpless and without a grave. The warden there is Charon. Those whom the waves carry are the buried. Nor may he bear them over the dreadful banks and hoarse-voiced waters before their bones have found a resting-place. A hundred years they roam and flit about these shores. Then only are they admitted and revisit the longed-for pools."

The son of Anchises paused and stayed his steps, pondering much, and pitying in his soul their cruel lot. There he spots, doleful and bereft of death's honor, Leucaspis and Orontes, captain of the Lycian fleet, whom, while voyaging together from Troy over windy waters, the south wind overwhelmed, engulfing alike ship and sailors.

Lo! there passed the helmsman, Palinurus, who of late, on the Libyan voyage, while he marked the stars, had fallen from the stern, flung forth in the midst of the waves. When at last amid the deep gloom Aeneas recognized the sorrowful form, he first accosts him thus: "What god, Palinurus, tore you from us and plunged you beneath the open ocean? O tell me! For Apollo, never before found false, with this one answer tricked my soul, for he foretold that you would escape the sea and reach Ausonian shores. Lo! is it thus his promise holds?" But he replied: "Neither did the tripod of Phoebus[64] fail you, my captain, son of Anchises, nor did a god plunge me in the deep. For by chance the helm to which, as my charge, I clung, steering our course, was violently torn from me, and I, dropping

headlong, dragged it with me. By the rough seas I swear that I felt such fear not for myself, but for your ship, lest, stripped of its gear and bereft of its helmsman, it might fail amid such surging waves. Three stormy nights over the measureless seas the south wind drove me wildly on the water. Just on the fourth dawn, aloft on the crest of a wave, I sighted Italy. Little by little I swam shoreward, and even now was grasping at safety, but as, weighted by dripping garb, I caught with bent fingers at the rugged cliff-peaks, a barbarous nation assailed me with the sword, in ignorance deeming me a prize. Now the waves hold me, and the winds toss me on the beach. Oh, by heaven's sweet light and air, I beseech you, by your father, by the rising hope of Iulus, snatch me from these woes, unconquered one! Either cast earth on me, for you can if you seek again the harbor of Velia or, if there is a way, if your goddess-mother shows you one (for I know you do not cross these great streams and the Stygian marsh without divine favor), give your hand to one so unhappy, and take me with you across the waves, that at least in death I may find a quiet resting place!"

So had he spoken, and the soothsayer thus began: "Whence, O Palinurus, this wild longing of yours? Shall you, unburied, view the Stygian waters and the Furies' stern river, and, without being ordered, draw near the bank? Cease to dream that heaven's decrees may be turned aside by prayer. But hear and remember my words, to solace your hard lot, for the neighboring people, in their cities far and wide, shall be driven by celestial portents to appease your dust, and shall establish a tomb, and to the tomb pay solemn offerings. And the place shall forever bear the name of Palinurus." By these words his cares are banished, and grief is driven for a time from his gloomy heart. He rejoices in the land bearing his name.

So they pursue the journey they had begun, and draw near the river. But when, even from the Stygian wave, the boatman saw them passing through the silent wood and turning their feet towards the bank, he first, unhailed, accosts and rebukes them: "Whoever you are that come to our river in arms, O tell me, even

64 I.e., Apollo's oracle.

from there, why you come, and check your steps. This is the land of Shadows, of Sleep and drowsy Night. I may not carry living bodies in the Stygian boat. And in truth it brought me no joy that I took Alcides[65] in his journey over the lake, or Theseus and Pirithous, though sons of gods and invincible in valor. The one sought to drag in chains, by force, even from the monarch's throne, the warder of Tartarus, and tore him off trembling.[66] The others tried to carry off our queen from the chamber of Dis."[67] The Amphrysian[68] sooth-sayer spoke briefly in reply: "No such trickery is here. Do not be troubled. Our weapons offer no force. The huge doorkeeper may from his cave frighten the bloodless shades with endless howls. Proserpina may in purity stay within her uncle's[69] threshold. Trojan Aeneas, famous for piety and arms, descends to his father, to the lowest shades of Erebus. If the picture of such piety in no way moves you, then see this bough!" She shows the bough, hidden in her robe. Thereon, after his anger, his swelling breast subsides. No more is said, but he, marveling at the dread gift, the fateful wand so long unseen, turns his blue barge and nears the shore. Then he routs out other souls that sit on the long benches, and clears the gangways and takes aboard giant Aeneas. The seamy craft groaned under the weight, and through its chinks took in a marshy flood. At last, across the water, he lands seer and soldier unharmed on the ugly mire and gray sedge.

Huge Cerberus makes these realms ring with his triple-throated baying, his monstrous bulk crouching in a cavern opposite. Seeing the snakes now bristling on Cerberus's necks, the seer flung him a morsel drowsy with honey and drugged meal. He, opening his triple throat in ravenous hunger, catches it when thrown and, with monstrous frame relaxed, sinks to earth and stretches his bulk over the entire den. The guardian buried in sleep, Aeneas wins the entrance, and swiftly leaves the bank of that stream from which none returns.

At once voices and sore wailing are heard—the souls of infants weeping, whom the black day swept off and plunged in bitter death, on the very threshold of the sweet life they did not share, torn from the breast. Near them were those condemned to die on a false charge. Yet these places are not given without a jury chosen by lot, not without a judge: Minos, presiding, shakes the urn from which he calls a court of the silent, and learns men's lives and misdeeds. The region thereafter is held by those sad souls who in innocence brought about their own death and, loathing the light, flung away their lives. How gladly now, in the air above, would they hear both want and harsh distress! Fate endures. The unlovely marsh with its dreary water enchains them and Styx imprisons them with his ninefold circles.

Not far from here, spread out on every side, are shown the Mourning Fields; such is the name they bear. Here those whom stern Love has consumed with cruel wasting are hidden in withdrawn walks, embowered in a myrtle grove. The pangs do not leave them even in death. In this region he sees Phaedra[70] and Procris,[71] and sad Eriphyle,[72] pointing to the wounds her cruel son had dealt, and Evadne[73] and Pasiphae. With them goes Laodamia,[74] and Caeneus, once a youth, now a woman, and again turned back by Fate into her form of old.[75] Among them, with her

---

65  I.e., Hercules.

66  Hercules went down to the underworld and dragged back in chains Cerberus, the fierce three-headed dog which guarded the place.

67  Theseus and Pirithous tried to carry off Proserpina from the underworld. Pluto foiled their attempt.

68  Apollo was the shepherd of Amphrysus.

69  Pluto was Proserpina's uncle as well as her husband.

70  Phaedra fell in love with her own stepson. He spurned her advances, and she in revenge procured his banishment, which led to his death. In remorse, Phaedra hanged herself.

71  Procris doubted the loyalty of her husband, who accidentally killed her.

72  Eriphyle was murdered by her son because she betrayed her husband, his father.

73  Evadne's husband was killed by a thunderbolt from Jupiter. She threw herself on the burning ashes and burned to death herself.

74  When Laodamia's husband went to the Trojan war, she in her grief had a wooden statue of him made and placed in her bed. When the statue was burned, she threw herself in the flames and burned up with it.

75  Caeneus began life as a woman, but was allowed by Jupiter to turn into a man.

wound still fresh, Phoenician Dido was wandering in the great forest. As soon as the Trojan hero stood near and knew her, a dim form amid the shadows—just as, early in the month, one sees or fancies one has seen the moon rise amid the clouds—he shed tears, and spoke to her in tender love: "Unhappy Dido! Then the tale brought to me was true, that you were no more, and had sought your doom with the sword? Was I, alas!, the cause of your death? I swear by the stars, by the world above, and whatever is sacred in the grave below, O queen, I parted from your shores unwillingly. But the gods' decrees, which now constrain me to pass through these shades, through squalid and forsaken lands, and through abysmal night, drove me with their behests, nor could I know my going would bring you such deep distress. Stay your step and do not withdraw from our view. Whom do you flee? The last word Fate suffers me to say to you is this!"

Aeneas tried to soothe the wrath of the fiery, fierce-eyed queen with such speech amid springing tears. She, turning away, kept her looks fixed on the ground and no more changes her countenance as he tries to speak than if she were set in hard flint or Marpesian rock. At length she flung herself away and, still his foe, fled back to the shady grove, where Sychaeus, her husband of former days, responds to her sorrows and gives her love for love. Yet nonetheless, dazed by her unjust doom, Aeneas follows after her with tears, and pities her as she goes.

From there he toils along the way that offered itself. And now they reached the farthest fields, where the renowned in war dwell apart. Here Tydeus meets him; here Parthenopaeus, famed in arms, and the pale shade of Adrastus; here, much wept for on earth above and fallen in war, the Dardan chiefs, whom as he beheld, all in long array, he moaned: Glaucus and Medon and Thersilochus, the three sons of Antenor, and Polyboetes, priest of Ceres, and Idaeus, still keep-ing his chariot and his arms. All around, right and left, stand the souls in throngs. To have seen him once is not enough. They delight to linger on, to pace beside him, and to learn the causes of his coming. But the Danaan princes and Agamemnon's battalions,[76] as soon as they saw the man and his arms flashing amid the gloom, trembled with mighty fear. Some turn to flee, as of old they sought the ships. Some raise a shout—faintly—the cry they attempt mocks their gaping mouths.

And here he saw Deiphobus, son of Priam, his whole frame mangled, his face cruelly torn—his face and both hands—his ears wrenched from despoiled brows, and his nostrils lopped by a shameful wound. Indeed, he barely knew the quivering form that tried to hide its awful punishment. Then, with familiar accents, unhailed, he addressed him:

"Deiphobus, strong in battle, you scion of Teucer's high lineage: who chose to wreak a penalty so cruel? Who had power to deal with you this way? Rumor told me that on that last night, weary with endless slaughter of Pelasgians,[77] you had sunk upon a heap of mingled carnage. Then I myself set up an empty tomb upon the Rhoetean shore, and with loud cry called three times upon your spirit. Your name and arms guard the place. You, my friend, I could not see, nor did you lie, as I departed, in your native land."

To this the son of Priam answered, "You have left nothing undone, my friend. You have paid Deiphobus and the dead man's shade everything due. But my own fate and the Laconian woman's[78] death-dealing crime overwhelmed me in these woes. Lo! it was she who left these memorials! For how we spent that last night amid deluding joys, you know—and all too well must you remember! When the fateful horse leapt over the heights of Troy, and brought armed infantry to weight its womb,[79] she feigned a solemn dance and led the Phrygian wives around the city, shrieking in

76  I.e., the dead Greeks who had fought against Troy in the Trojan war.
77  The Pelasgians were said to be the oldest people among the Greeks.
78  The Laconian woman was Helen, who had married Deiphobus after the death of Paris.
79  Aeneas before book IV had told Dido about how the Greeks had succeeded in taking Troy by offering the city an enormous statue of a horse and pretending to end the war and go home. The Trojans fell for the ruse, and brought the horse into the city. The Greeks, however, had concealed their leading warriors inside the horse. Those Greeks were thus able to surprise the Trojans at night, and open the gates to attacking soldiers from outside.

their Bacchic rites. She herself in the midst held a mighty torch and called the Danaans from the castle-height. Careworn and sunk in slumber, I was then in our ill-starred bridal chamber, sleep weighing upon me as I lay—sweet and deep, the very image of death's peace. Meanwhile, this peerless wife takes every weapon from the house—she had even withdrawn my trusty sword from under my head. She calls Menelaus[80] into the house and flings wide the door, hoping, I do not doubt, that her lover would find inside a great favor, and so the fame of old misdeeds might be blotted out. Why linger? They burst into my chamber. With them comes their fellow-counselor of sin, the son of Aeolus.[81] You gods, pay back the Greeks with like penalties, if I pray for vengeance with pious lips! But come, tell in turn what chance has brought you here, alive. Do you come driven in your ocean-wanderings, or by divine command? Or what fortune wearies you, that you should visit these sad, sunless dwellings, this land of disorder?"

During such exchange of talk, Dawn, with her rosy chariot, had now crossed mid-heaven in her course, and perhaps they would have spent all the allotted time in this way, if the Sibyl beside him had not given warning with these brief words: "Night is coming, Aeneas. We are wasting the hours in weeping. Here is the place where the road parts in two directions: there to the right, as it runs under the walls of great Dis, is our way to Elysium, but the left wreaks the punishment of the wicked, and sends them on to pitiless Tartarus." Deiphobus replied: "Do not be angry, great priestess. I will go my way; I will fill my spot among the shades and go back to the darkness. Go, our glory, go; enjoy a happier fate!" That is all he said and, as he spoke, he turned his steps.

Suddenly Aeneas looks back, and under a cliff on the left sees broad fortifications, surrounded with a triple wall and encircled with a rushing flood of torrential flames—Tartarean Phlegethon, that rolls along thundering rocks. The huge gate and pillars of solid adamant[82] stand in front so that no power of man, no, not even the sons of heaven, may uproot them in war. There stands the iron tower, soaring high, and Tisiphone,[83] sitting girt with bloody pall, keeps sleepless watch over the portal night and day. Groans and the sound of the savage lash, the clank of iron and dragging of chains are heard from within. Aeneas stopped, rooted to the spot in terror of the din. "What forms of crime are these? Say, O maiden! With what penalties are they scourged? What cry so loud rises up?" Then the seer thus began to speak: "Famed chieftain of the Teucrians, no pure soul may tread the accursed threshold. But when Hecate set me over the groves of Avernus, she taught me the gods' penalties and guided me through all. Gnosian Rhadamanthus holds here his iron sway. He chastises, and hears the tale of guilt, exacting confession of crimes, whenever anyone in the world above, rejoicing in vain deceit, has put off atonement until death's late hour. Immediately avenging Tisiphone, girt with the lash, leaps on the guilty to scourge them, and with left hand brandishing her grim snakes, calls on her savage sister band. Then at last, grating on their harsh, jarring hinges, the infernal gates open. Do you see what sentry sits in the doorway? What shape guards the threshold? The monstrous Hydra, even fiercer, with her 50 black gaping throats, dwells within. Then Tartarus itself yawns steeply down, stretching into the gloom twice as far as is yonder sky's upward view to heavenly Olympus. Here the ancient sons of Earth, the Titan's brood, hurled down by the thunderbolt, writhe in the lowest abyss.[84] Here, too, I saw the twin sons of Aloeus, giant in stature, whose hands tried to tear down high Heaven and thrust down Jove from his realm above. I saw also Salmoneus, who paid a cruel penalty while aping Jove's fires and the thunders of Olympus. He, borne by four horses and brandishing a torch, rode triumphant through the Greek peoples and his city in the heart of Elis, claiming as his own the homage due to the god. Madman! to mimic the storm-clouds and

---

80    Her Greek husband, whom she had left when she went with Paris.
81    I.e., Ulysses (the Greek Odysseus), whose father was Laertes, but who was rumored to be the grandson of Aeolus.
82    A substance thought to be the hardest stone, sometimes referring to diamond.
83    One of the Furies.
84    In Greek myth, the Titans were a group of giants who unsuccessfully rebelled against the gods.

inimitable thunder with brass and the tramp of horn-footed horses! But the Almighty Father launched his bolt amid thick clouds—no firebrands nor pitch-pines' smoky glare did he use—and drove him headlong with a furious whirlwind. Likewise one might see Tityos,[85] nursling of Earth, the universal mother. His body is stretched over nine full acres, and a monstrous vulture with crooked beak gnaws at his deathless liver and vitals fruitful for anguish. It lodges and gropes for its feast deep within the breast, nor is any respite given to the flesh that grows anew. Why tell of the Lapithae, Ixion[86] and Pirithous, over whom hangs a black rock that now, yes now, would seem to slip and fall? High festal seats gleam with frames of gold, and before their eyes is spread a banquet in royal splendor. Yet, reclining hard by, the eldest Fury keeps their hands from touching anything from the table, springing forth with uplifted torch and thunderous cries.

"Here were they who, while alive, hated their brothers, or struck a parent, and entangled a client in wrong or who brooded in solitude over wealth they had won, and set aside no portion for their kin (the largest number are such). Here are they who were slain for adultery or who followed impious warfare, and did not fear to break faith with their lords—all these, immured, await their punishment. Do not seek to learn that punishment, or what form of crime, or fate, overwhelmed them! Some roll a huge stone, or hang outstretched on spokes of wheels. Hopeless, Theseus sits and forever shall sit and Phlegyas,[87] most unblest, gives warning to all and with loud voice bears witness amid the gloom: 'Be warned. Learn to be just and not to slight the gods!' This one sold his country for gold, and fastened on her tyrant lord. He made and unmade laws for a bribe. This one forced his daughter's bed and a marriage forbidden. All dared a monstrous sin, and attained what they dared. Even if I had a hundred tongues, a hundred mouths, and voice of iron, I could not sum up all the forms of crime, or rehearse all the tale of torments."

So spoke the aged priestess of Phoebus, then adding: "But come now, take your way and fulfill the task in hand. Let us hasten. I make out the ramparts reared by Cyclopean[88] forges and the gates with fronting arch, where they order us to lay the appointed gifts." She ended, and advancing side by side along the dusky way, they hasten over the mid-space and come to the doors. Aeneas wins the entrance, sprinkles his body with fresh water, and plants the bough full on the threshold.

At length, with this done and the task of the goddess fulfilled, they came to a land of joy, the green pleasant places and happy seats of the Blissful Groves. Here an ampler air clothes the plains with bright light, and they have their own sun and stars. Some disport their limbs on the grassy wrestling-ground, vie in sports, and grapple on the yellow sand; some dance and chant songs. There, too, the long-robed Thracian priest matches their measures with the seven clear notes, striking them now with his fingers, now with his ivory quill. Here is Teucer's old line, that most beautiful family, high-souled heroes born in happier years—Ilus and Assaracus and Dardanus, Troy's founder. From afar Aeneas marvels at their phantom arms and chariots. Their lances stand fixed in the ground, and their steeds, unyoked, browse freely over the plain. The selfsame pride in chariot and arms that was theirs in life, the selfsame care in keeping sleek steeds, attends them when hidden beneath the earth. Lo! he sees others, right and left, feasting on the grass, and chanting in chorus a joyous paean within a fragrant laurel grove, from which, in the world above, the full flood of the Eridanus river[89] rolls amid the forest.

Here is the band of those who suffered wounds, fighting for fatherland; those who while alive were priests and pure, good bards, whose songs were fit for Phoebus; or they who ennobled life by discovering truths and they who by service have won remembrance among men. The brows of all of them are

reward / punishment

85  He assaulted the goddess Latona.
86  He assaulted Juno.
87  In Greek legend, he destroyed Apollo's temple at Delphi.
88  The Cyclopes were the assistants to Vulcan, god of the forge.
89  I.e., the Po river, in Italy. It runs underground very near its source.

bound with a snowy band. These, as they streamed round, the Sibyl thus addressed, Musaeus[90] above all, for he is at the center of the vast throng that gazes up to him, as with high shoulders he towers aloft: "Say, happy souls, and you best of bards, what land, what place holds Anchises? We have come and have sailed across the great rivers of Erebus for his sake."

And to her the hero thus made brief reply: "None of us has a fixed home. We dwell in shady groves, and live on cushioned river banks and in meadows fresh with streams. But, if the wish in your heart so inclines, surmount this ridge, and I will soon set you on an easy path." He spoke and walked ahead, and from above points out the shining fields. Then they leave the mountain tops.

Indeed, deep in a green vale, father Anchises was surveying with earnest thought the imprisoned souls that were to pass to the light above and, as it chanced, was telling the full tale of his people and beloved children, their fates and fortunes, their works and ways. And he, as he saw Aeneas coming towards him over the grass, eagerly stretched forth both hands, while tears streamed from his eyes and a cry fell from his lips: "Have you come at last, and has the love your father looked for vanquished the toilsome way? Is it given to me to see your face, my son, and hear and utter familiar tones? Even so I mused and thought the hour would come, counting the days to it, nor has my yearning failed me. Over what lands, what wide seas have you journeyed to my welcome! What dangers have tossed you, O my son! How I feared the realm of Libya might give you harm!"

But he replied: "Your shade, father, your sad shade, meeting me so often, drove me to seek these portals. My ships ride the Tuscan sea. Grant me to clasp your hand, grant me, O father, and do not withdraw from my embrace!"

So he spoke, his face wet with flooding tears. Three times he strove to throw his arms about his neck; three times the form, vainly clasped, fled from his hands, just like light winds, and most like a winged dream.

Meanwhile, in a retired vale, Aeneas sees a sequestered grove and rustling forest thickets, and the river of Lethe drifting past those peaceful homes. About it hovered unnumbered peoples and tribes, just as when, in the meadows, in cloudless summertime, bees light on many-hued blossoms and stream around lustrous lilies and all the fields murmur with the humming. Aeneas is thrilled by the sudden sight and, not knowing, asks the cause—what is that river there, and who are the men thronging the banks in such a host? Then father Anchises replied:

"They are spirits to whom second bodies are owed by Fate, and at the water of Lethe's stream they drink up soothing drink and long forgetfulness. These in truth I have long yearned to tell and show you to your face, yes, to count this, my children's seed, so you may rejoice with me the more at finding Italy."

"But, father, must we think that any souls pass up from here to yonder sky, and return a second time to sluggish bodies? What means, alas! their mad longing for the light?" "I will surely tell you, my son, and not hold you in doubt," replies Anchises, and reveals each truth in order.

"First, heaven and earth, and the watery plains, the shining orb of the moon and Titan's star are all sustained by a spirit within, and by mind, pervading its members, swaying the whole mass and mingling with its mighty frame. From these are created human beings and beasts, the life of winged things, and the strange shapes Ocean bears beneath his glassy floor. The source of those life-seeds is fiery and their vigor is divine, so far as harmful bodies do not clog them, nor earthly limbs and mortal frames dull them—hence their fears and desires, their griefs and joys. Nor do they, pent up in the gloom of their dark dungeon, discern the light. No, when at their last day of life has fled, still not all the evil, alas! not all the plagues of the body leave them utterly. It is inevitable that many faults, long linked in growth, should in a mysterious way become deeply ingrained. Therefore the souls are schooled with penalties, and pay punishment for old wicked deeds. Some are hung stretched out to the empty winds. From some the stain of guilt is washed away under swirling floods or burned out in fire. Each of us suffers his own spirit. Then we are sent through

90   A mythical poet.

wide Elysium, a few of us to abide in the joyous fields until the passing of the days, when time's cycle is complete, takes out the inbred taint and leaves the ethereal sense and pure flame of spirit unsoiled. All these, when they have rolled time's wheel through a thousand years, the god summons in a vast throng to the river of Lethe, so that, bereft of memory, they may revisit the vault above and conceive a desire to return again to the body."

Anchises ceased, and drew his son and, with him, the Sibyl into the midst of the concourse and murmuring throng, then chose a mound from which, face to face, he might scan the whole long line, and note their countenances as they came.

"Come now, I will set forth what glory shall hereafter attend the Dardan line, what children of Italian stock await you, illustrious souls and heirs of our name, and teach you your destiny. The youth you see over there, who leans on a headless spear, holds by lot a place nearest the light, and who shall rise first into the air of heaven, mingling with Italian blood, is Silvius, an Alban name, your last-born child, whom late in your old age your wife Lavinia shall bring forth in the woodland, a king and father of kings. From him shall our nation have sway in Longa Alba.[91] Next is Procas, glory of the Trojan race, and Capys and Numitor,[92] and he who shall renew your name, Silvius Aeneas, like you peerless in piety or in arms, if he ever wins the Alban throne. What youths! What mighty strength, lo! they display, and bear brows shaded with the civic oak! These, I tell you, shall rear Nomentum and Gabii and Fidenae's city; these shall crown hills with Collatia's turrets, with Pometii, and the Fort of Inuus, with Bola and Cora. These shall then be names that now are nameless lands.

"Yet more, a child of Mars shall join his grand sire, even Romulus, whom his mother Ilia shall bear of the blood of Assaracus. Do you see how the twin plumes stand upon his crest,[93] and how his father himself by his own token even now marks him for the world above? Lo! under his auspices, my son, that glorious Rome shall bound her empire by earth, her pride by heaven, and with a single city's wall shall enclose her seven hills, blessed in her brood of men, just as the Berecyntian Mother,[94] turret-crowned, rides in her chariot through the Phrygian cities, glad in her offspring of gods, and clasping a hundred of her children's children, all denizens of heaven, all tenants of the heights above. Now turn your two eyes here: behold this people, your own Romans. Here is Caesar,[95] and all Iulus's seed, destined to pass beneath the sky's mighty vault. This, this is he, whom you so often hear promised to you, Augustus Caesar, son of a god, who shall again set up the Golden Age amid the fields where Saturn once reigned, and shall spread his empire past the Garamantians[96] and the Indians, to a land that lies beyond the stars, beyond the paths of the year and the sun, where heaven-bearing Atlas turns the sphere, inset with gleaming stars, on his shoulders. Against his coming even now the Caspian realms and Maeotian[97] land shudder at Heaven's oracles, and the mouths of sevenfold Nile are in tumult of terror. Nor, in truth, did Alcides range over such space of earth, though he pierced the bronze-footed deer, or brought peace to the woods of Erymanthus, and made Lerna tremble at his bow. Nor did triumphant Bacchus, who guides his tiger-drawn chariot with vine-leaf reins, driving down from Nysa's lofty crest. And do we still hesitate to enlarge our prowess by deeds, or does fear forbid our settling on Ausonian land?

"But who is he, set apart, crowned with olive-sprays, and bearing the sacrifice? I know the locks and hoary chin of that king of Rome, who, called from the poor land of lowly Cures[98] to sovereign might, shall

---

91   Alba Longa, in central Italy.
92   Grandfather of Romulus (the founder of the city of Rome) and Remus.
93   I.e., two plumes of feathers are on his helmet. Mars, the god of war, wears such a helmet.
94   I.e., Cybele, a goddess of Asia Minor. She is sometimes depicted wearing a crown of city walls and fortifications.
95   I.e., Julius Caesar. He adopted his nephew Octavian, later known as Augustus. Julius Caesar was declared a god after his death, making Octavian the son of a god. The Romans, one may note, spelled "Julius" "Iulius."
96   A people of north Africa.
97   An area near the Crimea.
98   A town near Rome.

contrived?

base the infant city on his laws.[99] To him shall then succeed Tullus, who shall break his country's peace, and rouse to arms a slothful folk and ranks long unused to triumphs. Hard on him follows over-boastful Ancus, even now rejoicing overmuch in the people's breath.[100] Will you see, too, the Tarquin kings, and the proud soul of avenging Brutus,[101] and the *fasces*[102] regained? He shall be first to win a consul's power and cruel axes, and when his sons stir up new war, the father, for fair freedom's sake, shall call them to their doom[103]—unhappy one, however posterity extols that deed! Yet love of country and boundless passion for renown shall prevail.

"Behold also, a great way off, the Decii and Drusi,[104] and Torquatus of the cruel axe,[105] and Camillus bringing home the standards.[106] But they whom you see gleaming in equal arms, souls harmonious now, while wrapped in night, alas! if they but reach the light of life, what mutual war, what battles and carnage shall they arouse!: the father coming down from Alpine ramparts, and the fortress of Monoecus, his daughter's spouse arrayed against him with the armies of the East.[107] O my sons, do not make a home within your hearts for such warfare, nor turn your country's vigor and valor upon her very vitals! And forgive first, you who draw your family from heaven. Cast the sword from your hand, you blood of mine!

"Over there is one who, famed for the Achaeans[108] he has slain, triumphant over Corinth, shall drive a victor's chariot to the lofty Capitol.[109] That one over there shall uproot Argos and Agamemnon's Mycenae, indeed, and even one born of Aeacus, seed of Achilles the strong in battle, taking vengeance for his Trojan sires and Minerva's outraged temple.[110] Who would leave you in silence, great Cato,[111] or you, Cossus?[112] Who would leave in silence the Gracchan family,[113] or

---

99  This is Numa, Rome's second king.

100  I.e., in popular praise.

101  According to legend and possibly in fact, Rome was ruled by kings in its early days. The last of the kings were the Tarquins. The fall of the monarchy was said to have been brought about by the rape of a Roman aristocrat named Lucretia by the son of King Tarquin the Proud. When Tarquin failed to punish his son, Lucretia killed herself to inspire others against tyranny. One of those so inspired was Brutus, who led the movement to drive Tarquin from Rome, thus ending the monarchy and founding the Roman Republic. (This Brutus is not to be confused with the Brutus who later took part in the assassination of Julius Caesar.)

102  The *fasces* were the rods which symbolized office at Rome.

103  Brutus's sons attempted to overthrow the Republic and restore the monarchy. Brutus had them executed.

104  Two prominent families in Roman politics. Three members of the Decii, in three different battles, acted out the *devotio*, whereby the Romans believed that a soldier who goes ahead of the Roman lines and throws himself against the enemy and dies thus assures a Roman victory.

105  While consul, (Titus Manlius) Torquatus (fourth century BC) put his own son to death for disobeying military orders.

106  Marcus Furius Camillus, although exiled by the Romans, was willing to take up the office of dictator (a temporary office of supreme authority for emergencies) when asked. He fought the Gauls who had sacked Rome in 390 BC and recaptured the standards which the Gauls had taken, thus restoring Rome's honor.

107  This refers to the civil war between Pompey and Julius Caesar (first century BC). The fortress of Monoecus is in modern Monaco, then southern Gaul, a center of Caesar's power. Pompey, who had married Caesar's daughter, drew his support from the eastern part of the empire.

108  I.e., Greeks.

109  This is the consul L. Mummius (second century BC), who destroyed the Greek city of Corinth at the behest of the Senate. Unlike other generals, he took none of the spoils of war.

110  The Roman commander L. Aemilius Paulus defeated Perseus, the last king of Macedon, in 168 BC. Perseus claimed descent from Achilles, the grandson of Aeacus. Of the very rich spoils from Macedon, which now fell under Roman rule, Paulus took nothing except Perseus's library.

111  The senator Cato the elder (234-149 BC) was a byword among the Romans for rectitude.

112  Aulus Cornelius Cossus (fifth century BC) was said to have been one of the few Romans to slay an enemy commander in combat and take his armor.

113  The family of Tiberius and Gaius Gracchus (second century BC), would-be Roman reformers.

the pair of Scipio's line, two thunderbolts of war, the bane of Libya?[114] or you, Fabricius, poor, yet powerful?[115] or you, Serranus, sowing the seed in your furrow?[116] To where do you hurry my weary steps, O Fabii?[117] You are Maximus, who alone, by delaying, restores our state. Others, I do not doubt, shall beat out breathing bronze with softer lines; shall draw forth living features from marble; shall plead their causes better; with the rod shall trace the paths of heaven and tell the rising of the stars. Remember, O Roman, these shall be yours arts: to rule the nations with your *imperium*,[118] to join peace with law, to spare the humbled, and to tame in war the proud!"

Thus spoke father Anchises, and, as they marvel, he continues: "Lo! how Marcellus advances, glorious in his splendid spoils, and towers triumphant over all! He, an *eques*,[119] shall support the Roman realm, when turned over in utter confusion. He shall strike down Carthaginian and insurgent Gaul, and a third time hang up the captured arms to father Quirinus!"[120]

And now Aeneas saw coming with him a youth of wondrous beauty and brilliant in his arms—but his face was sad and his eyes downcast: "Who, father, is he who thus attends him on his way? A son, or one of the mighty stock of his children's children? What a rumbling in the encircling crowd! What noble presence in himself! But black night hovers about his head with its mournful shade."[121]

Then father Anchises with welling tears began: "O my son, do not ask of the vast sorrow of your people. The fates shall but show him to earth, nor allow him to stay longer. O gods, you deemed the Roman stock would be too mighty if these gifts were to last. What wailing of men shall that famous field raise by Mars's mighty city![122] What funeral-state, O Tiber, shall you see, as you glide past the new-built tomb! No youth of Ilian stock shall exalt so greatly with his promise his Latin forefathers, nor shall the land of Romulus ever take such pride in any of her sons. Alas for piety! alas for old-fashioned honor, and the hand invincible in war! None would have advanced unscathed against him in arms, whether he met the foe on foot, or dug his spurs into the flanks of his foaming horse. Ah! pitiable boy, if you could somehow burst the harsh bonds of fate, you shall be Marcellus! Give me lilies with full hands. Let me scatter purple flowers. Let me at least heap these gifts over my offspring's shade and fulfill an unavailing duty."

Thus they range freely through the whole region, surveying all in the broad, misty plains. And when Anchises had led his son over every scene, and fired his soul with love of fame that was to be, he tells him then of the wars he must thereafter wage, and

114 Publius Cornelius Scipio Africanus (236-183 BC) defeated Hannibal in the second Punic War. His adopted son, Publius Scipio Aemilianus (second century BC), destroyed Carthage at the end of the third Punic War.

115 Fabricius Caius Luscinus, a Roman commander of the third century who, despite his great poverty, steadfastly refused bribes.

116 C. Atilius Regulus (third century BC) was nicknamed *Serranus* (*serere* means "to sow") because he learned that he was to be consul while sowing his fields. He was captured by Carthage during the first Punic War. The Carthaginians sent him back to Rome to propose a peace favorable to Carthage after swearing oaths to return if the Romans did not agree. He went to Rome and advised that the Carthaginian offer be refused. Faithful to his oaths, he then returned to Carthage, where the Carthaginians tortured and executed him when they discovered what he had done.

117 A prominent Roman family, whose most famous member, Quintus Fabius Maximus (third century BC) helped save Rome during the second Punic War by delaying battle, thus earning the nickname *Cunctator* ("Delayer").

118 *Imperium*: the Roman term for the power of command.

119 I.e., a member of the Roman class below the Senators. *Eques* is often translated as "knight."

120 A Roman general of the third century BC who fought the Gauls and the Carthaginians, and was one of the few to slay an enemy commander in battle and take his armor. *Quirinus* was another name for Mars, the god of war, to whom the armor was dedicated. *Quirinus* could also refer to Romulus.

121 Aeneas is looking at the shade of Marcellus (first century BC), Augustus's very dear nephew, who died at the age of 20. Augustus is said to have wept when Vergil read this passage aloud.

122 The famous field is the "Field of Mars," where Augustus built his Mausoleum in 27 BC, in which Marcellus was also evidently laid. The city of Mars is Rome.

instructs him of the Laurentine peoples and the city of Latinus,[123] and how he is to flee or face each toil.

There are two gates of Sleep, of which one is said to be of horn, and through it an easy exit is given to true shades. The other gleams of the sheen of polished ivory, but through it false dreams are sent by the spirits to the world above. There then with these words Anchises attends both his son and the Sibyl, and dismisses them by the ivory gate. Aeneas speeds his way to the ships and revisits his comrades and then sails straight along the shore for Caieta's haven.[124] The anchor is cast from the prow; the sterns rest upon the beach.

12  [*Aeneas has come to Latium in central Italy, where he has found Latinus, king of the Latins. Aeneas is destined to marry Latinus's daughter, Lavinia. Lavinia, however, is engaged to be married to Turnus, king of the Rutulians, a neighboring people. When Latinus breaks off this engagement to Lavinia so she can marry Aeneas, Juno has Lavinia's mother, Amata, and Turnus stirred into a rage. Turnus and Amata in turn fire up the Latins against the marriage to Aeneas, which Latinus favors, and Latinus loses control over his people. Turnus then leads the Latins, Rutulians, and other peoples in a war against Aeneas and his Trojans. Aeneas, however, has gotten as allies the Arcadians, a Greek people who have settled in Italy and live a simple, rustic life under their king, Evander. Evander, an old man, remains at home, but has sent his men, including his beloved son Pallas, to fight beside the Trojans. Turnus killed Pallas in battle, taking from Pallas his baldric and belt. This war has been going on for some time, and has recently been going against the Latins. When book 12 begins, the Latins and Turnus are consulting King Latinus, who has been against the war all along, about what to do.*]

When Turnus sees the Latins crushed and faint of heart through war's reverse, his own pledge now claimed,[125] and himself the mark of every eye, forthwith he blazes with unappeasable wrath and raises his spirit high. Just as a lion, only when wounded in the

breast by the grievous stroke of huntsmen in Punic fields, wakes to war, joyously tosses from his neck his shaggy mane, and snaps, undaunted, the robber's implanted dart, roaring with blood-stained mouth: just so the fury swells in Turnus's kindling soul. Then he accosts the king, and with these wild words begins: "No delay lies with Turnus! There is no need for the coward sons of Aeneas to recall their words or to renounce their pact! I go to meet him. Bring the holy rites, father, and frame the covenant. Either with this arm will I hurl the Dardan, the Asian runaway, to Tartarus—let the Latins sit and see it—and with my single sword refute the nation's shame or let him be lord of the vanquished, let Lavinia pass to him as bride!"

To him Latinus with a calm heart replied: "O youth of matchless spirit, the more in fierce valor you excel, all the more heedfully must I ponder and with fear weigh every chance. You have your father Daunus's realms, have many towns which your hand has taken. Latinus, too, has gold and good will. There are other unwed women in Latium and Laurentum's fields, and of no ignoble birth. Suffer me to utter this hard saying, stripped of all disguise, and nonetheless drink it into your soul: all gods and men foretold that it was forbidden for me to ally my child to any of her old-time wooers. Overborne by love of you, overborne by kindred blood and the tears of my sorrowing queen, I broke all fetters, snatched the betrothed from her promised husband, and drew the unholy sword.[126] From that day, Turnus, you see what perils, what wars pursue me, what heavy burdens you above all bear. Twice vanquished in mighty battle, we scarce guard within our walls the hopes of Italy. Tiber's streams are still warm with our blood, the boundless plains still white with our bones. Why do I drift back so often? What madness turns my purpose? If, with Turnus dead, I am ready to link them to me as allies, why not rather end the strife while he still lives? What will your Rutulian kinsmen say, what the rest of Italy, if—Fortune refute the word—I should betray you to

123  Aeneas is looking at the shade of Marcellus (first century BC), Augustus's very dear nephew, who died at the age of 20. Augustus is said to have wept when Vergil read this passage aloud.
124  Caieta, Aeneas's childhood nurse, had died and been buried there earlier in the *Aeneid*, thus giving the place, modern "Gaeta," its name.
125  Turnus has said he is willing to resolve the conflict by a single combat between himself and Aeneas.
126  Latinus seems to overstate here his role in this move, to judge by Vergil's earlier account.

death, while you woo our daughter in marriage? Think on war's changes and chances; pity your aged father, whom now his native Ardea keeps far away from us in sorrow!"

His words in no way bend the fury of Turnus. Still higher his fury mounts, more inflamed by the healing. As soon as he could speak, he began: "Give up the care you have on my behalf, most gracious lord, I pray, and suffer me to barter death for fame. I too, father, can scatter darts and no weakling steel from this right hand, and from those wounds too flows blood. His goddess-mother will be too far from him to shelter the runaway, woman-like, with a cloud, and to conceal herself in empty shadows."[127]

But the queen,[128] dismayed by the new terms of conflict, wept, and clung to her fiery son-in-law to be, ready to die: "Turnus, by these my tears, by anything of reverence for Amata that yet may touch your heart: you are now our only hope, you the comfort of my sad old age. The honor and sovereignty of Latinus rests in your hands. All our sinking house rests on you. I beg one favor: forbear to fight the Trojans. Whatever perils await you in that combat of yours, also await me, Turnus. I will leave this hateful light along with you, nor in captivity see Aeneas as my son." Lavinia heard her mother's words, her burning cheeks steeped in tears, while a deep blush kindled its fire, and spread over her glowing face. Just as when one stains Indian ivory with crimson dye, or as when white lilies blush with many a blended rose—such hues her virgin features showed. Love throws Turnus into turmoil, and he fastens his looks upon the virgin. Then, fired yet more for the fray, he briefly addresses Amata:

"No, I beseech you, do not send me off, O my mother, with tears, nor with such an omen, as I go to stern war's conflicts. Nor truly has Turnus freedom to delay his death. Idmon, be my herald and bear my message to the Phrygian king—a message he will not welcome: as soon as tomorrow's Dawn, riding in her crimson chariot, reddens in the sky, let him not lead Teucrians against Rutulians—let Teucrian arms and Rutulians have rest—let us with our own blood settle the war; on that field let Lavinia be wooed and won!"

These words said, withdrawing home with haste, he calls for his steeds, and rejoices to see them neighing before his face—the steeds that Orithyia herself gave as a glory to Pilumnus, for they excelled the snow in whiteness, the gales in speed. The eager charioteers stand around, patting with hollow palms their sounding chests, and combing their flowing manes. Next he binds upon his shoulders a corslet stiff with gold and pale mountain bronze; withal, he fits for wear sword and shield and the horns of his ruddy crest. The divine Lord of Fire[129] had himself wrought the sword for his father Daunus and dipped it, all glowing, in the river Styx. Then, his mighty spear, spoil of Auruncan Actor,[130] which stood leaning upon a giant column in the hall, he seizes with his strong hand, and shakes it quivering, while he cries aloud: "Now, O spear, that never failed my call, now the hour has come! Mighty Actor once bore you. Now the hand of Turnus wields you. Grant me to lay low the body, with strong hand to tear and rend away the corslet of this Phrygian half-man, and to defile his locks, curled with heated iron and bedrenched in myrrh, in the dust!" Such is the frenzy driving him. From his whole face shoot fiery sparks and his eager eyes flash flame—just as a bull, before the battle begins, begins a fearful bellowing, and, trying to throw wrath into his horns, charges a tree trunk; he lashes the winds with his blows, and paws the sand in a prelude to the fray.

Meanwhile, Aeneas, fierce in the arms his mother gave,[131] no less whets his valor and stirs his heart with wrath, rejoicing that the war is settled by the offered agreement. Then he comforts his comrades, and sad Iulus's fear, teaching them of fate, and orders that a firm answer be taken to King Latinus to declare the terms of peace.

---

127 In the *Iliad*, Aeneas's mother attempts to rescue him in battle by hiding him in her cloak. At other points in the same work Apollo and Poseidon rescue him by means of a mist.

128 I.e., Amata.

129 I.e., Vulcan, god of the forge.

130 Actor had been a defender of the Trojan camp against Turnus.

131 Aeneas's mother, Venus, has procured for him armor made by Vulcan.

Scarcely was the next day's dawn sprinkling the mountaintops with light, the Sun's horses first rising from the deep flood, and breathing light from uplifted nostrils, when Rutulians and Teucrians marched out and made ready the area for the combat under the great city's walls, and in the midst hearths and grassy altars to their common deities. Others, in *limus*[132] and their brows bound with verbana were bringing fountain-water and fire. The Ausonian host moved forth, and troops, close-banded, pour from the crowded gates. On this side streams forth all the Trojan and Tyrrhenian host in diverse armament, accoutered in steel, just as though harsh battle-strife called them. Nor less, amid their thousands, the captains dart to and fro, brilliant in gold and purple: Mnestheus of the line of Assaracus, and brave Asilas, and Messapus, tamer of horses, seed of Neptune. As soon as, on the given signal, each has retired to his own ground, they plant their spears in the earth, and rest their shields against them. Then, eagerly streaming forth, mothers and the unarmed throng, and feeble old men, have gone to towers and house tops; others stand upon the lofty gates.

But Juno, from the hill-summit now called Alban— at that time the mount had neither name nor fame nor honor—looking forth, gazed upon the plain, upon the double lines of Laurentum and Troy, and upon the city of Latinus. She immediately spoke, goddess to goddess, to Turnus's sister, mistress of the pools and sounding rivers—such dignity Jupiter, heaven's high king, gave her in return for the theft of her virginity: "O nymph, glory of rivers, to my heart most dear, you know how I have preferred you above all Latin women that have mounted to high-souled Jove's thankless bed, and to you I have gladly given a place in heaven. Learn, Juturna, the grief that will be yours, so that you may not blame me. Where Fortune seemed to permit, and the Fates suffered Latium's state to prosper, I shielded Turnus and your city. Now I see the youth confront unequal destiny, and the day of doom and the enemy's stroke draw near. My eyes cannot look upon this battle, this treaty. If you dare anything

of more present help for your brother's sake, go on; it is your part. Perhaps better days shall remain for the unhappy."

She had scarcely spoken, when Juturna's eyes streamed with tears, and three, indeed, four times, her hand struck her comely breast. "This is no time for tears," cries Saturnian Juno. "Hurry, and if there is any way, snatch your brother from death. Or awaken battle and dash from their hands the treaty they have framed. It is I who tell you to dare." Having thus exhorted, she left Juturna doubtful and distracted in soul, with a cruel wound.

Meanwhile the kings ride forth, Latinus in mighty pomp drawn in a four-horse chariot, 12 golden rays circling his gleaming brows, emblem of his ancestral Sun, while Turnus comes behind a snow-white pair, his hand brandishing two spears with broad heads of steel. On this side father Aeneas, source of the Roman stock, ablaze with a starry shield and celestial arms, and, close by, Ascanius, second hope of mighty Rome, issue from the camp, while a priest in spotless raiment has brought the young of a bristly boar and an unshorn sheep, two years old, and set the beasts beside the blazing altars. The heroes, turning their eyes to the rising sun, sprinkle salted meal from their hands, mark the foreheads of the victims with the knife, and from goblets pour libations on the altars. Then good Aeneas, drawing his sword, prays: "Now let the Sun be witness to my call, and this Earth, for whose sake I have been able to endure such travails, and the Almighty Father, and you his consort, Saturnia—now kindlier, now at last, I pray, O goddess; and you, famed Mavors,[133] you the father that wields all warfare under your sway; I call on Founts and Floods, on all the majesty of high heaven and powers that are in the blue seas: if by chance victory falls to Turnus the Ausonian, it is agreed that the vanquished will withdraw to Evander's city. Iulus shall leave the soil, nor shall the sons of Aeneas ever later return for renewed war, or attack this realm with the sword. But if victory grants that the battle be ours—as I rather think, and so rather may the gods confirm it with their power!—I

---

132 The *limus* was an apron worn by priests.
133 I.e., Mars, the god of war.

will not order the Italians to be subject to Teucrians, nor do I seek the realm for my own. Let both nations, unconquered, enter upon an everlasting agreement, under equal terms. I will give gods and their rites; let Latinus, as my father-in-law, keep the sword and his accustomed power of command. The Teucrians shall raise walls for me, and Lavinia give the city her name.

Thus spoke Aeneas and after him Latinus, lifting eyes to heaven, and outstretching his right hand to the stars: "By these same Powers I swear, Aeneas, by Earth, Sea, Stars, Latona's two-fold offspring,[134] and two-faced Janus,[135] and the might of gods below, and the shrines of cruel Dis: may the great Sire hear my words, who sanctions treaties with his thunderbolt! I touch the altars, I have these fires and gods that stand between us as witness: no time shall break this peace and truce for Italy, however things shall turn out, nor shall any force turn aside my will, not even if it floods the earth in a deluge, plunging land into water, and dissolves Heaven into Tartarus. This is so just as this scepter" (for happily in his hand he bore his scepter) "shall never sprout with light leafage into branch or shade, once it is cut in the forest from the lower stem, bereft of its mother, and beneath the steel has shed its leaves and twigs. Once a tree, now the craftsman's hand has encased it in proper bronze and given it to Latin fathers to bear." With such words they sealed faith between them, amid the gazing leading men. Then over the flame they duly slay the hallowed beasts, and tear out the live entrails, and pile the altars with laden chargers.

But the battle had long seemed unequal to the Rutulians, and their hearts, swayed to and fro, had long been in turmoil and now more so, the more closely they scan its ill-matched strength. Turnus enlarges the unrest by advancing with noiseless tread and humbly adoring the altar with downcast eyes— enlarges it by his wasted cheeks and by the pallor of his youthful frame. As soon as his sister Juturna saw these whispers spread, and the hearts of the throng wavering in doubt, she plunges into the midmost ranks, in the feigned likeness of Camers—of a noble ancestral house, his father's worth of glorious renown, he himself most valiant in arms—into the midmost ranks, knowing her task well, and scatters diverse rumors, and so cries: "Are you not ashamed, Rutulians, for all of a host like ours to set at hazard one single life? Are we not their match in numbers or in might? See that all of them are here, Trojans and Arcadians, and the fate-led bands of Etruria, hostile to Turnus. If only every other man of us join battle, each of us would find barely one foe. Turnus, indeed, shall mount on fame to the gods, to whose altars he vows his life, and shall move living on the lips of men. But we, our country lost, shall bow to haughty masters— we, who today sit listless upon the fields!"

By such words the warriors' resolve is kindled yet more and more, and a murmur creeps from rank to rank. Even the Laurentines, even the Latins are changed. They who of late had hoped for rest from the fray, and safety for their fortunes, now long for arms, and pray that the agreement may be undone, pitying Turnus's unjust fate. To these Juturna adds another and mightier impulse, and in high heaven shows a sign—none was more potent to confound Italian minds and cheat them with its miracle. For, flying through the red sky, Jove's golden bird[136] was chasing the fowls of the shore and the clamorous rout of their winged troop, when, swooping suddenly to the water, shameless, he snatches up a stately swan in his crooked talons. The Italians become all alert, when lo! one and all, wondrous to behold, the birds clamorously wheel their flight and, darkening the sky with wings, in a serried cloud drive their foe through the air, until, overborne by the onset and the sheer weight, the bird gave way, dropped the booty from his talons into the stream, and sped far into the clouds.

Then in truth the Rutulians hail the omen with a cheer and spread out their hands. And first of all Tolumnius the augur cries: "This it was, this, that my vows have often sought! I accept it, I acknowledge the gods. With me, me at your head, snatch up the sword, O hapless people, whom, like frail birds, a shameless alien frightens with war, and rudely ravages your

---

134 Latona, a goddess, was the mother of Apollo and Diana.
135 A god with two faces, one looking forward, one backward, associated with doorways and with beginnings and endings.
136 An eagle.

coasts. He too will take to flight and spread sail far across the deep. Close ranks with one accord, and defend in battle the king thus snatched from you!"

He spoke, and, darting forward, hurled his spear full against the foe; the whistling cornel-shaft, unerring, sings, and splits the air. With the deed at once rises a mighty shout, the crowds are all confusion, and their hearts are heated with turmoil. The spear flies on, where, as it happened, nine brothers, of beautiful form, stood in its path—the many borne to Arcadian Gylippus by one faithful Tuscan wife. It pierces one of them—a youth of comely form and gleaming armor—clean through the ribs, near the waist where the stitched belt chafes the belly and the buckle bites the linked sides, and stretches him on the yellow sand. But his brothers—a gallant band, and fired by grief—some draw their swords, some seize steel missiles, and rush blindly on. Against them charge the Laurentine columns; from their side again pour in thickly Trojans and Agyllines and Arcadians with blazoned arms. Thus all are ruled by one passion, to let the sword decide. Lo! they have stripped the altars. A thickening storm of javelins flies and the iron rain falls through the whole sky. Bowls and hearth-fires are carried off. Latinus himself takes flight, bearing back his defeated gods, the covenant now void. The others rein their chariots or leap upon their horses and are on the scene with drawn swords.

Messapus,[137] eager to destroy the agreement, on a charging horse frightens Tuscan Aulestes,[138] a king and wearing a king's emblem. He rushes backward and, poor man, whirled upon the altars behind, is thrown on to his head and shoulders. But Messapus flashes forth like fire, spear in hand and, aloft on his horse, strikes heavily down upon him with the massive shaft, although Aulestes pleads much. Then he dies, Messapus saying: "He has it;[139] here is a nobler victim given to the mighty gods!" The Italians crowd around and strip his warm limbs of their armor. Standing in the path, Corynaeus[140] snatches up a charred brand from the altar, and as Ebysus[141] comes up and aims a blow, dashes flames in his face; his mighty beard blazed up, and sent forth a smell of fire. Then pursuing the stroke, he clutches in his left hand the locks of his bewildered foe, and with a thrust of his bended knee forces his body to the ground, and there strikes his side with his unyielding sword. Podalirius,[142] pursuing with naked steel, towered over the shepherd Alsus[143] as he rushes amid the darts in the front line. But Alsus, swinging back his axe, fully severs the middle of his enemy's brow and chin, and drenches his armor with widely spattered gore. Stern repose and iron slumber press upon his eyes, and their orbs close in everlasting night.

But pious Aeneas, with head bared, was stretching forth his unarmed hand, and calling loudly to his men: "Where are you rushing? Why this sudden outburst of strife? O curb your rage! The agreement is already made, and all its terms are fixed. The right to do battle is mine alone. Give way to me and banish fears; this hand shall prove the treaty true; these rites already make Turnus mine!" Amid these cries, amid such words, lo! a whizzing arrow winged its way against him. No one knows what hand launched it, who sent it, or who—chance or god—brought Rutulians such honor. The fame of that high deed is hidden, and no one boasted of wounding Aeneas.

As soon as Turnus saw Aeneas withdrawing from the ranks, and his captains in confusion, he glows with the fire of sudden hope, calls for horses, calls for arms, with a bound leaps proudly into his chariot, and firmly grasps the reins. In his swift course he gives many a brave man's body to death. He tumbles many a man half-slain, or crushes whole ranks beneath his chariot or, seizing spear after spear, showers them upon those fleeing—just as when, at full speed, by the streams of

---

137 An ally of Turnus.
138 An ally of Aeneas.
139 I.e., he has his death blow. Among the Romans the expression was used by spectators when a gladiator received a blow.
140 A Trojan.
141 A Latin.
142 A Trojan.
143 A Latin.

icy Hebrus[144] blood-stained Mars thunders with his shield, and, rousing war, gives rein to his frenzied steeds; they outstrip the South and the West wind over the open plain; farthest Thrace moans with the beating of their hoofs, and around him speed black Terror's forms, and Anger, and Ambush, attendants on the god. With a like eagerness, Turnus goads his sweat smoking horses amid the fray, piteously trampling on the slain foe. The galloping hooves splash bloody dew, and kick up the gore and mingled sand. And now he has given Sthenelus to death, and Thamyrus, and Pholus, the last two in hand-to-hand fighting, the first from afar; from afar the sons of Imbrasus, Glaucus and Lades, whom Imbrasus himself had nurtured in Lycia and equipped with like arms, either to fight hand to hand or on horseback to outstrip the winds.

Elsewhere Eumedes rides to the middle of the fray, war-famed son of ancient Dolon, renewing his grandfather's name and his father in his heart and hand, who of old dared to ask for the chariot of Peleus's son as his price for going as a spy to the Danaan camp.[145] But the son of Tydeus pays him a very different price, and he no longer sets his hopes upon Achilles's horses. Turnus spots him afar on the open plain, and, first following him with a light javelin through the long space between them, then halts his twin-yoked horses and leaps from his chariots. Now he descends on the fallen, dying man, and, planting his foot on his neck, seizes the sword from his hand, dyes the glittering blade deep in his throat, and to this adds these words: "Lo! Trojan, lie there, and measure out the fields and that Hesperia you sought in war. Such is the reward of those who dare to tempt me with the sword; so they build their walls!" Then with the cast of his spear he sends Asbytes to bear him company, and also Chloreus and Sybaris, Dares and Thersilochus, and Thymoetes, who had been flung from the neck of his restive horse. And as when the blast of the Edonian Northwind roars on the deep Aegean, and drives the billows toward shore, where the winds swoop, the clouds scud through the sky, so wherever Turnus

cleaves a path, the ranks give way, and lines turn and run. His own speed bears him on, and the breeze, as his chariot meets it, tosses his flying plume. Phegeus would not brook his onset and his fiery rage. He flung himself before the chariot and with his right hand wrenched aside the jaws of the furious steeds, foaming on the bits. While he is dragged along, clinging to the yoke, the broad spear-head reaches his unguarded side, rends the two-plated corslet where it lodged, and with its wound just grazes the surface of the flesh. Yet he, with shield before him, turned and was making for his foe, seeking succor from his drawn sword, when the wheel and axle, whirling onward, struck him headlong and flung him to the ground, and Turnus, following, with a sweep of steel between the helmet's lowest rim and the breastplate's upper edge, struck off his head, and left the trunk upon the sand.

And while Turnus thus victoriously deals havoc over the plains, Mnestheus and loyal Achates, and Ascanius by their side, set down Aeneas in the camp, all bleeding and halting every other step upon his long spear. Raging, he struggles to pluck out the head of the broken shaft, and calls for the nearest road to relief, insisting they cut the wound, tear open to the bottom the weapon's lair with a broad sword, and send him back to battle. And now Iapyx, Iasus's son, dearest beyond others to Phoebus, to whom once Apollo himself, smitten with love's sting, gladly offer his own arts, his own powers—his power of augury, his lyre and swift arrows—drew near. He, to defer the fate of a father sick unto death, chose rather to know the virtues of herbs and the practice of healing, and to ply, inglorious, the silent arts. Bitterly chafing, Aeneas stood propped on his mighty spear, amid a great gathering of warriors along with sorrowing Iulus, himself unmoved by their tears. The old man, with robe rolled back, and dressed in Paeonian fashion, with healing hand and Phoebus's potent herbs makes much ado— in vain. He pulls at the dart with his hands and tugs at the steel with gripping tongs in vain. No Fortune guides his path, in no way does Apollo's counsel help,

---

144 A river in Thrace, north of Greece.

145 In the *Iliad* the Trojan Dolon scouted out the Greek camp, demanding the chariot of Achilles (the son of Peleus) as his prize in return. He was caught by Odysseus (called Ulysses by the Romans) and Diomedes (the son of Tydeus) and revealed the plans of the Trojans. Diomedes then killed him.

and more and more the fierce alarm swells over the plains, and disaster draws closer. Now they see the sky borne on columns of dust. On come the horsemen, and shafts fall thick amid the camp. The dismal cries of men that fight and men that fall beneath the stern War god's hand mount to heaven.

But Venus, smitten by her son's cruel pain, with a mother's care, plucks from Cretan Ida[146] a stalk of dittany, clothed with downy leaves and a purple flower. That herb is not unknown to wild goats, when winged arrows have lodged in their flank. Venus, her face veiled in a dim mist, carried this down. She secretly steeps it in the river water they had poured into a bright-brimming ewer, and also sprinkles in it ambrosia's healthful juices and fragrant panacea. In ignorance, aged Iapyx washed the wound with this water and suddenly all pain fled from the body and deep in the wound blood stopped flowing. And now, following his hand, without constraint, the arrow fell out, and newborn strength returned, as before. "Quick bring him arms! Why are you standing around?" loudly cries Iapyx, the first to fire their spirit against the foe. "This does not come by mortal aid, not by masterful art, nor does my hand save you, Aeneas. A mightier one—a god—works here, and sends you back to mightier deeds." He, eager for the fray, had sheathed his legs in gold, right and left, and, scorning delay, is brandishing his spear. As soon as the shield is fitted to his side, and the corslet to his back, he clasps Ascanius in armed embrace and, lightly kissing his lips through the helmet, he cries: "Learn valor from me, my son, and true toil; learn good fortune from others. Today my hand shall shield you in war and lead you to great rewards. Soon, when your years have grown to ripeness, see that you are mindful of this and, as you recall the pattern of your kin, let your father Aeneas and your uncle Hector stir your soul!"

These words uttered, he passed forth from the gates in his might, his hand brandishing a massive spear. Antheus and Mnestheus rush with him in a ser-

ried column, and the entire throng streams from the forsaken camp. Then the plain is a turmoil of blinding dust, and the startled earth trembles under the tramping of feet. From the facing rampart Turnus saw them coming. The Ausonians saw, and a cold shudder ran through their inmost marrow. First, before all the Latins, Juturna heard and knew the sound, and, quaking in fear, retreated. Aeneas wings his way, and sweeps his dark column over the open plain. When a tempest bursts, and a storm cloud moves towards land through mid-ocean, the hearts of poor farmers (alas!) know it from far away and shudder—it will bring ruin to trees and havoc to crops, it will ruin all far and wide; the winds fly before it, and send their voices toward shore. In the same way the Rhoeteian chief[147] brings up his band full against the foe. Each and all gather densely to his side in close-packed columns. Thymbraeus[148] strikes mighty Osiris[149] with the sword, Mnestheus slays Arcetius, Achates Epulo, Gyas Ufens; even the augur Tolumnius, who first had hurled his spear full against the foe, also falls. A shout rises to heaven, and in turn the routed Rutulians, amid clouds of dust, turn their backs in flight across the fields. Aeneas himself does not deign to lay low the fugitives in death, nor does he assail those who meet him foot to foot or wield their darts. He summons Turnus alone to battle, with searching glance, tracking through the thick gloom.

Stricken in heart by that fear, Juturna the manwoman flings Metiscus, Turnus's charioteer, from amid his reins, and leaves him afar, fallen from the post. She herself takes his place and guides with her hands the flowing thongs, assuming all that Metiscus had—his voice, his body, his arms. Just as when a black swallow flits through a rich lord's ample mansion and wings her way through stately halls, gleaning for her chirping nestlings tiny crumbs and scraps of food, and twitters now in the empty courts, now about the watery pools, so Juturna is carried by the horses through the enemy's midst, and winging her way in the swift chariot scours the whole field. And

---

146  A mountain of the island of Crete.
147  Rhoetia was an area near Troy.
148  A Trojan.
149  A Latin and not, it seems, to be confused with the Egyptian god of the same name.

now here, and now there, she displays her triumphant brother, yet does not allow him to close in combat, but flits far away. Nonetheless, Aeneas threads the winding maze to meet him, and tracks his steps, and amid the scattered ranks calls him with a loud cry. As often as he cast eyes on his foe and strove by running to match the flight of the winged horses, Juturna turned and wheeled her chariot. Ah, what to do? Vainly he tosses on a shifting tide, and conflicting cares call his mind this way and that. Against him Messapus, who now in his left hand carried two tough shafts tipped with steel, lightly advancing, levels one and whirls it with an unerring stroke. Aeneas halted, and gathered himself behind his shield, sinking upon his knee. Yet the swift spear bore off his helmet-peak, and dashed from his head the topmost plumes. Then indeed his anger swells. Overcome by the treachery, when he sees that the steeds and chariot of his foe are withdrawn afar, having often appealed to Jove and the altars of the broken agreement, he now at last plunges into the middle, and the tide of war terribly awakes grim indiscriminate slaughter; he flings loose all the reins of anger.

What god can now unfold for me so many horrors, who in song can tell such diverse deaths, and the fall of commanders, whom now Turnus, now the Trojan hero, drives in turn all over the plain? Was it your will, O Jupiter, that nations which thereafter would dwell in everlasting peace should clash in so much violence? Aeneas, meeting Rutulian Sucro—this combat first brought the Trojan onset to a halt—with a brief delay strikes him on the flank, and drives the cruel steel through the ribs that fence the chest where death comes fastest. Turnus dismounts Amycus and his brother Diores, and, assailing them on foot, strikes the one with long spear as he advances, the other with his sword. Then, hanging from his chariot the severed heads of the two, he bears them off, dripping with blood. Aeneas sends Talos and Tanais and brave Cethegus to death, three in one onslaught, and sad Onites, of Echionian name, whose mother was Peridia. Turnus slays the brothers sent from Lycia and Apollo's

fields, and young Menoetes of Arcadia, who loathed warfare in vain; his craft and humble home had been near fish-haunted Lerna's streams, nor had he known the portals of the great, but his father sowed on hired soil. And like fires launched from opposing sides upon a dry forest and thickets of crackling laurel, or as when rivers roar and race seaward in swift descent from mountain heights, foaming, each leaving its own path waste, with no less fury both of them, Aeneas and Turnus, sweep through the battle. Now, now anger surges within them. Their hearts are bursting, not knowing how to yield; now, with all their force, they rush for wounds.

Murranus, as he boasts of his grandsires, and his grandsires' sires of ancient name, and a whole line traced through Latin kings, is dashed down headlong with a stone mightily whirled by Aeneas, and tumbles on the ground. The wheels rolled him along under the reins and yoke, and over him rush the hoofs of the steeds that do not remember their lord, trampling him down with many a beat. The other,[150] as Hyllus rushes on with boundless fury at heart, meets him and whirls a dart at his gold-bound brow; piercing the helmet, the spear stood fast in his brain. Nor did your right hand, Cretheus, you bravest of the Greeks, save you from Turnus, nor did his gods shield their Cupencus when Aeneas came; he put his breast in the weapon's path, and the brazen buckler's stay, alas! did not avail him. You too, Aeolus, the Laurentine plains saw sink, and spread your frame abroad over the earth—you fall, whom neither the Argive battalions[151] nor Achilles, destroyer of Priam's realms, could lay low. Here was your end set by death. Your stately home was at the foot of Ida, your stately home was at Lyrnesus, but your grave is in Laurentine soil. The whole lines, turning to the fray— all the Latins and all the Greeks, Mnestheus and valiant Serestus; Messapus, tamer of horses, and brave Asilas; the Tuscan battalion and Evander's Arcadian squadrons—each doing his all, strain with utmost force of strength with no stint, no stay. They struggle in measureless conflict.

150 I.e., Turnus.
151 I.e., the Greeks during the Trojan war.

Now Aeneas's most beautiful mother inspired him with the thought of advancing on the walls, flinging his column on the town, and confounding the Latins with sudden disaster. While he, tracking Turnus here and there throughout the host, swept his glance this way and that, he views the city free from that fierce warfare, peaceful and unharmed. Immediately a vision of greater battle fires his heart. He calls his captains, Mnestheus and Sergestus, and brave Serestus, and plants himself on a mound, where the rest of the Teucrian host crowd thickly around, yet do not drop shield or spear. Standing in their midst on the mounded height he cries: "Let nothing delay my command; Jupiter stands with us. Nor let anyone, I pray, be slower to advance because the venture is so sudden. This very day will I overthrow that city, the cause of war, the very seat of Latinus's realm, and lay its smoking roofs level with the ground unless they consent to receive our yoke, and to submit to us as vanquished. Indeed, am I to wait until it pleases Turnus to enter battle with me, and until, once beaten, he chooses to meet me a second time? This, fellow-citizens, is the head, this the sum, of the accursed war. Bring firebrands with speed, and in fire reclaim the treaty." He ceased—and lo! with hearts alike contending to outdo the others, all form a wedge and advance in a serried mass to the walls. In a moment ladders and sudden flames are seen. Some rush to the several gates and cut down the foremost guards; others hurl their steel and veil the sky with javelins. In the van, Aeneas uplifts his hand to the walls, loudly reproaches Latinus, and calls the gods to witness that again he is forced into battle, that twice the Italians became his foes, and that this treaty is the second broken. Strife rises among the startled citizens: some give orders to unbar the town and throw wide the gates to the Dardans, and would drag the king himself to the ramparts; others bring arms, and hasten to defend the walls, just as when some shepherd has tracked bees to their lair in a rocky covert, and filled it with stinging smoke, and they within, startled for their safety, scurry to and fro through the waxen fortress, and with loud buzzings whet their rage, and the black stench rolls through their dwelling, the rocks within hum with a hidden murmur, and smoke issues to the empty air.

Another fate befell the laboring Latins, and shook the whole city to its foundation with grief. When from her palace the queen sees the foe approach, the walls assailed, flames mounting to the roofs, yet sees Rutulian ranks nowhere, no troops of Turnus to meet them, alas!, she thinks her warrior has been slain in combat and, her mind distraught by sudden anguish, cries out that she is the guilty source and spring of sorrows, and uttering many a wild word in the frenzy of grief, resolved to die, rends her purple robes, and from a lofty beam fastens the noose of a hideous death. A soon as the unhappy Latin women learned of this disaster, first her daughter Lavinia, her hand tearing her flowery tresses and rosy cheeks, and then all the throng around her, rave madly. The wide halls ring with lamentations. From there the woeful rumor spreads throughout the town. Hearts sink. Latinus goes about in torn clothes, dazed at his wife's fate and his city's ruin, defiling his hoary hairs with showers of unclean dust.

Meanwhile Turnus, battling on the plain's far edge, is pursuing a few stragglers, slacker now and less and less exultant in the triumph of his horses. The breeze carried to him that cry blended with unknown terrors, and the sound and joyless murmur of the town in turmoil struck his straining ears. "Ah me! what is this great sorrow that shakes the walls? What is this cry speeding from the distant town?" So he speaks, and in a frenzy draws in the reins and halts. Thereon his sister, changed to the form of his charioteer Metiscus, as she guided chariot and horses and reins, meets him with these words: "Turnus, we should pursue the sons of Troy here, where victory first opens a path. There are others whose hands can guard their homes. Aeneas falls upon the Italians with turmoil of battle. Let our hands also deal fierce havoc among his Teucrians! You will not come off the worse in the number of men slain nor in honor of war." To this Turnus replied: "Sister, I recognized you long since you first craftily marred the agreement and flung yourself into this war. Now you hide your divinity in vain. But who willed that you be sent down from Olympus to bear such sore toils? Was it so that you would see your poor brother's cruel death? For what can I do? Or what fortune can now assure me of safety? I have seen Murranus—no other dearer was left to me—as he loudly called upon me, fall before my very eyes, a mighty soul, and laid low by a mighty wound. Luckless Ufens has fallen so that he might not view our shame; the Teucrians hold his corpse and armor. The razing of their homes—the one thing lacking to my lot—shall I endure it, nor refute Drances's taunts[152] with my sword? Shall I turn my back, and shall this land see Turnus in flight? Is death all so sad? Be kind to me, you Shades, since the gods above have turned their faces from me. A stainless soul, and ignorant of that reproach, I will descend to you, never unworthy of my mighty sires of old!"

He had scarcely spoken, when lo! Saces, carried on a foaming horse, speeds through the enemy's midst. Wounded full in the face by an arrow, and, rushing on, he calls for help by the name on Turnus: "Turnus, our last hope lies in you! Pity your people! Aeneas thunders in arms, and threatens to overthrow Italy's highest towers and give them to destruction. Even now firebrands are flying to the roofs. To you the Latins turn their looks, to you their eyes. King Latinus himself mutters in doubt, whom to call his sons, or towards what alliance to incline. Moreover the queen, whose trust was all in you, has fallen by her own hand, and fled in terror from the light. Messapus and valiant Atinas alone sustain our lines before the gates. Around these on either side stand serried squadrons, and a harvest of steel bristles with drawn swords, yet you wheel your chariot over the deserted green." Aghast and bewildered by the changeful picture of disaster, Turnus stood gazing mutely. Within that single heart surges mighty shame, and madness mingled with grief, and love stung by fury, and the consciousness of worth. As soon as the shadows scattered and light dawned afresh on his mind, he turned his blazing eyeballs wrathfully upon the walls and from his chariot looked back upon the spacious city.

But lo! from storey to storey a rolling spire of flame was eddying heavenward, and fastening upon a tower, a tower that he himself had reared of jointed beams and set on wheels and slung with lofty gangways. "Now, my sister, now Fate triumphs. Stop delaying; let us follow where the god and cruel Fortune call! I am resolved to meet Aeneas, resolved to bear all its bitterness in death. No longer, my sister, shall you behold me shamed. With this madness suffer me before the end, I pray, to be a madman," he said, and leapt quickly from his chariot to the field, and rushing through foes and through spears, leaves his sorrowing sister, and burst in rapid course amid their columns. And just as when a rock rushes headlong from a mountaintop, torn away by the blast—whether the whirling storm has washed it free, or time stealing on with lapse of years has loosened it—down the steep side with a mighty rush sweeps the reckless mass, and bounds over the earth, rolling along with it trees, herds, and men, so amid the scattered ranks Turnus rushes to the city walls, where the ground is drenched deepest with spilled blood, and the air is shrill with spears. Then he beckons with his hand and begins aloud: "Hold back now, Rutulians, and you Latins, stay your darts. Whatever fortune is here is mine. It is better that I alone in your stead atone for the agreement, and decide the issue with the sword." All drew apart from the center and gave him room.

But father Aeneas, hearing Turnus's name, forsakes the walls, forsakes the lofty fortress, flings aside all delay, breaks off all tasks and, exultant with joy, thunders terribly with his arms—as big as Athos, as big as Eryx or as big as Father Apennine himself[153] when he roars with his quivering oaks, and joyously lifts heavenward his snowy head. Now indeed, all—Rutulians, and Trojans, and Italians, both they who held the lofty ramparts, and they whose ram battered the walls below—eagerly turned their eyes, and doffed the armor from their shoulders. Latinus himself is amazed that these two mighty men, born in far distant climes, are met together and make decision with the sword. And they, as soon as the ground was clear on the open plain, dash swiftly forward, first hurling their spears from afar, and rush on the fray with shields and clanging brass. The earth groans. Then they shower blow on blow with the sword, chance and valor blending into

---

152 Drances, depicted in an earlier book of the *Aeneid* as a spiteful coward, was an advisor to Latinus. He had argued that Turnus should give up his claims to Lavinia in favor of Aeneas, stating that Turnus had often before led the Latins into war and misery.
153 Athos, Eryx, and the Appenines: all mountains.

one. And just as on mighty Sila[154] or on Taburnus's height,[155] when two bulls charge, brow to brow, in mortal battle, the keepers fall back in terror, and the whole herd stands mute with dread, and the heifers dumbly ponder who shall be lord of the forest, whom all the herds shall follow; they with mighty force deal mutual wounds, gore with butting horns, and bathe neck and shoulders in streaming blood; all the woodland re-echoes with the bellowing: just so Trojan Aeneas and the Daunian hero clash, shield on shield. The mighty crash fills the sky. Jupiter himself holds up two scales in an even balance, and lays therein the diverse destinies of both, whom the strife dooms, and with whose weight death sinks down.

Now Turnus springs forth, deeming it safe, raises his uplifted sword to his full height, and strikes. The Trojans and expectant Latins cry out loud. Both hosts are on tiptoe with excitement. But the traitorous sword snaps, and its fiery lord would have fallen in mid stroke, had not flight come to his aid. He flees faster than the east wind, as soon as he saw an unknown hilt in his defenseless hand. Fame tells that in his headlong haste, when first mounting behind his yoked horses for battle, he left his father's blade behind and in his haste snatched up the steel of Metiscus, his charioteer. That served for long that served, while the straggling Teucrians turned their backs. But when it met the god-wrought armor of Vulcan, the mortal blade, like brittle ice, flew asunder at the stroke. The fragments glitter on the yellow sand. So Turnus madly flees here and there over the plain, and now this way and now that entwines wavering circles, for the Teucrians enclosed him in a crowded ring on all sides, and here a waste fen, there steep ramparts encircle him.

Nor less, though at times his knees, retarded by the arrow-wound, impede him and deny their speed, does Aeneas pursue, and hotly press, foot to foot, upon his panting foe, just as when a hunting hound has caught a stag, pent in by a stream, or hedged about by the terror of crimson feathers,[156] and, run-ning and barking, presses him close. The stag, in terror of the snares and lofty bank, flees to and fro in a thou-sand ways, but the keen Umbrian[157] hound clings close with jaws agape, and now, now grips, or, as though he gripped, snaps his jaws, and baffled, bites on nothing. Then indeed the din rises; banks and pools around make answer, and all heaven thunders with the tumult. Turnus, even as he flees, even then, upbraids all the Rutulians, calling each by name, and clamoring for the sword he knew. Aeneas in turn threatens death and instant doom should anyone draw near, and frightens his trembling foes with threats to raze the town and, though wounded, press-es on. Five circles they cover at full speed, and unweave as many this way and that. They are not seeking trivial booty or a sports prize, but strive for Turnus's life and blood.

By chance there had stood here a bitter-leaved wild olive tree, sacred to Faunus, a tree revered of old by mariners, on which, when saved from the waves, they were accustomed to fasten their gifts to the god of Laurentum and to hang up their votive raiments. But the Teucrians, heeding nothing, had shorn the sacred stem, so they might fight in a clear field. Here stood the spear of Aeneas; its force had carried it there, and was holding it fast in the tough root. The Dardan stooped and wanted to pull out the steel perforce, and pursue with a javelin the one he could not catch by speed of foot. Then indeed Turnus, frantic with terror, cried: "Faunus, I beg you, have mercy, and you, most gracious Earth, hold the steel tight, if ever I cultivated your honors which, by contrast, Aeneas's men have defiled by war." He spoke, and to no fruitless vow did he invoke the aid of heaven. For although Aeneas wrestled and lingered over the stubborn stem for a long time, no strength availed him to unlock the oaken bite. While he fiercely tugs and strains, the Daunian goddess, changing once again into the form of chario-teer Metiscus, runs forward and restores the sword to her brother. But Venus, angry that such license is granted the bold nymph, drew nigh, and plucked the

---

154  A wood near the Appenine mountains.
155  Taburnus: a mountain in Italy.
156  Red feathers were used on hunting nets.
157  Umbria, in northern Italy, produced hunting dogs.

weapon from the deep root. At full height, in arms and heart renewed—one trusting to his sword, one fiercely towering with his spear—both breathless, they stand facing the War god's strife.

Meanwhile the king of almighty Olympus accosts Juno, as she gazes on the fray from a golden cloud: "What shall be the end now, O wife? What remains at the end? You yourself know, and acknowledge that you know, that Aeneas, as Hero of the land, is claimed of heaven, and the Fates exalt him to the stars. What are you planning? Or in what hope do you linger in the chill clouds? Was it appropriate that by a mortal's wound a god should be profaned? Or that the lost sword—for without you what could Juturna do?—should be restored to Turnus, and the vanquished gain fresh force? Cease now, and bend to our entreaties, that such great grief may not consume you in silence, nor to me may bitter cares so often return from your sweet lips. The end is reached. To chase the Trojans over land or sea, to kindle monstrous war, to mar a home with mourning and blend weddings with woe; you have had this power. I forbid you to attempt more!" Thus Jupiter began. Thus, with a downcast look, the goddess, child of Saturn, replied:

"Because I knew, great Jove, that such was your pleasure, I have, though reluctant, left Turnus and the earth. Otherwise, you would not see me now, alone on my airy throne, enduring fair and foul, but I would take my stand clothed in flame, close to the very ranks, and drag the Teucrians into deadly conflict. As for Juturna, I advised her (I admit) to help her poor brother, and for his life's sake sanctioned still greater deeds of daring, but not to level the arrow, not to bend the bow. I swear this by the inexorable fountainhead of the Styx, sole name of dread ordained for gods above. And now I yield, yes, yield, and leave the strife in loathing. But I ask one thing, banned by no law of fate, for Latium's sake, for your own kin's[158] greatness: when they make peace, sealed with happy bridal rites—so be it!—and join in laws and treaties, do not command the native Latins to change their ancient name, nor to become Trojans and be called Teucrians,

nor to change their tongue and alter their attire. Let Latium still exist, let Alban kings endure through the ages, let there exist a Roman stock strong in Italian valor. Troy has fallen, and fallen let her be, together with her name!"

Smiling on her, the creator of men and things replied: "You are a true sister of Jove, Saturn's other child; such waves of anger surge deep within your breast! But come, allay the rage thus vainly stirred: I grant your wish; yield to me, conquered and content. Ausonia's sons shall keep their fathers' speech and customs, and as it is, so shall be their name; the Teucrians shall but sink down, merged in the mass. I will add their sacred customs and rites and make all to be Latins of one tongue. From this shall arise a nation, blended with Ausonian blood, which you shall see surpass humanity and surpass gods in godliness, nor shall any nation celebrate your worship with equal zeal." Juno assented to this, and joyfully changed her purpose. Meanwhile, she passes from heaven, and leaves the cloud.

This done, the Father revolves another purpose in his heart, and prepares to withdraw Juturna from her brother's side. Men tell of twin fiends, named the Dread Ones, whom with hellish Megaera untimely Night bore in one and the same birth, wreathing them alike with snaky coils and clothing them with wings of wind. These wait by the throne of Jove, and on the threshold of the grim monarch, and whet the fears of feeble mortals, whenever heaven's king aims at diseases and awful death, or frightens guilty towns with war. Jove sent one of these swiftly down from high heaven, and ordered her to meet Juturna as a sign. She wings her way, and darts to earth in a swift whirlwind, just like an arrow shot from a string through a cloud, which, armed with gall and poison, a Parthian—a Parthian or a Cydonian[159]—has launched and speeds on, a shaft beyond all cure; whizzing, it leaps through the swift shadows, unknown to any. Thus sped the child of Night, and sought the earth. As soon as she sees the Ilian ranks and Turnus's troops, suddenly shrinking to the shape of that small bird which,

158 Latinus was descended from Saturn, Jupiter's father.
159 The Parthians were an eastern people known for their archery. Cydonia was on the island of Crete.

perched at night on tombs or deserted roofs, often chants her late, ill-omened song amid the shadows, the fiend, thus changed in form, flits before the face of Turnus, screaming to and fro, and wildly beats his buckler with her wings. A strange numbness unknits his limbs with dread. His hair stood up in terror and the voice stuck in his throat.

But when from afar Juturna recognized the dread one's whizzing wings, unhappy, she rends her loosened tresses, marring, in sisterly grief, her face with nails and her breast with clenched hands: "What now, my Turnus, can your sister do for you? Or what more awaits me, that have endured so much? With what art may I prolong your day? Can I face such a portent? Now, now I leave the field. Do not frighten my fluttering soul, you ill-boding birds! I know your beating wings, and their dreadful sound, nor do I fail to see the haughty mandates of high-hearted Jove. Is this his return for my virginity? Why did he give me eternal life? Why am I bereft of the law of death? Now surely I could end such anguish, and pass at my poor brother's side amid the shadows! I immortal! No, will anything of mine will be sweet to me without you, my brother? O what deepest earth can open wide enough for me, and send me down, a goddess, to the deepest shades?" So saying, she veiled her head in a mantle of gray and with many moans plunged into the deep river.

Aeneas presses on against the foe, brandishing his massive, tree-like spear, and, in wrathful spirit, cries: "What more delay is there now? Or why, Turnus, do you still draw back? We must fight not with swift feet, but hand-to-hand in fierce arms. Change yourself into all shapes, indeed, muster all your powers of courage or of skill. Wing your flight, if you will, to the stars aloft or hide yourself within earth's hollow prison!" The other, shaking his head: "Your fiery words, fierce one, do not daunt me. It is the gods who daunt me, and the enmity of Jove." He speaks no more. Then glancing around, he spies a giant stone, a giant stone and an ancient one, which by chance lay upon the plain, set up as a landmark in order to prevent disputes regarding the fields. Twice six chosen men, men of such frames as earth now begets, could barely lift it upon their shoulders. But the hero, with hurried grasp, seized and hurled it at his foe, rising to his height and at swiftest speed. But he does not recognize himself as he runs, nor as he moves, as he raises his hands, or throws the mighty stone; his knees totter, his blood is frozen cold. Indeed, the hero's stone itself, whirled through the empty void, did not cross the entire space, nor did it carry its blow home. And just as in dreams at night, when languorous sleep has weighed down our eyes, we seem to strive vainly to press on our eager course, and in mid-effort sink helpless; our tongue lacks power, our accustomed strength fails our limbs, nor voice nor words ensue, so it was for Turnus. By whatever valor he sought to win his way, the dread goddess denies him progress. Then shifting fancies whirl through his soul. He gazes on his Rutulians and the town, he falters in fear, and trembles at the threatening lance. He sees neither where he may escape, nor with what force he can bear against the foe, nor is his chariot anywhere, nor the charioteer, his sister.

As he wavers, Aeneas brandishes the fateful spear, seeking fortune with his eyes, and then hurls it from afar with all his strength. Never did a stone shot from a siege engine roar so loud, never did great bursts from a thunderbolt thus crash. The spear flies on like a black whirlwind, bearing destruction, and pierces the corslet's rim and the sevenfold shield's utmost circle; whizzing, it passes right through the thigh. Huge Turnus sank under the blow, with the knee beneath him bent down to earth. The Rutulians all up spring with a groan. The whole hill re-echoes round about, and far and near the wooded uplands send back the sound. He, in lowly suppliance, with eyes raised up and pleading hands cries: "Indeed, I have earned it, and I do not ask for mercy. Use your chance. If any thought of a parent's grief can touch you, I beg you—in Anchises you, too, had such a father—pity Daunus's old age, and give me back, or, if it pleases you, give back my lifeless body, to my kin. You are victorious, and the Ausonians have seen me, defeated, stretch forth my hands. Lavinia is yours to marry. Do not press your hatred further."

Fierce in arms, Aeneas stood with restless eyes, and stayed his hand. And now, as he paused, these words began more and more to sway him, when lo! high on the shoulder was seen the luckless baldric, and there flashed the belt with its well-known studs—the belt of young Pallas, whom Turnus had struck and stretched vanquished on the earth, and now wore on his shoulders his enemy's fatal badge. The other, as soon as his eyes drank in the trophy, that memorial of cruel grief, fired with fury and was terrible in his wrath: "Are you, you clad in my loved one's spoils, to be snatched from my hands in this way? It is Pallas, Pallas who with this stroke sacrifices you, and takes atonement from your guilty blood!" He buries the sword deep in Turnus's breast with fiery zeal. But the other's limbs grew slack and chill, and with a moan his life, resentful, passed to the shades below.

# 18

# AUGUSTUS,
## *THE DEEDS OF THE DIVINE AUGUSTUS*

Octavian, better known as Augustus, became the dominant power in the Roman world with his victory over Marc Antony and Cleopatra at the battle of Actium in 31 BC. He continued to enjoy that position until his death in AD 14. This period is traditionally seen as marking the end of the Roman Republic and its replacement with a monarchy, the Roman empire. Augustus ordered the inscription below to be set up before his mausoleum shortly before his death. It is named after the first Latin words of the preface (*Res gestae*), added after Augustus's death. Although the original inscription does not survive in Rome, copies in Latin and in Greek do exist in various parts of the former empire. The most complete copy is from Ankara, in modern Turkey.

---

Below is a copy of the deeds of the divine Augustus,[1] by which he subjected the whole world to the dominion of the Roman people, and of the amounts which he expended upon the Republic and the Roman people, as engraved upon two bronze columns which are set up at Rome.

1 In my twentieth year, acting upon my own judgment, and at my own expense, I raised an army by means of which I restored to liberty the Republic which had been oppressed by the tyranny of a faction. On account of this, the Senate by honorific decrees, admitted me to its order in the consulship of Gaius Pansa and Aulus Hirtius,[2] and at the same time gave me consular rank in the expression of opinion,[3] and gave me *imperium*.[4] It also voted that I, as propraetor[5] together with the consuls, should see to it that the Republic suffer no harm. In the same year, moreover, when both consuls had perished in war, the people made me consul and triumvir for organizing the Republic.[6]

2 I drove those who killed my father[7] into exile, avenging their crime by lawful judgments, and after-

---

1  After his death, the Senate decreed that Augustus be recognized as a god.

2  I.e., in 43 BC. The Romans commonly dated events according to who was consul at the time. Consuls served one-year terms.

3  I.e., in the Senate Octavian would vote when the consuls did, and so before other senators.

4  I.e., legal power to command.

5  A governor of a province.

6  In 43 BC the Romans voted that Octavian, Marc Antony, and a relatively insignificant figure named Lepidus serve as "triumvirs to organize the Roman Republic." That vote, which thus created what is known to historians as the Second Triumvirate, was, like so many elections of the time, largely a sham.

7  I.e., Julius Caesar, who adopted his nephew Octavian as his son and heir.

wards, when they waged war against the Republic, I twice defeated them in battle.[8]

3  I undertook civil and foreign wars by land and sea throughout the whole world, and as victor I showed mercy to all surviving citizens who asked for pardon. Foreign peoples, who could be pardoned with safety, I preferred to preserve rather than to destroy. About 500,000 Roman citizens took the military oath of allegiance to me. Of these I have settled in colonies[9] or sent back to their municipalities upon the expiration of their terms of service, somewhat over 300,000, and to all these I have allotted lands or granted money for farms. I have captured 600 ships, besides those which were smaller than triremes.[10]

4  I have triumphed twice in the ovation, and three times in the curule triumph,[11] and I have been saluted as imperator[12] 21 times. After that, when the Senate decreed many more triumphs for me, I declined them. I deposited laurel wreaths in the Capitol in fulfillment of vows which I had also made in battle.[13] On account of enterprises brought to a succesful conclusion by land or sea, or by my lieutenants under my auspices, the Senate decreed that there should be a thanksgiving to the immortal gods 55 times. The number of days, moreover, on which thanksgiving was rendered in accordance with the decree of the Senate was 890. In my triumphs there have been led before my chariot nine kings, or children of kings. When I wrote these words I had been consul 13 times, and was in the thirty-seventh year of the tribunician power.[14]

5  I did not accept the dictatorship, which was offered to me by the people and the Senate,[15] both when I was absent and when I was present, during the consulship of Marcus Marcellus and Lucius Arruntius. At a time of the greatest shortage of grain I did not refuse responsibility for the food supply, which I administered so that in a few days, at my own expense, I freed the whole people from the anxiety and danger in which they then were. I did not accept the annual and perpetual consulship offered to me at that time.

6  During the consulship of Marcus Vinucius and Quintus Lucretius, and afterwards in that of Publius and Cnaeus Lentulus, and a third time in that of Paullus Fabius Maximus and Quintus Tubero,[16] by the consent of the Senate and the Roman people,[17] I was voted the sole charge of the laws and of morals, with the fullest authority, but I accepted no offer of an office which was contrary to the customs of the country. I accomplished the measures of which the Senate at that time wished me to take charge in virtue of my possession of the tribunician power. In this office I associated with myself a colleague five times, with the consent of the Senate.

7  For 10 years in succession I was one of the triumvirs for organizing the Republic. Up to the day on which I write these words I have been princeps of the Senate[18] for 40 years. I have been pontifex maximus, augur, a member of the quindecemviral college of the sacred rites, of the septemviral college of the banquets, an Arval Brother, a member of the Titian sodality, and a fetial.[19]

---

8  Referring to the two battles which took place at Philippi in 42 BC.
9  I.e., settlements of Roman citizens in territory under Roman control, but not incorporated into Rome itself.
10  I.e., ships with three tiers of rowers.
11  A triumph was an honor bestowed by the Senate on a military commander who had won an important victory for Rome. The ovation was a lesser kind of triumph; the curule triumph was a greater one.
12  An honorary title given to a military commander who had defeated an enemy of Rome. Most of these occasions refer to victories obtained by commanders serving under Octavian's auspices.
13  This was a long-standing custom for generals hailed with the title *imperator*.
14  Octavian enjoyed the authority of a tribune, an elected official who had the power to veto government action and legislation, and whose person was regarded as sacrosanct.
15  In 22 BC. The office of dictator under the Republic was a position of supreme power to be held on a temporary basis in emergencies. Before his death, Julius Caesar had declared himself dictator for life.
16  I.e., in 19, 18, and 11 BC.
17  "The Senate and the Roman People" was a designation frequently used for the Roman state.
18  A traditional, honorary position under the Republic, roughly meaning "first person of the Senate." The *princeps* of the Senate spoke first in Senate debates.
19  These were all various priestly offices.

8   In my fifth consulship, by order of the people and the Senate, I increased the number of the patricians.[20] Three times I have revised the list of members of the Senate. In my sixth consulship, with Marcus Agrippa as colleague, I made a census of the people. I performed the lustration[21] after 41 years. In this lustration the number of Roman citizens was 4,063,000. Again assuming the consular power in the consulship of Gaius Censorinus and Gaius Asinius,[22] I alone performed the lustration. At this census the number of Roman citizens was 4,230,000. A third time, assuming the consular power in the consulship of Sextus Pompeius and Sextus Appuleius,[23] with Tiberius Caesar as colleague, I performed the lustration. At this lustration the number of Roman citizens was 4,937,000. By new legislation I have restored many customs of our ancestors which had now begun to fall into disuse, and I have myself also committed to posterity many examples to be imitated.

9   The Senate decreed that every fifth year vows for my good health should be performed by the consuls and priests. In accordance with these vows, games have been often celebrated during my lifetime, sometimes by the four chief colleges of priests, sometimes by the consuls. Also, the whole body of citizens, both individually and as municipalities, have constantly sacrificed at every shrine for my good health.

10   By a decree of the Senate my name has been included in the hymn sung by the Salian priests, and it has been enacted by law that I should be sacrosanct, and that as long as I live I should be invested with the tribunician power. I refused to be made *pontifex maximus* in the place of a colleague still living, when the people offered me that priesthood which my father held. I accepted that office after several years, when he

who had seized it during a time of civil disturbance was dead, and at the assembly of citizens for my election, during the consulship of Publius Sulpicius and Gaius Valgius,[24] so great a multitude assembled as, it is said, had never before been in Rome.

11   Close to the temples of Honor and Virtue, near the Capena gate, the Senate consecrated in honor of my return an altar to Fortune the Restorer, and upon this altar it ordered that the priests and the Vestal virgins[25] should offer sacrifice yearly on the anniversary of the day on which I returned into the city from Syria, in the consulship of Quintus Lucretius and Marcus Vinucius, and it called the day the Augustalia, from our name.

12   By a decree of the Senate at the same time a part of the praetors[26] and tribunes of the people, with the consul Quintus Lucretius and leading citizens, were sent into Campania[27] to meet me, an honor which up to this time has been decreed to no one but me. When I returned from Spain and Gaul after successfully arranging the affairs of those provinces, in the consulship of Tiberius Nero and Publius Quintilius,[28] the Senate voted that in honor of my return an altar of the Augustan Peace should be consecrated in the Campus Martius,[29] and upon this altar it ordered that the magistrates and priests and Vestal virgins offer sacrifices on each anniversary.

13   The temple of Janus Quirinus,[30] which it was the purpose of our fathers to close when there was peace won by victory throughout the whole empire of the Roman people on land and sea, and which, before I was born, from the foundation of the city, was reported to have been closed twice in all, the Senate three times ordered to be closed while I was princeps.

---

20   A class of distinguished aristocratic families; the designation had by this time little legal or social significance.
21   I.e., the ceremony of ritual purification at the closing of the census. This was in 28 BC.
22   I.e., 8 BC.
23   I.e., AD 14.
24   I.e., 13 BC.
25   A female priestly order.
26   One of the magistracies of the Republic.
27   A region of Italy.
28   I.e., 13 BC.
29   The field of Mars, where that god's altars and various temples were located.
30   The temple of this double-faced god was opened in time of war.

14 My sons, Gaius and Lucius Caesar, whom fortune snatched from me in their youth, the Senate and Roman people, in order to do me honor, designated as consuls in the fifteenth year of each, with the intention that they should enter upon that office after five years, and the Senate decreed that from the day in which they were introduced into the forum[31] they should share in the public discussion. Moreover, the whole body of the Roman equestrians[32] gave them the title, princepes[33] of the youth,[34] and gave to each a silver buckler and spear.

15 To each of the Roman plebs[35] I paid 300 sesterces in accordance with the last will of my father,[36] and in my own name, when consul for the fifth time,[37] I gave 400 sesterces from the spoils of the wars; again, moreover, in my tenth consulship I gave from my own estate 400 sesterces to each man as a gift; in my eleventh consulship I made distributions of food 12 times, buying grain at my own expense; in the twelfth year of my tribunician power I three times gave 400 sesterces to each man. These my donations have never been made to fewer than 250,000 people. In my twelfth consulship and the eighteenth year of my tribunician power I gave to 320,000 of the city plebs 60 denarii apiece. In the colonies of my soldiers, when consul for the fifth time, I gave to each man 1,000 sesterces from the spoils of war; about 120,000 people in the colonies received that triumphal donation. When consul for the thirteenth time I gave 60 denarii to the plebs who were at that time receiving public grain; these people were a little more than 200,000 in number.

16 For the lands which I assigned to soldiers in my fourth consulship,[38] and afterwards in the consulship of Marcus Crassus and Cnaeus Lentulus,[39] the augur, I paid money to the municipalities. I paid about 600,000,000 sesterces for Italian lands, and about 260,000,000 for lands in the provinces. Of all those who have established colonies of soldiers in Italy or in the provinces I am the first and only one within the memory of my age to do this. And afterward, in the consulship of Tiberius Nero and Cnaeus Piso, and also in that of Gaius Antistius and Decimus Laelius, and in that of Gaius Calvisius and Lucius Pasienus, and in that of Lucius Lentulus and Marcus Messala, and in that of Lucius Caninius and Quintus Fabricius,[40] I gave gratuities in money to the soldiers whom I sent back to their municipalities at the expiration of their terms of service, and for this purpose I freely spent 400,000,000 sesterces.

17 I have aided the public treasury from my own means four times, to such extent that I have furnished to those in charge of the treasury 150,000,000 sesterces. And in the consulship of Marcus Lepidus and Lucius Arruntius,[41] I paid 170,000,000 sesterces from my own estate into the military treasury which was established by my advice so that from it gratuities might be given to soldiers who had served a term of 20 or more years.

18 Beginning with that year in which Cnaeus and Publius Lentulus were consuls,[42] when the provincial taxes failed, I furnished aid sometimes to 100,000 people, and sometimes to more, by supplying grain or money for the tribute from my own land and property.

19 I built the Senate House and the adjacent Chalcidicum; the temple of Apollo on the Palatine hill, with its porticoes; the temple of the divine Julius;[43]

---

31 And so became adults.
32 The social group next below senators.
33 Plural of *princeps*.
34 That is, first among the youth—another honorary title.
35 A legal category which included most Roman citizens.
36 I.e., Julius Caesar.
37 I.e., 29 BC.
38 I.e., 30 BC.
39 I.e., 14 BC.
40 These various consulships are to be found in the years 7 to 2 BC.
41 I.e., AD 6.
42 I.e., 18 BC.
43 Julius Caesar was declared a god by the Senate after his death.

the Lupercal; the portico to the Circus of Flaminius, which I allowed to bear the name Portico Octavia, from his name who constructed the earlier one in the same place; the Pulvinar at the Circus Maximus; the temples of Jupiter the Vanquisher and Jupiter the Thunderer on the Capitoline hill; the temple of Quirinus; the temples of Minerva and Juno the Queen and of Jupiter Freedom on the Aventine hill; the temple of the Lares on the highest point of the Sacred Way; the temple of the divine Penates on the Velian hill; the temple of Youth; and the temple of the Great Mother on the Palatine hill.

20   I restored the Capitol and the Pompeian theater at enormous expense for each work, without any inscription of my name. I restored aqueducts which were crumbling in many places because of age, and I have doubled the water which bears the name Marcian[44] by turning a new spring into its course. I finished the Julian Forum and the basilica[45] which was between the temple of Castor and the temple of Saturn, works begun and almost completed by my father,[46] and when that same basilica was consumed by fire, I began its reconstruction on an enlarged site, inscribing it with the names of my sons, and if I do not live to complete it, I have given orders that it be completed by my heirs. In accordance with a decree of the Senate, while consul for the sixth time,[47] I restored 82 temples of the gods, passing over none which was at that time in need of repair. In my seventh consulship I constructed the Flaminian way from the city to Ariminum, and all the bridges except the Mulvian and Minucian.

21   Upon private ground I have built with the spoils of war the temple of Mars the Avenger and the Augustan Forum. Beside the temple of Apollo, I built upon ground, bought for the most part at my own expense, a theater, to bear the name of my son-in-law, Marcel-lus. From the spoils of war I have consecrated gifts in the Capitol, and in the temple of the divine Julius, and in the temple of Apollo, and in the temple of Vesta, and temple of Mars the Avenger; these gifts have cost me about 100,000,000 sesterces. In my fifth consulship[48] I remitted to the municipalities and Italian colonies the 35,000 pounds given to me as crown gold[49] on the occasion of my triumphs, and thereafter, as often as I was proclaimed imperator, I did not accept the crown gold which the municipalities and colonies as kindly as before voted to give me.

22   I have given gladiatorial exhibitions three times in my own name, and five times in that of my sons or grandsons; in these exhibitions about 10,000 people have fought. Twice in my own name, and three times in that of my grandson, I have offered the people the spectacle of athletes gathered from all quarters. I have celebrated games 4 times in my own name, and 23 times in the turns of other officials. On behalf of the college of quindecemvirs,[50] I, as master of the college, with my colleague Agrippa, celebrated the Secular Games in the consulship of Gaius Furnius and Gaius Silanut. When consul for the thirteenth time, I first celebrated the Martial games, which since that time the consuls have given in successive years. I have given hunts of African wild beasts in the circus, the forum, the amphitheatres 26 times in my own name, or in that of my sons and grandsons, and about 3,500 beasts have been killed.

23   I gave the people the spectacle of a naval battle beyond the Tiber river, where the grove of the Caesars is now. For this purpose an excavation was made that was 1,800 feet long and 1,200 feet wide. In this contest 30 beaked ships, triremes or biremes,[51] were engaged, besides more of smaller size. About 3,000 men fought in these vessels in addition to the rowers.

---

44   I.e., water in the Marcian aqueduct.
45   A kind of large public building.
46   I.e., Julius Caesar.
47   I.e., 28 BC.
48   I.e., 29 BC.
49   It had been the custom for commanders receiving triumphs to be given golden crowns as gifts by communities affected by the victory; this came to be replaced simply by a gift of the gold itself.
50   A priestly order.
51   I.e., a ship with two tiers of oars.

24 In the temples of all the cities of the province of Asia, I, as victor, replaced the ornaments of which he with whom I was at war[52] had taken private possession when he despoiled the temples. I removed silver statues of me on foot, on horseback and in a chariot, which stood in the city, about 80 in number, and out of their money value, I placed golden gifts in the temple of Apollo in my own name, and in the names of those who had offered me the honor of the statues.

25 I have freed the sea from pirates.[53] In that war I delivered to their masters for punishment about 30,000 slaves who had fled from their masters and taken up arms against the Republic. The whole of Italy voluntarily took an oath of allegiance to me, and demanded me as leader in that war in which I was victorious at Actium. The provinces of Gaul, Spain, Africa, Sicily, and Sardinia swore the same allegiance to me. There were more than 700 senators who at that time fought under my standards, and among these, up to the day on which these words are written, 83 have either before or since been made consuls, and about 170 have been made priests.

26 I have extended the boundaries of all the provinces of the Roman people which were bordered by nations not yet subject to our sway. I have reduced to a state of peace the Gallic and Spanish provinces, and Germany (the lands enclosed by the ocean from Gades to the mouth of the Elbe). I have brought into a state of peace the Alps from the region nearest the Adriatic as far as the Tuscan Sea, without waging an unjust war upon any people. My fleet has navigated the ocean from the mouth of the Rhine as far as the boundaries of the Cimbri, where before that time no Roman had ever penetrated by land or sea, and the Cimbri and Charydes and Semnones and other German peoples of that area, through their representatives, sought my friendship and that of the Roman people. By my command and under my auspices two armies at almost the same time have been led into

Ethiopia and into Arabia, which is called "the Happy," and very many of the enemy of both peoples have fallen in battle, and many towns have been captured. Into Ethiopia the advance was as far as Nabata, which is next to Merce. In Arabia the army penetrated as far as the confines of the Sabaei, to the town of Mariba.

27 I have added Egypt to the empire of the Roman people.[54] I could have made a province out of greater Armenia when its king Artaxes was killed, but I preferred, after the example of our predecessors, to deliver that kingdom to Tigranes, the son of king Artavasdes, and grandson of King Tigranes, and I did this through Tiberius Nero, who was then my son-in-law. And afterwards, when the same people became turbulent and rebellious, they were subdued by Gaius, my son, and I gave the sovereignty over them to King Ariobarzanes, the son of Artabazes, king of the Medes, and after his death to his son Artavasdes. When he was killed I sent into that kingdom Tigranes, who was sprung from the royal family of the Armenians. I recovered all the provinces across the Adriatic Sea, which extend toward the east, and Cyrenaica, at that time for the most part in the possession of kings, together with Sicily and Sardinia, which had been engaged in a servile war.[55]

28 I have established colonies of soldiers in Africa, Sicily, Macedonia, the two Spains, Achaea,[56] Asia, Syria, Gallia Narbonensis[57] and Pisidia. Italy also has 28 colonies established under my auspices, which within my lifetime have become very famous and populous.

29 After conquering the enemy, I recovered from Spain and Gaul, and from the Dalmatians, many military standards which had been lost by other leaders. I compelled the Parthians to give up to me the spoils and standards of three Roman armies and, as suppliants, to seek the friendship of the Roman people. Those standards, moreover, I have deposited in the sanctuary which is in the temple of Mars the Avenger.

52 I.e., Marc Antony.
53 Evidently a reference to the war at sea against Sextus Pompey, son of Pompey the Great, in 36 BC.
54 On the other hand, Egypt also seems to have been treated as pertaining specifically to Augustus and his successors.
55 Referring to the war with Sextus Pompey (see above, at n 52).
56 I.e., in Greece.
57 In southern Gaul.

30   The Pannonian peoples, whom before I became princeps, no army of the Roman people had ever attacked, were defeated by Tiberius Nero, at that time my son-in-law and legate,[58] and I brought them under subjection to the empire of the Roman people, and extended the boundaries of Illyricum to the bank of the Danube river. When an army of the Dacians crossed this river, it was defeated and destroyed, and afterwards my army, led across the Danube, compelled the Dacian people to submit to the sway of the Roman people.

31   Kings from India have often sent embassies to me, a thing never before seen in the case of any leader of the Romans. Our friendship has been sought by means of ambassadors by the Bastarnac and the Scythians, and by the kings of the Sarmatae, who are on either side of the Tanais, and by the kings of the Albani, the Hiberi, and the Medes.

32   To me have betaken themselves as suppliants the kings of the Parthians, Tiridates, and later, Phraates, the son of King Phraates; of the Medes, Artavasdes of the Adiabeni, Artaxares; of the Britons, Dumnobellaunus and Tincommius; of the Sicambri, Maelo; and of the Marcomanian Suevi, [first part of the name unclear]rus. Phraates, the son of Orodes and king of the Parthians, sent all his children and grandchildren into Italy to me, not because he had been conquered in war, but rather seeking our friendship by means of his children as pledges. Since I have been princeps, very many other peoples, who had never before exchanged embassies and friendship with the Roman people, have come to know the good faith of the Roman people.

33   The peoples of the Parthians and of the Medes, through ambassadors—the chief men of those peoples—asked for, and received, their kings from me: the Parthians, Vonones, the son of King Phraates, and grandson of King Orodes; the Medes, Ariobarzanes, the son of King Artavasdes, and grandson of King Ariobarzanes.

34   In my sixth and seventh consulships,[59] when I had put an end to the civil wars, after having obtained complete control of affairs by universal consent, I transferred the Republic from my own power to the disposition of the Senate and Roman people. In return for this favor on my part, I received by decree of the Senate the title *Augustus*,[60] the door-posts of my house were publicly decked with laurels, a civic crown was fixed above my door,[61] and in the Julian Senate House was placed a golden shield, which, by its inscription, bore witness that it was given to me by the Senate and Roman people on account of my valor, clemency, justice, and piety. After that time I excelled all others in dignity, but I held no more *potestas*[62] than those who were also my colleagues in any office.

35   While I was consul for the thirteenth time,[63] the Senate, the equestrian order, and the entire Roman people gave me the title of father of the fatherland, and decreed that it should be inscribed in the vestibule of my house and in the Julian Senate House, and in the Augustan Forum beneath the chariot which had been, by decree of the Senate, set up in my honor. When I wrote these words I was in my seventy-sixth year.[64]

---

58   I.e., Tiberius Nero was serving as a lieutenant to Augustus.

59   I.e., 28-27 BC.

60   An honorary title, whose meaning is difficult to render—perhaps to be rendered as "one full of *auctoritas*," i.e., the quality which means that, although one does not have the power to compel, one should be taken seriously.

61   A civic crown was a reward for any soldier who had saved the life of a citizen.

62   Latin: power, the ability to compel.

63   I.e., 2 BC.

64   After this was added a short, apparently posthumous, account of sums spent and buildings built by Augustus.

# 19

# PLINY THE YOUNGER, *LETTERS*

Gaius Plinius Caecilius Secundus, better known as Pliny the Younger (*c.* 61-113) made his career as a lawyer before entering on a series of public offices in the Roman empire. A senator, his career culminated in his appointment as governor of Bithynia-Pontus, in what is today Turkey, *c.* 111-113. Writing letters was often seen as a literary art, and Pliny collected and published his letters during his own lifetime, a few of which appear here. His letters to the Emperor Trajan (98-117) and that emperor's replies, however, were published only after his death.

---

### 19.1
#### PLINY TO JUNIUS MAURICUS:

You desire me to look out for a proper husband for your niece; it is with justice that you enjoin me that office. You know the high esteem and affection I bore that great man, her father, and with what noble instructions he nurtured my youth, and taught me to deserve those praises he was pleased to bestow upon me. You could not give me, then, a more important, or more agreeable, commission, nor could I be employed in an office of higher honor than that of choosing a young man worthy of being father of the grandchildren of Rusticus Arulenus, a choice I should be long in determining, were I not acquainted with Minutius Aemilianus, who seems formed for our purpose. He loves me with all that warmth of affection which is usual between young men of equal years (as indeed I have the advance of him by but a very few), and reveres me at the same time, with all the deference due to age. In a word, he is no less desirous to model himself by my instructions than I was by those of yourself and your brother.

He is a native of Brixia,[1] one of those towns in Italy which still retain much of the old modesty, frugal simplicity, and even rusticity, of manner. He is the son of Minutius Macrinus, whose humble desires were satisfied with standing at the head of the equestrian order,[2] for although he was nominated by the divine Vespasian[3] in the number of those whom that princeps[4] dignified with the praetorian office,[5] yet, with an inflexible greatness of mind, he resolutely preferred an honorable repose to the ambitious, shall I call them, or exalted, pursuits, in which we public men

---

1  Now Brescia, in what was then "Cisalpine Gaul."
2  Traditionally the rank next below that of senator, sometimes referred to as the "knights" in modern English translations.
3  Roman emperor (69-79); he was declared a god by the Senate after his death.
4  A difficult term to translate: "the first citizen" or "first among equals." When Augustus received this title from the Senate, it did not clearly have legal significance. All his successors were also called *princeps.*
5  I.e., to the office of praetor, a judicial office which dated to the Republic.

are engaged. His grandmother, on the mother's side, is Serrana Procula, of Patavium[6]—you are no stranger to the character of its citizens. Yet Serrana is looked upon, even among these correct people, as an exemplary instance of strict virtue. Acilius, his uncle, is a man of almost exceptional gravity, wisdom, and integrity. In short, you will find nothing throughout his family unworthy of yours. Minutius himself has plenty of vivacity, as well as application, together with a most amiable and becoming modesty. He has already, with considerable credit, passed through the offices of quaestor, tribune, and praetor[7] so that you will be spared the trouble of soliciting for him those honorable employments. He has a fine, well-bred countenance, with a ruddy, healthy complexion, while his whole person is elegant and comely and his bearing is graceful and senatorial—advantages, I think, by no means to be slighted, and which I consider as the proper compensation for a virgin's innocence. I think I *may* add that his father is very rich. When I contemplate the character of those who require a husband of my choosing, I know it is unnecessary to mention wealth, but when I reflect upon the prevailing manners of the age, and even the laws of Rome, which rank a man according to his possessions, it certainly claims *some* regard; and, indeed, in establishments of this nature, where children and many other circumstances are to be duly weighed, it is a matter that well deserves to be taken into the account.

You will be inclined, perhaps, to suspect that affection has had too great a share in the character I have been drawing, and that I have heightened it beyond the truth. But I will stake all my credit that you will find everything far beyond what I have represented. I love the young fellow indeed (as he justly deserves) with all the warmth of a most ardent affection. But for that very reason, I would not attribute more to his merit than I know it will bear.

## 19.2
### PLINY TO HIS PRISCUS:[8]

Just as I know that you eagerly embrace every opportunity of obliging me, so there is no man to whom I would rather be obligated. I apply to you, therefore, in preference to anyone else, for a favor which I very much desire to obtain. You, who command a large army, have many opportunities to exercise your generosity, and the length of time you have enjoyed that post must have enabled you to provide for all of your own friends. I hope you will now turn your eyes upon some of mine, as indeed there are but few. Your generous disposition, I know, would be better pleased if the number were greater, but one or two will suffice for my modest desires; at present I will name only Voconius Romanus. His father was of great distinction among the Roman equestrians, and his stepfather, or, I might more properly call him, his second father (for his affectionate treatment of Voconius entitles him to that designation), was still more conspicuous. His mother was one of the most considerable ladies of upper-Spain: you know what character the people of that province have, and how remarkable they are for their strictness of manners. As for himself, he has lately held the position of flamen.[9]

Now from the time that we were students together I have felt very tenderly attached to him. We lived under the same roof, in town and country, we joked together, we shared each other's serious thoughts; for where indeed could I have found a truer companion than he? In his conversation, and even in his very voice and countenance, there is a rare sweetness; as at the bar, he displays talents of a high order: acuteness, elegance, ease and skill. And he writes such letters that, were you to read them, you would imagine they had been dictated by the Muses themselves.

Even in the earlier part of our lives, I warmly

---

6   Now Padua, in what was then "Cisalpine Gaul."
7   Offices dating to the Republic.
8   Perhaps to Javolenus Priscus.
9   A priestly position.

embraced every opportunity of doing him all the good services which then lay in my power, as I have lately obtained for him from our most gracious princeps the privilege granted to those who have three children,[10] a favor which, though Caesar very rarely bestows it, and always with great caution, yet he conferred it at my request, in such a manner as to give it the air and grace of being his own choice. The best way of showing that I think he deserves the kindnesses he has already received from me is by increasing them, especially as he always accepts my services so gratefully as to deserve more. Thus I have shown you what manner of man Romanus is, how thoroughly I have proved his worth, and how much I love him. Let me entreat you to honor him with your patronage in a way suitable to the generosity of your heart and the eminence of your station. But above all let him have your affection, for even if you were to confer on him the utmost in power to bestow, you can give him nothing more valuable than your friendship. That you may see he is worthy of it, even to the closest degree of intimacy, I send you this brief sketch of his tastes, his character, his whole life. I should continue my intercessions on his behalf, but I know you prefer not being pressed, and I have already repeated them in every line of this letter, for to show a good reason for what one asks is true intercession, and of the most effective kind. Farewell.

### 19.3
#### TO ACILIUS:

The atrocious treatment of Larcius Macedo, a man of praetorian rank, lately received at the hands of his slaves is so extreme that it deserves a place in public history rather than in a private letter, although it must be at the same time acknowledged that there was a haughtiness and severity in his behaviour towards them which showed that he little remembered, indeed almost entirely forgot, the fact that his own father had once been in that station of life. He was bathing in his villa at Formiae,[11] when he found himself suddenly surrounded by his slaves; one seizes him by the throat,

another strikes him on the mouth, while others trampled on his chest, stomach, and even other parts which I need not mention. When they thought the breath must be quite out of his body, they threw him down upon the heated pavement of the bath, to test whether he was still alive; he lay there motionless, either really senseless or only feigning to be so, upon which they concluded he was actually dead. They brought him out in this condition, pretending that he had been suffocated by the heat of the bath. Some of his more trusty slaves received him, and his mistresses came about him shrieking and crying. The noise of their cries and the fresh air, together, brought him a little to himself; he opened his eyes, moved his body, and showed them (as he now safely might) that he was not quite dead. The murderers immediately made their escape, but most of them have been caught again, and they are after the rest. He was with great difficulty kept alive for a few days, and then expired, having, however, the satisfaction of finding himself as amply revenged in his lifetime as he would have been after his death. Thus you see to what affronts, indignities, and dangers we are exposed. Leniency and kind treatment are no safeguard, for it is malice and not reflection which arms such ruffians against their masters. So much for this piece of news. And what else? Nothing else, or you would hear it, for I have yet more paper, and time too (as it is holiday time for me) to spare for more, and I can tell you one further circumstance relating to Macedo, which now occurs to me. As he was in a public bath at Rome, a remarkable, and (judging from the manner of his death) an ominous, accident happened to him. A slave of his, in order to make way for his master, laid his hand gently upon a Roman equestrian, who, turning around suddenly, struck, not the slave who had touched him, but Macedo, with so violent a blow by his open palm that he almost knocked him down. Thus the bath by a kind of gradation proved fatal to him, being first the scene of an indignity he suffered, afterwards the scene of his death.

Farewell.

---

10 The law allowed those who had three children priority in holding some public offices and allowed them to hold them at a younger age than otherwise.

11 In central Italy.

### 19.4
#### TO THE IMPERATOR[12] TRAJAN:

When by your gracious indulgence, master,[13] I was appointed to preside at the treasury of Saturn,[14] I immediately renounced all engagements of the bar (as indeed I never blended business of that kind with the functions of the state), that all my attention might be devoted to the post to which I was appointed. For this reason, when the province of Africa petitioned the Fathers[15] that I might undertake their cause against Marius Priscus,[16] I excused myself from that office, and my excuse was allowed. But when afterwards the consul elect proposed that the senate should apply to us again, and endeavor to prevail with us to yield to its inclinations, and suffer our names to be thrown into the urn, I thought it most agreeable to that tranquillity and good order which so happily distinguishes your times not to oppose (especially in so reasonable an instance) the will of that most illustrious assembly. And, as I am desirous that all my words and actions may receive the sanction of your exemplary virtue, I hope you approve of my compliance.

### 19.5
#### TRAJAN TO PLINY:

You acted as became a good citizen and a worthy senator, by paying obedience to the just demand of that most illustrious assembly, and I have full confidence that you will faithfully discharge the business you have undertaken.

### 19.6
#### PLINY TO THE IMPERATOR TRAJAN:

Having been attacked last year by a very severe and dangerous illness, I employed a physician, whose care and diligence, master, I cannot sufficiently reward, but by your gracious assistance. I entreat you therefore to make him a citizen of Rome, for as he is the freedman of an alien lady, he is, consequently, himself also an alien. His name is Harpocras; his patroness (who has been dead a considerable time) was Thermuthis, wife of Theon. I further entreat you to bestow full Roman citizenship upon Hedia and Antonia Harmeris, the freedwomen of Antonia Maximilla, a lady of great merit. It is at her desire I make this request.

### 19.7
#### PLINY TO THE IMPERATOR TRAJAN:

I thank you, master, for your ready compliance with my desire, in granting full Roman citizenship to the freedwomen of a lady to whom I am allied, and also for making Harpocras, my physician, a citizen of Rome. But when, in accordance to your directions, I gave an account of his age and estate, I was informed by those who are better skilled in the affair than I pretend to be, that, as he is an Egyptian, I ought first to have obtained for him the citizenship of Alexandria[17] before he was made a citizen of Rome. I confess, indeed, as I was ignorant of any difference in this case between Egypt and other countries, I contented myself with only informing you that he had been

---

12  "Imperator" had been, since the Republic, a traditional honorary title given to an outstanding general. It was routinely carried by Augustus and his successors. It eventually became so associated with them that it came to mean "emperor." By Trajan's time, "imperator" was the first to appear in an emperor's list of titles.

13  "Master" ("dominus" in Latin) was a title of address which Augustus had avoided.

14  The main government treasury under the Republic. By this time it had declined in importance relative to the treasury of Augustus's successors.

15  I.e., the Senate.

16  Marius Priscus, the former governor of the province, was being charged with extortion and taking bribes. He was convicted. Another letter of Pliny states that this trial took place in the Senate, with Trajan presiding as consul.

17  Alexandria, officially termed "Alexandria by Egypt," was the Greek city founded in Egypt by Alexander the Great.

freed by a foreign lady deceased long ago. However, it is an ignorance I cannot regret because it affords me an opportunity of receiving from you a double obligation in favor of the same person. That I may legally therefore enjoy the benefit of your goodness, I beg you would be pleased to grant him the citizenship of the city of Alexandria, as well as that of Rome. And that your gracious intentions may not meet with any further obstacles, I have taken care, as you directed, to send an account to your freedman of his age and possessions.

## 19.8

### TRAJAN TO PLINY:

It is my resolution, in pursuance of the maxim observed by the principes[18] my predecessors, to be extremely cautious in granting the citizenship of the city of Alexandria. However, since you have obtained from me Roman citizenship for your physician Harpocras, I cannot refuse you this other request. You must let me know to what district he belongs, that I may give you a letter to my friend Pompeius Planta, governor of Egypt.

## 19.9

### PLINY TO THE IMPERATOR TRAJAN:

It is my invariable rule, master, to refer to you in all matters where I feel doubtful. For who is more capable of removing my scruples or informing my ignorance? Having never been present at any trials concerning those who profess Christianty, I am unacquainted not only with the nature of their crimes and the measure of their punishment, but also how far it is proper to enter into an examination concerning them. Whether, therefore, any difference is usually made with respect to ages, or no distinction is to be observed between the young and the adult; whether repentance entitles them to a pardon, or, if a man has been once a Christian, it avails nothing to desist from his error; whether the very profession of Christianity,

unaccompanied any criminal act, or only the crimes themselves inherent in the profession are punishable—on all these points I am in great doubt. Meanwhile, the method I have observed towards those who have been brought before me as Christians is this: I asked them whether they were Christians; if they admitted it, I repeated the question twice, and threatened them with punishment; if they persisted, I ordered them to be at once punished, for I was persuaded, whatever the nature of their opinions might be, a contumacious and inflexible obstinacy certainly deserved correction. There were others also brought before me similarly infatuated, but being Roman citizens, I directed that they be sent to Rome.[19] But since this crime was spreading (as is usually the case) while it was actually under prosecution, several instances of the same nature occurred. Anonymous information was laid before me containing a charge against several persons, who upon examination denied they were Christians, or had ever been so. They repeated after me an invocation to the gods, and offered wine and incense before your statue (which for that purpose I had ordered to be brought, together with those of the gods) and even reviled the name of Christ. Whereas, it is said, there is no forcing those who are really Christians into any of these actions, I thought it proper therefore to discharge them.

Some among those who were accused by a witness in person at first confessed themselves to be Christians, but immediately after denied it. The rest admitted that indeed that they had been of that number formerly, but had now (some above three, others more, and a few above 20 years ago) renounced that error. They all did reverence before your statue and the images of the gods, uttering curses against the name of Christ. They affirmed that the whole of their guilt, or their error, was that they met on a stated day before it was light, and addressed a form of prayer to Christ, as to a divinity, binding themselves by a solemn oath, not for the purposes of any wicked design, but never to commit any fraud, theft, or adultery, never to falsify their word, nor deny a trust when they should be

---

18  Plural of *princeps*.
19  Technically, Roman citizens could not be tried in capital cases except by the body of Roman citizens.

called upon to deliver it up; after which it was their custom to separate, and then reassemble, to eat in common a harmless meal. From this custom, however, they desisted after the publication of my edict, by which, according to your commands, I forbade the meeting of any assemblies. After receiving this account, I judged it so much the more necessary to endeavor to extort the real truth, by putting two female slaves, who were said to officiate in their religious rites, under torture. But all I could discover was evidence of an absurd and extravagant superstition. I deemed it expedient, therefore, to adjourn all further proceedings, in order to consult you. For it appears to be a matter highly deserving your consideration, more especially as great numbers must be involved in the danger of these prosecutions, which have already extended, and are still likely to extend, to persons of all ranks and ages, and even of both sexes. In fact, this contagious superstition is not confined to the cities only, but has spread its infection among the neighboring villages and country. Nevertheless, it still seems possible to restrain its progress. The temples, at least, which were once almost deserted, begin now to be frequented; the sacred rites, after a long intermission, are again revived, while there is a general demand for the victims, which till lately found very few purchasers.[20] From all this it is easy to conjecture what numbers might be reclaimed if a general pardon were granted to those who shall repent of their error.

19.10

TRAJAN TO PLINY:

You have adopted the right course, my dear Secundus, in investigating the charges against the Christians who were brought before you. It is not possible to lay down any general rule for all such cases. Do not go out of your way to look for them. If indeed they should be brought before you, and the crime is proved, they must be punished, with, however, the restriction that where the party denies he is a Christian, and shall make it evident that he is not, by invoking our gods, let him (notwithstanding any former suspicion) be pardoned upon his repentance. Anonymous information ought not to be received in any sort of prosecution. Doing so would introduce a very dangerous precedent, and is quite foreign to the spirit of our age.

---

20  Animals sacrificed to the gods were then sold as meat. Christians were forbidden to consume such meat.

# 20

# Papyri from Oxyrhynchus

The dry sands of Egypt have preserved many papyri—i.e., pieces of papyrus paper, rarely complete, which people in Egypt either lost or threw away over the centuries. Thousands of such papyri dating from the time of Roman rule have been recovered from Oxyrhynchus. Oxyrhynchus served as the capital of the Oxyrhynchite nome, one of the roughly 30 territorial divisions of Egypt; these nomes dated back to Egypt's old kingdom. The writing on most of the papyri which have been found is in Greek, as is the case with all those which appear below except where noted.

---

### 20.1
#### PETITION OF SYRA, DAUGHTER OF THEON FOR THE RETURN OF HER DOWRY (20-50)

To Heraclides, priest, chief justice, superintendent of the chrematistae[1] and the other courts, from Syra, daughter of Theon. I married Sarapion, bringing him by cession a dowry amounting to 200 drachmae of silver. As he was destitute of means I received him into my parents' house, and I for my part conducted myself blamelessly in all respects. But Sarapion, having squandered my dowry as he pleased, continually ill-treated and insulted me, using violence towards me, and depriving me of the necessities of life; finally he deserted me, leaving me in a state of destitution. I therefore beg you to order him to be brought before you, in order that he may be compelled perforce to pay back my dowry increased by half its amount. This petition is without prejudice to any other claims which I have or may have against him.

### 20.2
#### NOTICE TO CHAEREAS THE STRATEGUS[2] OF A TRANSFER OF CATTLE (23)

To Chaereas, strategus, from Cerinthus, slave of Antonia, daughter of Drusus. I wish to transfer from the Oxyrhynchite to the Cynopolite nome for the sake of pasturage 320 sheep and 160 goats and the lambs and kids that may be produced, which I have on the register in the Oxyrhynchite nome in the present ninth year of Tiberius Caesar Augustus. I therefore present this memorandum in order that you may write to the strategus of the Cynopolite nome to register the aforesaid sheep and goats....[3]

I, Cerinthus, slave of Antonia, daughter of Drusus, have presented this in the ninth year of Tiberius Caesar Augustus, on Mechir[4] 8.[5]

Chaereas to Hermias, strategus of the Cynopolite nome, many greetings. Cerinthus, slave of Antonia,

---

1   A court at Alexandria.
2   The chief official of a nome.
3   This portion of the document breaks off.
4   Roughly the Egyptian month of January.
5   This sentence is written in Latin in a second hand.

daughter of Drusus, has presented to me a return, wishing to....[6]

### 20.3
#### PETITION OF TRYPHON, SON OF DIONYSIUS, AGAINST HIS WIFE DEMETROUS (30-35)

To Alexandrus, strategus, from Tryphon, son of Dionysius, of the city of Oxyrhynchus. I married Demetrous, daughter of Heraclides, and I for my part provided for my wife in a manner that exceeded my resources. But she became dissatisfied with our union, and finally left the house carrying off property belonging to me, a list of which is added below. I beg, therefore, that she be brought before you in order that she may receive what she deserves, and return to me my property. This petition is without prejudice to the other claims which I have or may have against her. The stolen articles are: a ...[7] worth 40 drachmae....[8]

### 20.4
#### REPORT OF A LAWSUIT CONCERNING THE IDENTITY OF A CHILD (49-50)

From the minutes of Tiberius Claudius Pasion, strategus. The ninth year of Tiberius Claudius Caesar Augustus Germanicus Imperator,[9] Pharmouthi[10] 3. In court, Pesouris versus Saraeus.

Aristocles, advocate for Pesouris, said: "Pesouris, my client, in the seventh year of our sovereign Tiberius Claudius Caesar, picked up from the gutter a boy foundling, named Heraclas. He put it in the defendant's charge. This nurse[11] was there for the son of Pesouris. She received her wages for the first year when they became due, she also received them for the second year. In proof of my assertions there are the documents in which she acknowledges receipt. The foundling was being starved, and Pesouris took it away. Thereupon Saraeus, waiting her opportunity, made an incursion into my client's house and carried the foundling off. She now justifies its removal on the ground that it was freeborn. I have here, firstly, the contract with the nurse; I have also, secondly, the receipt of the wages. I demand their recognition."

Saraeus: "I weaned my own child and the foundling belonging to these people was placed in my charge. I received from them my full wages of 8 staters. Then the foundling died and I was left with the money. They now wish to take away my own child."

Theon: "We have the papers relating to the foundling."

The strategus: "Since from its features the child appears to be that of Saraeus, if she and her husband will make a written declaration that the foundling entrusted to her by Pesouris died, I give judgment in accordance with the decision of our lord the praefect,[12] that she have her own child on paying back the money she has received."

### 20.5
#### PETITION TO THE PRAEFECT FROM THE HUSBAND OF SARAEUS REGARDING THE ABOVE CASE (49-50, PROBABLY A FEW MONTHS AFTER THE ABOVE DOCUMENT)

To Gnaeus Vergilius Capito, from Tryphon, son of Dionysius, of the city of Oxyrhynchus. Syrus, son of Syrus, entrusted to the keeping of my wife Saraeus, daughter of Apion, in the seventh year of Tiberius Claudius Caesar Augustus Germanicus Imperator, on my security, a boy foundling named Heraclas, whom he had picked up from the gutter, to be nursed. The foundling died, and Syrus tried to carry off into slav-

---

6   The document breaks off. This paragraph is in a third hand.
7   Words are missing.
8   The document breaks off.
9   Imperator: a term today usually translated as "emperor," in the Roman Republic it was an honorary title given to certain victorious generals.
10   Roughly the Egyptian month of April.
11   I.e., wetnurse.
12   The emperor's sole representative in Egypt, who had sweeping powers. This official is not to be confused with the military officers of the same title outside Egypt.

ery my infant son Apion. I accordingly applied to Pasion, the strategus of the nome, by whom my son Apion was restored to me in accordance with what you, my benefactor, had commanded, and the minutes entered by Pasion. Syrus, however, refuses to comply with the judgment, and hinders me in my trade. I therefore come to you, my preserver, in order to obtain my rights. Farewell.

## 20.6

### RECORD OF THE SALE OF A HOUSE BY PNEPHEROS, SON OF PAPONTOS, TO TRYPHON, SON OF DIONYSIUS

(55)

Copy. The second year of Nero Claudius Caesar Augustus Germanicus Imperator, on the 6th of the month Audnaeus[13]=Sebastus, at Oxyrhynchus in the Thebaid,[14] before the agoranomi[15] Andromachus and Diogenes. Tryphon, son of Dionysius, about ...[16] years old, of middle height, fair, with a long face and a slight squint, and having a scar on his right wrist, has bought from his mother Thamounis's cousin, Pnepheros, son of Papontos, also an inhabitant of Oxyrhynchus, about 65 years old, of middle height, fair, having a long face and a scar above his ...[17] eyebrow and another on his right knee, (the document being drawn up in the street) one half of a three-storied house inherited from his mother, together with all its entrances and exits and appurtenances, situated by the Serapeum[18] at Oxyrhynchus in the southern part of the street called Temgenouthis to the west of the lane leading to "Shepherds' Street," its boundaries being, on the south and east, public roads, on the north, the house of the aforesaid Thamounis, mother of Tryphon the buyer, on the west, the house of Tausiris, sister of Pnepheros the seller, separated by a blind alley, for the sum of 32 talents

of copper; and Pnepheros undertakes to guarantee the half share which is sold perpetually in every respect with every guarantee.

## 20.7

### DECLARATION OF BACCHE REGARDING HER SALE OF SARAPOUS (77)

To the agoranomi ...[19] from Bacche, citizen, daughter of Hermon, with her guardian Diognetus, son of Dionysius, of the Epiphanean deme.[20] I swear by the Emperor Caesar Vespasianus Augustus that I have sold to Heliodora, daughter of Heliodora, with her guardian who is her husband Apollonius, son of Dionysius, son of Dionysius also called Didymus, the slave Sarapous who belongs to me, and is about eight years old and without blemish apart from epilepsy and leprosy;[21] and I swear that she is my property and is not mortgaged, and has not been alienated to other persons in any respect, and that I have received the price, 640 silver drachmae, and will guarantee the contract. If I swear truly may it be well with me, but if falsely, the reverse.

[Signature of Diognetus on behalf of Bacche, and date.]

## 20.8

### REPORT OF A PURCHASE OF LAND BY MARCUS PORCIUS

(90)

To Epimachus and Theon, keepers of the archives, from Zoilus, son of Apollonius, son of Ptollion, his mother being Ptolema, daughter of Ischurion, an inhabitant of the village of Enepta in the middle toparchy.[22] I register for Marcus Porcius, who happens to be away, in obedience to the orders of the lord

---

13  A Macedonian month, roughly November.
14  The nomes of Egypt were grouped into three large districts, of which the Thebaid was the southernmost.
15  Market regulators, and one of the chief officials of the nome's capital town.
16  Word(s) missing.
17  Portion missing.
18  A temple of Serapis, a god created under the Pharoah Ptolemy I out of aspects of Greek and Egyptian gods.
19  Words missing.
20  A district of the city.
21  This clause is in most such contracts; slaves were not guaranteed against being subject to epilepsy or leprosy.
22  An administrative district within a nome.

praefect Mettius Rufus, a piece of unwooded land which at present belongs to Marcus, in the village of Petne in the same toparchy in the southern part of the village, which he bought from Tiberius Julius Basilides through Tiberius Julius Philetas in accordance with his rights over it.

## 20.9

### AGREEMENT BETWEEN AGATHODAEMON AND GAIUS JULIUS GERMANUS CONCERNING THE SALE OF DIOSCOROUS (129)

The thirteenth year of the Emperor Caesar Trajanus Hadrianus Augustus, Payni[23] 29, at Oxyrhynchus in the Thebaid. Agathodaemon, also called Dionysius, son of Dionysius, son of Dionysius, his mother being Hermione, of Oxyrhynchus, agrees with Gaius Julius Germanus, son of Gaius Julius Domitianus, the agreement being executed in the street, that he hereby assents to the autograph[24] contract, made on Tybi[25] 25 of the present 13th year, for the sale to Julius Germanus of a slave named Dioscorous, about 25 years old, with no distinguishing marks, which slave was his by purchase, having previously belonged to Heraclides also called Theon, son of Machon, son of Sosicosmius also called Althaeeus. This slave Julius Germanus then took from him just as she was, free from blemish except epilepsy and marks of punishment, at the price of 200 drachmae of silver, which sum Agathodaemon also called Dionysius thereupon received from Julius Germanus in full together with the autograph contract. In consequence of this contract Julius Germanus paid the tax upon the sale of the said slave Dioscorous on Phamenoth[26] 3 of the same year, in accordance with the receipt issued to him. Agathodaemon also called Dionysius is the guarantor of the said slave Dioscorous in all respects, as the autograph contract states. If the terms of it should be broken or it in

any other way be rendered invalid, Julius Germanus has the right to demand....[27]

## 20.10

### LEASE OF LAND BY DIONYSIA, DAUGHTER OF CHAEREMON, TO PSENAMOUNIS, SON OF THONIS (142)

Dionysia, daughter of Chaeremon, with her guardian who is her son Apion also called Dionysius, son of Diogenes, both of Oxyrhynchus, has leased to Psenamounis, son of Thonis and Seoeris, from Paberke in the eastern toparchy, a Persian of the Epigone,[28] for six years dating from the present sixth year of our sovereign Antoninus Caesar, 38 arourae belonging to her and previously cultivated by Psenamounis under another lease, on these conditions. For the first five years fixed by the agreement the lessee may sow and gather whatever crops he chooses with the exception of woad and coriander;[29] in the last year he shall sow and gather the same crops as those appointed for him in the last year of the previous lease. The rent of the whole leasehold during the six years is fixed at 190 artabae of wheat a year and a money payment of 12 drachmae a year, which shall all be free of every risk, the land tax being paid by the lessor, who shall also be the owner of the crops until the rent is paid. If in any of the years there should be a failure of water, an allowance shall be made to the lessee. He shall also, when the lease is guaranteed to him, measure into the public granary from the amount fixed as the rent for the year the yearly grain tax on the buildings, at his own expense, and he shall pay this deposit to the lessor free of all adulteration every year at the time of the first measuring, an equivalent allowance being made to him. The remainder of the yearly rent together with the money payment he shall always pay to the lessor in the month of Payni at the granary of Paberke: new, clean, unadulterated, sifted wheat, with no bar-

---

23  Roughly the Egyptian month of June.
24  I.e., handwritten by the parties.
25  Roughly the Egyptian month of January.
26  Roughly the Egyptian month of March.
27  The document breaks off here.
28  I.e., a descendant of a Persian settler who has married an Egyptian.
29  This last word is unclear.

ley in it, similar to that which is delivered at the public granary, measured by the bronze-rimmed measure containing four choenices used for payments to the lessor or her agents. Any arrears owed by the lessee shall be paid with the addition of half their amount. The lessor shall have the right of execution upon both the person and all the property of the lessee, and the lessor shall not be permitted to let the property to anyone else or to cultivate it herself within the six years. This lease is valid. The sixth year of the Emperor Caesar Titus Aelius Hadrianus Antoninus Augustus Pius, Phaophi[30] 5.

I, Psenamounis, son of Thonis, have taken the land on lease for the six years at a yearly rental of 190 artabae of wheat and a money payment of 12 drachmae, and I will make all the payments aforesaid. I, Theon, son of Theon and Ophelia, signed for him, as he is illiterate, on the same date.

### 20.11

### RECEIPT FROM CHOSION, SON OF SARAPION, CONCERNING WAGES OF TANENTERIS, DAUGHTER OF THONIS (187)

Chosion, son of Sarapion, son of Harpocration, his mother being Sarapias, of Oxyrhynchus, to Tanenteris, daughter of Thonis, son of Thonis, her mother being Zoilous, of the same city, with her guardian Demetrius, son of Horion and Arsinoë, of the same city, greeting. I acknowledge the receipt from you through Heliodorus and his associate overseers of the bank at the Serapeum near the city of Oxyrhynchus, for which Epimachus made the promise of payment, of 400 drachmae in imperial coin for wages, oil, clothes, and all other expenses during the two years in which my slave Sarapias nursed your daughter Helena known as her father's child, who, when you took her back had been weaned and had received every attention;

and I acknowledge that I neither have nor shall have any complaint or charge to make against you either in connection with this transaction or any other matter whatever up to the present time. This receipt is valid.

### 20.12

### PETITION OF TABESAMMON, DAUGHTER OF AMMONIUS, REGARDING APPOINTMENT OF A GUARDIAN (211)

To Maximus, priest, exegetes[31] in office and councillor, from Tabesammon, the daughter of Ammonius otherwise called Cassius, of Oxyrhynchus, her mother being Diophantis, a citizen. As I am borrowing for my pressing needs a sum of money at interest, amounting to 6,000 drachmae, upon the security of property consisting of a piece of vine land and all its appurtenances near the village of Oinaru, I make the request through you, being aware ...[32] that the royal scribe, the acting strategus, is absent, that I may have assigned to me as my guardian for this transaction only Amoitas, son of Ploution and Demetrous, of the aforesaid city of Oxyrhynchus, who is present and gives his consent. I have paid the appointed tax for making such a request.

### 20.13

### TWO PETITIONS TO CLODIUS CULCIANUS, PRAEFECT (303)

To his excellency Culcianus, praefect of Egypt, from Aurelius Demetrius, son of Nilus, late chief priest of Arsinoë. Knowing your care for honest citizens, my lord praefect, I make my petition to you with full confidence that I shall obtain justice from your highness. In the seventeenth=the sixteenth[33]=the ninth year of this auspicious reign, Aurelius Sota, ex-gymnasiarch[34] of Arsinoë, acknowledged in two bonds the receipt of a fully secured deposit from me, the first

---

30  Roughly the Egyptian October.
31  An official who presided over a board of town magistrates for the year.
32  The document is defective here.
33  Both are dates of the emperor's reign, whose accession was calculated in Egypt in a manner different from that of the rest of the empire.
34  The gymnasiarch was the city magistrate who ensured supplies for the gymnasium, a social and educational center for Greek men in a city.

bond which was made in the month of Tybi, being for 2 talents of silver; the second, which was in Phamenoth, for 20 talents of silver. These sums he, by the terms of the aforesaid contracts, undertook to repay without an action at law or any delay or quibble. When therefore I asked him for the money while Heron was strategus, he attempted, owing to my being illiterate, to commit a fraud to my detriment. When he was detected in this and was in danger of being prosecuted before your highness, he entreated that he be allowed to settle his debts without the trouble of an action. Up to the present moment he is still putting off the payment, taking a mean advantage of my forbearance, while I am in debt to the most sacred treasury not only on account of the deficit in connection with the duty which I have performed as superintendent of the grain supply, but also in connection with both my private estate and the municipal post which I undertook, and I have no other resources than this money in question. On all these accounts therefore I beg and entreat you to instruct, if you will, the strategus or any other magistrate whom you may sanction, that Sotas shall be compelled by seizure of the securities provided in his written bonds now at length to make repayment, or that, if he is recalcitrant, he shall be summoned before your highness to answer for his previous fraud also. Thus I shall be enabled to recover my property and acknowledge my gratitude to your excellency. Farewell. I, Aurelius Demetrius presented this petition. The nineteenth=eighteenth year, Phamenoth 4.[35]

To his excellency Clodius Culcianus, praefect of Egypt, from the most noble Aurelia[36] ..., and inhabitant of Arsinoë. You extend help, my lord praefect, and you render to all their due, but especially to women on account of their natural weakness. Therefore I myself make petition to your highness in the full confidence that I shall obtain assistance from you.

Having large estates in the Arsinoite nome, and paying a considerable sum in taxes (I refer to payments for public purposes and supplies for the soldiers), and being a defenseless widow, for my sons are in the army and are absent on foreign service, I engaged as my assistant and business manager first one Secundus and subsequently Tyrranus besides, that they would preserve my good name. But they behaved dishonestly and robbed me....[37]

## 20.14

### DECLARATION OF AURELIUS PAMBECHIS TO THE CHIEF OF THE TREASURY OF OXYRHYNCHUS (560)

In the thirty-fourth year of the reign of our most godly and pious sovereign Flavius Justinian, eternal Augustus and Imperator, which is the nineteenth year after the consulship of Flavius Basilius the most illustrious, Choiak[38] 17, the indiction.[39] To his worshipful lordship the superintendent of the public treasury-office of this city of Oxyrhynchus, the son of the sainted Abraham of the illustrious city of Oxyrhynchus, from Aurelius Pambechis, son of the sainted Menas and Maxima, whose own signature follows, of the same city, greeting. Whereas I presented an appeal to your worship to become my surety with the most illustrious Apphouas, assistant of the village of Sephtha, if he accepted me as his deputy for one year reckoned from the present month Choiak of the current two hundred thirty seventh=the two hundred sixth year,[40] and of the present ninth indiction, and whereas your worship did this in accordance with my request, your worship at the same time made the reasonable demand to receive from me a written agreement proper to such an appeal. I have accordingly been constrained to enter upon the present appellant's agreement, wherein I agree not to permit your worship to suffer any damage, loss, annoyance, or trouble on my account in

---

35  The date appears in a second hand.
36  Portion missing. This petition appears in third hand.
37  The document breaks off.
38  Roughly the Egyptian December.
49  A cycle of fifteen years.
40  I.e., the two hundred thirty seventh and the two hundred sixth years after some today unknown events; these events were frequently used to date documents at Oxyrhyncus, but do not appear to have been used in documents from elsewhere.

this connection, whether in court or out of court, but on the contrary to guarantee you against annoyance, trouble, loss and damage. But if the contingency which I deprecate should occur, and your worship should suffer loss or annoyance or trouble, or I should permit you to be reminded of your suretyship for me by any person whatsoever, you are to have the power to distrain[41] upon all my property, personal and real, until you have received satisfaction. To all this I swear the oath by Heaven and the Emperor that I will abide by and observe these conditions and will in no way break them; and I pledge for the observance of this appellant's agreement my property present and future, whether held by myself or my family....[42]

---

41 I.e., to seize and enjoy the income from.
42 The document breaks off.

# 21

# Inscription from Mactar

A number of inscriptions (i.e., words carved into stone) survive from the ancient world, most of them in fragments. Below is one from the town of Mactar, in the Roman province of Numidia (modern Algeria), North Africa; it dates to about 260-270. This inscription is in verse.

---

I was born poor of a poor family
and we had neither house nor property.
From the time I was born I lived my life harvesting
   the fields;
there was no pause for them or for me.
And when the year produced the ripened wheat,
I was the first to plunge into the grain.
When the sickle-bearing teams of men went into the
   field
seeking the grain in Jovian or Cirtian Numidia[1]
I went into the fields first and before them all,
leaving their compact ranks behind me.
For twice sixty months I toiled in the fierce sun,
and for this work, I was eventually made factor.[2]
For eleven years I led the team of harvesters,
and our hands cut the Numidian fields.

This labor and a frugal life allowed me
to become a landowner with a house and an estate,
a house that lacks no riches.
And my life has gathered the fruits of office as well.
Indeed I myself have been enrolled into the city senate,
and I was adlicted[3] by that body to sit in that council.
From a poor farm boy even I myself have become
   censor.[4]
I have fathered children and dear grandchildren,
and I have passed my years recognized for the worth
   of my life,
years which no evil tongue has besmirched with
   slander.
Learn, o mortals, to live without slanders.
Living thus, I have merited to die without deception.

---

1 Two regions of Numidia. Cirta was a city in Numidia.

2 I.e., contractor.

3 I.e., chosen by the city council to be a decurion, a man of substance selected to carry out certain aspects of Roman administration in the locality, and from which class the emperor chose members of the city council or senate.

4 Presumably a local office similar to that of the censor at Rome in relation to the Roman Senate, and so charged with determining that those who were decurions were indeed wealthy enough to qualify.

# 22

# BOOK OF MATTHEW 3–9.32

Written *c.* 80-85, the book of Matthew makes up part of the texts sacred to Christians as the New Testament. Early Christians seem to have given special consideration to the book of Matthew, which includes what is known as the "Sermon on the Mount," among the writings which they considered authoritative. Like most of the books of the New Testament, its author is unknown, although there is a tradition that it was written by Jesus's disciple Matthew mentioned in chapter 9. Modern scholars think it unlikely, however, that this Matthew in fact wrote the work. Whoever did so relied on earlier material, including that part of the New Testament called the *Book of Mark*.

3   And in those days comes John the Baptist, preaching in the wilderness of Judaea, saying, "Repent, for the kingdom of heaven is at hand." For this is he that was spoken of by Isaiah the prophet, saying, "The voice of one crying in the wilderness, make ready the way of the Lord, make his paths straight."[1] Now John himself had his raiment of camel's hair, and a leather belt about his loins, and his food was locusts and wild honey. Then Jerusalem, and all Judaea, and all the region round about Jordan went out to him, and they were baptized by him in the river Jordan, confessing their sins. But when he saw many of the Pharisees[2] and Sadducees[3] coming to his baptism, he said to them, "You offspring of vipers, who warned you to flee from the wrath to come? Bring forth therefore fruit worthy of repentance, and do not think to say within yourselves, 'We have Abraham[4] as our father,' for I say to you that God is able from these stones to raise up children to Abraham. And even now is the ax laid to the root of the trees; every tree therefore that does not bring forth good fruit is cut down, and cast into the fire. I indeed baptize you with water for repentance, but he that comes after me is mightier than I, whose shoes I am not worthy to bear; he shall baptize you with the Holy Ghost and with fire; his winnowing fan is in his hand, and he will thoroughly cleanse his threshing-floor, and he will gather his wheat into the garner, but the chaff he will burn up with unquenchable fire."

Then comes Jesus from Galilee to the Jordan to John, to be baptized by him. But John would have hindered him, saying, "I have need to be baptized by you, and you come to me?" But Jesus answering said to him, "Suffer me now, for thus it becomes us to fulfill all righteousness." Then he suffers him. And Jesus, when he was baptized, went up immediately from the water, and lo, the heavens were opened to him, and he saw the spirit of God descending as a dove, and com-

1   Old Testament, Isaiah 40.3.
2   A Jewish group which stressed strict adherence to the ritual Jewish law laid down in the Old Testament.
3   A Jewish group associated with the Temple and its priests.
4   The founder of the Hebrews.

ing upon him, and lo, a voice out of the heavens, saying, "This is my beloved son, in whom I am well pleased."

4     Then was Jesus led up by the Spirit into the wilderness to be tempted by the Devil. And when he had fasted 40 days and 40 nights, he afterward hungered. And the tempter came and said to him, "If you are the son of God, command that these stones become bread." But he answered and said, "It is written, 'Man shall not live by bread alone, but by every word that proceeds out of the mouth of God.'"[5] Then the devil took him into the holy city, and he set him on the pinnacle of the Temple,[6] and said to him, "If you are the son of God, cast yourself down: for it is written, 'He shall give his angels charge concerning you, and on their hands they shall bear you up, lest it should happen that you dash your foot against a stone.'"[7] Jesus said to him, "Again it is written, 'You shall not tempt the Lord your God.'"[8] Again, the Devil took him to an exceedingly high mountain, and showed him all the kingdoms of the world, and the glory of them, and he said to him, "All these things will I give you, if you will fall down and worship me." Then Jesus said to him, "Get you away, Satan, for it is written, 'You shall worship the Lord your God, and him only shall you serve.'"[9] Then the devil left him and behold, angels came and ministered to him.

Now when he heard that John was imprisoned, he withdrew into Galilee, and leaving Nazareth, he came and dwelled in Capernaum, which is by the sea, in the borders of Zebulun and Naphtali, that it might be fulfilled which was spoken by Isaiah the prophet, saying, "The land of Zebulun and the land of Naphtali, toward the sea, beyond Jordan, Galilee of the gentiles, the people which sat in darkness saw a great light, and to them which sat in the region and shadow of death, to them did light spring up."[10]

From that time Jesus began to preach, and to say,

"Repent, for the kingdom of heaven is at hand."

And walking by the sea of Galilee, he saw two brethren, Simon who is called Peter, and Andrew his brother, casting a net into the sea, for they were fishers. And he said to them, "Follow me, and I will make you fishers of men." And they immediately left the nets, and followed him. And going on from there he saw another two brethren, James the son of Zebedee, and John his brother, in the boat with Zebedee their father, mending their nets, and he called them. And they immediately left the boat and their father, and followed him.

And Jesus went about in all of Galilee, teaching in their synagogues,[11] and preaching the gospel of the kingdom, and healing all manner of disease and all manner of sickness among the people. And the report of him went forth into all Syria, and they brought to him all that were sick, afflicted with diverse diseases and torments, possessed with devils, and epileptic, and palsied; and he healed them. And there followed him great multitudes from Galilee and Decapolis and Jerusalem and Judaea and from beyond Jordan.

5     And seeing the multitudes, he went up into the mountain, and when he had sat down, his disciples came to him, and he opened his mouth and taught them, saying,

"Blessed are the humble in spirit, for theirs is the kingdom of heaven.

Blessed are they that mourn, for they shall be comforted.

Blessed are the meek, for they shall inherit the earth.

Blessed are they that hunger and thirst after righteousness, for they shall be satisfied.

Blessed are the merciful, for they shall obtain mercy.

Blessed are the pure in heart, for they shall see God.

---

5   Old Testament, Deuteronomy 8.3.
6   I.e., the Jewish temple, in Jerusalem.
7   Old Testament, Psalms 91.11,12.
8   Old Testament, Deuteronomy 6.16.
9   Old Testament, Deuteronomy 6.13.
10  Old Testament, Isaiah 9.1,2.
11  I.e., Jewish communities of worship.

Blessed are the peacemakers, for they shall be called sons of God.

Blessed are they that have been persecuted for righteousness' sake, for theirs is the kingdom of heaven.

Blessed are you when they shall reproach you, and persecute you, and say all manner of evil against you falsely, for my sake. Rejoice, and be exceedingly glad, for great is your reward in heaven, for they thus persecuted the prophets which were before you.

You are the salt of the earth. But if the salt has lost its savor, wherewith shall it be salted? It is thenceforth good for nothing, but to be cast out and trodden under foot of men.

You are the light of the world. A city set on a hill cannot be hidden. Neither do men light a lamp, and put it under the bushel, but on the stand, and it shines on all that are in the house. Even so let your light shine before men, that they may see your good works, and glorify your Father which is in heaven.

Do not think that I came to destroy the law or the prophets; I came not to destroy, but to fulfill. For truly I say to you, until heaven and earth pass away, one jot or one tittle shall in no way pass away from the law, until all things are accomplished. Whosoever therefore shall break one of these least commandments, and shall teach others to do so, shall be called least in the kingdom of heaven; but whosoever shall do and teach them, he shall be called great in the kingdom of heaven.

For I say to you that unless your righteousness shall exceed the righteousness of the scribes[12] and Pharisees, you shall in no way enter into the kingdom of heaven. You have heard that it was said to them of old, 'You shall not kill; and whosoever shall kill shall be in danger of the judgment.'[13] But I say to you that everyone who is angry with his brother shall be in danger of the judgment, and whosoever shall abuse his brother shall answer for it in court, and whosoev-

er shall say, 'You fool,' to him shall answer for it in the fire of hell. If therefore you are offering your gift at the altar, and there remember that your brother has anything against you, leave there your gift before the altar, and go your way, first be reconciled to your brother, and then come and offer your gift. Agree with your adversary quickly, while you are with him in the way, lest the adversary deliver you to the judge, and the judge deliver you to the officer, and you be cast into prison. Truly I say to you, you shall by no means come out thence until you have paid the last farthing. You have heard that it was said, 'You shall not commit adultery,'[14] but I say to you that every one that looks on a woman to lust after her has committed adultery with her already in his heart. And if your right eye causes you to stumble, pluck it out, and cast it from you, for it is profitable for you that one of your members should perish, and not your whole body be cast into hell. And if your right hand causes you to stumble, cut it off, and cast it from you, for it is profitable for you that one of your members should perish, and not your whole body go into hell. It was said also, 'Whosoever shall put away his wife, let him give her a writing of divorce,'[15] but I say to you, that everyone that puts away his wife, except for the cause of fornication, makes her an adulteress, and whosoever shall marry her when she is put away commits adultery. Again, you have heard that it was said to them of old, 'You shall not swear falsely, but shall perform your oaths to the Lord,'[16] but I say to you, swear not at all, neither by heaven, for it is the throne of God, nor by the earth, for it is the footstool of his feet, nor by Jerusalem, for it is the city of the great King; neither shall you swear by your head, for you cannot make one hair white or black. But let your speech be, 'Yes, yes; No, no,' and whatsoever is more than these is of the evil one. You have heard that it was said, 'An eye for an eye, and a tooth for a tooth,'[17] but I say to you, do not resist him that is evil, but whosoever smites

---

12   Highly educated experts in Jewish law.
13   Old Testament, Exodus 20.13. Only the first clause is to be found there.
14   Old Testament, Exodus 20.14.
15   Old Testament, Deuteronomy 24.1, Jeremiah 3.8, Malachi 2.14-16.
16   There is some confusion regarding this portion of the text.
17   Old Testament, Exodus 21.24, Leviticus 24.20, Deuteronomy 19.21.

you on your right cheek, turn to him the other also. And if any man would go to law with you, and take away your coat, let him have your cloak also. And whosoever shall compel you to go one mile, go with him two. Give to him that asks you, and do not turn away from him that would borrow from you. You have heard that it was said, 'You shall love your neighbor, and hate your enemy,'[18] but I say to you, love your enemies, and pray for them that persecute you, that you may be sons of your Father which is in heaven, for he makes his sun rise on the evil and the good, and sends rain on the just and the unjust. For if you love them that love you, what reward have you? Do not even the publicans[19] do the same? And if you salute your brethren only, what do you do more than others? Do not even the gentiles do the same? You therefore shall be perfect, as your heavenly Father is perfect.

6  Take heed that you do not do your righteousness before men, to be seen by them, or else you have no reward with your Father which is in heaven. When therefore you do alms, do not sound a trumpet before you, as the hypocrites do in the synagogues and in the streets, that they may have glory from men. Truly I say to you, they have received their reward. But when you do alms, do not let your left hand know what your right hand does, that your alms may be in secret, and your Father which sees in secret shall recompense you. And when you pray, you shall not be as the hypocrites, for they love to stand and pray in the synagogues and in the corners of the streets, that they may be seen by men. Truly I say to you, they have received their reward. But you, when you pray, enter into your inner chamber, and having shut your door, pray to your Father which is in secret, and your Father which sees in secret shall recompense you. And in praying do not use vain repetitions, as the gentiles do, for they think that they shall be heard for their much speaking. Do not therefore be like them, for your Father knows what things you need before you ask him. Therefore pray after this manner:

Our Father which are in heaven,
Hallowed be your name,
Your kingdom come,
Your will be done,
As in heaven, so on earth.
Give us this day
Our daily bread.
And forgive us our debts,
As we also have forgiven our debtors.
And bring us not into temptation,
But deliver us from the evil one.

For if you forgive others their trespasses, your heavenly Father will also forgive you. But if you do not forgive others their trespasses, neither will your Father forgive your trespasses. Moreover when you fast, do not be, as the hypocrites, of a sad countenance, for they disfigure their faces, that they may be seen by others to fast. Truly I say to you, they have received their reward. But you, when you fast, anoint your head, and wash your face, that you not be seen by men to fast, but by your Father which is in secret, and your Father, which sees in secret, shall recompense you.

Do not lay up for yourselves treasures upon the earth, where moth and rust consume, and where thieves break through and steal, but lay up for yourselves treasures in heaven, where neither moth nor rust consumes, and where thieves do not break through or steal.

For where your treasure is, there will your heart be also. The lamp of the body is the eye; if therefore your eye is good, your whole body shall be full of light, but if your eye is evil, your whole body shall be full of darkness. If therefore the light that is in you is darkness, how great is the darkness! No man can serve two masters, for either he will hate the one, and love the other, or else he will hold to one, and despise the other. You cannot serve God and mammon.[20] Therefore I say to you, do not be anxious for your life, what you shall eat, or what you shall drink; nor yet for your body, what you shall put on. Is not the life more than the

18  The first clause is from Old Testament, Leviticus 19.18.
19  In the Roman world, public contractors, most usually ones who collected taxes.
20  I.e., wealth.

food, and the body than the raiment? Behold the birds of the heavens, that they do not sow, neither do they reap nor gather into barns, and your heavenly Father feeds them. Are you not of much more value than they? And which of you by being anxious can add one cubit to his stature? And why are you anxious concerning raiment? Consider the lilies of the field, how they grow: they do not toil, neither do they spin; yet I say to you, that even Solomon[21] in all his glory was not arrayed like one of these. But if God so clothes the grass of the field, which today is, and tomorrow is cast into the oven, shall he not much more clothe you, O you of little faith? Therefore do not be anxious, saying, 'What shall we eat?' or 'What shall we drink?' or, 'Wherewithal shall we be clothed?'—for after all these things the Gentiles seek—for your heavenly Father knows that you have need of all these things. But seek first his kingdom, and his righteousness, and all these things shall be added to you. Do not therefore be anxious for the morrow, for the morrow will be anxious for itself. Sufficient to the day is the evil thereof.

7   Do not judge, that you not be judged. For with what judgment you judge, you shall be judged, and with what measure you use, it shall be measured to you. And why do you behold the mote that is in your brother's eye, but not consider the beam that is in your own eye? Or how will you say to your brother, 'Let me cast out the mote out of your eye,' and lo, the beam is in your own eye? You hypocrite, cast out first the beam out of your own eye, and then shall you see clearly to cast out the mote out of your brother's eye. Do not give that which is holy to the dogs, neither cast your pearls before the swine, lest they trample them under their feet, and turn and rend you. Ask, and it shall be given you;

   Seek, and you shall find;
   Knock, and it shall be opened to you,
   For everyone that asks receives,
   And he that seeks finds,
   And to him that knocks it shall be opened.

   Or what man is there of you, who, if his son shall ask him for a loaf, will give him a stone; or if he shall ask for a fish, will give him a serpent? If you then,

being evil, know how to give good gifts to your children, how much more shall your Father which is in heaven give good things to them that ask him?

   All things therefore whatsoever you would that others should do to you, even so do also to them, for this is the law and the prophets.

   Enter in by the narrow gate. For wide is the gate, and broad is the way that leads to destruction, and many are they that enter in thereby. For narrow is the gate, and straitened the way, that leads to life, and few are they that find it.

   Beware of false prophets, which come to you in sheep's clothing, but inwardly are ravening wolves. By their fruits you shall know them. Do men gather grapes of thorns, or figs of thistles? Even so every good tree brings forth good fruit, but the corrupt tree brings forth evil fruit. A good tree cannot bring forth evil fruit, neither can a corrupt tree bring forth good fruit. Every tree that does not bring forth good fruit is cut down, and cast into the fire. Therefore by their fruits you shall know them.

   Not everyone that says to me, 'Lord, Lord,' shall enter into the kingdom of heaven, but he that does the will of my Father which is in heaven. Many will say to me in that day, 'Lord, Lord, did we not prophesy by your name, and by your name cast out devils, and by your name do many mighty works?' And then will I profess to them, 'I never knew you; depart from me, you that work iniquity.' Everyone therefore which hears these words of mine, and does them, shall be likened to a wise man, which built his house upon the rock; the rain descended, and the floods came, and the winds blew, and beat upon that house, and it did not fall, for it was founded upon the rock. And everyone that hears these words of mine, and does not do them, shall be likened to a foolish man, which built his house upon the sand; the rain descended, and the floods came, and the winds blew, and smote upon that house, and it fell, and great was its fall."

   And it came to pass, when Jesus ended these words, the multitudes were astonished at his teaching, for he taught them as one having authority, and not as their scribes.

---

21   One of the most powerful of the Hebrew kings.

8   And when he had come down from the mountain, great multitudes followed him. And behold, there came to him a leper and worshipped him, saying, "Lord, if you will it, you can make me clean." And he stretched forth his hand, and touched him, saying, "I will it; be made clean." And immediately his leprosy was cleansed. And Jesus said to him, "See you tell no man, but go your way, show yourself to the priest, and offer the gift that Moses commanded, for a testimony to them."

And when he was entered into Capernaum, there came to him a centurion,[22] beseeching him, and saying, "Lord, my servant lies in the house sick with the palsy, grievously tormented." And he said to him, "I will come and heal him." And the centurion answered and said, "Lord, I am not worthy that you should come under my roof, but only say the word, and my servant shall be healed. For I also am a man under authority, having under myself soldiers, and I say to this one, 'Go,' and he goes, and to another, 'Come,' and he comes, and to my servant, 'Do this,' and he does it." And when Jesus heard it, he marvelled, and said to them that followed, "Truly I say to you, I have not found so great faith, no, not in Israel. And I say to you that many shall come from the east and the west, and shall sit down with Abraham, and Isaac, and Jacob, in the kingdom of heaven, but the sons of the kingdom[23] shall be cast forth into the outer darkness; there shall be the weeping and gnashing of teeth." And Jesus said to the centurion, "Go your way; as you have believed, so let it be done to you." And the servant was healed in that hour.

And when Jesus had come into Peter's house, he saw his wife's mother lying sick with a fever. And he touched her hand, and the fever left her, and she arose, and ministered to him. And when evening had come, they brought to him many possessed with devils, and he cast out the spirits with a word, and healed all that were sick, that it might be fulfilled which was spoken by Isaiah the prophet, saying, "He himself took our infirmities, and bore our diseases."[24]

Now when Jesus saw great multitudes about him, he gave commandment to depart to the other side. And there came a scribe, and said to him, "Master, I will follow you whithersoever you go." And Jesus said to him, "The foxes have holes, and the birds of the heaven have nests, but the son of man has nowhere to lay his head." And another of the disciples said to him, "Lord, suffer me first to go and bury my father." But Jesus said to him, "Follow me, and leave the dead to bury their own dead."

And when he had entered into a boat, his disciples followed him. And behold, there arose a great tempest in the sea, insomuch that the boat was covered with the waves, but he was asleep. And they came to him, and awoke him, saying, "Save us, Lord; we are perishing." And he said to them, "Why are you fearful, O you of little faith?" Then he arose, and rebuked the winds and the sea, and there was a great calm. And the men marvelled, saying, "What manner of man is this, that even the winds and the sea obey him?"

And when he had come to the other side into the country of the Gadarenes, there met him two possessed with devils, coming forth out of the tombs, exceedingly fierce, so that no man could pass by that way. And behold, they cried out, saying, "What have we to do with you, you son of God? Have you come hither to torment us before the time?" Now there was far off from them a herd of many swine feeding. And the devils besought him, saying, "If you cast us out, send us away into the herd of swine." And he said to them, "Go." And they came out, and went into the swine, and behold, the whole herd rushed down the steep into the sea, and perished in the waters. And they that fed them fled, and went away into the city, and told everything, and what had befallen them that were possessed with devils. And behold, all the city came out to meet Jesus, and when they saw him, they besought him that he would depart from their borders.

9   And he entered into a boat, and crossed over, and came into his own city. And behold, they brought to

---

22   A kind of Roman military officer.
23   I.e., of Israel.
24   Old Testament, Isaiah 53.4.

him a man sick with paralysis, lying on a bed, and Jesus, seeing their faith, said to the one sick with the palsy, "Son, be of good cheer; your sins are forgiven." And behold, certain of the scribes said within themselves, "This man blasphemes." And Jesus, knowing their thoughts, said, "Wherefore do you think evil in your hearts? For which is easier, to say, 'Your sins are forgiven' or to say, 'Arise, and walk'? But that you may know that the son of man has power on earth to forgive sins," then he said to the sick with paralysis, "Arise, and take up your bed, and go to your house." And he arose, and departed to his house. But when the multitudes saw it, they were afraid, and glorified God, which had given such power to men.

And as Jesus passed by from there, he saw a man, called Matthew, sitting at the place of taxes, and he said to him, "Follow me." And he arose, and followed him. And it came to pass, as he sat at the table in the house, behold, many publicans and sinners came and sat down with Jesus and his disciples. And when the Pharisees saw it, they said to his disciples, "Why does your master eat with the publicans and sinners?" But when he heard it, he said, "They that are whole have no need of a physician, but they that are sick do. But go and learn what this means, I desire mercy, and not sacrifice, for I came not to call the righteous, but sinners."

Then the disciples of John come to him, saying, "Why do we and the Pharisees fast often, but your disciples do not fast?" And Jesus said to them, "Can the sons of the bridechamber mourn, as long as the bridegroom is with them? But the days will come when the bridegroom shall be taken away from them, and then they will fast. And no man puts a piece of undressed cloth upon an old garment, for that which should fill it up takes from the garment, and a worse rent is made. Neither do they put new wine into old wineskins, else the skins burst, and the wine is spilled and

the skins perish, but they put new wine into fresh wine-skins, and both are preserved."

While he spoke these things to them, behold, there came a ruler, and worshipped him, saying, "My daughter is even now dead; but come and lay your hand upon her, and she shall live." And Jesus arose, and followed him, and so did his disciples. And behold, a woman, who had had a flow of blood for 12 years, came behind him, and touched the border of his garment, for she said within herself, "If I but touch his garment, I shall be made whole." But Jesus turning and seeing her said, "Daughter, be of good cheer; your faith has made you whole." And the woman was made whole from that hour. And when Jesus came into the ruler's house, and saw the flute-players, and the crowd making a tumult, he said, "Make way, for the damsel is not dead, but sleeps." And they laughed him to scorn. But when the crowd was put forth, he entered, and took her by the hand, and the damsel arose. And the fame hereof went forth into all that land.

And as Jesus passed by from there, two blind men followed him, crying out, and saying, "Have mercy on us, you son of David."[25] And when he had come into the house the blind men came to him, and Jesus said to them, "Do you believe that I am able to do this?" They said to him, "Yes, Lord." Then he touched their eyes, saying, "According to your faith let it be done to you." And their eyes were opened. And Jesus sternly charged them, saying, "See that no man knows it." But they went forth, and spread abroad his fame in all that land.

And as they went forth, behold, there was brought to him a dumb man possessed with a devil. And when the devil was cast out, the dumb man spoke, and the multitudes marvelled, saying, "It was never so seen in Israel." But the Pharisees said, "By the prince of the devils he casts out devils." ...

25  I.e., the Hebrew King David.

# 23

# JOHN, *BOOK OF REVELATION 15–20*

Written at various times *c.* 60-100, the *Book of Revelation* makes up part of the Christian sacred texts known to Christians as the New Testament in their Bible. Although the author gives his name (John), this information helps little in identifying him. In the work, John states that he had received a series of visions of things which would soon occur. He introduces them by saying that these things were shown to him by an angel, who was acting as an agent of Jesus, who had received the revelation from God. When chapter 15 opens, John has already recounted a series of remarkable visions concerning the future.

---

15   And I saw another sign in heaven, great and marvellous, <u>seven angels having seven plagues,</u> which are the last, for in them is finished the wrath of God.

   And I saw as it were a glassy sea mingled with fire, and them that come victorious from the beast,[1] and from his image, and from the number of his name, standing by the glassy sea, having harps of God. And they sing the song of Moses the servant of God,[2] and the song of the Lamb,[3] saying,

Great and marvelous are your works, O Lord God, the Almighty;
Righteous and true are your ways, you King of the ages.
Who shall not fear, O Lord,
And glorify your name?
For only you are holy,

For all the nations shall come and worship before you,
For your righteous acts have been made manifest.

   And after these things I looked, and the temple of the tabernacle of the testimony in heaven was opened, and there came out from the temple the seven angels that had the seven plagues, arrayed with precious stone, pure and bright, and with golden bands girt about their breasts. And one of the four living creatures gave to the seven angels seven golden bowls full of the wrath of God, who lives forever and ever. And the temple was filled with smoke from the glory of God, and from his power, and none was able to enter into the temple, until the seven plagues of the seven angels should be finished.

16   And I heard a great voice out of the temple, saying to the seven angels, "Go, and pour out the seven bowls of the wrath of God into the earth."

---

1   Identified with the devil.
2   Who led the Hebrews out of captivity in Egypt and received the Hebrew law from God (Old Testament, Exodus).
3   I.e., Jesus.

And the first went, and poured out his bowl into the earth, and it became a noisome and grievous sore upon the men which had the mark of the beast,[4] and which worshipped his image.

And the second poured out his bowl into the sea, and it became blood as of a corpse, and every living soul died, even the things that were in the sea.

And the third poured out his bowl into the rivers and the fountains of the waters, and it became blood. And I heard the angel of the waters saying, "You, which are and which was, are righteous, you Holy One, because you did thus judge, for they poured out the blood of saints and prophets, and blood you have given them to drink; they are worthy." And I heard the altar saying, "Yea, O Lord God, the Almighty, true and righteous are your judgments."

And the fourth poured out his bowl upon the sun, and it was given to it to scorch men with fire. And they were scorched with great heat, and they blasphemed the name of the God which had the power over these plagues, and they did not repent to give him glory.

And the fifth poured out his bowl upon the throne of the beast, and his kingdom was darkened, and they gnawed their tongues for pain, and they blasphemed the God of heaven because of their pains and their sores, and they did not repent of their works.

And the sixth poured out his bowl upon the great river, the river Euphrates, and the water thereof was dried up, that the way might be made ready for the kings that come from where the sun rises. And I saw coming out of the mouth of the dragon, and out of the mouth of the beast, and out of the mouth of the false prophet, three unclean spirits, as it were frogs, for they are spirits of devils, working signs, which go forth to the kings of the whole world, to gather them together to the war of the great day of God, the Almighty.

Behold, I come as a thief.

Blessed is he that watches, and keeps his garments, Lest he walk naked, and they see his shame.

And they gathered them together into the place which is called in Hebrew "Armageddon."

And the seventh poured out his bowl upon the air, and there came forth a great voice out of the temple, from the throne, saying, "It is done," and there were lightning and voices and thunder, and there was a great earthquake, such as was not since humanity was upon the earth, so great an earthquake, so mighty. And the great city was divided into three parts, and the cities of the nations fell, and Babylon the great was remembered in the sight of God, to give to her the cup of the wine of the fierceness of his wrath. And every island fled away, and the mountains were not found. And great hail, every stone about the weight of a talent, came down out of heaven upon men, and they cursed God because of the plague of the hail, for the plague thereof was exceedingly great.

17 And there came one of the seven angels that had the seven bowls, and spoke with me, saying, "Come hither, I will show you the judgment of the great harlot that sits upon many waters, with whom the kings of the earth committed fornication, and they that dwell in the earth were made drunk with the wine of her fornication." And he carried me away in the Spirit into a wilderness, and I saw a woman sitting upon a scarlet-colored beast, full of names of blasphemy, having seven heads and ten horns. And the woman was arrayed in purple and scarlet, and decked with gold and precious stone and pearls, having in her hand a golden cup full of abominations, even the unclean thing of her fornication, and upon her forehead a name written: "Mystery, Babylon the Great, Mother of Harlots and of the Abominations of the Earth."

And I saw the woman drunk with the blood of the saints, and with the blood of the martyrs of Jesus. And when I saw her, I wondered with a great wonder. And the angel said to me, "Wherefore did you wonder? I will tell you the mystery of the woman, and of the beast that carries her, which has the seven heads and the ten horns. The beast that you saw was, and is not, and is about to come up out of the abyss, and to go into perdition. And they that dwell on the earth shall wonder, they whose names have not been written in the book of life from the foundation of the world, when they behold the beast, how that he was, and is not, and shall come. Here is the mind which has wisdom. The seven heads are seven mountains, on which

4 Identified with the devil.

the woman sits,[5] and they are seven kings; the five are fallen, the one is, the other has not yet come; and when he comes, he must continue a little while. And the beast that was, and is not, is himself also an eighth, and is of the seven, and he goes into perdition. And the ten horns that you saw are ten kings, which have received no kingdom as yet; but they receive authority as kings, with the beast, for one hour. These have one mind, and they give their power and authority to the beast. These shall war against the Lamb, and the Lamb shall overcome them, for he is Lord of lords, and King of kings, and they also shall overcome that are with him, called and chosen and faithful." And he said to me, "The waters which you saw, where the harlot sits, are peoples, and multitudes, and nations, and tongues. And the ten horns which you saw, and the beast, these shall hate the harlot, and shall make her desolate and naked, and shall eat her flesh, and shall burn her utterly with fire. For God did put in their hearts to do his mind, and to come to one mind, and to give their kingdom to the beast, until the words of God should be accomplished. And the woman whom you saw is the great city which reigns over the kings of the earth."

18   After these things I saw another angel coming down out of heaven, having great authority, and the earth was lit with his glory. And he cried with a mighty voice, saying, "Fallen, fallen has Babylon the great, and has become a habitation of devils, and a hold of every unclean spirit, and a hold of every unclean and hateful bird. For by the wine of the wrath of her fornication all the nations have fallen, and the kings of the earth committed fornication with her, and the merchants of the earth waxed rich by the power of her wantonness."

And I heard another voice from heaven, saying, "Come forth, my people, out of her, that you have no fellowship with her sins, and that you receive nothing of her plagues, for her sins have reached even to heaven, and God has remembered her iniquities. Render to her even as she rendered, and double to her the double according to her works; in the cup which she min-

gled,[6] mingle double for her. Howevermuch she glorified herself, and waxed wanton, so much give her of torment and mourning, for she said in her heart, 'I sit as a queen, and am no widow, and shall in no way see mourning.' Therefore in one day shall her plagues come—death, and mourning, and famine, and she shall be utterly burned with fire, for strong is the Lord God which judged her. And the kings of the earth, who committed fornication and lived wantonly with her, shall weep and wail over her, when they look upon the smoke of her burning, standing far off for the fear of her torment, saying, 'Woe, woe, the great city, Babylon, the strong city! For in one hour has your judgment come.' And the merchants of the earth weep and mourn over her, for no one buys their merchandise any more—merchandise of gold, and silver, and precious stone, and pearls, and fine linen, and purple, and silk, and scarlet; and all kinds of citron wood, and every vessel of ivory, and every vessel made of most precious wood, and of brass, and iron, and marble; and cinnamon, and spice, and incense, and ointment, and frankincense, and wine, and oil, and fine flour, and wheat, and cattle, and sheep; and merchandise of horses and chariots and slaves; and souls of men. And the fruits which your soul lusted after have gone from you, and all things that were dainty and sumptuous have gone from you, and you shall find them no more at all. The merchants of these things, who were made rich by her, shall stand far off for the fear of her torment, weeping and mourning, saying, 'Woe; woe, the great city, she that was arrayed in fine linen and purple and scarlet, and decked with gold and precious stone and pearls! For in one hour so great riches are made desolate.' And every shipmaster, and everyone that sails anywhere, and mariners, and as many as gain their living by sea, stood far off, and cried out as they looked upon the smoke of her burning, saying, 'What city is like the great city?' And they cast dust on their heads, and cried, weeping and mourning, saying, 'Woe, woe, the great city, wherein were made rich all that had their ships in the sea by reason of her costliness! For in one hour she is made desolate.' Rejoice

---

5   Babylon was very much an enemy city for the Hebrews in the Old Testament; the city of Rome sat on seven hills.
6   Wine was generally drunk mixed with water in the ancient world.

over her, you heaven, and you saints, and you apostles, and you prophets, for God has judged your judgment on her."

And a strong angel took up a stone as it were a great millstone, and cast it into the sea, saying, "Thus with a mighty fall shall Babylon, the great city, be cast down, and shall be found no more at all. And the voice of harpers and minstrels and flute players and trumpeters shall be heard no more at all in you; and no craftsman, of whatsoever craft, shall be found any more at all in you; and the voice of a millstone shall be heard no more at all in you; and the light of a lamp shall shine no more at all in you; and the voice of the bridegroom and of the bride shall be heard no more at all in you, for your merchants were the princes of the earth, for with your sorcery were all the nations deceived. And in her was found the blood of prophets and of saints, and of all that have been slain upon the earth."

19    After these things I heard as it were a great voice of a great multitude in heaven, saying, "Hallelujah; salvation, and glory, and power belong to our God, for true and righteous are his judgments, for he has judged the great harlot, which corrupted the earth with her fornication, and he has avenged the blood of his servants at her hand." And a second time they say, "Hallelujah." And her smoke goes up forever and ever. And the four and twenty elders and the four living creatures fell down and worshipped God that sits on the throne saying, "Amen; Hallelujah."

And a voice came forth from the throne, saying, "Give praise to our God, all you his servants, you that fear him, the small and the great." And I heard as it were the voice of a great multitude, and as the voice of many waters, and as the voice of mighty thunder, saying, "Hallelujah, for the Lord our God, the Almighty, reigns. Let us rejoice and be exceedingly glad, and let us give the glory to him, for the marriage of the Lamb has come, and his wife has made herself ready. And it was given to her that she should array herself in fine linen, bright and pure, for the fine linen is the righteous acts of the saints."

And he said to me, "Write, 'Blessed are they which are bidden to the marriage supper of the Lamb.'" And he said to me, "These are true words of God." And I fell down before his feet to worship him. And he said

to me, "See that you do not do it; I am a fellow-servant with you and with your brethren that hold the testimony of Jesus. Worship God, for the testimony of Jesus is the spirit of prophecy."

And I saw heaven opened, and behold, a white horse, and he that sat thereon, called, "Faithful and True," and in righteousness he judges and makes war. And his eyes are a flame of fire, and upon his head are many crowns, and he has a written name, which no one knows but he himself. And he is arrayed in a garment sprinkled with blood, and his name is called the Word of God. And the armies which are in heaven followed him upon white horses, clothed in fine linen, white and pure. And out of his mouth proceeds a sharp sword, that with it he should smite the nations, and he shall rule them with a rod of iron, and he treads the winepress of the fierceness of the wrath of Almighty God. And he has on his garment and on his thigh a written name, "King of kings and Lord of lords."

And I saw an angel standing in the sun, and he cried with a loud voice, saying to all the birds that fly in mid-heaven, "Come and be gathered together to the great supper of God, that you may eat the flesh of kings, and the flesh of captains, and the flesh of mighty men, and the flesh of horses and of them that sit thereon, and the flesh of all men, both free and slave, and small and great."

And I saw the beast, and the kings of the earth, and their armies, gathered together to make war against him that sat upon the horse, and against his army. And the beast was taken, and with him the false prophet that wrought the signs in his sight, wherewith he deceived them that had received the mark of the beast, and them that worshipped his image, they both were cast alive into the lake of fire that burns with brimstone, and the rest were killed with the sword of him that sat upon the horse, even the sword which came forth out of his mouth, and all the birds were filled with their flesh.

20    And I saw an angel coming down out of heaven, having the key of the abyss and a great chain in his hand. And he laid hold of the dragon, the old serpent, which is the Devil and Satan, and bound him for a thousand years, and cast him into the abyss, and shut it, and sealed it over him, that he should deceive the nations no more, until the thousand years should

be finished; after this he must he loosed for a little time.

And I saw thrones, and they sat upon them, and judgment was given to them, and I saw the souls of them that had been beheaded for the testimony of Jesus, and for the word of God, and such as had not worshipped the beast, nor his image, and had not received the mark upon their forehead and upon their hand; they lived, and reigned with Christ a thousand years. The rest of the dead did not live until the thousand years should be finished. This is the first resurrection. Blessed and holy is he that has part in the first resurrection; over these the second death has no power, but they shall be priests of God and of Christ, and shall reign with him a thousand years.

And when the thousand years are finished, Satan shall be loosed out of his prison, and shall come forth to deceive the nations which are in the four corners of the earth, Gog and Magog, to gather them together to the war, the number of whom is as the sand of the sea. And they went up over the breadth of the earth, and compassed the camp of the saints about, and the beloved city, and fire came down out of heaven, and devoured them. And the devil that deceived them was cast into the lake of fire and brimstone, where are also the beast and the false prophet, and they shall be tormented day and night forever and ever.

And I saw a great white throne, and him that sat upon it, from whose face the earth and the heaven fled away, and there was found no place for them. And I saw the dead, the great and the small, standing before the throne, and books were opened, and another book was opened, which is the book of life, and the dead were judged out of the things which were written in the books, according to their works. And the sea gave up the dead which were in it, and death and Hades[7] gave up the dead which were in them, and they were judged, each according to their works. And death and Hades were cast into the lake of fire. This is the second death, even the lake of fire. And anyone not found written in the book of life was cast into the lake of fire.

---

7  In Greek tradition, the god of the dead, sometimes also used to refer to the place where the dead reside.

# 24

# PERPETUA AND OTHERS, *THE MARTYRDOM OF SAINT PERPETUA*

*The Martyrdom of Saint Perpetua*, which actually describes several martyrs' deaths, presents itself as a composite text, written by at least three people—Perpetua herself, Saturus, and some unknown Christian. The martyrdoms it recounts took place at Carthage, in Roman North Africa, in 203.

---

If ancient illustrations of faith which both testify to God's grace and tend to humanity's edification are collected in writing, so that by their being read, as though the deeds had been revived, may honor God and strengthen humanity, why should not new instances also be collected, that shall be equally suitable for both purposes? Indeed, these modern examples will one day become ancient and necessary for posterity, although in their present time they are esteemed of less authority, by reason of the presumed veneration for antiquity. But if they judge the one power of the Holy Spirit according to the times and seasons, let them see to it, since some things of later date must be esteemed greater because they are nearer to the very last times, in accordance with the exuberance of grace shown to the final periods determined for the world. For "in the last days, says the Lord, I will pour out my Spirit upon all flesh, and their sons and their daughters shall prophesy. And upon my servants and my handmaidens I will pour out of my Spirit, and your young men shall see visions, and your old men shall dream

dreams."[1] And thus we—who both acknowledge and revere modern visions, just as we do modern prophecies, as equally promised to us, and consider the other powers of the Holy Spirit as an agency of the Church for which also He was sent, administering all gifts in all, even as the Lord distributed to everyone as well—needfully collect them in writing, and, in reading them, commemorate them to God's glory, so that no weakness or despondency of faith may suppose that divine grace was among only the ancients, whether respecting martyrs or revelations; God always carries into effect what He has promised, as testimony to unbelievers and as a benefit to believers. And we therefore declare also to you, brethren and little children, what we have heard and handled so that those of you who were concerned in these matters may be reminded of them again to the glory of the Lord, and that those of you who know them by report may have communion with the blessed martyrs, and through them with the Lord Jesus Christ, to whom be glory and honor, for ever and ever. Amen.

---

1  Old Testament, Joel 2.28, 29.

The young catechumens,[2] Revocatus and his fellow-slave Felicitas, Saturninus and Secundulus, were apprehended. And among them also was Vivia Perpetua, nobly born, liberally educated, married honorably, having a father and mother and two brothers, one of whom, like herself, was a catechumen, and an infant son at the breast. She herself was about 22 years of age. From this point onward she shall herself narrate the whole course of her martyrdom, as she left it described by her own hand and with her own mind.

"While," she says, "we were still with the persecutors, and my father, for the sake of his affection for me, was trying to turn me away, and to cast me down from the faith, I said, 'Father, do you see, let us say, this vessel lying here to be a little pitcher, or something else?' And he said, 'I see it to be so.' And I replied to him, 'Can it be called by any name other than what it is?' And he said, 'No.' 'So neither can I call myself anything else than what I am—a Christian.' Then my father, provoked at this word 'Christian,' threw himself upon me, as if he would tear my eyes out. But he only annoyed me, and went away overcome by the devil's arguments. Then, in a few days after I had been without my father, I gave thanks to the Lord, and his absence became a source of consolation to me. In that same interval of a few days we were baptized, and to me the Spirit declared that after the water of baptism I should seek nothing else except for bodily endurance. After a few days we are taken into the dungeon, and I was very much afraid, because I had never felt such darkness. O terrible day! O the fierce heat because of the crowds! O harsh handling by the soldiers! I was very unusually distressed by my anxiety for my infant. Present there Tertius and Pomponius, the blessed deacons who ministered to us, and had arranged by means of a gratuity that we might be refreshed by being sent out for a few hours into a pleasanter part of the prison. Then going out of the dungeon, all attended to their own needs. I suckled my child, which was now feeble with hunger.[3] In my anxiety for it, I addressed my mother and comforted my brother, and commended my son to their care. I

was languishing because I had seen them languishing on my account. I suffered such cares for many days, and I obtained leave for my infant to remain in the prison with me, and immediately I grew strong and was relieved from distress and anxiety about my infant, and the prison became like a palace to me, so that I preferred being there to being elsewhere.

"Then my brother said to me, 'My dear sister, you are already in a position of great honor, such that you may ask for a vision, and that it may be made known to you whether this is to result in passion[4] or escape.' And I, who knew that I was privileged to converse with the Lord, for whom I had suffered so much, confidently promised him, and said, 'Tomorrow I will tell you.' And I asked, and this was what was shown me: I saw a marvelously high golden ladder, reaching up even to heaven, and very narrow, so that persons could only ascend it one by one, and on the sides of the ladder was fixed every kind of iron weapon. There were swords, lances, hooks, and daggers, so that anyone going up carelessly, or not looking upwards, would be torn to pieces, and the flesh would cleave to the iron weapons. And under the ladder itself crouched a dragon of wondrous size, who lay in wait for those who ascended, and frightened them from the ascent. And Saturus, who had subsequently delivered himself up freely on our account (not having been present at the time that we were taken prisoners) went up first. And he reached the top of the ladder, and turned towards me, and said to me, 'Perpetua, I am waiting for you; but be careful that the dragon does not bite you.' And I said, 'In the name of the Lord Jesus Christ, he shall not hurt me.' And from under the ladder itself, as if in fear of me, the dragon slowly lifted up his head, and as I trod upon the first step, I trod upon his head. And I went up, and I saw an immense extent of garden and, in the midst of the garden, a tall, white-haired man sitting in the dress of a shepherd, milking sheep, and many thousand white-robed ones were standing around. And he raised his head, and looked at me, and said to me, 'Child, you are welcome here.' And he called me, and he gave me as it were a little

---

2  People in their period of instruction as Christians.
3  Her baby seems not have been with her the whole time, but brought to her now.
4  That is, suffering and martyrdom.

piece[5] from the milk as he was milking, and I received it with joined hands, and I ate it, and all who stood around said 'Amen.' And at the sound of their voices I was awakened, still tasting a sweetness which I cannot describe. And I immediately related this to my brother, and we understood that it was to be a passion, and we ceased henceforth to have any hope in this world.

"After a few days there prevailed a report that we were to be examined. And then my father came to me from the city, worn out with anxiety. He came up to me, so he might cast me down, saying, 'Have pity, my daughter, on my gray hairs. Have pity on your father, if I am worthy to be called a father by you. If with these hands I have brought you up to this flower of your time, if I have preferred you to all your brothers, do not deliver me up to the scorn of men. Have regard to your brothers, have regard to your mother and your aunt, have regard to your son, who will not be able to live after you. Lay aside your courage, and do not bring us all to destruction; for none of us will speak freely if you should suffer anything.' My father said these things in his affection, kissing my hands, and throwing himself at my feet, and with tears he called me not 'Daughter,' but 'Lady.' And I grieved over my father's gray hairs, that he alone of all my family would not rejoice over my passion. And I comforted him, saying, 'Whatever God wills to happen on that scaffold will happen. For know that we are not in our own power, but in that of God.' And he departed from me in sorrow.

"Another day, while we were at dinner, we were suddenly taken away to be heard, and we arrived at the forum. At once the rumor spread through the neighborhood of the forum, and an immense number of people were gathered together. We mounted the platform. The rest were interrogated, and confessed. Then they came to me, and my father immediately appeared with my boy, and withdrew me from the step, and said in a supplicating tone, 'Have pity on your baby.' And the acting governor, Hilarianus, who had just received the power of life and death in the place of the deceased governor, Minucius Timinianus,

said, 'Spare the gray hairs of your father, spare the infancy of your boy, offer sacrifice for the well-being of the emperors.' And I replied, 'I will not do so.' Hilarianus said, 'Are you a Christian?' And I replied, 'I am a Christian.' And as my father stood there to cast me down from that faith, he was ordered by Hilarianus to be thrown down, and was struck with a rod. And my father's misfortune grieved me as if I myself had been beaten, I so grieved for his wretched old age. The governor then passed judgment on all of us, and condemned us to the wild beasts, and we cheerfully went down to the prison. Then, because my child had been used to suckling from me, and to stay with me in the prison, I sent Pomponius the deacon to my father to ask for the infant, but my father would not give him. And even as God willed it, the child no long desired my breasts, nor did my breasts cause me uneasiness, lest I should be tormented by care for my baby and by the pain of my breasts at the same time.

"After a few days, while we were all praying, a word suddenly came to me in the middle of our prayer, and I spoke the name of Dinocrates; I was amazed that that name had never come into my mind until then, and I was grieved as I remembered his misfortune. And I felt myself immediately to be worthy, and to be called on to ask on his behalf. And I began earnestly to make supplication, and to cry with groaning to the Lord on his behalf. Without delay, on that very night, I was shown this vision: I saw Dinocrates going out from a gloomy place, where also there were several others, and he was parched and very thirsty, with a filthy countenance and pallid color, and the wound on his face which he had when he died. This Dinocrates had been my brother in the flesh, seven years old, who died miserably of disease, his face being so eaten out with cancer that his death caused loathing to all. I then prayed for him, and between us there was a large space, so that neither of us could approach to the other. And moreover, in the same place where Dinocrates was, there was a pool full of water, whose rim was higher than the height of the boy, and Dinocrates raised himself up as if to drink. And I was grieved that, although that pool held water,

---

5   I.e., cheese, it seems.

still, on account of the height to its rim, he could not drink. And I woke up, and knew that my brother was in suffering. But I trusted that my prayer would bring help to his suffering; and I prayed for him every day until we passed over into the prison of the camp, for we were to fight in the camp-show. Then was the birthday of Geta Caesar, and I prayed for my brother day and night, groaning and weeping that he might be granted to me.

"Then, on the day on which we remained in fetters, I was shown this vision: I saw that that place which I had formerly observed to be in gloom was now bright; and Dinocrates, well clad with a clean body, refreshed. And where there had been a wound, I saw a scar; and that pool which I had seen before, I now saw with its margin lowered even to the boy's navel. And one could draw water from the pool unceasingly, and upon its rim was a goblet filled with water; and Dinocrates drew near and began to drink from it, and the goblet did not fail. And when he was satisfied, he went away from the water to play joyously, in the manner of children, and I awoke. Then I understood that he had been transferred from the place of punishment.

"Again, after a few days, Pudens, a soldier and assistant overseer of the prison, who began to regard us in great esteem, perceiving that the great power of God was in us, admitted many brethren to see us, so both we and they might be mutually refreshed. And when the day of the games drew near, my father, worn with suffering, came in to me, and began to tear out his beard, and to throw himself on the earth, and to cast himself down on his face, and to curse his years, and to utter such words as might move all creation. I grieved for his unhappy old age.

"The day before that on which we were to fight, I saw in a vision that Pomponius the deacon came hither to the gate of the prison, and knocked vehemently. I went out to him, and opened the gate for him; and he was clothed in a richly ornamented white robe, and he had on curious shoes. And he said to me, 'Perpetua, we are waiting for you; come!' And he held out his hand to me, and we began to go through rough and winding places. Scarcely at length had we arrived breathless at the amphitheater, when he led me into the middle of the arena, and said to me, 'Do not fear: I am here with you, and I am laboring with you,' and departed. And I gazed upon an immense assembly in astonishment. And because I knew that I was condemned to the wild beasts, I marveled that wild beasts were not let loose upon me. Then there came forth against me a certain Egyptian, horrible in appearance, with his assistants, to fight with me. And handsome youths came to me, to be my helpers and encouragers, and I was stripped, and became a man. Then my helpers began to rub me with oil, as is the custom for a contest; and I beheld that Egyptian on the side rolling in the dust. And a certain man came forth, of wondrous height, so that he stood over even the top of the amphitheater; and he wore a loose tunic and a purple robe between two bands over the middle of the breast; and he had on curious shoes, made of gold and silver; and he carried a rod, as if he were a trainer of gladiators, and a green branch upon which were golden apples. And he called for silence, and said, 'If this Egyptian overcomes this woman, he shall kill her with the sword; and if she shall defeat him, she shall receive this branch.' Then he departed. And we drew near to one another, and began to hit each other. He tried to lay hold of my feet, while I struck at his face with my heels; and I was lifted up in the air, and began thus to thrust at him as if spurning the earth. But when I saw that there was some delay in the fight, I joined my hands so as to intertwine my fingers, I took hold of his head, he fell on his face, and I trod upon his head. And the people began to shout, and my supporters to sing. And I drew near to the trainer and took the branch; and he kissed me, and said to me, 'Daughter, peace be with you,' and I began to go gloriously to the Sanavivarian gate.[6] Then I woke up, and perceived that I was not to fight with beasts, but against the devil. Still I knew that victory awaited me. I have completed this account up to the day before the exhibition; but let whoever wishes to do so write about what passed at the games themselves."

Moreover, also the blessed Saturus related his

---

6  I.e., the gate by which gladiators who survived because of popular acclaim exited the arena.

vision, which he himself committed to writing: "We had suffered," he says, "and we had left the flesh, and we were beginning to be carried into the east by four angels whose hands did not touch us. And we did not float on our backs, but as if ascending a gentle slope. And being set free, we at length saw the first boundless light; and I said, 'Perpetua' (for she was at my side), 'this is what the Lord promised to us; we have received the promise.' And while we were carried by those same four angels, there appeared to us a vast space which was like a pleasure garden, with rose-trees and every kind of flower. And the height of the trees was like that of a cypress, and their leaves were falling incessantly. Moreover, four other angels appeared in the pleasure garden, brighter than the previous ones, who, when they saw us, honored us, and said to the rest of the angels, 'Here they are! Here they are!' with admiration. And those four angels who carried us, being greatly afraid, put us down, and we passed over on foot the space of a furlong in a broad path. There we found Jocundus and Saturninus and Artaxius, who having suffered the same persecution, had been burned alive; and Quintus, who, also a martyr, had died in the prison. And we asked them where the rest were. And the angels said to us, 'Come first, enter, and greet your Lord.'

"And we came near to a place whose walls seemed as if they were built of light; and before whose gate stood four angels, who clothed those who entered with white robes. And being thus clothed, we entered and saw the boundless light, and heard united voices saying without ceasing, 'Holy! Holy! Holy!' And in the midst of that place we saw what seemed to be a white haired man, snow-white, sitting, with a youthful countenance, and did not see his feet. And at his right hand and at his left were four elders, and behind them stood a great many other elders. We entered with great wonder, and stood before the throne; and the four angels raised us up, and we kissed Him, and He passed His hand over our face. And the rest of the elders said to us, 'Let us stand,' and we stood and made peace. And the elders said to us, 'Go and enjoy.' And I said, 'Perpetua, you have what you wish.' And she said to me, 'Thanks be to God, that joyous as I was in the flesh, I am now more joyous here.'

"And we went forth, and saw before the entrance Optatus the bishop at the right hand, and Aspasius the priest, at the left, separate and sad; and they cast themselves at our feet, and said, 'Restore peace between us, because you have gone forth and have left us thus.' And we said to them, 'Are you not our father, and are you not our priest? Why do you cast yourselves at our feet?" And we were moved, and we embraced them; and Perpetua began to speak with them in Greek, and we drew them apart in the pleasure garden under a rose-tree. And while we were speaking with them, the angels said to them, 'Leave them alone, so they can refresh themselves; and if you have any dissensions between you, forgive one another.' And they thus confounded Optatus and Aspasius. And they said to Optatus, 'Rebuke your people, because they come to you as if returning from the circus, contending about conflicts there.' And then it seemed to us as if they would shut the doors. And in that place we began to recognize many brethren and, moreover, martyrs. We were all nourished with an indescribable odor, which satisfied us. Then, I awoke joyously."

The above were the more eminent visions of the blessed martyrs Saturus and Perpetua themselves, which they themselves committed to writing. But God called Secundulus to an earlier exit from this world while he has still in the prison, not without favor, so he might escape the beasts. Nevertheless, even if his soul did not know the sword, assuredly his flesh did.

But respecting Felicitas (for the Lord's favor approached her in the same way), when she had already gone eight months with child (for she had been pregnant when she was apprehended), as the day of the games was drawing near, she was in great grief lest her martyrdom be delayed on account of her pregnancy, since it is illegal for pregnant women to be publicly punished, and lest she should later shed her sacred and guiltless blood among the wicked. Moreover, also, her fellow-martyrs were painfully saddened lest they should leave so excellent a friend, and as it were companion, alone on the path to the same hope. Therefore, joining together their united cries, three days before the games they poured forth their prayer to the Lord. Immediately after their prayer, her pains came upon her, and when in labor she was suffering a great deal from the difficulty natural to an eight-months' delivery, a servant of one of the jailers said to her, "You who are in such suffering now, what will you do when you are thrown to the beasts, which you despised when you refused to sacrifice?" And she replied, "Now I am the one who suffers what I suffer, but then there will be another in me, who will suffer for me, because I also am about to suffer for Him." Thus she gave birth to a little girl, which a certain sister brought up as her daughter.

Since, therefore, the Holy Spirit permitted, and by permitting willed, that the proceedings of those games should be committed to writing, although we are unworthy to complete the description of so great a glory, we nonetheless obey as it were the command of the most blessed Perpetua, nay, her sacred trust, and add one more testimony concerning her constancy and her loftiness of mind. While they were treated with more severity by the tribune, because, from the intimations of certain deceitful men, he feared lest they should be withdrawn from the prison by some sort of magic spells, Perpetua answered to his face, and said, "Why do you not at least permit us to be refreshed, being as we are most noble, belonging to Caesar, and to fight on his birthday? Or is it not to your glory if we are fatter when we are brought forward?" The tribune shuddered and blushed, and commanded that they should be kept with more humanity, so that permission was given to their brethren and others to go in and be refreshed with them; now even the keeper of the prison believed.

Moreover, on the day before, when in that last meal, which they call the free meal,[7] they had so far as they were able not as a free feast, but of as a love feast, they uttered with that same firmness words to the people, threatening the judgment of the Lord, bearing witness to the happiness of their passion, laughing at the curiosity of the people who came together. Saturus said, "Tomorrow is not enough for you, for you to behold with pleasure what you hate. Friends today, enemies tomorrow. Yet note our faces well, so you may recognize them on the day of judgment." Thus all left the place astonished, and from these things many believed.

The day of their victory dawned, and they proceeded from the prison into the amphitheater, as if to heaven, joyous and with brilliant countenances; if they trembled, it was with joy, and not with fear. Perpetua followed with a placid look, and with the step and gait of a wife Christ, beloved of God, casting down the gaze of all with the luster of her eyes. Moreover, Felicitas, rejoiced that she had born her child in safety, so that she might fight with the wild beasts, going from the blood of childbirth to more blood, from the midwife to the gladiator, to wash after childbirth with a second baptism. And when they were brought to the gate, and were made to put on the clothing—the men, that of the priests of Saturn, and the women, that of those who were consecrated to Ceres—that noble-minded woman resisted even to the end with constancy. For she said, "We have come thus far of our own will, so that our liberty might not be restrained. For this reason, we have yielded our lives, that we might not do any such thing as this; we have agreed on this with you." Injustice acknowledged justice; the tribune yielded to their being brought as simply as they were. Perpetua sang psalms, already treading the head of the Egyptian under foot; Revocatus, and Saturninus, and Saturus uttered threats against the people watching. When they came within sight of Hilarianus, they said by gestures and nods, "You judge us, but God will judge you." At this the people, exasperated, demanded that they should be tormented with scourges as they passed along the gauntlet. And they indeed rejoiced that they should have incurred any one of their Lord's sufferings.

But He who had said, "Ask, and you shall receive,"[8] gave to them when they asked: the death which each one had wished for. For when at any time they had discussed among themselves their wish in respect of their martyrdom, Saturninus indeed had said that he wished to be thrown to all the beasts; so he doubtless would wear a more glorious crown. Therefore at the beginning of the games, he and Revocatus made trial of a leopard and, moreover upon the scaffold they were harassed by the bear. Saturus, how-

---

7   At which the condemned had their choice of food.
8   New Testament, John 16.24.

ever, held nothing in greater abomination than a bear, but believed that he would be put an end to with one bite of a leopard. Therefore, when a wild boar was supplied, it was the huntsman who had supplied that boar who was gored by that same beast, and died the day after the shows. Saturus was only dragged, and when he had been tied up on the bridge near a bear, the bear would not come forth from his den. And so Saturus for the second time was recalled unhurt.

Moreover, for the young women the devil prepared a very fierce cow, provided especially for that purpose contrary to custom, rivalling their sex also with that of the beasts. And so, stripped and enclosed in nets, they were led forth. The populace shuddered as they saw one young woman of a delicate frame, and another with breasts still dropping with milk after her recent childbirth. So, being recalled, they are unbound. Perpetua was led in first. She was tossed, and fell on her loins; and when she saw her tunic torn from her side, she drew it over to cover her thighs, more mindful of her modesty than of her suffering. Then she called for a pin, and pinned up her dishevelled hair, for it was not becoming for a martyr to suffer with dishevelled hair, lest she should seem to mourn in her glory. So she rose up, and when she saw Felicitas crushed, she approached and gave her her hand, and lifted her up. And both of them stood together, and the brutality of the populace being appeased, they were recalled to the Sanavivarian gate. Then Perpetua was received by a certain Rusticus, who was still a catechumen, and who kept close to her. She, as if aroused from sleep, so deeply had she been in the Spirit and in an ecstasy, began to look around her, and to say to the amazement of all, "I cannot tell when we are to be led out to that cow." And when she had heard what had already happened, she did not believe it until she had perceived certain signs of injury in her body and in her dress, and had recognized the catechumen. Then she had that catechumen and her brother approach and addressed them, saying, "Stand steadfast in the faith, and love one another, all of you, and do not be offended at my suffering."

The same Saturus at the other entrance exhorted the soldier Pudens, saying, "Assuredly I am here, as I have promised and foretold, for up to this moment I have felt no beast's touch. And now believe with your whole heart. Behold, I am going forth to that beast, and I shall die with one bite from the leopard." And immediately at the end of the games the leopard was set loose. With one bite of his he was bathed with so much blood that as he was returned the people shouted out to him the testimony of his second baptism: "Saved and washed, saved and washed." Manifestly he who had been glorified in such a spectacle was assuredly saved. Then to the soldier Pudens he said, "Farewell, and be mindful of my faith; and do not let these things disturb you, but confirm you." And at the same time he asked for a little ring from Pudens's finger, and returned it to him bathed in his wound, leaving to him an inherited token and the memory of his blood. And then, lifeless, he was cast down with the rest to the usual place for slaughtering. And when the populace called for them to be brought into their midst, so the people might make their eyes partners in the murder as the sword penetrated the bodies, they rose up of their own accord, and went to where the people wished; but they first kissed one another, so they might consummate their martyrdom with the kiss of peace. The rest indeed, immoveable and in silence, received the sword-thrust, especially Saturus, who also had first ascended the ladder, and first gave up his spirit, for he also was waiting for Perpetua. But Perpetua, so she might taste some pain, was pierced between the ribs, and cried out loudly, and she herself guided the wavering right hand of the youthful gladiator to her throat. Perhaps such a woman could not have been slain unless she herself had willed it, because she was feared by the impure spirit.

O most brave and blessed martyrs! O truly called and chosen to the glory of our Lord Jesus Christ! Whoever magnifies, and honors, and adores that glory, assuredly ought to read these examples, no less than the ancient ones, for the edification of the Church, so that new examples of virtue also may testify that one and the same Holy Spirit is always operating even now, and all-powerful God the Father, and His Son Jesus Christ Our Lord, whose is the glory and infinite power for ever and ever. Amen.

# 25

# AUGUSTINE, *CONFESSIONS*

Saint Augustine of Hippo was born in Thagaste, in Roman North Africa, in 354. Although his mother, Monica, was a Christian, his father was not. At one point of his life he was a member of the radical dualist sect of the Manichaeans. Ultimately, however, he converted to Christianity in 387, becoming perhaps the most influential Christian writer after Saint Paul. In 396 he became bishop of the North African town of Hippo, where he died in 430, while the town was under seige by the Vandals. He wrote his autobiography, the *Confessions*, in 397-8.

---

BOOK 1

1   You are great, O Lord, and greatly to be praised; great is Your power, and to Your wisdom there is no end.[1] And man, being a part of Your creation, desires to praise You—man, who carries about with him his mortality, the witness of his sin, even the witness that You "resist the proud."[2] Yet man, this part of Your creation, desires to praise You. You move us to delight in praising You, for You have formed us for Yourself, and our hearts are restless until they find rest in You. Lord, teach me to know and understand which of these should be first: to call on You for help, or to praise You, and likewise in order to know You, to call upon You for help. But who is there that calls upon You for help without knowing You? For one that does not know You may call upon You as other than You are. Or perhaps we call on You that we may know You. "But how shall they call on Him in whom they have not believed? Or how shall they believe without a preacher?"[3] And those who seek the Lord shall praise Him.[4] For those who seek shall find Him,[5] and those who find Him shall praise Him. Let me seek You, Lord, in calling on You, and call on You in believing in You; for You have been preached unto us. O Lord, my faith calls on You, that faith which You imparted to me, which You breathed into me through the incarnation of Your Son, through the ministry of Your preacher.

2   And how shall I call upon my God—my God and my Lord? For when I call on Him I ask Him to come into me. And what place is there in me into which my God can come—into which God can come, even He who made heaven and earth? Is there anything in me, O Lord my God, that can contain You? Do indeed the very heaven and the earth, which You have made, and in which You made me, contain You? Or, as nothing could exist without You, does whatever exists contain

---

1   Referring to Old Testament Psalms 145.3; 147.5.
2   New Testament, 1 Peter 5.5.
3   New Testament, Romans 10.14.
4   Referring to Old Testament, Psalms 145.3; 147.5.
5   Referring to New Testament, Matthew 7.8.

You? Why, then, do I ask You to come into me, since I indeed exist, and could not exist if You were not in me? Because I am not yet in hell, though You are even there, for "if I go down into hell You are there."[6] I could not therefore exist, could not exist at all, O my God, unless You were in me. Or should I not rather say that I could not exist unless I were in You from whom are all things, by whom are all things, in whom are all things? Even so, Lord; even so. Where do I call You to, since You are in me, or from where can You come into me? For where outside heaven and earth can I go that from there my God, who has said, "I fill heaven and earth,"[7] may come into me?

3 Since, then, You fill heaven and earth, do they contain You? Or, as they do not contain You, do You fill them, with yet something remaining left over? And where do You pour forth that which remains of You when heaven and earth are filled? Or, indeed, is there no need that You who contains all things should be contained of any, since those things which You fill, You fill by containing them? For the vessels which You fill do not sustain You, since should they even be broken, You would not be poured forth. And when You are poured forth on us,[8] You are not cast down, but we are uplifted, nor are You dissipated, but we are drawn together. But, as You fill all things, do You fill them with Your whole self, or, as even all things cannot altogether contain You, do they contain a part, and do all at once contain the same part? Or has each its own proper part—the greater more, the smaller less? Is, then, one part of You greater, another less? Or is it that You are wholly everywhere while nothing altogether contains You?

4 What, then, are You, O my God—what, I ask, but the Lord God? For who is Lord but the Lord? Or who is God save our God?[9] Most high, most excellent, most potent, most omnipotent; most piteous and most just; most hidden and most near; most beauteous and most strong, stable, yet incomprehensible; unchangeable, yet changing all things; never new, never old; making all things new, yet bringing old age upon the proud who do not realize it; always working, yet ever at rest; gathering, yet needing nothing; sustaining, pervading, and protecting; creating, nourishing, and developing; seeking, and yet possessing all things. You love, and yet do not burn; are jealous, yet are free from care; repent, and have no sorrow; are angry, yet are serene; change Your ways, yet leave Your plans unchanged; recover what You find, having yet never lost anything; are never in want, while You rejoice in gain; never covetous, though requiring a larger repayment for what You give.[10] That You may owe, more than enough is given to You; yet who has anything that is not Yours? You pay debts while owing nothing. And when You forgive debts, you lose nothing. Yet, O my God, my life, my holy joy, what is this that I have said? And what says anyone who speaks of You? Yet woe to them that keep silence, seeing that even they who say most are as the dumb.

BOOK 2

[*Augustine has attended school at Thagaste and Madaura. He has received training in Christianity, but has not been baptized.*]

3 And for that year my studies were interrupted, while after my return from Madaura (a neighboring city, where I had begun to go in order to learn grammar and rhetoric[11]), the expenses for a further residence at Carthage were provided for me; and that was rather by the determination than the means of my father, who was but a poor freeman of Thagaste.[12] To whom do I narrate this? Not to You, my God; but before You to my own kind, even to that small part of the human race who may chance to come upon my writings. And to what end? That I and all who read the same may reflect out of what depths we are to cry

---

6   Old Testament, Psalms 139.8.
7   Old Testament, Jeremiah 23.24.
8   Referring to New Testament, Acts 2.18.
9   Referring to Old Testament, Psalms 18.31.
10  Referring to New Testament, Matthew 25.27.
11  "Rhetoric" did not refer only to the art of public speaking, but also to other elements of Latin literary study.
12  Also in North Africa.

out to You.[13] For what comes nearer to Your ears than a confessing heart and a life of faith? For who did not extol and praise my father, in that he went even beyond his means to supply his son with all the necessities for a distant journey for the sake of his studies? For many far richer citizens did not act similarly for their children. But yet this same father did not trouble himself about how I grew towards You, nor about how chaste I was, so long as I was skillful in speaking—however barren I was to Your tilling, O God, who are the sole true and good Lord of my heart, which is Your field.

But while, in that sixteenth year of my age, I resided with my parents, having been on holiday from school for a time (this idleness being imposed upon me by my parents' necessitous circumstances), the thorns of lust grew thick over my head, and there was no hand to pluck them out. Moreover when my father, seeing me at the baths, perceived that I was becoming a man, and was stirred with a restless youthfulness, he, as if from this anticipating future descendants, joyfully told it to my mother, rejoicing in that intoxication wherein the world so often forgets You, its Creator, and falls in love with Your creature instead of You, from the invisible wine of its own perversity turning and bowing down to the most infamous things. But in my mother's breast You had even then begun building Your temple, and the commencement of Your holy habitation, whereas my father was only a catechumen[14] as yet, and that but recently. She then started up with a pious fear and trembling. Although I had not yet been baptized, she feared those crooked ways in which they walk who turn their back to You, and not their face.[15]

Woe is me! And dare I affirm that You held Your peace, O my God, while I strayed farther from You? Did You then hold Your peace to me? And whose words were they but Yours which by my mother, Your faithful handmaid, You poured into my ears, none of which sank into my heart to make me do it? For she desired and, I remember, privately warned me, with great solicitude, "not to commit fornication; but above all things never to defile another man's wife." These appeared to me but womanish counsels, which I would blush to obey. But they were Yours, and I did not know it, and I thought that You held Your peace, and that it was she who spoke, through whom You did not hold Your peace to me, and in her person was despised by me, her son, "the son of Your handmaid, Your servant."[16] But I did not know this, and rushed on headlong with such blindness that among my equals I was ashamed to be less shameless, when I heard them pluming themselves upon their disgraceful acts, indeed, and glorying all the more in proportion to the greatness of their baseness. I took pleasure in doing it, not for the pleasure's sake only, but for the praise. What is worthy of being despised but vice? But I made myself out to be worse than I was, in order that I might not be despised. When in anything I had not sinned as the sinners, I would affirm that I had done what I had not, so that I would not appear weak for being more innocent, or of less esteem for being more chaste.

Behold with what companions I walked the streets of Babylon,[17] in whose filth I was rolled, as if in cinnamon and precious ointments. And that I might cling the more tenaciously to its very center, my invisible enemy trod me down, and seduced me, I being easily seduced. Nor did the mother of my flesh, who herself had by this time fled "out of the midst of Babylon"[18] (although she remained in its outskirts), in counseling me to chastity, so bear in mind what she had been told about me by her husband that she attempted to restrain within the limits of conjugal affection (if it could not be cut away to the quick) what she knew to be destructive in the present and dangerous in the future. Instead, she took no heed of this, for she was afraid that a wife would prove a hindrance and a clog

---

13  Referring to Old Testament, Psalms 130.1.
14  I.e., an adult receiving instruction in Christianity, but not yet baptized.
15  Referring to Old Testament, Jeremiah 2.27.
16  Old Testament, Psalms 116.16.
17  The city which, in the Old and especially New Testaments, stood for sin.
18  Old Testament, Jeremiah 51.6.

to my hopes—not those hopes of the future world, which my mother had in You, but the hope regarding my education, which both my parents were too anxious that I should acquire. He was anxious because he had little or no thought of You, and but vain thoughts for me, while she was so because she calculated that those usual courses of learning would not only be no drawback, but rather a furtherance towards my attaining You. For thus I conjecture, recalling as well as I can the dispositions of my parents. The reins on me, meanwhile, were slackened beyond the restraint of due severity that I might play, indeed, even to dissoluteness, in whatsoever I fancied. And in all there was a mist, shutting out from my sight the brightness of Your truth, O my God, and my iniquity displayed itself as from very "fatness."[19]

4 Theft is punished by Your law, O Lord, and by the law written in men's hearts, which iniquity itself cannot blot out. For what thief will suffer a thief? Even a rich thief will not suffer him who is driven to it by want. Yet I had a desire to commit robbery, and did so, compelled neither by hunger, nor poverty, but through a distaste for well-doing, and a lustiness for wrong-doing. For I pilfered what I already had enough of, and much better. Nor did I desire to enjoy what I pilfered, but the theft and sin itself. There was a pear-tree close to our vineyard, heavily laden with fruit, which was tempting neither for its color nor its flavor. Some of us wanton young fellows went to shake and rob this tree, late one night (having, according to our disgraceful habit, prolonged our games in the streets until then), and carried away great loads of pears, not to eat ourselves, but to fling to the very swine, having eaten only some of them; doing this pleased us all the more because it was not permitted. Behold my heart, O my God; behold my heart, which You had pity upon when it was in the bottomless pit. Behold now, let my heart tell You what it was seeking there: that I should be gratuitously wanton, having no inducement to evil but the evil itself. It was foul, and I loved it. I loved to perish. I loved my own error—not that for which I erred, but the error itself. Base soul, falling from Your firmament to utter destruction, seeking nothing through the shame but the shame itself!

BOOK 3

*[At school in Carthage, Augustine has been associating with a group of dissolute youth.]*

4 Among such as these, at that unstable period of my life, I studied books of eloquence, wherein I was eager to be eminent from a damnable and inflated purpose, even a delight in human vanity. In the ordinary course of study, I came upon a certain book of Cicero,[20] whose language, though not his heart, almost all admire. This book of his contains an exhortation to philosophy, and is called *Hortensius*. This book, in truth, changed my feelings, and turned my prayers to You, O Lord, and made me have other hopes and desires. Suddenly every vain hope became worthless to me and, with an incredible warmth of heart, I yearned for an immortal wisdom, and began now to arise[21] that I might return to You. Not, then, to improve my language—which I appeared to be purchasing with my mother's means, in that my nineteenth year, my father having died two years before—not to improve my language did I have recourse to that book; nor did it persuade me by its style, but its content.

How ardent was I then, my God, how ardent to fly from earthly things to You! Nor did I know how You would deal with me, for with You is wisdom. In Greek the love of wisdom is called "philosophy," with which that book inflamed me. There are some who seduce through philosophy, using a great, and alluring, and honorable name to color and adorn their own errors. And almost all who in that and former times were such are censured and pointed out in that book. There is also disclosed that most salutary admonition of Your Spirit, by Your good and pious servant: "Beware that any man spoil you through philosophy and vain deceit, after the tradition of men, after the rudiments of the world, and

---

19 Old Testament, Psalms 73.7.
20 The politician, philosopher, and master Latin prose stylist of the first century BC.
21 Referring to New Testament, Luke 15.18.

not after Christ: for in Him dwells all the fullness of the Godhead bodily."[22] And since at that time (as You, O Light of my heart, know) the words of the apostle were unknown to me, I was delighted with that exhortation, in so far only as I was thereby stimulated, and enkindled, and inflamed to love, seek, obtain, hold, and embrace, not this or that sect, but wisdom itself whatever it may be. That the name of Christ was not in it alone checked my ardor. For this name, according to Your mercy, O Lord, this name of my Savior, Your Son, my tender heart had piously drunk in, deeply treasured even with my mother's milk; whatsoever was without that name, though never so erudite, polished, and truthful, did not completely take hold of me.

5   I resolved, therefore, to direct my mind to the Holy Scriptures, that I might see what they were. And behold, I perceive something not comprehended by the proud, not disclosed to children, but lowly as you approach, sublime as you advance, and veiled in mysteries. And I was not of the number of those who could enter into it, or bend my neck to follow its steps. For I did not feel the same as when now I speak when I turned towards those Scriptures; they appeared to me unworthy to be compared with the dignity of Cicero, for my inflated pride shunned their style, nor could the sharpness of my wit pierce their inner meaning. Yet, truly, they were such as would develop little children. But I scorned to be a little child. Swollen with pride, I looked upon myself as a great man.

### BOOK 4

[*Augustine, back in Thagaste, had begun to teach, when a close friend died. He then returned to Carthage and taught there.*]

6   But why do I speak of these things?[23] For this is not the time to question, but rather to confess to You. Miserable I was, and miserable is every soul fettered by the friendship of perishable things—it is torn to pieces when it loses them, and then is sensible of the misery which it had before it ever lost them. Thus was it at that time with me; I wept most bitterly, and found rest in bitterness. Thus was I miserable, and that life of misery I accounted dearer than my friend. For though I would willingly have changed it, yet I was even more unwilling to lose it than him. Indeed, I did not know whether I was willing to lose it even for him, as is handed down to us (if not an invention) concerning Pylades and Orestes,[24] that they would gladly have died one for another, or both together, it being worse than death to them not to live together. But there had sprung up in me some kind of feeling, too, contrary to this, for it was both exceedingly wearisome to me to live, and dreadful to die. I suppose the more I loved him, so much the more did I hate and fear, as a most cruel enemy, that death which had robbed me of him. I imagined it would suddenly annihilate all men, as it had power over him. Thus, I remember, it was with me. Behold my heart, O my God! Behold and look into me, for I remember it well, O my Hope! who cleanses me from the uncleanness of such feelings, directing my eyes towards You, and plucking my feet out of the net.[25] For I was astonished that other mortals lived, since he whom I loved as if he would never die, was dead. And I wondered still more that I, who was to him a second self, could live when he was dead. Well did one say of his friend, "You half of my soul,"[26] for I felt that my soul and his soul were but one soul in two bodies.[27] Consequently, my life was a horror to me because I would not live in half. And therefore, perchance, I was afraid to die, so that he whom I had so greatly loved would not die completely.

7   O madness, which does not know how to love men as men should be loved! O foolish man that I then was, enduring with so much impatience the lot of man! So I

---

22   New Testament, Colossians 2.8,9.

23   Augustine has been discussing the death of his friend and the weeping it produced in him.

24   In Greek legend Pylades was the great friend of Orestes, and assisted him in the assassination of Clytemnestra, Orestes's mother, in revenge for her murder of Agamemnon, her husband and Orestes's father. Pylades followed Orestes into exile; their friendship was proverbial.

25   Referring to Old Testament, Psalm 25.15.

26   Horace, Latin poet (first century BC).

27   This description is from the Latin poet Ovid (43 BC–?AD 17).

fretted, sighed, wept, tormented myself, and took nei-ther rest nor advice. For I bore about with me a torn and polluted soul, impatient of being borne by me, and I could find no place for it to rest—not in pleasant groves, not in sport or song, not in fragrant spots, or in magnificent banquetings, or in the pleasures of the bed and the couch, or, finally, in books and songs, did it find repose. All things looked terrible, even the very light itself; whatever was not what he was, was repul-sive and hateful, except groans and tears, for in those alone found I a little repose. But when my soul was withdrawn from them, a heavy burden of misery weighed me down. To You, O Lord, should it have been raised, for You to heal it. I knew this, but was nei-ther willing nor able, all the more since, in my thoughts of You, You were not any solid or substantial thing to me. For You were not Yourself, but an empty phan-tasm, and my error was my god. If I attempted to dis-charge my burden thereon, so it might find rest, it sank into emptiness, and came rushing down again upon me, and I remained to myself an unhappy place, from which I could neither stay nor depart. For where could my heart fly from my heart? Where could I fly from my own self? Where not follow myself? And yet I fled from my country; for so should my eyes look less for him where they were not accustomed to see him. And thus I left the town of Thagaste, and came to Carthage.

8    Times lose no time, nor do they idly roll through our senses. They work strange operations on the mind. Behold, they came and went from day to day, and by coming and going they disseminated in my mind other ideas and other remembrances, and little by little patched me up again with the former kind of delights, to which that sorrow of mine yielded. But yet there succeeded, not certainly other sorrows, yet the causes of other sorrows. For from where had that for-mer sorrow so easily penetrated to the marrow, but that I had poured out my soul upon the dust, in loving one who must die as if he were never to die? But what revived and refreshed me especially was the consola-tions of other friends, with whom I did love what

instead of You I loved. And this was a monstrous fable and protracted lie, by whose adulterous contact our soul, which lay itching in our ears, was being pollut-ed. But that fable would not die to me so often as any of my friends died. There were other things in them which laid hold of my mind more—to discourse and jest with them; to indulge in an interchange of kind-nesses; to read together pleasant books; to trifle together, and to be earnest together; to differ at times without ill-humor, as one would do with one's own self, and even by the infrequency of these differences to give zest to our more frequent consentings, some-times teaching, sometimes being taught, longing for the absent with impatience, and welcoming that one's arrival with joy. These and similar expressions, ema-nating from the hearts of those who loved and were beloved in return, by the countenance, the tongue, the eyes, and a thousand pleasing movements, were so much fuel to melt our souls together, and out of many to make only one.

9    This is what is loved in friends, and so loved that a person's conscience accuses itself if one does not exchange love for love, expecting nothing from one's loved one but indications of love. Hence that mourn-ing if a loved one dies, and gloom of sorrow, that steeping of the heart in tears, all sweetness turned into bitterness, and upon the loss of the life of the dying, the death of the living. Blessed be the one who loves You, and his friend in You, and one's enemy for Your sake. For that person alone loses no one dear to him to whom all are dear in Him, who cannot be lost. And who is this but our God, the God that created heaven and earth, and fills them,[28] because by filling them He created them? None loses You but one who leaves You. And one who leaves You, where does that person go, or where does that person flee, but from You well pleased to You angry? For where does not such a per-son find Your law in his own punishment? "And Your law is the truth,"[29] and truth is You.[30]

10    "Turn us again, O Lord God of Hosts, cause Your face to shine; and we shall be saved."[31] For toward

---

28    Referring to Old Testament, Genesis 1.1.
29    Old Testament, Jeremiah 23.24.
30    Referring to New Testament, John 14.6.
31    Old Testament, Psalms 80.19.

wherever the soul of man turns itself, unless towards You, it is clasped to sorrows, indeed, even when it is clasped to beautiful things outside You and itself. And yet such beautiful things would not be unless they were from You. They rise and set and, by rising, they begin, as it were, to be; they grow, so that they may become perfect; and when perfect, they wax old and perish. Not all wax old, but all perish. Therefore when they rise and tend to be, the more rapidly they grow that they may be, so much the more they hasten not to be. This is the law they follow. Thus much have You given them, because they are parts of things which do not exist all at the same time, but by departing and succeeding they together make up the universe, of which they are parts. And even thus is our speech accomplished by signs emitting a sound. But this, again, is not perfected unless one word passes away when it has sounded its part, in order that another may succeed it. Let my soul praise You out of all these things, O God, the Creator of all, but let not my soul be affixed to these things by the glue of love, through the senses of the body. For they go where they were to go, so that they might no longer be, and they rend the soul with pestilent desires, because it longs to be, and yet loves to rest in what it loves. But in these things no place is to be found; they do not stay, but flee, and who is able to follow them with the senses of the flesh? Or who can grasp them, even when they are near? For the sense of the flesh is tardy because it is the sense of the flesh, and its boundary is itself. It suffices for that for which it was made, but it is not sufficient to prevent things from running their course from their appointed starting place to the appointed end. For in Your word, by which they were created, they hear the command, "Here is your beginning and here is your end."

11    Be not foolish, O my soul, and do not deaden the ear of your heart with the tumult of your folly. Hearken also: the word itself invokes you to return, and there is the place of imperturbable rest, where the word will not keep from you love if your love will not keep from the word. Behold, these things pass away so that others may succeed them, and so this lower universe will be made complete in all its parts. "But do I depart anywhere?" says the word of God. There fix your habitation. There commit whatever you have from there, O my soul. At all events now you are tired out with deceits. Commit to truth whatsoever you have from the truth, and you shall lose nothing, and all that is decayed in you shall flourish again, and all your diseases shall be healed,[32] and your perishable parts shall be reformed and renewed, and united to you. Nor shall they drag you down with them into the earth, but they shall remain with you, and continue forever before God, who remains and continues for ever.[33]

Why, then, be perverse and follow your flesh? Rather let it be converted and follow you. Whatever you feel by the flesh, is but in part. You are ignorant of the whole, of which these are portions, and yet they delight you. But had the senses of your flesh been capable of comprehending the whole (for your punishment has been justly limited to a portion of the whole) you would want that whatsoever exists at the present time should pass away, that so the whole might please you more. For you hear what we speak by the same fleshly sense and yet you would not wish that the syllables should keep sounding, but fly away, so that others might replace them, and the whole utterance be heard. Thus it always is when any single thing is composed of many, all of which do not exist at the same time: all together would delight more than they each do individually. But far better than these is He who made all. He is our God, and He does not pass away, for there is nothing to succeed Him. If bodies please you, praise God for them, and turn your love back upon their Creator, so you do not displease in those things which please you.

BOOK 5

8    You[34] dealt with me, therefore, so that I would be persuaded to go to Rome, and teach there what I was then teaching at Carthage. And how I was persuaded to do this, I will not fail to confess to You, for in this

---

32   Referring to Old Testament, Psalms 103.3.
33   Referring to New Testament, 1 Peter 1.23.
34   I.e., God.

also the profoundest workings of Your wisdom and Your ever present mercy to us must be pondered and avowed. It was not my desire to go to Rome because of the greater advantages and dignities which were guaranteed to me by the friends who persuaded me into this (although even at this period I was influenced by these considerations), but my principal and almost sole motive was that I had been informed that the youths studied more quietly there, and were kept under the control of more rigid discipline, so that they did not capriciously and impudently rush into the school of a master not their own, into whose presence they were forbidden to enter unless with his consent. At Carthage, on the contrary, there was a shameful and intemperate license among the students. There they burst in rudely, and, with almost furious gesticulations, break up any system which one may have instituted for the good of the pupils. They perpetrate many outrages with astounding recklessness, which would be punishable by law if they were not maintained by custom, that custom showing them to be the more worthless, in that they now do according to law, what by Your unchangeable law will never be lawful. And they fancy they do it with impunity, whereas the very blindness whereby they do it is their punishment, and they suffer far greater things than they do. The manners, then, which as a student I would not adopt, I was compelled as a teacher to endure from others. So I was too glad to go where all who knew anything about it assured me that similar things were not done. But You, "my refuge and my portion in the land of the living,"[35] goaded me while at Carthage, so that I might thereby be withdrawn from there, and exchange my worldly habitation for the preservation of my soul. While I was at Rome, You offered me enticements by which to attract me there, using men enchanted with this dying life—the one doing insane actions, and the other making assurances of vain things. And in order to correct my footsteps, you secretly employed their and my perversity. For both they who disturbed my tranquillity were blinded by a shameful madness, and they who lured me else-where smacked of the earth. And I, who hated real misery here, sought fictitious happiness there.

But the cause of my going from the one place and to the other, You, O God, knew, yet did not reveal, either to me or to my mother, who grievously lamented my journey, and went with me as far as the sea. But I deceived her, when she violently restrained me, either in order to keep me or accompany me; I pretended that I had a friend whom I could not leave until he had a favorable wind to set sail. And I lied to my mother—and such a mother!—and got away. For this also You have in mercy pardoned me, saving me, thus full of abominable pollutions, from the waters of the sea, for the water of Your grace, whereby, when I was purified, the fountains of my mother's eyes should be dried, from which for me she day by day watered the ground under her face. And yet, refusing to go back without me, it was with difficulty I persuaded her to remain that night in a place quite close to our ship, where there was a shrine dedicated to the memory of the blessed Cyprian. That night I secretly left, but she was not backward in prayers and weeping. And what was it, O Lord, that she, with such an abundance of tears, was asking of You, but that You would not permit me to sail? But You, mysteriously counseling and hearing the real purpose of her desire, did not grant what she then asked, in order to make me what she was always asking. The wind blew and filled our sails, and withdrew the shore from our sight, and she, wild with grief, was there the next morning, and filled Your ears with complaints and groans, which You disregarded, while, by the means of my longings, You were hastening me on to the end of all longing, and You used her too great love of me as a just lash of sorrow. Like all mothers, though even more than others, she loved to have me with her, and did not know not what joy You were preparing for her by means of my absence. Being ignorant of this, she wept and mourned, and in her agony was seen the inheritance of Eve, seeking in sorrow what in sorrow she had brought forth. And yet, after scolding my perfidy and cruelty, she again continued her intercessions for me with You, returned to her accustomed place, and I to Rome.

---

35   Old Testament, Psalms 103.5.

BOOK 6

*[Augustine, although he had ceased to be a Manichaean, was not quite converted to Christianity, as he had trouble conceiving God as something other than a physical substance.]*

5   From this belief, however, being led to prefer the catholic[36] doctrine, I felt that it was with more moderation and honesty that it commanded things to be believed that were not demonstrated (whether it was that they could be demonstrated, but not to everyone, or could not be demonstrated at all), than was the method of the Manichaeans, where our credulity was mocked by audacious promises of knowledge, and then so many most fabulous and absurd things were forced upon belief because they were not capable of demonstration. After that, O Lord, You, little by little, with a most gentle and most merciful hand, leading and calming my heart, persuaded me, taking into consideration what a multiplicity of things which I had never seen, nor was present when they were enacted, like so many of the things in secular history, and so many accounts of places and cities which I had not seen. Unless we believe so many accounts from friends, so many from physicians, so many now from these people, now from those, we would do nothing at all in this life. Lastly, with how unalterable an assurance I did believe I knew to what parents I was born, which it was impossible for me to know except by hearsay. Taking all this into consideration, You persuaded me that those who believed Your books (which, with so great authority, You have established among nearly all nations) are not to be blamed, but those who did not believe them and that those who should say to me, "How then do you know that those Scriptures were imparted to mankind by the Spirit of the one true and most true God?" were not to be listened to. For that was the thing that I needed to believe most of all, since no wranglings of blasphemous questions, of which I had read so many among the self-contradicting philosophers, could once wring the belief from me that You are, though I did not know

what You are, or that the government of human affairs belongs to You.

Thus much I believed, at one time more strongly than another, yet I always believed both that You were, and cared about us, although I was ignorant of both what was to be thought of Your substance, and what way led, or led back to You. Seeing, then, that we were too weak by unaided reason to find out the truth, and for this reason needed the authority of the holy writings, I had now begun to believe that You would by no means have given such excellent authority to those Scriptures throughout all lands had it not been Your will thereby to be believed in, and thereby sought. For now, having heard many of those things in the Scriptures which before appeared incongruous to me, and used to offend me, expounded reasonably, I referred to the depth of the mysteries, and the Scriptures' authority seemed to me all the more venerable and worthy of religious belief, for, while it was visible for all to read, they reserved the majesty of their secrets within their profound significance, stooping to cater to all in the great plainness of their language and lowliness of style, yet exercising the application of the learned, so they might receive all into their common bosom, and although few pass through the Scriptures' narrow openings to reach You, yet many more do than if the Scriptures did not stand upon such a height of authority or lure multitudes within their bosom by their holy humility. I meditated upon these things, and You were with me. I sighed, and You heard me. I vacillated, and You guided me. I roamed through the broad way[37] of the world, and You did not desert me.

6   I longed for honors, gain, and wedlock, and You mocked me. In these desires I underwent most bitter hardships, You being the more gracious the less You allowed anything which was not You to grow sweet to me. Behold my heart, O Lord, who willed that I should recall all this, and confess to You. Now let my soul cleave to You, which You have freed from that fast-holding bird-trap of death. How wretched it was! And You irritated the feeling of my heart's wound that, forsaking all else, it might be converted to You—who are

---

36   I.e., correct, or orthodox.
37   Referring to New Testament, Matthew 7.13.

above all, and without whom all things would be nothing—be converted and be healed. How wretched was I at that time, and how did You deal with me, to make me sensible of my wretchedness on that day on which I was preparing to recite a speech of praise for the emperor, in which I was to deliver many lies, and the lies were to be applauded by those who knew I lied. My heart panted with these cares, and boiled over with the fever of consuming thoughts. While walking along one of the streets of Milan, I observed a poor beggar (at that time, I imagine, with a full belly), joking and full of joy. And I sighed, and spoke to the friends around me of the many sorrows resulting from our madness, for that by all exertions such as ours (such as those in which I then labored, carrying the burden of my own unhappiness spurred by desires, and increasing the burden by carrying it) we aimed to reach only that very joyousness which the beggar had already reached and, perhaps, we would never reach it! For the joy of temporary happiness, which he had obtained through a few begged coins, I schemed to get by many wretched and tortuous maneuvers. For he did not have true joy, but I, with my ambitions, was seeking joy even less true. And in truth, he was joyous and I was anxious. He was free from care, I was full of alarm. But if anyone were to ask me whether I wanted to be merry or fearful, I would reply, "Merry." Again, if I were asked whether I would like to be as he was, or I was then, I would choose to be myself, even facing cares and anxiety, but out of perversity; for was it so in truth? For I should not prefer myself to him because I happened to be more learned than he, given that I took no delight in that, but sought instead to please others by my learning, and not to instruct them, but only to please. For which reason, You broke my bones with the rod of Your correction.[38]

Away with those from my soul, then, who say to it, "It makes a difference from where a person's joy is derived. That beggar rejoiced in drunkenness; you longed to rejoice in glory." What glory, O Lord?: glory which is not in You. For even as the beggar's was no true joy, so mine was no true glory, and it subverted my soul more. The beggar would digest his drunkenness that night, but I had slept many nights with mine, and had risen again with it, and was to sleep again and again to rise with it, I do not know how often. It does indeed "make a difference from where a person's joy is derived." I know it is so, and that joy of a faithful hope is incomparably beyond such vanity. Indeed, at that time, the beggar was beyond me, for he was truly the happier man, not only because he was fully steeped in mirth and I was torn to pieces with cares, but he, by giving good wishes, had gotten wine, whereas I, by lying, was following after pride. I said at the time much to this effect to my dear friends, and I often noticed in them how I fared, and I found that it went ill with me, and fretted, doubling that very ill. And if any prosperity smiled upon me, I loathed to seize it, for almost before I could grasp it, it would fly away.

14    And many of us friends, consulting on and abhorring the turbulent vexations of human life, had considered living, and now almost decided to live, at rest, and separate from human turmoil. This end was to be obtained in the following way: we were to bring together whatever we could procure individually, and set up a common household, so that, through the sincerity of our friendship, nothing would belong more to one of us than to another, but the whole, coming from all of us, would belong as a whole to each of us, and the whole to all of us together. It seemed to us that this society might consist of 10 persons, some of whom were very rich, especially Romanianus,[39] from my own town, an intimate friend of mine from his childhood, whom grave business matters had then brought up to Court, and who was the most earnest of us all for this project, and whose voice was of great weight in commending it because his estate was far more ample than that of the rest. We had arranged, too, that two officers should be chosen yearly, to provide all necessary things, while the rest were left undisturbed. But when we began to consider whether the wives which some of us had already, and others hoped to have, would permit this, this entire plan, which was being so well framed, broke to pieces in our hands, and was utterly wrecked and cast aside.

---

38    Referring to Old Testament, Proverbs 22.15.
39    A cousin of Augustine's friend, Alypius.

From this we fell again to sighs and groans, and our steps to follow the broad and beaten ways[40] of the world, for many thoughts were in our heart, but Your counsel stands forever.[41] Out of which counsel You mocked ours, and prepared Your own, aiming to give us meat in due season, and to open Your hand, and to fill our souls with blessing.[42]

15  Meanwhile my sins were being multiplied, and my mistress being torn from my side as an impediment to my marriage, my heart, which cleaved to her, was racked, and wounded, and bleeding. And she went back to Africa, making a vow to You never to know another man, leaving with me my natural son by her. But I, unhappy one, who could not imitate a woman, impatient of delay, since it was not until two years' time I was to obtain the woman I sought[43]—being not so much a lover of marriage as a slave to lust—procured another woman (not a wife, though), so that by the bondage of a lasting habit the disease of my soul might be maintained, and kept up in its vigor, or even increased, into the kingdom of marriage. Nor was that wound of mine as yet cured which had been caused by the separation from my former mistress, but after inflammation and most acute anguish it festered, and the pain became numbed, but more desperate.

16  Unto You be praise, unto You be glory, O Fountain of mercies! I became more wretched, and You nearer. Your right hand was ever ready to pluck me out of the mire, and to cleanse me, but I was ignorant of it. Nor did anything recall me from a yet deeper abyss of carnal pleasures, but the fear of death and of Your future judgment, which, amid all my fluctuations of opinion, never left my breast. And in disputing with my friends, Alypius and Nebridius, concerning the nature of good and evil, I would have held that Epicurus[44] had, in my judgment, won the palm, had I not believed that after death there remained a life for the soul, and places of punishment, which Epicurus refused to believe. And I demanded, "Supposing us to be immortal, and to be living in the enjoyment of perpetual bodily pleasure, and without any fear of losing it, why, then, should we not be happy, or why should we search for anything else?"—not knowing that this very thing was a part of my great misery: that, being thus sunk and blinded, I could not discern that light of honor and beauty to be embraced for its own sake, which cannot be seen by the eye of the flesh, it being visible only to the inner man. Nor did I, unhappy one, consider out of what vein it emanated, that even these things, loathsome as they were, I with pleasure discussed with my friends. Nor could I, even in accordance with what were then my notions of happiness, make myself happy without friends, amid no matter how great an abundance of carnal pleasures. And these friends assuredly I loved for their own sakes, and I knew myself to be loved by them for my own sake. O crooked ways! Woe to the audacious soul which hoped that, if it forsook You, it would find some better thing! It has turned and returned, on back, sides, and belly, and all was hard, and You alone provide rest. And behold, You are near, and deliver us from our wretched wanderings, and establish us in Your way, and comfort us, and say, "Run; I will carry you, indeed, I will lead you, and there also will I carry you."

### BOOK 8

11  Thus was I sick and tormented, accusing myself more severely than was my habit, tossing and turning in my chain[45] by which I now was barely held, but still was held, until that chain was utterly broken. And You, O Lord, pressed upon me in my inward parts by

---

40  Referring to New Testament, Matthew 7.13.

41  Referring to Old Testament, Psalms 33.11.

42  Referring to Old Testament, Psalms 145.15,16.

43  A marriage had been arranged by this time between Augustine and a girl below marriageable age.

44  Epicurus was a Hellenistic philosopher who influenced later Romans. He held that the soul does not survive after death, and that people should pursue pleasure. Although the term "epicurean" does not suggest it, Epicurus held that the highest pleasures were not sensual.

45  I.e., his sinful habits.

a severe mercy, redoubling the lashes of fear and shame, so that I would not give way again, and that same slender remaining tie not being broken off, it should recover strength, and enchain me the faster. For I said mentally, "Lo, let it be done now, let it be done now." And as I spoke, I all but came to a resolve. I all but did it, yet did it not do it. Yet I did not go back to my old condition, but took up my position hard by, and drew breath. And I tried again, and lacked but very little to reach it, and then somewhat less, and then all but touched and grasped it, and yet did not reach it, nor touched, nor grasped it, hesitating to die unto death, and to live unto life. The worse way, to which I had been habituated, prevailed more with me than the better way, which I had not tried. And the nearer the moment in which I was to become another man approached, the more horror struck into me. But it did not drive me back or turn me aside, but kept me in suspense.

The very trifle of trifles, and vanities of vanities, my old mistresses, still enthralled me. They shook my fleshly garment, and whispered softly, "Are you leaving us? And from that moment will we no longer be with you, forever? And from that moment will this or that be unlawful for you, forever?" And what did they suggest to me in the words "this or that"? What is it that they suggested, O my God? Let Your mercy avert it from the soul of Your servant. What impurities did they suggest! What shame! And now I far less than half heard them, not openly showing themselves and contradicting me, but muttering, as it were, behind my back, and furtively plucking at me as I was departing, to make me look back upon them. Yet they delayed me, so that I hesitated to tear myself away and shake myself free from them, and to leap over to where I was called. An unruly habit was saying to me, "Do you think you can live without them?"

But now it said this very faintly. From the direction toward which I had set my face, and toward which I trembled to go, appeared to me the chaste dignity of Continence, cheerful, but not dissolutely gay, honestly luring me to come and doubt nothing, and extending her holy hands, full of a multiplicity of good examples, to receive and embrace me. There were there so many young men and maidens, a multitude of youths and of every age, grave widows and old virgins, and Continence herself was in all of them, not barren, but a fruitful mother of children, of joys, born of you, O Lord, her Husband. And she smiled to me with an encouraging mockery, as if to say, "Can you not do what these youths and maidens can? Or think that one or another of them do it by themselves, and not in the Lord their God? Why do you stand in your own strength, and so not stand at all? Cast yourself upon Him, and do not be afraid. He will not withdraw so you will fall. Cast yourself upon him without fear. He will receive you, and heal you." And I blushed without measure, for I still heard the mutterings of those trifles, and remained undecided. And she again seemed to say, "Shut up your ears against those unclean, earthly parts of yours, that they may be mortified.[46] They tell you of delights, but not as the law of the Lord your God does."[47] This controversy in my heart was nothing but self against self. Alypius, sitting close beside me, waited in silence for the result of my unaccustomed emotion.

12   But when a profound reflection had, from the hidden depths of my soul, drawn together and heaped up all my misery before the sight of my heart, there arose in me a mighty storm, accompanied by as mighty a shower of tears. So I might pour forth that shower fully, I stole away from Alypius, for it seemed to me that solitude was more fit for the business of weeping. So I retired to such a distance that even his presence could not be oppressive to me. Thus it was with me at the time, and he perceived it, for I had said something, I believe, in which the sound of my voice appeared choked with weeping, and I got up in that state. He then remained where we had been sitting, completely astonished. I flung myself down (how, I do not know) under a certain fig tree, giving full vent to my tears, and the streams of my eyes gushed out, an acceptable sacrifice to You.[48] And, indeed not in these words, but to this effect, I said a great deal to You: "But how long,

---

46   Referring to New Testament, Colossians 3.5.
47   Referring to Old Testament, Psalms 119.85.
48   Referring to New Testament, 1 Peter 2.5.

O Lord?"[49] "How long, Lord? Will You be angry forever? Oh, do not remember former iniquities against us,"[50] for I felt I was enthralled by them. I sent up these sorrowful cries: "How long, how long? Tomorrow and tomorrow? Why not now? Why is not there an end to this uncleanness this hour?"

I was saying these things, and weeping in the most bitter contrition of my heart when, lo, I heard a voice like that of a boy or girl (I do not know which) coming from a neighboring house, chanting, and frequently repeating, "Pick up and read, pick up and read." My countenance immediately changed, and I began very earnestly to consider whether it was usual for children to sing such words in any kind of game—nor could I remember ever having heard them do so. So, restraining my torrent of tears, I rose up, interpreting the words in no way other than as a command to me from Heaven to open the book[51] and to read the first chapter I came upon. For I had heard that Anthony,[52] accidentally coming in while the gospel was being read, received the admonition that what was being read was addressed to him: "Go and sell what you have, and give to the poor, and you will have treasure in heaven, and come follow me."[53] By such a divine statement he was immediately converted to You. So I quickly returned to where Alypius was sitting, for there I had put down the volume of the apostles when I had gotten up. I grasped the book, opened it, and in silence read the first paragraph on which my eyes fell: "Not in rioting and drunkenness, not in lust and wantonness, not in strife and envy, but put on the Lord Jesus Christ, and do not provide for the flesh to fulfill its lusts."[54] I would read no further, nor did I need to, for instantly, as the sentence ended, all the gloom of doubt vanished away, by means, as it were, of a light of security infused into my heart.

Closing the book, then, and marking the spot with my finger or in some other way, I now with a tranquil countenance made it known to Alypius. And he thus disclosed to me what was wrought in him, which I did not know. He asked to look at what I had read. I showed him; and he looked even further than I had read, and I did not know what followed. Truly, it was this: "Him that is weak in the faith, receive,"[55] which he applied to himself, as he told me. He was strengthened by this admonition. By a good resolution and purpose, very much in accord with his character (wherein, for the better, he was always very different from me), without any restless delay he joined me. From there, we went in to my mother. We made it known to her—she rejoiced. We related how it came to pass—she leaped for joy, and triumphed, and blessed You, who are "able to do exceeding abundantly above all that we ask or think,"[56] for she perceived You to have given her more for me than she used to ask by her pitiful and most doleful groanings. For You converted me to Yourself, so that I sought neither a wife, nor any other of this world's hopes, standing in that rule of faith in which You, so many years before, had showed me to her in a vision. You turned her grief into a gladness[57] much more plentiful than she had desired, and much dearer and chaster than having the grandchildren of my body, which she used to crave.

BOOK 9

[*Augustine and Monica are waiting for a ship to take from the Italian port of Ostia home to Africa. Augustine's mother has been telling him that she looks for no more joys in this life except that Augustine become a Christian before she dies.*]

11   I do not well remember what reply I made to her. However, scarcely five days after, or not much more,

---

49   Old Testament, Psalms 6.3.
50   Old Testament, Psalms 79.5,8.
51   A New Testament.
52   Saint Anthony, a leading founder of monasticism in the fourth century.
53   New Testament, Matthew 19.21.
54   New Testament, Romans 13.13,14.
55   New Testament, Romans 14.1.
56   New Testament, Ephesians 3.20.
57   Referring to Old Testament, Psalms 30.11.

she was prostrated by fever; and while she was sick, she one day sank into a swoon, and was for a short time unconscious of visible things. We hurried up to her; but she soon regained her senses, and gazing on me and my brother as we stood by her, she said to us inquiringly, "Where was I?" Then looking intently at us stupefied with grief, "Here," she said, "you will bury your mother." I was silent, and refrained from weeping; but my brother said something, wishing her, as the happier lot, to die in her own country and not abroad. She, when she heard this, with anxious countenance arrested him with her eye, as savoring such things, and then gazing at me, said, "Behold what he says" and soon after to us both she said, "Lay this body anywhere, do not let care for it trouble you at all. I ask only this: that you will remember me at the Lord's altar, wherever you may be." And when she had given forth this statement in such words as she could, she was silent, being in pain with her increasing sickness.

But, as I reflected on Your gifts, O You invisible God, which You instill into the hearts of Your faithful ones, from which such marvelous fruits spring, I rejoiced and gave thanks to You, calling to mind what I knew before, how she had always burned with anxiety respecting her burial-place, which she had provided and prepared for herself next to the body of her husband. For as they had lived very peacefully together, her desire had also been (so little is the human mind capable of grasping divine things) that this should be added to that happiness, and be talked of among men, that after her wandering beyond the sea, it had been granted her that they both, so united on earth, should lie in the same grave. But I did not know when this uselessness had, through the bounty of Your goodness, begun to be no longer in her heart, and I was full of joy admiring what she had thus disclosed to me, though indeed in our conversation in the window also, when she said, "What am I still doing here?" she appeared not to desire to die in her own country. I heard afterwards, too, that at the time we were at Ostia, with a maternal confidence, she one day, when I was absent, was speaking with certain of my friends on the condemning of this life, and the blessing of death. When they—amazed at the courage which You had given to her, a woman—asked her whether she did not dread leaving her body at such a distance from her own city, she replied, "Nothing is far to God, nor need I fear that He should be ignorant at the end of the world of the place from which He is to raise me up." On the ninth day, then, of her sickness, the fifty-sixth year of her age, and the thirty-third of mine, was that religious and devout soul set free from the body.

12   I closed my eyes, and a great sadness flowed into my heart, and it was passing into tears when, by a violent effort of mind, my eyes dried—woe was me in such a struggle! As soon as she had breathed her last, the boy Adeodatus[58] burst out into wails, but became quiet after he was stopped by all of us. In the same manner my own childish feeling, which was, through the youthful voice of my heart, finding its escape through tears, was restrained and silenced, for we did not consider it fitting to celebrate that funeral with tearful complaints and moanings; they who die unhappy or who die entirely are customarily mourned in such a way. But she died neither unhappy nor entirely. We were assured of this by the witness of her good life, by her "faith unfeigned,"[59] and other sufficient grounds.

What, then, was that which grievously pained me within, but that newly made wound, from having that most dear and sweet habit of living together suddenly broken off? I was indeed full of joy in her testimony when, in her final illness, flattering my dutifulness, she called me "kind" and recalled, with great feeling of love, that she had never heard any harsh or reproachful sound come out of my mouth against her. But yet, O my God, who made us, how can the honor which I paid to her be compared with her slavery for me? As, then, I was left destitute of so great a comfort in her, my soul was stricken, and that life, as it were, torn apart—that life which had made but one life out of her life and mine.

---

58  Augustine's son.
59  New Testament, 1 Timothy 1.5.

The boy being then restrained from weeping, Evodius took up the Psalter[60] and began to sing the Psalm "I will sing of mercy and judgment unto You, O Lord,"[61] with the whole house responding. When they heard what we were doing, many brethren and religious women came together, and while they whose office it was made ready for the funeral, I, in a convenient part of the house, discussed matters suitable for the occasion with those who thought I should not be left alone. These true words mitigated the anguish which You knew, though my hearers, who listened intently, were unconscious of it, and thought I was devoid of any sense of sorrow. But in Your ears, where none of them heard, I blamed the softness of my feelings, and restrained the flow of my grief, which yielded a little, but then returned, though not as a new flood of tears, or as a change of countenance, although I knew what I repressed in my heart. And as I was exceedingly annoyed that these human things had such power over me, which in the due order and destiny of our natural condition must necessarily come to pass, I sorrowed for my sorrow with a new sorrow, and was wasted by a double sadness.

So, when the body was carried forth, we both went and returned without tears. For neither in those prayers which we poured forth to You when the sacrifice of our redemption[62] was offered to You for her (the dead body now being placed next to the grave before it is laid in it, as is customary) nor in their prayers did I shed tears. Yet I was most grievously sad in secret all day, and with a troubled mind I entreated You, as I was able, to heal my sorrow. You did not do so, but fixed, I believe, in my memory by this one lesson the power of the bonds of all habit, even on a mind which now fed on not a fallacious word. It also appeared to me a good thing to go and bathe, as I had heard that the word "bath"[63] comes from the Greek

*balaneion*[64] because it drives trouble from the mind. Lo, this also I confess to Your mercy, "Father of the fatherless,"[65] that I bathed, and felt the same as I had before I had done so. For the bitterness of my grief did not leave my heart. Then I slept, and on waking up found my grief much reduced, and as I lay alone on my bed, there came into my head those verses of Your Ambrose,[66] for You are

Maker of all things! God most high!
Great Ruler of the starry sky!
Who, robing day with beauteous light,
Has clothed in soft repose the night,
That sleep may wearied limbs restore,
And fit for toil and use once more;
May gently soothe the careworn breast,
And lull our anxious griefs to rest.[67]

And then little by little did I bring back my former thoughts of Your handmaid, her devout conversation towards You, her holy tenderness and attentiveness towards us, which was suddenly taken away from me; it was pleasant to me to weep in Your sight, for her and for me, concerning her and concerning myself. I set free the tears which before I repressed, so they might flow at their will, spreading them beneath my heart; and it rested in them, for Your ears were nigh me—not those of man, who would have put a scornful interpretation on my weeping. But now in writing I confess it to You, O Lord! Read it who will, and interpret how he will. If he finds me to have sinned in weeping for my mother during so small a part of an hour (that mother who was for a while dead to my eyes, who had for many years wept for me, that I might live in Your eyes) let him not laugh at me, but rather, if he is a man of noble charity, let him weep for my sins against You, the Father of all the brethren of Your Christ.

---

60  A book of psalms from the Old Testament, arranged for use in church services.
61  Old Testament, Psalms 101.5.
62  I.e., the communion (the ritual consumption of bread and wine).
63  The Latin is "balneum."
64  Greek: "bath."
65  Old Testament, Psalms 66.5.
66  St. Ambrose, the bishop of Milan, who had helped Augustine toward his conversion.
67  The translation is by J.D. Chambers, 1854.

13   But, my heart being now healed of that wound, in so far as it could be convicted of a carnal[68] affection, I pour out to You, O our God, on behalf of Your handmaid, tears of a far different sort, even that which flows from a spirit broken by the thoughts of the dangers of every soul that dies in Adam. And although she, having been "made alive" in Christ[69] even before she was freed from the flesh, had so lived as to praise Your name both by her faith and conversation, yet I dare not say that from the time You regenerated her by baptism, no word went forth from her mouth against Your precepts.[70] And it has been declared by Your Son, the Truth, that "Whoever shall say to his brother, 'You fool,' shall be in danger of hell fire."[71] And woe even to the praiseworthy life of man, if, putting away mercy, You should investigate it. But because You do not narrowly inquire after sins, we hope with confidence to find some place of indulgence with You. But whosoever recounts his true merits to You, what is it that he recounts to You but Your own gifts? Oh, if men would know themselves to be men; and that "he that glorieth" would "glory in the Lord!"[72]

O my Praise and my Life, You God of my heart, I therefore, putting aside for a little her good deeds, for which I joyfully give thanks to You, do now beseech You for the sins of my mother. Listen to me, through that Medicine of His wounds who hung on the cross, and who, sitting at Your right hand, "makes intercession for us."[73] I know that she acted mercifully, and from the heart forgave her debtors their debts; forgive her her debts also,[74] whatever she contracted during so many years since the water of salvation. Forgive her, O Lord, forgive her, I beseech You; "do not enter into judgment"[75] with her. Let Your mercy be exalted above Your justice[76] because Your words are true, and You have promised mercy to "the merciful"[77] which You gave them to be who will "have mercy" on whom You will "have mercy," and will "have compassion" on whom You have had compassion.[78]

And I believe You have already done that which I ask You; but "accept the free will offerings of my mouth, O Lord."[79] For she, when the day of her dissolution was near at hand, took no thought to have her body sumptuously covered, or embalmed with spices; nor did she covet a choice monument, or desire her paternal burial-place. She did not entrust these things to us, but only desired to have her name remembered at Your altar, which she had served without the omission of a single day; whence she knew that the holy sacrifice was dispensed, by which the handwriting that was against us is blotted out,[80] by which the enemy was triumphed over who, summing up our offenses, and searching for something to bring against us, found nothing in Him[81] in whom we conquer. Who will restore to Him the innocent blood? Who will repay Him the price with which He bought us, so as to take us from Him? Your handmaid bound her soul by the bond of faith to the sacrament of our ransom. Let none separate her from Your protection. Let not the "lion" and the "dragon" introduce himself by force or fraud.[82] For she will not reply that she owes nothing, lest she be convicted and gotten the better of by the

---

68   Referring to New Testament, Romans 8.7.
69   Referring to New Testament, 1 Corinthians 15.22.
70   Referring to New Testament, Matthew 12.36.
71   New Testament, Matthew 5.22.
72   New Testament, 2 Corinthians 10.17.
73   New Testament, Romans 8.34.
74   Referring to New Testament, Matthew 18.35.
75   Old Testament, Psalms 143.2.
76   Referring to New Testament, James 2.13.
77   New Testament, Matthew 5.7.
78   New Testament, Romans 9.15.
79   Old Testament, Psalms 119.108.
80   Referring to New Testament, Colossians 2.14.
81   Referring to New Testament, John 14.30.
82   Old Testament, Psalms 91.13.

wily deceiver, but she will answer that her "sins are forgiven"[83] by Him to whom no one is able to repay that price which He, owing nothing, laid down for us.

May she therefore rest in peace with her husband, before or after whom she married none, whom she obeyed, with patience bringing forth fruit[84] to You, that she might gain him also for You. And inspire, O my Lord my God, inspire Your servants, my brethren, Your sons my masters, who with voice and heart and writings I serve, that as many of them as read these confessions may at Your altar remember Monica, Your handmaid, together with Patricius, her sometime husband, by whose flesh You introduced me into this life, in what manner I do not know. May they with pious affection be mindful of my parents in this transitory light, of my brethren that are under You our Father in our Catholic mother, and of my fellow-citizens in the eternal Jerusalem, which the wandering of Your people sighs for from their departure until their return. That so my mother's last entreaty to me may, through my confessions more than through my prayers, be more abundantly fulfilled through the prayers of many.

### BOOK 10

30   Truly, You command that I should be continent from the "lust of the flesh, and the lust of the eyes, and the pride of life."[85] You have commanded me to abstain from concubinage. As to marriage itself: You have advised something better than You have allowed. And because You gave it, it was done, and done before I became a dispenser of Your sacrament. But there are still in my memory—of which I have spoken much—the images of such things as my habits had fixed there. Though weak, these images rush into my thoughts when I am awake, but in sleep they do so not only so as to give pleasure, but even to obtain consent, and what very nearly resembles reality. Indeed,

the illusion of the image prevails to such an extent, both in my soul and in my flesh, that the false images persuade me, when sleeping, to what the true are not able when waking. Am I not myself at that time, O Lord my God? And there is yet so much difference between myself and myself in that instant in which I pass back from waking to sleeping, or return from sleeping to waking. Where, then, is reason which, when I am awake, resists such suggestions? And if the things themselves are forced on it, I remain unmoved. Is it shut up with the eyes? Or is it put to sleep with the bodily senses? But from there, then, does it come to pass that even in slumber we often resist, and, bearing our purpose in mind, and continuing most chastely in it, yield no assent to such allurements? And there is yet so much difference that, when it happens otherwise, upon awaking, we return to peace of conscience, and by this same diversity we discover that it was not we that did it, while we still feel sorry that in some way it was done in us.

Is not Your hand able, O Almighty God, to heal all the diseases of my soul,[86] and by Your more abundant grace to quench even the lascivious motions of my sleep? You will increase in me, O Lord, Your gifts more and more, that my soul may follow me to You, disengaged from the snare of concupiscence, that it may not be in rebellion against itself, and even in dreams not simply, through sensual images, commit those deformities of corruption, even to the pollution of the flesh, but that it may not even consent to them. For it is no great thing for the Almighty, who is "able to do ... above all that we ask or think,"[87] to bring it about that no such influence—not even so slight a one as a sign might restrain—should afford gratification to the chaste affection even of one sleeping, and that not only in this life, but at my present age. But what I still am in this species of my ill, have I confessed unto my good Lord, rejoicing with trembling[88] in that which You have given me, and bewailing that in which I am still

---

83   New Testament, Matthew 9.2.
84   Referring to New Testament, Luke 8.15.
85   New Testament, 1 John 2.16.
86   Referring to Old Testament, Psalms 103.3.
87   New Testament, Ephesians 3.20.
88   Referring to Old Testament, Psalms 2.11.

imperfect, trusting that You will perfect Your mercies in me, even to the fullness of peace, which both that which is within and that which is without shall have with You, when death is swallowed up in victory.[89]

31 There is another daily evil, which I wish were "enough."[90] For by eating and drinking we repair the daily decay of the body, until You destroy both food and stomach, when You shall destroy my need with an amazing satiety, and shall clothe this corruptible nature with an eternal, incorruptible one.[91] But now this need is sweet to me, and against this sweetness I fight, so I will not be enthralled. I carry on a daily war by fastings, often "bringing my body into subjection,"[92] and my pains are expelled by pleasure. For hunger and thirst are in some way pains. They consume and destroy like a fever, unless the medicine of nourishment relieves us. Such cure is at hand through the comfort we receive of Your gifts, with which land and water and air serve our infirmity; our calamity is called pleasure.

You taught me this much: that I should bring myself to take food as medicine. But during the time that I am passing from the uneasiness of want to the calmness of satiety, even in the very passage that snare of concupiscence lies in wait for me. For the passage itself is pleasure, nor is there any other way of passing there, to where necessity compels us to pass. And whereas health is the reason for eating and drinking, there joins itself as a handmaid a perilous delight, which mostly tries to precede it, in order that I may do for her sake what I say I do, or desire to do, for health's sake. Nor do both have the same limit. For what is sufficient for health is too little for pleasure. And often it is doubtful whether it is the necessary care of the body which still asks for nourishment, or whether a sensual snare of desire offers its ministry. In this uncertainty my unhappy soul rejoices, and therein prepares an excuse as a defense, glad that what may be sufficient for the moderation of health does not appear, so that under the pretense of health it may conceal the business of pleasure. I endeavor to resist these temptations daily, and I summon Your right hand to my assistance, and refer my excitements to You, because as yet I have no resolve in this matter.

I hear the voice of my God commanding, do not let "your hearts be overcharged with surfeiting and drunkenness."[93] "Drunkenness," is far from me. May You have mercy so that it will not come near me. But eating to excess sometimes creeps up on Your servant. May You have mercy, that it may be far from me. For no one can be continent unless You give it.[94] You give us many things which we pray for, and whatever good we receive before we prayed for it, we receive from You, and we also receive as Your gift the fact that we afterwards know this. I was never a drunkard, but I have known drunkards to be made sober men by You. It was Your doing, then, that they who were never drunkards might not be so, just as it was from You that they who have been so heretofore might not remain so always. And it was from You that the gift that both might know from whom it came. I heard another voice of Yours, "Go not after your lusts, but keep yourself from your appetites."[95] And by Your favor have I also heard this saying, which I have much delighted in, "Neither if we eat, are we the better; neither if do not we eat, are we the worse,"[96] which is to say, that neither shall the one make me have plenty, nor the other to be wretched. I heard also another voice, "For I have learned, in whatever state I am, to be content with it; I know both how to be abased, and I know how to have much.... I can do all things through Christ which strengthens me."[97] (Behold speaking here a sol-

89 Referring to New Testament, Corinthians 15.54.
90 New Testament, Matthew 6.34.
91 Referring to New Testament, 1 Corinthians 15.54.
92 New Testament, 1 Corinthians 9.27.
93 New Testament, Luke 21.34.
94 Referring to Apocrypha, Wisdom 8.21.
95 Referring to Apocrypha, Ecclesiasticus 18.30.
96 New Testament, 1 Corinthians 8.8.
97 New Testament, Philippians 4.11-14.

dier of the celestial army, not dust as we are.) But remember, O Lord, "that we are dust,"[98] and You created man out of dust[99] and he "was lost, and is found."[100] Nor could he do this of his own power, seeing that he[101] whom I so loved, saying these things through Your inspiration, was of that same dust. "I can," he says, "do all things through Him which strengths me."[102] Strengthen me, that I may be able. Give what You command and command what You will. He confesses to have received Your gifts, and when he glories, he glories in the Lord.[103] I have heard another begging to receive gifts, saying, "Take from me the greediness of the belly,"[104] by which it appears, O my holy God, that You give when what You command to be done is done.

You have taught me, good Father, that "to the pure all things are pure,"[105] but "it is evil for that man who eats with offense,"[106] "and that every creature of Yours is good, and nothing to be refused, if it is received with thanksgiving,"[107] and that "meat does not commend us to God,"[108] and that no man should "judge us in meat or drink,"[109] and that he that eats, let him not despise him that does not, and let not him that does not eat judge him that eats.[110] I have learned these things, thanks and praise be to You, O my God and Master, who knocks at my ears

and enlightens my heart; deliver me from all temptation. It is not the uncleanness of meat that I fear, but the uncleanness of lust. I know that permission was granted to Noah to eat every kind of flesh[111] that was good for food; that Elias was fed with flesh;[112] that John, endowed with a wonderful abstinence, was not polluted by the living creatures (that is, the locusts) on which he fed.[113] I know, too, that Esau was deceived by a longing for lentils,[114] and that David blamed himself for desiring water,[115] and that our King[116] was tempted not by flesh, but bread.[117] And the people in the wilderness, therefore, also deserved reproof not because they desired flesh, but because, in their desire for food, they murmured against the Lord.[118]

Placed, then, in the midst of these temptations, I strive daily against longing for food and drink. For this is not of such a nature as that I am able to resolve to cut it off once for all, and not touch it afterwards, as I was able to do with concubinage. The bridle of the throat, therefore, is to be held in between slackness and tightness. And who, O Lord, is he who is not in some degree carried away beyond the bounds of necessity? Whoever he is, he is great; let him magnify Your name. But I am not such a one, "for I am a sinful man."[119] Yet I also magnify Your name, and He who

---

98  Old Testament, Psalms 103.14.
99  Referring to Old Testament, Genesis, 3.19.
100 New Testament, Luke, 15.32.
101 I.e., Saint Paul the apostle, earlier quoted by Augustine.
102 New Testament, Philippians 4.13.
103 Referring to New Testament, 1 Corinthians 1.31.
104 Apocrypha, Ecclesiasticus 23.6.
105 New Testament, Titus 1.15.
106 New Testament, Romans 14.20.
107 New Testament, 1 Timothy 4.4.
108 New Testament, 1 Corinthians 8.8.
109 New Testament, Colossians 2.16.
110 Referring to New Testament, Romans 13.23.
111 Referring to Old Testament, Genesis 9.3.
112 Referring to Old Testament, 1 Kings 17.6.
113 Referring to New Testament, Matthew 3.4.
114 Referring to Old Testament, Genesis 25.34.
115 Referring to Old Testament, 2 Samuel 23.15-17.
116 I.e., Jesus.
117 Referring to New Testament, Matthew 4.3.
118 Referring to Old Testament, Numbers 11.
119 New Testament, Luke 5.8.

has "overcome the world"[120] intercedes with You for my sins, accounting me among the "feeble members" of His body,[121] because Your eyes saw that of him which was imperfect, and in Your book all shall be written.[122]

32 I am not much troubled by the attractions of odors. When absent I do not seek them, and when present I do not refuse them, and I am prepared to be always without them. At any rate, thus I appear to myself—perhaps I am deceived. For that also is a lamentable darkness in which my capacity is hidden in me, so that my mind, making inquiry into itself concerning its own powers, does not venture readily to believe itself because that which is already in it is, for the most part, concealed, unless experience reveals it. And no one ought to feel secure[123] in this life, the whole of which is called a temptation, so that one who could be made better from worse may not also from better be made worse. Our sole hope, our sole confidence, our sole assured promise, is Your mercy.

33 The delights of the ear had more powerfully inveigled and conquered me, but You unbound and liberated me. Now, hymns of praise to You, when sung with a sweet and trained voice, I do somewhat enjoy, yet not so as to cling to them, but so as to free myself when I wish. But with the words which are their life do they, so that they may gain admission into me, strive after a place of some honor in my heart; I can hardly assign them a fitting one. Sometimes I appear to myself to give them more respect than is fitting, as I perceive that our minds are more devoutly and earnestly elevated into a flame of piety by the holy words themselves when they are thus sung, than when they are not. I also am aware that all feelings of our spirit, by their own diversity, have their appropriate measures in the voice and singing, wherewith I do not know by what secret relationship they are stimulated. But the gratification of my flesh, to which the mind ought never to be given over so as to be para-

lyzed, often beguiles me, while the senses do not follow reason so as to follow her patiently, but having gained admission merely for her sake, they strive even to run on before her, and be her leader. Thus in these things I sin unknowingly, but afterwards do I know it.

Sometimes, again, avoiding very earnestly this same deception, I err out of too great preciseness, sometimes so much as to wish that every tune of the pleasant songs to which David's Psalter is often sung be banished, both from my ears and those of the Church itself. That path to me seemed safer which I remembered to have been often related to me concerning Athanasius, bishop of Alexandria, who obliged the reader of the psalm to use so slight an inflection of voice that it was more like speaking than singing. Notwithstanding that, when I call to mind the tears I shed at the songs of Your Church, at the outset of my recovered faith, and how even now I am moved not by the singing but by what is sung, when they are sung with a clear and skilfully modulated voice, I then acknowledge the great utility of this custom. Thus I vacillate between dangerous pleasure and proven soundness, being inclined rather (though I pronounce no irrevocable opinion upon the subject) to approve of the use of singing in church, so that by the delights of the ear weaker minds may be stimulated to devotion. Yet when it happens that I am more moved by the singing than by what is sung, I confess I have sinned criminally, and then I would rather not have heard the singing. See now the condition I am in! Weep with me, and weep for me, you who so control your inward feelings that good results ensue. As for you who do not act thus, these things do not concern you. But You, O Lord my God, give ear, behold and see, and have mercy upon me, and heal me[124]—You, in whose sight I become a puzzle to myself; "this is my infirmity."[125]

34 There remain the delights of these eyes of my flesh. May I make my confessions concerning them in the hearing of the ears of Your temple, those fraternal

---

120 New Testament, John 16.33.
121 Referring to New Testament, 1 Corinthians 12.22.
122 Referring to Old Testament, Psalms 139.16.
123 Referring to Old Testament, Job 7.1.
124 Referring to Old Testament, Psalms 6.2.
125 Old Testament, Psalms 77.10.

and devout ears, and so conclude this discussion of the temptations of "the lust of the flesh"[126] which still assail me, groaning and desiring to be sheltered by my house from heaven.[127] The eyes delight in fair and varied forms, and bright and pleasing colors. Do not allow these to take possession of my soul. Instead let God possess it—He who made these things "very good"[128] indeed. He is my good, not these. And these move me while I am awake, during the day, nor is rest from them granted me, as there is from the voices of melody, sometimes, in silence. For that queen of colors, light, flooding all that we look upon, wherever I am during the day, gliding past me in manifold forms, soothes me when I am busy with other things, and do not notice it. And it insinuates itself so strongly that if it is suddenly withdrawn, it is looked for longingly, and if long absent, saddens the mind.

O You Light, which Tobias saw,[129] when, his eyes being closed, he taught his son the way of life, himself going before with the feet of charity, never going astray. Or that which Isaac saw, when his fleshly "eyes were dim, so that he could not see"[130] by reason of old age. It was permitted him, not to bless his sons knowingly, but in blessing them to know them. Or that which Jacob saw, when he too, blind through great age, with an enlightened heart, in the persons of his own sons, threw light upon the races of the future people, presignified in them, and laid his hands, mystically crossed, upon his grandchildren by Joseph, not as their father, looking outwardly, corrected them, but as he himself distinguished them.[131] This is the light, the only one, and all those who see and love it are one. But that corporeal light of which I was speaking seasons the life of the world for her blind lovers with a tempting and fatal sweetness. But they who know how to praise You for it, "Maker of all things! God most

high!" take it up in Your hymn, and are not taken up with it in their sleep. I desire that I be thus. I resist seductions of the eyes, so my feet with which I advance on Your way will not be entangled. I raise my invisible eyes to You, so You would be pleased to "pluck my feet out of the net."[132] You continually pluck them out, for they are ensnared. You never cease to pluck them out, but I constantly remain fast in the snares set all around me because You "that keep Israel shall neither slumber nor sleep."[133]

What numberless things, made by diverse arts and manufactures, both in our apparel, shoes, vessels, and every kind of work, in pictures, too, and sundry images, and these going far beyond necessary and moderate use and holy signification, have men added for the enthrallment of the eyes. Following outwardly what they make, forsaking inwardly Him by whom they were made, indeed, and destroying that which He made in them! But I, O my God and my Joy, do hence also sing a hymn to You, and offer a sacrifice of praise to my Sanctifier because those beautiful patterns, which through the medium of men's souls are conveyed into their artistic hands, emanate from that Beauty which is above our souls, for which my soul sighs day and night. But as for the makers and followers of those outward beauties, they derive from that Beauty the way of judging them, but not of using them. And though they do not see Him, yet He is there, that they might not go astray, but keep their strength for You,[134] and not dissipate it upon delicious weariness. And I, though I both say and perceive this, impede my course with such beauties. But You rescue me, O Lord, You rescue me, "for Your loving kindness is before my eyes."[135] For I am taken miserably, and You rescue me mercifully. Sometimes, when I come upon these hesitatingly, I do not perceive Your rescue

126  New Testament, 1 John 2.16.
127  Referring to New Testament, 2 Corinthians 5.2.
128  Old Testament, Genesis 1.31.
129  Referring to Apocrypha, Tobit 4.
130  Old Testament, Genesis 27.1.
131  Referring to Old Testament, Genesis 43.13-19.
132  Old Testament, Psalms 25.15.
133  Old Testament, Psalms 121.4.
134  Referring to Old Testament, Psalms 58.10.
135  Old Testament, Psalms 26.3.

of me. At other times, when held fast by them, I perceive your rescue of me with pain.

35   In addition to this there is another form of temptation, more complex in its peril. For besides that concupiscence of the flesh which lies in the gratification of all senses and pleasures, in which its slaves who "are far from You perish,"[136] there pertains to the soul, through the same senses of the body, a certain vain and curious longing, cloaked under the name of knowledge and learning, not of having pleasure in the flesh, but in inquisitiveness. This longing, since it originates in an appetite for knowledge, and the sight being the chief among the senses in the acquisition of knowledge, is called in divine language, "the lust of the eyes."[137] For seeing belongs properly to the eyes. Yet we apply this word to the other senses also when we exercise them in the search for knowledge. For we do not say, "listen how it glows," "smell how it glistens," "taste how it shines," or "feel how it flashes," since all these are said to be seen. And yet we say not only, "see how it shines," which the eyes alone can perceive, but also, "see how it sounds," "see how it smells," "see how it tastes," "see how hard it is." Thus the general experience of the senses, as was said before, is termed "the lust of the eyes" because the other senses, by way of similitude, whenever they seek out knowledge, take possession of the function of seeing, in which the eyes hold preeminence.

But by this pleasure and inquisitiveness are more clearly distinguished: when pleasure or curiosity is pursued by the senses, pleasure follows after objects that are beautiful, melodious, fragrant, savory, or soft; but curiosity, for inquisitiveness's sake, seeks the contrary of these—not with a view of undergoing discomfort, but from the passion of inquiring about and knowing them. For what pleasure is there to see, in a lacerated corpse, that which makes you shudder? And yet if it lies near, we flock to it, to be made sad and turn pale. Even in sleep they fear that they should see it, as though when awake someone compelled them to go and see it, or any report of its beauty had attracted them! Thus also is it with the other senses, which it

would be tedious to discuss further. All those strange sights exhibited in the theater come from this malady of curiosity. Hence we proceed to search out the secret powers of nature (which is beside our end), which it does not profit us to know, and concerning which men desire nothing but to know. Hence, too, with that same end of perverted knowledge, we consult magical arts. Hence, again, even in religion itself, is God tempted, when signs and wonders are eagerly asked of Him, not desired for any saving end, but simply for enjoyment.

In so vast a wilderness, replete with snares and dangers, lo, I have lopped off many of them, and expelled from my heart, as You, O God of my salvation, enabled me to do. And yet when dare I say—since so many things of this kind buzz around our daily life—when dare I say that no such thing makes me intent to see it, or creates in me vain solicitude? It is true that the theaters never carry me away now, nor do I now care to know the courses of the stars, nor has my soul at any time consulted departed spirits; I abhor all sacrilegious oaths. O Lord my God, to whom I owe all humble and single-hearted service, with what subtlety of suggestion does the enemy influence me to require some sign from You! But by our King, and by our pure and chaste country of Jerusalem, I beseech You, that as any consent to such thoughts is far from me, so may it always be farther and farther. But when I entreat You for the salvation of anyone, the end I aim at is far different, and You who do what You will, grant me, as you will grant me, that I willingly "follow" You.[138]

Nevertheless, in how many most minute and contemptible things is our curiosity daily tempted, and who can number how often we succumb? How often, when people are narrating idle tales, do we begin by tolerating them, lest we should give offense to the weak, and then gradually we listen willingly! I do not nowadays go to the circus to see a dog chasing a hare, but if by chance I pass such a race in the fields, it possibly distracts me even from some serious thought, and draws me after it—not that I turn the body of my

---

136  Old Testament, Psalms 63.27.
137  New Testament, 1 John 2.16.
138  New Testament, John 21.22.

beast aside, but I turn aside the inclination of my mind. And if You, by demonstrating to me my weakness, do not speedily warn me, either through the sight itself or by some reflection to rise to You, or wholly to despise and pass it by, I, vain one, am absorbed by it. How is it, when sitting at home, a lizard catching flies, or a spider entangling them as they rush into her nets, often stops me? Is the feeling of curiosity not the same because these are such tiny creatures? From them I proceed to praise You, the wonderful Creator and Disposer of all things, but it is not this that first attracts my attention. It is one thing to get up quickly, and another not to fall, and my life is full of such things. My only hope is in Your exceedingly great mercy, for when this heart of ours is made the receptacle of such things, and bears crowds of this abounding vanity, then are our prayers often interrupted and disturbed thereby. While in Your presence we direct the voice of our heart to Your ears, this so great a matter is broken off by the influx of I know not what idle thoughts.

36   Shall we, then, also count this inquisitiveness among those things to be lightly esteemed, or shall anything restore us to hope except Your complete mercy since You have begun to change us? You know to what extent You have already changed me, You who first healed me of the lust of vindicating myself, so You might forgive all my remaining "iniquities," and heal all my "diseases," and redeem my life from corruption, and crown me with "loving-kindness and tender mercies," and satisfy my desire with "good things," You who restrained my pride with Your fear, and subdued my neck to Your "yoke."[139] And now I bear it, and it is "light"[140] to me, because so You have promised, and made it, and so in truth it was, although I did not know it when I feared to take it up. But, O Lord—You who alone reigns without pride because You are the only true Lord, who has no lord—has this third kind of temptation left me, or can it leave me during this life?

The desire to be feared and loved by men, with no other view than that I may experience a joy therein which is no joy, is a miserable life, and unseemly ostentation. Hence especially it arises that we do not love You, nor devoutly fear You. And therefore You resist the proud, but give grace to the humble.[141] You thunder upon the ambitious designs of the world, and "the foundations of the hills" tremble.[142] Because now certain offices of human society render it necessary to be loved and feared by men, the adversary of our true blessedness presses hard upon us, everywhere scattering his snares of "well done, well done," that while acquiring them eagerly, we may be caught unawares, and disunite our joy from Your truth, and fix it on the deceits of men, and take pleasure in being loved and feared, not for Your sake, but in Your place. By this means, we, being made the adversary, he may have us as his, not in harmony of love, but in the fellowship of punishment, who aspired to exalt his throne in the north[143] that dark and cold we might serve him, who imitates You in perverse and distorted ways. But we, O Lord, lo, we are Your "little flock."[144] Possess us, stretch Your wings over us, and let us take refuge under them. Be our glory; let us be loved for Your sake, and Your word feared in us. They who desire to be commended by men when You blame, will not be defended of men when You judge, nor will they be delivered when You condemn. But, not when the sinner is praised in the desires of his soul, nor when he is blessed who acts unjustly, but a man is praised for some gift that You have bestowed upon him, and he is more gratified at the praise for himself, than that he possesses the gift from You for which he is praised, such a one is praised while You blame. And better truly is he who praised than the one who was praised. For the gift of God in man was pleasing to the one, while the other was better pleased with the gift of man than that of God.

37   By these temptations, O Lord, we are daily tried. Indeed, we are unceasingly tried. Our daily "furnace"[145] is the human tongue. And in this respect also

139  Old Testament, Psalms 103.3-5.
140  New Testament, Matthew 11.30.
141  Referring to New Testament, 1 Peter 5.5.
142  Old Testament, Psalms 18.7.
143  Referring to Old Testament, Isaiah, 14.13,14.
144  New Testament, Luke 12.32.
145  Old Testament, Isaiah 48.10 and Proverbs 27.21.

You command us to be continent. Give what You command, and command what You will. Regarding this matter, You know the groans of my heart and the rivers of my eyes. For I am not able to ascertain how far I am clean of this plague, and I stand in great fear of my "secret faults,"[146] which Your eyes perceive, though mine do not. For in other kinds of temptations I have some sort of power of examining myself, but in this, hardly any. For, both as regards the pleasures of the flesh and an idle curiosity, I see how far I have been able to hold my mind in check when I do without them, either voluntarily or by reason of their not being at hand, for then I inquire of myself how much more or less troublesome it is to me not to have them. This is also true of riches, which are sought in order that they may minister to some one of these three "lusts,"[147] or to two, or all of them. If the mind is not able to see clearly, when it has riches, whether it despises them, they may be cast on one side, that the mind may thus prove itself. But if we desire to test our power of doing without praise, do we need to live so wickedly and immoderately that everyone who knows us shall detest us? What greater madness than this can be either said or conceived? But if praise both is accustomed to be and ought to be the companion of a good life and of good works, we should as little forego its companionship as a good life itself. But unless a thing is absent, I do not know whether I shall be contented or troubled at being without it.

What, then, do I confess to You, O Lord, about this kind of temptation? What, except that I am delighted with praise, but more with the truth itself than with praise? For were I to have my choice, whether I had rather, being mad, or astray on all things, be praised by all men, or, being firm and well-assured in the truth, but blamed by all, I see which I would choose. Yet would I be unwilling that the approval of another should even add to my joy for any good I have. Yet I admit that it does increase it and, more than that, that dispraise diminishes it. And when I am disquieted at this misery of mine, an excuse presents itself to me, the value of which You, God, know, for it renders me uncertain. For since it is not continency alone that You have enjoined upon us, that is, from what things to hold back our love, but righteousness also, that is, upon what to bestow it, and have wished us to love not You only, but also our neighbor[148]—often, when gratified by well-observed praise from my neighbor, I appear to myself to be gratified by the proficiency or future promise of my neighbor, and again to be sorry concerning evil in him when I hear him dispraise either that which he does not understand or which is good. For I am sometimes grieved at praise of me, either when those things which I am displeased at in myself are praised in me, or when even lesser and trifling goods in me are more valued than they should be. But, again, how do I know whether I am thus affected, because I am unwilling that he who praises me should differ from me concerning myself—not as being moved with consideration for him, but because the same good things which please me in myself are more pleasing to me when they also please another? For, in a way, I am not praised when my judgment of myself is not praised, since either those things which are displeasing to me are praised, or those more so which are less pleasing to me. Am I then uncertain of myself in this matter?

Behold, O Truth, in You do I see that I ought not to be moved at my own praises for my own sake, but for my neighbor's good. And whether it is so, in truth I do not know. For concerning this I know less of myself than You do. I beseech You now, O my God, to reveal to me myself also, that I may confess to my brethren, who are to pray for me, what I find weak in myself. Once again let me more diligently examine myself. If, in my own praise, I am moved with consideration for my neighbor, why am I less moved if some other person is unjustly dispraised than if I am? Why am I more irritated at that reproach which is cast upon me, than at that which is with equal injustice cast upon another in my presence? Am I ignorant of this also? Or does it remain that I deceive myself,[149] and do not put the

---

146 Old Testament, Psalms 19.12.
147 New Testament, 1 John 2.16.
148 Referring to Old Testament, Leviticus 19.18.
149 Referring to New Testament, Galatians 6.3.

"truth"[150] before You in my heart and tongue? Put such madness far from me, O Lord, lest my mouth be to me the oil of sinners, to anoint my head.[151]

38   "I am poor and needy,"[152] yet I am better while in secret groanings I displease myself and seek Your mercy, until what is lacking in me is renewed and made complete, even up to that peace of which the eye of the proud is ignorant. Yet in the word which proceeds out of the mouth, and actions known to others, there is a most dangerous temptation—the love of praise, which, for the establishment of a certain reputation, gathers together sought-after good opinion. It tempts, even when within I reprove myself for it, on the very ground that it is reproof. Often one glories more vainly in the very scorn of vainglory, wherefore it is not any longer scorn of vainglory whereof it glories, for he does not truly condemn it when he inwardly glories.

39   Within also, within is another evil, arising out of the same kind of temptation, whereby they who please themselves in themselves become empty, although they do not please, or displease, or aim at pleasing, others. But in pleasing themselves, they much displease You, not merely taking pleasure in bad things as if they were good, but in Your good things as though they were their own, or even as if in Yours, yet as though of their own merits, or even as if though of Your grace, yet not with friendly rejoicing, but as envying that grace to others. In all these and similar perils and labors You perceive the trembling of my heart, and I feel my wounds, inflicted by me, to be cured by You.

---

150  New Testament, 1 John 1.8.
151  Referring to Old Testament, Psalms 141.5.
152  Old Testament, Psalms 109.22.

# 26

# TACITUS, *DE GERMANIA*

Tacitus (*c.* 55-120), a senator who eventually rose to be governor of the Roman province of Asia, wrote several works, including ones on Roman history, in which he criticized the rule of the emperors. He had himself had some experience on Rome's frontier with the Germans, as well as access to earlier accounts written by Romans, some of which are now lost. His own *De Germania* (*Concerning Germany*) is the fullest early written account of the Germanic peoples to survive.

---

1 Undivided Germany is separated from the Gauls, Rhaetians, and Pannonians by the Rhine and Danube rivers and from the Sarmatians and Dacians by mutual fear or mountains; the rest of it is surrounded by the ocean, which enfolds wide peninsulas and islands of vast expanse, some of whose people and kings have but recently become known to us: war has lifted the curtain.

The Rhine, rising from the inaccessible and precipitous crest of the Rhaetian Alps, after turning west for a reach of some length is lost in the North Sea. The Danube pours from the sloping and not very lofty ridge of Mount Abnoba, and visits several peoples on its course, until at length it emerges by six of its channels into the Pontic Sea; the seventh mouth is swallowed in marshes.

2 As for the Germans themselves, I should suppose them to be native to the area and only very slightly blended with new arrivals from other races or regions; for in ancient times people who sought to migrate reached their destination by sea and not by land; while, in the second place, the great ocean on the further side of Germany—at the opposite end of the world, so to speak, from us—is rarely visited by ships

from our world. Besides, even apart from the perils of an awful and unknown sea, who would have left Asia or Africa or Italy to look for Germany? With its wild scenery and harsh climate it is pleasant neither to live in nor look upon unless it be one's home.

Their ancient hymns—the only record of history which they possess—celebrate a god Tuisto, sprung from the soil, and his son Mannus as the founders of their race. To Mannus they ascribe three sons, from whose names the tribes of the seashore came to be known as Ingaevones, the central tribes as Herminones, and the rest as Istaevones. Some authorities, using the license which pertains to antiquity, claim more sons for the god and a larger number of race names: Marsi, Gambrivii, Suebi, Vandilii. These are, they say, real and ancient names, while the name of "Germany" is new. The first tribes in fact to cross the Rhine and expel the Gauls, though now called Tungri, were then styled Germans, so little by little the name—a tribal, not a national, name—prevailed, until the whole people were called by the artificial name of "Germans," first only by the victorious tribe in order to intimidate the Gauls, but afterwards among themselves also.

3  The authorities also record how Hercules[1] appeared among the Germans, and on the eve of battle the natives chant "Hercules, the first of brave men." They use as well another chant—"barritus" is the name they use for it—to inspire courage; and they forecast the results of the coming battle from the sound of the cry. Intimidation or timidity depends on the concert of the warriors; the chant seems to them to mean not so much unison of voices as union of hearts; the object they specially seek is a certain volume of hoarseness, a crashing roar, their shields being brought up to their lips, that the voice may swell to a fuller and deeper note by means of the echo.

To return. Ulysses[2] also—in the opinion of some authorities—was carried during his long and legendary wanderings into this ocean, and reached the lands of Germany. Asciburgium, which stands on the banks of the Rhine and has inhabitants today, was founded, they say, and named by him; further, they say that an altar dedicated by Ulysses, who added to his own inscription that of his father Laertes, was once found at the same place, and that certain monuments and barrows, marked with Greek letters, are still extant on the borderland between Germany and Rhaetia. I have no intention of furnishing evidence to establish or refute these assertions; everyone according to his temperament may minimize or magnify their credibility.

4  Personally, I agree with those who hold that in the peoples of Germany there has been given to the world a nation untainted by intermarriage with other peoples, a peculiar people and pure, like no one but themselves; whence it comes that their physique, in spite of their vast numbers, is identical: fierce blue eyes, red hair, tall frames. They are powerful too, but only spasmodically; they have no fondness for feats of endurance or for hard work. Nor are they well able to bear thirst and heat; they are accustomed, thanks to the climate and the soil, to cold and hunger.

5  There is some variety in the appearance of the country, but in general it is a land of bristling forests and unhealthy marshes; the rainfall is heavier on the side of Gaul; the winds are higher on the side of Noricum and Pannonia.

It is fertile in cereals, but unkind to fruit bearing trees; it is rich in flocks and herds, but for the most part they are undersized. Even the cattle lack natural beauty and majestic brows. The pride of the people is rather in the number of their beasts, which constitute the only form of wealth they value.

The gods have denied them gold and silver, whether in mercy or in wrath I find it hard to say. Not that I would assert that Germany has no veins bearing gold or silver, for who has explored there? At any rate, they are not affected, like their neighbors, by the use and possession of such things. One may see among them silver vases, given as gifts to their commanders and chieftains, but treated as of no more value than earthenware. Although the border tribes for purposes of trade treat gold and silver as precious metals, and recognize and collect certain coins of our money, the tribes of the interior practice barter in the simpler and older fashion. The coinage which appeals to them is the old and long familiar: the denarii with milled edges,[3] showing the two-horsed chariot. They prefer silver to gold—not that they have any feeling in the matter, but because a number of silver pieces is easier to use for people whose purchases consist of cheap objects of general utility.

6  Even iron is not plentiful among them, as may be gathered from the style of their weapons. Few have swords or the longer kind of lance; they carry short spears, in their language "frameae," with a narrow and small iron head, so sharp and so handy in use that they fight with the same weapon, as circumstances demand, both at close quarters and at a distance. The mounted man is content with a shield and framea; the infantry launch showers of spears as well, each man a volley, and are able to hurl these great distances, for they wear no outer clothing, or at most a light cloak.

---

1  The Roman name for the Greek hero, Heracles.

2  The Roman name for Odysseus, the hero of Homer's Greek epic, the *Odyssey*. Odysseus wandered for 10 years trying to return home after the Trojan war.

3  Denarii were Roman coins. The kind with milled edges and two-horsed chariots were in use in the last century of the Roman Republic.

Their garb is for the most part quite plain; only shields are decorated, each with a few colors. Few have breastplates; scarcely one or two at most have metal or hide helmets. The horses are conspicuous for neither beauty nor speed; but then neither are they trained like our horses to run in shifting circles: the Germans ride them forwards only or to the right, with but one turn from the straight, dressing the line so closely as they wheel that no one is left behind. In general there is more strength in their infantry, and accordingly cavalry and infantry fight in one body; the swift footed infantryman, whom they pick out of the whole body of warriors and place in front of the line, are well adapted to cavalry battles. The number of these men is fixed—100 from each canton, and among themselves "the Hundred" is the precise name they use. What was once a number only has become a title and a distinction. The battle line itself is arranged in wedges. To retire, provided you press on again, they treat as a question of tactics, not of cowardice; they carry off their dead and wounded even in drawn battles. To have abandoned one's shield is the height of disgrace. The man so dishonored cannot be present at religious rites or attend a council; many survivors of war have ended their infamy with a noose.

7 They choose their kings on the grounds of birth, their generals on the basis of courage. The authority of their kings is not unlimited or arbitrary; their generals control them by example rather than command, the troops admiring their energy and the conspicuous place they take in front of the line. But anything beyond this—capital punishment, imprisonment, even a blow—is permitted only to the priests, and then not as a penalty or under the general's orders, but in obedience to the god whom they believe accompanies them on campaign. Certain totems, in fact, and emblems are fetched from groves and carried into battle. The strongest incentive to courage lies in this, that neither chance nor casual grouping makes the squadron or the wedge, but family and kinship. Close

at hand, too, are their dearest, so that they hear the wailing voices of women and cries of children. Here are the witnesses who are in each man's eyes most precious, here the praise he covets most. The warriors take their wounds to mother and wife, who do not shrink from counting the hurts and demanding a sight of them; they give to the combatants food and encouragement.

8 Tradition relates that some battles that seemed lost have been restored by the women, by their incessant prayers and by the baring of their breasts; for so it is brought home to the men that slavery, which they dread much more keenly on their women's account, is close at hand. It follows that the loyalty of those tribes is more effectively guaranteed if you hold, among other hostages, girls of noble birth.

Further, they conceive that in women is a certain uncanny and prophetic sense; they neither scorn to consult them nor slight their answers. In the reign of Vespasian[4] of happy memory we saw Velaeda treated as a deity by many during a long period; but in ancient times they also reverenced Albruna and many other women—in no spirit of flattery, nor for the manufacture of goddesses.

9 Of the gods, they most worship Mercury,[5] to whom on certain days they count even the sacrifice of human life lawful. Hercules and Mars[6] they appease with such animal life as is permissible. A section of the Suebi sacrifices also to Isis;[7] the cause and origin of this foreign worship I have not succeeded in discovering, except that the emblem itself, which takes the shape of a Liburnian galley, shows that the ritual is imported.

Apart from this they deem it incompatible with the majesty of the heavenly host to confine the gods within walls, or to mold them into any likeness of the human face. They consecrate groves and coppices,[8] and they give divine names to that mysterious presence which is visible only to the eyes of faith.

10 To divination and casting lots they pay as much

---

4 In the years 68-79.
5 The Roman god of merchants and luck.
6 The Roman god of war.
7 An Egyptian goddess widely worshiped in the Roman world.
8 A thicket of shrubs or small trees.

attention as anyone. The method of drawing lots is uniform. A bough is cut from a nut bearing tree and divided into slips. These are distinguished by certain runes and spread casually and at random over white cloth. Afterwards, should the inquiry be official the priest of the *civitas*,[9] if private the father of the family in person, after prayers to the gods and with eyes turned to heaven takes up one slip at a time till he has done this on three separate occasions. After taking the three he interprets them according to the runes which have already been stamped on them. If the message is a prohibition, no inquiry on the same matter is made during the same day; if the message gives permission, further confirmation is required by means of divination. Among the Germans divination by consultation of the cries and flight of birds is well known. Another form of divination peculiar to them is to seek the omens and warnings furnished by horses.

In the same groves and coppices are fed certain white horses, never soiled by mortal use. These are yoked to a sacred chariot and accompanied by the priest and king, or other chief of the civitas, who then observe their neighing and snorting. On no other form of divination is more reliance placed, not merely by the people but also by their leaders. The priests they regard as the servants of the gods, but the horses are their confidants.

They have another method of taking divinations, by means of which they probe the issue of serious wars. A member of the tribe at war with them is somehow or other captured and pitted against a selected champion of their own countrymen, each in his tribal armor. The victory of one or the other is taken as a presage.

11 On small matters the chiefs consult, on larger questions the community, but with this limitation: even when the decision rests with the people, the matter is considered first by the chiefs. They meet, unless there is some unforeseen and sudden emergency, on days set apart—when the moon is either new or full. They regard these times as the most auspicious for the transaction of business. They count not days as we do, but by nights, and their decisions and proclamations are subject to this principle; the night, that is, seems to take precedence over the day.

It is a foible of their freedom that they do not meet at once and when commanded, but waste two or three days by dilatoriness in assembling. When they are finally ready to begin, they take their seats carrying arms. Silence is called for by the priests, who then have the power to force obedience. Then a king or a chief is listened to, in order of age, birth, glory in war, or eloquence. Such figures command attention through the prestige which belongs to their counsel rather than any prescriptive right to command. If the advice tendered is displeasing, the people reject it with groans; if it pleases them, they clash their spears. The most complimentary expression of assent is this martial approbation.

12 At this assembly it is also permissible to lay accusations and to bring capital charges. The nature of the death penalty differs according to the offense: traitors and deserters are hung from trees; cowards, poor fighters and notorious evil livers are plunged in the mud of marshes with a hurdle on their heads. These differences of punishment follow the principle that crime should be blazoned abroad by its retribution, but shameful actions hidden. Lighter offenses have also a measured punishment. Those convicted are fined a certain number of horses or cattle. Part of the fine goes to the king or the *civitas*; part is paid to the person who has brought the charge or to his relatives. At the same gatherings are selected chiefs, who administer law through the cantons and villages; each of them has 100 assessors from the people to act as his responsible advisors.

13 They do no business, public or private, without arms in their hands; yet the custom is that no one takes arms until the *civitas* has endorsed this competence. Then in the assembly itself one of the chiefs or his father or his relatives equip the young man with shield and spear. This corresponds with them to the toga, and is youth's first public distinction; before that he was merely a member of the household, now he becomes a member of the *res publica*.[10] Conspicuously high birth, or great services on the part of their ances-

---

9  *Civitas*: a Latin word that is sometimes translated as "city," as "state," as "the body of citizens."

10  *Res publica*: in Latin, literally "the public thing"—what Romans both under the Republic and later called their own state.

tors, may win the chieftain's approval even for the very young men. They mingle with the others, men of maturer strength and tested by long years, and have no shame to be seen among the chief's retinue. In the retinue itself degrees are observed at the chief's discretion; there is great rivalry among the retainers to decide who shall have the first place with the chief, and among the chieftains as to who shall have the largest and most enthusiastic retinue. It is considered desirable to be surrounded always with a large band of chosen youths—glory in peace, in war protection. Nor is this only so with a chief's own people; with neighboring *civitates*[11] also it means name and fame for a man that his retinue be conspicuous in number and character. Such men are in demand for embassies, and are honored with gifts; often, by the mere terror of their name, they are able to break the back of opposition in war.

14  When the battlefield is reached it is a reproach for a chief to be surpassed in prowess and a reproach for his retinue not to equal the prowess of its chief. Much worse, though, is to have left the field and survived one's chief; this means lifelong infamy and shame. To protect and defend the chief and to devote one's own feats to his glorification is the gist of their allegiance. The chief fights for victory, but the retainers for the chief.

Should it happen that the community where they are born has been drugged with long years of peace and quiet, many of the high born youth voluntarily seek those tribes which are at the time engaged in some war; for rest is unwelcome to the race, and they distinguish themselves more readily in the midst of uncertainties: besides, you cannot keep up a great retinue except by war and violence. It is the generous chief that the warriors expect to give them a particular war horse or murderous and masterful spear. Banquetings and a certain rude but lavish outfit take the place of salary. The material for this generosity comes through war and foray. You will not so readily persuade a German to plough the land and wait for the year's returns as to challenge the enemy and earn wounds. Besides, it seems limp and slack to get with

the sweating of your brow what you can gain with the shedding of your blood.

15  When they are not warring, they spend much time hunting, but more in idleness—creatures who eat and sleep, the best and bravest warriors doing nothing, having handed over the charge of their home, hearth and estate to the women and the old men and the weakest members of the family. For themselves they vegetate by that curious incongruity of temperament which makes of the same men such lovers of slumber and such haters of quiet.

It is the custom in their *civitates* for each man to bestow upon the chief unasked some portion of his cattle or crops. It is accepted as a compliment, but also serves the chief's needs. The chiefs appreciate still more the gifts of neighboring tribes, which are sent not merely by individuals but by the community—selected horses, heavy armor, bosses and bracelets; by this time we have taught them to accept money also.

16  It is well known that none of the German tribes lives in cities, that individually they do not permit houses to touch each other. They live separated and scattered, according as spring water, meadow, or grove appeals to each man. They lay out their villages not, after our fashion, with buildings contiguous and connected; everyone keeps a clear space around his house, whether it be a precaution against the chances of fire or just ignorance of building. They have not even learned to use quarry-stone or tiles—the timber they use for all purposes is unshaped, and stops short of all ornament or attraction. Certain buildings are smeared with a stucco bright and glittering enough to be a substitute for paint and frescoes. They are in the habit also of opening pits in the earth and piling dung in quantities on the roof, as a refuge from the winter or a root house, because such places lessen the harshness of frost. If an enemy comes, he lays waste the open, but the hidden and buried houses are either missed outright or escape detection just because they require a search.

17  For clothing all wear a cloak, fastened with a clasp, or, in its absence, a thorn. They spend whole days on the hearth around the fire with no other cov-

---

11   Latin: plural of *civitas*.

ering. The richest men are distinguished by the wearing of underclothes—not loose, like those of Parthians and Sarmatians, but drawn tight, throwing each limb into relief.

They wear also the skins of wild beasts, the tribes adjoining the riverbank in casual fashion, the inland tribes with more attention, since they cannot depend on traders for clothing. The beasts for this purpose are selected, and the hides so taken are checkered with the pied skins of the creatures native to the outer ocean and its unknown waters.

The women have the same dress as the men, except that very often long linen garments, striped with purple, are in use for the women. The upper part of this costume does not widen into sleeves; their arms and shoulders are therefore bare, as is the adjoining portion of the breast.

18   Nonetheless, the marriage tie with them is strict; you will find nothing in their character to praise more highly. They are almost the only barbarians who are content with a wife apiece. The very few exceptions have nothing to do with passion, but consist of those with whom polygamous marriage is eagerly sought for the sake of their high birth.

As for the dowry, it is not the wife who brings it to the husband, but the husband to the wife. The parents and relations are present to approve these gifts—gifts not devised for ministering to female fads or for the adornment of the person of the bride, but oxen, a horse and bridle, a shield and spear or sword. It is to share these things that the wife is taken by the husband, and she in turn brings some piece of armor to her husband. Here is the gist of the bond between them, here in their eyes its mysterious sacrament, the divinity which hedges it. Thus the wife may not imagine herself released from the practice of heroism, released from the chances of war; she is warned by the very rites with which her marriage begins that she comes to share with her husband hard work and peril. Her fate will be the same as his in peace and in panic, her risks the same. This is the moral of the yoked oxen, of the bridled horse, of the exchange of arms; so she must live and so she must die. The things she takes she is to hand over inviolate to her children, fit to be taken by her daughters-in-law and passed on again to her grandchildren.

19   So their life is one of fenced-in chastity. There is no arena with its seductions, no dinner tables with their provocations to corrupt them. Of the exchange of secret letters men and women alike are innocent. Adultery is very rare among these people. Punishment is prompt and is the husband's prerogative: the wife's hair is close-cropped, she is stripped of her clothes, her husband drives her from his house in the presence of his relatives and pursues her with blows through the length of the village. For lost chastity there is no pardon; neither beauty nor youth nor wealth will find the sinner a husband. No one laughs at vice there; no one calls seduction the spirit of the age. Better still are those tribes where only maids marry and where a woman makes an end, once and for all, with the hopes and vows of a wife. So they take one husband only, just as one body and one life, in order that there may be no second thoughts, no belated fancies, and in order that their excessive desire may be not for the man, but for marriage. To limit the number of their children or to put to death any of the later children is considered abominable. Good habits have more force with them than good laws elsewhere.

20   The children in every house grow up amid nakedness and squalor into that girth of limb and frame which is to our people a marvel. Its own mother suckles each at her breast; children are not passed on to nursemaids and wet nurses.

Nor can master be recognized from servant by having been spoiled in his upbringing. Master and servant live in the company of the same cattle and on the same mud floor until years separate the freeborn and character claims her own.

The virginity of young men is long preserved, and their powers are therefore inexhaustible. Nor for the girls is there any hot-house forcing; they pass their youth in the same way as the boys. Their stature is as tall; when they reach the same strength they are mated, and the children reproduce the vigor of the parents. Sisters' children mean as much to their uncle as to their father; some tribes regard this blood tie as even closer and more sacred than that between son and father, and in taking hostages make it the basis of their demand, as though they thus secure loyalty more surely and have a wider hold on the family.

However, so far as succession is concerned, each

man's children are his heirs, and there is no will. If there are no children, the nearest degrees of relationship for the holding of property are brothers, paternal uncles, and maternal uncles. The more relations a man has and the larger the number of his connections by marriage, the more influence he has in his old age; it does not pay to have no ties.

21 It is incumbent to take up the feuds of one's father or kinsman no less than his friendships. But such feuds do not continue unappeasable; even homicide may be atoned for by a fixed number of cattle and sheep. The whole family thereby receives satisfaction to the public advantage, for feuds are more dangerous among a free people.

No race indulges more lavishly in hospitality and entertainment. To close the door against any human being is a crime. Everyone according to his means welcomes guests generously. Should there not be enough, he who is your host goes with you next door, without an invitation, but it makes no difference; you are received with the same courtesy. Stranger or acquaintance, no one distinguishes them where the right of hospitality is concerned. It is customary to speed the parting guest with anything he fancies. There is the same readiness in turn to ask of him; gifts are the Germans' delight, but they neither count upon what they have given, nor are bound by what they have received.

22 On waking from sleep, which they generally prolong in the day, they wash, usually in warm water, since winter bulks so large in their lives. After washing they take a meal, seated apart, each at his own table. Then, arms in hand, they proceed to business, or, just as often, to revelry. To drink heavily day and night is a reproach to no man. Brawls are frequent, as you would expect among heavy drinkers; these seldom terminate with abuse, more often in wounds and bloodshed. Nevertheless the mutual reconciliation of enemies, the forming of family alliances, the appointment of chiefs, the question even of war or peace, are usually debated at these banquets, as though at no other time were the mind more open to obvious, or better warmed to larger, thoughts. The people are without craft or cunning, and expose in the freedom of revelry the heart's secrets; so every mind is bared to nakedness. On the next day the matter is handled afresh. So the principle of each debating season is justified: deliberation comes when people are incapable of pretense, but decision when they are secure from illusion.

23 For drink they use a liquid distilled from barley or wheat after fermentation has given it a certain resemblance to wine. The tribes nearest the river also buy wine. Their diet is simple: wild fruit, fresh venison, curdled milk. They banish hunger without sauce or ceremony, but there is not the same temperance in facing thirst: if you humor their drunkenness by supplying as much as they crave, they will be vanquished through their vices as easily as on the battlefield.

24 Their shows are all of one kind, and the same whatever the gathering may be: naked youths, for whom this is a form of professional acting, jump and bound between swords and upturned spears. Practice has made them dexterous and graceful. Yet they do not perform for hire or gain: however daring be the sport, the spectator's pleasure is the only price they ask.

Gambling, one may be surprised to find, they practice in all seriousness in their sober hours, with such recklessness in winning or losing that, when all else has failed, they stake personal liberty on the last and final throw.

The loser faces voluntary slavery; though he may be the younger and the stronger man, he will still allow himself to be bound and sold. Such is the Germans' persistence in wrong-doing, or their good faith, as they themselves style it. Slaves so acquired they trade, in order to deliver themselves as well as the slave from the humiliation involved in such victory.

25 Their other slaves are not organized in our fashion: that is, by a division of the services of life among them. Each of them remains master of his own house and home: the master requires from the slave a certain quantity of grain or cattle or clothing. The slave so far is subservient; but the other services of the household are discharged by the master's wife and children. To beat a slave or coerce him with hard labor and imprisonment is rare. If slaves are killed, it is not usually to preserve strict discipline, but in a fit of fury like an enemy, except that there is no penalty to be paid.

Freedmen are not much above slaves. Rarely are they of any weight in the household, never in politics, except among those peoples which have kings. Then they climb above the freeborn and above the nobles; in other *civitates* the disabilities of the freedman are the evidence of freedom.

26   To charge interest, let alone interest at high rates, is unknown, and the principle of avoiding usury is accordingly better observed than if there had been actual prohibition.

Land is taken up by a village as a whole, in quantity according to the number of cultivators. They then distribute it among themselves on the basis of rank, such distribution being made easy by the amount of land available. They change the arable land yearly, and there is still land to spare, for they do not strain the fertility and resources of the soil by tasking them through the planting of vineyards, the setting apart of meadows, or the irrigation of vegetable gardens. Grain is the only harvest required of the land. Accordingly the year itself is not divided into as many parts as with us—winter, spring, summer have a meaning and a name; the gifts of autumn and its name are alike unknown.

27   In burial there is no ostentation. The only ceremony is to burn the bodies of their notables with special kinds of wood. They build a pyre, but do not load it with clothes or spices. The man's armor and some of his horses also are added to the fire. The tomb is a mound of turf; the difficult and tedious tribute of a monument they reject as too heavy on the dead. Weeping and wailing they put away quickly; sorrow and sadness linger. Lamentation becomes women—men must restrain their emotion.

So much in general we have ascertained concerning the origin of the undivided Germans and their customs. I shall now set forth the habits and customs of the several nations, and the extent to which they differ from each other, and explain what tribes have migrated from Germany to the Gallic provinces.

28   That the fortunes of Gaul were once higher than those of Germany is recorded on the supreme authority of Julius of happy memory.[12] Therefore it is easy to believe that the Gauls at one time crossed over into Germany; small chance there was of the river preventing each tribe, as it became powerful, from seizing new land, which had not yet been divided into powerful kingdoms. Accordingly the country between the Hercynian forest and the rivers Rhine and Moenus was occupied by the Helvetii, and the country beyond by the Boii, both Gallic races. The name Boihaemum still testifies to the old traditions of the place, though here has been a change of occupants.

Whether, however, the Aravisci migrated into Pannonia from the Osi, or the Osi into Germany from the Aravisci, must remain uncertain, since their speech, habits, and type of character are still the same. Originally, in fact, there was the same misery and the same freedom on either bank of the river, the same advantages and the same drawbacks.

The Treveri and Nervi conversely go out of their way in their ambition to claim a German origin, as though this illustrious ancestry delivers them from any affinity with the indolent Gaul.

On the river bank itself are planted certain peoples who are unquestionably German: Vangiones, Triboci, Nemetes. Not even the Ubii, though they have earned the right to be a Roman colony and prefer to be called "Agrippinenses" after the name of their founder, blush to own their German origin. They originally came from beyond the river. After they had given proof of their loyalty, they were placed in charge of the bank itself, in order to block the way to others, not in order to be under supervision.

29   Of all these races the most manly are the Batavi, who occupy only a short stretch of the river bank, but with it the island in the stream. They were once a tribe of the Chatti, and on account of a rising at home they crossed the river onto lands which later became part of the Roman Empire. Their distinction persists and the emblem of their ancient alliance with us; they are not insulted, that is, by the exaction of tribute, and there is no tax farmer to oppress them. Immune from burdens and contributions, and set apart for fighting purposes only, they are reserved for war to be, as it were, our arms and weapons. Equally loyal are the tribe of the Mattiaci; for the greatness of the Roman nation has projected the awe felt for our Empire

---

12   I.e., Julius Caesar (first century BC).

beyond the Rhine, and beyond the long established frontier. So by site and territory they belong to their own bank, but by sentiment and thought they act with us, and are similar in all respects to the Batavi, except that hitherto both the soil and the climate of their land make them more lively.

I should not count among the people of Germany, though they have established themselves beyond the Rhine and Danube, the tribes who cultivate "the tithe-lands." All the wastrels of Gaul, plucking courage from misery, took possession of that disputed land. Later, since the frontier line has been drawn and the garrisons pushed forward, these lands have been counted as an outlying corner of the Empire and a part of the Roman province.

30  Beyond these people are the Chatti. The front of their settlements begins with the Hercynian forest. The land is not so low and marshy as the other *civitates* of the level German plain; yet even where the hills cover a considerable territory, they gradually fade away, and so the Hercynian forest, after escorting its Chatti to the full length of their settlement, drops them in the plain. This tribe has hardier bodies than the others, close knit limbs, a forbidding expression, and more strength of the intellect. There is much method in what they do, for Germans at least, and much shrewdness. They elect magistrates and listen to the man elected; know their place in the ranks and recognize opportunities; reserve their attack; have a time for everything; entrench at night; distrust luck, but rely on courage; and—the rarest thing of all, and usually attained only through Roman discipline—depend on the initiative of the general rather than on that of the soldier. Their whole strength lies in their infantry, whom they load with iron tools and baggage, in addition to their arms. Other Germans may be seen going to battle, but the Chatti go to war. Forays and casual fighting are rare with them. The latter method no doubt is part of the strength of cavalry—to win suddenly, that is, and as suddenly to retire. For the speed of cavalry is near allied to panic, but the deliberate action of infantry is more likely to be resolute.

31  One ceremony that is practiced by other German peoples only occasionally, depending on preference, has with the Chatti become a convention: to let the hair and beard grow when a youth has attained man-hood, and to remove this manly facial garb only after an enemy has been slain. Standing above the bloody spoil, they dismantle their faces again, and advertise that then and not before have they paid the price of their birthpangs, and are worthy of their kin and country. Cowards and weaklings remain unkempt. The bravest also wear a ring of iron—the badge of shame on other occasions among this people—as a symbolic band from which each man frees himself by the slaughter of an enemy. This symbolism is very popular, and men already growing gray still wear this uniform for the pointing finger of friend and foe. Every battle begins with these men; the front rank is made up of them and is a curious sight. But, even in peace they do not allow a tamer life to enervate them. None of them has a house or land or any business. Wherever they go they are entertained; they waste the possessions of others and are indifferent to their own, until age and loss of blood make them unequal to such demanding heroism.

32  Next to the Chatti come the Usipi and Tencteri, on the Rhine banks where the river has ceased to shift its bed and has become fit to serve as a boundary. The Tencteri, in addition to the general reputation of the race as warriors, excel in the accomplishments of trained horsemen. Even the fame of the Chattan infantry is not greater than that of their cavalry. Their ancestors established the precedent, and succeeding generations vie with them. Horsemanship is the diversion of children, the center of competition for youth, and the abiding interest of age. Horses descend with servants, house, and regular inheritance. The heir to the horse, however, is not as in other things the eldest son but the confident soldier and the better man.

33  Next to the Tencteri one originally came across the Bructeri. The Chamavi and Angrivarii are said to have trekked there recently, after the Bructeri had been expelled or cut to pieces by the joint action of neighboring peoples. Whether this was from disgust at their arrogance or from the attractions of plunder, or because Heaven leans to the side of Rome cannot be said. But Heaven did not grudge us a dramatic battle; over 60,000 men fell, not before the arms and spears of Rome, but—what was even a greater triumph for us—merely to delight our eyes. Long may such behavior last, I pray, and persist among the German nations—if

they feel no love for us, at least may they feel hatred for each other. Now that the destinies of the Empire have passed their zenith, Fortune can guarantee us nothing better than discord among our foes.

34   The Angrivarii and Chamavi are surrounded to the south by the Dulgubnii and the Chasuarii and other tribes not so well known to history. To the north follow the Frisii; they are called the Greater or Lesser Frisii according to the measure of their strength. These two tribes border the Rhine down to the ocean, and also fringe the great lakes which the fleets of Rome navigate. In that quarter we have even reached the ocean itself, and beyond our range are rumored to stand the pillars of Hercules. Did Hercules really visit those shores, or is it only that we have agreed to credit all marvels everywhere to him? Nor did Drusus Germanicus[13] lack audacity as an explorer but Ocean[14] vetoed inquiry into either itself or Hercules. Soon the attempt was abandoned, and it came to be judged more reverent to believe in the works of deities than to comprehend them.

35   Thus far we have been enquiring into Western Germany. At this point the country falls away with a great bend towards the north. First in this area come the Chauci. Though they start next to the Frisii and occupy part of the seaboard, they also border on all of the tribes just mentioned, and finally edge away south as far as the Chatti. This vast block of territory is not merely held by the Chauci but filled by them. They are the noblest of the German tribes, and prefer to protect their vast domain by justice alone. They are neither grasping nor lawless; in peaceful seclusion they provoke no wars and despatch no raiders on marauding forays. The special proof of their great strength is, indeed, just this: that they do not depend for their superior position on injustice. Yet they are ready with arms, and, if circumstances should require, with armies, men, and horse in abundance. So, even though

they keep the peace, their reputation does not suffer.

36   Bordering the Chauci and the Chatti are the Cherusci. For long years they have been unassailed and have encouraged an abnormal and languid peacefulness. It has been a pleasant rather than a sound policy. With lawlessness and strength on either side of you, you will find no true peace; where might is right, self-control and righteousness are titles reserved for the stronger. Accordingly, the Cherusci, who were once styled just and generous, are now described as indolent and shortsighted, while the good luck of the victorious Chatti has been credited to them as wisdom. The fall of the Cherusci dragged down the Fosi also, a neighboring tribe. They share the adversity of the Cherusci on even terms, though they have only been dependents in their prosperity.

37   This same "sleeve" or peninsula of Germany is the home of the Cimbri, who dwell nearest the ocean. They are a small *civitas* today, but rich in memories. Broad traces of their ancient fame are still extant—a spacious camp on each bank [of the Rhine], by the circuit of which you can even today measure the size and skill of the nation and get some sense of that mighty trek.

Our city was in its six hundred and fortieth year when the Cimbrian armies were first heard of, in the consulship of Caecilius Metellus and Papirius Carbo. If we count from that date to the second consulship of the Emperor Trajan,[15] the total amounts to about 210 years. For that length of time the conquest of Germany has been in process. Between the beginning and end of that long period there have been many mutual losses. Neither Samnite nor Carthaginian,[16] neither Spain nor Gaul, nor even the Parthians have taught us more lessons. The German fighting for liberty has been a keener enemy than the absolutism of Arsaces.[17] What has the East to taunt us with, apart from the overthrow of Crassus[18]—the

---

13   The brother of the Emperor Tiberius (14-37).

14   The Greeks and Romans believed the world's continents were surrounded by a single body of water, "Ocean."

15   Emperor 98-117.

16   The Samnites nearly defeated the Romans in Italy, 343-290 BC. The Carthaginians fought the Romans in the Punic Wars of the third and second centuries BC. Rome came close to destruction in the second Punic War.

17   Arsaces was the founder of the Parthian kingdom to the east of the Mediterranean, for many years an opponent of Rome.

18   Crassus, the Roman politician and general associated with Pompey and Julius Caesar, was destroyed with his army by the Parthians in 53 BC.

East which itself lost Pacorus and fell at the feet of Ventidius?[19]

But the Germans routed or captured Carbo and Cassius and Aurelius Scaurus and Servilius Caepio and Gnaeus Mallius,[20] and wrested five consular armies in one campaign from the people of Rome, and even from a Caesar wrested Varus[21] and three legions with him. Nor was it without paying the price that Marius smote them in Italy, and Julius of happy memory in Gaul, and Drusus, Nero, and Germanicus[22] in their own homes. Soon after that the great tragedy threatened by Gaius Caesar turned into a farce. Then came peace until, on the opportunity offered by our own dissensions and by civil war, the Germans carried the legions' winter quarters by storm and even aspired to the Gallic provinces. Finally they were repulsed, and they have in recent years gratified us with more triumphs[23] than victories.

38   Now I must speak of the Suebi, who do not comprise only one tribe, as with the Chatti and the Tencteri. Rather they occupy the greater part of Germany, and are still distinguished by special national names, though styled in general Suebi. One mark of the race is to comb the hair back over the side of the face and tie it low in a knot behind. This distinguishes the Suebi from other Germans, and the free born of the Suebi from the slave. In other tribes, whether from some relationship to the Suebi or, as often happens, from imitation, the same thing may be found, but it is rare and confined to the period of youth. Among the Suebi, even till the hair is gray they twist the rough locks backward, and often knot them on the very crown. The chieftains wear theirs somewhat more ornamentally, and are to this extent interested in appearances, but innocently so. It is not for making love or being made love to, but rather that men who are to face battle are—in the eyes of their foes—more terrifying with these adornments heightening their stature.

39   The Semnones are described as the most ancient and best-born tribe of the Suebi; this is confirmed by religious rite. At fixed seasons all the tribes of the same blood gather with their delegations at a certain forest that is hallowed by visions beheld by their ancestors and by the awe of the ages. After publicly offering up a human life, they celebrate the grim "initiation" of their barbarous worship. There is a further tribute which they pay to the grove; no one enters it until he has been bound with a chain. He puts off his freedom, and advertises in his person the might of the deity. If he chances to fall, he must not be lifted up or rise—he must writhe along the ground until he is out again. The whole superstition comes to this: that it was here where the race arose, here where dwells the god who is lord of all things; everything else is subject to him. The prosperity of the Semnones enforces the idea; they occupy 100 cantons, and their magnitude leads them to consider themselves the head of the Suebi.

40   The Langobardi, conversely, are distinguished by lack of number. Set in the midst of numberless and powerful tribes, they find safety not in submissiveness, but in peril and pitched battle. Then come the Reudigni and the Aviones, and the Anglii and the Varini, the Eudoses and Suardones and Nuithones. These tribes are protected by forests and rivers. There is nothing noteworthy about them individually, except that they worship in common Nerthus, or Mother Earth, and conceive her as intervening in human affairs, and riding in procession through the cities of men. In an island of the ocean is a holy grove, and in it a consecrated chariot, covered with robes. A single priest is permitted to touch it; he interprets the presence of the goddess in her shrine, and follows with deep reverence as she rides away, drawn by cows. Then come days of rejoicing, and all places keep holiday, as many as she thinks worthy to receive and entertain her. They make no war, take no arms. Every weapon is put away; peace and quiet rules until the same priest returns the goddess to her

---

19   Ventidius was a Roman general who defeated and slew Pacorus, the son of the king of the Parthians, in 38 BC.

20   All Roman generals and politicians active in the late second century BC.

21   One of the Emperor Augustus's generals, who was slaughtered along with three legions by the Germans.

22   Drusus was the brother of the Emperor Tiberius, and Germanicus was Tiberius's adopted son. By "Nero" here Tacitus means the Emperor Tiberius.

23   A Roman "triumph" was a ceremonial welcome at Rome for a victorious general on his return.

temple, when she has had her fill of the society of mortals. After this the chariot and the robes, and, if you are willing to credit it, the deity in person, are washed in a sequestered lake. Slaves perform this duty and are then immediately swallowed by the same lake—hence a mysterious terror and ignorance full of piety as to what it may be which men behold only to die.

41   These sections on the Suebi extend into the more secluded parts of Germany. Nearer to us—to follow the course of the Danube, as before I followed the Rhine—comes the state of the Hermunduri. They are loyal to Rome, and with them alone among Germans business is transacted not on the river bank, but far within the frontier in the most thriving colony of the province of Rhaetia. They cross the river everywhere without supervision, and while we let other peoples see only our fortified camps, to them we have thrown open our houses and homes because they do not covet them. Among the Hermunduri rises the River Albis—a river once famous, now a name only.

42   Next to the Hermunduri are the Naristi and then the Marcomani and the Quadi. The fame and strength of the Marcomani are outstanding; their very home was won by their bravery, through the expulsion in ancient times of the Boii. Nor are the Naristi and Quadi inferior to them. These tribes are, so to speak, the brow of Germany, so far as Germany is wreathed by the Danube. The Marcomani and the Quadi retained kings of their own race down to our time—the noble houses of Maroboduus and Tudrus. Now they submit to foreign kings also, but the force and power of their kings rest on the influence of Rome. Occasionally they are assisted by our armed intervention—more often by subsidies, out of which they get as much help.

43   Behind them are the Marsigni, Cotini, Osi, and Buri, enclosing the Marcomani and Quadi from the rear. Among these, the Marsigni and Buri in language and culture recall the Suebi. As for the Cotini and Osi, the Gallic tongue of the first and the Pannonian of the second prove them not to be Germans; so does their submission to tribute. This tribute is imposed upon them as foreigners in part by the Sarmatae, in part by the Quadi. The Cotini, to their shame, even

have iron mines to work. All these peoples have little level land, but occupy the summits and ridges of mountains. In fact, a continuous range parts and cuts Suebia in two.

Beyond the range are many races. The most widely diffused name is that of the Lugii, which extends over several states. It will be sufficient to have named the strongest: Harii, Helvecones, Manimi, Elisii, Nahanar-vali. Among the Nahanarvali one is shown a grove, the seat of a prehistoric ritual. A priest presides in female dress; but according to the Roman interpreta-tion the gods recorded in this fashion are Castor and Pollux. That at least is the spirit of the godhead here recognized, whose name is the Alci. No images are in use; there is no sign of foreign superstition. Neverthe-less they worship these deities as brothers and as youths.

But to return. The Harii, apart from the strength in which they surpass the peoples just enumerated, are fierce in nature, and augment this natural feroci-ty by the help of art and season. They blacken their shields and dye their bodies; they choose pitchy nights for their battles; by sheer panic and darkness they strike terror like an army of ghosts. No enemy can face this novel and, as it were, phantasmagorical vision. In every battle, after all, the eye is conquered first.

Beyond the Lugii is the monarchy of the Gotones. The hand upon the reins closes somewhat tighter here than among the other tribes of Germans, but not so tight yet as to destroy freedom. Then immediately fol-lowing them and on the ocean are the Rugii and the Lemovii. The distinguishing features of all these tribes are round shields, short swords, and a submissive bearing before their kings.

44   Beyond these tribes the states of the Suiones, on the ocean, possess not merely arms and men but pow-erful fleets. The style of their ships differs in this respect: there is a prow at each end, with a beak ready to be driven forwards. They neither work a ship with sails, nor add oars in banks to the side; the gearing of the oars is detached as on certain rivers, and reversible as occasion demands for movement in either direction.

Among these peoples respect is paid to wealth, and one man is accordingly supreme, with no restrictions and with an unchallenged right to obedience. Nor is there any general carrying of arms here, as among the other Germans. Rather they are locked up in charge of a custodian, who is a slave. The ocean forbids sudden inroads from enemies; and, besides, bands of armed men, with nothing to do, easily become riotous. It is not in the king's interest to put a noble or a free men or even a freedman in charge of the arms.

45 Beyond the Suiones is another sea, sluggish and almost motionless, with which the earth is girdled and bounded. Evidence for this is furnished by the brilliance of the last rays of the sun, which remain so bright from his setting to his rising again as to dim the stars. Faith adds further that the sound of the sun's emergence is audible and the forms of his horses visible with the spikes of his crown.

So far (and here rumor speaks the truth), and so far only, does Nature reach.

We must now turn to the right-hand shore of the Suebic Sea. Here it washes the tribes of the Aestii; there customs and dress are Suebic, but their language is nearer British.

They worship the mother of the gods. As an emblem of that superstition they wear the figures of wild boars; this boar takes the place of arms or of any other protection, and guarantees to the votary of the goddess a mind at rest even in the midst of foes. They use swords rarely, clubs frequently. Grain and other products of the earth they cultivate with a patience out of keeping with the lethargy customary to Germans. They ransack the sea also, and are the only people who gather in the shallows and on the shore itself amber, which they call in their tongue "glaesum."

Nor have they, being barbarians, inquired or learned what substance or process produces it. It lay there long among the rest of the flotsam and jetsam of the sea, until Roman luxury gave it a name. To the natives it is useless. It is gathered crude and is forwarded to Rome unshaped; the barbarians are astonished to be paid for it. Yet you may infer that it is the gum of trees; certain creeping and even winged creatures are continually found embedded in it. They have been entangled in its liquid form, and, as the material hardens, are imprisoned. I should suppose

therefore that just as in the secluded places in the East, where frankincense and balsam are exuded, so in the islands and lands of the West there are groves and glades more than ordinarily luxuriant. These are tapped and liquified by the rays of the sun as it approaches, and ooze into the nearest sea, whence by the force of tempests they are stranded on the shores opposite. If you try the qualities of amber by setting fire to it, it kindles like a torch, feeds an oily and odorous flame, and soon dissolves into something like pitch and resin.

Adjacent to the Suiones come the tribes of the Sitones, resembling them in all other respects, and differing only in this, that among them the woman rules. To this extent they have fallen lower not merely than free men but even than slaves.

46 Here Suebia ends. As for the tribes of the Peucini, Venedi, and Fenni, I am in doubt whether to count them as Germans or Sarmatians. Though the Peucini, whom some men call Bastarnae, in language, culture, fixity of habitation, and house-building, conduct themselves as Germans, all are dirty and lethargic. The faces of the chiefs, too, owing to intermarriage, wear to some extent the degraded aspect of Sarmatians while the Venedi have contracted many Sarmatian habits; they are robbers, infesting all the hills and forests which lie between the Peucini and the Fenni.

And yet these peoples are preferably entered as Germans, since they have fixed abodes, and carry shields, and delight to use their feet and to run fast, all of which are traits opposite to those of the Sarmatians, who live in wagons and on horseback.

The Fenni live in astonishing barbarism and disgusting misery: no arms, no horses, no fixed homes; herbs for their food, skins for their clothing, earth for their bed. Arrows are all their wealth and for want of iron they tip them with bone. This same hunting is the support of the women as well as of the men, for they accompany the men freely and claim a share of the spoil. Nor have their infants any shelter against wild beasts and rain, except the covering afforded by a few intertwined branches. To these the hunters return, these are the refuge of age; and yet the people think it happier so than to groan over field labor, be encumbered with house-service, and be forever exchanging their own and their neighbors' goods with alternate hopes and fears. Unconcerned towards men, unconcerned towards Heaven, they have achieved a consummation very difficult: they have nothing even to ask for.

Beyond this all else that is reported is legendary: that the Hellusii and Oxiones have human faces and features, the limbs and bodies of beasts. It has not been so ascertained, and I shall leave it an open question.

# 27

# Sidonius Apollinaris, *Letters*

Sidonius Apollinaris was born into a family of senatorial rank in the Roman province of Gaul and died about sixty years later, in 489. He had a political career at the highest reaches of Roman government, being associated with the Emperor Avitus (455-6). After this career ended, he was invited to become bishop of his city of Clermont in 472, an invitation he accepted. A collection of about 100 of his letters and some of his poems survive him.

---

### 27.1
#### TO HIS FRIEND DONIDIUS [461-7]:

To your question why, having got as far as Nîmes, I still leave your hospitality expectant, I reply by giving the reason for my delayed return. I will even dilate upon the causes of my dilatoriness, for I know that what I enjoy is your enjoyment too. The fact is, I have passed the most delightful time in the most beautiful country in the company of Tonantius Ferreolus and Apollinaris, the most charming hosts in the world. Their estates march together; their houses are not far apart, and the extent of intervening ground is just too far for a walk and just too short to make the ride worth while. The hills above the houses are under vines and olives; they might be Nysa and Aracynthus,[1] famed in song. The view from one villa[2] is over a wide flat country, that from the other over woodland; yet different though their situations are, the eye derives equal pleasure from both. But enough of sites; I have now to unfold the order of my entertainment. Sharp scouts were posted to look out for our return; and not only

were the roads patrolled by men from each estate, but even winding short-cuts and sheep-tracks were under observation, to make it quite impossible for us to elude the friendly ambush. Into this of course we fell, no unwilling prisoners; and our captors instantly made us swear to dismiss every idea of continuing our journey until a whole week had elapsed. And so every morning began with a flattering rivalry[1] between the two hosts, as to which of their kitchens should first smoke for the refreshment of their guest; nor, though I am personally related to one, and connected through my relatives with the other, could I manage by alternation to give them quite equal measure, since age and the dignity of prefectorian rank[3] gave Ferreolus a prior right of invitation over and above his other claims. From the first moment we were hurried from one pleasure to another. Hardly had we entered the vestibule of either house when we saw two opposed pairs of partners in the ball-game repeating each other's movements as they turned in wheeling circles; in another place one heard the rattle of dice boxes and the shouts of the contending players; in yet another, were books in abundance

---

1 Two mountains.
2 I.e., a country residence of a Roman aristocrat.
3 A high rank in Roman government. Earlier in his career, Sidonius had been prefect of Rome.

ready to your hand; you might have imagined your-self among the shelves of some grammarian, or the tiers of the Athenaeum,[4] or a bookseller's towering cases. They were so arranged that the devotional works were near the ladies' seats; where the master sat were those ennobled by the great style of Roman elo-quence. The arrangement had this defect, that it sepa-rated certain books by certain authors in manner as near to each other as in matter they are far apart. Thus Augustine writes like Varro,[5] and Horace like Pruden-tius,[6] but you had to consult them on different sides of the room. Turranius Rufinus's interpretation of Adamantius Origen[7] was eagerly examined by the readers of theology among us; according to our sever-al points of view, we had different reasons to give for the censure of this Father by certain of the clergy as too trenchant a controversialist and best avoided by the prudent; but the translation is so literal and yet ren-ders the spirit of the work so well, that neither Apuleius's version of Plato's *Phaedo*, nor Cicero's of the *Ctesiphon* of Demosthenes,[8] is more admirably adapted to the use and rule of our Latin tongue. While we were engaged in these discussions as fancy prompted each, appears an envoy from the cook to warn us that the moment of bodily refreshment is at hand. And in fact the fifth hour had just elapsed, prov-ing that the man was punctual, had properly marked the advance of the hours upon the water-clock. The dinner was short, but abundant, served in the fashion affected in senatorial houses where inveterate usage prescribes numerous courses on very few dishes, though to afford variety, roast alternated with stew. Amusing and instructive anecdotes accompanied our potations; wit went with the one sort, and learning with the other. To be brief, we were entertained with decorum, refinement, and good cheer. After dinner, if we were at Vorocingus (the name of one estate) we walked over to our quarters and our own belongings. If at Prusianum, as the other is called, [the young] Tonantius and his brothers turned out of their beds for

us because we could not be always dragging our gear about; they are surely the elect among the nobles of our own age. The siesta over, we took a short ride to sharpen our jaded appetites for supper. Both of our hosts had baths in their houses, but in neither did they happen to be available; so I set my own servants to work in the rare sober interludes which the convivial bowl, too often filled, allowed their sodden brains. I made them dig a pit at their best speed either near a spring or by the river; into this a heap of red-hot stones was thrown, and the glowing cavity then cov-ered over with an arched roof of wattled hazel. This still left gaps, and to exclude the light and keep in the steam given off when water was thrown on the hot stones, we laid coverings of Cilician goats' hair over all. In these vapor-baths we passed whole hours with lively talk and repartee; all the time the cloud of hiss-ing steam enveloping us induced the healthiest per-spiration. When we had perspired enough, we were bathed in hot water; the treatment removed the feeling of repletion, but left us languid; we therefore finished off with a bracing douche from fountain, well or river. For the river Gardon runs between the two properties; except in time of flood, when the stream is swollen and clouded with melted snow, it looks red through its tawny gravels, and flows still and pellucid over its pebbly bed, teeming none the less with the most deli-cate fish. I could tell you of suppers fit for a king; it is not my sense of shame, but simply want of space which sets a limit to my revelations. You would have a great story if I turned the page and continued on the other side, but I am always ashamed to disfigure the back of a letter with an inky pen. Besides, I am on the point of leaving here, and hope, by Christ's grace, that we shall meet very shortly; the story of our friends' banquets will be better told at my own table or yours—provided only that a good week's interval first elapses to restore me to the healthy appetite for which I long. There is nothing like thin living to give tone to a system disordered by excess. Farewell.

---

4   A center of learning at Rome.
5   I.e., the fourth-century Christian theologian and bishop writes like the Roman scholar of that name of the first century BC.
6   I.e., the poet of the late first century BC writes like the Latin Christian poet of *c*. 348-410.
7   Turranius Rufinus was a fourth-century translator of the works of Origen, the Greek Christian theologian, into Latin.
8   Demosthenes, the Greek orator of the fourth century BC, gave a speech of this name.

## 27.2
### TO THE LORD BISHOP LUPUS[9] [472]:

I render you the observance always due to the incomparable eminence of your apostolic life, still always due, however regularly paid. But I have a further object, to commend to your notice a long-standing trouble of the bearers of this letter, in whose case I have recently become interested. They have journeyed a great distance into Auvergne at this unfavorable season, and the journey has been undertaken in vain. A female relative of theirs was carried off during a raid of the "Vargi,"[10] as the local bandits are called. They received trustworthy information, and following an old but reliable clue, discovered that some years ago she had been brought here before being removed elsewhere. As a matter of fact, the unfortunate woman had been sold in open market before their arrival, and is now actually under the roof and the control of my man of affairs. A certain Prudens, rumored to be now resident in Troyes, had attested the contract for the vendors, whose names are unknown to us; his signature is to be seen on the deed of purchase as that of a suitable witness of the transaction. By the fortunate fact of your presence, you will be able, if you think fit, to see the parties confronted, and use your personal influence to investigate the whole course of the outrage. I gather from what the bearers say that the offense is aggravated by the death of a man upon the road as a sequel to the abduction. But as the aggrieved parties who wish to bring this scandalous affair to light are anxious for the remedy of your judgment and for your neighborly aid, it seems to me that it would no less become your character than your position to bring about an equitable arrangement, thus affording the one side some comfort in affliction, and saving the other from an impending danger. Such a qualified decision would be most beneficial to all concerned; it would diminish the misery of one party and the guilt of the other, while it would give both of them a greater feeling of security. Otherwise, in regions and times like these of ours, the last state of the dispute may well prove no better than the beginning. Deign to keep me in remembrance, my Lord Bishop.

## 27.3
### TO HIS FRIEND MAGNUS FELIX [473]:

The bearer of this is Gozolas, a Jew, and a client of your excellency, a man I should like if I could only overcome my contempt for his sect. I write in great anxiety. Our town lives in terror of a sea of tribes which find in it an obstacle to their expansion and surge in arms all round it. We are exposed as a pitiful prey at the mercy of rival peoples, suspected by the Burgundians, almost in contact with the Goths.[11] We have to face at once the fury of our assailants and the envy of our defenders.[12] But of this more later. Only let me know that all goes well with you, and I shall be content. For though we may be punished in the sight of all men for some obscure offense, we are still generous enough of heart to desire for others all prosperity. If a man cannot wish others well in evil times he is no better than a captive; the enemy that takes him is his own unworthy nature. Farewell.

## 27.4
### TO HIS BROTHER-IN-LAW ECDICIUS[13] [474]:

There never was a time when my people of Clermont needed you so much as now; their affection for you is a ruling passion for more than one reason. First, because a man's native soil may rightly claim the chief place in his affection; secondly, because you were not only your countrymen's joy at birth, but the desire of their hearts while yet unborn. Perhaps of no other man in this age can the same be said; but the proof of the statement is that as your mother's pregnancy advanced, the citizens with one accord fell to checking every day as it went by. I will not dwell on

---

9   Bishop of Troyes, in Gaul.
10  Other sources indicate this was a Germanic term for "outlaws."
11  I.e., the Visigoths.
12  The Burgundians, another Germanic tribe, were at this point allied with the Romans in the province against Visigoths.
13  Ecdicius was also the son of the Emperor Avitus.

those common things which yet so deeply stir a man's heart, as that here was the grass on which as an infant you crawled, or that here were the first fields you trod, the first rivers you swam, the first woods through which you broke your way in the hunt. I will not remind you that here you first played ball and cast the dice, here you first knew sport with hawk and hound, with horse and bow. I will forget that your schooldays brought us a veritable confluence of learners and the learned from all quarters, and that if our nobles were imbued with the love of eloquence and poetry, if they resolved to forsake the barbarous Celtic dialect, it was to your personality that they owed all. Nothing so kindled their universal regard for you as this, that you first made Romans of them and never allowed them to relapse again. And how should the vision of you ever fade from any patriot's memory as we saw you in your glory upon that famous day, when a crowd of both sexes and every rank and age lined our half-ruined walls to watch you cross the space between us and the enemy? At midday, and right across the middle of the plain, you brought your little company of eighteen safe through some thousands of the Goths,[14] a feat which posterity will surely deem incredible. At the sight of you, nay, at the very rumor of your name, those seasoned troops were smitten with stupefaction; their captains were so amazed that they never stopped to note how great their own numbers were and yours how small. They drew off their whole force to the brow of a steep hill; they had been besiegers before, but when you appeared they dared not even deploy for action. You cut down some of their bravest, whom gallantry alone had led to defend the rear. You never lost a man in that sharp engagement, and found yourself sole master of an absolutely exposed plain with no more soldiers to back you than you often have guests at your own table. Imagination may better conceive than words describe the procession that streamed out to you as you made your leisurely way towards the city, the greetings, the shouts of applause, the tears of heartfelt joy. One saw you receiving in the press a veritable ovation on this glad return; the courts of your spacious house were crammed with people. Some kissed away the dust of battle from your person, some took from the horses the bridles slimed with foam and blood, some inverted and ranged the sweat-drenched saddles; others undid the flexible cheek-pieces of the helmet you longed to remove, others set about unlacing your greaves. One saw folk counting the notches in swords blunted by much slaughter, or measuring with trembling fingers the holes made in cuirasses by cut or thrust. Crowds danced with joy and hung upon your comrades; but naturally the full brunt of popular delight was borne by you. You were among unarmed men at last; but not all your arms would have availed to extricate you from them. There you stood, with a fine grace suffering the silliest congratulations; half torn to pieces by people madly rushing to salute you, but so loyally responsive to this popular devotion that those who took the greatest liberties seemed surest of your most generous acknowledgements. And finally I shall say nothing of the service you performed in raising what was practically a public force from your private resources, and with little help from our magnates. I shall not tell of the chastisement you inflicted on the barbaric raiders, and the curb imposed upon an audacity which had begun to exceed all bounds; or of those surprise attacks which annihilated whole squadrons with the loss of only two or three men on your side. Such disasters did you inflict upon the enemy by these unexpected onsets, that they resorted to a most unworthy device to conceal their heavy losses. They decapitated all whom they could not bury in the short night-hours, and let the headless lie, forgetting in their desire to avoid the identification of their dead, that a trunk would betray their ruin just as well as a whole body. When, with morning light, they saw their miserable artifice revealed in all its savagery, they turned at last to open obsequies; but their precipitation disguised the ruse no better than the ruse itself had concealed the slaughter. They did not even raise a temporary mound of earth over the remains; the dead were neither washed, shrouded, nor interred; but the imperfect rites they received

---

14  I.e., the Visigoths.

befitted the manner of their death. Bodies were brought in from every where, piled on dripping carts and, since you never paused a moment in following up the rout, they had to be taken into houses which were then hurriedly set alight, till the fragments of blazing roofs, falling in upon them, formed their funeral pyres. But I run on beyond my proper limits. My aim in writing was not to reconstruct the whole story of your achievements, but to remind you of a few among them, to convince you how eagerly your friends here long to see you again; there is only one remedy, at once quick and efficacious, for such fevered expectancy as theirs, and that is your prompt return. If, then, the entreaties of our people can persuade you, sound the retreat and start homeward at once. The intimacy of kings is dangerous;[15] court it no more; the most distinguished of mankind have well compared it to a flame, which illuminates things at a short distance but consumes them if they come within its range. Farewell.

---

15  Ecdicius has probably been at the court of a Burgundian king.

# BENEDICT OF NURSIA, *THE RULE*

Very little is known of the life of Saint Benedict of Nursia (*c.* 480-547). The only early source regarding his life is the biography written by Pope Gregory the Great (589-604) who states that Benedict, an Italian, became a hermit in reaction against the corruption he found in the schools at Rome. He went on to found a number of monasteries. He himself at times served as abbot, not always enjoying good relations with his monks; some tried to assassinate him, but he was miraculously saved when a pitcher containing poisoned wine shattered. The Benedictine *Rule* was clearly based on earlier rules, but had become the standard one in the West by the middle of the ninth century.

---

PROLOGUE

Listen, my son, and turn the ear of your heart to the precepts of your Master. Receive readily and faithfully carry out the advice of a loving Father, so that by the work of obedience you may return to Him, whom you have left by the sloth of disobedience. Therefore, my words are intended for you, whosoever you may be, who, giving up your own will, take the all-powerful and excellent arms of obedience to fight under the Lord Christ, the true King.

First, beg of Him with most earnest prayer to finish the good work begun, that He who now has deigned to count us among His children may never be grieved by our evil deeds. For at all times we must so serve Him with the good things He has given us, that He may not, as an angry father, disinherit His children, nor as a dread lord, provoked by our evil deeds, deliver us to everlasting punishment as wicked servants who refuse to follow Him to glory.

Let us, therefore, arise at once, the Scripture stirring us up, saying, "It is now the hour for us to rise from sleep."[1] And, our eyes now open to the divine light, let us with wondering ears listen to the divine voice, daily calling to us and warning us, "Today if you shall hear His voice, do not harden your hearts";[2] and again, "He that has ears, let him hear what the Spirit says to the Churches."[3] And what does He say? "Come, you children, and hearken unto Me: I will teach you the fear of the Lord."[4] "Run while you have the light of life, that the darkness of death does not overtake you."[5]

---

1  New Testament, Romans 13.11.
2  Old Testament, Psalms 95.7-8.
3  New Testament, Revelation 2.7.
4  Old Testament, Psalms 34.11.
5  New Testament, John 12.35.

And our Lord, seeking His workman among the multitude of those to whom He thus speaks, says again, "Who is the man that will have life, and desires to see good days?"[6] And if you, hearing this, reply, "I am he," God says to you, "If you desire to possess true and everlasting life, 'restrain your tongue from evil, and your lips that speak no guile. Fall away from evil and do good; seek after peace and pursue it.'"[7] And when you have done this, "My eyes shall be on you, and My ears shall be open to your prayers. And before you can call upon Me, I will say to you, 'Behold, I am present.'"[8] What can be more agreeable, dearest brethren, than this voice of our Lord inviting us? Behold how in His loving kindness He shows us the way of life!

Therefore, with our loins girt by faith, and by the practice of good works under the guidance of His Gospel, let us walk in the path He has marked out for us, that we may deserve to see Him who has called us into His kingdom.

If we would live in the shelter of this kingdom, we can reach it only by speeding on the way of good works (by this path alone is it to be attained). But let us, with the prophet, ask our Lord, and say to Him, "Lord, who shall dwell in Your tabernacle? or who shall rest on Your holy mountain?"[9] And when we have so asked, let us hear our Lord's answer, pointing out to us the way to this His dwelling, and saying, "He that walks without blemish and works justice, he that speaks truth in his heart, that has not forged guile with his tongue, he that has not done evil to his neighbor, and has not reproached him."[10] He that, casting out of the inmost thoughts of his heart the suggestions of the evil-minded devil trying to lead him astray, has brought them all to nothing; he that taking hold of his thoughts while in their birth has dashed them against the rock, which is Christ. They who, fearing the Lord, are not lifted up by their good observance, but knowing that all that is good in them comes not from themselves but from the Lord, extol His work in them, saying with the prophet, "Not to us, O Lord, not to us, but to Your name give glory."[11] Thus the Apostle Paul imputed nothing of his preaching to himself, saying, "By the grace of God I am what I am."[12] And again he says, "He that glories, let him glory in the Lord."[13]

Hence also our Lord in the Gospel says, "He that hears these My words and does them, I will liken him to a wise man that has built his house upon a rock. The floods came, the winds blew and beat against that house, and it did not fall, because it was founded upon a rock."[14] In fulfillment whereof our Lord daily looks for deeds in us complying with His holy admonitions. Therefore the days of this our life are lengthened for a while for the mending of our evil deeds, according to the words of the apostle, "Do you not know that the patience of God leads you to repentance?"[15] For our loving Lord says, "I do not will the death of the sinner, but that he be converted and live."[16]

So questioning the Lord, brethren, we have heard on what conditions we may dwell in His temple, and if we fulfill these we shall be heirs of the kingdom of heaven. Therefore our hearts and bodies must be prepared to fight under the holy obedience of His commands, and we must beg our Lord to supply by the help of His grace what by nature is not possible to us. And if, fleeing from the pains of hell, we will to attain to everlasting life, we must, while time yet serves and while we live in the flesh and the light is still on our path, hasten to do now what will profit us for all eternity.

6   Old Testament, Psalms 34.12.
7   Old Testament, Psalms 34.13-14.
8   Old Testament, 2 Chronicles 7.15; Isaiah 65.24.
9   Old Testament, Psalms 115.1.
10  Old Testament, Psalms 15.2-3.
11  Old Testament, Psalms 151.1.
12  New Testament, 1 Corinthians 15.10.
13  New Testament, 2 Corinthians 10.17.
14  New Testament, Matthew 7.24-25.
15  New Testament, Romans 2.4.
16  Old Testament, Ezekiel 33.11.

We are, therefore, now about to institute a school for the service of God, in which we hope nothing harsh or burdensome will be ordained. But if we proceed in certain things with some little severity, sound reason so advising for the amendment of vices or the preserving of charity,[17] do not for fear of this forthwith flee from the way of salvation, which is always narrow in the beginning. In living our life, however, and by the growth of faith, when the heart has been enlarged, we run down the path of God's commandments with unspeakable loving sweetness, so that never leaving His school, but persevering in the monastery until death in His teaching, we share by our patience in the sufferings of Christ, and so merit to be partakers of His kingdom.

## 1

### OF THE KINDS OF MONKS

It is recognized that there are four kinds of monks. The first are the cenobites, that is, those who live in a monastery under a rule and an abbot. The second kind is that of anchorites, or hermits, who not in the first fervor of conversion, but after long trial in the monastery, and already taught by the example of many others, have learned to fight against the devil, and are well prepared to go forth from the ranks of the brotherhood to the single combat of the desert. They can now, by God's help, safely fight against the vices of their flesh and against evil thoughts individually, with their own hand and arm and without the encouragement of a companion. The third and worst kind of monk is that of the sarabaits, who have not been tried under any rule or schooled by an experienced master, as gold is tried in the furnace, but, soft as lead and still in their works cleaving to the world, are known to lie to God by their tonsure.[18] These in twos or threes, or more frequently singly, are penned in, without a shepherd, not in our Lord's fold, but in their own. The pleasure of carrying out their particular desires is their law, and they call holy whatever they dream of or choose, but what they do not like, that they deem unlawful.

The fourth class of monks is called the gyrovagues.[19] These move about all their lives through various countries, staying as guests for three or four days at different monasteries. They are always on the move and never settle down, and are slaves to their own wills and to the enticements of gluttony. In every way they are worse than the sarabaits, and of their wretched way of life it is better to be silent than to speak.

Leaving these therefore aside, let us by God's help set down a Rule for cenobites, who are the best kind of monks.

## 2

### WHAT THE ABBOT SHOULD BE

To be fit to rule a monastery, an abbot should always remember what he is called, and in his acts illustrate his high calling. For in a monastery he is considered to take the place of Christ, since he is called by His name as the apostle says, "You have received the spirit of the adoption of sons, whereby we cry, Abba, Father."[20] Therefore the abbot should neither teach, ordain, nor require anything against the command of our Lord (God forbid!), but in the minds of his disciples let his orders and teaching be mingled with the leaven of divine justice.

The abbot should always be mindful that at the dread judgment of God there will be inquiry both as to his teaching and as to the obedience of his disciples. Let the abbot know that any lack of goodness which the master of the household shall find in his flock will be accounted the shepherd's fault. On the other hand, he shall be acquitted in so far as he shall have shown all the watchfulness of a shepherd over a restless and disobedient flock, and if as their pastor he shall have employed every care to cure their corrupt ways, he shall be declared guiltless in the Lord's judgment, and he may say with the prophet, "I have not hidden Your

---

17  I.e., love.
18  The shaved crown of the head of a monk.
19  I.e., wanderers.
20  New Testament, Romans 8.15.

justice in my heart; I have told Your truth and Your salvation, but they turned away and despised me."[21] And then in the end death shall be inflicted as a just punishment upon the sheep which have not responded to his care. When, therefore, anyone shall receive the name of abbot, he ought to rule his disciples with a twofold teaching, that is, he should first show them in deeds rather than words all that is good and holy. To such as are understanding, indeed, he may expound the Lord's behests by words; but to the hard-hearted and to the simple-minded he must manifest the divine precepts in his life. Thus, what he has taught his disciples to be contrary to God's law, let him show in his own deeds that such things are not to be done, lest preaching to others "he himself becomes a castaway,"[22] and God says to him thus sinning, "Why do you declare My commandments, and take My testament in your mouth? You have hated discipline, and cast My words behind you."[23] And "You, who saw the mote in your brother's eye, have you not seen the beam that is in your own?"[24]

Let him make no distinction of persons in the monastery. Let not one be loved more than another, except such as are found to excel in obedience or good works. Let not the freeborn be put before the slaveborn in religion, unless there is other reasonable cause for it. If upon due consideration the abbot shall see such cause, he may place him where he pleases; otherwise let all keep their own places, because "whether slave or free, we are all one in Christ,"[25] and bear an equal burden of service under one Lord, "for with God there is no partiality among persons."[26] For one thing only are we preferred by Him: if we are found better than others in good works and more humble. Let the abbot therefore have equal love for all, and let all, according to their deserts, be under the same discipline.

The abbot in his teaching should always observe that apostolic rule which says, "Reprove, entreat, rebuke."[27] That is to say, as occasions require he ought to mingle encouragement with reproofs. Let him manifest the sternness of a master and the loving affection of a father. He must reprove the undisciplined and restless severely, but he should exhort such as are obedient, quiet and patient, for their better profit. We charge him, however, to reprove and punish the stubborn and negligent. Let him not shut his eyes to the sins of offenders; but, as soon as they begin to show themselves and to grow, he must use every means to root them up utterly, remembering the fate of Eli, the priest of Shiloh.[28] To the more virtuous and of greater understanding, indeed, he may for the first or second time use words of warning, but in dealing with the stubborn, the hard-hearted, the proud and the disobedient, even at the very beginning of their sin, let him chastise them with whips and with bodily punishment, knowing that it is written, "The fool is not corrected with words,"[29] and again, "Strike your son with a rod and you shall deliver his soul from death."[30]

The abbot ought always to bear in mind what he is and what he is called; he ought to know that to whom more is entrusted, from him more is exacted. Let him recognize how difficult and how hard a task he has undertaken, to rule souls and to make himself a servant to the temperaments of many. One must be led by gentle words, another by sharp reproof, another by persuasion, and thus shall he so shape and adapt himself to the character and intelligence of each that he shall not only suffer no loss in the flock entrusted to his care, but may even rejoice in its good growth. Above all things, let him not slight or make little of the souls committed to his care, heeding more fleeting, worldly, and frivolous things; but let him remember always that he has undertaken the government of souls, of which he shall

---

21  Old Testament, Psalms 40.10; Isaiah 1.2.
22  New Testament, 1 Corinthians 9.27.
23  Old Testament, Psalms 50.16-17.
24  New Testament, Matthew 7.3.
25  New Testament, Galatians 3.28.
26  New Testament, Romans 2.11.
27  New Testament, 2 Timothy 4.2.
28  Referring to Old Testament, 1 Samuel 4.
29  Old Testament, Proverbs 29.19.
30  Old Testament, Proverbs 23.14.

also have to give an account. And that he may not complain of the want of temporal means, let him remember that it is written, "Seek first the kingdom of God, and His justice, and all things shall be given to you,"[31] and again, "Nothing is wanting to such as fear Him."[32]

He should know that whoever undertakes the government of souls must prepare himself to account for them. And however great the number of the brethren under him may be, let him understand for certain that at the day of judgment he will have to give to our Lord an account of all their souls as well as of his own. In this way, by fearing the inquiry concerning his flock which the Shepherd will hold, he is solicitous on account of others' souls as well as of his own, and thus while reclaiming other men by his corrections, he frees himself also from all vice.

3
OF TAKING COUNSEL OF THE BRETHREN

Whenever any weighty matters have to be transacted in the monastery, let the abbot call together the whole community and himself propose the matter for discussion. After hearing the advice of the brethren, let him consider it in his own mind, and then do what he shall judge most expedient. We ordain that all must be called for counsel, because the Lord often reveals to a younger member what is best. And let the brethren give their advice with all humble subjection, and not presume stiffly to defend their own opinion. Let them rather leave the matter to the abbot's discretion, so that all submit to what he shall deem best. As it becomes disciples to obey their master, so does it behoove the master to dispose of all things with forethought and justice.

In all things, therefore, everyone shall follow the Rule as their master, and let no one rashly depart from it. In the monastery no one is to be led by the desires of his own heart, neither shall anyone within or without the monastery presume to argue wantonly with his abbot. If he presumes to do so, let him be subjected to punishment according to the Rule.

The abbot, however, must himself do all things in the fear of God and according to the Rule, knowing that he shall undoubtedly have to give an account of his whole government to God, the most just Judge.

If anything of less importance has to be done in the monastery, let the abbot take advice of the seniors only, as it is written, "Do all things with counsel, and you shall not afterwards repent of it."[33]

4
THE INSTRUMENTS OF GOOD WORKS[34]

1 To love the Lord God with all our heart, with all our soul, with all our strength.
2 To love our neighbor as ourself.
3 Not to kill.
4 Not to commit adultery.
5 Not to steal.
6 Not to be covetous.
7 Not to bear false witness.
8 To respect everyone.
9 Not to do to another what one would not have done to oneself.
10 To deny oneself in order to follow Christ.
11 To chastise the body.
12 Not to be fond of pleasures.
13 To love fasting.
14 To relieve the poor.
15 To clothe the naked.
16 To visit the sick.
17 To bury the dead.
18 To come to the help of those in trouble.
19 To comfort those in sadness.
20 To become a stranger to the ways of the world.
21 To prefer nothing to the love of Christ.
22 Not to give way to wrath.
23 Not to harbor anger for any time.
24 Not to foster deceit in one's heart.

31  New Testament, Matthew 6.33.
32  Old Testament, Psalms 34.9.
33  Apocrypha, Ecclesiasticus 32.24.
34  Roughly a third of the precepts in this chapter are quotations from the Old or New Testaments; the sources are not noted in individual notes here.

25 Not to make a false peace.

26 Not to depart from charity.

27 Not to swear at all, lest one forswears.

28 To speak the truth with heart and lips.

29 Not to return evil for evil.

30 Not to do an injury, but patiently to suffer an injury when done to oneself.

31 To love one's enemies.

32 Not to speak ill of those who speak ill of one, but rather to speak well of them.

33 To suffer persecution for justice's sake.

34 Not to be proud.

35 Not to be given to wine.

36 Not to be a great eater.

37 Not to be given to sleep.

38 Not to be slothful.

39 Not to be a grumbler.

40 Not to be a detractor.

41 To put one's trust in God.

42 When one sees any good in oneself, to attribute it to God, not to oneself.

43 That one recognizes that one does evil, and to attribute it to oneself.

44 To fear the day of judgment.

45 To be afraid of hell.

46 To desire everlasting life with complete spiritual longing.

47 To have the vision of death before one's eyes daily.

48 To watch over the actions of one's life every hour of the day.

49 To know for certain that God sees one everywhere.

50 To dash at once against Christ (as against a rock) evil thoughts which rise up in the mind,

51 And to reveal all such to one's spiritual father.

52 To guard one's lips from uttering evil or wicked words.

53 Not to be fond of much talking.

54 Not to speak idle words or such as move to laughter.

55 Not to love much or boisterous laughter.

56 Willingly to hear holy reading.

57 Often to devote oneself to prayer.

58 Daily with tears and sighs to confess to God in prayer one's past offenses, and to avoid them in the future.

59 Not to give way to the desires of the flesh and to hate one's own will.

60 In all things to obey the abbot's commands, even if he himself (which God forbid) should act otherwise, remembering our Lord's precept, "Do what they say, but do not do what they do."

61 Not to wish to be called holy before one is so, but to be holy first so as to be called such with truth.

62 Daily in one's acts to keep God's commandments.

63 To love chastity.

64 To hate no one.

65 Not to be jealous or envious.

66 Not to love wrangling.

67 To show no arrogant spirit.

68 To revere the old.

69 To love the young.

70 To pray for one's enemies for the love of Christ.

71 To make peace with an adversary before the sun sets.

72 Never to despair of God's mercy.

Behold: these are the tools of our spiritual craft; when we shall have made use of them constantly day and night, and shall have proved them at the day of judgment, that reward shall be given us by our Lord, which He has promised, "Which the eye has not seen, nor the ear heard, nor has it entered into the heart of man to conceive what God has prepared for those that love Him."[35] Steadfastly abiding in the community, the workshop where all these instruments are made use of is the cloister[36] of the monastery.

## 5
### OF OBEDIENCE

The first degree of humility is prompt obedience. This is required of all who, whether by reason of the holy

---

35 New Testament, 1 Corinthians 2.9.

36 I.e., the portion of the monastery closed off from outsiders.

servitude to which they are pledged, or through fear of hell, or to attain to the glory of eternal life, hold nothing more dear than Christ. Such disciples do not delay in doing what is ordered by their superior, just as if the command had come from God. Of such our Lord says, "At the hearing of the ear he has obeyed me."[37] And to the teachers He likewise says, "He that hears you, hears me."[38]

For this reason such disciples, surrendering forthwith all they possess, and giving up their own will, leave unfinished what they were working at, and with the ready foot of obedience in their acts follow the word of command. Thus, as it were, at the same moment comes the order of the master and the finished work of the disciple; with the speed of the fear of God both go jointly forward and are quickly effected by such as ardently desire to walk in the way of eternal life. These take the narrow way, of which the Lord says, "Narrow is the way which leads to life."[39] That is, they live not as they themselves will, neither do they obey their own desires and pleasures, but following the command and direction of another and, abiding in their monasteries, their desire is to be ruled by an abbot. Without doubt such as these carry out that saying of our Lord, "I came not to do my own will but the will of Him Who sent me."[40]

This kind of obedience will be both acceptable to God and pleasing to men when what is ordered is not done out of fear, or slowly and coldly, grudgingly, or with reluctant protest. Obedience shown to superiors is indeed given to God, Who Himself has said, "He that hears you, hears Me."[41] What is commanded should be done by those under obedience, with a good will, since "God loves a cheerful giver."[42] If the disciple obeys unwillingly and grumbles in word as well as in heart, it will not be accepted by God, Who considers the heart of a grumbler, even if he does what was ordered. For a work done in this spirit shall have no reward; rather the doer shall incur the penalty appointed for grumblers if he does not amend and does not make satisfaction.

## 6

### OF SILENCE

Let us do as the prophet says, "I have said, I will keep my ways, that I not offend with my tongue. I have been watchful over my mouth; I held my peace and humbled myself and was silent from speaking even good things."[43] Here the prophet shows that, for the sake of silence, we are at times to abstain even from good talk. If this is so, how much more needful is it that we refrain from evil words on account of the penalty of the sin. Because of the importance of silence, therefore, let permission to speak be seldom given, even to perfect disciples, although their talk is of good and holy matters and tends to edification, since it is written, "In much speaking, you shall not escape sin."[44] The master, indeed, should speak and teach; the disciple should hold his peace and listen.

Whatever, therefore, has to be asked of the superior, let it be done with all humility and with reverent submission. But as to coarse, idle words, or such as move to laughter, we utterly condemn and ban them in all places. We do not allow any disciple to speak them.

## 7

### OF HUMILITY

Brethren, Holy Scripture cries out to us, saying, "Everyone who exalts himself shall be humbled, and he who humbles himself shall be exalted."[45] In this it tells us that every form of self-exaltation is a kind of

---

37  Old Testament, Psalms 18.44.
38  New Testament, Luke 10.16.
39  New Testament, Matthew 7.14.
40  New Testament, John 6.38.
41  New Testament, Luke 10.16.
42  New Testament, 2 Corinthians 9.7.
43  Old Testament, Psalms 39.1-2.
44  Old Testament, Proverbs 10.19.
45  New Testament, Luke 14.11.

pride, which the prophet declares he carefully avoided, where he says, "Lord, my heart is not exalted, neither are my eyes lifted up; neither have I walked in great things, nor in wonders above myself." And why? "If I did not think humbly, but exalted my soul: as a child weaned from his mother, so will You reward my soul."[46]

Wherefore, brethren, if we would scale the summit of humility, and swiftly gain the heavenly height which is reached by our lowliness in this present life, we must set up a ladder of climbing deeds like that which Jacob saw in his dream, whereon angels were descending and ascending.[47] Without doubt that descending and ascending is to be understood by us as signifying that we descend by exalting ourselves and ascend by humbling ourselves. But the ladder itself thus set up is our life in this world, which by humility of heart is lifted by our Lord to heaven. Our body and soul we may indeed call the sides of the ladder in which our divine vocation has set the diverse steps of humility and discipline we have to ascend.

The first step of humility, then, is reached when a man, with the fear of God always before his eyes, does not allow himself to forget, but is ever mindful of all God's commandments. He remembers, moreover, that those who scorn God fall into hell for their sins, and that eternal life awaits those who fear Him. And warding off at each moment all sin and defect in thought and word, of eye, hand or foot, of self-will, let such a one bestir himself to prune away the lusts of the flesh.

Let him think that he is seen at all times by God from heaven, and that wheresoever he may be, all his actions are visible to the eye of God and at all times are reported by the angels. The prophet shows us this when he says that God is ever present to our thoughts: "God searches the hearts and minds,"[48] and again, "The Lord knows the thoughts of men, that they are vain."[49] He also says, "You have understood my thoughts afar,"[50] and again, "The thought of man shall confess to you."[51] In order, then, that the humble brother may be careful to avoid wrong thoughts, let him always say in his heart, "Then shall I be without blemish before Him, if I shall keep myself from my iniquity."[52]

We are forbidden to do our own will, since Scripture tells us, "Leave your own will and desire."[53] And again, "We beg of God in prayer that His will may be done in us."[54]

Rightly are we taught therefore not to do our own will, if we take heed of what the Scripture teaches: "There are ways which to men seem right, the end whereof plunges even into the deep pit of hell."[55] And again, when we fear what is said about the negligent, "They are corrupted, and made abominable in their pleasures."[56] But regarding the desires of the flesh, we ought to believe that God is present with us, as the prophet says, speaking to the Lord, "O Lord, all my desire is before You."[57]

We have therefore to beware of evil desires, since death stands close by the door of pleasure. It is for this reason that Scripture bids us, "Do not follow your lusts."[58] If, therefore, the eyes of the Lord behold both the good and the bad; if He is ever looking down from heaven upon the sons of men to find one who thinks of God or seeks Him; and if day and night what we do is made known to Him—for these reasons, by the

46  Old Testament, Psalms 131.1-2.
47  A reference to the Old Testament, in which the Hebrew Jacob dreamed of this ladder (Genesis 28).
48  Old Testament, Psalms 7.9.
49  Old Testament, Psalms 94.11.
50  Old Testament, Psalms 139.2.
51  Old Testament, Psalms 76.10.
52  Old Testament, Psalms 18.23.
53  Apocrypha, Ecclesiasticus 18.30.
54  New Testament, Matthew 6.10.
55  Old Testament, Proverbs 16.9.
56  Old Testament, Psalms 14.1.
57  Old Testament, Psalms 38.9.
58  Apocrypha, Ecclesiasticus 18.30.

angels appointed to watch over us, we should always take heed, brethren, lest God may sometime or other see us, as the prophet says in the Psalm, "inclined to evil and become unprofitable servants."[59] Even though He spares us for a time, because He is loving and waits for our conversion to better ways, let us fear that He may say to us hereafter, "These things you have done and I held my peace."[60]

The second step of humility is reached when anyone not loving self-will takes no heed to satisy his own desires, but copies in his life what our Lord said, "I came not to do My own will but the will of Him Who sent Me."[61] Similarly we read that "self-will engenders punishment, and necessity purchases a crown."[62]

The third step of humility is reached when a man, for the love of God, submits himself with all obedience to a superior, imitating our Lord, of whom the apostle says, "He was made obedient even to death."[63]

The fourth step of humility is reached when anyone in the exercise of his obedience patiently and with a quiet mind bears all that is inflicted on him, things contrary to nature, and even at times unjust, and in suffering all these he neither wearies nor gives over the work, since the Scripture says, "He only that perseveres to the end shall be saved"[64] and also "Let your heart be comforted, and expect the Lord."[65] And in order to show that for our Lord's sake the faithful man ought to bear all things, no matter how contrary to nature they may be, the psalmist, in the person of the sufferers, says, "For you we suffer death all the day long; we are considered as sheep for the slaughter."[66] Secure in the hope of divine reward they rejoice, saying, "But in all things we overcome by the help of Him Who has loved us."[67]

Elsewhere also Scripture says, "You have tested us, O Lord; You have tried us, as silver is tried, with fire. You have brought us into the snare; You have laid tribulation upon our backs."[68] And to show that we ought to be subject to a superior it goes on, "You have placed men over our heads."[69] And, moreover, they fulfill the Lord's command by patience in adversity and injury, who, "when struck on one cheek, offer the other"; when one "takes away their coat, leave go their cloak also," and who "being compelled to carry a burden one mile, go two";[70] who, with Paul the apostle, suffer "false brethren," and "bless those who speak ill of them."[71]

The fifth step of humility is reached when a monk manifests to his abbot, by humble confession, all the evil thoughts of his heart and his secret faults. The Scripture urges us to do this where it says, "Reveal your way to the Lord and hope in Him."[72] It also says, "Confess to the Lord because He is good, because His mercy endures forever."[73] And the prophet also says, "I have made known to You my offense, and my injustices I have not hidden. I have said I will declare openly against myself my injustices to the Lord; and You have pardoned the wickedness of my heart."[74]

The sixth step of humility is reached when a monk is content with all that is mean and vile, and in regard

---

59  Old Testament, Psalms 14.1.
60  Old Testament, Psalms 50.21.
61  New Testament, John 6.38.
62  *Acts of the Martyrs.*
63  New Testament, Philippians 2.8.
64  New Testament, Matthew 10.22.
65  Old Testament, Psalms 27.14.
66  Old Testament, Psalms 44.22.
67  New Testament, Romans 8.37.
68  Old Testament, Psalms 66.10,11.
69  Old Testament, Psalms 66.12.
70  New Testament, Matthew 5.39-41.
71  New Testament, 2 Cornithians 11.26; 1 Corinthians 4.12.
72  Old Testament, Psalms 37.5.
73  Old Testament, Psalms 106.1.
74  Old Testament, Psalms 32.5.

to everything enjoined him accounts himself a poor and worthless workman, saying with the prophet, "I have been brought to nothing, and did not know it. I have become as a beast before You, and I am always with You."[75]

The seventh step of humility is reached when a man not only confesses with his tongue that he is most lowly and inferior to others, but in his inmost heart believes so. Such a one, humbling himself, exclaims with the prophet, "I am a worm and no man, the reproach of men and the outcast of the people,"[76] "I have been exalted and am humbled and confounded,"[77] and again, "It is good for me that You have humbled me, that I may learn Your commandments."[78]

The eighth step of humility is reached when a monk does nothing but what the common rule of the monastery, or the example of his seniors, enforces.

The ninth step of humility is reached when a monk restrains his tongue from talking, and, practicing silence, does not speak till a question is asked him, since Scripture says, "In much speaking, you shall not escape sin,"[79] and "a talkative man shall not prosper upon the earth."[80]

The tenth step of humility is attained when one is not easily and quickly moved to laughter, for it is written, "The fool lifts his voice in laughter."[81]

The eleventh step of humility is reached when a monk, in speaking, does so quietly and without laughter, humbly, gravely and in a few words and not with a loud voice, for it is written, "A wise man is known by a few words."[82]

The twelfth step of humility is reached when a monk not only has humility in his heart, but even shows it also exteriorly to all who behold him. Thus, whether he is in the oratory[83] at the work of God,[84] in the monastery, or in the garden, on a journey, or in the fields, or wheresoever he may be, sitting, standing or walking, always let him, with head bent and eyes fixed on the ground, bethink himself of his sins and imagine that he is arraigned before the dread judgment of God. Let him be ever saying to himself, with the publican in the Gospel, "Lord, I a sinner am not worthy to lift my eyes to heaven,"[85] and with the prophet, "I am bowed down and humbled on every side."[86]

When all these steps of humility have been mounted, the monk will presently attain to that love of God which is perfect and casts out fear. By means of this love everything which before he had observed not without fear, he shall now begin to do by habit, without any trouble and, as it were, naturally. He acts now not through fear of hell, but for the love of Christ, out of a good habit and a delight in virtue. All this our Lord will vouchsafe to work by the Holy Spirit in His servant, now cleansed from vice and sin.

## 8

### OF THE DIVINE OFFICE[87] AT NIGHT

In the winter—that is, from the first of November until Easter—the brethren shall get up at the eighth hour of the night by reasonable calculation, so that having rested till a little more than half the night, they may rise refreshed. Let the time that remains after Matins[88] be used, by those brethren who need it, for the study

---

75    Old Testament, Psalms 73.22,23.
76    Old Testament, Psalms 22.6.
77    Old Testament, Psalms 88.1-5.
78    Old Testament, Psalms 119.71.
79    Old Testament, Proverbs 10.19.
80    Old Testament, Psalms 140.11.
81    Apocrypha, Ecclesiasticus 20.23.
82    Old Testament, Proverbs 10.14.
83    The room designated for communal prayer, where the communion was also held.
84    I.e., the divine office, or course of prayers sung at certain regular times, or hours, over the course of a day in the monastery.
85    New Testament, Luke 18.13.
86    Old Testament, Psalms 38.8.
87    See above, n 83.
88    I.e., the first morning prayer, at about 2 a.m.

of the Psalter[89] or lessons. From Easter to the aforesaid first of November, let the hour for saying Matins be so arranged that after a brief interval, during which the brethren may go forth for the necessities of nature, Lauds,[90] which are to be said at daybreak, may presently follow.

## 9

### HOW MANY PSALMS ARE TO BE SAID IN THE NIGHT HOURS

In the winter season, the night office should begin with the words, "O Lord, You shall open my lips and my mouth shall declare Your praise,"[91] and these are to be said three times. After this the third Psalm is to be said with a *Gloria*,[92] after which the ninety-fourth Psalm, with an antiphon,[93] is to be recited or sung, followed by a hymn, and then six psalms with their antiphons. When these are ended and a versicle said, let the abbot give a blessing, and then, all being seated, let three lessons[94] from the book placed on the lectern be read by the brethren in turns. Between these lessons three responsories are to be sung, two without a *Gloria*. After the third lesson, however, let the chanter add the *Gloria* to the responsory, and as soon as he begins it let all rise from their seats out of honor and reverence to the Holy Trinity.

Let the divinely inspired books of the Old and New Testament be read at Matins, together with their expositions from the best known orthodox and catholic Fathers.

After these three lessons, with their responsories, let six other psalms be sung with the *Alleluia*.[95] A lesson from the Apostle is then to be said by heart, and a verse with the prayer of the Litany, that is, *Kyrie eleison*[96]—and so let the Night Office end.

## 10

### HOW THE NIGHT OFFICE IS TO BE SAID IN THE SUMMER

From Easter to the first day of November, the same number of psalms as above appointed are to be said. On account of the short nights of summer, however, the lessons are not to be read from the book, but in place of the three lessons let one from the Old Testament be said by heart and followed by a short responsory. Let all the rest be done as we have arranged above, so that, without counting the third and ninety-fourth Psalm, there may never be less than 12 psalms at Matins.

## 11

### HOW THE NIGHT OFFICE IS TO BE CELEBRATED ON SUNDAYS

On Sunday let the brethren rise earlier for Matins, in which the following order is to be observed: when six psalms and the versicle have been sung, as we have before arranged, let all sit down on the benches in the proper order and let four lessons be read from the book with their responsories, in the manner before prescribed. To the fourth responsory only let the chanter add the *Gloria*, and when he begins it, let all rise at once out of reverence. After these lessons, six other psalms follow in order with their antiphons and a versicle as before. Then let four other lessons be read with their responsories in the same way as the former, and then three canticles out of the Prophets,[97] appointed by the abbot; these canticles are to be sung with *Alleluia*.

When the versicle has been said, and the abbot has given the blessing, four more lessons from the New Testament are to be read, in the same order as before.

---

89  The book of psalms used in church services.
90  I.e., the second hour of prayer.
91  Old Testament, Psalms 51.15.
92  I.e., "glory be to the Father."
93  A verse of a psalm sung by one group in response to another.
94  I.e., passages read aloud from the Bible or some other Christian book.
95  In Christian worship, an expression of joy; originally a Hebrew ejaculation signifying praise.
96  I.e., "Lord have mercy."
97  From the Old Testament.

After the fourth responsory let the abbot begin the hymn "We praise you God," and when that is finished he shall read a lesson from the Gospel, with reverence and fear, while all stand. At the conclusion of this let all answer "Amen," and let the abbot immediately go on with the hymn "May praise be to You"; after the blessing let them begin Lauds.

This method of singing Matins on Sundays is to be observed always, in summer as well as in winter, unless perchance (which God forbid) they get up late, and the lessons or responsories have to be somewhat shortened. Let great care be taken that this shall not happen; but if it does, let him to whose carelessness it is due make full satisfaction to God in the oratory.

12

HOW LAUDS ARE TO BE SOLEMNIZED

At Lauds on Sunday let the sixty-sixth Psalm be first said straight on, and without an antiphon. After this, the fiftieth is to be said with *Alleluia*, with the one-hundred-seventeenth and the sixty-second. Then follow the "Blessings" and the "Praises" psalms, a lesson from the Apocalypse, said by heart, a responsory and hymn, the versicle and the canticle from the Gospel with the litanies, and so conclude.

13

HOW LAUDS ARE TO BE CELEBRATED ON ORDINARY DAYS

On ordinary week days let Lauds be celebrated as follows: the sixty-sixth Psalm is to be said, as on Sunday, straight on without any antiphon, and somewhat slowly, to allow all to be in their places for the fiftieth Psalm, which is to be said with an antiphon. After this come two other psalms according to custom: that is, on Monday, the fifth and thirty-fifth; on Tuesday, the forty-second and fifty-sixth; on Wednesday, the sixty-third and sixty-fourth; on Thursday, the eighty-seventh and eighty-ninth; on Friday, the seventy-fifth and

ninety-first; on Saturday, the one-hundred-forty-second and the Canticle of Deuteronomy, which must be divided into two *Glorias*. But on other days let a canticle out of the Prophets be said, each on its proper day, according to the custom of the Roman Church. After these let the "Praises" psalms follow, then a lesson of the Apostle, said by heart, the responsory, hymn and versicle, the canticle from the Gospel, the litanies, and the office is completed.

Lauds and Vespers[98] are never to be finished without the Lord's prayer at the end. This is said by the prior (that is, the superior) aloud, so that all may hear, because of the thorns of scandal which are always cropping up: that the community, by reason of the pledge given in this prayer, in the words, "Forgive us our trespasses as we forgive them that trespass against us,"[99] may purge themselves from this kind of vice. In saying the other hours, however, the last part of the prayer only is said aloud that all may answer, "But deliver us from evil."[100]

14

HOW MATINS IS TO BE SAID ON THE FEAST DAYS
OF SAINTS[101]

On saints' feast days and on all solemnities let Matins be said in the manner we have ordered for Sunday, except that the psalms, antiphons and lessons are said which are proper to the day itself. The method of saying them, however, shall remain as before prescribed.

15

AT WHAT SEASONS *ALLELUIA* IS TO BE SAID

From the holy feast of Easter until Pentecost *Alleluia* is to be always said both with the psalms and in the responsories. From Pentecost till the beginning of Lent, let it be said every night at Matins only with the last six psalms. On every Sunday out of Lent let the Canticles, Lauds, Prime, Tierce, Sext and None[102] be

---

98  An hour of the divine office, sung at sundown.
99  New Testament, Matthew 6.12.
100  New Testament, Matthew 6.13.
101  I.e., the days on which saints were celebrated, usually the days of their deaths.
102  Hours of the divine office: Prime: *c.* 6 a.m.; Tierce: *c.* 9 a.m.; Sext: *c.* noon; None: *c.* 3 p.m.

said with *Alleluia*, but Vespers with antiphons. Responsories, however, except from Easter until Pentecost, are never to be said with *Alleluia*.

## 16
### HOW THE DIVINE OFFICE IS TO BE SAID

The prophet says, "Seven times a day have I sung Your praises."[103] This sacred number of seven will be kept by us if we perform the duties of our service in the hours of Lauds, Prime, Tierce, Sext, None, Vespers and Compline.[104] It was of these day hours the prophet said, "Seven times a day I have sung Your praises," for of the night watches the same prophet says, "At midnight I arose to confess to You."[105] At these times, therefore, let us give praise to our Creator for His just judgments, that is, at Lauds, Prime, Tierce, Sext, None, Vespers and Compline, and at night let us rise to confess to Him.

## 17
### HOW MANY PSALMS ARE TO BE SAID IN THESE HOURS

We have already settled the order of the psalmody for Matins and for Lauds, let us now arrange for the hours which follow. At Prime three psalms are to be said separately, that is, not under one *Gloria*. After the verse, "O God, come to my assistance,"[106] and before the psalms are begun, the hymn of each hour is to be said. At the end of the three psalms a lesson is recited, then with the versicle and *Kyrie eleison* the hour is concluded. The hours of Tierce, Sext and None are to be said in the same way, that is, the verse, the hymns of these hours, three psalms, the lesson and versicle, and with *Kyrie eleison* they are concluded.

If the community is large, the hours shall be sung with antiphons, but if it is small, they are to be sung without. Vespers shall be said with four psalms and antiphons, after which a lesson is to be recited, then a responsory, hymn, versicle, canticle from the Gospel,

and it is concluded by the litanies and the Lord's Prayer. Compline shall consist in the saying of three psalms straight through and without antiphons, followed by the hymn of the hour, a lesson, versicle, a *Kyrie eleison*, and shall conclude with the blessing.

## 18
### THE ORDER IN WHICH THE PSALMS ARE TO BE SAID

Let the verse, "O God, come to my assistance; O Lord, make haste to help me,"[107] with a *Gloria*, always come first, followed by the hymn of each hour. Then, on Sundays, at Prime, four divisions of the one-hundred-eighteenth Psalm are to be said, and at the other hours of Tierce, Sext and None three divisions of the same. On Monday, at Prime, the first, second and third Psalms are recited, and so on each day till Sunday, three other psalms in order up to the nineteenth Psalm, the ninth and seventeenth Psalm being each divided in two by a *Gloria*. In this way the Sunday Matins may always begin with the twentieth Psalm.

On Mondays, at Tierce, Sext and None, let the remaining nine divisions of the one-hundred-eighteenth Psalm be said, three at each hour. The one-hundred-eighteenth Psalm being finished on the two days, Sunday and Monday, therefore on Tuesday, at Tierce, Sext and None the three psalms at each hour shall be the nine from the one-hundred-nineteenth to the one-hundred-twenty-seventh. And these same psalms are to be repeated at the hours till Sunday. A uniform order of the hymns, lessons and versicles is to be likewise observed, so that the one-hundred-eighteenth Psalm is always begun on Sunday.

Four psalms are to be sung each day at Vespers. These begin with the one-hundred-ninth Psalm and conclude with the one-hundred-forty-seventh, omitting those already set apart for the various other hours, that is to say, from the one-hundred-seventeenth Psalm to the one-hundred-twenty-seventh; the one-hundred-thirty-third and the one-hundred-forty-second. All the

---

103  Old Testament, Psalms 119.164.
104  The last hour of the divine office, sung at nightfall.
105  Old Testament, Psalms 119.62.
106  Old Testament, Psalms 70.1.
107  Old Testament, Psalms 70.1.

rest are to be said at Vespers, and because this leaves three psalms short, the longest of them, namely, the one-hundred-thirty-eighth, the one-hundred-forty-third, and the one-hundred-fortyfourth, are to be divided. The one-hundred-sixteenth, however, since it is brief, is to be joined to the one-hundred-fifteenth.

The order of the psalms for Vespers being thus arranged, let the other parts, such as the lessons, responsories, hymns, versicles and canticles, be used as before directed. At Compline the same psalms are repeated every day, namely, the fourth, the ninetieth and the one-hundred-thirty-third.

The order of the psalmody for the day office being thus settled, all the rest of the psalms are to be equally portioned to the seven night offices. Those that are too long are to be divided into 2, and 12 psalms are to be arranged for each night. If this distribution of the psalms displeases anyone, we specially desire him to arrange otherwise, if he thinks something else would be better, provided that care be taken that every week the whole Psalter of 150 psalms is sung, and that at Matins on Sunday it is begun again. Monks, indeed, show themselves in their service too negligent and undevout who sing less than the Psalter, with the usual canticles, once a week, when we read that our holy Fathers courageously performed in one day what I would that we who are tepid may do in a whole week.

## 19
### HOW ONE SHOULD PERFORM THE OFFICE

We believe that the Divine Presence is everywhere, and that the eyes of the Lord behold both the good and the bad in all places. Especially do we believe without any doubt that this is so when we assist at the divine office. Let us therefore always be mindful of what the prophet says: "Serve the Lord in fear"[108] and again, "Sing His praises with understanding"[109] and, "In the sight of angels I will sing praise to You."[110] Wherefore let us consider how it behooves us to be in the sight of God and the angels, and so let us take our part in the psalmody that mind and voice accord together.

## 20
### OF REVERENCE AT PRAYER

If, when we wish to obtain some favor from those who have the power to help us, we do not dare to ask except with humility and reverence, how much more reason is there that we should present our petitions to the Lord God of the universe in all lowliness of heart and purity of devotion. We may know for certain that we shall be heard, not because we use many words, but on account of the purity of our hearts and our tears of sorrow. Our prayer, therefore, should be short and pure, unless by some inspiration of divine grace it is prolonged. All prayer made by the community in common, however, should be short, and when the superior has given the sign, let all rise together.

## 21
### THE DEANS OF THE MONASTERY

If the community is large, let brethren of good repute and holy lives be chosen from amongst them and appointed deans. These shall carefully watch over their deaneries in all things relating to the commandments of God and the injunctions of the abbot. Deans are to be chosen on whom the abbot may safely rely to share his burdens, and the choice is not to be determined by their rank but by the worthiness of their lives and their proved learning. And if perchance any one of these deans, being puffed up by pride, is found blameworthy, and after being corrected three times will not amend, then let him be put out of office and another more worthy be substituted. We direct the same in the case of the prior.[111]

## 22
### HOW MONKS ARE TO SLEEP

All shall sleep in separate beds and each shall receive,

---

108 Old Testament, Psalms 2.11.
109 Old Testament, Psalms 47.7.
110 Old Testament, Psalms 138.1.
111 A superior office to that of the deans, second only to the abbot.

according to the appointment of his abbot, bedclothes fitted to the condition of his life. If it is possible, let them all sleep in a common dormitory, but if their great number will not allow this, they may sleep in tens or twenties, with seniors to have charge over them. Let a candle be constantly burning in the room until morning, and let the monks sleep clothed and wearing belts or cords; but they are not to have knives by their sides in their beds, lest by accident they injure themselves while sleeping. In this way the monks shall always be ready to rise quickly when the signal is given and hurry each one to come before his brother to the divine office, and yet with all gravity and modesty.

The younger brethren are not to have their beds next to each other, but amongst those of the elders. When they rise for the divine office, let them gently encourage one another because of the excuses made by those that are drowsy.

### 23
#### OF EXCOMMUNICATION FOR OFFENSES

If any brother be found stubborn, disobedient, proud, grumbling, or in any way acting contrary to the holy Rule, or despises the orders of his seniors, let him, according to the precept of our Lord, be secretly admonished by those seniors, once or twice. If he will not amend, let him be publicly reproved before all. But if even then he does not correct his faults, let him, if he understands the nature of the punishment, be subject to excommunication. But if he is obstinate, he is to undergo corporal punishment.

### 24
#### THE MANNER OF EXCOMMUNICATION

The mode of excommunication or punishment should be proportionate to the fault, and the gravity of the fault shall depend on the judgment of the abbot. If any brother is detected in small faults, let him be excluded from eating at table with the rest. The punishment of one thus separated from the common table shall be of

this kind: in the oratory he shall intone neither psalm nor antiphon; neither shall he read any lesson until he has made satisfaction. He shall take his portion of food alone, after the brethren have had their meal, and in such quantity and at such time as the abbot shall think fit, so that if, for example, the brethren take their meal at the sixth hour, let him take his at the ninth; if the brethren take theirs at the ninth, let him have his in the evening, until such time as by due satisfaction he obtains pardon.

### 25
#### OF GRAVER FAULTS

Let the brother who is guilty of some graver fault be excluded both from the common table and from the oratory. None of the brethren shall talk to him or consort with him. Let him be alone at the work which is set him; let him remain in penance and sorrow, and keep before his mind that terrible sentence of the apostle where he says, "Such a one is delivered over to Satan for the destruction of the flesh, that his spirit may be saved in the day of our Lord."[112] Let him take his food alone, in such quantity and at such time as the abbot shall think fit. Let no one bless him as he passes by, nor bless the food that is given him.

### 26
#### OF THOSE WHO MEET WITH THE EXCOMMUNICATED
#### WITHOUT PERMISSION FROM THE ABBOT

If any brother shall presume, without the abbot's order, to have contact in any way with an excommunicated brother, to talk with him or send him any message, let him suffer the same penalty of excommunication.

### 27
#### WHAT CARE THE ABBOT SHOULD HAVE
#### FOR THE EXCOMMUNICATED

Let the abbot take every possible care of the offending brethren, for "They that are well do not need the

---

112  New Testament, 1 Corinthians 5.5.

physician, but they that are sick."[113] Like a wise physician, therefore, he ought to make use of every remedy; he should send some of the older and wiser brethren as comforters, to console, as it were, in secret their wayward brother, and urge him to make humble satisfaction. And let them comfort him that he be not overwhelmed by too great sorrow, but as the apostle says, "Let charity be confirmed in him and let all pray for him."[114]

The abbot ought to take the greatest care and to use all prudence and industry to lose none of the sheep entrusted to him. Let him know that he has undertaken the care of souls that are sick, and not act as a tyrant over such as are well. Let him fear the reproach of the prophet in whom God speaks thus, "What you saw to be fat, that you took for yourselves, and what was diseased, that you threw away."[115] Let him copy the loving example of the Good Shepherd, who, leaving 99 sheep in the mountains, went to seek the one that had gone astray, and on whose infirmity He took such compassion that He deigned to lay it on His shoulders and carry it back to the flock.[116]

### 28
#### OF THOSE WHO, BEING CORRECTED, DO NOT AMEND

If any brother does not amend after being often corrected for any fault, and even excommunicated, let a sharper punishment be administered to him, that is, let him be corrected by whipping. And if even after this he shall not correct himself, or, being puffed up by pride (which God forbid), shall attempt to defend his doings, then let the abbot act like a wise physician. If after applying the compresses and ointments of exhortation, the medicine of the Holy Scripture, and the final cautery of excommunication and scourging, he finds that his labors have had no effect, then let him try what is more than all this, his own prayer and

those of the brethren for him that the Lord, who can do all things, may work the cure of the sick brother. If he is not healed by this means, then let the abbot use the severing knife, according to that saying of the apostle, "Put away the evil one from among you,"[117] and again, "If the faithless one departs, let him depart,"[118] lest one diseased sheep should infect the whole flock.

### 29
#### WHETHER BRETHREN WHO LEAVE THE MONASTERY MUST BE RECEIVED BACK

If the brother, who, through his own bad conduct, leaves or is expelled from the monastery, shall desire to return, he must first promise full amendment of the fault for which he left it. He may then be received back in the lowest place, that by this his humility may be tested. If he shall again leave, he may he received back until the third time, but he shall know that after this all possibility of returning will be denied to him.

### 30
#### HOW YOUNG CHILDREN ARE TO BE CORRECTED

Every age and state of intelligence ought to be governed in the way suitable to it. Thus the faults of those who are children or youths, or who cannot understand the seriousness of the penalty of excommunication, shall be punished by rigorous fasting or corrected by sharp whips so they may be healed.

### 31
#### WHAT MANNER OF MAN THE CELLARER[119] OF THE MONASTERY SHOULD BE

Let one of the community be chosen as cellarer of the monastery who is wise, mature in character, temper-

---

113 New Testament, Matthew 9.12.
114 New Testament, 2 Corinthians 2.8.
115 Old Testament, Ezekiel 34.3-4.
116 An episode from the New Testament, Luke 15. Jesus is the good shepherd.
117 New Testament, 1 Corinthians 5.13.
118 New Testament, 1 Corinthians 7.15.
119 The monastic officer in charge of keeping provisions.

ate, not a great eater, not arrogant or quarrelsome, or insolent, and not a dawdler, nor wasteful, but one who fears God and is as a father to the community. Let him have charge of everything; do nothing without the abbot's order; see to what is commanded, and not make the brethren sad. If any of them shall perchance ask something unreasonable, he must not vex him by contemptuously rejecting his request, but humbly and reasonably refuse what he wrongly asks.

Let him look after his own soul, mindful of the apostolic principle, that "he that ministers well shall secure a good standing for himself."[120] Let him take every care of the sick, of children, of guests, and of the poor, knowing that without doubt he shall have to render an account of all these on the judgment day.

Let him look upon all the vessels and goods of the monastery as if they were the consecrated chalices of the altar. He must not think anything can be neglected; he must not be covetous, nor a prodigal waster of the goods of the monastery, but let him do everything with forethought and according to the direction of his abbot.

Above all things, let him have humility and give a gentle answer to those to whom he can give nothing else, for it is written, "A good word is above the best."[121] Let him take charge of all the abbot shall commit to him, but let him not meddle with anything which is forbidden him. Let him provide the brethren with their appointed allowance of food without impatience or delay, so that they are not driven to offend, being mindful of the divine word which declares the punishment he deserves "Who shall scandalize one of these little ones. It would be better for him that a millstone should be hanged about his neck, and that he should he drowned in the depth of the sea."[122] If the community is large, let him be given helpers, by whose aid he may without worry perform the office committed to him. What is given let it be given, and what is asked for let it be asked at suitable times, so that no one is troubled or distressed in the house of God.

## 32
### CONCERNING THE TOOLS AND OTHER GOODS OF THE MONASTERY

Let the abbot appoint brethren, of whose life and moral conduct he is sure, to keep the tools, the clothes, or other property of the monastery. To these he shall allot the various things to be kept and collected, as he shall deem expedient. The abbot shall hold a list of these things so that, as the brethren succeed each other in their appointed work, he may know what he gives and what he receives back. If anyone shall treat the property of the monastery in a slovenly or careless way, let him be corrected; if he does not amend let him be subjected to the discipline of the Rule.

## 33
### WHETHER MONKS OUGHT TO HAVE ANYTHING OF THEIR OWN

Above all others, let this vice be uprooted in the monastery. No one, without leave of the abbot, shall presume to give, or receive, or keep as his own, anything whatever: neither book, nor writing tablets, nor pen—nothing at all. For monks can claim no dominion, even over their own bodies or wills. All that is necessary, however, they may hope from the father of the monastery, but they shall keep nothing which the abbot has not given or allowed. All things are to be common to all, as it is written, "Neither did anyone say or think that anything was his own."[123] Hence if anyone shall be found given to this most wicked vice, let him be admonished once or twice, and if he does not amend, let him be subjected to correction.

---

120  New Testament, 1 Timothy 3.13.
121  Apocrypha, Ecclesiasticus 18.17.
122  New Testament, Matthew 18.6.
123  New Testament, Acts 4.32.

## 34

### WHETHER ALL OUGHT TO RECEIVE NECESSARY THINGS UNIFORMLY

It is written, "Distribution was made to every one, according as he had need."[124] By this we do not mean that there is to be a personal preference (which God forbid), but a consideration for infirmities. In this way, let him who needs less thank God and not be distressed, and let him who requires more be humiliated because of his infirmity and not puffed up by the mercy that is shown him, so all the members shall be in peace. Above all things, do not let the pestilence of grumbling, for whatever cause, by any word or sign, be manifested. If anyone shall be found faulty in this, let him be subjected to most severe punishment.

## 35

### OF THE WEEKLY SERVERS IN THE KITCHEN

The brethren are so to serve each other that no one is excused from the work of the kitchen unless by reason of health, or because he is occupied in some matter of great utility, for thence great reward is obtained and charity is exercised. Let the weaker brethren, however, have help so that they may not do their work in sadness, and let all generally be helped according to the circumstances of the community or the circumstances of the place. If the community is large, the cellarer may be eased from the service of the kitchen, and any others who (as we have said) are engaged in matters of greater utility. Let the rest serve one another in charity. On Saturday, he who ends his weekly service must clean up everything. He must wash the towels with which the brethren wipe their hands and feet, and he who finishes his service, and he who enters on it, are to wash the feet of all. He shall give back to the cellarer all the vessels used in his ministry, cleaned and unbroken, and the cellarer shall hand them to the one entering on his office, that he may know what he gives and what he receives.

An hour before the meal these weekly servers may receive a drink of water and a piece of bread over and above the appointed allowance, so that they may serve the brethren at meal time without grumbling or too great fatigue. On solemn days, however, let them wait until after mass. Immediately after Lauds on Sunday both the incoming and outgoing servers for the week shall cast themselves on their knees in the presence of all and ask for their prayers. Let him who finishes his week say this verse, "Blessed are You, O Lord God, who helped me and consoled me,"[125] and when this has been said three times, let him receive a blessing. He who enters on his office shall then follow and say, "O God, come to my assistance; O Lord, make haste to help me,"[126] and this also shall be repeated by all three times, and having received his blessing, let him enter on his service.

## 36

### OF SICK BRETHREN

Before all things and above all things, special care must be taken of the sick, so that truly they be looked after as if it were Christ Himself who was served. He Himself has said, "I was sick, and you visited Me; and what you did to one of these, My least brethren, you did to Me."[127]

But let the sick themselves bear in mind that they are served for the honor of God, and should not grieve their brethren who serve them by their superfluous demands. These, nevertheless, must be borne with patience, since from such a more abundant reward is obtained. Let the abbot, therefore, take the greatest care that the sick suffer no neglect.

For them let a separate cell be set apart with an attendant who is God-fearing, diligent and painstaking. Let baths be granted to the sick as often as it shall be expedient, but to those in health, and especially to the young, they shall be seldom permitted. Also for the recovery of their strength the eating of meat may be allowed to the sick and those of very weak health.

---

124  New Testament, Acts 4.35.
125  Old Testament, Psalms 86.17; Apocrypha, Daniel 3.52.
126  Old Testament, Psalms 70.1.
127  New Testament, Matthew 25.36, 40.

As soon, however, as they shall mend, they must all in the accustomed manner abstain from flesh. Let the abbot take special care that the sick not be neglected by the cellarer or the attendants, because he is responsible for what is done amiss by his disciples.

## 37
### OF THE ELDERLY AND CHILDREN

Although human nature itself inclines us to show pity and consideration to age, that is, to the elderly and to children, still it is proper that the authority of the Rule should provide for them. Let their weakness be always taken into account, and let the full rigor of the Rule as regards food be in no way maintained in their regard. There is to be a kind consideration for them, and permission is to be given them to anticipate the regular hours.

## 38
### THE READER FOR THE WEEK

There ought always to be reading while the brethren eat at table. Yet no one shall presume to read there from any book taken up haphazardly, but whoever is appointed to read for the whole week is to enter on his office on Sunday. Let the brother when beginning his service after mass and communion ask all to pray for him, that God may preserve him from the spirit of pride. And let the following verse be repeated three times by all in the oratory, he, the reader, first beginning: "O Lord, You will open my lips, and my mouth shall declare Your praise"[128]; then, having received a blessing, let the reader enter upon his office. The greatest silence shall be kept, so that no whispering or noise, except the voice of the reader alone, may be heard there.

Whatever is required for eating and drinking the brethren shall minister to each other so that no one need ask for anything. Yet should anything be wanted, it ought to be demanded by an audible sign rather than by word. Let no one ask any question there about what is being read or about anything else, lest occasion be given to the evil one, unless, perhaps, the superior shall wish to say something briefly for the purpose of edification. The brother who is reader for the week may take a drink of wine before beginning to read, on account of holy communion, and lest it may be too long for him to fast. He shall eat afterwards with the weekly servers and kitchen helpers. The brethren, however, are not all to read or sing according to their rank, but only those who may edify the hearers are to do so.

## 39
### OF THE AMOUNT OF FOOD

We believe that it is enough to satisfy just needs if in the daily meals, at both the sixth and ninth hours, there are at all seasons of the year two cooked dishes, so that he who cannot eat from one may make his meal of the other. Therefore two dishes of cooked food must suffice for all the brethren, and if there is any fruit or young vegetables, these may be added to the meal as a third dish. Let a pound weight of bread suffice for each day, whether there is one meal or two, that is, for both dinner and supper. If there is to be supper, a third of the pound is to be kept back by the cellarer and given to the brethren at that meal.

If, however, the community has been occupied in any great labor, it shall be at the will, and in the power of the abbot, if he thinks fit, to increase the allowance, so long as every care is taken to guard against excess, and that no monk be incapacitated by indigestion. For nothing is more contrary to the Christian spirit than gluttony, as our Lord declares, "Take heed that your hearts be weighed down with indulgence."[129] And the same quantity shall not be given to young children, but a lesser amount than to those older, frugality being maintained in everything. All but the very weak and sick are to abstain wholly from eating the flesh of four-footed animals.

---

128 Old Testament, Psalms 51.15.
129 New Testament, Luke 21.34.

## 40

### OF THE AMOUNT OF DRINK

"Everyone has his own gift from God, one this, another that."[130] For this reason, the amount of other people's food cannot be determined without some misgiving. Still, having regard to the weak state of the sick, we think that a pint of wine a day is sufficient for anyone. But let those to whom God gives the gift of abstinence know that they shall receive their proper reward. If either local circumstances, the amount of labor, or the heat of summer requires more, it can be allowed at the will of the prior, care being taken in all things that gluttony and drunkenness do not creep in.

Although we read that "wine is not the drink of monks at all," yet, since in our time they cannot be persuaded of this, let us at least agree not to drink to satiety, but sparingly, "Because wine makes even the wise go astray."[131]

## 41

### THE HOURS AT WHICH THE BRETHREN ARE TO TAKE THEIR MEALS

From the holy feast of Easter until Pentecost, the brethren shall have their first meal at the sixth hour and their supper at night. But from Pentecost, throughout the summer, if the monks do not have to work in the fields, nor are oppressed by any great heat, let them fast on Wednesdays and Fridays until None; on the other days they may dine at the sixth hour. Dinner at the sixth hour shall be the rule at the discretion of the abbot, if they have work in the fields, or the heat of the summer is great. Let the abbot so temper and arrange everything that souls may be saved, and that what the brethren do may be done without just complaint.

From September 13 until the beginning of Lent, the brethren shall always take their meal at the ninth hour. During Lent, however, until Easter, their meal shall be towards evening, but this evening meal shall be so arranged that while eating they shall not need lamps, and all things are finished in daylight. Indeed, at all times of the year let the hour of meals, whether of dinner or supper, be so arranged that all things are done by daylight.

## 42

### THAT NO ONE SHALL SPEAK AFTER COMPLINE

Monks should practice silence at all times, but especially during the night hours. On all days, therefore, whether it is a fast day or otherwise, this shall be the practice. If it is not a fast day, as soon as they shall have risen from supper, let all sit together while one of them reads the *Conferences*,[132] or *Lives of the Fathers*, or some other book to edify the hearers. He shall not, however, read the Heptateuch, or Books of Kings,[133] for at that hour it will not profit weak understandings to listen to this part of Scripture; at other times, however, they may be read. If it is a fast day, let the brethren, when Vespers is over, and after a brief interval, come to the reading of the *Conferences*, as we have said. Four or five pages are to be read, or as many as time will allow, that during the reading all may come together, even such as have had some work given them to do. When all, therefore, are gathered together, let them say Compline, and on coming out from Compline no one shall be permitted to speak at all. If anyone shall be found breaking this rule of silence, he shall be punished severely, unless the needs of a guest require it, or the abbot shall order something of someone. But even this shall be done with the greatest gravity and moderation.

## 43

### OF THOSE WHO COME LATE TO THE DIVINE OFFICE OR TO TABLE

As soon as the signal for the divine office is heard, each one must lay aside whatever work he may be

---

130 New Testament, 1 Corinthians 7.7.

131 Apocrypha, Ecclesiasticus 19.2.

132 A record of conversations with Christian hermits in Egypt produced by Cassian in the fifth century. Cassian had spent his earlier career as an ascetic in Egypt before founding a monastery in southern Gaul.

133 Parts of the Old Testament. The Heptateuch is the first seven books of the Old Testament.

engaged upon and hasten to it, with all speed, but still with gravity, so as not to cause any frivolity. Nothing, therefore, shall be put before the divine office. If anyone shall come to Matins after the *Gloria* of the ninety-fourth Psalm, which on this account we wish to be said slowly and leisurely, he shall not take his place in the choir, but go last of all, or to some place set apart which the abbot may appoint for those that so fail, so they might be seen by him and all the brethren, until the divine office is over and he shall have done penance and made public satisfaction.

We have judged it fitting that these should stand last, or in some place apart, in order that, being seen by all, for very shame they may amend. For if they remain outside the oratory someone will, perhaps, return to sleep, or at least sit outside by himself, or, setting himself to idle talk, give an occasion to the evil one. Let such a one, therefore, come inside, so that he may not lose all, but make amends during the rest of the office. At the day hours one who does not come to the work of God until after the opening verse and the *Gloria* of the first Psalm said after the verse shall stand last, according to the rule laid down above. He is not to presume to join the choir of singers until he has made satisfaction, unless, indeed, the abbot, by his permission, allows him to do so, but even then on the condition that he shall afterwards make satisfaction for his omission.

He who does not come to table before the verse, so that all may say it, and praying together, sit down to table at the same time, must be corrected once or twice if this is through his own fault or bad habit. If he does not after this amend, he is not to be allowed to share in the common table, but he is to be separated from the company of all the rest and eat alone. Until he makes satisfaction and mends his ways, let his portion of wine be taken away from him. He who is not present at the verse which is said after meals is to undergo the same punishment. Let no one presume to take food or drink before or after the regular time, but if something is offered to anyone by the superior, and he refuses it, and afterwards wishes to have what he had rejected, or some other thing, let him get neither this nor anything else till he makes proper satisfaction.

## 44
### HOW THOSE WHO ARE EXCOMMUNICATED ARE TO MAKE SATISFACTION

He who has been excluded from the oratory and the table for grievous offenses is to prostrate himself before the door of the oratory, in silence, at the time when the divine office is being celebrated; with his face to the ground, let him lie at the feet of all who leave the place. This he shall continue to do until the abbot shall judge that he has made satisfaction. Then, when the abbot ordains, let him cast himself down, first at the feet of the abbot and then at those of the brethren, that they may pray for him.

Afterwards, if the abbot shall so direct, let him be received into the choir and into the place he shall appoint him. Even so, he may not presume to intone a psalm or to read a lesson, or to do anything else in the oratory, unless the abbot again orders it. Moreover, after each hour, when the divine office is ended, let him cast himself on the ground in his place, and in this way make satisfaction until such time as the abbot tells him to cease. Those who are excluded from the table only shall make satisfaction in the oratory as long as the abbot shall direct, and shall continue to do this till he blesses them and declares it to be sufficient.

## 45
### OF THOSE WHO BLUNDER IN THE ORATORY

If anyone, while reciting a psalm, responsory, antiphon or lesson, makes any mistake, and does not at once make humble satisfaction for it before all, let him be subjected to greater punishment, as being one who is unwilling to correct by humility what he has done amiss through negligence. For such a fault let children be whipped.

## 46
### OF SUCH WHO OFFEND IN OTHER WAYS

If anyone, while engaged in any work, either in the kitchen, in the cellar, in serving others, in the bakehouse, in the garden, or in any other occupation or place, shall do anything amiss, break or lose anything, or offend in any way whatsoever, and does not come at once to the abbot and community of his own accord to confess his offense and make satisfaction, if afterwards it shall become known by another, he shall be more severely punished. If, however, it is a secret sin, let him manifest it only to the abbot, or to his spiritual seniors, who know how to heal their own wounds and not to disclose and make public those of others.

## 47
### OF LETTING THE HOUR OF DIVINE OFFICE BE KNOWN

Let the duty of giving warning of the time of the divine office, both night and day, be that of the abbot. Either he himself shall give the signal or he shall assign this task to some careful brother, so that all things are done at their fixed time. After the abbot, those appointed are to intone the psalms and antiphons in turns. No one, however, shall presume either to sing or read except such as can do so to the edification of the hearers. Let him to whom the abbot shall enjoin this duty do it with humility, gravity and fear.

## 48
### OF DAILY MANUAL LABOR

Idleness is an enemy of the soul. Because this is so, the brethren ought to be occupied at specified times in manual labor, and at other fixed hours in holy reading. We therefore think that both these may be arranged for as follows: from Easter October 1, on coming out from Prime, let the brethren labor till about the fourth hour. From the fourth till close upon the sixth hour, let them employ themselves in reading. On rising from table after the sixth hour, let them rest on their beds in strict silence; but if anyone shall wish to read, let him do so in such a way as not to disturb anyone else.

Let None be said somewhat before the time, about the middle of the eighth hour, and after this all shall work at what they have to do till evening. If, however, the nature of the place or poverty requires them to labor at gathering in the harvest, let them not grieve at that, for then are they truly monks when they live by the labor of their hands, as our fathers and the apos-

tles did. Let everything, however, be done with moderation for the sake of the faint-hearted.

From October 1 till the beginning of Lent let the brethren be occupied in reading till the end of the second hour. At that time Tierce shall be said, after which they shall labor at the work enjoined them till None. At the first signal for the hour of None, all shall cease to work, so as to be ready when the second signal is given. After their meal they shall be employed in reading or on the psalms.

On the days of Lent, from the morning till the end of the third hour, the brethren are to have time for reading, after which let them work at what is set them to do till the close of the tenth hour. During these Lenten days let each one have some book from the library which he shall read through carefully. These books are to be given out at the beginning of Lent.

It is very important that one or two seniors be appointed to go about the monastery at such times as the brethren are free to read, in order to see that no one is slothful, given to idleness or foolish talking instead of reading, and so not only makes no profit himself but also distracts others. If any such be found (which God forbid), let him be corrected once or twice, and if he does not amend, let him be subjected to the discipline of the Rule in such a way that the rest may take warning. Moreover one brother shall not associate with another at unsuitable hours.

On Sunday also, all, except those who are assigned to various offices, shall have time for reading. If, however, anyone is so negligent and slothful as to be unwilling or unable to read or meditate, he must have some work given to him, so as not to be idle. For weak brethren, or those who are sick, some work or craft shall be found to keep them from idleness, and yet not such as to crush them by heavy labor or to drive them away. The weakness of such brethren must be taken into consideration by the abbot.

## 49
### OF THE OBSERVANCE OF LENT

The mode of a monk's life ought to follow the Lenten observance at all times. Since few, however, are capable of this, we exhort everyone in these days of Lent to guard their lives in all purity, and during this holy season to wash away every negligence of other times. This we shall worthily accomplish if we restrain ourselves from every vice, and give ourselves to tearful prayer, to reading, to heartfelt sorrow, and to abstinence. In these days of Lent, therefore, let us of our own accord add something to our usual yoke of service, such as private prayer, and abstinence from food and drink. Let everyone of his own will with joy of the Holy Spirit offer to God something above the allotted measure, that is, let him deny his body in food, drink, sleep, talking or laughter, and with spiritual joy await the holy feast of Easter—on this condition, however: that each one inform his abbot what it is that he is offering, for what is done without leave of the spiritual father will be reckoned presumption and vainglory, and merit no reward. All things, therefore, must be done with the approval of the abbot.

## 50
### OF THE BRETHREN WHO WORK AT A DISTANCE FROM THE ORATORY OR ARE ON A JOURNEY

Those brethren who work at a distance and cannot come to the oratory at the appointed hours, with the abbot judging that this is the case, shall say the divine office where they are working, kneeling in the fear of God. In the same way, those who are sent on a journey shall not omit the customary hours, but keep them as best they may, and not fail to accomplish this duty of their service.

## 51
### OF THE BRETHREN WHO GO ONLY A SHORT DISTANCE

The brother who is sent on an errand and expects to return to his monastery the same day shall not presume to eat outside his house, even though he is asked to do so by anyone, unless he is so ordered by his abbot. If he does otherwise, let him be excommunicated.

## 52
### CONCERNING THE ORATORY OF THE MONASTERY

Let the oratory be what its name signifies,[134] and let nothing else be done or discussed there. When the work of God is ended, let all depart in strict silence, in the reverence of God, so that the brother who may wish to pray privately may not be hindered by the misconduct of another. If any brother wishes to pray privately, let him go into the oratory, without ostentation, and say his prayers, not with a loud voice, but with tears and an earnest heart. Therefore, as has been said, no one is allowed to remain in the oratory after the divine office is ended, unless for the purpose of prayer, lest some other brother be hindered by him.

## 53
### ON THE RECEPTION OF GUESTS

Let all guests who come be received as Christ would be, because He will say, "I was a stranger, and you took Me in."[135] And let due honor be shown to all, especially to those who are of the household of the Faith, and to pilgrims. As soon, therefore, as a guest is announced, let him be met by the prior or the brethren, with all marks of charity. And let them first pray together, that so they may associate in peace. The kiss of peace, however, is not to be given till after prayer, on account of the deceptions practiced by the devil. And in the salutation itself let true humility be shown to all guests coming and going. By bowed head, or body prostrate on the ground, all shall adore Christ in them, Who, indeed, is received in their persons.

Let guests, after their reception, be conducted to prayer, and then the superior, or anyone he may order, shall sit with them. Let the Divine Law be read in the presence of the guest for his edification, and after this let all courtesy be shown to him. For the guest's sake, a superior may break his fast, unless it is a strict day when the fast may not be broken. The brethren, how-

134  I.e., a place for prayer.
135  New Testament, Matthew 25.35.

ever, shall keep the accustomed fasts. Let the abbot pour water on the hands of the guests, and let him and all the community wash their feet. After this, let them say the verse, "We have received Your mercy, O God, in the midst of Your temple."[136] Let special care be taken of the poor and pilgrims, because in them Christ is more truly received, for the very awe of the rich secures respect for them.

Let the kitchen of the abbot and the guests be separate, so that strangers, who are never absent from a monastery, coming in at irregular hours, may not disturb the community. Let two of the brethren, who can perform their duties well, take charge of this kitchen for a year at a time. When they need it they shall be given assistance, so that they may serve without grumbling. In like manner, when they have lighter work, let them labor where they are told. And, indeed, not only in their regard, but also in respect to all the other officers of the monastery let this consideration always be shown: when they need help, let them have it, and when, on the other hand, they are free, they shall do what they are ordered to do. Also, let the charge of the guest-place be assigned to a brother whose soul the fear of God possesses. A sufficient number of beds are to be prepared there, and let the house of God be wisely ruled by wise men.

No one, unless so ordered, may associate with or speak to the guests. If anyone shall meet or see them, after such humble salutation as we have above enjoined, having asked their blessing, let him pass on, saying he is not permitted to talk with any guest.

## 54
### WHETHER A MONK MAY RECEIVE LETTERS OR PRESENTS

It is by no means lawful, without the abbot's permission, for any monk to receive or give letters, presents, and gifts of any kind to anyone, whether parent or someone else, and not even to one of the brethren. If anything is sent to a monk from his parents, he shall not venture to receive it unless the abbot is told first. If he orders it to be accepted, he may appoint the person

to whom it shall be given. And let not the brother, to whom perchance it was sent, be grieved, lest an opening be given to the devil. He who shall dare to do otherwise shall be subjected to the discipline of the Rule.

## 55
### OF THE CLOTHES AND SHOES OF THE BRETHREN

Let clothing suitable to the locality and the temperature be given to the brethren, for in cold regions more is needed, and less in warm. The determination of all these things is in the hands of the abbot. We believe, however, that in ordinary places it will be enough for each monk to have a cowl and tunic, in winter the cowl being heavier, in summer of thinner or old cloth. He should have also a scapular[137] for work, and shoes and stockings for the feet.

Monks must not grumble at the color or coarseness of these things; they shall be such as can be procured in the district where they live, or such as can be bought at the cheapest price.

Let the abbot see to their dimensions, that they not be too short, but of the proper length for those who use them. When receiving new clothes the monks shall always give back the old ones at the same time, to be put away in the clothes-room for the poor. For it is sufficient that a monk have two tunics and two cowls, for night wear as well as for the convenience of washing. Anything beyond this is superfluous, and must be removed. Their shoes also, and whatever is worn out, they shall return on getting new things. Those who are sent on a journey shall get underclothing from the wardrobe, which, on their return, when washed, they shall put back. Let their cowls and tunics on such occasions be somewhat better than those in ordinary use. These they shall receive from the wardrobe when starting and put back on their return.

A mattress, blanket, coverlet and pillow are to suffice for bedding. The beds shall be frequently searched by the abbot to guard against the vice of hoarding. And if anyone is found in possession of something not allowed by the abbot, let him be subjected to the

---

136 Old Testament, Psalms 48.9.
137 A kind of cloak made of two strips of cloth joined across the shoulders, symbolizing the yoke of Christ.

severest punishment. And to uproot this vice of appropriation, let all that is necessary be furnished by the abbot, that is, cowl, tunic, shoes, stockings, belt, knife, pen, needle, handkerchief and writing tablets. By this every pretext of necessity will be taken away. The abbot, however, should always bear in mind that sentence in the Acts of the Apostles, "And distribution was made to everyone according to his need."[138] He should, therefore, consider the infirmities of such as need something, and not regard the ill will of the envious. In all his decisions, let him ponder upon the retribution of God.

## 56
### THE ABBOT'S TABLE

The abbot shall always take his meals with the guests and strangers. But when there are few guests, he may invite any of the brethren he may choose. Let him see, however, that one or two of the seniors are always left with the community, for the sake of discipline.

## 57
### OF THE ARTISANS OF THE MONASTERY

Let such craftsmen as be in the monastery ply their trade in all lowliness of mind, if the abbot allows it. But if any is puffed up by his skill in his craft, and thinks the monastery is indebted to him for it, such a one shall be shifted from his handicraft, and not attempt it again till such time as, having learned a low opinion of himself, the abbot shall order him to resume. If anything of the fruit of their labors is sold, let those who handle the affair see to it that they do not dare to practice any fraud therein.

Let them remember Ananias and Saphira,[139] lest they, or any who practice any fraud in regard to the possessions of the monastery, suffer the death of their souls as did they of their bodies. In settling the prices, however, do not let the vice of greed creep in, but let the things be sold somewhat cheaper than they can be by laymen, that in all things God may be glorified.

## 58
### THE MANNER OF ADMITTING NEW BRETHREN

Anyone on first coming to the religious life should not find the entrance made easy, but as the apostle says, "Test the spirits to see if they are of God."[140] If, however, the newcomer continues to knock at the door, and for four or five days shows a patient bearing, both of the harshness shown to him and of the difficulty made about admitting him, and persists in his petition, he shall then be allowed to enter the guest-place for a few days. After that let him enter the novitiate, where he shall meditate and eat and sleep.

And let a senior, such as has the skill of winning souls, be appointed to watch carefully over him, to discover whether he truly seeks God and is eager for the divine office, for obedience and humiliation. Let all the rigor and austerity of our journey to God be put clearly before him. If he promises to continue in steadfast perseverance, at the end of two months the entire Rule shall be read to him, and let him be told, "See the law under which you wish to fight; if you can observe it, enter; if you cannot, you are free to depart."

If he still perseveres, let him be brought back to the novitiate and again tested in all patience. And after the lapse of six months, let the Rule be read to him again, that he may fully know the kind of life upon which he is entering. If he still perseveres, after four months the Rule shall be read to him once more. If after due deliberation he shall then promise to keep all the law and to do whatever is commanded of him, let him be received into the community, knowing that he is now under the law of the Rule, so that he can henceforth neither leave the monastery nor withdraw his neck from the yoke of the Rule which, after so long a deliberation, he was free to have taken or refused.

When he is to be admitted into the community, let him in the presence of the entire community in the oratory promise before God and His saints stability,[141] amendment of manners, and obedience, in order that if at any time he shall act otherwise, he may know that

---

138  New Testament, Acts 4.35.
139  A reference to the New Testament, Acts 5.1-10.
140  New Testament, 1 John 4.1.
141  I.e., to remain a member of the monastery.

he shall be condemned by Him Whom he mocks. He shall draw up the form of his promise in the name of the saints, whose relics are reposing there, and of the abbot there present. Let him write out this form himself, or at least, if he is illiterate, another at his request must write it for him, and to this the novice himself shall set his mark and with his own hand lay it upon the altar.

After he has placed it there, let the novice immediately begin the verse, "Uphold me, O Lord, acccording to Your word, and I shall live, and let me not be confounded in my expectation."[142] This verse the community shall repeat three times, adding at the end, "Glory be to the Father." Then the brother novice shall cast himself at the feet of all, asking their prayers, and from that time he shall be counted as one of the community. If he has any property he must first either give it to the poor, or by formal gift make it over to the monastery without any reservation for himself, since he must know that he has henceforth no power, even over his own body. Let him, therefore, forthwith be divested in the oratory of his own garments and be clothed in those of the monastery. The clothes he has taken off, however, are to be kept in the wardrobe, so that if (which God forbid) he should, by the persuasion of the devil, resolve to leave the monastery, he may be stripped of his monastic dress and expelled. The form of profession which the abbot took from him at the altar he shall not receive back, but it shall be kept in the monastery.

## 59

### OF THE SONS OF NOBLES OR OF THE POOR WHO ARE OFFERED TO GOD

If any nobleman shall offer his son to God in the monastery, let the parents, if the child himself is underage, make the petition for him, and together with the oblation[143] wrap the formal promise and the hand of the boy in the altar cloth and thus dedicate him to God. With regard to any property, let the par-

ents promise in the document under oath that they will never either give or furnish him with this means of obtaining anything whatever, either themselves or by any other person or by any means. Or, if they will not do this, and desire to give some alms to the monastery as a free gift, let them hand over to the place what they wish, reserving, if they please, the income for themselves. Let all these matters be so managed that the child have no expectations by which he may be deceived and perish (which God forbid), as by experience we have learned is sometimes the case. Let those who are poorer act in the same way. But such as have nothing whatever shall simply make the promise and offer their son before witnesses with the oblation.

## 60

### OF PRIESTS WHO WISH TO LIVE IN THE MONASTERY

If anyone in the ranks of the priesthood shall ask to be received into a monastery, let him not obtain permission too quickly. If, however, he persists in his request, he shall understand that he will have to keep the Rule in all rigor, and that no mitigation will be allowed to him, according to what is written, "Friend, for what have you come?"[144] Nevertheless, let him be allowed to stand next after the abbot, to give the blessing or to say mass, provided the abbot orders him. If not, he may not presume to do anything, knowing that he is subject to the discipline of the Rule, and is specially obliged to set an example of humility to all. If it happens there is an appointment to be made in the monastery or some other matter to be dealt with, he should remember that his proper place is what he has according to the time of his entry to the monastery, not that which is given him out of respect for the priesthood. But if any clerics manifest the same desire to be admitted into the monastery, let them be put into a middle rank, but only if they promise observance of the Rule and of their stability therein.

---

142 Old Testament, Psalms 119.116.
143 I.e., offering.
144 New Testament, Matthew 26.50.

## 61

### OF RECEIVING VISITING MONKS

If any visiting monk, coming from a distant place, desires to dwell in the monastery as a guest and, content with the customs he finds there, does not trouble the house by superfluous wants, but is simply content with what he finds, let him be received for as long a time as he desires to remain. And if he reasonably and with loving humility criticizes something, or points out anything amiss, let the abbot prudently consider it, lest the Lord shall have sent him there for that purpose. If, also, after a time he shall wish to make his stay permanent, such a desire should not be refused, particularly since during the time he has lived as a guest his manner of life could be known.

If in that period he shall have been found troublesome or full of vice, not only should he not be incorporated with the community, but he should even be told frankly to leave, lest others be corrupted by his ill doing. But if he does not deserve to be sent away, not only if he shall ask, shall he be received into the ranks of the community, but he should even be induced to stay, that others may be taught by his example, because in every place we serve a common Lord, and fight under the same King.

And if the abbot shall find such a monk deserving, he may even put him into a somewhat higher rank. And the abbot may raise above the rank of his entry into religion, not only any monk, but also any of the aforesaid priests or clerics, if he shall consider that their lives deserve it. Let the abbot, however, beware never to receive permanently any monk of a known monastery without the consent of his own abbot, or without letters of commendation from him, for it is written, "What you would not have done to you, do not do to another."[145]

## 62

### THE PRIESTS OF THE MONASTERY

If any abbot desires to have a priest or deacon ordained, let him choose from his monks one who is worthy to fill the office of priesthood. Let the monk, however, who is ordained beware of haughtiness and pride, and let him not presume to do anything except what is ordered by the abbot, remembering that he is now much more subject to the discipline of the Rule. Let him not make his priesthood an excuse for forgetting obedience and the rigor of the Rule; rather he should strive on account of it to draw more and more towards God.

He shall, moreover, always keep the place he had when he came to the monastery, except in his service at the altar, or if on account of the holiness of his life, by the wish of the community and the will of the abbot, he is moved up to a higher place. Even then, let him understand that he must keep the rules prescribed for him by the deans or prior, and if he presumes to act otherwise, he shall be judged not as a priest but as a rebel. If, after frequent warnings, he shall not amend his ways, even the bishop shall be brought in to witness the fact. And if after this he does not amend, and his faults become notorious, let him be expelled from the monastery, if his contempt is such that he will not submit and obey the Rule.

## 63

### THE ORDER OF THE COMMUNITY

The brethren shall take their places according to the date of their entry, the merit of their lives, or the appointment of their abbot. And the abbot must not disturb the flock committed to him, or, as it were, by any arbitrary use of his power, ordain anything unjustly. But let him always remember that he will have to render an account to God of all his judgments and of all his works.

Wherefore, in the order he shall appoint, or in that which they hold amongst themselves, let the brethren receive the kiss of peace, approach communion, intone a psalm and stand in choir. In all places, without exception, order shall not be decided by age, for this shall not be a prejudice to anyone since Samuel and Daniel, though children, were judges of the priests.[146] With the exception therefore of those who, as we have

---

145 Compare New Testament, Matthew 7.12.
146 A reference to Old Testament, 1 Samuel 3; and Apocrypha, Daniel 13.44-62.

said, for some weighty reason, the abbot shall advance, or for certain causes shall put in a lower place, let all the rest remain in the order of their entry. For example, one who shall come to the monastery at the second hour of the day shall know that he is junior to him who has come at the first hour, no matter what his age or dignity may be. In regard to children, let them be kept by all under discipline in every way.

Let the juniors, therefore, honor their seniors, and the seniors love the juniors. In addressing each other in person no one shall call another by his mere name, but let the senior call the junior, "brother," and the junior call the senior, "father." But, because the abbot is held to take the place of Christ, he shall be called "lord" and "abbot," not out of consideration for himself, but for the honor and love of Christ. He, however, should remember and so conduct himself as to be worthy of such an honor.

Wherever the brethren meet each other, the junior shall ask a blessing from the senior. When a senior passes by, let the junior rise and make place for him to sit down; neither shall the junior presume to sit unless the senior bids him so to do, in order to fulfill what is written, "In honor they prevent one another."[147]

Little children or youths shall keep their respective places in the oratory and at table, under discipline. Outside, or indeed anywhere, watch shall be kept over them, till they come to an age of understanding.

## 64

### THE ELECTION OF THE ABBOT

In the election of an abbot, let the following points be always borne in mind: that he who is made abbot be the choice of the whole community, in the fear of God, or be the choice of a part of the community, however small, acting with greater wisdom. Let him who is created abbot be chosen because of his virtuous life and his wisdom, even if he is the last in the community. And if the whole community (which God forbid) unanimously choose one who supports them in their evil practices, and their vicious lives become known to the bishop (to whose diocese the monastery belongs), or to the abbots or Christians of the neighborhood, they shall annul the choice of these bad men and appoint a worthy steward of God's house, knowing that for this they shall receive a good reward, provided they do it with pure intention and through zeal for God, just as, on the other hand, they sin if they neglect to do it.

Let him who has been created abbot always reflect upon the weighty burden he has taken up and remember to Whom he shall give an account of his stewardship. Let him know also that it is better for him to profit others than to rule over them. He must therefore be learned in the divine law so that he may know when to "bring forth new things and old."[148] He must be chaste, sober, merciful, and always exalt mercy above justice, that he may obtain mercy. He shall hate vice and love the brethren. Even in his correction he shall act with prudence and not try too much, lest while too violently scouring off the rust, the vessel itself is broken. Let him always bear in mind his own frailty, and remember that "the bruised reed must not be broken."[149]

In saying this we do not propose that he should allow vices to spring up, but, as we have declared before, seek to root them out prudently and with charity, in the way he shall think proper in each case. Let him aim at being loved rather than feared. He must not be worried or anxious, neither should he be too exacting or obstinate, or jealous, or overly suspicious, for then he will never be at rest. Even in what he orders, whether it relates to God or to worldly matters, let him be prudent and considerate. In all that he enjoins he should be discreet and moderate, meditating on the prudence of holy Jacob, who says, "If I drive my flocks too hard, they will all die in one day."[150] Wherefore, adopting these and like principles of discretion, the mother of virtues, let him so temper all things that the strong may have their scope and the weak be not scared. And especially let him keep the

---

147 New Testament, Romans 12.10.
148 New Testament, Matthew 13.52.
149 Old Testament, Isaiah 42.3.
150 Old Testament, Genesis 33.13.

present Rule in all things, so that when he shall have well administered it he may hear from our Lord what the good servant heard who gave grain to his fellow-servants in due season: "Amen, I say to you, over all his goods will he place him."[151]

## 65
### THE PRIOR OF THE MONASTERY

It often happens that by the appointment of a prior grave scandals arise in monasteries. There are some who, puffed up by the evil spirit of pride, and esteeming themselves to be like abbots, take it on themselves to act the tyrant, to foster scandals and promote discord in the community. This is especially the case in places where the prior is appointed by those who appoint the abbot of the monastery. How foolish this custom is may easily be seen. From the very commencement of the appointment a pretext for pride is given to the prior, since his imagination suggests to him that he is now released from the power of his abbot, for (as it seems to say) "You are appointed by those who created the abbot." Hence arise envy, quarrels, detractions, rivalries and disorders. And while the abbot and the prior are at variance, it must of necessity follow that their souls are endangered by the quarrel, and that those under them, by taking sides, are going to destruction. The guilt of this danger chiefly weighs on those who were the authors of such appointments.

Therefore we foresee that for the preservation of peace and charity it is expedient that the ordering of his monastery depend on the will of the abbot and, as we have before arranged, if it be possible, let all the work of the monastery be managed by deans, as we have directed, in order that, where many are entrusted with the work, no one may become proud.

But if the circumstances of the place require a prior, or the community shall with reason and humility ask for one, and the abbot shall think it expedient, with the advice of the brethren who have the fear of God, let him nominate whomsoever he shall himself choose as prior. Let this prior, moreover, reverently do whatever shall be enjoined him by his abbot, never acting against his will or directions, because the higher he is raised above the others, the more careful he must be to keep the precepts of the Rule. If this prior shall be found to be inclined to vice, or carried away by the haughtiness of pride, or a proved despiser of the holy Rule, let him be warned four times; if he does not amend, let him fall under the punishment of the discipline of the Rule. If even then he is not corrected, he shall be deposed from his position of prior, and another who is worthy shall be put in his place. If after this he shall not be quiet and obedient in the community, let him even be put out of the monastery. The abbot nevertheless shall bear in mind that he will have to give an account of all his judgments to God, lest his soul may burn with the flame of envy and jealousy.

## 66
### THE PORTER OF THE MONASTERY

Let there be stationed at the gate of the monastery some wise old man who knows how to give and receive an answer, and whose age will not allow him to wander from his post. This porter should have his cell near the door, that those who arrive may always find him there to give an answer.

As soon as anyone shall knock, or some poor man shall call for help, let him reply, "Thanks be to God," or invoke a blessing. And let him in the meekness of God's fear hasten to reply with zealous charity. If the porter stands in need of help, let him have a junior brother with him. The monastery, however, itself ought, if possible, to be so constructed as to contain within it all necessities, that is, water, a mill, a garden and places for the various crafts which are exercised within a monastery, so that there is no occasion for monks to wander outside, since this is in no way good for their souls. We wish this rule to be read frequently in the community so that no brother may plead ignorance as an excuse.

---

151 Old Testament, Matthew 24.47.

## 67

### OF BRETHREN WHO ARE SENT ON A JOURNEY

When brethren are about to be sent on a journey, let them commend themselves to the prayers of all the brethren and of the abbot, and at the closing prayer of the divine office let a commemoration be made of all the absent brethren. When they come back from a journey, on the day of their return, at all the canonical hours when the divine office is finished, the brethren shall prostrate themselves on the ground and beg the prayers of all for any faults they may have fallen into on the road, by the sight or hearing of evil things, or by idle talk. And let no one dare to relate to another what he shall have seen or heard outside the monastery because this is most detrimental. If anyone shall presume to do this, he must be subjected to the punishment prescribed in the Rule. In like manner shall he be punished who shall presume to break the enclosure of the monastery, or go anywhere, or do anything, however trifling, without the abbot's permission.

## 68

### WHEN A BROTHER IS ORDERED TO DO IMPOSSIBLE THINGS

If anything hard or impossible is enjoined on a brother, let him receive the injunctions of him who orders him in all mildness and obedience. If he shall see that the burden altogether exceeds the measure of his strength, let him patiently and at the proper time state, without show of pride, resistance, or contradiction, the reason for this impossibility. If, after his suggestion, the will of the superior shall still remain unchanged, let the subordinate monk know that this is best for him and, trusting in God's help, through love of Him, let him obey.

## 69

### THAT IN THE MONASTERY NO ONE IS TO PRESUME TO DEFEND ANOTHER

Special care must be taken that under no pretext shall one monk presume to defend or uphold another in a monastery, even though they may be very closely related by blood. In no way whatsoever let monks dare to do this, because from it an occasion of the gravest scandal may arise. If anyone shall transgress in this way he shall be severely punished.

## 70

### THAT NO ONE SHALL PRESUME TO STRIKE ANOTHER AT RANDOM

In the monastery every occasion of presumption should be avoided. We ordain that no one shall be allowed to excommunicate or strike any of his brethren unless the abbot has given him authority to do so. Those who offend in this matter shall be reprimanded before all, that the rest may be inspired with fear. But over children, till they are 15 years old, let all exercise strict discipline and care, yet this also must be done with moderation and discretion. He, however, who shall presume to do so to those above this age, without the abbot's order, or shall be severe to children beyond discretion, shall be subjected to the discipline of the Rule, since it is written, "What you would not have done to you, do not do to another."[152]

## 71

### THAT THE BRETHREN MUST BE OBEDIENT TO EACH OTHER

The excellent virtue of obedience is to be shown by all, not to the abbot only, but to the brethren who shall also mutually obey each other, knowing that by this path of obedience they shall go to God. The commands of the abbot, or other superiors constituted by him, having the first place (for to these we do not allow any unofficial orders to be preferred), the juniors shall obey their seniors with all charity and diligence. If anyone is found to be contentious, let him be punished.

If a brother is rebuked for even the least thing by the abbot, or by any superior, or if he shall perceive that the mind of any superior is, however slightly, moved against him, or in anger with him, let him without delay prostrate himself at his feet, and remain offering satisfaction until the feeling is removed and he receives

---

152 New Testament, Matthew 7.12.

a blessing. If anyone is found to be too proud to do this, let him be expelled from the monastery.

## 72
### OF THE GOOD ZEAL OF MONKS

As there is an evil and bitter emulation which separates from God and leads to hell, so too there is a good spirit of emulation which frees from vices and leads to God and everlasting life. Let monks therefore practice this emulation with most fervent love; that is to say, let them "in honor prevent one another,"[153] let them bear most patiently with each other's infirmities, whether of body or of manner. Let them contend with one another in their obedience. Let no one follow what he thinks most profitable to himself, but rather what is best for another. Let them show brotherly charity with a chaste love. Let them fear God and love their abbot with sincere and humble affection, and set nothing whatever before Christ, Who can bring us to eternal life.

## 73
### THAT ALL PERFECTION IS NOT CONTAINED
### IN THIS RULE

We have written this Rule that, by its observance in monasteries, we may show that we have in some measure uprightness of manners or the beginning of religious life. But for such as hasten onward to the perfection of holy life there are the teachings of the holy fathers, the observance whereof leads one to the heights of perfection. For what page or what passage of the divinely inspired books of the Old and the New Testament is not a most perfect rule for temporal life? Or what book is there of the holy catholic fathers that does not proclaim this, that by a direct course we may come to our Creator? Also, what else are the *Conferences* of the fathers, their *Institutes*,[154] their *Lives*, and the *Rule of our Holy Father St. Basil*,[155] but examples of the virtues, of the good living, and obedience of monks? But to us who are slothful, and lead bad and negligent lives, they are matter for shame and confusion.

Therefore, whoever you are who hastens forward to the heavenly country, accomplish first, by the help of Christ, this little Rule written for beginners, and then at length shall you come, under God's guidance, to the lofty heights of doctrine and virtue, which we have spoken of above.

---

153  New Testament, Romans 12.10.
154  A work by Cassian on Egyptian monasticism.
155  An austere *Rule* for Eastern monastic communities founded by Saint Basil in the fourth century.

# LIFE OF BALTHILD

This life of Saint Balthild (died *c.* 680) was probably written by a nun of the monastery of Chelles, in Frankia, where Balthild ended her life. It is an example of one of the largest surviving genres of medieval writing, that of hagiography, or the biography of saints. It was read to the community of Chelles annually, on Balthild's feast day.

---

Here Begins the Prologue to the Life of Lady Balthild the Queen

1   Most beloved brothers,[1] I have been commanded by the prelate[2] Christ, to accomplish a simple and pious work. My lack of skill and experience prevents me from setting forth an exquisite narrative in learned language. But the power of heartfelt love more strongly commands us not to be puffed up with vain glory and simply bring the truth to light. For we know that the lord Jesus Christ asked for fruit from the fig tree, not leaves. And likewise we have determined that the fruit of truth shall not be hidden but shine forth upon a candlestick for the advancement and edification of many. Though less skilled in scholarship, we are all the more eager to cultivate a plain and open style so as to edify the many people who, like prudent bees seeking sweet nectar from the flowers, seek from simple words the burgeoning truth that edifies but does not flatter and puff up the one who hears it. Thus may the compendium of piety be thrown open to those who desire to imitate her. Therefore in what follows we have shown forth the truth as best we can, not for detractors but rather for the faithful.

Here Begins the Life of the Blessed Queen Balthild

2   The blessed Lord, "who will have all men to be saved, and to come unto the knowledge of the truth," works "all in all" both "to will and to do."[3] By the same token, among the merits and virtues of the saints, praise should first be sung of Him Who made the humble great and raised the pauper from the dunghill and seated him among the princes of his people. Such a one is the woman present to our minds, the venerable and great lady Balthild the queen. Divine Providence called her from across the seas.[4] She, who came here as God's most precious and lofty pearl, was sold at a cheap price. Erchinoald,[5] a Frankish magnate and most illustrious man, acquired her and in his service the girl

---

1   Presumably addressed to male subordinates of the nuns at Chelles. It is not clear why the work is addressed to them here.
2   I.e., a higher official of the clergy, such as a bishop.
3   New Testament, 1 Timothy 2.4; 1 Corinthians 12.6; Philippians 2.13.
4   From England.
5   Mayor of the palace, or chief household officer, of the king of Neustria, one of the Frankish kingdoms. Such mayors of the palace often acted as the power behind the throne, wielding more effective power than the king.

behaved most honorably. And her pious and admirable manners pleased this prince and all his servants. For she was kind-hearted and sober and prudent in all her ways, careful and plotting evil for none. Her speech was not frivolous nor her words presumptuous but in every way she behaved with utmost propriety. And since she was of the Saxon race, she was graceful in form with refined features, a most seemly woman with a smiling face and serious gait. And she so showed herself just as she ought in all things, that she pleased her master and found favor in his eyes. So he determined that she should set out the drinking cup for him in his chamber and, honored above all others as his housekeeper, stand at his side always ready to serve him. She did not allow this dignity to make her proud but rather kept her humility. She was all obedience to her companions and amiable, ministering with fitting honor to her elders, ready to draw the shoes from their feet and wash and dry them. She brought them water to wash themselves and prepared their clothing expeditiously. And she performed all these services with good spirits and no grumbling.

3   And from this noble conduct, the praise and love of her comrades for her increased greatly. She gained such happy fame that, when the said lord Erchinoald's wife died, he hoped to unite himself to Balthild, that faultless virgin, in a matronal bed. But when she heard of this, she fled and most swiftly took herself out of his sight. When she was called to the master's chamber she hid herself secretly in a corner and threw some vile rags over herself so that no one could guess that anyone might be concealed there. Thus for the love of humility, the prudent and astute virgin attempted to flee as best she could from vain honors. She hoped that she might avoid a human marriage bed and thus merit a spiritual and heavenly spouse. But doubtless Divine Providence brought it about that the prince, unable to find the woman he sought, married another wife. Thereafter it happened, with God's approval, that Balthild, the maid who escaped marriage with a lord, came to be espoused to Clovis, son of the former King Dagobert. Thus by virtue of her humility she was raised to a higher rank. Divine dispensation deter-

mined to honor her in this station so that, having scorned the king's servant, she came to be coupled with the king himself and bring forth royal children. And these events are known to all for now her royal progeny rule the realm.

4   She upon whom God conferred the grace of prudence obeyed the king with vigilant care as her lord, acted as a mother to the princes, as a daughter to priests, and as a most pious nurse to children and adolescents. And she was amiable to all, loving priests as fathers, monks as brothers, a pious nurse to the poor. And she distributed generous alms to every one. She guarded the princes' honor by keeping their intimate counsels secret. She always exhorted the young to strive for religious achievement and humbly and assiduously suggested things to the king for the benefit of the church and the poor. For, desiring to serve Christ in the secular habit at that time, she frequented daily prayers commending herself with tears to Christ, the King of heaven. The pious king, impressed by her faith and devotion, delegated his faithful servant the abbot Genesius as her helper. Through his hands, she ministered to priests and poor alike, feeding the needy and clothing the naked and taking care to order the burial of the dead, funneling large amounts of gold and silver through him to convents of men and virgins. Afterwards that servant of Christ, Genesius, by Christ's order, was ordained bishop of Lyon in Gaul. But at that time, he was busy about the palace of the Franks. And as we have said, by King Clovis's order, Lady Balthild followed the servant of God's advice in providing alms through him to every poor person in many places.

5   What more? In accordance with God's will, her husband King Clovis migrated from the body and left his sons with their mother. Immediately after him her son Clothar took up the kingdom of the Franks, maintaining peace in the realm, with the most excellent princes, Chrodebert, bishop of Paris, Lord Ouen and Ebroin, mayor of the palace with the rest of the elders and many others. Then to promote peace, by command of Lady Balthild with the advice of the other elders, the people of Austrasia[6] accepted her son

---

6   Another of the Frankish kingdoms.

Childeric as their king and the Burgundians were united with the Franks. And we believe, under God's ordinance, that these three realms then held peace and concord among themselves because of Lady Balthild's great faith.

6   Then following the exhortations of good priests, by God's will working through her, Lady Balthild prohibited the impious evil of the simoniac heresy, a depraved custom which stained the church of God, whereby episcopal orders were obtained for a price. She proclaimed that no payment could be exacted for receipt of a sacred rank. Moreover, she, or God acting through her, ordained that yet another evil custom should cease, namely, that many people determined to kill their children rather than nurture them, for they feared to incur the public exactions which were heaped upon them by custom, which caused great damage to their affairs. In her mercy, that lady forbade anyone to do these things. And for all these deeds, a great reward must surely have awaited her.

7   Who can count how many and how great her services were to religious communities? She showered great estates and whole forests upon them for the construction of their cells and monasteries. And at Chelles, in the region of Paris, she built a great community of virgins as her own special house of God. There she established the maiden Bertilla, God's serving girl, as the first to hold the place of their mother. And there in turn the venerable lady Balthild had determined she would finally go to live under the rule of religion and to rest in peace and in truth she fulfilled her desire with willing devotion. Whatever wonders God works through His saints and His chosen ones should not be passed over, for they contribute to His praise. For, as Scripture says, "God does wonders in his saints."[7] For His Holy Spirit, the Paraclete, dwells within and cooperates with the benevolent heart as it is written: "All things work together for good to them that love God."[8] And thus it was spoken truly of this great woman. As we said, neither our tongue nor any others, however learned as I believe, can give voice to all the good she did. How much consolation and help did she lavish on the houses of God and on the poor for the love of Christ and how many advantages and comforts did she confer on them? And what of the monastery called Corbie in the parish of Amiens that she built at her own expense? There the venerable man, Lord Theofredus, now a bishop but then the abbot, ruled a great flock of brothers whom Lady Balthild had requested from the most saintly Lord Waldebert, then abbot of the monastery of Luxeuil, who wondrously had them sent to that same convent which all agree in praising to this very day.

8   What more? At Jumièges, the religious man Lord Philibert, was given a great wood from the fisc[9] where his community has settled and other gifts and pastures were also conceded from the fisc for the building of this same monastery. And how many great farms and talents of gold and silver did she give to Lord Lagobert at Curbio? She took off a girdle from her regalia, which had encircled her own holy loins and gave it to the brothers to devote to alms. And she dispensed all this with a benign and joyous soul, for as the scripture says: "The Lord loveth a cheerful giver."[10] And likewise to Fontanelle and Logium, she conceded many things. As to Luxeuil and the monasteries in Burgundy, who can tell how many whole farms and innumerable gifts of money she gave? And what did she do for Jouarre, whence she gathered the Lady Bertilla abbess of Chelles and other sacred virgins? How many gifts of wealth and land? And similarly she often directed gifts to holy Fara's monastery. And she granted many great estates to the basilicas[11] of the saints and monasteries of the city of Paris, and enriched them with many gifts. What more? As we have said, we cannot recount these things one by one, not even half of them and to give an account of all the blessings she conferred is utterly beyond our powers.

9   We should not pass over, however, what she did in her zealous love of God for the older basilicas of the

---

7   Old Testament, Psalms 37.34.
8   New Testament, Romans 8.28.
9   I.e., land which in theory pertained permanently to the king.
10   New Testament, 2 Corinthians 9.7.
11   I.e., churches.

saints, Lord Denis and Lord Germanus and Lord Médard and Saint Peter or the Lord Anianus, and Saint Martin, or wherever something came to her notice. She would send orders and letters warning bishops and abbots that the monks dwelling in those places ought to live according to their holy rule and order. And that they might agree more freely, she ordered their privileges confirmed and granted immunities[12] that it might please them all the more to beseech Christ the highest King to show mercy to the king and give peace. And let it be remembered, since it increases the magnitude of her own reward, that she prohibited the sale of captive Christian folk to outsiders and gave orders through all the lands that no one was to sell captive Christians within the borders of the Frankish realm. What is more, she ordered that many captives should be ransomed, paying the price herself. And she installed some of the captives she released and other people in monasteries, particularly as many men and women of her own people as possible and cared for them. For as many of them as she could persuade thereto, she commended to holy communities and bade that they might pray for her. And even to Rome, to the basilicas of Peter and Paul, and the Roman poor, she directed many and large gifts.

10    And as we have said before, it was her own holy intention to convert to[13] this monastery of religious women which she had built at Chelles. But the Franks delayed much for love of her and would not have permitted this to happen except that there was a commotion made by the wretched Bishop Sigobrand whose pride among the Franks earned him his mortal ruin. Indeed, they formed a plan to kill him against her will. Fearing that the lady would act heavily against them, and wish to avenge him, they suddenly relented and permitted her to enter the monastery. There can be no doubt that the princes' motives were far from pure. But the lady, considering the will of God rather than their counsel, thought it a dispensation from God so that, whatever the circumstances, she might have the chance to fulfill her holy plan under Christ's rule. And conducted by several elders, she came to her aforesaid

monastery of Chelles and there she was received into the holy congregation by the holy maidens, as was fitting, honorably and with sufficient love. But at first she had no small complaint against those whom she had so sweetly nurtured. For they suspected her of false motives or else simply attempted to return evil for good. Hastily conferring with the priests about this, she mercifully indulged them in the delay and begged that they would forgive the commotion in her heart. And afterwards by the largesse of God, peace was fully restored between them.

11    And indeed, she loved her sisters with the most pious affection as her own daughters and she obeyed their most holy abbess as a mother. She showed herself as a servant and lowliest bondwoman to them from holy devotion, even while she still ruled over the public palace, and had often visited the community. One example of her great humility was the way she would valiantly take care of the dirtiest cleaning jobs for the sisters in the kitchen, personally cleaning up the dung from the latrine. And she did all this gladly and in perfect joy of spirit, doing such humble service for Christ's sake. For who would believe that one so sublime in power would take care of things so vile? Only if she were driven by the fullest love of Christ could it be expected. And she prayed constantly, persistently, devoutly, tearfully. She frequently attended divine reading and gave constant comfort to the sick through holy exhortation and frequent visits. Through the achievement of charity, she grieved with the sorrowful, rejoiced with the joyful and, that all might be comforted, she often made suggestions for their improvement humbly to the lady abbess. And that lady amiably gave heed to her petitions for truly in them as in the apostles, there was but one heart and one soul, and they loved each other tenderly in Christ.

12    Then the lady Balthild became physically ill of body and suffered wearily from pain in the bowels caused by a serious infection, and but for the doctors' efforts she would have died. But she always had more confidence in celestial medicine for her health. So, with a holy and pious conscience, she never ceased to

---

12    Exemptions from certain aspects of royal authority.
13    I.e., enter.

thank God for chastising. She gave her astute advice at all times and—example of great humility—she provided a pattern of piety in her service to her sisters. She often consulted with the mother of the monastery as to how they might always call on the king and queen and their honored nobles with gifts, as was customary, that the house of God might continue to enjoy the good fame with which it began. Thus it would not lose but always remain in loving affection with all its friends and grow stronger in the name of God, as it is written: "It is fitting to have good report of them which are without."[14] Particularly, she urged them always to care for the poor and for guests with the utmost zeal, out of love and mercy and the mother of the monastery heard her salutary admonitions willingly for love of Christ and did all with gladness of heart. Nor did she ever cease to carry out all this and to increase the rewards of her community.

13   And as her glorious death approached, a clear vision was shown to her. Before holy Mary's altar, a ladder stood upright whose height reached the heavens. Angels of God were going up and down and there the Lady Balthild made her ascent. Through this revelation, she was clearly given to understand that her sublime merit, patience and humility, would take her to the heights of the eternal King who would swiftly reward her with an exalted crown. The lady knew, from this clear vision, that it would not be long before she would migrate from her body and come where she had already laid up her best treasures. And she ordered that this be concealed from her sisters so that until her passing the vision was not revealed lest it cause painful grief to the sisters or the mother of the monastery. But she on her part devoted herself with ever greater piety and good spirits to holy prayer, commending herself ever more zealously, humbly, and in contrition of heart to the celestial King, the Lord Jesus Christ. As much as she could, she concealed the weight of her pain and consoled Lady Bertilla and the rest of the sisters saying that her illness was not serious, that she was convalescent, dissimulating what was to come so that afterwards they took comfort in believing that the blow fell suddenly and she went unexpectedly from life.

14   And when the lady felt her end to be truly near, she raised her holy mind to Heaven. And having made certain that she would be awarded the great prize that the blessed receive, she vehemently forbade her attendants to say how sick she was to the other sisters or to the abbess who was ill herself lest she be distracted by a multitude of even heavier sorrows. At the time there was an infant, her goddaughter whom she wished to take with her. And she was suddenly snatched from her body and preceded her to the tomb. Then full of faith, she crossed herself. Raising pious eyes and holy hands to heaven, the saint's soul was released from the chains of her flesh in peace. And immediately her chamber glittered brightly with the light of divine splendor. And no doubt with that light, a chorus of angels and her faithful old friend Bishop Genesius came to receive that most holy soul as her great merits deserved.

15   For a little while, the sisters attending her stifled their sorrowful groans. They said nothing of her death and, as she had ordered, remained silent and told only those priests who commended her most blessed soul to the Lord. But when the abbess and all the congregation learned what had happened they asked tearfully how this universally desired jewel could have been snatched away so suddenly without warning, without knowing the hour of her departure. And stupefied, they all prostrated themselves on the ground in grief and with profuse tears and fearful groans, gave thanks to the pious Lord and praised Him together. Then they commended her holy soul to Christ, the pious King, that He might escort her to holy Mary in the chorus and company of the saints. Then they buried her with great honor and much reverence as was proper. And Lady Bertilla the Abbess, with solicitous striving for piety, earnestly commended her to the holy priests in several churches that her holy name be carefully commemorated in the sacred oblations. And they still celebrate her merits in many places.

---

14   New Testament, 1 Timothy 3.7.

16  To her followers, she left a holy example of humility and patience, mildness and overflowing zest for loving; nay more, infinite mercy, astute and prudent vigilance, pure confessions. She showed that everything should be done as a result of consultation and that nothing should be done without consent but that all actions should be temperate and rational. She left this rule of piety as a model to her companions and now for her holy virtues and many other merits she has received the prize of the crown that the Lord set aside for her long ago. So she is happy among the angels in the Lord's sight and as His spouse rejoices forever among the white-garbed flock of virgins enjoying the immense and everlasting joy she had always desired. And in order to make known her sublime merits to the faithful, God in his goodness has effected many miracles at her holy tomb. For whoever came there seized by fever, or vexed with demons, or worn with toothache, if they had faith, was immediately cured through divine virtue and her holy intercession from whatever plague or illness. Safe and sound, they went out in the Lord's name as was manifested not long ago in the case of a certain boy.

17  A certain venerable man, Bishop Leudegund, came from Provence, a faithful friend to the monastery of Chelles. His son was possessed by a demon so violent that his companions could only control him if his hands and feet were bound, for with great cruelty he tore apart all he could reach. But when they brought him into the place of her holy sepulchre and laid him half-alive on the pavement, the ferocious demon grew stiff and terrified with fear of God and fell silent. Divine power made him flee from the boy forthwith. And the boy rose up confidently, crossed himself and, giving thanks to God, returned to his own unharmed and in his right mind.

18  Now let us recall that there have been other noble queens in the realm of the Franks who worshipped God: Clothild, King Clovis's queen of old,[15] niece of King Gundobad. Her husband was a mighty pagan but she drew him, with many other Frankish leaders, to Christianity and the Catholic faith by holy exhortations. She led them to construct a church in honor of Saint Peter at Paris, and she built the original community of virgins for Saint George at Chelles and in honor of the saints and to store up her future reward she founded many others which she endowed with much wealth. And likewise we are told of Queen Ultragotha of the most Christian king Childebert, that she was a comforter of the poor and helper of the monks who served God. And also, there was the most faithful handmaid Radegund, King Clothar's queen of elder time, whom the grace of the Holy Spirit enkindled so that she relinquished her husband during his life and consecrated herself to the Lord Christ under the holy veil. And we may read in her acts of all the good she did for Christ her spouse.

19  But it is only right that we meditate instead on her who is our subject here, Lady Balthild whose many good deeds have been done in our time and whose acts are best known to us. We have commemorated a few of these many acts and cannot think her merits inferior to those who came before her for we know she surpassed them in zealous striving for what is holy. For after performing many good deeds to the point of evangelical perfection, she at last surrendered herself freely to holy obedience and happily ended her life as a religious, a true *monacha*.[16] Her sacred obit and holy feast are celebrated on the third calends of February.[17] She lies entombed in Chelles, her monastery, while truly she reigns gloriously with Christ in Heaven in perpetual joy never, we trust, to forget her faithful friends. And as well as we could, if not as much as we ought, in fervent charity we have striven to follow your orders. Forgive our lack of skill and for our sins of negligence we pray for charity's sake that you ask the good Lord to exonerate us. May the peace of the Lord be with you to Whom be glory from everlasting to everlasting. Amen.

---

15  This Clovis (481-511) is regarded as the first king of the Franks.

16  Latin: a feminine form of *monachus*, or monk.

17  I.e., January 30.

# 30

# EINHARD, *LIFE OF CHARLEMAGNE*

Einhard (*c.* 770-840) was raised as a monk, and after 791 was educated in the palace school of Charles, king of the Franks (better known as Charles the Great, or Charlemagne). He served both Charlemagne and, after Charlemagne's death in 814, his successor, Louis the Pious, in various governmental capacities. Einhard wrote his life of Charlemagne between 829 and 836, after retiring from Louis's service in the 820s.

---

### EINHARD'S PREFACE

Since I have taken upon myself to narrate the public and private life, and no small part of the deeds, of my lord and foster-father, the most excellent and most justly renowned King Charles, I have condensed the matter into as brief a form as possible. I have been careful not to omit any fact that could come to my knowledge, but at the same time not to offend by a repetitive style those minds that despise everything modern, if one can possibly avoid offending by a new work men who seem to despise also the masterpieces of antiquity, the works of most learned and luminous writers. Very many of them, I have no doubt, are men devoted to a life of literary leisure, who feel that the affairs of the present generation ought not to be passed by, and who do not consider everything done today as unworthy of mention and deserving to be given over to silence and oblivion, but are nevertheless seduced by lust of immortality to celebrate the glorious deeds of other times by some sort of composition rather than to deprive posterity of the mention of their own names by not writing at all.

Be this as it may, I see no reason why I should refrain from entering upon a task of this kind since no man can write with more accuracy than I of events that took place around me, and of facts concerning which I had personal knowledge, ocular demonstration, as the saying goes, and I have no means of ascertaining whether or not anyone else has the subject in hand. In any event, I would rather commit my story to writing, and hand it down to posterity in partnership with others, so to speak, than to allow the most glorious life of this most excellent king, the greatest of all the princes of his day, and his illustrious deeds, hard for men of later times to imitate, to be wrapped in the darkness of oblivion.

But there are still other reasons, neither unwarrantable nor insufficient, in my opinion, that urge me to write on this subject, namely, the care that King Charles bestowed upon me in my childhood, and my constant friendship with him and his children after I took up my abode at court. In this way he strongly endeared me to himself, and made me greatly his debtor in death as well as in life, so that were I, unmindful of the benefits conferred upon me, to keep silence concerning the most glorious and illustrious deeds of a man who claims so much at my hands, and allow his life to lack due eulogy and written memorial, as if he had never lived, I should deservedly appear ungrateful, and be so considered, albeit my powers are feeble, scanty, indeed next to nothing, and not at all adapted to write and set forth a life that would tax the eloquence of a Tully.[1]

I submit the book. It contains the history of a very great and distinguished man, but there is nothing in it to wonder at besides his deeds, except the fact that I, who am a barbarian, and very little versed in the Roman language, seem to suppose myself capable of writing gracefully and respectably in Latin, and to carry my presumption so far as to disdain the sentiment that Cicero is said to have expressed in the first book of the *Tusculan Disputations* when speaking of the Latin authors. His words are: "It is an outrageous abuse both of time and literature for a man to commit his thoughts to writing without having the ability either to arrange them or elucidate them, or attract readers by some charm of style." This pronouncement of the famous orator might have deterred me from writing if I had not made up my mind that it was better to risk the opinions of the world, and put my little talents for composition to the test, than to slight the memory of so great a man for the sake of sparing myself.

1   The Merovingian family, from which the Franks used to choose their kings, is commonly said to have lasted until the time of Childeric,[2] who was deposed, shaved[3] and thrust into a monastery by command of the Roman Pontiff Stephen.[4] But although, to all outward appearances, it ended with him, it had long since been devoid of vital strength, and was conspicuous only from bearing the empty epithet "royal"; the real power and authority in the kingdom lay in the hands of the chief officer of the court, the so-called mayor of the palace, and he was at the head of affairs. There was nothing left for the king to do but to be content with his name of king, his flowing hair, and long beard, to sit on his throne and play the ruler, to give ear to the ambassadors that came from all quarters, and to dismiss them as if on his own responsibility, using words that were, in fact, suggested to him or

even imposed upon him. He had nothing that he could call his own beyond this vain title of king and the precarious support allowed by the mayor of the palace in his discretion, except a single country estate that brought him but a very small income. There was a dwelling house upon this, and a small number of servants attached to it, sufficient to perform the necessary offices. When he had to go abroad, he used to ride in a cart, drawn by a yoke of oxen, driven, peasant fashion, by a ploughman; he rode in this way to the palace and to the general assembly of the people that met once a year for the welfare of the kingdom, and he returned in like manner. The mayor of the palace took charge of the government and everything that had to be planned or executed at home and abroad.

2   At the time of Childeric's deposition, Pepin, the father of King Charles, held this office of mayor of the palace, one might almost say by hereditary right, for Pepin's father, Charles, had received it at the hands of his father, Pepin, and filled it with distinction. It was this Charles that crushed the tyrants who claimed to rule the whole Frank land as their own, and that utterly routed the Saracens,[5] when they attempted the conquest of Gaul, in two great battles—one in Aquitania, near the town of Poitiers, and the other on the River Berre, near Narbonne—and compelled them to return to Spain. This honor was usually conferred by the people only upon men eminent from their illustrious birth and ample wealth. For some years, ostensibly under King Childeric, Pepin, the father of King Charles, shared the duties inherited from his father and grandfather most amicably with his brother, Carloman. The latter, then, for unknown reasons, renounced the heavy cares of an earthly crown and retired to Rome. Here he exchanged his worldly garb for a cowl, and built a monastery on Mt. Oreste, near the Church of St. Sylvester, where he enjoyed for several years the seclusion that he desired, in company with certain others who had the same object in view. But so many distinguished Franks made the pilgrim-

---

1   I.e., Marcus Tullius Cicero, Roman writer and politician of the first century BC.

2   Childeric III (743-751).

3   I.e., the hair on his head was cut.

4   Actually, Pope Zacharias was the pope concerned here. Pope Stephen later met with the succeeding monarch, Pepin, and consecrated him.

5   I.e., the Moslems, who at this point had already largely conquered what is today Spain.

age to Rome to fulfill their vows, and insisted upon paying their respects to him, as their former lord, on the way, that the repose which he so much loved was broken by these frequent visits, and he was driven to change his abode. Accordingly, when he found that his plans were frustrated by his many visitors, he abandoned the mountain, and withdrew to the monastery of St. Benedict, on Monte Cassino, in the province of Samnium, and passed the rest of his days there in the exercises of religion.

3 Pepin, however, was raised, by decree of the Roman Pontiff, from the rank of mayor of the palace to that of king, and ruled alone over the Franks for 15 years or more. He died of dropsy, in Paris, at the close of the Aquitanian war, which he waged with William, duke of Aquitania, for nine successive years, and left two sons, Charles and Carloman, upon whom, by the grace of God, the succession devolved.

The Franks, in a general assembly of the people, made them both kings, on condition that they should divide the whole kingdom equally between them, Charles to take and rule the part that had belonged to their father, Pepin, and Carloman the part which their uncle, Carloman, had governed. The conditions were accepted, and each entered into possession of the share of the kingdom that fell to him by this arrangement; but peace was maintained between them only with the greatest difficulty, because many of Carloman's party kept trying to disturb their good understanding, and there were some even who plotted to involve them in a war with each other. The event, however, showed the danger to have been imaginary rather than real, for at Carloman's death his widow fled to Italy with her sons and her principal adherents, and without reason, despite her husband's brother, put herself and her children under the protection of Desiderius, king of the Lombards. Carloman had succumbed to disease after ruling two years in common with his brother, and at his death Charles was unanimously elected King of the Franks.

4 It would be folly, I think, to write a word concerning Charles's birth and infancy, or even his boyhood, for nothing has ever been written on the subject, and there is no one alive now who can give information about it. Accordingly, I have determined to pass that by as unknown, and to proceed at once to discuss his character, his deeds, and such other facts of his life as are worth telling and setting forth, and shall first give an account of his deeds at home and abroad, then of his character and pursuits, and lastly of his administration and death, omitting nothing worth knowing or necessary to know.

5 His first undertaking in a military way was the Aquitanian war, begun by his father, but not brought to a close; because he thought that it could be readily carried through, he took it up while his brother was still alive, calling upon him to render aid. The campaign once opened, he conducted it with the greatest vigor, notwithstanding that his brother withheld the assistance that he had promised, and Charles did not desist or shrink from his self-imposed task until, by his patience and firmness, he had completely gained his ends. He compelled Hunold, who had attempted to seize Aquitania after Waifar's death, and renew the war then almost concluded, to abandon Aquitania and flee to Gascony. Even here he gave him no rest, but crossed the River Garonne, built the castle of Fronsac, and sent ambassadors to Lupus, duke of Gascony, to demand the surrender of the fugitive, threatening to take him by force unless he were promptly given up to him. Thereupon Lupus chose the wiser course, and not only gave Hunold up, but submitted himself, with the province which he ruled, to the king.

6 After bringing this war to an end and settling matters in Aquitania (his associate in authority had meantime departed this life), he was induced, by the prayers and entreaties of Hadrian, bishop of the city of Rome,[6] to wage war on the Lombards. His father before him had undertaken this task at the request of Pope Stephen, but under great difficulties, for certain leading Franks, from whom he usually took counsel, had so vehemently opposed his design as to declare openly that they would leave the king and go home. Nevertheless, the war against the Lombard King Astolf[7] had been taken up and very quickly

---

6  I.e., the pope.
7  His kingdom lay in central Italy.

concluded. Now, although Charles seems to have had similar, or rather just the same grounds for declaring war that his father had, the war itself differed from the preceding one alike in its difficulties and its result. Pepin, to be sure, after besieging King Astolf a few days in Pavia, had compelled him to give hostages, to restore to the Romans the cities and castles that he had taken, and to take an oath that he would not attempt to seize them again; but Charles did not cease, after declaring war, until he had exhausted King Desiderius by a long siege, and forced him to surrender at his discretion; driven his son Adalgis, the last hope of the Lombards, not only from his kingdom, but from all Italy; restored to the Romans all that they had lost; subdued Hruodgaus, duke of Friuli, who was plotting revolution; reduced all Italy to his power, and set his son Pepin as king over it.

At this point I should describe Charles's difficult passage over the Alps into Italy, and the hardships that the Franks endured in climbing the trackless mountain ridges, the heaven-aspiring cliffs and ragged peaks, if it were not my purpose in this work to record the manner of his life rather than the incidents of the wars that he waged. Suffice it to say that this war ended with the subjection of Italy, the banishment of King Desiderius for life, the expulsion of his son Adalgis from Italy, and the restoration of the conquests of the Lombard kings to Hadrian, the head of the Roman Church.

7   At the conclusion of this struggle, the Saxon war, that seems to have been only laid aside for the time, was taken up again. No war ever undertaken by the Frank nation was carried on with such persistence and bitterness, or cost so much labor, because the Saxons, like almost all the tribes of Germany, were a fierce people, given to the worship of devils, and hostile to our religion, and did not consider it dishonorable to transgress and violate all law, human and divine. Then there were peculiar circumstances that tended to cause a breach of peace every day. Except in a few places, where large forests or mountain ridges intervened and made the bounds certain, the line between ourselves and the Saxons passed almost in its whole extent through an open country, so that there was no end to the murders, thefts and arsons on both sides. In this way the Franks became so embittered that they at last

resolved to make reprisals no longer, but to come to open war with the Saxons. Accordingly, war was begun against them, and was waged for 33 successive years with great fury—more, however, to the disadvantage of the Saxons than of the Franks. It could doubtless have been brought to an end sooner, had it not been for the faithlessness of the Saxons. It is hard to say how often they were conquered, and, humbly submitting to the king, promised to do what was enjoined upon them, gave without hesitation the required hostages, and received the officers sent them from the king. They were sometimes so much weakened and reduced that they promised to renounce the worship of devils, and to adopt Christianity, but they were no less ready to violate these terms than prompt to accept them, so that it is impossible to tell which came easier to them to do; scarcely a year passed from the beginning of the war without such changes on their part. But the king did not suffer his high purpose and steadfastness—firm alike in good and evil fortune—to be turned from the task that he had undertaken; on the contrary, he never allowed their faithless behaviour to go unpunished, but either took the field against them in person, or sent his counts with an army to wreak vengeance and exact righteous satisfaction. At last, after conquering and subduing all who had offered resistance, he took 10,000 of those that lived on the banks of the Elbe, and settled them, with their wives and children, in many different bodies here and there in Gaul and Germany. The war that had lasted so many years was at length ended by their accepting the terms offered by the king: renunciation of their national religious customs and the worship of devils, acceptance of the sacraments of the Christian faith and religion, and union with the Franks to form one people.

8   Charles himself fought but two pitched battles in this war, although it was long protracted—one on Mount Osning, at the place called Detmold, and again on the bank of the river Hase, both in the space of little more than a month. The enemy were so routed and overthrown in these two battles that they never afterwards ventured to take the offensive or to resist the attacks of the king, unless they were protected by a strong position. A great many of the Frankish as well as of the Saxon nobility, men occupying the highest

posts of honor, perished in this war, which came to an end only after the lapse of 32 years. The wars that were declared against the Franks in the meantime, and skillfully conducted by the king, were so many and grievous that one may reasonably question whether his fortitude or his good fortune is to be more admired. The Saxon war began two years before the Italian war, but although it went on without interruption, business elsewhere was not neglected, nor was there any shrinking from other equally arduous contests. The king, who excelled all the princes of his time in wisdom and greatness of soul, did not allow difficulty to deter him or danger to daunt him from anything that had to be taken up or carried through, for he had trained himself to bear and endure whatever came, without yielding in adversity, or trusting to the deceitful favors of fortune in prosperity.

9    In the midst of this vigorous and almost uninterrupted struggle with the Saxons, he covered the frontier by garrisons at the proper points, and marched over the Pyrenees into Spain at the head of all the forces that he could muster. All the towns and castles that he attacked surrendered, and up to the time of his homeward march he sustained no loss whatsoever; but on his return through the Pyrenees he had cause to rue the treachery of the Gascons. That region is well adapted for ambushes by reason of the thick forests that cover it; as the army was advancing in the long line of march necessitated by the narrowness of the road, the Gascons, who lay in ambush on the top of a very high mountain, attacked the rear of the baggage train and the rear guard in charge of it, and hurled them down to the very bottom of the valley. In the struggle that ensued, they cut them off to a man; they then plundered the baggage, and dispersed with all speed in every direction under cover of approaching night. The lightness of their armor and the nature of the battle ground stood the Gascons in good stead on this occasion, whereas the Franks fought at a disadvantage in every respect because of the weight of their armor and the unevenness of the ground. Eggihard, the king's steward, Anselm, count Palatine, and Roland, governor of the March of Brittany, with very many others, fell in this engagement. This ill turn could not be avenged for the time being because the enemy scattered so widely after carrying out their

plan that not the least clue could be had as to their whereabouts.

10    Charles also subdued the Bretons, who live on the seacoast, in the extreme western part of Gaul. When they refused to obey him, he sent an army against them, and compelled them to give hostages, and to promise to do his bidding. He afterwards entered Italy in person with his army, and passed through Rome to Capua, a city in Campania, where he pitched his camp and threatened the Beneventans with hostilities unless they submitted to him. Their duke, Aragis, escaped the danger by sending his two sons, Rumold and Grimold, with a great sum of money to greet the king, begging him to accept them as hostages, and promising for himself and his people compliance with all the king's commands, on the single condition that his personal attendance should not be required. The king took the welfare of the people into account rather than the stubborn disposition of the duke, accepted the offered hostages, and released him from the obligation to appear before him in consideration of his handsome gift. He retained only the younger son as hostage, and sent the elder back to his father, and returned to Rome, leaving commissioners with Aragis to exact the oath of allegiance, and to administer it to the Beneventans. He stayed in Rome several days in order to pay his devotions at the holy places, and then came back to Gaul.

11    At this time, suddenly, the Bavarian war broke out, but came to a speedy end. It was due to the arrogance and folly of Duke Tassilo. His wife, a daughter of King Desiderius, desired to avenge her father's banishment through the agency of her husband, and accordingly induced him to make a treaty with the Huns, the neighbors of the Bavarians on the east, and not only to leave the king's commands unfulfilled, but to challenge him to war. Charles's high spirit could not brook Tassilo's insubordination, for it seemed to him to pass all bounds; accordingly he immediately summoned his troops from all sides for a campaign against Bavaria, and appeared in person with a great army on the river Lech, which forms the boundary between the Bavarians and the Alemanni. After pitching his camp upon its banks, he determined to put the duke's disposition to the test by an embassy before entering the province. Tassilo did not

think that it was for his own or his people's good to persist, so he surrendered himself to the king, gave the hostages demanded, among them his own son Theodo, and promised by oath not to give ear to anyone who should attempt to turn him from his allegiance. So this war, which appeared likely to be very grievous, came very quickly to an end. Tassilo, however, was afterward summoned to the king's presence, and not allowed to depart, and the government of the province that he had had in charge was no longer entrusted to a duke, but to counts.

12   After these uprisings had been thus quelled, war was declared against the Slavs who are commonly known among us as Wilzi, but properly, that is to say in their own tongue, are called Welatabians. The Saxons served in this campaign as auxiliaries among the tribes that followed the king's standard at his summons, but their obedience lacked sincerity and devotion. War was declared because the Slavs kept harassing the Abodriti, old allies of the Franks, by continual raids, in spite of all commands to the contrary. A gulf of unknown length, but nowhere more than a hundred miles wide, and in many parts narrower, stretches off towards the east from the Western Ocean. Many tribes have settlements on its shores—the Danes and Swedes, whom we call Northmen, on the northern shore and all the adjacent islands—but the southern shore is inhabited by the Slavs and Aïsti, and various other tribes. The Welatabians, against whom the king now made war, were the chief of these. But in a single campaign, which he conducted in person, he so crushed and subdued them that they did not think it advisable thereafter to refuse obedience to his commands.

13   The war against the Avars, or Huns, followed, and, except for the Saxon war, was the greatest that was waged; he took it up with more spirit than any of his other wars, and made far greater preparations for it. He conducted one campaign in person in Pannonia, of which the Huns then had possession. He entrusted all subsequent operations to his son, Pepin, and the governors of the provinces, even to counts and lieutenants. Although they most vigorously prose-

cuted the war, it came to a conclusion only after a seven years' struggle. The utter depopulation of Pannonia, and the site of the khan's[8] palace, now a desert, where not a trace of human habitation is visible, bear witness how many battles were fought in those years, and how much blood was shed. The entire body of the Hun nobility perished in this contest, and all its glory with it. All the money and treasure that had been amassing for years was seized, and no war in which the Franks have ever engaged within the memory of man brought them such riches and such booty. Up to that time the Huns had passed for a poor people, but so much gold and silver was found in the khan's palace, and so much valuable spoil taken in battle, that one may well think that the Franks took justly from the Huns what the Huns had formerly taken unjustly from other nations. Only two of the chief men of the Franks fell in this war— Eric, duke of Friuli, who was killed in Tarsatch, a town on the coast of Liburnia, by the treachery of the inhabitants, and Gerold, governor of Bavaria, who met his death at Pannonia, slain with two men that were accompanying him, by an unknown hand while he was marshalling his forces for battle against the Huns, and riding up and down the line encouraging his men. This war was otherwise almost a bloodless one so far as the Franks were concerned, and ended most satisfactorily, although by reason of its magnitude it was long protracted.

14   The Saxon war next came to an end as successful as the struggle had been long. The Bohemian and Linonian wars that next broke out could not last long; both were quickly carried through under the leadership of the younger Charles. The last of these wars was the one declared against the Northmen called Danes. They began their careers as pirates, but afterward took to laying waste the coasts of Gaul and Germany with their large fleet. Their king Godfred was so puffed with vain aspirations that he counted on gaining empire over all Germany, and looked upon Saxony and Frisia as his provinces. He had already subdued his neighbors the Abodriti, and made them tributary, and boasted that he would shortly appear with a great

8   The khan was the political leader of the Huns.

army before Aix-la-Chapelle, where the king held his court. Some faith was put in his words, empty as they sound, and it is supposed that he would have attempted something of the sort if he had not been prevented by a premature death. He was murdered by one of his own bodyguard, and so ended at once his life and the war that he had begun.

15   Such are the wars, most skillfully planned and successfully fought, which this most powerful king waged during the 47 years of his reign. He so largely increased the Frankish kingdom, which was already great and strong when he received it at his father's hands, that more than double its former territory was added to it. The authority of the Franks was formerly confined to that part of Gaul included between the Rhine and the Loire, the Ocean and the Balearic Sea; to that part of Germany which is inhabited by the so-called Eastern Franks, and is bounded by Saxony and the Danube, the Rhine and the Saale—this stream separates the Thuringians from the Sorabians; and to the country of the Alemanni and Bavarians. By the wars above mentioned he first made tributary Aquitania, Gascony, and the whole of the region of the Pyrenees as far as the River Ebro,[9] which rises in the land of the Navarrese, flows through the most fertile districts of Spain, and empties into the Balearic Sea, beneath the walls of the city of Tortosa. He next reduced and made tributary all Italy from Aosta to Lower Calabria,[10] where the boundary line runs between the Beneventans and the Greeks,[11] a territory more than a thousand miles long; then Saxony, which constitutes no small part of Germany, and is reckoned to be twice as wide as the country inhabited by the Franks, while about equal to it in length; in addition, both Pannonias, Dacia beyond the Danube, and Istria, Liburnia, and Dalmatia, except the cities on the coast, which he left to the Greek emperor for friendship's sake, and because of the treaty that he had made with him. In sum, he vanquished and made tributary all the wild and barbarous tribes dwelling in Germany between the Rhine and the Vistula, and the Ocean and the Danube, all of which speak very much the same language, but differ widely from one another chiefly in customs and dress. The chief among them are the Welatabians, the Sorabians, the Abodriti, and the Bohemians, and he had to make war upon these, but the rest, by far the larger number, submitted to him of their own accord.

16   He added to the glory of his reign by gaining the good will of several kings and nations; so close, indeed, was the alliance that he contracted with Alfonso, king of Galicia and Asturias, that the latter, when sending letters or ambassadors to Charles, invariably styled himself Charles's man. His munificence won the kings of the Scots also to pay such deference to his wishes that they never gave him any title other than lord, or themselves than subjects or slaves; there are letters from them extant in which these feelings in his regard are expressed.[12] His relations with Aaron, king of the Persians, who ruled over almost the whole of the East, India excepted, were so friendly that this prince preferred his favor to that of all the kings and potentates of the earth, and held that to him alone marks of honor and munificence were due. Accordingly, when the ambassadors sent by Charles to visit the most holy sepulcher and place of resurrection of our Lord and Savior presented themselves before him with gifts, and made known their master's wishes, he not only granted what was asked, but gave possession of that holy and blessed spot. When they returned, he dispatched his ambassadors with them, and sent magnificent gifts, besides stuffs, perfumes, and other rich products of the Eastern lands. A few years before this, Charles had asked him for an elephant, and he sent the only one that he had. The emperors of Constantinople, Nicephorus, Michael, and Leo, made advances to Charles, and sought friendship and alliance with him by several embassies; even when the Greeks suspected him of designing to wrest the empire from them, because of his assumption of the title emperor, they made a close alliance with him, so he might have no cause of offense. In fact, the power

---

9   Einhard exaggerates regarding this southern extent.
10   Einhard exaggerates regarding Calabria.
11   Parts of southern Italy were still in Byzantine hands.
12   These letters do not survive.

of the Franks was always viewed by the Greeks and Romans with a jealous eye, whence the Greek proverb "Have the Frank for your friend, but not for your neighbor."

17   This king, who showed himself so great in extending his empire and subduing foreign nations, and was constantly occupied with plans to that end, undertook also very many works calculated to adorn and benefit his kingdom, and brought several of them to completion. Among these, the most deserving of mention are the great church of the Holy Mother of God at Aix-la-Chapelle, built in the most admirable manner, and a bridge over the Rhine at Mayence, half a mile long, the breadth of the river at this point. This bridge was destroyed by fire the year before Charles died, but, owing to his death so soon after, could not be repaired, although he had intended to rebuild it in stone. He began two palaces of beautiful workmanship—one near his manor called Ingelheim, not far from Mayence, the other at Nimeguen, on the Waal, the stream that washes the south side of the island of the Batavians. But, above all, sacred edifices were the object of his care throughout his whole kingdom, and whenever he found them falling into ruin from age, he commanded the bishops and clergy in charge of them to repair them, and made sure by commissioners that his instructions were obeyed. He also fitted out a fleet for the war with the Northmen; the vessels required for this purpose were built on the rivers that flow from Gaul and Germany into the North Sea. Moreover, since the Northmen continually overran and laid waste the Gallic and German coasts, he caused watch and ward to be kept in all the harbors, and at the mouths of rivers in all the harbors, and at the mouths of rivers large enough to admit the entrance of vessels, to prevent the enemy from disembarking; in the South, in Narbonensis and Septimania, and along the whole coast of Italy as far as Rome, he took the same precautions against the Moors, who had recently begun their piratical practices. Hence, Italy suffered no great harm in his time at the hands of the Moors, nor Gaul and Germany from the Northmen, except that the Moors got possession of the Etruscan town of Città Vecchia by treachery, and sacked it, and the Northmen harried some of the islands in Frisia off the German coast.

18   Thus did Charles defend and increase as well as beautify his kingdom, as is well known, and here let me express my admiration of his great qualities and his extraordinary constancy alike in good and evil fortune. I will now forthwith proceed to give the details of his private and family life.

After his father's death, while sharing the kingdom with his brother, he bore his unfriendliness and jealousy most patiently, and, to the wonder of all, could not be provoked to be angry with him. Later he married a daughter of Desiderius, king of the Lombards, at the instance of his mother, but he repudiated her at the end of a year for some unknown reason, and married Hildegard, a woman of high birth, of Suabian origin. He had three sons by her—Charles, Pepin, and Louis—and as many daughters—Hruodrud, Bertha, and Gisela. He had three other daughters besides these—Theoderada, Hiltrud, and Ruodhaid—two by his third wife, Fastrada, a woman of east Frankish (that is to say, German) origin, and the third by a concubine, whose name for the moment escapes me. At the death of Fastrada, he married Liutgard, an Alemannic woman, who bore him no children. After her death he had three concubines—Gersuinda, a Saxon, by whom he had Adaltrud; Regina, who was the mother of Drogo and Hugh; and Ethelind, by whom he had Theodoric. Charles's mother, Berthrada, passed her old age with him in great honor; he entertained the greatest veneration for her, and there was never any disagreement between them except when he divorced the daughter of King Desiderius, whom he had married to please her. She died soon after Hildegard, after living to see three grandsons and as many granddaughters in her son's house, and he buried her with great pomp in the basilica[13] of St. Denis, where his father lay. He had an only sister, Gisela, who had consecrated herself to a religious life from girlhood, and he cherished as much affection for her as for his mother. She also died a few years before him in the monastery where she had passed her life.

---

13   A kind of church, typically Roman in structure.

19  The plan that he adopted for his children's education was, first of all, to have both boys and girls instructed in the liberal arts, to which he also turned his own attention. As soon as their years admitted, in accordance with the customs of the Franks, the boys had to learn horsemanship, and to practice war and hunting, and the girls to familiarize themselves with cloth-making, and to handle distaff and spindle, that they might not grow lazy through idleness, and he fostered in them every virtuous sentiment. He lost only three of all his children before his death, two sons and one daughter: Charles who was the eldest, Pepin, whom he had made king of Italy, and Hruodrud, his oldest daughter, whom he had betrothed to Constantine, emperor of the Greeks. Pepin left one son, named Bernard, and five daughters: Adelaide, Atula, Guntrada, Berthaid, and Theoderada. The king gave a striking proof of his fatherly affection at the time of Pepin's death: he appointed the grandson to succeed Pepin, and had the granddaughters brought up with his own daughters. When his sons and his daughter died, he was not so calm as might have been expected from his remarkably strong mind, for his affections were no less strong, and moved him to tears. Again, when he was told of the death of Hadrian, the Roman Pontiff, whom he had loved most of all his friends, he wept as much as if he had lost a brother, or a very dear son. He was by nature most ready to contract friendships, and not only made friends easily, but clung to them persistently, and cherished most fondly those with whom he had formed such ties. He was so careful of the training of his sons and daughters that he never took his meals without them when he was at home, and never made a journey without them; his sons would ride at his side, and his daughters follow him, while a number of his bodyguard, detailed for their protection, brought up the rear. Strange to say, although they were very handsome women, and he loved them very dearly, he was never willing to marry any of them to a man of their own nation or to a foreigner, but kept them all at home until his death, saying that he could not dispense with their society. Hence, though otherwise happy, he experienced the malignity of fortune[14] as far as they were concerned; yet he concealed his knowledge of the rumors current in regard to them, and of the suspicions entertained of their honor.

20  By one of his concubines he had a son, handsome in face, but hunchbacked, named Pepin, whom I omitted to mention in the list of his children. When Charles was at war with the Huns, and was wintering in Bavaria, this Pepin shammed sickness, and plotted against his father in company with some of the leading Franks, who seduced him with vain promises of the royal authority. When his deceit was discovered, and the conspirators punished, his head was shaved, and he was allowed, in accordance with his wishes, to devote himself to a religious life in the monastery of Prüm. A formidable conspiracy against Charles had previously been set on foot in Germany, but all the traitors were banished, some of them without mutilations, others after their eyes had been put out. Only three of them lost their lives; they drew their swords and resisted arrest, and, after killing several men, were cut down, because they could not otherwise be overpowered. It is supposed that the cruelty of Queen Fastrada was the primary cause of these plots, and they were both due to Charles's apparent acquiescence in his wife's cruel conduct, and deviation from the usual kindness and gentleness of his disposition. All the rest of his life he was regarded by everyone with the utmost love and affection, so much so that not the least accusation of unjust rigor was ever made against him.

21  He liked foreigners, and was at great pains to take them under his protection. There were often so many of them, both in the palace and the kingdom, that they might reasonably have been considered a nuisance; but he, with his broad humanity, was very little disturbed by such annoyances because he felt himself compensated for these great inconveniences by the praises of his generosity and the reward of high renown.

22  Charles was large and strong, and of lofty stature, though not disproportionately tall (his height is well known to have been seven times the length of his foot); the upper part of his head was round, his eyes

---

14  Two of his daughters, unmarried as Einhard says, are known to have had children.

very large and animated, nose a little long, hair fair, and face laughing and merry. Thus his appearance was always stately and dignified, whether he was standing or sitting, although his neck was thick and somewhat short, and his belly rather prominent; but the symmetry of the rest of his body concealed these defects. His gait was firm, his whole carriage manly, and his voice clear, but not so strong as his size led one to expect. His health was excellent, except during the four years preceding his death, when he was subject to frequent fevers; at the last he even limped a little with one foot. Even in those years he consulted his own inclinations rather than the advice of physicians, who were almost hateful to him because they wanted him to give up roasts, to which he was accustomed, and to eat boiled meat instead. In accordance with the national custom, he took frequent exercise on horseback and in hunting, accomplishments in which scarcely any peoples in the world can equal the Franks. He enjoyed the exhalations from natural warm springs, and often practiced swimming, at which he was so adept that none could surpass him. Hence it was that he built his palace at Aix-la-Chapelle, and lived there constantly during his latter years until his death. He used to invite not only his sons to his bath, but his nobles and friends, and now and then a troop of his retinue or bodyguard, so that a hundred or more persons sometimes bathed with him.

23   He used to wear the national, that is to say, Frankish, dress—a linen shirt and linen breeches next to his skin, and above these a tunic fringed with silk, while hose fastened by bands covered his lower limbs, and shoes his feet, and he protected his shoulders and chest in winter by a close fitting coat of otter or marten skins. Over all this he flung a blue cloak, and he always had a sword girt about him, usually one with a gold or silver hilt and belt; he sometimes carried a jeweled sword, but only on great feast days or at the reception of ambassadors from foreign nations. He despised foreign costumes, however handsome, and never allowed himself to be robed in them, except twice in Rome, when he put on the Roman tunic, the chlamys, and shoes, the first time at the request of

Pope Hadrian, the second to gratify Leo, Hadrian's successor. On great feast days he made use of embroidered clothes and shoes bedecked by a golden buckle, and he appeared crowned with a diadem of gold and gems, but on other days his dress varied little from the common dress of the people.

24   Charles was temperate in eating, and particularly so in drinking, for he abominated drunkenness in anybody, much more in himself and those of his household. But he could not easily abstain from food, and often complained that fasts injured his health. He very rarely gave entertainments, only on great feast days, and then to large numbers of people. His meals ordinarily consisted of four courses, not counting the roast, which his huntsmen used to bring in on the spit; he was more fond of this than any other dish. While at the table, he listened to reading or music. The subjects of the readings were the stories and deeds of olden times: he was fond, too, of St. Augustine's[15] books, and especially of the one entitled *The City of God*. He was so moderate in the use of wine and all sorts of drink that he rarely allowed himself more than three cups in the course of a meal. In summer, after the midday meal, he would eat some fruit, drain a single cup, put off his clothes and shoes, just as he did for the night, and rest for two or three hours. He was in the habit of awaking and rising from bed four or five times during the night. While he was dressing and putting on his shoes, he not only gave audience to his friends, but if the count of the palace told him of any suit in which his judgment was necessary, he had the parties brought before him forthwith, heard the case, and gave his decision, just as if he were sitting in the judgment seat. This was not the only business that he transacted at this time, but he performed any duty of the day whatever, whether he had to attend to the matter himself, or to give commands concerning it to his officers.

25   Charles had the gift of ready and fluent speech, and could express whatever he had to say with the utmost clearness. He was not satisfied merely with command of his native language, but gave attention to the study of foreign ones, and in particular was such a

---

15   Leading Christian theologian of the late fourth and early fifth centuries.

master of Latin that he could speak it as well as his native tongue, but he could understand Greek better than he could speak it. He was so eloquent, indeed, that he might have passed for a teacher of eloquence. He most zealously cultivated the liberal arts, held those who taught them in great esteem, and conferred great honors upon them. He took lessons in grammar from the deacon Peter of Pisa, at that time an aged man. Another deacon, Albin of Britain, surnamed Alcuin, a man of Saxon extraction, who was the greatest scholar of the day, was his teacher in other branches of learning. The king spent much time and labor with him studying rhetoric, dialectic,[16] and especially astronomy; he learned to reckon, and used to investigate the motions of the heavenly bodies most curiously, with an intelligent scrutiny. He also tried to write, and used to keep tablets and blanks in bed under his pillow, so in leisure hours he might accustom his hand to form the letters; however, as he did not begin his efforts in due season, but late in life, they met with ill success.

26   He cherished with the greatest fervor and devotion the principles of the Christian religion, which had been instilled into him from infancy. Hence it was that he built the beautiful church at Aix-la-Chapelle, which he adorned with gold and silver and lamps, and with rails and doors of solid brass. He had the columns and marbles for this structure brought from Rome and Ravenna,[17] for he could not find such as were suitable elsewhere. He was a constant worshipper at this church as long as his health permitted, going morning and evening, even after nightfall, besides attending mass, and he took care that all the services there conducted should be administered with the utmost possible propriety, very often warning the sacristans not to let any improper or unclean thing be brought into the building or remain in it. He provided it with a great number of sacred vessels of gold and silver and with such a quantity of clerical robes that not even the doorkeepers who fill the humblest office in the church were obliged to wear their everyday clothes when in the exercise of their duties. He was at great pains to improve the church reading and the singing of psalms, for he was well skilled in both, although he neither read in public nor sang, except in a low tone and with others.

27   He was very forward in relieving the poor, and in that wholly voluntary generosity which the Greeks call alms, so much so that he not only made a point of giving in his own country and his own kingdom, but when he discovered that there were Christians living in poverty in Syria, Egypt, and Africa, at Jerusalem, Alexandria, and Carthage, he had compassion for their needs, and used to send money over the seas to them. The reason that he zealously strove to make friends with kings beyond the seas was that he might get help and relief to the Christians living under their rule. He cherished the Church of St. Peter the Apostle at Rome above all other holy and sacred places, and heaped its treasury with a vast wealth of gold, silver, and precious stones. He sent great and countless gifts to the popes, and throughout his whole reign the wish that he had nearest at heart was to re-establish the ancient authority of the city of Rome under his care and by his influence, and to defend and protect the Church of St. Peter, and to beautify and enrich it out of his own resources above all other churches. Although he held it in such veneration, he only went to Rome to pay his vows and make his supplications 4 times during the whole 47 years that he reigned.

28   When he made his last journey there,[18] he also had other ends in view. The Romans[19] had inflicted many injuries upon the Pontiff Leo, tearing out his eyes and cutting out his tongue, so that he had been compelled to call upon the king for help. Charles accordingly went to Rome, to set in order the affairs of the church, which were in great confusion, and passed the whole winter there. It was then that he received the titles of Emperor and Augustus, to which he at first had such an aversion that he declared that he would not have set foot in the church the day that they were conferred, although it was a great feast day, if he

---

16   I.e., the art of rational argument.
17   Ravenna had been the residence of the Roman emperors in the West in the fifth century.
18   In 800.
19   I.e., the inhabitants of the city of Rome.

could have foreseen the design of the pope. He bore very patiently with the jealousy which the Roman emperors showed upon his taking these titles, for they took this step very ill; and by dint of frequent embassies and letters, in which he addressed them as brothers, he made their haughtiness yield to his magnanimity, a quality in which he was unquestionably much their superior.

29   It was after he received the imperial title that, finding the laws of his people very defective (the Franks have two sets of laws, very different in many particulars), he decided to add what was wanting, to reconcile the discrepancies, and to correct what was vicious and wrongly cited in them. However, he went no further in this matter than to supplement the laws with a few capitularies,[20] and those were imperfect; but he caused the unwritten laws of all the tribes that came under his rule to be compiled and reduced to writing. He also had the old barbarous songs that celebrate the deeds and wars of the ancient kings written out for transmission to posterity. He began a grammar of his native language. He gave the months names in his own tongue, in place of the Latin and barbarous names by which they were formerly known among the Franks. He likewise designated the winds by 12 appropriate names; there were hardly more than 4 distinctive ones in use before. He called January, Wintarmanoth; February, Hornung; March, Lentzinmanoth; April, Ostarmanoth; May, Winnemanoth; June, Brachmanoth; July, Heuvimanoth; August, Aranmanoth; September, Witumanoth; October, Windumemanoth; November, Herbistmanoth; December, Heilagmanoth. He styled the winds as follows; Subsolanus, Ostroniwint; Eurus, Ostsundroni: Euroauster, Sundostroni; Auster, Sundroni; Austro-Africus, Sundwestroni; Africus, Westsundroni; Zephyrus, Westroni; Caurus, Westnordroni; Circius, Nordwestroni; Septentrio, Nordroni; Aquilo, Nordostroni; Vulturnus, Ostnordroni.

30   Toward the close of his life, when he was broken by ill health and old age, he summoned Louis, king of Aquitania, his only surviving son by Hildegard, and gathered together all the chief men of the whole kingdom of the Franks in a solemn assembly. He appointed Louis, with their unanimous consent, to rule with himself over the whole kingdom, and constituted him heir to the imperial title.[21] Placing the diadem upon his son's head, he bade him be proclaimed Emperor and Augustus. This step was hailed by all present with great favor, for it really seemed as if God had prompted him to it for the kingdom's good; it increased the king's dignity, and struck no little terror into foreign nations. After sending his son back to Aquitania, although weak from age he set out to hunt, as usual, near his palace at Aix-la-Chapelle, and passed the rest of the autumn hunting, returning there about the first of November. While wintering there, he was seized, in the month of January, with a high fever, and took to his bed. As soon as he was taken sick, he prescribed for himself abstinence from food, as he always used to do in case of fever, thinking that the disease could be driven off, or at least mitigated, by fasting. Besides the fever, he suffered from a pain in the side, which the Greeks called pleurisy. But he still persisted in fasting, and in keeping up his strength only by drinks taken at very long intervals. He died on January 28, the seventh day from the time he took to his bed, at nine o'clock in the morning, after partaking of the holy communion, the seventy-second year of his age and the forty-seventh of his reign.

31   His body was washed and cared for in the usual manner, and was then carried to the church, and interred amid the greatest lamentations of all the people. There was some question at first about where to lay him because in his lifetime he had given no directions as to his burial; but at length all agreed that he could nowhere be more honorably entombed than in the very church that he had built in the town at his own expense, for the love of God and our Lord Jesus Christ, and in honor of the holy and eternal Virgin, his mother. He was buried there the same day that he died, and a gilded arch was erected above his tomb with his image and an inscription. The words of the inscription were as follows: "In this tomb lies the body

20   Legal pronoucements on various issues.
21   In 813.

of Charles, the great and orthodox emperor, who gloriously extended the kingdom of the Franks, and reigned prosperously for 47 years. He died at the age of more than seventy, in the year of our Lord 814, the seventh Indiction,[22] on the twenty-eighth day of January."

32  Very many omens had foretold his approaching end, a fact that he had recognized as well as others. Eclipses both of the sun and moon were very frequent during the last three years of his life, and a black spot was visible on the sun for the space of seven days. The gallery between the church and the palace, which he had built at great pains and labor, fell in sudden ruin to the ground on the day of the Ascension of our Lord. The wooden bridge over the Rhine at Mayence, which he had caused to be constructed with admirable skill, at the cost of ten years' hard work, so that it seemed as if it might last forever, was so completely consumed in three hours by an accidental fire that not a single splinter of it was left, except what was under water. Moreover, one day in his last campaign into Saxony against Godfred, king of the Danes, Charles himself saw a ball of fire fall suddenly from the heavens with a great light, just as he was leaving camp before sunrise to set out on the march. It rushed across the clear sky from right to left, and everybody was wondering what was the meaning of the sign, when the horse which he was riding gave a sudden plunge, head foremost, and fell, and threw him to the ground so heavily that his cloak buckle was broken and his sword belt shattered, and after his servants had hastened to him and relieved him of his arms, he could not rise without their assistance. He happened to have a javelin in his hand when he was thrown, and this was struck from his grasp with such force that it was found lying at a distance of 20 feet or more from the spot. Again, the palace at Aix-la-Chapelle frequently trembled, the roofs of whatever buildings he lived in kept up a continual crackling noise, the church in which he was afterwards buried was struck by lightning, and the gilded ball that adorned the pinnacle of the roof was shattered by the thunderbolt and hurled upon the bishop's house next

door. In this same church, on the margin of the cornice that ran around the interior, between the upper and lower tiers or arches, a legend was inscribed in red letters, stating who was the builder of the church, the last words of which were *Charles, Princeps*.[23] The year that he died it was remarked by some, a few months before his death, that the letters of the word *Princeps* were so effaced as to be no longer decipherable. But Charles despised, or pretended to despise, all these omens, as having no reference whatever to him.

33  It had been his intention to make a will, so he might give some share in the inheritance to his daughters and the children of his concubines, but it was begun too late and could not be finished. Three years before his death, however, he made a division of his treasure, money, clothes, and other movable goods in the presence of his friends and servants, and called them to witness it, so their voices might ensure the ratification of the disposition thus made. He had a summary drawn up of his wishes regarding this distribution of his property, the terms and text of which are as follows:

"In the name of the Lord God, the Almighty Father, Son, and Holy Ghost. This is the inventory and division dictated by the most glorious and most pious Lord Charles, Emperor Augustus, in the 811th year of the Incarnation of our Lord Jesus Christ, in the 43rd year of his reign in France and 37th in Italy, the 11th of his empire, and the 4th Indiction, which considerations of piety and prudence have determined him, and the favor of God enabled him, to make of his treasures and money ascertained this day to be in his treasure chamber. In this division he especially desires to provide not only that the largess of alms which Christians usually make of their possessions shall be made for himself in due course and order out of his wealth, but also that his heirs shall be free from all doubt, and know clearly what belongs to them, and be able to share their property by suitable partition without litigation or strife. With this intention and to this end he first divided all his substance and movable goods ascertained to be in his treasure chamber on the day

---

22  A cycle of fifteen years.
23  *Princeps* was a title held by Roman emperors, beginning with Augustus.

aforesaid in gold, silver, precious stones, and royal ornaments into three lots, and has subdivided and set off two of the said lots into 21 parts, leaving the third undivided. The first two lots have been thus subdivided into 21 parts because there are in his kingdom 21 recognized metropolitan cities,[24] and in order that each archbishopric may receive by way of alms, at the hands of his heirs and friends, one of the said parts, and that the archbishop who shall then administer its affairs shall take the part given to it, and share the same with his suffragans[25] in such manner that one third shall go to the church, and the remaining two-thirds be divided among the suffragans. The 21 parts into which the first two lots are to be distributed, according to the number of recognized metropolitan cities, have been set apart from one another, and each has been put aside by itself in a box labeled with the name of the city for which it was destined. The names of the cities to which these alms or largess are to be sent are as follows: Rome, Ravenna, Milan, Friuli, Grado, Cologne, Mayence, Salzburg, Trèves, Sens, Besançon, Lyons, Rouen, Rheims, Arles, Vienne, Moutiers-en-Tarantaise, Embrun, Bordeaux, Tours, and Bourges. The third lot, which he wishes to be kept undivided, is to be bestowed as follows: while the first two lots are to be divided into the parts aforesaid, and set aside under seal, the third lot shall be employed for the owner's daily needs, as property which he shall be under no obligation to part with in order to fulfill any vow, and this as long as he shall be in the flesh, or consider it necessary for his use. But upon his death, or voluntary renunciation of the affairs of this world, this said lot shall be added to the aforesaid 21 parts; the second shall be assigned to his sons and daughters, and to the sons and daughters of his sons, to be distributed among them in just and equal partition; the third, in accordance with the custom common among Christians, shall be devoted to the poor; and the fourth shall go to the support of the male and female servants on duty in the palace. It is his wish that to this said third lot of the whole amount, which consists, as well as the rest, of gold and silver, shall be added all the vessels and utensils of brass, iron, and other metals, together with the arms, clothing, and other movable goods, costly and cheap, adapted to diverse uses, such as hangings, coverlets, carpets, woolen stuffs, leather articles, pack-saddles, and whatsoever shall be found in his treasure chamber and wardrobe at that time, in order that thus the parts of the said lots may be augmented, and the alms distributed reach more persons. He ordains that his chapel—that is to say, its church property, as well that which he has provided and collected as that which came to him by inheritance from his father—shall remain entire, and not be disserviced by any partition whatever. If, however, any vessels, books, or other articles are found therein which are certainly known not to have been given by him to the said chapel, whoever wants them shall have them on paying their value at a fair estimation. He likewise commands that the books which he has collected in his library in great numbers shall be sold for fair prices to such as want them, and the money received therefrom be given to the poor. It is well known that among his other property and treasures there are three silver tables, and one very large and massive golden one. He directs and commands that the square silver table, upon which there is a representation of the city of Constantinople, shall be sent to the church of St. Peter the Apostle at Rome, with the other gifts to be sent there; that the round one, adorned with a delineation of the city of Rome, shall be given to the bishopric of the church at Ravenna; that the third, which far surpasses the other two in weight and in beauty of workmanship, and is made in three circles, showing the plan of the whole universe, drawn with skill and delicacy, shall go, together with the golden table, the fourth mentioned above, to increase that lot which is to be devoted to his heirs and to alms.

This deed, and the dispositions thereof, he has made and appointed in the presence of the bishops, abbots, and counts able to be present, whose names are hereto subscribed: Bishops—Hildebald, Ricolf, Arno, Wolfar, Bernoin, Laidrad, John, Theodulf, Jesse, Heito, Waltgaud. Abbots—Fredugis, Adalung,

---

24   I.e., cities with archbishops.
25   Bishops subordinate to an archbishop.

Angilbert, Irmino. Counts—Walacho, Meginher, Otulf, Stephen, Unruoch, Burchard, Meginhard, Hatto, Rihwin, Edo, Ercangar, Gerold, Bero, Hildiger, Rocculf."

Charles's son Louis, who by the grace of God succeeded him, after examining this summary, took pains to fulfill all its conditions most religiously as soon as possible after his father's death.

# 31

# THE DOOMS OF KING ALFRED

King Alfred the Great (871-899) lived in challenging times. Rome's political control over its province of Britain had ended centuries before his reign, and had been replaced by seven Anglo-Saxon kingdoms, of which Alfred's kingdom of Wessex was one. However, in Alfred's day Norse invaders had toppled six of these kingdoms, leaving Alfred as the only Anglo-Saxon, or English, king. Alfred began the long process of reconquering England from the Norse. This process ended in a unified English kingdom, although Alfred did not live to see it. Alfred's "dooms," or laws, written in Anglo-Saxon (an early form of English, although as intelligible to the modern English speaker as, say, Swedish) were probably produced in about the middle of his reign.

---

The Lord spoke these words to Moses, and thus said, "I am the Lord your God. I led you out of the land of the Egyptians, and out of their bondage.

1 Do not love other, strange gods above me.
2 Do not utter my name idly, for you shall not be guiltless towards me if you utter my name idly.
3 Remember to hallow the restday.[1] Work six days for yourselves, and on the seventh rest. For in six days Christ made the heavens and the earth, the seas, and all creatures that are in them, and rested on the seventh day, and therefore the Lord hallowed it.
4 Honor your father and your mother whom the Lord has given you, so you may be the longer living on earth.
5 Do not kill.
6 Do not commit adultery.

7 Do not steal.
8 Do not speak false witness.
9 Do not covet your neighbor's goods unjustly.
10 Do not make for yourself gold or silver gods...."[2]

[A number of specific laws follow, as well as a recital of how Jesus came to earth not to break the commandments, but increase them, and how the apostles had spread his teaching to other nations, quoting the New Testament.]

After this, it transpired that many nations received the faith of Christ. Then there were many synods[3] of holy bishops and also of other exalted witan[4] assembled throughout the earth, and also among them English after they had received the faith of Christ. They then ordained, out of that mercy which Christ had taught, that secular lords, with their permission,

---

1 I.e., the sabbath.
2 The source up to this point is a version of Old Testament, Exodus 20.1-17.
3 I.e., church councils.
4 I.e., counsellors.

might without sin take for almost every misdeed, for the first offense, the money compensation which they then ordained, except in cases of treachery against a lord, to which they dared not declare any mercy because almighty God adjudged none to them who despised him, nor did Christ the son of God adjudge any to the one who sold him to death,[5] and he commanded that a lord should be loved as oneself. They then in many synods ordained a compensation for many human misdeeds, and they wrote in many synod-books one doom at one place, another doom at another.

I, then, King Alfred, gathered these dooms together and commanded many of them which our forefathers held, which seemed good to me, to be written down; many of those which did not seem good to me I rejected, by the counsel of my *witan*,[6] and commanded them to be obeyed in another way, for I dare not set down in writing much of my own, for it is unknown to me what might please those who come after us. So I have gathered together here those dooms which seem to me the most just, from whatever time I found them—from the days of my kinsman Ine,[7] of Offa king of the Mercians,[8] or of Aethelberht,[9] who first among the English received baptism— and I have rejected others.

I, then, Alfred, king of the West Saxons, have shown these to my entire *witan*, and it seemed good to them for them all to be obeyed.

1   To start, we teach that it is most needful that every man warily keep his oath and his pledge. If anyone is constrained to either of these wrongfully, either to promise treason against his lord, or to any unlawful aid, then is it more just to belie one's engagement than to fulfill it. But if he pledges himself to that which it is lawful to fulfill and in that belies himself, let him sub-

missively deliver up his weapon and his goods to the keeping of his friends, and be in prison for 40 days on a king's estate. Let him there suffer whatever the bishop may prescribe to him, and let his kinsmen feed him, if he himself has no food. If he has no kinsmen and no food, let the king's reeve[10] feed him. If he must be forced to come, and will not come otherwise, and if they bind him, let him forfeit his weapons and his property. If he is slain, let him lie uncompensated. If he flees before the time ends, and he is taken, let him be in prison 40 days, as he should have been before. But if he escapes, let him be outlawed, and be excommunicated from all Christ's churches. If, however, there is a secular security for him, he is to pay for the violation of the security as the law directs him, and for the violation of the pledge as his confessor may prescribe to him.

2   If anyone, for whatever crime, seeks refuge in any of the monasteries to which the king's food rent is incident, or to some other privileged community which is worthy of reverence, let him have a space of three days to protect himself, unless he is willing to come to terms. If during this space, anyone harms him by blows, or by bonds, or wounds him, let him make amends for each of these according to regular usage, with *wergeld*[11] as with a fine, and to the brotherhood[12] 120 shillings, as compensation for the violation of sanctuary, and let him forfeit his own claim against the criminal.

3   If anyone breaks the security given by the king, let him make compensation for the charge, as the law directs him, and for the breach of the security, with 5 pounds of pure pennies. For the breach of security or protection given by an archbishop, let him make compensation with 3 pounds; for any other bishop or an ealdorman,[13] the compensation is to be 2 pounds.

---

5   I.e., Judas, who betrayed Jesus for a gift of silver.

6   These counsellors would have included the chief landed magnates of the kingdom and Alfred's military retainers.

7   King of Wessex (688-726).

8   Mercia was another of the Anglo-Saxon kingdoms. Offa was king 757-796.

9   King of the Anglo-Saxon kingdom of Kent (560-616).

10   An official, such as a bailiff.

11   *Wergeld* was the price one had to pay the kin of a person one has slain in order to have peace.

12   I.e., the monastic community.

13   The king's representative in the shire, the territories into which the kingdom was divided. The ealdorman was generally an aristocrat. He would soon be replaced in the shires by the sheriff.

4   If anyone plots against the king's life, himself or by harboring exiles or his men,[14] let him be liable for his life and in all that he has. If he desires to prove himself true, let him do so according to the king's *wergeld*.[15] So also we ordain for all degrees, whether *ceorl*[16] or *earl*.[17] As to him who plots against his lord's life, let him be liable, for his life and all that he has, or let him prove himself true according to his lord's *wergeld*.

5   We also ordain this sanctuary for every church which has been blessed by a bishop: if a man under a feud flees to and reaches one, no one shall drag him out for 7 days if, despite hunger, he can live, unless he fights his way out. But if anyone does so, then let him be liable to pay compensation for violation of the security given by the king and of the church's sanctuary—and more if he commits more wrong there. If the brethren have further need of their church, let them keep him in another house, and let that not have more doors than the church. Let the church's chief take care that no one gives him food during this time. If he himself is willing to deliver up his weapons to his foes, let them keep him 30 days, and let them give notice of him to his kinsmen. It is also church sanctuary if any man seeks a church for any offenses which have not yet been discovered, and there confesses himself in God's name; it is to be half forgiven. As to one who steals on a Sunday, or at Christmas, or at Easter, or on Holy Thursday in Rogation days;[18] for each of these we will that the compensation be double, as during the fast of Lent.[19]

6   If anyone steals anything in a church, let him pay the simple compensation and the fine such as belongs to that compensation, and let the hand with which he did it be struck off. If he wills to redeem the hand, and that is allowed him, let him pay as appropriate for his *wergeld*.

7   If anyone fights in the king's hall, or draws his weapon, and is taken, let it be in the king's decision: either death or life, as he may be willing to grant him.

If he escapes, and is taken again, let him pay compensation for himself according to his *wergeld*, and pay a fine for the offense as well, according to what he has done.

8 If anyone carries off a nun from a monastery without the king's or the bishop's leave, let him pay 120 shillings, half to the king, half to the bishop and the lord of the nun's church. If she lives longer than he who carried her off, let her not have anything of his property. If she bears a child, let that child not have any more of the property than the mother. If anyone slays her child, let him pay to the king the maternal kindred's share of the compensation; let the share of the paternal kindred be given to them.

9   If a man kills a woman with her child, while the child is in her, let him pay for the woman her full *wergeld* and pay for the child half a *wergeld*, according to the *wergeld* of the father's kin. Let the fine be always 60 shillings, until the simple compensation rises to 30 shillings. After the simple compensation has risen to that, let the fine be 120 shillings. Formerly there was a distinct fine for a gold-thief, and a mare-thief, and a bee-thief, and many fines were greater than others; now all are alike, except for a man-thief, which is 120 shillings.

10   If a man lies with the wife of a 1,200-*wergeld* man, let him make compensation with the husband with one 120 shillings. To a 600-*wergeld* man, let him make compensation with 100 shillings. To a *ceorl*, let him make compensation with 40 shillings.

11   If a man seizes hold of the breast of a *ceorl* woman, let him make compensation to her with 5 shillings. If he throws her down and does not lie with her, let him make compensation with 10 shillings. If he lies with her, let him make compensation with 60 shillings. If another man had lain with her before, then let the compensation be half that. If she is charged therewith, let her clear herself with 60 hides[20] or forfeit half the

---

14   Presumably the king's men who are out of favor.
15   I.e., swearing an oath to pay the *wergeld* of the king.
16   A free peasant.
17   The highest-ranking aristocrat.
18   The week before Easter.
19   The 40 days before Easter.
20   A unit of land.

compensation. If this befalls a woman more nobly born, let the compensation increase according to her *wergeld*.

12  If a man burns or cuts down another's wood without permission, let him pay for every great tree with 5 shillings, and afterwards for each tree, as many of them as may be, with 5 pence; the fine will be 30 shillings.

13  If at their common work one man slays another unwillfully,[21] let the tree be given to the kindred, and let them have it from the land within 30 days or let him who owns the wood take possession of it.

14  If a man is born dumb or deaf, so that he cannot acknowledge or confess his offenses, let the father make compensation for his misdeeds.

15  If a man fights or draws his weapon before an archbishop, let him make compensation with 150 shillings. If this happens before another bishop or an ealdorman, let him make compensation with 100 shillings.

16  If a man steals a cow or a stud-mare, and drives off the foal or the calf, let him pay with a shilling for the foal or calf, and for the mothers according to their worth.

17   If anyone commits his small one to another's keeping, and the small one dies during such keeping, let him who feeds him prove himself innocent of treachery, if anyone accuses him of anything.

18   If anyone, with lewd intent, seizes a nun either by her clothing or by her breast without her permission, let the compensation be double, as we have before ordained concerning a lay woman. If a betrothed woman commits fornication, if she is of *ceorl*ish degree, let compensation be made to the person offering security with 60 shillings, and let it be in livestock, cattle only, and in that let no human being be given; if she is a 600-*wergeld* woman, let him pay 100 shillings to the person offering security; if she is a 1,200-*wergeld* woman, let him make compensation to the person offering security with 120 shillings.

19  If anyone lends his weapon to another so he may kill someone therewith, they may join together if they wish in paying the *wergeld*. If they do not join together, let him who lent the weapon pay a third of the *wergeld* and a third of the fine. If he is willing to justify himself, that he knew of no ill-intention in the loan, he may do so. If a sword-polisher receives another man's weapon to polish, or a smith receives a man's material, let them both return it as sound as either of them received it, unless either of them had before agreed that he should not be liable for compensation in this regard.

20  If a man entrusts cattle to another man's monk,  without permission of the monk's lord, and it escapes, let him who owned it, forfeit it.

21  If a priest kills another man, let everything in his home which he had bought be surrendered, and let the bishop secularize him;[22] then let him be surrendered from the church, unless his lord wishes to pay for his *wergeld*.

23  If a dog tears or bites a man, for the first misdeed let 6 shillings be paid. If the owner gives the dog food, he shall pay 12 shillings for the second time, and for the third, 30 shillings. If, in any of these misdeeds, the dog dies, let this compensation nevertheless take place. If the dog does more misdeeds, and the owner keeps him, let him make compensation for wounds according to the full *wergeld*.

24  If an ox wounds a man, let the ox be surrendered or the owner make compensation.

25   If a man rapes a *ceorl*'s female slave, let him make compensation to the *ceorl* with 5 shillings, and let the fine be 60 shillings. If a male slave rapes a female slave, let him make compensation with his testicles.

26  If a man rapes an underage woman, let the compensation be that for a full-grown person.

27  If a man without paternal relatives fights and slays a man, but he has maternal relatives, let them pay a third of the *wergeld*, and his associates a third, and for the other third, let him flee. If he has no maternal relatives, let his associates pay half; for the other half let him flee.

28  If a man kills a man thus circumstanced—that he

---

21  By allowing a tree to fall on him.
22  I.e., strip him of the status of priest.

has no relatives—let half be paid to the king, half to his associates.

29  If anyone with a band of men slays an unoffending 200-*wergeld* man, let him who acknowledges the death-blow pay *wergeld* and compensation, and let everyone who was of the band pay 30 shillings as compensation.

30  If it is a 600-*wergeld* man, let every man pay 60 shillings as compensation, and the slayer pays the *wergeld* and the full fine.

31  If it is a 1,200-*wergeld* man, let each of them pay 120 shillings, and the slayer pays *wergeld* and fine. If a band of men does this, and afterwards denies it on oath, let them all be accused, and let them then all together pay the *wergeld* and all pay one fine such as pertains to the *wergeld*.

32  If a man commits public slander and it is proven against him, let him make compensation with no lighter thing than having his tongue cut out, which must not be redeemed at any cheaper rate than is estimated in accordance with his *wergeld*.

33  If anyone accuses another on account of a pledge sworn before God, and wishes to complain that that person has not fulfilled any of those promises which he gave him, let the plaintiff make his announcement in 4 churches, and if the other wishes to prove himself innocent, let him do so[23] in 12 churches.

34  It is also directed that traders bring the men whom they take up with them before the king's reeve at the public meeting, and let it be stated how many of them there are; let them take such men with them as they may be able afterwards to present for justice at the public meeting, and when they need to take more men up with them on their journey, let them always declare it to the king's reeve, in presence of the meeting, as often as they need to.

35  If anyone binds an unoffending *ceorl*, let him make compensation with 10 shillings. If anyone scourges him, let him make compensation with 20 shillings. If he imprisons him, let him make compensation with 30 shillings. If, in order to insult him, he shaves the *ceorl*'s head, let him make compensation

with 10 shillings. If without binding him, he shaves him like a priest,[24] let him make compensation with 30 shillings. If he shaves off his beard, let him make compensation with 20 shillings. If he binds him, and then shaves him like a priest, let him make compensation with 60 shillings.

36  It is moreover decreed that if a man has a spear over his shoulder, and any man impales himself on it, that he pay the compensation without the fine. If he impales himself before the man's face, let him pay the *wergeld*. If he is accused of intending the deed, let him clear himself in accordance with the fine and with that let the fine be satisfied if the point of the spear is three fingers higher than the hindmost part of the shaft; if the point and the hindmost part of the shaft are both on a level, that is to be considered safe.

37  If a man from one district wishes to seek a lord in another, let him do it with the knowledge of the ealdorman whom he before served in his shire. If he does it without his knowledge, let him who receives him as his man pay 120 shillings as fine; let him, however, pay half to the king in the shire where he served before and half in that into which he comes. If he has done any wrong where he was before, let him who has received him as his man make compensation for it, and let the fine to the king be 120 shillings.

38  If a man fights before one of the king's ealdormen in the public meeting, let him make compensation with *wergeld* and fine, as it is right, and before doing so, pay 120 shillings to the ealdorman as compensation. If he disturbs the public meeting by drawing his weapon, 120 shillings to the ealdorman as fine. If anything of this happens before a lieutenant of the king's ealdorman, or a king's priest, 30 shillings as fine.

39  If anyone fights in a *ceorl*'s house, let him make compensation to the *ceorl* with 6 shillings. If he draws his weapon and does not fight, let it be half that. If, however, either of these happens to a 600-*wergeld* man, let it increase to threefold the compensation due to a *ceorl*; if it happens to a 1,200-*wergeld* man, the compensation is to be double that due to the 600-*wergeld* man.

---

23  Presumably by swearing an oath.
24  A mark of clerical status was the tonsure, a shaved area at the top of the head.

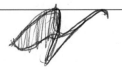

40   Forced entry into the king's residence shall be 120 shillings. An archbishop's shall be 90 shillings; any other bishop's, and an ealdorman's, 60 shillings; a 1,200-*wergeld* man's, 30 shillings; a 600-*wergeld* man's, 15 shillings. A *ceorl*'s, 5 shillings. If any of this happens when the army is summoned, or during the fast of Lent, let the compensation be double. If anyone during Lent ignores holy law among the people[25] without permission, let him make compensation with 120 shillings.

41   Regarding the man who has bookland[26] which his kindred left him, we ordain that he must not give it away from his kindred if there is a document or witness to the effect that doing so was forbidden by those men who first acquired the land and by those who gave it to him; and then let this be declared[27] in the presence of the king and of the bishop, before his kinsmen.

42   We also command that the man who knows his foe to be at home not fight before he demands justice from him. If he has such power that he can beset his foe, and besiege him within, let him keep him within for 7 days, and not attack him if he will remain within. And then, after 7 days, if he surrenders, and gives up his weapons, let him be kept unharmed for 30 days, and let notice concerning him be given to his kinsmen and his friends. If, however, he flees to a church, then let it be handled according to the sanctity of the church, as we have before said above. But if he does not have sufficient power to besiege him, let him ride to the ealdorman, and ask him for help. If he will not aid him, let him ride to the king before he fights. In like manner also, if a man comes upon his foe, and he did not before know him to be at home, if he is willing to give up his weapons, let him be kept for 30 days, and let notice concerning him be given to his friends; if he will not give up his weapons, then he may attack him. If he is willing to surrender, and to give up his weapons, and anyone after that attacks him, let that person pay *wergeld* as well as compensation for wounds, according to what he has done, and

he shall pay the fine and let him forfeit his right to avenge his kin. We also declare that a man may fight for his lord should anyone attack his lord, without incurring the feud; thus also may a lord fight for his man. In the same way, a man may fight for his born kinsman, if a man attacks the kinsman wrongfully, except against his lord—that we do not allow. And a man may fight without incurring the feud if he finds another with his lawful wife, behind closed doors, or under one covering, or with his lawfully-born[28] daughter, or with his lawfully-born sister, or with his mother, who was given to his father as his lawful wife.

43   Let these days be given to all freemen, but not to slaves or the unfree: 12 days at Christmas, and the day on which Christ overcame the devil, and the commemoration day of St. Gregory, and the 7 days before Easter and 7 days after, and 1 day at the feast of St. Peter and St. Paul, and during the harvest the whole week before the feast of St. Mary, and 1 day at the celebration of All Saints. The 4 Wednesdays in Lent are to be given to all slaves for them to sell to anyone whom they choose whatever anyone has given them in God's name, or what they in any of their own time may have deserved to receive.

44   For compensation of a head wound: if the bones are both pierced, let 30 shillings be given. If the outer bone is pierced, let 15 shillings be given as compensation.

45   If within the hair there is a wound an inch long, let 1 shilling be given as compensation. If outside the hair there is a wound an inch long, 2 shillings as compensation.

46   If either ear is struck off, let 30 shillings be given as compensation. If the hearing is impaired, so that he cannot hear, let 60 shillings be given as compensation.

47   If a man knocks out another's eye, let him pay him 66 shillings, 6 pennies, and a third of a penny as compensation. If it remains in the head, and he cannot see anything with it, let one third of the compensation be retained.

---

25   I.e., publicly.
26   Land granted (especially by the king) with a written document.
27   By whoever is contesting the land.
28   I.e., legitimate.

48   If a man strikes off another's nose, let him make compensation with 60 shillings.

49   If a man knocks out another's tooth in the front of his head, let him make compensation for it with 8 shillings; if it is the canine tooth, let 4 shillings be paid as compensation. A man's grinder is worth 15 shillings.

50   If a man strikes another's cheeks so that they are broken, let him make compensation with 15 shillings. If a man's chin-bone is broken, let 12 shillings be paid as compensation.

51   If a man's windpipe is pierced, let compensation be made with 12 shillings.

52   If a man's tongue is removed from his head by another man's deeds, that shall be handled in the same ways as eye-compensation.

53   If a man is wounded on the shoulder so that the joint-oil[29] flows out, let compensation be made with 30 shillings.

54   If the arm is broken above the elbow, there shall be 15 shillings as compensation.

55   If both bones of the arm are broken, the compensation is 30 shillings.

56   If the thumb is struck off, for that the compensation shall be 30 shillings. If the nail is struck off, for that the compensation shall be 5 shillings.

57   If the shooting finger[30] is struck off, the compensation is 15 shillings; for its nail it is 4 shillings.

58   If the middlemost finger is struck off, the compensation is 12 shillings, and its nail's compensation is 2 shillings.

59   If the gold finger[31] is struck off, the compensation will be 17 shillings, and for its nail 4 shillings as compensation.

60   If the little finger is struck off, the compensation shall be 9 shillings, and for its nail, 1 shilling, if that is struck off.

61   If a man is wounded in the belly, let 30 shillings be paid him as compensation; if he is wounded right through, for each orifice, 20 shillings.

62   If a man's thigh is pierced, let 30 shillings be paid him as compensation; if it is broken, the compensation is likewise 30 shillings.

63   If the skin is pierced beneath the knee, the compensation shall be 12 shillings; if it is broken beneath the knee, let 30 shillings be paid him as compensation.

64   If the big toe is struck off, let 20 shillings be paid him as compensation; if it is the second toe, let 15 shillings be paid as compensation; if the middlemost toe is struck off, there shall be 9 shillings as compensation; if it is the fourth toe, there shall be 6 shillings as compensation; if the little toe is struck off, let 5 shillings be paid him.

65   If a man is so severely wounded in the genitals that he cannot beget a child, let compensation be made to him for that with 80 shillings.

66   If a man's arm, with the hand, is entirely cut off before the elbow, let compensation be made for it with 80 shillings. For every wound before the hair, and before the sleeve, and beneath the knee, the compensation is doubled.

67   If the loin is maimed, there shall be 60 shillings as compensation; if it is pierced, let 15 shillings be paid as compensation; if it is pierced through, then there shall be 30 shillings as compensation.

68   If a man is wounded in the shoulder, let compensation be made with 80 shillings, if the man is alive.

69   If a man maims another's hand outwardly,[32] let 20 shillings be paid him as compensation if he can be healed; if half of it flies off, then 40 shillings shall be paid as compensation.

70   If a man breaks another's rib, but the skin is unbroken, let 10 shillings be paid as compensation; if the skin is broken and the bone is taken out, let 15 shillings be paid as compensation.

71   If a man strikes out another's eye or his hand or his foot off, like compensation goes to all: 6 pennies and 66 shillings and the third part of a penny.

72   If a man's skin is struck off at the knee, there shall be 80 shillings as compensation.

73   If a man fractures another's shoulder, let 20 shillings be paid him as compensation.

---

29   I.e., synovia, a liquid which lubricates the joint.
30   I.e., the forefinger.
31   I.e., ring finger.
32   The sense here is unclear.

74   If it is broken inwardly, and the bone is taken out, let an additional 15 shillings be paid as its compensation.

75   If a man ruptures the great sinew,[33] if it can be healed so that it is sound, let 12 shillings be paid as compensation. If the man is lame on account of the wounded sinew and he cannot be cured, let 30 shillings be paid as compensation.

76   If the small sinew[34] is ruptured, let 6 shillings be paid him as compensation.

77   If a man ruptures the tendons on another's neck, and wounds them so severely that he has no power over them, and lives despite such wounding, let 100 shillings be given him as compensation, unless the *witan* decrees to him a greater and more just compensation.

33   I.e., the Achilles tendon?
34   Presumably some tendon or muscle in the foot.

# 32

## GREGORY VII, HENRY IV, AND THE GERMAN BISHOPS, *DOCUMENTS*

In February, 1075, Pope Gregory VII forbade lay investiture, that is, the investing of bishops and other clergy with church office by lay people. This declaration came in the midst of a long-simmering dispute over who should be the bishop of Milan in northern Italy. When Gregory had been elected pope in 1073, the Holy Roman Emperor, Henry IV, distracted by political problems in Germany, promised to accept Gregory's decision about the bishopric. After Gregory's announcement of 1075, Henry renewed his support for a candidate who could be expected to be loyal to him, in opposition to another candidate supported by the papacy. Henry's move brought the letter labelled 32.2 from Gregory.

---

### 32.1
#### GREGORY VII, THE *DICTATUS PAPAE*

*The* Dictatus Papae *("the statements of the pope") of March, 1075, which survives in the record of Gregory's official correspondence, is of uncertain origin, but it is thought that its statements were meant to be chapter titles for a collection of canon (i.e., church) law which would support the various positions listed.*

That the Roman church was founded by God alone.

That the Roman pontiff[1] alone can with right be called universal.

That he alone can depose or reinstate bishops.

That, in a council, his legate,[2] even if of a lower grade, is above all bishops, and can pass sentence of deposition against them.

That the pope may depose the absent.

That, among other things, we ought not to remain in the same house with those excommunicated by him.

That for him alone is it lawful, according to the needs of the time, to make new laws, to assemble together new congregations, to make an abbey of a canonry;[3] and, on the other hand, to divide a rich bishopric and unite the poor ones.

That he alone may use the imperial insignia.[4]

That all princes shall kiss the feet of the pope alone.

That his name alone shall be recited in the churches.

That this title is unique in the world.

That it may be permitted to him to depose emperors.

---

1  I.e., the pope.
2  I.e., his appointed representative.
3  I.e., a community of secular clergy, that is, clergy who are not governed by a monastic rule.
4  I.e., the symbols of the position of Roman emperor.

That he may be permitted to transfer bishops if need be.

That he has power to ordain a cleric of any church he may wish.

That he who is ordained by him may preside over another church, but may not hold a subordinate position to others, and that such a one may not receive a higher grade from any bishop.

That no synod[5] shall be called a general one without his order.

That no chapter and no book shall be considered canonical without his authority.

That a sentence passed by him may be retracted by no one, and that he himself, alone of all, may retract it.

That he himself may be judged by no one.

That no one shall dare to condemn one who appeals to the apostolic see.[6]

That to the latter should be referred the more important cases of every church.

That the Roman church has never erred, nor will it err to all eternity, the Scriptures bearing witness.

That the Roman pontiff, if he has been canonically ordained, is undoubtedly made a saint by the merits of St. Peter, St. Ennodius, bishop of Pavia, bearing witness, and many holy fathers agreeing with him, as is contained in the decrees of St. Symmachus the pope.

That, by his command and consent, it may be lawful for subordinates to bring accusations.

That he may depose and reinstate bishops without assembling a synod.

That he who is not at peace with the Roman church shall not be considered catholic.[7]

That he may absolve subjects from their fealty to wicked men.

### 32.2
#### LETTER OF GREGORY VII TO HENRY IV, HOLY ROMAN EMPEROR (DECEMBER, 1075)

Bishop Gregory, servant of the servants of God, to King Henry, greeting and apostolic benediction—that is, if he is obedient to the apostolic see as becomes a Christian king. Considering and carefully weighing with what judgment we shall have to render account for the ministry entrusted to us by St. Peter, chief of the apostles, it is with hesitation that we have sent to you the apostolic benediction, for you are said knowingly to exercise fellowship with those excommunicated by a judgment of the apostolic see and by sentence of a synod. If this is true, you know yourself that you may receive the favor neither of the divine nor of the apostolic benediction unless, those who have been excommunicated being first separated from you, and compelled to do penance, you, with condign repentance and satisfaction, seek absolution and indulgence for your transgression. Therefore, we counsel your highness that, if you do feel yourself guilty in this matter, you seek the advice of some canonical bishop with speedy confession, who, with our permission, enjoining on you a proper penance for this fault, shall absolve you and shall endeavor by letter to inform us truly, with your consent, the measure of your penitence.

For the rest it seems strange enough to us that, although you send us so many and such devoted letters, and although your Highness shows such humility through the words of your legates[8]—calling yourself the son of holy mother church and of ourselves, subject in the faith, unique in affection, foremost in devotion—although, finally, you commend yourself with all devotion of sweetness and reverence, you nonetheless in stubborn deeds show yourself contrary to the canonical and apostolic decrees in those matters which the religion of the church enjoins as the chief ones. For, not to mention other things, in the affair of Milan the actual outcome of the matter shows plainly how you carry out—and with what intent you made them—the promises made to us through your mother and through our colleagues the bishops whom we sent to you. And now, indeed, inflicting wound upon wound, contrary to the establishments of the apostolic see, you have given the sees of Fermo and Spoleto—if

---

5  I.e., church council.

6  A "see" is a bishopric. The "apostolic see" is the bishopric of Rome, i.e., the papacy. The term "apostolic" is often used to denote the papacy.

7  Orthodox.

8  I.e., Henry's ambassadors to the pope.

indeed a church could be given or granted by a man—to certain persons not even known to us, whom, unless they are previously well known and proven, it is not lawful even to consecrate.

Since you confess yourself to be a son of the church, it would have become your royal dignity to look more respectfully upon the master of the church—that is, St. Peter, the chief of the apostles. To him, if you are of the Lord's flock, you were given over by the Lord's voice and authority to be fed, Christ himself saying, "Peter, feed my sheep."[9] And again, "To you are given over the keys of the kingdom of Heaven, and whatsoever you shall bind upon earth shall be bound also in Heaven; and whatsoever you shall loose upon earth shall be loosed also in Heaven."[10] Inasmuch as in his seat and apostolic ministration we, however sinful and unworthy, act as the representative of his power, surely he himself has received whatever, through writing or in bare words, you have sent to us. And at the very time when we are either perusing the letters or listening to the voices of those who speak, he himself is discerning, with subtle inspection, in what spirit the instructions were issued. Wherefore your Highness should have seen to it that no defect of good will should have been found towards the apostolic see in your words and messages. And, in those things through which the Christian faith and the state of the church chiefly progress towards eternal salvation, you should not have denied the reverence due, not to us, but to God Almighty, disregarding the fact that the Lord saw fit to say to the apostles and their successors, "Who hears you, hears me; and who scorns you, scorns me."[11] For we know that he who does not refuse to show faithful obedience to God, does not scorn to observe our commands—which we have spoken according to the decrees of the holy fathers—even as if he had heard them from the lips of the apostle himself. For if, out of reverence for the chair of Moses, the Lord ordered the apostles to observe whatever the scribes and Pharisees sitting above them should say, it is not to be doubted but that the apostolic and evangelic teaching, the seat and foundation of which is Christ, should be received—and observed—by the faithful, with full veneration, from the lips of those who have been chosen for the service of preaching.

In this year, at a synod being assembled around the apostolic see over which the heavenly dispensation willed that we should preside, at which, moreover, some of your faithful subjects were present, seeing that the good order of the Christian religion has now for some time been falling away, and that the chief and proper methods of saving souls had long fallen into abeyance and, through the persuasion of the devil had been trampled under foot, we, struck by the danger and the clearly approaching ruin of the Lord's flock, reverted to the decrees and to the teachings of the holy fathers, decreeing nothing new, nothing of our own invention. We decreed that, error being abandoned, the first and only rule of ecclesiastical discipline was again to be followed, and the well-worn way of the saints to be resought. Nor indeed do we know of any other entrance to salvation and eternal life which lies open to the sheep of Christ and their shepherds, except the one which, as we have learned in the gospel and in every page of the divine Scriptures, was shown by Him who said, "I am the door, he who enters through me shall be saved and shall find pasture,"[12] was preached by the apostles and followed by the holy fathers. This decree,[13] moreover, which some, preferring human to divine honors, call an unbearable weight and immense burden, we, however, by a more suitable word, call a necessary truth and light for regaining salvation, and we judge that it should be devoutly received and observed, not only by you and by those of your kingdom, but by all the princes and peoples of the world who confess and cherish Christ, although we much desire—and it would have most become you—that, as you surpass others in glory,

---

9  New Testament, John 21.17.

10  New Testament, Matthew 16.19. Peter is regarded here as the first bishop of Rome, and thus, the first pope.

11  New Testament, Luke 10.16.

12  New Testament, John 10.9.

13  I.e., Gregory's edict against lay investiture.

honor and valor, so you should be superior in your devotion to Christ. Nevertheless, lest these things should seem burdensome beyond measure or wrong to you, we sent word to you through your faithful servants that the changing of an evil custom should not alarm you; that you should send to us wise and religious men from your land, who, if they could, by any reasoning, demonstrate or prove in what, saving the honor of the eternal King and without danger to our soul, we might moderate the decree as passed by the holy fathers, we would yield to their counsels. In this matter, indeed, even if you had not been so amicably admonished by us, it would nevertheless have been only right that you should, by negotiation, have inquired of us in cases where we oppressed you or stood in the way of your prerogatives before you violated apostolic decrees. But of how much worth you consider either our commands or the observance of justice is shown by those things which you afterwards did and had done.

But since, inasmuch as the still long-suffering patience of God invites you to amend your ways, we have hopes that, your understanding being increased, your heart and mind can be bent to the obedience of the mandates of God. We warn you with fatherly love, that, recognizing the dominion of Christ over you, you reflect how dangerous it is to prefer your own honor to His, and that you do not impede, by your present detraction from it, the liberty of the church which He considered worthy to join to Himself as His spouse in celestial union, but that you begin, with faithful devotion, to lend it the aid of your valor, in order that it may best increase to the honor of God Almighty and of St. Peter, by whom also your glory may deserve to be increased. All of which, in return for the victory recently conferred upon you over your enemies, you should recognize to be now most clearly due from you to them, so that, when they reward you with noteworthy prosperity, they may see you the more devout for the benefits granted. And, in order that the fear of God, in whose hand and power is every kingdom and empire, may remain fixed in your heart more deeply

than our admonition, bear in mind what happened to Saul after the victory which, by the prophet's order, he enjoyed, and how he was rebuked by God when he boasted of his victory, not carrying out the commands of that same prophet; but what favor followed David for the merit of humility amid the distinctions of valor.[14]

Finally, we keep silent regarding the things which we have seen and noted in your letter. Nor will we give you a sure reply until your legates, Radbod, Adalbert and Odescalcus, and those whom we sent with them, shall return to us and more fully reveal your will to us in those matters which we entrusted to them to discuss with you.

Given at Rome on the sixth day before the Ides of January, in the 14th indiction.

## 32.3
### LETTER OF HENRY IV TO GREGORY VII
### (JANUARY 24, 1076)

Henry, king not through usurpation but through the holy ordination of God, to Hildebrand,[15] at present not pope but false monk. You have merited such a greeting through your disturbances, inasmuch as there is no grade in the church which you have omitted to make a partaker not of honor but of confusion, not of benediction but of malediction. For, to mention a few outstanding cases out of many, not only have you not feared to lay hands upon the rulers of the holy church, the anointed of the Lord—namely the archbishops, bishops and priests—but you have trodden them under foot like slaves ignorant of what their master is doing. You have won favor from the common herd by crushing them; you have looked upon all of them as knowing nothing, upon yourself alone, moreover, as knowing all things. You have used this knowledge, however, not for edification but for destruction, so that with reason we believe that St. Gregory,[16] whose name you have usurped for yourself, was prophesying concerning you when he said: "The pride of him who is in power increases the more, the greater the number of those sub-

---

14 Referring, respectively, to Old Testament, 1 Samuel 15 and 1 Samuel 16-18.
15 Gregory's name before he became pope.
16 Pope Gregory the Great (590-604).

ject to him, and he thinks that he himself can do more than all." And we, indeed, have endured all this, being eager to guard the honor of the apostolic see. You, however, have understood our humility to be fear, and have not, accordingly, shunned to rise up against the royal power conferred upon us by God, daring to threaten to divest us of it. As if we had received our kingdom from you! As if the kingdom and the empire were in yours and not in God's hand! And this, although our Lord Jesus Christ did call us to the kingdom, He did not, however, call you to the priesthood. For you have ascended by the following steps: by wiles, namely, which the profession of monk abhors, you achieved money; by money, favor; by the sword, the throne of peace.[17] And from the throne of peace you have disturbed peace; inasmuch as you have armed subjects against those in authority over them and inasmuch as you, who were not called, have taught that our bishops called of God are to be despised; inasmuch as you have usurped for laymen the bishops' ministry over their priests, allowing them to depose or condemn those whom they themselves had received as teachers from the hand of God through the laying on of hands of the bishops.[18] On me also who, although unworthy to be among the anointed, has nevertheless been anointed to the kingdom, you have lain your hand. I, who, as the tradition of the holy Fathers teaches, am subject to the  judgment of God alone, and am not to be deposed for any crime unless, God forbid, I should stray from the faith. For the wisdom of the holy fathers committed even Julian the apostate[19] not to themselves, but to God alone, to be judged and to be deposed. For himself the true pope, Peter, also exclaims, "Fear God, honor the king."[20] But you who do not fear God, dishonor in me His appointed one. Wherefore St. Paul, when he has not spared an angel of Heaven if he shall have preached otherwise, has not excepted you also who teach otherwise upon earth. For he says, "If anyone, either I or an angel from Heaven, should preach a gospel other than that which has been preached to you, he shall be damned."[21] Therefore, condemned by this curse and by the judgment of all our bishops and by our own, descend and relinquish the apostolic see which you have usurped. Let another ascend the throne of St. Peter, who shall not practice violence under the cloak of religion, but shall teach the sound doctrine of St. Peter. I, Henry, king by the grace of God, say to you, together with all our bishops: Descend! Descend!

## 32.4

### LETTER OF BISHOPS IN GERMANY TO GREGORY VII (JANUARY 24, 1076)

Siegfried archbishop of Mainz, Udo of Trier, William of Utrecht, Herman of Metz, Henry of Liège, Richert of Verdun, Bido of Touls, Hozeman of Speier, Burchard of Halberstadt, Werner of Strassburg, Burchard of Basel, Otto of Constance, Adalbero of Würzburg, Rupert of Bamberg, Otto of Regensburg, Egilbert of Freising, Ulrich of Eichstaatt, Frederick of Münster, Eilbert of Minden, Hezilo of Hildesheim, Benno of Osnabrück, Eppo of Naumburg, Imadus of Paderborn, Tiedo of Brandenburg, Burchard of Lausanne, Bruno of Verona, to Brother Hildebrand.

Athough it was well known to us, when you first invaded the government of the church, what an unlawful and nefarious thing you, with your well known arrogance, presumed to do contrary to right and justice, we nevertheless thought it best to veil the vicious beginnings of your elevation by a certain excusatory silence. We had hoped that such wicked beginnings would be rectified, and to some degree obliterated, by the probity and zeal of the rest of your reign. But now, as the lamentable state of the universal church proclaims and bemoans, you stubbornly and sadly fulfill the promises of your evil beginnings through the still worse progress of your actions and decrees. For although our Lord and Savior impressed upon His faithful followers the special advantages of peace and charity—in testimony of which too many

---

17　Modern scholarship, one may note, does not support these charges.
18　I.e., the consecration of a priest by a bishop.
19　Julian the apostate (fourth century) was the only pagan Roman emperor after Constantine. He attempted to restore the worship of the gods and to demote Christianity.
20　New Testament, 1 Peter 2.17.
21　New Testament, Galatians 1.8.

proofs exist to be comprised in the extent of a letter—you, on the contrary, striving after profane novelties, delighting more in a widely known than in a good name, being swelled with unheard of pride, have, like a standard-bearer of schism, torn with proud cruelty and cruel pride all the members of the church, which, following the apostle, were enjoying a quiet and tranquil life before your times. With raging madness you have scattered through all the churches of Italy, Germany, Gaul and Spain the flame of discord which, through your ruinous factions, you started in the Roman church. For by taking away from the bishops, as much as you could, all the power which is known to have been divinely conferred upon them through the grace of the holy Spirit, which manifests itself chiefly in ordinations, and by giving over to the fury of the people all the administration of ecclesiastical affairs—seeing that now no one is bishop or priest over anyone unless he has bought this by most unworthy assent from your magnificence—you have disturbed, with wretched confusion, all the vigor of the apostolic institution[22] and that most beautiful distribution of the members of Christ which the Teacher of the nations so often commends and inculcates. And thus, through your boasted decrees—we cannot speak of this without tears—the name of Christ has almost perished. Moreover, who, on account of the very indignity of the thing, is not astounded that you should usurp and arrogate to yourself a certain new and unlawful power in order to destroy rights which are the due of the whole brotherhood? For you assert that if even the mere rumor of a sin of any one of our parishioners reaches you, no one of us shall have any power of binding or loosing; only you, or him whom you specially delegate for this purpose will have that power. Does anyone learned in the sacred Scriptures not see that this decree is more than mad? Since, therefore, we have decided that it is worse than any evil to tolerate longer that the church of God should be so seriously endangered—indeed, almost ruined—through these and other workings of your presump-

tions, we have agreed, by common consent of all of us, to make known to you that about which we have hitherto kept silent: why it is that you neither now may, nor at any time can, preside over the apostolic see. You yourself, in the time of the Emperor Henry of blessed memory,[23] bound yourself by an oath in person, never while that emperor lived, or his son our master the most glorious king who is now at the head of affairs, to accept the papacy, or, so far as you could prevent it, to permit anyone else to receive it without the assent and approbation either of the father during his life, or of the son so long as he too should live. And there are very many bishops who can today bear witness to this oath, having seen it at that time with their own eyes and heard it with their own ears. Remember also, how, when the ambition of securing the papacy tickled some of the cardinals, you yourself, in order to remove rivalry, bound yourself by an oath, on the condition and with the understanding that they should do the same, never to accept the papacy. See how faithfully you have observed both these oaths! Moreover, when, in the time of Pope Nicholas,[24] a synod was held with 125 bishops in session, this was established and decreed: that no one should ever become pope except by election of the cardinals, with the approbation of the people and through the consent and authority of the king. And you yourself were the author, the sponsor, and the signer of this decree. Furthermore you have filled the whole church, as it were, with the stench of a most grave charge concerning overly familiar living together and cohabitation with another person's wife. Our sense of shame suffers more than our case on this account, although this general complaint has resounded everywhere: that all the decrees of the apostolic see have been set in motion by women—in a word, that through this new senate of women the whole circle of the church is administered. For no amount of complaining suffices concerning the injuries and insults against the bishops whom you most unworthily call sons of harlots and the like. Since, therefore, your accession has been inaugurated

---

22    Here the bishops seem to refer to the doctrine of "apostolic succession," by which every bishop claimed authority as a successor of the apostles. The doctrine, still maintained by some modern churches, was orthodox in the medieval church.
23    The Holy Roman Emperor Henry III (1039-1056).
24    Nicholas II (1059-1061).

by such perjuries; since, through the abuse of your innovations, the church of God is in danger through so severe a storm; and since you have defiled your life and conduct with such manifold infamy, we renounce the obedience which we never promised to you, nor shall we in future at all observe it. And since, as you have publicly proclaimed, not one of us has been a bishop to you thus far, so also you shall henceforth be pope to none of us.

## 32.5
### FIRST DEPOSITION AND BANNING OF THE EMPEROR HENRY IV BY GREGORY VII (FEBRUARY 22, 1076)

O St. Peter, chief of the apostles, I beg that you incline to us your holy ears, and hear me your servant whom you have nourished from infancy, and whom, until this day, you have freed from the hand of the wicked, who have hated and do hate me for my faithfulness to you. You, and my mistress the mother of God, and your brother Saint Paul are witnesses for me among all the saints that your holy Roman church drew me to its head against my will, that I had no thought of ascending your see through force, and that I would rather have ended my life as a pilgrim than, by secular means, to have seized your throne for the sake of earthly glory. And therefore I believe it to be through your grace and not through my own deeds that it has pleased and does please you that the Christian people, who have been especially committed to you, should obey me. And especially to me, as your representative and by your favor, has the power been granted by God of binding and loosing in Heaven and on earth. On the strength of this belief therefore, for the honor and security of your church, in the name of Almighty God, Father, Son and Holy Ghost, I withdraw, through your power and authority, from Henry the king, son of Henry the emperor, who has risen against your church with unheard of insolence, the rule over the whole kingdom of the Germans and over Italy. And I absolve all Christians from the bonds of the oath which they have made or shall make to him, and I forbid anyone to serve him as king. For it is fitting that he who strives to lessen the honor of your church should himself lose the honor which belongs to him. And since he has scorned to obey as a Christian, and has not returned to God, whom he had deserted—holding intercourse with the excommunicated, practicing manifold iniquities, spurning my commands which, as you bear witness, I issued to him for his own salvation, separating himself from your church and striving to rend it—I, in your place, bind him with the chain of anathema. And, leaning on you, I so bind him that the people may know and have proof that you are Peter, and on your rock the Son of the living God has built His church, and the gates of Hell shall not prevail against it.[25]

---

25  Referring to the episode in which Jesus says to Peter, "upon this rock I will build my church, and the gates of hell shall not prevail against it" (Matthew 16.18).

# 33

# SPEECH OF URBAN II AT THE COUNCIL OF CLERMONT: TWO ACCOUNTS

## 33.1

### ACCOUNT OF FULCHER OF CHARTRES

*In 1095 Pope Urban II attended the church council held at the French town of Clermont. The exact text of his speech at the council does not survive. The efforts for which Urban called became the First Crusade (1096-1099). One of the four surviving descriptions of the council is that of Fulcher of Chartres, who may have been in attendance, and who took part in the crusade as a chaplain to Stephen, count of Blois. He recounted the events at the council in his history of the crusade, composed at least several years after its conclusion.*

Most beloved brethren, moved by the exigencies of the times, I, Urban, wearing by the permission of God the papal tiara, and spiritual ruler of the whole world, have come here to you, the servants of God, as a messenger to disclose the divine admonition. I desire that those whom I have believed to be the faithful servants of God shall show themselves such, and that there shall be no shameful dissimulation. But if there is in you, contrary to God's law, any deformity or crookedness, because you have lost the moderation of reason and justice, I will earnestly strive to root out the fault. For the Lord has placed you over His family as stewards in order that you may feed its members with pleasant tasting food suited to the time. You will be happy indeed, if when He requires of you an account,

He shall find that you have been faithful in your stewardships. You are also called shepherds; be not hirelings. Be true shepherds and have your crooks always in your hands. Fall not asleep , but watch in all places over the flock committed to your charge. For if, through your carelessness or negligence, any wolf snatches away a sheep, you will not only lose the reward prepared for you in the presence of your Lord, but also, having been first bitterly tortured by remorse for your crimes, you will be savagely hurled into the deadly abode.

In the words of the Gospel, "Ye are the salt of the earth."[1] But if you fail in your duty, how, we ask, can it be salted? Oh, how admirable is that salting! Truly, you must strive by the salt of wisdom to correct these foolish people, hastening open-mouthed after the pleasures of this world, lest putrefied by sins and unsalted, they may be a stench in the nostrils when the Lord wills on some future day to address them. For if, through your neglect of duty, He shall find in them any worms, that is, sins, He will in contempt order them to be hurled into the abyss of unclean things. And because you are unable to make good to Him so great a loss, He will certainly drive you, condemned by His judgment, from the presence of His love.

But for this reason the distributor of this salt ought to be wise, prudent, modest, pacific, learned, watchful, pious, just, equitable, pure. For how can the

---

1   New Testament, Matthew 5.13.

unlearned make others learned, the immodest make others modest, the impure make others pure? If anyone hates peace, how can he be a peace-maker? Or if one's own hands are unclean, how can he cleanse the impurities of another? We read also that "if the blind lead the blind, both shall fall into the ditch."[2] Accordingly first correct yourselves, so that without reproach you may be able to correct those under your charge.

If you wish to be the friends of God, do willingly the things which you believe to be agreeable to Him. Look to it especially that the rules of the church are vigorously maintained, so that simoniacal heresy[3] in no way takes root among you; take heed lest purchasers and venders alike, struck by the chastisement of the Lord, be miserably driven through narrow ways to confusion and destruction. Keep the church and those in its service entirely free from all secular power, cause the tithes due to God from all the fruits of the field to be faithfully paid; let them not be sold or held back. If anyone shall lay hands on a bishop, let him be considered as wholly an outlaw. Of anyone shall seize or despoil monks, priests, nuns, and their servants, or pilgrims or merchants, let him be anathematized. Let robbers, incendiaries and their accomplices be shut out from the church and stricken with the anathema. Therefore we must, as Gregory says, especially consider how he, who steals the property of another, is to be punished, if he who from his own possessions does not employ a part in alms, incurs the damnation of hell. For so it befel Dives mentioned in the Gospel, who forsooth was punished not for having stolen the property of another, but because he was a bad steward of what had be intrusted to him.[4]

By these evils, therefore, as has been said, dearly beloved brethren, you have seen the world troubled for a long time to such an extent that in some places in your provinces, as has been reported to us—perhaps through your weakness in administering justice—

hardly anyone can venture to travel upon the highways, by night or day, without danger of attack by thieves or robbers; and no one is sure that his property at home or abroad will not be taken from him by the violence or craft of the wicked. Therefore, let us re-enact the law made by our holy ancestors long ago and commonly called "the Truce."[5] I most earnestly exhort you that each one should strenuously do all in his power to have it observed in his bishopric. But if anyone misled by pride or cupidity breaks it voluntarily, let him be anathematized by the authority of God and by the sanction of the decrees of this council.

[*Here Urban paused and the council enacted the decrees which he desired, and which all who were present took oath to obey faithfully. The pope then proceeded:*]

Since, Oh sons of God, you have promised the Lord more earnestly than heretofore to maintain peace in your midst and faithfully to sustain the laws of the church, there remains for you, newly fortified by the correction of the Lord, to show the strength of your integrity in a certain other duty, which is not less your concern than the Lord's. For you must carry succor to your brethren dwelling in the East, and needing your aid, which they have so often demanded. For the Turks, a Persian people, have attacked them, as many of you know, and have advanced into the territory of Romania[6] as far as that part of the Mediterranean which is called the Arm of St. George;[7] and occupying more and more the lands of those Christians, have already seven times conquered them in battle, have killed and captured many, have destroyed the churches and devastated the kingdom of God. If you permit them to remain for a time unmolested, they will extend their sway more widely over many faithful servants of the Lord.

Wherefore, I pray and exhort, nay not I, but the

---

2  New Testament, Matthew 15.14.

3  Simony was the sin of purchasing church office.

4  A reference to New Testament, Luke 16. "Dives" (Latin: "Wealthy") is the name that became attached to the rich man who turned away the beggar Lazarus in this chapter.

5  I.e., the Truce of God, a movement to ban warfare on certain holy days.

6  I.e., "Roman" territory.

7  I.e., the Dardanelles, where Europe meets Asia in modern Turkey.

Lord prays and exhorts you, as heralds of Christ, by frequent exhortation, to urge men of all ranks, knights and foot-soldiers, rich and poor, to hasten to exterminate this vile race from the lands of our brethren, and to bear timely aid to the worshippers of Christ. I speak to those who are present, I proclaim it to the absent, but Christ commands. Moreover, the sins of those who set out thither, if they lose their lives on the journey, by land or sea, or in fighting against the heathen, shall be remitted in that hour; this I grant to all who go, through the power of God vested in me.

Oh, what a disgrace if a race so despised, degenerate, and slave of the demons, should thus conquer a people fortified with faith in omnipotent God and resplendent with the name of Christ! Oh, how many reproaches will be heaped upon you by the Lord Himself if you do not aid those who like yourselves are counted of the Christian faith! Let those who have formerly been accustomed to contend wickedly in private warfare against the faithful, fight against the infidel and bring to a victorious end the war which ought long since to have been begun. Let those who have hitherto been robbers now become soldiers of Christ. Let those who have formerly contended against their brothers and relatives now fight as they ought against the barbarians. Let those who have formerly been mercenaries at low wages, now gain eternal rewards. Let those who have been striving to the detriment both of body and soul, now labor for a two-fold reward. What shall I add? On this side will be the sorrowful and poor, on the other the joyful and rich; here the enemies of the Lord, there His friends. Let not those who are going delay their journey, but having arranged their affairs and collected the money necessary for their expenses, when the winter ends and the spring comes, let them with alacrity start on their journey under the guidance of the Lord.

### 33.2
#### ACCOUNT OF ROBERT THE MONK

*In 1095 Pope Urban II attended the church council held at the French town of Clermont. The exact text of his speech to the council does not survive. The efforts for which Urban called became the First Crusade (1096-1099). Robert the Monk wrote his history roughly ten years after the crusade; he seems to have relied on witnesses for his account of the Council of Clermont.*

Oh, race of Franks, race from across the mountains, race chosen and beloved by God—as shines forth in very many of your works—set apart from all nations by the situation of your country, as well as by your catholic faith and the honor of the holy church! To you our discourse is addressed and for you our exhortation is intended. We wish you to know what a grievous cause has led us to your country, what peril threatening you and all the faithful has brought us.

From the confines of Jerusalem and the city of Constantinople a horrible tale has gone forth and very frequently has been brought to our ears, namely, that a race from the kingdom of the Persians, an accursed race, a race utterly alienated from God, a generation forsooth which has not directed its heart and has not entrusted its spirit to God, has invaded the lands of those Christians and has depopulated them by the sword, pillage and fire; it has led away a part of the captives into its own country, and a part it has destroyed by cruel tortures; it has either entirely destroyed the churches of God or appropriated them for the rites of its own religion. They destroy the altars, after having defiled them with their uncleanness. They circumcise the Christians, and the blood of the circumcision they either spread upon the altars or pour into the vases of the baptismal font. When they wish to torture people by a base death, they perforate their navels, and dragging forth the extremity of the intestines, bind it to a stake; then with flogging they lead the victim around until the viscera having gushed forth the victim falls prostrate upon the ground. Others they bind to a post and pierce with arrows. Others they compel to extend their necks and then, attacking them with naked swords, attempt to cut through the neck with a single blow. What shall I say of the abominable rape of the women? To speak of it is worse than to be silent. The kingdom of the Greeks[8] is now dismembered by them and deprived of

---

8   I.e., the Byzantine Empire.

territory so vast in extent that it can not be traversed in a march of two months. On whom therefore is the labor of avenging these wrongs and of recovering this territory incumbent, if not upon you? You, upon whom above other nations God has conferred remarkable glory in arms, great courage, bodily activity, and strength to humble the hairy scalp of those who resist you.

Let the deeds of your ancestors move you and incite your minds to manly achievements; the glory and greatness of King Charles the Great,[9] and of his son Louis, and of your other kings, who have destroyed the kingdoms of the pagans, and have extended in these lands the territory of the holy church. Let the holy sepulcher of the Lord our Savior, which is possessed by unclean nations, especially incite you, and the holy places which are now treated with ignominy and irreverently polluted with their filthiness. Oh, most valiant soldiers and descendants of invincible ancestors, be not degenerate, but recall the valor of your progenitors.

But if you are hindered by love of children, parents, and wives, remember what the Lord says in the Gospel, "He that loveth father or mother more than me, is not worthy of me."[10] "Every one that hath forsaken houses, or brethren, or sisters, or father, or mother, or wife, or children, or lands for my name's sake shall receive an hundredfold and shall inherit everlasting life."[11] Let none of your possessions detain you, nor solicitude for your family affairs, since this land which you inhabit, shut in on all sides by the seas and surrounded by the mountain peaks, is too narrow for your large population; nor does it abound in wealth; and it furnishes scarcely food enough for its cultivators. Hence it is that you murder and devour one another, that you wage war, and that frequently you perish by mutual wounds. Let therefore hatred depart from among you, let your quarrels end, let wars cease, and let all dissensions and controversies slumber. Enter upon the road to the holy sepulcher;

wrest that land from the wicked race, and subject it to yourselves. That land which as the Scripture says "floweth with milk and honey,"[12] was given by God into the possession of the children of Israel.

Jerusalem is the navel of the world; the land is fruitful above others, like another paradise of delights. This the Redeemer of the human race has made illustrious by His advent, has beautified by residence, has consecrated by suffering, has redeemed by death, has glorified by burial. This royal city, therefore, situated at the center of the world, is now held captive by His enemies, and is in subjection to those who do not know God, to the worship of the heathens. She seeks therefore and desires to be liberated, and does not cease to implore you to come to her aid. From you especially she asks succor, because, as we have already said, God has conferred upon you above all nations great glory in arms. Accordingly undertake this journey for the remission of your sins, with the assurance of the imperishable glory of the kingdom of heaven.

When Pope Urban had said these and very many similar things in his urbane discourse, he so influenced to one purpose the desires of all who were present, that they cried out, "God wills it! God wills it!" When the venerable Roman pontiff heard that, with eyes uplifted to heaven he gave thanks to God and, with his hand commanding silence, said:

Most beloved brethren, today is manifest in you what the Lord says in the Gospel, "Where two or three are gathered together in my name there am I in the midst of them."[13] Unless the Lord God had been present in your spirits, all of you would not have uttered the same cry. For, although the cry issued from numerous mouths, yet the origin of the cry was one. Therefore I say to you that God, who implanted this in your breasts, has drawn it forth from you. Let this then be your war-cry in combats, because this word is given to you by God. When an armed attack is made upon the enemy, let this one cry be raised by all the soldiers of God: God wills it! God wills it!

---

9  I.e., Charlemagne (768-814).

10  New Testament, Matthew 10.37.

11  New Testament, Matthew 19.29.

12  A description repeatedly used in the Old Testament to describe the land of Israel (e.g., Exodus 3.08).

13  New Testament, Matthew 18.20.

And we do not command or advise that the old or feeble, or those unfit for bearing arms, undertake this journey; nor ought women to set out at all, without their husbands or brothers or legal guardians. For such are more of a hindrance than aid, more of a burden than advantage. Let the rich aid the needy; and according to their wealth, let them take with them experienced soldiers. The priests and clerks of any order are not to go without the consent of their bishop; for this journey would profit them nothing if they went without permission of these. Also, it is not fitting that laymen should enter upon the pilgrimage without the blessing of their priests.

Whoever, therefore, shall determine upon this holy pilgrimage and shall make his vow to God to that effect and shall offer himself to Him as a living sacrifice, holy, acceptable unto God, shall wear the sign of the cross of the Lord on his forehead or on his breast. When, truly, having fulfilled his vow he wishes to return, let him place the cross on his back between his shoulders. Such, indeed, by the two-fold action will fulfill the precept of the Lord, as He commands in the Gospel, "He that taketh not his cross and followeth after me, is not worthy of me."[14]

---

14   New Testament, Matthew 10.38.

# 34

# TWO LETTERS FROM CRUSADERS

### LETTER OF ANSELM OF RIBEMONT TO MANASSES II, ARCHBISHOP OF REIMS

*Anselm of Ribemont took part in the First Crusade (1096-1099). He wrote the following letter during the siege of Antioch, in the Middle East, about February 10, 1098. He died after Antioch's fall.*

To his reverend lord M., by God's grace archbishop of Reims, A. of Ribemont, his vassal and humble servant, greeting.

Inasmuch as you are our lord and as the kingdom of France is especially dependent upon your care, we tell to you, our father, the events which have happened to us and the condition of the army of the Lord. Yet, in the first place, although we are not ignorant that the disciple is not above his master, nor the servant above his lord, we advise and beseech you in the name of our Lord Jesus to consider what you are and what the duty of a priest and bishop is. Provide therefore for our land, so that the lords may keep peace among themselves, the vassals may in safety work on their property, and the ministers of Christ may serve the Lord, leading quiet and tranquil lives. I also pray you and the canons of the holy mother church of Reims, my fathers and lords, to be mindful of us, not only of me and of those who are now sweating in the

service of God, but also of the members of the army of the Lord who have fallen in arms or died in peace.

But passing over these things, let us return to what we promised. Accordingly, after the army had reached Nicomedia, which is situated at the entrance to the land of the Turks, we all, lords and vassals, cleansed by confession, fortified ourselves by partaking of the body and blood of our Lord, and proceeding thence beset Nicaea on the second day before the Nones of May.[1] After we had for some days besieged the city with many machines and various engines of war, the craft of the Turks, as often before, deceived us greatly. For on the very day on which they had promised that they would surrender, Soliman and all the Turks, collected from neighboring and distant regions, suddenly fell upon us and attempted to capture our camp. However the count of St. Gilles, with the remaining Franks, made an attack upon them and killed an innumerable multitude. All the others fled in confusion. Our men, moreover, returning in victory and bearing many heads fixed upon pikes and spears, furnished a joyful spectacle for the people of God. This was on the seventeenth day before the Kalends of June.[2]

Beset moreover and routed in attacks by night and day, they surrendered unwillingly on the thirteenth day before the Kalends of July.[3] Then the Christians entering the walls with their crosses and imperial standards, reconciled the city to God, and both within

1  May 7.
2  May 16.
3  June 19.

the city and outside the gates cried out in Greek and Latin, "Glory to Thee, O God." Having accomplished this, the princes of the army met the emperor who had come to offer them his thanks, and having received from him gifts of inestimable value, some withdrew, with kindly feelings, others with different emotions.

We moved our camp from Nicaea on the fourth day before the Kalends of July[4] and proceeded on our journey for three days. On the fourth day the Turks, having collected their forces from all sides, again attacked the smaller portion of our army, killed many of our men and drove all the remainder back to their camps. Bohemond, count of the Romans,[5] count Stephen, and the count of Flanders commanded this section. When these were thus terrified by fear, the standards of the larger army suddenly appeared. Hugh the Great and the duke of Lorraine were riding at the head, the count of St. Gilles and the venerable bishop of Puy followed. For they had heard of the battle and were hastening to our aid. The number of the Turks was estimated at 260,000. All of our army attacked them, killed many and routed the rest. On that day I returned from the emperor, to whom the princes had sent me on public business.

After that day our princes remained together and were not separated from one another. Therefore, in traversing the countries of Romania[6] and Armenia we found no obstacle, except that after passing Iconium, we, who formed the advance guard, saw a few Turks. After routing these, on the twelfth day before the Kalends of November,[7] we laid siege to Antioch, and now we captured the neighboring places, the cities of Tarsus and Laodicea and many others, by force. On a certain day, moreover, before we besieged the city, at the "Iron Bridge" we routed the Turks, who had set

out to devastate the surrounding country, and we rescued many Christians. Moreover, we led back the horses and camels with very great booty.

While we were besieging the city, the Turks from the nearest redoubt daily killed those entering and leaving the army. The princes of our army, seeing this, killed 400 of the Turks who were lying in wait, drove others into a certain river and led back some as captives. You may be assured that we are now besieging Antioch with all diligence, and hope soon to capture it. The city is supplied to an incredible extent with grain, wine, oil, and all kinds of food.

I ask, moreover, that you and all whom this letter reaches pray for us and for our departed brethren. Those who have fallen in battle are: at Nicaea, Baldwin of Ghent, Baldwin *Chalderuns,* who was the first to make an attack upon the Turks and who fell in battle on the Kalends of July,[8] Robert of Paris, Lisiard of Flanders, Hilduin of *Mansgarbio,*[9] Ansellus of *Caium,*[10] Manasses of *Claromonte,*[11] *Laudunensis.*

Those who died from sickness: at Nicaea, Guy of *Vitreio,* Odo of *Vernolio,*[12] Hugh of Reims; at the fortress of Sparnum, the venerable abbot Roger, my chaplain; at Antioch, Alard of *Spiniaeco,* Hugh of *Calniaco.*

Again and again I beseech you, readers of this letter, to pray for us, and you, my lord archbishop, to order this to be done by your bishops. And know for certain that we have captured for the Lord 200 cities and fortresses. May our mother, the western church, rejoice that she has begotten such men, who are aspiring for her so glorious a name and who are so wonderfully aiding the eastern church. And in order that you may believe this, know that you have sent to me a tapestry by Raymond "*de Castello.*"[13] Farewell.

---

4   June 25.
5   This should be Normans.
6   I.e., Roman Territory.
7   October 21.
8   July 1.
9   Mazingarbe.
10  Anseau of Caien.
11  Clermont.
12  Verneuil (?).
13  I.e., "of the castle."

## 34.2

### LETTER FROM STEPHEN, COUNT OF BLOIS TO ADELE, HIS WIFE

*As Count of Blois, Stephen was one of those French nobles sometimes called the "princes" because of the extent of their territories and their practical independence from higher political authority. He was also married to Adele, the daughter of William the Conqueror, king of England. While on the First Crusade (1096-1099), he wrote the following letter during the siege of Antioch, in the Middle East, on March 29, 1098.*

Count Stephen to Adele, his sweetest and most amiable wife, to his dear children, and to all his vassals of all ranks, his greeting and blessing.

You may be very sure, dearest, that the messenger whom I sent to give you pleasure, left me before Antioch safe and unharmed, and through God's grace in the greatest prosperity. And already at that time, together with all the chosen army of Christ, endowed with great valor by Him, we had been continuously advancing for 23 weeks toward the home of our Lord Jesus. You may know for certain, my beloved, that of gold, silver, and many other kind of riches I now have twice as much as your love had assigned to me when I left you. For all our princes with the common consent of the whole army, against my own wishes, have made me up to the present time the leader, chief, and director of their whole expedition.

You have certainly heard that after the capture of the city of Nicaea we fought a great battle with the perfidious Turks and by God's aid conquered them. Next we conquered for the Lord all Romania[14] and afterwards Cappadocia. And we learned that there was a certain Turkish prince Assam, dwelling in Cappadocia; thither we directed our course. All his castles we conquered by force and compelled him to flee to a certain very strong castle situated on a high rock. We also gave the land of that Assam to one of our chiefs and in order that he might conquer the above-mentioned Assam, we left there with him many soldiers of Christ. Thence, continually following the wicked Turks, we drove them through the midst of Armenia, as far as the great river Euphrates. Having left all their baggage and beasts of burden on the bank, they fled across the river into Arabia.

The bolder of the Turkish soldiers, indeed, entering Syria, hastened by forced marches night and day, in order to be able to enter the royal city of Antioch before our approach. The whole army of God learning this gave due praise and thanks to the Lord. Hastening with great joy to the aforesaid chief city of Antioch, we besieged it and very often had many conflicts there with the Turks; and seven times with the citizens of Antioch and with the innumerable troops coming to its aid, whom we rushed to meet, we fought with the fiercest courage, under the leadership of Christ. And in all these seven battles, by the aid of the Lord God, we conquered and most assuredly killed an innumerable host of them. In those battles, indeed, and in very many attacks made upon the city, many of our brethren and followers were killed and their souls were borne to the joys of paradise.

We found the city of Antioch very extensive, fortified with incredible strength and almost impregnable. In addition, more than 5,000 bold Turkish soldiers had entered the city, not counting the Saracens, Publicans, Arabs, Turcopolitans, Syrians, Armenians, and other different races of whom an infinite multitude had gathered together there. In fighting against these enemies of God and of our own we have, by God's grace, endured many sufferings and innumerable evils up to the present time. Many also have already exhausted all their resources in this very holy passion. Very many of our Franks, indeed, would have met a temporal death from starvation, if the clemency of God and our money had not succored them. Before the above-mentioned city of Antioch, indeed, throughout the whole winter we suffered for our Lord Christ from excessive cold and enormous torrents of rain. What some say about the impossibility of bearing the heat of the sun throughout Syria is untrue, for the winter there is very similar to our winter in the west.

When truly Caspian,[15] the emir of Antioch—that is, prince and lord—perceived that he was hard pressed

---

14  I.e., "Roman" territory.
15  Bagi Seian.

by us, he sent his son Sensodolo[16] by name, to the prince who holds Jerusalem, and to the prince of Calep, Rodoam,[17] and to Docap,[18] prince of Damascus. He also sent into Arabia to Bolianuth and to Carathania to Hamelnuth. These five emirs with 12,000 picked Turkish horsemen suddenly came to aid the inhabitants of Antioch. We, indeed, ignorant of all this, had sent many of our soldiers away to the cities and fortresses. For there are 165 cities and fortresses throughout Syria which are in our power. But a little before they reached the city, we attacked them at three leagues' distance with 700 soldiers, on a certain plain near the "Iron Bridge." God, however, fought for us, His faithful, against them. For on that day, fighting in the strength that God gives, we conquered them and killed an innumerable multitude—God continually fighting for us—and we also carried back to the army more than 200 of their heads, in order that the people might rejoice on that account. The emperor of Babylon[19] also sent Saracen messengers to our army with letters, and through these he established peace and concord with us.

I love to tell you, dearest, what happened to us during Lent. Our princes had caused a fortress to be built before a certain gate which was between our camp and the sea. For the Turks daily issuing from this gate killed some of our men on their way to the sea. The city of Antioch is about five leagues' distance from the sea. For this reason they sent the excellent Bohemond and Raymond, count of St. Gilles, to the sea with only 60 horsemen, in order that they might bring mariners to aid in this work. When, however, they were returning to us with those mariners, the Turks collected an army, fell suddenly upon our two leaders and forced them to a perilous flight. In that unexpected flight we lost more than 500 of our foot-soldiers—to the glory of God. Of our horsemen, however, we lost only two, for certain.

On that same day truly, in order to receive our brethren with joy, and ignorant of their misfortunes, we went out to meet them. When, however, we approached the above-mentioned gate of the city, a mob of horsemen and foot-soldiers from Antioch, elated by the victory which they had won, rushed upon us in the same manner. Seeing these, our leaders sent to the camp of the Christians to order all to be ready to follow us into battle. In the meantime our men gathered together and the scattered leaders, namely, Bohemond and Raymond, with the remainder of their army, came up and narrated the great misfortune which they had suffered.

Our men, full of fury at these most evil tidings, prepared to die for Christ and, deeply grieved for their brethren, rushed upon the sacrilegious Turks. They, enemies of God and of us, hastily fled before us and attempted to enter their city. But by God's grace the affair turned out very differently; for, when they wanted to cross a bridge built over the great river *Moscholum*, we followed them closely as possible, killed many before they reached the bridge, forced many into the river, all of whom were killed, and we also slew many upon the bridge and very many at the narrow entrance to the gate. I am telling you the truth, my beloved, and you may be very certain that in this battle we killed 30 emirs, that is princes, and 300 other Turkish nobles, not counting the remaining Turks and pagans. Indeed, the number of Turks and Saracens killed is reckoned at 1,230, but of ours we did not lose a single man.

While on the following day (Easter) my chaplain Alexander was writing this letter in great haste, a party of our men lying in wait for the Turks fought a successful battle with them and killed 60 horsemen, whose heads they brought to the army.

These which I write to you are only a few things, dearest, of the many which we have done, and because I am not able to tell you, dearest, what is in my mind, I charge you to do right, to carefully watch over your land, to do your duty as you ought to your children and your vassals. You will certainly see me just as soon as I can possibly return to you. Farewell.

---

16  Chems Eddaulah.
17  Rodoanus.
18  Deccacus Ibn Toutousch.
19  I.e., the Moslem ruler of Egypt, whose capital, Cairo, was referred to as "Babylon."

# 35

# MARIE DE FRANCE, *ELIDUC*

A *lay* is a short French poem, generally one telling a story. *Eliduc* is found in a collection of lays surviving from *c.* 1160-1170 which only in the sixteenth century were attributed, along with other works, to someone named Marie de France. Modern scholars debate who this woman was, and for the sake of convenience the name is still used to designate the author of the lays. She seems to have been connected with England. Marie's lays were written for an unidentified king.

---

I will tell you the story of a most ancient Breton[1] lay, even as I have heard it, and as I believe it to be true. There lived in Brittany a knight called Eliduc, who was noble and courteous, brave and high-hearted, indeed, the most valiant man in the realm. He had married a lady of high lineage, a gentle dame, and of good discretion, and lived with her a long time in faithful love. But at last it happened that he sought service in a war abroad, and there came to love a damsel called Guilliadun, daughter to a king and queen, and withal the fairest maid in her land. Now Eliduc's wife was called Guildeluc, and from these two, the lay is named *Guildeluc and Guilliadun*. It was called *Eliduc* at first, but the name has been changed because the story has to do chiefly with the two ladies. And now I will tell you truly how the adventure befell, whereof the lay was made.

Eliduc was very dear to his lord, the king of Lesser Britain,[2] and rendered him such faithful service that whenever the king had to be absent, Eliduc for his prowess was made warden of the land. And still bet-ter fortune befell him, for he had the right to hunt in the royal forests, so that no forester dared gainsay him or begrudge him at any time. But for envy of his good fortune—as often befalls others—he was brought into disfavor with his lord, being so accused and slandered that he was banished from court without a hearing, yet did not know why. Again and again he entreated the king to show him justice, and not hearken to false charges, inasmuch as he had served him with good will. Since the king would hear nothing of it, he had to depart; so Eliduc went home, and summoning all his friends, told them of the king's anger—it was an ill return for his faithful service! As the peasant says in the proverb, when he chides his ploughman, "Lord's favor is no fief"; so he is wise and prudent who, with all due loyalty to his lord, expends his love upon his good neighbors. The knight said further that he would not remain in the land, but would journey overseas to the realm of Loengre, and there take his pleasure for a while. His wife he would leave in his domain, com-mending her to the charge of his vassals and his

---

1  I.e., from Brittany, a province of what is today France.
2  I.e., Brittany.

friends. In this purpose he remained, and arrayed himself richly, his friends grieving sorely at his departure. He took ten knights with him, and his wife conducted him on the way. When it came to their parting she made exceedingly great lamentation, but he assured her that he would keep good faith with her. Thereupon he set forth, held straight on his way until he came to the sea, crossed over and arrived at Totnes.[3]

There were many kings in that land, and they were at strife and war with one another. Among them was one who lived near Exeter, a powerful man, but of very great age. He had no son to inherit after him, but only a daughter of an age to wed, and because he would not give her in marriage to his neighbor, this other was making war upon him, and laying waste all his land, even besieging him in a castle so closely that he had no man who dared sally against the foe, or engage in *mêlée* or combat.

Upon hearing of this war, Eliduc decided to go no further, but to remain in the land, and aid as much as he could this king who was so wronged, humiliated, and hard pressed. So he sent messengers with letters to say that he had departed from his own country and had come to help the king; but if the king did not wish to retain him, the knight asked for safe conduct through the realm, that he might go further to seek service.

The king looked kindly upon the messengers, and entertained them well. Calling his constable, he gave commands immediately that an escort be prepared to conduct the knight there, and that hostels be made ready where the strangers might lodge, and he further set at their disposal as much as they would spend for a month.

The escort was arrayed and sent for Eliduc, and he was received with great honor, for he was very welcome to the king. He was lodged with a kind and worthy burgess, who gave up to him his fair tapestried chamber. Here Eliduc had a splendid feast served, and invited the needy knights who sojourned in the city. Furthermore, he admonished all his men that none should be so forward as to take a gift or money for the first 40 days.

On the third day after his arrival, there arose cries in the city that the foe had arrived and were spread throughout the land, and would advance to the very gates and assail the town.

Eliduc, hearing the clamor of the frightened folk, armed himself at once, and bade his comrades do likewise. There were 40 mounted knights dwelling in that town (though some were wounded and many had been captured), and when they saw Eliduc mounting his horse, all who were able came out of their hostels armed, and went forth from the gate with him, waiting for no summons. "Lord," they said, "we will go with you, and do as you shall do."

He replied: "I thank you. Is there none among you here who knows a narrow pass suitable for an ambush, where we may take them unawares? True, if we wait for them here, we shall probably fight, but to no advantage if any knows better counsel."

And they said: "Lord, in faith, in the thicket hard by yonder wood is a narrow road, by which they usually return when they have been plundering, riding unarmed on their palfreys. Again and again they return there, thus putting themselves in jeopardy of a speedy death, so that they might easily be overcome and put to shame and worsted."

Eliduc answered: "Friends, I give you my word that he who does not venture often where he expects to lose shall never win much, nor attain to great renown. Now you are all the king's men, and should keep good faith with him. Come with me where I shall go, and do as I shall do, and I promise you faithfully that you shall come to no harm as long as I can aid you. If we gain anything, it will be to our glory to have weakened our foes."

They took his pledge, and guided him to the forest, where they placed themselves in ambush along the road until the enemy should return. Eliduc commanded in all things, devising and explaining how they should leap out suddenly with loud cries.

As soon as the enemy had come to the narrow pass Eliduc shouted to his comrades to act worthily. And they gave hard blows, sparing not at all, so that the foe, taken by surprise, was quickly confused and scat-

---

3    In Devonshire, on the southern coast of Britain.

tered, and in a little while vanquished. Their constable was captured and so many other knights that the squires had much to do to take charge of them. There were 25 men of this land, and they took prisoner 30 of those from abroad, and as much armor as they liked. It was marvelous booty, and the knights returned home rejoicing in their exploit.

The king, meanwhile, was on a tower, in great fear for his men, and complaining bitterly of Eliduc, for he supposed, or at least dreaded, that through treason he might have led the knights of that city into danger. And when they came back all encumbered with booty and prisoners, so that they were many more at their homecoming than when they went forth, the king did not know them, and so was in doubt and suspense. He gave commands that the gates be closed, and that soldiers be stationed on the walls to shoot, and to hurl darts at them. But all this was needless, for they sent a squire spurring in advance, to tell of the stranger's achievement, how he had vanquished the foe, and how nobly he had borne himself—there never was such a knight!—and how the constable had been captured, and 29 others, besides many wounded and many slain.

The king rejoiced marvelously at these tidings, and descended from the tower to meet Eliduc, and to thank him for his good service. He in turn delivered up his prisoners, and divided the booty among the other knights. For his own use he kept only three horses that he liked especially. All his share he distributed and gave out among the prisoners as well as among the other folk.

After this feat of which I have told you, the king greatly loved and cherished him, and for a whole year retained him in his service, and likewise his comrades. Moreover, after receiving Eliduc's oath, the king made him warden of the land.

Now Eliduc was courteous and discreet, a goodly knight, and strong and openhanded; hence, the king's daughter heard him talked of and his virtues recounted. Accordingly, by one of her trusty chamberlains she prayed and commanded him to visit her, that they might have friendly speech together, and become acquainted—indeed, she marveled greatly that he had not come to her before.

Eliduc answered that he would most gladly go to make her acquaintance. Attended by a single knight,

he mounted his horse and rode to her bower, where he sent the chamberlain before, and followed when his coming had been announced.

With sweet courtesy, with gentle manner and with noble bearing, he spoke as one skilled in speech, and thanked the fair lady Guilliadun, in that she had been pleased to summon him to her presence. She took him by the hand, and they sat down together upon a couch, speaking of many things. She looked at him attentively, studying his face, his stature and his bearing, and said to herself, "There is no fault in him." And all at once, as she was praising him in her heart, Love flung his dart at her, bidding her love the knight, whereupon she grew pale and sighed. But she would not put her thought into speech, lest he hold her too lightly.

He tarried there a long while, but at last took his leave—though she granted it unwillingly—and returned to his hostel. He was very pensive and sadly distraught for thinking of the fair princess, how she had so sweetly called him, and how she had sighed. His only regret was that he had been in the land so long, and had not seen her often. But even as he said this he repented, reminding himself of his wife, and how he had promised to keep good faith with her.

On the other hand, the maid, as soon as she beheld him, loved him more than any other in the world, and wished to have him for her lover. All night she lay awake, and had neither sleep nor rest. The next morning she arose, and going to a window, called her chamberlain and told him of her condition, saying: "By my faith, it is ill with me! I have fallen into a bad situation! I love the new knight, Eliduc, so that I have no rest at night, nor can I close my eyes in sleep. If he would return my love and be my betrothed, I would do all he wills, and he indeed might win great good thereby, for he would be king of this land! But if he will not love me, I must die of grief for the very love of his wisdom and his courtesy!"

When she had said what she desired, the chamberlain whom she had called gave her excellent counsel—let no man think ill of it! "Lady," he said, "since you love him, send to him and tell him so. It would be well, perhaps, to send him a belt or ribbon or ring, and if he should accept it gratefully and be joyous at the message, you would be sure of his love. There is no emperor under heaven who, if you would love him, ought not to be truly glad!"

And when the damsel had heard this counsel, she answered: "How shall I know by my gift whether he will love me? Never have I seen a knight, whether he loved or hated, who had to be entreated to keep willingly the present one sent him. I should hate bitterly to be a jest to him! Still, one may know somewhat by his manner—make ready, and go!"

"I am all ready," he said.

"Give him a golden ring, and my belt. Greet him from me a thousand times!"

The chamberlain turned away, leaving her in such a state that she all but called him back; but yet she let him go, and began to lament in this way: "Alas! now is my heart captive for a stranger from another land! I do not know if he is of high degree, yet if he should leave here suddenly, I would be left mourning. I have set my heart's desire foolishly, for I have never spoken with him except yesterday, and now I have sent to entreat his love. I think that he will blame me, yet if he is gentle, he will show me grace! Now everything is at risk, and if he does not care for my love, I shall be in such sorrow that never again in my life shall I have joy!"

While she was thus bemoaning herself, the chamberlain hastened and came to Eliduc. As had been devised, he greeted the knight according to the maiden's bidding, and gave him the little ring and the belt. Eliduc thanked him, put the gold ring on his finger, and girt himself with the belt. But there was no further speech between them, except that the knight proffered gifts, of which the chamberlain would have none.

Returning to his lady, whom he found in her bower, he greeted her on the knight's behalf and thanked her for her present.

"Come," she said, "hide nothing from me. Will he love me with true love?"

"As I think," he answered. "The knight is not wanton, but I judge him rather as courteous and discreet in knowing how to hide his heart. I greeted him for you and gave him your gifts, whereupon he girt himself with your belt, drawing it close about him, and put the little ring on his finger. Nor said I more to him, nor he to me."

"Did he not receive it in token of love? If not, I am undone!"

He answered: "By my faith, I do not know; yet, listen to me: unless he wished you well, he would have none of your gifts."

"You speak folly!" said she. "I know well that he does not hate me, for I have never wronged him in anything, except in loving him tenderly, and if for that he hates me, he deserves to die! Never by you, or by any other, will I ask anything of him until I myself speak to him and show how love for him sways me. But I do not know whether he remains?"

The chamberlain answered: "Lady, the king has retained him under oath to serve faithfully for a year; hence, you may have time enough to show him your pleasure."

When she heard that he would remain, she was exceeding joyful and glad at heart. She knew nothing of the sorrow that came upon him as soon as he had beheld her, for his only joy was in thinking of her, and he held himself to be in a bad situation since he had promised his wife, before he left his domain, to love none but her. Now his heart was in sore conflict, for he wished to keep his faith, yet in no way could he doubt that he loved the maiden Guilliadun, so sweet to gaze upon and to speak with, to kiss and to embrace. But he would not seek her love, since it would be dishonorable to his wife, and to the king as well.

For all this, he was so tormented for love that he mounted his horse presently, and rode away with his companions to the castle. But the reason of his going was not so much to speak with the king as to see the maiden, if he could.

Now the king had risen from dinner and entered into his daughter's bower, where he was playing chess with a knight from overseas, and from across the chessboard the princess was watching the game. As Eliduc came forward, the king showed him great favor, and bade him sit by his side; then, turning to his daughter, he said "Damsel, acquaint yourself with this knight, and show him all honor, for there is none more worthy among 500!"

Upon her father's command, the maiden turned joyfully to greet Eliduc, and they sat far off from the others. Love so overcame them that she dared say no word to him and he could scarcely speak to her. Yet he

thanked her for her gift, which was to him the dearest thing he had. Thereupon she said that she was glad at heart: she had sent him the ring and the belt because she loved him so well that she would willingly take him for her husband, and if this might not be, truly she would never have a living man! But now, let him show his heart!

"Lady," he said, "I thank you for the grace of your love, which fills me with joy! That I stand so high in your favor makes me glad beyond telling, yet the future does not rest with me, for, although I am bound to remain a year with the king, having given my oath not to depart until his war is ended, after that, I ought to return to my own land without delay, if you will grant me leave."

The maiden answered: "My love, I thank you! You are so very wise and courteous, that before that time you will have devised what you will do with me. I love and trust you above everything!"

Thus they promised themselves, and at that time spoke no more. Eliduc returned to his dwelling full of joy, for he had done much and might speak with his lady as often as he liked, and between them was the fullness of love's joy.

Accordingly, he entered into the war with such zeal that he seized and took captive the lord who fought against the king, and set free all the land. He was praised far and wide for his prowess, for his wisdom, and for his generosity, and fair fortune befell him.

Now while these things were happening, his own lord had sent three messengers forth from the land to seek Eliduc, for he was harassed in war, endangered and hard situated, so that he was losing all his castles, and all his land was being laid waste. He had often repented of banishing Eliduc through foolish hearkening to evil counsel, and he had cast out of the land the traitors who had accused and slandered and wronged the knight, and sent them forever into exile. Now in his sore distress he sent for his vassal, commanding and adjuring him by the bond of homage between them, to come to his lord's aid in this time of sore need.

At these tidings Eliduc was sorrowful for the maiden whom he loved so much, and who loved him with all her heart. His hope and intent was that their love might continue to show itself in the giving of fair gifts

and in speaking together, without foolish trifling or dalliance; but she thought to have him for her lord, if she might keep his love, for she did not know that he had a wife.

"Alas!" he cried, "that ever I came here; too long have I been in this land! Would I had never seen it! I have come to love the princess Guilliadun so dearly, and she loves me so well, that if we must part, one of us will die, or perhaps both! And yet I must go, for my lord has summoned me by letter, and I am bound to him by oath, and then again my wife! Now it behoves me to take heed, for I must depart without fail, and if I were to wed my love, the Church would interfere. Everything goes ill with me! God—how hard is this parting! But whoever may judge it wrong, I will always deal rightly with her, doing her will and following her counsel. The king, her father, has peace now, and looks for no further war; hence, for my lord's need I must ask leave before the end of my time for abiding in this land. I will go speak to the maid, and show her all my case; and when she has told me her will, I will do it as far as I may."

He tarried no longer, but went at once to the king to ask leave, relating to him what had happened and reading the letter from his lord, who was so hard-pressed. And when the king heard that Eliduc might by no means remain, he became sorrowful and troubled in thought, and offered a large part of his possessions, one-third of his heritage and of his treasure; if only Eliduc would remain, he would give him cause to be grateful all his life.

"O God," said Eliduc, "since my lord is now so oppressed, and has summoned me from afar, I must go hence to help him, nor by any means remain. But if you have need of my service, I will return to you gladly with a strong force of knights."

For this the king thanked him, and with all courtesy gave him leave to depart, setting at his disposal all the treasures of his mansion, gold and silver, dogs and horses, rich and beautiful silk. Of these took he moderately. Thereupon he added to the king, as was fitting, that he would like to say farewell to his daughter, if it pleased him. The king answered, "With all my heart," and sent forward a page to open the chamber door.

Eliduc went with him, and when the lady saw the knight, she called him by name, and said he was 6,000 times welcome. He asked her counsel in this matter, briefly showing the need for his journey, but before he had told her all, or taken leave, or even asked it, she turned pale and swooned for grief. Seeing this, Eliduc began to lament, and kissed her often, weeping sorely, and held her in his arms until she had recovered from her swoon.

"O God," he said, "my sweet love, try to bear what I tell you. You are my life and my death, and in you is all my comfort! And though I must return to my land, and have already taken leave of your father, I consult you on account of the promise between us, and, whatsoever befalls me, I will do your will!"

"Take me with you," she cried, "since you will not stay longer! Or if you will not, I must kill myself, for never more shall I have joy or contentment!"

Eliduc answered tenderly that indeed he loved her with true love: "Sweet, I am bound to your father by oath, from now until the term which was set, and if I took you with me, I should belie my faith to him. I promise you faithfully and swear that if you will grant me leave and respite now, and set a day afterwards, and if you wish me to return, nothing in the world shall hinder me, if I be alive and well. My life is all in your hands!"

When she perceived his great love, she granted him a term, and set a day when he should come and take her with him. In bitter grief they exchanged gold rings, and with sweet kisses parted. Eliduc went down to the sea, and with a good wind was quickly across.

Upon his return his lord rejoiced greatly, and likewise his friends and his kinsmen and many other folk, and above all his good wife, who was so fair and wise and gentle. But he was always thinking upon the love that overmastered him, and showed no joy or pleasure at all—indeed, he might never be glad again until he saw his beloved.

He acted very secretively, and his wife grieved in her heart, and often mourned by herself, for she did not know what this might mean. Again and again she asked him if he had not heard from someone that she had been false to him or had sinned against him while he was out of the land. She would most gladly prove her innocence before his folk, whenever he pleased. "Wife," he said, "I charge you with no sin or misdeed whatsoever. But in the land where I have been, I

promised and swore to the king that I would return to him, for he has great need of me. If my lord had peace, I would not stay here eight days longer. I must endure great anxiety before I may return, indeed, never until that time shall I take pleasure in anything that I see, for I would not break my pledge."

With this the lady let be. He went to his lord and so much aided and supported him that by his counsel the king saved all the land. But when the time appointed by the maiden drew near, he made ready for his departure, and having brought the enemy to terms, he arrayed himself for the journey, and likewise those he would take with him. These were only his two nephews whom he loved especially, the trusty chamberlain who had brought the message, and his squires; he had no desire for other comrades. These few he made promise and swear to keep silence on this undertaking.

He put out to sea at once, and was quickly across in the land where he was so eagerly expected.

Now, for prudence's sake, Eliduc took lodging far from the harbor, so that he might not be seen or recognized, and arrayed his chamberlain to bear word to the princess, that he had kept her command, and had now arrived, and when the darkness of evening had fallen, she should come forth from the city with the chamberlain, and he himself would meet her.

The chamberlain changed his dress for a disguise and went on foot all the way to the city where the king's daughter was. He devised a means to be admitted to her bower, and greeting the maiden, said that her lover had come. Upon hearing these tidings she was all startled and confused, wept tenderly for joy, and often kissed the messenger. He said further that at dusk she must go with him, for all day he had been planning their flight. In the darkness of evening they set out from the city, the chamberlain and herself—no more than they two. She had great fear of being seen, for she was clad in a silken robe, delicately embroidered with gold, and had wrapped about her only a short mantle.

But her lover had come to meet her, and was awaiting them a bow shot's length from the gate, by the hedge that enclosed a fair wooded park. When the chamberlain brought her up, Eliduc dismounted to kiss her, and they had exceedingly great joy together.

Soon, however, he placed her on a horse, mounted, took the reins, and rode away at full speed. When they arrived at Totnes harbor, they embarked at once, he and his own men only, and the lady Guilliadun. At first they had a favoring breeze to waft them across, and calm weather; but even as they were nearing the shore, there came a storm at sea, and a wind arose before them, which drove them far from their haven, broke and split their mast and tore all their sail. Devoutly they called on God, on St. Nicholas and St. Clement, and Our Lady, the Virgin Mary, that she entreat her Son to save them from death, and bring them safe to land. One hour backwards, another forwards, thus they coasted along, for they were in the heart of the tempest. And presently one of the sailors cried aloud: "What shall we do? Lord, you have here with you the one for whose sake we perish! We shall never come to land, for you have a lawful wedded wife, and yet bear away this other, against God and the law, against right and honor! Let us cast her into the sea, and we may arrive at once!"

At these words Eliduc in his wrath all but hurt the fellow. "You whore's son!" he cried, "wretch! foul traitor! be still! If I could leave my lady, you would pay dearly for this!"

He held the princess in his arms, soothing her as best he could both for her terror of the sea and for her woe in hearing that her lover had a wife in his own land. But she fell forward in a swoon, and continued in that state, entirely pale and colorless, neither reviving nor breathing. He truly thought that she was dead, and fell into bitter grief. He arose and went to the sailor who had spoken, struck him with an oar and stretched him prone, then hurled him overboard, head foremost into the sea, where the waves swept the body away. Thereupon the knight took the helm, and so steered the ship and held it firm, that he made the haven and came to land, and when they had arrived safely, he cast anchor and put down the gangway.

And still the maid lay with the look of death upon her, so that Eliduc in his heavy grief longed to lie dead by her side. But he asked counsel of his comrades as to where he should take her, for he would not part from

her until she should be buried with great honor and fair service, as became a king's daughter, in holy ground. His men were all perplexed and had nothing to say, so the knight considered what he should do. He remembered that near his dwelling, itself so close to the sea that it could be reached by midday, in the great forest which stretched around it for 30 leagues, a holy hermit had had a cell and chapel for 40 years. Now since he knew this good man, he resolved to take the maid there and bury her in his chapel, and to give enough land to found an abbey, and to place therein a convent of monks or nuns or canons, who would pray for her unceasingly, "God grant her sweet mercy!"

So he had his horses brought, mounted with his men, and taking an oath from them not to betray him, rode away on his palfrey with his lady in his arms. They journeyed straight on, until they came to the chapel in the wood, where they knocked and called, but found no one to answer, or to open to them, so that Eliduc had to make one of his men climb over the wall to unbar and open the door. Within they found the newly made tomb of the holy man, who had died eight days before. At this the knight was sorely troubled and distressed, and when his men would have made the lady's grave, he stopped them, saying: "This must not be until I have taken counsel with the wise folk of the land, as to how I shall sanctify the place as an abbey or a church. Let us lay her before the altar here, and commend her to God."

He bade them forthwith bring robes and prepare a couch, on which he placed the maiden whom he thought dead. But when he came to the parting, he thought he would die of grief. He kissed her eyes and her face, saying: "Dear, please God, never more will I bear arms or live out my life in the world! Fair love, alas that you ever saw me; sweet dear, alas that you came with me! Pretty, now perhaps you would have been queen, were it not for the true and loyal love with which you loved me. My heart aches sorely for you! On the day that I bury you I shall put on the cowl,[4] and at your tomb day after day cry out anew my grief!"

At last he left the maiden, and made fast the door of the chapel, and then he sent a messenger to his

---

4   I.e., become a monk.

dwelling to announce to his wife that he was on his way home, but was weary and travelworn.

Upon hearing these tidings she rejoiced greatly and, arraying herself to meet her lord, received him in all kindness; yet she got but little joy from him, for his looks were so forbidding that none dared accost him, and he spoke no loving word.

He was in the house two days, and after mass in the morning went forth alone on the road to the forest chapel, where the damsel lay. He found her neither revived nor seeming to breathe; yet he marveled in seeing her still white and red, with no loss of her fair color, except that she was a little pale. In his bitter anguish he wept and prayed for her soul, and having prayed, returned home.

One day, when he went forth from the church, his wife set a squire to watch him, promising to give horse and arms if he would follow his lord and see where he went. And as she bade him, he followed unperceived through the wood, saw Eliduc enter the chapel and heard his mourning. When the knight came out again, the squire returned to his lady, and told her of all the cries of grief and lamentation that her lord had made in the hermitage. All her heart was stirred, and she said: "Let us go at once and search through the hermitage. My lord must go, I think, to the king's court. This hermit has been dead for some time, and though I know well that my husband loved him, he never would do thus for his sake, nor feel such lasting grief." For the time she let be; but that same day, after noon, when Eliduc went to the king's court, she came with her squire to the hermitage. When she entered the chapel, and saw the bed with the maiden, who was like a freshly blooming rose, she put aside the robes and gazed upon the slender body, the long white hands with graceful fingers, slim and shapely, and then she knew truly why her lord was in such grief. Calling the squire, she showed him the marvel.

"See," she said, "this woman like a jewel in her fairness! She is my lord's loved one, for whom he is all sorrowful. In faith, I do not wonder at it, since so lovely a woman is dead! As much for pity as for love, I shall never again have joy!"

She began to weep and moan for the maiden. As she sat lamenting by the bedside, a weasel ran from under the altar, and because it passed over the corpse, the squire struck it with his staff and killed it. He threw it upon the floor, but it lay there only while one might run a league before its mate sped thither and saw it. And when, after running about the dead weasel's head, and lifting it with its foot, the little creature could not get its mate to rise, it gave signs of grief, and sped out of the chapel among the herbs in the wood. Here it seized in its teeth a flower, crimson in hue, and returned at once to place it in the mouth of its mate. Within the hour the weasel came to life. When the lady saw this, she cried to the squire, "Stop it! Strike it, good lad! Let it not escape!"

He threw his staff so that the weasel dropped the flower, whereupon the lady rose and, picking up the pretty blossom, placed it in the maiden's mouth. And presently, as she waited there, the damsel revived and breathed, saying as she opened her eyes, "Dear God, I have slept long!"

The lady gave thanks to God, and asked the maid who she was, and she answered: "Lady, I am from Logres, daughter to a king in that land. I loved dearly a good knight, Eliduc, and he brought me away with him; but he did wrong in beguiling me, for he has a wedded wife, and neither told me of her, nor ever made sign of such a thing. And when I heard talk of this wife, I swooned in my grief, and he, most unknightly, has abandoned me all desolate in a strange land. He has betrayed me, though I do not know why. Foolish is she who puts her trust in man."

"Fair maid," answered the other, "there is no living thing in all the world that can give him joy! One may say truly that since he believes you dead, he has fallen into strange despair; every day he has come to look upon you, though deeming to find you lifeless. I am his wife, and indeed my heart is heavy for him. Because he showed such great grief, I longed to know where he went, came after him, and found you. I have great joy in finding you alive, and will take you back with me and restore you to your loved one. As for myself, I will release him from his vows, and veil my head!"[5]

---

5  I.e., become a nun.

Thus the lady comforted her and took her away, at the same time sending a squire to go for his lord. He journeyed until he came to him, and, greeting him courteously, told him what had happened. Thereupon, Eliduc waited for no companion, but mounted at once, and rode home that same night. When he found his lady alive he rendered thanks sweetly to his wife, and was more glad than he had ever been before. Again and again he kissed the maiden, and she him most tenderly, and they had very great joy together.

When his wife saw their happiness, she accosted her lord and asked his leave to depart and be a nun in God's service; further, she asked him to give her part of his land whereon she might build an abbey, and said that he should marry the one whom he loved so much, since it was neither well nor fitting to maintain two wives, nor would the law permit it.

Eliduc granted this, and parted from her in all kindness, saying that he would do all she wished, and would give her some of his land. Thus near the castle in a wood hard by the chapel and the hermitage, she built her church and monastic dwellings, and added thereto land enough and rich possessions, so that she might be well content to live there. When it was all finished, she veiled her head, and took with her 30 nuns to establish the new order of her life.

Eliduc wedded his lady, and on that day held a feast with great honor and splendid service. They lived together many years in perfect love, giving great alms and doing much good, until at length they turned themselves wholly to God.

Thereupon, with good counsel and care, Eliduc built a church also near the castle but on the other side, and bestowed upon it the greater part of his land, and all his gold and silver. He placed there men of good religion to establish the order of the house, and when all things were ready, after no long delay, he gave himself also to the service of almighty God. He placed his beloved lady with his former wife, by whom she was received honorably as a sister, was admonished to serve God, and instructed in the rules of the order. Together they prayed God to show sweet mercy to their friend, and he prayed for them, sending messengers to know how it was with them and how each did. They strove, each of them, to love God with good faith, and so made a fair ending, by the grace of the True and Holy God.

The chivalrous Bretons of old times made a lay of the adventure of these three, that it might not be forgotten.

# 36

## *MAGNA CARTA*

After a brief civil war between King John of England (1199-1216) and many of his barons (that is, his greater tenants holding land in return for military service), the defeated king was forced to issue Magna Carta in 1215. "Magna Carta" means "large charter," in contrast to the shorter charter concerning the Royal Forest[1] which John was also forced to issue. Magna Carta did not bring a permanent end to the trouble between John and his barons, some of whom were again in rebellion by the time of his death. Magna Carta was often reissued, without certain clauses (e.g., those concerning the council of barons), by later kings in the Middle Ages.

---

John, by the grace of God, king of England, lord of Ireland, duke of Normandy and Aquitaine, count of Anjou, to the archbishops, bishops, abbots, earls, barons,[2] judges, foresters,[3] sheriffs,[4] stewards, servants, and to all his bailiffs and faithful subjects, greeting. Know that we, by the will of God and for the safety of our soul, and of the souls of all our predecessors and our heirs, to the honor of God and for the exalting of the holy church and the bettering of our realm, by the counsel of our venerable fathers, Stephen, archbishop of Canterbury, primate of all England and cardinal of the holy Roman church, Henry, archbishop of Dublin, the bishops William of London, Peter of Winchester, Jocelin of Bath and Glastonbury, Hugh of Lincoln, Walter of Worcester, William of Coventry and Benedict of Rochester, Master Pandulf, subdeacon and member of the household of the lord pope, Brother Aymeric, master of the knights of the Temple[5] in England, and of the noble men, William Marshall, earl of Pembroke, William, earl of Salisbury, William, earl of Warren, William, earl of Arundel, Alan de Galloway, constable of Scotland, Warin son of Gerold, Peter son of Herbert, Hubert de Burgh, seneschal of Poitou, Hugh de Neville, Matthew son of Herbert, Thomas Basset, Alan Basset, Philip d'Aubigny, Robert de Ropsley, John Marshall, John son of Hugh, and others of our faithful subjects:

1   First of all have granted to God, and, for us and for our heirs forever, have confirmed, by this our present charter, that the English church shall be free and shall have its rights intact and its liberties uninfringed upon. And thus we will that it be observed, as is

---

1   The Royal Forest was land set aside under the special jurisdiction of the king, who had extraordinary rights over it. By this time Forest land was often under cultivation.
2   All the preceding categories of persons were also John's barons.
3   Officials in charge of the Royal Forest.
4   The king's officials in charge of each shire, or county, of England.
5   A crusading monastic order.

apparent from the fact that we, spontaneously and of our own free will, before discord broke out between ourselves and our barons, granted and by our charter confirmed—and obtained confirmation from the lord pope Innocent—freedom of elections, which is considered most important and most necessary to the church of England, and which we ourselves shall observe, and we will that it be observed with good faith by our heirs forever. We have also granted to all free persons of our realm, on the part of ourselves and our heirs forever, all the liberties written below, to have and to hold, to them and to their heirs, from us and from our heirs.

2   If any one of our earls or barons, or of others holding from us in chief through military service, shall die, and if, at the time of his death, his heir is of full age and owes a relief,[6] he shall have his inheritance by the old relief: namely the heir or the heirs of an earl, by 100 pounds for the whole barony of an earl; the heir or heirs of a baron, by 100 pounds for the whole barony; the heir or heirs of a knight, by 100 shillings at most for a whole knight's fee;[7] and whoever will owe less shall give less, according to the ancient custom of fees.

3   But if the heir of any of the above persons shall be underage and in wardship, when he comes of age he shall have his inheritance without relief and without fine.

4   The custodian of the land of such an heir who is underage shall take none but reasonable revenue from the land of the heir, and reasonable customs and services and do so without destruction and waste of men or goods. And if we shall have committed the custody of any such land to the sheriff or to any other man who ought to be responsible to us for its revenue, and he causes destruction or waste to what is in his charge, we will fine him, and the land shall be handed over to two lawful and discreet men of that fee who shall answer to us, or to whomever we shall have referred them, regarding that revenue. And if we shall have

given or sold to anyone the custody of any such land, and he shall have caused destruction or waste to it, he shall lose that custody, and it shall be given to two lawful and discreet men of that fee, who likewise shall answer to us, as has been explained.

5   Moreover, so long as the custodian has custody of the land, the custodian shall from the revenue of that land maintain the houses, parks, preserves, fish ponds, mills, and other things pertaining to it, and he shall restore to the heir when he comes to full age his whole land stocked with ploughs and means of farming, according as the season of farming requires and the issues of the land will reasonably permit.

6   Heirs may marry without disparagement,[8] so, nevertheless, that, before the marriage is contracted, it shall be announced to the relations by blood of the heir himself.

7   After the death of her husband, a widow shall immediately, and without difficulty, have her marriage portion and her inheritance, nor shall she give anything in return for her dower,[9] her marriage portion, or her inheritance which she and her husband held on the day of the death of that husband. And she may remain in the house of her husband for 40 days after his death, within which time her dower shall be assigned to her.

8   No widow shall be forced to marry when she prefers to live without a husband; but, however, that she shall thus give security not to marry without our consent, if she holds from us, or the consent of the lord from whom she holds, if she holds from another.

9   Neither we nor our bailiffs shall seize any land or rent for any debt, so long as the chattels of the debtor suffice to pay the debt, nor shall the sponsors of that debtor be distrained[10] so long as that chief debtor has enough to pay the debt. But if the chief debtor fails in paying the debt, not having the wherewithal to pay it, the sponsors shall answer for the debt. And, if they wish, they may have the lands and revenues of the

---

6   A gift or payment an heir customarily made to a lord before obtaining the land.

7   In theory, a land-holding suitable to support one knight.

8   Being married as a ward to a socially unsuitable person.

9   That portion of her husband's lands set aside for a widow to hold from her husband's death until her death, at which time the land went to her husband's heirs.

10   I.e., to have one's lands seized and the revenue collected.

debtor until satisfaction has been given them for the debt previously paid for him, unless the chief debtor shall show that he is free in that respect towards those same sponsors.

10 If anyone shall have taken any sum, great or small, as a loan from the Jews, and shall die before that debt is paid, that debt will not bear interest so long as the heir, from whomever he may hold, is underage. And if the debt falls into our hands,[11] we shall take nothing save the chattels contained in the deed.

11 And if anyone dies owing a debt to the Jews, his wife shall have her dower, and shall pay nothing of that debt. But if children of that dead man survive, and they are underage, the necessities shall be provided for them according to the nature of the dead man's holdings, and the debt shall be paid from the residue, saving the service due to the lords.[12] The like shall be done concerning debts that are due to others besides Jews.

12 No scutage[13] or aid[14] shall be imposed in our kingdom unless by the common counsel of our kingdom, except for ransoming our person, knighting our eldest son, and marrying once our eldest daughter. And for these purposes there shall be only a reasonable aid. In like manner shall be done concerning aids from the city of London.

13 And the city of London shall have all its old liberties and free customs both by land as well as by water. Moreover, we will and grant that all other cities and boroughs, and towns and ports, shall have all their liberties and free customs.

14 And, in order to have the common counsel of the realm in the matter of assessing an aid otherwise than in the aforesaid cases, or of assessing a scutage, we shall cause the archbishops, bishops, abbots, earls, and greater barons to be summoned by means of our letters under seal, and we shall cause to be summoned in general, through our sheriffs, bailiffs, all those who hold from us in chief[15] to meet on a fixed day and a fixed place, with at least 40 days' notice. And in all those letters of summons we shall state the cause of the summons. And when a summons has thus been made, the business shall be proceeded with on the day appointed according to the counsel of those who shall be present, even if not all who were summoned have come.

15 We will not allow anyone henceforth to take an aid from his freemen except for the ransom of his person, and the knighting of his eldest son, and the marrying, once, of his eldest daughter and, for these purposes, there shall be only a reasonable aid.

16 No one shall be distrained to do more service for a knight's fee, or for another free holding, than is due from it.

17 Common pleas[16] shall not follow our court but shall be held in a certain fixed place.

18 Assizes of novel disseisin, of mort d'ancestor, and of darrein presentment[17] shall not be held save in their own counties, and in this way: we, or if we are absent from the kingdom, our chief justiciar,[18] shall send two judges through each county four times a year; they, with four knights from each county, chosen by the county, shall hold the aforesaid assizes in the county on the day and at the place of the county court.

19 And if on the day of the county court the aforesaid assizes cannot be held, a sufficient number of knights and free tenants from among those who were present at the county court on that day shall remain, so that through them the judgments may be suitably given, according to whether there is much or little business.

20 A free person shall be amerced[19] for a small

---

11 The king was by law the heir of all Jews in the kingdom.
12 I.e., the lord or lords of the deceased.
13 A payment made to a lord instead of furnishing military service.
14 Often a rendering of money to help one's lord.
15 I.e., the barons.
16 I.e., routine legal cases heard according to the standardized forms of the Common Law.
17 These are all actions, or types of lawsuits, in the Common Law. Speaking very roughly, novel disseisin concerns who has legal possession of land; mort d'ancestor concerns inheritance of land; darrein presentment concerns who has the right to nominate candidates for the position of priest of a parish to the local bishop.
18 The king's chief governmental official.
19 I.e., fall "into the mercy" of a court or a lord, and so be fined.

offense only according to the nature of that offense. And for a great offense he shall be amerced according to the magnitude of the offense, saving his livelihood; and a merchant, in the same way, saving his merchandise; and a villein,[20] in the same way, if he falls into our mercy, shall be amerced, saving his means of farming. And none of the aforesaid fines shall be imposed save upon the oath of upright men from the neighborhood.

21   Earls and barons shall not be amerced except through their peers, and only according to the nature of the offense.

22   No cleric shall be amerced for his lay tenement except according to the manner of the other persons aforesaid, and not according to the size of his ecclesiastical benefice.[21]

23   Neither a town nor a man shall be forced to build bridges over rivers, with the exception of those who, from of old and by law, ought to do it.

24   No sheriff, constable, coroners,[22] or other bailiffs of ours shall hold the pleas of our crown.[23]

25   All counties, hundreds, wapentakes, and ridings[24]—our demesne manors[25] being excepted—shall continue according to the old farms,[26] without any increase at all.

26   If anyone holding a lay fee from us dies, and our sheriff or bailiff can show our letters patent[27] containing our summons for the debt which the dead man owed to us, our sheriff or bailiff may be allowed to attach and enroll[28] the chattels of the dead man to the value of that debt, through the supervision of lawful men. This shall be done in such a way, however, that nothing shall be removed until the debt is paid which

was plainly owed to us, and the residue shall be left to the executors that they may carry out the will of the dead man. And if nothing is owed to us by him, all the chattels shall go to the use prescribed by the deceased, except for the reasonable portions of his wife and children.

27   If any free person shall have died without a will, his chattels shall be distributed through the hands of his near relatives and friends, under the supervision of the church, saving to anyone the debts which the dead man owed him.

28   No constable or other bailiff of ours shall take the grain or other chattels of anyone unless he immediately renders money for them, or can be allowed a delay in that regard by the will of the seller.

29   No constable shall force any knight to pay money for castle guard[29] if he is willing to perform that guard in person, or, if for a reasonable cause he is not able to perform it himself, through another proven man. And if we shall have led or sent him on a military expedition, he shall be excused his guard service according to the amount of time during which, through us, he shall have been in military service.

30   No sheriff or bailiff of ours, or anyone else, shall take the horses or carts of any freeman for transport, unless by the will of that free man.

31   Neither we nor our bailiffs shall take another's wood for castles or for other private uses, unless by the will of the one to whom the wood belongs.

32   We shall not hold the lands of those convicted of felony longer than a year and a day; and then the lands shall be restored to the lords of the fees.

33   Henceforth, all the fish traps in the Thames and

---

20   I.e., a serf.
21   I.e., an endowed, revenue-producing church office.
22   Coroners were royal officials charged with investigating certain deaths.
23   I.e., the more serious judicial business, largely crime.
24   The counties or shires were the largest territorial divisions of English royal government. The hundreds, etc., were various subdivisions of these.
25   Royal manors in the king's own hand.
26   The king granted out the revenues to various shires etc. in return for a lump sum payment, or "farm," to be made at regular periods to the king in return.
27   Letters sealed, but open, so they can be read.
28   I.e., seize and record.
29   Some tenants held land on condition of supplying such service.

Medway, and throughout all England, except on the seacoast, shall be done away with entirely.

34  Henceforth the writ which is called *Praecipe*[30] shall not be given to anyone for any holding so as to cause a free man to lose his court.

35  There shall be one measure of wine throughout our whole kingdom, and one measure of ale and one measure of wheat—namely, the London quart—and one width of dyed and russet[31] and halberjet[32] cloth—namely, two ells below the selvage.[33] And with weights, moreover, it shall be as with measures.

36  Henceforth, nothing shall be given or taken for a writ of inquest[34] in a matter concerning life or limb but it shall be conceded for free, and shall not be denied.

37  If anyone holds of us in fee-farm, or in socage, or in burgage,[35] and holds land of another person by military service, we shall not, by reason of that fee-farm, or socage, or burgage, have the wardship of his heir or of his land which is held as a fee from another. Nor shall we have the wardship of that fee-farm, or socage, or burgage unless that fee-farm owes military service. We shall not, by reason of some petty-serjeanty[36] which someone holds of us through the service of giving us knives or arrows or the like, have the wardship of his heir or of the land which he holds of another person by military service.

38  No bailiff, on his own simple assertion, shall henceforth put anyone on trial, without producing faithful witnesses regarding the matter.

39  No free man shall be taken, or imprisoned, or disseised,[37] or outlawed, or exiled, or in any way destroyed—nor will we go or send against him—except by the lawful judgment of his peers or by the law of the land.

40  To no one will we sell, to no one deny or delay right or justice.

41  All merchants may safely and securely go out of England, and come into England, and stay and pass through England, by land as well as by water, for the purpose of buying and selling, free from all evil taxes, subject to the ancient and right customs, except in time of war, and if they are of the land at war against us. And if such merchants are found in our land at the beginning of the war, they shall be held without harm to their bodies and goods, until it shall be known to us or our chief justiciar how the merchants of our land who at that time are to be found in the land at war against us are treated. And if ours are safe there, the others shall be safe in our land.

42  Henceforth any person, saving loyalty to us, may go out of our kingdom and return to it, safely and securely, by land and by water, except for a brief period in time of war, on account of the common interest of the kingdom. But prisoners and outlaws are excepted according to the law of the kingdom, as are people of a land at war against us, and merchants with regard to whom shall be done as aforesaid.

43  If anyone holds from any escheat[38]—as from the honors[39] of Wallingford, Nottingham, Boulogne, Lancaster, or the other escheats which are in our hands and are baronies—and shall die, his heir shall not give a relief, nor shall he perform for us other service than he would perform for a baron if that barony were in the hand of a baron, and we shall hold it in the same way in which the baron has held it.

---

30  A royal writ was a brief letter conveying a command. In order to begin a lawsuit in a court held by a royal judge, one had to obtain a writ from the king ordering the judge or some other person to act. Most such writs came in standardized forms, and were named after a characteristic word or few words which appeared in that kind of writ. The writ *Praecipe* ordered the recipient to return disputed land to the person who had procured the writ or else come to the king's court to be sued for the land by that person. This writ could effectively remove a dispute from a lord's court to the king's court.

31  A coarse wool cloth, often reddish in color.

32  It is not clear what kind of cloth this was.

33  I.e., the edge of the cloth which is finished so that it will not unravel.

34  A writ ordering an inquiry into a matter of fact by questioning a local jury of people from the neighborhood.

35  These are three forms of land tenure for free people which did not involve military service.

36  A category of land tenure through some kind of minor military service.

37  I.e., put out of legal possession.

38  I.e., a fee which has reverted to a lord.

39  A collection of lands held by or from a great lord and which are seen as a unit.

44   Persons dwelling outside the Forest[40] henceforth shall not come before the Forest judges through common summonses, unless they are sued or are the sponsors of some person or persons attached for matters concerning the Forest.

45   We will not make judges, constables, sheriffs, or bailiffs, except such as know the law of the kingdom, and are minded to observe it well.

46   All barons who have founded abbeys for which they have charters of the kings of England, or ancient right of tenure, shall have, as they ought to have, custody of those abbeys when vacant.[41]

47   All Forests constituted as such in our time shall immediately be annulled, and the same shall be done for river banks enclosed by us to be places of defense in our time.

48   All evil customs concerning Forests and warrens,[42] and concerning foresters and game keepers, sheriffs and their servants, river banks and their guardians, shall be immediately investigated in each county through 12 sworn knights from that county, and shall be entirely eradicated by them so that they shall never be recalled, within 40 days after the inquiry has been made; concerning these, we, or if we are not in England, our justiciar, will first be informed.

49   We shall immediately return all hostages and charters which were delivered to us by Englishmen as security for peace or faithful service.

50   We shall entirely remove from their offices the relatives of Gerard de Athée, so that they shall henceforth have no office in England: Engelard de Cigogné, Peter, Andrew and Guy de Chanceaux, Guy de Cigogné, Geoffrey de Martigny and his brothers, Philip Mark and his brothers, and Geoffrey, his nephew, and all of their following.

51   And immediately after peace is restored we shall remove from the kingdom all alien knights, crossbowmen, serjeants, and mercenaries who have come with horses and arms to the harm of the kingdom.

52   If anyone has been disseised by us, or removed, without a legal judgment of his peers, from his lands, castles, liberties or right, we shall immediately restore them to him. And if a dispute shall arise concerning this matter, it shall be settled according to the judgment of the 25 barons who are mentioned below concerning the security of the peace. But with regard to all those things of which anyone was disseised or dispossessed by King Henry our father[43] or King Richard our brother[44] without legal judgment of his peers, which we have in our hand or which others hold, and for which we are to give warranty:[45] we shall have respite until the usual term for crusaders,[46] excepting those concerning which a suit was begun or an inquiry made by our order before we took the cross.[47] But when we return from our pilgrimage, or if, by chance, we desist from our pilgrimage, we shall immediately then show full justice regarding them.

53   We shall have the same respite, moreover, and in the same manner, in the matter of showing justice with regard to Forests to be annulled and Forests to remain which Henry our father or Richard our brother constituted, and in the matter of wardships of lands which belong to the fee of another—wardships of which kind we have hitherto enjoyed by reason of the fee which someone held from us in military service—and in the matter of abbeys founded in the fee of someone other than us, in which the lord of the fee may say that he has jurisdiction. And when we return, or if we desist from our pilgrimage, we shall immediately show full justice to those complaining with regard to these matters.

54   No one shall be taken or imprisoned on account

---

40   See above, n 1.

41   When the position of abbot was vacant, the founder of a monastery often had the right to the lands and revenues of the office of abbot or those of the monastery itself during the vacancy .

42   Land set aside for hunting.

43   Henry II (1153-1189).

44   Richard I (1189-1199).

45   The guarantee of protection in the landholding a lord gave a tenant.

46   Crusaders were given a respite from being sued, thus allowing them to go on crusade without having to defend their holdings in court at home.

47   "To take the cross" was to commit oneself to going on crusade.

of the appeal of a woman concerning the death of anyone except her husband.

55  All fines imposed by us unjustly and contrary to the law of the land, and all amercements made unjustly and contrary to the law of the land, shall be entirely remitted, or they shall be dealt with according to the judgment of the 25 barons mentioned below concerning the security of the peace, or according to the judgment of the majority of them together with the aforesaid Stephen, archbishop of Canterbury, if he can be present, and with others whom he may wish to summon with him for this purpose. And if he cannot be present, the business shall nevertheless proceed without him in such a way that, if one or more of the said 25 barons shall be concerned in a similar complaint, they shall be removed as to this particular decision, and, in their place, for this purpose alone, others shall be substituted who shall be chosen and sworn by the remainder of those 25.

56  If we have disseised or dispossessed Welshmen of their lands or liberties or other things without legal judgment of their peers, in England or in Wales, they shall immediately be restored to them. And if a dispute shall arise concerning this, then action shall be taken upon it in the March[48] through judgment of their peers—concerning English holdings according to the law of England, concerning Welsh holdings according to the law of Wales, concerning holdings in the March according to the law of the March. The Welsh shall do likewise with regard to us and our subjects.

57  But with regard to all those things of which anyone of the Welsh was, by King Henry our father or King Richard our brother, disseised or dispossessed without legal judgment of his peers, which we have in our hands or which others hold, and for which we are to give warranty: we shall have respite until the usual term for crusaders, excepting those concerning which a suit was begun or an inquiry made by our order before we took the cross. But when we return from our pilgrimage, or if, by chance, we desist from our pilgrimage, we shall immediately then show full justice regarding them, according to the laws of Wales and the aforesaid districts.

58  We shall immediately return the son of Llywelyn[49] and all the Welsh hostages, and the charters delivered to us as security for the peace.

59  We shall act towards Alexander, king of the Scots, regarding the restoration of his sisters, hostages, and his liberties and his lawful right, as we shall act towards our other barons of England, unless it ought to be otherwise according to the charters which we hold from William, his father, the former king of the Scots. And this shall be done through judgment of his peers in our court.

60  Moreover, all the subjects of our realm, clergy as well as laity, shall, as far as pertains to them, observe, with regard to their subjects, all these aforesaid customs and liberties which we have decreed shall, as far as pertains to us, be observed in our realm with regard to our subjects.

61  Since, however, we have made all these aforesaid concessions for the sake of God, and for the bettering of our realm, and for the more ready healing of the discord which has arisen between us and our barons, wishing that they enjoy these things forever, entirely and with a firm stability, we make and grant to them the following security: namely, that the barons may elect at their pleasure 25 barons from the kingdom, who ought, with all their strength, to observe, maintain and cause to be observed the peace and liberties which we have granted to them and confirmed by this our present charter. This is done in such a way that if we, or our justiciar, or our bailiffs, or any one of our servants transgress against anyone in any respect, or shall have broken any of the articles of peace or security, and our transgression has been shown to 4 barons of the aforesaid 25, those 4 barons shall come to us, or, if we are abroad, to our justiciar, showing us our error, and they shall ask us to cause that error to be amended without delay. And if we do not amend that error, or, we being abroad, if our justiciar does not amend it within 40 days from the time when it was shown to us or, we being abroad, to our justiciar, the aforesaid 4

---

48  A region along the border between England and Wales in which the king's barons had a special jurisdiction, and which thus produced a distinctive body of law.

49  Llywelyn was the leading political power in Wales beyond John's clear jurisdiction. Earlier in his career he had declared himself to be John's vassal, probably without the intention of being much subject to John in practice.

barons shall refer the matter to the remainder of the 25 barons, and those 25 barons, with the commune[50] of the whole land, shall distrain and oppress us in every way in their power, namely, by taking our castles, lands and possessions, and in every other way that they can, excepting the persons of ourselves, our queen and our children, until amends have been made according to their judgment. And when amends have been made, they shall maintain themselves toward us as they had done previously. And whoever in the land wishes to do so, shall swear that in carrying out all the aforesaid measures he will obey the mandates of the aforesaid 25 barons, and that, with them, he will oppress us to the extent of his power. And, to anyone who wishes to do so, we publicly and freely give permission to swear, and we will never prevent anyone from swearing. Moreover, as to all those in the land who shall be unwilling, themselves and of their own accord, to swear to the 25 barons as to distraining and oppressing us with them: such ones we shall make swear by our mandate, as has been said. And if any one of the 25 barons dies, or leaves the country, or in any other way is prevented from carrying out the aforesaid measures, the remainder of the aforesaid 25 barons shall choose another in his place, according to their judgment, who shall be sworn in the same way as the others. Moreover, in all things entrusted to those 25 barons to be carried out, if those 25 shall be present and chance to disagree among themselves with regard to some matter, or if some of them, having been summoned, shall be unwilling or unable to be present, that which the majority of those present shall decide or decree shall be considered binding and valid, just as if all the 25 had consented to it. And the aforesaid 25 shall swear that they will faithfully observe all the foregoing, and will cause it to be observed to the extent of their power. And we shall obtain nothing from anyone, either through ourselves or through another, by which any of those concessions and liberties may be revoked or diminished. And if any such thing shall have been obtained, it shall be in vain and invalid, and we shall never make use of it, either ourselves or through another.

62   And we have fully remitted and pardoned all the ill-will, anger and rancor which has arisen between us and our subjects, clergy and laity, from the time of the struggle. Moreover we have fully remitted to all, clergy and laity, and—as far as pertains to us—have pardoned fully all the transgressions committed on the occasion of that same struggle, from Easter of the sixteenth year of our reign until the re-establishment of peace. In witness of which, moreover, we have caused to be drawn up for them letters patent of lord Stephen, archbishop of Canterbury, lord Henry, archbishop of Dublin, and the aforesaid bishops and master Pandulf, regarding that security and the aforesaid concessions.

63   Wherefore, we will and firmly decree that the English church shall be free, and that the subjects of our realm shall have and hold all the aforesaid liberties, rights and concessions, duly and in peace, freely and quietly, fully and entirely, for themselves and their heirs, from us and our heirs, in all matters and in all places, forever, as has been said. Moreover, it has been sworn, on our part, as well as on the part of the barons, that all these above mentioned provisions shall be observed with good faith and without evil intent. The witnesses are the above mentioned and many others. Given by our hand, in the meadow called Runnymede between Windsor and Staines, on the 15th day of June, in the 17th year of our reign.

---

50   In politics, a commune was generally a body of associates who had taken an oath for common action.

# 37

# CANONS OF THE FOURTH LATERAN COUNCIL

Pope Innocent III (1198-1215) is widely considered one of the most influential popes of the Middle Ages. In 1213 he summoned about 1,200 higher clergy to meet at Rome for the Fourth Lateran Council, held in 1215. He also summoned representatives from the major secular powers of the Western world, although they were to act solely as observers. The council issued the canons, or church laws, which appear below. It is generally held that they were ultimately the products of Innocent and those close to him.

---

1  We firmly believe and openly confess that there is only one true God, eternal and immense, omnipotent, unchangeable, incomprehensible, and ineffable, Father, Son, and Holy Spirit—three Persons indeed, but one essence, substance, or nature absolutely simple, the Father proceeding from no one, but the Son from the Father only, and the Holy Spirit equally from both, always without beginning and end, the Father begetting, the Son begotten, and the Holy Spirit proceeding, consubstantial[1] and coequal, co-omnipotent and coeternal, the one principle of the universe, Creator of all thing invisible and visible, spiritual and corporeal, who from the beginning of time and by His omnipotent power made from nothing creatures both spiritual and corporeal, namely angelic and mundane, and then human, as it were, common, composed of spirit and body. The devil and other demons were indeed created by God good by nature, but they became bad through themselves; humanity, however, sinned at the suggestion of the devil. This Holy Trinity—in its common essence undivided and in personal properties divided—gave, through Moses, the holy prophets, and other servants, the doctrine of salvation to the human race at the most opportune intervals of time.

And finally, Jesus Christ, the only begotten Son of God made flesh by the entire Trinity, conceived with the cooperation of the Holy Spirit of Mary, ever Virgin, made true humanity, composed of a rational soul and human flesh, one Person in two natures, pointed out more clearly the way of life. Who according to His divinity is immortal and impassable,[2] according to His humanity was made passable and mortal, suffered on the cross for the salvation of the human race, and being dead descended into hell, rose from the dead, and ascended equally in both natures; He will come at the end of the world to judge the living and the dead and will render to the reprobate and to the elect according to their works, who all shall rise with their own bodies which they now have that they may receive according to their merits, whether good or bad, the latter

---

1  I.e., having the same substance.
2  I.e., incapable of suffering.

eternal punishment with the devil, the former eternal glory with Christ.

There is one Universal Church of the faithful, outside of which there is absolutely no salvation, in which there is the same priest and sacrifice, Jesus Christ, whose body and blood are truly contained in the sacrament of the altar under the forms of bread and wine—the bread being changed by divine power into the body, and the wine into the blood so that to realize the mystery of unity we may receive from Him what He has received from us. And no one can perform this sacrament except the priest who has been duly ordained in accordance with the keys of the Church, which Jesus Christ Himself gave to the Apostles and their successors.

But the sacrament of baptism, which by the invocation of each Person of the Trinity, namely, of the Father, Son, and Holy Spirit, is effected in water, duly conferred on children and adults in the form prescribed by the Church by anyone whatsoever, leads to salvation. And should anyone after the reception of baptism have fallen into sin, by true repentance he can always be restored. Not only virgins and those practicing chastity, but also those united in marriage, through the right faith and through works pleasing to God, can merit eternal salvation.

2  We condemn, therefore, and reject the book or tract which Abbot Joachim[3] published against Master Peter Lombard[4] concerning the unity or essence of the Trinity, calling him heretical and insane because he said in his *Sentences* that the Father, Son, and Holy Spirit are some supreme entity in which there is no begetting, no begotten, and no proceeding, whence he

asserts that he[5] attributed to God not so much a trinity as quaternity, namely three Persons and that common essence as a fourth, clearly protesting that there is no entity that is Father, Son, and Holy Spirit, neither is it essence or substance or nature, although he concedes that the Father, Son and Holy Spirit are one essence, one substance, and one nature. But he says that such a unity is not a true and proper unity, but rather a collective one or one by way of similitude, as many men are called one people and many faithful one Church, according to the words: "The multitude of believers had but one heart and one soul";[6] and "He who is joined to the Lord, is one spirit";[7] similarly, "He that plants and he that waters, are one";[8] and, "So we being many, are one body in Christ."[9] Again in the Book of Kings: "My people and your people are one."[10] To strengthen this teaching he cites that most important word which Christ spoke concerning the faithful in the Gospel: "I will, Father, that they may be one, as we also are one, that they may be made perfect in one."[11] For the faithful of Christ, he says, are not one in the sense that they are some one thing that is common to all, but in the sense that they constitute one Church by reason of the unity of the Catholic faith and one kingdom by reason of the union of indissoluble charity, as we read in the canonical Epistle of St. John: "There are three who give testimony in heaven: the Father, the Word, and the Holy Spirit; and these three are one."[12] And immediately it is added: "And there are three who give testimony on earth: the spirit, the water, and the blood; and these three are one,"[13] as it is found in some books.

But we, with the approval of the holy and general

---

3  Joachim, abbot of Fiore, who in the late twelfth century foretold a future "age of the Holy Spirit," which would supersede the need for the Church and the New Testament; he also maintained that his own time was the "age of the Son" (i.e., of the New Testament), which itself had superseded the "age of the Father" (i.e., the Old Testament).
4  A leading twelfth-century scholastic.
5  I.e., Peter Lombard.
6  New Testament, Acts 4.32.
7  New Testament, 1 Corinthians 6.17.
8  New Testamant, 1 Corinthians 3.8.
9  New Testament, Romans 12.5.
10  Old Testament, 1 Kings 22.4, 2 Kings 3.7.
11  New Testament, John 17.22.
12  New Testament, 1 John 5.7.
13  New Testament, 1 John 5.8.

council, believe and confess with Peter[14] that there is one supreme entity, incomprehensible and ineffable, which is truly Father, Son, and Holy Spirit, together three persons and each one of them singly. And thus in God there is only trinity, not quaternity, because each of three persons is the entity, namely, substance, essence, or divine nature, which alone is the principle of the universe and besides which there is no other. And that entity is not the one begetting or the one begotten or the one proceeding, but it is the Father who begets, the Son who is begotten, and the Holy Spirit who proceeds, in order that there may be distinctions in the Persons and unity in the nature. Though, therefore, the Father is one being, the Son is another, and the Holy Spirit is another, yet they are not different, but that which is the Father is the Son and the Holy Spirit, absolutely the same, since according to the orthodox and Catholic faith they are believed to be consubstantial. For the Father begetting the Son from eternity imparted to Him His own substance, as He Himself testifies: "That which my Father has given me, is greater than all."[15] And it cannot be said that He gave to Him a part of His substance and retained a part for Himself, since the substance of the Father is indivisible, that is, absolutely simple. But neither can it be said that the Father in begetting transferred His substance to the Son, as if He gave it to the Son without retaining it for Himself, otherwise He would cease to be a substance. It is evident, therefore, that the Son in being begotten received without any diminution the substance of the Father, and thus the Father and Son have the same substance, and thus the Father and Son as well as the Holy Spirit proceeding from both are the same entity. When therefore the Truth[16] prays to the Father for the faithful, saying: "I will that they be one in us, even as we are one,"[17] this term "one" is understood first for the faithful, as implying a union of charity in grace, then for the divine persons, as implying a unity of identity in nature; as the Truth says in another place: "Be you perfect, as your heavenly Father is perfect";[18] as if He would say more clearly: be perfect by the perfection of grace as your heavenly Father is perfect by the perfection of nature, namely, each in his own way, because between the Creator and the creature[19] there cannot be a likeness so great that the unlikeness is not greater. If therefore anyone presumes to defend or approve the teaching of the aforesaid Joachim on this point, let him be repressed by all as a heretic.

In this, however, we do not wish to derogate in anything from the monastery of Fiore, which Joachim himself founded, since therein is both the regular life[20] and salutary observance, but chiefly because the same Joachim ordered that his writing be submitted to us to be approved or corrected by the judgment of the Apostolic See,[21] dictating a letter which he subscribed with his own hand, in which he firmly confesses that he holds that faith which the Roman Church holds, which by the will of God is the mother and mistress of all the faithful. We also reject and condemn the perverse teaching of the impious Amaury de Bene,[22] whose mind the father of lies has so darkened that his teaching is to be regarded not so much heretical as insane.

3 We excommunicate and anathematize every heresy that raises itself against the holy, orthodox and Catholic faith which we have above explained, condemning all heretics under whatever names they may be known, for while they have different faces, they are nevertheless bound to each other by their tails, since in all of them vanity is a common element. Those condemned, being handed over to the secular rulers or

---

14  Peter Lombard.
15  New Testament, John 10.29.
16  I.e., Jesus.
17  New Testament, John 17.22.
18  New Testament, Matthew 5.48.
19  I.e., created thing.
20  I.e., life according to the Benedictine Rule.
21  I.e., the papacy.
22  Burned in 1209. He had claimed that the Holy Spirit had made him incapable of sin, and so he did not require the sacraments of the Church.

their bailiffs, let them be abandoned, to be punished with due justice, clerics being first degraded from their orders.[23] As to the property of the condemned, if they are laymen, let it be confiscated; if clerics, let it be applied to the churches from which they received revenues. But regarding those who are only suspected, due consideration being given to the nature of the suspicion and the character of the person, unless they prove their innocence by a proper defense, let them be anathematized and avoided by all until they have made suitable satisfaction. But if they have been under excommunication for one year, then let them be condemned as heretics. Secular authorities, whatever office they may hold, shall be admonished and induced and if necessary compelled by ecclesiastical censure, that as they wish to be esteemed and numbered among the faithful, so for the defense of the faith they ought publicly to take an oath they will strive in good faith and to the best of their ability to exterminate in the territories subject to their jurisdiction all heretics pointed out by the Church, so that whenever anyone shall have assumed authority, whether spiritual or temporal, let him be bound to confirm this decree by oath. But if a temporal ruler, after having been requested and admonished by the Church, should neglect to cleanse his territory of this heretical foulness, let him be excommunicated by the metropolitan[24] and the other bishops of the province. If he refuses to make satisfaction within a year, let the matter be made known to the supreme pontiff,[25] that he may declare the ruler's vassals absolved from their allegiance and may offer the territory to be ruled by Catholics,[26] who on the extermination of the heretics may possess it without hindrance and preserve it in the purity of faith. The right, however, of the chief ruler is to be respected so long as he offers no obstacle in this matter and permits freedom of action. The same law is to be observed in regard to those who

have no chief rulers. Catholics who have girded themselves with the cross for the extermination of the heretics shall enjoy the indulgences and privileges granted to those who go in defense of the Holy Land.

We decree that those who give credence to the teachings of the heretics, as well as those who receive, defend, and patronize them, are excommunicated, and we firmly declare that after any one of them has been branded with excommunication, if he has deliberately failed to make satisfaction within a year, let him incur by the same law the stigma of infamy and let him not be admitted to public offices or deliberations, and let him not take part in the election of others to such offices or use his right to give testimony in a court of law. Let him also be intestable,[27] that he may not have the free exercise of making a will, and let him be deprived of the right of inheritance. Let no one be urged to give an account to him in any matter, but let him be urged to give an account to others. If he happens to be a judge, let his decisions have no force, nor let any case be brought to his attention. If he is an advocate, let his assistance by no means be sought. If a notary, let the instruments drawn up by him be considered worthless, for, the author being condemned, let them enjoy a similar fate. In all similar cases we command that the same be observed. If, however, he be a cleric, let him be deposed from every office and benefice,[28] that the greater the fault the graver may be the punishment inflicted.

If anyone refuses to avoid such persons after they have been ostracized by the Church, let them be excommunicated till they have made suitable satisfaction. Clerics shall not give the sacraments of the Church to such pestilential people, nor shall they presume to give them Christian burial, or to receive their alms or offerings; otherwise they shall be deprived of their office, to which they may not be restored without a special indult[29] of the Apostolic See. Similarly, all

23  I.e., clergy are first to be stripped of their standing as clergy.
24  A metropolitan was an archbishop; the territory he governed was a province, in which might be included one or more dioceses, each governed by a bishop.
25  I.e., the pope. A pontiff is a bishop.
26  I.e., orthodox Christians.
27  Unable to make a valid will.
28  A church office which yields revenue.
29  Permission.

regulars,[30] on whom also this punishment may be imposed, let their privileges be nullified in that diocese in which they have presumed to perpetrate such excesses.

But since some, under "the appearance of godliness, but denying the power thereof," as the Apostle says,[31] arrogate to themselves the authority to preach, as the same Apostle says, "How shall they preach unless they be sent?"[32] all those prohibited or not sent, who, without the authority of the Apostolic See or of the Catholic bishop of the locality, shall presume to usurp the office of preaching either publicly or privately, shall be excommunicated and unless they amend, and the sooner the better, they shall be visited with a further suitable penalty. We add, moreover, that every archbishop or bishop should himself or through his archdeacon[33] or some other suitable persons, twice or at least once a year make the rounds of his diocese in which report has it that heretics dwell, and there compel three or more men of good character or, if it should be deemed advisable, the entire neighborhood, to swear that if anyone knows of the presence there of heretics or others holding secret assemblies, or differing from the common way of the faithful in faith and morals, they will make them known to the bishop. The latter shall then call together before him those accused, who, if they do not purge themselves of the matter of which they are accused,[34] or if after the rejection of their error they lapse into their former wickedness, shall be canonically punished. But if any of them by damnable obstinacy should disapprove of the oath and should perchance be unwilling to swear, from this very fact let them be regarded as heretics.

We wish, therefore, and in virtue of obedience strictly command, that to carry out these instructions effectively the bishops exercise throughout their dioceses a scrupulous vigilance if they wish to escape canonical punishment. If from sufficient evidence it is apparent that a bishop is negligent or remiss in cleansing his diocese of the ferment of heretical wickedness, let him be deposed from the episcopal office and let another, who will and can confound heretical depravity, be substituted.

4   Though we wish to favor and honor the Greeks who in our days are returning to the obedience of the Apostolic See[35] by permitting them to retain their customs and rites in so far as the interests of God allow us, in those things, however, that are a danger to souls and derogatory to ecclesiastical propriety, we neither wish nor ought to submit to them. After the Church of the Greeks with some of her accomplices and supporters had severed herself from the obedience of the Apostolic See, to such an extent did the Greeks begin hating the Latins that among other things which they impiously committed derogatory to the Latins was this, that when Latin priests had celebrated upon their altars, they would not offer the sacrifice upon those altars until the altars had first been washed, as if by this they had defiled. Also, those baptized by the Latins the Greeks rashly presume to rebaptize, and even now, as we understand, there are some who do not hesitate to do this. Desirous, therefore, of removing such scandal from the Church of God, and advised by the holy council, we strictly command that they do not presume to do such things in the future, but conform themselves as obedient children to the Holy Roman Church, their mother, that there may be "one fold and one shepherd." If anyone shall presume to act contrary to this, let him be excommunicated and deposed from every office and ecclesiastical benefice.

5   Renewing the ancient privileges of the patriarchal sees,[36] we decree with the approval of the holy and ecumenical council that after the Roman Church,

---

30   Members of the regular clergy, or monastics, so called because they live under a *regula*, or rule.
31   New Testament, 2 Timothy 3.5.
32   New Testament, Romans 10.15.
33   In theory, the chief assistant of a bishop.
34   I.e., swear, perhaps with companions, that they are not guilty of the charges.
35   I.e., those in the east, previously considered Greek Orthodox, who have accepted papal jurisdiction.
36   I.e., the sees of those archbishops who were recognized as "patriarchs." So far as the papacy was concerned, only the popes, who were also patriarchs, had a higher standing.

which by the will of God holds over all others preeminence of ordinary[37] power as the mother and mistress of all the faithful, that of Constantinople shall hold first place, that of Alexandria second, that of Antioch third, and that of Jerusalem fourth, the dignity proper to each to be observed; so that after their bishops have received from the Roman pontiff the pallium,[38] which is the distinguishing mark of the plenitude of the pontifical office, and have taken the oath of fidelity and obedience to him, they may also lawfully bestow the pallium upon their suffragans,[39] receiving from them the canonical profession of faith for themselves, and for the Roman Church the pledge of obedience. They may have the standard of the cross carried before them everywhere, except in the city of Rome and wherever the supreme pontiff or his legate[40] wearing the insignia of the Apostolic dignity is present. In all provinces subject to their jurisdiction appeals may be taken to them when necessary, saving the appeals directed to the Apostolic See, which must be humbly respected.

6   In accordance with the ancient provisions of the holy Fathers, the metropolitans must not neglect to hold with their suffragans the annual provincial synods.[41] In these they should be actuated with a genuine fear of God in correcting abuses and reforming morals, especially the morals of the clergy, familiarizing themselves anew with the canonical rules, particularly those that are enacted in this general council, that they may enforce their observance by imposing due punishment on transgressors. That this may be done more effectively, let them appoint in each and every diocese prudent and upright persons, who throughout the entire year shall informally and without any jurisdiction diligently investigate such things

as need correction or reform and faithfully present them to the metropolitan, suffragans, and others in the following synod, so that they may give prudent consideration to these and other matters as circumstances demand; and in reference to those things that they decree, let them enforce observance, publishing the decisions in the episcopal synods to be held annually in each diocese. Whoever shall neglect to comply with this salutary statute, let him be suspended from his office and benefices until it shall please his superior to restore him.

7   By an unbreakable decree we ordain that prelates[42] make a prudent and earnest effort to correct the excesses and reform the morals of their subjects, especially of the clergy, lest their blood be demanded at their hands. But that they may perform the duty of correction and reform unhindered, we decree that no custom or appeal shall stand in the way of their efforts, unless they shall have exceeded the form to be observed in such cases. The abuses, however, of the canons of the cathedral church,[43] the correction of which has by custom belonged to the chapter, shall, in those churches in which such a custom has hitherto prevailed, by the advice or command of the bishop be corrected within a reasonable time specified by the bishop. Otherwise the bishop, having in mind the interests of God, opposition notwithstanding, shall not delay to correct them by means of ecclesiastical censure according as the care of souls demands. Nor shall he neglect to correct the excesses also of the other clerics assisting the canons according as the care of souls requires, due order, however, being observed in all things. If the canons, without a manifest and reasonable cause, chiefly through contempt for the bishop, discontinue divine services, the bishop

---

37   An ecclesiastical judge with broad jurisdiction which inheres permanently in the office the judge holds—such as a bishop in his diocese—held "ordinary jurisdiction." A delegated judge was one appointed by an ordinary, most usually the pope, himself sometimes called "the universal ordinary."

38   A kind of stole.

39   I.e., subordinate bishops.

40   Officially designated personal representative of the pope.

41   I.e., a council of the clergy.

42   I.e., high church officials, such as bishops.

43   The canons of a cathedral church, or headquarters church of a diocese, were collectively called a "chapter." Although in origin the bishop's chief assistants in managing the diocese, by this time the chapter generally claimed a large measure of independence from the bishop's jurisdiction.

may, if he wishes, perform divine services in the cathedral church, and on his complaint the metropolitan, as delegated by us in this matter, shall so punish them with ecclesiastical censure that for fear of a repetition of the punishment they will not presume to do such things in the future. Let the prelates of the churches, therefore, be diligently on their guard that they do not convert this salutary decree into a means of personal profit or other objectionable conduct, but let them enforce it earnestly and faithfully if they wish to escape canonical punishment, for in this matter the Apostolic See, on the authority of the Lord, will be most vigilant.

8   How and when a prelate ought to proceed in the inquiry and punishment of the excesses of subjects[44] is clearly deduced from the authority of the New and Old Testaments, from which the canonical decrees were afterward drawn, as we have long since clearly pointed out and now with the approval of the holy council confirm. For we read in the Gospel that the steward who was accused to his master of wasting his goods, heard him say: "How is it that I hear this of you? Give an account of your stewardship, for now you can be steward no longer."[45] And in Genesis the Lord said: "I will go down and see whether they have done according to the cry that is come to me."[46] From these authorities it is clearly proved that not only when a subject but also when a prelate is guilty of excesses and these should come to the ears of the superior through complaint and report, not indeed from spiteful and slanderous persons, but from those who are prudent and upright persons, and not only once but often, he must in the presence of the seniors of the church carefully inquire into the truth of such reports, so that if they prove to be true, the guilty party may be duly punished without the superior being both accuser and judge in the matter. But, while this is to be observed in regard to the subjects, the

observance must be stricter in reference to prelates, who are, as it were, a target for the arrow. Because they cannot please all, since by their very office they are bound not only to rebuke but also at times to loose and bind,[47] they frequently incur the hatred of many and are subject to insidious attacks. The holy fathers, therefore, wisely decreed that accusations against prelates must be accepted with great reserve lest, the pillars being shattered, the edifice itself fall unless proper precaution be exercised, by which recourse not only to false but also malicious incrimination is precluded. They wished so to protect prelates that on the one hand they might not be unjustly accused, and on the other hand, that they might be on their guard, lest they should become haughtily delinquent; finding a suitable remedy for each disease in the provision that a criminal accusation which calls for diminution of the chief, that is, degradation, is by no means to be accepted, unless a legal written instrument[48] comes first. But when anyone shall have been accused on account of his excesses, so that the reports and whisperings arising therefrom cannot any longer be ignored without scandal or tolerated without danger, then steps, inspired not by hatred but by charity, must be taken without scruple toward an inquiry and punishment of his excesses. If it is a question of a grave offense, though not one that calls for degradation from the order, the accused must be deprived absolutely of all administrative authority, which is in accordance with the teaching of the Gospel, namely, that the steward who cannot render a proper account of his office as steward be deprived of his stewardship. He about whom inquiry is to be made must be present, unless he absents himself through stubbornness, and the matter to be investigated must be made known to him, that he may have opportunity to defend himself. Not only the testimony of the witnesses but also their names must be made known to him, that he may be

---

44   Evidently clerical subordinates.
45   New Testament, Luke 16.2.
46   Old Testament, Genesis 18.21.
47   A reference to New Testament, Matthew 16.19, where Jesus announces that Peter will have the power to "bind and loose." The pope is seen as the successor of Peter, the first bishop of Rome.
48   Such an instrument would name the accuser.

aware who testified against him and what was their testimony and, finally, legitimate exceptions and replies must be admitted, lest by the suppression of names and by the exclusion of exceptions the boldness of the defamer and the false witness be encouraged. The diligence of the prelate in correcting the excesses of his subjects ought to be in proportion to the blame-worthiness of allowing the offense to go unpunished. Against such offenders, to say nothing of those who are guilty of notorious crimes, there can be a threefold course of procedure, namely, by accusation, by denun-ciation, and by inquiry, in all of which, however, prop-er precaution must be exercised lest perhaps by undue haste grave detriment should result. The accusation must be preceded by the legal written instrument, denunciation by the loving warning, and the inquiry by the public proclamation; such moderation to be always used so that the mode of the judgment be gov-erned by the mode of the trial. The foregoing, howev-er, does not apply to regular clerics, who, when a rea-son exists, can be removed from their charges more easily and expeditiously.

9   Since in many places within the same city and dio-cese there are people of different languages having one faith but various rites and customs, we strictly command that the bishops of these cities and dioceses provide suitable men who will, according to the dif-ferent rites and languages, celebrate the divine offices[49] for them, administer the sacraments of the Church and instruct them by word and example. But we absolutely forbid that one and the same city or dio-cese have more than one bishop, one body, as it were, with several heads, which is a monstrosity. But if by reason of the aforesaid conditions an urgent necessity should arise, let the bishop of the locality after due deliberation appoint a prelate acceptable to those peo-ples, who shall act as vicar in the aforesaid matters and be subject to him in all things. If anyone shall act otherwise, let him consider himself excommunicated,

and if even then he will not amend, let him be deposed from every ecclesiastical ministry, and if need be, let the secular arm[50] be employed, that such insolence may be curbed.

10   Among other things that pertain to the salvation of the Christian people, the food of the word of God is above all necessary, because as the body is nourished by material food, so is the soul nourished by spiritual food, since "not in bread alone does man live, but in every word that proceeds from the mouth of God."[51] It often happens that bishops, on account of their man-ifold duties or bodily infirmities, or because of hostile invasions or other reasons, to say nothing of lack of learning, which must be absolutely condemned in them and is not to be tolerated in the future, are them-selves unable to minister the word of God to the peo-ple, especially in large and widespread dioceses. Wherefore we decree that bishops provide suitable men, powerful in work and word, to exercise with fruitful result the office of preaching, who in place of the bishops, since these cannot do it, diligently visiting the people committed to them, may instruct them by word and example. And when they are in need, let them be supplied with the necessities, lest for want of these they may be compelled to abandon their work at the very beginning. Wherefore we command that in cathedral churches as well as in conventual churches[52] suitable men be appointed whom the bishops may use as coadjutors and assistants, not only in the office of preaching, but also in hearing confessions, imposing penances, and in other matters that pertain to the sal-vation of souls. If anyone neglects to comply with this, he shall be subject to severe punishment.

11   Since there are some who, on account of the lack of necessary means, are unable to acquire an educa-tion or to meet opportunities for perfecting them-selves, the Third Lateran Council[53] in a salutary decree provided that in every cathedral church a suit-able benefice be assigned to a master[54] who shall

---

49   Prayers.
50   I.e., secular authorities.
51   New Testament, Matthew 4.4.
52   I.e., monastic churches.
53   Held in 1179.
54   One who has studied in the schools, just now becoming universities, and attained a degree.

instruct for free the clerics of that church and other poor students, by means of which benefice the material needs of the master might be relieved and to the students a way opened to knowledge. But, since in many churches this is not observed, we, confirming the aforesaid decree, add that, not only in every cathedral church but also in other churches where means are sufficient, a competent master be appointed by the prelate with his chapter, or elected by the greater and more discerning part of the chapter, who shall instruct for free and to the best of his ability the clerics of those and other churches in the art of grammar[55] and in other branches of knowledge. In addition to a master, let the metropolitan church have also a theologian, who shall instruct the priests and others in the Sacred Scriptures and in those things especially that pertain to the care of souls. To each master let there be assigned by the chapter the revenue of one benefice, and to the theologian let as much be given by the metropolitan, not that they thereby become canons, but they shall enjoy the revenue only so long as they hold the office of instructor. If the metropolitan church cannot support two masters, then it shall provide for the theologian in the aforesaid manner, but for the one teaching grammar, let it see to it that a sufficiency is provided by another church of his city or diocese.

12　In every ecclesiastical province there shall be held every three years, saving the right of the diocesan ordinaries,[56] a general chapter of abbots and of priors having no abbots, who have not been accustomed to hold such chapters. This shall be held in a monastery best adapted to this purpose and shall be attended by all who are not canonically impeded, with this restriction, however, that no one bring with him more than six horses and eight persons. In inaugurating this new arrangement, let two neighboring abbots of the Cistercian order[57] be invited to give them counsel and opportune assistance, since among them the holding of such chapters is of long standing. These two Cistercians shall without hindrance choose from those present two whom they consider the most competent, and these four shall preside over the entire chapter, so that no one of these four may assume the authority of leadership; should it become expedient, they may be changed by prudent deliberation. Such a chapter shall be held for several consecutive days according to the custom of the Cistercian order. During its deliberations, careful attention is to be given to the reform of the order and to regular observance, and what has been enacted with the approval of the four shall be observed inviolably by all, excuses, contradictions, and appeals to the contrary notwithstanding. In each of these chapters the place for the holding of the following one is to be determined. All those in attendance, even if for want of room many must occupy other houses, must live the common life and bear proportionately all common expenses. In the same chapter religious and prudent persons should be appointed who, in our name, shall visit every abbey in the province, not only of monks but also of nuns, according to a form prescribed for them, correcting and reforming those things that need correction and reform, so that, if they should know that the rector[58] of a locality ought to be removed from office, let them make it known to his bishop, that he may procure his removal; but if he should neglect to do it, then the appointed visitors shall refer the matter to the attention of the Apostolic See. We wish and command that canons regular[59] observe this according to their order. But if in this new arrangement a difficulty should arise which cannot be disposed of by the aforesaid persons, let it be referred without scandal to the judgment of the Apostolic See. In the meantime, let the other things that have been accomplished by amicable deliberation be inviolably observed. Moreover, the diocesan ordinaries must strive so to reform the monasteries subject to them, that when the aforesaid visitors come to them they will find in them more that is worthy of commendation than of correction, taking special care lest the monasteries be oppressed by them with undue

55　This would have been Latin grammar.
56　I.e., bishops with ordinary jurisdiction within a diocese.
57　The Cistercian order was a reformed organization of monasteries begun in the twelfth century.
58　Cleric given charge of a parish, and enjoying the revenues from that parish.
59　Canons who followed a rule.

burdens. For, while we wish that the rights of superiors be respected, we do not on that account wish that injury be sustained by inferiors. We strictly command diocesan bishops and persons attending the chapters that with ecclesiastical censure—every appeal being denied—they restrain advocates, patrons, vicegerents, rulers, consuls, nobles, and soldiers, and all others, from molesting the monasteries either in persons or properties, and if it happens that these persons should so molest the monasteries, let the aforesaid bishops and chapter members not neglect to compel these latter to make satisfaction, that the monasteries may serve Almighty God more freely and peacefully.

13   Lest too great a diversity of religious orders[60] lead to grave confusion in the Church of God, we strictly forbid anyone in the future to found a new order, but whoever should wish to enter an order, is to choose one already approved. Similarly, one who wishes to found a new monastery must accept a rule already approved. We forbid also anyone to presume to be a monk in different monasteries, or that one abbot preside over several monasteries.

14   That the morals and general conduct of clerics may be better reformed, let all strive to live chastely and virtuously, particularly those in sacred orders, guarding against every vice of desire, especially that on account of which the anger of God came from heaven upon the children of unbelief, so that in the sight of Almighty God they may perform their duties with a pure heart and chaste body. But lest the facility to obtain pardon be an incentive to do wrong, we decree that whoever shall be found to indulge in the vice of incontinence,[61] shall, in proportion to the gravity of their sin, be punished in accordance with the canonical statutes, which we command to be strictly and rigorously observed, so that those whom divine fear does not restrain from evil, may at least be withheld from sin by a temporal penalty. If, therefore, anyone suspended for this reason shall presume to celebrate the divine mysteries,[62] let him not only be deprived of his ecclesiastical benefices, but for this twofold offense let him be deposed forever. Prelates who dare support such in their iniquities, especially in view of money or other temporal advantages, shall be subject to a like punishment. But if those, who according to the practice of their country have not renounced the conjugal bond, fall by the vice of impurity, they are to be punished more severely, since they can use matrimony lawfully.[63]

15   All clerics shall carefully abstain from drunkenness. Wherefore, let them accommodate the wine to themselves, and themselves to the wine. Nor shall anyone be encouraged to drink, for drunkenness banishes reason and incites lust. We decree, therefore, that that abuse be absolutely abolished by which in some localities the drinkers bind themselves each to drink an equal portion of drink as the others, and he in their judgment is the hero of the day who outdrinks the others. Should anyone be culpable in this matter, unless he heeds the warning of the superior and makes suitable satisfaction, let him be suspended from his benefice or office.

We forbid hunting and catching birds to all clerics; wherefore, let them not presume to keep dogs or birds for these purposes.

16   Clerics shall not hold secular offices or engage in secular and, above all, dishonest pursuits. They shall not attend the performances of mimics and buffoons, or theatrical presentations. They shall not visit taverns except in case of necessity, namely, when on a journey. They are forbidden to play games of chance or be present at them. They must have an appropriate head and tonsure[64] and apply themselves diligently to the study of the divine offices and other useful subjects. Their garments must be worn clasped at the top and neither too short nor too long. They are not to use red or green garments or curiously sewed together gloves, or beak-shaped shoes or gilded bridles, saddles, pectoral ornaments,[65] spurs, or

60   I.e., monastic organizations following different rules.
61   I.e., illicit sexual relations.
62   I.e., perform the sacraments, such as the mass.
63   This presumably refers to those priests who, formerly of the Greek Orthodox church, had recognized the jurisdiction of the papacy. The Greek Orthodox permitted priests to marry.
64   The tonsure was the shaved top of the head which signalled clerical status.
65   Ornaments worn by horses.

anything else indicative of superfluity. At the divine office in the church they are not to wear cappas[66] with long sleeves, and priests and dignitaries may not wear them elsewhere except in case of danger when circumstances should require a change of outer garments. Buckles may under no condition be worn, nor sashes having ornaments of gold or silver, nor rings, unless it be in keeping with the dignity of their office. All bishops must use in public and in the church outer garments made of linen, except those who are monks, in which case they must wear the habit of their order. In public they must not appear with open mantles, but these must be clasped either on the back of the neck or on the bosom.

17 It is a matter for regret that there are some minor clerics and even prelates who spend half of the night in banqueting and in unlawful gossip, not to mention other abuses, and in giving the remainder to sleep. They are scarcely awakened by the daily concerts of the birds. Then they hasten through matins[67] in a hurried and careless manner. There are others who say mass scarcely four times a year and, what is worse, do not even attend mass, and when they are present they are engaged outside in conversation with lay people to escape the silence of the choir, so that, while they readily lend their ears to unbecoming talk, they regard with utter indifference things that are divine. These and all similar things, therefore, we absolutely forbid under penalty of suspension, and strictly command in virtue of obedience that they celebrate diligently and devoutly the daily and nightly offices[68] so far as God gives them strength.

18 No cleric may pronounce a sentence of death, or execute such a sentence, or be present at its execution. If anyone in consequence of this prohibition should presume to inflict damage on churches or injury on ecclesiastical persons, let him be restrained by ecclesiastical censure. Nor may any cleric write or dictate letters destined for the execution of such a sentence. Wherefore, in the chanceries[69] of the princes[70] let this matter be committed to laymen and not to clerics. Neither may a cleric act as judge in the case of the Rottarii,[71] archers, or other men of this kind devoted to the shedding of blood. No subdeacon, deacon, or priest shall practice that part of surgery involving burning and cutting. Neither shall anyone in judicial tests or ordeals by hot or cold water or hot iron bestow any blessing;[72] the earlier prohibitions in regard to trial by combat remain in force.

19 We do not wish to leave uncorrected the practice of certain clerics who convert churches into storehouses for their own household goods and also for those of others, so that the churches have the appearance of the houses of lay people rather than of the house of God, not considering that the Lord does not permit the carrying of a vessel through the temple. There are also others who not only neglect to keep the churches clean, but also leave the vessels, vestments, pails, and corporeal things so unclean that sometimes they are a source of aversion. Wherefore, "since the zeal of the house of God has eaten us up,"[73] we strictly forbid that household goods be placed in the churches, unless by reason of hostile invasion, sudden fire, or other urgent reasons it should become necessary to store them there. When, however, the necessity no longer exists, let them be returned to their proper place. We command also that the aforesaid churches, vessels, corporeal things, and vestments be kept clean and bright. For it is absurd to tolerate in sacred things a filthiness that is unbecoming even in profane things.

---

66 A cappa was a kind of long cloak.

67 Morning prayers.

68 Prayers.

69 A chancery was a writing office.

70 I.e., of secular rulers.

71 Bands of robbers.

72 In the ordeal, an accused person's guilt or innocence was determined by, for example, having the accused person's hand plunged in hot water, bandaged, and examined after three days to see whether the wound was healing properly. If not, the accused was presumed guilty. A priest's blessing was considered essential to the process.

73 New Testament, John 2.17.

20   We decree that in all churches the chrism[74] and the eucharist[75] be kept in properly protected places provided with locks and keys, so that they may not be reached by rash and indiscreet persons and used for impious and blasphemous purposes. But if he to whom such guardianship pertains should leave them unprotected, let him be suspended from office for a period of three months. And if through his negligence an execrable deed should result, let him be punished more severely.

21   All the faithful of both sexes shall after they have reached the age of discretion faithfully confess all their sins at least once a year to their own parish priest and perform to the best of their ability the penance imposed, receiving reverently at least at Easter the sacrament of the eucharist, unless it happens at the advice of their own priest they may for a good reason abstain for a time from its reception; otherwise they shall be cut off from the Church[76] during life and deprived of Christian burial in death. Wherefore, let this salutary decree be published frequently in the churches, that no one may find in the plea of ignorance a shadow of excuse. But if anyone for a good reason should wish to confess one's sins to another priest, let that person first seek and obtain permission from that person's own priest, since otherwise he cannot loose or bind him.

Let the priest be discreet and cautious, that he may pour wine and oil into the wounds of the one injured after the manner of a skillful physician, carefully inquiring into the circumstances of the sinner and the sin, from the nature of which he may understand what kind of advice to give and what remedy to apply, making use of different experiments to heal the sick one. But let him exercise the greatest precaution that he does not in any degree by word, sign, or any other manner make known the sinner, but should he need more prudent counsel, let him seek it cautiously without any mention of the person. He who dares to reveal a sin confided to him in the tribunal of penance, we decree that he be not only deposed from the priestly office, but also relegated to a monastery of strict observance to do penance for the remainder of his life.

22   Since bodily infirmity is sometimes caused by sin, the Lord saying to the sick man whom he had healed, "Go and sin no more, lest some worse thing happen to you,"[77] we declare in the present decree and strictly command that when physicians of the body are called to the bedside of the sick, before all else they admonish them to call for the physician of souls, so that after spiritual health has been restored to them, the application of bodily medicine may be of greater benefit, for the cause being removed, the effect will pass away. We publish this decree for the reason that some, when they are sick and are advised by the physician in the course of the sickness to attend to the salvation of their soul, give up all hope and yield more easily to the danger of death. If any physician shall transgress this decree after it has been published by the bishops, let him be cut off from the Church until he has made suitable satisfaction for his transgression. And since the soul is far more precious than the body, we forbid under penalty of anathema that a physician advise a patient to have recourse to sinful means for the recovery of bodily health.

23   That the ravenous wolf may not invade the Lord's flock that is without a pastor, that a widowed church may not suffer grave loss in its properties, that danger to souls may be averted, and that provision may be made for the security of the churches, we decree that a cathedral or regular church must not be without a bishop for more than three months. If within this time an election has not been held by those to whom it pertains, though there was no impediment, the electors lose their right of voting, and the right to appoint devolves upon the next immediate superior. Let the one upon whom this right to appoint devolves, having God before his eyes, not delay more than three months to provide canonically and with the advice of the chapter and other prudent men the widowed church with a suitable pastor, if he wishes to escape canonical punishment. This pastor is to be chosen from the wid-

---

74   Holy oil.
75   The bread and wine used in the mass or communion.
76   I.e., excommunicated.
77   New Testament, John 5.14.

owed church itself, or from another in case a suitable person is not found therein.

24   Since, on account of the different forms of elections which some endeavor to employ, many impediments arise and great danger threatens widowed churches, we decree that when an election is to take place and all are present who ought, wish, and are able to be present, let three trustworthy members of the assembly be chosen who shall with care collect secretly and one by one the votes of all, and when these have been written down, he is to be considered elected who has obtained all or the majority of the votes of the chapter, absolutely no appeal being allowed. Or the authority of making the choice may be entrusted to some confidential persons, who in the place of all may provide a pastor for the widowed church. An election in any other form is not valid, unless it happens that there is absolute unanimity among the electors, as if by divine inspiration. Whoever shall attempt to hold an election contrary to the aforesaid form shall for this time be deprived of his vote. We absolutely forbid that anyone appoint a representative in the matter of an election, unless he is canonically prevented and cannot come, in which case, if need be, let him declare himself to that effect on oath, and then he may choose one of his colleagues at the assembly to represent him. We also disapprove of clandestine elections, and decree that as soon as an election has been held, it must be solemnly made public.

25   Whoever shall presume to consent to the election of oneself through the abusive intervention of the secular authorities, contrary to canonical liberty, shall lose the advantage gained therefrom and shall be ineligible in the future, nor may that person be chosen or raised to any other dignity without a dispensation. Those who presume to hold an election of this kind (that is, those who allow themselves to be influenced by secular authorities), which we declare to be by right of the same invalid, let them be absolutely suspended from offices and benefices for a period of three years, and during this time let them be deprived of the right of voting.

26   Nothing is more injurious to the Church of God than the selection of unworthy prelates for the direction of souls. Wishing, therefore, to apply the necessary remedy to this evil, we decree by this unbreakable ordinance that when anyone has been elected for the guidance of souls, he to whom the confirmation of the election belongs shall carefully investigate the process and the circumstances of the election as well as the person of the one elected, and only when everything proves to be satisfactory may he confirm the election. If through carelessness the contrary takes place, then not only is the one unworthily promoted to be removed, but the one who furthered the promotion[78] is to be punished. The latter's punishment, we decree, shall consist in this: that when it is agreed that through negligence he confirmed a person who lacks sufficient knowledge or is wanting in integrity of morals or is not of legitimate age, not only is he to lose the right of confirming the first successor of such a person but, that he may not in some case escape punishment, he is also to be deprived of the revenues of his benefice until he is deemed worthy of a pardon. If, however, the evidence shows that his action was inspired by malice, a severer punishment is to be imposed on him. Bishops also, if they wish to escape canonical punishment, shall take the necessary precaution to promote to holy orders[79] and ecclesiastical dignities only such as are qualified to discharge worthily the office committed to them. Those who are directly subject to the Roman pontiff must appear personally before him for confirmation if this can be done conveniently; otherwise, they may send some suitable persons from whom may be ascertained the necessary information regarding the process of the election and the person of the one elected, so that only after a thorough investigation by the pope will those elected obtain the plenitude of their office, provided, of course, there is no canonical obstruction. Those who live at a great distance, that is, outside of Italy, if they have been elected unanimously, may in the meantime, and by way of exception on account of the needs of the churches, administer the respective offices in matters spiritual and temporal, so, however, that they alienate

---

78   I.e., the one who furthered the promotion by wrongly confirming the election.
79   I.e., to the clerical ranks of subdeacon, deacon, or priest.

absolutely nothing belonging to the churches. Let them receive consecration or benediction as has so far been the custom.

27 Since the direction of souls is the art of arts, we strictly command that bishops, either themselves or through other qualified men, diligently prepare and instruct those to be elevated to the priesthood in the divine offices and in the proper administration of the sacraments of the Church. If in the future they presume to ordain ignorant and raw men (a defect that can easily be discovered), we decree that both those ordaining and those ordained be subject to severe punishment. In the ordination of priests especially, it is better to have a few good ministers than many who are no good, for if the blind lead the blind both will fall into the pit.[80]

28 There are some who urgently seek permission to resign and, after obtaining such permission, neglect to do so. But since in requesting a resignation they seemed to have had in view the needs of the churches over which they preside or their own salvation, neither of which we wish to be impeded, whether by the sophistries of self-seekers or by mere instability, we decree that they be compelled to resign.

29 With much foresight it was prohibited in the Lateran Council[81] that no one should, contrary to the sacred canons, accept several ecclesiastical dignities or several parish churches; otherwise the one receiving should lose what he received, and the one who bestowed should be deprived of the right of bestowal. But since, on account of the boldness and avarice of some, the aforesaid statute has thus far produced little or no fruit, we, wishing to meet the situation more clearly and emphatically, declare in the present decree that whoever shall accept a benefice to which is annexed the care of souls after having previously obtained another such benefice, shall automatically be deprived of the first one, and if it happens he should attempt to retain it, let him be deprived of the other one also. He to whom the bestowal of the first benefice belongs may freely confer it, after the incumbent has

accepted a second, on anyone whom he may deem worthy; should he delay to do so beyond a period of six months, then in accordance with the decree of the Lateran Council, let not only its bestowal devolve on another, but also let him be compelled to indemnify the church in question from his own resources equal to the amount of the revenues drawn from it during its vacancy.[82] The same we decree is to be observed in regard to dignities, adding that no one may presume to have several dignities in the same church, even though they do not have the care of souls annexed. Only in the case of eminent and learned persons who are to be honored with major benefices, can the Apostolic See, if need be, grant a dispensation.

30 It is a very inconsistent and grave matter that some bishops, when they can promote suitable men to ecclesiastical benefices, do not fear to choose unworthy ones, who lack integrity of morals and sufficient knowledge, following the carnal and inordinate affections for their kindred rather than the judgment of reason. No one of sound mind is ignorant of the great detriment that thus accrues to churches. Wishing, therefore, to cure this disease, we command that unworthy persons be rejected and suitable ones, who will and can render to God and the churches an acceptable service, be chosen, and let a careful investigation in regard to this matter be made in the annual provincial synod. Anyone who has been found culpable after the first and second warning, let him be suspended from conferring benefices by the synod, and in the same synod let a prudent and upright person be appointed who may take the place of the one suspended. The same is to be observed in regard to the chapters that prove delinquent in this matter. An offense of this kind on the part of a metropolitan must be made known by the synod to a higher superior. That this salutary provision may be more effectively observed, such a sentence of suspension may by no means be removed except by the authority of the Roman pontiff or by the patriarch of the one suspended, that in this matter also the four patriarchal sees may be specially honored.

---

80 Referring to New Testament, Matthew 15.14.
81 I.e., the Third Lateran Council.
82 While vacant, a benefice's revenues often went to the authority who had the right to nominate to that benefice.

31 To destroy that worst of corruptions that has grown up in many churches, we strictly forbid that the sons of canons, especially the illegitimate ones, be made canons in the same secular churches in which their fathers have been appointed. Such appointments, we decree, are invalid; those who presume to make them, let them be suspended from their benefices.

32 In some localities a vice has grown up, namely, that patrons of parochial churches[83] and some other persons (including bishops) arrogate to themselves the revenues of those churches, leaving to the priests attached to them such a meager portion as to deprive them of a decent subsistence. For we have learned from a source the authority of which is unquestionable that in some places the parochial clergy receive for sustenance only a fourth of a fourth, that is, one sixteenth of the tithes.[84] Whence it is that in these localities there seldom is found a parish priest who possesses more than a very limited knowledge of letters. Since, therefore, the mouth of the ox that threshes should not be muzzled, and he who serves the altar should live by the altar, we decree that no custom on the part of a bishop, patron, or anybody else shall stand in the way of priests receiving a sufficient portion.

He who has a parish church must serve it himself and not entrust its administration to a vicar, unless it happens there is a parish church annexed to a prebend or dignity,[85] in which case we grant that he who has such a prebend or dignity, since it behooves him to serve in the major church, may ask to have appointed for the parochial church a suitable and irremovable vicar, who, as was said before, shall enjoy a suitable portion of the revenues of that church; otherwise by the authority of this decree let him be deprived of it and let it be conferred on another who will and can fulfill the aforesaid requirements. We also absolutely forbid that anyone presume to confer fraudulently on another a pension as a benefice from the revenues of a church that ought to have its own priest.

33 The procurations[86] which by reason of visitation are due to bishops, archdeacons, and others, also to legates and nuncios[87] of the Apostolic See, are, except in a case of manifest and urgent necessity, to be demanded only when they personally conduct the visitation, and then they must observe the restrictions made by the Lateran Council in regard to the number of horses and persons accompanying them. This restriction being observed, should the legates and nuncios of the Apostolic See find it necessary to make a delay in any place, to avoid being too great a burden on the place, let them receive moderate procurations from other churches or persons who have not yet been burdened in the way of supplying such sustenance so that the number of procurations may not exceed the number of days of the delay, and should some procuration by itself not suffice, let two or more be united in one. Moreover, those conducting the visitation shall not seek their own interests, but those of Jesus Christ, devoting themselves to preaching, exhortation, correction, and reform, that they may bring back fruit that does not perish. Whoever shall presume to act contrary to this decree, shall not only return what he received, but to the church that he so oppressed he shall also make compensation equivalent to his injustice.

34 Since very many prelates, that they may provide papal legates and others with procurations and the like, extort from their subjects more than they hand over to the legates and, chasing after gain to their own damnation, seek among their subjects plunder rather than help, we forbid that this be done in the future. If it happens that anyone should presume to act contrary to this decision, he shall not only restore what he has thus extorted, but he shall also be compelled to give an

---

83 I.e., persons who have the right to nominate to the bishop someone to hold the position of parish priest. The bishop was then to examine the candidate, and put him in the position if the candidate was suitable and all is else was proper.

84 Tithes, in rough theory a tenth of the produce of the parish, were a tax which went to the priest of the parish.

85 I.e., the revenue of a parish church goes to a member of a cathedral chapter or some other collegiate church.

86 Payments or hospitality legally due a bishop or other officials when they come to the neighborhood in order to conduct a visitation, that is, visit in order to inspect and, usually, to correct.

87 I.e., representatives.

equal amount to the poor. If the superior with whom a complaint in regard to this matter has been lodged proves negligent in the execution of this decree, let him be subject to canonical punishment.

35   That proper respect may be shown to judges and that the interests of litigants in the matter of labor and expenses may be duly considered, we decree that when anyone proceeds against an adversary before a competent judge, that person shall not without good reason appeal to a higher judge before sentence is pronounced, but shall continue the case before the same judge (that is, of the first instance), even if that person claims to have sent a message to the superior judge or has received letters from the same, as long as the letters have not been given to the delegated judge. But if that person thinks he has sufficient ground for an appeal, he must make known this ground to the same judge, and, if it be found legal, let it be made known to the superior judge; if the superior judge finds the ground for an appeal insufficient, he must return the appellant to the judge of the first instance, who shall condemn him to pay the expenses also of the other party. Otherwise let him proceed, excepting, of course, the ordinances governing more important cases, which must be referred to the Apostolic See.

36   When an ordinary or delegated judge has produced a threatening or temporary decision, the execution of which would be oppressive to one of the litigants, but following prudent counsel he refrains from carrying into effect this threatening or temporary decision, he can proceed with the principal matter, even if an appeal has been taken from such a threatening or temporary decision (provided he is not suspected from another legitimate source), so that the progress of the case may not be delayed by trifling circumstances.

37   Some, abusing the good will of the Apostolic See, attempt to obtain from it letters whereby their disputes may be referred to judges residing at a remote distance. This they do to fatigue the accused with labor and expenses, that thus the accused may be compelled to yield in the matter under dispute or by payment be freed from the vexations of the plaintiff. Since however a legal trial ought not to open the door to injustice, as is forbidden by the law, we decree that no one may by means of Apostolic letters be summoned before a judge who is distant more than two days from

his diocese, except with the consent of both parties and with express mention of this decree.

There are also others who, turning themselves to a new kind of commercialism, that they may revive old complaints or introduce new questions, fabricate cases, on the strength of which they seek letters from the Apostolic See without a mandate from the lord for whom they act, which letters they offer for sale either to the accused parties that with their aid that person may not be exposed to the loss of labor and expenses, or to the plaintiff that with these he may fatigue his opponents by undue vexations. Since, however, disputes are to be restricted in number rather than multiplied, we decree that if anyone shall in the future presume to seek Apostolic letters upon any question without a specific mandate from the lord for whom he is acting, such letters shall be regarded as invalid, and he shall be punished as a falsifier, unless perchance it is a question of persons from whom a mandate ought not be legally required.

38   Since against the false assertion of an unjust judge the innocent party sometimes cannot prove the truth of a denial, because by the very nature of things there is no direct proof of one denying a fact, that falsity may not prejudice the truth, and injustice may not prevail over justice, we decree that in an ordinary as well as extraordinary inquiry let the judge always employ either a public person (if one can be had) or two competent men who shall faithfully take down in writing all the acts of the inquiry, namely, citations and delays, refusals and exceptions, petitions and replies, interrogations and confessions, the depositions of witnesses and presentation of documents, temporary decisions, appeals, renunciations, decisions, and other acts which take place must be written down in convenient order, the time, places, and persons to be designated. A copy of everything thus written is to be handed to each of the parties. The originals are to remain in possession of the writers, so that if a dispute should arise in regard to any action of the judge, the truth can be established by a reference to these documents. This provision is made to protect the innocent party against judges who are imprudent and dishonest. A judge who neglects to observe this decree, if on account of this neglect some difficulty should arise, let him be duly punished by a superior judge; nor is there any

presumption in favor of doing things his way unless it is evident from legitimate documents in the case.

39 It often happens that a thief transfers to another what he has unjustly taken, and the one robbed is rendered helpless in any process against the possessor to obtain restitution because the claim of possession having vanished on account of the difficulty or lack of proof, the right of ownership ceases. Wherefore, notwithstanding the rigor of the civil law, we decree that if anyone in the future shall knowingly accept such an article, thus becoming a participant in the theft—for after all, there is little difference, especially when it is a question of danger to the soul, whether one holds unjustly or takes what belongs to another— the one robbed is to be assisted to obtain restitution from such a possessor.

40 It sometimes happens that the plaintiff to whom, in consequence of the contumaciousness of the opposing party, the possession of the object in dispute is judicially awarded, cannot on account of the violence or deceit of the accused obtain actual possession for a whole year, and thus, since in the opinion of many he is not after the lapse of a year to be regarded as the owner, the malice of the accused gains the advantage. Therefore, that the condition of the disobedient may not be better than that of the obedient, we decree that in the aforesaid case, even after the lapse of a year, the plaintiff is the true owner.

In general we forbid that decisions in ecclesiastical matters be referred to a layman, because it is not becoming that a layman should arbitrate in such matters.

41 Since "all that is not of faith is sin,"[88] we decree through synodical judgment that no prescriptive right,[89] whether canonical or civil, is valid unless it rests on good faith because in a general way any law or custom that cannot be maintained without mortal sin is to be repealed. Wherefore it is essential that one who holds a prescriptive right should not be aware that the object belongs at another time to another person.

42 As desirous as we are that lay persons do not usurp the rights of clerics, we are no less desirous that clerics abstain from arrogating to themselves the rights of lay persons. Wherefore, we forbid all clerics so to extend in the future their jurisdiction under the pretext of ecclesiastical liberty to the detriment of secular justice, but let them be content with the laws and customs thus far approved, that the things that are Caesar's may be rendered to Caesar, and those that are God's may by a just division be rendered to God.[90]

43 Some lay persons attempt to usurp too much of divine right when they compel ecclesiastical men who are under no obligation to them in secular matters to take an oath of fidelity to them. Wherefore, since according to the Apostle, "To the Lord the servant stands or falls,"[91] we forbid by the authority of the sacred council that such clerics be forced by secular persons to take an oath of this kind.

44 Since no power to dispose of ecclesiastical properties has been given to lay persons, even though they are pious, their duty being to obey, not to command, we regret that in some of them charity has grown so cold that they do not fear in their laws, or rather monstrosities, to attack the immunity of ecclesiastical liberty, which not only the holy fathers, but also the secular rulers, have fortified with many privileges, presuming illicitly that power not only in the matter of the alienation of fiefs and also of ecclesiastical possessions and of the usurpation of jurisdictions, but also in the matter of mortuaries and other things that seem annexed to the spiritual right. Wishing, therefore, in this matter to secure churches against loss and to provide against such injustice, we decree, with the approval of the sacred council, that laws of this kind and appropriations of fiefs or other ecclesiastical properties made without the legitimate consent of ecclesiastical persons under pretext of lay power, do not hold, since they cannot be called laws but rather want of law or destruction and usurpation of jurisdiction, and those having recourse to such presumptions are to be checked by ecclesiastical censure.

---

88  New Testament, Romans 14.23.
89  A right established by custom or unbroken possession.
90  A reference to New Testament, Matthew 22.21.
91  New Testament, Romans 14.4.

45 In some provinces, patrons, vicegerents, and advocates[92] of churches have so far advanced in insolence that not only do they create difficulties and mischief when vacant churches are to be provided with competent pastors, but they also presume to administer the possessions and other ecclesiastical goods at their own will, and what is worse, they do not fear to put the prelates to death. Since, therefore, what has been ordained as a means of defense must not be perverted into an instrument of destruction, we expressly forbid patrons, advocates, and vicegerents in the future to extend their jurisdiction in the aforesaid matter beyond what is permitted them by law, and should they act contrary to this, let them be restrained by canonical penalties. With the approval of the holy council we decree that if patrons, advocates, feudal tenants, vicegerents, or other beneficiaries should presume either themselves or through others to kill or mutilate the rector of some church or another cleric of that church, the patrons shall lose absolutely their right of patronage, the advocates their office of counselor, the feudal tenants their fief, the vicegerents their vicegerency, and beneficiaries their benefice. That the punishments may not be impressed upon the memory less deeply than the excesses, not only shall their heirs be deprived of all favors accruing to them from the aforesaid offices, but to the fourth generation the posterity of such shall be absolutely excluded from the clerical state, nor may they hold the office of prelate in religious houses, unless by an act of mercy they have received a dispensation.

46 Against magistrates and rulers of cities and others who strive to oppress churches and ecclesiastical persons with taxes and other exactions, the Lateran Council, desiring to protect ecclesiastical immunity, prohibited actions of this kind under penalty of anathema, commanding that transgressors and their abettors be punished with excommunication until they make suitable satisfaction. But, if the bishop with his clergy should perceive such necessity or utility, and without compulsion decide that the aid of the churches ought to be enlisted to meet the needs where the resources of lay people do not suffice, let the aforesaid lay people accept such assistance humbly, devoutly, and with gratitude. However, on account of the boldness of some, let them first consult the Roman pontiff, to whom it belongs to attend to common needs. But, if even this does not allay the malice of some toward the Church of God, we add that the laws and enactments which have been promulgated by excommunicated persons in this matter or by their orders shall be considered null and void and at no time whatever be regarded as valid. But, since fraud and deception ought not to protect anyone, let no one be deceived by the illusion that, although a ruler may incur anathema during the period of his incumbency, yet on the expiration of his term of office there will be no compulsion to make due satisfaction. For both he who refuses to make satisfaction and his successor, if they do not make satisfaction within a month, we decree that they remain bound by ecclesiastical censure until they have made suitable satisfaction, since he who is successor in the honor assumes the burden.

47 With the approval of the holy council, we prohibit the promulgation of the sentence of excommunication against anyone without a previous warning and in the presence of suitable persons by whom, if need be, such admonition can be proved. Should anyone act contrariwise, even if the sentence of excommunication is a just one, let him know that he is forbidden entrance to the church for a period of one month, which punishment, however, is to be altered should it be deemed advisable. Let also proper precaution be taken against excommunicating anyone without a just and reasonable cause; should this perchance have happened and he who imposed the sentence does not care to withdraw it without complaint, then the one injured may take his complaint of unjust excommunication to a superior, who, if there is no danger in delay, shall send him back to the excommunicator with the command that he absolve him within a specified time. Otherwise he himself, should it seem fit, after the presentation of a sufficient reason, will grant him the required absolution either personally or through another. When it is an evident case against the excommunicator of unjust excommunication, let him be con-

---

92  I.e., lay people officially designated as protectors of a church or monastery. Many such advocates claimed various rights over the institution thus protected.

demned to pay all the expenses and to repair all the damages incurred by the one unjustly excommunicated; if, however, the gravity of his fault demands it, let him be punished in accordance with the judgment of the superior, since it is not a trivial fault to impose such a punishment on an innocent person, unless it happens that he erred for a credible reason, especially if he has a laudable reputation. But if against the sentence of excommunication no reasonable proof was offered by the complainant, then for the unjust annoyance of his complaint let him be condemned to pay the expenses and repair the damages, or else let him be punished in accordance with the decision of the superior, unless it happens credible error likewise excuses him, and in regard to the matter for which he was excommunicated, let him be compelled to make satisfaction through an adequate pledge, or let the original sentence be reimposed even for the purpose of forcing him to make condign satisfaction. But if the judge, recognizing his error, is prepared to revoke such a sentence, and he on whom it was imposed appeals against such a revocation unless satisfaction is made, let him not heed the appeal unless it is an error about which there can be a just doubt, and then on the receipt of a satisfactory pledge that he will obey the summons of him to whom the appeal has been made, or of one delegated by him, let him absolve the one excommunicated, and thus he will in no way incur the penalties prescribed; let him be careful, however, not to forge an error to the detriment of another if he wishes to escape canonical punishment.

48  By a special prohibition it has been provided that a sentence of excommunication be promulgated against no one without a previous warning. Wishing to forestall any attempt on the part of the one thus warned to avoid, under pretext of deceitful refusal or appeal, the inquiry of the one giving the admonition, we decree that, should he assert that he entertains a suspicion in regard to the judge, let him in the presence of the judge indicate the cause of his just suspicion, and let him with his opponent, or if he has no opponent, with the judge, conjointly choose arbiters, or if together they cannot agree, let them choose without ill will two, he one and the judge the other, who may inquire into the cause of the suspicion; and if they cannot come to an agreement, let them ask for a third

party, so that what two of them decide may obtain greater weight. Let them know also that, by reason of a strict precept enjoined by us in virtue of obedience under witness of the divine Judge, they are bound to execute this faithfully. If the true cause of the suspicion has not been proved by them within a reasonable period of time, let the judge use his jurisdiction. But if it has been legitimately proved, then let the judge with the consent of the one who suspected him commit the matter to a competent person, or let him submit it to the superior, that the latter may take such action in his regard as should be taken.

Moreover, in case the one warned should resort to an appeal, let no heed be given to a provocation of this kind if from the evidence of the case or from his confession or from another source his guilt has been clearly established, since the remedy of appeal was not instituted for the defense of iniquity but for the protection of the innocent. If his guilt is doubtful, that he may not impede the process of the judge by recourse to a frivolous appeal, let him explain in the judge's presence the probable ground of the appeal, namely, such a ground as, if proved, would be regarded as valid. If he has an opponent, the cause of the appeal is to be continued within a period fixed by the same judge, due consideration being given to the distance, time, and nature of the business; if he does not care to continue it, then, notwithstanding the appeal, let the judge proceed with it. If there is no opponent and the cause of the appeal has been proved before the superior judge, let the latter excercise his jurisdiction. But if the appellant fails in his proof, then the case is to be returned to the judge from whom he deceitfully appealed.

These two aforesaid decrees, however, we do not wish to be applied to regular clergy, who have their own special observances.

49  Under threat of the divine Judge we absolutely forbid that anyone, impelled solely by greed, dare bind one with the chain of excommunication or absolve one so bound, especially in those regions where it is customary, when the one excommunicated is absolved, to impose a pecuniary punishment on him, and we decree that when it is agreed that the sentence of excommunication was an unjust one, the excommunicator will be compelled by ecclesiastical

censure to restore the money thus extorted, and unless he was deceived by credible error, let him make full compensation for the injury sustained. If he fails to do this, let other penalties be imposed.

50   It must not be deemed reprehensible if human statutes change sometimes with the changing of time, epecially when urgent necessity or common interest demands it, since God himself has changed in the New Testament some things that He had decreed in the Old. Since, therefore, the prohibition against the contracting of marriage in the second and third degree of affinity, and that against the union of the offspring from second marriages to a relative of the first husband, frequently constitute a source of difficulty and sometimes are a cause of danger to souls, that by a cessation of the prohibition the effect may cease also, we, with the approval of the holy council, revoking previous enactments in this matter, decree in the present statute that such persons may in the future contract marriage without hindrance. The prohibition also is not in the future to affect marriages beyond the fourth degree of consanguinity and affinity; since in degrees beyond the fourth a prohibition of this kind cannot be generally observed without grave inconvenience. This number four agrees well with the prohibition of corporal wedlock of which the Apostle says that "the wife has not power of her own body, but the husband; and in like manner the husband also has not power of his own body, but the wife"[93] because there are four humors in the body, which consists of four elements. Since therefore the prohibition of conjugal union is restricted to the fourth degree,[94] we wish that it remain so in perpetuity, notwithstanding the decrees already issued relative to this matter either by others or by ourselves, and should any persons presume to contract marriage contrary to this prohibition, no number of years shall excuse them, since duration of time does not palliate the gravity of sin but rather aggravates it, and their crimes are the graver the longer they hold their unhappy souls in bondage.

51   Since the prohibition of the conjugal union in the

three last degrees has been revoked, we wish that it be strictly observed in the other degrees. Whence, following in the footsteps of our predecessors, we absolutely forbid clandestine marriages, and we forbid also that a priest presume to witness such. Wherefore, extending to other localities generally the particular custom that prevails in some, we decree that when marriages are to be contracted, they must be announced publicly in the churches by the priests during a suitable and fixed time, so that if legitimate impediments exist, they may be made known. Let the priests nevertheless investigate whether any impediments exist. But when there is ground for doubt concerning the contemplated union, let the marriage be expressly forbidden until it is evident from reliable sources what ought to be done in regard to it. But if anyone should presume to contract a clandestine or forbidden marriage of this kind within a prohibited degree, even through ignorance, the children from such a union shall be considered illegitimate, nor shall the ignorance of the parents be pleaded as an extenuating circumstance in their behalf, since they by contracting such marriages appear not as wanting in knowledge but rather as pretending ignorance. In like manner the children shall be considered illegitimate if both parents, knowing that a legitimate impediment exists, presume to contract such a marriage in the sight of the church[95] in disregard of every prohibition. As to the parochial priest who deliberately neglects to forbid such unions or any regular priest who presumes to witness them, let them be suspended from office for a period of three years and, if the nature of their offense demands it, let them be punished more severely. On those also who presume to contract such marriages in a lawful degree, a condign punishment is to be imposed. If anyone maliciously presents an impediment for the purpose of frustrating a legitimate marriage, let that person not escape ecclesiastical punishment.

52   Through some necessity the common mode of procedure in computing the degree of consanguinity

---

93   New Testament, 1 Corinthians 7.4.
94   Effectively the canon prohibits marriage between persons who share great-great grandparents, but undoes earlier restrictions on marriage between people more distantly related.
95   I.e., not clandestinely.

and affinity has been replaced by another, namely, hearsay testimony, since on account of the shortness of human life, eye-witnesses cannot be had in the matter of reckoning to the seventh degree. But, since we have learned from many instances and from experience that, in consequence of this, legitimate marriages are beset with many dangers, we decree that in this matter hearsay witnesses shall not be received in the future, since the prohibition now does not extend beyond the fourth degree, unless they be reputable persons to whom uprightness is a precious asset and who before the dispute arose obtained their testimony from those gone immediately before, not from one indeed, since that person would not suffice if alive, but from two at least, who must have been reliable persons, beyond suspicion and of good faith, since it would be absurd to admit them if their informants were worthy only of rejection. Not even if one person has obtained testimony from many, or if an unreliable person has obtained it from people of good faith, must they be admitted as many and suitable witnesses, since even in the ordinary judicial processes the statement of one witness does not suffice, even though the witness shines in all the splendor of a governing dignity, and, moreover, legitimate acts are denied to persons of a disreputable character. Witnesses of this kind must declare on oath that in giving their testimony they are not actuated by hatred, fear, love, or self-interest; let them designate persons by their names or by a satisfactory description or circumlocution, and distinguish by a clear counting up each degree on both sides, and let them include in their oath that they obtained their information from their predeccessors and believe it to be so. But neither do such witnesses suffice unless they declare on oath that they have seen persons who belonged to at least one of the aforesaid degrees and who acknowledged themselves blood relatives. For it is more tolerable that some who have been united contrary to human laws be separated than that those who have been legitimately united separate in violation of the laws of God.

53  In some localities there dwell people who according to their rites are not accustomed to pay tithes, though they are considered Christians.[96] To these some owners entrust the cultivation of their estates, in order to defraud the churches of tithes and thus realize greater profits. Wishing, therefore, to safeguard the churches against loss in this matter, we decree that the owners may entrust to such people and in such a manner the cultivation of their estates, but they must without argument pay to the churches the tithes in full, and to this let them be compelled, if necessary, by ecclesiastical censure. All tithes due by reason of the divine law or by reason of an approved local custom must be paid.

54  Since it is not in the power of man that the seed yield a return to the sower, because according to the words of the Apostle, "Neither he that plants is anything, nor he that waters; but God who gives the increase,"[97] the decayed seed producing much fruit, some impelled too much by avarice strive to defraud in the matter of tithes, deducting from the profits and first fruits taxes and other expenses on which at times they thus escape the payment of tithes. But since the Lord, as a sign of His universal dominion, formerly reserved tithes to Himself by a special title, we, wishing to safeguard the churches against loss and souls against danger, decree that by the prerogative of general dominion the payment of tithes precedes the payment of taxes and other expenses, or at least they to whom the taxes and other expenses are paid but from which the tithes have not been deducted should be compelled by ecclesiastical censure to pay the tithes to the churches to which they are legally due, since the obligation that attaches to a thing passes with the thing from one possessor to another.

55  Lately the abbots of the Cistercian order assembled in general chapter wisely decided, in reference to our warning, that in the future the brethren of that order shall purchase no property on which tithes are due to the churches, unless it is for the purpose of establishing new monasteries. And if such possessions have been given to them through the pious generosity

---

96  Referring to Christians in the East.
97  New Testament, 1 Corinthians 3.7.

of the faithful or bought for them for the purpose of founding new monasteries, they may commit their cultivation to others by whom the tithes will be paid to the churches, lest by reason of their privileges the churches be further oppressed.[98] We decree, therefore, that from strange lands or from lands that they may acquire in the future, though they cultivate them with their own hands or at their own expense, they pay the tithes to the churches to which they were formerly paid, unless they make some other arrangement with those churches. We therefore, holding this decree acceptable and accepted, wish it to be extended also to other regulars who enjoy similar privileges, and we ordain that the prelates of the churches be more willing and energetic in punishing evil doers and strive to observe their privileges better and more perfectly.

56  We understand that many regular and secular clerics, when sometimes they lease houses or grant fiefs, make a contract prejudicial to parish churches, namely, that the administrator or feudal tenants pay the tithes to them and choose burial among them. But, since this is prompted by avarice, we absolutely condemn a contract of this kind and declare that whatever has been received by means of such a contract must be returned to the parish church.

57  That the privileges which the Roman Church has granted to some religious[99] may be maintained in their entirety, we take occasion to make clear some things in regard to them, lest being misunderstood they lead to abuse, by reason of which they may be rightly revoked, because one who abuses the benefits which privileges confer deserves to lose them. The Apostolic See has granted permission to some regulars that to those who have become members of their order, ecclesiastical burial may not be denied if the churches to which they belong should be under interdict,[100] provided they themselves are not excommunicated or interdicted by name, and they may, therefore, take their brethren, whom the prelates of the churches

are not permitted to bury from their churches, to their own churches for burial, if they (the deceased brethren) were not nominally under excommunication or interdict. By "brethren" we understand both those who, having lived in the world, gave themselves to their order and accepted its habit, and those who gave their possessions to the order, retaining for their own maintenance during life only the products of the possessions, who, however, may be buried from noninterdicted churches of regulars or others in which they may choose to be buried; it is not, however, to be understood of those who join their fraternity and contribute annually no more than two or three *denarii*,[101] for this would upset ecclesiastical order and discipline. Yet these also obtain a certain remission granted to them by the Apostolic See.

That other privilege also that has been granted to some regulars, namely, that when any of their brethren who have been sent by them to collect alms, arrives in any city, fortified town, or village, if it happens that place is under interdict, in view of their joyful arrival, the churches may be opened once a year for the celebration of the divine offices for those not under excommunication, we wish to be understood thus: that in each city, fortified town, or village, only one church of the same order may, as has been said, be opened to the brethren once a year, for though the statement, "that on their joyful arrival the churches may be opened," is plural, yet it is not to be understood as referring to the churches of the same place separately, but to the churches of the aforesaid places collectively; otherwise, if they should visit each church of the same place, the interdict would be too much disregarded. Whoever shall presume to act contrary to these enactments, let him be subject to severe penalties.

58  The privilege that has been granted to some religious we concede also to bishops, that, when the entire territory is under interdict, those excommuni-

---

98 One of the privileges of the Cistercian order was that the Cistercians did not have to pay tithes on produce from land held by the order.

99 I.e., regular clergy, or clergy under a monastic rule.

100 The church, as punishment, could declare certain areas under "interdict," i.e., that no church services could take place in that area.

101 A *denarius* was a small unit of currency, one pence.

cated and interdicted being excluded, they may some-times with the doors closed, in a low voice and with-out the ringing of bells, perform the divine offices, unless this is expressly covered by the interdict. But we grant this to those only who in no way shared in the cause of the interdict, that they may not execute treachery or fraud, bringing such a profit to iniquitous loss.

59   What has been forbidden by the Apostolic See to some religious orders, we wish and command to be extended to all, namely, that no religious may, without the permission of the abbot and of the greater part of his chapter,[102] provide security to anyone or borrow money from anyone beyond an amount fixed by com-mon agreement. Otherwise the convent is not held in any degree responsible for such things, unless per-chance it is evident that his action would redound to the advantage of the convent.[103] Let anyone who pre-sumes to act contrary to this be subject to severe disci-pline.

60   From different parts of the world complaints of bishops come to us in regard to grave excesses of some abbots, who, not content within their own spheres, extend their hands to those things that concern the episcopal office, deciding matrimonial cases, impos-ing public penances, granting letters of indul-gences,[104] and similar things, from which it sometimes happens that the episcopal authority is looked upon by many as something of trifling importance. Wishing, therefore, in these matters to safeguard the dignity of the bishops and the welfare of the abbots, we absolute-ly forbid in the present decree that abbots presume to overreach themselves in such matters if they wish to escape canonical penalties, unless they can, by a spe-cial concession or other legitimate reason, defend themselves in matters of this kind.

61   In the Lateran Council, regulars were forbidden to receive churches and tithes from lay hands without the consent of the bishops, and under no circum-stances to admit to divine services those excommuni-cated or under interdict by name. Wishing to curb this evil more effectively and provide that transgressors meet with condign punishment, we decree that in churches that do not belong to them by full right, they present to the bishops priests to be appointed in accor-dance with the statutes of that council, that they may be responsible to them in those things that pertain to the care of souls; in temporal affairs, however, let them render a satisfactory account to the monasteries. Let them not dare remove those who have been appoint-ed without the approval of the bishops. We add, more-over, that care be taken to nominate to the bishop such priests as are known for their uprightness and ability or whom the probable testimony of the bishops rec-ommends.

62   From the fact that some expose for sale and promiscuously exhibit the relics of saints, great injury is sustained by the Christian religion. That this may not occur hereafter, we ordain in the present decree that in the future old relics may not be exposed for sale or exhibited outside of a case. And let no one pre-sume to venerate new relics publicly unless they have been approved by the Roman pontiff. In the future prelates shall not permit those who come to their churches for the purpose of venerating saints to be deceived by worthless fabrications or false docu-ments as has been done in many places for the sake of gain. We also forbid that seekers of alms, some of whom, misrepresenting themselves, preach certain abuses, be permitted to preach, unless they exhibit genuine letters either from the Apostolic See or of the diocesan bishop, in which case they may not preach anything to the people except what is contained in those letters. We give, herewith, a form which the Apostolic See commonly uses in granting such letters, that the diocesan bishops may model their own upon it. The form is the following:

Because, as the Apostle says, "we shall all stand before the tribunal of Christ,"[105] to receive just as we

---

102  I.e., the meeting of the community the abbot governs.
103  I.e., the community the abbot governs.
104  Letters which stated what remission of sins would accrue to those who undertook certain actions. The theology of indul-gences required that the sinner be contrite for the indulgence to be effective.
105  New Testament, Romans 14.10.

have done in the body, whether it has been good or bad, it is needful that we prepare for the last judgment by works of mercy, and also to sow in the earth what, with God having returned it multiplied, we ought to collect in heaven, holding in this a firm hope and trust because "one who sowes sparingly will also reap sparingly,"[106] and one who sowes with blessings, shall reap blessings and shall reap eternal life. Since the resources of this or that hospital do not suffice for the sustenance of the brothers and the poor,[107] we warn and exhort you all in the Lord, and enjoin you for remission of sins, that you give, from the goods given to you by God, pious alms to those hospitals as charitable support, so that their need may be addressed by your assistance, which you will have made through inspiration from God, and you will be able to arrive at eternal joy.

Those who are assigned to collect alms must be upright and discreet, must not seek lodging for the night in taverns or in other unbecoming places, nor incur useless and extravagant expenses, and must avoid absolutely the wearing of the habit of a false religious.

Since, through indiscreet and superfluous indulgences which some prelates of churches do not hesitate to grant, contempt is brought on the keys of the Church, and the penitential discipline is weakened, we decree that on the occasion of the dedication of a church an indulgence of not more than one year be granted, whether it be dedicated by one bishop only or by many, and on the anniversary of the dedication the remission granted for penances enjoined is not to exceed 40 days. We command also that in each case this number of days be made the rule in issuing letters of indulgences which are granted from time to time, since the Roman pontiff who possesses the plenitude of power customarily observes this rule in such matters.

We have learned with certainty that in many places and by many persons exactions and base extortions are made for the consecration of bishops, the blessing of abbots, and the ordination of clerics, and that a tax is fixed as to how much this one or that one is to receive and how much this one or that one is to pay, and what is worse, some endeavor to defend such baseness and depravity by an appeal to custom of long standing. Therefore, wishing to abolish such abuse, we absolutely condemn customs of this kind, which ought rather to be called corruption, firmly decreeing that neither for those conferring nor for the things conferred shall anyone presume to demand or to extort something under any pretext whatsoever. Otherwise both the one who has received and the one who has given a price of this kind shall share the condemnation of Giezi and Simon.[108]

64   Since the stain of simony[109] has so infected female monastics that scarcely any are received into the community without a price, doing this on the plea of poverty in order to conceal that evil, we strictly forbid that this be done in the future, decreeing that whoever in the future shall be guilty of such irregularity, both the one receiving and the one received, whether subject or superior, shall, without hope of restoration, be removed from their monastery to one of stricter observance to do penance for the remainder of their life. Those female monastics, however, who have been so received before the publication of this decree, are to be removed from the monasteries which they entered in a wrong manner and placed in others of the same order. But if, on account of a lack of room, it happens they cannot be conveniently placed elsewhere, lest they should to their own loss become wanderers in the world, let them be received anew by means of a special dispensation in the same monastery, and from the priority of places which they held in the community let them be assigned to lower ones. We decree that this is to be observed also with regard to monks and other

---

106  New Testament, 2 Corinthians 9.6.

107  A "hospital," a semi-monastic institution in the Middle Ages, served poor sick people, and the poor generally.

108  Simon (see New Testament, Acts 8.9-24) gave his name to the sin of "simony," or the sale of church office. For Giezi (or Gehazi), see Old Testament, 2 Kings 5.20-27.

109  See previous note.

regulars. But, lest they should attempt to excuse themselves on grounds of simplicity or ignorance, we command the bishops to see to it that this decree is published every year throughout their dioceses.

65   We have heard it said of some bishops that on the death of rectors of churches they place the churches under interdict and will not allow any persons to be appointed to the vacancies until a certain sum of money has been paid them. Moreover, when a soldier or cleric enters a monastery or chooses to be buried among the religious, although he has left nothing to the religious institution, difficulties and villainy are forced into service until something in the nature of a gift comes into their hands. Since, therefore, according to the Apostle, we must abstain not only from evil but also from every appearance of evil, we absolutely forbid exactions of this kind. If any transgressor is found, let that person restore double the amount exacted; this is to be placed faithfully at the disposal of those localities to whose detriment the exactions were made.

66   It has frequently come to the ears of the Apostolic See that some clerics demand and extort money for burials, nuptial blessings, and similar things, and, if it happens that their cupidity is not given satisfaction, they fraudulently interpose fictitious impediments. On the other hand, some laymen, under the pretext of piety but really on heretical grounds, strive to suppress a laudable custom introduced by the pious devotion of the faithful in behalf of the church (that is, of giving freely something for ecclesiastical services rendered). Wherefore, we forbid that such evil exactions be made in these matters and, on the other hand, command that pious customs be observed, decreeing that the sacraments of the Church be administered freely and that those who endeavor maliciously to change a laudable custom be restrained by the bishops of the locality when once the truth is known.

67   The more Christians are restrained from the practice of usury, the more they are oppressed in this matter by the treachery of Jews, so that in a short time they exhaust the resources of Christians. Wishing, there-

fore, in this matter to protect Christians against cruel oppression by Jews, we ordain in this decree that if in the future under any pretext Jews extort from Christians oppressive and immoderate interest, contact with Christians shall be denied them until they have made suitable satisfaction for their excesses. Christians also, every appeal being set aside, shall, if necessary, be compelled by ecclesiastical censure to abstain from all commercial intercourse with them. We command the princes not to be hostile to Christians on this account,[110] but rather to strive to hinder the Jews from practicing such excesses. Lastly, we decree that the Jews be compelled by the same punishment to make satisfaction for the tithes and offerings due to the churches, which Christians were accustomed to supply from their houses and other possessions before these properties, under whatever title, fell into the hands of Jews, that thus the churches may be safeguarded against loss.

68   In some provinces a difference of dress distinguishes Jews and Saracens[111] from Christians, but in others confusion has developed to such a degree that no difference is discernible. Whence it happens sometimes through error that Christians mingle with the women of Jews and Saracens, and, on the other hand, Jews and Saracens mingle with those of the Christians. Therefore, that such ruinous commingling through error of this kind may not serve as a refuge for further excuse for excesses, we decree that such people of both sexes (that is, Jews and Saracens) in every Christian province and at all times be distinguished in public from other people by a difference of dress, since this was also enjoined on them by Moses. On the days of the Lamentations and on Passion Sunday[112] they may not appear in public, because some of them, as we understand, on those days are not ashamed to show themselves more ornately attired and do not fear to amuse themselves at the expense of Christians, who in memory of the sacred passion go about attired in robes of mourning. That we most strictly forbid, lest they should presume in some measure to burst forth

---

110  Some secular rulers were the special protectors of Jews in their territories. Such protection often entailed special access to Jewish financial resources.

111  I.e., Moslems.

112  Christian holy days associated with Jesus's crucifixion.

suddenly in contempt of the Redeemer.[113] And, since we ought not to be ashamed of Him who blotted out our offenses, we command that the secular princes restrain presumptuous persons of this kind by condign punishment, lest they presume to blaspheme in some degree the One crucified for us.

69  Since it is absurd that a blasphemer of Christ exercise authority over Christians, we on account of the boldness of transgressors renew in this general council what the Synod of Toledo[114] wisely enacted in this matter, prohibiting Jews from being given preference in the matter of public offices, since in such capacity they are most troublesome to Christians. But if anyone should commit such an office to them, let that person, after previous warning, be restrained by such punishment as seems proper by the provincial synod which we command to be held every year. The official, however, shall be denied commercial and other intercourse with Christians until, in the judgment of the bishop, all that person acquired from Christians from the time that person assumed office has been restored for the needs of the Christian poor, and let that person lose the office, irreverently assumed, with shame. The same we extend also to pagans.

70  There are some, we understand, who having voluntarily approached the waters of holy baptism, do not entirely cast off the old person so they may more perfectly put on the new one, because, retaining remnants of the former rite, they obscure by such a mixture the beauty of the Christian religion. But since it is written, "Accursed is the one who goes on the two ways"[115] and "a garment that is woven together of wool and linen"[116] should not be put on, we decree that such persons be in every way restrained by the prelates from the observance of the former rite, so that, having given themselves of their own free will to the Christian religion, salutary coercive action may preserve them in its observance, since not to know the way of the Lord is a lesser evil than to retrace one's steps after it is known.

71  Desiring with an ardent desire to liberate the Holy Land from the hands of the infidels, we decree with the advice of prudent men who are fully familiar with the circumstances of the times, and with the approval of the council, that all who have taken the cross[117] and have decided to cross the sea, hold themselves prepared so that they may, on June 1 of the year after next, come together in the Kingdom of Sicily, some at Brundusium and others at Messina, where, God willing, we will be present personally to order and to bestow on the Christian army the divine and Apostolic blessing. Those who decide to make the journey by land should strive to hold themselves prepared for the same time; for their aid and guidance we shall in the meantime appoint a competent legate *a latere*.[118] Priests and other clerics who are with the Christian army, subjects as well as prelates, must be diligent in prayer and exhortation, teaching the crusaders by word and example that they have always before their eyes the fear and love of God, lest they say or do something that might offend the majesty of the eternal King. And should any have fallen into sin, let them quickly rise again through true repentance, practicing humility both interiorly and exteriorly, observing moderation in food as well as in clothing, avoiding dissension and rivalry, and divesting themselves of all malice and ill will, that being thus fortified with spiritual and material arms, they may fight with greater success against the enemies of the faith, not indeed relying on their own strength, but putting their trust in the power of God. To the clerics we grant for a period of three years as complete an enjoyment of their benefices as if they actually resided in them,[119] and they may, if necessary, even give them as pledges during this time. Therefore, that this undertaking may not be impeded or retarded, we strictly command all

---

113  I.e., Jesus.
114  In 589.
115  Apocrypha, Ecclesiasticus 2.14.
116  Old Testament, Deuteronomy 22.11.
117  "Taking the cross" meant to commit oneself to go on a crusade.
118  An especially empowered papal representative.
119  The canon law imposed legal limits on clergy being absent from a benefice that required care of souls.

prelates that each one in his own territory induce those who have laid aside the crusader's cross to resume it, and carefully to admonish them and others who have taken the cross, as well as those who happen to be engaged for this purpose, to renew their vows to God, and if necessary to compel them by excommunication and interdict to abandon all delay.

Moreover, so that nothing connected with the affairs of our Lord Jesus Christ be omitted, we wish and command that patriarchs, archbishops, bishops, abbots, and others who have the care of souls, diligently explain the meaning of the crusade to those committed to them, entreating—through the Father, Son, and Holy Spirit, one, only true, and eternal God—kings, dukes, princes, marquises, counts, barons, and other prominent men, as well as cities, villages, and towns, that those who cannot go personally to the Holy Land furnish a suitable number of soldiers and, for a period of three years, in proportion to their resources, will bear the necessary expenses connected therewith for the remission of their sins, as we have made known in the general letters already sent over the world and as will be expressed in greater detail below. In this remission we wish not only those to participate who for this purpose furnish their own ships, but those also who undertake to build ships. To those declining to render aid, if it happens that any should be found to be so ungrateful to God, the Apostolic See firmly protests that on the last day they will be held to render an account to us in the presence of a terrible Judge. Let them first consider with what security they can appear in the presence of the only begotten Son of God, Jesus Christ, into whose hands the Father has given all things, if in this matter they refuse to serve Him who was crucified for sinners, by whose favor they live, by whose benefits they are sustained, and by whose blood they were redeemed.

But, lest we should seem to place grave and unbearable burdens on the shoulders of the people, we ourselves donate to the cause what we have been able to save by strict economy, 30,000 pounds, besides a ship to convey the crusaders from Rome and its vicinity, and 3,000 marks silver, the remnant of alms received from the faithful. The remainder we have given to Albert, patriarch of Jerusalem, and to the masters of the Temple and Hospital for the necessities of the Holy Land. With the approval of the council we further decree that absolutely all clerics, subjects as well as superiors, shall, in aid of the Holy Land and for a period of three years, pay into the hands of those appointed by the Apostolic See for this purpose one-twentieth part of ecclesiastical revenues, some religious orders only being excepted and those clerics also who take or already have taken the crusader's cross and are about to set out personally. We and our brethren, the cardinals of the Holy Roman Church, will pay one-tenth of our revenues. All are bound to the faithful observance of this under penalty of excommunication, so that those who deliberately commit fraud in this matter will incur that penalty.

Since by the just judgment of the heavenly King it is only right that those who are associated with a good cause should enjoy a special privilege, we exempt the crusaders from collections, taxes, and other assessments. Their persons and possessions, after they have taken the cross, we take under the protection of Blessed Peter[120] and our own, decreeing that they stand under the protection of the archbishops, bishops, and all the prelates of the Church. Besides, special protectors will be appointed, and, till their return or till their death shall have been certified, they shall remain unmolested, and if anyone shall presume the contrary, let him be restrained by ecclesiastical censure.

In the case of crusaders who are bound under oath to pay interest, we command that their creditors be compelled to cancel the oath given and to cease exacting interest. Should any creditor force the payment of interest, we command that the creditor be similarly forced to make restitution. We command also that Jews be compelled by the secular power to cancel interest, and, until they have done so, intercourse with them must be absolutely denied them by all Christians under penalty of excommunication. For those who cannot before their departure pay their debts to the Jews, the secular princes shall provide such a delay that from the time of their

---

120 I.e., Saint Peter.

departure until their return or until their death is known, they shall not be embarrassed with the inconvenience of paying interest. If a Jew has received security (for example, a piece of ground) for such a debt, he must, after deducting his own expenses, pay to the owner the income from such security. Prelates who manifest negligence in obtaining justice for the crusaders and their servants shall be subject to severe penalty.

Since the corsairs and pirates too vehemently impede assistance to the Holy Land by capturing and robbing those who go there and those returning, we excommunicate them and their principal abettors and protectors, forbidding under threat of anathema that anyone knowingly hold intercourse with them in any contract of buying and selling, and enjoin upon the rulers of cities and their localities that they check and turn them away from this iniquity. And since an unwillingness to disturb the perverse is nothing else than to favor them, and is also an indication of secret association with them on the part of those who do not resist manifest crime, we wish and command that severe ecclesiastical punishment be imposed by prelates on their persons and lands. We excommunicate and anathematize, moreover, those false and ungodly Christians who furnish the enemies of Christ and the Christian people with arms, iron, and wood for the construction of ships; those also who sell them ships and who in the ships of the Saracens hold the post of pilot, or in any other way give them aid or advice to the detriment of the Holy Land; and we decree that their possessions be confiscated and they themselves become the slaves of their captors. We command that this sentence be publicly announced in all maritime cities on all Sundays and festival days, and that to such people the church be not opened until they return all that they have obtained from so reprehensible a traffic, and give the same amount of their own in aid of the Holy Land. In case they are not able to pay, then let them be punished in other ways, so that by their chastisement others may be deterred from undertaking similar pursuits.

Furthermore, under penalty of anathema, we forbid all Christians for a period of four years to send their ships to Eastern lands inhabited by the Saracens, in order that a greater number of ships may be available to those who wish to go to the aid of the Holy Land, and that to the Saracens may be denied the benefits that they usually reap from such commercial intercourse.

Although tournaments have been, under certain penalties, generally forbidden by different church councils, since however at this time they are a serious obstacle to the success of the crusade, we strictly prohibit them under penalty of excommunication for a period of three years.

But, since for the success of this undertaking it is above all else necessary that princes and Christian people maintain peace among themselves, we decree with the advice of the holy council that for four years peace be observed in the whole Christian world, so that through the prelates discordant elements may be brought together in the fullness of peace, or at least to the strict observance of the truce. Those who refuse to acquiesce in this are to be compelled by excommunication and interdict, unless the malice that inspired their wrongdoings was such that they ought not to enjoy such peace. But, if by chance they despise ecclesiastical censure, they have every reason to fear lest by the authority of the Church the secular power will be invoked against them as disturbers of the affairs of the One crucified.

We, therefore, by the mercy of the omnipotent God, trusting in the authority of the Blessed Apostles Peter and Paul, in virtue of that power of binding and loosing which God has conferred on us, though unworthy, grant to all who aid in this work personally and at their own expense a full remission of their sins about which they are profusely contrite at heart and which they have orally confessed, and promise them when the just shall receive their reward an increase of eternal happiness. To those who do not personally go to the Holy Land, but at their own expense send there as many suitable men as their means will permit, and to those also who go personally but at the expense of others, we grant a full remission of their sins. Participants of this remission are, moreover, all those who in proportion to their means contribute to the aid of the Holy Land, or in regard to what has been said give opportune advice and assistance. Finally, to all who in a spirit of piety aid in bringing to a successful issue this holy undertaking, this holy and general council imparts the benefits of its prayers and blessings that they may advance worthily to salvation.

Amen.

# 38

# Court Rolls of the Abbots
# of Ramsey and Battle

A manor has been defined as a "collection of rights." More commonly, it is defined as an estate whose lord receives labor service and other renders from peasant tenants. Abbots, like other medieval lords, commonly maintained manor courts, to which the serfs of the manor were obliged to come. Such lords might also hold other sorts of courts. A number of documents recording the courts' proceedings, called "rolls" because they were rolled up for storage, survive from the thirteenth century and later. Excerpts from the court rolls of two English abbots appear below. In theory the law of the English royal courts, the Common Law, was not available to serfs, who appeared only in the manor court.

---

### 38.1

### COURT ROLL OF THE ABBOT OF RAMSEY
### FOR THE MANOR OF ELTON

Elton. On the day of Saint Clement[1] in the said year.[2]

Names of the jurors: Robert at Cross, Reginald Blackman, Henry the reeve's[3] son, Roger Gamel, Geoffrey of Brington, John Duning, Henry Reaper, Philip Child, Hugh Achard, Geoffrey in the Nook, Henry Godswein, Jocelin.

For chevage[4] they give 18s.[5] 4d.[6] Those of the homage of John of Elton[7] give for the same 2s.

John Page and John Franceys[8] were pledges that Henry Smith would pay 2s. to John son of Alexander in the Lane at the most recent Nativity of the Virgin,

---

1. November 23.
2. 1278.
3. The reeve was a manorial official. It is not clear, however, whether in this document "reeve" denotes a last name rather an office.
4. Adult males were to be members of a "tithing," i.e., a group of men who had to appear in court and report infractions of the law (a procedure known as "view of frankpledge"), and to ensure the presence in court of other members of the tithing. However, members of a tithing could pay a small head tax, the chevage, instead of appearing in court. This system was a function of the lowest public courts, answerable to the king. Often, however, view of frankpledge was in the hands of a lord of a manor.
5. I.e., shillings. 20 shillings made up a pound.
6. I.e., denarii (Latin: pence). 12 pence made up a shilling.
7. John of Elton held a manor from the abbot of Ramsey within the larger manor of Elton. Those paying the 2s. are John's tenants.
8. Another source indicates that these two men held land by freehold (i.e., not as serfs).

and nothing was paid, so let both be in mercy.[9] Their fines are pardoned. He finds better pledges, namely, William of Barnwell[10] and Reginald Benet's son, and is to pay 12d. on Sunday next after Saint Catherine's day[11] and the rest at Christmas.

Due from Richard Bele's son: 6d. for renting to the lord Robert the Chaplain the house of Maud his sister without the license of the lord; pledge: John Godswein and by the same pledge etc.

Due from Henry Godswein for coming late to mow the lord's crop in autumn—see below; pledge: Roger Gamel. From Henry Achard for the same: pardoned. From Ralph Cobbler for the same: 6d.; from Alexander Gilbert's son for the same: 6d.; each is pledge for the other.

From Henry Godswein: 6d. because he would not work at the second boon-day[12] in autumn; and because he obstructed the boon-work, ordering all to go home before the proper time and without the leave of the bailiffs, to the damage of the lord: 6s. 8d., and for bad reaping in his boon-works on the lord's fields; pledges: John Godswein, Roger Gamel and Geoffrey of Brington.

From Richard in the Nook for being slow about doing the carrying due from him as boon-work: 6d. From Henry the reeve's son for the same: 6d. From Philip Noppe for the same: he is poor. Each is pledge for the other.

It is found by the jurors that Andrew the reeve falsely accused Gilbert Gamel so that the charge came to the ears of the bailiffs, the said charge being that Geoffrey feigned that he was sick and was at work in his own barn and doing other work in his yard. Therefore Andrew is in mercy for 12d.; pledge: Michael the reeve.

From Robert at Cross for his beasts doing damage in the lord's field which had been sown with barley: 6d.; pledge: Roger Gamel.

William of Barnwell was pledge that William Freeman[13] would pay 6d. to Ralph Hubert, and he has paid nothing. Therefore let him make satisfaction at Christmas to the said Ralph and be in mercy for 6d. for the wrongful detention; pledge: Michael the reeve.

The jurors say that Alexander at Cross, Gilbert son of Richard the reeve, and Henry son of Henry Bovebrook have badly beaten Gilbert son of Reginald Wyse. Therefore let them make satisfaction to him for his injuries and be in mercy for the trespass.[14] Alexander's fine: 6d.; pledge: Richard the reeve; Gilbert's fine: 6d.; pledge: Richard his father; Henry's fine: 6d.; pledge: Richard the reeve; the damages are assessed at 12d.

And they say that Elias Carpenter has wrongfully planted trees upon a boundary.

And they say that Maggie Carter has born a child to Richard son of Thomas Male out of wedlock. Fine on both of them: 6d.

And Agnes daughter of Philip Saladin has raised the hue[15] against Thomas Morborne who attempted to copulate with her.

And they say that Gilbert Child has withdrawn himself from the fulling mill.[16] Therefore he is in mercy: he is poor.

And they say that John Bovebrook has omitted to pay the toll of flax. Therefore he is in mercy for 6d.; pledge: Henry Newbond.

Due from John Bovebrook for not producing Thomas of Morborne whom he had replevied[17] to answer the charge of attempted rape on the daughter of Philip Saladin, 6d.; pledge: Henry Newbond, and let Thomas be arrested if he is found.

---

9   I.e., be fined by the court.
10  Another freeholder (see above n 9).
11  Saint Catherine's day: November 25.
12  A day on which a serf is obliged to work for the lord.
13  Both men are freeholders (on which, see n 8).
14  I.e., for the transgression against him.
15  A person who observes a crime was expected to "raise the hue and cry," i.e., cry out or otherwise raise the alarm. Neighbors were then expected to respond with help.
16  Where newly woven cloth was softened with water.
17  I.e., had taken possession of his animals in order to force him into living up to his obligation, or at least to appear in court.

And Agnes Cuttyle has born a child out of wedlock: she is poor.

And they say that Geoffrey of Brington omitted to perform a service of ploughing half an acre due to the lord. Therefore he is amerced[18] 6d.; pledge: Henry the reeve's son.

And they say that Reginald Boneyt[19] near Westereston has taken to himself to form part of the rod[20] that he holds three furrows subtracted from all the sulungs[21] which abut upon that rod; also at Arnewassebroc he has appropriated to the headland[22] that he holds three furrows from all the sulungs that abut upon that headland. Therefore this is to be put right and he is in mercy for his trespass for 6d.; pledges: William Barnwell and John Page.[23]

And they say that a cow has come as a waif and is in the abbot's yard.

They say as they have said before that the men of Water Newton have diverted a water-course at Follewellemor and at [illegible]mor. This must be discussed.

They say as they have said before that the men of Fotheringhay castle have made a purpresture[24] at Yarwellton upon John Page and upon the abbot at Wynewobesholm.[25] This must be discussed.

And they say that Fabian and Ralph Imbert's son are butchers, but each of them gives two fowls.[26]

They say as they have said before that the men of Morborne and Haddon have diverted a water-course

at Billingbrook. Therefore let this be put right and a day is given for having it put right before the hundred court[27] on the feast of Saint Mary's Conception.[28]

They say as they have said before that Jordan Mustard, the born serf of the lord, dwells at Alwalton, where he has married a wife of the homage of [the abbot] of Peterborough and has there a half-virgate[29] of land of the villeinage[30] of the said Abbot. Order is therefore given to Reginald Page and his tithing to produce the same man, etc.

They say as they have said before that John son of Richard Dunning is a tanner and dwells at Heyham, but he gives two capons every year by way of acknowledgment; and because he is well-to-do and has many goods, order was given to Hugh Achard and his tithing at the last view [of frankpledge] to produce him at the present court. And Hugh has not done this; therefore he and his tithing are in mercy. This amercement is forgiven.

It is presented by the said jurors that Reginald Benet's[31] son wrongfully refuses to be one of the 12 jurors, alleging that he is a freeman, whereas in truth Alice his sister made fine with Stephen of Elton the then farmer [of the manor][32] for leave to marry, and Cristiana and Athelina his sisters likewise made fine with William of Wald the then farmer. Therefore the said Reginald is in mercy for his contempt, 6d.

They also say that William of Barnwell[33] wrongfully alleges himself free and therefore refuses to be one

---

18  I.e., fined.

19  A freeholder.

20  Land five and a half yards square.

21  A sulung was in theory the amount of land one plough team could cultivate in a year; different parts of the country defined this acreage differently.

22  Land at the edge or head of a furrow.

23  These two men are freeholders.

24  I.e., have seized or encroached upon something to which others have common rights.

25  The words "Yarwellton ... Wynewobesholm" are unclear in the source.

26  Serfs customarily made certain renders of goods, including fowls, to their lord.

27  One of the lowest public courts, responsible to the king.

28  December 8.

29  The size of a virgate varied; it was about 30 acres.

30  I.e., held by serf tenure. A "villein" in England was a serf.

31  Reginald was a freeholder.

32  I.e., a person to whom the manor was farmed out; the "farmer" paid the abbot a lump sum in return for the right to collect and keep all the revenue produced by the manor for a certain period of time.

33  William was a freeholder.

of the jurors, whereas in truth he ought to pay merchet[34] at the lord's will when he wishes to give his daughter in marriage, and so did John the Freeman, ancestor of Elias the Freeman; he gave merchet for giving his daughter in marriage to one Roger Crudde at Nassington. Therefore William [is in mercy] for 6d.

They also say that John Page[35] deprives the lord of his due ploughing service between Easter and Whitsuntide on seven Fridays, namely, on each such day the ploughing of half an acre. The amercement is pardoned, for afterwards he discharged the service.

Michael the reeve complains of Richer Jocelin's son and Richard the reeve, and his wife, that when he was in the churchyard of Elton on the Sunday next before the feast of All Saints[36] in this year, there came the said Richer, Richard, and Richard's wife, who insulted him before the whole parish with vile words, charging him with collecting his own hay by means of the labor services due to the abbot, and with reaping his own crop in autumn by means of boon-works done by the abbot's customers,[37] and with ploughing his own land in Eversholmfield by means of ploughs "booned" from the vill,[38] and with releasing the customers from their labors and carrying services on condition of their letting and handing over their land to him at a cheap rate, and of taking gifts from the richer tenants as a consideration for not turning them into tenants at money rents and with obliging the poorer tenants to become payers of money rent. And the said Richard and Richer are present and defend etc., and ask that [the truth] be inquired by [the?] 12 jurors. These come and say that of none of the charges is he [Michael] guilty. Therefore let the said Richard and Richer make satisfaction to the said Michael, and be in mercy for the trespass. Richard's fine is 2s.; pledge: William Jacob's son. Richer's fine is 12d.; pledge: Jocelin. And Michael's damages are assessed and he is to receive 10s. from Richard Reeve; but Michael releases all save 2s....

Sum total: 38s. 10d.

## 38.2
### COURT ROLL OF THE ABBOT OF BATTLE FOR THE MANOR OF BRIGHTWALTHAM.

*The roll is organized according to the vills which made up the manor.*

Lawday. Court of [the manor of] Brightwaltham held on Monday following Ascension day[39] in the twenty-first year of King Edward.[40]

... Conholt. The tithingman of Conholt with his whole tithing present that all is well save that William of Mescombe has stopped up a certain [watercourse?] wrongfully. Therefore he is in mercy.[41] Also they say that Edith of Upton has cut down trees in the enclosure and the seisin[42] of the lord contrary to a prohibition, and they say that she has no property and has fled into foreign parts.[43]

Adam Scot is made tithingman and sworn to a faithful exercise of his office.

(b)[44] John son of Hugh Poleyn enters on the land which Randolph Tailor held saving the right of everyone and gives for entry-money 4 marks[45] and will pay 1 mark at Michaelmas in the twenty-second year of King Edward, 1 mark at Christmas next following, 1 mark at Easter, and 1 mark at Michaelmas next

---

34   Merchet was a payment by a female serf (or her parent) to the lord in order to marry, especially when marrying someone not of the manor. The Common Law held that payment of merchet demonstrated status as a serf.
35   A freeholder.
36   I.e., November 1.
37   Tenants by customary service; another term for serfs.
38   A village which made up part of a manor.
39   The sixth Thursday after Easter.
40   1293.
41   The margin indicates the sum of 12d.
42   I.e., lawful possession.
43   The margin reads "amercement 12d."
44   "b" here seems to indicate that this paragraph should be read after the next, which is labelled "a."
45   A mark was worth 13s. 4d.

following, and for the due making of all these payments the said Hugh Poleyn finds sureties, namely, Adam Scot, John Gosselyn, William of Mescombe, John Gyote. And because the said John is a minor, the wardship[46] of the said lands and holdings is delivered to his father the said Hugh Poleyn until he is of full age, on the terms of his performing the services due and accustomed for the same. Also there is granted to the said Hugh the crop now growing on the sown land, and the heriot[47] due on this entry, for a half-mark payable at next Michaelmas on the security of the above-named sureties.

(a) Hugh Poleyn gives the lord 2s. so that he may have the judgment of the court as to his right in a certain holding in Upton which J. son of Randolph Tailor claims as his right. And upon this the whole vill of Brightwaltham, sworn along with the whole vill of Conholt, say upon their oath that Hugh Poleyn has better right to hold the said holding than anyone else has, and that he is the next heir by right of blood.

[[48]The Conholt case as to the tenure of Edith wife of Robert Tailor according to the inquest made by the jurors. One Alan Poleyn held a holding in Conholt upon servile terms[49] and had a wife, Cristina by name. The said Alan died when Richard was the farmer of the manor. Thereupon came the friends of the said Cristina and procured for her a part of the land by way of dower,[50] making a false suggestion and as though the land were of free status; and this was to the great prejudice of the lord Abbot. Upon this came one Richard Meyn and married the said Cristina and begot upon her one Randolph. Then Richard died, and the said Cristina of her own motion enfeoffed[51] Randolph

her son of the said holding. Then Cristina died, and Randolph, being in seisin of the said holding, married Edith, the present plaintiff; and after Randolph's death Edith married Robert Tailor. Now you can see and give your counsel about the right of the said Edith. And know this, that if I had at hand the court rolls of the time when William of Lewes (was steward) I could certify the facts and I could show you many strange things that were improvidently done.]

Hartley. The whole tithing of Hartley comes as it ought to come and presents that all is well.

Brightwaltham. The tithingman of Brightwaltham with his whole tithing present that all is well, except that William of Westwood has made a default. They say also that John son of Richard at Cross dwells at Bromham[52] and is not in a tithing. Therefore his father is ordered to produce him at the next court. They say also that Henry Smith struck the lord Robert the chaplain and drew blood, and then to conceal his fault raised the hue. Therefore he is in mercy; pledges: John Atgreen, Richard Young and Thomas Smith. They also present that Cristina widow of Ralph Smith has received a guest contrary to the court. Therefore she is in mercy; pledge: Richard Smoker.

Agnes, Maud's daughter, at the instance of her friends, gives the lord 12d. for permission to marry; she gives no more because she is very poor....

Court of Brightwaltham held on Wednesday next after the feast of Saint Peter at Chains[53] in the twenty-second year of King Edward.[54]

... It is prohibited to all the lord's tenants to give in any way sheaves of grain to anyone of the vill or from outside it on pain of a half mark.

---

46  I.e., the lord's right to custody of the land and the right to enjoy its revenue while the holder is a minor.

47  A payment to a lord when a serf entered into a holding on a manor. The payment of heriot was viewed by the Common Law as evidence of being a serf.

48  The words in brackets are on a strip of parchment attached to the roll. This may be a portion of a letter from the abbot's steward concerning the above case.

49  I.e., as a serf.

50  I.e., in the Common Law, a portion (two thirds) of a husband's freehold set aside for a widow on his death, in which she holds a lifetime interest.

51  I.e., granted as a freehold.

52  Another manor of the abbot.

53  I.e., August 1.

54  1294. Perhaps, however, this entry should be dated to the king's twenty-first year.

Inquest is made by the steward on Tuesday after Saint Matthew's day[55] as to the abduction of sheep and other trespasses committed in the manor of Brightwaltham in the said year. By this inquest it is found that John Sket bought from the reeve three sheep and when a price had been agreed between them the said John pastured the sheep in the lord's pasture. Therefore he is in mercy. Pledges: John Parlefrens and Richard Young. [Amercement is] 40d.

Richard Fette is in mercy for receiving sheaves of grain in autumn upon the delivery of the reeve against the prohibition of the steward; pledge: the whole vill.

And the jurors [of the said inquest] further say that the sheep were neither abducted nor brought back again by any malice, but owing to the negligence of William Wachel the shepherd, many sheep were wandering about the country hither and thither; and therefore the said John[56] is in mercy; pledge: the whole vill.

They say that John Atgreen, John of Southwood, Thomas Smith and Richard Young are the best and most competent men of the whole vill for the purpose of filling and executing the office of reeve. And of these the steward has chosen Thomas Smith for the office. Afterwards the said Thomas made fine that he might be absolved from the office of reeve and gives the lord 40s....

They say also that John surnamed Lord is a good man needful to the lord for the keeping of the ewes. And the whole vill undertook for him that he shall keep them well and truly and with all diligence and will answer for him. They say also that John son of John Atgreen is needful to the lord for keeping the lord's muttons; and he is admitted [to the office] and the whole vill undertakes for him. They say also that Thomas Bagge is needful for holding one plough and Richard Uhtred for driving it. As to the other teams, whether of oxen or of horses, they say that it is well

that those men should stay with the lord who were with him in the past year.

View of frankpledge[57] on Wednesday next [before or after] the feast of Saint Matthew in the twenty-first year of King Edward.

Richard of Fulrith tithingman of Hartley with his whole tithing present that Gervase May, John Cooper, John at Moor and Nicholas Sharie are missing [from the frankpledge]; they undertake to produce them at the next court. And because they make insufficient presentment, they are in mercy.[58]

Prohibition is made that none of the tenants of Hartley upon pain of l00s. are to go to the hundred court or the county court[59] at the summons of any outside bailiff, and if hereafter they do so, although they may have been distrained into doing it, if they are convicted of it they shall incur the said penalty....

Geoffrey Willam tithingman of Brightwaltham and his whole tithing present that ... Thomas Miller laid violent hands on Alice daughter of Ralph and that she raised the hue. And because Geoffrey the tithingman presents that there was no violence but that [Thomas and Alice] were playing, and this is not likely since the hue was raised, let the said tithingman be in mercy, and let Thomas Miller be in mercy for the trespass; pledges: Richard his father and Richard Young.

They further present that Warin Agodehalf[60] does not pay obedience as he ought to his tithingman[61] as regards contributions and other matters. And the said Warin comes into full court and says that he is of free status by the service of 1d. a year. And it is found by the court that his father was of servile status and the father's issue must continue of the same status. And because against right he says that he is free, whereas he is a serf, therefore he is in mercy, both as to this false claim [of freedom] and as to the main matter [the charge originally made against him]. Pledge: the whole tithing....

---

55  I.e., September 21.
56  Apparently an error for William.
57  See above, n 4.
58  The margin indicates 12d.
59  The abbot of Battle held an exemption from being sued in these courts.
60  A document of 1284 refers to him as "the villein of the lord." He also holds an acre of freehold.
61  Or, perhaps, "his tithing."

Court of Brightwaltham held on Thursday next after the exaltation of the holy cross[62] in the same year.[63]

Robert of Evershole is in mercy for renting his land to Ralph Tailor and others for a term of years without license. Pledges for the amercement: John Woodward and John Atgreen.

John Woodward is in mercy for counterpleading the lord in his court. Pledges: John Atgreen and Robert of Evershole.

Ralph the reeve is in mercy for accepting the land of Robert of Evershole for a term of years without license. Pledges: Richard Young and William Parlefrens....

John Atgreen is elected by all the virgaters[64] to guard the wood and swine of the lord ... and it is enjoined on him that if he finds the beasts of any persons in the lord's woods he shall forthwith go and impound them, on pain of 40s.

To this court came the whole community of the villeins of Brightwaltham and of its mere and spontaneous will surrendered to the lord all the right and claim that the said villeins have heretofore claimed by reason of common in the lord's wood called Hemele and the surrounding adjacent lands, to the intent that neither the said villeins nor those who hereafter shall hold their holdings shall henceforth be able to exact, demand or have any right or claim by reason of common in the said wood and surrounding adjacent lands. And in return for this surrender the lord of his special grace has remitted to them the common that he had in the field called Eastfield which lies along the road which runs from the Red Pit to the lord's wood called Hemele. And he has further remitted to them the common that he had in the wood of the said villeins called Trendale, to the intent that the said lord shall have no beasts pasturing in the said common or in the said wood. And the lord has also granted that at the time of pannage[65] as soon as the lord ever shall enter his said wood of Hemele for the purpose of pannaging his pigs, they [the said villeins] also may enter with their pigs until the day of Saint Martin[66] and shall give for pannage according to the age of the pigs as is more fully contained in the Register [of the Abbey], namely, for a pig of full age a penny, and for a younger pig a halfpenny....

---

62  I.e., September 14.
63  The date is unclear; probably 1294.
64  A social group made up of the middling ranks of peasants.
65  The foraging of swine in a wood.
66  November 11.

# 39

# THOMAS AQUINAS,
## *SUMMA CONTRA GENTILES*

A Dominican friar, Saint Thomas Aquinas (1225-1274) taught theology at the University of Paris and at the papal court. He wrote the *Summa Contra Gentiles* in the years 1259-1264. Evidence from the early fourteenth century suggests that the work was intended for use by Christian missionaries in Spain.

BOOK I: GOD

*1   In what consists the office of a wise man*

"My mouth shall meditate truth, and my lips shall hate wickedness" ([Old Testament] Proverbs 8).

The general use which, in the Philosopher's opinion,[1] should be followed in naming things has resulted in those men being called wise who direct things themselves and govern them well. Wherefore among other things which men conceive of the wise man, the Philosopher reckons that "it belongs to the wise man to direct things." Now the rule of all things directed to the end of government and order must be taken from their end, for then a thing is best disposed when it is fittingly directed to its end, since the end of everything is its good. Wherefore in the arts we observe that the art which governs and rules another is the one to which the latter's end belongs. Thus, the medical art rules and directs the art of the druggist because health, which is the object of medicine, is the end of all drugs which are made up by the druggist's art. The same may be observed in the art of sailing in relation to the art of shipbuilding, and in the military art in relation

to the equestrian art and all warlike appliances. These arts which govern others are called master-arts, that is principal arts, for which reason their craftsmen, who are called master-craftsmen, are awarded the name of wise men. Since, however, these same craftsmen, through being occupied with the ends of certain individual things, do not attain to the universal end of all things, they are called wise this or that, in which sense it is said "As a wise architect, I have laid the foundation" ([New Testament] 1 Corinthians 3); whereas the name of being wise simply is reserved to him alone whose consideration is about the end of the universe, which end is also the beginning of the universe. Wherefore, according to the Philosopher, it belongs to the wise man to consider the highest causes.

Now the last end of each thing is that which is intended by the first author or mover of that thing, and the first author and mover of the universe is an intellect, as we prove further on. Consequently, the last end of the universe must be the good of the intellect, and this is truth. Therefore truth must be the last end of the whole universe, and the consideration thereof must be the chief occupation of wisdom. And for this reason divine Wisdom, clothed in flesh,

---

1   For Aquinas, "the Philosopher" is always Aristotle (fourth century BC).

declares that He came into the world to make known the truth, saying, "For this was I born, and for this cause came I into the world, that I should give testimony to the truth" ([New Testament] John 18). Moreover the Philosopher defines the First Philosophy as being the knowledge of truth—not of any truth, but of that truth which is the source of all truth, of that, namely, which relates to the first principle of being of all things. Wherefore its truth is the principle of all truth, since the disposition of things is the same in truth as in being.

Now it belongs to the same thing to pursue one contrary and to remove the other. Thus medicine, which effects health, removes sickness. Hence, just as it belongs to a wise man to meditate and disseminate truth, especially about the first principle, so does it belong to him to refute contrary falsehood.

Wherefore the twofold office of the wise man is fittingly declared from the mouth of Wisdom in the words quoted above, namely, to meditate and publish the divine truth, which is the truth in itself, as signified by the words, "My mouth shall meditate truth" and to refute the error contrary to truth, as signified by the words, "and my lips shall hate wickedness," by which is denoted falsehood opposed to divine truth, which falsehood is contrary to religion that is also called godliness, wherefore the falsehood that is contrary thereto receives the name of ungodliness.

## 2   The author's intention in this work

Now of all human pursuits, that of wisdom is the most perfect, the most sublime, the most profitable, the most delightful. It is the most perfect, since in proportion as a man devotes himself to the pursuit of wisdom, so much does he already share in true happiness. Wherefore, the wise man says, "Blessed is the man that shall continue in wisdom" ([Apocrypha] Ecclesiasticus 14). It is the most sublime because thereby especially does man approach a likeness to God, Who made all things in wisdom. Wherefore, since likeness

is the cause of love, the pursuit of wisdom especially unites man to God by friendship. Hence it is said that "wisdom is an infinite treasure to men, which they that use, become the friends of God" ([Apocrypha] Wisdom 7). It is the most profitable, because by wisdom itself man is brought to the kingdom of immortality, "for the desire of wisdom brings to the everlasting kingdom" ([Apocrypha] Wisdom 6). And it is the most delightful because her conversation hath no bitterness, nor her company any tediousness, but joy and gladness ([Apocrypha] Wisdom 8.16).

Wherefore, taking heart from God's loving kindness to assume the office of a wise man, although it surpasses our own powers, the purpose we have in view is, in our own weak way, to declare the truth which the Catholic faith professes, while weeding out contrary errors. For, in the words of Hilary, "I acknowledge that I owe my life's chief occupation to God, so that every word and every thought of mine may speak of Him."[2] But it is difficult to refute the errors of each individual, for two reasons. First, because the sacrilegious assertions of each erring individual are not so well known to us that we are able from what they say to find arguments to refute their errors. For the Doctors of old[3] used this method in order to confute the errors of the heathens, whose opinions they were able to know, since either they had been heathens themselves, or had lived among heathens and were conversant with their teachings. Secondly, because some of them, like the Mohammedans[4] and pagans, do not agree with us as to the authority of any Scripture whereby they may be convinced, in the same way as we are able to dispute with the Jews by means of the Old Testament, and with heretics by means of the New, whereas the former accept neither. Wherefore it is necessary to have recourse to natural reason, to which all are compelled to assent. And yet this is deficient in the things of God.

And while we are occupied in the inquiry about a particular truth, we shall show what errors are exclud-

2   St. Hilary, theologian (fourth century).
3   I.e., the doctors of the church, the leading theologians of Christianity's first few centuries after the apostles.
4   I.e., Moslems. Moslems generally consider the term "Mohammedan" an insult in that it can imply they worship Mohammed, a human being, rather than Allah, or God. It is not clear that Aquinas means the term in an offensive sense.

ed thereby, and how demonstrable truth is in agreement with the faith of the Christian religion.

### 3   In what way it is possible to make known the divine truth

Since, however, not every truth is to be made known in the same way, and "it is the part of an educated man to seek for conviction in each subject only so far as the nature of the subject allows," as the Philosopher most rightly observes as quoted by Boethius,[5] it is necessary to show first of all in what way it is possible to make known the aforesaid truth.

Now in those things which we hold about God there is truth in two ways. For certain things that are true about God wholly surpass the capability of human reason, for instance that God is three and one, while there are certain things to which even natural reason can attain, for instance that God exists, that God is one, and others like these, which even the philosophers proved demonstratively of God, being guided by the light of natural reason.

It is most clearly evident that certain divine truths wholly surpass the capability of human reason. For since the principle of all the knowledge which reason acquires about a thing is the understanding of that thing's essence, because according to the Philosopher's teaching the principle of a demonstration is what a thing is, it follows that our knowledge about a thing will be in proportion to our understanding of its essence. Wherefore, if the human intellect comprehends the essence of a particular thing, for instance a stone or a triangle, no truth about that thing will surpass the capability of human reason. But this does not happen to us in relation to God, because the human intellect is incapable by its natural power of attaining to the comprehension of His essence since our intellect's knowledge, according to the mode of the present life, originates from the senses, so that things which are not objects of the senses cannot be comprehended by the human intellect, except in so far as knowledge of them is gathered from sensibles.[6] Now sensibles

cannot lead our intellect to see in them what God is, because they are effects unequal to the power of their cause. And yet our intellect is led by sensibles to the divine knowledge so as to know that God exists, and other such truths about God, which need to be ascribed to the first principle. Accordingly some divine truths are attainable by human reason, while others altogether surpass the power of human reason.

Again, the same is easy to see from the differences among intellects. For if one of two men perceives a thing with his intellect with greater subtlety, the one whose intellect is of a higher degree understands many things which the other is altogether unable to grasp, as instanced in a yokel who is utterly incapable of grasping the subtleties of philosophy. Now the angelic intellect surpasses the human intellect more than the intellect of the cleverest philosopher surpasses that of the most uncultured. For an angel knows God through a more excellent effect than does man, for as much as the angel's essence, through which he is led to know God by natural knowledge, is more excellent than sensible things, even than the soul itself, by which the human intellect mounts to the knowledge of God. And the divine intellect surpasses the angelic intellect much more than the angelic surpasses the human. For the divine intellect by its capacity equals the divine essence, wherefore God perfectly understands of Himself what He is, and He knows all things that can be understood about Him, whereas the angel does not know what God is by his natural knowledge because the angel's essence, by which he is led to the knowledge of God, is an effect unequal to the power of its cause. Consequently, an angel is unable by his natural knowledge to grasp all that God understands about Himself. Nor again is human reason capable of grasping all that an angel understands by his natural power. Accordingly, just as a man would show himself to be a most insane fool if he declared the assertions of a philosopher to be false because he was unable to understand them, so, and much more, a man would be exceedingly foolish were he to suspect of falsehood the things revealed by God

---

5   Boethius (c. 480-524), a Christian, wrote several philosophical works.
6   I.e., things which are perceived by means of the senses.

through the ministry of His angels because they cannot be the object of reason's investigations.

Furthermore, the same is made abundantly clear by the deficiency which every day we experience in our knowledge of things. For we are ignorant of many of the properties of sensible things, and in many cases we are unable to discover the nature of those properties which we perceive by our senses. Much less, therefore, is human reason capable of investigating all the truths about that most sublime essence.

With this the saying of the Philosopher is in accord where he says that "our intellect in relation to those primary things which are most evident in nature is like the eye of a bat in relation to the sun."

To this truth Holy Scripture also bears witness. For it is written, "Peradventure you will comprehend the steps of God and will find out the Almighty perfectly?" ([Old Testament] Job 11) and "Behold God is great, exceeding our knowledge" ([Old Testament] Job 36) and "We know in part" ([New Testament] 1 Corinthians 13).

Therefore, all that is said about God, though it cannot be investigated by reason, must not be forthwith rejected as false, as the Manicheans[7] and many unbelievers have thought.

### 4    That the truth about divine things which is attainable by reason is appropriately offered to humanity as an object of belief

Since, then, the truth of the knowable things about God is twofold, one to which the inquiry of reason can attain, the other which surpasses the whole range of human reason, both are fittingly proposed by God to man as an object of belief. We must first show this with regard to that truth which is attainable by the inquiry of reason, so it does not appear to some that, since it can be attained by reason, it is useless to make it an object of faith by supernatural inspiration. Now three disadvantages would result if this truth were left solely to the inquiry of reason. One is that few people

would have knowledge of God because very many are hindered from gathering the fruit of diligent inquiry, which is the discovery of truth, for three reasons. Some indeed on account of an indisposition of temperament, by reason of which many are naturally indisposed to knowledge, so that no efforts of theirs would enable them to reach to the attainment of the highest degree of human knowledge, which consists in knowing God. Some are hindered by the needs of daily affairs. For there must be among humanity some who devote themselves to the conduct of temporal affairs, who would be unable to devote so much time to the leisure of contemplative research as to reach the summit of human inquiry, namely the knowledge of God. And some are hindered by laziness. For in order to acquire the knowledge of God in those things which reason is able to investigate, it is necessary to have a previous knowledge of many things since almost the entire consideration of philosophy is directed to the knowledge of God. For this reason metaphysics, which is about divine things, is the last of the parts of philosophy to be studied. Wherefore it is not possible to arrive at the inquiry about the aforesaid truth except after a most laborious study. Few are willing to take upon themselves this labor for the love of knowledge, the natural desire for which has nevertheless been instilled into the mind of man by God.

The second disadvantage is that those who would arrive at the discovery of the aforesaid truth would scarcely succeed in doing so after a long time. First, because this truth is so profound, that it is only after long practice that the human intellect is enabled to grasp it by means of reason. Secondly, because many things are required beforehand, as stated above. Thirdly, because at the time of youth, the mind, when tossed about by the various movements of the passions, is not fit for the knowledge of so sublime a truth, whereas "calm gives prudence and knowledge," as stated in the *Physics*.[8] Hence mankind would remain in the deepest darkness of ignorance if the path of reason were the only available way to the

---

7    The Manicheans were an ancient group, opposed by St. Augustine in the fourth century, who held that all physical matter is evil, and is created by an evil force independently of God, who being good, created only spirit, which was also wholly good. Evil and good were thus in constant conflict.

8    Aristotle's *Physics*.

knowledge of God, for the knowledge of God, which especially makes people perfect and good, would be acquired only by the few, and by these only after a long time.

The third disadvantage is that much falsehood is mingled with the investigations of human reason, on account of the weakness of our intellect in forming its judgments, and by reason of the admixture of phantasms. Consequently, many would remain in doubt about even those things which are most truly demonstrated, through ignoring the force of the demonstration. This is especially so when they perceive that different things are taught by the various men who are called wise. Moreover, among the many demonstrated truths, there is sometimes a mixture of falsehood that is not demonstrated, but assumed for some probable or sophistic reason which at times is mistaken for a demonstration. For these reasons, it was necessary that definite certainty and pure truth about divine things should be offered to man by the way of faith.

Accordingly, divine mercy has made this salutary commandment, that even some things which reason is able to investigate must be held by faith, so that all may share in the knowledge of God easily, and without doubt or error.

Hence it is written "That henceforward you walk not as also the Gentiles walk in the vanity of their mind, having their understanding darkened" ([New Testament] Ephesians 4) and "All your children shall be taught of the Lord" ([Old Testament] Isaiah 54).

### 5 That those things which cannot be investigated by reason are appropriately proposed to humanity as an object of faith

It may appear to some that those things which cannot be by reason ought not to be proposed to man as an object of faith because divine wisdom provides for each thing according to the mode of its nature. We must, therefore, prove that it is necessary also for those things which surpass reason to be proposed by God to man as an object of faith.

For no man tends to do a thing by his desire and endeavor unless it be previously known to him. Wherefore, since man is directed by divine providence to a higher good than human frailty can attain in the present life, as we shall show later, it was necessary for his mind to be asked to rise somewhat higher than those things to which our reason can reach in the present life, so that he might learn to aspire, and by his endeavors to tend to something surpassing the whole state of the present life. And this pertains especially to the Christian religion, which alone promises spiritual and eternal goods. For this reason it proposes many things surpassing the thought of man, whereas the old law,[9] which contained promises of temporal things, proposed few things that are above human inquiry. It was with this motive that the philosophers, in order to wean men from sensual pleasures to virtue, took care to show that there are other goods of greater account than those which appeal to the senses, the taste of which things affords much greater delight to those who devote themselves to active or contemplative virtues.

Again it is necessary for this truth to be proposed to man as an object of faith in order that he may have truer knowledge of God. For then alone do we know God truly, when we believe that He is far above all that man can possibly think of God, because the divine essence surpasses man's natural knowledge, as stated above. Hence by the fact that certain things about God are proposed to man which surpass his reason, he is strengthened in his opinion that God is far above what he is able to conceive.

There results also another advantage from this, namely, the checking of presumption which is the mother of error. For there are people who presume so far on their wits that they think themselves capable of measuring the whole nature of things by their intellect, in that they esteem all things true which they see, and false which they do not see. Accordingly, in order that man's mind might be freed from this presumption, and seek the truth humbly, it was necessary that certain things far surpassing his intellect should be proposed to man by God.

---

9    I.e., the Hebrews' sacred text, the Old Testament.

Yet another advantage is made apparent by the words of the Philosopher in the *Ethics*. For when a certain Simonides maintained that man should neglect the knowledge of God, and apply his mind to human affairs, and declared that "a man ought to know human things, and a mortal, mortal things," the Philosopher contradicted him, saying that "a man ought to devote himself to immortal and divine things as much as he can." Hence he says in *Concerning Animals* that though it is but little that we perceive of higher substances, yet that little is more loved and desired than all the knowledge we have of lower substances. He also says in *On the Heavens and the Earth* that when questions about the heavenly bodies can be answered by a short and probable solution, it happens that the hearer is very much rejoiced. All this shows that, however imperfect the knowledge of the highest things may be, it bestows very great perfection on the soul. Consequently, although human reason is unable to grasp fully those things that are above reason, it nevertheless acquires much perfection, if at least it hold things, in any way whatever, by faith.

Wherefore it is written "Many things are shown to you above the understanding of men" ([Apocrypha] Ecclesiasticus 3), and "The things ... that are of God no man knows, but the Spirit of God: but to us God hath revealed them by His Spirit" ([New Testament] 1 Corinthians 2).

### 7   That the truth of reason is not in opposition to the truth of the Christian faith

Now though the aforesaid truth of the Christian faith surpasses the ability of human reason, nevertheless those things which are naturally instilled in human reason cannot be opposed to this truth. For it is clear that those things which are implanted in reason by nature are most true, so much so that it is impossible to think they are false. Nor is it lawful to deem false that which is held by faith, since it is so evidently confirmed by God. Seeing, then, that the false alone is opposed to the true, as evidently appears if we examine their definitions, it is impossible for the aforesaid truth of faith to be contrary to those principles which reason knows naturally.

Again, the same thing which the disciple's mind receives from a teacher is contained in the knowledge of the teacher, unless he teaches insincerely, which it would be wicked to say of God. Now the knowledge of naturally known principles is instilled in us by God, since God Himself is the author of our nature. Therefore the divine Wisdom also contains these principles. Consequently, whatever is contrary to these principles is contrary to the divine Wisdom, wherefore it cannot be from God. Therefore, those things which are received by faith from divine revelation cannot be contrary to our natural knowledge.

Moreover, our intellect is hindered by contrary arguments, so that it cannot advance to the knowledge of truth. Wherefore, if conflicting knowledges were instilled into us by God, our intellect would thereby be hindered from knowing the truth. And this cannot be ascribed to God.

Furthermore, things that are natural are unchangeable so long as nature does not change. Now contrary opinions cannot be together in the same knower at the same time. Therefore, God does not instill into man any opinion or belief contrary to natural knowledge.

Hence, the Apostle says "The word is nigh to you even in your heart and in your mouth. This is the word of faith which we preach" ([New Testament] Romans 10). Yet, because it surpasses reason, some look upon it as though it were contrary to reason, which is impossible.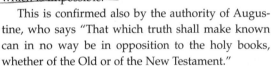

This is confirmed also by the authority of Augustine, who says "That which truth shall make known can in no way be in opposition to the holy books, whether of the Old or of the New Testament."

From this we may evidently conclude that whatever arguments are alleged against the teachings of faith, they do not rightly proceed from the first self-evident principles instilled by nature. Wherefore they lack the force of demonstration, and are either probable or sophistical arguments, and consequently it is possible to solve them.

### 13   Arguments in proof of God's existence

Having shown, then, that it is not futile to endeavor to prove the existence of God, we may proceed to set forth the arguments whereby both philosophers and Catholic doctors have proved that there is a God. In the first place, we shall give the arguments by which Aristotle sets out to prove God's existence. He aims at proving this from the point of view of movement, in two ways.

The first way is as follows. Whatever is in motion is moved by another. It is clear to the senses that something, the sun for instance, is in motion. Therefore it is set in motion by something else moving it. Now that which moves it is itself either moved or not. If it is not moved, then the point is proved that we must postulate an unmoved mover, and this we call God. If, however, it is moved, it is moved by another mover. Either, therefore, we must proceed to infinity, or we must come to an unmoved mover. But it is not possible to proceed to infinity. Therefore, it is necessary to postulate an immovable mover.

This argument contains two propositions that need to be proved: namely that whatever is in motion is moved by another, and that it is not possible to proceed to infinity in movers and things moved.

The first of these is proved by the Philosopher in three ways. First, if a thing moves itself, it must have the principle of its movement in itself or else it would clearly be moved by another. Again it must be moved primarily, that is, it must be moved by reason of itself and not by reason of its part, as an animal is moved by the movement of its foot, for in the latter way not the whole but the part would be moved by itself, and one part by another. Again it must be divisible and have parts, since whatever is moved is divisible, as is proved in the *Physics*.

These things being supposed, he argues as follows. That which is stated to be moved by itself is moved primarily. Therefore if one of its parts is at rest, it follows that the whole is at rest. For if, while one part is at rest, another of its parts were in motion, the whole itself would not be moved primarily, but its part which is in motion while another is at rest. Now nothing that is at rest while another is at rest is moved by itself, for that which is at rest as a result of another

thing being at rest must be in motion as a result of the other's motion, and hence it is not moved by itself. Hence, that which was stated to be moved by itself is not moved by itself. Therefore, whatever is in motion must be moved by another....

Another argument[10] can be drawn from the words of Aristotle. For in *Metaphysics* 2 he shows that those things which excel in being as true excel in being and in *Metaphysics* 4 he shows that there is something supremely true from the fact that we see that, of two false things, one is falser than the other, wherefore it follows that one also is truer than the other. Now this is by reason of approximation to that which is simply and supremely true. Wherefore, we may further conclude that there is something that is supremely being. And this we call God.

Another argument in support of this conclusion is adduced by Damascene[11] from the government of world, and the same reasoning is indicated by the Commentator on the *Physics*.[12] It runs as follows. It is impossible for contrary and discordant things to accord in one order always or frequently except by someone's governance, whereby each and all are made to tend to a definite end. Now we see that in the world things of different natures accord in one order, not seldom and fortuitously, but always or for the most part. Therefore it follows that there is someone by whose providence the world is governed. And this we call God.

BOOK II: CREATION

2   *That the consideration of creatures[13] is useful for building up our faith*

This meditation on the divine works is indeed necessary in order to build up man's faith in God.

First, because through meditating on His works we are able somewhat to admire and consider the divine wisdom. For things made by art[14] are indications of

---

10   For the existence of God.
11   I.e., St. John Damascene (eighth century), a theologian of the Eastern Orthodox Church.
12   The Commentator is Abu-al-Walid Mohammed ibn-Ahmed ibn-Rushd (twelfth century), better known in the West as Averroës. Active in Islamic Spain, he wrote commentaries on Aristotle, among other works.
13   I.e., created things.
14   I.e., by design.

the art itself, since they are made in likeness to the art. Now God brought things into being by His wisdom. For this reason it is said in the psalm, "You have made all things in wisdom."[15] Hence, we are able to gather the wisdom of God from the consideration of His works, since by a kind of communication of His likeness it is spread abroad in the things He has made. For it is said, "He poured her out, namely wisdom, upon all His works" ([Apocrypha] Ecclesiasticus 1), wherefore the psalmist, after saying "Your knowledge has become wonderful to me: it is high, and I cannot reach it," and after referring to the aid of the divine enlightening, when he says, "Night shall be my light," etc., confesses himself to have been helped to know the divine wisdom by the consideration of the divine works, saying, "Wonderful are Your works, and my soul knows right well."[16]

Secondly, this consideration leads us to admire the sublime power of God, and consequently begets in men's hearts a reverence for God. For we must conclude that the power of the maker transcends the things made. Wherefore it is said, "If they," namely, the philosophers, "admired their power and their effects," namely of the heavens, stars, and elements of the world, "let them understand ... that He that made them is mightier than they" ([Apocrypha] Wisdom 13). Also it is written, "The invisible things of God ... are clearly seen, being understood by the things that are made: His eternal power also and divinity" ([New Testament] Romans 1). And this admiration makes us fear and revere God. Hence it is said, "Great is Your name in might. Who shall not fear You, O King of nations?" ([Old Testament] Jeremiah 10).

Thirdly, this consideration inflames the souls of men to the love of the divine goodness. For whatever goodness and perfection is generally apportioned among various creatures is all united together in Him universally, as in the source of all goodness, as we proved in the First Book. Wherefore, if the goodness, beauty, and sweetness of creatures are so alluring to the minds of men, the fountainhead of the goodness of God Himself, in comparison with the rivulets of goodness which we find in creatures, will draw the entranced minds of men wholly to itself. Hence it is said in the psalm, "You have given me, O Lord, a delight in Your doings; and in the works of Your hands I shall rejoice,"[17] and elsewhere it is said of the children of men, "They shall be inebriated with the plenty of Your house," that is of all creatures, "and You shall make them drink of the torrent of Your pleasure. For with You is the fountain of life."[18] Again, it is said against certain men, "By these good things that are seen," namely creatures that are good by a kind of participation, "they could not understand Him that is" ([Apocrypha] Wisdom 13) good, namely, indeed, that is goodness itself, as we have shown in the First Book.

Fourthly, this consideration bestows on man a certain likeness to the divine perfection. For it was shown in the First Book that God, by knowing Himself, beholds all other things in Himself. Since, then, the Christian faith teaches man chiefly about God, and makes him know creatures by the light of divine revelation, there results in man a certain likeness to the divine wisdom. Hence it is said, "But we all beholding the glory of the Lord with open face, are transformed into the same image" ([New Testament] 2 Corinthians 3).

Accordingly, it is evident that the consideration of creatures helps to build up the Christian faith. Wherefore it is said, "I will ... remember the works of the Lord, and I will declare the things I have seen: by the words of the Lord are His works" ([Apocrypha] Ecclesiasticus 42).

## BOOK III: PROVIDENCE

### 1 Prologue

"The Lord is a great God and a great King above all gods." "For the Lord will not reject His people." "For in His hands are all the ends of the earth and the heights of the mountains are His. For the sea is His

---

15   Old Testament, Psalms 104.24.
16   Old Testament, Psalms 139.14.
17   Old Testament, Psalms 92.4.
18   This and the previous quotation: Old Testament, Psalms 36.8.

and He made it, and His hands formed the dry land" ([Old Testament] Psalms 94-95).

We have shown in the preceding books that there is one First Being, possessing the full perfection of all being, whom we call God, and who of the abundance of His perfection bestows being on all that exists, so that He is proved to be not only the first of beings, but also the beginning of all. Moreover, He bestows being on others, not through natural necessity, but according to the decree of His will, as we have shown above. Hence it follows that He is the Lord of the things made by Him since we dominate over those things that are subject to our will. And this is a perfect dominion that He exercises over things made by Him, forasmuch as in their making He needs neither the help of an extrinsic agent, nor matter as the foundation of His work[19] since He is the universal efficient cause of all being.

Now everything that is produced through the will of an agent is directed to an end by that agent because the good and the end are the proper object of the will, wherefore whatever proceeds from a will must be directed to an end. And each thing attains its end by its own action, which action needs to be directed by him who endowed things with the principles whereby they act.

Consequently, God, who in Himself is perfect in every way, and by His power endows all things with being, must be the Ruler of all, Himself ruled by none. Nor is anything to be exempted from His rule, since there is nothing that does not owe its being to Him. Therefore, as He is perfect in being and causing, so is He perfect in ruling.

The effect of this ruling is seen to differ in different things, according to the difference of natures. For some things are so produced by God that, being intelligent, they bear a resemblance to Him and reflect His image, wherefore not only are they directed, but they direct themselves to their appointed end by their own actions. And if in thus directing themselves they are subject to the divine ruling, they are admitted by that divine ruling to the attainment of their final end. But they are excluded therefrom if they direct themselves otherwise.

There are other things which, bereft of intelligence, do not direct themselves to their end, but are directed by another. Some of these, being incorruptible, even as they are not able to suffer defects in their natural being, so neither do they wander, in their own action, from the direction to their appointed end, but are subject, without fail, to the ruling of the supreme ruler. Such are the heavenly bodies, whose movements are invariable. Others, however, being corruptible, are able to suffer defects in their natural being. Yet this defect exists to the advantage of another thing, since when one thing is corrupted, another is generated. Likewise, they fail from their natural direction in their own actions, yet this failing is compensated by some resultant good. From this it is clear that not even those things which are seen to wander from the direction of the supreme ruling escape from the power of the supreme ruler. These corruptible bodies, even as they are created by God, so too are they perfectly subject to Him. Wherefore, considering this, the Psalmist, filled with the divine spirit, in order to give us an illustration of the divine government, first describes to us the perfection of the supreme governor—as to His nature when he says, "God"; as to His power, when he says, "a great Lord," implying that He needs no one for His power to produce its effect; as to His authority, when he says, "A great king above all gods," since, although there be many rulers, yet all are subject to His rule. Secondly, he describes to us the manner of this government. As regards intellectual beings, which, if they submit to His rule, receive from Him their last end which is Himself, wherefore he says, "For the Lord will not reject His people." As regards things corruptible which, albeit at times they wander from their proper mode of action, never escape the power of the supreme ruler, he says, "Because in His hands are all the ends of the earth." And as regards the heavenly bodies, which transcend the highest summits of the earth, that is of corruptible bodies, and always maintain the order of the divine government, he says, "And the mountain heights are His." Thirdly, he assigns the reason of this universal government, for the things that God made must

---

19  I.e., God did not require pre-existing matter on which to impose the forms, but God created matter too.

needs be governed by Him. To this he refers when he says, "For the sea is His," etc.

Since, then, in the First Book we have treated of the perfection of the divine nature, and, in the Second, of the perfection of the divine power, inasmuch as He is the creator and lord of all, it remains for us in this Third Book to treat of His perfect authority or dignity, inasmuch as He is the end and governor of all. We must therefore proceed in this way, so as first to treat of Him as the end of all things; secondly of His universal government, inasmuch as He governs every creature: thirdly, of that special government, whereby He governs creatures endowed with intelligence.

### 3   That every agent[20] acts for a good

Hence we must go on to prove that every agent acts for a good.

For that every agent acts for an end clearly follows from the fact that every agent tends to something definite. Now that to which an agent tends definitely must be befitting to that agent since the latter would not tend to it unless on account of some fittingness to it. But that which is fitting to a thing is good for it. Therefore every agent acts for a good.

Furthermore, the end is that wherein the appetite[21] of the agent or mover is at rest, as also the appetite of that which is moved. Now it is the very notion of good to be the termination of appetite, since good is the object of every appetite. Therefore all action and movement is for a good.

Again, all action and movement would seem to be directed in some way to being,[22] either for the preservation of being in the species or in the individual or for the acquisition of being. Now this itself, that is, being, is a good: and for this reason all things desire being. Therefore all action and movement is for a good....

Again, that which results from the agent's action beside his intention is said to happen by chance or luck. Now we observe in the works of nature that either always or more often that which happens is best. Thus, in plants the leaves are so placed as to protect the fruit; and the parts of an animal are so disposed as to conduce to the animal's safety. Wherefore, if this happens beside the intention of the natural agent, it will be the result of chance or luck. But that is impossible because things that happen always or frequently are not casual or fortuitous, but those which occur seldom. Therefore the natural agent tends to that which is best and much more evidently is this so with the intellectual agent. Therefore every agent intends a good in acting....

Hence the philosophers, in defining the good, said, "The good is the object of every appetite"[23]; and Dionysius says that "all things desire the good and the best."[24]

### 79   That the lower intellectual substances are ruled by the higher

Because some intellectual creatures are higher than others, as we have shown, the lower intellectual nature must be governed by the higher.

Again, the more universal powers move the particular powers, as already stated. And the higher intellectual natures have more universal forms, as we have proved. Therefore they rule the lower intellectual natures.

Besides, the intellectual faculty that is nearer to the principle is always found to be the ruler of the intellectual faculty that is more distant from the principle. This is evident both in speculative and in practical science. For the speculative science that receives its principles of demonstration from another is said to be subalternate to it, and the practical science that is nearer to the end, which is the principle in practical matters, is the master science in comparison with the more distant. Since, then, some intellectual substances are

---

20   I.e., thing that acts.

21   I.e., the element of a thing which desires or is drawn to something else.

22   I.e., to existence.

23   Citing Aristotle.

24   This quotation is of the Pseudo-Dionysius, a fifth-century Christian follower of Plato, whose writings were credited in the Middle Ages to an earlier Christian martyr, St. Dionyius (or Denis) (third century).

nearer to the first principle, namely God, as we have shown, they will be the rulers of the others.

Moreover, the higher intellectual substances receive the influence of divine wisdom more perfectly, since each one receives something according to its mode. Now all things are governed by divine wisdom, so that those which have the greater share of divine wisdom govern those which have the smaller share. Therefore, the lower intellectual substances are governed by the higher.

Wherefore, the higher spirits are called both angels, inasmuch as they direct the lower spirits, by message as it were, for angels are called messengers; and ministers, since as by their operation they execute, even in corporeal things, the order of divine providence—because a minister is like an animate instrument according to the Philosopher. This is what is said in the Psalm, "Who makes your angels spirits: and your ministers a burning fire" ([Old Testament] Psalms 104).

### 80   Of the order among the angels

Since corporeal things are governed by spiritual ones, as we have proved, and since there is order of a kind among corporeal things, it follows that the higher bodies are governed by the higher intellectual substances, and the lower bodies by the lower intellectual substances. And seeing that the higher a substance is, the more universal is its power, while the power of an intellectual substance is more universal than the power of a body, the higher intellectual substances have powers entirely independent of any corporeal power, and consequently they are not united to bodies, whereas the lower intellectual substances have powers confined to certain limits and dependent on certain corporeal organs for their exercise, and consequently they need to be united to bodies. And just as the higher intellectual substances have a more universal power, so too they receive from God more perfectly the divine disposal of things, in that they are acquainted with the scheme of order, even as regards individuals, through receiving it from God. This manifestation of the divine governance, made by God, reaches to the uttermost intellectual substances; thus it is said, "Is there any numbering of his soldiers? and

upon whom shall not his light arise?" ([Old Testament] Job 25). On the other hand, the lower intelligences do not receive this manifestation so perfectly, as to be able to know thereby every detail of the order of divine providence left to their execution, but only in a general way. The lower their position, the less detailed knowledge of the divine government do they receive through this first manifestation received from above. This is so much so that the human intellect, which is the lowest in point of natural knowledge, has a knowledge of only certain most general things. Accordingly, the higher intellectual substances receive immediately from God the perfection of the knowledge in question. The other, lower intellectual substances need to receive this perfection through them, just as we have said above that the general knowledge of the disciple is brought to perfection by means of the specific knowledge of the master. Hence it is that Dionysius, speaking of the highest intellectual substances which he assigns to the first hierarchy or holy sovereignty, says that "they are not sanctified by means of other substances, but that they are placed by God Himself immediately around Him, and as far as possible close to His immaterial and incomprehensible beauty on which they gaze, and in which they contemplate the intelligible reasons for His works." By these, he says, the inferior ranks of heavenly substances are instructed....

Accordingly, there is a certain order among the intelligences who take from God Himself immediate and perfect cognizance of the order of divine providence. The first and highest perceive the ordered scheme of providence in the last end itself, which is the divine goodness. Some of them, however, do so more clearly than others. These are called Seraphim, i.e., fiery or setting on fire, because fire is used to designate intensity of love or desire, which are concerned with the end. Hence Dionysius says that this name indicates both their fervent and quivering activity towards God, and their leading lower things to God as their end.

The second place belongs to those who acquire perfect knowledge of the scheme of providence in the divine form. These are called Cherubim, which signifies fullness of knowledge, for knowledge is made complete through the form of the thing known.

Wherefore, Dionysius says that their name indicates that they contemplate the highest operative power of the divine beauty.

The third grade is of those who contemplate the disposition of divine judgments in itself. They are called Thrones because the throne signifies judicial power, according to this: "You have sat on the throne, who judges justice."[25] Hence, Dionysius says that this name signifies that they are "God-bearers and adapted for the obedient fulfillment of all divine undertakings."

What has been said must, however, be understood, not as though the divine goodness, essence, and knowledge of the disposition of things were three distinct things, but in the sense that according to what we have been saying we may look at the matter in question from different points of view.

Again, there must be order among even the lower spirits who receive from the higher spirits perfect knowledge of the divine order to be fulfilled by them. Because the higher ones are also more universal in their power of understanding, they acquire their knowledge of the order of providence from more universal principles and causes, but those beneath them do so from more particular causes. For a man who could consider the entire physical order in the heavenly bodies would be of a higher intelligence than one who needed to turn his mind to lower things in order to perfect his knowledge. Accordingly, those who are able to know perfectly the order of providence from the universal causes which stand midway between God, the supremely universal cause, and particular causes, are themselves between those who are able to consider the aforesaid order in God Himself and those who need to consider it in particular causes. Dionysius assigns these to the middle hierarchy which, as it is governed by the highest, so, says he, does it govern the lowest.

Again, among these intellectual substances also there must be some kind of order since the universal disposition of providence is divided, first, among many executors, which belongs to the order of Dominations because to command what others execute belongs to one having dominion. Hence Dionysius says that domination signifies "a certain liberty free from servile condition and any subjection." Secondly, it is distributed by the operator and executor in reference to many effects. This is done by the order of Virtues whose name, as Dionysius says in the same passage, designates a certain strength and virility in carrying out the divine operations, without so much as swerving through weakness, from the divine movement. Hence, it is evident that the principle of universal operation belongs to this order, so that apparently the movement of the heavenly bodies belongs to this order also, from which, as from universal causes, particular effects ensue in nature, wherefore they are called "powers of heaven" where it is said, "The powers of heaven shall be moved" ([New Testament] Luke 21). To the same spirits apparently belongs the execution of those divine works which are done outside the order of nature. For these are the highest of God's ministries, for which reason Gregory[26] says that the "Virtues are those spirits through whom miracles are frequently wrought." And if there be anything else of a universal and prominent nature in the fulfillment of the divine ministry, it is fittingly ascribed to this order. Thirdly, the universal order of providence, once established in its effects, is guarded from confusion by curbing the things which might disturb that order. This belongs to the order of Powers. Wherefore, Dionysius says in the same place that the name Powers implies "a well-established order, without confusion, in the divine undertakings," and so Gregory says that it belongs to this order "to check contrary powers."

The lowest of superior intellectual substances are those who receive the knowledge of the order of divine providence in relation to particular causes. These are placed in immediate authority over human affairs. Of them Dionysius says, "This third rank of spirits presides, in consequence, over the human hierarchy." By human affairs we must understand all lower natures and particular causes that are subordi-

---

25 Old Testament, Psalms 9.7-8.
26 St. Gregory the Great, Christian writer and pope (590-604).

nated to man and serve for his use, as we have already explained. Among these also there is a certain order. For in human affairs there is a common good, namely the good of the city or of the nation, and this apparently belongs to the order of Principalities. Hence Dionysius says in the same chapter that the name Principality indicates "leadership in a sacred order." Hence, mention is made of "Michael the Prince of the Jews," of a "Prince of the Persians, and of a Prince of the Greeks" ([Old Testament] Daniel 10). And thus the government of kingdoms and the change of supremacy from one nation to another must belong to the ministry of this order. It would also seem part of their office to instruct those men who are in positions of authority in matters pertaining to the administration of their office.

There is also a kind of human good, not pertaining to the community, but belonging to an individual by himself, yet useful not to one only, but to many, for instance those things which all and each one must believe and observe, such as the articles of faith, the divine worship, and the like. This belongs to the Archangels of whom Gregory says that "they announce the greater things." Thus we call Gabriel an Archangel because he announced the Incarnation of the Word to the Virgin, which is an article of faith for all.

There is also a human good that belongs to each person individually. This pertains to the order of Angels of whom Gregory says that they announce minor matters. Hence they are called guardian angels: "He has given His angels charge over you, to keep you in all your ways" ([Old Testament] Psalms 91). Wherefore Dionysius says that the Archangels are between the Principalities and Angels because they have something in common with both, with the Principalities "inasmuch as they lead the lower angels," and rightly so, because in human affairs matters of restricted interest must be regulated according to those that are of common interest. And so with the Angels, because they announce to the Angels, and through the Angels, to us, for it is the duty of the latter to announce to men what concerns each individual. For this reason the lowest order has received as proper the name common to all because its duty is to announce to us immediately. And so the name Archangel is, as it were, composed of both names, since Archangel means a Principal Angel.

Gregory assigns the ordering of the heavenly spirits differently. He places the Principalities among the spirits of the second rank, immediately after the Dominations and places the Virtues among the lowest, above the Archangels. But to one who considers the matter carefully, the difference is very small. For, according to Gregory, the Principalities are not placed over nations but over good spirits, as holding the principal place in the execution of the divine ministry because, he says, "to be a principal is to stand in a higher place than others." According to the explanation given above, we said that this belonged to the Virtues. As to the Virtues, according to Gregory they are assigned to certain particular operations when, in some special case, outside the usual order of things, miracles have to be wrought. In this way they are fittingly numbered among the lowest angels.

Both explanations have the authority of the Apostle. For he says, "Sitting Him, namely Christ, on his right hand in heavenly places, above all principality, and power, and virtue, and dominion" ([New Testament] Ephesians 1), where it is clear that in the ascending order he places the Powers above the Principalities, and the Virtues above these, and the Dominations above the last named. This is the order adopted by Dionysius. Whereas speaking of Christ to the Colossians he says, "Whether thrones or dominations or principalities or powers, all things were created by Him and in Him" ([New Testament] Colossians 1). Here we see that, beginning with the Thrones, in the descending order, he places the Dominations under them, beneath these the Principalities, and lower still the Powers. This is the order adopted by Gregory.

Mention is made of the Seraphim ([Old Testament] Isaiah 6); of Cherubim ([Old Testament] Ezekiel 1); of the Archangels, when Michael the archangel disputes with the devil, etc. ([New Testament] Jude 9); and of the Angels in the Psalms, as already observed.

In all ordered powers there is this in common: that the lower all work by virtue of the higher. Hence what we have stated as belonging to the order of Seraphim, all the lower angels accomplish by virtue thereof, and the same applies to the other orders.

## 81    Of the ordering of human beings among themselves and other things

In comparison with other intellectual substances, the human soul holds the lowest place because, as we have already stated, when it is first created it receives knowledge of the order of divine providence only in a general way, whereas, in order to acquire perfect knowledge of that order in individual matters, it needs to start from these very things in which the order of divine providence is already established in detail. Consequently, the human soul needs bodily organs, so as to be able to receive knowledge from things having bodies. And yet, on account of the weakness of its intellectual light, it is unable to acquire perfect knowledge of things that concern humanity without the help of higher spirits, God so disposing that the lower spirits reach perfection through the higher, as we have already proved. Since, however, man has some share of intellectual light, dumb animals which have none at all are subject to man, according to the order of divine providence. Hence it is said, "Let us make man to our own image and likeness," that is to say, inasmuch as he is an intelligent being, and "let him have dominion over the fishes of the sea, and the fowls of the air, and the beasts of the earth" ([Old Testament] Genesis 1). Dumb animals, though bereft of intellect, yet, since they have some kind of knowledge, are placed by the order of divine providence above plants and other things devoid of knowledge. Hence it is said, "Behold I have given you every herb bearing seed upon the earth, and all trees that have in themselves seed of their own kind, to be your meal, and to all the beasts of the earth" ([Old Testament] Genesis 1).

Among those that are wholly bereft of knowledge, one thing is placed before another according as one is more capable of action than another. For they have no share in the disposition of providence, but only in the execution.

And since man has both intelligence, and sense, and bodily powers, these things are dependent on one another, according to the disposition of divine providence, in likeness to the order to be observed in the universe. For bodily power is subject to the powers of sense and intellect, as carrying out their commands, and the sensual power is subject to the intellectual, and is controlled by its rule.

In the same way, we find order among men. For those who excel in intelligence are naturally rulers, whereas those who are less intelligent, but strong in body, seem made by nature for service, as Aristotle says in his *Politics*. The statement of Solomon is in agreement with this: "The fool shall serve the wise" ([Old Testament] Proverbs 11); as are also the words of Exodus: "Provide out of all the people wise men such as fear God ... who may judge the people at all times" ([Old Testament] Exodus 18).

And in the works of one man there is disorder through the intellect being obsequious to the sensual faculty, while the sensual faculty, through indisposition of the body, is drawn to the movement of the body, as instanced in those who limp. So too, in human government, disorder results from a man being set in authority, not on account of his excelling in intelligence, but because he has usurped the government by bodily force, or has been appointed to rule through motives of sensual affection. Nor does Solomon omit to mention this disorder, for he says, "There is an evil that I have seen under the sun, as it were by an error proceeding from the face of the prince; a fool set in high dignity" ([Old Testament] Ecclesiastes 10). Now divine providence does not exclude a disorder of this kind, for it results, by God's permission, from the fault of the inferior agents, even as we have said of other evils. Nor is the natural order wholly perverted by such a disorder, for the government of fools is weak, unless it be strengthened by the counsels of the wise. Hence it is said, "Designs are strengthened by counsels and wars are to be arranged by governments" ([Old Testament] Proverbs 20) and "A wise man is strong, and a knowing man, stout and valiant: because war is managed by due ordering, and there shall be safety when there are many counsels" ([Old Testament] Proverbs 24). And since the counselor rules him who receives his counsel, and, in a sense, governs him, it is said that "a wise servant shall rule over foolish sons" ([Old Testament] Proverbs 17).

It is therefore evident that divine providence imposes order on all things, and thus the Apostle says truly that "the things which are of God are well ordered" ([New Testament] Romans 13).

### 121　That the divine law directs humanity according to reason regarding corporeal and sensible things

Just as the human mind can be raised to God by corporeal and sensible things, provided one makes right use of them for God's honor, even so their abuse either wholly withdraws the mind from God, if the will places its end in lower things, or distracts the mind's intention from God, when we are too attached to those things. Now the divine law was given chiefly that man might adhere to God. Therefore, it pertains to the divine law to direct man in his love and use of corporeal and sensible things.

Again, just as the mind of man is subordinate to God, so is the body subordinate to the soul, and the lower powers to reason. Now it belongs to divine providence, which God sets before man under the form of the divine law, that everything should keep to its own order. Therefore, humanity should be directed by the divine law in such a way that the lower powers are subject to reason, the body to the soul, and external things are employed for human needs.

Furthermore, every law that is framed correctly promotes virtue. Now virtue is the rule of reason over both interior feelings and the use of corporeal things. Therefore, this should be prescribed by the divine law.

Moreover, every lawgiver should legislate for those things that are necessary for the observance of the law. Since, then, the law is proposed to reason, human beings would not obey the law unless all that is in human beings is subject to reason. Therefore, it is for the divine law to command that all that is in human beings be subject to reason.

Hence it is said, "May your service be reasonable" ([New Testament] Romans 12), and "This is the will of God, your sanctification" ([New Testament] 1 Thessalonians 4).

With this discussion, we refute the error of those who assert that there is no sin except when our neighbor is injured or scandalized.

### 122　How, according to divine law, simple fornication is a sin, and that matrimony is natural

Hence, it is clear how futile is the reasoning of those who say that simple fornication is not a sin. For they say, "Take, for instance, a woman who is not married, or under any authority, paternal or otherwise. If, with her consent, a man has intercourse with her, he does her no wrong since she pleases herself, and has the disposal of her own body. He does not wrong a third party because, in this supposition, she is under no one's authority. Therefore there is no sin."

Nor, seemingly, is it enough to reply that he does a wrong to God because we do not wrong God unless we wrong our own good as stated above. But this would not seem to be contrary to man's good. Consequently no wrong, seemingly, is done to God.

Likewise, it does not seem adequate to reply that the man wrongs his neighbor by scandalizing him. For one may be scandalized at something that is not a sin in itself, so that it becomes a sin accidentally. But the point at issue is whether simple fornication is a sin, not accidentally, but in itself.

Accordingly, we must seek the solution from what has been said above. For it has been stated that God cares for everything concerning what is good for it. Now, it is good for everything that it obtain its end, and its evil is that it turns from its end. This applies to a thing's parts as well as to the whole, so that every part of a human being, even a human being's every act, should reach its appropriate end. Now, although semen is superfluous for the preservation of the individual, it is necessary for the propagation of the species. Other superfluities, such as excrement, urine, sweat, and the like, are not necessary for anything, and so it is only their discharge that is good for man. Semen, however, has another end in view since it is emitted for the purpose of generation, which is the object of coition. Moreover, generation would be in vain, if due nourishment were not to follow because the offspring would not survive if deprived of due nourishment. Hence, the emission of semen should be ordered in such a way that appropriate generation and rearing of the offspring may follow. It is, therefore, clearly contrary to man's good that semen be emitted in such a way that generation cannot ensue and, if this is done deliberately, it must be a sin. I mean here that if it is done in a way that is directly opposed to generation, such as every emission of semen without the natural union of male and female. Hence, sins of this kind are said to be against nature. If, however, it is accidental that generation cannot ensue, it is not on this account contrary to nature, or sinful, for instance if the woman is sterile.

In like manner, it must be contrary to man's good if, though semen is emitted so that generation can ensue, the proper upbringing of the offspring is hindered. For it must be observed that in those animals in which the female alone suffices for the rearing of the offspring (dogs for instance), the male and female do not remain together after coition. On the other hand, in all cases in which the female does not suffice to rear the offspring, the male and female remain together after coition, as long as may be necessary for the rearing and development of the young. We have an instance of this in certain birds, whose young are unable to seek food as soon as they are hatched. For since the bird does not feed its young on milk (which is ready at hand through being prepared by nature, as in the case of quadrupeds) and needs to go in search of food for them, and besides this fosters them by incubation, the female alone would not suffice for all this. Wherefore, divine providence has given the male of such animals the natural instinct to remain with the female for the rearing of the offspring. Now it is clear that in the human species the female is far from sufficing alone for the rearing of the children since the needs of human life require many things that one person alone cannot provide. It is, therefore, in keeping with human nature that the man remain with the woman after coition, and not leave her at once, indulging in promiscuous intercourse, as do those who have the habit of fornication.

Nor is this argument weakened because some woman has sufficient wealth to rear her offspring by herself. Because natural rectitude in human acts depends not on what is accidentally in one individual but on that which is proper to the whole species. Again, we must observe that, in the human species, the offspring needs not only nourishment for its body, as with other animals, but also instruction for its soul. For other animals have their natural forethought which enables them to provide for themselves. Human beings, however, live by reason, which can attain to forethought only after long experience, so that children need to be instructed by their parents, who are experienced.

Moreover, children are not capable of this instruction as soon as they are born, but only after a long time, and especially when they reach the age of discretion. Besides, this instruction requires a long time. And even then, on account of the assaults of the passions whereby the judgment of prudence is perverted, they need not only instruction, but correction. Now a woman is insufficient for these things. In fact, there is more need for a man for such things, for his reason is more developed for instruction, and his arm is stronger for punishment. Consequently, a short space of time, such as suffices for birds, is not sufficient for the education of the offspring in the human species, and a great part of life is required for the purpose. So that, as in all animals, it behooves the male to remain with the female as long as the father is needed by the offspring. It is natural in the human race that the man should have not a short-lived but a lasting fellowship with a particular woman. This fellowship is called matrimony. Therefore, matrimony is natural to human beings and intercourse in fornication, which is outside matrimony, is contrary to humanity's good. For this reason it must be a sin.

Moreover, the emission of semen without the requisite intention of procreation and education must not be thought a slight sin, thinking that it is a small sin, or none at all, to use some part of one's body for some other purpose than that for which nature intended it, for instance, if one walks on one's hands, or uses one's feet to do what the hands should do. Such actions little harm the good of humanity. But the inordinate discharge of semen perverts a natural good, the preservation of the species. Wherefore, after the sin of murder, whereby human nature is deprived of actual existence, this kind of sin, whereby the generation of human nature is hindered, holds, it seems, the second place.

The foregoing conclusions are confirmed by divine authority. That the discharge of semen in such a way that no offspring can ensue is unlawful is clear from the words of Leviticus, "You shall not lie with mankind as with womankind ... you shall not copulate with any beast" ([Old Testament] Leviticus 18) and of [New Testament] 1 Corinthians [6], "Nor the effeminate, nor liers with mankind ... shall possess the kingdom of God."

Again, that fornication and all intercourse with other than one's own wife is unlawful is evident from the words of Deuteronomy, "There shall be no whore among the daughters of Israel, nor whoremonger among the sons of Israel" ([Old Testament] Deuteronomy 23), and of Job, "Take heed to keep yourself ... from all fornication, and beside your wife never endure to know a crime" ([Old Testament] Job 4) and of [New Testament] 1 Corinthians [6], "Flee fornication."

Hereby we exclude the error of those who deny that there is a greater sin in the emission of semen than in the discharge of other superfluities, and of those who said that fornication is no sin.

*123   That matrimony should be indissoluble*

If one considers the matter rightly, it will be seen that the foregoing arguments not only show that the fellowship of male and female in human nature, which we call matrimony, should be lasting, but also that it should endure throughout life.

For possessions are directed to the preservation of the natural life. Since the natural life which cannot be preserved in the person of an undying father is preserved, by a kind of succession, in the person of the son, it is naturally appropriate that the son succeed in things belonging to the father. Therefore, it is natural that the father's care for his son should endure to the end of his life. If, then, the father's care for his son causes, even among birds, the continued fellowship of male and female, the natural order demands that in the human species father and mother should remain together to the end of life.

It would seem also contrary to equity for the aforesaid fellowship to be dissolved. For the female requires the male, not only for procreation, as in other animals, but also for governance because the male excels both in intelligence and in strength. Now, the woman is taken into partnership with the man for the purpose of procreation. Consequently, when the woman ceases to be fruitful and beautiful, this is an obstacle to her being associated with another man. Hence, if a man, after taking a wife in her youth, while she is yet beautiful and fruitful, can put her away when she has aged, he does her an injury, contrary to natural equity.

Again, it is clearly inappropriate that a woman be allowed to put away a man since she is naturally subject to the man's authority, and one who is subject to another is not free to withdraw oneself from that authority. Hence, it would be contrary to the natural order if a wife could leave her husband. Consequently, if the husband could leave his wife, there would not be just fellowship between husband and wife, but a kind of slavery on the part of the latter.

Also, there is in man a certain natural anxiety to be assured of his offspring. This is necessary because the child needs the father's authority for a long time. Hence, whatever prevents him from being assured of having children is contrary to the natural instinct of the human species. Now, if the husband may put away his wife, or the wife leave her husband and take another man, thus copulating first with one, and afterwards with another, the certainty of offspring would be hindered. Therefore, it is contrary to the natural instinct of the human species that husband and wife be separated. In consequence, the union of male and female in the human race must be not only long lasting, but indissoluble.

Moreover, the greater the friendship, the more stable and lasting it is. Now, there seems to be the greatest friendship between husband and wife, for they are made one not only in the act of carnal intercourse, which even among dumb animals causes an agreeable fellowship, but also as partners in the whole intercourse of daily life, so that, to indicate this, "man must leave father and mother" ([Old Testament] Genesis 2) for his wife's sake. Therefore, it is right that matrimony should be altogether indissoluble. It must also be observed that among natural acts generation alone is directed to the common good since eating and the discharge of other superfluities regard the individual, whereas procreation concerns the preservation of the species. Hence, as the law is made for the common good, whatever regards procreation should be regulated, before other things, by laws both divine and human. Now positive laws should be based on natural instinct, if they are human, even as in demonstrative sciences, all human discoveries must be founded on principles known naturally. And if laws are divine, not only do they express the instinct of nature, but they also supply the defect of natural instinct, just as the things that God reveals are beyond the grasp of natural reason. Since, then, the natural instinct of the human species is that the union of male and female be indissoluble, and that one man be united to one woman, this must be ordered by human law. Moreover, the divine law adds a kind of supernatural reason taken from the representation of the indissoluble union of Christ and the Church, which is union of one with one. Wherefore, disorder in the act of generation is not only contrary to the natural instinct, but it also transgresses both divine and human law. Hence, this kind of disorder is more sinful than that which may occur in taking food, or in similar things.

And since in man all other things should be subordinate to what is best in him, the union of male and female is ordered by law not only because of its relationship to the procreation of children, as in other animals, but also because of its relationship to good morals, which right reason regulates, both regarding individuals and individuals as members either of a private family, or of the civil community. Now, the indissolubility of the union of male and female belongs to good morals because their mutual love will be the more constant if they know that they are indissolubly united. They will also be more carefully provident in the conduct of the household when they realize that they are always to remain together in possession of the same things. Again, this precludes the origin of quarrels which must arise between the husband and his wife's relatives, if he were to put his wife away and those who are connected through affinity have a greater regard for one another. Moreover, it removes the occasions of adultery which would occur were the husband free to put away his wife, or vice versa, for this would encourage the seeking of further marriage.

Hence it is said, "But I say to you that the wife depart not from her husband" ([New Testament] Matthew 5, 19; 1 Corinthians 7).

Hereby we condemn the custom of putting a wife away. Nevertheless, this was permitted to the Jews in the Old Law by reason of the hardness of their heart because, namely, they were prone to wife-murder. Hence, the lesser evil was allowed, in order to avoid the greater.

## 124  *That matrimony should be the union of one man with one woman*

It is also to be observed, it seems, that all animals that are used to copulation have a natural instinct to resist another's intercourse with their mate, for which reason animals fight on account of copulation. And as regards all animals, there is one common reason for this: because every animal desires to indulge at will in the pleasure of copulation, just as in the pleasure of eating, and this freedom ceases if many males have access to one female, or vice versa, just as an animal is deprived of the free enjoyment of its food if another animal despoils it of the food it desires to consume. Hence, animals fight both for food and for copulation. But with regard to men there is a special reason because, as already stated, man naturally desires to be assured of his offspring, and this assurance would be altogether nullified in the case of promiscuous copulation. Therefore, the union of one man with one woman comes from a natural instinct.

A difference, however, is to be noted here. Both the foregoing arguments hold regarding one woman not being united to several men. But the second argument does not hold as regarding one man not being joined to several women since the certainty of having offspring is not removed if one man is joined to several women. The first argument, however, holds against this, for just as freedom of access to the woman is denied if she has another man, so too the same freedom is denied the woman if the man has several women. Hence, as certainty of having offspring is the chief good sought from marriage, no human law or custom has permitted polyandry.[27] This was considered to be wrong even among the ancient Romans, of whom Maximus Valerius relates that they deemed that not even on account of barrenness should the marriage bond be severed.

---

27  The practice of one woman having more than one husband.

Again, in every animal species where the father has a certain care for his offspring, one male has but one female, as may be seen in birds, where both unite in feeding their young, for one male would not suffice to rear the progeny of several females. On the other hand, where the male animal does not take care of the offspring, we find indifferently union of one male with several females, or of one female with several males. Such is the case with dogs, hens, and so forth. Since, then, of all animals the male of the human species is preeminent in the care of his offspring, it is clearly natural to man that one man should have one wife and vice versa.

Besides, equality is a condition of friendship. Hence, if a woman may not have several husbands, because this removes the certainty of offspring, and if it were lawful for a man to have several wives, the friendship of a wife for her husband would not be freely bestowed, but, as it were, servile. And this argument is confirmed by experience since where men have several wives, the wives are treated as servants.

Furthermore, in perfect friendship it is impossible to be friends with many, according to the Philosopher in the *Ethics*. Hence, if the wife has but one husband, while the husband has several wives, the friendship will not be equal on either side, and consequently it will be not a freely bestowed, but, as it were, a servile friendship.

Moreover, as we have already stated, matrimony among men should be so ordered as to be consistent with good morals. Now it is contrary to good morals that one man have several wives, for this leads to discord in the family, as shown by experience. Therefore, it is not right for one man to have several wives.

Hence it is said, "They shall be two in one flesh" ([Old Testament] Genesis 2).

By these arguments, polygamy stands condemned, as is also the opinion of Plato, who said that wives should be possessed in common, which opinion was adopted by Nicolas, one of the seven deacons.[28]

### 125   *That marriage should not be contracted between relatives*

For these reasonable motives the laws have decreed that certain persons belonging to a common stock should be debarred from marriage.

Because, as marriage is the union of different persons, those who should consider themselves as one through having a common ancestor are rightly debarred from marriage, that they may have a greater regard for each other through realizing that for that reason they are one.

Again, since in the relations between husband and wife there is a certain natural shame, relations should be forbidden between those who, through being united in blood, should revere each other. This motive seems to be indicated in the law, where it is said, "You shall not uncover the nakedness of your sister" ([Old Testament] Leviticus 18), and so on.

Furthermore, humans being too much given to the pleasure of copulation corrupts good morals because, since, more than any other, this pleasure absorbs the mind, and so the reason would be hindered in things pertaining to rectitude. Now an abuse of pleasure would result if man were allowed to be united in copulation with those in whose society he must live, such as sisters and other relatives. For it would be impossible to remove the occasion of intercourse with such persons. It was therefore in keeping with good morals that the laws should forbid such unions.

Moreover, the pleasure of copulation entirely corrupts the judgment of prudence. Therefore, frequency of that pleasure is contrary to good morals. Now, this pleasure is increased by the mutual love of those who are thus united. Hence it would be contrary to good morals for relatives to marry, for then there would be in them the love arising from community of blood and nourishment in addition to the love of desire and, in consequence, through multiplicity of loves the soul would be all the more a slave to pleasures.

Besides, it is most necessary in human society that friendship be among many. Now friendships among

---

28   An incident discussed by St. Augustine.

men are multiplied if marriage is contracted between persons of different stock. Therefore, it is appropriate for the laws to direct that marriage be contracted with those of different stock, and not between relatives.

Also, it is unsuitable that a person be united socially with those to whom he should naturally be subject. Now it is natural for a man to be subject to his parents. Therefore it is unfitting for one to marry one's parent, since marriage is a social union.

Hence it is said, "No man shall approach to her that is near of kin to him" ([Old Testament] Leviticus 18).

For these reasons, the custom of those who contract bonds of the flesh with persons of their kindred stands condemned. We must observe, however, that just as the natural inclination is to what occurs most frequently, so too is the law made to fit the majority of cases. The foregoing arguments are not invalidated by any possible exceptions, for the good of many should not be foregone for the sake of the good of one, since "the common good is ever more godlike than the good of one."[29] Lest, however, a problem that may occur in a single instance be altogether irremediable, lawgivers and the like have the power to dispense with the statutes that are made for the generality, according to the requirements of a particular case. If the law is made by man, those who have the same power can dispense therein. But if the law is of God, dispensation can be granted by divine authority, just as in the old law, polygamy, concubinage, and divorce were, it seems, allowed by dispensation.

### 126 That not all carnal intercourse is sinful

Just as it is contrary to reason to indulge in carnal intercourse so as to frustrate the begetting and rearing of children, so is it in keeping with reason to make use of it in a manner consistent with procreation and upbringing. Now, the divine law forbids only those things that are contrary to reason, as we have shown above. Therefore it is unreasonable to say that all carnal intercourse is sinful.

Again, since the parts of the body are instruments of the soul, the end of each part, as of any other instrument, is its use. Now, the use of certain parts of the body is carnal intercourse. Therefore carnal intercourse is the end of certain parts of the body. But that which is the end of any natural thing cannot be evil in itself since that which is according to nature is directed to an end by divine providence, as stated above. Therefore, carnal intercourse cannot possibly be evil in itself.

Furthermore, natural inclinations are implanted in things by God, who moves all things. Therefore the natural inclination of a species cannot be to that which is evil in itself. Now, in all perfect[30] animals there is a natural inclination to carnal intercourse. Therefore carnal intercourse cannot be evil in itself.

Moreover, that which is a necessary condition for something good and very good, is not evil in itself. But the preservation of the animal species cannot last except by means of generation by carnal intercourse. Therefore, carnal intercourse cannot be evil in itself.

Hence it is said, "A virgin sins not if she marries" ([New Testament] 1 Corinthians 7).

Hereby we refute the error of those who say that all carnal intercourse is unlawful, wherefore they utterly condemn matrimony and nuptials. Some of them are led to this assertion because they believe that bodies were made not by a good, but by an evil force.

### 127 That no food is in itself sinful for one to eat

Even as sexual activity, so also food, may be made use of without sin, if the order of reason is observed. And a thing is done according to the order of reason when it is directed in a befitting manner to its appropriate end. Now, the end appropriate to the consumption of food is the preservation of the body by nourishment. Therefore, one may partake of any food that is appropriate to this purpose. Therefore, no food is in itself sinful for one to take.

Again, it is not in itself sinful to use a thing that is not evil in itself. Now, no food is evil by nature

---

29 Aristotle, *Nichomachean Ethics.*

30 I.e., whole and grown.

because everything, in its nature, is good, as we have proved above. A certain food may, however, be bad for a certain person, as being harmful to the well being of that person's body. Therefore no food, considered as a thing of such and such a nature, is sinful for one to eat, but it may be sinful if one uses it unreasonably, so as to injure one's health.

Moreover, to put a thing to the use for which it is intended is not, in itself, a sin. Now, plants are intended for animals. Of animals, some are intended for others and all things are intended for man, as we have already proved. Therefore, it is not sinful in itself to make use of either plants or of the flesh of animals, whether for food or for any other purpose useful to man.

Besides, the defect of sin spreads from the soul to the body, and not vice versa because sin is a disorder of the will. Now food concerns the body immediately, and not the soul. Therefore, the consumption of food cannot be sinful in itself, except in so far as it is contrary to rectitude of the will. This happens in one way, through incompatibility with the end for which food is taken, for instance when, for the sake of the pleasure afforded thereby, a man partakes of a food injurious to his health, whether because of the kind of food, or by reason of the quantity consumed.

In another way, this may happen through the food being inconsistent with the condition either of the consumer or of those among whom he lives. For instance, if a man is so fastidious about his food that he goes beyond his means or makes himself unusual by not conforming to the manner of food customary to those around him. In a third way, this may happen if certain foods are forbidden by law for some special reason. Thus, in the old law, certain foods were prohibited on account of their signification; in Egypt it was forbidden of old to eat beef so that agriculture would not be hindered. Or again, because certain regulations forbid the use of certain foods in order to tame the flesh. Hence our Lord said, "Not that which goes into the mouth defiles a man" ([New Testament] Matthew 15). Again,

it is said, "Whatsoever is sold in the shambles, eat: asking no questions for conscience's sake" ([New Testament] 1 Corinthians 10). And again, "Every creature of God is good, and nothing to be rejected that is received with thanksgiving" ([New Testament] 1 Timothy 4).

Hereby we refute the error of those who say the use of certain foods is illicit in itself, of whom the Apostle says, "In the last times some shall depart from the faith: forbidding to marry, to abstain from meats, which God has created to be received with thanksgiving."[31]

Since, then, the use of food and sexual activity is not unlawful in itself, and can be unlawful only when it evades the order of reason, and whereas external possessions are necessary for the consumption of food, the rearing of children, support of the family, and other bodily needs, it follows that the possession of wealth also is not unlawful in itself, if the order of reason is observed. In such a way, namely, that human beings possess justly what they have, that they do not make wealth the end of the will, that they use wealth correctly, for their own and others' good. Hence the Apostle, as above in [New Testament] 1 Timothy [6], does not condemn the rich, but lays down for them a definite rule for the use of riches, when he says "Charge the rich of this world not to be high-minded, nor to trust in the uncertainty of riches ... to do good, to be rich in good works, to give easily, to communicate to others." Again it is said, "Blessed is the rich man that is found without blemish and that has not gone after gold, nor put his trust in money nor in treasures" ([Apocrypha] Ecclesiasticus 31).

Hereby we also refute the error of those who, as Augustine states in *On Heresies*, "most arrogantly called themselves Apostolics, because they admitted to their community neither married men, nor possessors of property, such as are in the Catholic Church, as well as monks, and clergy in great number. The reason why they are heretics is because they sever themselves from the Church, and consider that those who use these things which they themselves do not use are without hope."

---

31   New Testament, 1 Timothy 4.

# 40

# RALPH OF SHREWSBURY, *LETTER*

Ralph of Shrewsbury, bishop of Bath and Wells (in southern England), sent the letter below to his immediate administrative subordinates in the diocese on August 17, 1348. Other sources suggest the plague had already reached England earlier that month. Ralph had enjoyed a distinguished academic career in canon law and theology before becoming bishop. The letter survives in a copy kept in the record of his administration of the diocese.

---

*spiritual*

Omnipotent God, from whose throne proceed thunder, lightning, and other scourges which he sends to scourge his sons so he may receive them into salvation, etc.

Since the disaster of such a pestilence has come from the eastern parts to a neighboring kingdom, it is greatly to be feared, and being greatly to be feared, it is to be prayed devoutly and without ceasing that such a pestilence not extend its poisonous growth to the inhabitants of this kingdom, and torment and consume them.

Therefore, to each and all of you we mandate, with firm enjoining, that in your churches you publicly announce this present mandate in the vulgar tongue[1] at opportune times, and that in the bowels of Jesus Christ you exhort your subordinates—regular,[2] secular,[3] parishioners, and others—or have them exhorted by others, to appear before the Face of the Lord in confession, with psalms and other works of charity.

Remember the destruction that was deservedly pronounced by prophetic utterance on those who, doing penance, were mercifully freed from the destruction threatened by the judgment of God, for they had said, "Who can know if God will turn and forgive, and turn aside from his fierce anger, that we shall not perish,"[4] and there follows "and God saw their works, that they were converted from their evil way, and God took mercy."[5] Thus, for a penitent people, the most benificent Lord healthfully turned his wrath into gentleness, annihilation in the harshness of banishment into life, destruction into conversion; but he did the reverse to obstinate people and a nation hard of heart, not desiring to repent, just as is proved in the old histories concerning Pharaoh and the five cities of the Sodomites[6] and others who

---

1  In the language spoken by ordinary people rather than in Latin.
2  I.e., those who have sworn to obey a rule (Latin: "regula"), and so monks, nuns, and friars.
3  I.e., clergy who are not regular clergy.
4  Old Testament, Jonah 3.9.
5  Old Testament, Jonah 3.10.
6  A reference to Old Testament, Exodus 7-14 and Genesis 19.

perished eternally on account of their final impenitence.

You are to make processions and stations[7] in individual churches—collegiate,[8] regular, and parish—at the very least on all sixth days,[9] in which you shall lead the people, wherefore they, after falling prostrate before the eyes of divine mercy, may be in terror concerning their sins and repent, and also that they may not omit to expiate them more quickly with devout prayers, that the mercies of God may quickly begin before us and he may avert from his people such a pestilence and the harshness of scourges, and that on account of his mercy he may concede peace among the Catholic kingdoms and healthful air, if it pleases him, as the Psalms say: "Do not remember our iniquities, let your mercies speedily prevent us."[10]

---

7  Ceremonial stopping points in the processions.
8  Churches served by a body of priests.
9  On Fridays.
10  Old Testament, Psalms 79.8. "Prevent" means "come before."

# 41

# CITY OFFICIALS OF COLOGNE, *LETTER*

*1 year*

Many cities within the Holy Roman Empire (roughly modern Germany) were largely self governing. The letter below was from one such city to another, and dates to January 12, 1349 and so followed the progress of the Black Death through Germany. It survives in a copy kept by the Cologne city government.

*social*

...[1] , judges, ... , officials, and ... , councillors of the city of Cologne, to their very dear friends, the circumspect, prudent, and discreet men, the lords the city master Conrad von Winterthur, ... , officials, and ... , councillors of the city of Strasburg, with all promptitude for mutual gratification, and a sincere heart to celebrate together in prosperity and to sympathize together in adversity.

Very dear friends, all sorts of rumors are now flying about against Judaism and the Jews prompted by this unexpected and unparalleled mortality of Christians, which, alas, has raged in various parts of the world and is still woefully active in several places. Throughout our city, as in yours, many-winged Fame clamors that this mortality was intially caused, and is still being spread, by the poisoning of springs and wells, and that the Jews must have dropped some poisonous substances into them. When it came to our knowledge that serious charges had been made against the Jews in several small towns and villages on the basis of this mortality, we sent numerous letters to you and to other cities and towns to uncover the truth about these rumors, and set a thorough investigation in train. But we have been unable to get the whole story, either from you or anywhere else—just as you have recently written to us to say that you have still not arrived at the truth of the matter.

If a massacre of the Jews be allowed in the major cities (something which we are determined to prevent in our city, if we can, so long as the Jews are found to be innnocent of these or similar actions) it could lead to the sort of outrages and disturbances which would whip up a popular revolt among the common people—and such revolts have in the past brought cities to misery and desolation. In any case we are still of the opinion that this mortality and its attendant circumstances are caused by divine vengeance and nothing else. Accordingly we intend to forbid any harassment of the Jews in our city because of these flying rumors, but to defend them faithfully and keep them safe, as our predecessors did—and we are convinced that you ought to do the same.

We know what prudence you show in all your dealings, and it is by way of friendship that we urge you to proceed sensibly and cautiously in this Jewish business, as right and reason demand, and to take steps to guard against any popular rising from which a massacre of the Jews and other disturbances might

---

1  Ellipses indicate names left out of the surviving copy.

arise; and that the rage which the common people feel against the Jews should be checked before it spreads down the Rhine. You should take the decision to protect the Jews in your city, and keep them safe—as your predecessors did—until the truth is known. For should an uprising occur in your city against the Jews, experience tells us that it will surely spread to every other city and town. It therefore behooves you and us and all the major cities to proceed with prudence and caution in this matter, for the man who does not keep a wary eye on what the future may bring often falls into unexpected dangers.

Farewell. If you have obtained any definite information, either from kings and princes or from the Jews themselves, let us know it in writing by this messenger.

Given on the twelfth day of the month of January.

# 42

# THE STATUTE OF LABORERS

*3 years*

The Statute of Laborers was issued by the English parliament in 1351. It is preserved here in the body of a letter from King Edward III (1327-1377) to the archbishop of Canterbury.

*Laws*

Edward by the grace of God, etc., to the reverend father in Christ, William, by the same grace archbishop of Canterbury, primate of all England, greeting. Because a great part of the people and especially of the workers and servants has now died in the pestilence, some, seeing the needs of the masters and the scarcity of servants, are not willing to serve unless they receive excessive wages, and others, rather than gain their living through labor, prefer to beg in idleness. We, considering the grave inconveniences which might come from such a shortage, especially of ploughmen and such laborers, have held deliberation and discussion concerning this with the prelates[1] and nobles and other learned men sitting by us, by whose consenting counsel we have seen fit to ordain that every man and woman of our kingdom of England, of whatever condition, whether serf or free, who is able bodied and below the age of 60 years, not living from trade or carrying on a definite craft, or having private means of living or private land to cultivate, and not serving another—if such a person is sought after to serve in a suitable service appropriate to that person's status, that person shall be bound to serve whomever has seen fit so to offer such employment, and shall take only the wages, liveries,[2] reward or salary usually given in that place in the twentieth year of our reign in England,[3] or the usual year of the five or six preceding ones. This is provided so that in thus retaining their service, lords are preferred before others by their serfs or land tenants, so that such lords nevertheless thus retain as many as shall be necessary, but not more. And if any man or woman, being thus sought after for service, will not do this, the fact being proven by two faithful men before the sheriffs or the bailiffs of our lord the king, or the constables of the town where this happens to be done, immediately through them, or some one of them, that person shall be taken and sent to the next jail, and remain there in strict custody until offering security for serving in the aforesaid form. And if a reaper or mower, or other worker or servant, of whatever standing or condition, who is retained in the service of anyone, departs from the said service before the end of the agreed term without permission or reasonable cause, that person shall undergo the penalty of imprisonment, and let no one, under the same penalty, presume to receive or retain such a person for service. Let no one, moreover, pay or permit to be paid to anyone more wages, livery,

1 Chief officials of the church, such as bishops and abbots.
2 Payments in food or clothing.
3 1347-1348.

reward or salary than was customary, as has been said. Nor let anyone in any other manner exact or receive them, under penalty of paying to one who feels aggrieved from this double the sum that has thus been paid or promised, exacted or received. And if such a person is not willing to prosecute, then the sum is to be given to any one of the people who shall prosecute in this matter. And such prosecutions shall take place in the court of the lord of the place where such a case happens. And if the lords of the towns or manors presume of themselves or through their servants in any way to act contrary to this our present ordinance, then in the counties, wapentakes and ridings[4] suit shall be brought against them in the aforesaid form for triple the sum thus promised or paid by them or their servants. And if it happens that prior to the present ordinance anyone shall have covenanted with anyone thus to serve for more wages, that person shall not be bound by reason of the said covenant to pay more than what at another time was accustomed to be paid to such a person and, indeed, shall not presume to pay more, under the aforesaid penalty.

Likewise saddlers, skinners, tawyers,[5] cordwainers, tailors, smiths, carpenters, masons, tilers, shipwrights, carters and all other artisans and laborers shall not take for their labor and handiwork more than what, in the places where they happen to labor, was customarily paid to such persons in the said twentieth year and in the other usual years preceding, as has been said. And anyone who takes more shall be committed to the nearest jail in the aforesaid manner.

Likewise, let butchers, fishmongers, innkeepers, brewers, bakers, those dealing in foodstuffs and all other vendors of any victuals, be bound to sell such victuals for a reasonable price, having regard for the price at which such victuals are sold in the adjoining places, so that such vendors may have moderate gains, and not excessive ones, according as the distance of the places from which such victuals are carried may seem reasonably to require. And if anyone sells such victuals in another manner, and is convicted of it in the aforesaid way, that person shall pay double what was received to the injured party, or in default of the injured party, to another who shall be willing to prosecute in this behalf. And the mayor and bailiffs of the cities and boroughs, merchant towns and others, and of the maritime ports and places shall have power to inquire concerning each and every one who shall in any way err against this, and to levy the aforesaid penalty for the benefit of those at whose suit such delinquents shall be convicted. And in case the same mayor and bailiffs neglect to carry out the aforesaid, and are convicted of this before judges to be assigned by us, then the same mayor and bailiffs shall be compelled through the same judges to pay a wronged person so wronged, or to another person prosecuting in such a person's place, three times the price of the thing thus sold, and notwithstanding that, they shall be grievously punished on our part too.

And because many sturdy beggars refuse to labor so long as they can live from begging alms, giving themselves up to idleness and sin and, at times, to robbery and other crimes, let no one, under the aforesaid pain of imprisonment, presume, under color of piety or alms, to give anything to those who can very well work, or to cherish them in their sloth, so that thus they may be compelled to work for the necessities of life.

---

4   The shires or counties were the major territorial divisions of England. Wapentakes and ridings were further subdivisions. Each had a court.

5   I.e., producers of white leather.

# 43

## ENGLISH STATUTE OF 1363 ON FOOD AND CLOTHING

Like other English statutes, the following statute was produced by king and parliament in 1363. It covers various matters.

*Laws*

King Edward,[1] at his parliament held at Westminster on the Friday in the Octaves of Saint Michael in the thirty-seventh year of his reign,[2] at the request of the Commons, and by the assent of the prelates,[3] dukes, earls, barons,[4] and other great men assembled there, has ordained the things written below in the following form.

First, that the Magna Carta, the Charter of the Forest,[5] and the statutes and ordinances made in times past, and especially the statutes made at the last parliament, be kept and duly executed according to their form....

Item. Regarding the great dearth of poultry which is in many places of the realm, it is ordained that the price of a young capon[6] shall not be above 3 pence, and that of an old one, 4 pence, or that of a hen 2 pence or that of a pullet[7] 1 pence or that of a goose 4 pence.

And in the places where the prices of such foods are less, they will not be raised by this ordinance. In the towns and markets of the highlands, they shall be sold for a lower price, as may be agreed between seller and buyer. Judges will be specially assigned duly to carry out these arrangements....

Item. Great mischief has happened to the king, the great men, and the commons because the merchants called "grocers" monopolize all kinds of saleable merchandise within the realm, putting the scarcest merchandise up for sale by covenant and arrangement made among themselves (called "the Fraternity and Guild of Merchants") and keeping back the other merchandise until it is scarce.

Regarding this mischief, it is ordained that no English merchant deal in more than one kind of ware or

*price fixing*

---

1 Edward III, king of England 1327-1377.

2 I.e., October 6, 1363. The dates of medieval documents are often indicated in only an indirect way, if at all. The thirty-seventh year of Edward III's rule ran January 25, 1363-January 24, 1364. The day of Saint Michael (i.e., Saint Michael's "feast day") was always September 29. The "octaves" were the eighth day after a saint's day, counting the saint's day itself. In 1363, the octaves of Saint Michael fell on Friday, October 6.

3 Greater members of the clergy.

4 "Dukes, earls, barons": i.e, the nobility.

5 I.e., the royal charter concerning the Forest (royal land set aside under its own law). The charter was issued at the same time as Magna Carta (in 1215).

6 A rooster castrated to make better eating.

7 A young hen.

merchandise, either through himself or another person or through any kind of covenant, but will deal in only one kind, which the merchant shall choose between the next Feast of Candlemas and the one following. And those who have wares and merchandise in their hands other than what they have chosen may put them up for sale before the next feast of the birth of St. John. If anyone breaks this ordinance in any way and is attainted for it, that person will forfeit to the king the merchandise used in that way, in the manner that follows hereafter and, moreover, will pay a fine to the king, according to the magnitude of the transgression.

And regarding how this ordinance will be put into execution, it is ordained that, concerning every kind of merchandise, good and lawful people shall be chosen and put on oath to survey that this ordinance be kept and executed—that is, two merchants dealing in each kind of merchandise in every town and borough[8] and two merchants in each county. They will redress violations, and concerning those they cannot redress they will notify the chancellor[9] and the King's Council. Commissions will also be made to certain people, to whom and when it shall please the king, to inquire by oath of six sworn men in cities, boroughs, and counties, where necessary, regarding violators of this ordinance as well as surveyors (in case they are negligent, or are in a covenant with violators) and, moreover, thereupon to hear and determine this business daily, and to punish the violators and surveyors, that is, the violators as ordained above, and the surveyors according to the discretion of the judges, and to try them by a jury of 12 in case they put themselves on the country[10] regarding the accusation. And whoever shall sue on behalf of the king in such a case shall have the case heard, and shall receive the fourth penny of the forfeiture that is obtained by the suit.

Item. It is ordained that artisans and craftspeople shall each be members of one craft only, which each will choose between the coming Feast of Candelmas and the next one after. Two of every craft shall be chosen to investigate whether anyone practices a craft other than the one chosen, and judges will be assigned to inquire according to procedure to hear such cases and punish regarding this business, as in the article aforesaid. Violators of this article shall be punished by imprisonment for half a year and, moreover, will pay fine and ransom according to the magnitude of the violation, and the surveyors will be handled according to the discretion of the judges, as before. But the intent of the king and his council is that women, that is to say, brewers, bakers, carders,[11] spinners, and workers of wool, as well as of linen cloth and silk, embroiderers and cutters of wool and all others who do manual work may freely work as they have done before, without any accusation or restraint from this ordinance....

[*The statute then regulates the work of goldsmiths.*]

Item. Regarding the outrageous and excessive apparel of diverse people, violating their estate and degree, to the great destruction and impoverishment of the whole land, it is ordained that grooms[12] (both servants of lords and those employed in crafts) shall be served meat or fish once a day, and the remaining occasions shall be served milk, butter, and cheese, and other such food, according to their estate. They shall have [from lords or employers] clothes for their wear worth no more than two marks, and they shall wear no cloth of higher price which they have bought themselves or gotten in some other way. Nor shall they wear anything of silver, embroidered items, nor items of silk, nor anything pertaining to those things. Their wives, daughters, and children shall be of the same condition in their clothing and apparel, and they shall wear no veils worth more than 12 pence a veil.

Item. Artisans and yeomen[13] shall not take or wear cloth for their clothing or stockings of a higher

---

8   A community with certain rights recognized by a charter issued by the king.
9   One of the king's chief administrative officials.
10  A defendant could in some matters choose among various kinds of trial. To "put oneself on the country" was to choose trial by jury.
11  People who straightened wool fibers, a prelude to spinning.
12  In the original French, "garçons," or boys. These were not, however, necessarily children.
13  In the countryside, the social level below that of a gentleman.

price than 40 shilllings for the whole cloth,[14] by way of purchase or by any other means. Nor may they take or wear silk, silver, or jewelled cloth, nor shall they take or wear silver or gold belts, knives, clasps, rings, garters, or brooches, ribbons, chains, or any manner of silk apparel which is embroidered or decorated. And their wives, daughters and children are to be of the same condition in their dress and apparel. And they are to wear no veils made of silk, but only of yarn made within the kingdom, nor are they to wear any manner of fur or of budge,[15] but only of lamb, rabbit, cat, or fox.

Item. Esquires[16] and all manner of gentlepersons of less than the estate of a knight who do not have land or receive rents of 100 pounds a year in value, will not take or wear cloth for their clothing or stockings priced more than 4 1/2 marks for the whole cloth, acquired either by purchase or otherwise. And they shall wear no cloth of gold or silver, or any kind of embroidered clothing or rings, clasps, brooches of gold, or ribbons, belts or any other apparel or harness[17] of gold or silver, or any with jewels, or any kind of fur. And their wives, daughters, and children shall be of the same condition as to their wear and apparel, without any turned back facing or fur linings. And they shall wear no kind of apparel of gold or silver or with jewels. But esquires who have land or rent worth 2 marks a year or more may take and wear cloth priced at 5 marks for the whole cloth, and cloth of silk and silver, ribbon, belts, and other apparel reasonably garnished with silver. And their wives, daughters, and children may wear fur facing made of miniver, but no ermine or lettice,[18] nor any kind of jewelled cloth, except for on their heads.

Item. Merchants, citizens, and burgesses, producers, master craftspeople, both in the city of London and elsewhere, who have goods and chattels certainly worth 500 pounds, as well as their wives and children, may take and wear apparel in the same way as esquires and gentlemen who have land renting at the value of 100 pounds a year. The same merchants, citizens, and burgesses who have chattels worth 1,000 pounds, and their wives and children, may take and wear apparel in the same way as esquires and gentlemen who have land and rents valued at 200 pounds a year. No groom, yeoman, merchant's servant, or craftsperson shall wear apparel other than what is ordained above for grooms and yeomen of lords.

Item. Knights who have land or rent valued up to 200 marks a year shall take and wear clothes of cloth valued at 6 marks for the whole cloth, and nothing of more expensive cloth. And they shall not wear cloth of gold or mantles or gowns furred with pure miniver[19] or ermine, or any apparel embroidered with jewels or anything else. Their wives, daughters, and children will be of the same condition. And they shall not wear ermine facings or lettice or any jewelled apparel, except on their heads. All knights and ladies, however, who have land or rent of more than 400 marks a year, up to the sum of 1,000 marks, shall wear what they like, except ermine and lettice, and apparel with jewels and pearls, unless on their heads.

Item. Clergy who have any rank in a church, cathedral, college,[20] or schools, or a cleric of the king who has an estate that requires fur, will wear and use it according to the constitution of the same. All other clergy who have 200 marks from land a year will wear and do as knights who receive the same rent. Other clergy with the same rent will wear what the esquires who have 100 pounds in rent wear. All of them, both clergy and knights, may wear fur in winter, and in the same manner will wear linure[21] in summer.

Item. Carters, ploughmen, ploughdrivers, cowherds, shepherds, swineherds, and all other keepers of animals, wheat threshers and all manner of people of the estate of a groom occupied in husbandry, and all

---

14   Whole cloth: i.e., cloth before it has in any way been cut up for use or to be sold in smaller quantities.
15   An expensive, imported black lamb fleece.
16   Those who have the right to a coat of arms.
17   I.e., belts or buckles.
18   Fur of a snow weasel; it was a cheaper approximation of ermine.
19   I.e., miniver with the gray fur removed—a more expensive fur than mixed gray and white miniver.
20   A community of secular clergy, which may or may not be educational in nature.
21   A thin, fine linen.

other people who do not have 40 shillings' worth of goods or chattels will not take or wear any kind of cloth but blanket,[22] and russet worth 12 pence, and shall wear belts of linen according to their estate. And domestic servants shall come to eat and drink in the manner pertaining to them, and not excessively. And it is ordained that if anyone wears or does contrary to the above, that person will forfeit to the king all the apparel thus worn against this ordinance.

Item. In order to maintain this ordinance and keep it in all points without exception, it is ordained that all makers of cloth within the realm, both men and women, shall confirm that they make their cloth according to the price set by this ordinance. And all the clothmakers shall buy and sell their varieties of cloth according to the same price, so that a great supply of such cloths will be made and put up for sale in every city, borough, and merchant town and elsewhere in the realm, so that no lack of supply of such cloths shall cause the violation of this ordinance. And to that end the said clothmakers will be constrained in any way that shall seem best to the king and his council. And this ordinance on new apparel shall take effect at the next Candlemas.

---

22   A white or undyed woolen cloth used for clothing.

# 44

# CATHERINE OF SIENA, *DIALOGUE*

Catherine of Siena (1347-1380) was the daughter of a wool dyer in Siena. One of her confessors states that Catherine was only seven years old when she vowed to remain a virgin for life, a decision which caused immense conflict with her parents in her teenage years. She joined a group of women, probably mostly widows who, although they lived at home, were affiliated with the Dominican order. Her mysticism and her extreme asceticism brought her to the attention of the church authorities, who were not uniformly friendly. Eventually, however, she became an advisor to Pope Gregory XI and played a role in that pope's decision to return to Rome from Avignon. She composed the *Dialogue*, which records a conversation in Italian between the Christian God and Catherine, toward the end of her life. God is speaking as Book 55 opens.

---

55   "I have now shown you the general method that every rational creature should follow in order to come out of the sea of the world without being drowned, and escape eternal damnation. I have also shown you the three general steps, that is, the three powers of the soul and how one cannot ascend one without ascending them all. And I have spoken to you of those words of My Truth: 'Where two or three or more are gathered together in My name,' telling you that this means the gathering together of the three steps, that is, of the three powers of the soul, which three powers, being united, have with them the two principal commandments of the Law, that is, love of Me and of the neighbor. Then, the staircase being mounted, that is, gathered together in My Name, as I have said, man immediately thirsts for the Living Water and sets off and passes over the Bridge, following the doctrine of My Truth, Who is this Bridge, and runs, in reply to His Voice, which called you, as I told you, above, in the Temple, inviting you all, saying, 'Whoever thirsts, let him come to Me and drink, for I am the Fountain of the Water of Life.'[1] I have explained to you what He meant, and how these words are to be understood, in order that you may better see the abundance of my love and the confusion of those who, deceived by what appears to be pleasure, run the way of the devil, who invites them to the water of death.

"Now you have seen and heard what you asked of Me, and I have told you what method should be held so as not to drown in the river, namely, to mount by the Bridge, carrying the heart and the affection like a vessel to Me, Who will give drink to him who asks of Me and to keep the way of the crucified Christ with perseverance, until death. This is that method which every man should follow, no matter what his condition is. No man can draw back, saying 'I have such

---

1   See Old Testament, Isaiah 55.1; New Testament, Revelation 21.6.

and such a position or children or other worldly reasons, for which I draw back from following, for I have already told you that every condition is pleasing and acceptable to Me, provided it be held with a holy and good will, for everything is good and perfect and made by Me, Who am Supreme Good, and I did not create nor give anything by which man could be brought to death, but everything was made to lead him to life. I ask an easy thing of you, for nothing is so easy and delightful as love, and what I require of you is none other than love of Me and of the neighbor. This you can fulfill in every time and in every place and in every condition, provided it be held to the praise and glory of My Name. You know that I told you that it was through their delusion and walking without the Light, being clothed in self-love, and possessing and loving things and creatures without Me that some pass through this life in torture, being insupportable to themselves and, unless they rise above themselves, in the aforesaid way, they will arrive at eternal damnation.

"Now I have told you what general method everyone should hold to come out of the river.

56    "As I have told you above how they ought to walk who live in common charity, that is, observing the commandments and counsels in thought, now I wish to tell you of those who have begun to mount the staircase and want to follow the perfect way, that is, to observe the commandments and counsels in act, in three states, which states I will show you now, explaining them in particular. There are three degrees and states of the soul—as there are three steps, which steps I explained to you in general as the powers of the soul—of which one state is imperfect, one more perfect, and the other most perfect. The first state is to Me as that of a mercenary servant, the second as of a faithful servant, and the other as of a son who loves Me without any self-concern. These are the three states of the soul, which can and do belong to many creatures and sometimes all to one creature. They can and do belong to one creature when, with perfect solicitude, he runs by the aforesaid way, using his time in such a way that, from the servile state he arrives at the free

state, and from the free state, at the filial. Arise above yourself and open the eye of your intellect and behold these travelling pilgrims as they pass, some imperfectly and others perfectly, on the way of the commandments, and some most perfectly keeping the way of the counsels. You will see, then, from where imperfection comes and from where perfection comes and how greatly the soul who has not rooted out of herself the roots of self-love is deceived. For in every state in which man may be, it is necessary to destroy this self-love."

57    Then that soul, tormented with intense desire, gazing into the sweet Divine mirror, saw creatures setting out to attain their end in diverse ways and with diverse considerations. She saw that many began to mount, feeling themselves pricked by servile fear, that is, fearing their own personal pain, and she saw others, practicing this first state, arriving at the second state, but few she saw who arrived at the greatest perfection.

58    Then the goodness of God, wishing to satisfy the desire of that soul, said, "Do you see those? They have arisen with servile fear from the vomit of mortal sin, but if they do not arise with love of virtue, servile fear alone is not sufficient to give eternal life. But love with holy fear is sufficient, because the law is founded in love and holy fear. The old law was the law of fear that was given by Me to Moses, by which law they who committed sin suffered the penalty of it. The new law is the law of love, given by the Word of My only begotten Son, and is founded in love alone. The new law does not break the old law, but rather fulfills it, as said of My Truth, 'I come not to destroy the law, but to fulfill it.'[2] And He united the law of fear with that of love. Through love was taken away the imperfection of the fear of the penalty, and the perfection of holy fear remained, that is, the fear of offending, not on account of one's own damnation, but of offending Me, Who am Supreme Good, so that the imperfect law was made perfect with the law of love. Wherefore, after the chariot of the fire of My only-begotten Son came and brought the fire of My charity into your humanity with abundance of mercy, the penalty of the sins com-

2   New Testament, Matthew 5.17.

mitted by humanity was taken away; that is, he who offended was no longer punished suddenly, as was given and ordained of old in the law of Moses.

"There is, therefore, no need for servile fear, and this does not mean that sin is not punished, but that the punishment is reserved, unless, that is to say, the person punish himself in this life with perfect contrition. For in the other life the soul is separated from the body; wherefore, while man lives is his time for mercy, but when he is dead, comes the time of justice. He ought, then, to arise from servile fear, and arrive at love and holy fear of Me; otherwise, there is no remedy against his falling back again into the river and reaching the waters of tribulation and seeking the thorns of consolation, for all consolations are thorns that pierce the soul who loves them inordinately.

59 "I told you that no one could go by the Bridge or come out of the river without climbing the three steps, which is the truth. There are some who climb imperfectly and some perfectly and some climb with the greatest perfection. The first are those who are moved by servile fear and have climbed so far being imperfectly gathered together; that is to say, the soul, having seen the punishment which follows her sin, climbs and gathers together her memory to recollect her vice, her intellect to see the punishment which she expects to receive for her fault, and her will to move her to hate that fault. And let us consider this to be the first step and the first gathering together of the powers of the soul, which should be exercised by the light of the intellect with the pupil of the eye of holy faith, which looks not only at the punishment of sin but at the fruit of virtue and the love which I bear to the soul, so that she may climb with love and affection, stripped of servile fear. And doing so, such souls will become faithful and not unfaithful servants, serving Me through love and not through fear, and if, with hatred of sin, they employ their minds to dig out the root of their self-love with prudence, constancy, and perseverance, they will succeed in doing so. But there are many who begin their course climbing so slowly and render their debt to Me by such small degrees and with such negligence and ignorance that they suddenly faint, and every little breeze catches their sails and turns their prow backwards. Wherefore, because they imperfectly climb to the first Step of the Bridge of Christ crucified, they do not arrive at the second step of His Heart.

60 "Some there are who have become faithful servants, serving Me with fidelity without servile fear of punishment, but rather with love. This very love, however, if they serve Me with a view to their own profit or the delight and pleasure which they find in Me, is imperfect. Do you know what proves the imperfection of this love? The withdrawal of the consolations which they found in Me and the insufficiency and short duration of their love for their neighbor, which grows weak by degrees and often disappears. Towards Me their love grows weak when, on occasion, in order to exercise them in virtue and raise them above their imperfection, I withdraw from their minds My consolation and allow them to fall into battles and perplexities. This I do so that, coming to perfect self-knowledge, they may know that of themselves they are nothing and have no grace and accordingly in time of battle fly to Me, as their Benefactor, seeking Me alone with true humility, for which purpose I treat them thus, withdrawing from them consolation indeed, but not grace. At such a time these weak ones of whom I speak relax their energy, impatiently turning backwards, and sometimes abandon, under color of virtue, many of their exercises, saying to themselves, 'This labor does not profit me.' All this they do because they feel themselves deprived of mental consolation. Such a soul acts imperfectly, for she has not yet unwound the bandage of spiritual self-love, for had she unwound it, she would see that, in truth, everything proceeds from Me, that no leaf of a tree falls to the ground without My providence, and that what I give and promise to My creatures, I give and promise to them for their sanctification, which is the good and the end for which I created them. My creatures should see and know that I wish nothing but their good through the blood of My only-begotten Son, in which they are washed from their iniquities. By this blood they are enabled to know My Truth: how, in order to give them eternal life, I created them in My image and likeness and re-created them to grace with the blood of My Son, making them sons of adoption. But since they are imperfect, they make use of Me only for their own profit, relaxing their love for their neighbor. Thus, those in the first state come to naught

through the fear of enduring pain, and those in the second, because they slacken their pace, ceasing to render service to their neighbor and withdrawing their charity if they see their own profit or consolation withdrawn from them. This happens because their love was originally impure, for they gave to their neighbor the same imperfect love which they gave to Me, that is to say, a love based only on desire of their own advantage. If, through a desire for perfection, they do not recognize this imperfection of theirs, it is impossible that they should not turn back. For those who desire Eternal Life, a pure love, prescinding from themselves, is necessary, for it is not enough for eternal life to flee sin from fear of punishment or to embrace virtue from the motive of one's own advantage. Sin should be abandoned because it is displeasing to Me, and virtue should be loved for My sake. It is true that, generally speaking, every person is first called in this way, but this is because the soul herself is at first imperfect, from which imperfection she must advance to perfection, either while she lives, by a generous love to Me with a pure and virtuous heart that takes no thought for herself or, at least, in the moment of death recognizing her own imperfection with the purpose, had she but time, of serving Me, irrespectively of herself. It was with this imperfect love that Saint Peter loved the sweet and good Jesus, My only begotten Son, enjoying most pleasantly His sweet conversation, but when the time of trouble came, he failed, and so disgraceful was his fall that not only could he not bear any pain himself, but his terror of the very approach of pain caused him to fall, and deny the Lord with the words, 'I have never known Him.'[3] The soul who has climbed this step with servile fear and mercenary love alone falls into many troubles. Such souls should arise and become sons and serve Me, irrespective of themselves, for I, who am the Rewarder of every labor, render to each man according to his state and his labor; wherefore, if these souls do not abandon the exercise of holy prayer and their other good works but go on with perseverance to increase their virtues, they will arrive at the state of filial love because I respond to them with the same love with which they love Me, so that, if they love Me as a servant does his master, I pay them their wages according to their deserts, but I do not reveal Myself to them because secrets are revealed to a friend, who has become one thing with his friend and not to a servant. Yet it is true that a servant may so advance by the virtuous love which he bears to his master as to become a very dear friend, and so do some of these of whom I have spoken, but while they remain in the state of mercenary love, I do not manifest Myself to them. If they, through displeasure at their imperfection and love of virtue, dig up with hatred the root of spiritual self-love and mount to the throne of conscience, reasoning with themselves so as to quell the motions of servile fear in their heart and to correct mercenary love by the light of the holy faith, they will be so pleasing to Me that they will attain to the love of the friend. And I will manifest Myself to them, as My Truth said in these words: 'He who loves Me shall be one thing with Me and I with him, and I will manifest Myself to him and we will dwell together.'[4] This is the state of two dear friends, for though they are two in body, yet they are one in soul through the affection of love, because love transforms the lover into the object loved, and where two friends have one soul, there can be no secret between them; wherefore My Truth said, 'I will come and we will dwell together,'[5] and this is the truth.

61   "Do you know how I manifest Myself to the soul who loves Me in truth and follows the doctrine of My sweet and amorous Word? In many is My virtue manifested in the soul in proportion to her desire, but I make three special manifestations. The first manifestation of My virtue, that is to say, of My love and charity in the soul, is made through the Word of My Son and shown in the blood which He spilled with such fire of love. Now this charity is manifested in two ways: first, in general to ordinary people, that is, to those who live in the ordinary grace of God. It is

---

3   Referring to New Testament, Matthew 26.69-75, Mark 14.66-72, Luke 22.54-62, John 18.25-27.
4   New Testament, John 14.21, 23.
5   See New Testament, John 14.23.

manifested to them by the many and diverse benefits which they receive from Me. The second mode of manifestation, which is developed from the first, is peculiar to those who have become My friends in the way mentioned above and is known through a sentiment of the soul, by which they taste, know, prove, and feel it. This second manifestation, however, is in men themselves when they manifest Me through the affection of their love. For though I am no Acceptor of creatures, I am an Acceptor of holy desires and Myself in the soul in that precise degree of perfection which she seeks in Me. Sometimes I manifest Myself (and this is also a part of the second manifestation) by endowing men with the spirit of prophecy, showing them the things of the future. This I do in many and diverse ways, according as I see need in the soul herself and in other creatures. At other times the third manifestation takes place. I then form in the mind the presence of the Truth, My only begotten Son, in many ways, according to the will and the desire of the soul. Sometimes she seeks Me in prayer, wishing to know My power, and I satisfy her by causing her to taste and see My virtue. Sometimes she seeks Me in the wisdom of My Son, and I satisfy her by placing His wisdom before the eye of her intellect, sometimes in the clemency of the Holy Spirit, and then My Goodness causes her to taste the fire of Divine charity and to conceive the true and royal virtues, which are founded on the pure love of her neighbor.

62 "You see now how truly My Word spoke when He said: 'He who loves Me shall be one thing with Me.' Because, by following His doctrine with the affection of love, you are united with Him, and, being united with Him, you are united with Me, because We are one thing together. And so it is that I manifest Myself to you, because We are one and the same thing together. Wherefore if My Truth said, 'I will manifest Myself to you,' He said the truth, because in manifesting Himself He manifested Me and, in manifesting Me He manifested Himself. But why did He not say, 'I will manifest My Father to you'? For three reasons in particular. First, because He wished to show that He and

I are not separate from each other, on which account He also made the following reply to Saint Philip when he said to Him, 'Show us the Father, and it is enough for us.'[6] My Word said, 'Who sees Me sees the Father, and who sees the Father sees Me.'[7] This He said because He was one thing with Me, and that which He had, He had from Me, I having nothing from Him; wherefore, again, He said to Judas, 'My doctrine is not Mine, but My Father's who sent Me'[8] because My Son proceeds from Me, not I from Him, though I with Him and He with Me are but one thing. For this reason He did not say, 'I will manifest the Father' but 'I will manifest Myself,' being one thing with the Father. The second reason was because, in manifesting Himself to you, He did not present to you anything He had not received from Me, the Father. These words, then, mean the Father has manifested Himself to Me because I am one thing with Him, and I will manifest to you, by means of Myself, Me and Him. The third reason was because I, being invisible, could not be seen by you until you should be separated from your bodies. Then, indeed, will you see Me, your God, and My Son, the Word, face to face. From now until after the general Resurrection when your humanity will be conformed with the humanity of the Eternal Word, according to what I told you in the treatise of the Resurrection, you can see Me with the eye of the intellect alone, for as I am, you cannot see Me now. Wherefore I veiled the Divine nature with your humanity so that you might see Me through that medium. I, the Invisible, made Myself, as it were, visible by sending you the Word, My Son, veiled in the flesh of your humanity. He manifested Me to you. Therefore it was that He did not say, 'I will manifest the Father to you' but rather, 'I will manifest Myself to you,' as if He should say, 'According as My Father manifests Himself to Me, will I manifest Myself to you, for in this manifestation of Himself, He manifests Me.' Now therefore you understand why He did not say, 'I will manifest the Father to you,' both because such a vision is impossible for you while yet in the mortal body and because He is one thing with Me.

---

6  New Testament, John 14.8.
7  New Testament, John 14.9.
8  New Testament, John 7.16 (Jesus speaks to the Jews here).

63  "You have now seen how excellent is the state of him who has attained to the love of a friend. Climbing with the foot of affection, he has reached the secret of the Heart, which is the second of the three steps figured in the Body of My Son. I have told you what was meant by the three powers of the soul, and now I will show you how they signify the three states, through which the soul passes. Before treating of the third state, I wish to show you how a man becomes a friend and how, from a friend, he grows into a son, attaining to filial love, and how a man may know if he has become a friend. And first of how a man arrives at being a friend. In the beginning, a man serves Me imperfectly through servile fear, but by exercise and perseverance, he arrives at the love of delight, finding his own delight and profit in Me. This is a necessary stage through which he must pass who would attain to perfect love, to the love that is of friend and son. I call filial love perfect because thereby a man receives his inheritance from Me, the Eternal Father, and because a son's love includes that of a friend, which is why I told you that a friend grows into a son. What means does he take to arrive at that point? I will tell you. Every perfection and every virtue proceeds from charity, and charity is nourished by humility, which results from the knowledge and holy hatred of self, that is, sensuality. To arrive at that point, a man must persevere and remain in the cellar of self-knowledge in which he will learn My mercy in the blood of My only begotten Son, drawing My divine charity to Himself with this love, exercising himself in the extirpation of his perverse self-will, both spiritual and temporal, hiding himself in his own house, as did Peter, who, after the sin of denying My Son, began to weep. Yet his lamentations were imperfect and remained so until after the 40 days, that is, until after the Ascension.[9] But when My Truth returned to Me, in His humanity, Peter and the others concealed themselves in the house, awaiting the coming of the Holy Spirit, which My Truth had promised them. They remained barred in from fear because the soul always fears until she arrives at true love. But when they had persevered in fasting and in humble and continual prayer until they had received the abundance of the Holy Spirit, they lost their fear and followed and preached concerning the crucified Christ. So also the soul who wishes to arrive at this perfection, after she has risen from the guilt of mortal sin, recognizing it for what it is, begins to weep from fear of the penalty, whence she rises to the consideration of My mercy, in which contemplation she finds her own pleasure and profit. This is an imperfect state, and I, in order to develop perfection in the soul after the 40 days, that is, after these two states, withdraw Myself from time to time, not in grace but in feeling. My Truth showed you this when He said to the disciples, 'I will go and will return to you.'

"Everything that He said was said primarily and in particular to the disciples but referred in general to the whole present and future, to those, that is to say, who should come after. He said, 'I will go and will return to you,' and so it was, for when the Holy Spirit returned upon the disciples, He also returned, as I told you above, for the Holy Spirit did not return alone but came with My power and the wisdom of the Son, who is one thing with Me, and with His own clemency, which proceeds from Me the Father and from the Son. Now, as I told you, in order to raise the soul from imperfection, I withdraw Myself from her sentiment, depriving her of former consolations. When she was in the guilt of mortal sin, she had separated herself from Me, and I deprived her of grace through her own guilt because that guilt had barred the door of her desires. Wherefore the sun of grace did not shine, not through its own defect but through the defect of the creature who bars the door of desire. When she knows herself and her darkness, she opens the window and vomits her filth by holy confession. Then I, having returned to the soul by grace, withdraw Myself from her by sentiment, which I do in order to humiliate her and cause her to seek Me in truth, and to prove her in the light of faith, so that she comes to prudence. Then, if she love Me without thought of self and with lively faith and with hatred of her own sensuality, she rejoices in the time of trouble, deeming herself unworthy of peace and quietness of mind. Now comes the second of the three things of which I told you, that is to say,

---

9   I.e., when Christ bodily entered heaven on the fortieth day after his resurrection from the dead.

how the soul arrives at perfection and what she does when she is perfect. This is what she does. Though she perceives that I have withdrawn Myself, she does not, on that account, look back but perseveres with humility in her exercises, remaining barred in the house of self-knowledge and continuing to dwell therein, awaits with lively faith the coming of the Holy Spirit, that is of Me, who am the fire of charity. How does she await me? Not in idleness but in watching and continued prayer, and not only with physical but also with intellectual watching, that is, with the eye of her mind alert and watching with the light of faith, she extirpates, with hatred, the wandering thoughts of her heart, looking for the affection of My charity and knowing that I desire nothing but her sanctification, which is certified to her in the blood of My Son. As long as her eye thus watches, illumined by the knowledge of Me and of herself, she continues to pray with the prayer of holy desire, which is a continued prayer, and also with actual prayer, which she practices at the appointed times, according to the orders of Holy Church. This is what the soul does in order to rise from imperfection and arrive at perfection, and it is to this end, namely that she may arrive at perfection, that I withdraw from her, not by grace but by sentiment. Once more do I leave her, so that she may see and know her defects, so that, feeling herself deprived of consolation and afflicted by pain, she may recognize her own weakness and learn how incapable she is of stability or perseverance, thus cutting down to the very root of spiritual self-love, for this should be the end and purpose of all her self-knowledge, to rise above herself, mounting the throne of conscience and not permitting the sentiment of imperfect love to turn again in its death-struggle, but with correction and reproof, digging up the root of self-love with the knife of self-hatred and the love of virtue.

64   "And I would have you know that just as every imperfection and perfection is acquired from Me, so is it manifested by means of the neighbor. And simple souls, who often love creatures with spiritual love, know this well, for if they have received My love sin-cerely without any self-regarding considerations, they satisfy the thirst of their love for their neighbor equally sincerely. If a man carries away the vessel which he has filled at the fountain and then drinks of it, the vessel becomes empty, but if he keeps his vessel standing in the fountain while he drinks, it always remains full. So the love of the neighbor, whether spiritual or temporal, should be drunk in Me, without any self-regarding considerations. I require that you should love Me with the same love with which I love you. This indeed you cannot do, because I loved you without being loved. All the love which you have for Me you owe to Me, so that it is not of grace that you love Me but because you ought to do so. While I love you of grace and not because I owe you My love. Therefore to Me, in person, you cannot repay the love which I require of you, and I have placed you in the midst of your fellows, that you may do to them that which you cannot do to Me, that is to say, that you may love your neighbor of free grace, without expecting any return from him, and what you do to him I count as done to Me, which My Truth showed forth when He said to Paul, My persecutor, 'Saul, Saul, why persecutest you Me?'[10] This He said, judging that Paul persecuted Him in His faithful.[11] This love must be sincere, because it is with the same love with which you love Me that you must love your neighbor. Do you know how the imperfection of spiritual love for the creature is shown? It is shown when the lover feels pain if it appear to him that the object of his love does not satisfy or return his love or when he sees the beloved one's conversation turned aside from him or himself deprived of consolation or another loved more than he. In these and in many other ways can it be seen that his neighborly love is still imperfect and that, though his love was originally drawn from Me, the Fountain of all love, he took the vessel out of the water in order to drink from it. It is because his love for Me is still imperfect that his neighborly love is so weak and because the root of self-love has not been properly dug out. Wherefore I often permit such a love to exist so that the soul may in this way come to the knowledge

---

10   New Testament, Acts 27.14.
11   According to the New Testament, before his conversion to Christianity, St. Paul, under his first name ("Saul"), had persecuted Christians.

of her own imperfection, and for the same reason I withdraw myself from the soul by sentiment that she may be thus led to enclose herself in the house of self-knowledge, where is acquired every perfection. After which I return into her with more light and with more knowledge of My Truth in proportion to the degree in which she credits to grace the power of slaying her own will. And she never ceases to cultivate the vine of her soul, and to root out the thorns of evil thoughts, replacing them with the stones of virtues, cemented together in the blood of the crucified Christ, which she has found on her journey across the Bridge of Christ, My only begotten Son. For I told you, if you remember, that upon the Bridge, that is, upon the doctrine of My Truth, were built up the stones, based upon the virtue of His blood, for it is in virtue of this blood that the virtues give life.

66    "Know, dearest daughter, how by humble, continual, and faithful prayer, the soul acquires, with time and perseverance, every virtue. Wherefore should she persevere and never abandon prayer, either through the illusion of the devil or her own fragility, that is to say, either on account of any thought or movement coming from her own body, or of the words of any creature. The devil often places himself upon the tongues of creatures, causing them to chatter nonsensically, with the purpose of preventing the prayer of the soul. All of this she should pass by, by means of the virtue of perseverance. Oh, how sweet and pleasant to that soul and to Me is holy prayer made in the house of knowledge of self and of Me, opening the eye of the intellect to the light of faith and the affections to the abundance of My charity, which was made visible to you through My visible only-begotten Son, who showed it to you with His blood! Which blood inebriates the soul and clothes her with the fire of divine charity, giving her the food of the Sacrament (which is placed in the tavern of the mystical body of the holy Church) that is to say, the food of the body and blood of My Son, wholly God and wholly man, administered to you by the hand of My vicar, who holds the key of the blood. This is that tavern, which I mentioned to you, standing on the Bridge, to provide food and com-

fort for the travelers and the pilgrims, who pass by the way of the doctrine of My Truth, lest they should faint through weakness. This food strengthens little or much, according to the desire of the recipient, whether he receives sacramentally or virtually. He receives sacramentally when he actually communicates with the blessed sacrament. He receives virtually when he communicates, both by desire of communion and by contemplation of the blood of the crucified Christ, communicating, as it were, sacramentally, with the affection of love, which is to be tasted in the blood which, as the soul sees, was shed through love. On seeing this the soul becomes inebriated and blazes with holy desire and satisfies herself, becoming full of love for Me and for her neighbor. Where can this be acquired? In the house of self-knowledge with holy prayer, where imperfections are lost, even as Peter and the disciples, while they remained in watching and prayer, lost their imperfection and acquired perfection. By what means is this acquired? By perseverance seasoned with the most holy faith.

"But do not think that the soul receives such ardor and nourishment from prayer, if she pray only vocally, as do many souls whose prayers are rather words than love. Such as these give heed to nothing except to completing psalms and saying many paternosters.[12] And when they have once completed their appointed tale, they do not appear to think of anything further, but seem to place devout attention and love in merely vocal recitation, which the soul is not required to do, for in doing only this, she bears but little fruit, which pleases Me but little. But if you ask Me whether the soul should abandon vocal prayer, since it does not seem to all that they are called to mental prayer, I should reply 'No.' The soul should advance by degrees, and I know well that, just as the soul is at first imperfect and afterwards perfect, so also is it with her prayer. She should nevertheless continue in vocal prayer, while she is yet imperfect, so as not to fall into idleness. But she should not say her vocal prayers without joining them to mental prayer, that is to say, that while she is reciting, she should endeavor to elevate her mind in My love, with the consideration of her own defects and of the blood of My only-begotten

---

12    A "paternoster" is the prayer which begins "Our Father Who art in heaven...(New testament, Matthew 6.9,13)."

Son, wherein she finds the breadth of My charity and the remission of her sins. And this she should do so that self-knowledge and the consideration of her own defects should make her recognize My goodness in herself and continue her exercises with true humility. I do not wish defects to be considered in particular, but in general, so that the mind may not be contaminated by the remembrance of particular and hideous sins. But, as I said, I do not wish the Soul to consider her sins, either in general or in particular, without also remembering the blood and the broadness of My mercy, for fear that otherwise she should be brought to confusion. And together with confusion would come the devil, who has caused it, under color of contrition and displeasure of sin, and so she would arrive at eternal damnation, not only on account of her confusion but also through the despair which would come to her because she did not seize the arm of My mercy. This is one of the subtle devices with which the devil deludes My servants, and in order to escape from his deceit and to be pleasing to Me, you must enlarge your hearts and affections in My boundless mercy with true humility. You know that the pride of the devil cannot resist the humble mind, nor can any confusion of spirit be greater than the broadness of My good mercy, if the soul will only truly hope therein. Wherefore it was, if you remember rightly, that once, when the devil wished to overthrow you by confusion, wishing to prove to you that your life had been deluded and that you had not followed My will, you did that which was your duty, which My goodness (which is never withheld from him who will receive it) gave you strength to do, that is, you rose, humbly trusting in My mercy and saying, 'I confess to my Creator that my life has indeed been passed in darkness, but I will hide myself in the wounds of the crucified Christ and bathe myself in His blood, and so shall my iniquities be consumed and with desire will I rejoice in my Creator.' You remember that then the devil fled, and turning around to the opposite side, he endeavored to inflate you with pride, saying, 'You are perfect and pleasing to God, and there is no more need for you to afflict yourself or to lament your sins.' And once more I gave you the light to see your true path, namely, humiliation of yourself, and you answered the devil with these words: 'Wretch that I am, John the Baptist never sinned and was sanctified in his mother's womb. And I have committed so many sins and have hardly begun to know them with grief and true contrition, seeing Who God is, Who is offended by me, and who I am, who offend Him.' Then, the devil, not being able to resist your humble hope in My goodness, said to you: 'Cursed that you are, for I can find no way to take you. If I put you down through confusion, you rise to Heaven on the wings of mercy, and if I raise you on high, you humble yourself down to Hell, and when I go into Hell, you persecute me, so that I will return to you no more, because you strike me with the stick of charity.' The soul, therefore, should season the knowledge of herself with the knowledge of My goodness, and then vocal prayer will be of use to the soul who makes it, and pleasing to Me, and she will arrive, from the vocal imperfect prayer, exercised with perseverance, at perfect mental prayer. But if she simply aims at completing her tale and abandons mental prayer for vocal, she will never arrive at it. Sometimes the soul will be so ignorant that, having resolved to say so many prayers vocally, and I, visiting her mind, sometimes in one way and sometimes in another, in a flash of self-knowledge or of contrition for sin, sometimes in the broadness of My charity and sometimes by placing before her mind in diverse ways, according to My pleasure and the desire of the soul, the presence of My Truth, she (the soul), in order to complete her tale, will abandon My visitation, that she feels, as it were, by conscience, rather than abandon that which she had begun. She should not do so, for in so doing, she yields to a deception of the devil. The moment she feels her mind disposed by My visitation, in the many ways I have told you, she should abandon vocal prayer. Then, once my visitation is done, if there is time, she can resume the vocal prayers which she had resolved to say, but if she has not time to complete them, she ought not on that account to be troubled or suffer annoyance and confusion of mind, of course provided that it was not the divine office[13] which clerics and religious[14] are bound

---

13  I.e., prayers said by clergy and monastics according to the time of day.
14  "Religious": those in the monastic life.

and obliged to say under penalty of offending Me, for they must, until death, say their office. But if they, at the hour appointed for saying it, should feel their minds drawn and raised by desire, they should so arrange as to say it before or after My visitation, so that the debt of rendering the office be not omitted. But in any other case, vocal prayer should be immediately abandoned for the said cause. Vocal prayer, made in the way that I have told you, will enable the soul to arrive at perfection, and therefore she should not abandon it, but use it in the way that I have told you.

"And so, with exercise in perseverance, she will taste prayer in truth, and the food of the blood of My only-begotten Son, and therefore I told you that some communicated virtually with the body and blood of Christ, although not sacramentally—that is, they communicate in the affection of charity, which they taste by means of holy prayer, little or much, according to the affection with which they pray. They who proceed with little prudence and without method taste little, and they who proceed with much, taste much. For the more the soul tries to loosen her affection from herself and fasten it in Me with the light of the intellect, the more she knows, and the more she knows, the more she loves, and loving much, she tastes much. You see then that perfect prayer is not attained through many words, but through affection of desire, the soul raising herself to Me with knowledge of herself and of My mercy, seasoned the one with the other. Thus she will exercise together mental and vocal prayer, for even as the active and contemplative life is one, so are they. Although vocal or mental prayer can be understood in many and diverse ways, for I have told you that a holy desire is a continual prayer, in this sense that a good and holy will disposes itself with desire to the occasion actually appointed for prayer in addition to the continual prayer of holy desire; wherefore vocal prayer will be made at the appointed time by the soul who remains firm in a habitual holy will, and will sometimes be continued beyond the appointed time, according as charity commands for the salvation of the neighbor, if the soul sees him to be in need, and also her own necessities according to the state in which I have placed her. Each one, according to his condition, ought to exert himself for the salvation of souls, for this exercise lies at the root of a holy will,

and whatever he may contribute, by words or deeds, towards the salvation of his neighbor, is virtually a prayer, although it does not replace a prayer which one should make oneself at the appointed season, as My glorious standard-bearer Paul said, in the words, 'He who ceases not to work ceases not to pray.' It was for this reason that I told you that prayer was made in many ways, that is, that actual prayer may be united with mental prayer if made with the affection of charity, which charity is itself continual prayer. I have now told you how mental prayer is reached by exercise and perseverance and by leaving vocal prayer for mental when I visit the soul. I have also spoken to you of common prayer, that is, of vocal prayer in general, made outside of ordained times, and of the prayers of goodwill, and how every exercise, whether performed in oneself or in one's neighbor with good-will, is prayer. The enclosed soul should therefore spur herself on with prayer, and when she has arrived at friendly and filial love, she does so. Unless the soul keeps to this path, she will always remain tepid and imperfect and will only love Me and her neighbor in proportion to the pleasure which she finds in My service.

90  "You have now seen the various states of tears and the difference between them, according as it has pleased My Truth to satisfy your desire. With regard to the first tears of those who are in the state of death, in the guilt, namely, of mortal sin, you have seen that their sorrow, proceeding in general from their heart on account of the conception of the principle of the affection which causes tears, is corrupt and miserable sorrow, and indeed their every work is corrupt. The second stage is that of those who are beginning to learn their own evil through the penalty which follows their guilt. This is a general beginning, generously given by Me to the fragile, who ignorantly drown in the river, loathing the doctrine of My Truth. But there are many who know their evil without servile fear (fear, that is, of the penalty due to their guilt), who abandon sin with a great self-hatred, which makes them deem themselves worthy of punishment, and who in their simple goodness devote themselves to serving Me, their Creator, grieving over the offense which they have done Me. It is true that he who abandons sin with very great self-hatred is more apt for perfection than the others (those actuated by servile fear), yet

both classes may arrive thereat by exercise, though the former will arrive first.

"One of the latter class should take care not to remain in servile fear, and one of the former should beware of tepidity, that he does not grow cold within through not exercising his simple goodness. This is a common vocation.

"The third and fourth stages are of those who, having arisen out of fear, have arrived at love and hope, tasting My Divine mercy, receiving many gifts and consolations from Me, on account of which the eye weeps in order to satisfy the feeling of the heart. But because this sorrow is imperfect and mingled with the sorrow of spiritual self-love, as I have said, the soul must, by exercise in virtue, reach the fourth stage, where, having grown by her desires, she unites and conforms herself to My will to such a point that she can neither wish nor desire other than what I wish in the matter of love to her neighbor, from which she extracts the grief of love in herself for the offenses and losses inflicted on her neighbor. This stage is united with the fifth and ultimate perfection in which the soul unites herself to the Truth, and the fire of holy desire is increased, from which desire the devil flees, for he can persecute the soul no more, neither by injuring her, for she has grown patient in the love of her neighbor, nor by spiritual or temporal consolation, because through self-hatred and true humility she despises both. True indeed it is that the devil, for his part, never sleeps, thus reading a lesson to you negligent ones, who sleep through the time of merit. But all his watching cannot hurt such as these, because he cannot endure the heat of their love, nor the odor of the union which they have made with Me, the sea pacific, while a soul thus united to Me cannot be deceived. So he avoids such a soul, as a fly avoids the boiling kettle from fear of the fire. The following however happens to the soul before she has reached perfection. The devil, seeing that she seems tepid, enters into her with many and diverse temptations. But the soul, being in the sea of knowledge, heat, and hatred of guilt, resists, binding the will, for fear it should consent, with the bands of hatred of sin and love of virtue. Let every soul that experiences many temptations rejoice, for through them lies the road to this glorious and sweet state. For I have already told you that by knowledge and hatred of yourselves and knowledge of Me, you could arrive at perfection. At no time does the soul know so well whether I am in her or no as in the time of battle. You ask, in what way? I will tell you. If she knows well, seeing herself in battle, that she cannot liberate herself or resist the perverse will, for she has nothing of her own with which to do so (she can indeed resist the perverse will, in the sense of not consenting to it, but in no other sense), and then she learns that she herself is nothing, for were she anything in her own power, she could cause this battle, which is against her will, to cease. Thus she humbles herself with true self-knowledge and, with the light of the most holy faith, runs to Me, the Eternal God, through Whose Goodness she is able to preserve a good and holy will that does not consent in the time of battle or yield to the miseries with which it is assailed. You are then quite right to comfort yourselves with the doctrine of the sweet and amorous Word, My only-begotten Son, in the time of your troubles and adversities and temptations from men or devils, for these increase your virtue and cause you to arrive at great perfection.

99  "When the soul has arrived at the attainment of the general light, of which I have spoken, she should not remain contented, because as long as you are pilgrims in this life you are capable of growth, and he who does not go forward, by that very fact, is turning back. She should either grow in the general light, which she has acquired through My Grace, or anxiously strive to attain to the second and perfect light, leaving the imperfect and reaching the perfect. For if the soul truly has light, she will wish to arrive at perfection. In this second perfect light are to be found two kinds of perfection; for they may be called perfect who have abandoned the general way of living of the world. One perfection is that of those who give themselves up wholly to the castigation of the body, doing great and severe penance. These, in order that their sensuality may not rebel against their reason, have placed their desire rather in the mortification of the body than in the destruction of their self-will, as I have explained to you in another place. These feed their souls at the table of penance and are good and perfect, if their penance be illuminated by discretion and founded on Me, if, that is to say, they act with true

knowledge of themselves and of Me, with great humility and wholly conformed to the judgment of My will and not to that of the will of man. But if they were not thus clothed with My will, in true humility, they would often offend against their own perfection, esteeming themselves the judges of those who do not walk in the path. Do you know why this would happen to them? Because they have placed all their labor and desire in the mortification of the body rather than in the destruction of their own will. Such as these wish always to choose their own times and places and consolations, after their own fashion, and also the persecutions of the world and of the devil, as I have narrated to you in speaking of the second state of perfection.

"They say, cheating themselves with the delusion of own self-will, which I have already called their spiritual will, 'I wish to have that consolation and not these battles, or these temptations of the devil, not, indeed, for my own pleasure but in order to please God the more and in order to retain Him the more in my soul through grace because it seems to me that I should possess Him more and serve Him better in that way than in this.' And this is the way the soul often falls into trouble and becomes tedious and insupportable to herself, thus injuring her own perfection. Yet she neither perceives it nor that, within her, lurks the stench of pride, and there she lies. Now, if the soul were not in this condition, but were truly humble and not presumptuous, she would be illuminated to see that I, the primary and sweet truth, grant condition and time and place and consolations and tribulations as they may be needed for your salvation and to complete the perfection to which I have elected the soul. And she would see that I give everything through love and that therefore, with love and reverence, should she receive everything, which is what the souls in the second state do, and by doing so, arrive at the third state. Of whom I will now speak to you, explaining to you the nature of these two states which stand in the most perfect light.

100  "Those who belong to the third state, which immediately follows the last, having arrived at this glorious light, are perfect in every condition in which they may be, and receive every event which I permit to happen to them with due reverence, as I have mentioned to you when speaking of the third and unitive state of the soul. These deem themselves worthy of the troubles and stumbling blocks caused them by the world and of the privation of their own consolation and indeed of whatever circumstance happens to them. And inasmuch as they deem themselves worthy of trouble, so also do they deem themselves unworthy of the fruit which they receive after their trouble. They have known and tasted in the light My eternal will, which wishes nothing else but your good, and gives and permits these troubles in order that you should be sanctified in Me. Wherefore the soul having known My will, clothes herself with it and fixes her attention on nothing else except seeing in what way she can preserve and increase her perfection to the glory and praise of My Name, opening the eye of her intellect and fixing it in the light of faith upon the crucified Christ, My only-begotten Son, loving and following His doctrine, which is the rule of the road for perfect and imperfect alike. And see how My truth, the lamb, Who became enamored of her when He saw her, gives the soul the doctrine of perfection. She knows what this perfection is, having seen it practiced by the sweet and amorous Word, My only-begotten Son, Who was fed at the table of holy desire, seeking the honor of Me, the Eternal Father, and your salvation. And inflamed with this desire, He ran with great eagerness to the shameful death of the Cross and accomplished the obedience which was imposed on Him by Me, His Father, not shunning labors or insults or withdrawing on account of your ingratitude or ignorance of so great a benefit, or because of the persecutions of the Jews, or on account of the insults, derision, grumbling, and shouting of the people. But all this He passed through like the true captain and knight that He was, Whom I had placed on the battlefield to deliver you from the hands of the devil, so that you might be free and drawn out of the most terrible slavery in which you could ever be and also to teach you His road, His doctrine, and His rule, so that you might open the Door of Me, eternal life, with the key of His precious blood, shed with such fire of love, with such hatred of your sins. It was as if the sweet and amorous Word, My Son, should have said to you, 'Behold, I have made the road and opened the door with My blood.' Do not then be negligent to follow, laying yourselves down to rest in self-love and ignorance of the road, presuming

to choose to serve Me in your own way, instead of in the way which I have made straight for you by means of My truth, the incarnate Word, and built up with His blood. Rise up then, promptly, and follow Him, for no one can reach Me, the Father, if not by Him; He is the way and the door by which you must enter into Me, the sea of peace.

"When therefore the soul has arrived at seeing, knowing, and tasting in its full sweetness this light, she runs, as one enamored and inflamed with love, to the table of holy desire; she does not see herself in herself, seeking her own consolation either spiritual or temporal, but like one who has placed his all in this light and knowledge and has destroyed his own will, she shuns no labor from whatever source it comes but rather, enduring the troubles, the insults, the temptations of the devil, and the murmurings of men, eats at the table of the most holy Cross, the food of the honor of Me, the eternal God, and of the salvation of souls, seeking no reward either from Me or from creatures, because she is stripped of mercenary love, that is of love for Me based on interested motives, and is clothed in perfect light, loving Me in perfect purity, with no other regard than for the praise and glory of My name, serving neither Me for her own delight, nor her neighbor for her own profit, but purely through love alone. Such as these have lost themselves, and have stripped themselves of the old man, that is of their own sensuality and having clothed themselves with the new man, the sweet Christ Jesus, My Truth, follow Him manfully. These are they who sit at the table of holy desire, having been more anxious to slay their own will than to slay and mortify their own body. They have indeed mortified their body, though not as an end in itself but as a means which helps them to stay their own will, as I said to you when explaining that sentence that I wished few words and many deeds, and so ought you to do. Their principal desire should be to slay their own will, so that it may not seek or wish anything else than to follow My sweet truth, the crucified Christ, seeking the honor and glory of My name and the salvation of souls. Those who are in this sweet light know it and remain constantly in peace and quiet, and no one scandalizes them, for they have cut away that thing by which stumbling-blocks are caused, namely their own will. And all the persecutions with which the world and the devil can attack them slide under their feet, standing, as they do, in the waters of many tribulations and temptations, and do not hurt them, for they remain attached to Me by the umbilical cord of fiery desire. Such a man rejoices in everything, nor does he make himself judge of My servants or of any rational creature, but rejoices in every condition and in every manner of holiness which he sees, saying: 'Thanks be to You, eternal Father, Who has in Your house many mansions.'[15] And he rejoices more in the different ways of holiness which he sees than if he were to see all travelling by one road, because in this way he perceives the greatness of My Goodness become more manifest and thus rejoicing, draws from all the fragrance of the rose. And not only in the case of good but even when he sees something evidently sinful, he does not fall into judgment but rather into true and holy compassion, interceding with Me for sinners and saying, with perfect humility, 'Today it is your turn, and tomorrow it will be mine unless the divine grace preserves me.'

"Enamor yourself, dearest daughter, of this sweet and excellent state and gaze at those who run in this glorious light and holiness, for they have holy minds and eat at the table of holy desire and, with the light, have arrived at feeding on the food of souls, that is, the honor of Me, the Eternal Father, being clothed with burning love in the sweet garment of My Lamb, My only-begotten Son, namely His doctrine. These do not lose their time in passing false judgments, either on My servants or the servants of the world, and they are never scandalized by any murmurings of men, either for their own sake or that of others. That is to say, in their own case they are content to endure anything for My name's sake, and when an injury is done to someone else, they endure it with compassion for this injured neighbor and without murmuring against him who caused the injury or him who received it, because their love is not disordered but has been ordered in Me, the eternal God.

---

15   Referring to New Testament, John 14.2.

"And since their love is so ordered, these souls, my dearest daughter, never take offense from those they love nor from any rational creature, their will being dead and not alive; wherefore they never assume the right to judge the will of men but only the will of My clemency. These observe the doctrine which, as you know, was given you by My truth at the beginning of your life, when you were thinking in what way you could arrive at perfect purity and were praying to Me with a great desire of doing so. You know what was replied to you, while you were asleep, concerning this holy desire and that the words resounded not only in your mind but also in your ear. So much so, that if you remember truly, you returned to your waking body, when My truth said, 'Will you arrive at perfect purity and be freed from stumbling-blocks, so that your mind may not be scandalized by anything?' Unite yourself always to Me by the affection of love, for I am the supreme and eternal purity. I am that fire which purifies the soul, and the closer the soul is to Me, the purer she becomes, and the further she is from Me, the more does her purity leave her, which is the reason men of the world fall into such iniquities, for they are separated from Me, while the soul who, without any medium, unites herself directly to Me participates in My purity. Another thing is necessary for you to arrive at this union and purity, namely, that you should never judge the will of man in anything that you may see done or said by any creature whatsoever, either to yourself or to others. You should consider My will alone, both in them and in yourself. And if you should see evident sins or defects, draw out of those thorns the rose; that is to say, offer them to Me with holy compassion. In the case of injuries done to yourself, judge that My will permits this in order to prove virtue in yourself and in My other servants, esteeming that he who acts thus does so as the instrument of My will, perceiving, moreover, that such apparent sinners may frequently have a good intention, for no one can judge the secrets of the heart of man. That which you do not see you should not judge in your mind, even though it may externally be open mortal sin, seeing nothing in others but My will, not in order to judge but, as has been said, with holy compassion. In this way you will arrive at perfect purity, because acting thus, your mind will not be scandalized either in Me or in your neighbor. Otherwise you fall into contempt of your neighbor, if you judge his evil will towards you instead of My will acting in him. Such contempt and scandal separate the soul from Me and prevent perfection and in some cases, deprive one of grace, more or less according to the gravity of one's contempt and the hatred which that one's judgment has conceived against one's neighbor.

"A different reward is received by the soul who perceives only My will, which, as has been said, wishes nothing else but your good, so that everything which I give or permit to happen to you, I give so that you may arrive at the end for which I created you. And because the soul remains always in the love of her neighbor, she remains always in Mine, and thus remains united to Me. Wherefore, in order to arrive at purity, you must entreat Me to do three things: to grant you to be united to me by the affection of love, retaining in your memory the benefits you have received from Me; and with the eye of your intellect to see the affection of My love, with which I love you inestimably; and in the will of others to discern My will only and not their evil will, for I am their judge, not you, and in doing this, you will arrive at all perfection.

"This was the doctrine given to you by My truth, if you remember well. Now I tell you, dearest daughter, that such as these, who have learned this doctrine, taste the earnest of eternal life in this life, and if you have well retained this doctrine, you will not fall into the snares of the devil, because you will recognize them in the case about which you have asked Me.

"But nevertheless, in order to satisfy your desire more clearly, I will tell you and show you how men should never discern by judgment, but with holy compassion.

101 "Why did I say to you that they received the earnest of eternal life? I say that they receive the earnest-money, but not the full payment, because they wait to receive it in Me, the Eternal Life, where they have life without death and satiety without disgust and hunger without pain, for from that divine hunger pain is far away, and though they have what they desire, disgust is far from satiety, for I am the flawless food of life. It is true that, in this life, they receive the earnest and taste it in this way, namely that the soul

begins to hunger for the honor of the eternal God and for the food of the salvation of other souls, and being hungry, she eats, that is to say, nourishes herself with love of her neighbor, which causes her hunger and desire, for the love of the neighbor is a food which never satiates him who feeds on it, the eater being insatiable and always remains hungry. So this earnest-money is a commencement of a guarantee which is given to man, in virtue of which he expects one day to receive his payment, not through the perfection of the earnest-money in itself, but through faith, through the certitude which he has of reaching the completion of his being and receiving his payment. Wherefore this enamored soul, clothed in My truth, having already received in this life the earnest of My love, and of her neighbor's, is not yet perfect, but expects perfection in immortal life. I say that this earnest is not perfect, because the soul who tastes it has not, as yet, the perfection which would prevent her feeling pain in herself or in others: in herself, through the offense done to Me by the law of perversity, which is bound in her members and struggles against the spirit, and in others by the offense of her neighbor. She has indeed, in a sense, a perfect grace, but not that perfection of My saints who have arrived at Me, eternal life, for, as has been said, their desires are without suffering and yours are not. These servants of Mine, as I have said to you in another place, who nourish themselves at this table of holy desire, are blessed and full of grief, even as My only-begotten Son was, on the wood of the holy cross, because, while His flesh was in grief and torment, His soul was blessed through its union with the divine nature. In like manner these are blessed by the union of their holy desire towards Me, clothed, as has been said, in My sweet Will, and they are full of grief through compassion for their neighbor and because they afflict their own self-love, depriving it of sensual delights and consolations.

102 "Now listen, dearest daughter, in order that you might understand better that which you desired to know, I have spoken to you of the general light, which you all must have, in whatever state you be, speaking of those who live in ordinary charity. And I have also spoken of those who are in the perfect light, which light I distinguished in two instances, first, that of those who, having left the world, applied themselves

to the mortification of the body, and of those who, in all things, destroyed their own will; these latter were the perfect souls who nourish themselves at the table of holy desire. I will now speak particularly to you, and in speaking to you and in satisfying your desire, I shall also speak to others. I wish that you should do three things in particular, so that ignorance may not prevent the perfection to which I call you. And I will tell you the first thing I wish you to do in order that the devil, hidden in the cloak of love of the neighbor, may not nourish within your soul the root of presumption, for, by this means, you would fall into false judgments, which I have forbidden you, ordering you to judge aright, whereas you would judge wrongly, returning to your human point of view, for the devil would often cause you to see what was true in order to lead you into falsehood. This he would do in order to make you judge the minds and intentions of My rational creatures, which fall, as I have told you, under My judgment alone. This, then, is the first of the three things which I wish you to do and observe, namely, that you should never deliver a judgment, except under a certain condition, but under that condition I wish you to do it. The condition is this: unless I have expressly manifested to you in your mind, not once, nor twice, but several times your neighbor's fault, you should say nothing in particular to the one who seems to you to fall into it, but rather in general correct the vices of those who come to visit you and plant the virtues lovingly and with benignity, but with a certain sternness in your benignity, according as you shall see need. And if it should appear to you that I have shown to you many times the defects of others, unless you see that it was an express revelation from Me, as has been said, you should say nothing in particular, but devote yourself to the surer way, so as to dispel the delusion and malice of the devil, for with the blade of this desire to judge, he might wound you, causing you often to judge your neighbors falsely, and, thus, often to scandalize them.

"Wherefore, let silence dwell in your mouth or holy conversation about virtue and the contemptibleness of sin, and attribute that vice, which you seem to recognize in others to yourself at the same time as to them, and if in truth, these people should have fallen into that vice, they will correct themselves better, seeing themselves so sweetly treated, and will be obliged, by your pleasant warnings, to correct themselves, and will themselves tell you that very thing which you were on the point of saying to them. Thus you will remain in safety and will have cut away the road under the devil's feet, who will not be able to delude you or prevent the perfection of your soul. I will too that you should know that you should not trust all you see, but rather cast it behind you and refuse to look at it, looking only at yourself and recognizing in yourself My bounty and My goodness. Thus do they, who have arrived at the last state, of which I spoke to you. They constantly turn to the valley of self-knowledge, and do not, on that account, diminish the height of their union with Me. And this is the first of the three things which, as I told you, I wish you to do, in order to serve Me in truth.

103   "If at any time it should happen to you, as in the case of which you asked Me the explanation, that you should be praying in particular for one of My creatures and that during your prayer, you should see in him for whom you pray a ray of grace, and in another, none at all, both persons being servants of Mine, you should not judge him who appears to you to have a confused and darkened mind, to be in a state of grave sin, because often your judgment would be false; and I wish you to know that often, when praying for one and the same person, you will sometimes see him full of light and of a holy desire before Me (in so good a state will he appear to you, that your soul will grow fat therewith, which is the effect of love by which you all participate in each other's good). And sometimes you will see the same person, far away in mind from Me, and filled with darkness and temptations, so that it will seem to you a weariness to pray for that person—to hold that person before Me. This happens sometimes through the defect of the person for whom you have prayed, but more often, not through his defect, but because I, the eternal God, have withdrawn Myself from that soul, as I often do, to bring that soul to greater perfection, according to what I told you when speaking of the states of the soul. I may have withdrawn, not My grace, but the feeling of it, its sweetness and consolation, deprived of which the mind remains barren, dry, and in grief, which grief I manifest to the soul who is praying, on account of the grace and love which I have to the soul who receives the fruit of the prayer, so that the one who is praying may help that person to disperse the clouds which are in that person's mind.

"See then, sweetest and dearest daughter, how ignorant and worthy of reprehension would be the judgment which you or another might make at the sight alone of this soul. You would judge that vice was there because I showed her to you full of darkness, whereas you see that such a soul is not deprived of grace, but only of the feeling of My sweetness which I have given her. I wish, therefore, you and My other servants should also wish, that you should give yourselves up to perfect self-knowledge, so that you may perfectly recognize My goodness in you, and leave this and every other judgment to Me, for judgment is Mine and not yours.

"Abandon judgment, which is Mine, and take up rather compassion, with hunger for My honor and salvation of souls. Preach virtue with yearning desire and reprove vice in yourself and in others, as I have shown you. In this way will you come to Me, in truth, and will show that you have kept in mind and observed the doctrine, which was given you by My truth—namely, to make My will the subject of your judgments, and not that of man.

"This must you do if you will possess virtue in all its purity and will stand in the last and most perfect light, eating at the table of holy desire of the food of souls, to the glory and praise of My Name.

107   "Now I have told you, dearest daughter, and fully explained to you, illuminating the eye of your intellect, about the deceptions the devil might practice upon you, and I have satisfied your desire in that which you asked Me, because I do not despise the desire of My servants. Also I not only give to all who ask, but I invite you all to ask, and he displeases Me much, who does not knock, in truth, at the door of the wisdom of My only-begotten Son, following His doctrine, the following of which doctrine is a knocking, calling to Me, the eternal Father, with the voice of holy desire, with humble and continual prayers. And I am that Father Who gives you the bread of grace by means of this sweet door, My Truth. And sometimes, to test your desires and your perseverance, I pretend not to understand you, but I really understood you

well, and give you that state of mind that you need, because I give you that hunger and the voice with which you cry to Me, and I, seeing your constancy, fulfill your desires when they are ordered and directed to Me. It was to such asking as this that My truth invited you, when He said, 'Cry out and you shall be answered, knock and it shall be opened to you, ask and it shall be given to you.'[16] And so I say to you that I will that you should never relax the desire of asking for My help, neither lower your voice from crying to Me that I may have mercy on the world, nor cease from knocking at the door of My Truth, following in His Footsteps, and delight thyself in the cross with Him, eating the food of souls to the glory and praise of My name, and lament, with anxiety of heart, over the death of the human generation, that you see led to misery so great that your tongue is not sufficient to relate it. On account of this lamenting and crying will I have mercy on the world, and it is this which I demand from My servants, and which will be a sign to Me, that they love Me in truth, and, as I told you, I will not despise their desires."

108  Then that soul, as if, in truth, inebriated, seemed beside herself, as if the feelings of the body were alienated through the union of love which she had made with her Creator, and as if, in elevation of mind, she had gazed into the eternal truth with the eye of her intellect and having recognized the truth, had become enamored of it and said, "O Supreme and eternal goodness of God, who am I, miserable one, that You, supreme and eternal Father, have manifested to me Your Truth, and the hidden deceits of the devil and the deceitfulness of personal feeling, so that I, and others in this life of pilgrimage, may know how to avoid being deceived by the devil or ourselves! What moved You to do it? Love, because you loved me, without my having loved You. O, fire of Love! Thanks, thanks be to You, eternal Father! I am imperfect and full of darkness, and You, perfection and light, have shown to me perfection and the resplendent way of the doctrine of Your only-begotten Son. I was dead, and You have brought me to life. I was sick, and You have given me

medicine, not only the medicine of the blood which You gave for the diseased human race in the person of Your Son, but also a medicine against a secret infirmity of which I knew nothing; in this precept, that in no way can I judge any rational creature and particularly Your servants, upon whom often I, as one blind and sick with this infirmity, passed judgment under the pretext of Your honor and the salvation of souls. Wherefore I thank You, supreme and eternal Good, that in the manifesting of Your truth and the deceitfulness of the devil and our own passions, You have made me know my infirmity. Wherefore I beseech You, through grace and mercy, that from today henceforward, I may never again wander from the path of Your doctrine, given by Your goodness to me and to whoever wishes to follow it, because without You nothing is done. To You then, eternal Father, do I have recourse and flee, and I do not beseech You for myself alone, Father, but for the whole world, and particularly for the mystical body of the holy Church, that this truth given to me, miserable one, by You, eternal Truth, may shine in Your ministers. I also beseech You especially for all those whom You have given me and whom You have made one thing with me and whom I love with a particular love, because they will be my refreshment to the glory and praise of Your Name, when I see them running on this sweet and straight road, pure and dead to their own will and opinion and without any passing judgment on their neighbors, or causing them any scandal or murmuring. And I pray You, sweetest love, that not one of them may be taken from me by the hand of the infernal devil, so that at last they may arrive at You, their end, eternal Father.

"Also I make another petition to You for my two fathers,[17] the supports whom You have placed on the earth to guard and instruct me, miserable infirm one, from the beginning of my conversion until now, that You unite them and of two bodies make one soul, and that they attend to nothing else than to complete in themselves and in the mysteries that You have placed in their hands the glory and praise of Your Name and the salvation of souls, and that I, an unworthy and

---

16  New Testament, Matthew 7.7; Luke 11.9.
17  I.e., Catherine's confessors.

miserable slave, and no daughter, may behave to them with due reverence and holy fear, for love of You, in a way that will be to Your honor and their peace and quiet and to the edification of the neighbor. I now know for certain, eternal truth, that You will not despise the desire of the petitions that I have made to You, because I know, from seeing what it has pleased You to manifest and still more from proof, that You are the acceptor of holy desires. I, Your unworthy servant, will strive, according as You will give me grace, to observe Your commandments and Your doctrine. Now, O Eternal Father, I remember a word which you did say to me in speaking of the ministers of the holy Church, to the effect that You would speak to me more distinctly, in some other place, of the sins which they commit today; wherefore if it should please Your goodness to tell me aught of this matter, I will gladly hear it, so as to have material for increasing my grief, compassion, and anxious desire for their salvation. For I remember that You said that on account of the endurance and tears, the grief and sweat and prayers of Your servants, You would reform the holy church and comfort her with good and holy pastors. I ask You this in order that these sentiments may increase in me."

109  Then the eternal God, turning the eye of His mercy upon this soul, not despising her desire, but granting her requests, proceeded to satisfy the last petition, which she had made concerning His promise, saying, "O best beloved and dearest daughter, I will fulfill your desire in this request in order that, on your side, you may not sin through ignorance or negligence. For a fault of yours would be more serious and worthy of graver reproof now than before, because you have learned more of My truth. Wherefore, apply yourself attentively to pray for all rational creatures, for the mystical body of the holy Church, and for those friends whom I have given you, whom you love with particular love, and be careful not to be negligent in giving them the benefit of your prayers and the example of your life and the teaching of your words, reproving vice and encouraging virtue according to your power.

"Concerning the supports which I have given you, of whom you did speak to Me, know that you are, in truth, a means by which they may each receive, according to their needs and fitness. And as I, your Creator, grant you the opportunity, for without Me you can do nothing, I will fulfill your desires, but do not you fail, or they either, in your hope in Me. My Providence will never fail you, and every man, if he is humble, shall receive that which he is fit to receive and every minister that which I have given him to administer, each in his own way, according to what he has received and will receive from My goodness."

# 45

# BARDUCCIO DI PIERO CANIGIANI, *LETTER*

Barduccio di Piero Canigiani was a follower of Saint Catherine of Siena, who died in 1380. On her death, he wrote this letter to Sister Catherine Petriboni in the monastery of San Piero a Monticelli near Florence.

Dearest Mother in Christ Jesus, and Sister in the holy memory of our blessed mother Catherine, I, Barduccio, a wretched and guilty sinner, recommend myself to your holy prayers as a feeble infant, orphaned by the death of so great a mother.[1] I received your letter and read it with much pleasure, and communicated it to my afflicted mothers here, who, supremely grateful for your great charity and tender love towards them, recommend themselves greatly, for their part, to your prayers, and beg you to recommend them to the prioress and all the sisters that they may be ready to do all that may be pleasing to God concerning themselves and you. But since you, as a beloved and faithful daughter, desire to know the end of our common mother, I am constrained to satisfy your desire, and although I know myself to be but little fitted to give such a narration, I will write in any case what my feeble eyes have seen, and what the dull senses of my soul have been able to comprehend.

This blessed virgin and mother of thousands of souls, at about the feast of the Circumcision,[2] began to feel so great a change both in soul and body that she was obliged to alter her mode of life, the action of taking food for her sustenance becoming so loathsome to her that it was only with the greatest difficulty that she could force herself to take any, and, when she did so, she swallowed nothing of the substance of the food, but had the habit of rejecting it. Moreover, not one drop of water could she swallow for refreshment, from which came to her a most violent and tedious thirst, and so great an inflammation of her throat that her breath seemed to be fire, with all which, however, she remained in very good health, robust and fresh as usual. In these conditions we reached Sexagesima Sunday,[3] when, about the hour of vespers,[4] at the time of her prayer, she had so violent a stroke that from that day onwards she was no longer in health. Towards the night of the following Monday, just after I had written a letter, she had another stroke so terrific that we all mourned her as dead, remaining under it for a long time without giving any sign of life. Then, rising, she stood for an equal space of time, and did

---

1   Catherine of Siena had had no biological children.
2   January 1, the day commemorating the circumcision of Christ.
3   The second Sunday before the beginning of Lent (the 40 days preceding Easter).
4   Evening worship service.

not seem the same person as she who had fallen. From that hour began new travail and bitter pains in her body, and, Lent having arrived, she began, in spite of her infirmity, to give herself with such application of mind to prayer that the frequency of the humble sighs and sorrowful plaints which she exhaled from the depth of her heart appeared to us a miracle. I think, too, that you know that her prayers were so fervent that one hour spent in prayer by her reduced that dear tender frame to greater weakness than would be suffered by one who persists for two whole days in prayer. Meanwhile, every morning, after communion, she arose from the earth in such a state that anyone who had seen her would have thought her dead, and was thus carried back to bed. Thence, after an hour or two, she would arise afresh, and we would go to Saint Peter's, although a good mile distant, where she would place herself in prayer, so remaining until vespers, finally returning to the house so worn out that she seemed a corpse. These were her exercises up till the third Sunday in Lent, when she finally succumbed, conquered by the innumerable sufferings, which daily increased and consumed her body, and the infinite afflictions of the soul which she derived from the consideration of the sins which she saw being committed against God and from the dangers ever more grave to which she knew the Holy Church to be exposed, on account of which she remained greatly overcome, and both internally and externally tormented. She lay in this state for eight weeks, unable to lift her head, and full of intolerable pains, from the soles of her feet to the crown of her head, to such an extent that she would often say, "These pains are truly physical, but not natural; for it seems that God has given permission to the devils to torment this body at their pleasure." And, in truth, it evidently was so, for, if I were to attempt to explain the patience which she practiced under this terrible and unheard-of agony, I would fear to injure, by my explanations, facts which cannot be explained. This only will I say: every time that a new torment came upon her, she would joyously raise her eyes and her heart to God and say, "Thanks to You, O eternal Spouse, for granting such graces afresh every day to me, Your miserable and most unworthy hand-maid!" In this way her body continued to consume itself until the Sunday before the Ascension. But by that time it was reduced to such a state that it seemed like a corpse in a picture, though I do not speak of the face, which remained ever angelical and breathed forth devotion, but of the bosom and limbs, in which nothing could be seen but the bones, covered by the thinnest skin, and so feeble was she from the waist downwards that she could not move herself, even a little, from one side to another. In the night preceding the aforesaid Sunday, about two hours or more before dawn, a great change was produced in her, and we thought that she was approaching the end. The whole family was then called around her, and she, with singular humility and devotion, made signs to those who were standing near that she desired to receive Holy Absolution for her faults and the pains due to them, and so it was done. After which she became gradually reduced to such a state that we could observe no other movement than her breathing, continuous, sad, and feeble. On account of this it seemed right to give her extreme unction,[5] which our abbot of Sant' Antimo did, while she lay as it were deprived of feeling. After this unction she began altogether to change, and to make various signs with her head and her arms as if to show that she was suffering from grave assaults of demons, and remained in this calamitous state for an hour and a half, half of which time having been passed in silence, she began to say, "I have sinned! Oh Lord, have mercy on me!" And this, as I believe, she repeated more than 60 times, raising each time her right arm, and then letting it fall and strike the bed. Then, changing her words, she said as many times again, but without moving her arms, "Holy God, have mercy on me!" Finally she employed the remainder of the above-mentioned time with many other formulas of prayer, both humble and devout, expressing various acts of virtue, after which her face suddenly changed from gloom to angelic light, and her tearful and clouded eyes became serene and joyous, in such a manner that I could not doubt that, like one saved from a deep sea, she was restored to herself, which cir-

---

5   The final priestly ritual for a dying person.

cumstance greatly mitigated the grief of her sons and daughters who were standing around in the affliction you can imagine. Catherine had been lying on the bosom of Mother Alessia and now succeeded in rising and, with a little help, began to sit up, leaning against the same mother. In the meantime we had put before her eyes a pious picture, containing many relics and various pictures of the saints. She, however, fixed her eyes on the image of the cross set in it, and began to adore it, explaining in words certain of her most profound feelings of the goodness of God, and while she prayed, she accused herself in general of all her sins in the sight of God, and, in particular, said, "It is my fault, O eternal Trinity, that I have offended You so miserably with my negligence, ignorance, ingratitude, and disobedience, and many other defects. Wretch that I am! For I have not observed Your commandments, either those which are given in general to all, or those which Your goodness laid upon me in particular! Oh mean creature that I am!" Saying this, she struck her breast, repeating her confession, and continued, "I have not observed Your precept, with which You commanded me to seek always to give You honor, and to spend myself in labors for my neighbor, while I, on the contrary, have fled from labors, especially where they were necessary. Did You not command me, oh, my God! to abandon all thought of myself and to consider solely the praise and glory of Your Name in the salvation of souls, and with this food alone, taken from the table of the most holy Cross, to comfort myself? But I have sought my own consolation. You always invited me to bind myself to You alone by sweet, loving, and fervent desires, by tears and humble and continuous prayers for the salvation of the whole world and for the reformation of the holy Church, promising me that, on account of them, You would use mercy with the world, and give new beauty to Your Spouse. But I, wretched one, have not corresponded with Your desire, but have remained asleep in the bed of negligence. Oh, unhappy that I am! You have placed me in charge of souls, assigning to me so many beloved sons that I would love them with singular love and direct them to You by the way of Life,

but I have been to them nothing but a mirror of human weakness; I have had no care of them; I have not helped them with continuous and humble prayer in Your presence, nor have I given them sufficient examples of the good life or the warnings of salutary doctrine. Oh, mean creature that I am! With how little reverence have I received Your innumerable gifts, the graces of such sweet torments and labors which it pleased You to accumulate on this fragile body, nor have I endured them with that burning desire and ardent love with which You sent them to me. Alas! oh, my Love, through Your excessive goodness You chose me as Your spouse, from the beginning of my childhood, but I was not faithful enough; in fact, I was unfaithful to You, because I did not keep my memory faithful to You alone and to Your most high benefits; nor have I fixed my intelligence on the thought of them only or disposed my will to love You immediately with all its strength." Of these and many other similar things did that pure dove accuse herself, rather, as I think, for our example than for her own need, and then, turning to the priest, said, "For the love of the crucified Christ, absolve me of all these sins which I have confessed in the presence of God, and of all the others which I cannot remember." That done, she asked again for the plenary indulgence,[6] saying that it had been granted her by Pope Gregory and Pope Urban, saying this as one as hungered for the blood of Christ. So I did what she asked, and she, keeping her eyes ever fixed on the crucifix, began to adore it afresh with the greatest devotion, and to say certain very profound things which I, for my sins, was not worthy to understand, and also on account of the grief with which I was laboring and the anguish with which her throat was oppressed, which was so great that she could hardly utter her words, while we, placing our ears to her mouth, were able to catch one or two now or again, passing them on from one to the other. After this she turned to certain of her sons, who had not been present at a memorable discourse which, many days previously, she had made to the whole family, showing us the way of salvation and perfection, and laying upon each of us the particular task

---

6   A full remission of sins which would keep Catherine in purgatory.

which he was to perform after her death. She now did the same to these others, begging most humbly pardon of all for the slight care which she seemed to have had of our salvation. Then she said certain things to Lucio and to another, and finally to me, and then turned herself immediately to prayer.

Oh! had you seen with what humility and reverence she begged and received many times the blessing of her most sorrowful mother,[7] all that I can say is that it was a bitter sweet to her. How full of tender affection was the spectacle of the mother, recommending herself to her blessed child, and begging her to obtain a particular grace from God—namely, that in these melancholy circumstances she might not offend Him. But all these things did not distract the holy virgin from the fervor of her prayer; and, approaching her end, she began to pray especially for the Catholic Church, for which she declared she was giving her life. She prayed again for Pope Urban VI, whom she resolutely confessed to be the true pope,[8] and strengthened her sons never to hesitate to give their life for that truth. Then, with the greatest fervor, she asked all her beloved children whom the Lord had given her to love Him alone, repeating many of the words which our Savior used when He recommended the disciples to the Father, praying with such affection that, at hearing her, not only our hearts, but the very stones might have been broken. Finally, making the sign of the cross, she blessed us all, and thus contin-

ued in prayer to the end of her life for which she had so longed, saying, "You, O Lord, call me, and I come to You, not through my merits, but through Your mercy alone, which I ask of You, in virtue of Your blood!" and many times she called out, "Blood, blood!" Finally, after the example of the Savior, she said, "Father, into Your Hands I commend my soul and my spirit," and thus sweetly, with a face all shining and angelical, she bent her head, and gave up the ghost.

Her death occurred on the Sunday at the hour of Sext,[9] but we kept her unburied until the hour of Compline[10] on Tuesday, without any odor being perceptible, her body remaining so pure, intact, and fragrant, that her arms, her neck, and her legs remained as flexible as if she were still alive. During those three days the body was visited by crowds of people, and lucky he thought himself who was able to touch it. Almighty God also worked many miracles in that time, which in my hurry I omit. Her tomb is visited devoutly by the faithful, like those of the other holy bodies which are in Rome, and Almighty God is granting many graces in the name of His blessed spouse, and I do not doubt that there will be many more, and we are made great by hearing of them. I say no more. Recommend me to the prioress and all the sisters, for I have, at present, the greatest need of the help of prayer. May Almighty God preserve you and help you to grow in His grace.

---

7   With whom Catherine had had very great conflicts over whether Catherine would marry; Catherine insisted on not doing so.
8   Urban VI (1378-89) was the first of the Italian line of popes in the Great Schism. A rival line of popes was established at Avignon.
9   A point in the monastic schedule of prayer: about noon.
10  A point in the monastic schedule of prayer: after sunset.

# 46

# Petrarch,
## *Letters of Familiar Intercourse*

Francesco Petrarch (1304-74) was perhaps the best known poet of his time. He wrote in Italian and, especially, in Latin. Born in Italy, he spent some of his early years at Avignon, the papal residence in southern France. Some of his *Letters of Familar Intercourse*, written in Latin, appear below.

---

### 46.1
#### TO HIS FRIEND SOCRATES,[1]

What now, brother? We have tried almost everything, and nowhere have we found peace. When may we hope for that, and where shall we seek it? Time, as the saying goes, has slipped between our fingers. Our early hopes are buried with our friends. The year 1348[2] has left us solitary and bereaved and has taken from us what all the wealth of Ormus and of Ind could never replace.

Such final losses are irreparable, and the wounds inflicted by death can never be healed. There is but one source of consolation; we shall soon follow those who have gone before. How long we must wait we do not know. But this we do know; it cannot be for long, and the delay, however short, will not be without its trials. Yet let us, here at the outset at least, refrain from lamentation.

I do not know, brother, what anxieties are weighing upon you or what your present preoccupations may be. As for me, I am making up my bundles and, as those on the verge of departure are wont to do, I am trying to decide what to take with me, what to distribute among my friends, and what to throw into the fire. At any rate, I have nothing to sell. I possess, or rather am burdened by, more than I supposed. I found, for example, a vast store of scattered and neglected writings of different kinds in the house. I have laboriously exhumed boxes, buried in dust, and bundles of manuscript, half-destroyed by time. The importunate mouse, as well as the insatiable bookworm, have plotted against me, and, a devotee of Pallas,[3] I have been entangled in the toils of Pallas's enemy, the spider. There is, however, no obstacle which may not be overcome by persistent effort. Surrounded by the confused masses of letters and manuscripts I began, following my first impulse, to consign everything to the flames,

---

1  This is Petrarch's pet name for his contemporary friend, Ludovico.
2  The year of the Black Death.
3  Another name for Athena, Greek goddess of wisdom. She was challenged to a weaving contest by Arachne; when the two performed equally well, Arachne hanged herself, whereupon Athena turned Arachne into a spider.

with a view to escaping from the inglorious task of assorting the papers. Then, as one thought springs from another, it occurred to me that, like a traveler weary by reason of the long road, I might well look back as from a height, and step by step review the history of my younger days.

This counsel prevailed. It seemed to me, if not an exalted undertaking, at least not a disagreeable one, to recall the shifting feelings and sentiments of earlier times. But, taking up the disordered papers at random, I was astonished to see how distorted and blurred the past appeared to me, not of course that it, but rather that my mental vision, had changed, so that I hardly recognized my former self. Still, some things that I happened upon called up pleasant reminiscences of long ago. Some of the productions moved with the free step of prose, some were held in check by Homeric reins (I have rarely used those of Isocrates), others, destined to charm the ear of the people, also obeyed their own appropriate laws. The last mentioned style of verse, revived, it is said, not many generations ago, among the Sicilians, spread in a short time throughout Italy, and even beyond.[4] This kind of poetry was held in great repute by the earliest writers among the Greeks and Romans, and the common people of Rome and Athens are said to have been accustomed to the rhythmical lyrics only.

This chaotic medley kept me busy for several days, and, although I felt the potent charm and natural partiality which are associated with all one's own productions, the love for my more important works finally got the upper hand. These had suffered a long interruption and were still uncompleted, although they were anxiously awaited by not a few. The shortness of life was borne in upon me. I feared, I must confess, its snares and pitfalls. What indeed is more transient than life, and what more certain than death? It occurred to me to ask what foundation I had laid, and what would remain to me for all my toil and vigils. It seemed a rash, an insane thing, to have undertaken such long and enduring labors in the course of so brief and uncertain an existence, and thus to scatter my

talents, which would scarcely suffice for the successful accomplishment of a single undertaking. Moreover, as you well know, another task awaits me more glorious than these in proportion as actions merit more enduring praise than words.

But why dwell longer upon this matter? It will perhaps seem incredible to you, but it is none the less true, that I committed to Vulcan[5] for correction a thousand or more scattered poems of all kinds and letters of friendly intercourse, not because I found nothing in them to my liking, but because they involved more work than pleasure. I did this, however, with a sigh, as I am not ashamed to confess. But with a mind so occupied it was necessary to resort even to somewhat harsh measures for relief, just as an overburdened ship must sometimes be lightened by the sacrifice of valuable cargo.

After disposing of these I noticed, lying in a corner, a few papers which had been preserved rather by accident than intention, or had, at some former time, been copied by my assistants, and so in one way or the other had escaped the perils of advancing age. I say a few—I fear they will seem a great many to the reader, and far too numerous to the copyist. I was more indulgent to these, and allowed them to live, not so much on account of their worthiness as of my convenience, for they did not involve any additional labor of my own. As I considered them with regard to the natural inclinations of two of my friends, the prose fell to you, while the verse I decided to dedicate to our friend Barbato. I recollected that this used to be your preference, and that I had promised to follow your wishes. My mood was such that I was on the point of destroying everything which I came across, not even sparing those writings just mentioned, when you both seemed to appear to me, one on my right and one on my left, and, grasping my hands, you admonished me in a friendly manner not to do violence at once to my good faith and your anticipations. This was the chief reason why these were spared, for otherwise, believe me, they would have gone up in smoke like the rest.

---

4   In this and the previous sentence Petrarch refers to ancient forms of verse.
5   The Roman god of, among other things, fire.

You will read your portion of what remains, such as it is, not only patiently, but even eagerly. I do not venture to repeat the boast of Apuleius of Madaura, "Reader, you have but to listen to be charmed,"[6] for on what grounds could I venture to promise pleasure to the reader? But, you at least will read the letters, my good Socrates, and, as you are very fond of your friends, you may discover some charm in them. Your partiality for the author will make his style pleasing (indeed what beauty of style is likely to be perceived by an unfriendly judge?); it is vain to adorn what already delights. If anything gratifies you in these letters of mine, I freely concede that it is not really mine but yours—that is to say, the credit is due not to my ability but to your good will. You will find no great eloquence or vigor of expression in them. Indeed I do not possess these powers, and if I did, in ever so high a degree, there would be no place for them in this kind of composition. Even Cicero,[7] who was renowned for these abilities, does not manifest them in his letters, nor even in his treatises, where, as he himself says, the language is characterized by a certain evenness and moderation. In his orations, on the other hand, he displayed extraordinary powers, pouring out a clear and rapid stream of eloquence. This oratorical style Cicero used frequently for his friends, and against his enemies and those of the republic. Cato[8] resorted to it often on behalf of others, and for himself four and forty times. In this mode of composition I am wholly inexperienced, for I have been far away from the responsibilities of state. And while my reputation may sometimes have been assailed by slight murmurs, or secret whisperings, I have so far never suffered any attack in the courts which I must avenge or parry. Hence, as it is not my profession to use my weapons of speech for the defense of others, I do not frequent the tribunals, nor have I ever learned to loan my tongue. I have, indeed, a deep repugnance for such a life, for I am by nature a lover of silence and solitude, an enemy of the courts, and a condemner of wealth. It

was fortunate for me that I was freed from the necessity of resorting to a weapon which I might not have been able to use if I had tried. I have therefore made no attempt to employ an oratorical style, which, even if it had been at my disposal, would have been uncalled for in this instance. But you will accept this homely and familiar language in the same friendly spirit as you do the rest, and take in good part a style well adapted to the sentiments we are accustomed to express in ordinary conversation.

All my critics, however, are not like you, for they do not all think the same, nor do they all love me as you do. But how can I hope to please everybody, when I have always striven to gratify a few only? There are three poisons which kill sound criticism: love, hate, and envy. Beware lest through too much love you should make public what might better be kept concealed. As you are guided by love, so others may be influenced by other passions. Between the blindness of love and that of jealousy there is indeed a great difference in origin, but not always in effect. Hate, to which I have assigned a middle place, I neither merit nor fear. Still it can easily be so arranged that you may keep and read my trifling productions for your own exclusive pleasure, thinking of nothing except the incidents in our lives and those of our friends which they recall. Should you do this, it would be most gratifying to me. In this way your request will have been satisfied and my reputation will be safe. Beyond this I do not deceive myself with the vain hope of favor. For how can we imagine even a friend, if he is not an alter ego, reading without weariness such a mass of miscellaneous and conflicting recollections? There is no unity in the themes or composition of the letters, and with the various matters treated went varying moods, which were rarely happy and usually despondent. Epicurus,[9] a philosopher held in disrepute among the vulgar but esteemed by those better able to judge, confined his correspondence to two or three persons— Idomeneus, Polyaenus, and Metrodorus. Cicero wrote

---

6  The line is from the ancient Roman writer's *The Golden Ass*.
7  Roman politician, model Latin prose stylist, and orator of the first century BC.
8  I.e., Cato the elder, the ancient Roman politician and writer.
9  Greek philosopher of the Hellenistic period.

to hardly more, to Brutus, Atticus, and the other two Ciceros, his brother and son. Seneca[10] wrote to few except his friend Lucilius. It obviously renders felicitous letter-writing a simple matter if we know the character of our correspondent and get used to his particular mind, so that we can judge what he will be glad to hear and what we may properly communicate. But my lot has been a very different one, for heretofore almost my whole life has been passed in journeying from place to place. I might compare my wanderings with those of Ulysses;[11] certainly were we only on the same plane in reputation and in the fame of our adventures, I might claim that he had not wandered farther or been cast upon more distant shores than I. He was already well advanced in years when he left his native land, and, since nothing is long in our lives, the experiences of his old age were necessarily brief indeed. I, on the other hand, was conceived and born in exile, costing my mother such grievous pangs, and in such critical circumstances, that not only the midwives but the physicians long believed her to be dead. Thus I began to encounter dangers before I was born, and attained the threshold of life under the auspices of death. The event is commemorated by the no means insignificant city of Arezzo, to which my father, driven from his country, had taken refuge, together with many another worthy man.[12] Thence I was taken in my seventh month and carried about all over Tuscany[13] by a certain sturdy youth, who wrapped me up in a cloth, just as Metabus did Camilla,[14] and bore me suspended from a knotty staff, so as not to injure my tender body by any rough contact. But once, in crossing the Arno (I delight to recall with you the beginnings of my tribulations), his horse stumbled and he fell into the water, and while striving to save the burden entrusted to him, he nearly sacrificed his own life in the raging flood.

Our wanderings through Tuscany finally ended at Pisa. From here, however, I was dragged away again, in my seventh year, and in our journey to France by sea we were wrecked by winter storms, not far from Marseilles, and I was on the verge of being summoned away anew from the vestibule of life. But I am straying from my subject. From then until now I have had little or no opportunity to stop and take breath. How many and how various the dangers and apprehensions I have suffered in my migrations no one, after myself, better knows than you. Hence, I have felt free to recall these events, so that you may keep in mind that I was born among perils and among perils have grown old, if old I am, and there are not worse trials ahead. Although similar vicissitudes may be common to everyone entering this life, since existence is a warfare—no more, a battle—each nevertheless has his peculiar experiences, and the fighting differs greatly in kind. Each has his own burdens to bear, but it still makes a great difference what these burdens are.

Well then, to return to the matter in hand, since amid the tempests of life I have never for long cast anchor in any one port, I have naturally made innumerable acquaintances. I do not know many true friends, for friends are not only exceedingly few, but difficult to distinguish. It has fallen to my lot, in consequence, to write to a great many who differed so widely from one another in mind and condition that on re-reading my letters it sometimes seemed to me as if I had said in one precisely the opposite from what I had in another. Yet anyone who has been in a similar position will readily admit that I was almost forced into such contradictions. The first care indeed in writing is to consider to whom the letter is to be sent; then we may judge what to say and how to say it. We address a strong man in one way and a weak one in another. The inexperienced youth and the old man

---

10  Roman philosopher and writer of the second century.

11  The Roman term for Homer's character, Odysseus, who wandered for 10 years on his way home from the Trojan war.

12  The authorities at Arezzo had decreed that no changes be made to the otherwise undistinguished house in which Petrarch had been born.

13  A region of Italy north of Rome.

14  Petrarch refers to a legend recounted in Vergil's *Aeneid* (first century BC), in which Metabus, fleeing his pursuers, bound his infant daughter Camilla to a staff and hurled the staff, and Camilla with it, across a river. Metabus himself was then able to cross.

who has fulfilled the duties of life, he who is puffed up with prosperity and he who is stricken with adversity, the scholar distinguished in literature and the man incapable of grasping anything beyond the commonplace: each must be treated according to his character or position. There are infinite varieties among men; minds are no more alike than faces. And as the same stomach does not always relish the same kind of food, the same mind is not always to be fed upon the same kind of writing. So the task becomes a double one, for not only have we to consider the person to whom we propose to write, but how those things we are planning to say are likely to affect him when he reads them. Owing to these difficulties I have often been forced into apparent contradictions. And in order that unfavorable critics may not turn this against me, I have relied in a measure upon the kind aid of the flames for safety, and for the rest, upon your keeping the letters secret and suppressing my name.

But friends are lynx-eyed, and nothing is likely to escape them; so that if you cannot keep the letters from the few who still remain, be sure to urge them to destroy immediately any of my communications that they may possess, lest they be disturbed by any changes which I have made in the words or matter. These changes are due to the fact that, since it never occurred to me that you would ask or that I would consent to have the letters brought together in a single collection, I was accustomed, in order to avoid labor, to repeat now and then something I had said in a previous letter, using my own as my own, as Terence says. Now that letters sent off years ago to the most distant regions are brought together at once in a single place, it is easy to perceive deformities in the whole body which were not apparent in the separate parts. Phrases which pleased when they occurred but once in a letter, begin to annoy one when frequently repeated in the same collection. Accordingly they must be retained in one and expunged from the others. Many things, too, which related to everyday cares and which deserved mention when I wrote, would now weary even the most eager reader, and were therefore omitted. I recollect that Seneca laughed at Cicero for including trivial matters in his letters, and yet I am much more prone in my epistles to follow Cicero's example than Seneca's. Seneca, indeed, gathered into his letters pretty much all the moral reflections which he had published in his various books. Cicero, on the other hand, treats philosophical subjects in his books, but fills his letters with miscellaneous news and the gossip of the day. Let Seneca think as he likes about this; as for me, I must confess that I find Cicero's letters very agreeable reading. They relax the tension produced by weighty matters, which if long continued strains the mind, though if occasionally interrupted it becomes a source of pleasure.

I cannot sufficiently wonder at the boldness of Sidonius,[15] although I may be a bit rash myself in denouncing this boldness when I do not very well understand his sarcasms, either because of my slow wit or his obscure style, or, as is not impossible, by reason of some error in the text. One thing, however, is clear; Cicero is ridiculed, and by a Sidonius! What liberty! or effrontery, I would say, did I not fear to exasperate those whom I have already offended by calling him bold. Here is one of the Latin people who finds it in his heart to attack Cicero. Nor does he speak of some single weakness, for if that were all I should have to ask pardon for both Seneca and myself. Human frailty, indeed, can hardly escape criticism. But this Sidonius has dared to make sport of Cicero's eloquence, of his whole style and his method in general. This Avernian[16] orator does not simply imagine himself, as he says, a brother of the Latin orator, which would be audacious enough, but he assumes the role of a rival, and, what is worse, of a scoffer. He would deprive him of the renown which all but a few of his contemporaries and fellow-citizens unanimously concede to him: even those few were doubtless warped in their judgment and goaded on by envy, the constant attendant upon contemporary fame. But neither time nor place afford any extenua-

---

15  Sidonius Apollinaris, Roman of the fifth century BC, author of various works. It seems that Petrarch is working here from a corrupt version of Sidonius's letters.
16  The Avernus was a putrid lake in Italy, which, in ancient Roman legend, lay at the entrance of the land of the dead. Sidonius also became bishop of Clermont (in modern France), which was known as "Averni" in ancient times.

tion in the case of Sidonius. Consequently I wonder more and more what manner of person this was who thus attacked the undoubted prince of orators, although he was himself a disciple of oratory, and belonged to another age, and was born in another land. Upon turning the whole matter over in my mind, I find it impossible to accept in the case of so learned a man the excuse of ignorance, and to ascribe his perverted opinions to a weakness of the head rather than of the heart. I may be mistaken in this matter, as in many others, but if I am I rejoice that I am mistaken in company with many, and those by far the most distinguished, judges in believing that Cicero leaves all fault-finders far behind, and that to him belongs the palm for prose eloquence. From this point of view the moral and intellectual perversity of those who deny him preeminence becomes as clear as day.

Sidonius brings forward, it is true, a certain Julius Titianus and certain Frontoniani, of whom I have never heard, as the authorities for his sarcasms. To these, and to all those holding such views, I make one and the same reply, namely, that Seneca was right when he said, "Whatever strength or advantage Roman eloquence may have to oppose to the arrogance of Greece was developed by Cicero." Moreover, Quintilian,[17] among the many glorious things which he says of Cicero, well observes, "He was sent by the special gift of providence, with such extraordinary powers that in him eloquence might manifest all her resources." And after many proofs of this, he continues,

> It was therefore but right that his contemporaries should declare with one accord that he reigned supreme in the courts. With succeeding generations it has come to pass that Cicero is no longer regarded as the name of a man, but of eloquence itself. To him, therefore, let us look, placing him before us as our model. When a student comes to admire Cicero greatly, he may know that he is making progress.

I hold moreover that, conversely, it is quite true that one to whom Cicero's style is displeasing either knows nothing of the highest eloquence or hates it.

Anxious as I was to hasten on, I could not pass over this calumny altogether. To return again to the letters, you will find many written in a familiar style to friends, including yourself, sometimes referring to matters of public or private interest, sometimes relating to bereavements, which form (alas!) an ever recurring theme, or to other matters which circumstances brought into prominence. I have discussed almost nothing else, except when I have spoken of my state of mind, or have imparted some bit of news to my friends. I approve, you see, what Cicero says in his first letter to his brother, that it is the proper aim of a letter to inform the one to whom it is addressed of something of which he was ignorant. These considerations account for the title which I have selected. For, on thinking over the matter, although the simple rubric "epistles" was quite appropriate, I rejected it, both because many older writers had chosen it, and because I myself had applied it to the verses to my friends which I mentioned above, and consequently disliked to resort to it a second time. So I chose a new name, and entitled the volume *Letters of Familiar Intercourse*, letters, that is, in which there is little anxious regard to style, but where homely matters are treated in a homely manner. Sometimes, when it was not inappropriate, there may be a bit of simple narration or a few moral reflections, such as Cicero was accustomed to introduce into his letters.

To say so much about a small matter is justified by the fear of censorious critics, who, instead of producing work of their own to be judged, set themselves up as the judges of others' talents—a most audacious and impudent set, whose only safety lies in holding their tongues. Sitting upon the shore with folded hands, we are safe in expressing any opinions we please upon the art of navigation. By keeping the letters secret you will at least shield these crude productions, that I have carelessly thrown off, from such impudence. If I ever put the last touches to this work, I will send you, not a Phidian Minerva,[18] as Cicero

---

17    Quintilian (first century) was regarded as an authoritative teacher of, and writer on, rhetoric.

18    Phidias was the sculptor of the fifth century BC who made the renowned statue of Athena (the Roman Minerva) for the Parthenon in Athens.

says, but an image, in some sort, of my mind and character, hewn out with great labor. When it reaches you, place it in some safe niche.

So far, so good. The next matter I would gladly say nothing about, but a serious ailment is not easily concealed; its very symptoms betray it. I am ashamed of a life which has lapsed into weakness. As you will see, and as the order of the letters testifies, the language of my earlier years was sober and strong, betokening a valiant heart. I not only stood firm myself, but often consoled others. The succeeding letters become day by day weaker and more dispirited, nor do the lamentations with which they are filled have a sufficiently manly tone. It is these that I would ask you to guard with special care. For what would others say to sentiments which I myself cannot re-read without a blush? Was I indeed a man in my youthful days, only to become a child when I reached maturity?

With a disingenuousness which I reprehend and deplore, I conceived the plan of changing the order of the letters, or concealing from you entirely those that I condemn. Neither subterfuge would have deceived you, since you possess the originals of these melancholy missives, and are aware of the year and day upon which each was written. Consequently, I must arm myself with excuses. I have grown weary in the long and arduous battle. While courage and valor stood by me, I made a stand myself and encouraged others to resist. But when, by reason of the strength of the enemy and the fierceness of his onset, I began to lose my footing, and my spirits began to droop, that fine, bold tone promptly deserted me, and I descended to those weak laments which are so displeasing. My affection for my friends may perhaps extenuate my offense, for while they remained unharmed I never groaned on account of any wound of fortune. But when almost all of them were hurried away in a single great catastrophe, nay when the whole world seemed about to perish, it would have been inhuman, rather than courageous, to remain unmoved. Before that who ever heard me complain of exile, disease, litigation, elections, or the whirl of public affairs? Who ever heard a tearful regret for my father's house, for lost fortune, diminished fame, squandered money, or absent friends? Cicero, however, shows such a want of manliness in the way he writes of such grievances that his sentiments often offend as much as his style delights me. Add to this his litigious epistles, and the complaints and insults which, with the utmost fickleness, he directs against distinguished men whom he himself has but just been lauding to the skies! On reading these I was so shocked and discomposed that I could not refrain in my irritation from writing to him and pointing out what offended me in his writings, as if he were a friend and contemporary. Ignoring the space of time which separates us, I addressed him with a familiarity springing from my sympathy with his genius. This letter suggested others of the kind. For instance, on re-reading, after some years, Seneca's tragedy, *Octavia*, I felt the same impulse to write to him, and later I wrote, on various themes, to Varro, Vergil,[19] and others. A few of these, which I have inserted in the latter part, produce the utmost astonishment in the mind of the reader, were he not forewarned. The rest I burned up in that general holocaust noted above.

Just as Cicero was absorbed in his trials, so was I at one time in mine. But today—that you may know my present temper—it would not be inappropriate to attribute to me that serenity which comes, as Seneca says, even to the most untried, the serenity of despair itself. Why indeed fear, when one has so many times striven with death itself? "The one safety the defeated have is to hope for safety."[20] You will see me work and speak with growing courage from day to day. If I should hit upon any subject worthy of my pen, the style itself will be more vigorous. Many themes will undoubtedly offer themselves. My writing and my life, I foresee, will come to an end together.

But while my other works are finished, or bid fair to be, these letters, which I began in an irregular fashion in my early youth, and am now bringing together in my old age and arranging in a volume—this work the love of my friends will never permit me to finish,

---

19   Varro: Roman writer. For Vergil, see n 14.
20   Quoting Vergil's *Aeneid*, where the Trojan Aeneas describes how the Greeks destroyed Troy.

since I must conscientiously reply to their messages, nor can I ever persuade them to accept the often repeated excuse of my other occupations. When you shall learn that I have at last begged to be freed from that duty, and have brought this work to an end, then you may know that I am dead and freed from all life's burdens. In the meantime I shall continue to follow the path which I have entered upon, not looking for its end until darkness comes upon me. Pleasant work will take the place of repose with me. Moreover, having placed the weakest of my forces in the center, as orators and generals are accustomed to do, I shall take care that, as I showed a solid front in beginning my book, so my rear-guard too shall not be wanting in courage. Indeed, I may make better head against the attacks and buffets of fortune, thanks to a gradual process of hardening which has gone on through life. In short, although I dare not assert how I shall demean myself in the stress of circumstances, I am firmly resolved not to succumb to any trial hereafter. "Beneath the crash of worlds undaunted he appears." You may picture me thus armed with the good thoughts of Vergil and Horace,[21] which I used often to read and praise in my earlier years, and which, in my latter days of calamity, stern necessity has forced me to make my own.

My communion with you has been very pleasant, and I have, in my enjoyment, been led half unconsciously to prolong it. It brought back your face over land and sea, and kept you with me until evening. I took up my pen this morning, and the day and this letter are coming to an end together.

Well, this which I dedicate to you, my brother, is a fabric, so to speak, of many colored threads. But should I ever find a resting place, and the leisure I have always sought in vain (and there is the promise of such a change), I intend to weave for you a more worthy and certainly more uniform web. I should be glad to think that I am among the few who can promise and confer fame; but you can lift yourself into the light without my aid, borne on the wings of your own genius. However, if I am able to rise, in spite of all

the difficulties which beset me, you hereafter shall assuredly be my Idomeneus, my Atticus, and my Lucilius.

Farewell.

46.2

TO TOMASSO DA MESSINA:

It is hazardous to engage an enemy who longs rather for battle than for victory. You write to me of a certain old logician who has been greatly excited by my letter, as if I condemned his art. With a growl of rage, he loudly threatened to make war in turn upon our studies, in a letter for which, you say, you have waited many months in vain. Do not wait longer; believe me, it will never come. He retains some traces of decency, and this is a confession that he is ashamed of his style or an acknowledgment of his ignorance. The most implacable in contests with the tongue will not resort to the pen. They are reluctant to show how ill-armed they are, and so follow the Parthian[22] system of warfare, carried on during a rapid retreat, by letting fly a shower of winged words and committing their shafts to the wind.

It is foolhardy, as I have said, to accept an engagement with these fellows upon their own terms. It is indeed from the fighting itself that they derive their chief pleasure. Their object is not to discover the truth, but to prolong the argument. But you know Varro's proverb: "Through over-long contention the truth is lost." You need not fear, then, that these warriors will come out into the open fields of honest discussion, whether with tongue or pen. They belong to the class of whom Quintilian speaks in his *Institutes of Oratory*, whom one finds wonderfully warm in disputation, but once get them away from their caviling, they are as helpless, in a serious juncture, as certain small animals which are active enough in a narrow space, but are easily captured in a field. Hence their reluctance to engage in an open contest. As Quintilian goes on to say, their tergiversations indicate their weakness. They seek, like an indifferent runner, to escape by dodging.

---

21   Roman poet (first-century BC).
22   The Parthian empire was an opponent of the Roman.

This is what I would impress upon you, my friend; if you are seeking virtue or truth, avoid persons of that stripe altogether. But how shall we escape from these maniacs, if even the isles of the sea are not free from them? So neither Scylla nor Charybdis[23] has prevented this pest from finding its way into Sicily?[24] Nay, this ill is now rather peculiar to islands, as we shall find if we add the logicians of Britain to the new Cyclopes about Aetna.[25] Is this the ground of the striking similarity between Sicily and Britain, which I have seen mentioned in Pomponius Mela's *Cosmographia*?[26] I had thought that the resemblance lay in the situation of the countries, the almost triangular appearance of both, and perhaps in the perpetual contact which each enjoys with the surrounding sea. I never thought of logicians; I had heard of the Cyclopes, and then of the tyrants, both savage inhabitants. But I was unaware of the coming of this third race of monsters, armed with two-edged arguments, and fiercer than the burning shores of Taormina itself.

There is one thing which I myself long ago observed, and of which you now warn me anew. These logicians seek to cover their teachings with the splendor of Aristotle's name. They claim that Aristotle was accustomed to argue in the same way.[27] They would have some excuse, I readily confess, if they followed in the steps of illustrious leaders, for even Cicero says that it would give him pleasure to err with Plato, if err he must. But they all deceive themselves. Aristotle was a man of the most exalted genius, who not only discussed but wrote upon themes of the very highest importance. How can we otherwise explain so vast an array of works, involving such prolonged labor, and prepared with supreme care amid such serious preoccupations, especially those connected with the guardianship of his fortunate pupil,[28] and within the compass, too, of a life by no means long? (For he died at about 63, the age which all writers deem so unlucky.) Now why should these fellows diverge so widely from the path of their leader? Why is not the name of "Aristotelians" a source of shame to them rather than of satisfaction, for no one could be more utterly different from that great philosopher than a man who writes nothing, knows but little, and constantly indulges in much vain declamation? Who does not laugh at their trivial conclusions, with which, although educated men, they weary both themselves and others? They waste their whole lives in such contentions. Not only are they good for nothing else, but their perverted activity renders them actually harmful. Disputations such as they delight in are made a subject of mirth by Cicero and Seneca, in several passages. We find an example in the case of Diogenes,[29] whom a contentious logician addressed as follows: "What I am, you are not." Upon Diogenes conceding this, the logician added, "But I am a man." As this was not denied, the poor quibbler propounded the conclusion, "Therefore you are not a man." "The last statement is not true," Diogenes remarked, "but if you wish it to be true, begin with me in your major premise." Similar absurdities are common enough with them. What they hope to gain from their efforts, whether fame or amusement, or some light upon the way to live righteously and happily, they may know; to me, I confess, it is the greatest of mysteries. Money, certainly, does not appeal at least to noble minds as a worthy reward of study. It is for the mechanical trades to strive for lucre; the higher arts have a more generous end in view.

On hearing such things as these, those of whom we are speaking grow furious. Indeed the chatter of the disputatious man usually verges closely on anger. "So you set yourself up to condemn logic," they cry. Far from it; I know well in what esteem it was held by that sturdy and virile sect of philosophers, the Stoics,[30] whom our Cicero frequently mentions, especially in

---

23  Two monsters which, according to ancient legend, threatened sailors passing between Sicily and Italy.
24  Tomasso da Messina's name indicates an origin in Sicily.
25  The Cyclopes were, according to Greek legend, monsters who lived near Mount Aetna in Sicily.
26  The Roman writer Pomponius composed his *Cosmographia*, a work on geography, in the first century.
27  Aristotle (fourth century BC) composed works on logic much studied in the high and late Middle Ages.
28  Aristotle had for a time been the tutor of the young Alexander the Great.
29  Greek philosopher (fourth century BC).
30  A school of philosophy active in Greece and Rome.

his work *De Finibus*. I know that it is one of the liberal studies, a ladder for those who are striving upwards, and by no means a useless protection to those who are forcing their way through the thorny thickets of philosophy. It stimulates the intellect, points out the way of truth, shows us how to avoid fallacies, and finally, if it accomplishes nothing else, makes us ready and quick-witted.

All this I readily admit, but because a road is proper for us to traverse, it does not immediately follow that we should linger on it forever. No traveler, unless he be mad, will forget his destination on account of the pleasures of the way. His characteristic virtue lies, on the contrary, in reaching his goal as soon as possible, never halting on the road. And who of us is not a traveler? We all have our long and arduous journey to accomplish in a brief and untoward time—on a short, tempestuous, wintry day as it were. Dialectics[31] may form a portion of our road, but certainly not its end—it belongs to the morning of life, not to its evening. We may have done once with perfect propriety what it would be shameful to continue. If as mature men we cannot leave the schools of logic because we have found pleasure in them as boys, why should we blush to play odd and even, or prance upon a shaky reed, or be rocked again in the cradle of our childhood? Nature, with cunning artifice, escapes from dull monotony by her wondrous change of seasons, with their varying aspects. Shall we look for these alternations in the circuit of the year, and not in the course of a long life? The spring brings flowers and the new leaves of the trees, the summer is rich in its harvest, autumn in fruit, and then comes winter with its snows. In this order the changes are not only tolerable but agreeable. But if the order were to be altered, against the laws of nature, they would become distasteful. No one would suffer with equanimity the cold of winter in summer time, or a raging sun during the months where it does not belong.

Who would not scorn and deride an old man who sported with children, or marvel at a grizzled and gouty stripling? What is more necessary to our training than our first acquaintance with the alphabet itself, which serves as the foundation of all later studies? But, on the other hand, what could be more absurd than a grandfather still busy over his letters?

Use my arguments with the disciples of your ancient logician. Do not deter them from the study of logic; urge them rather to hasten through it to better things. Tell the old fellow himself that it is not the liberal arts which I condemn, but only hoary-headed children. Even as nothing is more disgraceful, as Seneca says, than an old man just beginning his alphabet, so there is no spectacle more unseemly than a person of mature years devoting himself to dialectics. But if your friend begins to vomit forth syllogisms, I advise you to take flight, bidding him argue with Enceladus.[32] Farewell.

46.3

TO MARCUS TULLIUS CICERO[33]:

If my earlier letter gave you offense—for, as you often have remarked, the saying of your contemporary in the Andria is a faithful one, that compliance begets friends, truth only hatred—you shall listen now to words that will soothe your wounded feelings and prove that the truth need not always be hateful. For, if censure that is true angers us, true praise, on the other hand, gives us delight.

You lived then, Cicero, if I may be permitted to say it, like a mere man, but spoke like an orator, wrote like a philosopher. It was your life that I criticized; not your mind, nor your tongue; for the one fills me with admiration, the other with amazement. And even in your life I feel the lack of nothing but stability, and the love of quiet that should go with your philosophic professions, and abstention from civil war, when liberty had been extinguished and the republic buried and its dirge sung.

See how different my treatment of you is from yours of Epicurus, in your works at large, and especially in the *De Finibus*. You are continually praising his life, but you ridicule his talents. I ridicule in you

31  The art of logical argumentation.
32  The most powerful of the giants who attacked the gods of Greek and Roman myth.
33  This *is* the Cicero of the first century BC.

nothing at all. Your life does awaken my pity, as I have said; but your talents and your eloquence call for nothing but congratulation. O great father of Roman eloquence! not I alone but all who deck themselves with the flowers of Latin speech render thanks unto you. It is from your wellsprings that we draw the streams that water our meadows. You, we freely acknowledge, are the leader who marshals us; yours are the words of encouragement that sustain us; yours is the light that illumines the path before us. In a word, it is under your auspices that we have attained to such little skill in this art of writing as we may possess.

You have heard what I think of your life and your genius. Are you hoping to hear of your books also— what fate has befallen them, how they are esteemed by the masses and among scholars? They still are in existence, glorious volumes, but we of today are too feeble a folk to read them, or even to be acquainted with their mere titles. Your fame extends far and wide; your name is mighty, and fills the ears of men, yet those who really know you are very few, be it because the times are unfavorable, or because men's minds are slow and dull, or, as I am the more inclined to believe, because the love of money forces our thoughts in other directions. Consequently, right in our own day, unless I am much mistaken, some of your books have disappeared, I fear beyond recovery. It is a great grief to me, a great disgrace to this generation, a great wrong done to posterity. The shame of failing to cultivate our own talents, thereby depriving the future of the fruits that they might have yielded, is not enough for us. We must waste and spoil, through our cruel and insufferable neglect, the fruits of your labors too, and of those of your fellows as well, for the fate that I lament in the case of your own books has befallen the works of many another illustrious man.

It is of yours alone, though, that I would speak now. Here are the names of those among them whose loss is most to be deplored: the *Republic*, the *Praise of Philosophy*, the treatises on the *Care of Property*, on the *Art of War*, on *Consolation*, on *Glory*, although in the case of this last my feeling is rather one of hopeful uncertainty than of certain despair. And then there are huge gaps in the volumes that have survived. It is as if indolence and oblivion had been worsted, in a great battle, but we had to mourn noble leaders slain, and others lost or maimed. This last indignity very many of your books have suffered, but more particularly the *Orator*, the *Academics*, and the *Laws*. They have come forth from the fray so mutilated and disfigured that it would have been better if they had perished outright.

Now, in conclusion, you will wish me to tell you something about the condition of Rome and the Roman Republic: the present appearance of the city and whole country, the degree of harmony that prevails, what classes of citizens possess political power, by whose hands and with what wisdom the reins of empire are swayed, and whether the Danube, the Ganges, the Ebro, the Nile, the Don, are our boundaries now, or whether in very truth the man has arisen who "bounds our empire by the ocean-stream, our fame by the stars of heaven," or "extends our rule beyond Garama and Ind," as your friend the Mantuan[34] has said. Of these and other matters of like nature I do not doubt you would very gladly hear. Your filial piety tells me so, your well-known love of country, which you cherished even to your own destruction.[35] But indeed it were better that I refrained. Trust me, Cicero, if you were to hear of our condition today you would be moved to tears, in whatever circle of heaven above, or Erebus below,[36] you may be dwelling. Farewell, forever.

Written in the world of the living, on the left bank of the Rhone, in Transalpine Gaul,[37] in the same year, but in the month of December, the nineteenth day.

---

34  I.e., Vergil, who was from the Italian town of Mantua.
35  Cicero virulently criticized the rising power of Marc Antony in the late Republic, for which he was put to death.
36  In Roman mythology, the portion of the land of the dead, which was below the earth, in which virtuous shades reside.
37  Petrarch was writing in the French city of Avignon.

# 47

# NICCOLÒ MACHIAVELLI, *THE PRINCE*

Niccolò Machiavelli (1469-1527) lived at a time when much of Italy was governed by independent city states. The governments of many of them had fallen into the hands of men who had seized or inherited power. Machiavelli himself served in the government of the republic of Florence, one of the most powerful of the city states, and was especially involved in its diplomatic and military affairs. However, Florence's defeat in 1512 brought the powerful Medici family to supreme power there, and Machiavelli was imprisoned and then exiled to a family farm, where he wrote *The Prince*, while he sought to re-enter the Florentine civil service. He attained that goal in a minor way soon before his death. *The Prince* is one of various works, ranging from drama to history, produced by Machiavelli.

---

### DEDICATION

To the Magnificent Lorenzo di Piero de Medici[1]:

It is customary for such as seek a prince's favor to present themselves before him with those things of theirs which they themselves most value, or in which they perceive him chiefly to delight. Accordingly, we often see horses, armor, cloth of gold, precious stones, and the like costly gifts offered to princes as worthy of their greatness. Desiring in like manner to approach your Magnificence with some token of my devotion, I have found among my possessions none that I so much prize and esteem as a knowledge of the actions of great men, acquired in the course of a long experience of modern affairs and a continual study of antiquity. Which knowledge most carefully and patiently pondered over and sifted by me, and now reduced to this little book, I send to your Magnificence. And

though I deem the work unworthy of your greatness, yet am I bold enough to hope that your courtesy will dispose you to accept it, considering that I can offer you no better gift than the means of mastering in a very brief time all that in the course of so many years, and at the cost of so many hardships and dangers, I have learned and know.

I have not adorned or amplified this work with rounded phrases, swelling and high-flown language, or any other of those extrinsic attractions and allurements with which many authors are accustomed to set off and grace their writings since it is my desire that it should either pass wholly unhonored, or that the truth of its matter and the importance of its subject should alone recommend it.

Nor would I have it thought presumption that a person of very mean and humble station should venture to discourse and lay down rules concerning the

---

1   A member of the ruling Medici family.

government of princes. For as those who make maps of countries place themselves low down in the plains to study the character of mountains and elevated lands, and place themselves high up on the mountains to get a better view of the plains, so in like manner to understand the people a man should be a prince, and to have a clear notion of princes he should belong to the people.

Let your Magnificence, then, accept this little gift in the spirit in which I offer it; wherein, if you diligently read and study it, you will recognize my extreme desire that you should attain to that eminence which fortune and your own merits promise you. Should you from the height of your greatness sometime turn your eyes to these humble regions, you will become aware how undeservedly I have to endure the keen and unremitting malignity of fortune.

### 1 OF THE VARIOUS KINDS OF PRINCEDOM, AND OF THE WAYS IN WHICH THEY ARE ACQUIRED

Governments by which men are or ever have been ruled, have been and are either republics or princedoms. Princedoms are either hereditary, in which the sovereignty is derived through an ancient line of ancestors, or they are new. New princedoms are either wholly new as that of Milan to Francesco Sforza;[2] or they are like limbs joined on to the hereditary possessions of the prince who acquires them, as the kingdom of Naples to the dominions of the king of Spain.[3] The states thus acquired have either been used to live under a prince or have been free; and he who acquires them does so either by his own arms or by the arms of others, and either by good fortune or by merit.

### 2 OF HEREDITARY PRINCEDOMS

Of republics I shall not now speak, having elsewhere spoken of them at length. Here I shall treat exclusively of princedoms, and, filling in the outline traced out above, shall proceed to examine how such states are to be governed and maintained.

I say, then, that hereditary states, accustomed to the family of their princes, are maintained with far less difficulty than new states, since all that is required is that the prince shall not depart from the usages of his ancestors, trusting for the rest to deal with events as they arise. So that if an hereditary prince is of average address, he will always maintain himself in his princedom, unless deprived of it by some extraordinary and irresistible force; and even if so deprived he will recover it, should any, even the least, mishap overtake the usurper. We have in Italy an example of this in the duke of Ferrara, who never could have withstood the attacks of the Venetians in 1484, nor those of Pope Julius in 1510, had not his authority in that state been consolidated by time. For since a prince by birth has fewer occasions and less need to give offense, he ought to be better loved, and will naturally be popular with his subjects unless outrageous vices make him odious. Moreover, the very antiquity and continuance of his rule will efface the memories and causes which lead to innovation. For one change always leaves a dovetail into which another will fit.

### 3 OF MIXED PRINCEDOMS

But in new princedoms difficulties abound. And, first, if the princedom is not wholly new, but joined onto the old dominions of the prince, so as to form with them what may be termed a mixed princedom, changes will come from a cause common to all new states, namely, that men, thinking to better their condition, are always ready to change masters, and in this expectation will take up arms against any ruler; wherein they deceive themselves, and find afterwards by experience that they are worse off than before. This again results naturally and necessarily from the circumstance that the prince cannot avoid giving offense to his new subjects, either in respect to the troops he quarters on them, or to some other of the numberless vexations attendant on a new acquisition. And in this way you may find that you have enemies in all those whom you have injured in seizing the princedom, yet

---

2 Francesco Sforza (1401-1466) began as a mercenary, and by force became duke of the Italian city state of Milan in 1450, thus establishing a dynasty.

3 The king of Spain gained control of Naples in 1504.

cannot keep the friendship of those who helped you to gain it; since you can neither reward them as they expect, nor yet, being under obligations to them, use violent remedies against them. For however strong you may be in respect to your army, it is essential that in entering a new province you should have the good-will of its inhabitants.

Hence it happened that Louis XII of France,[4] speedily gaining possession of Milan, as speedily lost it, and that on the occasion of its first capture, Lodovico Sforza[5] was able with his own forces only to take it from him. For the very people who had opened the gates to the French king, when they found themselves deceived in their expectations and hopes of future benefits, could not put up with the insolence of their new ruler. It is true that when a state rebels and is conquered again, it will not afterwards be lost so easily. For the prince, using the rebellion as a pretext, will not scruple to secure himself by punishing the guilty, bringing the suspected to trial, and otherwise strengthening his position in the points where it was weak. So that if to recover Milan from the French it was enough on the first occasion that a Duke Lodovico should raise alarms on the frontiers, to wrest it from them a second time the whole world had to be ranged against them, and their armies destroyed and driven out of Italy. And this for the reasons above assigned. And yet, for a second time, Milan was lost to the king. The general causes of its first loss have been shown. It remains to note the causes of the second, and to point out the remedies which the French king had, or which might have been used by another in like circumstances, to maintain his conquest more successfully than he did.

I say, then, that those states which upon their acquisition are joined on to the old dominions of the prince who acquires them are either of the same province and tongue as the people of these dominions, or they are not. When they are, there is great ease in retaining them, especially when they have not been accustomed to live in freedom. To hold them securely it is enough to have rooted out the line of the reigning prince because, if in other respects the old condition of things is continued, and there is no disagreement between their customs, men live peaceably with one another, as we see to have been the case in Brittany, Burgundy, Gascony, and Normandy, which have so long been united to France. For although there is some slight difference in their languages, their customs are similar, and they can easily get on together. He, therefore, who acquires such a state, if he means to keep it, must see to two things: first, that the blood of the ancient line of princes is destroyed; second, that no change is made in respect to laws or taxes; for in this way the newly acquired state speedily becomes incorporated with the hereditary one.

But when states are acquired in a country differing in language, usages, and laws, difficulties multiply, and great good fortune, as well as address, is needed to overcome them. One of the best and most efficacious methods for dealing with such a state is for the prince who acquires it to go and dwell there in person, since this will tend to make his tenure more secure and lasting. This course has been followed by the Turk with regard to Greece, who, had he not, in addition to all his other precautions for securing that province, himself come to live in it, could never have kept his hold of it. For when you are on the spot, disorders are detected in their beginnings and remedies can be readily applied; but when you are at a distance, they are not heard of until they have gathered strength and the case is past cure. Moreover, the province in which you take up your abode is not pillaged by your officers; the people are pleased to have a ready recourse to their prince, and have all the more reason if they are well disposed, to love, if disaffected, to fear him. A foreign enemy desiring to attack that state would be cautious how he did so. In short, where the prince resides in person, it will be extremely difficult to oust him.

Another excellent expedient is to send colonies into one or two places, so that these may become, as it were, the keys of the province; for you must either do this, or else keep up a numerous force of men-at-arms and foot soldiers. A prince need not spend much on colonies. He can send them out and support them at little or no

---

4  Louis XII of France (1498-1515) invaded Italy in 1499 in order to enforce his claims to Milan and Naples, and continued to be involved in Italian politics until his death.
5  Ruler of Milan (1481-1500).

charge to himself, and the only persons to whom he gives offense are those whom he deprives of their fields and houses to bestow them on the new inhabitants. Those who are thus injured form but a small part of the community, and remaining scattered and poor, can never become dangerous. All others, being left unmolested, are in consequence easily quieted, and at the same time are afraid to make a false move, lest they share the fate of those who have been deprived of their possessions. In a few words, these colonies cost less than soldiers, are more faithful, and give less offense, while those who are offended, being, as I have said, poor and dispersed, cannot cause harm. And let it here be noted that men are either to be kindly treated, or utterly crushed, since they can revenge lighter injuries, but not graver ones. Wherefore the injury we do to a man should be of a sort to leave no fear of reprisals.

But if instead of colonies you send troops, the cost is vastly greater, and the whole revenue of the country is spent in guarding it; so that the gain becomes a loss, and much deeper offense is given, since in shifting the quarters of your soldiers from place to place the whole country suffers hardship, which as all feel it, all are made enemies; and enemies who remaining, although vanquished, in their own homes, have power to cause harm. In every way, therefore, this mode of defense is as disadvantageous as that by colonizing is useful.

The prince who establishes himself in a province whose laws and language differ from those of his own people ought also to make himself the head and protector of his feebler neighbors, and endeavor to weaken the stronger, and must see that by no accident shall any other stranger as powerful as himself find an entrance there. For it will always happen that some such person will be called in by those of the province who are discontented, either through ambition or fear, as we see of old the Romans brought into Greece by the Aetolians,[6] and in every other country that they entered, invited there by its inhabitants. And the usual course of things is that as soon as a formidable stranger enters a province, all the weaker powers side with him, moved thereto by the ill will they bear towards him who has hitherto kept them in subjection. So that in respect to these lesser powers, no trouble is needed to gain them over, for at once, together, and of their own accord, they throw in their lot with the government of the stranger. The new prince, therefore, has only to see that they do not increase too much in strength, and with his own forces, aided by their goodwill, can easily subdue any who are powerful, so as to remain supreme in the province. He who does not manage this matter well, will soon lose whatever he has gained, and while he retains it, will find in it endless troubles and annoyances.

In dealing with the countries of which they took possession, the Romans diligently followed the methods I have described. They planted colonies, conciliated weaker powers without adding to their strength, humbled the great, and never suffered a formidable stranger to acquire influence. A single example will suffice to show this. In Greece the Romans took the Achaeans[7] and Aetolians into their pay; the Macedonian monarchy was humbled; Antiochus[8] was driven out. But the services of the Achaeans and Aetolians never obtained for them any addition to their power; no persuasions on the part of Philip[9] could induce the Romans to be his friends on the condition of sparing him humiliation; nor could all the power of Antiochus bring them to consent to his exercising any authority within that province. And in thus acting the Romans did as all wise rulers should, who have to consider not only present difficulties but also future ones, against which they must use all diligence to provide. For these, if they are foreseen while yet remote, admit of easy remedy, but if their approach is awaited, they are already past cure, the disorder having become hopeless, realizing what the physicians tell us of hectic fever, that in its beginning it is easy to cure, but hard to recognize, whereas, after a time, not having been detected and treated at the first, it becomes easy to recognize, but impossible to cure.

---

6   A state in Greece in the late Hellenistic period.
7   Another state in Greece in the late Hellenistic period.
8   Antiochus III of the Seleucid kingdom (223-187 BC), who worked at extending his influence into the Greek mainland.
9   Philip V of Macedon (220-179 BC), who followed Macedonian tradition in working to dominate the Greek mainland.

And so it is with state affairs. For the distempers of a state being discovered while yet inchoate, which can be done only by a sagacious ruler, may easily be dealt with; but when, from not being observed, they are suffered to grow until they are obvious to everyone, there is no longer any remedy. The Romans, therefore, foreseeing evils while they were yet far off, always provided against them, and never suffered them to take their course for the sake of avoiding war; since they knew that war is not so to be avoided, but is only postponed to the advantage of the other side. They chose, therefore, to make war with Philip and Antiochus in Greece, that they might not have to make it with them in Italy, although for a while they might have escaped both. This they did not desire, nor did the maxim "leave it to time," which the wise men of our own day have always on their lips, ever recommend itself to them. What they looked to enjoy were the fruits of their own valor and foresight. For time, driving all things before it, may bring with it evil as well as good.

But let us now go back to France and examine whether she has followed any of those methods of which I have made mention. I shall speak of Louis[10] and not of Charles,[11] because from the former having held longer possession of Italy, his manner of acting is more plainly seen. You will find, then, that he has done the direct opposite of what he should have done in order to retain a foreign state.

King Louis was brought into Italy by the ambition of the Venetians, who hoped by his coming to gain for themselves a half of the state of Lombardy. I will not blame this coming, nor the part taken by the king, because, desiring to gain a footing in Italy, where he had no friends, but on the contrary, owing to the conduct of Charles, every door was shut against him, he was driven to accept such friendships as he could get. And his designs might easily have succeeded had he not made mistakes in other particulars of conduct.

By the recovery of Lombardy, Louis at once regained the credit which Charles had lost. Genoa made submission; the Florentines came to terms; the marquis of Mantua, the duke of Ferrara, the Bentivogli,[12] the countess of Forli, the lords of Faenza, Pesaro, Rimini, Camerino, and Piombino, the citizens of Lucca, Pisa, and Siena, all came forward offering their friendship. The Venetians, who to obtain possession of a couple of towns in Lombardy had made the French king master of two-thirds of Italy, had now cause to repent the rash game they had played.

Let anyone, therefore, consider how easily King Louis might have maintained his authority in Italy had he observed the rules which I have noted above, and secured and protected all those friends of his, who being weak, and fearful, some of the church, some of the Venetians, were of necessity obliged to attach themselves to him, and with whose assistance, for they were many, he might readily have made himself safe against any other powerful state. But no sooner was he in Milan than he took a contrary course, in helping Pope Alexander[13] to occupy the Romagna—not perceiving that in seconding this enterprise he weakened himself by alienating friends and those who had thrown themselves into his arms, while he strengthened the church by adding great temporal power to the spiritual power which of itself confers so mighty an authority. Making this first mistake, he was forced to follow it up, until at last, in order to curb the ambition of Pope Alexander, and prevent him becoming master of Tuscany, he was obliged to come himself into Italy.

And as though it were not enough for him to have aggrandized the church and stripped himself of friends, he had in his desire to possess the kingdom of Naples to divide it with the king of Spain—thus bringing into Italy, where before he had been supreme, a rival to whom the ambitious and discontented in that province might have recourse. And whereas he might have left in Naples a king willing to hold it as his tributary, he displaced him to make way for another strong enough to effect his expulsion. The wish to acquire is no doubt a natural and common sentiment, and when men attempt things within their power,

10 Louis XII of France, for whom, see above, n 4.
11 Charles VIII of France (1483-1498), who invaded Italy in 1494 claiming the kingdom of Naples.
12 The leading family of the city state of Bologna.
13 Alexander VI (1492-1503).

they will always be praised rather than blamed. But when they persist in attempts that are beyond their power, mishaps and blame ensue. If France, therefore, with her own forces could have attacked Naples, she should have done so. If she could not, she ought not to have divided it. And if her partition of Lombardy with the Venetians may be excused as the means whereby a footing was gained in Italy, this other partition is to be condemned as not justified by the like necessity.

Louis, then, had made these five blunders: he had destroyed weaker states; he had strengthened a prince already strong; he had brought into the country a very powerful stranger; he had not come to reside; and he had not sent colonies. And yet all these blunders might not have proved disastrous to him while he lived, had he not added to them a sixth in depriving the Venetians of their dominions. For had he neither aggrandized the church, nor brought Spain into Italy, it might have been at once reasonable and necessary to humble the Venetians; but after committing himself to these other courses, he should never have consented to the ruin of Venice. For while the Venetians were powerful they would always have kept others back from an attempt on Lombardy, as well because they never would have agreed to that enterprise on any terms save of themselves being made its masters, as because others would never have desired to take it from France in order to hand it over to them, nor would ever have ventured to defy both. And if it be said that King Louis ceded the Romagna to Alexander, and Naples to Spain, in order to avoid war, I answer that for the reasons already given, you ought never to suffer your designs to be crossed in order to avoid war, since war is not so to be avoided, but is only deferred to your disadvantage. And if others should allege the king's promise to the pope to undertake that enterprise on his behalf, in return for the dissolution of his marriage, and for the cardinal's hat conferred on d'Amboise,[14] I answer by referring to what I say further on concerning the faith of princes and how it is to be kept.

King Louis, therefore, lost Lombardy from not following any one of the methods pursued by others who have taken provinces with the resolve to keep them. Nor is this anything strange, but only what might reasonably and naturally be looked for. And on this very subject I spoke to d'Amboise at Nantes, at the time when Duke Valentino, as Cesare Borgia,[15] son to Pope Alexander, was vulgarly called, was occupying the Romagna. For, on the cardinal saying to me that the Italians did not understand war, I answered that the French did not understand statecraft, for had they done so, they never would have allowed the church to grow so powerful. And the event shows that the aggrandizement of the church and of Spain in Italy has been brought about by France, and that the ruin of France has been wrought by them. Whence we may draw the general axiom, which never or rarely errs, that "he who is the cause of another's greatness is himself undone," since he must work either by address or force, each of which excites distrust in the person raised to power.

4 WHY THE KINGDOM OF DARIUS,[16] CONQUERED BY ALEXANDER, DID NOT, ON ALEXANDER'S DEATH, REBEL AGAINST HIS SUCCESSORS

Alexander the Great, having achieved the conquest of Asia in a few years, and dying before he had well entered in possession, it might have been expected, having regard to the difficulty of preserving newly acquired states, that on his death the whole country would rise in revolt. Nevertheless, his successors were able to keep their hold, and found in doing so no difficulty other than what arose from their own ambition and mutual jealousies.

If anyone thinks this strange and asks the cause, I answer that all the princedoms of which we have record have been governed in one or other of two ways: either by a sole prince, all others being his servants permitted by his grace and favor to assist in governing the kingdom as his ministers, or else, by a

14  Cardinal Georges d'Amboise (1460-1510), Louis XII's chief minister.
15  Cesare Borgia (*c.* 1476-1507) was Alexander VI's son by that pope's mistress. Alexander attempted to establish him as a territorial ruler in Italy, but these plans failed after Alexander's death in 1503.
16  Darius, king of Persia (336-330 BC) lost his empire to the conquests of Alexander the Great.

prince with his barons who hold their rank, not by the favor of a superior lord, but by antiquity of blood, and who have states and subjects of their own who recognize them as their rulers and entertain for them a natural affection. States governed by a sole prince and by his servants vest in him a more complete authority because throughout the land none but he is recognized as sovereign, and if obedience is yielded to any others, it is yielded as to his ministers and officers for whom personally no special love is felt.

Of these two forms of government we have examples in our own day in the Turk and the king of France. The whole Turkish empire is governed by a sole prince, all others being his slaves. Dividing his kingdom into *sanjaks*,[17] he sends there different governors whom he shifts and changes at his pleasure. The king of France, on the other hand, is surrounded by a multitude of nobles of ancient descent, each acknowledged and loved by subjects of his own, and each asserting a precedence in rank of which the king can deprive him only at his peril.

He, therefore, who considers the different character of these two states, will perceive that it would be difficult to gain possession of that of the Turk, but that once won it might be easily held. The obstacles to its conquest are that the invader cannot be called in by a native nobility or expect his enterprise to be aided by the defection of those whom the sovereign has around him. And this is for the various reasons already given, namely, that all being slaves and under obligations, they are not easily corrupted, or if corrupted can render little assistance, being unable, as I have already explained, to carry the people with them. Whoever, therefore, attacks the Turk must reckon on finding a united people, and must trust rather to his own strength than to divisions on the other side. But were his adversary once overcome and defeated in the field so that he could not repair his armies, no cause for anxiety would remain, except in the family of the prince; this being extirpated, there would be no one else to fear, for since all else are without credit with the people, the invader, as before his victory he had noth-ing to hope from them, so after it has nothing to dread.

But the contrary is the case in kingdoms governed like that of France, into which, because men who are discontented and desirous of change are always to be found, you may readily procure an entrance by gaining over some baron of the realm. Such persons, for the reasons already given, are able to open the way to you for the invasion of their country and to render its conquest easy. But afterwards the effort to hold your ground involves you in endless difficulties, in respect to those who have helped you, as well as to those whom you have overthrown. Nor will it be enough to have destroyed the family of the prince, since all those other lords remain to put themselves at the head of new movements, whom being unable either to content or to destroy, you lose the state whenever occasion serves them.

Now, if you examine the nature of the government of Darius, you will find that it resembled that of the Turk, and, consequently, that it was necessary for Alexander, first of all, to defeat him utterly and strip him of his dominions; after which defeat, Darius having died, the country, for the causes above explained, was permanently secured to Alexander. And had his successors continued united they might have enjoyed it undisturbed, since there arose no disorders in that kingdom save those of their own creating.

But kingdoms ordered like that of France cannot be retained with the same ease. Hence the repeated risings of Spain, Gaul, and Greece against the Romans, resulting from the number of small princedoms of which these provinces were made up. For while the memory of these lasted, the Romans would never think their tenure safe. But when that memory was worn out by the authority and long continuance of their rule, they gained a secure hold, and were able afterwards, in their contests among themselves,[18] each to carry with him some portion of these provinces, according as each had acquired influence there; for these, on the extinction of the line of their old princes, came to recognize no lords other than the Romans.

---

17   In the empire of the Ottoman Turks, a territorial unit within a minor province; each *sanjak* had a governor appointed by the sultan.

18   Apparently a reference to the civil wars of the last century of the Roman republic.

Bearing all this in mind, no one need wonder at the case in which Alexander was able to lay a firm hold on Asia, nor that Pyrrhus[19] and many others found difficulty in preserving other acquisitions; since this arose, not from the less or greater merit of the conquerors, but from the different character of the states with which they had to deal.

## 5 HOW CITIES OR PROVINCES WHICH BEFORE THEIR ACQUISITION HAVE LIVED UNDER THEIR OWN LAWS ARE TO BE GOVERNED

When a newly acquired state has been accustomed, as I have said, to live under its own laws and in freedom, there are three methods whereby it may be held. The first is to destroy it; the second, to go and reside there in person; the third, to suffer it to live on under its own laws, subjecting it to a tribute, and entrusting its government to a few of the inhabitants who will keep the rest your friends. Such a government, since it is the creature of the new prince, will see that it cannot stand without his protection and support, and must therefore do all it can to maintain him; and a city accustomed to live in freedom, if it is to be preserved at all, is more easily controlled through its own citizens than in any other way.

We have examples of all these methods in the histories of the Spartans and the Romans. The Spartans held Athens and Thebes by creating oligarchies in these cities,[20] yet lost them in the end. The Romans, to retain Capua, Carthage, and Numantia, destroyed them and never lost them. On the other hand, when they thought to hold Greece as the Spartans had held it, leaving it its freedom and allowing it to be governed by its own laws, they failed, and had to destroy many cities of that province before they could secure it. For, in truth, there is no sure way of holding other than by destroying, and whoever becomes master of a city accustomed to live in freedom and does not destroy it, may reckon on being destroyed by it. For if it should rebel, it can always justify itself under the name of liberty and its ancient laws, which no length of time or any benefits conferred will ever cause it to forget; and do what you will, and take what care you may, unless the inhabitants are scattered and dispersed, this name, and the old order of things, will never cease to be remembered, but will at once be turned against you whenever misfortune overtakes you, as when Pisa rose against the Florentines after a hundred years of servitude.[21]

If, however, the newly acquired city or province has been accustomed to live under a prince, and his line is extinguished, it will be impossible for the citizens, used, on the one hand, to obedience, and deprived, on the other, of their old ruler, to agree to choose a leader from among themselves; as they do not know how to live as free men, and are therefore slow to take up arms, a stranger may readily gain them over and attach them to his cause. But in republics there is a stronger vitality, a fiercer hatred, a keener thirst for revenge. The memory of their former freedom will not let them rest, so that the safest course is either to destroy them, or to go and live in them.

## 6 OF NEW PRINCEDOMS WHICH A PRINCE ACQUIRES WITH HIS OWN ARMS AND BY MERIT

Let no man marvel if in what I am about to say concerning princedoms wholly new, both as regards the prince and the form of government, I cite the highest examples. For since men for the most part follow in the footsteps and imitate the actions of others, and yet are unable to adhere exactly to those paths which others have taken, or attain to the virtues of those whom they would resemble, the wise man should always follow the roads that have been trodden by the great, and imitate those who have most excelled, so that if he cannot reach their perfection, he may at least acquire something of its savor—acting in this like the skillful archer, who seeing that the object he would hit is distant, and knowing the range of his bow, takes aim much above the destined mark, not designing that his arrow should strike so high,

---

19  King (306-272 BC) of the Hellenistic state of Epirus.
20  Following Sparta's victory over these cities in the fifth century BC.
21  In 1494, when Florence faced the army of a hostile Charles VIII of France.

but that flying high it may alight at the point intended.

I say, then, that in entirely new princedoms where the prince himself is new, the difficulty of maintaining possession varies with the greater or lesser ability of him who acquires possession. And, because the mere fact of a private person rising to be a prince presupposes either merit or good fortune, it will be seen that the presence of one or other of these two conditions lessens, to some extent, many difficulties. And yet, he who is less beholden to fortune has often in the end the better success; and it may be for the advantage of a prince that, from his having no other territories, he is obliged to reside in person in the state which he has acquired.

Looking first to those who have become princes by their merit and not by their good fortune, I say that the most excellent among them are Moses,[22] Cyrus,[23] Romulus,[24] Theseus,[25] and the like. And though perhaps I ought not to name Moses, he being merely an instrument for carrying out the divine commands, he is still to be admired for those qualities which made him worthy to converse with God. But if we consider Cyrus and the others who have acquired or founded kingdoms, they will all be seen to be admirable. And if their actions and the particular institutions of which they were the authors are studied, they will be found not to differ from those of Moses, instructed though he was by so great a teacher. Moreover, on examining their lives and actions, we shall see that they were debtors to fortune for nothing beyond the opportunity which enabled them to shape things as they pleased, without which the force of their spirit would have been spent in vain, as on the other hand, opportunity would have offered itself in vain had the capacity for turning it to account been wanting. It was necessary, therefore, that Moses should find the children of Israel in bondage in Egypt, and oppressed by the Egyptians, in order that they might be disposed to follow him, and so escape from their servitude. It was

fortunate for Romulus that he found no home in Alba, but was exposed at the time of his birth, to the end that he might become king and founder of the city of Rome. It was necessary that Cyrus should find the Persians discontented with the rule of the Medes, and the Medes enervated and effeminate from a prolonged peace. Nor could Theseus have displayed his great qualities had he not found the Athenians disunited and dispersed. But while it was their opportunities that made these men fortunate, it was their own merit that enabled them to recognize these opportunities and turn them to account, to the glory and prosperity of their country.

They who come to the princedom, as these did, by prowess, acquire with difficulty, but keep with ease. The difficulties which they have in acquiring arise mainly from the new laws and institutions which they are forced to introduce in founding and securing their government. And let it be noted that there is no more delicate matter to take in hand, or more dangerous to conduct, or more doubtful in its success, than to set up as a leader in the introduction of changes. For he who innovates will have for his enemies all those who are well off under the existing order of things, and only lukewarm supporters in those who might be better off under the new one. This lukewarm temper arises partly from the fear of adversaries who have the laws on their side, and partly from the incredulity of mankind, who will never admit the merit of anything new until they have seen it proved by the event. The result, however, is that whenever the enemies of change make an attack, they do so with all the zeal of partisans, while the others defend themselves so feebly as to endanger both themselves and their cause.

But to get a clearer understanding of this part of our subject, we must see whether these innovators can stand alone, or whether they depend for aid upon others—in other words, whether to carry out their ends they must resort to entreaty, or can prevail by force. In the former case they always fare badly and bring noth-

---

22  Who, according to the Old Testament, led the Hebrews out of Egypt and to Israel, receiving the Hebrew laws from God in the process.
23  Who led the Persians in overthrowing the Medes, thus becoming the first king (550-529 BC) of the Persian empire.
24  The mythical founder of Rome.
25  In myth, an early king of Athens.

ing to a successful issue, but when they depend upon their own resources and can employ force, they seldom fail. Hence it comes that all armed prophets have been victorious, and all unarmed prophets have been destroyed.

For, besides what has been said, it should be borne in mind that the temper of the multitude is fickle, and that while it is easy to persuade them of a thing, it is hard to fix them in that persuasion. Wherefore, matters should be so ordered that when men no longer believe of their own accord, they may be compelled to believe by force. Moses, Cyrus, Theseus, and Romulus could never have made their ordinances be observed for any length of time had they been unarmed, as was the case, in our own days, with the Friar Girolamo Savonarola,[26] whose new institutions came to nothing as soon as the multitude began to waver in their faith, since he did not have the means to keep those who had been believers steadfast in their belief, or to make unbelievers believe.

Such persons, therefore, have great difficulty in carrying out their designs, but all their difficulties are on the road, and may be overcome by courage. Having conquered these, and coming to be held in reverence, and having destroyed all who were jealous of their influence, they remain powerful, safe, honored, and prosperous.

To the great examples cited above, I would add one other, of less note indeed, but assuredly bearing some proportion to them, and which may stand for all others of a like character. I mean the example of Hiero the Syracusan.[27] He rose from a private station to be prince of Syracuse, and he too was indebted to fortune only for his opportunity. For the Syracusans, being oppressed, chose him to be their captain, which office he so discharged as deservedly to be made their king. For even while a private citizen his merit was so remarkable that one who writes of him says he lacked nothing that a king should have save the kingdom.

Doing away with the old army, he organized a new one, abandoned existing alliances and assumed new allies, and with an army and allies of his own, was able on that foundation to build what superstructure he pleased, having trouble enough in acquiring but none in preserving what he had acquired.

## 7 OF NEW PRINCEDOMS ACQUIRED BY THE AID OF OTHERS AND BY GOOD FORTUNE

They who from a private station become princes by mere good fortune, do so with little trouble, but have much trouble to maintain themselves. They meet with no hindrance on their way, being carried as it were on wings to their destination, but all their difficulties overtake them when they alight. Of this class are those on whom states are conferred either in return for money, or through the favor of him who confers them; as it happened with many in the Greek cities of Ionia and the Hellespont who were made princes by Darius[28] so they might hold these cities for his security and glory, and as happened in the case of those emperors[29] who, from a private station attained the imperial dignity by corrupting the army. Such princes are wholly dependent on the favor and fortunes of those who have made them great, than which supports none could be less stable or secure, and they lack both the knowledge and the power that would enable them to maintain their position. They lack the knowledge because, unless they have great parts and force of character, it is not to be expected that, having always lived in a private station, they should have learned how to command. They lack the power since they cannot look for support from attached and faithful troops. Moreover, states suddenly acquired, like all else that is produced and that grows up rapidly, can never have such root or hold that the first storm which strikes them shall not overthrow them—unless, indeed, as I have said already, they who thus suddenly become

---

26 A passionate preacher and denouncer of vice, his sermons stirred up religious feeling at Florence which made him virtual ruler of the city in the 1490s. He fell from power and was eventually executed as a heretic.
27 Tyrant of the Greek city of Syracuse in Sicily (fifth century BC).
28 Darius, king of Persia, took over many Greek city states in what is today Western Turkey and the islands off it (here referred to as Ionia) and the Hellespont, where one crosses from Asia into Europe.
29 I.e., Roman emperors.

princes have a capacity for learning quickly how to defend what fortune has placed in their lap, and can lay those foundations after they rise which by others are laid before.

Of each of these methods of becoming a prince, namely, by merit and by good fortune, I shall select an instance from times within my own recollection, and shall take the cases of Francesco Sforza and Cesare Borgia. By suitable measures and singular ability, Francesco Sforza rose from private life to be duke of Milan, preserving with little trouble what it cost him infinite efforts to gain. On the other hand, Cesare Borgia, vulgarly spoken of as Duke Valentino, obtained his princedom through the favorable fortunes of his father, and with these lost it, although, so far as in him lay, he used every effort and practiced every expedient that a prudent and able man should, who desires to strike root in a state given him by the arms and fortune of another. For, as I have already said, he who does not lay his foundations at first, may, if he is of great parts, succeed in laying them afterwards, though with inconvenience to the builder and risk to the building. And if we consider the various measures taken by Duke Valentino, we shall perceive how broad were the foundations he had laid whereon to rest his future power.

I think these are not superfluous to examine, since I do not know what lessons I could teach a new prince that would be more useful than the example of his actions. And if the measures taken by him did not profit him in the end, it was through no fault of his, but from the extraordinary and extreme malignity of fortune.

In his efforts to aggrandize the duke his son, Alexander VI had to face many difficulties, both immediate and remote. In the first place, he saw no way to make him lord of any state which was not a state of the church, while, if he sought to take for him a state belonging to the church, he knew that the duke of Milan and the Venetians would withhold their consent, Faenza and Rimini being already under the protection of the latter. Further, he saw that the arms of Italy, and those more especially of which he might

have availed himself, were in the hands of men who had reason to fear his aggrandizement, that is, of the Orsini, the Colonna,[30] and their followers. These therefore he could not trust. It was consequently necessary that the existing order of things should be changed, and the states of Italy thrown into confusion, in order that he might safely make himself master of some part of them; and this became easy for him when he found that the Venetians, moved by other causes, were plotting to bring the French once more into Italy. This design he accordingly did not oppose, but furthered by annulling the first marriage of the French king.

King Louis therefore came into Italy at the instance of the Venetians, and with the consent of Pope Alexander, and no sooner was he in Milan than the pope got troops from him to aid him in his enterprise against the Romagna, which province, moved by the reputation of the French arms, at once submitted. After thus obtaining possession of the Romagna, and after quelling the Colonna, Duke Valentino desired to follow up and extend his conquests. Two causes, however, held him back, namely, the doubtful fidelity of his own forces, and the waywardness of France. For he feared that the Orsini, of whose arms he had made use, might fail him, and not merely prove a hindrance to further acquisitions, but take from him what he had gained, and that the king might serve him the same turn. How little he could count on the Orsini was made plain when, after the capture of Faenza, he turned his arms against Bologna, and saw how reluctantly they took part in that enterprise. The king's mind he understood, when, after seizing on the dukedom of Urbino, he was about to attack Tuscany, from which design Louis compelled him to desist. Whereupon the duke resolved to depend no longer on the arms or fortune of others. His first step, therefore, was to weaken the factions of the Orsini and Colonna in Rome. Those of their following who were of good birth, he gained over by making them his own gentlemen, assigning them a generous provision, and conferring upon them commands and appointments suited to their rank, so that in a few months their old

30  Two powerful noble families of the city of Rome.

partisan attachments died out, and the hopes of all rested on the duke alone.

He then awaited an occasion to crush the chiefs of the Orsini, for those of the house of Colonna he had already scattered, and a good opportunity presenting itself, he turned it to the best account. For when the Orsini came at last to see that the greatness of the duke and the church involved their ruin, they assembled a council at Magione in the Perugian territory, whence resulted the revolt of Urbino, commotions in the Romagna, and an infinity of dangers to the duke, all of which he overcame with the help of France. His credit thus restored, the duke trusting no longer either to the French or to any other foreign aid, that he might not have to confront them openly, resorted to stratagem, and was so well able to disguise his designs that the Orsini, through the mediation of Signor Paolo[31] (whom he did not fail to secure by every friendly attention, furnishing him with clothes, money, and horses), were so won over as to be drawn in their simplicity into his hands at Sinigaglia. When the leaders were thus disposed of, and their followers made his friends, the duke had laid sufficiently good foundations for his future power since he held all the Romagna together with the dukedom of Urbino, and had ingratiated himself with the entire population of these states, who now began to see that they were well off.

And since this part of his conduct merits both attention and imitation, I shall not pass over it in silence. After the duke had taken the Romagna, finding that it had been ruled by feeble lords, who thought more of plundering than correcting their subjects, and gave them more cause for division than for union, so that the country was overrun with robbery, tumult, and every kind of outrage, he judged it necessary, with a view to render it peaceful and obedient to his authority, to provide it with good government. Accordingly he set over it Messer Remiro d'Orco, a stern and prompt ruler, who being entrusted with the fullest powers, in a very short time, and with much credit to himself, restored it to tranquillity and order. But afterwards apprehending that such unlimited authority might become odious, the duke decided that it was no longer needed, and established in the center of the province a civil tribunal, with an excellent president, in which every town was represented by its advocate. And knowing that past severities had generated ill feeling against himself, in order to purge the minds of the people and gain their goodwill, he sought to show them that any cruelty which had been done had originated not with him, but in the harsh disposition of his minister. Availing himself of the pretext which this afforded, he one morning caused Remiro to be beheaded, and exposed in the market place of Cesena with a block and bloody ax by his side. The barbarity of this spectacle at once astounded and satisfied the populace.

But, returning to the point from which we diverged, I say that the duke, finding himself fairly strong and in a measure secured against present dangers, being furnished with arms of his own choosing and having to a great extent gotten rid of those which, if left near him, might have caused him trouble, had to consider, if he desired to follow up his conquests, how he was to deal with France, since he saw he could expect no further support from King Louis, whose eyes were at last opened to his mistake. He therefore began to look about for new alliances, and to waver in his adherence to the French, then occupied with their expedition into the kingdom of Naples against the Spaniards, at that time laying siege to Gaeta; his object was to secure himself against France, and in this he would soon have succeeded had Alexander lived.

Such was the line he took to meet present exigencies. As regards the future, he had to apprehend that a new head of the church might not be his friend, and might even seek to deprive him of what Alexander had given. This he thought to provide against in four ways. First, by exterminating all who were kin to those lords whom he had despoiled of their possessions, that they might not become instruments in the hands of a new pope. Second, by gaining over all the Roman nobles, so as to be able with their help to put a bridle, as the saying is, in the pope's mouth. Third, by bringing the college of cardinals, so far as he could,

---

31 Leader of the Orsini.

under his control. And fourth, by establishing his authority so firmly before his father's death, as to be able by himself to withstand the shock of a first onset.

Of these measures, at the time when Alexander died, he had already effected three, and had almost carried out the fourth. For of the lords whose possessions he had usurped, he had put to death all whom he could reach, and very few had escaped. He had gained over the Roman nobility, and had the majority in the college of cardinals on his side.

As to further acquisitions, his design was to make himself master of Tuscany. He was already in possession of Perugia and Piombino, and had assumed the protectorship of Pisa, on which city he was about to spring; taking no heed of France, as indeed he no longer had occasion, since the French had been deprived of the kingdom of Naples by the Spaniards under circumstances which made it necessary for both nations to buy his friendship. Pisa taken, Lucca and Siena would soon have yielded, partly through jealousy of Florence, partly through fear, and the position of the Florentines must then have been desperate.

Had he therefore succeeded in these designs, as he was succeeding in that very year in which Alexander died, he would have won such power and reputation that he might afterwards have stood alone, relying on his own strength and resources, without being beholden to the power and fortune of others. But Alexander died five years from the time he first unsheathed the sword, leaving his son with the state of the Romagna alone consolidated, with all the rest unsettled, between two powerful hostile armies, and sick almost to death. And yet such were the fire and courage of the duke, so well did he know how men must either be conciliated or crushed, and so solid were the foundations he had laid in that brief period, that had these armies not been upon his back, or had he been in sound health, he would have surmounted every difficulty.

How strong his foundations were may be seen from this: that the Romagna waited for him for more than a month, and that although half dead, he

remained in safety in Rome, where though the Baglioni,[32] the Vitelli,[33] and the Orsini came to attack him, they met with no success. Moreover, since he was able if not to make whom he liked pope, at least to prevent the election of any whom he disliked, had he been in health at the time when Alexander died, all would have been easy for him. But he told me himself on the day on which Julius II[34] was created, that he had foreseen and provided for everything else that could happen on his father's death, but had never anticipated that when his father died he too would be at death's door.

Taking all these actions of the duke together, I can find no fault with him; indeed, it seems to me reasonable to put him forward, as I have done, as a pattern for all such as rise to power by good fortune and the help of others. For with his great spirit and high aims he could not act otherwise than he did, and nothing but the shortness of his father's life and his own illness prevented the success of his designs. Whoever, therefore, on entering a new princedom, judges it necessary to rid himself of enemies, to conciliate friends, to prevail by force or fraud, to make himself feared yet not hated by his subjects, respected and obeyed by his soldiers, to crush those who can or ought to injure him, to introduce changes in the old order of things, to be at once severe and affable, magnanimous and generous, to do away with a mutinous army and create a new one, to maintain relations with kings and princes on such a footing that they must see it as their interest to aid him, and dangerous to offend him, can find no brighter example than in the actions of this prince.

The one thing for which he may be blamed was the creation of Pope Julius II, in respect to whom he chose badly. Because, as I have said already, though he could not secure the election he desired, he could have prevented any other; and he ought never to have consented to the creation of any one of those cardinals whom he had injured, or who on becoming pope would have reason to fear him, for fear is as dangerous an enemy as resentment. Those whom he had offended were, among others, San Pietro ad Vincula,

---

32  Who ruled Perugia, a city under papal dominion.
33  A noble, mercenary family in the papal states.
34  Pope Julius II (1503-1513) sought to increase the papacy's territorial position in Italy.

Colonna, San Giorgio, and Ascanio; all the rest, excepting d'Amboise and the Spanish cardinals (the latter from their connection and obligations, the former from the power he derived through his relations with the French court), would on assuming the pontificate have had reason to fear him. The duke, therefore, ought, in the first place, to have labored for the creation of a Spanish pope. Failing that, he should have agreed to the election of d'Amboise, but never to that of San Pietro ad Vincula. And he deceives himself who believes that, with the great, recent benefits cause old wrongs to be forgotten.

The duke, therefore, erred in the part he took in this election, and his error was the cause of his ultimate downfall.

### 8 OF THOSE WHO BY THEIR CRIMES COME TO BE PRINCES

But since from private life a man may also rise to be a prince in one or other of two ways, neither of which can be referred wholly either to merit or to fortune, it is fit that I notice them here, though one of them may fall to be discussed more fully in treating of republics.

The ways I speak of are, first, when the ascent to power is made by paths of wickedness and crime; second, when a private person becomes ruler of his country by the favor of his fellow citizens. The former method I shall make clear by two examples, one ancient, the other modern, without entering further into the merits of the matter, for these, I think, should be enough for anyone who is driven to follow them.

Agathocles the Sicilian[35] came, not merely from a private station, but from the very dregs of the people, to be king of Syracuse. Son of a potter, through all the stages of his fortunes he led a foul life. His vices, however, were conjoined with such great vigor both of mind and body that, becoming a soldier, he rose through the various grades of the service to be praetor of Syracuse. Once established in that post, he resolved to make himself prince, and to hold by violence and without obligation to others the authority which had been spontaneously entrusted to him. Accordingly,

after imparting his design to Hamilcar, who with the Carthaginian armies was at that time waging war in Sicily, he one morning assembled the people and senate of Syracuse as though to consult with them on matters of public importance, and on a prearranged signal caused his soldiers to put to death all the senators and the wealthiest of the commons. These being thus gotten rid of, he assumed and retained possession of the sovereignty without opposition on the part of the people. Although twice defeated by the Carthaginians, and afterwards besieged, he was able not only to defend his city, but leaving a part of his forces for its protection, to invade Africa with the remainder, and so in a short time to raise the siege of Syracuse, reducing the Carthaginians to the utmost extremities, and compelling them to make terms whereby they abandoned Sicily to him and confined themselves to Africa.

Whoever examines this man's actions and achievements will discover little or nothing in them which can be ascribed to fortune, seeing, as has already been said, that it was not through the favor of any, but by the regular steps of the military service, gained at the cost of a thousand hardships and hazards, that he reached the princedom which he afterwards maintained by so many daring and dangerous enterprises. Still, to slaughter fellow citizens, to betray friends, to be devoid of honor, pity, and religion, cannot be counted as merits, for these are means which may lead to power, but which confer no glory. Wherefore, if in respect to the valor with which he encountered and extricated himself from difficulties, and the constancy of his spirit in supporting and conquering adverse fortune, there seems no reason to judge him inferior to the greatest captains that have ever lived, his unbridled cruelty and inhumanity, together with his countless crimes, forbid us to number him with the greatest men; but, at any rate, we cannot attribute to fortune or to merit what he accomplished without either.

In our own times, during the papacy of Alexander VI, Oliverotto of Fermo, who some years before had been left an orphan, and had been brought up by his maternal uncle Giovanni Fogliani, was sent while still

---

35  Tyrant and then king (316-289 BC) of the Greek city of Syracuse in Sicily.

a lad to serve under Paolo Vitelli, in the expectation that a thorough training under that commander might qualify him for high rank as a soldier. After the death of Paolo, he served under his brother Vitellozzo, and in a very short time, being of a quick wit, hardy and resolute, he became one of the first soldiers of his company. But thinking it beneath him to serve under others, with the countenance of the Vitelli and the connivance of certain citizens of Fermo who preferred the slavery to the freedom of their country, he formed the design to seize that town.

He accordingly wrote to Giovanni Fogliani that after many years of absence from home, he desired to see him and his native city once more, and to look a little into the condition of his patrimony; and as his one endeavor had been to make a name for himself, in order that his fellow citizens might see that his time had not been misspent, he proposed to return honorably attended by a hundred horsemen from among his own friends and followers; and he begged Giovanni graciously to arrange for his reception by the citizens of Fermo with corresponding marks of distinction, as this would be creditable not only to himself, but also to the uncle who had brought him up.

Giovanni, accordingly, did not fail in any proper attention to his nephew, but caused him to be splendidly received by his fellow citizens, and lodged him in his house, where Oliverotto having passed some days, and made the necessary arrangements for carrying out his wickedness, gave a formal banquet, to which he invited his uncle and all the first men of Fermo. When the repast and the other entertainments proper to such an occasion had come to an end, Oliverotto artfully turned the conversation to matters of grave interest by speaking of the greatness of Pope Alexander and Cesare his son, and of their enterprises. When Giovanni and the others were replying to what he said, he suddenly rose up, observing that these were matters to be discussed in a more private place, and so withdrew to another chamber, where his uncle and all the other citizens followed him, and where they had no sooner seated themselves, than soldiers rushing out from places of concealment put Giovanni and all the rest to death.

After this butchery, Oliverotto mounted his horse, rode through the streets, and besieged the chief magistrate in the palace, so that all were constrained by fear to yield obedience and accept a government of which he made himself the head. And all who from being disaffected were likely to stand in his way, he put to death, while he strengthened himself with new ordinances, civil and military, to such purpose that for the space of a year during which he retained the princedom, he not merely kept a firm hold of the city, but grew formidable to all his neighbors. And it would have been as impossible to unseat him as it was to unseat Agathocles, had he not let himself be overreached by Cesare Borgia on the occasion when, as has already been told, the Orsini and Vitelli were entrapped at Sinigaglia—where he too being taken, one year after the commission of his parricidal crime, was strangled along with Vitellozzo, whom he had assumed for his master in villainy as in valor.

It may be asked how Agathocles and some like him, after numberless acts of treachery and cruelty, have been able to live long in their own countries in safety, and to defend themselves from foreign enemies, without being plotted against by their fellow citizens, whereas many others, by reason of their cruelty, have failed to maintain their position even in peaceful times, not to speak of the perilous times of war. I believe that this results from cruelty being well or ill employed. Those cruelties we may say are well employed, if it be permitted to speak well of evil things, which are done once and for all under the necessity of self-preservation, and are not afterwards persisted in, but so far as possible modified to the advantage of the governed. Ill employed cruelties, on the other hand, are those which from small beginnings increase rather than diminish with time. They who follow the first of these methods, may, by the grace of God and man, find, as did Agathocles, that their condition is not desperate; but by no possibility can the others maintain themselves.

Hence we may learn the lesson that, on seizing a state, the usurper should make haste to inflict what injuries he must at a stroke, that he may not have to renew them daily, but be enabled by their discontinuance to reassure men's minds, and afterwards win them over by benefits. Whosoever, either through timidity or from following bad counsels, adopts a contrary course, must keep the sword always drawn, and can put no trust in his subjects, who suffering from continued and constantly renewed severities, will never yield him their confidence. Injuries, therefore, should be inflicted all at once, that their ill savor being less lasting, they may the less offend, whereas, benefits should be conferred little by little, so that they may be more fully relished.

But, above all things, a prince should so live with his subjects that no vicissitude of good or evil fortune shall oblige him to alter his behavior because, if a need to change comes through adversity, it is then too late to resort to severity, while any leniency you may use will be thrown away, for it will be seen to be compulsory and gain you no thanks.

## 11 OF ECCLESIASTICAL PRINCEDOMS[36]

It now only remains for me to treat of ecclesiastical princedoms, concerning all the difficulties in respect to which precede their acquisition. For they are acquired by merit or good fortune, but are maintained without either, being upheld by the venerable ordinances of religion, which are all of such a nature and efficacy that they secure the authority of their princes in whatever way they may act or live. These princes alone have territories which they do not defend, and subjects whom they do not govern. Yet their territories are not taken from them through not being defended, neither are their subjects concerned at not being governed, or led to think of throwing off their allegiance, nor is it in their power to do so. Accordingly these princedoms alone are secure and happy. But inasmuch as they are sustained by agencies of a higher nature than the mind of man can reach, I forbear to speak of them, for since they are set up and supported by God himself, he would be a rash and presumptuous man who should venture to discuss them.

Nevertheless, should anyone ask me how it comes about that the temporal power of the church, which before the time of Alexander was looked on with contempt by all the potentates of Italy, and not only by those so styling themselves, but by every baron and lordling however insignificant, has now reached such a pitch of greatness that the king of France trembles before it, and that it has been able to drive him out of Italy and to crush the Venetians, though the causes are known, it seems to me not superfluous to call them in some measure to recollection.

Before Charles of France passed into Italy, that country was under the control of the pope, the Venetians, the king of Naples, the duke of Milan, and the Florentines. Two chief objects had to be kept in view by all these powers: first, that no armed foreigner should be allowed to invade Italy; second, that no one of their own number should be suffered to extend his territory. Those whom it was especially needed to guard against were the pope and the Venetians. To hold back the Venetians it was necessary that all the other states should combine, as was done for the defense of Ferrara; while to restrain the pope, use was made of the Roman barons, who being divided into two factions, the Orsini and Colonna, had constant cause for feud with one another, and standing with arms in their hands under the very eyes of the pontiff, kept the papacy feeble and insecure.

And although there arose from time to time a courageous pope like Sixtus,[37] neither his prudence nor his good fortune could free him from these embarrassments. The cause of this was the shortness of the lives of the popes. For in 10 years, which was the average duration of a pope's life, he could barely succeed in humbling one of these factions—so that if, for instance, one pope had almost exterminated the Colonna, he was followed by another, who being the enemy of the Orsini, had no time to rid himself of them, but so far from completing the destruction of the Colonna, restored them to life. This led to the temporal authority of the popes being little esteemed in Italy.

Then came Alexander VI, who more than any of his predecessors showed what a pope could effect with money and arms, achieving by the instrumentality of Duke Valentino, and by taking advantage of the coming of the French into Italy, all those successes which I

36  Machiavelli refers here to territories such as the papal states in central Italy or those territories in Germany governed by their bishops in all matters, secular as well as religious.

37  Pope Sixtus IV (1471-1484).

...ed in speaking of the actions of the ...ugh his object was to aggrandize not ...t the duke, what he did turned to the ...f the church, which after his death, and ...uke had been put out of the way, became the ...is labors.

...ter him came Pope Julius, who found the church strengthened by the possession of the whole of the Romagna, and the Roman barons exhausted and their factions shattered under the blows of Pope Alexander. He found also a way opened for the accumulation of wealth, which before the time of Alexander no one had followed. Julius not only used but added to these advantages. He undertook the conquest of Bologna, the overthrow of the Venetians, and the expulsion of the French from Italy, in all which enterprises he succeeded, and with the greater glory to himself in that whatever he did was done to strengthen the church and not to aggrandize any private person. He succeeded, moreover, in keeping the factions of the Orsini and Colonna within the same limits as he found them, and, though some seeds of insubordination may still have been left among them, two causes operated to hold them in check: first, the great power of the church, which overawed them, and second, their being without cardinals, who had been the cause of all their disorders. For these factions while they have cardinals among them can never be at rest, since it is they who foment dissension both in Rome and out of it, in which the barons are forced to take part, the ambition of the prelates[38] thus giving rise to tumult and discord among the barons.

His Holiness, Pope Leo,[39] has consequently found the papacy most powerful, and from him we may hope that, as his predecessors made it great with arms, he will render it still greater and more venerable by his benignity and other countless virtues.

## 13 OF AUXILIARY, MIXED, AND CITIZEN ARMS

The second sort of unprofitable arms[40] are auxiliaries, by whom I mean troops brought to help and protect you by a potentate whom you summon to your aid— as when in recent times Pope Julius II, observing the pitiful behavior of his mercenaries at the enterprise of Ferrara, turned to auxiliaries, and arranged with Ferdinand of Spain to be supplied with horse and foot soldiers.

Auxiliaries may be excellent and useful soldiers for themselves, but are always harmful to him who calls them in, for if they are defeated, he is undone, if victorious, he becomes their prisoner. Ancient histories abound with instances of this, but I shall not pass from the example of Pope Julius, which is still fresh in men's minds. It was the height of rashness for him, in his eagerness to gain Ferrara, to throw himself without reserve into the arms of a stranger. Nevertheless, his good fortune came to his rescue, and he did not have to reap the fruits of his ill considered conduct. For after his auxiliaries were defeated at Ravenna, the Swiss[41] suddenly descended and, to their own surprise and that of everyone else, swept the victors out of the country, so that he neither remained a prisoner with his enemies, they being put to flight, nor with his auxiliaries, because victory was won by arms other than theirs. The Florentines, being wholly without soldiers of their own, brought 10,000 French men-at-arms to the siege of Pisa, thereby incurring greater peril than in any previous time of trouble. To protect himself from his neighbors, the emperor of Constantinople[42] summoned 10,000 Turkish soldiers into Greece, who, when the war was over, refused to leave, and this was the beginning of the servitude of Greece to the Infidel.

Let him, therefore, who would deprive himself of every chance of success, have recourse to auxiliaries,

---

38  I.e., high church officials.
39  Pope Leo X (1513-1521) of the Medici family, who worked to promote the family's interests.
40  In chapter 12 Machiavelli discussed mercenaries.
41  I.e., Swiss mercenaries hired by the pope.
42  I.e., the Byzantine Emperor John VI (1347-1354), who became emperor after winning a civil war with Turkish help, and who later brought in the Turks when engaged in another civil war.

these being far more dangerous than mercenary arms, bringing ruin with them ready made. For they are united, and wholly under the control of their own officers; whereas, before mercenaries, even after gaining a victory, can do you harm, more time and better opportunities are needed because, as they are made up of separate companies, raised and paid by you, he whom you place in command cannot at once acquire such authority over them as will be injurious to you. In short, with mercenaries your greatest danger is from their inertness and cowardice, with auxiliaries from their valor. Wise princes, therefore, have always eschewed these arms, and trusted rather to their own, and have preferred defeat with the latter to victory with the former, counting that as no true victory which is gained by foreign aid.

I shall never hesitate to cite the example of Cesare Borgia and his actions. He entered the Romagna with a force of auxiliaries, all of them French men-at-arms, with whom he took Imola and Forli. But it appearing to him afterwards that these troops were not to be trusted, he had recourse to mercenaries from whom he thought there would be less danger, and took the Orsini and Vitelli into his pay. But finding these likewise while under his command to be fickle, false, and treacherous, he got rid of them, and fell back on troops of his own raising. And we may readily discern the difference between these various kinds of arms by observing the different degrees of reputation in which the duke stood while he depended upon the French alone, when he took the Orsini and Vitelli into his pay, and when he fell back on his own troops and his own resources; for we find his reputation always increasing, and that he was never so well thought of as when everyone perceived him to be sole master of his own forces.

I am unwilling to leave these examples, drawn from what has taken place in Italy and in recent times, and yet I must not omit to notice the case of Hiero of Syracuse, who is one of those whom I have already named. He, as I have before related, being made captain of their armies by the Syracusans, saw at once that a force of mercenary soldiers, supplied by men resembling our Italian *condottieri*,[43] was not serviceable; and as he would not retain and could not disband them, he caused them to be entirely cut to pieces, and afterwards made war with native soldiers only, without other aid.

And here I would call to mind a passage in the Old Testament as bearing on this point. When David offered himself to Saul to go forth and fight Goliath the Philistine champion, Saul to encourage him armed him with his own armor, which David, as soon as he had put it on, rejected, saying that with these untried arms he could not prevail, and that he chose rather to meet his enemy with only his sling and his sword. In a word, the armor of others is too wide or too narrow for us; it falls off us, or it weighs us down.

Charles VII,[44] the father of Louis XI, who by his good fortune and valor freed France from the English, saw this necessity of strengthening himself with a citizen army, and drew up ordinances regulating the service both of men-at-arms and of foot soldiers throughout his kingdom. But afterwards his son, King Louis, did away with the citizen infantry, and began to hire Swiss mercenaries. This blunder, having been followed by subsequent princes, has been the cause, as the result shows, of the dangers into which the kingdom of France has fallen, for, by enhancing the reputation of the Swiss, the whole of the citizen troops of France has deteriorated. For from their infantry being done away with, their men-at-arms are made wholly dependent on foreign assistance, and being accustomed to cooperate with the Swiss, have grown to think they can do nothing without them. Hence the French are no match for the Swiss, and without them cannot succeed against others.

The armies of France, then, are mixed, being partly citizen and partly mercenary. Armies thus composed are far superior to mere mercenaries or mere auxiliaries, but far inferior to purely citizen forces. And this example is in itself conclusive, for the realm of France would be invincible if the military ordinances of Charles VII had been retained and extended. But from

---

43  Italian mercenary companies.
44  King of France (1422-1461), in whose reign the English were largely swept out of France in the Hundred Years' War.

want of foresight men make changes which, tasting good at first, do not betray their hidden venom, as I have already observed respecting hectic fever. Nevertheless, the ruler is not truly wise who cannot discern evils before they develop themselves, and this is a faculty given to few.

If we look for the causes which first led to the overthrow of the Roman Empire, they will be found to have had their source in the employment of Gothic[45] mercenaries, for from that hour the strength of the Romans began to wane, and all the prowess which went from them passed to the Goths. And, to be brief, I say that without citizen arms no princedom is safe, but on the contrary is wholly dependent on fortune, being without the strength that could defend it in adversity. And it has always been the deliberate opinion of the wise that nothing is so infirm and fleeting as a reputation for power not founded upon a citizen army, by which I mean one composed of subjects, citizens, and dependants, all others being mercenary or auxiliary.

The methods to be followed for organizing a citizen army may readily be ascertained, if the rules above laid down by me, and by which I abide, are well considered, and attention is given to the manner in which Philip, father of Alexander the Great, and many other princes and republics have armed and organized their forces.

### 14  OF THE DUTY OF A PRINCE IN RESPECT TO MILITARY AFFAIRS

A prince, therefore, should have no care or thought but for war, and for the regulations and training it requires, and should apply himself exclusively to this as his peculiar province. For war is the sole art looked for in one who rules, and is of such efficacy that it not merely maintains those who are born princes, but often enables men to rise to that eminence from a private station; while, on the other hand, we often see that when princes devote themselves to pleasure rather than to arms, they lose their dominions. And as neglect of this art is the prime cause of such calamities,

so to be proficient in it is the surest way to acquire power. Francesco Sforza, from his renown in arms, rose from private life to be duke of Milan, while his descendants, seeking to avoid the hardships and fatigues of military life, from being princes fell back into private life. For among other causes of misfortune which your not being armed brings upon you, it makes you despised, and this is one of those reproaches against which, as shall presently be explained, a prince ought most carefully to guard.

There is comparison between an armed and an unarmed man, and it is contrary to reason to expect that the armed man should voluntarily submit to him who is unarmed, or that the unarmed man should stand secure among armed retainers. For with contempt on one side, and distrust on the other, it is impossible that men should work well together. Wherefore, as has already been said, a prince who is ignorant of military affairs, besides other disadvantages, can neither be respected by his soldiers, nor can he trust them. A prince, therefore, ought never to allow his attention to be diverted from warlike pursuits, and should occupy himself with them even more in peace than in war. This he can do in two ways, by practice or by study.

As to practice, he ought, besides keeping his soldiers well trained and disciplined, to be constantly engaged in hunting, that he may inure his body to hardships and fatigue, and gain at the same time a knowledge of places, by observing how the mountains slope, the valleys open, and the plains spread, acquainting himself with the characters of rivers and marshes, and giving the greatest attention to this subject. Such knowledge is useful to him in two ways: for first, he learns thereby to know his own country, and to understand better how it may be defended; and next, from his familiar acquaintance with its localities, he readily comprehends the character of other districts when obliged to observe them for the first time. For the hills, valleys, plains, rivers, and marshes of Tuscany, for example, have a certain resemblance to those elsewhere, so that from a knowledge of the natural features of that province, similar knowledge in respect

---

45  The Goths were one among the Germanic peoples from beyond the empire.

to other provinces may readily be gained. The prince who is wanting in this kind of knowledge is wanting in the first qualification of a good captain, for by it he is taught how to surprise an enemy, how to choose an encampment, how to lead his army on a march, how to array it for battle, and how to post it to the best advantage for a siege.

Among the commendations which Philopoemon,[46] prince of the Achaeans, has received from historians is this: that in times of peace he was always thinking of methods of warfare, so that when walking in the country with his friends he would often stop and talk with them on the subject. "If the enemy," he would say, "were posted on that hill, and we found ourselves here with our army, which of us would have the better position? How could we most safely and in the best order advance to meet them? If we had to retreat, what direction should we take? If they retired, how should we pursue?" In this way he put to his friends, as he went along, all the contingencies that can befall an army. He listened to their opinions, stated his own, and supported them with reasons, and from his being constantly occupied with such meditations, it resulted that, when in actual command, no complication could ever present itself with which he was not prepared to deal.

As to the mental training of which we have spoken, a prince should read histories, and in these should note the actions of great men, observe how they conducted themselves in their wars, and examine the causes of their victories and defeats, so as to avoid the latter and imitate them in the former. And above all, he should, as many great men of past ages have done, assume for his models those persons who before his time have been renowned and celebrated, whose deeds and achievements he should constantly keep in mind, as it is related that Alexander the Great sought to resemble Achilles,[47] Caesar Alexander, and Scipio[48] Cyrus. And anyone who reads the life of this last named hero, written by Xenophon,[49] recognizes afterwards in the life of Scipio how much this imitation

was the source of his glory, and how nearly in his chastity, affability, kindliness, and generosity, he conformed to the character of Cyrus as Xenophon describes it.

A wise prince, therefore, should pursue such methods as these, never resting idle in times of peace, but strenuously seeking to turn them to account, so that he may derive strength from them in the hour of danger, and find himself ready, should fortune turn against him, to resist her blows.

## 15 OF THE QUALITIES IN RESPECT TO WHICH MEN, AND MOST OF ALL PRINCES, ARE PRAISED AND BLAMED

It now remains for us to consider what ought to be the conduct and bearing of a prince in relation to his subjects and friends. And since I know that many have written on this subject, I fear it may be thought presumptuous in me to write of it also—the more so because in my treatment of it I depart from the views that others have taken.

But since it is my object to write what shall be useful to whosoever understands it, it seems to me better to follow the real truth of things than an imaginary view of them. For many republics and princedoms have been imagined that were never seen or known to exist in reality. And the manner in which we live, and that in which we ought to live, are things so far apart, that he who leaves the one for the other is more likely to destroy than to save himself since anyone who would act up to a perfect standard of goodness in everything must be ruined among so many who are not good. It is essential, therefore, for a prince who desires to maintain his position to have learned how to be other than good, and to use or not to use his goodness as necessity requires.

Laying aside, therefore, all fanciful notions concerning a prince, and considering those only that are true, I say that all men when they are spoken of, and princes more than others from their being set so high, are characterized by some one of those qualities which

---

46  General of the Achaean League in Greece (*c.* 253-183 BC).
47  The mythical Greek hero of the *Iliad*.
48  I.e., Scipio Africanus (238-183 BC), who led the Romans to victory against Carthage.
49  Greek historical writer of the fourth century BC.

attract either praise or blame. Thus one is accounted generous, another miserly (which word I use, rather than *avaricious*, to denote the man who is too sparing of what is his own, *avarice* being the disposition to take wrongfully what is another's); one is generous, another greedy; one cruel, another tender hearted; one is faithless, another true to his word; one effeminate and cowardly, another high spirited and courageous; one is courteous, another haughty; one impure, another chaste; one simple, another crafty; one firm, another flexible; one grave, another frivolous; one devout, another unbelieving; and the like. Everyone, I know, will admit that it would be most laudable for a prince to be endowed with all of the above qualities that are reckoned good. But since it is impossible for him to possess or constantly practice them all, the conditions of human nature not allowing it, he must be discreet enough to know how to avoid the infamy of those vices that would deprive him of his government, and, if possible, be on his guard also against those which might not deprive him of it; though if he cannot wholly restrain himself, he may with less scruple indulge in the latter. He need never hesitate, however, to incur the reproach of those vices without which his authority can hardly be preserved. For if he considers the whole matter, he will find that there may be a line of conduct having the appearance of virtue, to follow which would be his ruin, and that there may be another course having the appearance of vice, by following which his safety and well being are secured.

### 16  OF GENEROSITY AND MISERLINESS

Beginning, then, with the first of the qualities noted above, I say that it may be a good thing to be reputed generous, but, nevertheless, that generosity without the reputation of it is harmful because, though it is worthily and rightly used, still if it is not known, you do not escape the reproach of its opposite vice. Hence, to have credit for generosity with the world at large, you must never neglect sumptuous display, the result being that a prince of a generous disposition will consume his whole substance in things of this sort and,

after all, be obliged, if he would maintain his reputation for generosity, to burden his subjects with extraordinary taxes, and to resort to confiscations and all the other shifts whereby money is raised. But in this way he becomes hateful to his subjects, and growing impoverished, is held in little esteem by any. So that in the end, having by his generosity offended many and obliged few, he is worse off than when he began, and is exposed to all his original dangers. Recognizing this, and endeavoring to retrace his steps, he at once incurs the infamy of miserliness.

A prince, therefore, since he cannot without injury to himself practice the virtue of generosity so that it may be known, will not, if he is wise, greatly concern himself though he may be called miserly. Because in time he will come to be regarded as more and more generous, when it is seen that through his parsimony his revenues are sufficient; that he is able to defend himself against any who make war on him; that he can engage in enterprises against others without burdening his subjects; and thus exercise generosity towards all from whom he does not take, whose number is infinite, while he is miserly in respect to those only to whom he does not give, whose number is few.

In our own days we have seen no princes accomplish great results save those who have been accounted miserly. All others have been ruined. Pope Julius II, after availing himself of his reputation for generosity to arrive at the papacy, made no effort to preserve that reputation when making war on the king of France, but carried on all his numerous campaigns without levying from his subjects a single extraordinary tax, providing for the increased expenditure out of his long-continued savings. Had the present king of Spain[50] been accounted generous, he never could have engaged or succeeded in so many enterprises.

A prince, therefore, if he is enabled thereby to forbear from plundering his subjects, to defend himself, to escape poverty and contempt, and the necessity of becoming rapacious, ought to care little if he incurs the reproach of miserliness, for this is one of those vices which enable him to reign.

---

50   King Ferdinand of Aragon (1479-1516), whose marriage to Queen Isabella of Castile (1474-1504) created a unified Spain.

And should any object that Caesar[51] by his generosity rose to power, and that many others have been advanced to the highest dignities from their having been generous and so reputed, I reply, "Either you are already a prince or you seek to become one; in the former case generosity is harmful, in the latter it is very necessary that you be thought generous. Caesar was one of those who sought the sovereignty of Rome, but if after obtaining it he had lived on without retrenching his expenditure, he must have ruined the empire." And if it be further urged that many princes reputed to have been most generous have achieved great things with their armies, I answer that a prince spends either what belongs to himself and his subjects, or what belongs to others, and that in the former case he ought to be sparing, but in the latter ought not to refrain from any kind of generosity. Because for a prince who leads his armies in person and maintains them by plunder, pillage, and forced contributions, dealing as he does with the property of others this generosity is necessary, since otherwise he would not be followed by his soldiers. Of what does not belong to you or to your subjects you should, therefore, be a lavish giver, as were Cyrus, Caesar, and Alexander, for to be generous with the property of others does not detract from your reputation, but adds to it. What injures you is to give away what is your own. And there is no quality so self-destructive as generosity, for while you practice it you lose the means whereby it can be practiced, and become poor and despised, or else, to avoid poverty, you become rapacious and hated. For generosity leads to one or other of these two results, against which, beyond all others, a prince should guard.

Wherefore it is wiser to put up with the name of being miserly, which breeds ignominy, but without hate, than to be obliged, from the desire to be reckoned generous, to incur the reproach of rapacity, which breeds hate as well as ignominy.

## 17 OF CRUELTY AND CLEMENCY, AND WHETHER IT IS BETTER TO BE LOVED OR FEARED

Passing to the other qualities above referred to, I say that every prince should desire to be accounted merciful and not cruel. Nevertheless, he should be on his guard against the abuse of this quality of mercy. Cesare Borgia was reputed cruel, yet his cruelty restored the Romagna, united it, and brought it to order and obedience; so that if we look at things in their true light, it will be seen that he was in reality far more merciful than the people of Florence, who, to avoid the imputation of cruelty, suffered Pistoia[52] to be torn to pieces by factions.

A prince should therefore disregard the reproach of being thought cruel where it enables him to keep his subjects united and obedient. For he who quells disorder by a very few signal examples will in the end be more merciful than he who from too great leniency permits things to take their course and so to result in rapine and bloodshed. For these hurt the whole state, whereas the severities of the prince injure individuals only.

And for a new prince, of all others, it is impossible to escape a name for cruelty, since new states are full of dangers. Wherefore Vergil, by the mouth of Dido,[53] excuses the harshness of her reign on the plea that it was new, saying

Res dura, et regni novitas me talia cogunt
Moliri, et late fines custode tueri.[54]

Nevertheless, the new prince should neither be too ready of belief, nor too easily set in motion; nor should he himself be the first to raise alarms, but should so temper prudence with kindliness that too great confidence in others shall not throw him off his guard, nor groundless distrust render him unbearable.

And here comes in the question whether it is better to be loved rather than feared, or feared rather than

---

51   I.e., Julius Caesar (first century BC).
52   A city under Florence's control, and which was torn by internal conflict in 1501-1502.
53   In the Roman epic, Vergil's *Aeneid*, Dido founded the north African city of Carthage.
54   Latin: "A hard fate and the newness of my rule compel me to do such things and guard a wide domain."

loved. It might perhaps be answered that we should wish to be both. But since love and fear can hardly exist together, if we must choose between them, it is far safer to be feared than loved. For of men it may generally be affirmed that they are thankless, fickle, false, studious to avoid danger, greedy for gain, devoted to you while you are able to confer benefits upon them, and ready, as I said before, while danger is distant, to shed their blood, and sacrifice their property, their lives, and their children for you; but in the hour of need they turn against you. The prince, therefore, who without otherwise securing himself builds wholly on their promises, is undone. For the friendships which we buy with a price, and do not gain by greatness and nobility of character, though they are fairly earned, are not made good, but fail us when we have occasion to use them.

Moreover, men are less careful how they offend him who makes himself loved than him who makes himself feared. For love is held by the tie of obligation, which, because men are a sorry breed, is broken on every whisper of private interest. But fear is bound by the apprehension of punishment which never relaxes its grasp.

Nevertheless, a prince should inspire fear in such a fashion that, if he does not win love, he may escape hate. For a man may very well be feared and yet not hated, and this will be the case so long as he does not meddle with the property or with the women of his citizens and subjects. And if constrained to put any to death, he should do so only when there is manifest cause or reasonable justification. But, above all, he must abstain from the property of others. For men will sooner forget the death of their father than the loss of their patrimony. Moreover, pretexts for confiscation are never hard to find, and he who has once begun to live by rapine always finds reasons for taking what is not his, whereas reasons for shedding blood are fewer, and sooner exhausted.

But when a prince is with his army, and has many soldiers under his command, he must disregard the reproach of cruelty, for without such a reputation in its captain, no army can be held together or kept under any kind of control. Among other things remarkable in Hannibal, this has been noted: that having a very great army, made up of men of many different nations and brought to fight in a foreign country, no dissension ever arose among the soldiers themselves, or any mutiny against their leader, either in his good or in his evil fortunes. This we can only ascribe to the transcendent cruelty, which, joined with numberless great qualities, rendered him at once venerable and terrible in the eyes of his soldiers, for without this reputation for cruelty these other virtues would not have produced the like results.

Unreflecting writers, indeed, while they praise his achievements, have condemned the chief cause of them. But that his other merits would not by themselves have been so efficacious we may see from the case of Scipio, one of the greatest captains, not only of his own time, but of all times of which we have record, whose armies rose against him in Spain from no other cause than his too great leniency in allowing them a freedom inconsistent with military strictness. This was the weakness with which Fabius Maximus taxed him in the Senate House, calling him the corrupter of the Roman soldiery. Again, when the Locrians[55] were shamefully outraged by one of his lieutenants, he neither avenged them, nor punished the insolence of his officer. This was from the natural easiness of his disposition, so that it was said in the Senate by one who sought to excuse him that there were many who knew better how to refrain from doing wrong themselves than how to correct the wrongdoing of others. This temper, however, would in time have marred the name and fame even of Scipio, had he continued in it, and retained his command. But living as he did under the control of the Senate, this harmful quality was not merely disguised, but came to be regarded as a glory.

Returning to the question of being loved or feared, I sum up by saying that since his being loved depends upon his subjects, while his being feared depends upon himself, a wise prince should build on what is his own, and not on what rests with others. Only, as I have said, he must do his utmost to escape hatred.

## 18  HOW PRINCES SHOULD KEEP FAITH

Everyone understands how praiseworthy it is in a prince to keep faith, and to live uprightly and not

---

55   A people of Sicily.

craftily. Nevertheless, we see from what has taken place in our own days that princes who have set little store by their word, but have known how to overreach men by their cunning, have accomplished great things, and in the end gotten the better of those who trusted to honest dealing.

Let it be known, then, that there are two ways of contending, one in accordance with the laws, the other by force, the first of which is proper to men, the second to beasts. But since the first method is often ineffectual, it becomes necessary to resort to the second. A prince should, therefore, understand how to use well both the man and the beast. And this lesson has been covertly taught by the ancient writers, who relate that Achilles and many others of these old princes were given over to be brought up and trained by Chiron the Centaur,[56] since the only meaning of their having for instructor one who was half man and half beast is that it is necessary for a prince to know how to use both natures, and that the one without the other has no stability.

But since a prince should know how to use the beast's nature wisely, he ought, among beasts, to choose both the lion and the fox. For the lion cannot guard himself from traps, or the fox from wolves. He must therefore be a fox to discern traps, and a lion to drive off wolves.

To rely wholly on the lion is unwise, and for this reason a prudent prince neither can nor ought to keep his word when to keep it is harmful to him and the causes which led him to pledge it are removed. If all men were good, this would not be good advice, but since they are dishonest and do not keep faith with you, you, in return, need not keep faith with them, and no prince was ever at a loss for plausible reasons to cloak a breach of faith. Of this numberless recent instances could be given, and it might be shown how many solemn treaties and engagements have been rendered inoperative and idle through want of faith in princes, and that he who was best known to play the fox has had the best success.

It is necessary, indeed, to put a good color on this nature, and to be skillful in simulating and dissem-

bling. But men are so simple, and governed so absolutely by their present needs, that he who wishes to deceive will never fail in finding willing dupes. One recent example I will not omit. Pope Alexander VI had no care or thought but how to deceive, and always found material on which to work. No man ever had a more effective manner of asseverating, or made promises with more solemn protestations, or observed them less. And yet, because he understood this side of human nature, his frauds always succeeded.

It is not essential, then, that a prince should have all the qualities which I have enumerated above, but it is most essential that he should seem to have them. I will even venture to affirm that if he has and invariably practices them all, they are harmful, whereas the appearance of having them is useful. Thus, it is well to seem merciful, faithful, humane, religious, and upright, and also to be so; but the mind should remain so balanced that if it were needful not to be so, you would be able and know how to change to the contrary.

And you are to understand that a prince, and most of all a new prince, cannot observe all those rules of conduct in respect to which men are accounted good, being often forced, in order to preserve his princedom, to act in opposition to good faith, charity, humanity, and religion. He must therefore keep his mind ready to shift as the winds and tides of fortune turn, and, as I have already said, he ought not to quit good courses if he can help it, but should know how to follow evil courses if he must.

A prince should therefore be very careful that nothing ever escapes his lips which is not replete with the five qualities above named, so that to see and hear him, one would think him the embodiment of mercy, good faith, integrity, humanity, and religion. And there is no virtue which it is more necessary for him to seem to possess than this last because men in general judge rather by the eye than by the hand, for everyone can see, but few can touch. Everyone sees what you seem, but few know what you are, and these few dare not oppose themselves to the opinion of the many, who have the majesty of the state to back them up.

---

56   In ancient Greek myth, a creature which was half man and half horse.

Moreover, in the actions of all men, and most of all of princes, where there is no tribunal to which we can appeal, we look to results. Wherefore if a prince succeeds in establishing and maintaining his authority, the means will always be judged honorable and be approved by everyone. For the vulgar are always taken by appearances and by results, and the world is made up of the vulgar, the few only finding room when the many have no longer ground in which to stand.

A certain prince[57] of our own days, whose name it is as well not to mention, is always preaching peace and good faith, although the mortal enemy of both— and both, had he practiced them as he preaches them, would, more often than once, have lost him his kingdom and authority.

## 24  WHY THE PRINCES OF ITALY
### HAVE LOST THEIR STATES

The lessons taught above if prudently followed will make a new prince seem like an old one, and will soon seat him in his place more firmly and securely than if his authority had the sanction of time. For the actions of a new prince are watched much more closely than those of a hereditary prince, and when seen to be good are far more effective than antiquity of blood in gaining men over and attaching them to his cause. For men are more nearly touched by things present than by things past, and when they find themselves well off as they are, enjoy their happiness and seek no further. Indeed, they are ready to do their utmost in defense of the new prince, provided he is not wanting in other respects. In this way there accrues to him a twofold glory, in having laid the foundations of the new princedom, and in having strengthened and adorned it with good laws and good arms, with faithful friends and great deeds—as, on the other hand, there is a double disgrace in one who has been born to a princedom losing it by his own want of wisdom.

And if we contemplate those lords who in our own times have lost their dominions in Italy, such as the king of Naples, the duke of Milan, and others, in the first place we shall see that in respect to arms they have, for reasons already dwelled on, been all alike defective; and next, that some of them have either had the people against them, or if they have had the people with them, have not known how to secure themselves against their nobles. For without such defects as these, states powerful enough to keep an army in the field are never overthrown.

Philip of Macedon, not the father of Alexander the Great, but he who was vanquished by Titus Quintius,[58] had no great state as compared with the strength of the Romans and Greeks who attacked him. Nevertheless, being a prince of a warlike spirit, and skillful in gaining the goodwill of the people and in securing the fidelity of the nobles, he maintained himself for many years against his assailants, and in the end, though he lost some towns, succeeded in saving his kingdom.

Let those princes of ours, therefore, who, after holding them for a length of years, have lost their dominions, not blame fortune but their own inertness. For never having reflected in tranquil times that there might come a change (and it is human nature when the sea is calm not to think of storms), when adversity overtook them, they thought not of defense but only of escape, hoping that their people, disgusted with the arrogance of the conqueror, would some day recall them.

This course may be a good one to follow when all others fail, but it would be the height of folly, trusting to it, to abandon every other, since none would wish to fall on the chance of someone else being found to lift him up. It may not happen that you will be recalled by your people, or if it happens, it gives you no security. It is an ignoble resource, since it does not depend on you for its success, and those modes of defense are alone good, certain, and lasting which depend upon yourself and your own worth.

## 25  WHAT FORTUNE CAN EFFECT IN HUMAN AFFAIRS,
### AND HOW SHE MAY BE WITHSTOOD

I am not ignorant that many have been and are of the opinion that human affairs are so governed by fortune

---

57  Thought to be King Ferdinand of Spain.
58  I.e., Philip V of Macedon (220-179 BC). His defeat by the Romans ended Macedon's dominance over Greece.

and by God that men cannot alter them by any prudence of theirs, and indeed have no remedy against them, and for this reason have come to think that it is not worthwhile to labor much about anything, but that they must leave everything to be determined by chance.

Often when I turn the matter over, I am in part inclined to agree with this opinion, which has had the readier acceptance in our own times from the great changes in things which we have seen, and every day see happen contrary to all human expectation. Nevertheless, that our free will may not be not wholly set aside, I think it may be the case that fortune is the mistress of one half our actions, and yet leaves the control of the other half, or a little less, to ourselves. And I would liken her to one of those wild torrents which, when angry, overflow the plains, sweep away trees and houses, and carry off soil from one bank to throw it down upon the other. Everyone flees before them, and yields to their fury without the least power to resist. And yet, though this is their nature, it does not follow that, in seasons of fair weather, men cannot, by constructing dykes and barriers, take such precautions as will cause them when again in flood to pass off by some artificial channel, or at least prevent their course from being so uncontrolled and destructive. And so it is with fortune, who displays her might where there is no organized strength to resist her, and directs her onset where she knows that there is neither barrier nor embankment to confine her.

And if you look at Italy, which has been at once the seat of these changes and their cause, you will perceive that it is a field without embankment or barrier. For if, like Germany, France, and Spain, it had been guarded with sufficient skill, this inundation, if it ever came upon us, would never have wrought the violent changes which we have witnessed.

I think this is enough to say generally touching resistance to fortune. But confining myself more closely to the matter at hand, I note that one day we see a prince prospering and the next day overthrown, without detecting any change in his nature or character. This, I believe, comes chiefly from a cause already dwelled upon, namely, that a prince who rests wholly on fortune is ruined when she changes. Moreover, I believe that he will prosper most whose mode of acting best adapts itself to the character of the times, and conversely that he will be unprosperous with whose mode of acting the times do not accord. For we see that men in these matters which lead to the end that each has before him, namely, glory and wealth, proceed by different ways, one with caution, another with impetuosity, one with violence, another with subtlety, one with patience, another with its contrary, and that by one or other of these different courses each may succeed.

Again, of two who act cautiously, you shall find that one attains his end, the other does not, and that two of different temperaments, the one cautious, the other impetuous, are equally successful. All of this happens from no cause other than that the character of the times accords or does not accord with their methods of acting. And hence it comes, as I have already said, that two operating differently arrive at the same result, and of two operating similarly, the one succeeds and the other does not. On this likewise depend the vicissitudes of fortune. For if to one who conducts himself with caution and patience, time and circumstances are propitious, so that his method of acting is good, he goes on prospering; but if these change, he is ruined, because he does not change his method of acting.

For no man is found so prudent as to know how to adapt himself to these changes, both because he cannot deviate from the course to which nature inclines him, and because, having always prospered while adhering to one path, he cannot be persuaded that it would be good for him to forsake it. And so when occasion requires the cautious man to act impetuously, he cannot do so and is undone; whereas, had he changed his nature with time and circumstances, his fortune would have been unchanged.

Pope Julius II proceeded with impetuosity in all his undertakings, and found time and circumstances in such harmony with his mode of acting that he always obtained a happy result—witness his first expedition against Bologna, when Messer Giovanni Bentivoglio[59] was yet living. The Venetians

---

59  Who took power in Bologna, a city in the Romagna, holding it until being driven out by Julius II when he asserted his control over the territory in 1506.

were not favorable to the enterprise; neither was the king of Spain. Negotiations respecting it with the king of France were still open. Nevertheless, the pope, with his wonted hardihood and impetuosity, marched in person on the expedition, and by this movement brought the king of Spain and the Venetians to a halt, the latter through fear, the former from his eagerness to recover the entire kingdom of Naples; at the same time, he dragged after him the king of France, who, desiring to have the pope for an ally in humbling the Venetians, on finding him already in motion saw that he could not refuse him his soldiers without openly offending him. By the impetuosity of his movements, therefore, Julius effected what no other pontiff endowed with the highest human prudence could. For had he, as any other pope would have done, put off his departure from Rome until terms had been settled and everything duly arranged, he never would have succeeded. For the king of France would have found a thousand pretexts to delay him, and the others would have menaced him with a thousand alarms. I shall not touch upon his other actions, which were all of a like character, and all of which had a happy issue since the shortness of his life did not allow him to experience reverses. But if times had overtaken him, rendering a cautious line of conduct necessary, his ruin must have ensued, since he never could have departed from those methods to which nature inclined him.

To be brief, I say that since fortune changes and men stand fixed in their old ways, they are prosperous so long as there is congruity between them, and the reverse when there is not. Of this, however, I am well persuaded: that it is better to be impetuous than cautious. For fortune is a woman who to be kept under must be beaten and roughly handled, and we see that she suffers herself to be more readily mastered by those who so treat her than by those who are more timid in their approach. And always, like a woman, she favors the young, because they are less scrupulous and fiercer, and command her with greater audacity.

## 26 AN EXHORTATION TO LIBERATE ITALY FROM THE BARBARIANS

Turning over in my mind all the matters which have been considered above, and debating with myself whether in Italy at the present hour the times are such as might serve to confer honor on a new prince, and whether fit circumstances now offer an opportunity to a prudent and valiant leader to bring about changes glorious for himself and beneficial to the whole Italian people, it seems to me that so many conditions combine to further such an enterprise that I know of no time so favorable to it as the present. And if, as I have said, it was necessary in order to display the valor of Moses that the children of Israel should be slaves in Egypt, and to know the greatness and courage of Cyrus that the Persians should be oppressed by the Medes, and to illustrate the excellence of Theseus that the Athenians should be scattered and divided, so at this hour, to prove the worth of some Italian hero, it was required that Italy should be brought to her present abject condition, to be more a slave than the Hebrews, more oppressed than the Persians, more disunited than the Athenians, without a head, without order, beaten, spoiled, torn in pieces, overrun, and abandoned to destruction in every form.

But though, heretofore, glimmerings may have been discerned in this man or that, whence it might be conjectured that he was ordained by God for her redemption, nevertheless it has afterwards been seen in the further course of his actions that fortune has disowned him; so that our country, left almost without life, still waits to know who it is that is to heal her bruises, to put an end to the devastation and plunder of Lombardy, to the rapacity and extortion in Naples and Tuscany, and to stanch those wounds of hers which long neglect has changed into running sores.

We see how she prays God to send someone to rescue her from these barbarous cruelties and oppressions. We see too how ready and eager she is to follow any standard if there were only someone to raise it. But at present we see no one except in your illustrious house (pre-eminent by its virtues and good fortune, and favored by God and by the church whose headship it now holds[60]),

---

60  See above, n 39.

who could undertake the part of a deliverer.

But for you this will not be too hard a task, if you keep before your eyes the lives and actions of those whom I have named above. For although these men were singular and extraordinary, after all they were but men, not one of whom had so great an opportunity as now presents itself to you. For their undertakings were not more just than this, nor more easy, nor was God more their friend than yours. The justice of the cause is conspicuous, "iustum enim est bellum quibus necessarium, et pia arma ubi nulla nisi in armis spes est."[61] Everywhere there is the strongest disposition to engage in this cause, and where the disposition is strong the difficulty cannot be great, provided you follow the methods observed by those whom I have set before you as models.

But further, we see here extraordinary and unexampled proofs of divine favor. The sea has been divided; the cloud has attended you on your way; the rock has flowed with water; the manna has rained from heaven; everything has concurred to promote your greatness. What remains to be done must be done by you, since in order not to deprive us of our free will and such share of glory as belongs to us, God will not do everything himself.

Nor is it to be marveled at if none of those Italians I have named has been able to effect what we hope to see effected by your illustrious house, or that amid so many revolutions and so many warlike movements it should always appear as though the military virtues of Italy were spent, for this comes from her old system being defective, and from no one being found among us capable of creating a new one. Nothing confers such honor on the reformer of a state as do the new laws and institutions which he devises, for these, when they stand on a solid basis and have a greatness in their scope, make him admired and venerated. And in Italy material is not wanting for improvement in every form. If the head is weak, the limbs are strong, and we see daily in single combats, or where few are engaged, how superior are the strength, dexterity, and intelligence of Italians. But when it comes to armies, they are nowhere, and this from no other reason than the defects of their leaders. For those who are skillful in arms will not obey, and everyone thinks himself skillful, since hitherto we have none among us so raised by merit or by fortune above his fellows that they should yield him the palm. And hence it happens that for the long period of 20 years, during which many wars have taken place, whenever there has been a purely Italian army it has always been beaten. To this testify, first the battle of Taro, then those of Alessandria, Capua, Genoa, Vaila, Bologna, and Mestre.[62]

If, then, your illustrious house should seek to follow the example of those great men who saved their country in past ages, it is above all things necessary, as the true foundation of every such attempt, to be provided with citizen troops, since you can have no braver, truer, or more faithful soldiers; and although every single man of them is good, collectively they will be better, seeing themselves commanded by their own prince, and honored and esteemed by him. That you may be able, therefore, to defend yourself against the foreigner with Italian valor, the first step is to provide yourself with an army such as this.

And although the Swiss and the Spanish infantry are each thought formidable, there are yet defects in both, by reason of which troops trained on a different system might not merely withstand them, but be certain of defeating them. For the Spaniards cannot resist cavalry and the Swiss will give way before infantry if they find them as resolute as themselves at close quarters. From which it has been seen, and may be seen again, that the Spaniards cannot sustain the onset of the French men-at-arms and that the Swiss are broken by the Spanish foot. And although of this last we have no complete instance, we have yet an indication of it in the battle of Ravenna,[63] where the Spanish infantry confronted the German companies who have the same discipline as the Swiss. On this occasion the Spaniards

---

61  Latin, quoting the Roman historian Livy (59 BC-AD 17): "for that war is just which is necessary, and those arms are sacred from which we derive our only hope."

62  All these took place between 1495 and 1513.

63  In 1512.

by their agility and with the aid of their bucklers forced their way under the pikes,[64] and stood ready to close with the Germans, who were no longer in a position to defend themselves, and had they not been charged by cavalry, they must have put the Germans to utter rout. Knowing, then, the defects of each of these kinds of troops, you can train your men on some different system to withstand cavalry and not to fear infantry. To effect this will not require the creation of any new forces, but simply a change in the discipline of the old. And these are matters in the reforming of which the new prince acquires reputation and importance.

This opportunity then, for Italy at last to look on her deliverer, ought not to be allowed to pass away. With what love he would be received in all those provinces which have suffered from the foreign inundation, with what thirst for vengeance, with what fixed fidelity, with what devotion, and what tears, no words of mine can declare. What gates would be closed against him? What people would refuse him obedience? What jealousy would stand in his way? What Italian but would yield him homage? This barbarian tyranny stinks in everyone's nostrils.

Let your illustrious house therefore take upon itself this enterprise with all the courage and all the hopes with which a just cause is undertaken, so that under your standard our country may be ennobled, and under your auspices the words of Petrarch[65] will be fulfilled:

Brief will be the strife
When valor arms against barbaric rage;
For the bold spirit of the bygone age
Still warms Italian hearts with life.

---

64  I.e., the long spears with metal heads which massed infantry held, rather than threw against the enemy, in the sixteenth century.
65  Italian humanist poet and scholar of the fourteenth century.

# 48

## DESIDERIUS ERASMUS, *LETTERS*

Born in Holland *c.* 1466, Desiderius Erasmus entered a semi-monastic life by becoming an Augustinian canon as a youth. He later left the order by papal permission, going on to become something of a celebrity traveller in Western Europe. He was a leading scholar of Greek, producing a new Greek edition of the New Testament and many other works, including *In Praise of Folly*, which criticized religious ritual. Although widely looked to as an ally by Protestants, he ultimately supported the Catholic church. He died in 1536.

---

### 48.1
#### LETTER TO ANNE OF BORSELLE, MARCHIONESS OF VEER
#### (PARIS, JANUARY 27, 1501)

*At the time of this letter Erasmus was far from financial security. His friend Jacobus Battus, the tutor to Anne of Borselle's son in classical languages, had introduced Erasmus into that widowed noblewoman's circle, and had been trying to use his influence with her on Erasmus's behalf. In the end, however, Erasmus was not to secure her patronage.*

Three Annas have been commended to posterity by ancient literature: one, called Perenna, who for her signal devotion to her sister Dido[1] was believed by antiquity to have been received among the gods; another, the wife of Elkanah,[2] for whom it is praise enough that, by the divine blessing, she gave birth in her old age to Samuel, not to be of service to herself, but to be a devout priest of God, and an incorruptible judge of his people; the third, the parent of the virgin mother, the grandmother of Jesus, God and man, who requires no further eulogy. The first has been consecrated by Roman muses to immortality. The second has been extolled in the Hebrew annals. The third is worshiped by Christian piety, and has been celebrated by the eloquent verse of Rodolphus Agricola and Baptista Mantuanus.[3] May Heaven grant such virtue to my writings that posterity, not unacquainted with your pious, chaste, and stainless heart, may number a fourth Anna with the other three. So shall it be, if only our feeble genius be equal to your merit....

I may venture to confess that I am the more attracted to you because I see that deity of Rhamnus,[4] whom I have always found most unkind to me, is not altogether well disposed to you, for a fellowship even in misfortunes is often a means of knitting people

---

1  Dido was the queen of Carthage in the Roman epic, Vergil's *Aeneid*.
2  In the Old Testament, a Hebrew whose wife, Hannah (Anna), remained childless into old age, and then gave birth to three children, including the Hebrew leader Samuel.
3  Respectively, a fifteenth-century Dutch scholar, artist, and advocate of classical studies, and a fifteenth-century Latin poet from Italy.
4  A community in Greece famous in antiquity for its statue of the goddess Nemesis (i.e., Revenge).

together. But what comparison can be drawn between us? Your rank is almost placed beyond the risks of Fortune, who yet sometimes gives you a pinch; but against me she rages with a constancy which is the one quality not like herself, as if she had entered into a sworn conspiracy against my letters.[5] As I trace these lines it comes into my mind (for to whom should I disclose my sorrows, if not to the only person both able and willing to heal them?), it comes into my mind, I say, that the sun rose this morning on the anniversary of the day when my little capital, the sustenance of my studies, was shipwrecked on the British shore, ever since which time I have been involved in a chain of misfortunes without a single break to the present day. For as soon as that British Charybdis[6] had restored me naked to the continent, first a cruel storm made our journey a most distressing one, and then the swords of robbers threatened to cut our throats. Then came fever, and afterwards the plague, which however did not touch me, but only drove me away. Add to these the domestic cares which one's life daily produces in abundance.

But I am ashamed, so help me heaven, that I, a man in some degree fortified by the protection of learning, and armed with the precepts of philosophy, should lose my courage, while you, whom nature has made a woman, and who have been born in the highest station and brought up in the greatest luxury, have still something to suffer, and bear it in no womanly spirit. I should remember too, that however Fortune may thunder against me, there is no excuse for my abandoning letters or allowing my heart to fail, so long as you shine before my eyes as a cynosure of security. We cannot be deprived of letters by Fortune, and those little means which my leisure requires, your wealth, abundant as your liberality, can easily supply. The poverty of Maro and Flaccus[7] was relieved by the

unstinted generosity of Maecenas;[8] the lucubrations of Pliny were encouraged by the favor of Vespasian....[9] In short, not to count the sands, as the Greeks say, every genius has found his Maecenas, and they seem to me to have made no contemptible return for their patrons, whose memory their books have consecrated to eternity. For my part I would not, in my senses, change my foster-mother for any Maecenas or any Caesar; as for the return I may make, whatever my poor genius can do shall be exerted to the utmost, that future ages may know that there existed at this extremity of the world one lady by whose beneficence good letters, corrupted by the ignorance of the unskillful, ruined by the default of princes, neglected by the indifference of mankind, were encouraged to raise their head; who found the learning of Erasmus—such as it was—deserted by those who had made noble promises, despoiled by a tyrant, beset by all the chances of Fortune, and would not suffer it to die of want. Proceed as you have begun, regard my learning as a suppliant depending upon you and imploring your aid, not only in the name of our various fortunes, but also for the love of true Theology, that excellent queen, whom the inspired psalmist describes, according to the interpretation of Jerome,[10] as standing on the king's right hand, not mean and ragged as she is now seen in the schools of sophists, but in clothing of gold, wrought about with diverse colors, to whose rescue from degradation my nightly studies are devoted.

With this object in view, I have long felt the necessity of two things: to visit Italy, so that my little learning may derive an authority from the celebrity of the place, and to take the title of doctor.[11] The one is as absurd as the other. For they who cross the sea do not change their minds, as Horace[12] says, nor will the shadow of a name make me a whit more learned. But it is no use acting a good play to be hissed by the entire

---

5 I.e., Erasmus's written works, and literature more generally.
6 In classical mythology, a sea monster which attacked sailors and was later changed by the gods into a dangerous whirlpool.
7 I.e., Vergil and Horace, two leading Roman poets of the first century BC.
8 A close adviser to the Roman Emperor Augustus, and a great patron of literary talent.
9 Pliny the elder (first century), author of an encyclopedia of natural history among other works, and uncle of Pliny the younger, best known for his letters, was supported by the Roman Emperor Vespasian (69-79).
10 Leading Christian theologian and translator of the Bible into Latin (c. 341-420).
11 I.e., of letters; not a medical degree.
12 See above, n 7.

audience, and we must put on the lion's skin to force the conviction of our competence upon the minds of those who judge a man by a title, and not by his books, which indeed they do not understand. With such monsters have I to contend, and the struggle requires another Hercules. If therefore you will arm your Erasmus to fight against these portents with equal authority as well as equal courage, not we only, but literature itself will owe its very being to you. But he must be armed with the armor of Homer's Glaucus,[13] not what he gave, but what he received. The meaning of this riddle may be learned from a letter of Battus, to whom I have disclosed all my circumstances, with an effrontery contrary to my habits and character, and to that virgin modesty which is proper to letters; but as it has been said, necessity is a hard taskmaster.

I send you herewith another *Anna*, a poem, or rather some verses I made when quite a boy, which may show you the ardent veneration which from my youthful days I have cherished for that saint. I also send some invocations, with which, as with magic charms, not the crescent moon, but she who bore the Sun of Righteousness, may be called down from heaven....[14]

I have for some time had in hand a work upon *Epistles*, and also on the *Varying of Discourse*, which is destined to aid the studies of your son Adolf, and another on *Letters*, intended to be consecrated to yourself. If these are completed later than I have wished, you will not find fault with my backwardness, but with my ill-fortune, or if you like, you will attribute it to the difficulty of the work. For to publish bad books is mere madness, and to produce good ones is the most difficult thing in the world. Farewell, and regard our muses as under your special protection.

### 48.2

TO JACOBUS BATTUS (PARIS, JANUARY 27, 1501)

That buffoon has delivered me your second letter, which is no less absurd and insulting than the former one. Unless I am much mistaken, some evil genius, angry at finding friends so attached to one another, is plotting to break off our loving union. It shall certainly never happen by my fault; pray see that it does not by yours. In the first place, what was the use of Lewis running back here, as if there were a thousand nobles to send, and not merely eight francs? Could not that little sum have been sent by someone else? And then, when you did send, why think it right to keep back anything out of so small an amount? Were you afraid that if I had enough cash I would forget my duty? Or were one or two pieces to be reserved as a reason for sending another embassy? For as to your difficulty about the letter,[15] trust me: the whole business might have been completed just as easily without this letter, if your courage had not failed. Besides, you might have asked for this very letter by the other messenger, and you will never understand what inconvenience is caused by this running backwards and forwards.

There are three or four months out of the solid year that fever leaves me for study and therefore I must put my heart into my work. I have been extending, or rather recasting, the book on *Letter-writing*, which I formerly planned, and I find I have set myself a heavy and laborious task; in the meantime this fellow comes in with your letters full of reproaches, and with even the small sum of money docked! This so disturbed me that I was on the point of throwing away what I had in hand, and intending to send the lad back without any letters, if James Tutor had not with a great deal of persuasion induced me to change my purpose. But may I die if I ever in my life wrote anything with so much repugnance as the nonsense, or rather Gnathonisms,[16] which I have written for the lady, the provost and the abbot. I dare say you will fall afoul of my "moroseness." You do not understand that there is no severer fatigue than that of a mind wearied with writing, nor consider that in this place I ought to satisfy those whose favors I am actually enjoying.

---

13   In Homer's *Iliad*, the addled Glaucus exchanges his golden armor for iron.
14   I.e., Mary, the virgin mother of Jesus, rather than Diana, the virgin moon goddess of the Romans. Anna is honored as the mother of Mary.
15   A letter which Battus had asked Erasmus to write to the marchioness of Veer, presumably the above letter.
16   The character Gnatho was a fawning parasite in the play *The Eunuch* by the Roman writer Terence (second century BC).

A year has gone by since the money was promised, and meantime your letters bring me nothing but empty hope. "Do not despair, I will diligently attend to your interests," and such phrases, of which I am sick, have been dinned over and over again into my ears. And now at last you deplore the condition of my lady's fortune! You seem to me to be sick with another person's disease. She plays the fool with her N. and you make a face. She has nothing forsooth to give! One thing I plainly see: if she gives nothing for these reasons, she will never give anything at all, for great people are never without such excuses as those. How little will it matter, in the countless number of expenses that are merely thrown away, if she gives me 200 francs? She has means to keep those cowled libertines and good for nothing scoundrels—you know whom I mean—and not to maintain the leisure of one who can write books which even posterity may value, if I may speak somewhat boastfully of myself. She has fallen, I fear, into some trouble. It is her own fault, as she has chosen to associate with that insignificant coxcomb, rather than with a grave and serious companion suitable to her sex and age. But what, I beseech you, does it matter to her fortune, if I receive 200 francs, which she would not remember seven hours after they are given?

The gist of the matter is this: to obtain the money, either in cash or so that I may receive it through a banker here at Paris. You have now written her several letters about it, all containing messages, hints, and suggestions. What can be more useless? You ought to have waited, if not for the best, at any rate for some fair opportunity, and then having set about the thing discreetly, you should have carried it out in a resolute way. This is what even at this late hour must be done. I am sure you will get the matter through, if you attempt it courageously. You may be a little more bold in the cause of a friend without compromising my modesty. How much is to be told to N. you will determine yourself. But before you go or send, let me have the remaining gold pieces by some safe messenger, and if I may ask it, to save me from want, four or five of yours, which you will recover out of the lady's

money. Only look how that little sum has melted away. I received eight francs, for that is what I got in exchange for the nobles, and out of those the boy has taken off two or not much less, not to mention his board. You say you have two angels[17] left, and out of these the messenger who brings them must be allowed something.

That John, whom you sent to England, has run away, and if I am not mistaken, has played the thief. Augustine has gone to Orleans on horseback after him. I see we shall have everything upset here. Lewis will tell you the rest. Farewell, my dear Battus, and take in good part what I have written, not from excitement or panic, but most plainly, as to the best of friends.

You will treat the boy Lewis, not as you might that ninny Adrian, who could take no harm, but as one gifted with superior intelligence, and likely to be of much use to you in many ways. He will relieve your solitude, and you will have a person to read to, to chat with about letters, and with whom, in fine, you may keep yourself in practice. Therefore, about the coat: although I do not contest the matter, still, if you do give it to him, it will be very acceptable and not unfair. Farewell.

### 48.3
TO POPE LEO X (LONDON, AUGUST 8, 1516)

I thought I would be abundantly fortunate, most blessed Father, if your Holiness had only not condemned the temerity, or importunity, with which I ventured unbidden to address a letter to the eminence of papal dignity and, what is more august, to the incomparable majesty of Leo. But this audacity has, I find, turned out most happily for me. Your more than paternal kindness has surpassed both my hopes and my wishes. Without any solicitation you have sent two letters, in one of which you distinguish me and my studies with a testimonial as complete as it is authoritative, and in the other you recommend me no less lovingly than earnestly to the king's majesty.[18] It is the

17   A kind of gold coin.
18   Henry VIII of England.

highest object to deserve the approbation of the Almighty, and next to this I certainly think it is, to be commended by the oracular voice of the supreme pontiff,[19] still more by that of Leo, that is to say, of him who, invested with the highest of all human dignities, graces it in turn by every kind of excellence and learning. If those dispatches had reached me in time, as I was then at Basel,[20] no perils of travel could have deterred me from flying to the feet of your Holiness. But having returned to my native land, while advancing years somewhat impede my movements, I am also kept back by the liberality of the government, and tied to home by the extraordinary affection of my country, the most illustrious Prince Charles, Catholic king, the incomparable light and glory of this our age, in whose dominions I was born, and by whose father Philip I was not only known but loved, having invited me to his court, while I was abroad, with the promise of an annual salary, and that without my either soliciting or expecting it, and immediately upon my return having conferred on me an ample and honorable benefice.[21] On the other hand I have found by the surest proofs how much the king of England's early predilection for me, how much the good will of the most reverend cardinal of York,[22] and the archbishop of Canterbury's[23] old interest on my behalf have been increased by the commendation of your Holiness, which was both more agreeable to me and more effectual with them, inasmuch it was not extorted by any asking on my part, but spontaneously bestowed.

Seeing myself therefore so much indebted to your Holiness, I have conceived the wish of becoming still more obliged. Indeed I shall be glad to owe my whole fortune and the sum of my felicity to Leo alone, and it is to my mind no inconsiderable part of happiness to be indebted without grudging. What my request is will be orally explained by the reverend father the bishop of Worcester, the resident envoy of the king of England at the court of your Holiness, and will be signified by letter by Andreas Ammonius, your Holiness' nuncio[24] in England, in which matter I do not doubt I shall experience that goodness which your letter freely promises, and which I am also led to expect from the benevolence of your character, whereby you recall the image of Christ, whose worthy vicegerent you are, especially as the business is of such a nature as not so much to concern my own credit, to which you have a sincere regard, as the general interest of the world, for which your solicitude is ever on the watch. I might have misemployed the recommendation of the greatest princes to obtain the favor I am seeking, but I prefer to owe whatever benefit it may be to your goodness alone....

The New Testament in Greek and Latin, revised by us, together with our annotations, has been published for some time, under the safeguard of your auspicious name. I do not know whether the work pleases everyone, but I find that up to this time it has certainly been approved by the most approved and principal theologians, and among the first by that incomparable prelate,[25] Christopher, bishop of Basel, who witnessed its printing. For by this labor we do not intend to tear up the old and commonly accepted edition, but to emend it in some places where it is corrupt, and to make it clear where it is obscure, and this not by the dreams of my own mind, nor, as they say, with unwashed hands, but partly by the evidence of the earliest manuscripts, and partly by the opinion of those whose learning and sanctity have been confirmed by the authority of the Church—I mean Jerome, Hilary, Ambrose, Augustine, Chrysostom, and Cyril.[26] In the meantime we are always prepared either to give our reasons, without presumption, for anything which we have rightly taught, or to correct,

---

19  I.e., the pope.
20  In Switzerland.
21  An income-producing church office.
22  Thomas Wolsey, the King's chief minister.
23  William Warham.
24  I.e., a papal diplomatic representative.
25  I.e., high church official.
26  All fathers of the church, i.e., authoritative Christian writers of the church's early centuries.

without grudging, any passage where as men we have unwittingly fallen into error. We sent one volume to Rome last winter, still fresh and warm from the press, which I suppose was delivered to your Holiness; I would send the other now, if I did not know that there is no place in the world where the work is not by this time within reach of everybody. Although the greatest pains have been bestowed upon it, so far as the limit of time allowed by the prince, and the condition of my health admitted, yet I shall never be tired out, and will never rest, until I have made it so complete and so correct that it may appear not altogether unworthy of the great pontiff and great personage to whom it is dedicated.

The revised Jerome will be published next September. It will be, I think, an auspicious revival, and is expected with much interest by all the learned. And in future no page will be produced by Erasmus which will not carry with it some praise of Leo....

Farewell, and may Christ long save your Holiness, to illustrate and propagate His religion, and to relieve the troubles of mankind.

### 48.4

#### TO LAMBERTUS GRUNNIUS, APOSTOLIC SECRETARY
#### (AUGUST, 1516)

*This letter is widely regarded as a barely disguised, slightly fictionalized piece of autobiography. Its addressee, a papal official, also seems to have been a fiction, and Erasmus is to be regarded as the author of "Grunnius's" reply (below).*

Hitherto, most erudite Lambert, often as my interference has been solicited, I have been glad to keep clear of suits of this kind, as I could not bear to be burdensome to any of my friends. But in this instance a special sense of duty has induced me to undertake a novel advocacy, and to solicit one of my best friends on behalf of another friend. I therefore first of all beg this favor of you: that you will condescend to become acquainted with the whole course of the transaction, being confident that, if this request is granted, you will approve my interest in the matter, and will also glad-ly accord your own, not merely to our friendship, for which I am sure there is nothing you would not do, but to the cause itself. For the matter at stake is not goat's wool, as the saying goes, but the safety of a supremely gifted character, which will be buried alive and utterly lost unless we come to the rescue. Would that the nature of the whole proceeding were as well known to you as it is to me! In that case, I am quite sure that with three words I should gain your judgment in my client's favor. Nevertheless I will draw you such a genuine picture of the whole affair that nothing, or at any rate little that is worth knowing, may escape your attention. For the person whose cause I plead has been so well known to me from boyhood that I am scarcely better known to myself; as to most of the facts of the case, I have not merely heard them, but have seen them with my own eyes. It is so shameful a story that I can scarcely recall the circumstances without tears, and it may be, such is the kindness of your nature, that your eyes will not be dry while you read them. Indeed it is part of our religion not only to rejoice with those that rejoice, but to weep with those that weep.

I am sure, my excellent friend, that you know well and detest heartily the obstinate temper of a sort of Pharisees,[27] who not only, according to the testimony of the Gospel, compass seas and lands, but find their way into every prince's court, into every rich man's house, into every school, into every drinking party, to entice some proselyte into their net, and use artifices that can hardly be believed to ensnare the simplicity of boys and girls. They know their age, how liable it is to injury and fraud, and are intent on dragging them into a kind of life from which, once caught, they cannot extricate themselves, and which is therefore more miserable than servitude, inasmuch as a slave bought under the hammer may deserve so well of his master as to become a freedman.

For my own part I do not care to find fault with anyone's plan of life, nor will I defend those who, having heedlessly thrown themselves into the ditch, turn bad into worse by taking refuge, not in liberty, but in a license of sinning. There is however so great a vari-

---

27  A Jewish group led by the Scribes; they criticized Jesus for appearing to violate the Hebrew ritual law of the Old Testament.

ety in men's bodies and minds that the same conditions do not suit everybody, and no more unhappy a fate can befall persons of signal ability than to be inveigled or forced into a kind of life from which they cannot extricate themselves. For human happiness depends mainly upon this: that everyone should apply himself to that for which he is naturally fitted. There are some people whose devotion to celibacy or monasticism is no more likely to succeed than if you brought an ass into an Olympic race, or "an ox to the appointment,"[28] as the saying goes. But I have said enough by way of preface. You shall now hear the story of this young man's misfortune, and of the detestable persistence of those kidnappers.

There are two brothers, Florence and his elder brother, Antony. When very young, they lost their mother, and their father, dying soon after, left them a slender patrimony, which would however have been abundantly sufficient for the completion of their studies if the rapacity of the kinsfolk who were present at his death had not diminished the amount. For not a farthing of ready money was found. But what was left in landed property or in bills, not so freely exposed to those harpies' claws, was in any case enough to pay the cost of a liberal education, if again a good deal had not been lost by the carelessness of the guardians. You know how few people there are who are honestly vigilant in a matter in which they are not themselves interested. But in this case the guardians had set their hearts on educating their wards for a monastery, reckoning it an act of signal piety if their living was thus secured. And being themselves this way disposed, they were encouraged—especially one of them, a schoolmaster under whom the boys had in their early childhood learned the rudiments of Grammar—by the advice of one warden, a supercilious man with a great reputation for piety. The schoolmaster was, according to common estimation, a pious and harmless man; that is to say, he had not lost his character by gambling or lewdness or drunkenness or other offenses, but living for himself and very parsimonious, he was not remarkable for good sense, and had no regard for any

learning beyond the little he had himself acquired. When Florence, in his fourteenth year, wrote him a letter in a somewhat polished style, he roughly answered that if he was going to send him such letters, he had better add a commentary; for his own part he had always been accustomed to write plainly and point by point—that was the expression he used. He seems, like a great many persons I know, to have been disposed to think that he was offering a most acceptable sacrifice to God if he induced any of his pupils to adopt a monastic life, and he is accustomed to boast of the number of young people whom year by year he has succeeded in gaining for St. Francis, St. Dominic, St. Augustine, St. Benedict or St. Bridget.[29]

Accordingly, when the boys were ripe for a university—for they were well grounded in grammar and had learned a great part of the *Dialectic* of Petrus Hispanus,[30] still fearing they might imbibe from this learning something of a worldly spirit and refuse the yoke, he had them sent away to one of the houses of the so-called Collationary Brethren, who are building their nests all over the world, and earning a living by the education of boys. These teachers, if they find in any boy a more generous and lively spirit, such as commonly distinguishes the happiest intellects, make it their main endeavor, by means of blows, threats, reproaches and various other devices, to break it and cast it down (they call this "taming"), and fit it for monastic life. On this account they are in high favor with the Dominicans and Franciscans, who say their orders would soon come to an end unless a seed-plot were grown for them in the houses of these Brethren. For it is out of their squads that the friars enlist their own recruits. I myself think that they have among them persons who are not at all bad; but deficient as they are in the best authors, living in their own darkness and with certain rites and customs of their own, having little opportunity of comparing themselves with others, and compelled to spend a good part of the day in stated tasks of prayer and work, I do not see how they are in a position to educate boys in a liberal way; at any rate it is shown by experience that there is

---

28 Old Testament, Proverbs 7.22.

29 I.e., the various religious orders founded by, or named for, these figures.

30 A thirteenth-century scholastic.

no school that produces youths less elegantly taught or inferior in character.

Under these teachers our two brothers lost two years and more. In the case of the younger, the time was certainly lost, as he was more advanced than his teachers in the studies which they professed. Of one of them Florence declares that he has not seen anywhere a monster more ignorant or more conceited. Such persons are often placed in charge of boys, not being chosen by the judgment of learned men, but by the discretion of a patriarch, who generally knows nothing of letters. There was one, however, who always seemed to be specially pleased with Florence's character, and who, when he heard of his intended return to his country, endeavored in private conversation to induce him to join their society, mentioning many attractions which are inviting to boys. I wish he had succeeded; in that case Florence would either have stayed with them of his own accord out of love of religion, or if circumstances led to his departure, he might without hindrance have returned to his original freedom. For this class of men possesses one main advantage as a vestige of primitive religion: that they are not bound by indissoluble vows. Indeed, if the judgment of truly pious and spiritual persons prevailed over the opinion of dullards, there would be in future no indissoluble vows, save those of baptism, especially in the present condition of human malice, or shall we call it imbecility? When, however, this brother followed up his advances with frequent exhortations, adding from time to time flattering speeches and presents and caresses, the boy made answer in no boyish fashion, saying that he had not yet knowledge enough either of the kind of life or of himself, but that when he was of riper age he would consider the matter. The brother, not being quite a fool or knave, gave up the pursuit; but I know some of that society who have tried, not only by intimidation and blandishments, but even by appeals to heaven which make one shudder—I would almost say by exorcisms and enchantments—to stupefy the minds of rich and well-born boys, not 14 years of age, and induce them, without the knowledge of their parents, to devote themselves to the brotherhood. If this is not kidnapping, what is?

Accordingly, when Antony and Florence had returned to their old home, their guardians, who had not dealt with their estate, scanty as it was, in the most scrupulous way, began to make arrangements for carrying out the monastic scheme, partly in order to be sooner relieved of their trust, and partly because the schoolmaster, as I have said before, thought that he should propitiate the deity with a most acceptable sacrifice if he slew two sheep upon his altar. This person was now the sole manager of the estate, one of the other guardians having caught the plague and died suddenly, leaving his accounts unsettled, and the other, a merchant, not taking much interest in the matter.

Florence, perceiving them to be acting as if they had the will of their wards in absolute bondage, took counsel with his brother, who was his elder by nearly 3 years (he himself being scarcely more than 15), whether he was really disposed to consent to be bound by knots which he could not afterwards untie. Antony frankly admitted that he was not attracted by any love of religion, but dragged on by fear of his guardians.

"What," said Florence, "can be more silly than your conduct, if from any foolish shame and fear of men, from whom at any rate you need not be afraid of blows, you throw yourself into a kind of life, the nature of which you do not know, and from which, when you have once entered it, you cannot withdraw?"

At this point Antony began to plead their means, which were both slender in themselves and diminished by their guardians' negligence. "There is nothing to fear," said Florence. "We will scrape together what is left, and when we have made up a little sum, we will go to the university. We shall not be without friends; many who have nothing at all are maintained by their own industry, and finally God will aid those whose intentions are honest."

This answer was so agreeable to Antony that he pointed out himself many hopeful considerations which had not occurred to the younger boy. It was therefore resolved between them that the monastic question should be put off to a later period, when after spending three or four years in the schools,[31] they

31   I.e., at university.

might from their age and experience be better able to see what was best. This conclusion was accepted without hesitation by both brothers, but the elder was still tormented by doubt as to what answer was to be given to the guardians, who without ascertaining the wishes of their wards, were beginning in good earnest to carry out their own plan. A form of answer was hit upon which was approved by Antony; he begged only that the younger boy would be spokesman, and answer in the name of both, being himself more timid in speech, as he was less forward in learning. Florence agreed to this demand, but strongly insisted on his brother's adherence to his resolution; "for if," he said, "you desert me after the answer has been given, the whole catastrophe will fall on my head. You had better change your mind now, if you think you can be driven from your position either by blandishments or by harsh words. Take my word for it, the thing we are doing is no laughing matter." Antony then pledged his word in the most solemn way that he would abide by his own declaration.

When some days had passed, the guardian came, and after a long preface about his affection for his wards and his extraordinary zeal and vigilance on their behalf, began to congratulate them on his having found them a place among those who have a double title to the name of canons. The boy Florence, answering according to their agreement for both, thanked the guardian for all the pains he had taken, but said that his brother and he did not think it prudent for them, young and inexperienced as they were, to attach themselves to any scheme of life, not having as yet sufficient knowledge of themselves or of the nature of the proposed undertaking. They therefore thought it would be better, if after some years spent in study, this question were taken up at a more seasonable time.

The guardian, had he been a really pious man with a fair share of evangelical wisdom, might well have been pleased with so mature an answer from so young a person; indeed, if he had seen his wards too much inclined out of youthful ardor in the direction he expected, he ought to have held them back, and refused to act immediately upon the faith of a passing

impulse. His conduct was quite different. He fired up, as if he had received a blow, and although he generally appeared to be a person of mild character, on this occasion he had no control over his temper, and was scarcely restrained by shame from violence. With a supremely contemptuous air he called Florence a scapegrace, and said that "he had not the spirit" (you recognize the monkish expression); he renounced the guardianship, and refused to be answerable to those from whom he had bought their provisions, protesting that there was no balance remaining, and they must see where they could get their food for themselves.

These and many other reproaches, with which he belabored the boy, made him drop some tears—but not the purpose he had deliberately taken up. "We accept," he said, "the renunciation of the guardianship, and relieve you from your care of us." This was the conclusion of the interview.

The guardian, finding that he made no way by threats and wrangling, fetches in his brother, the merchant already mentioned, a singularly courteous and fairspoken gentleman. The interview takes place in his garden, where the boys are invited to sit down; cups are brought in, and after some friendly conversation, the old proposal is introduced more carefully and in a different fashion. The guardians were all amiability. They told many fibs about the marvelous felicity of that state of life; they pointed to brilliant hopes of future grandeur; added entreaties, and what not. Under this influence the elder youth began to waver, having apparently forgotten his repeated oaths of constancy, while the younger nevertheless persevered in his resolution. To cut the matter short, the traitor betrayed his brother, and submitted to the yoke, quietly purloining whatever ready money there was, a proceeding that was no novelty on his part. His story had a fine ending. As he was inert in mind, so he was robust of body, attentive to business and in that respect sharp and cunning, thievish in money matters, a brave tippler and an arrant rake, in fine so unlike his brother that you might suppose him a changeling. For indeed to him he was never anything but his evil genius. Not long after, he took the same part among his companions as Iscariot[32]

---

32   I.e., Jesus's disciple Judas, who betrayed him.

among the apostles. When, however, he saw his brother caught in the trap, he was touched by the stings of conscience, and lamented that he had enticed him into the net and brought him to destruction. It was the confession of Judas! Would that he had hanged himself like his prototype, before he would have been guilty of so impious a crime!

Florence, like most of those who are born for literature, was unskillful and careless in ordinary business. Upon such subjects his simplicity was marvelous, whereas you may find some boys grown up in cunning while still children in years. The vigor of his mind was shown only in study, and its efforts were all exerted in the direction towards which he was by nature impelled, having been a student from his early infancy. Of a delicate constitution, but not unfitted for intellectual pursuits, he had scarcely entered his sixteenth year. It should be added that he was then in feeble health, having been suffering for more than a year with a quartan fever, contracted from the sordid and illiberal fashion in which he had been brought up. Which way should a lad of this sort turn, betrayed and abandoned as he was, without any knowledge of affairs, and not free from sickness? Was not force enough exerted to constrain the will of a child? He nevertheless persisted in the decision which he had deliberately adopted.

Meanwhile, that stupid guardian, intent on carrying out his plan, brings upon the scene a variety of characters of diverse conditions and also of diverse sex: monks, half-monks, cousins male and cousins female, young persons and old, known and unknown, among whom were some such natural fools that, if they had not been distinguished by the dress of their holy profession, they might have roamed the streets as clowns with foolscaps and bells. There were others too, whom I judge to have erred rather from superstition than from any malicious intention; but what does it matter to a dying man, whether he is slaughtered by folly or by malice? In these circumstances, how many engines were brought to bear upon the resolution of a boy? One drew a charming picture of monastic tranquillity, picking out every favorable point—a quartan fever might be praised in this way—adding a liberal supply of lies, and suppressing all the contrary facts. Another, in tragic vein, magnified the perils of the world, as if monks were outside the world, as they sometimes draw pictures of themselves sailing in a well-guarded ship while everyone else is tossed about in the waves, and on the point of perishing unless they throw out a spar or rope to save him. A third gave a lively description of the tortures of hell, as if there were no thoroughfare between a convent[33] and the realms below. Another struck terror by legendary examples, of which they have a plentiful supply; while stories were related of miraculous visions, as silly as those told by old wives about ghosts and goblins.

Some plied the boy with tales of a different kind, about the monk with whom Christ discoursed for several hours every day, or about Catherine of Siena,[34] who in her childhood was so much a spouse or lover of Christ that they walked backwards and forwards in her chamber, and sometimes said their prayers together. They laid special stress upon the communion of good works, as if they had themselves an excess of them, and did not sometimes stand, even more than the laity, in need of divine mercy, or as if there were not in the whole body of Christ a participation of all that is done right. Not to prolong my story, every kind of engine was brought to bear on the mind of a simple boy, abandoned by the treachery of a brother, and broken in health; the siege being pressed with as much care, zeal and watchfulness as if there had been a wealthy city to be taken. So important did it seem to these more than Pharisees, to consign one poor youth, alive and breathing, to the grave.

There were some among them who were acting in the interest of their own order, for which they are so much concerned that they quarrel with one another most fiercely on that score, regarding our common profession of Christianity as scarcely of any account. The boy was clever, and well-read, with a faculty of speech beyond his years, and they hoped that his tal-

33   I.e., the residential community of a religious order.
34   An Italian saint and mystic of the fourteenth century.

ents would confer no small distinction on their society. This was the meaning of their pious zeal.

There were many incidents, most learned Grunnius, which, to avoid tiring you, I purposely omit. Your knowledge of the world will enable you from what I have related to guess the rest. Florence, meanwhile, was between the altar and the knife, as it is said in the Proverbs,[35] and while he was looking around to see whether any deity would appear to offer some hope of escape, he happened to pay a visit at a college[36] of canons near the town where he then lived. There he fell in with a former comrade some years older than himself, named Cantelius, with whom he had been brought up as a child. This young man was of a shrewd turn of mind, with his own interest always in view, but at the same time of a haughty temper. He had been induced to enter a convent not so much by religious feeling as by a regard for his appetite and a love of ease. He had not been successful as a student, being skillful only in singing, an art that he had practiced from his earliest years. On his return from Italy, where he had chased Fortune in vain, he found his parents bewailing the narrowness of their circumstances and the multitude of their children, and consequently took refuge in a cowl,[37] for which there is this to be said: that it provides a fairly comfortable subsistence for many a creature that would otherwise starve.

In this interview Cantelius did not fail to observe how accomplished a scholar Florence had become. His next thought was for himself, and, being of a mercurial turn, he set to work with incredible ardor to persuade the other to share his profession, drawing an attractive picture of the monastic life, and exaggerating its sacred tranquillity, freedom and concord, representing it, in short, as a fellowship of angels, and especially repeating and impressing on his friend what an abundance there was of books and what leisure for study. He knew the bait with which the lad's mind might be caught. If you had heard him, you

might have thought it was not a monastery he was describing, but the muses'[38] bower.

Florence, with all the sincerity of his character, loved Cantelius with a childish and passionate love, which was strengthened by their unexpected reunion, as boys of that age often conceive a violent affection for some of their schoolfellows. He did not yet know men's characters, but judged of others by himself, while Cantelius left no stone unturned, using every means to bewitch the boy's mind, but without producing any effect.

After his return from that visit, Florence had to meet a fresh attack from his other assailants, who had armed themselves with more powerful engines than ever. They now insisted on the desperate state of his fortune, the displeasure of all his friends, and finally on the prospect before him of the most cruel sort of death—starvation—if he did not "renounce the world." Such is the language they use, applying this word of reproach to those whom Christ has with His own blood redeemed from the world, and claiming, as peculiar to monks, that which is the common privilege of all Christians. Having for some time been more worried than convinced by their arguments, he paid another visit to Cantelius, merely for the sake of having some discussion with him. It was now that worthy's object, to which he directed his utmost efforts, to secure a companion who would give him lessons in secret and without cost. Florence, on the other hand, was singularly disposed to form attachments, and prompt to comply with the wishes of any friend. The result was that, there being no end to those deafening arguments, and no gleam of hope appearing elsewhere, he betook himself to a convent—not the one proposed by his guardian, but that in which he had happened to find a foster-brother.[39] The situation of the house was so damp and unhealthy that it was scarcely fit for rearing bullocks, not to speak of a delicate constitution like his; but at that age he had not learned to take account either of food or climate or

---

35 Erasmus uses this saying in his work, *Adages*.
36 I.e., community.
37 I.e., the habit of monk.
38 The muses were minor Greek goddesses of various fine, literary, and scientific arts.
39 Presumably Cantelius.

locality. And indeed he did not go to the convent with the intention of adopting the monastic life, but to escape for a while that deafening clamor, and in the hope that the mere lapse of time might bring better counsel.

Cantelius meanwhile was busy in his own interest, turning to a selfish account the good nature and simplicity of his comrade. For Florence would sometimes lead him through the grammar of a whole play of Terence[40] in a single night, so that in those stolen lessons they ran through the principal authors in a few months, a practice which involved no small danger to a sickly constitution. But this was nothing to Cantelius, who chuckled over the opportunity that had befallen him, having no genuine love for anybody but himself.

During this period, as it was not desired that Florence should draw back from his position, there was no indulgence that was not allowed him. The boy was cheered by the pleasant companionship of the younger inmates of the convent; songs were sung; games were played; verses were capped;[41] he was not compelled to fast, nor roused from his bed for the nightly services. No one found fault; no one scolded; all were kind and cheerful. In this way many months glided by unheeded. But when the day drew near for putting off the lay, and putting on the religious habit, Florence, coming to himself again, began to sing his old song, and sent for his guardians in order to claim his liberty.

Upon their arrival the old threats were harshly repeated; he was bidden to look at the utterly desperate condition of his affairs if he did not persevere in what he had so well begun, and Cantelius, who was interested in retaining his free instructor, took an earnest part in the discussion. I beseech you to tell me whether this is not a case of mere violence practiced on a boy, naturally simple, inexperienced and heedless. But I must not shrink from narrating the conclusion. In spite of his remonstrances, the sacred robe was thrust upon him when they knew his mind had undergone no change.

This done, blandishments and indulgence were again employed to tempt his boyish humor; again, almost a whole year passed without serious thought. But by this time he had fairly found out that this sort of life was suited neither to his mind nor to his body. His mind had no pleasure but in study, and for study in that place there was neither honor nor use. For the rest, he had no distaste for religion, but was not so much attracted by the services and ceremonies which well nigh make up their whole life. Moreover, those who are thrust into these societies are mostly persons of sluggish intellect, half idiots at their birth, more concerned with their belly than with books, and if there should appear among them an extraordinary genius with a natural capacity for learning, it is their business to keep it down and prevent it from finding any outlet. And it almost comes to this: that the stupidest and most obstinate man, provided he is hale and strong, is of most account in that herd. Only think for a moment what a torture it is for a man of natural refinement to pass his whole life in such company, from which he has no hope of release, unless by some chance he is put in charge of a community of nuns, a sort of slavery as miserable as can be. For besides the constant care of a flock of women, he will have to sit every day at prolonged meals, not without some risk of compromising his character; it also is not uncommon for them to send back their patriarch, broken by years and unfit for service, to his old stable, where he feels all the more wretched for having lived for some time an easy life.

The lad's constitution was naturally so unsuited for fasting that his health had often been affected by a meal being put off to a later hour than usual, when he had himself been unconscious of his weakness and thought of nothing of the kind, until warned by a sharp pain in the stomach and a failure in the action of the heart. This will perhaps appear ridiculous to some coarse animals, who would wax fat and kick even if fed upon hay. But expert doctors are not unaware that this is a peculiarity of a body specifically light, and of subtle spirits, for which cases they prescribe food easy

---

40   A Roman playwright (second century BC).
41   To cap a verse is to reply to a verse just quoted with another which starts with the previous verse's last or first letter, or which rhymes with the previous verse.

to digest, taken frequently and in small quantities, whereas you may find others who have only to fill their stomachs once, and they will go on without trouble as long as vultures. The same constitutions are observed by physicians to be intolerant of cold, winds, and fogs, and to be affected by climate even sooner than by food. The young man was subject to another special inconvenience, which from his tender years to the present day he has never been able to shake off. He cannot go to sleep except late in the evening and, if once roused, does not sleep again for several hours. How often does he regret that he is not permitted to enjoy those golden hours in familiar talk, and that the most delightful part of the day is lost in sleep! How often has he tried to drive nature out by force, and tried in vain! Again, it is not without injury to his health that he can keep a night watch without a meal. When young he had so great a dislike for fish, that the mere smell of it gave him a feverish headache.[42] With such a character and such a constitution, what was he to do in a monastery, especially in a situation like that?

Now, as these facts were not unknown to those reverend fathers, I would ask you whether, if they had had a grain of charity[43] in them, they ought not to have come forward themselves to help an ignorant or heedless boy, and to have warned him in some such terms as these. "Son, it is foolish to strive in vain. Our institution is not suited for you, nor you for it. While that course is still open, choose another kind of life. Christ dwells everywhere, not only here. Religion may be pursued in any dress, if the heart is not wanting. We will help you to return to freedom with the sanction of your guardians and friends. In this way you will neither be a burden to us, nor we a curse to you." This would have been an utterance worthy of truly religious men. But no one gave a note of warning; on the contrary, they employed every device to prevent that luckless fish from escaping out of the net. One repeated that it was Satan's fashion in such a crisis to use every wile to trip up the young soldier of Christ;[44] he had only to sustain the conflict bravely,

and his future path would be easy and even pleasant; the adviser had himself gone through the same experience, and now seemed to be living in paradise. Another suggested a fresh scruple by pointing out the risk of St. Augustine being offended and sending some great calamity in return for the despite done him by abandoning his habit, and called to mind several terrible examples of this danger: how one had caught an incurable disease, another had been struck dead by lightning, another killed by the bite of a viper. It was added that putting on the habit was a tacit profession, and to turn back now was scarcely a lighter offense in the sight of God or less disgraceful in that of man than if he deserted the order after he had openly sworn his commitment. There was no kind of weapon they did not use against the lad, but none distressed him more than the fear of loss of character. "It is too late," they said, "to turn tail now; you have put your hand to the plough, and it is wicked to look back. If you lay aside the habit which you have received before a number of witnesses, you will be forever the talk of mankind." In this argument they gave a dismal importance to the word "apostate." "Where shall an apostate go?" they said. "You can never live in the sight of good men. You will be execrated by monks, and hated by laymen!"

The boy's character had in it a sort of virgin shyness, so that he shrank less from death than from disgrace. On the other hand, he was urged on by his guardians and friends, some of whom had by their own dishonesty diminished his fortune. To sum up the matter, their pertinacity was successful. The lad, in spite of the abhorrence which he felt, and the reluctance which he expressed, was forced to accept the halter, just as prisoners taken in battle hold out their hands to be tied, or slaves overcome by continued tortures do, not what they will, but what their masters choose.

However Florence had subdued his mind, no man can mold his own body. For a time he did what prisoners often do; he consoled himself, as far as he was allowed, with study. For even this had to be done by

---

42 Monks were generally forbidden meat.
43 I.e., love appropriate to a Christian.
44 A phrase traditionally used to describe a monk.

stealth, whereas drunkenness was openly permitted. It was therefore with literature that he beguiled the weariness of his captivity, until an unexpected event, like a stage god,[45] revealed some hope of deliverance. He was summoned by a wealthy bishop to become one of his household, and from there he advanced a step further and proceeded to a famous university. But for this course of events, so transcendent a character might have rotted in idleness, luxury and conviviality. Not that the young man brings any charge against the society in which he lived but that his own nature was not in sympathy with it, for what is life to one man may be death to another. And such is his bashfulness and modesty that he is never heard to say anything unfriendly of his old associates; but more is sometimes expressed by silence and reserve than by a multitude of words.

It must be understood, however, that none of these steps was taken except by the permission, or rather the command, of the bishop of the diocese, and also by permission of the provost of his order, both domestic and general,[46] and finally with the acquiescence of the whole society. And although his conscience was free, and he knew that he was not bound by an enforced vow, yet he so far yielded for the time, partly to his own natural bashfulness, which was so excessive as to be often a misfortune to him, and partly to the invincible scruples of unenlightened and superstitious persons, that he abstained from changing his dress, although invited to do so by his bishop.

It happened some time later that his love of study led him to travel to a distant country. When there he wore a linen scarf, after the French fashion, over his robe, assuming that it was not unusual there. But owing to this costume, he was twice in danger of losing his life, because the surgeons of that place who attend cases of plague wear a white linen cloth on the left shoulder hanging down before and behind, in order that they may be easily distinguished and avoided by persons meeting or following them; indeed the surgeons themselves would be stoned by passers-by if they did not find their way by the least frequented lanes, the people of that country having such a dread of death that they are up in arms even at the smell of incense because it is used at funerals. On one occasion, when Florence was going to call on a learned friend, he fell in with two profligates—or else bravoes—who came towards him with their swords drawn, and threatened to kill him had not a lady, who was fortunately passing, told them it was not a surgeon's but a clergyman's dress. Even then they did not cease to growl, nor sheath their swords, until he knocked at the door of the house which was close by and obtained admission.

Another day he was visiting some comrades from his own country, when all of a sudden he found himself in the midst of a crowd armed with sticks and stones, shouting furiously to each other, "Kill the dog, kill the dog." While this was going on, a priest came up, who did nothing but smile at him and say inaudibly and in Latin, "Asses, asses." While the crowd was still around him, a young man of elegant appearance, in a purple cloak, came out of the palace; Florence fled to his side as to a sanctuary. For he was quite ignorant of the language of the people, and was still wondering what they meant, when the young man addressed him. "If," he said, "you do not take off that linen affair, you will certainly be stoned some day. Take warning by what I tell you." Accordingly, without altogether disusing the scarf, he hid it under his robe.

Good heavens, what a disturbance has arisen out of a matter of no consequence at all! This exclamation will shock some foolish people, who think the whole sum and substance of religion consists in dress. I admit that this should not be lightly cast aside. And yet the Carthusians[47] often change theirs for that of a merchant in order to travel more safely to synod,[48] and our canons, either for the sake of study or on occasion of a journey, change or hide their distinctive garment without special permission, and without incurring any censure. For there is not the same scrupulosity about this linen vestment as about others,

---

45  In ancient theater, a god in a play who is introduced into a scene to intervene in human affairs.
46  I.e., both the local provost and the one set over the order as a whole.
47  One of the strictest of monastic orders.
48  A meeting of clergy.

for the so-called canons formerly were not monks, and now they are an intermediate class; monks where it is an advantage to be so, not monks where it is not. But it is a horrible crime for a Dominican or Franciscan friar to throw aside his habit. For a Dominican cloak brings safety and prosperity to a rich man's whole household, and if it is worn by boys for some years in fulfillment of a mother's vow, it guards them from diseases and accidents! And the Franciscan shirt, put on a man, even after he is dead, saves him from hell.

The papal decretal[49] is not launched against those who lay aside their dress for creditable reasons, but against those who do so in order to join more freely with lay persons in practices which are common in the world. For the linen robe does not specially belong to monks, but to bishops, and perhaps formerly to the clergy generally. And Augustine in his own Rule does not prescribe any form of dress, and indeed rather condemns a distinct costume, while he advises that the habit of the clergy should not be such as to attract attention, and that they should work to please, not by their clothes but by their character—although it is plain that the Rule was written, not for men but for women, but I am now dealing with those who take it to have been written for men. And finally this costume is that worn by the Roman pontiff,[50] when most pontifically arrayed.

All this was not unknown to Florence; but still in order to fulfill all righteousness, he took the advice of friends, and obtained without difficulty from the pope a permission to wear any symbol of his calling upon any part of his body at his own discretion.

When he was recalled to the patrons that he had in another country—persons not of the lowest degree either in learning or condition—he resumed French dress, which, with the exception of the linen scarf, does not differ from that of a secular priest, for by this ignominious adjective the lawful ministers of the church instituted by the apostles and by Christ are now distinguished. This he did not do without the advice of persons of consideration. But when he went into the streets in his old costume, he was warned by

his dearest friends that it was quite inadmissible in that country, and that he must put the linen affair out of sight. You will say he might have adopted the entire dress of the canons of that nation. But that is as tiresome as anything can be, for while with your right hand you have to hold up a flowing tail, there is a cowl of the amplest dimensions to be kept in place with your left. For this fashion is thought there uncommonly fine, being quite after the pattern of cardinals. Then again, he was often compelled by business to move from one country to another, and so to become an octopus in dress, for the costume which is respectable in one place appears monstrous in another. And finally he was a guest in other people's houses, and had to pass some time every day in company with men of rank, who are apt to be critical in matters of this kind. It was at last thought best by his sincerest friends that, as his own conscience was free, every scruple having been entirely removed by the pope's authority, he should be restored to his liberty, for fear of providing busybodies with a worse scandal by his being obliged so often to give up the dress, and assume it again. I will add this: that the kind of life into which the young man has been thrust is so free as to be not far removed from that of secular persons; I am not speaking of a stolen freedom, but of that conceded by those who have had authority in the matter.

I will not discuss the question of monastic vows, the importance of which is much exaggerated by some, whereas this kind of obligation—not to say bondage—is not found either in the New Testament or in the Old. And whereas the sabbath, according to the authority of Christ, is made for man and not man for the sabbath, much more ought such human constitutions give way whenever they impede the welfare of man, especially that of his soul, whereas our Lord speaks of that of the body, the talk being about hunger and the man that was healed on the sabbath day. But these people are your real Pharisees, who if an ox or an ass falls into a pit, drag it out in violation of God's sabbath, while they allow a man to perish altogether for the sake of a sabbath of their own.

---

49   I.e., papal decision which is legally binding in future cases.
50   I.e., the pope.

I will not allege here how great is the number of monasteries in which there is so utter an absence of pious discipline that the brothels are modest and well conducted in comparison, nor again how many there are in which there is no religion at all except ceremonies and outward show. The latter are almost worse than the former, for while they lack the spirit of Christ, it is incredible what a conceit they have of themselves by reason of those Pharisaical observances, placing the whole of religion in externals and beating boys to death every day on account of those ceremonies; although for their own part they go through them with remarkable weariness, and would not do so at all if they did not think that the sight attracted the admiration of the people. And finally how remarkably few convents there are in which the religious rule of life is heartily observed; even in these, if you open Silenus,[51] if you look into the matter more closely, and test it by the touchstone of true piety, it is grievous to think how very few persons you will find to be sincere. The crafty devices of Satan, the intricacies of the heart of man, the subtlety with which he imposes on himself and others, these are things by which the oldest and most experienced are frequently deceived, and they are the things which they require a boy to see through in a few months. And this is what is called profession.[52]

But suppose you find a convent which satisfies all requirements. What is a man to do when a change takes place in the persons who make it up, when a worthy patriarch is succeeded by one that is stupid, drunken and tyrannical, when good comrades give place to bad. Let him change, they say, his house or his order. But in such circumstances how grudgingly does a seceding member obtain leave to depart, and still more grudgingly will he be received by others who suspect that there is something horrible in the background from the fact that he has withdrawn from his old society. And if, when received, he gives the slightest offense, there is the ready question, "Why do you

not go back to your old home?" Besides, what an anxious discussion is raised about which is the stricter and which the laxer order, as each wishes his own order to be thought the strictest. So that after all, this vaunted facility of changing house and order comes to this: that the poor fellow undergoes a fresh risk of falling into a more cruel bondage.

Again, whereas the young members are for the most part enticed by fraud, and when captured are taught, not a spiritual, but a Pharisaical religion, and are brought under the bondage of men, a vast number become discontented with their profession. Consequently, those in authority, being afraid of the exposure of their orgies, have recourse to floggings, to curses, to the secular arm,[53] to walls, to gratings, to prisons, and even to death, to keep their members from leaving them. I pledge my word that Matthew, cardinal of Sion, at a great dinner in the hearing of a number of people, mentioned by name the place, the persons and the monastery in which a society of Dominicans buried alive a young man who had been induced to join them by stealth, and whose release was demanded with threats by his father, a person of knightly rank. There was another case in Poland, in which a nobleman who had fallen asleep in a church, probably after a full supper, saw two Franciscans buried alive after the midnight service. The papal authority upon this point, as to which it has perhaps granted them a special privilege, is regarded with some respect; but when the same authority relieves anyone from the religious habit, the bull[54] is torn up, and the person who has procured it is cast into prison. And whereas, after all this, they boast of Benedict, Basil, Jerome, Augustine, Dominic, Francis, Bruno, as the founders of their order, let them examine their lives, and see whether anything of the kind was ever instituted or done by them. They will find a very different policy. The entire purpose of these holy men was carried out by example, by wholesome teaching, by friendly counsel, by brotherly remonstrance. He

---

51  In Plato's *Symposium* (fourth century BC), the ugly Socrates, who contains truth and virtue, is described as a Silenus, or sculpture inside of which are small statues of gods.
52  I.e., taking the vow to become a member of a religious order.
53  I.e., secular government, which could be invoked to return a runaway monk or nun.
54  A solemn papal decree.

that was not reformed by these means was expelled from the society, even if he did not leave it of his own accord, so far were they from keeping anyone who wished to go.

I say nothing of so many human constitutions, so many forms of dress, so many prayers and ceremonies, among which that which is of the least importance, I mean dress, is made of the greatest. The man who in his religious habit indulges in daily drunkenness, who is a slave to his palate and his belly, who is too familiar with women both secretly and openly (not to speak of anything less decent still), who squanders in luxury the money of the church, who devotes his time to sorceries and other wicked arts—such a man is a good monk and is promoted to an abbacy, while he, who for any reason lays aside his dress, is execrated as an apostate. This name was in former times deservedly held in abomination because it was used to denote those who fell away from the profession of Christ to Judaism or paganism. But if you give it a wider scope, whoever is given up to the pleasures, pomps, riches and other lusts of the world, which he has abjured in baptism, is an apostate, and no better but rather more guilty, however much the odiousness of the offense is lightened by its frequency. And in the same way monks who live a godless life, as they are everywhere doing, are doubly apostates, because they have fallen away, first, from that holy profession in which they were enlisted as soldiers of Christ, and then from the manner of life which they have since professed. These are the persons against whom the odious name of apostate might well be launched, were they enwrapped in ten cowls.

Under conditions such as these, my Lambert, what a wickedness it is to drive youthful simplicity into the toils either by force or by strategem. If the religious orders are plainly corrupt, as most of them are, what else do they do but drag a boy to perdition. If they are neither hot nor cold, in what a wretched bondage do they entangle him! Even if they are recommended by an appearance of probity, when we consider how great a variety there is in men's minds and constitutions, how cleverly people impose upon each other,

how great is the simplicity of boyhood, and that the knot, as they will have it, is indissoluble, it is evident into what peril both of mind and body young men are thrown. It is argued that the age of puberty brings with it a power to discriminate between good and evil. But this stage is not reached in the same year by all constitutions, still less by all minds. Puberty, in the natural course of things, may make a man fit for marriage, but not so much for a monastic life. This has been tried by some persons of not less than 30 years of age with considerable experience of the world, who have drawn back before profession, asserting that they had no conception of what it was. In former times persons of 30 years were hardly admitted into the priesthood, and yet boys as soon as they have a few hairs on their chin are fit at once to become monks! Meanwhile, the inexperienced are taken in by an abuse of terms, such as "the world," as if monks were not of the world; "obedience," whereas the Scripture bids us obey God rather than man; "an indissoluble vow," when they have not yet been able to find the difference between a dissoluble and an indissoluble vow, except that Scotus[55] has discovered that a monk's vow cannot be set aside because it is made through man to God, for that which is made to God alone is easily set aside.

And here we may ask, considering that their whole status rests upon the authority of popes, how does it happen that they treat that authority with gross contempt whenever they choose? The pope releases many persons from monasticism, although he will not do so without good reason. But if he has power to do what he does, why in this particular case do they set his authority at nothing? If they deny his power to do what he does, do they not bring him in guilty of a frightful crime? So that whenever it is for their own convenience, the pope is the vicar of Christ and cannot do wrong; whenever they do not agree with him, what he does goes for nothing.

It is not, however, my present intention to do battle with the monastic orders. We will suppose that this or that calling in life is expedient or even necessary for this person or that, and that a lifelong engagement

---

55 Duns Scotus (c. 1265-1308), a scholastic theologian. His followers resisted the development of humanist studies.

may be allowed. But the more holy and arduous the profession is, so much the more circumspectly, deliberately and late in life should it be undertaken, early enough in my opinion, if it is done before the fortieth year. Other engagements are not valid unless it is plain that the person who made them was of sound mind, in his sober senses and free from terror or overwhelming anxiety. And is it to hold good in this instance, where a boy, by enticements, by threats, by misrepresentations, by alarms, has in spite of his own protest been forced into the halter? Is this a case of the effect of fear upon a man of robust character? It is much rather an instance of the effect of deception and terror upon a simple and inexperienced stripling. We may add that in many persons there is a natural simplicity, not only arising from age but from character. But in this matter no distinction is admitted; if puberty is reached, the vow holds fast, and so fast that by virtue of it the bride is abandoned before she is known. Can such be our laws?

Therefore, considering that Florence has been thrust into continued reluctance and protests, and has done nothing but wear the dress, having kept his conscience free, I hold him to be no more bound by any vow than if he had sworn an immoral oath to a band of pirates who were making an attempt on his life. And I do not doubt that the pope's goodness will be no less indignant against those man-stealers than favorable to the cause of our man.

You will say the pope may restore him to his freedom so far as human jurisdiction is concerned, his conscience being free by its own judgment, but he cannot keep men's tongues from wagging. And yet, when Christ, the truly supreme pontiff of the church, and his not degenerate disciple, Paul, teach us that no one is to be judged, especially in such things as do not constitute piety or impiety, surely the pope's authority ought to have so much influence as to turn suspicion into confidence, where to suspect evil is a fault. But what is to become of human affairs, if we are always to give way to the senseless opinions and scurrilous aspersions of such people! Paul would have us show indulgence to infirmity or to invincible conviction, but that only for a time. If we constantly give way to foolish and malicious judgments, what else is it but to sap the vigor of Christian piety? Christ so far gave way to Caesar as to pay the tribute money, so far to the Jews as to abstain from meats forbidden by the law, but in healing the woman who was "bowed together," in giving sight to the blind, in restoring the maimed limb, in plucking the ears of grain,[56] he disregarded them openly, and indeed purposely provoked a scandal among the Scribes and Pharisees. And if St. Paul had not done the same, where would Christianity be now?[57]

But what objection do these stupid people make against Florence? He has put off the linen robe. How do they know whether he still wears it underneath? And if he has put it off, what means have they of knowing for what reasons he did so, or by what authority it was done? If they do not know, why do they judge? And if they know that it was done by the pope's authority, why are they not afraid of condemning his judgment, which in other matters they desire to maintain inviolate? Where in this case is that marvelous and so much vaunted obedience, when they do not listen to Christ, and tear to pieces His vicar, the head of the Church? Where is that simplicity which they display with their faces bowed to the ground? Where is that spirit that is dead to the world? Not to speak of these, where is their humanity; where is their common sense? When so many sins, not to be here related, may be objected against them, in which they are daily all but publicly detected, for I will not stir up "the things not to be spoken or stirred,"[58] they still go on forever objecting to a change of dress as an inexpiable crime!

But what can be more inhuman than to cast in a man's teeth a calamity into which he has fallen by accident or by the malice of others? And what greater calamity could befall a youth of promise than to be thrust into such a life? But if he is lost to humanity,

---

56   Referring to the New Testament, Matthew 12.1-14; Luke 6.1-11, 13.10-17; John 5.2-18, 9.1-41.
57   St. Paul successfully advocated relaxing the requirements of the Jewish law of the Old Testament regarding matters such as circumcision and diet when converting non-Jews to Christianity.
58   The phrase appears in Greek.

who treats mere misfortune as a crime, what is to be said of a man who reproaches another for an evil which he has himself inflicted upon him? It is as if a clumsy surgeon called his patient a purblind idiot whose eyesight he had himself destroyed; or as if a pirate reviled a man as a slave, whom he had himself reduced to servitude. For it is not the man who has fallen into a pit that ought to be ashamed, but those who cast him into it. Florence has put off the robe, but it is you that forced him to put it on. Whoever found fault with a captive for escaping from pirates? Not even the pirates themselves, I should imagine! All the rest of the world wish him joy. And any person who violently deprives another of his liberty is to that man a pirate.

To conclude, my dear friend, if you are satisfied with my proof of Florence's case, I implore you earnestly to get his business completed with the utmost dispatch, and as much as possible in accordance with my views. To put you at ease about the costs, you may hold me answerable.

In what looks like a blank space at the bottom of this letter, I have set down some particulars which may perhaps be required for drawing up the bull. They are written in the code I sent you with my last letter, but will not be legible unless you hold the paper to the fire. I expect an answer by the courier who brings this, and who is to stay at Rome for a fortnight, or not much less. Farewell.

## 48.5
### LAMBERTUS GRUNNIUS TO ERASMUS

Dearest Erasmus, I have never undertaken any business more willingly than that which you have entrusted to me, and have scarcely ever concluded any with more satisfaction. My interest in the matter is not due so much to your friendship, to which I of course pay the utmost regard, as to the undeserved misfortunes of Florence. I read your letter through from beginning to end to the pope, in the presence of several cardinals and other eminent persons. The holy father was singularly delighted with your style, and you will hardly

believe how indignant he was against those veritable man-stealers. For the more favor he has for true religion, so much more heartily does he detest those persons who fill the world with either miserable or bad monks, not without serious damage to the Christian profession. It is spontaneous piety, he says, that Christ loves, not prisons full of slaves!

He has ordered the bull to be prepared forthwith, and without charge. Nevertheless, I have given the clerks and notaries three ducats to obtain it more quickly. You know what a voracious pack they are: whether you like it or not, they will not be satisfied without a few mouthfuls.

The courier by whom you wrote went off to Naples, saying he would return this way. What has happened I do not know, but he has not come back. In the meantime, the bearer, who is, if I am not mistaken, a safer man than the other, has offered himself at the right moment, and will deliver you the bull, with the exemplification and the pope's signature. I have arranged with him for half a ducat, and you are not to give more.

Farewell, and greet Florence lovingly in my name. He is now my Florence as well as yours. Given at Rome.

## 48.6
### ERASMUS TO CARDINAL WOLSEY
### (ANTWERP, MAY 18, 1517)

*Erasmus had enjoyed the patronage of both Cardinal Thomas Wolsey, King Henry VIII of England's chief minister, and of the king himself, both of whom had humanist interests. Wolsey was also a supporter of learning at Oxford University.*

Most reverend lord, not the least illustrious of the august order of cardinals, my not having as yet revisited the Maecenates[59] that I have in Britain, high in rank and indeed not few in number, has been occasioned by the burden of my studies, by which I am almost overwhelmed—"weight being heaped on weight, as wave climbs over wave"—to use the phrase

---

59 Plural of the name Maecenas.

of Naso.[60] And yet in the meantime it is my health, which is still too delicate for me to venture to trust myself to a sea voyage, that has been most at fault. I may add that my not having even by letter made my bow to your Eminence has been partly due to my being ashamed of intruding with my tattle upon one whose attention is occupied with weighty concerns both of church and kingdom, and partly to your own greatness, which is addressed with reverence even by the greatest men. But while the persons who pass from that side of the Channel to this have reported, with wonderful unanimity, with what zeal and with what success your wisdom and patriotism are striving to convert your country's image from brass into gold, I could not restrain myself from congratulating you upon the possession of those qualities, and *our* Britain upon possessing you. I now hear it further proclaimed that by your means among so many of the principal rulers of the world, a long desired peace has been knit together with the closest ties, while Pope Leo, most desirous as he was of peace, was negotiating only for a five years truce.

By your means all Britain is cleared of robbers and of vagabonds, so that it is now as free from noxious men as it is from poison and wild beasts. By your authority the perplexities of litigation are no less effectually untied than was the Gordian knot by Alexander the Great; the differences among noblemen are arranged; the monasteries are restored to their ancient discipline; the clergy are recalled to a more approved manner of life. Polite letters, which were struggling against the patrons of ancient ignorance, are supported by your favor, defended by your authority and fostered by your liberality, the most learned professors being by ample salaries invited to your aid. In the purchase of libraries, rich with every good author, you vie with Ptolemy Philadelphus[61] himself, more renowned for this possession than for his kingdom. The three tongues,[62] without which learning is incomplete, are

recalled at your command, for by the benefaction, which is now conferred upon the famous school of Oxford, I judge all Britain to be obliged; and indeed I trust that this brilliant example will before long awaken the minds of our princes also. I see, I see a truly golden age arising, if that temper of yours shall prevail with some proportion of our sovereigns! These most holy efforts will receive a due reward from Him under Whose auspices they are made; neither will posterity be ungrateful, when in a distant age that generous heart, born for the benefit of humanity, will still be celebrated alike by Latin and Greek eloquence. For myself, rejoicing, as I do, in the general felicity, I am not sorry that my own name is cast into the shade by more recent lights, when I see those around me, compared with whom I appear no wiser than a child. Enough for me to claim this praise, if indeed I can fairly do so—to be described as one of those who has done his best to drive out of this part of the world that barbarous ignorance of languages with which Italy was wont to reproach us. How far I have been successful in this, I do not know; that I have striven to do so I know, and striven not without some of that jealousy which accompanies and pursues exceptional efforts, as the shadow follows the light. But the majority is now more kind; only a few still hold out, too old to hope, too stupid to learn, or too arrogant to wish to know better!

These people see only too plainly that their own authority will fall to the ground if we have the Sacred Books[63] accessible in a corrected form, and seek their meaning at the fountainhead. And so high a value do they set upon their own importance, that they would rather have many things unknown, many things misread and cited amiss from the Divine Books, than appear to be ignorant themselves of any point. But inasmuch as they are conscious of their own inferiority in argument, and aware that, if they deal with books, they do nothing but betray their own ignorance

---

60    The Roman poet Ovid (*c.* 43 BC-AD 17). The phrase, however, has not been found among Ovid's works, but in the letters of Ovid's contemporary, the poet Horace.

61    A Hellenistic king of Egypt (third century BC) and patron of learning. His father and predecessor is credited with having established the library at Alexandria, the largest in the classical world.

62    Hebrew, Greek, and Latin.

63    I.e., the Bible.

and folly, making themselves a laughingstock to the learned, they have given up open fighting, and have recourse to stratagems, loading with their slanders literature and its defenders, and me above all, whom they judge to have had some influence in the revival of these studies. Whatever writing of an invidious nature may be published, they fasten it upon Erasmus, and here you will detect the very genius of calumny at work, when the cause of good letters is mixed up with the affairs of Reuchlin[64] or of [Martin] Luther, whereas they have no proper connection with each other.

For my own part, I never had any fancy for the Cabala or the Talmud;[65] and as for Reuchlin himself, I have only once met him at Frankfort, when nothing passed between us, except such friendly civilities as are usual between scholars. Not that I am ashamed to have joined in friendly correspondence with him; he has a letter of mine, in which, before I knew him by sight, I advised him to abstain from those plain terms of abuse of his opponents in which after the German fashion he indulges in his apology; so far is it from the truth that I have ever encouraged writings affecting anyone's good name!

Luther is no more known to me than to any stranger he might meet, and as for the man's books, I have not had time to turn over more than one or two pages. And yet it is pretended—so I am told—that he has had my help in his work! If he has written aright, no credit is due to me and, if the reverse, I deserve no blame, seeing that in all his lucubrations not a tittle is mine. Anyone who cares to investigate the matter will find this to be quite true. The man's life is by a wide and general consent approved, and it is no small presumption in his favor that his moral character is such that even his foes can find no fault with it. If I had had ample leisure to read his works, I do not claim so much authority as to pass judgment upon the writings of so important a person, although in these days you

find boys everywhere pronouncing with the greatest temerity that this proposition is erroneous and that heretical. And indeed we were at one time all the more inclined to find fault with Luther for fear of a prejudice that might arise against literature, upon which I did not wish a further burden to be laid. For I saw plainly enough how invidious an act it is to disturb the stability of things from which a rich harvest is reaped by priests or monks.

The first of these writings which came out were several propositions concerning papal pardons. These were followed by one or two pamphlets about confession and penance; when I became aware that some persons were intent upon their publication, I did my best to discourage it, that they might not strengthen the prejudice against good letters. This circumstance will be shown by the evidence even of those who are Luther's well-wishers. At last a whole swarm of pamphlets came out; no one saw me reading them; no one heard me give any opinion either for or against them. I am not so rash as to approve that which I have not read, nor such a sycophant as to condemn that which I do not know; although in these days this is commonly done by those who have least excuse for doing so.

Germany has now many young men who afford the greatest promise both of erudition and of eloquence, and by whose means she may sometime be able to make the same boast as is now fairly made by Britain. None of them is personally known to me except Eobanus, Hutten, and Beatus;[66] these, with all the weapons they have at their command, are waging war against the enemies of the languages[67] and of good letters. The freedom which they claim I might myself admit to be intolerable, if I did not know how atrociously they are attacked both publicly and privately. Their assailants, in their sermons, in their schools, in their convivial parties, allow the most odi-

---

64  Johann Reuchlin, German humanist and cabbalist (on which see below n 167), and critic of the Dominican friars.

65  Cabala: a mystical interpretation of the Old Testament originally, at least, by Jewish writers; Talmud: an authoritative body of rabbinical commentary on the Jewish Law.

66  Eobanus Hessus: a German humanist and Latin poet, and future supporter of Luther; Ulrich von Hutten: a German humanist, and future supporter of Luther and opponent of Erasmus; Beatus Rhenanus: a German humanist who supervised the publication of some of Erasmus's works.

67  Classical Greek and Latin.

ous and indeed seditious appeals to be made to the ignorant multitude, but they judge it to be an intolerable offense if any of their victims ventures to complain—when even the little bees have their sting with which they may wound an assailant, and the mice have teeth to use in their own defense. Whence comes this new race of gods, fixing the character of heretic on whomsoever they choose, and mingling earth and sky if anyone calls them sycophants? And while they do not hesitate to find a name for what even Orestes[68] is ashamed to mention, they demand of us not to be named themselves without some honorable preface, such confidence have they in the stupidity of the multitude, not to say of our princes.

For myself, little as I have been able to do in the pursuit of good letters, I have always loved them, and I give my support to their adherents, who are everywhere in favor with our nobility, if we except a few Midases,[69] whom someone will sometime take an opportunity of describing! And yet my favor extends only so far: that I support that which is in alliance with virtue, and if anyone will consider with what faults those authors were saturated who mainly assisted in the old revival of literature in Italy and France, he cannot fail to give his approval to the writers of our own time, whose moral character is such that they would rather be objects of imitation than of blame to their theological censors. And whatever they produce is suspected to be mine, even among you in England, if we may believe what is told us by the merchants who come to this country from yours! For my part, I will frankly confess that I cannot fail to admire literary genius, while I disapprove any license of the pen, whoever the author may be.

Some time since, Hutten amused himself with a book, the title of which was *Nemo*.[70] Everybody knows that the subject is a ludicrous one, and the theologians of Louvain,[71] who think themselves more sharpsighted than lynxes, insisted that it was mine! Presently there came out another publication called *Fever*, and that was mine too, when the whole character of the book, as well as its whole phraseology, is quite different from my work! ...

I have advised by letter all those young German writers to control their excessive freedom of language, and certainly to abstain from any attack upon persons of authority in the church, lest they should prejudice against literature those by whose patronage they might be able to stand up against their foes. What more am I to do? I can advise, but have no power to compel; I may temper my own style, but to control the pen of another is not in my power. The absurdest thing of all is that the work which was lately written by the bishop of Rochester against Lefèvre[72] was suspected to be mine, when there is so great a difference of style—and indeed I have no pretensions to the erudition of that divine prelate. There were also persons to be found who ascribed More's *Utopia*[73] to my authorship, everything new, whether I like it or not, being attributed to me!

Several months ago, an ill-starred and ridiculous booklet came out, the subject of which sufficiently shows that it was written upon the last vacancy of the papal see, but by what writer is not known, save that its contents show that, whoever it was, his sympathies were with the French.[74] The suspicion of its authorship goes the round of many different persons, especially among the Germans, the work being current among them under various titles. When I met with it here myself some years ago circulated in a

---

68  In Greek myth and literature, the son of Agamemnon and Clytemnestra; he murdered Clytemnestra in retaliation for her murder of Agamemnon.

69  In Greek myth, Midas was a king so fond of gold that he asked the gods to grant that all he touched be turned into that metal.

70  Latin: *No one.*

71  I.e., of the university there.

72  Lefèvre d'Etaples, French humanist and student of the Bible, who was to be condemned for heresy and find refuge with the queen of Navarre, a supporter of Protestantism.

73  Sir Thomas More's fictional account of an ideal society (sixteenth century).

74  This appears to be a reference to the *Julius Exclusus*, in which the dead Pope Julius II finds difficulty in obtaining admission into heaven, whose entry is guarded by Saint Peter. It seems the work was in fact written by Erasmus.

furtive way, and had some taste of its contents—for I galloped through it rather than read it—many persons can bear witness how hateful it was to me, and what pains I took that it should be hidden in eternal darkness, a thing that has been done by me more than once in the case of other publications, as many persons will admit. The facts are shown in a letter written by me to John Caesarius, which was published at Cologne from a copy furtively obtained. And I am told that there are some people in your parts who are trying to fix upon me the suspicion of being the author of this publication, so unwilling are those persons who regret the revival of learning and of better studies to leave anything untried that may help to carry out their purpose. The sole argument they rely upon is that of the style, which nevertheless is not much like mine, unless that is little known to myself. And yet what wonder would there be, if some expressions here and there agreed with my phraseology, when in these days my lucubrations pass through so many hands that, even in the books of those who are writing against me, I often recognize my own style, and have the sensation of being struck by a shaft winged with my own feathers. I have not hitherto composed—and do not intend to compose—any work to which I do not prefix my name. We did some fencing long ago in the *Moria*, but without drawing blood, though perhaps with more than enough freedom. At any rate, I have taken every precaution that nothing should proceed from me which would either corrupt the young by obscenity, or in any way hinder piety, give rise to sedition, or draw a black line across anyone's character. Whatever exertions I have hitherto made, have been made for the assistance of honorable studies and the advancement of the Christian religion, and all persons on every side are thankful for what has so been done, except a few theologians and monks who have no wish to be wiser or better than they are. May I lose the favor of Christ if I do not desire that whatever I have of talent or of eloquence should be wholly dedicated to His glory, to the Catholic church, and to sacred studies.

But of this personal matter I have said more than enough, and was going to write nothing at all, if a British merchant, on arriving here from home, had not persistently asserted that some persons had endeavored to impose this utterly false suspicion upon your Eminence, whose singular prudence nevertheless makes me quite confident that you will not listen or give any attention to such impudent calumnies. Indeed, if you will deign some time or other to try the experiment in a personal interview, you will find Erasmus devoted to the dignity of the Roman see, especially under the Tenth Leo, to whose piety he recognizes how much he owes, and also heartily attached to those persons who lend their services to the cause of letters and of religion, among whom your Eminence holds a principal place.

I am sending herewith a copy of my New Testament, which I shall deem to have received a great distinction, if you think it worthy of a place in your library.

# 49

# MARTIN LUTHER, *LETTERS*

Martin Luther (1483-1546) was a priest, Augustinian canon, and professor of theology and Biblical study at Wittenberg, in the Holy Roman Empire. In 1517 he issued his *95 Theses*, which attacked aspects of Christian belief and practice as they then stood, thus marking the start of what became the Protestant Reformation. He was excommunicated by the pope in 1520. In April of 1521 he was condemned by the Diet of Worms, an assembly of the leading territorial rulers of Germany under the presidency of the Holy Roman Emperor. He was protected, however, by Frederick, elector of Saxony, who gave him refuge in his castle at Wartburg; Luther returned to Wittenberg in 1522.

---

### 49.1
### LETTER OF MARTIN LUTHER TO GEORGE SPALATIN, DECEMBER 19, 1521

Greetings. Neither Capito's nor Erasmus's[1] opinion moves me in the least. They are only doing what I have expected. Indeed, I have been afraid that someday I should have trouble with one or the other of them, for I saw that Erasmus was far from the knowledge of grace. In everything he writes he is thinking of peace, not of the cross. Thus he thinks that everything must be discussed civilly and with a certain kindliness and courtesy; but Behemoth[2] cares nothing for that, and it will never bring him to reform. I remember that when he said of himself in the Preface to his New Testament,[3] "A Christian readily despises glory," I thought in my heart, "O Erasmus, you deceive yourself, I fear." It is a great thing to despise glory, but his way of despising it was to think lightly of it, not to bear contempt that others put upon him. But the despising of glory is nothing, if it is only in words; it is less than nothing, if it is only in thoughts; for Paul says, "The kingdom of God is in power."[4] Therefore I have never dared, nor can I now boast of anything except the word of truth, which the Lord has given me.

Their books do no good because they refrain from chiding and biting and giving offense. When the popes are civilly admonished, they think it flattery, and keep right on as before, as though they possessed a sort of right to be uncorrected and incorrigible (*jus incorrigibilitatis*[5]), content that they are feared and

---

1  Erasmus, one of the most important Catholic advocates of church reform, and Capito (also known as Wolfgang Fabricius Kopfel, a former Catholic priest) had been trying to reconcile Luther and his followers with the Catholic Church.
2  Old Testament: enormous creature; i.e. the Roman Catholic Church.
3  Erasmus had produced a new edition of the New Testament.
4  New Testament, 1 Corinthians 4.20.
5  Latin: The right not to be corrected.

that no man dares reproach them. They are the sort of people that your Plutarch[6] paints in his book on flattery; but Jeremiah speaks more gravely and terribly of them: "Cursed be he that doeth the work of the Lord deceitfully,"[7] for he is speaking of the work of the sword against the enemies of God. I, too, am afraid and my conscience troubles me, because I listened to you and to my friends at Worms, and held my spirit in check and did not show myself a second Elijah[8] to those idols. They would hear another story if I stood before them again. But enough of this.

Duke John the elder[9] knows at last where I am; so far he has not known; my host has told him in confidence, but he will be silent. I am well here, but I am growing sluggish and languid and cold in spirit, and am miserable. Until today I have been constipated for six days.... Christ be thanked! He has not left me without some relics of the holy cross.... I write this not for sympathy, but for congratulation, praying that I may be worthy to be fervent in spirit. For it is time to pray against Satan with all our might; he is threatening Germany with a fatal tragedy, and I fear the Lord will allow him to bring it about. I am sleepy and lazy both in prayer and in striving, so that I am displeased with myself and have become a burden to myself; perhaps it is because I am alone and you are not here to help me. I beg you, let us pray and watch that we enter not into temptation. I have nothing else to write just now; you know everything about everybody.

I am glad that Wittenberg is flourishing, and especially that it is flourishing when I am away, that the wicked may see it and be grieved, and his desire may perish.[10] May Christ perfect that which He has begun! I greatly wish that Philip,[11] too, would preach to the people somewhere in the city on festival days after dinner. His preaching would take the place of the drinking and the gambling, and people would grow used to the introduction of liberty and the restoration of the customs and manners of the early church. If we have broken all the laws of men and cast off their yokes from us, what difference ought it to make if he is not anointed or shorn and is a married man? He is, nevertheless, a true priest and is actually doing the work of a priest, unless it is not the office of a priest to teach the Word; but in that case Christ Himself would not be a priest, for He taught now in the synagogues, now in ships, now on the shore, now in the mountains; in a word, He was always and everywhere all things to all men. Since, therefore, Melanchthon is called of God and performs the ministry of the Word, as nobody can deny, what difference does it make if he is not called by those tyrannical bishops, not of churches, but of horses and courtiers? But I know what he thinks about it; he will not yield to my persuasion. Let him be called, therefore, and driven to it by the urgent command of the whole church. For if the church demands and requires it of him, he ought not and cannot say no. If I were there I would do my best with the city council and the people to have them ask him to lecture to them privately on the Gospel in German, as he has already begun to do in Latin, and thus, little by little, he would become a German bishop, as he is already a Latin bishop. I wish you would do what you can to bring this about, for the thing the people need above all things is the Word of God, and since he is rich in the Word above others, you can see that it is our duty to call him, that the Word may not be cheated of its fruit.

You will be able to get this through the city council very easily by the help of Lucas [Cranach] and Christian [Doering]. In this way, too, Christ will make up for my absence and silence by his preaching, to the confusion of Satan and his apostles. Origen[12] taught women privately; why should not he, too, undertake something of this sort, since he can do it and ought to, and especially since the people are famishing and in

---

6   Classical writer of the second century.
7   Old Testament, Jeremiah 48.10.
8   An Old Testament prophet who attacked idolatry among the Hebrews (Old Testament, 1 Kings).
9   The brother of the Elector of Saxony, Luther's protector.
10   A reference to Old Testament, Psalms 112.1.
11   Philip Melanchthon, a leading Protestant reformer.
12   Christian theologian of the third century.

want? I hope you will not listen too readily to his excuses, for he will get behind the most beautiful trifles—and it is right that he should, for he ought not to seek such a duty, but the church ought to urge him and call him, and even beseech him to serve it, and to do not what is useful for himself, but what is profitable for many. I beg you to use every effort to accomplish this one thing and get your friends to help you. Farewell, and remember me in your prayers.

Yours, Martin Luther

### 49.2
### LETTER OF MARTIN LUTHER TO PAUL SPERATUS,
### JUNE 13, 1522

*Paul Speratus (1484-1530) was a priest who became a Lutheran.*

Grace and peace in Christ. I received your letter with the questions, and one at the same time from Madame Julia von Stauffen,[13] and learned from them with the greatest pleasure that the Gospel is bearing fruit in your land, because the emperor's satellites, the sophists, are persecuting it with incredible fury in the Low Countries. But God has given them an omen of death, if perchance they may come to themselves and repent; for a sea monster has been cast ashore at Haarlem.[14] It is called a whale, and is 70 feet long and 35 feet wide. By all the precedents of antiquity this prodigy is a sure sign of God's wrath. The Lord have mercy on them and us.

To the questions of the Waldensians,[15] which you have put to me through their commissioners, I would reply as follows. In the first place, I wish that questions of this sort were done away with and suppressed, so far as possible, for they are unprofitable and dangerous to the common people, who are uneducated and fickle and are easily drawn away from the

things that are necessary—that is, from faith and love—into these new and strange matters. Satan is clever; he starts these things so that he may have a way of corrupting the simplicity that is in Christ, and introduces questions that are, as Paul says,[16] interminable. This is what he[17] did when he spread philosophy and ceremonies throughout the world, and none of the bishops resisted him, or stood for the liberty and purity of faith. Thus even now, among us, he is quibbling over the worship of saints and what the saints are conscious of in heaven, and I have it in mind to take the matter up with him, so far as the Lord permits. This is doubtless what has happened with the Waldensian brethren also. Do this, therefore! Urge, insist on, demand the things that are necessary: namely, faith and love, and if they do not first embrace these things, then denounce their frivolity, which occupies itself with these externalities, and not with the things that are necessary. For even the sacrament[18] itself is not so necessary that faith and love are to be let go on its account. It is foolish to quarrel over these cheap things and neglect the precious and salutary things.

Nevertheless, for fear they may think that importunate fools cannot be answered, I should say that a man is free to adore or invoke Christ in the sacrament, and he who does not adore Him commits no sin, neither does he commit sin who adores Him. Let this be the end of this contention. Do not allow either party to be coerced, and let no one adduce circumcision, or judge another. Hold this sort of contention over this matter in contempt, and by your contempt condemn it. Where faith and love are present there can be no sin either in adoring or in not adoring Christ in the sacrament; but if faith and love are not present, no one will be without sin, whether he adores Christ or not; no, no one will ever be without sin no matter what he does. For faith adores Christ, because it sets before it only Him whose body and blood it doubts not to be pre-

---

13  Luther misrepresents her name here. *Argula* von Stauffen was a married noblewoman who wrote on behalf of the Protestant movement.

14  A Dutch city.

15  A medieval heretical group which some claimed to follow during the early days of the Reformation.

16  New Testament, 1 Timothy 1.4.

17  I.e, Satan.

18  I.e., the mass, communion or Lord's supper.

sent. If the contentious are unwilling to call this "concomitance,"[19] let them call it something else and cease the contention, which in this matter is not seemly. For no one denies—not even the Brethren,[20] I take it—that the body and blood of Christ, who is the object of adoration, are present, and this is reason enough for using the term "concomitance." But if there are any who wish to discover how the Deity is contained in the sacrament by way of concomitance, show them that their curiosity is foolish and that they are rushing headlong into the mysteries of God with carnal imaginations; you will in this way keep them in the simplicity of faith and in the pure knowledge of the sacrament. For when these foolish and needless imaginings are admitted, they make people curious, faith becomes a secondary matter, and the way is open for all that filth about infinite space, the void, quantity, substance,[21] and all the other ravings of natural reason and philosophy. For this reason we must guard the simplicity of faith in these discussions. Again, faith and love do not adore Christ in the sacrament because they know that there is no command to adore Him there, and no sin in not adoring Him. Thus faith and love, in their liberty, pass through the midst of them and bring them all into agreement, allowing everybody to hold his own opinion. There is only one thing that faith and love forbid—that people shall strive with one another and judge one another; for they hate sects and schisms and will have freedom in all things.

The dispute about whether the body of Christ alone is present under the bread by virtue of the words [spoken by the priest], etc., is to be settled the same way. Judge for yourself whether there is any need to involve the ignorant multitude in these hair-splittings, when otherwise they can be guided by the sound and safe faith that under the bread there is the body of Him who is true God and true man. What is the use of wearying ourselves with the question how blood, humanity, Deity, hair, bones and skin are present by concomitance, for these things we do not need to know. These things neither teach nor increase faith, but only sow doubts and dissensions. Faith wishes to know nothing more than that under the bread is present the body, under the wine the blood of the Christ who lives and reigns. It holds fast to this simple truth and despises curious questions.

Thus, too, I would solve the question about adoring and invoking God dwelling in the saints. It is a matter of liberty, and it is not necessary either to do it or not to do it. To be sure, it is not so certain that God has His dwelling in many men as that He is present in the sacrament, but we do read in [New Testament,] 1 Corinthians that an unbeliever will fall on his face and worship God in the saints, if he hears them prophesying; and Abraham[22] saw three angels, and worshiped one Lord; and (to use your own illustration) what do we do when we "prefer one another in honor,"[23] except honor and adore God in ourselves? Let it be free, then, to call upon God in man or out of man, in creatures or out of them, for "I fill heaven and earth," saith the Lord.[24] Here faith goes the safest way, for in all things it sees only God, but we cannot say enough of this to unbelievers, or prove it to them because they are always worshiping themselves. Therefore, as I said before, teach them only to be sound in faith, and there will be no need for this kind of question, and the anointing by the Lord will teach them in all things; without it we can do nothing else than run into endless questionings.

Greet Martin Novilianus[25] for me. I have written to Madame Julia but not at length. The book on vows is long since out of print, but I have ordered that a new edition be printed. I have told the bearers of this letter to be sure to tell you what is going on here. Farewell in Christ, and pray for me.

---

19  A term for the physical presence of Christ's body and blood in the bread and wine of the mass.
20  I.e., Waldensians.
21  These terms derive from Aristotle (fourth century BC).
22  Founder of the Hebrew nation (Old Testament, Genesis 18).
23  New Testament, Romans 12.10.
24  Old Testament, Jeremiah 23.24.
25  A schoolmaster.

P.S.: When I was about to seal this letter I looked over your letter again to see if I had answered all your questions, and found the page in which you ask about the power of the words of institution in the sacrament. You think rightly that the power comes from the promise if, between ourselves, there is any power in the words. But you know, too, that it is faith alone that consecrates, and the priests are very often without faith when they consecrate, in which case, of course, their use of the words is not only a mockery and deception, but is even impious. Therefore, in order to be safe, we ought to learn that they also consecrate, and although a priest ought not to be such an unbeliever, nevertheless he can consecrate in the faith of the church when he acts by the command and authority of the church. For it is not he that speaks the words, but the church, and he is the minister of the words which the church speaks. From this you can readily draw further conclusions. Again farewell.

Martin Luther

### 49.3

LETTER OF MARTIN LUTHER TO GEORGE SPALATIN, APRIL 10, 1523

*A few nights before Luther wrote this letter, nine nuns left a convent at Nimbschen. Three others had escaped at about this time.*

Grace and peace. Nine fugitive nuns, a wretched crowd, have been brought me by honest citizens of Torgau. I mean Leonard Coppe[26] and his nephew and Wolf Dommitzsch;[27] there is therefore no cause for suspicion. I pity them much, but most of all the others who are dying everywhere in such numbers in their cursed and impure celibacy. This sex, so very, very weak, joined by nature or rather by God to the other, perishes when cruelly separated. O tyrants! O cruel parents and kinsmen in Germany! O Pope and bishops, who can curse you enough? Who can sufficiently execrate the blind fury which has taught and

enforced such things? But this is not the place to do so.

You ask what I shall do with them? First I shall inform their relatives and ask them to support the girls; if they will not I shall have the girls otherwise provided for. Some of the families have already promised me to take them; for some I shall get husbands if I can. Their names are: Magdalene von Staupitz, Elsa von Canitz, Ave Gross, Ave von Schonfeld and her sister Margaret, Laneta von Goltz, Margaret and Catharine Zeschau and Catharine von Bora.[28] Here are they, who serve Christ, in need of true pity. They have escaped from the cloister in miserable condition. I pray you also to do the work of charity and beg some money for me from your rich courtiers, by which I can support the girls a week or two until their kinsmen or others provide for them. For my Capernaans have no wealth but that of the Word, so that I myself could not find the loan of ten gulden for a poor citizen the other day. The poor, who would willingly give, have nothing; the rich either refuse or give so reluctantly that they lose the credit of the gift with God and take up my time begging from them. Nothing is too much for the world and its way. Of my annual salary I have only 10 or 15 gulden left, besides which not a penny has been given me by my brothers or by the city. But I ask them for nothing, to emulate the boast of Paul, despoiling other churches to serve my Corinthians free....

Farewell, and pray for me.

Martin Luther

### 49.4

LETTER OF MARTIN LUTHER TO WOLFGANG REISSENBUSCH, MARCH 27, 1525

*Wolfgang Reissenbusch was a school teacher at Lichtenberg who eventually entered the diplomatic service of the elector of Saxony.*

God's grace and peace in Christ. Honored Sir! I am moved by good friends and also by the esteem I bear

---

26   A town councillor and tax collector for the elector.
27   A member of a prominent family in Torgau.
28   Most of these women eventually married. Catharine von Bora married Luther himself in 1525.

you, to write this letter on the estate of matrimony, as I have often spoken of it with you before and have noticed that you would like to marry, or are rather forced and compelled to do so by God Himself who gave you a nature requiring it.

I do not think you should be hindered by the rule of the Order,[29] or by a vow, for you should be fully convinced that no vow can bind you or be valid except under two conditions. First, the vow must be possible of performance. For who will vow an impossible thing? Or who would demand it? Thus the Scripture limits all vows so as to be within our power, such as to give God cattle, sheep, houses, land and so forth. Now chastity is not in our power, as little as are God's other wonders and graces, but we are made for marriage as the Scripture says: "It is not good that man should be alone; I will make a help meet for him."[30]

Whoever, therefore, considers himself a man, and believes himself included in that general term, should hear what God his Creator decrees for him, saying that it is not good for him to be alone, but that he should multiply,[31] and, therefore, makes him a help meet to be with him and aid him so that he may not be alone. This is the Word of God, through Whose power seed is created in man's body and the burning desire for a woman kindled and kept alight, which cannot be restrained by vows or laws. For this is God's law and doing. Let him who will be alone cast off the name of man and prove himself an angel or spirit, for God does not permit such a condition to a man. We do right when we sing of holy virgins that their life is not human but angelic, that though in the flesh they could be without the flesh by God's high grace. Our body is in great part woman's flesh, for by them we were conceived and grew, were borne and nourished, so that no one can keep himself entirely free from them. This is God's ordinance, Who made it and had it so. Even the impotent we see are full of natural desire; yes, the more impotent they are the more they desire to be with women, which is natural, as we always desire most what we can least have.

Therefore we see that it is true that whoever will live alone undertakes an impossible task and runs counter to God's Word and the nature God gave him. Those who wrestle with God and nature fall and are full of fornication and every kind of uncleanness until they are drowned in their own vices and driven to despair. Therefore such a vow against God and nature is impossible and void. God condemns it, just as if someone should vow: I will be God's mother, or, I will make a heaven.

Secondly, for a vow to be valid, it must not be against God and the Christian faith, and everything is against that which relies on works and not on God's grace, as is said in [New Testament,] Hebrews, chapter 12. One must ground one's heart on faith and not on food (that is, on works and laws which relate to food, drink and the like). Of this sort are all monastic vows which build hearts and consciences on works and not on grace, by which reliance on works they lose and deny Christ and the faith.

I believe, honored sir, that you are convinced of what I say, and that you are not troubled by such scruples, but I fancy that human fear and timidity lie in your way, as it is said that he must be a bold man who dares to take a wife. There is, therefore, the greater need to encourage, counsel and urge you, making you eager and bold. Dear and honored sir, why should you torture yourself and strive with your own thoughts? It cannot be otherwise than that you think of these things. Thoughts come from the senses and are right merry. Your body urges you to marry and needs it; God wills and forces it. What will you do about it?

It would also be a fine, noble example if you married, that would help many feeble ones broaden their paths and give them more scope, so many others might escape the dangers of the flesh and follow you. What harm is it if people say, "So the Lichtenberg professor has taken a wife, has he?" Is it not a great glory and Christian virtue that you should thereby become a noble excuse for others doing the same? Christ was an example to us all how to bear reproach for con-

---

29 I.e., a religious order to which Reissenbusch had belonged.
30 Old Testament, Genesis 2.18.
31 Referring to Old Testament, Genesis 1.28, 2.18, passim.

science's sake. Do I say reproach? Only foolish fanatics think marriage a reproach, men who do not mind fornication but forbid what God commanded. If it is a shame to take a wife, why is it not a shame to eat and drink, for we have equal need of both, and God wills both?

Why should I say more? It is a pity that men should be so stupid as to wonder that a man takes a wife, or that anyone should be ashamed of it, while no one is ashamed of eating and drinking. Why should only this necessity be doubted and wondered at? Nothing is better than to comply with our senses as early and as fully as possible, and give ourselves to God's Word and work in whatever He wishes us to do, for, if we stand aside in unbelief and anger, He will punish us by giving us over to sin and hell.

Friend, let us not fly higher or try to be better than Abraham, David, Isaiah, Peter, Paul,[32] and all the patriarchs, prophets and apostles, as well as many holy martyrs and bishops, who all knew that they were created men by God and were not ashamed to be, and to be thought, men and, therefore, believed that they should not remain alone. Who is ashamed of marriage should also be ashamed to be and to be thought a man, and thinks he can do better than God. Adam's children are and remain men, and, therefore, they should and must let men be begotten by them.

Good heavens! We see daily how much trouble it costs to remain within marriage and keep conjugal faith, and yet we try to keep out of it as if we were men with neither flesh nor blood! This is the work of the world's god, the devil, who slanders and shames marriage but lets adulterers, harlots and rascals remain in honor. It is only reasonable to get married as a defense against him and his world, and to bear his reproaches for God's sake.

I beg, honored sir, that you will take my true Christian advice kindly, and act on it quickly, so that you may tempt God no longer. If you follow God's grace and promise, you thereby honor His Word and work and He will honor you in return. There will be one little hour of shame and then years of honor will follow. May Christ, our Lord, give you His grace that this my letter may by His Spirit become living and powerful in your heart, and bring forth fruit to the praise and honor of His name. Amen.

Your honor's devoted
Martin Luther

## 49.5
### LETTER OF MARTIN LUTHER TO GEORGE SPALATIN, OCTOBER 20, 1528

Grace and peace in Christ.... I believe you have heard the news, that by a great miracle the Duchess [Ursula] of Munsterberg has got away from the monastery at Freiberg; just now she is a member of my household, together with two virgins, Margaret Volkmar, daughter of a citizen of Leipzig, and Dorothea, daughter of a citizen of Freiberg, who brought to the monastery 1,400 guldens inherited from her father. She has left it behind her, and is now, with Mistress Ursula herself, a poor follower of the poor Christ; neither of them brought a farthing with her. Duke George is worrying our Prince;[33] what will come of it, I do not know. For she is a relative of Duke George, as I think you know, that is to say, their mothers were sisters. Nicholas von Minkwitz is said to be enlisting a great army, but where he will attack I do not know. I wonder what the princes[34] think that they see and allow such things, for it is to be feared that this spark will start a fire in Germany. Some say that he is leading them against the Wowaida,[35] others that he is preparing to move against the Margrave,[36] who is snoring peacefully. Bugenhagen has gone to Hamburg, Philip[37] to

---

32  Prominent figures of the Old and New Testaments.
33  The elector of Saxony, Luther's protector. Duke George, a defender of Catholicism, was head of the junior branch of the elector's family and ruled a neighboring territory of Saxony.
34  The various territorial rulers in Germany.
35  A Transylvanian ruler who was rival of the Holy Roman Emperor for the throne of Hungary.
36  One of the leading German princes.
37  Philip Melanchthon.

Thuringia.[38] On the day after St. Ursula's day we shall go at our part of the Visitation; I hope that you will do, or are already doing, the same. Christ be with us all and bless us. Amen. Greet Eberhard and Ehrhard and all the Hards that are with you.

Your Martin Luther

---

38  Luther appears to refer here to the activities of leading Protestant clergy conducting "visitations," i.e., examinations of the spiritual condition of the inhabitants of various districts.

# 50

# JOHN CALVIN, *LETTERS*

John Calvin is generally regarded as the leading Protestant reformer of the sixteenth century after Martin Luther. Born in 1509 and raised in France, the product of a humanist education, he became a Protestant in the 1520s and was exiled from Paris. Calvin then went to Switzerland, eventually settling in Geneva, where he became the leader of the Protestant movement there. After being driven out of the city in 1538 because of discontent with the rigor of his moral reforms, he returned three years later to great influence at Geneva, where he died in 1564. He wrote the letters below in Latin.

---

### 50.1

CALVIN TO THE DUCHESS OF FERRARA[1]

(GENEVA, OCTOBER, 1541)

Madame, I humbly beseech you that you would take in good part my boldness in writing these present words, deeming that, should you find therein too great a plainness, it proceeds not so much from rashness, or from overweening self-conceit, as from pure and true affection for your service in our Lord. For albeit that I do acknowledge myself a very unprofitable servant of the Church, it has, notwithstanding, been found expedient to employ me in that station, according to the grace which the Lord has imparted to me; it has even occurred to me that there was a need-be for my doing so, if I wished to acquit myself of my duty, not merely because I feel myself obliged, in regard to you, to seek, in so far as is possible for me, and in the way of duty, your welfare and advantage, howbeit that such motive is alone sufficient to stir me

up to action, but rather that, considering the state and preeminence in which the Lord has set you, it seems to us all, we whom the Lord by his goodness has called to be ministers of his holy word, ought to keep in special remembrance, to apply ourselves to the bestowal of some pains for you, and the more so because, more than most princely persons, you are able to promote and advance the kingdom of Christ. I have, besides, observed in you such fear of God and such disposed faithfulness of obedience, that independently of the high rank which he has vouchsafed you among men, I do so value the graces which he has put upon you, even to such a degree, that I would think myself accursed should I have omitted the occasions of any profitable service, in so far they might be presented to me. This is certainly what I can say without any feigning or flattery, but in sincerity of heart, and speaking as in his presence who knows all our secret thoughts.

Madame, by other worthy persons who have passed through here at different times, I have been

---

1 This was Renée of France, daughter of King Louis XII of France. As duchess of Ferrara (by marriage) she received Protestant reformers, including Calvin, and converted to Protestantism.

given to understand how Master Francis, whom you have appointed preacher to your household, after having acquitted himself well in preaching, as well at least as could be expected of him, had persuaded you that it would not be a bad thing, after having heard mass, to hold some sort of communion, which must be somehow the Supper of our Lord; this proceeding, which was not approved of by one of your ladies, who, according to the knowledge which she had received of God, did not wish against her conscience to meddle with what she considered to be wrong in itself, and has been the occasion, on the representation of the said Master Francis, to have some way or other turned away from her the goodwill which you have been wont to bear her; so that matters have reached such a height that you have intimated that all those who do as she does ought not to be supported, inasmuch as, by their importunity, they give birth to scandals to no purpose among the faithful. Wherefore, concluding that a thing of so much importance must not be concealed, seeing that you had been given to understand that matters were otherwise than they are, according as it has pleased the Lord to reveal himself to me in Scripture, I have thought it right to communicate to you what the Lord has given me of understanding in that matter. But while I have been in some doubt and hesitation about doing so, I have been given to understand, on the part of Madame de Pons,[2] that you wished very much to be more fully instructed, the more so that, besides the many difficulties which you see, on the other hand, it is very difficult to come to a satisfactory solution to them. This message has all the more confirmed me in my purpose to venture to try to give you a faithful exposition so far as I know, in order that afterward you may judge for yourself, and in so far as you shall have fully understood God's truth, that you may follow in all obedience, seeing that your zeal is not of the kind that rebels against it, but receives the truth in love and with all benign affection. Yet all this notwithstanding, Madame, before I begin, I beseech you not to take up any suspicion of me, as though I did this having been put up to it by some persons of your household, or to

favor anyone in particular, for I can assure you, before God, that I do so without having been requested by anyone, and only on the advertisement, as I have already assured you, of persons passing through this way who never thought that I could have the means of any direct communication. On the other hand, I would rather desire to be cast down into the lowest depths of the abyss than to twist about or wrest the truth of God in order to make it suit the hatred or to procure the favor of any creature whatsoever. But what makes me speak out is that I cannot bear that the word of God should be thus to you concealed, perverted, depraved, and corrupted in such essential things by those in whom you have some confidence, to whom you have given authority.

Touching Master Francis, to speak soberly, I would to a certainty put you upon your guard not to confide too unreservedly in his doctrine. Should I do so, I need have no reason to fear that perhaps you may entertain some bad opinion of me, as though I might speak from hatred or envy of this personage. For I have neither matter nor occasion of envy in any way toward him, and the hatred which, up to the present hour, I have felt toward him, is such that I have at all times, to the utmost of my power, made it my business to edify him in doing well. But when I perceive that anyone, owing to an ill-informed conscience, sets himself to overthrow the word of the Lord, and to extinguish the light of Truth, I could by no means pardon him, even were he my own father a hundred times over. As for this same individual, I have been aware, from having long known him, that whatsoever small understanding of the Scripture God has vouchsafed him, he has always made subserve his own profit and ambition, preaching wherever he saw that it would be a help to gratify his avarice, forbearing to preach wherever he found that it began to be troublesome to him; then for all that, as often as he could procure hearers, persons of credit to countenance him, and the wealthy to fill his wallet or his purse, who required him to give glory to God, he has taken the trouble to satisfy them by almost always selling them his word. On the other hand, again, wherever he met with any trouble or per-

---

2   A Calvinist noblewoman attached to the duchess.

secution, he had always his denial ready to escape from it to such a degree that one could not know in regard to him whether the holy and sacred word of God was but a sport and mockery, inasmuch as he turned it into a farce, playing at one time one character, and at another the part of another, according to the pastime he finds in it. As to his life, I do not touch upon that, except that one could desire that it were better in a minister of the word. I know, Madame, that the duty of a Christian man is not to detract from his neighbor, and that is what I have not wished to do, for had I desired to speak ill of him, I have plenty of other material concerning him which I conceal. But our Lord does not mean, when we see a wolf, under the color and appearance of a pastor, scattering his flock, that we should quail in silence through fear of speaking evil of him. He rather commands us to discover the perversity of those who, like the pestilence, corrupt by their infection, and mar the face of the Church. And as for myself, neither would I have taken that method here if I saw any better remedy, taking into account the mortal fury of that sort of people which I do thereby provoke against myself. For I have not at this day so fierce a warfare with any as with those who, under the shadow of the Gospel, wear a rough garment outwardly toward princes, amazing and entertaining them by their finesse and subtlety, enshrouded in some cloud, as it were, without ever leading them to the right object. But how could I do otherwise? If I do not address myself to them, it is because I see their heart to be so divested of all fear of God that speaking of his judgment to them is but a mere fable or a pleasant tale. But when I describe them such as they are, to make them aware that they could carry their abuse no farther, I find that by this method they are more restrained from further seduction and abuse. This very person I have often set about trying to bring back into the good way, so far even as to make him confess his iniquity, albeit, that impudently he would excuse himself before men, being convicted in his own conscience before God. Notwithstanding, with a horrible obstinacy and hardness of heart, he would persist in saying that he could not desist from doing that which he knew to be bad, except that on one occasion, after having seen some treatise of mine, with grievous imprecations on himself he protested that he would never assist at the mass because it was such a gross abomination. But I know my man so well that I scarcely count on his oath more than upon the chattering of a magpie. Howsoever, Madame, as I would not that he did persevere in ill-doing, to the great detriment of yourself and of the people of God, I feel constrained to warn you by my intimation, seeing that as regarded him, he would not profit by taking advantage of it. What I have told you about him is so certain that I do not wish you to believe it until you have first of all found out by experience that it is true, for if you pay attention, you will see at a glance that he preaches the word of God only in so far as he wishes to gratify you, in order to catch benefices[3] or other prey, and in the meantime not to displease anyone who can do him harm.

Now, Madame, having done with this personage, I come to the present matter. He gives you to understand that the mass is neither so wicked nor abominable, but that it is allowable to say it, and to the faithful to hear it, so that those who make this a matter of conscience are the disturbers of the Church, stirring up scandals among the weak, whom we are commanded to strengthen. As regards the first point, I doubt whether I ought to stop to argue it, inasmuch as I reckon that you are so fully resolved already that the mass is a sacrilege, the most execrable that one can imagine, that I fear to make myself appear ridiculous to you in taking the pains to prove to you a thing about which you can be in no way in doubt. And, besides, the small compass of a letter cannot comprise that which is enough to fill a large book. Yet, notwithstanding, I will touch briefly upon it and, as it were, in a cursory way, in order that you may not have any doubt. In so far as the mass is a sacrifice, appointed by men for the redemption and salvation of the living and the dead, as their canon maintains, it is an unbearable blasphemy by which the passion of Jesus Christ is quite overthrown and set aside, as if it were of no effect whatever. For we say that the faithful have been purchased by

---

3  Church positions which provide an income.

the blood of Jesus, have obtained thereby the remission of their sins, righteousness, and the hope of eternal life, and that belief must imply so far that the blessed Savior, in offering up himself to the Father, and presenting himself to be sacrificed, has offered himself as an eternal sacrifice by which our iniquities have been purged and cleansed, ourselves received into the grace of the Father, and made partakers of the heavenly inheritance, as the apostle declares very fully in the Epistle to the Hebrews.[4] If, then, the death of Jesus is not acknowledged as the only sacrifice which has been once made for all, in order that it might have an eternal efficacy, what more remains except that it be effaced entirely, as being altogether ineffectual? I know well that these liars, to cover their abomination, say that they make the same sacrifice which Jesus has made, but from that statement there arise several blasphemies. For that sacrifice could be made by no one except by Jesus himself. And the Apostle says that if Jesus is now sacrificed, it follows, that he must suffer still.[5] Therefore, you can see that one of two things must here take place: either to acknowledge the horrible blasphemy of the mass, and to detest it, or, in approving it, to trample under foot the cross of Jesus. How much it is contrary to the Supper of Christ, I leave you to consider with yourself, after you have read in Scripture the words of institution.[6] But the crowning desecration which they commit is the idolatry which they perpetrate by adoring a created thing instead of God, a thing which is altogether inexcusable. Taking these considerations into view, let us look well to it, since we can neither speak nor hear such things without grievously offending God by communicating in such abominations. For how can we pretend that we are not justly reproved for having consented to such iniquities since we do receive them with greater honor and reverence than we do the word of God? If you wish to know how far that is pleasing to the Lord God, he declares by his prophet Ezekiel, in the twentieth chapter,[7] where he tells the people of Israel that they love to practice open idolatry like the gentiles, that they made mention of God's name along with the name of their idols, as wishing to compass their own ends contrary to his statutes, by which he was to be served in worship, and by setting up their own foolish inventions, by which they were made to fall away from his word; on the other hand, the prophet telling them that God will scatter all those who swear by his name, avowing him as their God, while, at the same time, they witness against themselves in adoring something other than him alone. Should someone object that externals in religion are quite indifferent, that what is required is only that the heart within should be upright, to that our Lord answers that he will be glorified in our body, which he has purchased with his blood, that he requires the confession of the mouth, and that all our prayers should be consecrated to his honor, without being in any way contaminated or defiled by anything displeasing to him. But, because this would be too long to treat of here, as it ought to be, you can have recourse, for your more full information, to the treatise where I hope that you will find reasons enough to satisfy you. The scandal still remains, which your almoner says troubles the consciences of the weak, when anyone esteemed a believer holds the mass in such horror that he would not in any way come in contact with it, that he neither wished to find it here nor to meet with it elsewhere. But he does not consider that, in reference to those things which are either commanded or forbidden by God, although it might offend the whole world, we must not go beyond his ordinances. That which is commanded us, to support and strengthen our weak brethren, by doing nothing which may wound or offend them, refers to lesser things of no great consequence, which are of themselves indifferent and permitted of our Christian liberty, as the whole of Scripture shows. Besides, all those commands about not scandalizing our neighbor tend to his edification in well-doing, as St. Paul points out in the fifteenth of the Romans.[8] It follows, therefore, that

---

4  In the New Testament.
5  New Testament, 1 Hebrews 10.11-12.
6  New Testament, 1 Corinthians 11.23-26.
7  In the Old Testament.
8  In the New Testament.

we must not seek to please God in those things which do not tend to edification, but to destruction. And thence we have the doctrine of St. Paul in the First Epistle to the Corinthians, chapters 8 and 10,[9] where he says that if by any external action of ours our neighbor is built up in wrong-doing, albeit on our part there may have been no violation of conscience, we yet sin against God and destroy our brother. As is here the case: we know the mass to be cursed and execrable; we assist in it to content the ignorant; those who see us assisting in it conclude that we approve by so doing, and they then follow our example. St. Paul counts that a great crime, although we make no difficulty about it. Wherefore, Madame, I do beseech you not to permit that under the name of scandal anyone should beguile you; for there is not a more pernicious scandal in this world than when our Christian brother, by our example, is entrapped in ruin and driven forward into error. If we would avoid all scandal we must cast behind us Jesus Christ, who is the stone of offense at which the most part of the world trips and stumbles. And even thus has he been a scandal to the Jews and Israelites to whom he was sent, as always a large portion of that nation has been offended and stumbled in the worship of their God. We must, therefore, hold fast by this rule, that, in reference to things which are either command-ed or forbidden by God, it is mainly requisite in the doing or forbearing that he may not be deprived of his due obedience, even if we offend the whole world. But since it is so, that Christ and his Evangel[10] are a scan-dal to the evil-disposed and malignant, we must expect, if we would follow him, that they must always be a scandal to us. As for things which are free and indifferent, that is to say, which, according to our opportunity, we can either do or omit the doing of, we ought to suit ourselves to the convenience of our Chris-tian brethren, in order that our liberty may be subject to choice, and even in doing so, regard must be had so to support their infirmity as they may be built up in

God; for if, by our example, we lead them on and draw them in to do what they consider to be wrong, we are the means of their destruction. There are few, indeed, who have had experience of the truth of God, who do not know in some measure the iniquity of the mass. When they well know what sort of a thing it is, it is impossible that they should not desire to flee from it. While they scruple and are in doubt about it, whenev-er they perceive that we communicate,[11] they follow our example, without caring for being further resolved in the matter. Here is the worst scandal that can hap-pen, seeing that their consciences are wrung unto death. If what I hear is true, that he would have you to believe that affair to be so small in importance that German Churches make no question at all about it, that is, that those of one persuasion let alone and permit the other to have the mass, in this he inflicts a great dam-age and injury upon the Churches of God, in charging them with a practice which you will acknowledge to be false whenever you shall be pleased to make inquiry for yourself. For not only among the Churches which have received the Evangel, but in the judgment of pri-vate individuals, this article is quite agreed on: that the abomination of the mass must not continue. And to that effect Capito,[12] who is one of those who set them-selves to moderate the zeal of the others in these mat-ters, has written a book of late which he has dedicated to the king of England,[13] in which he teaches that it is the duty of Christian princes to abolish such execrable idolatry in their kingdoms if they wish to do their duty as might be expected of them. There is, in short, in our day no man of any renown who is not quite agreed on this point.

Well then, Madame, seeing that it has pleased the Lord God, of his goodness and infinite compassion, to visit you with the knowledge of his name, and to enlighten you with the truth of his holy Evangel, acknowledge your calling to which he has called you. For he has drawn us forth out of the depths of dark-

---

9   In the New Testament.
10  I.e., good news or gospel, as recounted in the New Testament.
11  I.e., partake of the communion.
12  Wolfgang Fabricius Kopfel, a former Catholic priest who became a Protestant and worked to unite Lutherans and Calvinists.
13  Henry VIII.

ness, where we were detained as captives, in order that we follow uprightly the light of his word, without falling away to one side or the other, and that we seek more and more to be instructed by him, so that we may profit more abundantly in that holy wisdom wherein he has made some beginning among us; and above all, to look to it carefully that we do not restrain his Spirit, as do those who shut their eyes and ears to the evident plain truth, being content to remain ignorant of that which the Lord would have them know and understand. It is not thus that he would have us do, from mere dread that the Lord would punish such contempt and ingratitude, but rather we ought to study to profit continually in the school of this good Master, until we shall have attained perfection in his doctrine, which will be when we are free from this weighing down and this earthly coil of the flesh, praying, with the good David,[14] that he would instruct us in the doing of his will. Surely, if we go forward advancing therein with zealous affection, he will so guide us that he will not let us go astray out of the right path. And although there are still some remains of ignorance in us, he will vouchsafe a more full revelation when there is need for it, seeing that he knows the right season better than we. The main point is to understand how his holy doctrine ought to become fruitful, and so bring forth fruit in us, and that is when it so transforms us by the renewal of our heart and mind that his radiant glory which consists in innocence, integrity, and holiness, relights the soul within us. If it be not thus with us, we take the name of God in vain when we glorify ourselves by making our boast that we know the Evangel. I do not say this to admonish you to do what you do not do at present, but with the purpose that the work of God, which is already begun in you, may be confirmed from day to day.

But only, as I have said at the beginning, I beseech you to pardon my simplicity. Should it be your pleasure to have more instruction in this argument, and especially how a Christian person ought to govern himself in regard to scandals, I will attempt, so far as the Lord shall enable me, to satisfy you. In the meantime, I send you a letter[15] on the subject, as you will see, if you think it worth your while to devote some hours to it at your leisure; besides that, a little tract which I have put together lately which, as I hope, by reason of its brevity, may serve as a help to consolation inasmuch as it contains complete enough doctrine. That the Lord may have care over you in your infirmity, and that he would manifest in the efficacy of his Spirit in such a way that you may be as much honored in his household as he is elevated in station and dignity among men.

50.2

## LETTER TO THE PRIEST OF CERNEX (1543)

Sir priest, we acknowledge that point of your letter to be very true, that the plague which we have in our town[16] is a scourge of God, and we confess that we are justly punished on account of our faults and demerits. We do not doubt also, that by this mean he admonishes us to examine ourselves, to lead and draw us to repentance. Wherefore, we take in good part what you have said, that it is time for us to return to God, to ask and to obtain pardoning mercy from him. We likewise see that throughout the whole of Christendom there is great trouble, that there is scarce a single corner which is not in some way afflicted in that respect, from which we must conclude that the wrath of God is greatly kindled against this poor world. And it is no wonder, for the causes are evident, and they are not far to seek, while one sees that such corruption everywhere prevails, and how vice of every kind is carried to the utmost pitch and reigns paramount. We do not say this to excuse ourselves, by hiding, as it were, in a crowd, but inasmuch as the wrath of God ought to be all the more dreadful in our apprehension when it is thus spread abroad over the whole earth, like a kind of deluge. Besides, when we have well considered the matter in every way, we can come to no other conclusion except that over and above the vice which reigns generally everywhere, there are among Christians two things

---

14  The Old Testament Hebrew king.
15  A copy of a letter Calvin had sent someone else.
16  Geneva was in the midst of an outbreak of plague in 1543.

which especially provoke the wrath of God: namely, that one party of them dishonors him by their idolatry and superstitions, and instead of receiving his holy word to bring them back into the straight road, not only despise and mock and flout, but have a hatred and horror of, and even persecute, the truth. On the other hand, we who know by his Evangel how we ought to serve and honor him do not make strict account in our discharge of duty so that the Word of life is as if it were idle and unproductive among us. We have no wish to justify ourselves by condemning others. For in so far as it has pleased God to withdraw us out of the horrible darkness wherein we were, and to enlighten us in the knowledge of the right way of salvation, we are so much the more blameable if we are negligent in doing our duty, as it is written, "The servant knowing the will of his master, and not doing it, shall be severely punished" ([New Testament] Luke 12). So that we ought not to be astonished if our Lord should punish us twofold on account of our ingratitude which is in us, when we do not walk as children of the light, and produce no fruit of that holy calling to which he has called us. Moreover, he threatens that judgment shall begin at his own house, that is to say, that he will correct his servants first of all ([New Testament] 1 Peter 4). But, nevertheless, we would rather consider, on the other hand, that seeing above all else he holds his own glory in highest commendation, he hates and chiefly holds in detestation the idolatries and superstitions by which he is dishonored, and which more grievously offend than every other thing. Think for a little on what takes place among you. They adore stone and wood; they invoke the dead; they trust in lying vanities; they would serve God by ceremonies foolishly invented without the authority of his word. The true doctrine is buried, and if anyone wishes to have it brought forth, he is cruelly persecuted. Do you think that God can bear with such pollutions and blasphemies against his own honor? St. Paul bears witness that God had sent the plague on Corinth because the Holy Supper had not been so reverently treated there as it ought ([New Testament] 1 Corinthians 11). Then what must we expect, seeing that it has already, for so long a period, been converted into such an execrable sacrifice as is your mass? There is no

need for a long proof of what we say. Consider attentively the institution [of the Lord's Supper] of our Lord, and make the comparison between it and your mass. You will find a greater distance between them than between the heaven and the earth. Thus, in truth, our duty would be to give glory to God all together with one accord by confessing our offenses, everyone for his own sin, according to his state and circumstances ([Old Testament] Daniel 9). Thus it is that on our part we should feel how grievous a sin it is for us not to receive his grace as it befits us to do, when he presents it to us, and that we do not live in higher perfection, considering the knowledge which he has given us of his Evangel, and the exhortations which are daily made to us by his commandment. Let those who, instead of the Word, follow their own fancies or human traditions consider that it is an abomination very displeasing to God—that of corrupting his service, as they have done, of adhering to false doctrine, of attributing the grace of his salvation to created things, of reversing the right use of the sacraments,[17] turning them quite upside down, of abusing and taking his name in vain, and along with that, of persecuting the witnesses of Jesus Christ, who dare venture to open their mouths against such abuses. And if some of them are at present in prosperity, let them by no means put their trust in that. For it is ever the fashion of hypocrites, and especially of idolaters, to glorify themselves when the hand of God does not press upon them, as if this were because they have so well deserved of God, while dishonoring him by their idolatrous mummeries, and by that they harden themselves in their impiety, flattering themselves and condemning others. But what does our Lord say? "I have done them," he says, "all the good which was possible, and they have thought that this was the wages of whoredom with their idols. Wherefore, I will take away all that I have given them, to discover their vileness, and constrain them to return to me."

Now, even at this very time, when we are seeking and searching to find out the misdeeds on account of which God punishes us, and in what we have offended, you allege against us that we have changed the divine service, and the order of the Church, which had been so well established and observed in this town.

---

17   Those ceremonies which, in Christian theology, involved God's grace.

This is not any new reproach, for it was made against Jeremiah in his time, as he relates in the forty-fourth chapter.[18] It is that the hypocrites complain that since they had left off the adoration of the queen of heaven,[19] they had had nothing but famine, war, and all poverty. Lactantius[20] also, an ancient doctor[21] of the Church, and St. Augustine[22] demonstrate that in their time all the afflictions which had happened in the world were imputed to the Evangel because it had brought about the abolition of the pagan superstitions, which were thought to be service to God. You will reply that it was not all alike; we hold that it was. What then is to be done? We must ascertain what is the truth upon the point, in order to pronounce a sound and correct opinion. Well, then, besides that our consciences speak peace to us before God as touching that, the thing itself can clearly answer for us before men. For no one has hitherto shown us that we had changed anything which was commanded by God, nor that we had introduced any novelty against his person, nor that we had declined from the truth to lay hold of some evil doctrine. On the contrary, it is well known that we have reformed our Church according to the pure doctrine of God, which is the rule to apply and to keep up a healthy state. It is true that it is rather an odious thing to alter what has been hitherto received. But the order which Our Lord has once delivered to us ought to be forever inviolable. Thus, when it has been forsaken for a season, it ought to be renewed and set up again, even if heaven and earth should commingle. There is no antiquity, no custom which can be set up or pleaded to the detriment of this doctrine: that the government of the Church established by the authority of God should be perpetual even to the end of the world, since he has willed and determined that it should be so. The reasons which have made us change are more than sufficiently urgent. The first point in Christianity is the true adoration of God. Now, we have come to know that the form of adoration which we have been in the habit of observing was false and perverted and, moreover, that it was not in the spirit of truth ([New Testament] John 4), but in that of external ceremonies, and even in superstitious practices. It is certain that then we did not adore God alone, but wood and stones instead of him, the pictures, the reliquaries[23] of the dead, and things of a like kind. To the adoration of God is conjoined the rule of worshipping him aright. And in what manner is it that he is invoked throughout the papacy, except with doubt and distrust, inasmuch as they know nothing about the office of Jesus Christ as our Advocate and Intercessor, by whom we obtain our requests ([New Testament] Romans 8; 1 Timothy 2.1; John 2; Hebrews 4)? Besides, what are the public prayers but murmurs and ululations, vain repetitions without understanding? Thirdly, how many blasphemies are there in it, in so far as the power of the sole Mediator is attributed to saints and saintesses, to obtain grace in their name and by their merits? After the invocation follows the service, as if we were instructed to serve God by the vain traditions of men. On the contrary, he wills and requires that we take for our rule his will alone throughout ([Old Testament] Deuteronomy 12; 1 Kings 15). As concerning the confidence and firm persuasion of our salvation, which is like, as it were, the foundation of all, instead of relying on his pure mercy, in order to have our consciences at rest, and give to him the glory which appertains to him, we were taught, like the rest of the world, to put our trust partly in ourselves, and partly in other created things. There is no need, however, to rehearse all the rest, for there would be no end of that. For, in short, it has come to this: that the grace of Jesus Christ was, as it were, buried out of our sight. When we have understood so much, and that it has been clearly proven to us that all that was abomination in the sight of God, what could we have done? Were we to withstand God, and to resist his truth? Had it merely been

---

18  In the Old Testament.

19  I.e., the Virgin Mary.

20  Fourth-century Christian writer.

21  I.e., an early learned theologian.

22  Leading Christian theologian of the late fourth and early fifth centuries.

23  A container which holds the relics, usually bones, of saints.

a matter of Church order, if it had been at all bearable, we might have been content to remain, but it was such a Babel[24] of confusion and disorder, that there remained no other remedy but that of an entire renovation. What shall we say of the sacraments, the observance and use of which had been altogether perverted from the ordinance of Jesus Christ our Lord? How many silly baptismal ceremonies had been sought out and invented by men, without the authority of God! And what is worse, the true and pure institution of our Lord was, as it were, abolished by such frivolous patchwork. In short, they set a greater value upon the anointing chrism[25] than the water, and at present it seems to be a settled point with you that our baptism is null because we have retained only what the Lord has commanded, and what the Apostles have observed and held fast in practice. As for the Holy Supper, it has been much more profaned. Our Lord has left us that as a pledge, on purpose that (we might be) certain that our souls are nourished from his body and from his blood, to make us partakers of all his benefits, and particularly so of his death and passion. In order that we may do this, we ought to distribute it according to the terms of his commandment, namely, in declaring the worth and efficacy of the mystery. On the contrary, they have converted it into a sacrifice, to make reconciliation anew with God by man's work, and not for the living only, but also for the dead. The priest, to make what he considers a due use of the sacrament, separates himself from the Church.[26] The whole is done and spoken in an unknown language, after the manner of enchanters with their charms. When Easter comes, again they give to the people only half of the sacrament, depriving them of the cup, against the express command of the Master. To consent to such sacrilege as that is not even to be thought of. And yet, nevertheless, they reproach us with having let down and abased this holy sacrament. But the thing speaks for itself: that we have restored it in complete integrity, where it had been corrupted and polluted in so many ways. St. Paul, wishing to correct an

abuse which had grown up among the Corinthians in reference to this sacrament, sends them back to the first institution of the ordinance by the Lord himself as to an inviolable statute ([New Testament] 1 Corinthians 11). What could we do, then, to correct the infinite abuses with which it had been contaminated, except to follow that same rule? Let them show us, if they can, if there is anything in the manner of our worship which is not conformable to the institution of our Lord, to the usage of the apostles, and we are ready to amend our fault. But when they accuse us without either rhyme or reason, that will not in the least disturb or excite us so as to make us renounce the true and settled institution. Wherefore, that which you impute to us as a fault, we hold and take to be a work of God, the best to which we have been able to attain. Yet nevertheless, we do not deny that we have come very far short in many respects, for which our Lord has good right to punish us, but this is in regard to our life not corresponding with his holy doctrine of which we make a profession.

In like manner, where you exhort us to return back to God in order to appease his wrath, you drive us back to the means which rather serve to provoke and inflame it the more. First of all, you would have us present the offering of the precious body and blood of our Lord Jesus. We are well aware that it is a customary practice among you, but in order to ascertain whether it is a work pleasing to God, inquiry ought to be made if it is according to his will. Besides, he does not say that we should offer his body, but that we should receive it ([New Testament] Matthew 26; Mark; Luke; Paul). "Take," he says, "eat." Instead of receiving the body of Jesus Christ, if we wish to make God believe that it is a sacrifice which we offer to him, where shall we find any approval of our fantasy? We would pray you seriously ponder this reason. You advise us to make an offering of the body of Christ by a priest for the purpose of obtaining grace. We reply that Christ never gave us his sacrament for that end, but that it is in order to receive him, in the intention of

---

24  Referring to the tower of Babel of the Old Testament (Genesis 11), whose destruction by God was followed by God making the languages of those who presumed to build it mutually unintelligible.

25  Holy oil.

26  I.e., from the congregation.

being partakers of that once-for-all and eternal sacrifice which he alone has offered, according to his office ([New Testament] Hebrews 7-10). We say, moreover, that it is to derogate from his dignity, inasmuch as he has been consecrated sacrificial priest, without successor or companion, to make offering of himself, because no one else could be worthy to perform an act of such excellence. For the office of sacrificing is to be Mediator, to make reconciliation between God and men. In whom shall we put our trust—in Jesus Christ, or in you—seeing that there is such contrariety? Then after that, you hold forth to us the beautiful general processions.[27] But what use is there for that, except that with great pomp and ceremony one would think of appeasing God? You will tell us that you would intend that they should devoutly engage in them. And what devotion is there to place reliance in candles and torches, in beautiful and sumptuous furnishings, in images, in reliquaries of the dead? Such, indeed, has always been the usage and wont of pagans, as appears from history. How such things comport with Christianity it is impossible to explain. We make no question about assembling together to make solemn prayer to God. But we ask what there is in these public general processions beyond the accoutrements full of pomp, lamps and luminaries, relics, and other things of a like kind? All that sort of thing smells of rank Judaism, and befits pagan rather than Christian worship. They shout well, indeed, and make an outcry, and they sing prettily. But to what end? It is in an unknown tongue,[28] and therefore against the express command of the Holy Spirit, who wills that the common prayers be made in the common language so that the rude and uninstructed may take part in them, and say "Amen" at the end ([New Testament] 1 Corinthians 14). You further exhort us to invoke the Virgin Mary and the saints, among whom you make special mention of Saint Peter, as our patron. But God calls us to himself alone, forbidding us to have recourse elsewhere ([Old Testament] Psalms 49), and with good right, for his chief glory lies in that we should call upon him alone in the name of Jesus Christ. But even

had there been no such reason for it there, we have many exhortations in Scripture pressing our return to God with prayer and supplication in time of pestilence, of war, and famine ([Old Testament] Isaiah 44,45; Jeremiah 45; Hosea 2). Never does there occur a single word about the invocation of the saints. It would therefore be very inconsiderate on our part were we to follow what you have told us, in turning away from the doctrine of God. Touching that of your calling Saint Peter our patron, it is the same thing with what the prophet speaks: "Israel, your gods are according to the number of your towns" ([Old Testament] Jeremiah 2), and at that time the intention of the people of Israel was not to invent many gods in order to abolish the worship of the true God, the Creator of the world. Forasmuch, however, as each town chose a patron in whom to trust, they are reproved by the prophet, for that every town had its own god. You would have us do the like at present. But it does not please God that we should take up with any other patron than Jesus Christ, who has taken us into his keeping, to recommend us to God his Father. If we have formerly been in this state of blindness of mind, the darkness has passed away ([New Testament] John 10). There is now an end of transgression, now that we have the shining light before our eyes. But you have known by experience, you say, how much that has profited you. It is no new thing, as we have said, to attribute God's benefits to our own foolish and perverted doings, as if by our idolatry we had merited the good things which he has sent us. The sorcerers, enchanters, soothsayers, and the like could say as much. But we have our certain rule, which is that reason goes before, and experience follows after. If we do thus, we shall not wander away from the right path, and shall neither decline on this side nor on that from what God commands us. And we shall find in truth and without deceit that his help is never wanting to those who put their whole trust and confidence in him. On the contrary, in seeking for other help, we shall sometimes think to profit by it, but we shall be disappointed in the end.

---

27  I.e., the ceremonial carrying about of the consecrated bread (in Catholic theology, Christ's body).
28  Latin.

Well, then, our Lord Jesus wishes to open your eyes to understand and to see what it is that he would say when he calls himself the only Savior, the only life, the only sanctification, the only wisdom, the only confidence of men: that it is in order that we may altogether acknowledge him to be such, that with good accord we glorify him, in heart as well as with the mouth, and equally in all our works, so that, as we have all received one baptism in his name, we might have the same confession of our Christianity.

### 50.3
#### TO AN UNKNOWN PERSON (APPARENTLY 1545)

And so, just as if the day for holding the Council had been appointed for the next month, you already make arrangements for your departure. This, however, is of itself a proof of how rashly and haphazardly everything is done among you, and nothing set about prudently or after deliberation, that when the most able persons in the whole kingdom should be selected, the matter has been entrusted to such incapable people, except, perchance, that while on other occasions they are the most sluggish of all, they are nonetheless on all occasions but too well prepared for mischief. Besides, I have an opinion that the expectation of a Council, which is said to be at its height among you, will prove to have been unfounded. The diet[29] of the Empire will meet in February. No serious deliberation, however, will begin before March. I know by experience the German method of doing business. Of this I can assure you as certainly as if I had been actually present. Our friends will insist from the first that, excluding Antichrist, they may at length establish something of order among themselves. On the other hand, those who are enchained in willing bondage to their Romish idol will deny that this is lawful or allowable for them to do. The emperor, that he may in part give some sort of satisfaction to our side, will promise fair, that he is ready to do everything, and may, perhaps, make a show of doing a little, but as soon as possible after having made a beginning, upon some pretense or other, which is never wanting to men of that sort, he will break away altogether. This will certainly be the final decision: that it is not lawful to determine anything in the matter of religion except by authority of the pope. As for the calling of a synod,[30] when that shall have begun to be mooted, by and by our side will begin to remonstrate that it is disgraceful that the settlement of religion should be entrusted to the professed enemies of God. They will cite Antichrist as a criminal and defendant; certainly, they will never permit him to be the judge. But by what means do you think they can be induced to come to Trent?[31] If even there were to be no let or hindrance on our side, since there is nothing that would be more agreeable to the emperor than, having turned the attention of every one to the Turkish war,[32] to leave the state of the Church for a while in suspense—will he not then, in this matter which accords so perfectly with his own views, be only too well inclined to make concessions which will gratify the pope? Even were we to suppose, for instance, that a Council has been summoned, that already everything is in readiness and all prepared, do we reckon that the idol will be in any way at a loss for some artifice or other whereby he may interrupt and throw all into disorder? What will then become of religion, torn and rent asunder and laid waste? What will become of the wretched Church rushing forward apparently to destruction? What will become of the Christian name? What will become of the glory of God? Assuredly, we must ask of him that he alone would take complete charge of all things and uphold the Church. Our friends are drowsy, nor is there any hope of their more vigorous and cordial action, unless the Lord awakens them from some quarter or another. Howbeit, the ungodly give them occasion enough of beginning to think of taking some heed to themselves. The canons of Cologne, with the whole rabble of the clergy, have done their utmost to get their archbishop

---

29   The assembly representing the various states which made up the Holy Roman Empire.
30   A council of clergy.
31   The council of Trent, held by the pope to reform the church and respond to the Protestant challenge.
32   That between the Holy Roman Emperor and the Ottoman Turks.

degraded from his station.[33] They have called meetings of the States, that they might have their allowance to substitute another in his place. This has been refused. They made the same application to the emperor; his answer was that he would not be found wanting on the occasion, provided they themselves did their duty. He was unwilling to grant their request openly. However, one may easily prognosticate from these roundabout proceedings that he would not be at all unwilling that they should make some disturbance about it, and should they proceed to any greater length, war is certain, in which the whole of Germany throughout will be much weakened and shaken to the foundations; for this, also, the Lord will provide and see to. This to my mind is the only consolation: that death can never be a misfortune to a Christian man. Meanwhile, I will lament as I ought for the calamities of the Church, and make myself wretched when I think of the condition of the godly—only, however, not so far as to be in despair. Were we only well agreed among ourselves, I would be much less anxious; but in the midst of those hostile preparations on the other side, that certain persons should find leisure enough for senseless quarrelling with one another, looks rather portentous. On the other hand, too, someone or other, in an elegy, has attacked Osiander,[34] a person who is himself rather wanting in good sense. In desiring to clear himself, he has so besprinkled his book with rancor that for myself I was mightily ashamed of him; but nothing has given me more vexation than that he insults the Zwinglians[35] in every third line. It is even after such a sort as this that we seem to have hired ourselves, both hand and tongue, to the ungodly, that we may afford them sport and pastime by tearing one another to pieces. Who is there that would not lose heart entirely where so many stumbling blocks are thrown our way? I do most readily acknowledge that there is no one so iron-hearted who would not be utterly cast down, unless he looks continually to the

Lord. And, therefore, I read the meaning of all this to be that it appears to be the Lord's will to test by every possible means whether our dependence is placed on men; for my own part, it is so far from overwhelming me, that, on the contrary, no slender confirmation thence arises of my faith. For while I see the Church marvellously steered by the Lord in the midst of those mighty waves, so that it cannot be overwhelmed; while these very tempests are at their height, until everything would seem as if about to mingle in wild disorder, yet I see that the noise of the waves is stilled, and in a moment they are calm; wherefore, then, may I not thence conceive good hope for the future? Let us therefore hasten forward in the race of our calling, leaning upon this confidence: that the Church, which has God as the perpetual Guardian of her safety, will at length surmount these perils; but because everyone does not have the same strength of mind, the more confidentially I put these matters in your confidence, all the more on that account you will be careful as to the few to whom you may communicate them.

With regard to what you asked in your last letter, I felt some sort of hesitation whether I ought to undertake the matter, for the journey is long, rugged, and toilsome. The post on horseback does not reach Wittenberg[36] in less than 20 days. To send anyone, as it might happen, without choosing a fit person, would be dangerous. One can place no dependence on light-headed fellows and vagabonds, and few others are to be found. To a person unacquainted with the language, the road will prove very toilsome, and there is scarcity everywhere on account of the late dearth. I myself am altogether unsupplied as to money; besides, although the season is not inconvenient, I am unable to sustain the burdens which already press upon me without being entirely exhausted. For in this time of dearth, with which for the last two years we have had to struggle, I found the incurring of debt was unavoidable. I do not, however, speak of this for the

---

33  The archbishop of Cologne, one of the princes of the Holy Roman Empire, had attempted to introduce a Protestant-inspired Catholic reform in his territory. He would be deposed by the Holy Roman Emperor in 1546. The canons of Cologne were the clergy of the cathedral.

34  A German Lutheran theologian.

35  Followers of the Protestant reformer Ulrich Zwingli, who was based at Zurich.

36  Luther's city.

sake of complaining. God has dealt with me very kindly, so much so that I am quite content with what I have. But I mention it so that you may understand that it is not easy for me to find persons here from whom I can take up money by loan; they are indeed all of them merchants, and themselves almost starving. Add to this what I have already said, that the time is unseasonable for consulting Luther, because his anger has scarce settled down from the heat of contention. Since, however, you insist so earnestly, and press me with so many protestations that I do so, my first and chief desire was to comply with your wishes. I have accordingly requested and obtained from an honorable and a not unlearned young man, that he will take this trouble on my account. I have translated my two treatises word for word into Latin, which have been sent along with my letters, that so they might be able to form an opinion. Nor have I asked any other favor, except that they would express freely and without reserve whatever they may think upon the question, only adding that it would be in no way agreeable to me should they feel any delicacy in so far as concerned myself. The messenger will scarcely have returned before two months, for he must be 40 days upon the road; I assign four days for rest, the remainder of the time for consultation.

Farewell.

### 50.4
### TO MELANCTHON[37] (JUNE 28, 1545)

Would that the fellow feeling which enables me to console you, and to sympathize with your heaviness, might also impart the power in some degree, at least, to lighten your sorrow. If the matter stands as the Zurichers[38] say it does, then they have just occasion for their writing. Your Pericles[39] allows himself to be carried beyond all due bounds by his love of thunder, especially seeing that his own case is by no means the better of the two. We all of us do acknowledge that we

are much indebted to him. Neither shall I submit myself unwillingly, but be quite content that he may hold the chief sway, provided that he can manage to conduct himself with moderation. Howbeit, in the Church we must always be upon our guard, lest we pay too great a deference to men. For it is all over with her when a single individual, be he whosoever you please, has more authority than all the rest, especially where this very person does not scruple to test how far he may go. Where there exists so much division and separation as we now see, it is indeed no easy matter to still the troubled waters and bring about composure. But were we all of the mind we ought to be, some remedy might, perhaps, be discovered; most certainly we convey a mean example to posterity when we of our own accord prefer entirely to throw away our liberty rather than to irritate a single individual by the slightest offense. But, you will say, his disposition is vehement, and his impetuosity is ungovernable—as if that very vehemence did not break forth with all the greater violence when all alike show themselves indulgent to him, and allow him to have his way, unquestioned. If this specimen of overbearing tyranny has sprung forth already as the early blossom in the springtide of a reviving Church, what must we expect in a short time, when affairs have fallen into a far worse condition? Let us therefore bewail the calamity of the Church, and not devour our grief in silence, but venture boldly to groan for freedom. Consider, besides, whether the Lord may not have permitted you to be reduced to these straits in order that you may be brought to a yet fuller confession upon this very article. It is indeed most true, as I acknowledge it to be, that which you teach, and also that hitherto, by a kindly method of instruction, you have studiously endeavored to recall the minds of men from strife and contention. I applaud your prudence and moderation. While, however, you dread, as you would some hidden rock, to meddle with this question from the fear of giving offense, you are leaving in perplexity and sus-

---

37   Philip Melancthon, a German Protestant reformer. Close to Luther, he was active in trying to reconcile Lutherans and Calvinists in order to reunite Protestantism.

38   The clergy of the Swiss city of Zurich, who followed the radical Protestantism of Ulrich Zwingli, had issued a doctrine which Luther bitterly attacked, to which the Zurich ministers had replied in kind.

39   I.e., Luther, here called by the name of the leading politician of classical Athens.

pense very many persons who require from you a somewhat more certain sound on which they can rest; besides, as I remember I have sometimes said to you, it is not over-creditable to us that we refuse to sign, even with ink, that very doctrine which many saints have not hesitated to leave witnessed with their blood. Perhaps, therefore, it is now the will of God thus to open up the way for a full and satisfactory declaration of your own mind that those who look up to your authority may not be brought to a stand, and kept in a state of perpetual doubt and hesitation. These, as you are aware, amount to a very great number of persons. Nor do I mention this so much for the purpose of arousing you to freedom of action as for the sake of comforting you; for indeed, unless I could entertain the hope that out of this vexatious collision some benefit shall have arisen, I would be utterly worn out by far deeper distress. Howbeit, let us wait patiently for a peaceable conclusion, such as it shall please the Lord to vouchsafe. In the meantime, let us run the race set before us with deliberate courage. I return you very many thanks for your reply, and at the same time, for the extraordinary kindness which Claude assures me had been shown to him by you.[40] I can form a conjecture what you would have been to myself, from your having given so kind and courteous a reception to my friend. I do not cease, however, to offer my chief thanks to God, who has vouchsafed to us that agreement in opinion upon the whole of that question about which we had both been examined; for although there is a slight difference in certain particulars, we are, notwithstanding, very well agreed upon the general question itself.

### 50.5
TO MONSIEUR DE FALAIS (GENEVA, MAY 18, 1547)

My lord,
Since your convenience has not permitted your coming here as we had hoped, it is enough if God gra-

ciously grants you health where you are. For although I might desire to be near you, nevertheless I prefer what is best for you. Concerning the man of whom Maldonado spoke to you, besides the knowledge which I have had of him while he has been here, I have made inquiry about him with his old master, Gallars, who tells me that he found him very faithful and serviceable. It is true that he would not reckon him qualified to manage great affairs unless one should instruct and set him his lesson, but in the carrying out of whatsoever he shall be commanded to do there will be nothing wanting, nay, he will even be vigilant. And even as regards the former quality, I do not undervalue him. For a staid and modest man is far better than one who is overbold and venturesome. You will decide according to the turn of your affairs, in order that the lord of Albiac may send him, and thus you may not remain long unprovided. Moreover, I hope that God has rid you of the annoyances by which that interferer[41] has been so long teasing you. That done, you may be altogether at ease about your house.

We are still on the lookout for news about the general state of the Church. If God intends so sorely to afflict us as to let loose that tyrant upon us who seeks only to ruin everything,[42] we must be quite prepared to suffer. Considering that God, who has charge over us, rules in the midst of his enemies, it becomes us to have patience, consoling ourselves in the certain hope that in the end he will confound them. But yet I hope that he will provide against these great troubles, supporting our weakness, and that he will check the boldness of those who triumph before the time and against himself.

Sir, having humbly commended myself to your kind favor, and that of Madame, and having presented to both of you the remembrances of my wife, I pray to our good Lord to guide you continually, to watch over you and to enlarge you in all his mercies. I abstain from entering upon the proposal which the lord of Maldonado has brought me about settling a church in that

40 Claude de Senaraclens had visited various reformers in Germany, and returned with expressions of their good will to Calvin.
41 Valeran Poulain, a French Protestant reformer active in Strasbourg.
42 The Holy Roman Emperor Charles V, an opponent of Protestantism, had just defeated the Protestant German princes at the battle of Muhlberg.

quarter,[43] for I do not know what to say about it except that I would desire that all may be well done.

Your servant and humble brother,

John Calvin

### 50.6
### TO VIRET[44] (JULY 2, 1547)

We must now fight in earnest. The wife of the comedian Caesar was again summoned to the Consistory,[45] on account of her forwardness.[46] While there, although she received no provocation, even in the form of too harsh a word, she vomited forth more venom than on any previous occasion. First of all, she denied the right of our court to take cognizance of her, even supposing she had been guilty of a delinquency. In the next place, she complained that she was deeply branded with ignominy by being compelled to appear in a place to which the depraved and criminal could alone by right be summoned. When one of the assessors sought to restrain her intemperate behavior, she turned her fury upon him. Abel then intervened and expressed his surprise that she had at first professed that she was too modest, or too little given to speaking, to be able to answer at greater length, whereas she was match in abuse for as many as there might be. At this her fury boiled all over. "No, indeed," she says, "but you are a reviler, who unscrupulously slandered my father. Begone, coarse swineherd, you are a malicious liar!" She would have almost overwhelmed us by her thunder had she not been forcibly taken out. The Senate[47] desired that she should be more closely imprisoned. She escaped by means of that matron who is wont to take under her patronage all bad causes. One of her sons accompanied her in her flight. Accidentally meeting Abel not far from the city gate, she insulted him afresh,

and even more shamelessly than before. Abel said nothing, but conducted himself with the greatest moderation, just as he had done in the Consistory. Next day a paper is found in the pulpit, threatening us with death unless we remain silent. I send a copy of it to you. The Senate, startled by such audacity, orders a rigorous inquiry to be made into the conspiracy. The investigation is committed to a few. Because many suspected Gruet, he was immediately arrested.[48] It was, however, a different hand; but while they were turning over his papers, much was discovered that was not less capital. There was a humble petition which he had planned to present to the people in the Assemblies, in which he contended that no offense should be punished by the laws except what was injurious to the state, for such was the practice of the Venetians, who were the highest authority in the matter of government; and that in truth there was danger, while this city submitted to be ruled by the brain of one man of melancholy temperament, of a thousand citizens being destroyed in the event of any outbreak. Letters were also found, chiefly written to André Philippe, and to others. In some he named me; at other times, he had enveloped me in figures of speech so clumsily contrived, however, that one could lay one's finger on what he meant to conceal. There were, besides, two pages in Latin, in which the whole of Scripture is laughed at, Christ insulted, the immortality of the soul called a dream and a fable, and finally the whole of religion torn to pieces. I do not think he is the author of it, but as it is in his handwriting, he will be compelled to appear in his defense, although it may be that he himself has thrown into the form of a memorandum, according to the turn of his own genius, what he heard from others, for there are mutilated sentences, crammed with solecisms and barbarisms. I do not know whether Jacoba, whose sister is the wife of Des Gallars,[49] has been

---

43   A Protestant church which had been erected in France.

44   Swiss Protestant reformer.

45   In Calvin's Protestant Geneva, the Consistory was the body of elders charged with maintaining moral discipline and Protestant orthodoxy in the church and the city.

46   The Consistory records show that Calvin had brought the complaint.

47   I.e., the Consistory.

48   Jacques Gruet, who had been a member of the Catholic clergy, and had become a Protestant, was an opponent of the clergy of Geneva. Under torture, he admitted the crimes Calvin discusses in this letter, as well as that of inciting the duke of Savoy to attack Geneva, and was condemned to death, being executed on July 26, 1547.

49   Nicolas des Gallars, a Genevan pastor and supporter of Calvin.

apprehended. There is, indeed, a decree of the Senate [for that purpose]. What Vandel's sentence will be is still doubtful; but he is in considerable danger. Such was the state of things when I wrote. You know that our Syndics[50] have little enough judgment, otherwise the Senate is exceedingly well disposed to the cause.

The brethren have replied to me regarding Sonnier that they mean to make no change in their former resolution; for I relaxed, as I had abstained from writing, with a view to spare him. He eagerly made reference to the minister De Coppet, who also wished to change his place. I advise you to examine whether there is any truth in this.

The statements contained in Bucer's[51] letter regarding those two victories are quite certain, for a friend of mine who had ascertained the truth of the whole matter passed through this way. He also informed me that tidings of a third victory had been brought away within two hours before he left Strasbourg; but he did not venture to assert this for certain. He further mentioned to me that when the Landgrave had come to Leipzig on the strength of the promise made to him, he returned without accomplishing the matter, and in despair, and that he was collecting a new army. The name of Henry was erroneously given in Bucer's letter; for the Landgrave still keeps him in fetters, or at least closely imprisoned. But Bucer was speaking of Erich, who professes the same doctrine as ourselves, and yet hires himself to the tyrant in disturbing the Church. I wish that your Senate could be induced to take the initiative in the stipulated treaty; for Pharaoh[52] wishes to be asked, and thinks it unbecoming to his dignity to solicit the weaker parties. But let them look to these and other matters that are now in course of arrangement. I desire nothing to be done, unless what I judge to be fitting and useful to you.

Farewell, brother and most sincere friend, along with your wife and your whole family. May the Lord always direct you and be present with you. You will salute the brethren respectfully in my name. I and my wife salute you and yours in the Lord.

Yours,

John Calvin

## 50.7
### TO VIRET (GENEVA, JULY 24, 1547)

There is nothing new in our affairs. The Syndics protract the ease of Gruet against the will of the Senate, which does not, however, as would be proper, utter any protest against the delay. For you know that few of them are judicious. I exercise my severity in dislodging common vices, and principally the sources of corruption among the youth. I conceal all sense of the dangers which good men from several quarters allege to exist, lest I should appear over solicitous about myself. The Lord will produce the result in the way that may please himself. Farewell, brother, and most sincere friend, as also your wife and family. May the Lord Jesus continually direct you, and be present with you. You will convey best greetings to the brethren and to your wife in my name. My wife salutes you and your family.

Yours,

Calvin

## 50.8
### TO THE FAITHFUL OF FRANCE (JULY 24, 1547)

May the electing love of God our Father, and the grace of our Lord Jesus Christ, rest always upon you by the communion of the Holy Spirit.

Very dear lords and brethren, I do not doubt that you have daily much news, from here as well as from Germany, which might prove a stumbling block to those who are not overmuch confirmed in our Lord Jesus Christ. But I trust in God he has so strengthened you that you shall not be shaken, either thereby or by any still greater marvel which may yet arise. And truly, if we are indeed built upon that solid stone which has been ordained for the foundation of the Church, we may well sustain more violent storms and

---

50  Geneva's secular ruling authority, made up of the chief laymen of the city.

51  Martin Bucer, Protestant reformer in Strasbourg (France), who worked to reconcile Protestant sects with each other.

52  I.e., the king of France, at the time engaged in a political alliance of convenience with the Swiss.

tempests without foundering. It is even expedient for us that such things should happen, that the firmness and constancy of our faith may be tested.

As for the state of Germany, our Lord has so abased the worldly pride of our people, and given all power and authority to him from whom we can look for nothing but ill, as that it indeed appears that he means himself to maintain his spiritual kingdom wheresoever he had already set it up. It is very true that according to the carnal mind it is in danger; yet in commending to himself the care of his poor Church and the kingdom of his Son, let us hope that he will provide for all, beyond what we can think. The danger hitherto has been that human means might dazzle our eyes. Now, however, since there is nothing to prevent our looking to his hand, and recalling to mind how he has preserved his Church in time past, let us not doubt but he will glorify himself in such a way that we shall be amazed. Meanwhile, we must never grow weary of fighting under the ensign of the cross of our Lord Jesus Christ, for that is worth more than all the triumphs of the world.

As regards the rumors of our troubles which have flown abroad, they seem, the greater part of them, in the first place, to have been improvised; because, were you upon the spot, you would not see a tenth part of what is told at a distance. It is true that we have many hard-headed and stiff-necked rebels, who on all occasions seek only to raise themselves, and by riotous courses to dissipate and abolish all order in the Church, and these, indeed, young as well as old. And the state of our young people, especially, is very corrupt; so that, when we will not allow them every license, they go from bad to worse. Of late, they were sorely enraged under cover of a small matter. It was because they were not allowed to wear slashed breeches,[53] which has been prohibited in the town for these 12 years past. Not that we would make too much of this, but we see that, by the loop-holes of the breeches, they wish to bring in all manner of disorders. We have protested, however, in the meantime, that the slashing of their breeches was but a mere piece of foppery, which was not worth speaking

about, but that we had quite another end in view, which was to curb and to repress their follies. During this little conflict, the devil has interjected others, so that there has been great murmuring. And because they perceived in us more courage than they could have wished, and more determination to resist them, the venom which some of them had concealed within their hearts burst forth. But this is nothing but smoke; for their threats are nothing else but a splutter of the pride of Moab,[54] who is powerless to execute what he thus presumes to threaten.

Howsoever that may be, you need not be astonished. There have been greater commotions stirred against Moses and against the prophets, though they had to govern the people of God, and such exercises are needful for us. Only beseech our Lord that he would vouchsafe us grace not to flinch, but that we may prefer obedience to him over our life if need be, and that we may be more afraid of offending him than of stirring up all the fury of the wicked against ourselves, and that at length it may please him to allay all the tumults which might otherwise break the courage of the unsettled, for it is that which weighs me down more than all the rest. This grace our Lord has vouchsafed us: that we have a right good will to remedy the evil, and all our brethren are well agreed to go forward earnestly in that which is our duty so that there is the same constancy in all. Nothing is needful, except that this good Lord continues to conduct his own work.

I entreat you, my dear brethren, continue steadfast on your part also, and let no fear alarm you, even although the dangers were more apparent than you have seen them hitherto. May the reliance which God commands us to have in his grace and in his strength always be to you an impregnable fortress; and for the holding fast the assurance of his help, may you be careful to walk in his fear although when we have made it our whole study to serve him, we must always come back to this conclusion, of asking pardon for our shortcomings. And inasmuch as you know well from experience how frail we are, always be diligent to continue in the practice which you have established, of

---

53    I.e., breeches which were slashed so as to allow cloth of another color, sewn into area opened by the slash, to be seen.
54    A reference to Old Testament, Numbers 22-24; Isaiah 16.6; Jeremiah 48.29-30.

prayer and bearing of the holy word, to exercise you, and to sharpen and confirm you more and more. Let nothing turn you aside, as sometimes there are many colorable pretexts adduced to justify the remission of such duties. I am convinced that it would be much better that all those who desire to honor God should assemble together and that everyone should call the others thither as by the sound of a trumpet. But yet, it is much better to have what you have, though it be but a part, than nothing at all. And so watching well against falling away, seek rather to advance in the way of proficiency, and make use of what God gives you, edifying one another, and in general all poor and ignorant ones by your good life, so that, by the same means, the wicked may be put to confusion. In so doing, you will perceive the hand of God upon you, to whom I pray that he would increase in you the graces which he has put within you; that he would strengthen you in true consistency; that, in the midst of dogs and of wolves, he would preserve you, and in every way glorify himself in you, after having commended me affectionately to your kind prayers.

Your humble brother and entire friend,
Charles d'Espeville[55]

50.9

TO THE PROTECTOR SOMERSET[56]<br>(GENEVA, OCTOBER 22, 1548)

My lord,
Although God has endowed you with singular prudence, largeness of mind, and other virtues required in that station wherein he has set you, and for the affairs which he has put into your hand, nevertheless, inasmuch as you deem me to be a servant of his Son, whom you desire above all else to obey, I feel assured that for the love of him you will receive with courtesy that which I write in his name, as indeed I have no other end in view save only that, in following out yet more and more what you have begun, you may advance his honor until you have established his kingdom in as great perfection as is to be looked for in the world. And as you read, you will perceive likewise that, without advancing anything of my own, the whole is drawn from his own pure doctrine. Were I to look merely at the dignity and grandeur of your position, there would seem to be no access whatever for a man of my quality. But since you do not refuse to be taught about the Master whom I serve, but rather prize above all else the grace which he has bestowed in numbering you among his disciples, I think I have no need to make you any long excuse or preface, because I deem you well disposed to receive whatsoever proceeds from him.

We have all reason to be thankful to our God and Father: that he has been pleased to employ you in so excellent a work as that of setting up the purity and right order of his worship in England by your means, and establishing the doctrine of salvation, that it may there be faithfully proclaimed to all those who shall consent to hear it; that he has vouchsafed you such firmness and constancy to persevere hitherto, in spite of so many trials and difficulties; that he has helped you with his mighty arm, in blessing all your counsels and your labors, to make them prosper. These are grounds of thankfulness which stir up all true believers to magnify his name. Seeing however, that Satan never ceases to heave up new conflicts, and that it is a thing in itself so difficult that nothing can be more so, to cause the truth of God to have peaceable dominion among men, who by nature are most prone to falsehood; while, on the other hand, there are so many circumstances which prevent its having free course; and most of all, that the superstitions of Antichrist, having taken root for so long time, cannot be easily uprooted from men's hearts—you have much need, I think, to be confirmed by holy exhortations. I cannot doubt, indeed, that you have felt this from experience, and shall therefore deal all the more frankly with you, because, as I hope, my deliberate opinion will correspond with your own desire. Were my exhortations even uncalled for, you would bear with the zeal and earnestness which has led me to offer them. I believe, therefore, that the need of them which you feel will

---

55  A pseudonym of Calvin.
56  I.e., Edward Seymour, duke of Somerset, and protector, or regent, of England, who governed the country while the Protestant King Edward VI, son of the deceased Henry VIII, was a child.

make them all the more welcome. However this may be, my lord, may it please you to grant me audience in some particular reformations which I propose to lay here briefly before you, in the hope that when you shall have listened to them, you will at least find some savor of consolation therein, and feel the more encouraged to prosecute the holy and noble enterprise in which God has hitherto been pleased to employ you.

I have no doubt that the great troubles which have fallen out for some time past must have been very severe and annoying to you, and especially as many may have found in them occasion of offense, forasmuch as they were partly excited under cover of the change of religion. Wherefore you must necessarily have felt them very keenly, on account of the apprehensions they may have raised in your mind, as well as of the murmurs of the ignorant or disaffected, and also of the alarm of the well-disposed. Certainly, the mere rumor which I heard from afar caused me heartfelt anxiety, until I was informed that God had begun to apply a remedy thereto. However, since perhaps they are not yet entirely allayed, or seeing that the devil may have kindled them anew, it will be well that you call to mind what the sacred history relates of good King Hezekiah, namely, that after he had abolished the superstitions throughout Judaea and reformed the state of the church according to the law of God, he was even then so pressed by his enemies that it almost seemed as if he was a lost and ruined man ([Old Testament] 2 Chronicles 32). It is not without reason that the Holy Spirit pointedly declares that such an affliction happened to him immediately after having re-established the true religion in his realm, for it may well have seemed reasonable to himself, that having striven with all his might to set up the reign of God, he should have peace within his own kingdom. Thus, all faithful princes and governors of countries are forewarned by that example that, however earnest they may be in banishing idolatry and in promoting the true worship of God, their faith may yet be tried by diverse temptations. So God permits, and wills it to be thus, to manifest the constancy of his people, and to lead them to look above the world. Meanwhile, the devil also does his work, endeavoring to ruin sound doctrine by indirect means, working as it were underground, forasmuch as he could not openly attain his end. But according to the admonition of St. James, who tells us that in considering the patience of Job, we must look to the end of it ([New Testament] James 5.11), so ought we, my lord, to look to the end which was vouchsafed to this good king. We see there that God was a present help in all his perplexities, and that at length he came off victorious. Wherefore, seeing that his arm is not shortened, and that, in the present day, he has the defense of the truth and the salvation of his own as much at heart as ever, never doubt that he will come to your aid, and that not once only, but in all the trials he may send you.

If the majority of the world opposes the Gospel and even strives with rage and violence to hinder its progress, we ought not to think it strange. It proceeds from the ingratitude of men, which has always shown itself, and always will, in drawing back when God comes near, and even in kicking against him when he would put his yoke upon them. More than that, because by nature they are wholly given to hypocrisy, they cannot bear to be brought to the clear light of the word of God, which lays bare their baseness and shame, nor to be drawn forth out of their superstitions, which serve them as a hiding-hole and shady cover. It is nothing new, then, if we meet with contradiction when we attempt to lead men back to the pure worship of God. And we have, besides, the clear announcement of our Lord Jesus, who tells us that he has brought a sword along with his Gospel. But let this not daunt us, nor make us shrink and be fearful, for at last, when men shall have rebelled most stoutly, and vomited forth all their rage, they shall be put to confusion in a moment, and shall destroy themselves by the fury of their own onset. That is a true saying, in the second Psalm, that God shall only laugh at their commotion, that is to say, that seeming to connive, he will let them bluster, as if the affair did not at all concern him. But it always happens that at length they are driven back by his power, wherewith if we are armed, we have a sure and invincible fortification, whatever plots the devil may plan against us, and shall know by experience in the end that even as the Gospel is the message of peace and of reconciliation between God and us, it will also avail us to pacify men; and in this way we shall understand that it is not in vain that Isaiah has said that when Jesus Christ shall rule in the midst of us by his doctrine, the swords shall be turned into ploughshares and the spears into pruning-hooks ([Old Testament] Isaiah 2. 4).

Albeit, however, the wickedness and opposition of men may be the cause of the sedition and rebellion which rises up against the Gospel, let us look to ourselves, and acknowledge that God chastises our faults by those who would otherwise serve Satan only. It is an old complaint that the Gospel is the cause of all the ills and calamities that befall mankind. We see, in fact, from history that shortly after Christianity had been spread abroad everywhere there was not, so to speak, a corner of the earth which was not horribly afflicted. The uproar of war, like a universal fire, was kindled in all lands. Land-floods on the one hand, and famine and pestilence on the other, a chaotic confusion of order and civil polity to such a degree that it seemed as if the world was presently about to be overturned. In like manner we have seen in our times, since the Gospel has begun to be set up, much misery—to such an extent, indeed, that everyone complains we have come upon an unhappy period, and there are very few who do not *groan* under this burden. While, then, we feel the blow, we ought to look upward to the hand of him who strikes, and ought also to consider why the blow is sent. The reason why he makes us thus feel his rod is neither very obscure nor difficult to understand. We know that the Word, by which he would guide us to salvation, is an invaluable treasure; with what reverence do we receive it when he presents it to us? Seeing, then, that we make no great account of that which is so precious, God has good reason to avenge himself on our ingratitude. We hear also what Jesus Christ announces that the servant knowing the will of his Master, and not doing it, deserves double chastisement ([New Testament] Luke 12.47). Since, therefore, we are so remiss in obeying the will of our God, who has declared it to us more than a hundred times already, let us not think it strange if his anger rages more severely against us, seeing that we are all the more inexcusable. When we do not cultivate the good

seed, there is much reason that the thorns and thistles of Satan should spring up to trouble and annoy us. Since we do not render to our Creator the submission which is due to him, it is no wonder that men rise up against us.

From what I am given to understand, my lord, there are two kinds of rebels who have risen up against the king[57] and the estates of the kingdom. The one, a fantastic sort of person, who, under color of the Gospel, would put all into confusion. The others are persons who persist in the superstitions of the Roman Antichrist.[58] Both alike deserve to be repressed by the sword which is committed to you, since they attack not only the king, but strive with God, who has placed him upon a royal throne, and has committed to you the protection of his person as well as of his majesty. But the chief point is to endeavor, as much as possible, that those who have some savor of a liking for the doctrine of the Gospel, so as to hold fast, should receive it with such humility and godly fear as to renounce self in order to serve God; for they ought seriously to consider that God would awaken them all, so that in good earnest they may profit far more from his Word than they have ever yet done. These madmen, who would have the whole world turned back into a chaos of licentiousness, are hired by Satan to defame the Gospel, as if it bred nothing but revolt against princes, and all sorts of disorder in the world. Wherefore, all the faithful ought to be deeply grieved. The Papists,[59] in endeavoring to maintain the corruptions and abominations of their Roman idol, show themselves to be the open enemies of the grace of Jesus Christ, and of all his ordinances. That ought likewise to occasion great sickness at heart among all those who have a single drop of godly zeal. And therefore they ought every one of them earnestly to consider that these are the rods of God for their correction. And why? Just because they do not set a proper value on the doctrine of salvation, herein lies the chief remedy for the silencing of such calumnies: that those who make profession of the Gospel be indeed renewed after the image of

---

57  Edward VI.
58  I.e., the pope.
59  A derogatory term for Catholics.

God, so as to make manifest that our Christianity does not occasion any interruption of the humanities of social life, and to give good evidence, by their temperance and moderation, that being governed by the word of God, we are not unruly people subject to no restraint, and so by an upright holy life shut the mouths of all the evil speakers. For by this means God, being pacified, shall withdraw his hand, and instead of, as at this day, punishing the contempt with which they have treated his word, he will reward their obedience with all prosperity. It would be well if all the nobility and those who administer justice were to submit themselves, in uprightness and all humility, to this great King, Jesus Christ, paying him sincere homage, and with unfeigned faith, in body, soul, and spirit, so that he may correct and beat down the arrogance and rashness of those who would rise up against them. Thus ought earthly princes to rule and govern, serving Jesus Christ, and taking order that he may have his own sovereign authority over all, both small and great. Wherefore, my lord, as you hold dear and in regard the estate of your royal nephew, as indeed you show plainly that you do, I beseech you, in the name of God, to apply your chief care and watchfulness to this end, that the doctrine of God may be proclaimed with efficacy and power so as to produce its fruit, and never to grow weary, whatsoever may happen, in following out fully an open and complete reformation of the Church. The better to explain to you what I mean, I shall arrange the whole under three heads.

The first shall treat of the sound instruction of the people; the second shall regard the rooting out of abuses which have prevailed hitherto; the third, the careful repression and correction of vice, and to take strict heed that scandals and loose conversation may not grow into a fashion, so as to cause the name of God to be blasphemed.

As concerning the first article, I do not mean to pronounce what doctrine ought to have place. Rather do I offer thanks to God for his goodness, that after having enlightened you in the pure knowledge of himself, he has given you wisdom and discretion to take measures that his pure truth may be preached. Praise be to God, you have not to learn what is the true faith of Christians, and the doctrine which they ought to hold, seeing that by your means the true purity of the faith

has been restored. That is, that we hold God alone to be the sole Governor of our souls; that we hold his law to be the only rule and spiritual director for our consciences, not serving him according to the foolish inventions of men. Also, that according to his nature he would be worshipped in spirit and in purity of heart. On the other hand, acknowledging that there is nothing but complete wretchedness in ourselves, and that we are corrupt in all our feelings and affections, so that our souls are a true abyss of iniquity, utterly despairing of ourselves; and that, having exhausted every presumption of our own wisdom, worth, or power of well-doing, we must have recourse to the fountain of every blessing, which is in Christ Jesus, accepting that which he confers on us, that is to say, the merit of his death and passion, that by this means we may be reconciled to God; that being washed in his blood we may have no fear lest our spots prevent us from finding grace at the heavenly throne; that being assured that our sins are pardoned freely by virtue of his sacrifice, we may lean, indeed rest, upon that for assurance of our salvation; that we may be sanctified by his Spirit, and so consecrate ourselves to obedience to the righteousness of God; that being strengthened by his grace, we may overcome Satan, the world, and the flesh; finally, that being members of his body, we may never doubt that God reckons us among the number of his children, and that we may confidently call upon him as *our* Father; that we may be careful to recognize and bear in mind this purpose in whatsoever is said or done in the Church, namely, that being separated from the world, we should rise to heaven with our Head and Savior. Seeing then that God has given you grace to re-establish the knowledge of this doctrine, which had been so long buried out of sight by Antichrist, I forbear from entering further on the subject.

What I have thus suggested as to the manner of instruction is only that the people be so taught as to be touched to the quick, and that they may feel that what the Apostle says is true, that "the word of God is a two-edged sword, piercing even through the thoughts and affections to the very marrow of the bones" ([New Testament] Hebrews 4). I speak thus, my lord, because it appears to me that there is very little preaching of a lively kind in the kingdom, but that the greater part deliver it by way of reading from a written discourse. I see very well the necessity which constrains you to that; for in the first place you do not have, as I believe, such well tested and competent pastors as you desire. Wherefore, you need forthwith to supply this want. Secondly, there may very likely be among them many flighty persons who would go beyond all bounds, sowing their own silly fancies, as often happens on occasion of a change. But all these considerations ought not to hinder the ordinance of Jesus Christ from having free course in the preaching of the Gospel. Now, this preaching ought not to be lifeless but lively, to teach, to exhort, to reprove, as Saint Paul says in speaking thereof to Timothy ([New Testament] 2 Timothy 3). So indeed, that if an unbeliever enters, he may be so effectually stopped and convinced as to give glory to God, as Paul says in another passage ([New Testament] 1 Corinthians 14). You are also aware, my lord, how he speaks of the lively power and energy with which they ought to speak who would show themselves as good and faithful ministers of God, who must not make a parade of rhetoric, only to gain esteem for themselves, but that the Spirit of God ought to sound forth by their voice, so as to work with mighty energy. Whatever may the amount of danger to be feared, that ought not to hinder the Spirit of God from having liberty and free run in those to whom he has given grace for the edifying of the Church.

True it is, nevertheless, that it is both right and fitting to oppose the levity of some fantastic minds, who allow themselves in too great license, and also to shut the door against all eccentricities and new doctrines; but the method to be taken, which God has pointed out to us, for dealing with such occurrences is well fitted to dispose of them. In the first place, there ought to be an explicit summary of the doctrine which all ought to preach, which all prelates and curates[60] swear to follow, and no one should be received to any ecclesiastical responsibility who does not promise to preserve such agreement. Next, that they have a common formula of instruction for little children and for ignorant persons, serving to make them familiar with sound doctrine, so that they may be able to discern the difference between it and the falsehood and corruptions which may be brought forward in opposition to it. Believe me, my lord, the Church of God will never preserve itself without a catechism, for it is like the seed to keep the good grain from dying out, and causing it to multiply from age to age. And therefore, if you desire to build an edifice which shall be of long duration, and which shall not soon fall into decay, make provision for the children being instructed in a good catechism, which may show them briefly, and in language appropriate to their tender age, wherein true Christianity consists. This catechism will serve two purposes, to wit, as an introduction to the whole people, so that everyone may profit from what shall be preached, and also to enable them to discern when any presumptuous person puts forward strange doctrine. Indeed, I do not say that it may not be good, and even necessary, to tie down the pastors and curates to a certain written form for the sake of supplementing the ignorance and deficiencies of some, as well as the better to manifest the conformity and agreement between all the churches; thirdly, to take away all ground of pretense for bringing in any eccentricity or newfangled doctrine on the part of those who seek only to indulge an idle fancy; as I have already said, the catechism ought to serve as a check upon such people. There is, besides, the form and manner of administration of the sacraments, also the public prayers. But whatever, in the meantime, the arrangements are in regard to these matters, care must be taken not to quench the efficacy which ought to attend the preaching of the Gospel. And the utmost care should be taken that so far as possible you have good trumpets, which shall sound into the very depths of the heart. For there is some danger that you may see no great profit from all the reformation which you shall have brought about, however sound and godly it may have been, unless this powerful instrument of preaching is developed more and more. It is not said without a meaning, that Jesus Christ "shall smite the earth with the rod of his mouth, and with the breath of his lips he shall slay the wicked" ([Old Testament] Isaiah 11.4). The way by which he is pleased to subdue

---

60 I.e., higher church officials (such as bishops) and those who act as local or parish priests.

us is by destroying whatsoever is contrary to himself. And herein you may also perceive why the Gospel is called the Kingdom of God. Even so, although the edicts and statutes of princes are good help for advancing and upholding the state of Christianity, yet God is pleased to declare his sovereign power by this spiritual sword of his word when it is made known by the pastors.

Not to tire you, my lord, I shall now come to the second point which I propose to touch upon, that is, the abolition and complete uprooting of the abuses and corruptions which Satan had aforetime mixed up with the ordinances of God. We know well that under the pope there is a bastard sort of Christianity, and that God will disavow it at the last day, seeing that he now condemns it by his word. If we desire to rescue the world from such an abyss, there is no better method than to follow the example of St. Paul, who, wishing to correct what the Corinthians had improperly added to the Supper of our Lord, tells them "I have received from the Lord that which I have delivered to you" ([New Testament] 1 Corinthians 11). From this we are bound to take a general instruction to return to the strict and natural meaning of the commandment of God, if we would have a sound reformation and one tried by him. For whatsoever mixtures men have brought in of their own devising have been just so many pollutions which turn us aside from the sanctified use of what God has bestowed for our salvation. Therefore, to lop off such abuses by halves will by no means restore things to a state of purity, for then we shall always have a dressed-up Christianity. I say this because there are some who, under pretense of moderation, are in favor of sparing many abuses, without meddling with them at all, and to whom it appears enough to have rooted out the principal one. But on the contrary, we see how fertile is the seed of falsehood, and that only a single grain is needed to fill the world with them in three days' time, to such an extent are men inclined and addicted thereto. Our Lord teaches quite another method of procedure, for

when David speaks of the idols, he says, "Their names will I not take up into my lips" ([Old Testament] Psalms 16) to intimate in what degree of detestation we ought to hold them. Above all, if we consider how we have offended God in the days of our ignorance, we ought to feel doubly bound to flee from the inventions of Satan, which have led us into the commission of evil, as from baits which serve only to seduce souls. On the other hand, we see, even when we remonstrate with men about their faults and errors, though we warn them as earnestly as possible, they are nevertheless so hardened that we can produce no effect. If, therefore, we were to leave them any remnant of abuse, that would serve only to nourish their obstinacy the more, and become a veil to darken all the doctrine which we might set before them. I willingly acknowledge that we must observe moderation, and that overdoing things is neither discreet nor useful, indeed, that forms of worship need to be accommodated to the condition and tastes of the people. But the corruptions of Satan and of Antichrist must not be admitted under that pretext. Therefore it is that Holy Scripture, when praising those kings who had cast down the idols and their worshippers, not having swept them entirely away, notes it as a blemish that nevertheless they had not cast down the chapelries and places of foolish devotion. Wherefore, my lord, seeing that God has brought you so far, take order, I beseech you, that so without any exception he may approve you as a repairer of his temple, so that the times of the king your nephew may be compared to those of Josiah,[61] and that you put things in such condition that he may only need to maintain the good order which God shall have prepared for him by your means. I will mention to you an instance of such corruptions, as, if they were allowed to remain, would become a little leaven to sour in the end the whole lump. In your country, some prayer is made for the departed on occasion of communicating in the Lord's Supper. I am well aware that it is not done in belief of the purgatory of the pope.[62] I am also aware that

61  Old Testament, 2 Kings 22-23.
62  The Catholic church held that souls of the dead who had sinned enough not to be worthy of immediate entry into heaven, but who did not merit hell, were held for some time in purgatory, where they did penance for their sins. The prayers of the living could shorten one's time in purgatory.

ancient custom can be pleaded for making some mention of the departed, for the sake of uniting together all the members of the one body. But there is a peremptory ground of objection against it: that the Supper of Jesus Christ is an action so sacred that it ought not to be soiled by any human inventions whatsoever. And besides, in prayer to God, we must not take an unbounded license in our devotions, but observe the rule which St. Paul gives us, which is that we must be founded upon the word of God ([New Testament] Romans 10); therefore, such commemoration of the dead, as suggesting a commending of them to his grace, is contrary to the due form and manner of prayer—it is a hurtful addition to the Supper of our Lord. There are other things which possibly may be less open to reproof which, however, are not to be excused, such as the ceremony of chrism and unction.[63] The chrism has been invented out of a frivolous humor by those who, not content with the institution of Jesus Christ, desired to counterfeit the Holy Spirit by a new sign, as if water were not sufficient for the purpose. What they call extreme unction has been retained by the inconsiderate zeal of those who have wished to follow the apostles without being gifted as they were. When the apostles used oil in the case of the sick, it was for healing them miraculously. Now, when the gift of miracles has ceased, the representation ought no longer to be employed. Wherefore, it would be much better that these things should be pruned away, so that you might have nothing which is not conformed to the word of God, and serviceable for the edification of the Church. It is quite true we ought to bear with the weak but in order to strengthen them, and to lead them to greater perfection. That does not mean, however, that we are to humor blockheads who wish for this or that, without knowing why. I know the consideration which keeps back many is that they are afraid too great a change could not be carried through. It is admitted that when we have to do with neighbors with whom we desire to cherish friendly feeling, one is disposed to gratify them by giving way in many things. In worldly matters, that may be quite bearable, wherein it is allowable to yield one to another, and to

forego one's right for the sake of peace; but it is not altogether the same thing in regard to the spiritual governance of the Church, which ought to be according to the ordinance of the word of God. Herein, we are not at liberty to yield up anything to men, nor to turn aside on either hand in their favor. Indeed there is nothing that is more displeasing to God than when we would, in accordance with our own human wisdom, modify or curtail, advance or retreat, otherwise than he would have us. Wherefore, if we do not wish to displease him, we must shut our eyes to the opinion of men. As for the dangers which may arise, we ought to avoid them so far as we can, but never by going aside from the straight road. While we walk uprightly, we have his promise that he will help us. Therefore, what remains for us is to do our duty, humbly committing the result to himself. And here we may perceive wherefore the wise men of this world are often disappointed in their expectation, because God is not with them, when, in distrust of him and his aid, they seek out crooked paths and such as he condemns. Do we then wish to feel that we have the power of God upon our side? Let us simply follow what he tells us. Above all, we must cling to this maxim: that the reformation of his Church is the work of his hand. Wherefore, in such matters, men must leave themselves to be guided by him. What is more, whether in restoring or in preserving the Church, he thinks fit, for the most part, to proceed according to a method both marvellous and beyond human conception. And, therefore, it would be unseemly to confine that restoration, which must be divine, to the measure of our understanding, and to bring that which is heavenly into subjection to what is earthly and of this world's fashion. I do not thus exclude the prudence which is so much needed to take all appropriate and right means, not falling into extremes either on the one side or upon the other, to gain over the whole world to God, if that were possible. But the wisdom of the Spirit, not that of the flesh, must overrule all; and having inquired at the mouth of the Lord, we must ask him to guide and lead us, rather than follow the bent of our own understanding. When we take this method, it will be easy to cut off much

---

63 In the Catholic tradition, unction, or extreme unction, is the anointing of a dying person by a priest, which was a means of conferring divine grace. Chrism is the holy oil used in such anointing.

occasion of temptation, which might otherwise stop our progress midway.

Wherefore, my lord, as you have begun to bring Christianity back to the place which belongs to it throughout the realm of England, not at all in self-confidence, but upheld by the hand of God, as hitherto you have had sensible experience of that powerful arm, you must not doubt that it shall continue with you to the end. If God upholds the kingdoms and the principalities of the infidels who are his enemies, far more certainly will he have in safeguard those who range themselves on his side and seek him as their superior.

I come now to the last point, which concerns the chastisement of vice and the repression of scandals. I have no doubt that there are both good and laudable laws and statutes of the kingdom to keep the people within the bounds of decency. But the great and boundless licentiousness which I see everywhere throughout the world constrains me to beseech you that you would earnestly turn your attention to keeping men within the restraint of sound and wholesome discipline. That, above all, you would hold yourself charged, for the honor of God, to punish those crimes of which men have been in the habit of making no very great account. I speak of this because sometimes larcenies, assault, and extortions are more severely punished because thereby men are wronged, whereas they will tolerate whoredom and adultery, drunkenness, and blaspheming of the name of God, as if these were things quite allowable, or at least of very small importance. Let us hear, however, what God thinks of them. He proclaims aloud how precious his name is to him. Meanwhile, it is as if torn in pieces and trampled under foot. It can never be that he will allow such shameful reproach to remain unpunished. More than this, Scripture clearly points out to us that by reason of blasphemies a whole country is defiled. As concerning adultery, we who call ourselves Christians ought to take great shame on ourselves that even the heathens have exercised greater rigor in their punishment of such than we do, seeing even that some among us only laugh at them. When holy matrimony, which ought to be a lively image of the sacred union which we have with the Son of God, is polluted, and the covenant, which ought to stand more firm and indis-

soluble than any in this world, is disloyally rent asunder, if we do not lay to heart that sin against God, it is a token that our zeal for God is very low indeed. As for whoredom, it ought to be quite enough for us that St. Paul compares it to sacrilege, inasmuch as by its means the temples of God, which our bodies are, are profaned. Be it remembered also that whoremongers and drunkards are banished from the kingdom of God, on such terms that we are forbidden to converse with them, from which it clearly follows that they ought not to be endured in the Church. We see herein the cause why so many rods of judgment are this very day lifted up over the earth. For the more easily men pardon themselves in such enormities, the more certainly will God take vengeance on them. Wherefore, to prevent his wrath, I entreat you, my lord, to hold a tight rein, and to take order that those who hear the doctrine of the Gospel approve their Christianity by a life of holiness. For as doctrine is the soul of the Church for quickening, so discipline and the correction of vices are like the nerves to sustain the body in a state of health and vigor. The duty of bishops and curates is to keep watch over that, to the end that the Supper of our Lord may not be polluted by people of scandalous lives. But in the authority where God has set you, the chief responsibility returns upon you, who have a special charge given you to set the others in motion, on purpose that everyone discharges his duty, and diligently looks to it, so that the order which shall have been established may be duly observed.

Now, my lord, in accordance with the protestation which I made above, I shall make no further excuse, neither of the tiresomeness of my letter, nor on account of my having thus freely laid open to you what I had so much at heart. For I feel assured that my affection is well known to you, while in your wisdom, and as you are well versed in the Holy Scriptures, you perceive from what fountain I have drawn all that is herein contained. Wherefore, I do not fear to have been troublesome or importunate to you, in making manifest, according as I could, the hearty desire I have that the name of God may always be more and more glorified by you, which is my daily supplication, beseeching him that he would please to increase his grace in you, to confirm you by his Spirit in a true, unconquerable constancy, upholding you against all enemies, having yourself with your whole household under his holy protection, enabling you successfully to administer the charge which is committed to you so that the king may have whereof to praise this gracious God for having had such a governor in his childhood, both for his person and for his kingdom.

Whereupon I shall make an end, my lord, very humbly commending me to your kind favor.

### 50.10
### TO HENRY BULLINGER[64] (MAY 7, 1549)

As time does not permit me to reply to your letter now, I am merely desirous of telling you that I have scarcely received anything more pleasant from you, as it served to alleviate a very trying domestic grief which, occasioned by the death of my wife a little before, was causing me very much sorrow. For I am very glad that hardly anything, or at least very little, hinders us from agreeing now even in words. And, certainly if you think you can so arrange matters, I make no objection against endeavors being made to come here that you may the better become acquainted with all the sentiments of my mind. Nor shall it ever be owing to me that we do not unite in a solid peace, as we all unanimously profess the same Christ. But I have, at present, another reason for writing you.

You partly indicate what has kept you back from joining in the French alliance.[65] I confess the godly have just cause of alarm in the example of Jehoshaphat,[66] who bound himself in an unfortunate alliance with a wicked king, to his own ruin and that of his kingdom. Yet I do not so understand it that he was punished because he made a league with the king of Israel, but rather because he espoused a bad and impious cause, in order to gratify that king's desire. Ambition was inciting him to an unprovoked attack upon the Syrians; Jehoshaphat complied with his wishes and rashly took up arms. Add to this that they went forth to battle, the Lord through Micaiah forbidding them. This example does not, therefore, so weigh with me that I should pronounce all alliance whatever with the wicked to be unlawful. For I reflect that Abraham was not hindered by any religious scruples from making a covenant with Abimelech.[67] Isaac, David,[68] and others did the same, and received neither reproof nor punishment. I can, however, so far conclude that alliances of this nature are not to be sought after, seeing they must always be attended with very great danger. But if we be at all incited—I should rather say urged—to it by a just motive, I see no reason why we should be altogether averse to it.

Moreover, as regards the alliance in question, I cannot hold that it should be so avoided for this cause, unless the present aspect of the times should compel me to adopt an opposite conclusion. You have to do with a professed enemy of Christ, and one who is daily venting his rage against our brethren. He is too little deserving of trust that could wish that both we and Christ would be annihilated. It is absurd that we should enter into friendly alliance with one who is at war with all the servants of Christ without distinction that we should seize, as that of an ally, a hand polluted with innocent blood. And, certainly I should be unwilling to come to any conclusion on the matter, unless it were the express and distinct wish of the pious brethren. For his ferocity is indeed extraordinary. Besides, I am suspicious of the war with England. For I do not think it right to furnish any aid against a kingdom in which Christ is worshipped, and the very injustice of the cause, also, is another obstacle.

But, again, when I consider how our cause has been weakened, how great are the calamities which still impend, threatening almost the ruin of the Church, I fear much that if we neglect those aids which it is not unlawful to employ, we may fall into a state rather of excessive carelessness than of devout trustfulness. Nor, in truth, am I ignorant that God is

---

64 A Swiss Protestant and follower of Zwingli, who in this year came to an agreement with Calvin on the communion.
65 At this time the Catholic king of France was negotiating for an alliance with the Swiss. At Zurich, Bullinger opposed such an alliance.
66 Old Testament, 1 Kings 22.
67 Old Testament, Genesis 20-21.
68 Other Hebrew figures of the Old Testament.

especially present with us, and powerfully succors us when we are destitute of all human aid. I know, also, that there is nothing harder, when he reveals himself through some Egyptian shade,[69] than to keep the eye from turning aside, for if they are not fixed on the one God, they rove wickedly and perniciously. We must, therefore, endeavor zealously to counteract these dangers. Meanwhile, however, we should be on our guard, lest if in this, our critical condition, we reject what, without offending God, could have aided us, we may afterwards feel, to our loss, that we were too careless. My first fear is that our Pharaoh, shut out from all hope of contracting friendship with you, may betake himself to Antiochus.[70] However much they may have weighty grounds of disagreement, this latter is a wonderful master at contriving pretexts, and those who at present hold sway at our court would desire nothing more than to incline the mind of a youth, both inexperienced and not sufficiently sagacious, to accept peace on any terms whatever. Certainly, if he has not already concluded it, he will do so in a short time. Nor will there be wanting those who will urge him on. And I would there were none among us who would hold themselves and us as slaves to Antiochus, should an opportunity occur for doing so. He will, in truth, attempt everything, the other not only approving of it, but also, in the meantime, assisting in it because he will suppose that in this way he is avenging his repulse. Meanwhile, cruelty will be kindled everywhere through the kingdom itself, for he will, as women are wont, direct his own rage at another—a consideration, certainly, not to be accounted last by us of this place. If I wished to regard my own life or private concerns, I should immediately betake myself elsewhere. But when I consider how very important this corner is for the propagation of the kingdom of Christ, I have good reason to be anxious that it should be carefully watched over; and, in this respect, it is for your advantage, and quiet partly depends upon it. What man, imbued with wicked schemes, when he has

been estranged from you, will not be moved by despair? But you think that we are wanting in men of discontented and revolutionary character, or in those suffering from want, who have, for a long period, extended their hands to him. However, as often as I reflect particularly upon our wretched brethren who lie crushed under that fearful tyranny, my mind becomes soft and more disposed to this [alliance], as it the more unquestionably appears beneficial for the alleviation of their sufferings. Why is the rage of the tyrant to be removed when he has seen that he is despised and scorned? Is it that thereby the wicked are to have the greater license for tormenting the innocent? Thus, if any alliance does intervene, not only will Pharaoh himself be, for the present, somewhat softened, and the executioners rendered less daring, but it will, indeed, be possible also to extinguish the flames.

I beseech and solemnly implore you then, my dear Bullinger, to ponder in time all these considerations; and if you come to any agreement, strive earnestly to have remembered your brethren whose condition is so wretched and awful. For although I know you have their welfare sufficiently at heart, and am certain that when the matter is raised, you will, of your own accord, be solicitous about it, yet I did not wish to neglect my duty. Indeed, such is his fierceness that no fixed law can be laid down for you. I hope it is possible to show, however, that some sort of moderation may be exhibited.

Farewell, excellent man, and much esteemed brother in the Lord. Salute especially Theodore, Pellican, Gualter, Vuerduler, and the rest of the fellow ministers. Present my respects to your colleagues, and to Des Gallars among the rest. I pray the Lord Jesus that he may continue to guide and sustain you by his Spirit; may he bless you and your labors. I have to thank you greatly for the volume of discourses which Haller sent in your name.

Yours,

John Calvin

---

69  A reference to the Egyptians, who in the Old Testament kept the Hebrews enslaved.

70  I.e., the Holy Roman Emperor, Charles V. In the Old Testament, Antiochus is a Hellenistic king who persecuted Jews for refusing to worship gods other than their own.

## 50.11
### TO MELANCTHON (NOVEMBER 28, 1552)

Nothing could have come to me more seasonably at this time than your letter, which I received two months after its dispatch. For, in addition to the very great troubles with which I am so sorely consumed, there is almost no day on which some new pain or anxiety does not occur. I should, therefore, be in a short time entirely overcome by the load of evils under which I am oppressed, if the Lord did not by his own means alleviate their severity; among which it was no slight consolation to me to know that you are enjoying tolerable health, such at least as your years and the delicate state of your body admit of, and to be informed, by your own letter, that your affection for me had undergone no change. It was reported to me that you had been so displeased by a rather free admonition of mine which, however, ought to have affected you far otherwise—that you tore the letter to pieces in the presence of certain witnesses. But even if the messenger was not sufficiently trustworthy, still, after a long period of time, his fidelity was established by various proofs, and I was compelled to suspect something. Wherefore I have learned the more gladly that up to this time our friendship remains safe, which assuredly, as it grew out of a heartfelt love of piety, ought to remain sacred and inviolable forever. But it greatly concerns us to cherish faithfully and constantly to the end the friendship which God has sanctified by the authority of his own name, seeing that herein is involved either great advantage or great loss even to the whole Church. For you see how the eyes of many are turned upon us, so that the wicked take occasion from our dissensions to speak evil, and the weak are only perplexed by our unintelligible disputations. Nor, in truth, is it of little importance to prevent the suspicion of any difference having arisen between us from being handed down in any way to posterity, for it is worse than absurd that parties should be found disagreeing on the very principles after we have been compelled to make our departure from the world. I know and confess, moreover, that we occupy widely different positions; still, because I am not ignorant of the place in his theater to which God has elevated me, there is no reason for my concealing that our friendship could not be interrupted without great injury to the Church. And that we may act independent of the conduct of others, reflect, from your own feeling of the thing, how painful it would be for me to be estranged from that man whom I both love and esteem above all others, and whom God has not only nobly adorned with remarkable gifts in order to make him distinguished in the eyes of the whole Church, but has also employed as his chief minister for conducting matters of the highest importance. And surely it is indicative of a marvelous and monstrous insensibility that we so readily set at nothing that sacred unanimity by which we ought to be bringing back into the world the angels of heaven. Meanwhile, Satan is busy scattering here and there the seeds of discord, and our folly is made to supply much material. At length he has discovered fans of his own for fanning into a flame the fires of discord. I shall refer to what happened to us in this Church, causing extreme pain to all the godly; and now a whole year has elapsed since we were engaged in these conflicts. Certain worthless wretches, after stirring up strife amongst us, in reference to the free election of God, and the sad bondage of the human will, and after creating a public disturbance, had nothing more plausible to urge in defense of their grievous opposition than the authority of your name. And after they had found out how easy it was for us to refute whatever arguments they adduced, they tried to crush us, forsooth, by this artifice—by asking if we were willing openly to disagree with you. And yet, such was the moderation observed by us that least of all did they extort what they were adroitly seeking to obtain. Therefore, all my colleagues and myself openly professed to hold the same opinion on that doctrine which you hold. Not a word escaped us in the whole discussion either less honorable towards yourself than was seemly, or calculated to diminish confidence in you. Meanwhile, nevertheless, such indefinite and reserved expression of opinion cannot but pain me exceedingly, and it cannot but pain me that opportunity is being left to the evil-disposed for harassing the Church after our death as often as they please, while the conflicting parties will array against each other the opinions of those who ought to have spoken one and the same thing as with one mouth. It is neither surprising, nor a thing greatly to be lamented, that Osiander has withdrawn himself from us; yet he withdrew only after a violent attack. For you were long ago aware that he belonged to that race of wild animals which are never tamed; and I always ranked him amongst the number of those who were a disgrace to us. And assuredly, the very first day that I saw him, I abhorred the wicked disposition and abominable manners of the man. As often as he felt inclined to praise the agreeable and excellent wine, he had these words in his mouth, "I am that I am"[71] and also, "This is the Son of the living God,"[72] which he manifestly produced as mockeries of the Deity. Wherefore, I have the more frequently wondered that such a despicable person should at all be encouraged by your indulgence. In truth, I was particularly astonished on reading a passage in a certain preface of yours, where, after the proof of his folly at Worms, you commended him rather more than enough. But let him retire; it is an advantage to us to have gotten rid of him. I would rather that certain others were retained. Nevertheless—to pass by these also—the opposition, which is too plainly manifest in our modes of teaching, pains me not a little. I for my part am well aware that if weight is due the authority of men, it would be far more just that I should subscribe to your opinions than you to mine. But that is not the question, nor is it even a thing to be desired by the pious ministers of Christ. This, in all truth, we ought both to seek, namely, to come to an agreement on the pure truth of God. But, to speak candidly, religious scruples prevent me from agreeing with you on this point of doctrine, for you appear to discuss the freedom of the will in too philosophical a manner; and in treating of the doctrine of election,[73] you seem to have no other purpose save that you may suit yourself to the common feeling of mankind. And it cannot be attributed to hallucination that you, a man acute and wise, and deeply versed in Scripture, confound the election of God with his promises, which are universal. For nothing is more certain than that the Gospel is addressed to all promiscuously, but that the Spirit of faith is bestowed on the elect alone, by peculiar privilege. The promises are universal. How does it happen, therefore, that their efficacy is not equally felt by all? For this reason: because God does not reveal his arm to all. Indeed, among men but moderately skilled in Scripture, this subject does not need to be discussed, seeing that the promises of the Gospel make offer of the grace of Christ equally to all, and God, by the external call, invites all who are willing to accept salvation. Faith, also, is a special gift. I think I have clearly expounded this whole question, involved and intricate though it is, in a book only very recently published. Indeed, the matter is so obvious that no one of sound judgment can feel persuaded otherwise than that you are giving out what is quite different from your real inclination. It increases my anxiety, and at the same time my grief, to see you in this matter to be almost unlike yourself, for I heard, when the whole formula of the agreement of our Church with that of Zurich was laid before you, you instantly seized a pen and erased that sentence which cautiously and prudently makes a distinction between the elect and the reprobate. Which procedure, taking into consideration the mildness of your disposition, not to mention other characteristics, greatly shocked me. Accordingly, I do not ask you to endure the reading of my book, or even a part of it, because I think it would be useless to do so. Would that we might have an opportunity of talking over these matters face to face! I am not ignorant of your candor, of your transparent openness and moderation; as for your piety, it is manifest to the angels and to the whole world. Therefore, this whole question would be easily, as I hope, arranged between us; wherefore, if an opportunity should present itself, I would desire nothing more than to pay you a visit. But if it shall indeed turn out as you apprehend, it will be no slight comfort to me in sad and grievous circumstances to see you and embrace you before I take my departure from this world. Here we enjoy least of all that repose which you fancy we enjoy. There is much trouble, annoyance, and even disorder among us. The enemy who is continually imperilling our lives by new dangers is in full view. We are at a distance of three days' journey from

---

71  Words spoken by God in the Old Testament, Exodus 3.14.

72  New Testament, John 6.69.

73  I.e., the choice of God of who will enter heaven.

Burgundy. The French forces are but an hour's march from our gates. But because nothing is more blessed than to fight under the banner of Christ, there is no reason why these obstacles should prevent you from paying me a visit. Meanwhile, you will greatly oblige me by informing me of your own and the Churches' condition.

Farewell, most distinguished sir and heartily esteemed brother. May the Lord protect you by his power, guide you by his Spirit, and bless your pious labors. My colleague, and many pious and judicious men, reverently salute you.

John Calvin

# 51

# ARTICLES OF THE CATHOLIC LEAGUE

The sixteenth century was marked by on-and-off civil war between French Calvinists, known as Huguenots, and France's Catholic majority. In 1576 a peace was put together, prompting the formation of the Catholic League under the leadership of Henri de Lorraine, the duke of Guise (1550-1588), the head of one of the three leading noble families in France.

---

In the name of the Holy Trinity, Father, Son, and Holy Ghost, our only true God, to whom be glory and honor.

1   The association of Catholic princes, lords, and gentlemen is intended to be and shall be formed for the purpose of establishing the law of God in its entirety, to restore and maintain the holy service of the same according to the form and manner of the Holy Catholic Apostolic Roman church, abjuring and renouncing all errors to the contrary.

2   To maintain King Henry, the third of this name,[1] by the grace of God, and his successors, most Christian kings,[2] in the state, splendor, authority, duty, service and obedience which are due him from his subjects, as is contained in the articles which shall be presented to him at the meeting of the Estates,[3] which he swears and promises to protect at his consecration and coronation, solemnly asserting that he will do nothing prejudicial to that which shall be ordained by the said Estates.

3   To restore to the provinces of this kingdom and the Estates of the same the ancient rights, prerogatives, franchises and liberties, such as they were in the time of Clovis, the first Christian king,[4] and still better and more profitable ones, if such are to be found, under the protection above named.

4   In case there be any hindrance, opposition or rebellion against that which has been stated above, let it come from whatsoever source it may, the said associates shall be bound and obliged to make use of all their possessions and means and their very selves, even to death, in order to punish, chastise and fall upon those who have sought to constrain and hinder them, and to see to it that all the provisions above related shall be put into execution in reality and in fact.

5   In case any of the associates, their subjects, friends and allies should be molested, oppressed and made subject to investigation in the cases above mentioned by any person whatsoever, the said associates shall be bound to make use of their persons, goods, and means for the purpose of obtaining revenge upon those who have been guilty of the said oppressions and annoyances, whether by way of judicial process or by force

---

1   1574-1589.
2   A traditional title of the kings of France.
3   I.e., the Estates-General, the most important of the representative assemblies in France.
4   King of the Franks (481-511). He converted to Christianity in 496.

of arms, making no exception of any person whatsoever.

6 If it should come to pass that any of the associates, after having sworn an oath to the said association, should wish to retire or withdraw from the same under any pretext whatsoever (which may God forbid), such persons, falling away from their agreements, shall be injured in person and possessions, in all ways which may be devised, as enemies of God, rebels, violators of the public peace, without the said associates being disturbed or subject to investigation, either in public or in private.

7 The said associates shall swear absolute and ready obedience and service to the head who shall be selected, to follow him and give counsel and comfort, as much for the support and preservation of the said association as for the destruction of those who set themselves against it, without respect to persons, and defaulting and dilatory members shall be punished by authority of the head and according to regulations laid down by him, to which the said associates shall submit themselves.

8 Notice shall be given to all Catholics in incorporated towns and villages and they shall be summoned secretly by the local governors to enter into the said association and to furnish their due proportion of arms and men for the purpose of the same, each according to his power and ability.

9 That those who are unwilling to enter into the said association shall be considered enemies of the same and be subject to all sorts of injuries and annoyances.

10 It is forbidden to the said associates to enter into disputes or feuds among themselves without permission of the head, by whose decision offenders shall be punished, as much for the purpose of obtaining honorable satisfaction as in other cases.

11 If for the protection or the greater security of the said associates any treaty should be made with the provinces of this realm, it shall be in the form above indicated and under the same conditions whether the association be extended to the said towns or demanded by them, unless the heads shall hold another opinion.

12 I swear by God the Creator, upon the Gospels, and upon penalty of anathema and eternal damnation, that I have entered into this holy Catholic association according to the form of the agreement which has now been read to me, loyally and sincerely, be it to command, to obey, or to serve, and I promise upon my life and my honor not to spare myself up to the last drop of my blood, and that I will not oppose the association or withdraw from it on account of any command, pretext, or excuse, whatever may be the occasion.

# 52

# MICHEL DE MONTAIGNE, *ESSAYS*

Michel de Montaigne (1533-1592), a French nobleman and officer of the royal courts, retired to private life in 1571. During that retirement he composed his *Essays* (which literally means "attempts"), thus inventing that literary form. Two of these essays follow below.

## 52.1

### *ON CANNIBALS*

When King Pyrrhus[1] invaded Italy, having viewed and considered the order of the army the Romans sent out to meet him, he said, "I do not know what kind of barbarians" (for so the Greeks called all other nations) "these may be, but the disposition of this army, that I see, has nothing of barbarism in it." The Greeks said as much of the army which Flaminius[2] brought into their country, and Philip,[3] beholding from a height the order and distribution of the Roman camp formed in his kingdom by Publius Sulpicius Galba, spoke to the same effect. By these incidents it appears how cautious men ought to be of taking things upon trust from vulgar opinion, and that we are to judge by the eye of reason, and not from common report.

I long had a man in my house who lived 10 or 12 years· in the New World, discovered in these latter days, and in that part of it where Villegaignon landed,[4] which he called "Antarctic France." This discovery of so vast a country seems to me to be worth very great consideration. I cannot be sure whether in the future another might not be found, since so many wiser men than we have been deceived in this. I am afraid our eyes are bigger than our bellies, and that we have more curiosity than capacity, for we grasp at all, but catch nothing but wind.

Plato brings in Solon,[5] telling a story that he had heard from the priests of Sais in Egypt, that of old, and before the Deluge, there was a great island called Atlantis, situated exactly at the mouth of the Straits of Gibraltar, which contained more countries than both Africa and Asia put together. The kings of that country, who not only possessed that isle, but extended their dominion so far into the continent that they held Africa as far as Egypt, and extending in Europe to Tuscany, attempted to encroach even upon Asia, and to subjugate all the nations that border upon the Mediterranean Sea, as far as the Black Sea. To that effect they overran all Spain, the Gauls, and Italy, so far as to penetrate into Greece, where the Athenians stopped them. But sometime after, both the Athenians, and they and their island, were swallowed by the Flood.

---

1   King (*c*. 306-272 BC) of the Greek kingdom of Epirus.
2   A Roman commander.
3   A Hellenistic king of Macedon.
4   I.e., Brazil, in 1557.
5   Plato, the Greek philosopher (4th century BC), discussing Solon, an earlier statesman of Athens, in his dialogue, *Critias*.

It is very likely that this extreme irruption and inundation of water made wonderful changes and alterations in the habitations of the earth, as it is said that the sea then divided Sicily from Italy

> Haec loca, vi quondam, et vasta convulsa ruina,
> Dissiluisse ferunt, quum protenus utraque tellus
> Una foret[6]

and Cyprus from Syria, the isle of Euboea from the land of Boeotia, and elsewhere united lands that were separate before, by filling up the channel between them with sand and mud:

> Sterilisque diu palus, aptaque remis,
> Vicinas urbes alit, et grave sentit aratrum.[7]

But there is no great likelihood that this isle was this New World so lately discovered, for that almost touched upon Spain, and it would have been an unbelievable effect of an inundation, to have tumbled back so prodigious a mass, above 1,200 leagues. Besides, our modern navigators have already almost discovered it to be no island, but *terra firma*,[8]—a continent—with the East Indies on the one side, and the lands under the two poles on the other side, or, if it is separate from them, it is by so narrow a strait and channel, that it none the more deserves the name of an island for that.

It should seem that in this great body there are two sorts of motions, the one natural, and the other feverish, as there are in ours. When I consider the impression that our river of Dordogne has made in my time on the right bank of its descent, and that in 20 years it has gained so much, and undermined the foundations of so many houses, I perceive it to be an extraordinary agitation. For had it always followed this course, or were hereafter to do it, the aspect of the world would be totally changed. But rivers alter their course, some-

times beating against the one side, and sometimes the other, and sometimes quietly keeping the channel. I do not speak of sudden inundations, the causes of which everybody understands. In Médoc, by the seashore, my brother, the Lord of Arsac, sees an estate he had there buried under the sands which the sea vomits before it, where the tops of some houses are yet to be seen, and where his rents and domains are converted into pitiful barren pasturage. The inhabitants of this place affirm that of late years the sea has driven so vehemently upon them that they have lost above four leagues of land. These sands are her harbingers, and we now see great heaps of moving sand that march half a league before her and occupy the land.

The other testimony from antiquity, to which some would apply this discovery of the New World, is in Aristotle,[9] at least if that little book of unheard-of miracles is his. He there tells us that certain Carthaginians, having crossed the Atlantic Sea beyond the Straits of Gibraltar, and sailed a very long time, discovered at last a great and fruitful island, all covered over with wood, and watered with several broad and deep rivers, far remote from all *terra firma*, and that they, and others after them, lured by the goodness and fertility of the soil, went there with their wives and children, and began to plant a colony. But the senate of Carthage, perceiving their people to diminish little by little, issued an express prohibition, that none, upon pain of death, should transport themselves there, and also drove out these new inhabitants, fearing, it is said, lest in process of time the emigrants should so multiply as to supplant Carthage and ruin their state. But this relation of Aristotle no more agrees with our newfound lands than the other.

This man that I had was a plain, ignorant fellow, and therefore the more likely to tell truth, for your better bred sort of men are much more curious in their observation, it is true, and discover a great deal more, but then they elaborate upon it, and in order to give

---

6  Latin: "These lands, they say, once with violence and vast desolation convulsed, burst asunder, which erstwhile were one" (Vergil, Roman poet of the first century BC).

7  Latin: "That once was a sterile marsh, and bore vessels on its bosom, now feeds neighboring cities, and admits the plough" (Horace, Roman poet of the first century BC).

8  I.e., "solid land," on a continent.

9  Greek philosopher (fourth century BC).

the greater weight to what they say and gain your belief they cannot forbear to alter the story a little. They never represent things to you simply as they are, but rather as they appeared to them, or as they would have them appear to you, and to gain the reputation of men of judgment, and the better to induce your belief, are willing to help out the business with something more than is really true, something of their own invention. Now in this case, we should either have a man of irreproachable veracity, or one so simple that he does not have the wherewithal to contrive, and to give a color of truth to false relations, and who can have no ends in forging an untruth. Such a person was my man and, besides, he has at diverse times brought to me several seamen and merchants who took the same voyage at the same time. I shall therefore content myself with his information, without inquiring what the cosmographers say about the business.

We should have topographers to trace out for us the particular places where they have been; but for having had this advantage over us, to have seen the Holy Land, they would have the privilege, forsooth, to tell us stories about all the other parts of the world besides. I would have every one write what he knows, and as much as he knows, but no more, and that not in this only, but in all other subjects, for such a person may have some particular knowledge and experience of the nature of a particular river, or a particular fountain, who, as to other things, knows no more than what everybody does, and yet to bolster this little pittance of his, will undertake to write the whole science of physics—a vice from which great inconveniences derive.

Now, to return to my subject, I find that there is nothing barbarous and savage in this nation, by anything that I can gather, except that everyone gives the title of barbarism to everything that is not in use in his own country. Such, indeed, we have no other level of truth and reason than the example and idea of the opinions and customs of the place wherein we live. There always is the perfect religion, there the perfect government, there the most exact and accomplished usage of all things. They are savages in the same way

that we say fruits are wild, which nature produces from herself and by her own ordinary progress. In truth, however, we ought rather to call those wild whose natures we have changed by our artifice, and diverted from the common order. In the former, the genuine, most useful and natural virtues and properties are vigorous and sprightly; the latter we have helped make degenerate by accommodating them to the pleasure of our own corrupted palate. And yet for all this, our taste recognizes a flavor and delicacy in several fruits from those countries without art or culture, excellent even to us. Neither is it reasonable that art should gain pre-eminence over our great and powerful mother nature. We have so surcharged her with the additional ornaments and graces we have added to the beauty and riches of her own works by our inventions that we have almost smothered her. Yet, in other places, where she shines in her own purity and proper luster, she marvelously baffles and disgraces all our vain and frivolous attempts.

> Et veniunt hederae sponte sua melius;
> Surgit et in solis formosior arbutus antris;
> Et volucres nulla dulcius arte canunt.[10]

Our utmost endeavors cannot so much as imitate the nest of the least of birds, its structure, beauty, and convenience, or so much as imitate the web of a poor spider.

All things, says Plato, are produced either by nature, by fortune, or by art. The greatest and most beautiful by one or the other of the former, the least and the most imperfect by the last.

These nations, then, seem to me to be barbarous in that they have received but very little form and fashion from art and human invention, and consequently are not very far from their original simplicity. The laws of nature, however, govern them still, not being, as yet, much vitiated by any mixture of ours. They are in such purity that I am sometimes troubled that we were not sooner acquainted with these people, and that they were not discovered in those better times when there were men much more able to judge of

---

10  Latin: "The ivy grows best spontaneously, the arbutus best in shady caves, and wild notes of birds are sweeter than art can teach" (the Roman writer Propertius, who lived *c.* 50 BC–AD 15).

them than we are. I am sorry that Lycurgus[11] and Plato had no knowledge of them, for to my mind what we now see in those nations not only surpasses all the pictures with which the poets have adorned the golden age, and all their inventions in feigning a happy state of man, but, moreover, the fancy and even the wish and desire of philosophy itself. So native and so pure a simplicity as we by experience see to be in them could never enter into their imagination, neither could they ever believe that human society could have been maintained with so little artifice and human patchwork. I should tell Plato that it is a nation wherein there is no manner of traffic, no knowledge of letters, no science of numbers, no name of magistrate or political superiority, no use of service, riches or poverty, no contracts, no inheritances, no divisions of property, no properties, no employments but those of leisure, no respect of kindred, but common ties, no clothing, no agriculture, no metal, no use of wheat or wine. The very words that signify lying, treachery, dissimulation, avarice, envy, slander, pardon, are never heard of. How much would he find his imaginary Republic short of this perfection? "Viri a diis recentes."[12]

Hos natura modos primum dedit.[13]

As to the rest, they live in a country very pleasant and temperate so that, as my witnesses inform me, it is rare to hear of a sick person, and they moreover assure me that they never saw any natives paralytic, bleareyed, toothless, or crooked with age. The situation of their country is along the seashore, enclosed on the other side towards the land with great and high mountains, having about a hundred leagues in breadth between. They have great store of fish and flesh that have no resemblance to ours, which they eat without any cookery other than plain boiling, roasting, and broiling. The first person to ride a horse there, though in several other voyages he had contracted an acquaintance and familiarity with them, put them into

so terrible a fright, with his centaur[14] appearance that they killed him with their arrows before they could come to discover who he was. Their buildings are very long, and large enough to hold two or three hundred people, and made of the barks of tall trees, reared with one end upon the ground, and leaning to and supporting one another at the top like some of our barns, of which the coverings hang down to the very ground and serve for the side walls. They have wood so hard that they cut with it, and make their swords of it, and their grills of it to broil their meat. Their beds are of cotton, hung swinging from the roof, like our seaman's hammocks, every man his own, for the wives lie apart from their husbands. They rise with the sun, and so soon as they are up, eat for all day, for they have no more meals but that. They do not then drink, as Suidas[15] reports of some other people of the East that never drank at their meals, but they drink very often all day after, and sometimes to a rousing pitch. Their drink is made of a certain root, and is of the color of our claret, and they never drink it but lukewarm. It will not keep above two or three days. It has a somewhat sharp, brisk taste, is not at all heady, but very comfortable to the stomach. It is a laxative to strangers, but a very pleasant beverage to those accustomed to it. They make use, instead of bread, of a certain white compound, like preserved coriander. I have tasted it; the taste is sweet and a little flat. The whole day is spent in dancing. Their young men go hunting after wild beasts with bows and arrows. During this time some of their women are employed in preparing their drink, which is their chief employment. One of their old men, in the morning before they fall to eating, preaches to the whole family, walking from the one end of the house to the other, and several times repeating the same sentence till he has finished the round, for their houses are at least a hundred yards long. The chief topics of his discussion are valor towards their enemies and love towards their wives. At the end he never fails to put them in mind that it is

---

11   The mythical founder of the laws which governed Sparta.
12   Latin: "Men fresh from the gods" (Seneca, a Roman writer of the first century).
13   Latin: "These were the manners first taught by nature" (Vergil).
14   A creature in Greek myth which was half-human, half-horse.
15   A Byzantine literary commentator.

their wives who provide them their drink warm and well seasoned. The fashion of their beds, ropes, swords, and of the wooden bracelets they tie about their wrists, when they go to fight, and of the great canes, bored hollow at one end, by the sound of which they keep the cadence of their dances, are to be seen in several places, and amongst others, at my house. They shave all over, and much more neatly than we, without any razor other than one of wood or stone. They believe in the immortality of the soul, and that those who have merited well of the gods are lodged in that part of heaven where the sun rises, and the accursed in the west.

They have I do not know what kind of priests and prophets, who very rarely present themselves to the people, having their abode in the mountains. At their arrival, there is a great feast, and solemn assembly of many villages. Each house, as I have described, makes a village, and they are about a French league distant from one another. This prophet declaims to them in public, exhorting them to virtue and their duty, but all their ethics are comprised in these two articles: resolution in war and affection for their wives. He also prophesies to them events to come, and the issues they are to expect from their enterprises, and prompts them to, or diverts them from, war. But let him look to it, for if he fails in his divination, and anything happens otherwise than as he has foretold, he is cut into a thousand pieces if he is caught and condemned for a false prophet. For that reason, if any of them has been mistaken, he is heard of no more.

Divination is a gift of God, and therefore to abuse it ought to be a punishable imposture. Amongst the Scythians,[16] where their diviners failed in the promised effect, they were laid, bound hand and foot, upon carts loaded with furze and bavins, and drawn by oxen, on which they were burned to death. Only those who meddle with things subject to the conduct of human capacity are excusable in doing the best they can. But those other fellows who come to delude us with assurances of an extraordinary faculty beyond our understanding, ought they not to be punished when they do not make good the effect of their promise, and for the temerity of their imposture?

They have continual war with the nations that live further within the mainland, beyond their mountains, to which they go naked, and without arms other than their bows and wooden swords, fashioned at one end like the head of our javelins. The obstinacy of their battles is amazing, and they never end without great effusion of blood—for as to running away, they do not know what it is. Everyone brings home as a trophy the head of an enemy he has killed, which he fixes over the door of his house. After having a long time treated their prisoners very well, and given them all the attention they can think of, he to whom the prisoner belongs invites a great assembly of his friends. They having come, he ties a rope to one of the arms of the prisoner, of which, at a distance, out of his reach, he holds the one end himself, and gives to the friend he loves best the other arm to hold in the same manner. After this is done, these two, in the presence of all the assembly, despatch him with their swords. After that they roast him, everyone eats him, and some chops are sent to their absent friends. They do not do this, as some think, for nourishment, as the Scythians anciently did, but as a representation of an extreme revenge. This appears from the fact that, having observed the Portuguese, who were in league with their enemies, to inflict another sort of death upon any of them they took prisoners, which was to bury them in the earth to the waist, to shoot at the remaining part till it was stuck full of arrows, and then to hang them, they thought those people of the other world (as being men who had sown the knowledge of a great many vices amongst their neighbors, and who were much greater masters in all sorts of mischief than they) did not exercise this sort of revenge without a meaning, and that it must therefore be more painful than theirs. So they began to leave their old way and to follow this one. I am not sorry that we should here take notice of the barbarous horror of so cruel an action, but that, seeing so clearly into their faults, we should be so blind to our own. I believe there is more barbarity in eating a man alive than when he is dead; in tearing a body limb from limb by racks and torments that is still full

---

16   An ancient people discussed by the Greek historian Herodotus.

of sensation; in roasting it by degrees; in causing it to be bitten and worried by dogs and swine (as we have not only read, but lately seen, not amongst inveterate and mortal enemies, but among neighbors and fellow-citizens, and, which is worse, under color of piety and religion[17]), than to roast and eat him after he is dead.

Chrysippus and Zeno, the two heads of the Stoic sect,[18] were of opinion that there was no hurt in making use of our dead carcasses in any way whatsoever for our necessity, and in eating them too, as our own ancestors, who being besieged by Caesar in the city Alexia, resolved to bear the famine of the siege with the bodies of their old men, women, and other persons who were incapable of bearing arms.

Vascones, ut fama est, alimentis talibus usi
Produxere animas.[19]

And the physicians make no bones of employing it to all sorts of use, either to apply it outwardly or to give it inwardly for the health of the patient. But there never was any opinion so irregular as to excuse treachery, disloyalty, tyranny, and cruelty, which are our familiar vices. We may then call these people barbarous in respect to rules of reason, but not in respect to ourselves, who in all sorts of barbarity exceed them. Their wars are throughout noble and generous, and carry as much excuse and fair pretense as that human malady is capable of, having with them no other foundation than to show valor. Their disputes are not for the conquest of new lands, for those they already possess are so fruitful by nature as to supply them with all things necessary without labor or concern, and in such abundance that they have no need to enlarge their borders. And they are, moreover, happy in this: that they covet only so much as their natural necessities require; all beyond that is superfluous to them. Men of the same age call one another generally brothers, and those who are younger, children. The old men are fathers to all. These leave to their heirs in common the full possession of goods without any manner of divi-

sion or title other than what nature bestows upon her creatures in bringing them into the world. If their neighbors pass over the mountains to assault them, and obtain a victory, all the victors gain by it is glory only, and the advantage of having proved themselves the better in valor and virtue, for they never meddle with the goods of the conquered, but presently return into their own country, where they have no want of anything necessary, or of this greatest of all goods: to know happily how to enjoy their condition and to be content. And those on the coast do the same; they demand of their prisoners no other ransom than acknowledgment that they are overcome. But there is not one found in an age, who will not rather choose to die than make such a confession, or either by word or look step back from the grandeur of an invincible courage. There is not a man amongst them who would rather not be killed and eaten than so much as to open his mouth to beg not to be. They treat their prisoners with all liberality and freedom so that their lives may be so much the dearer to them, but also frequently entertain them with menaces of their approaching death, of the torments they are to suffer, of the preparations being made for it, of the mangling their limbs, and of the feast that is to be made, at which their carcass is to be the only dish. They do all this to no other end, but to extort some gentle or submissive word from them, or to frighten them so as to make them run away, to obtain this advantage: that they may be terrified, and that their constancy be shaken. Indeed, if rightly understood, it is in this point only that a true victory consists.

Victoria nulla est,
Quam quae confessos animo quoque subjugat
    hostes.[20]

The Hungarians, a very warlike people, never pretend more than to reduce the enemy to their discretion; for having forced this confession from them, they let them go without injury or ransom, excepting, at the

---

17  Montaigne refers here to the civil wars of religion in France.
18  An ancient school of Greek philosophy which later gained a substantial Roman following.
19  Latin: "It is said the Gascons appeased their hunger with such meats" (the Roman poet Juvenal of the first century).
20  Latin: "No victory is complete, which the conquered do not admit to be so" (the Roman writer Claudius of the third century BC).

most, to make them give their word never to bear arms against them again. We have sufficient advantages over our enemies that are borrowed and not truly our own. It is the quality of a porter, and no effect of virtue, to have stronger arms and legs. It is a dead and physical quality to have skill. It is a turn of fortune to make our enemy stumble or to dazzle him with the light of the sun. It is a trick of science and art, and one that may happen in a mean, base fellow to be a good fencer. The measure and value of a man consist in the heart and in the will; there his true honor lies. Valor is stability, not of legs and arms, but of the courage and the soul. It does not lie in the goodness of our horse or our arms, but in our own. He who falls, obstinate in his courage—"Si succiderit, de genu pugnat"[21]—he who, for any danger of imminent death, abates nothing of his assurance, who, dying, yet darts at his enemy a fierce and disdainful look, is overcome not by us but by fortune. He is killed, not conquered; the most valiant are sometimes the most unfortunate. There are defeats more triumphant than victories. Never could those four sister victories, the fairest the sun ever beheld, of Salamis, Plataea, Mycale, and Sicily venture to oppose all their united glories to the single glory of the discomfiture of King Leonidas and his men at the pass of Thermopylae.[22] Whoever ran with a more glorious desire and greater ambition to victory than did Captain Iscolas[23] to the certain loss of a battle? Who could have found out a more subtle invention to secure his safety, than he did to assure his destruction? He was set to defend a certain pass of the Peloponnesus[24] against the Arcadians. Discovering the nature of the place and the inequality of forces, and finding it utterly impossible for him to defend the pass, and seeing that all who fought the enemy must certainly die there, but on the other side, thinking it unworthy of his own virtue and magnanimity and of the Lacedaemonian[25] name to fail in any part of his duty, he chose a mean between these two extremes.

The youngest and most active of his men he preserved for the service and defense of their country, and sent them home. With the rest, whose loss would be of less concern, he resolved to hold the pass, and by their death to make the enemy buy their entry as dear as he possibly could. In the end, eventually surrounded on all sides by the Arcadians, after having made a great slaughter of the enemy, he and his men were all cut to pieces. Is there any trophy dedicated to the conquerors which was not much more due to these who were overcome? The part that true conquering is to play lies in the encounter, not in the result, and the honor of valor consists in fighting, not in winning.

But to return to my story: these prisoners are so far from discovering the least weakness, for all the terrors that can be represented to them that, on the contrary, during the two or three months they are kept, they always appear with a cheerful countenance and importune their masters to make haste to bring them to the test. They defy and rail at their captors, and reproach them for cowardice, and the number of battles they have lost against those of their own country. I have a song made by one of these prisoners, wherein he bids them all come and dine upon him, and welcome, for they shall thereby eat their own fathers and grandfathers, whose flesh has served to feed and nourish him. "These muscles," he says, "this flesh and these veins are your own: poor silly souls as you are, you little think that the substance of your ancestors' limbs is here yet; notice what you eat, and you will find in it the taste of your own flesh." In this song there is to be observed a capacity that is not at all barbarous. Those who depict these people dying after this manner represent the prisoner spitting in the faces of his executioners and making wry mouths at them. And it is most certain that to the very last gasp, they never cease to defy them both in word and gesture. In plain truth, these men are very savage in comparison to us. Of necessity, they must either be absolutely so or

---

21  Latin: "If his legs fail him, he fights on his knees" (Seneca).
22  Leonidas and his whole Spartan army were destroyed by a much larger Persian force at Thermopylae; the Spartans had refused to flee certain destruction. The four other battles noted here all took place in antiquity.
23  A Spartan commander.
24  In Greece.
25  I.e., Spartan.

else we are savages, for there is a vast difference between their manners and ours.

The men there have several wives, and have the greater number as they have the greater reputation for valor. And it is one very remarkable feature in their marriages, that the same care our wives have to hinder and divert us from friendship and familiarity with other women, their wives employ to promote their husbands' desires, and to procure them many spouses. Being above all things solicitous of their husbands' honor, it is their chief care to seek out and to bring in the most companions they can, inasmuch as it is a testimony of the husband's virtue. Most of our ladies will cry out that this is monstrous, whereas in truth it is not so, but a truly matrimonial virtue, and of the highest form. In the Bible, Sarah, with Leah and Rachel, the two wives of Jacob, gave the most beautiful of their handmaids to their husbands. Livia preferred the passions of Augustus to her own interest,[26] and the wife of King Deiotarus,[27] Stratonice, did not only give up a fair young maid that served her to her husband's embraces, but, moreover, carefully brought up the children he had by her, and assisted them in the succession to their father's crown.

And so that it may not be supposed that all this is done by a simple and servile obligation to their common practice, or by any authoritative impression of their ancient custom without judgment or reasoning and from having a soul so stupid that it cannot think anything else, I must here give you some evidence of their rational capacity. Besides what I repeated to you before, which was one of their songs of war, I have another, a love-song, that begins thus: "Stay, adder, stay, that by your pattern my sister may draw the fashion and work of a rich ribbon, that I may present to my beloved, by which means your beauty and the excellent order of your scales shall forever be preferred before all other serpents." In this the first couplet, "Stay, adder," etc., makes the burden of the song. Now I am conversant enough with poetry to judge this much: that not only is there nothing barbarous in this creation, but, moreover, that it is perfectly Anacreontic.[28] To which may be added that their language is soft, of a pleasing accent, and something bordering upon the Greek terminations.

Three of these people, not foreseeing how dear their knowledge of the corruptions of this part of the world will one day cost their happiness and repose, and that the effect of this interaction will be their ruin, as I suppose it already has in a very fair way (miserable men to suffer themselves to be deluded with desire of novelty and to have left the serenity of their own heaven, to come so far to gaze at ours!) were at Rouen[29] at the time that the late King Charles IX was there. The king himself talked to them a good while, and they were made to see our fashions, our pomp, and the form of a great city. After this, someone asked their opinion, and would know from them what, of all the things they had seen, they found most to be admired? To which they made answer, three things, of which I have forgotten the third, which bothers me, but I still remember the other two. They said that in the first place they thought it very strange that so many tall men wearing beards, strong, and well armed, who were around the king (it is likely they meant the Swiss of his guard) should be willing to obey a child, and that they did not instead choose one from among themselves to command. Secondly (they have a way of speaking in their language, to call men the half of one another), that they had observed that there were amongst us men loaded with all manner of commodities, while, in the meantime, their halves were begging at their doors, lean, and half-starved with hunger and poverty. They thought it strange that these needy halves were able to suffer so great an inequality and injustice, and that they did not take the others by the throats, or set fire to their houses.

I talked to one of them a great while, but I had so bad an interpreter, and one who was so prevented by his own ignorance from understanding my meaning, that I could get nothing out of him of any importance. Asking him what advantage he reaped from the supe-

---

26    Livia, wife of the Roman Emperor Augustus, is said to have procured sexual partners for him.
27    Roman client king of the Galatians (first century BC).
28    I.e., in the syle of Anacreon, a celebrated poet of the sixth century BC, known for his easy and epigrammatic verse.
29    A town in northern France.

riority he had among his own people (for he was a captain, and our mariners called him king), he told me: to march at the head of them to war. Demanding of him further how many men he had to follow him, he showed me a space of ground, to signify as many as could march in such a space, which might be four or five thousand men; and putting the question to him, whether or not his authority expired with the war, he told me this authority remained: that when he went to visit the villages subordinate to him, they cleared him paths through the thick of their woods, by which he might pass at his ease. All this does not sound very bad. But then, they wear no breeches.

### 52.2

*THAT IT IS FOLLY TO MEASURE TRUTH AND ERROR*
*BY OUR OWN CAPACITY*

It is not, perhaps, without reason that we attribute facility of belief and easiness of persuasion to simplicity and ignorance, for I fancy I have heard belief compared to the impression left by a seal upon the soul, and that the softer and less resisting the soul, the easier it is to impress. "Ut necesse est, lancem in libra, ponderibus impositis, deprimi, sic animum perspicuis cedere."[30] By how much the soul is more empty and without counterpoise, with so much greater facility it yields under the weight of the first persuasion. And this is the reason that children, the common people, women, and sick folks are most apt to be led by the ears. But then, on the other hand, it is a foolish presumption to slight and condemn all things as false that do not appear to us probable, which is the ordinary vice of such as fancy themselves wiser than their neighbors. I was myself once one of those, and if I heard talk of dead folks walking, of prophecies, enchantments, witchcraft, or any other story I had no mind to believe,

Somnia, terrores magicos, miracula, sagas,
Nocturnos lemures, portentaque Thessala.[31]

I presently pitied the poor people who were abused by these follies, whereas I now find that I myself was to be pitied at least as much as they. Not that experience has taught me anything to alter my former opinions, though my curiosity has endeavored that way. But reason has instructed me that thus resolutely to condemn anything as false and impossible is arrogantly and impiously to circumscribe and limit the will of God and the power of our mother nature within the bounds of my own capacity, than which no folly can be greater. If we give the names of monster and miracle to everything our reason cannot comprehend, how many such are continually presented before our eyes? Let us but consider through what clouds, groping in the dark as it were, our teachers lead us to the knowledge of most of the things around us; assuredly we shall find that it is custom rather than knowledge that takes away their strangeness.

Jam nemo, fessus saturusque vivendi,
Suspicere in coeli dignatur lucida templa;[32]

and that if those things were now newly presented to us, we should think them as incredible, if not more, than any others

Si nunc primum mortalibus adsint
Ex improviso, si sint objecta repente,
Nil magis his rebus poterat mirabile dici,
Aut minus ante quod auderent fore credere
    gentes?[33]

He who had never seen a river imagined the first he met with to be the sea, and the greatest things that

---

30  Latin: "As the scale of the balance must give way to the weight that presses it down, so the mind must of necessity yield to demonstration" (Cicero, Roman politician and writer of the first century BC).

31  Latin: "Dreams, magic terrors, marvels, sorceries, hobgoblins, and Thessalian prodigies" (Horace, Roman poet of the first century BC).

32  Latin: "Weary of the sight, now no one deigns to look up at heaven's lucid temples" (Lucretius, Roman poet and philosopher of the first century BC).

33  "If all these were now revealed for the first time to mortals, if they were thrown before them suddenly without preparation, what more wonderful than these things could be named, or such as the nations would have dared to believe beforehand?" (Lucretius).

have fallen within our knowledge we conclude to be the greatest that nature makes of their kind.

> Scilicet et fluvius qui non est maximus, ei
> Qui non ante aliquem majorem vidit; et ingens
> Arbor, homoque videtur, et omnia de genere omni
> Maxima quae vidit quisque, haec ingentia
>     fingit.[34]

"Consuetudine oculorum assuescunt animi, neque admirantur, neque requirunt rationes earum rerum, quas semper vident."[35] The novelty rather than the greatness of things tempts us to inquire into their causes. We should judge with more reverence, and with greater acknowledgment of our own ignorance and infirmity, of the infinite power of nature. How many unlikely things are there attested by people worthy of faith which, if we cannot persuade ourselves absolutely to believe, we ought at least to leave them in suspense. For to condemn them as impossible is by a rash presumption to pretend to know the utmost bounds of possibility. If we rightly understand the difference between the impossible and the unusual, and between that which is contrary to the order and course of nature, and contrary to the common opinion of men, in not believing rashly, and on the other hand, in not being too incredulous, we should observe the rule of "Ne quid nimis," enjoined by Chilo.[36]

When we find in Froissart[37] that the count of Foix knew in Béarn about the defeat of John, king of Castile, at Juberoth the next day after it happened, and the means by which he tells us he came to do so, we may be allowed to be a little merry at it, as also at what our annals report, that Pope Honorius, the same day that King Philip Augustus[38] died at Mantes performed his public obsequies at Rome, and commanded the like throughout Italy, the testimony of these authors not being, perhaps, of authority enough to restrain us. But what if Plutarch,[39] besides several examples that he produces out of antiquity, tells us he knows of certain knowledge that in the time of Domitian[40] the news of the battle lost by Antony in Germany was published at Rome, many days' journey distant, and dispersed throughout the whole world the same day it was fought; and if Caesar was of the opinion that it has often happened that the report has preceded the incident, shall we not say that these simple people have suffered themselves to be deceived along with the vulgar for not having been so clear-sighted as we? Is there anything more delicate, more clear, more sprightly, than Pliny's judgment,[41] when he is pleased to set it to work? Anything more remote from vanity? Setting aside his learning, of which I make less account, in which of these excellences do any of us excel him? And yet there is scarce a young schoolboy that does not convict him of untruth, and that pretends not to instruct him in the progress of the works of nature.

When we read in Bouchet the miracles of St. Hilary's relics, away with them; his authority is not sufficient to deprive us of the liberty of contradicting him. But generally and offhand to condemn all such stories seems to me a singular impudence. That great St. Augustine[42] testifies to having seen a blind child recover sight upon the relics of St. Gervaise and St. Protasius at Milan; a woman at Carthage cured of a cancer, by the sign of the cross made upon her by a woman newly baptized; Hesperius, a familiar friend of his, to have driven away the spirits that haunted his house with a little earth from the sepulcher of our

---

34 Latin: "A little river seems to him who has never seen a larger river, a mighty river; and so with other things—a tree, a man—anything appears greatest of the kind that never knew a greater" (Lucretius).

35 Latin: "Things grow familiar to men's minds by being often seen, so that they neither admire nor are inquisitive about things they see daily" (Cicero).

36 Latin: "Nothing in excess" (Chilo, a Spartan sage and statesman).

37 A French historian active in the fourteenth century.

38 King of France, 1180-1223.

39 Ancient writer of the second century.

40 Roman emperor (81-96).

41 Presumably Pliny the Elder, writer on natural science and other matters of the first century.

42 Christian theologian (354-430).

Lord, which earth, being also transported from there into the church, a paralytic to have there been suddenly cured by it; a woman in a procession, having touched St. Stephen's shrine with a nosegay, and rubbing her eyes with it, to have recovered her sight, lost many years before, and several other miracles of which he professes himself to have been an eyewitness. Of what shall we accuse him and the two holy bishops, Aurelius and Maximinus, both of whom he has attest to the truth of these things? Shall it be of ignorance, simplicity and facility, or of malice and imposture? Is any man now living so impudent as to think himself comparable to them in virtue, piety, learning, judgment, or any kind of perfection? "Qui ut rationem nullam afferent, ipsa auctoritate me frangerent."[43] It is a presumption of great danger and consequence, besides the absurd temerity it draws after it, to condemn what we do not comprehend. For after, according to your fine understanding, you have established the limits of truth and error, and that, afterwards, there appears a necessity upon you of believing stranger things than those you have contradicted, you are already obliged to give up these limits. Now what seems to me so much to disorder our consciences in the commotions we are now in concerning religion is the Catholics dispensing so much with their belief. They fancy they appear moderate and wise when they grant to their opponents some of the articles of belief in question; but, besides that they do not discern what advantage it is to those with whom we contend to begin to give ground and to retire, and how much this animates our enemy to follow up his argument. These articles which they select as things indifferent are sometimes of very great importance. We are either wholly and absolutely to submit ourselves to the authority of our ecclesiastical governance or totally throw off all obedience to it. It is not for us to determine what and how much obedience we owe to it. And this I can say, as having myself made trial of it, that having formerly taken the liberty of my own choice and fancy, and omitted or neglected certain rules of the discipline of our Church which seemed to me vain and strange, coming afterwards to discuss these matters with learned men, I have found those same things to be built upon very good and solid ground and strong foundations and that nothing but stupidity and ignorance makes us receive them with less reverence than the rest. Why do we not consider what contradictions we find in our own judgments; how many things were yesterday articles of our faith, that today appear no other than fables? Glory and curiosity are the scourges of the soul; the last prompts us to thrust our noses into everything, the other forbids us to leave anything doubtful and undecided.

---

43　Latin: "Who, though they should give me no reason for what they affirm, convince me solely by their authority" (Cicero).

# 53

# MARIE DE L'INCARNATION, *LETTERS*

A baker's daughter, Marie de l'Incarnation (1599-1672), married a silk maker at the age of seventeen. The marriage, which seems to have been a troubled one, ended with her husband's death in 1619. Marie, who had experienced mystical visions from childhood, embraced celibacy and stringent ascetic practices, eventually joining the Ursuline order in 1633. She left for New France in North America, in what is today Canada, in 1639. At Quebec she founded a convent, which she governed as its Superior, with a school for French and Native American girls, with the aim of converting the latter to Christianity. This work led her to compose the first dictionaries of Iroquois and Algonkian. She continued, however, to write letters to people in France, including her son, a monk.

---

### 53.1

### LETTER TO A LADY OF RANK
### (QUEBEC, SEPTEMBER 3, 1640)

... We have every reason then, Madame, to praise the Father of mercies for those he has so abundantly poured upon our Savages since, not content with having themselves baptized, they are beginning to become settled and to clear the land in order to establish themselves. It seems that the fervor of the primitive Church has descended to New France and that it illuminates the hearts of our good converts, so that if France will give them a little help towards building themselves small lodges in the village that has been commenced at Sillery, in a short time a much further progress will be seen.

It is a wonderful thing to see the fervor and zeal of the Reverend Fathers of the Company of Jesus.[1] To give heart to his poor Savages, the Reverend Father Vimont, the Superior of the mission, leads them to work himself and toils on the land with them. He then hears the children pray and teaches them to read, finding nothing lowly in whatever concerns the glory of God and the welfare of these poor people. The Reverend Father Le Jeune, the principal cultivator of this vineyard, continues to perform marvels there. He preaches to the people every day and has them do everything he wishes, for he is known to all these nations and is held among them as a man of miracles. And indeed he is indefatigable beyond anything that might be said in the practice of his ministry, in which he is seconded by the other Reverend Fathers, all of whom spare neither life nor health to seek those poor souls that the blood of Jesus Christ has redeemed.

There has been a great persecution among the Hurons in which one of the Fathers was almost martyred by the blow of a hatchet. A club was broken upon him in detestation of the faith he preached.

---

1   I.e., the Society of Jesus, or the Jesuits.

There has been a like conspiracy against the others, who were overjoyed to suffer. Despite all this, at least a thousand persons have been baptized. The devil has worked in vain. Jesus Christ will always be the Master—may he be praised forevermore....

It would take me too long to speak to you separately of them all but I shall tell you in general that these girls love us more than they love their parents, showing no desire to accompany them, which is most extraordinary in the Savages. They model themselves upon us as much as their age and their condition can permit. When we make our spiritual exercises, they keep a continual silence. They dare not even raise their eyes or look at us, thinking that this would interrupt us. But when we are finished, I could not express the caresses they give us, a thing they never do with their natural mothers....

It is a singular consolation to us to deprive ourselves of all that is most necessary in order to win souls to Jesus Christ, and we would prefer to lack everything rather than leave our girls in the unbearable filth they bring from their cabins. When they are given to us, they are naked as worms and must be washed from head to foot because of the grease their parents rub all over their bodies; and whatever diligence we use and however often their linen and clothing is changed, we cannot rid them for a long time of the vermin caused by this abundance of grease. A Sister employs part of each day at this. It is an office that everyone eagerly covets. Whoever obtains it considers herself rich in such a happy lot and those that are deprived of it consider themselves undeserving of it and dwell in humility. Madame our foundress performed this service almost all year; today it is Mother Marie de Saint-Joseph that enjoys this good fortune....

But after all it is a very special providence of this great God that we are able to have girls after the great number of them that died last year. This malady, which is smallpox, being universal among the Savages, it spread to our seminary, which in a very few days resembled a hospital. All our girls suffered this malady three times and four of them died from it. We all expected to fall sick, because the malady was a veritable contagion, and also because we were day and night succoring them and the small space we had forced us to be continually together. But Our Lord aided us so powerfully that none of us was indisposed.

The Savages that are not Christians hold the delusion that it is baptism, instruction, and dwelling among the French that was the cause of this mortality, which made us believe we would not be given any more girls and that those we had would be taken from us. God's providence provided so benevolently against this that the Savages themselves begged us to take their daughters, so that if we had food and clothing we would be able to admit a very great number, though we are exceedingly pressed for buildings. If God touches the hearts of some saintly souls, so that they will help us build close to the Savages as we have the design to do, we will have a great many girls. We are longing for that hour to arrive, so that we will be more perfectly able to do the things for which Our Lord sent us to this blessed country.

### 53.2
### LETTER TO HER SON
(QUEBEC, SEPTEMBER 4, 1641)

My very dear and well-loved son:

... For myself, my very dear son, what you say is true—I have found in Canada something quite other than I thought, but I mean this in another sense than you do. Travails here are so gentle and so easy for me to bear that I experience the words of Our Lord: My yoke is gentle and my burden is light.[2] I have not lost my pains in the thorny study of a foreign and savage tongue; it is so easy to me now that I have no trouble teaching our holy mysteries to our converts, whom we have had this year in great number—namely, more than fifty seminarians and more than seven hundred visits from passing Savages, all of whom we have assisted spiritually and corporally. The joy my heart receives in this holy employment wipes away all the fatigues I may from time to time experience, I assure you. So have no anxiety for me on this point.

---

2   New Testament, Matthew 11.29.

I see that you have none, but on the contrary I am very sensibly consoled by the good wish you make for me—namely, that I should be a martyr. Alas, my very dear son, my sins will deprive me of this great boon; I have done nothing until now that could have won the heart of God and obliged him to do me this honor....

53.3

LETTER TO HER SON
(QUEBEC, 1647)

My very dear and well-loved son:
Since I inform you every year of the graces and benedictions that God pours upon this new Church, it is right that I should also acquaint you with the afflictions he permits to befall it. He consoles us sometimes like a loving father and sometimes chastises us like a severe judge—and me, in particular, who incite his anger more than all others by my continual infidelities. He has made us feel the weight of his hand this year by an affliction that is very sensible to those zealous for the salvation of souls. This is the rupture of the peace by the perfidious Iroquois, whence has followed the death of a great number of Frenchmen and Christian Savages and, above all, of the Reverend Father Jogues.

What brought these barbarians to break a peace we believed so well established was the aversion several Huron captives gave them to our Faith and prayer by telling them it was these that had attracted all sorts of misfortunes upon their nation, that had infected them with contagious maladies and made their hunting and fishing more sterile than when they lived according to their ancient customs. Almost at the same time mortality attached itself to their nation and spread throughout their villages, where it harvested many of their people in a little time, and the contagion engendered a sort of worm in their corn, which devoured it almost completely. These mishaps easily persuaded the Iroquois that what the Huron captives said was true.

When the Reverend Father Jogues went to visit them to confirm the peace on behalf of Monsieur the Governor and all the Christians, both French and Savage, he left with his host, as a pledge for his return, a casket in which were some books and church furnishings. The barbarians believed that these were demons he had left among them and that they were the cause of their misfortunes....

Meanwhile Monsieur the Governor, who knew nothing of this reversal, readied some Frenchmen to go with some Hurons to visit them. The Reverend Father Jogues, who had already begun to sprinkle this ungrateful land with his blood, joined with them to give them advice and necessary assistance during the voyage. They departed from Trois-Rivières on the 24th of September 1646 and arrived in the country of the Agneronon Iroquois greatly fatigued on the 17th of October in the same year.

Upon their arrival they were treated in a manner they were not expecting. The barbarians did not even wait to mistreat them till they had entered the cabins but first stripped them quite naked, then greeted them with blows from fists and clubs, saying, "Do not be astonished at the treatment you are given, for you will die tomorrow. But console yourselves. You will not be burned but struck down with the hatchet and your heads placed on the palisade that encloses our village, so your brothers will see you again after we capture them."

This reception showed them very clearly that the spirits of the Iroquois were soured to such an extent that there was no hope of mercy. So they prepared themselves for death in the little time that remained to them. The next day passed quietly, however, which made them believe that the barbarians were slightly softened. But towards evening a Savage of the Bear clan took Father Jogues into his cabin to sup. Behind the door another barbarian was waiting and struck at him with a hatchet, so that he fell dead on the spot. As much was done to a young Frenchman named Jean de la Lande, a native of Dieppe, who had given himself to the Father to serve him. The barbarian at once cut off their heads and erected them as trophies on the palisade, then threw their bodies in the river.

Thus this great servant of God consummated his sacrifice. We honor him as a martyr and he is one indeed, since he was massacred in detestation of our holy Faith and of prayer, which these perfidious ones hold to be spells and enchantments. We can even say that he is thrice a martyr—as many times, that is to say, as he went to the Iroquois nations. The first time he did not die but suffered quite enough to die. The second time he did not suffer and died only in desire, his heart burning continually with the desire for martyrdom. But the third time God accorded him what he had for so long desired.

It seemed that God had promised him this great favor, for he wrote to one of his friends in a prophetic spirit, "I shall go and shall not return," and thence it appears that he was awaiting this blessed moment with a saintly impatience.

Oh, how sweet it is to die for Jesus Christ! It is for this reason that his servants so ardently desire to suffer. As the saints are always ready to do good to their enemies, we do not doubt that this one, being in heaven, asked God for the salvation of the man that had dealt him the mortal blow, for this barbarian was captured soon afterwards by the French and, after being converted to the Faith and receiving Holy Baptism, was put to death in the sentiments of a true Christian....

Before they went farther, they burned alive a Christian who had been dangerously wounded, lest he die on the way of too easy a death. We learned that, before they left the place, these barbarians, who are more cruel than the ferocious beasts, crucified a little child aged but three years, who had been baptized. They stretched his body upon a great piece of bark and pierced his feet and hands with sticks pointed like nails. Oh, how fortunate was that child to have deserved in his state of innocence a death like unto that of Jesus Christ! Who would not envy this holy infant, who was more fortunate, in my opinion, than those whose death honored the birth of our divine Savior?

The afflicted group was conducted to the country of the Iroquois where they were received like prisoners of war—that is to say, they were beaten with clubs and their sides pierced by blazing firebrands. Two great scaffolds were raised, one for the men, one for the women, where they were exposed quite naked to the laughter and taunts of the barbarians. They asked for Father Jogues—the Christians so they might confess, the catechumens[3] so they might be baptized. The only reply to their beseeching was mockery, but some captive Algonkin women quietly approached the

ignominious scaffolds and told the new prisoners that he had been killed by a blow from a hatchet and that his head was on the palisade. At these words they saw that they could not expect gentler treatment and that, having no priest to confess to, they could expect help and consolation in their suffering only from God.

Indeed, after they had been the plaything of old and young, they were taken down to be led to the three villages of the Agneronon Iroquois. In one their nails were torn out, in another their fingers were cut off, in the third they were burned, and everywhere they were beaten with clubs, which added new wounds continually to the old. The lives of the women, girls, and children were spared, but the men and the youths capable of bearing arms were distributed throughout the villages to be burned, boiled, and roasted.

The Christian I spoke of that made the public prayers was roasted and tortured with a most barbarous cruelty. They began to torment him before sundown, and throughout the night he was burned from his feet to his waist. Next day he was burned from the waist to the neck. They were waiting to burn his head on the night to come but, seeing that his strength was failing, his tormentors threw his body into the fire, where it was consumed. He was never heard to utter a word of complaint or give any sign of a downcast heart. Faith gave him strength within and enabled him to perform acts of resignation without. He raised his eyes incessantly to heaven, as to the place to which his soul aspired and must soon go. You may call him a martyr or by whatever other name it pleases you, but it is certain that prayer was the cause of his sufferings and that the reason he was tortured more cruelly than the others was that he prayed aloud at the head of all the captives....

53.4
LETTER TO HER SON
(QUEBEC, SEPTEMBER 24, 1654)

My very dear son:
... If this peace endures, as there is occasion to hope it will, this country will be very good and very suitable for the establishment of the French, who multiply

---

3   I.e., new initiates to Christianity.

greatly and get along quite well by cultivating the land, which is becoming good now that the great forests that made it so cold are being cut down. After three or four years' tillage, the farms are as good as, and in places better than, those in France. Beasts are raised for food and for milk products. This peace increases trade, especially in beaver, which are in very great number this year because there has been freedom to go everywhere to hunt without fear. But traffic in souls is the satisfaction of those that crossed the seas to seek them so as to gain them for Jesus Christ. It is hoped that there will come a great harvest from the initiative of the Iroquois.

Some very distant Savages say there is a very spacious river beyond their country that leads into a great sea that is held to be the China Sea. If with time this is found to be true, the way will be very much shortened, and the workers for the Gospel will be able to go easily into those vast and peopled kingdoms. Time will make us certain of all things.

This, then, is a little abridgement of the general affairs of the country. As for what concerns our Community and our seminary, everything is in quite a good state, thanks to Our Lord. We have some very good seminarians, whom the Iroquois ambassadors came to see each time they were on embassy here. As the Savages love singing, they were delighted, as I have already said, to hear our girls sing so well in the French style and, as a sign of affection for them, they reciprocated with a song in their own mode, which had not so ordered a measure.

We have some Huron girls that the Reverend Fathers have judged suitable to be reared by us as French girls for, as all the Hurons are now converted and live near the French, it is believed that with time they may intermarry, which will not be possible unless the girls are French in both tongue and manners.

It was suggested in the treaty of peace that the Iroquois should bring us some of their girls, and the Reverend Father Le Moyne was to have brought us five daughters of women chiefs when he returned from their country, but the occasion was not propitious. These women chiefs are women of rank among the savages, who have a deliberative voice in the councils and reach conclusions like the men, and it was they that delegated the first ambassadors to treat for peace.

In conclusion, the harvest will be large and I believe we shall have to find laborers. It is suggested and urged upon us that we establish ourselves at Montreal but we cannot consent to this unless a foundation is assured, for one finds nothing laid out in this country and nothing can be accomplished except at great expense. So, however willing we are to follow the inclination of those that call us there, prudence does not permit us to do so.

Help us praise God's goodness for his great mercies towards us and for not only giving us peace but wishing to make our greatest enemies his children so that they may share with us the blessings of so good a Father.

### 53.5
### LETTER TO HER SON
(QUEBEC, SEPTEMBER, 1661)

My very dear son:

… Since that time there has been nothing but massacres. The son of Monsieur Godefroy had set out from Trois-Rivières to go to the Attikamegues with a group of Algonkins when they were attacked and put to death by the Iroquois, after defending themselves valiantly and killing a great number of Iroquois.

These barbarians have made many like thrusts, but Montreal has been the chief scene of their carnage. Madame d'Ailleboust, who made a journey here, told me some utterly terrible things. She told me that several persons were killed in a surprise attack in the woods, without anyone's knowing where they were or what had become of them. No one dared go in search of them or even leave the settlement for fear of being involved in a like misfortune. Finally the place was discovered by means of some dogs that were seen to return each night, drunken and covered with blood. This made it believed they were tearing some dead bodies, which afflicted everyone sensibly.

Each one armed himself to go out to discover the truth. When they arrived at the place, they found here and there bodies cut in half, others all mangled and stripped of their flesh, with heads, legs, and hands scattered on all sides. Each one gathered up what he could so as to render the duties of Christian burial to the deceased. Madame d'Ailleboust, who told me this story, unexpectedly encountered a man who had the trunk of a human body pressed to his stomach and his hands full of legs and arms. This sight so startled her that she almost died of fright. But it was quite otherwise when those that carried the remains of the bodies went into the town, for then one heard only the lamentable cries of the wives and children of the deceased.

We have just learned that an ecclesiastic of the Company of the Gentlemen of Montreal, having just said Mass, withdrew a little distance away to tell his hours in silence and meditation, though still quite close to seven of their domestics who were at work. When he was least thinking of the mishap that befell him, sixty ambushed Iroquois discharged a volley of musket shots upon him. Although pierced by shots, he still had the courage to run to his people to warn them to withdraw, and immediately he fell dead. The enemies pursued him and were there as soon as he was. Our seven Frenchmen defended themselves as they retreated but could not prevent one of their number from being killed and another captured.

The barbarians then gave extraordinary howls as a sign of their joy at killing a Black Robe.[4] A renegade among them stripped the body and dressed himself in his robe and, putting a shirt over it for a surplice, paraded around the body in derision of what he had seen done in church at the obsequies of the dead. Then they cut off his head, which they carried off, retiring in haste lest they be pursued by the soldiers of the fort.

That is how these barbarians make war. They attack, then retire into the woods where the French cannot go.

We had baleful portents of all these misfortunes. After the departure of the vessels in 1660, signs appeared in the sky that terrified many people. A comet was seen, its rods pointed towards the earth. It appeared at about two or three o'clock in the morning and disappeared towards six or seven, with the day. In the air was seen a man of fire, enveloped in fire. A canoe of fire was also seen and, towards Montreal, a great crown likewise of fire. On the Island of Orleans a child was heard crying in its mother's womb.

As well, confused voices of women and children were heard in the air giving lamentable cries. On another occasion a thunderous and horrible voice was heard. All these mishaps caused such fear as you may imagine.

As well, it was discovered that there are sorcerers and magicians in this country. This became apparent in the person of a miller who came from France at the same time as Monseigneur our Prelate and whom His Highness forced to abjure heresy because he was a Huguenot.[5] This man wished to marry a girl that had travelled with her father and mother in the same vessel, saying that she had been promised to him, but, because he was a man of bad habits, no one would listen to him. After this refusal, he wished to obtain his ends by the ruses of his diabolic art. He caused demons or goblins to appear in the girl's house, and with them specters that caused her a great deal of distress and fear. However, no-one knew the cause of this invention until, the magician himself appearing, there was reason to believe this wretch had cast an evil spell, for he appeared to her day and night, sometimes alone and sometimes accompanied by two or three others, whom the girl called by name though she had never seen them before.

Monseigneur sent Fathers and went there himself to drive away the demons by the prayers of the Church. However, nothing improved and the din became louder than ever. Phantoms appeared, drums and flutes were heard playing, stones were seen to detach from the wall and fly about, and always the magician was there with his companions to trouble the girl. Their design was to make her marry that wretch, who wished it also but wished to corrupt her first.

The place is far from Quebec and it was a great fatigue to the Fathers to go so far to work their exorcism. So, seeing that the devils were trying to exhaust them with this travail and weary them with their antics, Monseigneur ordered the miller and the girl

---

4   I.e., a missionary Jesuit.
5   A term in France for a Protestant.

brought to Quebec. The former was put in prison and the latter shut up in the house of the Hospitalières. Thus the matter remains. Many extraordinary things came to pass which I shall not tell, to avoid tedium and make an end of the matter. The magician and the other sorcerers have not yet been willing to confess. Nor is anything said to them, for it is not easy to convict persons in crimes of this nature.

After this pursuit of sorcerers, all these regions were afflicted with a universal malady, of which it is believed they are the authors. This was a sort of whooping cough or mortal rheum which spread like a contagion in all the families so that not a single one has been free of it. Almost all the children of the Savages, and a great part of the French children, are dead from it. We had never yet seen a like mortality, for the malady terminated in pleurisy accompanied by fever. We were all attacked by it; our boarders, our seminarians, and our domestics were all at the extremity. In a word, I do not believe twenty persons in Canada were free from this sickness, which was so universal that there is a strong foundation for the belief that those wretches had poisoned the air.

Such then are the two scourges with which it has pleased God to try this new Church—one is that of which I have just spoken, for no one has ever seen so many persons die in Canada as died this year, and the other is the persecution of the Iroquois, which keeps the entire country in continual apprehension, for it must be confessed that if they had the skill of the French and knew our weakness they would already have exterminated us. But God blinds them in his goodness towards us, and I hope he will always favor us with his protection against our enemies, whoever they may be. I beseech you to pray him to do so.

53.6
LETTER TO HER SON
(QUEBEC, AUGUST 10, 1662)

My very dear son:
I spoke in another letter of a cross, which I said was heavier to me than all the hostilities of the Iroquois. Here is what it is. There are in this country Frenchmen so wretched and lacking in fear of God that they destroy all our new Christians by giving them very

violent liquors, such as wine and brandy, to extract beaver from them.

These liquors destroy all these poor people—the men, the women, the boys, and even the girls, for each is master in the cabin when it is a question of eating and drinking. They are immediately drunken and become almost mad. They run about naked with spears and other weapons and put everyone to flight, be it night or day. They run through Quebec, without anyone's being able to prevent them. Thence follow murders, violations, and monstrous and unheard-of crimes. The Reverend Fathers have done all they can to halt this evil, both on the French side and on the Savage; all their efforts have been in vain.

When our Savage day-pupils came to our classes, we pointed out the evil into which they would be precipitated if they followed the example of their kinsmen; they have not since set foot in our seminary. Such is the nature of the Savages. In the matter of behavior, they copy everything they see the people of their nation do, unless they are well strengthened in Christian morality.

An Algonkin chief, an excellent Christian and the first baptized in Canada, came to visit us and lamented, saying, "Onontio"—that is Monsieur the Governor "is killing us by permitting people to give us liquors."

We replied, "Tell him so he will forbid it."

"I have already told him twice," he answered, "and yet he does nothing. You beg him to forbid it. Perhaps he will obey you."

It is a deplorable thing to see the fatal mishaps that spring from this traffic. Monseigneur our Prelate has done everything that can be imagined to halt its course, as a thing that tends to nothing less than the destruction of faith and religion in these regions….

53.7
LETTER TO HER SON
(QUEBEC, AUGUST 9, 1668)

My very dear son:
… I wrote to you by all the ways, but as my letters may perish, I shall repeat here what I have said elsewhere about our employment, since you desire that I should discuss it with you….

The Savage girls lodge and eat with French girls, but it is necessary to have a special mistress for their instruction, and sometimes more, depending upon how many we have. I have just refused seven Algonkin seminarians to my great regret because we lack food, the officers having taken it all away for the King's troops, who were short. Never since we have been in Canada have we refused a single seminarian, despite our poverty, and the necessity of refusing these has caused me a very sensible mortification; but I had to submit and humble myself in our helplessness, which has even obliged us to return a few French girls to their parents. We are limited to sixteen French girls and three Savages, of whom two are Iroquois and one a captive to whom it is desired that we should teach the French tongue. I do not speak of the poor, who are in very great number and with whom we must share what we have left. But let us return to our boarding pupils.

Great care is taken in this country with the instruction of the French girls, and I can assure you that if there were no Ursulines they would be in continual danger for their salvation. The reason is that there are a great many men, and a father and mother who would not miss Mass on a feast-day or a Sunday are quite willing to leave their children at home with several men to watch over them. If there are girls, whatever age they may be, they are in evident danger, and experience shows they must be put in a place of safety.

In a word, all I can say is that the girls in this country are for the most part more learned in several dangerous matters than those of France. Thirty girls give us more work in the boarding-school than sixty would in France. The day-girls give us a great deal also, but we do not watch over their habits as if they were confined. These girls are docile, they have good sense, and they are firm in the good when they know it, but as some of them are only boarders for a little time, the mistresses must apply themselves strenuously to their education and must sometimes teach them in a single year reading, writing, calculating, the prayers, Christian habits, and all a girl should know.

Some of them are left with us by their parents till they are of an age to be provided, either for the world or for religion. We have eight, both professed

and novices, who did not wish to return to the world and do very well, having been reared in great innocence, and we have others that do not wish to return to their parents since they feel comfortable in God's house.

In the case of Savage girls, we take them at all ages. It will happen that a Savage, either Christian or pagan, wishes to carry off a girl of his nation and keep her contrary to God's law; she is given to us, and we instruct her and watch over her till the Reverend Fathers come to take her away. Others are here only as birds of passage and remain with us only until they are sad, a thing the Savage nature cannot suffer; the moment they become sad, their parents take them away lest they die. We leave them free on this point, for we are more likely to win them over in this way than by keeping them by force or entreaties. There are still others that go off by some whim or caprice; like squirrels, they climb our palisade, which is high as a wall, and go to run in the woods....

## 53.8
### LETTER TO HER SON
### (QUEBEC, SEPTEMBER 1, 1668)

My very dear son:

… If His Majesty desires this [that we should raise a number of little Native girls to be French], we are willing to do so, because of the obedience we owe him and, above all, because we are all prepared to do whatsoever will be for the greatest glory of God. However, it is a very difficult thing, not to say impossible, to make the little Savages French or civilized. We have more experience of this than anyone else, and we have observed that of a hundred that have passed through our hands we have scarcely civilized one. We find docility and intelligence in these girls but, when we are least expecting it, they clamber over our wall and go off to run with their kinsmen in the woods, finding more to please them there than in all the amenities of our French houses.

Such is the nature of the Savages; they cannot be restrained and, if they are, they become melancholy and their melancholy makes them sick. Moreover, the Savages are extraordinarily fond of their children and, when they know they are sad, they leave no stone unturned to get them back and we have to give them up.

We have had Hurons, Algonkins, and Iroquois; these last are the prettiest and the most docile of all. I do not know whether they will be more capable of being civilized than the others or whether they will keep the French elegance in which we are rearing them. I do not expect it of them, for they are Savages and that is sufficient reason not to hope....

# 54

# THE GRAND REMONSTRANCE AND PETITION FROM PARLIAMENT TO KING CHARLES I (DECEMBER 1, 1641) AND CHARLES'S REPLY (DECEMBER 23, 1641)

In 1629, Charles I, king of England and Scotland (1625-1649), called the last English parliament of his early reign. Having failed to come to agreement with it, he dissolved it, and did not call another for 11 years. This period, known as the "Personal Rule," came to an end in 1640 as a result of rebellion in Scotland two years before. Charles was forced to call one parliament (known as the "Short Parliament"), and then another (the "Long Parliament"), in order to obtain parliamentary grants of taxation to pay for an army to deal with the Scots. The second of these parliaments presented the king with the Grand Remonstrance and petition on December 1, 1641; it had been passed by 11 votes. Since the end of the Personal Rule, tight royal control over the press had come to an end, thus allowing the Grand Remonstrance to be printed widely in pamphlet form. The next year Charles and Parliament would be at war.

---

## 54.1
### THE GRAND REMONSTRANCE AND PARLIAMENT'S PETITION

Most Gracious Sovereign,

Your Majesty's most humble and faithful subjects the Commons in this present Parliament assembled, do with much thankfulness and joy acknowledge the great mercy and favor of God, in giving your Majesty a safe and peaceable return out of Scotland into your kingdom of England,[1] where the pressing dangers and distempers of the State have caused us with much earnestness to desire the comfort of your gracious presence, and likewise the unity and justice of your royal authority, to give more life and power to the dutiful and loyal counsels and endeavors of your Parliament, for the prevention of that eminent ruin and destruction wherein your kingdoms of England and Scotland are threatened. The duty which we owe to your Majesty and our country cannot but make us very sensible and apprehensive that the multiplicity, sharpness and malignity of those evils under which we have now many years suffered are fomented and cherished by a corrupt and ill-affected party, who amongst other their[2] mischievous devices

---

1  Charles had visited Scotland in August of 1641 to take advantage of a peace recently made with the Scots.
2  I.e., "their other."

for the alteration of religion and government, have sought by many false scandals and imputations, cunningly insinuated and dispersed amongst the people, to blemish and disgrace our proceedings in this Parliament, and to get themselves a party and faction amongst your subjects, for the better strengthening themselves in their wicked courses, and hindering those provisions and remedies which might, by the wisdom of your Majesty and counsel of your Parliament, be opposed against them.

For preventing whereof, and the better information of your Majesty, your Peers[3] and all other your loyal subjects, we have been necessitated to make a declaration of the state of the kingdom, both before and since the assembly of this Parliament, unto this time, which we do humbly present to your Majesty, without the least intention to lay any blemish upon your royal person, but only to represent how your royal authority and trust have been abused, to the great prejudice and danger of your Majesty, and of all your good subjects.

And because we have reason to believe that those malignant parties, whose proceedings evidently appear to be mainly for the advantage and increase of Popery,[4] is composed, set up, and acted by the subtle practice of the Jesuits[5] and other engineers and factors[6] for Rome, and to the great danger of this kingdom, and most grievous affliction of your loyal subjects, have so far prevailed as to corrupt diverse of your Bishops and others in prime pieces of the Church, and also to bring diverse of these instruments to be of your Privy Council, and other employments of trust and nearness about your Majesty, the Prince,[7] and the rest of your royal children.

And by this means have had such an operation in your counsel and the most important affairs and proceedings of your government, that a most dangerous division and chargeable preparation for war betwixt your kingdoms of England and Scotland, the increase of jealousies betwixt your Majesty and your most obedient subjects, the violent distraction and interruption of this Parliament, the insurrection of the Papists[8] in your kingdom of Ireland, and bloody massacre of your people, have been not only endeavored and attempted, but in a great measure compassed and effected.

For preventing the final accomplishment whereof, your poor subjects are enforced to engage their persons and estates to the maintaining of a very expensive and dangerous war, notwithstanding they have already since the beginning of this Parliament undergone the charge of £150,000 sterling, or thereabouts, for the necessary support and supply of your Majesty in these present and perilous designs. And because all our most faithful endeavors and engagements will be ineffectual for the peace, safety and preservation of your Majesty and your people, if some present, real and effectual course be not taken for suppressing this wicked and malignant party, we, your most humble and obedient subjects, do with all faithfulness and humility beseech your Majesty:

1    That you will be graciously pleased to concur with the humble desires of your people in a parliamentary way, for the preserving the peace and safety of the kingdom from the malicious designs of the Popish party;

For depriving the bishops of their votes in Parliament,[9] and abridging their immoderate power usurped over the clergy, and other your good subjects, which they have perniciously abused to the hazard of religion, and great prejudice and oppression to the laws of the kingdom, and just liberty of your people;

For the taking away such oppressions in religion, Church government and discipline, as have been brought in and fomented by them;

---

3    I.e., the House of Lords.
4    A term, generally derogatory, for Catholicism.
5    A clerical organization of the Catholic church, under direct papal authority, whose purpose was to reconvert lands lost to Catholicism in the Reformation.
6    I.e., agents.
7    The prince of Wales, heir to the throne.
8    "Papist" was a derogatory term for Catholics, referring to their affiliation with the papacy. A Catholic rebellion had broken out in Ireland in October, 1641.
9    English bishops were voting members of the House of Lords.

For uniting all such your loyal subjects together as join in the same fundamental truths against the Papists, by removing some oppressive and unnecessary ceremonies[10] by which diverse weak consciences have been scrupled, and seem to be divided from the rest, and for the due execution of those good laws which have been made for securing the liberty of your subjects.

2   That your Majesty will likewise be pleased to remove from your council all such as persist to favor and promote any of those pressures and corruptions wherewith your people have been grieved; and that for the future your Majesty will vouchsafe to employ such persons in your great and public affairs, and to take such to be near you in places of trust, as your Parliament may have cause to confide in;[11] that in your princely goodness to your people you will reject and refuse all mediation and solicitation to the contrary, how powerful and near soever.

3   That you will be pleased to forbear to alienate any of the forfeited and escheated[12] lands in Ireland which shall accrue to your Crown by reason of this rebellion, that out of them the Crown may be the better supported, and some satisfaction made to your subjects of this kingdom for the great expenses they are like to undergo [in] this war.

Which humble desires of ours being graciously fulfilled by your Majesty, we will, by the blessing and favor of God, most cheerfully undergo the hazard and expenses of this war, and apply ourselves to such other courses and counsels as may support your real[13] estate with honor and plenty at home, with power and reputation abroad, and by our loyal affections, obedience and service, lay a sure and lasting foundation of the greatness and prosperity of your Majesty, and your royal posterity in future times.

THE GRAND REMONSTRANCE

The Commons in this present Parliament assembled, having with much earnestness and faithfulness of affection and zeal to the public good of this kingdom, and His Majesty's honor and service, for the space of 12 months wrestled with great dangers and fears, the pressing miseries and calamities, the various distempers and disorders which had not only assaulted, but even overwhelmed and extinguished the liberty, peace and prosperity of this kingdom, the comfort and hopes of all His Majesty's good subjects, and exceedingly weakened and undermined the foundation and strength of his own royal throne, do yet find an abounding malignity and opposition in those parties and factions who have been the cause of those evils, and do still labor to cast aspersions upon that which hath been done, and to raise many difficulties for the hindrance of that which remains yet undone, and to foment jealousies between the King and Parliament, that so they may deprive him and his people of the fruit of his own gracious intentions, and their humble desires of procuring the public peace, safety and happiness of this realm.

For the preventing of those miserable effects which such malicious endeavors may produce, we have thought good to declare the root and the growth of these mischievous designs; the maturity and ripeness to which they have attained before the beginning of the Parliament; the effectual means which have been used for the extirpation of those dangerous evils, and the progress which hath therein been made by His Majesty's goodness and the wisdom of the Parliament; the ways of obstruction and opposition by which that progress hath been interrupted; the courses to be taken for the removing [of] those obstacles, and for the accomplishing of our most dutiful and faithful intentions and endeavors of restoring and establishing the ancient honor, greatness and security of this Crown and nation.

The root of all this mischief we find to be a malignant and pernicious design of subverting the fundamental laws and principles of government, upon which the religion and justice of this kingdom are

---

10   Ceremonies in church.

11   I.e., have confidence in.

12   Land which has "escheated," that is, land which was held from the king, and has returned to him, normally because the landholder has died or lost the land and has no heirs.

13   I.e., true.

firmly established. The actors and promoters hereof have been:

1 The Jesuited Papists, who hate the laws as the obstacles of that change and subversion of religion which they so much long for.

2 The Bishops and the corrupt part of the Clergy who cherish formality[14] and superstition as the natural effects and more probable supports of their own ecclesiastical tyranny and usurpation.

3 Such Councillors and Courtiers as for private ends have engaged themselves to further the interests of some foreign princes or states to the prejudice of His Majesty and the State at home.

The common principles by which they molded and governed all their particular counsels and actions were these:

First, to maintain continual differences and discontents between the King and the people, upon questions of prerogative[15] and liberty, that so they might have the advantage of siding with him, and under the notions of men addicted to his service, gain to themselves and their parties the places of greatest trust and power in the kingdom.

A second, to suppress the purity and power of religion and such persons as were best affected to it as being contrary to their own ends, and the greatest impediment to that change which they thought to introduce.

A third, to conjoin those parties of the kingdom which were most propitious to their own ends, and to divide those who were most opposite, which consisted in many particular observations.[16]

To cherish the Arminian[17] part in those points wherein they agree with the Papists, to multiply and enlarge the difference between the common Protestants and those whom they call Puritans,[18] to introduce and countenance such opinions and ceremonies as are fittest for accommodation with Popery, to increase and maintain ignorance, looseness and profaneness in the people; that of those three parties, Papists, Arminians and Libertines, they might compose a body fit to act such counsels and resolutions as were most conducible to their own ends.

A fourth, to disaffect the King to Parliaments by slander and false imputations, and by putting him upon other ways of supply,[19] which in show and appearance were fuller of advantage than the ordinary course of subsidies,[20] though in truth they brought more loss than gain both to the King and people, and have caused the great distractions under which we both suffer.

As in all compounded bodies the operations are qualified according to the predominant element, so in this mixed party, the Jesuited counsels, being most active and prevailing, may easily be discovered to have had the greatest sway in all their determinations, and if they be not prevented, are likely to devour the rest, or to turn them into their own nature.

In the beginning of His Majesty's reign the party began to revive and flourish again, having been somewhat damped[21] by the breach with Spain in the last year of King James,[22] and by His Majesty's marriage with France,[23] the interests and counsels of that State being not so contrary to the good of religion and

---

14   I.e., certain church ceremonies which dated to the Middle Ages.

15   Rights inhering in the crown.

16   I.e., occasions of observant care.

17   A Protestant group which held that Christians had free will in determining their own salvation and which stressed traditional ceremonies in church services which had their roots in the Middle Ages. William Laud, archbishop of Canterbury, held Arminian views.

18   A term whose meaning is much debated by historians. One definition is that Puritans were those who wished to see the Church of England (in their eyes) more thoroughly Protestant, indeed, Calvinist, in terms of doctrine and church ceremonies.

19   Revenue.

20   I.e., tax revenue approved by Parliament.

21   Discouraged.

22   James I of England and VI of Scotland, father of Charles I.

23   I.e., the French princess, Henrietta Maria.

the prosperity of this kingdom as those of Spain, and the Papists of England, having been ever more addicted to Spain than France, yet they still retained a purpose and resolution to weaken the Protestant parties in all parts, and even in France, whereby to make way for the change of religion which they intended at home.

1   The first effect and evidence of their recovery and strength was the dissolution of the Parliament at Oxford,[24] after there had been given two subsidies to His Majesty, and before they received relief in any one grievance many other more miserable effects followed.

2   The loss of the Rochel fleet,[25] by the help of our shipping, set forth and delivered over to the French in opposition to the advice of Parliament, which left that town without defense by sea, and made way, not only to the loss of that important place, but likewise to the loss of all the strength and security of the Protestant religion in France.

3   The diverting of His Majesty's course of wars from the West Indies, which was the most facile and hopeful way for this kingdom to prevail against the Spaniard, to an expenseful and successless attempt upon Cadiz,[26] which was so ordered as if it had rather been intended to make us weary of war than to prosper in it.

4   The precipitate breach with France, by taking their ships to a great value without making recompense to the English,[27] whose goods were thereupon imbarred and confiscated in that kingdom.

5   The peace with Spain without consent of Parliament, contrary to the promise of King James to both Houses, whereby the Palatine's cause was deserted[28] and left to chargeable[29] and hopeless treaties, which for the most part were managed by those who might justly be suspected to be no friends to that cause.

6   The charging of the kingdom with billeted soldiers in all parts of it, and the concomitant design of German horse, that the land might either submit with fear or be enforced with rigor to such arbitrary contributions as should be required of them.

7   The dissolving of the Parliament in the second year of His Majesty's reign, after a declaration of their intent to grant five subsidies.

8   The exacting of the like proportion of five subsidies,[30] after the Parliament dissolved, by commission of loan, and diverse gentlemen and others imprisoned for not yielding to pay that loan, whereby many of them contracted such sicknesses as cost them their lives.

9   Great sums of money required and raised by privy seals.[31]

10   An unjust and pernicious attempt to extort great payments from the subject by way of excise,[32] and a commission issued under the seal to that purpose.

11   The Petition of Right,[33] which was granted in full Parliament, blasted, with an illegal declaration to make it destructive to itself, to the power of Parliament, to the liberty of the subject, and to that purpose printed with it, and the Petition made of no use but to show the bold and presumptuous injustice of such ministers as durst break the laws and suppress the liberties of the kingdom, after they had been so solemnly and evidently declared.

12   Another Parliament dissolved 4 Car.,[34] the privi-

---

24   Charles's first parliament.

25   In 1627 the English sent a fleet to help the French Protestants of La Rochelle, then under seige by Louis XIII of France and Louis's chief minister, Cardinal Richelieu.

26   England and Spain, with its holdings in the Americas, were at war in the years 1624-1630. In 1626 an unsuccessful attack was made on the Spanish city of Cadiz.

27   England and France were at war 1626-1630.

28   Peace with Spain ended any English assistance to the Protestant Elector Palatine, a German prince then at war with Spain in the Thirty Years War (1618-1648).

29   Burdensome.

30   Financial grants to the Crown above customary Crown revenue.

31   I.e., by letters authorized by the seal under the king's tight control.

32   Taxes which the king collected by custom on certain goods produced domestically.

33   A petition presented by Parliament in 1628 complaining of billeted soldiers, imprisonment without specific charges, and other matters.

34   I.e., in the fourth year of King Charles's reign.

lege of Parliament broken by imprisoning diverse members of the House, detaining them close prisoners for many months together, without the liberty of using books, pen, ink or paper; denying them all the comforts of life, all means of preservation of health, not permitting their wives to come unto them even in the time of their sickness.

13   And for the completing of that cruelty, after years spent in such miserable durance,[35] depriving them of the necessary means of spiritual consolation, not suffering them to go abroad to enjoy God's ordinances in God's House, or God's ministers to come to them to minister comfort to them in their private chambers.

14   And to keep them still in this oppressed condition, not admitting them to be bailed according to law, yet vexing them with informations in inferior courts,[36] sentencing and fining some of them for matters done in Parliament; and extorting the payments of those fines from them, enforcing others to put in security of good behavior before they could be released.

15   The imprisonment of the rest, which refused to be bound, still continued, which might have been perpetual if necessity had not the last year brought another Parliament to relieve them, of whom one died by the cruelty and harshness of his imprisonment, which would admit of no relaxation, notwithstanding the imminent danger of his life did sufficiently appear by the declaration of his physician, and his release, or at least his refreshment, was sought by many humble petitions, and his blood still cries either for vengeance or repentance of those Ministers of State, who have at once obstructed the course both of His Majesty's justice and mercy.

16   Upon the dissolution of both these Parliaments, untrue and scandalous declarations were published to asperse their proceedings, and some of their members, unjustly; to make them odious, and color the violence which was used against them; proclamations set out to the same purpose; and to the great dejecting of the hearts of the people, forbidding them even to speak of Parliaments.

17   After the breach of the Parliament in the fourth [year] of His Majesty, injustice, oppression and violence broke in upon us without any restraint or moderation, and yet the first project was the great sums exacted through the whole kingdom for default of knighthood,[37] which seemed to have some color and shadow of a law, yet if it be rightly examined by that obsolete law which was pretended for it, it will be found to be against all the rules of justice, both in respect of the persons charged, the proportion of the fines demanded, and the absurd and unreasonable manner of their proceedings.

18   Tonnage and Poundage[38] hath been received without color or pretense of law; many other heavy impositions continued against law, and some so unreasonable that the sum of the charge exceeds the value of the goods.

19   The Book of Rates[39] lately enhanced to a high proportion, and such merchants that would not submit to their illegal and unreasonable payments were vexed and oppressed above measure; and the ordinary course of justice, the common birthright of the subject of England, wholly obstructed unto them.

20   And although all this was taken upon pretense of guarding the seas, yet a new unheard-of tax of ship-money was devised,[40] and upon the same pretense, by both which there was charged upon the subject near £700,000 some years, and yet the merchants have been left so naked to the violence of the Turkish pirates that

---

35   Imprisonment.

36   I.e., inferior to Parliament.

37   In the Middle Ages landowners with lands valued at £40 a year were, on penalty of fine, legally required to assume certain public duties associated with the status of knight. Such "distraint of knighthood" had long ceased to be enforced when Charles reimposed it as a way of raising money.

38   These were taxes on, respectively, wine and wool. For centuries parliament had granted them to a new king for life. Charles's first parliament had, however, granted them to him for only one year. Charles continued to collect them on the grounds that the revenue was inherent to the Crown.

39   Issued by the king from time to time to state the current values of goods for purpose of taxation by Poundage.

40   The king had traditionally had the right to collect this tax from coastal towns as a way of paying for naval defense. Charles had begun to collect ship money from inland towns.

many great ships of value and thousands of His Majesty's subjects have been taken by them, and do still remain in miserable slavery.

21   The enlargements of forests, contrary to *Carta de Foresta*,[41] and the composition thereupon.

22   The exactions of coat and conduct money[42] and diverse other military charges.

23   The taking away the arms of trained bands of diverse counties.

24   The desperate design of engrossing[43] all the gunpowder into one hand, keeping it in the Tower of London, and setting so high a rate upon it that the poorer sort were not able to buy it, nor could any have it without license, thereby to leave the several parts of the kingdom destitute of their necessary defense, and by selling so dear that which was sold to make an unlawful advantage of it, to the great charge and detriment of the subject.

25   The general destruction of the King's timber, especially that in the Forest of Deane, sold to Papists, which was the best storehouse of this kingdom for the maintenance of our shipping.

26   The taking away of men's right, under the color of the King's title to land, between high and low water marks.[44]

27   The monopolies of soap, salt, wine, leather, seacoal,[45] and in a manner of all things of most common and necessary use.

28   The restraint of the liberties of the subjects in their habitation, trades and other interests.

29   Their vexation and oppression by purveyors,[46] clerks of the market and saltpetre men.[47]

30   The sale of pretended nuisances, as building in and about London.

31   Conversion of arable into pasture, continuance of pasture, under the name of depopulation, have driven many millions out of the subjects' purses, without any considerable profit to His Majesty.

32   Large quantities of common and several grounds hath been taken from the subject by color of the Statute of Improvement, and by abuse of the Commission of Sewers,[48] without their consent, and against it.

33   And not only private interest, but also public faith, have been broken in seizing of the money and bullion in the mint, and the whole kingdom like to be robbed at once in that abominable project of brass money.

34   Great numbers of His Majesty's subjects, for refusing those unlawful charges, have been vexed with long and expensive suits; some fined and censured, others committed to long and hard imprisonments and confinements, to the loss of health in many, of life in some, and others have had their houses broken up, their goods seized; some have been restrained from their lawful callings.

35   Ships have been interrupted in their voyages, surprised at sea in a hostile manner by projectors,[49] as by a common enemy.

36   Merchants prohibited to unlade their goods in such ports as were for their own advantage, and forced to bring them to those places which were much for the advantage of the monopolizers and projectors.

37   The Court of Star Chamber[50] hath abounded in extravagant censures, not only for the maintenance

---

41   In the Middle Ages, the Royal Forest consisted of forest land thus designated, over which the king had special rights, whose infraction was punished by fine. These rights had largely fallen into disuse since then, but had been revived by Charles as a means of raising revenue. King John had been forced to grant the *Carta de Foresta*, or Charter of the Forest, at the same time he had been compelled to grant Magna Carta in 1215.

42   A levy on counties, in theory for supply of soldiers.

43   I.e., hoarding up.

44   The king could raise money by fining people for doing things on land to which he could claim title, e.g., land uncovered by the tidal lowering of the sea or along the Thames or Severn rivers.

45   The king sometimes granted monopolies on the manufacture or import of goods, either as a mark of favor or in return for money.

46   Purveyors were royal agents who confiscated or bought goods at prices arbitrarily set by the Crown.

47   Saltpetre men gathered nitrates from animal urine to make gunpowder.

48   Royally appointed commissions charged with maintaining and building drainage works and waterways.

49   I.e., schemers.

50   A royal court which, although it applied the Common Law, did not act according to the procedures of the Common Law. In the 1630s it had been especially active in applying corporal punishment.

and improvement of monopolies and their unlawful taxes, but for diverse other causes where there hath been no offense, or very small; whereby His Majesty's subjects have been oppressed by grievous fines, imprisonments, stigmatizings, mutilations, whippings, pillories, gags, confinements, banishments—after so rigid a manner as hath not only deprived men of the society of their friends, exercise of their professions, comfort of books, use of paper or ink, but even violated that near union which God hath established between men and their wives, by forced and constrained separation, whereby they have been bereaved of the comfort and conversation one of another for many years together, without hope of relief, if God had not by His overruling providence given some interruption to the prevailing power, and counsel of those who were the authors and promoters of such peremptory and heady courses.

38   Judges have been put out of their places for refusing to do against their oaths and consciences; others have been so awed that they durst not do their duties, and the better to hold a rod over them, the clause *Quam diu se bene gesserit* was left out of their patents, and a new clause *Durante bene placito* inserted.[51]

39   Lawyers have been checked for being faithful to their clients; solicitors and attorneys have been threatened, and some punished, for following lawful suits. And by this means all the approaches to justice were interrupted and foreclosed.

40   New oaths have been forced upon the subject against law.

41   New judicatories[52] erected without law. The Council Table[53] have by their orders offered to bind the subjects in their freeholds, estates, suits and actions.

42   The pretended Court of the Earl Marshal[54] was arbitrary and illegal in its being and proceedings.

43   The Chancery, Exchequer Chamber, Court of Wards,[55] and other English Courts have been grievous in exceeding their jurisdiction.

44   The estate of many families weakened, and some ruined by excessive fines, exacted from them for compositions of wardships.[56]

45   All leases of above a hundred years made to draw on wardship contrary to law.

46   Undue proceedings used in the finding of offices to make the jury find for the King.

47 The Common Law Courts, feeling all men more inclined to seek justice there, where it may be fitted to their own desire, are known frequently to forsake the rules of the Common Law, and straying beyond their bounds, under pretense of equity, to do injustice.

48 Titles of honor, judicial places, sergeantships at law,[57] and other offices have been sold for great sums of money, whereby the common justice of the kingdom hath been much endangered, not only by opening a way of employment in places of great trust, and advantage to men of weak parts, but also by giving occasion to bribery, extortion, partiality, it seldom happening that places ill-gotten are well used.

49   Commissions have been granted for examining the excess of fees, and when great exactions have been discovered, compositions have been made with delinquents, not only for the time past, but likewise for immunity and security in offending for the time to come, which under color of remedy hath but confirmed and increased the grievance to the subject.

50   The usual course of pricking[58] Sheriffs not observed, but many times Sheriffs made in an extraor-

---

51   Royal judges were appointed by means of letters patent—i.e., letters sealed with their contents open to all to read. Judges appointed *Quam diu se bene gesserit* had a legal right to have the king specify a reason should they be dismissed. Judges appointed *Durante bene placito* had no such right.
52   I.e., judicial authorities.
53   A kind of committee, made up of members of the king's Council, local gentry, nobles, and representatives from boroughs, set up in 1638 after the outbreak of resistance in Scotland.
54   A royal court hearing cases arising in physical proximity to the king.
55   All were royal courts.
56   The underage heir of a tenant who held a freehold—i.e., land held in perpetuity—of the king became the king's ward. The family could pay a fine to have custody of the heir and the heir's lands, thus making a "composition."
57   Sergeants at law were lawyers who had the right to represent clients in the highest of the Common Law courts.
58   I.e., selecting officials from a list of candidates.

dinary way, sometimes as a punishment and charge unto them; sometimes such were pricked out as would be instruments to execute whatsoever they would have to be done.

51   The Bishops and the rest of the Clergy did triumph in the suspensions, excommunications, deprivations, and degradations of diverse painful,[59] learned and pious ministers, in the vexation and grievous oppression of great numbers of His Majesty's good subjects.

52   The High Commission[60] grew to such excess of sharpness and severity as was not much less than the Romish Inquisition,[61] and yet in many cases by the Archbishop's[62] power was made much more heavy, being assisted and strengthened by authority of the Council Table.

53   The Bishops and their Courts were as eager in the country; although their jurisdiction could not reach so high in rigor and extremity of punishment, yet were they no less grievous in respect of the generality and multiplicity of vexations, which lighting upon the meaner sort of tradesmen and artificers did impoverish many thousands,

54   And so afflict and trouble others, that great numbers to avoid their miseries departed out of the kingdom, some into New England and other parts of America, others into Holland,

55   Where they have transported their manufactures of cloth, which is not only a loss by diminishing the present stock of the kingdom, but a great mischief by impairing and endangering the loss of that particular trade of clothing, which hath been a plentiful fountain of wealth and honor to this nation.

56   Those were fittest for[63] ecclesiastical preferment, and soonest obtained it, who were most officious in promoting superstition, most virulent in railing against godliness and honesty.

57   The most public and solemn sermons before His Majesty were either to advance prerogative above law, and decry the property of the subject, or full of such kind of invectives.

58   Whereby they might make those odious who sought to maintain the religion, laws and liberties of the kingdom, and such men were sure to be weeded out of the commission of the peace,[64] and out of all other employments of power in the government of the country.

59   Many noble personages were councillors[65] in name, but the power and authority remained in a few of such as were most addicted to this party, whose resolutions and determinations were brought to the table for countenance and execution, and not for debate and deliberation, and no man could offer to oppose them without disgrace and hazard to himself.

60   Nay, all those that did not wholly concur and actively contribute to the furtherance of their designs, though otherwise persons of never so great honor and abilities, were so far from being employed in any place of trust and power, that they were neglected, discountenanced, and upon all occasions injured and oppressed.

61   This faction was grown to that height and entireness of power, that now they began to think of finishing their work, which consisted of these three parts.

62   I. The government must be set free from all restraint of laws concerning our persons and estates.

63   II. There must be a conjunction between Papists and Protestants in doctrine, discipline and ceremonies; only it must not yet be called Popery.

64   III. The Puritans, under which name they include all those that desire to preserve the laws and liberties of the kingdom, and to maintain religion in the power of it, must be either rooted out of the kingdom with force, or driven out with fear.

65   For the effecting of this it was thought necessary to reduce Scotland to such Popish superstitions and

---

59   Diligent.

60   The highest church court in the country; it had ceased to be effective with the opening of the Long Parliament.

61   I.e., the Inquisition courts of the Catholic church.

62   I.e., that of the archbishop of Canterbury, William Laud.

63   I.e., most apt at obtaining.

64   A mainstay of local government in the shires or counties, traditionally staffed by local gentlemen.

65   Of the king.

innovations as might make them apt to join with England in that great change which was intended.

66 Whereupon new canons[66] and a new liturgy were pressed upon them, and when they refused to admit of them, an army was raised to force them to it,[67] towards which the Clergy and the Papists were very forward in their contribution.

67 The Scots likewise raised an army for their defense.

68 And when both armies were come together, and ready for a bloody encounter, His Majesty's own gracious disposition, and the counsel of the English nobility and dutiful submission of the Scots, did so far prevail against the evil counsel of others that a pacification was made, and His Majesty returned with peace and much honor to London.

69 The unexpected reconciliation was most acceptable to all the kingdom, except to the malignant party; whereof the Archbishop and the Earl of Strafford being heads, they and their faction began to inveigh against the peace, and to aggravate the proceedings of the states, which so incensed His Majesty, that he forthwith prepared again for war.

70 And such was their confidence, that having corrupted and distempered the whole frame and government of the kingdom, they did now hope to corrupt that which was the only means to restore all to a right frame and temper again.

71 To which end they persuaded His Majesty to call a Parliament, not to seek counsel and advice of them, but to draw countenance and supply from them, and to engage the whole kingdom in their quarrel.

72 And in the meantime continued all their unjust levies of money, resolving either to make the Parliament pliant to their will, and to establish mischief by a law, or else to break it, and with more color to go on by violence to take what they could not obtain by consent. The ground alleged for the justification of this war was this:

73 That the undutiful demands of the Parliaments in Scotland was a sufficient reason for His Majesty to take arms against them, without hearing the reason of those demands, and thereupon a new army was prepared against them, their ships were seized in all ports both of England and Ireland, and at sea, their petitions rejected, their commissioners refused audience.

74 This whole kingdom most miserably distempered with levies of men and money, and imprisonments of those who denied to submit to those levies.

75 The Earl of Strafford passed into Ireland, caused the Parliament there to declare against the Scots, to give four subsidies towards that war, and to engage themselves, their lives and fortunes, for the prosecution of it, and gave directions for an army of 8,000 foot and 1,000 horse to be levied there, which were for the most part Papists.

76 The Parliament[68] met upon the 13th of April, 1640. The Earl of Strafford and Archbishop of Canterbury, with their party, so prevailed with His Majesty that the House of Commons was pressed to yield a supply for maintenance of the war with Scotland before they had provided any relief for the great and pressing grievances of the people, which being against the fundamental privilege and proceeding of Parliament, was yet in humble respect to His Majesty so far admitted as that they agreed to take the matter of supply into consideration, and two several days it was debated.

77 Twelve subsidies were demanded for the release of ship-money alone; a third day was appointed for conclusion, when the heads of that party began to fear the people might close with the King in satisfying his desires of money; but that withal they were like to blast their malicious designs against Scotland, finding them very much indisposed to give any countenance to that war.

78 Thereupon they wickedly advised the King to break off the Parliament[69] and to return to the ways of confusion, in which their own evil intentions were most likely to prosper and succeed.

---

66 Church laws.

67 A reference to the Bishops' Wars of 1639 and 1640, sparked when Charles attempted to impose a version of the Church of England's *Book of Common Prayer* on his Presbyterian kingdom of Scotland.

68 The English parliament.

69 The Short Parliament.

79   After the Parliament ended the 5th of May, 1640, this party grew so bold as to counsel the King to supply himself out of his subjects' estates by his own power, at his own will, without their consent.

80   The very next day some members of both Houses had their studies and cabinets, yea, their pockets searched; another of them not long after was committed close prisoner for not delivering some petitions which he received by authority of that House.

81   And if harsher courses were intended (as was reported) it is very probable that the sickness of the Earl of Strafford, and the tumultuous rising in Southwark and about Lambeth[70] were the causes that such violent intentions were not brought into execution.

82   A false and scandalous Declaration against the House of Commons was published in His Majesty's name, which yet wrought little effect with the people, but only to manifest the impudence of those who were authors of it.

83   A forced loan of money was attempted in the City of London.

84   The Lord Mayor and Aldermen in their several wards enjoined to bring in a list of the names of such persons as they judged fit to lend, and of the sums they should lend. And such Aldermen as refused to do so were committed to prison.

85   The Archbishop and the other Bishops and Clergy continued the Convocation,[71] and by a new commission turned it into a provincial Synod, in which, by an unheard-of presumption, they made canons that contain in them many matters contrary to the King's prerogative, to the fundamental laws and statutes of the realm, to the right of Parliaments, to the property and liberty of the subject, and matters tending to sedition and of dangerous consequence, thereby establishing their own usurpations, justifying their altar-worship, and those other superstitious innovations which they formerly introduced without warrant of law.

86   They imposed a new oath upon diverse of His Majesty's subjects, both ecclesiastical and lay, for maintenance of their own tyranny, and laid a great tax on the Clergy for supply of His Majesty, and generally they showed themselves very affectionate to the war with Scotland, which was by some of them styled *Bellum Episcopale*,[72] and a prayer composed and enjoined to be read in all churches, calling the Scots rebels, to put the two nations in blood and make them irreconcileable.

87   All those pretended canons and constitutions were armed with the several censures of suspension, excommunication, deprivation, by which they would have thrust out all the good ministers, and most of the well-affected people of the kingdom, and left an easy passage to their own design of reconciliation with Rome.

88   The Popish party enjoyed such exemptions from penal laws as amounted to a toleration, besides many other encouragements and Court favors.

89   They had a Secretary of State, Sir Francis Windebanck, a powerful agent for speeding all their desires.

90   A Pope's Nuncio[73] residing here, to act and govern them according to such influences as he received from Rome, and to intercede for them with the most powerful concurrence of the foreign princes of that religion.

91   By his authority the Papists of all sorts, nobility, gentry, and clergy, were convocated after the manner of a Parliament.

92   New jurisdictions were erected of Romish Archbishops, taxes levied, another state molded within this state, independent in government, contrary in interest and affection, secretly corrupting the ignorant or negligent professors of our religion, and closely uniting and combining themselves against such as were found in this posture, waiting for an opportunity by force to destroy those whom they could not hope to seduce.

93   For the effecting whereof they were strengthened with arms and munitions, encouraged by superstitious prayers, enjoined by the Nuncio to be weekly made for the prosperity of some great design.

---

70   Where London militia had turned out and demonstrated support for Parliament.

71   A meeting of the English clergy to discuss matters of common concern; it did not have legislative powers, unlike a synod, which could make canon, or church, law.

72   Latin: the Episcopal War, or Bishops' War.

73   A papal diplomatic representative.

94   And such power had they at Court that secretly a commission was issued out, or intended to be issued to some great men of that profession, for the levying of soldiers, and to command and employ them according to private instructions, which we doubt were framed for the advantage of those who were the contrivers of them.

95   His Majesty's treasure was consumed, his revenue anticipated.

96   His servants and officers compelled to lend great sums of money.

97   Multitudes were called to the Council Table, who were tired with long attendances there for refusing illegal payments.

98   The prisons were filled with their commitments;[74] many of the Sheriffs summoned into the Star Chamber, and some imprisoned for not being quick enough in levying the ship-money; the people languished under grief and fear, no visible hope being left but in desperation.

99   The nobility began to weary of their silence and patience, and sensible of the duty and trust which belongs to them; and thereupon some of the most ancient of them did petition His Majesty at such a time, when evil counsels were so strong, that they had occasion to expect more hazard to themselves than redress of those public evils for which they interceded.

100   Whilst the kingdom was in this agitation and distemper, the Scots, restrained in their trades, impoverished by the loss of many of their ships, bereaved of all possibility of satisfying His Majesty by any naked supplication, entered with a powerful army into the kingdom, and without any hostile act or spoil in the country they passed, more than forcing a passage over the Tyne at Newburn, near Newcastle, possessed themselves of Newcastle, and had a fair opportunity to press on further upon the King's army.

101   But duty and reverence to His Majesty, and brotherly love to the English nation, made them stay there, whereby the King had leisure to entertain better counsels.

102   Wherein God so blessed and directed him that he summoned the Great Council of Peers to meet at York upon the 24th of September, and there declared a Parliament to begin the 3rd of November then following.

103   The Scots, the first day of the Great Council, presented an humble Petition to His Majesty, whereupon the Treaty was appointed at Ripon.

104   A present cessation of arms agreed upon, and the full conclusion of all differences referred to the wisdom and care of the Parliament.

105   As our first meeting, all oppositions seemed to vanish, the mischiefs were so evident which those evil counsellors produced that no man durst stand up to defend them; yet the work itself afforded difficulty enough.

106   The multiplied evils and corruption of 15 years, strengthened by custom and authority, and the concurrent interest of many powerful delinquents, were now to be brought to judgment and reformation.

107   The King's household was to be provided for—they had brought him to that want, that he could not supply his ordinary and necessary expenses without the assistance of his people.

108   Two armies were to be paid, which amounted very near to £80,000 a month.

109   The people were to be tenderly charged, having been formerly exhausted with many burdensome projects.

110   The difficulties seemed to be insuperable, which by the Divine Providence we have overcome. The contrarieties incompatible, which yet in a great measure we have reconciled.

111   Six subsidies have been granted and a Bill of poll-money,[75] which if it be duly levied, may equal six subsidies more, in all £600,000.

112   Besides we have contracted a debt to the Scots of £220,000, yet God hath so blessed the endeavors of this Parliament, that the kingdom is a great gainer by all these charges.

113   The ship-money is abolished, which cost the kingdom about £200,000 a year.

114   The coat and conduct-money, and other military

---

74   I.e., persons committed to prison.

75   A head tax.

charges are taken away, which in many countries[76] amounted to little less than the ship-money.

115   The monopolies are all suppressed, whereof some few did prejudice the subject, above £1,000,000 yearly.

116   The soap £100,000.

117   The wine £300,000.

118   The leather must needs exceed both, and salt could be no less than that.

119   Besides the inferior monopolies, which, if they could be exactly computed, would make up a great sum.

120   That which is more beneficial than all this is, that the root of these evils is taken away, which was the arbitrary power pretended to be in His Majesty of taxing the subject, or charging their estates without consent in Parliament, which is now declared to be against law by the judgment of both Houses, and likewise by an Act of Parliament.

121   Another step of great advantage is this, the living grievances, the evil counsellors and actors of these mischiefs have been so quelled.

122   By the justice done upon the Earl of Strafford, the flight of the Lord Finch and Secretary Windebank.

123   The accusation and imprisonment of the Archbishop of Canterbury, of Judge Berkeley; and

124   The impeachment of diverse other Bishops and Judges, that it is like not only to be an ease to the present times, but a preservation to the future.

125   The discontinuance of Parliaments is prevented by the Bill for a triennial Parliament, and the abrupt dissolution of this Parliament by another Bill, by which it is provided it shall not be dissolved or adjourned without the consent of both Houses.

126   Which two laws well considered may be thought more advantageous than all the former, because they secure a full operation of the present remedy, and afford a perpetual spring of remedies for the future.

127   The Star Chamber.

128   The High Commission.

129   The Courts of the President and Council in the North[77] were so many forges of misery, oppression and violence, and are all taken away, whereby men are more secured in their persons, liberties and estates than they could be by any law or example for the regulation of those Courts or terror of the Judges.

130   The immoderate power of the Council Table, and the excessive abuse of that power is so ordered and restrained, that we may well hope that no such things as were frequently done by them, to the prejudice of the public liberty, will appear in future times but only in stories, to give us and our posterity more occasion to praise God for His Majesty's goodness, and the faithful endeavors of this Parliament.

131   The canons and power of canon-making are blasted by the votes of both Houses.

132   The exorbitant power of Bishops and their courts are much abated by some provisions in the Bill against the High Commission Court, the authors of the many innovations in doctrine and ceremonies.

133   The ministers that have been scandalous in their lives have been so terrified in just complaints and accusations that we may well hope they will be more modest for the time to come; either inwardly convicted by the sight of their own folly, or outwardly restrained by the fear of punishment.

134   The forests are by a good law reduced to their right bounds.

135   The encroachments and oppressions of the Stannary Courts,[78] the extortions of the clerk of the market.

136   And the compulsion of the subject to receive the Order of Knighthood against his will, paying of fines for not receiving it, and the vexatious proceedings thereupon for levying of those fines, are by other beneficial laws reformed and prevented.

137   Many excellent laws and provisions are in preparation for removing the inordinate power, vexation and usurpation of Bishops, for reforming the pride and idleness of many of the clergy, for easing the people of unnecessary ceremonies in religion, for cen-

---

76   I.e., counties or shires.

77   This council exercised wide judicial and administrative powers on the king's behalf in five northern shires, or counties.

78   Special royal courts with jurisdiction over mining operations in certain areas of the country.

suring and removing unworthy and unprofitable ministers, and for maintaining godly and diligent preachers through the kingdom.

138   Other things of main importance for the good of this kingdom are in proposition, though little could hitherto be done in regard of the many other more pressing businesses, which yet before the end of this Session we hope may receive some progress and perfection.

139   The establishing and ordering the King's revenue, that so the abuse of officers and superfluity of expenses may be cut off, and the necessary disbursements for His Majesty's honor, the defense and government of the kingdom, may be more certainly provided for.

140   The regulating of courts of justice, and abridging both the delays and charges of law-suits.

141   The settling of some good courses for preventing the exportation of gold and silver, and the inequality of exchanges between us and other nations, for the advancing of native commodities, increase of our manufacturers, and well balancing of trade, whereby the stock of the Kingdom may be increased, or at least kept from impairing, as through neglect hereof it hath done for many years last past.

142   Improving the herring fishing upon our coasts, which will be of mighty use in the employment of the poor, and a plentiful nursery of mariners for enabling the kingdom in any great action.

143   The oppositions, obstructions and the difficulties wherewith we have been encountered, and which still lie in our way with some strength and much obstinacy, are these: the malignant party whom we have formerly described to be the actors and promoters of all our misery, they have taken heart again.

144   They have been able to prefer some of their own factors and agents to degrees of honor, to places of trust and employment, even during the Parliament.

145   They have endeavored to work in His Majesty ill impressions and opinions of our proceedings, as if we had altogether done our own work, and not his; and had obtained from him many things very prejudicial to the Crown, both in respect of prerogative and profit.

146   To wipe out this slander we think good only to say thus much: that all that we have done is for His Majesty, his greatness, honor and support, when we yield to give £25,000 a month for the relief of the Northern Counties; this was given to the King, for he was bound to protect his subjects.

147   They were His Majesty's evil counsellors, and their ill instruments that were actors in those grievances which brought in the Scots.

148   And if His Majesty please to force those who were the authors of this war to make satisfaction, as he might justly and easily do, it seems very reasonable that the people might well be excused from taking upon them this burden, being altogether innocent and free from being any cause of it.

149   When we undertook the charge of the army, which cost above £50,000 a month, was not this given to the King? Was it not His Majesty's army? Were not all the commanders under contract with His Majesty, at higher rates and greater wages than ordinary?

150   And have we not taken upon us to discharge all the brotherly assistance of £300,000, which we gave the Scots? Was it not toward repair of those damages and losses which they received from the King's ships and from his ministers?

151   These three particulars amount to above £1,100,000.

152   Besides, His Majesty hath received by impositions upon merchandise at least £400,000.

153   So that His Majesty hath had out of the subjects' purse since the Parliament began, £1,500,000, and yet these men can be so impudent as to tell His Majesty that we have done nothing for him.

154   As to the second branch of this slander, we acknowledge with much thankfulness that His Majesty hath passed more good Bills to the advantage of the subjects than have been in many ages.

155   But withal we cannot forget that these venomous councils did manifest themselves in some endeavors to hinder these good acts.

156   And for both Houses of Parliament we may with truth and modesty say thus much: that we have ever been careful not to desire anything that should weaken the Crown either in just profit or useful power.

157   The triennial Parliament for the matter of it, doth not extend to so much as by law we ought to have required (there being two statutes still in force for a Parliament to be once a year), and for the manner of it,

it is in the King's power that it shall never take effect, if he by a timely summons shall prevent any other way of assembling.

158   In the Bill for continuance of this present Parliament, there seems to be some restraint of the royal power in dissolving of Parliaments, not to take it out of the Crown, but to suspend the execution of it for this time and occasion only, which was so necessary for the King's own security and the public peace, that without it we could not have undertaken any of these great charges, but must have left both the armies to disorder and confusion, and the whole kingdom to blood and rapine.

159   The Star Chamber was much more fruitful in oppression than in profit, the great fines being for the most part given away, and the rest stalled[79] at long times.

160   The fines of the High Commission were in themselves unjust, and seldom or never came into the King's purse. These four Bills are particularly and more specially instanced.

161   In the rest there will not be found so much as a shadow of prejudice to the Crown.

162   They have sought to diminish our reputation with the people, and to bring them out of love with Parliaments.

163   The aspersions which they have attempted this way have been such as these:

164   That we have spent much time and done little, especially in those grievances which concern religion.

165   That the Parliament is a burden to the kingdom by the abundance of protections which hinder justice and trade; and by many subsidies granted much more heavy than any formerly endured.

166   To which there is a ready answer: if the time spent in this Parliament be considered in relation backward to the long growth and deep root of those grievances, which we have removed, to the powerful supports of those delinquents, which we have pursued, to the great necessities and other charges of the commonwealth for which we have provided,

167   Or if it be considered in relation forward to many advantages, which not only the present but future ages are like to reap by the good laws and other proceedings in this Parliament, we doubt not but it will be thought by all indifferent judgments that our time hath been much better employed than in a far greater proportion of time in many former Parliaments put together; and the charges which have been laid upon the subject, and the other inconveniences which they have borne, will seem very light in respect of the benefit they have and may receive.

168   And for the matter of protections, the Parliament is so sensible of it that therein they intended to give them whatsoever ease may stand with honor and justice, and are in a way of passing a Bill to give them satisfaction.

169   They have sought by many subtle practices to cause jealousies and divisions betwixt us and our brethren of Scotland, by slandering their proceedings and intentions towards us, and by secret endeavors to instigate and incense them and us one against another.

170   They have had such a party of Bishops and Popish lords in the House of Peers as hath caused much opposition and delay in the prosecution of delinquents, hindered the proceedings of diverse good Bills passed in the Commons' House concerning the reformation of sundry great abuses and corruptions both in Church and State.

171   They have labored to seduce and corrupt some of the Commons' House to draw them into conspiracies and combinations against the liberty of the Parliament.

172   And by their instruments and agents they have attempted to disaffect and discontent His Majesty's army, and to engage it for the maintenance of their wicked and traitorous designs; the keeping up of Bishops in votes and functions, and by force to compel the Parliament to order, limit and dispose their proceedings in such manner as might best concur with the intentions of this dangerous and potent faction.

173   And when one mischievous design and attempt of theirs to bring on the army against the Parliament and the City of London hath been discovered and prevented,

---

79   I.e., ordered to be paid in installments.

174   They presently undertook another of the same damnable nature, with this addition to it, to endeavor to make the Scottish army neutral, whilst the English army, which they had labored to corrupt and envenom against us by their false and slanderous suggestions, should execute their malice to the subversion of our religion and the dissolution of our government.

175   Thus they have been continually practicing to disturb the peace, and plotting the destruction even of all the King's dominions, and have employed their emissaries and agents in them, all for the promoting their devilish designs, which the vigilancy of those who were well affected hath still discovered and defeated before they were ripe for execution in England and Scotland.

176   Only in Ireland, which was farther off, they have had time and opportunity to mold and prepare their work, and had brought it to that perfection that they had possessed themselves of that whole kingdom, totally subverted the government of it, routed out religion, and destroyed all the Protestants whom the conscience of their duty to God, their King and country, would not have permitted to join with them, if by God's wonderful providence their main enterprise upon the city and castle of Dublin had not been detected and prevented upon the very eve before it should have been executed.

177   Notwithstanding they have in other parts of that kingdom broken out into open rebellion, surprising towns and castles, committed murders, rapes and other villainies, and shaken off all bonds of obedience to His Majesty and the laws of the realm.

178   And in general have kindled such a fire, as nothing but God's infinite blessing upon the wisdom and endeavors of this State will be able to quench it.

179   And certainly had not God in His great mercy unto this land discovered and confounded their former designs, we had been the prologue to this tragedy in Ireland, and had by this been made the lamentable spectacle of misery and confusion.

180   And now what hope have we but in God, when as the only means of our subsistence and power of reformation is under Him in the Parliament?

181   But what can we the Commons, without the conjunction of the House of Lords, and what conjunction can we expect there, when the Bishops and recusant[80] lords are so numerous and prevalent that they are able to cross and interrupt our best endeavors for reformation, and by that means give advantage to this malignant party to traduce our proceedings?

182   They infuse into the people that we mean to abolish all Church government, and leave every man to his own fancy for the service and worship of God, absolving him of that obedience which he owes under God unto His Majesty, whom we know to be entrusted with the ecclesiastical law as well as with the temporal, to regulate all the members of the Church of England, by such rules of order and discipline as are established by Parliament, which is his great council, in all affairs both in Church and State.

183   We confess our intention is, and our endeavors have been, to reduce within bounds that exorbitant power which the prelates have assumed unto themselves, so contrary both to the Word of God and to the laws of the land, to which end we passed the Bill for the removing them from their temporal power and employments, that so the better they might with meekness apply themselves to the discharge of their functions, which Bill themselves opposed, and were the principal instruments of crossing[81] it.

184   And we do here declare that it is far from our purpose or desire to let loose the golden reins of discipline and government in the Church, to leave private persons or particular congregations to take up what form of Divine Service they please, for we hold it requisite that there should be throughout the whole realm a conformity to that order which the laws enjoin according to the Word of God. And we desire to unburden the consciences of men of needless and superstitious ceremonies, suppress innovations, and take away the monuments of idolatry.

185   And the better to effect the intended reformation, we desire there may be a general synod of the most grave, pious, learned and judicious divines[82] of this island, assisted with some from foreign parts, professing the same religion with us, who may consider

---

80   I.e., Catholic.
81   I.e., preventing.
82   I.e., religious ministers.

of all things necessary for the peace and good government of the Church, and represent the results of their consultations unto the Parliament, to be there allowed of and confirmed, and receive the stamp of authority, thereby to find passage and obedience throughout the kingdom.

186 They have maliciously charged us that we intend to destroy and discourage learning, whereas it is our chiefest care and desire to advance it, and to provide a competent maintenance for conscionable and preaching ministers throughout the kingdom, which will be a great encouragement to scholars, and a certain means whereby the want, meanness and ignorance, to which a great part of the clergy is now subject, will be prevented.

187 And we intended likewise to reform and purge the fountains of learning, the two Universities, that the streams flowing from thence may be clear and pure, and an honor and comfort to the whole land.

188 They have strained to blast our proceedings in Parliament, by wresting the interpretations of our orders from their genuine intention.

189 They tell the people that our meddling with the power of episcopacy hath caused sectaries and conventicles,[83] when idolatrous and Popish ceremonies, introduced into the Church by the command of the Bishops have not only debarred the people from thence, but expelled them from the kingdom.

190 Thus with Elijah,[84] we are called by this malignant party the troublers of the State, and still, while we endeavor to reform their abuses, they make us the authors of those mischiefs we study to prevent.

191 For the perfecting of the work begun, and removing all future impediments, we conceive these courses will be very effectual, seeing the religion of the Papists hath such principles as do certainly tend to the destruction and extirpation of all Protestants, when they shall have opportunity to effect it.

192 It is necessary in the first place to keep them in such condition as that they may not be able to do us any hurt, and for avoiding of such connivance and favor as hath heretofore been shown unto them.

193 That His Majesty be pleased to grant a standing Commission to some choice men named in Parliament, who may take notice of their increase, their counsels and proceedings, and use all due means by execution of the laws to prevent all mischievous designs against the peace and safety of this kingdom.

194 Thus some good course be taken to discover the counterfeit and false conformity of Papists to the Church, by color whereof persons very much disaffected to the true religion have been admitted into place of greatest authority and trust in the kingdom.

195 For the better preservation of the law and liberties of the kingdom, that all illegal grievances and exactions be presented and punished at the sessions and assizes.[85]

196 And that Judges and Justices be very careful to give this in charge to the grand jury, and both the Sheriff and Justices to be sworn to the due execution of the Petition of Right and other laws.

197 That His Majesty be humbly petitioned by both Houses to employ such councillors, ambassadors and other ministers, in managing his business at home and abroad as the Parliament may have cause to confide in, without which we cannot give His Majesty such supplies for support of his own estate, nor such assistance to the Protestant party beyond the sea, as is desired.

198 It may often fall out that the Commons may have just cause to take exceptions at some men for being councillors, and yet not charge those men with crimes, for there be grounds of diffidence which lie not in proof.

199 There are others, which though they may be proved, yet are not legally criminal.

200 To be a known favorer of Papists, or to have been very forward in defending or countenancing some great offenders questioned in Parliament; or to speak contemptuously of either Houses of Parliament or parliamentary proceedings.

---

83 I.e., small Christian sects and gatherings which rejected the Church of England. "Sectary" and "conventicle" both had negative connotations.

84 A prophet who criticized the Hebrew king Ahab (Old Testament, 1 Kings 18).

85 Courts held in the counties or shires.

201   Or such as are factors or agents for any foreign prince of another religion; such are justly suspected to get councillors' places, or any other of trust concerning public employment for money; for all these and diverse others we may have great reason to be earnest with His Majesty, not to put his great affairs into such hands, though we may be unwilling to proceed against them in any legal way of charge or impeachment.

202   That all Councillors of State may be sworn to observe those laws which concern the subject in his liberty, that they may likewise take an oath not to receive or give reward or pension from any foreign prince, but such as they shall within some reasonable time discover to the Lords of His Majesty's Council.

203   And although they should wickedly forswear themselves, yet it may herein do good to make them known to be false and perjured to those who employ them, and thereby bring them into as little credit with them as with us.

204   That His Majesty may have cause to be in love with good counsel and good men, by showing him in an humble and dutiful manner how full of advantage it would be to himself to see his own estate settled in a plentiful condition to support his honor; to see his people united in ways of duty to him, and endeavors of the public good; to see happiness, wealth, peace and safety derived to his own kingdom, and procured to his allies by the influence of his own power and government.

### 54.2

### CHARLES I'S REPLY TO THE PETITION ACCOMPANYING THE GRAND REMONSTRANCE

We, having received from you, soon after our return out of Scotland, a long petition consisting of many desires of great moment, together with a declaration of a very unusual nature annexed thereunto, we had taken some time to consider of it, as befitted us in a matter of that consequence, being confident that your own reason and regard to us, as well as our express intimation by our comptroller, to that purpose, would have restrained you from the publishing of it till such time as you should have received our answer to it; but, much against our expectation, finding the contrary,

that the said declaration is already abroad in print, by directions from your House as appears by the printed copy, we must let you know that we are very sensible of the disrespect. Notwithstanding, it is our intention that no failing on your part shall make us fail in ours of giving all due satisfaction to the desires of our people in a parliamentary way; and therefore we send you this answer to your petition, reserving ourself in point of the declaration which we think unparliamentary, and shall take a course to do that which we shall think fit in prudence and honor.

To the petition, we say that although there are diverse things in the preamble of it which we are so far from admitting that we profess we cannot at all understand them, as of "a wicked and malignant party prevalent in the government"; of "some of that party admitted to our Privy Council and to other employments of trust, and nearest to us and our children"; of "endeavors to sow among the people false scandals and imputations, to blemish and disgrace the proceedings of the Parliament"; all, or any of them, did we know of, we should be as ready to remedy and punish as you to complain of, so that the prayers of your petition are grounded upon such premises as we must in no wise admit; yet, notwithstanding, we are pleased to give this answer to you.

To the first, concerning religion, consisting of several branches, we say that, for preserving the peace and safety of this kingdom from the design of the Popish party, we have, and will still, concur with all the just desires of our people in a parliamentary way; that, for the depriving of the Bishops of their votes in Parliament, we would have you consider that their right is grounded upon the fundamental law of the kingdom and constitution of Parliament. This we would have you consider; but since you desire our concurrence herein in a parliamentary way, we will give no further answer at this time.

As for the abridging of the inordinate power of the clergy, we conceive that the taking away of the High Commission Court hath well moderated that; but if there continue any usurpations or excesses in their jurisdictions, we therein neither have nor will protect them.

Unto that clause which concerneth corruptions (as you style them) in religion, in Church government, and in discipline, and the removing of such unneces-sary ceremonies as weak consciences might check at: that for any illegal innovations which may have crept in, we shall willingly concur in the removal of them; that, if our Parliament shall advise us to call a nation-al synod,[86] which may duly examine such ceremonies as give just cause of offense to any, we shall take it into consideration, and apply ourself to give due satisfac-tion therein; but we are very sorry to hear, in such gen-eral terms, corruption in religion objected, since we are persuaded in our consciences that no Church can be found upon the earth that professeth the true reli-gion with more purity of doctrine than the Church of England doth, nor where the government and disci-pline are jointly more beautified and free from super-stition, than as they are here established by law, which, by the grace of God, we will with constancy maintain (while we live) in their purity and glory, not only against all invasions of Popery, but also from the irreverence of those many schismatics and separatists, wherewith of late this kingdom and this city abounds, to the great dishonor and hazard both of Church and State, for the suppression of whom we require your timely aid and active assistance.

To the second prayer of the petition, concerning the removal and choice of councillors, we know not any of our Council to whom the character set forth in the petition can belong: that by those whom we had exposed to trial, we have already given you sufficient testimony that there is no man so near unto us in place or affection, whom we will not leave to the justice of the law, if you shall bring a particular charge and suf-ficient proofs against him; and of this we do again assure you, but in the meantime we wish you to for-bear such general aspersions as may reflect upon all our Council, since you name none in particular.

That for the choice of our councillors and ministers of state, it were to debar us that national liberty all freemen have; and as it is the undoubted right of the Crown of England to call such persons to our secret counsels, to public employment and our particular service as we shall think fit, so we are, and ever shall be, very careful to make election of such persons in those places of trust as shall have given good testi-monies of their abilities and integrity, and against whom there can be no just cause of exception where-on reasonably to ground a diffidence; and to choices of this nature, we assure you that the mediation of the nearest unto us hath always concurred.

To the third prayer of your petition concerning Ire-land, we understand your desire of not alienating the forfeited lands thereof to proceed from much care and love, and likewise that it may be a resolution very fit for us to take; but whether it be seasonable to declare resolutions of that nature before the events of a war be seen, that we much doubt of. Howsoever, we cannot but thank you for this care, and your cheerful engage-ment for the suppression of that rebellion; upon the speedy effecting whereof, the glory of God in the Protestant profession, the safety of the British there, our honor, and that of the nation, so much depends; all the interests of this kingdom being so involved in that business, we cannot but quicken your affections there-in, and shall desire you to frame your counsels to give such expedition to the work as the nature thereof and the pressures in point of time require; and whereof you are put in mind by the daily insolence and increase of those rebels.

For conclusion, your promise to apply yourselves to such courses as may support our royal estate with honor and plenty at home, and with power and repu-tation abroad, is that which we have ever promised ourself, both from your loyalties and affections, and also for what we have already done, and shall daily go adding unto, for the comfort and happiness of our people.

---

86   I.e., a meeting of the clergy which can make canon, or church laws.

# 55

# JOHN LOCKE,
## SECOND TREATISE OF GOVERNMENT

The *Second Treatise of Government* by the Englishman John Locke (1632-1704) was published in 1689. At the time, Locke expressed the hope that the work would justify the Glorious Revolution of 1688 and the coming of William of Orange (now William III of England) and his wife Mary to the thrones of England and Scotland. It appears, however, that Locke wrote the work in the years before 1688, starting as early as 1679, when the English political world was dominated by the Exclusion Crisis concerning whether the Catholic James (the future King James II) would be permitted to inherit the throne on the death of his older brother, King Charles II (1660-1685). Locke also seems to have added small portions after 1688, although it is unclear whether all of these can be identified. Selections from the first edition, which suffered from many typographical errors, appear below; there have been small amendments of punctuation and a few purely verbal changes which have been taken from later editions approved by Locke.

---

CHAPTER 1

1  It having been shown in the foregoing discourse:

*Firstly.* That Adam[1] had not, either by natural right of fatherhood or by positive donation from God, any such authority over his children, nor dominion over the world, as is pretended.

*Secondly.* That if he had, his heirs yet had no right to it.

*Thirdly.* That if his heirs had, there being no law of Nature nor positive law of God that determines which is the right heir in all cases that may arise, the right of succession, and consequently of bearing rule, could not have been certainly determined.

*Fourthly.* That if even that had been determined, yet the knowledge of which is the eldest line of Adam's posterity being so long since utterly lost, that in the races of mankind and families of the world, there remains not to one above another the least pretense to be the eldest house, and to have the right of inheritance.

All these premises having, as I think, been clearly made out, it is impossible that the rulers now on earth should make any benefit, or derive any the least shadow of authority from that which is held to be the fountain of all power, "Adam's private dominion and paternal jurisdiction"; so that he that will not give just occasion to think that all government in the world is

---

1  In the Old Testament, the first human being created by God.

the product only of force and violence, and that men live together by no other rules but that of beasts, where the strongest carries it, and so lay a foundation for perpetual disorder and mischief, tumult, sedition, and rebellion (things that the followers of that hypothesis so loudly cry out against), must of necessity find out another rise of government, another original[2] of political power, and another way of designing and knowing the persons that have it than what Sir Robert Filmer[3] hath taught us.

2   To this purpose, I think it may not be amiss to set down what I take to be political power, that the power of a magistrate over a subject may be distinguished from that of a father over his children, a master over his servant, a husband over his wife, and a lord over his slave. All which distinct powers happening sometimes together in the same man, if he be considered under these different relations, it may help us to distinguish these powers one from another, and show the difference betwixt a ruler of a commonwealth, a father of a family, and a captain of a galley.

3   Political power, then, I take to be a right of making laws, with penalties of death, and consequently all less penalties for the regulating and preserving of property, and of employing the force of the community in the execution of such laws, and in the defense of the commonwealth from foreign injury, and all this only for the public good.

### CHAPTER 2
### OF THE STATE OF NATURE

4   To understand political power aright, and derive it from its original, we must consider what estate all men are naturally in, and that is a state of perfect freedom to order their actions, and dispose of their possessions and persons as they think fit, within the bounds of the law of Nature, without asking leave or depending upon the will of any other man.

A state also of equality, wherein all the power and jurisdiction is reciprocal, no one having more than another, there being nothing more evident than that creatures of the same species and rank, promiscuously born to all the same advantages of Nature, and the use of the same faculties, should also be equal one amongst another, without subordination or subjection, unless the lord and master of them all should, by any manifest declaration of his will, set one above another, and confer on him, by an evident and clear appointment, an undoubted right to dominion and sovereignty.

5   This equality of men by Nature, the judicious Hooker[4] looks upon as so evident in itself, and beyond all question, that he makes it the foundation of that obligation to mutual love amongst men on which he builds the duties they owe one another, and from whence he derives the great maxims of justice and charity. His words are:

"The like natural inducement hath brought men to know that it is no less their duty to love others than themselves, for seeing those things which are equal, must needs all have one measure; if I cannot but wish to receive good, even as much at every man's hands, as any man can wish unto his own soul, how should I look to have any part of my desire herein satisfied, unless myself be careful to satisfy the like desire, which is undoubtedly in other men weak, being of one and the same nature? To have anything offered them repugnant to this desire must needs, in all respects, grieve them as much as me; so that if I do harm, I must look to suffer, there being no reason that others should show greater measure of love to me than they have by me showed unto them; my desire, therefore, to be loved of my equals in Nature, as much as possible may be, imposeth upon me a natural duty of bearing to themward fully the like affection. From which relation of equality between ourselves and them that are as ourselves, what several rules and canons natural reason hath drawn for direction of life no man is ignorant" (*Laws of Ecclesiastical Polity* i).

6   But though this be a state of liberty, yet it is not a state of license; though man in that state have an uncontrollable liberty to dispose of his person or possessions, yet he has not liberty to destroy himself, or so much as any creature in his possession, but where

---

2   I.e., origin.
3   Seventeenth-century English advocate of divine right monarchy and royal power.
4   Richard Hooker, sixteenth-century English theologian and author of *The Laws of Ecclesiastical Polity*.

some nobler use than its bare preservation calls for it. The state of Nature has a law of Nature to govern it, which obliges every one, and reason, which is that law, teaches all mankind who will but consult it, that being all equal and independent, no one ought to harm another in his life, health, liberty or possessions; for men being all the workmanship of one omnipotent and infinitely wise Maker; all the servants of one sovereign Master, sent into the world by his order and about his business; they are his property, whose workmanship they are made to last during his, not one another's pleasure. And, being furnished with like faculties, sharing all in one community of Nature, there cannot be supposed any such subordination among us that may authorize us to destroy one another, as if we were made for one another's uses, as the inferior ranks of creatures are for ours. Every one as he is bound to preserve himself, and not to quit his station willfully, so by the like reason, when his own preservation comes not in competition, ought he as much as he can to preserve the rest of mankind, and not unless it be to do justice on an offender, take away or impair the life, or what tends to the preservation of the life, the liberty, health, limb, or goods of another.

7  And that all men may be restrained from invading others' rights, and from doing hurt to one another, and the law of Nature be observed, which willeth the peace and preservation of all mankind, the execution of the law of Nature is in that state put into every man's hands, whereby every one has a right to punish the transgressors of that law to such a degree as may hinder its violation. For the law of Nature would, as all other laws that concern men in this world, be in vain if there were nobody that in the state of Nature had a power to execute that law, and thereby preserve the innocent and restrain offenders; and if any one in the state of Nature may punish another for any evil he has done, every one may do so. For in that state of perfect equality, where naturally there is no superiority or jurisdiction of one over another, what any may do in prosecution of that law, every one must needs have a right to do.

8  And thus, in the state of Nature, one man comes by a power over another, but yet no absolute or arbitrary power to use a criminal, when he has got him in his hands, according to the passionate heats or boundless extravagancy of his own will, but only to retribute[5] to him so far as calm reason and conscience dictate, what is proportionate to his transgression, which is so much as may serve for reparation and restraint. For these two are the only reasons why one man may lawfully do harm to another, which is that we call punishment. In transgressing the law of Nature, the offender declares himself to live by another rule than that of reason and common equity, which is that measure God has set to the actions of men for their mutual security, and so he becomes dangerous to mankind; the tie which is to secure them from injury and violence being slighted and broken by him, which being a trespass against the whole species, and the peace and safety of it, provided for by the law of Nature, every man upon this score, by the right he hath to preserve mankind in general, may restrain, or where it is necessary destroy things noxious to them, and so may bring such evil on any one who hath transgressed that law, as may make him repent the doing of it, and thereby deter him, and, by his example, others from doing the like mischief. And in this case, and upon this ground, every man hath a right to punish the offender, and be executioner of the law of Nature.

9  I doubt not but this will seem a very strange doctrine to some men; but before they condemn it, I desire them to resolve[6] me by what right any prince or state can put to death or punish an alien for any crime he commits in their country? It is certain their laws, by virtue of any sanction they receive from the promulgated will of the legislature, reach not a stranger. They speak not to him, nor, if they did, is he bound to hearken to them. The legislative authority by which they are in force over the subjects of that commonwealth hath no power over him. Those who have the supreme power of making laws in England, France, or Holland are, to an Indian, but like the rest of the world—men without authority. And therefore, if by the law of

---

5  I.e., repay.
6  I.e., answer.

Nature every man hath not a power to punish offenses against it, as he soberly judges the case to require, I see not how the magistrates of any community can punish an alien of another country, since, in reference to him, they can have no more power than what every man naturally may have over another.

10   Besides the crime which consists in violating the laws, and varying from the right rule of reason, whereby a man so far becomes degenerate, and declares himself to quit the principles of human nature and to be a noxious creature, there is commonly injury done, and some person or other, some other man, receives damage by his transgression; in which case, he who hath received any damage has (besides the right of punishment common to him, with other men) a particular right to seek reparation from him that hath done it. And any other person who finds it just may also join with him that is injured, and assist him in recovering from the offender so much as may make satisfaction for the harm he hath suffered.

11   From these two distinct rights (the one of punishing the crime, for restraint and preventing the like offense, which right of punishing is in everybody, the other of taking reparation, which belongs only to the injured party) comes it to pass that the magistrate, who by being magistrate hath the common right of punishing put into his hands, can often, where the public good demands not the execution of the law, remit the punishment of criminal offenses by his own authority, but yet cannot remit the satisfaction due to any private man for the damage he has received. That he who hath suffered the damage has a right to demand in his own name, and he alone can remit. The damnified[7] person has this power of appropriating to himself the goods or service of the offender by right of self-preservation, as every man has a power to punish the crime to prevent its being committed again, by the right he has of preserving all mankind, and doing all reasonable things he can in order to that end. And thus it is that every man in the state of Nature has a power to kill a murderer, both to deter others from doing the like injury (which no reparation can compensate) by the example of the punishment that attends it from everybody, and also to secure men from the attempts of a criminal who, having renounced reason, the common rule and measure God hath given to mankind, hath, by the unjust violence and slaughter he hath committed upon one, declared war against all mankind, and therefore may be destroyed as a lion or a tiger, one of those wild savage beasts with whom men can have no society nor security. And upon this is grounded that great law of Nature, "Whoso sheddeth man's blood, by man shall his blood be shed."[8] And Cain was so fully convinced that every one had a right to destroy such a criminal, that, after the murder of his brother, he cries out, "Every one that findeth me shall slay me,"[9] so plain was it writ in the hearts of all mankind.

12   By the same reason may a man in the state of Nature punish the lesser breaches of that law, it will, perhaps, be demanded, with death? I answer: Each transgression may be punished to that degree, and with so much severity, as will suffice to make it an ill bargain to the offender, give him cause to repent, and terrify others from doing the like.

Every offense that can be committed in the state of Nature may, in the state of Nature, be also punished equally, and as far forth as it may in a commonwealth. For though it would be beside my present purpose to enter here into the particulars of the law of Nature, or its measures of punishment, yet it is certain there is such a law, and that too as intelligible and plain to a rational creature and a studier of that law as the positive laws of commonwealths, nay, possibly plainer; as much as reason is easier to be understood than the fancies and intricate contrivances of men, following contrary and hidden interests put into words; for truly so are a great part of the municipal laws of countries, which are only so far right as they are founded on the law of Nature, by which they are to be regulated and interpreted.

13   To this strange[10] doctrine—viz.,[11] that in the state

---

7   I.e., indemnified.
8   Old Testament, Genesis 9.6.
9   Old Testament, Genesis 4.14.
10   I.e., foreign, new.
11   I.e., "videlicet" (Latin: "namely").

of Nature every one has the executive power of the law of Nature, I doubt not but it will be objected that it is unreasonable for men to be judges in their own cases, that self-love will make men partial to themselves and their friends; and, on the other side, ill-nature, passion, and revenge will carry them too far in punishing others, and hence nothing but confusion and disorder will follow, and that therefore God hath certainly appointed government to restrain the partiality and violence of men. I easily grant that civil government is the proper remedy for the inconveniences of the state of Nature, which must certainly be great where men may be judges in their own case, since it is easy to be imagined that he who was so unjust as to do his brother an injury will scarce be so just as to condemn himself for it. But I shall desire those who make this objection to remember that absolute monarchs are but men; and if government is to be the remedy of those evils which necessarily follow from men being judges in their own cases, and the state of Nature is therefore not to be endured, I desire to know what kind of government that is, and how much better it is than the state of Nature, where one man commanding a multitude has the liberty to be judge in his own case, and may do to all his subjects whatever he pleases without the least question or control of those who execute his pleasure and in whatsoever he doth, whether led by reason, mistake, or passion, must be submitted to? Which men in the state of Nature are not bound to do one to another. And if he that judges, judges amiss in his own or any other case, he is answerable for it to the rest of mankind.

14   It is often asked as a mighty objection, where are, or ever were, there any men in such a state of Nature? To which it may suffice as an answer at present, that since all princes and rulers of "independent" governments all through the world are in a state of Nature, it is plain the world never was, nor never will be, without numbers of men in that state. I have named all governors of "independent" communities, whether they are, or are not, in league with others; for it is not every compact that puts an end to the state of Nature between men, but only this one of agreeing together mutually to enter into one community, and make one body politic; other promises and compacts men may make one with another, and yet still be in the state of Nature. The promises and bargains for truck, etc., between the two men in Soldania,[12] in or between a Swiss and an Indian, in the woods of America, are binding to them, though they are perfectly in a state of Nature in reference to one another for truth, and keeping of faith belongs to men as men, and not as members of society.

15   To those that say there were never any men in the state of Nature, I will not only oppose the authority of the judicious Hooker (*Ecclesiastical Polity* i 10), where he says, "the laws which have been hitherto mentioned"—i.e., the laws of Nature—"do bind men absolutely, even as they are men, although they have never any settled fellowship, never any solemn agreement amongst themselves what to do or not to do; but for as much as we are not by ourselves sufficient to furnish ourselves with competent store of things needful for such a life as our Nature doth desire, a life fit for the dignity of man, therefore to supply those defects and imperfections which are in us, as living single and solely by ourselves, we are naturally induced to seek communion and fellowship with others; this was the cause of men uniting themselves as first in politic societies." But I, moreover, affirm that all men are naturally in that state, and remain so till, by their own consents, they make themselves members of some politic society, and I doubt not, in the sequel of this discourse, to make it very clear.

CHAPTER 3
OF THE STATE OF WAR

16   The state of war is a state of enmity and destruction; and therefore declaring by word or action, not a passionate and hasty, but sedate, settled design upon another man's life puts him in a state of war with him against whom he has declared such an intention, and so has exposed his life to the other's power to be taken away by him, or any one that joins with him in his defense, and espouses his quarrel; it being reasonable

---

12   Locke's reference to Soldania is thought to derive from Terry, *Voyage to East India* (1655).

and just I should have a right to destroy that which threatens me with destruction; for by the fundamental law of Nature, man being to be preserved as much as possible, when all cannot be preserved, the safety of the innocent is to be preferred, and one may destroy a man who makes war upon him, or has discovered an enmity to his being, for the same reason that he may kill a wolf or a lion, because they are not under the ties of the common law of reason, have no other rule but that of force and violence, and so may be treated as a beast of prey, those dangerous and noxious creatures that will be sure to destroy him whenever he falls into their power.

17    And hence it is that he who attempts to get another man into his absolute power does thereby put himself into a state of war with him; it being to be understood as a declaration of a design upon his life. For I have reason to conclude that he who would get me into his power without my consent would use me as he pleased when he had got me there, and destroy me too when he had a fancy to it; for nobody can desire to have me in his absolute power unless it be to compel me by force to that which is against the right of my freedom—i.e. make me a slave. To be free from such force is the only security of my preservation, and reason bids me look on him as an enemy to my preservation who would take away that freedom which is the fence to it; so that he who makes an attempt to enslave me thereby puts himself into a state of war with me. He that in the state of Nature would take away the freedom that belongs to any one in that state must necessarily be supposed to have a design to take away everything else, that freedom being the foundation of all the rest; as he that in the state of society would take away the freedom belonging to those of that society or commonwealth must be supposed to design to take away from them everything else, and so be looked on as in a state of war.

18    This makes it lawful for a man to kill a thief who has not in the least hurt him, nor declared any design upon his life, any farther than by the use of force, so to get him in his power as to take away his money, or what he pleases, from him; because using force, where he has no right to get me into his power, let his pretense be what it will, I have no reason to suppose that he who would take away my liberty would not, when he had me in his power, take away everything else. And, therefore, it is lawful for me to treat him as one who has put himself into a state of war with me—i.e., kill him if I can; for to that hazard does he justly expose himself whoever introduces a state of war, and is aggressor in it.

19    And here we have the plain difference between the state of Nature and the state of war, which however some men have confounded [them], are as far distant as a state of peace, goodwill, mutual assistance, and preservation; and a state of enmity, malice, violence and mutual destruction are one from another. Men living together according to reason without a common superior on earth, with authority to judge between them, is properly the state of Nature. But force, or a declared design of force upon the person of another, where there is no common superior on earth to appeal to for relief, is the state of war; and it is the want of such an appeal gives a man the right of war even against an aggressor, though he be in society and a fellow-subject. Thus, a thief whom I cannot harm, but by appeal to the law, for having stolen all that I am worth, I may kill when he sets on me to rob me but of my horse or coat, because the law, which was made for my preservation, where it cannot interpose to secure my life from present force, which if lost is capable of no reparation, permits me my own defense and the right of war, a liberty to kill the aggressor, because the aggressor allows not time to appeal to our common judge, nor the decision of the law, for remedy in a case where the mischief may be irreparable. Want of a common judge with authority puts all men in a state of Nature; force without right upon a man's person makes a state of war both where there is, and is not, a common judge.

CHAPTER 4

OF SLAVERY

22    The natural liberty of man is to be free from any superior power on earth, and not to be under the will or legislative authority of man, but to have only the law of Nature for his rule. The liberty of man in society is to be under no other legislative power but that established by consent in the commonwealth, nor under the dominion of any will, or restraint of any

law, but what that legislative[13] shall enact according to the trust put in it. Freedom, then, is not what Sir Robert Filmer tells us: "A liberty for every one to do what he lists, to live as he pleases, and not to be tied by any laws"; but freedom of men under government is to have a standing rule to live by, common to every one of that society, and made by the legislative power erected in it. A liberty to follow my own will in all things where that rule prescribes not, not to be subject to the inconstant, uncertain, unknown, arbitrary will of another man, as freedom of nature is to be under no other restraint but the law of Nature.

23   This freedom from absolute, arbitrary power is so necessary to, and closely joined with, a man's preservation, that he cannot part with it but by what forfeits his preservation and life together. For a man, not having the power of his own life, cannot by compact[14] or his own consent enslave himself to any one, nor put himself under the absolute, arbitrary power of another to take away his life when he pleases. Nobody can give more power than he has himself, and he that cannot take away his own life cannot give another power over it. Indeed, having by his fault forfeited his own life by some act that deserves death, he to whom he has forfeited it may, when he has him in his power, delay to take it, and make use of him to his own service; and he does him no injury by it. For, whenever he finds the hardship of his slavery outweigh the value of his life, it is in his power, by resisting the will of his master, to draw on himself the death he desires.

24   This is the perfect[15] condition of slavery, which is nothing else but the state of war continued between a lawful conqueror and a captive, for if once compact enter between them, and make an agreement for a limited power on the one side, and obedience on the other, the state of war and slavery ceases as long as the compact endures; for, as has been said, no man can by agreement pass over to another that which he hath not in himself—a power over his own life.

I confess, we find among the Jews, as well as other nations, that men did sell themselves; but it is plain this was only to drudgery, not to slavery; for it is evi-

dent the person sold was not under an absolute, arbitrary, despotical power, for the master could not have power to kill him at any time, whom at a certain time he was obliged to let go free out of his service; and the master of such a servant was so far from having an arbitrary power over his life that he could not at pleasure so much as maim him, but the loss of an eye or tooth set him free ([Old Testament] Exodus 21).

## CHAPTER 5
### OF PROPERTY

25   Whether we consider natural reason, which tells us that men, being once born, have a right to their preservation, and consequently to meat and drink and such other things as Nature affords for their subsistence, or "revelation," which gives us an account of those grants God made of the world to Adam, and to Noah and his sons, it is very clear that God, as King David says ([Old Testament] Psalm 115.16), "has given the earth to the children of men," given it to mankind in common. But, this being supposed, it seems to some a very great difficulty how any one should ever come to have a property in anything, I will not content myself to answer, that, if it be difficult to make out "property" upon a supposition that God gave the world to Adam and his posterity in common, it is impossible that any man but one universal monarch should have any "property" upon a supposition that God gave the world to Adam and his heirs in succession, exclusive of all the rest of his posterity; but I shall endeavor to show how men might come to have a property in several parts of that which God gave to mankind in common, and that without any express compact of all the commoners.

26   God, who hath given the world to men in common, hath also given them reason to make use of it to the best advantage of life and convenience. The earth and all that is therein is given to men for the support and comfort of their being. And though all the fruits it naturally produces, and beasts it feeds, belong to mankind in common, as they are produced by the

---

13   I.e., legislature.
14   I.e., agreement or contract.
15   I.e., complete.

spontaneous hand of Nature, and nobody has originally a private dominion exclusive of the rest of mankind in any of them, as they are thus in their natural state, yet being given for the use of men, there must of necessity be a means to appropriate them some way or other before they can be of any use, or at all beneficial, to any particular men. The fruit or venison which nourishes the wild Indian, who knows no enclosure, and is still a tenant in common,[16] must be his, and so his—i.e., a part of him, that another can no longer have any right to it before it can do him any good for the support of his life.

27　Though the earth and all inferior creatures be common to all men, yet every man has a "property" in his own "person." This nobody has any right to but himself. The "labor" of his body and the "work" of his hands, we may say, are properly his. Whatsoever, then, he removes out of the state that Nature hath provided and left it in, he hath mixed his labor with it, and joined to it something that is his own, and thereby makes it his property. It being by him removed from the common state Nature placed it in, it hath by this labor something annexed to it that excludes the common right of other men. For this "labor" being the unquestionable property of the laborer, no man but he can have a right to what that is once joined to, at least where there is enough, and as good left in common for others.

28　He that is nourished by the acorns he picked up under an oak, or the apples he gathered from the trees in the wood, has certainly appropriated them to himself. Nobody can deny but the nourishment is his. I ask, then, when did they begin to be his? When he digested? Or when he ate? Or when he boiled? Or when he brought them home? Or when he picked them up? And it is plain, if the first gathering made them not his, nothing else could. That labor put a distinction between them and common. That added something to them more than Nature, the common mother of all, had done, and so they became his private right. And will any one say he had no right to those acorns or apples he thus appropriated because he had not the consent of all mankind to make them

his? Was it a robbery thus to assume to himself what belonged to all in common? If such a consent as that was necessary, man had starved, notwithstanding the plenty God had given him. We see in commons, which remain so by compact, that it is the taking any part of what is common, and removing it out of the state Nature leaves it in, which begins the property, without which the common is of no use. And the taking of this or that part does not depend on the express consent of all the commoners. Thus, the grass my horse has bit, the turfs my servant has cut, and the ore I have digged in any place, where I have a right to them in common with others, become my property without the assignation or consent of anybody. The labor that was mine, removing them out of that common state they were in, hath fixed my property in them.

29　By making an explicit consent of every commoner necessary to any one's appropriating to himself any part of what is given in common, children or servants could not cut the meat which their father or master had provided for them in common without assigning to every one his peculiar part. Though the water running in the fountain be every one's, yet who can doubt but that in the pitcher is his only who drew it out? His labor hath taken it out of the hands of Nature where it was common, and belonged equally to all her children, and hath thereby appropriated it to himself.

30　Thus this law of reason makes the deer that Indian's who hath killed it; it is allowed to be his goods who hath bestowed his labor upon it, though, before, it was the common right of every one. And amongst those who are counted the civilized part of mankind, who have made and multiplied positive laws to determine property, this original law of Nature for the beginning of property, in what was before common, still takes place, and by virtue thereof, what fish any one catches in the ocean, that great and still remaining common of mankind; or what ambergris[17] any one takes up here is by the labor that removes it out of that common state Nature left it in, made his property who takes that pains about it. And even amongst us, the hare that any one is hunting is thought his who pursues her during the chase. For being a beast that is still

16　A term in Common Law, in which holders of land each have full use of it.
17　A secretion of sperm whales usually found floating in the ocean and used in the production of perfume.

looked upon as common, and no man's private possession, whoever has employed so much labor about any of that kind as to find and pursue her has thereby removed her from the state of Nature wherein she was common, and hath begun a property.

31   It will, perhaps, be objected to this, that if gathering the acorns or other fruits of the earth, etc., makes a right to them, then any one may engross as much as he will. To which I answer, not so. The same law of Nature that does by this means give us property, does also bound that property too. "God has given us all things richly."[18] Is the voice of reason confirmed by inspiration? But how far has he given it us—"to enjoy"? As much as any one can make use of to any advantage of life before it spoils, so much he may by his labor fix a property in. Whatever is beyond this is more than his share, and belongs to others. Nothing was made by God for man to spoil or destroy. And thus considering the plenty of natural provisions there was a long time in the world, and the few spenders, and to how small a part of that provision the industry of one man could extend itself and engross it to the prejudice of others, especially keeping within the bounds set by reason of what might serve for his use, there could be then little room for quarrels or contentions about property so established.

32   But the chief matter of property being now not the fruits of the earth and the beasts that subsist on it, but the earth itself, as that which takes in and carries with it all the rest, I think it is plain that property in that too is acquired [in the same way] as the former. As much land as a man tills, plants, improves, cultivates, and can use the product of, so much is his property. He by his labor does, as it were, enclose it from the common. Nor will it invalidate his right to say everybody else has an equal title to it, and therefore he cannot appropriate, he cannot enclose, without the consent of all his fellow-commoners, all mankind. God, when he gave the world in common to all mankind, commanded man also to labor, and the penury of his condition required it of him. God and his reason commanded him to subdue the earth—i.e., improve it for

the benefit of life and therein lay out something upon it that was his own, his labor. He that, in obedience to this command of God, subdued, tilled, and sowed any part of it, thereby annexed to it something that was his property, which another had no title to, nor could without injury take from him.

33   Nor was this appropriation of any parcel of land, by improving it, any prejudice to any other man, since there was still enough and as good left, and more than the yet unprovided could use. So that, in effect, there was never the less left for others because of his enclosure for himself. For he that leaves as much as another can make use of does as good as take nothing at all. Nobody could think himself injured by the drinking of another man, though he took a good draught,[19] who had a whole river of the same water left him to quench his thirst. And the case of land and water, where there is enough of both, is perfectly the same.

34   God gave the world to men in common, but since he gave it them for their benefit and the greatest conveniencies[20] of life they were capable to draw from it, it cannot be supposed he meant it should always remain common and uncultivated. He gave it to the use of the industrious and rational (and labor was to be his title to it), not to the fancy or covetousness of the quarrelsome and contentious. He that had as good left for his improvement as was already taken up needed not complain, ought not to meddle with what was already improved by another's labor; if he did it is plain he desired the benefit of another's pains, which he had no right to, and not the ground which God had given him, in common with others, to labor on, and whereof there was as good left as that already possessed, and more than he knew what to do with, or his industry could reach to.

35   It is true, in land that is common in England or any other country, where there are plenty of people under government who have money and commerce, no one can enclose or appropriate any part without the consent of all his fellow-commoners because this is left common by compact—i.e., by the law of the land, which is not to be violated. And, though it be common

---

18   New Testament, 1 Timothy 6.17.
19   I.e., drink.
20   I.e., conveniences.

in respect of some men, it is not so to all mankind, but is the joint propriety[21] of this country, or this parish. Besides, the remainder, after such enclosure, would not be as good to the rest of the commoners as the whole was, when they could all make use of the whole; whereas in the beginning and first peopling of the great common of the world it was quite otherwise. The law man was under was rather for appropriating. God commanded, and his wants forced him to labor. That was his property, which could not be taken from him wherever he had fixed it. And hence subduing or cultivating the earth and having dominion, we see, are joined together. The one gave title to the other. So that God, by commanding to subdue, gave authority so far to appropriate. And the condition of human life, which requires labor and materials to work on, necessarily introduces private possessions.

36　The measure of property Nature well set by the extent of men's labor and the conveniency of life. No man's labor could subdue or appropriate all, nor could his enjoyment consume more than a small part; so that it was impossible for any man, this way, to entrench upon the right of another or acquire to himself a property to the prejudice of his neighbor, who would still have room for as good and as large a possession (after the other had taken out his) as before it was appropriated. Which measure did confine every man's possession to a very moderate proportion, and such as he might appropriate to himself without injury to anybody in the first ages of the world, when men were more in danger to be lost by wandering from their company, in the then vast wilderness of the earth than to be straitened for want of room to plant in. And the same measure may be allowed still, without prejudice to anybody, full as the world seems. For, supposing a man or family, in the state they were at first, peopling of the world by the children of Adam or Noah, let him plant in some inland vacant places of America. We shall find that the possessions he could make himself, upon the measures we have given, would not be very large, nor, even to this day, prejudice the rest of mankind or give them reason to complain or think themselves injured by this man's

encroachment, though the race of men have now spread themselves to all the corners of the world, and do infinitely exceed the small number [there] was at the beginning. Nay, the extent of ground is of so little value without labor that I have heard it affirmed that in Spain itself a man may be permitted to plough, sow, and reap, without being disturbed, upon land he has no other title to, but only his making use of it. But, on the contrary, the inhabitants think themselves beholden to him who, by his industry on neglected, and consequently waste land, has increased the stock of corn,[22] which they wanted. But be this as it will, which I lay no stress on, this I dare boldly affirm, that the same rule of propriety—viz., that every man should have as much as he could make use of, would hold still in the world, without straitening anybody, since there is land enough in the world to suffice double the inhabitants, had not the invention of money, and the tacit agreement of men to put a value on it, introduced (by consent) larger possessions and a right to them; which, how it has done, I shall by and by show more at large.

37　This is certain, that in the beginning, before the desire of having more than men needed had altered the intrinsic value of things, which depends only on their usefulness to the life of man, or had agreed that a little piece of yellow metal, which would keep without wasting or decay, should be worth a great piece of flesh or a whole heap of corn, though men had a right to appropriate by their labor, each one to himself, as much of the things of Nature as he could use, yet this could not be much, nor to the prejudice of others, where the same plenty was still left, to those who would use the same industry.

Before the appropriation of land, he who gathered as much of the wild fruit, killed, caught, or tamed as many of the beasts as he could—he that so employed his pains about any of the spontaneous products of Nature as any way to alter them from the state Nature put them in, by placing any of his labor on them, did thereby acquire a propriety in them; but if they perished in his possession without their due use—if the fruits rotted or the venison putrefied before he could

---

21　I.e., property.
22　I.e., grain.

spend it, he offended against the common law of Nature, and was liable to be punished: he invaded his neighbor's share, for he had no right farther than his use called for any of them, and they might serve to afford him conveniencies of life.

38 The same measures governed the possession of land, too. Whatsoever he tilled and reaped, laid up and made use of before it spoiled, that was his peculiar right; whatsoever he enclosed, and could feed and make use of, the cattle and product was also his. But if either the grass of his enclosure rotted on the ground, or the fruit of his planting perished without gathering and laying up, this part of the earth, notwithstanding his enclosure, was still to be looked on as waste, and might be the possession of any other. Thus, at the beginning, Cain might take as much ground as he could till and make it his own land, and yet leave enough to Abel's sheep to feed on:[23] a few acres would serve for both their possessions. But as families increased and industry enlarged their stocks, their possessions enlarged with the need of them; but yet it was commonly without any fixed property in the ground they made use of till they incorporated, settled themselves together, and built cities, and then, by consent, they came in time to set out the bounds of their distinct territories and agree on limits between them and their neighbors, and by laws within themselves settled the properties of those of the same society. For we see that in that part of the world which was first inhabited, and therefore like to be best peopled, even as low down as Abraham's time,[24] they wandered with their flocks and their herds, which was their substance, freely up and down—and this Abraham did in a country where he was a stranger; whence it is plain that, at least, a great part of the land lay in common, that the inhabitants valued it not, nor claimed property in any more than they made use of; but when there was not room enough in the same place for their herds to feed together, they, by consent, as Abraham and Lot did ([Old Testament] Genesis 13.5), separated and enlarged their pasture where it best liked them. And for the same reason, Esau went from his father and his brother, and planted in Mount Seir ([Old Testament] Genesis 36.6).

41 There cannot be a clearer demonstration of anything than several nations of the Americans are of this, who are rich in land and poor in all the comforts of life; whom Nature, having furnished as liberally as any other people with the materials of plenty—i.e., a fruitful soil, apt to produce in abundance what might serve for food, raiment, and delight; yet, for want of improving it by labor, have not one hundredth part of the conveniencies we enjoy, and a king of a large and fruitful territory there feeds, lodges, and is clad worse than a day laborer in England.

47 And thus [by agreeing to regard certain precious metals as a means of exchange] came into the use of money, some lasting thing that men might keep without spoiling, and that, by mutual consent, men would take in exchange for the truly useful but perishable supports of life.

48 And as different degrees of industry were apt to give men possessions in different proportions, so this invention of money gave them the opportunity to continue and enlarge them. For supposing an island, separate from all possible commerce with the rest of the world, wherein there were but a hundred families, but there were sheep, horses, and cows, with other useful animals, wholesome fruits, and land enough for corn for a hundred thousand times as many, but nothing in the island, either because of its commonness or perishableness, fit to supply the place of money. What reason could any one have there to enlarge his possessions beyond the use of his family, and a plentiful supply to its consumption, either in what their own industry produced, or they could barter for like perishable, useful commodities with others? Where there is not something both lasting and scarce, and so valuable to be hoarded up, there men will not be apt to enlarge their possessions of land, were it never so rich, never so free for them to take. For I ask, what would a man value ten thousand or an hundred thousand acres of excellent land, ready cultivated and well stocked, too, with cattle, in the middle of the inland

---

23 Cain and Abel were sons of Adam.
24 Abraham, the first Hebrew patriarch of the Old Testament.

parts of America, where he had no hopes of commerce with other parts of the world, to draw money to him by the sale of the product? It would not be worth the enclosing, and we should see him give up again to the wild common of Nature whatever was more than would supply the conveniencies of life, to be had there for him and his family.

49   Thus, in the beginning, all the world was America, and more so than that is now; for no such thing as money was anywhere known. Find out something that hath the use and value of money amongst his neighbors, you shall see the same man will begin presently to enlarge his possessions.

50   But since gold and silver, being little useful to the life of man, in proportion to food, raiment, and carriage, has its value only from the consent of men—whereof labor yet makes in great part the measure—it is plain that the consent of men have agreed to a disproportionate and unequal possession of the earth—I mean out of the bounds of society and compact; for in governments the laws regulate it; they having, by consent, found out and agreed in a way how a man may, rightfully and without injury, possess more than he himself can make use of by receiving gold and silver, which may continue long in a man's possession without decaying for the overplus, and agreeing those metals should have a value.

CHAPTER 6

OF PATERNAL POWER

52   It may perhaps be censured as an impertinent criticism in a discourse of this nature to find fault with words and names that have obtained in the world. And yet possibly it may not be amiss to offer new ones when the old are apt to lead men into mistakes, as this of paternal power probably has done, which seems so to place the power of parents over their children wholly in the father, as if the mother had no share in it; whereas if we consult reason or revelation, we shall find she has an equal title, which may give one reason to ask whether this might not be more properly called parental power? For whatever obligation Nature and the right of generation lays on children, it must certainly bind them equal to both the concurrent causes of it. And accordingly we see the positive law of God everywhere joins them together without distinction, when it commands the obedience of children: "Honor thy father and thy mother" ([Old Testament] Exodus 20.12); "Whosoever curseth his father or his mother" ([Old Testament] Leviticus 20.9); "Ye shall fear every man his mother and his father" (Leviticus 19.3); "Children, obey your parents "([New Testament] Ephesians 6.1), etc., is the style of the Old and New Testament.

53   Had but this one thing been well considered without looking any deeper into the matter, it might perhaps have kept men from running into those gross mistakes they have made about this power of parents, which however it might without any great harshness bear the name of absolute dominion and regal authority, when under the title of "paternal" power, it seemed appropriated to the father, would yet have sounded but oddly, and in the very name shown the absurdity, if this supposed absolute power over children had been called parental, and thereby discovered that it belonged to the mother too. For it will but very ill serve the turn of those men who contend so much for the absolute power and authority of the father-hood, as they call it, that the mother should have any share in it. And it would have but ill supported the monarchy they contend for, when by the very name it appeared that that fundamental authority from whence they would derive their government of a single person only was not placed in one, but two persons jointly. But to let this of names pass.

54   Though I have said above (Chapter 2) "That all men by nature are equal," I cannot be supposed to understand all sorts of "equality." Age or virtue may give men a just precedency. Excellency of parts and merit may place others above the common level. Birth may subject some, and alliance or benefits others, to pay an observance to those to whom Nature, gratitude, or other respects, may have made it due; and yet all this consists with the equality which all men are in in respect of jurisdiction or dominion one over another, which was the equality I there spoke of as proper to the business in hand, being that equal right that every man hath to his natural freedom, without being subjected to the will or authority of any other man.

55   Children, I confess, are not born in this full state of equality, though they are born to it. Their parents have a sort of rule and jurisdiction over them when

they come into the world, and for some time after, but it is but a temporary one. The bonds of this subjection are like the swaddling clothes they are wrapt up in and supported by in the weakness of their infancy. Age and reason as they grow up loosen them, till at length they drop quite off, and leave a man at his own free disposal.

56 Adam was created a perfect man, his body and mind in full possession of their strength and reason, and so was capable from the first instance of his being to provide for his own support and preservation, and govern his actions according to the dictates of the law of reason God had implanted in him. From him the world is peopled with his descendants, who are all born infants, weak and helpless, without knowledge or understanding. But to supply the defects of this imperfect state till the improvement of growth and age had removed them, Adam and Eve, and after them all parents were, by the law of Nature, under an obligation to preserve, nourish and educate the children they had begotten, not as their own workmanship, but the workmanship of their own Maker, the Almighty, to whom they were to be accountable for them.

57 The law that was to govern Adam was the same that was to govern all his posterity, the law of reason. But his offspring having another way of entrance into the world, different from him, by a natural birth, that produced them ignorant, and without the use of reason, they were not presently under that law. For nobody can be under a law that is not promulgated to him; and this law being promulgated or made known by reason only, he that is not come to the use of his reason cannot be said to be under this law; and Adam's children being not presently as soon as born under this law of reason, were not presently free. For law, in its true notion, is not so much the limitation as the direction of a free and intelligent agent to his proper interest, and prescribes no farther than is for the general good of those under that law. Could they be happier without it, the law, as a useless thing, would of itself vanish; and that ill deserves the name of confinement which hedges us in only from bogs and precipices. So that however it may be mistaken, the end of law is not to abolish or restrain, but to preserve and enlarge freedom. For in all the states of created

beings, capable of laws, where there is no law there is no freedom. For liberty is to be free from restraint and violence from others, which cannot be where there is no law, and is not, as we are told, "a liberty for every man to do what he lists." For who could be free, when every other man's humor might domineer over him? But a liberty to dispose and order freely as he lists his person, actions, possessions, and his whole property within the allowance of those laws under which he is, and therein not to be subject to the arbitrary will of another, but freely follow his own.

58 The power, then, that parents have over their children arises from that duty which is incumbent on them, to take care of their offspring during the imperfect state of childhood. To inform the mind, and govern the actions of their yet ignorant nonage, till reason shall take its place and ease them of that trouble, is what the children want, and the parents are bound to. For God having given man an understanding to direct his actions, has allowed him a freedom of will and liberty of acting, as properly belonging thereunto within the bounds of that law he is under. But whilst he is in an estate wherein he has no understanding of his own to direct his will, he is not to have any will of his own to follow. He that understands for him must will for him too; he must prescribe to his will, and regulate his actions, but when he comes to the estate that made his father a free man, the son is a free man too.

59 This holds in all the laws a man is under, whether natural or civil. Is a man under the law of Nature? What made him free of that law? What gave him a free disposing of his property, according to his own will, within the compass of that law? I answer, an estate wherein he might be supposed capable to know that law, that so he might keep his actions within the bounds of it. When he has acquired that state, he is presumed to know how far that law is to be his guide, and how far he may make use of his freedom, and so comes to have it; till then, somebody else must guide him, who is presumed to know how far the law allows a liberty. If such a state of reason, such an age of discretion made him free, the same shall make his son free too. Is a man under the law of England? What made him free of that law—that is, to have the liberty to dispose of his actions and possessions, according to his own will, within the permission of that law? A

capacity of knowing that law; which is supposed, by that law, at the age of twenty-one, and in some cases sooner. If this made the father free, it shall make the son free too. Till then, we see the law allows the son to have no will, but he is to be guided by the will of his father or guardian, who is to understand for him. And if the father die and fail to substitute a deputy in this trust, if he hath not provided a tutor to govern his son during his minority, during his want of understanding, the law takes care to do it: some other must govern him and be a will to him till he hath attained to a state of freedom, and his understanding be fit to take the government of his will. But after that the father and son are equally free, as much as tutor and pupil, after nonage, equally subjects of the same law together, without any dominion left in the father over the life, liberty, or estate of his son, whether they be only in the state and under the law of Nature, or under the positive laws of an established government.

60   But if through defects that may happen out of the ordinary course of Nature any one comes not to such a degree of reason wherein he might be supposed capable of knowing the law, and so living within the rules of it, he is never capable of being a free man, he is never let loose to the disposure[25] of his own will; because he knows no bounds to it, has not understanding, its proper guide, but is continued under the tuition and government of others all the time his own understanding is incapable of that charge. And so lunatics and idiots are never set free from the government of their parents: "Children who are not as yet come unto those years whereat they may have, and innocents, which are excluded by a natural defect from ever having"; thirdly, "madmen, which, for the present, cannot possibly have the use of right reason to guide themselves, have, for their guide, the reason that guideth other men which are tutors over them, to seek and procure their good for them," says Hooker (*Ecclesiastical Polity* lib. i, section 7). All which seems no more than that duty which God and Nature has laid on man, as well as other creatures, to preserve their offspring till they can be able to shift for themselves, and will scarce

amount to an instance or proof of parents' regal authority.

61   Thus we are born free as we are born rational; not that we have actually the exercise of either: age that brings one, brings with it the other too. And thus we see how natural freedom and subjection to parents may consist together, and are both founded on the same principle. A child is free by his father's title, by his father's understanding, which is to govern him till he hath it of his own. The freedom of a man at years of discretion, and the subjection of a child to his parents, whilst yet short of it, are so consistent and so distinguishable that the most blinded contenders for monarchy, "by right of fatherhood," cannot miss of it; the most obstinate cannot but allow of it. For were their doctrine all true, were the right heir of Adam now known, and, by that title, settled a monarch in his throne, invested with all the absolute unlimited power Sir Robert Filmer talks of, if he should die as soon as his heir were born, must not the child, notwithstanding he were never so free, never so much sovereign, be in subjection to his mother and nurse, to tutors and governors, till age and education brought him reason and ability to govern himself and others? The necessities of his life, the health of his body, and the information of his mind would require him to be directed by the will of others and not his own; and yet will any one think that this restraint and subjection were inconsistent with, or spoiled him of, that liberty or sovereignty he had a right to, or gave away his empire to those who had the government of his nonage? This government over him only prepared him the better and sooner for it. If anybody should ask me when my son is of age to be free, I shall answer, just when his monarch is of age to govern. "But at what time," says the judicious Hooker (*Ecclesiastical Polity*, lib. i, section 6), "a man may be said to have attained so far forth the use of reason as sufficeth to make him capable of those laws whereby he is then bound to guide his actions; this is a great deal more easy for sense to discern than for any one, by skill and learning, to determine."

64   But what reason can hence advance this care of the parents due to their offspring into an absolute,

---

25   I.e., disposal.

arbitrary dominion of the father, whose power reaches no farther than by such a discipline as he finds most effectual to give such strength and health to their bodies, such vigor and rectitude to their minds, as may best fit his children to be most useful to themselves and others, and, if it be necessary to his condition, to make them work when they are able for their own subsistence; but in this power the mother, too, has her share with the father.

65   Nay, this power so little belongs to the father by any peculiar right of Nature, but only as he is guardian of his children, that when he quits his care of them he loses his power over them, which goes along with their nourishment and education, to which it is inseparably annexed, and belongs as much to the foster-father of an exposed child as to the natural father of another. So little power does the bare act of begetting give a man over his issue, if all his care ends there, and this be all the title he hath to the name and authority of a father. And what will become of this paternal power in that part of the world where one woman hath more than one husband at a time? Or in those parts of America where, when the husband and wife part, which happens frequently, the children are all left to the mother, follow her, and are wholly under her care and provision? And if the father die whilst the children are young, do they not naturally everywhere owe the same obedience to their mother, during their minority, as to their father, were he alive? And will any one say that the mother hath a legislative power over her children that she can make standing rules which shall be of perpetual obligation, by which they ought to regulate all the concerns of their property, and bound their liberty all the course of their lives, and enforce the observation of them with capital punishments? For this is the proper power of the magistrate, of which the father hath not so much as the shadow. His command over his children is but temporary, and reaches not their life or property. It is but a help to the weakness and imperfection of their nonage, a discipline necessary to their education. And though a father may dispose of his own possessions as he pleases when his children are out of danger of perishing for want, yet his power extends not to the lives or goods which either their own industry, or another's bounty, has made theirs, nor to their liberty neither, when they are once arrived to the enfranchisement of the years of discretion. The father's empire then ceases, and he can from thenceforward no more dispose of the liberty of his son than that of any other man. And it must be far from an absolute or perpetual jurisdiction from which a man may withdraw himself, having license from Divine authority to "leave father and mother and cleave to his wife."[26]

71   This shows the reason how it comes to pass that parents in societies, where they themselves are subjects, retain a power over their children and have as much right to their subjection as those who are in the state of Nature, which could not possibly be if all political power were only paternal, and that, in truth, they were one and the same thing; for then, all paternal power being in the prince, the subject could naturally have none of it. But these two powers, political and paternal, are so perfectly distinct and separate, and built upon so different foundations, and given to so different ends, that every subject that is a father has as much a paternal power over his children as the prince has over his. And every prince that has parents owes them as much filial duty and obedience as the meanest of his subjects do to theirs, and can therefore contain not any part or degree of that kind of dominion which a prince or magistrate has over his subject.

## CHAPTER 7
### OF POLITICAL OR CIVIL SOCIETY

77   God, having made man such a creature that, in His own judgment, it was not good for him to be alone, put him under strong obligations of necessity, convenience, and inclination, to drive him into society, as well as fitted him with understanding and language to continue and enjoy it. The first society was between man and wife, which gave beginning to that between parents and children, to which, in time, that between master and servant came to be added. And though all these might, and commonly did, meet

---

26   Old Testament, Genesis 2.24.

together, and make up but one family, wherein the master or mistress of it had some sort of rule proper to a family, each of these, or all together, came short of "political society," as we shall see if we consider the different ends, ties, and bounds of each of these.

78   Conjugal society is made by a voluntary compact between man and woman, and though it consist chiefly in such a communion and right in one another's bodies as is necessary to its chief end, procreation, yet it draws with it mutual support and assistance, and a communion of interests too, as necessary not only to unite their care and affection, but also necessary to their common offspring, who have a right to be nourished and maintained by them till they are able to provide for themselves.

79   For the end of conjunction between male and female being not barely procreation, but the continuation of the species, this conjunction betwixt male and female ought to last, even after procreation, so long as is necessary to the nourishment and support of the young ones, who are to be sustained by those that got them till they are able to shift and provide for themselves. This rule, which the infinite wise Maker hath set to the works of his hands, we find the inferior creatures steadily obey. In those vivaporous animals which feed on grass the conjunction between male and female lasts no longer than the very act of copulation, because the teat of the dam being sufficient to nourish the young till it be able to feed on grass, the male only begets, but concerns not himself for the female or young, to whose sustenance he can contribute nothing. But in beasts of prey the conjunction lasts longer, because the dam, not being able well to subsist herself and nourish her numerous offspring by her own prey alone (a more laborious as well as more dangerous way of living than by feeding on grass), the assistance of the male is necessary to the maintenance of their common family, which cannot subsist till they are able to prey for themselves, but by the joint care of male and female. The same is observed in all birds (except some domestic ones, where plenty of food excuses the cock from feeding and taking care of the young brood), whose young, needing food in the nest, the cock and hen continue mates till the young are able to use their wings and provide for themselves.

80   And herein, I think, lies the chief, if not the only reason, why the male and female in mankind are tied to a longer conjunction than other creatures—viz., because the female is capable of conceiving, and, *de facto*, is commonly with child again, and brings forth too a new birth, long before the former is out of a dependency for support on his parents' help and able to shift for himself, and has all the assistance due to him from his parents, whereby the father, who is bound to take care for those he hath begot, is under an obligation to continue in conjugal society with the same woman longer than other creatures, whose young, being able to subsist of themselves before the time of procreation returns again, the conjugal bond dissolves of itself, and they are at liberty till Hymen,[27] at his usual anniversary season, summons them again to choose new mates. Wherein one cannot but admire the wisdom of the great Creator, who, having given to man an ability to lay up for the future as well as supply the present necessity, hath made it necessary that society of man and wife should be more lasting than of male and female amongst other creatures, that so their industry might be encouraged, and their interest better united, to make provision and lay up goods for their common issue, which uncertain mixture, or easy and frequent solutions[28] of conjugal society would mightily disturb.

81   But though these are ties upon mankind which make the conjugal bonds more firm and lasting in man than the other species of animals, yet it would give one reason to inquire why this compact, where procreation and education are secured and inheritance taken care for, may not be made determinable,[29] either by consent, or at a certain time, or upon certain conditions, as well as any other voluntary compacts, there being no necessity, in the nature of the thing, nor to the ends of it, that it should always be for life—I mean, to such as are under no restraint of any positive law which ordains all such contracts to be perpetual.

27   The Greek god of marriage.
28   I.e., dissolutions.
29   I.e., able to be brought to an end.

82 But the husband and wife, though they have but one common concern, yet having different understandings, will unavoidably sometimes have different wills too. It therefore being necessary that the last determination (i.e., the rule) should be placed somewhere, it naturally falls to the man's share as the abler and the stronger. But this, reaching but to the things of their common interest and property, leaves the wife in the full and true possession of what by contract is her peculiar right, and at least gives the husband no more power over her than she has over his life; the power of the husband being so far from that of an absolute monarch that the wife has, in many cases, a liberty to separate from him where natural right or their contract allows it, whether that contract be made by themselves in the state of Nature or by the customs or laws of the country they live in, and the children, upon such separation, fall to the father or mother's lot as such contract does determine.

83 For all the ends of marriage being to be obtained under politic government, as well as in the state of Nature, the civil magistrate doth not abridge the right or power of either, naturally necessary to those ends—viz., procreation and mutual support and assistance whilst they are together, but only decides any controversy that may arise between man and wife about them. If it were otherwise, and that absolute sovereignty and power of life and death naturally belonged to the husband, and were necessary to the society between man and wife, there could be no matrimony in any of these countries where the husband is allowed no such absolute authority. But the ends of matrimony requiring no such power in the husband, it was not at all necessary to it. The condition of conjugal society put it not in him; but whatsoever might consist with procreation and support of the children till they could shift for themselves—mutual assistance, comfort, and maintenance—might be varied and regulated by that contract which first united them in that society, nothing being necessary to any society that is not necessary to the ends for which it is made.

84 The society betwixt parents and children, and the distinct rights and powers belonging respectively to them, I have treated of so largely in the foregoing chapter that I shall not here need to say anything of it; and I think it is plain that it is far different from a politic society.

85 Master and servant are names as old as history, but given to those of far different condition; for a free man makes himself a servant to another by selling him for a certain time the service he undertakes to do in exchange for wages he is to receive; and though this commonly puts him into the family of his master, and under the ordinary discipline thereof, yet it gives the master but a temporary power over him, and no greater than what is contained in the contract between them. But there is another sort of servant which by a peculiar name we call slaves, who being captives taken in a just war are, by the right of Nature, subjected to the absolute dominion and arbitrary power of their masters. These men having, as I say, forfeited their lives and, with it, their liberties, and lost their estates, and being in the state of slavery, not capable of any property, cannot in that state be considered as any part of civil society, the chief end whereof is the preservation of property.

86 Let us therefore consider a master of a family with all these subordinate relations of wife, children, servants and slaves, united under the domestic rule of a family, with what resemblance soever it may have in its order, offices, and number too, with a little commonwealth, yet is very far from it both in its constitution, power, and end; or if it must be thought a monarchy, and the paterfamilias[30] the absolute monarch in it, absolute monarchy will have but a very shattered and short power, when it is plain by what has been said before, that the master of the family has a very distinct and differently limited power both as to time and extent over those several persons that are in it; for excepting the slave (and the family is as much a family, and his power as paterfamilias as great, whether there be any slaves in his family or no) he has no legislative power of life and death over any of them, and

---

30 Latin: male head of household.

SOURCES • VOLUME I

none too but what a mistress of a family may have as well as he. And he certainly can have no absolute power over the whole family who has but a very limited one over every individual in it. But how a family, or any other society of men, differ from that which is properly political society, we shall best see by considering wherein political society itself consists.

87　Man being born, as has been proved, with a title to perfect freedom and an uncontrolled enjoyment of all the rights and privileges of the law of Nature, equally with any other man, or number of men in the world, hath by nature a power not only to preserve his property—that is, his life, liberty, and estate, against the injuries and attempts of other men, but to judge of and punish the breaches of that law in others, as he is persuaded the offense deserves, even with death itself, in crimes where the heinousness of the fact, in his opinion, requires it. But because no political society can be, nor subsist, without having in itself the power to preserve the property, and in order thereunto punish the offenses of all those of that society, there, and there only, is political society where every one of the members hath quitted this natural power, resigned it up into the hands of the community in all cases that exclude him not from appealing for protection to the law established by it. And thus all private judgment of every particular member being excluded, the community comes to be umpire, and by understanding indifferent[31] rules and men authorized by the community for their execution, decides all the differences that may happen between any members of that society concerning any matter of right, and punishes those offenses which any member hath committed against the society with such penalties as the law has established; whereby it is easy to discern who are, and are not, in political society together. Those who are united into one body, and have a common established law and judicature to appeal to, with authority to decide controversies between them and punish offenders, are in civil society one with another; but those who have no such common appeal, I mean on earth, are still in the state of Nature, each being, where there is no other, judge

for himself and executioner, which is, as I have before showed it, the perfect state of Nature.

88　And thus the commonwealth comes by a power to set down what punishment shall belong to the several transgressions they think worthy of it, committed amongst the members of that society (which is the power of making laws), as well as it has the power to punish any injury done unto any of its members by any one that is not of it (which is the power of war and peace); and all this for the preservation of the property of all the members of that society, as far as is possible. But though every man entered into society has quitted his power to punish offenses against the law of Nature in prosecution of his own private judgment, yet with the judgment of offenses which he has given up to the legislative, in all cases where he can appeal to the magistrate, he has given up a right to the commonwealth to employ his force for the execution of the judgments of the commonwealth whenever he shall be called to it, which, indeed, are his own judgments, they being made by himself or his representative. And herein we have the original of the legislative and executive power of civil society, which is to judge by standing laws how far offenses are to be punished when committed within the commonwealth; and also by occasional judgments founded on the present circumstances of the fact, how far injuries from without are to be vindicated, and in both these to employ all the force of all the members when there shall be need.

89　Wherever, therefore, any number of men so unite into one society as to quit every one his executive power of the law of Nature, and to resign it to the public, there and there only is a political or civil society. And this is done wherever any number of men, in the state of Nature, enter into society to make one people one body politic under one supreme government, or else when any one joins himself to and incorporates with any government already made. For hereby he authorizes the society, or which is all one, the legislative thereof, to make laws for him as the public good of the society shall require, to the execution whereof his own assistance (as to his own decrees) is due. And

---

31　I.e., impartial.

this puts men out of a state of Nature into that of a commonwealth, by setting up a judge on earth with authority to determine all the controversies and redress the injuries that may happen to any member of the commonwealth, which judge is the legislative or magistrates appointed by it. And wherever there are any number of men, however associated, that have no such decisive power to appeal to, there they are still in the state of Nature.

90    And hence it is evident that absolute monarchy, which by some men is counted for the only government in the world, is indeed inconsistent with civil society, and so can be no form of civil government at all, for the end of civil society being to avoid and remedy those inconveniencies of the state of Nature which necessarily follow from every man's being judge in his own case, by setting up a known authority to which every one of that society may appeal upon any injury received, or controversy that may arise, and which every one of the society ought to obey. Wherever any persons are who have not such an authority to appeal to, and decide any difference between them there, those persons are still in the state of Nature. And so is every absolute prince in respect of those who are under his dominion.

91    For he being supposed to have all, both legislative and executive, power in himself alone, there is no judge to be found, no appeal lies open to any one, who may fairly and indifferently, and with authority decide, and from whence relief and redress may be expected of any injury or inconveniency that may be suffered from him, or by his order. So that such a man, however entitled, Czar,[32] or Grand Signior,[33] or how you please, is as much in the state of Nature, with all under his dominion, as he is with the rest of mankind. For wherever any two men are who have no standing rule and common judge to appeal to on earth, for the determination of controversies of right betwixt them, there they are still in the state of Nature, and under all the inconveniencies of it, with only this woeful difference to the subject, or rather slave of an absolute prince: that whereas, in the ordinary state of Nature,

he has a liberty to judge of his right, according to the best of his power to maintain it; but whenever his property is invaded by the will and order of his monarch, he has not only no appeal, as those in society ought to have, but, as if he were degraded from the common state of rational creatures, is denied a liberty to judge of, or defend his right, and so is exposed to all the misery and inconveniencies that a man can fear from one, who being in the unrestrained state of Nature, is yet corrupted with flattery and armed with power.

92    For he that thinks absolute power purifies men's blood, and corrects the baseness of human nature, need read but the history of this, or any other age, to be convinced to the contrary. He that would have been insolent and injurious in the woods of America would not probably be much better on a throne, where perhaps learning and religion shall be found out to justify all that he shall do to his subjects, and the sword presently silence all those that dare question it. For what the protection of absolute monarchy is, what kind of fathers of their countries it makes princes to be, and to what a degree of happiness and security it carries civil society, where this sort of government is grown to perfection, he that will look into the late relation of Ceylon[34] may easily see.

93    In absolute monarchies, indeed, as well as other governments of the world, the subjects have an appeal to the law, and judges to decide any controversies, and restrain any violence that may happen betwixt the subjects themselves, one amongst another. This every one thinks necessary, and believes; he deserves to be thought a declared enemy to society and mankind who should go about to take it away. But whether this be from a true love of mankind and society, and such a charity as we owe all one to another, there is reason to doubt. For this is no more than what every man, who loves his own power, profit, or greatness, may, and naturally must do—keep those animals from hurting or destroying one another who labor and drudge only for his pleasure and advantage; and so are taken care of, not out of any love the master has for

---

32   The title of Russia's emperor.
33   "Great Lord."
34   A reference to a book of 1680 concerning that island (now called Sri Lanka) off the coast of India.

them, but love of himself, and the profit they bring him. For if it be asked what security, what fence is there in such a state against the violence and oppression of this absolute ruler, the very question can scarce be borne. They are ready to tell you that it deserves death only to ask after safety. Betwixt subject and subject, they will grant, there must be measures, laws, and judges for their mutual peace and security. But as for the ruler, he ought to be absolute, and is above all such circumstances; because he has a power to do more hurt and wrong, it is right when he does it. To ask how you may be guarded from harm or injury on that side, where the strongest hand is to do it, is presently the voice of faction and rebellion. As if when men, quitting the state of Nature, entered into society, they agreed that all of them but one should be under the restraint of laws; but that he should still retain all the liberty of the state of Nature, increased with power, and made licentious by impunity. This is to think that men are so foolish that they take care to avoid what mischiefs may be done them by polecats or foxes, but are content, nay, think it safety, to be devoured by lions.

### CHAPTER 8

OF THE BEGINNING OF POLITICAL SOCIETIES

95   Men being, as has been said, by nature all free, equal, and independent, no one can be put out of this estate and subjected to the political power of another without his own consent, which is done by agreeing with other men, to join and unite into a community for their comfortable, safe, and peaceable living, one amongst another, in a secure enjoyment of their properties, and a greater security against any that are not of it. This any number of men may do, because it injures not the freedom of the rest; they are left, as they were, in the liberty of the state of Nature. When any number of men have so consented to make one community or government, they are thereby presently incorporated, and make one body politic, wherein the majority have a right to act and conclude the rest.

96   For, when any number of men have, by the consent of every individual, made a community, they have thereby made that community one body, with a power to act as one body, which is only by the will and determination of the majority. For that which acts [as] any community, being only the consent of the individuals of it, and it being one body, must move one way, it is necessary the body should move that way whither the greater force carries it, which is the consent of the majority, or else it is impossible it should act or continue [as] one body, one community, which the consent of every individual that united into it agreed that it should; and so every one is bound by that consent to be concluded by the majority. And therefore we see that in assemblies empowered to act by positive laws where no number is set by that positive law which empowers them, the act of the majority passes for the act of the whole, and of course determines as having, by the law of Nature and reason, the power of the whole.

97   And thus every man, by consenting with others to make one body politic under one government, puts himself under an obligation to every one of that society to submit to the determination of the majority, and to be concluded by it; or else this original compact, whereby he with others incorporates into one society, would signify nothing, and be no compact if he be left free and under no other ties than he was in before in the state of Nature. For what appearance would there be of any compact? What new engagement if he were no farther tied by any decrees of the society than he himself thought fit and did actually consent to? This would be still as great a liberty as he himself had before his compact, or any one else in the state of Nature, who may submit himself and consent to any acts of it if he thinks fit.

98   For if the consent of the majority shall not in reason be received as the act of the whole, and conclude every individual, nothing but the consent of every individual can make anything to be the act of the whole, which, considering the infirmities of health and avocations of business, which in a number though much less than that of a commonwealth, will necessarily keep many away from the public assembly; and the variety of opinions and contrariety of interests which unavoidably happen in all collections of men, it is next impossible ever to be had. And, therefore, if coming into society be upon such terms, it will be only

like Cato's coming into the theater, *tantum ut exiret*.[35] Such a constitution as this would make the mighty leviathan[36] of a shorter duration than the feeblest creatures, and not let it outlast the day it was born in, which cannot be supposed till we can think that rational creatures should desire and constitute societies only to be dissolved. For where the majority cannot conclude the rest, there they cannot act as one body, and consequently will be immediately dissolved again.

99 Whosoever, therefore, out of a state of Nature unite into a community, must be understood to give up all the power necessary to the ends for which they unite into society to the majority of the community, unless they expressly agreed in any number greater than the majority. And this is done by barely agreeing to unite into one political society, which is all the compact that is, or needs be, between the individuals that enter into or make up a commonwealth. And thus, that which begins and actually constitutes any political society is nothing but the consent of any number of freemen capable of majority, to unite and incorporate into such a society. And this is that, and that only, which did or could give beginning to any lawful government in the world.

100 To this I find two objections made: 1. That there are no instances to be found in story[37] of a company of men, independent and equal one amongst another, that met together, and in this way began and set up a government. 2. It is impossible of right that men should do so, because all men, being born under government, they are to submit to that, and are not at liberty to begin a new one.

101 To the first there is this to answer: that it is not at all to be wondered that history gives us but a very little account of men that lived together in the state of Nature. The inconveniencies of that condition, and the love and want of society, no sooner brought any number of them together, but they presently united and incorporated if they designed to continue together. And if we may not suppose men ever to have been in the state of Nature, because we hear not much of them in such a state, we may as well suppose the armies of Salmanasser[38] or Xerxes[39] were never children, because we hear little of them till they were men and embodied in armies. Government is everywhere antecedent to records, and letters seldom come in amongst a people till a long continuation of civil society has, by other more necessary arts, provided for their safety, ease, and plenty. And then they begin to look after the history of their founders, and search into their original when they have outlived the memory of it. For it is with commonwealths as with particular persons, they are commonly ignorant of their own births and infancies; and if they know anything of it, they are beholden for it to the accidental records that others have kept of it. And those that we have of the beginning of any polities in the world, excepting that of the Jews, where God Himself immediately interposed, and which favors not at all paternal dominion, are all either plain instances of such a beginning as I have mentioned, or at least have manifest footsteps of it.

102 He must show a strange inclination to deny evident matter of fact, when it agrees not with his hypothesis, who will not allow that the beginning of Rome and Venice were by the uniting together of several men, free and independent one of another, amongst whom there was no natural superiority or subjection. And if Josephus Acosta's word may be taken,[40] he tells us that in many parts of America there was no government at all. "There are great and apparent conjectures," says he, "that these men," speaking of those of Peru, "for a long time had neither kings nor

---

35 Latin: "that he might leave it." The reference is to Cato the elder (234-139 BC), the Roman senator who was known as a strict moralist. The Romans regarded the stage as disreputable.
36 A great beast mentioned in the Old Testament, Isaiah 27.1.
37 I.e., history.
38 Assyrian king and conqueror discussed in the Old Testament (2 Kings 17).
39 Persian king of the fifth century BC; the Persian army with which he invaded Greece was famously large.
40 I.e., José de Acosta, sixteenth-century Spanish missionary to Latin America and author of *Historia Natural y Moral de las Indias*.

commonwealths, but lived in troops, as they do this day in Florida—the Cheriquanas, those of Brazil, and many other nations, which have no certain kings, but, as occasion is offered in peace or war, they choose their captains as they please" (lib. i. cap. 25). If it be said, that every man there was born subject to his father, or the head of his family, that the subjection due from a child to a father took not away his freedom of uniting into what political society he thought fit, has been already proved; but be that as it will, these men, it is evident, were actually free; and whatever superiority some politicians now would place in any of them, they themselves claimed it not; but, by consent, were all equal, till, by the same consent, they set rulers over themselves. So that their politic societies all began from a voluntary union, and the mutual agreement of men freely acting in the choice of their governors and forms of government.

CHAPTER 9
OF THE END OF POLITICAL SOCIETY AND GOVERNMENT

123   If man in the state of Nature be so free as has been said, if he be absolute lord of his own person and possessions, equal to the greatest and subject to nobody, why will he part with his freedom, this empire, and subject himself to the dominion and control of any other power? To which it is obvious to answer, that though in the state of Nature he hath such a right, yet the enjoyment of it is very uncertain and constantly exposed to the invasion of others; for all being kings as much as he, every man his equal, and the greater part no strict observers of equity and justice, the enjoyment of the property he has in this state is very unsafe, very insecure. This makes him willing to quit this condition which, however free, is full of fears and continual dangers; and it is not without reason that he seeks out and is willing to join in society with others who are already united, or have a mind to unite for the mutual preservation of their lives, liberties and estates, which I call by the general name—property.

124   The great and chief end, therefore, of men uniting into commonwealths, and putting themselves under government, is the preservation of their property; to which in the state of Nature there are many things wanting.

Firstly, there wants an established, settled, known law, received and allowed by common consent to be the standard of right and wrong, and the common measure to decide all controversies between them. For though the law of Nature be plain and intelligible to all rational creatures, yet men, being biased by their interest, as well as ignorant for want of study of it, are not apt to allow of it as a law binding to them in the application of it to their particular cases.

125   Secondly, in the state of Nature there wants a known and indifferent judge, with authority to determine all differences according to the established law. For every one in that state being both judge and executioner of the law of Nature, men being partial to themselves, passion and revenge is very apt to carry them too far, and with too much heat in their own cases, as well as negligence and unconcernedness, make them too remiss in other men's.

126   Thirdly, in the state of Nature there often wants power to back and support the sentence when right, and to give it due execution. They who by any injustice offended will seldom fail where they are able by force to make good their injustice. Such resistance many times makes the punishment dangerous, and frequently destructive to those who attempt it.

127   Thus mankind, notwithstanding all the privileges of the state of Nature, being but in an ill condition while they remain in it are quickly driven into society. Hence it comes to pass, that we seldom find any number of men live any time together in this state. The inconveniencies that they are therein exposed to by the irregular and uncertain exercise of the power every man has of punishing the transgressions of others, make them take sanctuary under the established laws of government, and therein seek the preservation of their property. It is this makes them so willingly give up every one his single power of punishing to be exercised by such alone as shall be appointed to it amongst them, and by such rules as the community, or those authorized by them to that purpose, shall agree on. And in this we have the original right and rise of both the legislative and executive power as well as of the governments and societies themselves.

128   For in the state of Nature to omit the liberty he has of innocent delights, a man has two powers. The

first is to do whatsoever he thinks fit for the preservation of himself and others within the permission of the law of Nature; by which law, common to them all, he and all the rest of mankind are one community, make up one society distinct from all other creatures, and were it not for the corruption and viciousness of degenerate men, there would be no need of any other, no necessity that men should separate from this great and natural community, and associate into lesser combinations. The other power a man has in the state of Nature is the power to punish the crimes committed against that law. Both these he gives up when he joins in a private, if I may so call it, or particular political society, and incorporates into any commonwealth separate from the rest of mankind.

129   The first power—viz., of doing whatsoever he thought fit for the preservation of himself and the rest of mankind, he gives up to be regulated by laws made by the society, so far forth as the preservation of himself and the rest of that society shall require; which laws of the society in many things confine the liberty he had by the law of Nature.

130   Secondly, the power of punishing he wholly gives up, and engages his natural force, which he might before employ in the execution of the law of Nature, by his own single authority, as he thought fit, to assist the executive power of the society as the law thereof shall require. For being now in a new state, wherein he is to enjoy many conveniencies from the labor, assistance, and society of others in the same community as well as protection from its whole strength, he is to part also with as much of his natural liberty, in providing for himself, as the good, prosperity, and safety of the society shall require, which is not only necessary but just, since the other members of the society do the like.

131   But though men when they enter into society give up the equality, liberty, and executive power they had in the state of Nature into the hands of the society, to be so far disposed of by the legislative as the good of the society shall require, yet it being only with an intention in every one the better to preserve himself, his liberty and property (for no rational creature can be supposed to change his condition with an intention to be worse), the power of the society or legislative constituted by them can never be supposed to extend farther than the common good, but is obliged to secure every one's property by providing against those three defects above mentioned that made the state of Nature so unsafe and uneasy. And so, whoever has the legislative or supreme power of any commonwealth, is bound to govern by established standing laws, promulgated and known to the people, and not by extemporary decrees, by indifferent and upright judges, who are to decide controversies by those laws; and to employ the force of the community at home only in the execution of such laws, or abroad to prevent or redress foreign injuries and secure the community from inroads and invasion. And all this to be directed to no other end but the peace, safety, and public good of the people.

CHAPTER 10

OF THE FORMS OF A COMMONWEALTH

132   The majority having, as has been showed, upon men's first uniting into society, the whole power of the community naturally in them, may employ all that power in making laws for the community from time to time, and executing those laws by officers of their own appointing, and then the form of the government is a perfect democracy; or else may put the power of making laws into the hands of a few select men, and their heirs or successors, and then it is an oligarchy; or else into the hands of one man, and then it is a monarchy; if to him and his heirs, it is a hereditary monarchy; if to him only for life, but upon his death the power only of nominating a successor, to return to them, an elective monarchy. And so accordingly of these the community make compounded and mixed forms of government, as they think good. And if the legislative power be at first given by the majority to one or more persons only for their lives, or any limited time, and then the supreme power to revert to them again, when it is so reverted the community may dispose of it again anew into what hands they please, and so constitute a new form of government; for the form of government depending upon the placing the supreme power, which is the legislative, it being impossible to conceive that an inferior power should prescribe to a superior, or any but the supreme make laws, according as the power of making laws is placed, such is the form of the commonwealth.

133   By "commonwealth" I must be understood all along to mean not a democracy, or any form of government, but any independent community which the Latins signified by the word *civitas*, to which the word which best answers in our language is "commonwealth," and most properly expresses such a society of men which "community" does not (for there may be subordinate communities in a government), and "city" much less. And therefore, to avoid ambiguity, I crave leave to use the word "commonwealth" in that sense, in which sense I find the word used by King James himself,[41] which I think to be its genuine signification, which, if anybody dislike, I consent with him to change it for a better.

CHAPTER 11

OF THE EXTENT OF THE LEGISLATIVE POWER

134   The great end of men's entering into society being the enjoyment of their properties in peace and safety, and the great instrument and means of that being the laws established in that society, the first and fundamental positive law of all commonwealths is the establishing of the legislative power, as the first and fundamental natural law which is to govern even the legislative itself is the preservation of the society and (as far as will consist with the public good) of every person in it. This legislative is not only the supreme power of the commonwealth, but sacred and unalterable in the hands where the community have once placed it. Nor can any edict of anybody else, in what form soever conceived, or by what power soever backed, have the force and obligation of a law which has not its sanction from that legislative which the public has chosen and appointed; for without this the law could not have that which is absolutely necessary to its being a law, the consent of the society, over whom nobody can have a power to make laws but by their own consent and by authority received from them; and therefore all the obedience, which by the most solemn ties any one can be obliged to pay, ultimately terminates in this supreme power, and is directed by those laws which it enacts. Nor can any

oaths to any foreign power whatsoever, or any domestic subordinate power, discharge any member of the society from his obedience to the legislative, acting pursuant to their trust, nor oblige him to any obedience contrary to the laws so enacted or farther than they do allow, it being ridiculous to imagine one can be tied ultimately to obey any power in the society which is not the supreme.

135   Though the legislative, whether placed in one or more, whether it be always in being or only by intervals, though it be the supreme power in every commonwealth, yet, first, it is not, nor can possibly be, absolutely arbitrary over the lives and fortunes of the people. For it being but the joint power of every member of the society given up to that person or assembly which is legislator, it can be no more than those persons had in a state of Nature before they entered into society, and gave it up to the community. For nobody can transfer to another more power than he has in himself, and nobody has an absolute arbitrary power over himself, or over any other, to destroy his own life, or take away the life or property of another. A man, as has been proved, cannot subject himself to the arbitrary power of another; and having, in the state of Nature, no arbitrary power over the life, liberty, or possession of another, but only so much as the law of Nature gave him for the preservation of himself and the rest of mankind, this is all he doth, or can give up to the commonwealth, and by it to the legislative power, so that the legislative can have no more than this. Their power in the utmost bounds of it is limited to the public good of the society. It is a power that hath no other end but preservation, and therefore can never have a right to destroy, enslave, or designedly to impoverish the subjects; the obligations of the law of Nature cease not in society, but only in many cases are drawn closer, and have, by human laws, known penalties annexed to them to enforce their observation. Thus the law of Nature stands as an eternal rule to all men, legislators as well as others. The rules that they make for other men's actions must, as well as their own and other men's actions, be conformable to the law of Nature—i.e., to the will of God, of which that is

---

a declaration, and the fundamental law of Nature being the preservation of mankind, no human sanction can be good or valid against it.

136 Secondly, the legislative or supreme authority cannot assume to itself a power to rule by extemporary arbitrary decrees, but is bound to dispense justice and decide the rights of the subject by promulgated standing laws, and known authorized judges. For the law of Nature being unwritten, and so nowhere to be found but in the minds of men, they who, through passion or interest, shall miscite or misapply it, cannot so easily be convinced of their mistake where there is no established judge; and so it serves not as it ought, to determine the rights and fence the properties of those that live under it, especially where every one is judge, interpreter, and executioner of it too, and that in his own case; and he that has right on his side, having ordinarily but his own single strength, hath not force enough to defend himself from injuries or punish delinquents. To avoid these inconveniencies which disorder men's properties in the state of Nature, men unite into societies that they may have the united strength of the whole society to secure and defend their properties, and may have standing rules to bound it by which every one may know what is his. To this end it is that men give up all their natural power to the society they enter into, and the community put the legislative power into such hands as they think fit, with this trust, that they shall be governed by declared laws, or else their peace, quiet, and property will still be at the same uncertainty as it was in the state of Nature.

137 Absolute arbitrary power, or governing without settled standing laws, can neither of them consist with the ends of society and government, which men would not quit the freedom of the state of Nature for, and tie themselves up under, were it not to preserve their lives, liberties, and fortunes, and by stated rules of right and property to secure their peace and quiet. It cannot be supposed that they should intend, had they a power so to do, to give any one or more an absolute arbitrary power over their persons and estates, and put a force into the magistrate's hand to execute his unlimited will arbitrarily upon them; this were to put themselves into a worse condition than the state of Nature, wherein they had a liberty to defend their right against the injuries of others, and were upon equal terms of force to maintain it, whether invaded by a single man or many in combination. Whereas by supposing they have given up themselves to the absolute arbitrary power and will of a legislator, they have disarmed themselves, and armed him to make a prey of them when he pleases; he being in a much worse condition that is exposed to the arbitrary power of one man who has the command of a hundred thousand than he that is exposed to the arbitrary power of a hundred thousand single men, nobody being secure, that his will who has such a command is better than that of other men, though his force be a hundred thousand times stronger. And, therefore, whatever form the commonwealth is under, the ruling power ought to govern by declared and received laws, and not by extemporary dictates and undetermined resolutions, for then mankind will be in a far worse condition than in the state of Nature if they shall have armed one or a few men with the joint power of a multitude, to force them to obey at pleasure the exorbitant and unlimited decrees of their sudden thoughts, or unrestrained, and till that moment, unknown wills, without having any measures set down which may guide and justify their actions. For all the power the government has, being only for the good of the society, as it ought not to be arbitrary and at pleasure, so it ought to be exercised by established and promulgated laws, that both the people may know their duty, and be safe and secure within the limits of the law, and the rulers, too, kept within their due bounds, and not be tempted by the power they have in their hands to employ it to purposes, and by such measures as they would not have known, and own not willingly.

138 Thirdly, the supreme power cannot take from any man any part of his property without his own consent. For the preservation of property being the end of government, and that for which men enter into society, it necessarily supposes and requires that the people should have property, without which they must be supposed to lose that by entering into society which was the end for which they entered into it; too gross an absurdity for any man to own. Men, therefore, in society having property, they have such a right to the goods, which by the law of the community are theirs, that nobody hath a right to take them, or any

part of them, from them without their own consent; without this they have no property at all. For I have truly no property in that which another can by right take from me when he pleases against my consent. Hence it is a mistake to think that the supreme or legislative power of any commonwealth can do what it will, and dispose of the estates of the subject arbitrarily, or take any part of them at pleasure. This is not much to be feared in governments where the legislative consists wholly or in part in assemblies which are variable, whose members upon the dissolution of the assembly are subjects under the common laws of their country, equally with the rest. But in governments where the legislative is in one lasting assembly, always in being, or in one man as in absolute monarchies, there is danger still, that they will think themselves to have a distinct interest from the rest of the community, and so will be apt to increase their own riches and power by taking what they think fit from the people. For a man's property is not at all secure, though there be good and equitable laws to set the bounds of it between him and his fellow-subjects, if he who commands those subjects have power to take from any private man what part he pleases of his property, and use and dispose of it as he thinks good.

139   But government, into whosesoever hands it is put, being as I have before showed, entrusted with this condition, and for this end, that men might have and secure their properties, the prince or senate, however it may have power to make laws for the regulating of property between the subjects one amongst another, yet can never have a power to take to themselves the whole, or any part of the subjects' property, without their own consent; for this would be in effect to leave them no property at all. And to let us see that even absolute power, where it is necessary, is not arbitrary by being absolute, but is still limited by that reason, and confined to those ends which required it in some cases to be absolute, we need look no farther than the common practice of martial discipline. For the preservation of the army, and in it of the whole commonwealth, requires an absolute obedience to the command of every superior officer, and it is justly death to disobey or dispute the most dangerous or unreasonable of them; but yet we see that neither the sergeant that could command a soldier to march up to the mouth of a cannon, or stand in a breach where he is almost sure to perish, can command that soldier to give him one penny of his money; nor the general that can condemn him to death for deserting his post, or not obeying the most desperate orders, cannot yet with all his absolute power of life and death dispose of one farthing of that soldier's estate, or seize one jot of his goods, whom yet he can command anything, and hang for the least disobedience. Because such a blind obedience is necessary to that end for which the commander has his power—viz., the preservation of the rest, but the disposing of his goods has nothing to do with it.

140   It is true governments cannot be supported without great charge,[42] and it is fit every one who enjoys his share of the protection should pay out of his estate[43] his proportion for the maintenance of it. But still it must be with his own consent—i.e., the consent of the majority, giving it either by themselves or their representatives chosen by them; for if any one shall claim a power to lay and levy taxes on the people by his own authority, and without such consent of the people, he thereby invades the fundamental law of property, and subverts the end of government. For what property have I in that which another may by right take when he pleases to himself?

141   Fourthly. The legislative cannot transfer the power of making laws to any other hands, for it being but a delegated power from the people, they who have it cannot pass it over to others. The people alone can appoint the form of the commonwealth, which is by constituting the legislative, and appointing in whose hands that shall be. And when the people have said, "We will submit, and be governed by laws made by such men, and in such forms," nobody else can say other men shall make laws for them; nor can they be bound by any laws but such as are enacted by those whom they have chosen and authorized to make laws for them.

---

42  I.e., expense.
43  I.e., from his property, especially landed property.

142   These are the bounds which the trust that is put in them by the society and the law of God and Nature have set to the legislative power of every commonwealth, in all forms of government. First: they are to govern by promulgated established laws, not to be varied in particular cases, but to have one rule for rich and poor, for the favorite at court, and the countryman at plough. Secondly: these laws also ought to be designed for no other end ultimately but the good of the people. Thirdly: they must not raise taxes on the property of the people without the consent of the people given by themselves or their deputies. And this properly concerns only such governments where the legislative is always in being, or at least where the people have not reserved any part of the legislative to deputies, to be from time to time chosen by themselves. Fourthly: [the] legislative neither must nor can transfer the power of making laws to anybody else, or place it anywhere but where the people have.

CHAPTER 13

OF THE SUBORDINATION OF THE POWERS
OF THE COMMONWEALTH

155   It may be demanded here, what if the executive power, being possessed of the force of the commonwealth, shall make use of that force to hinder the meeting and acting of the legislative, when the original constitution or the public exigencies require it? I say, using force upon the people, without authority, and contrary to the trust put in him that does so, is a state of war with the people, who have a right to reinstate their legislative in the exercise of their power. For having erected a legislative with an intent they should exercise the power of making laws, either at certain set times, or when there is need of it, when they are hindered by any force from what is so necessary to the society, and wherein the safety and preservation of the people consists, the people have a right to remove it by force. In all states and conditions the true remedy of force without authority is to oppose force to it. The use of force without authority always puts him that uses it into a state of war as the aggressor, and renders him liable to be treated accordingly.

156   The power of assembling and dismissing the legislative, placed in the executive, gives not the exec-utive a superiority over it, but is a fiduciary trust placed in him for the safety of the people in a case where the uncertainty and variableness of human affairs could not bear a steady fixed rule. For it not being possible that the first framers of the government should by any foresight be so much masters of future events as to be able to prefix so just periods of return and duration to the assemblies of the legislative, in all times to come, that might exactly answer all the exigencies of the commonwealth, the best remedy could be found for this defect was to trust this to the prudence of one who was always to be present, and whose business it was to watch over the public good. Constant, frequent meetings of the legislative, and long continuations of their assemblies, without necessary occasion, could not but be burdensome to the people, and must necessarily in time produce more dangerous inconveniencies, and yet the quick turn of affairs might be sometimes such as to need their present help; any delay of their convening might endanger the public; and sometimes, too, their business might be so great that the limited time of their sitting might be too short for their work, and rob the public of that benefit which could be had only from their mature deliberation. What, then, could be done in this case to prevent the community from being exposed some time or other to imminent hazard on one side or the other, by fixed intervals and periods set to the meeting and acting of the legislative, but to entrust it to the prudence of some who, being present and acquainted with the state of public affairs, might make use of this prerogative for the public good? And where else could this be so well placed as in his hands who was entrusted with the execution of the laws for the same end? Thus, supposing the regulation of times for the assembling and sitting of the legislative not settled by the original constitution, it naturally fell into the hands of the executive, not as an arbitrary power depending on his good pleasure, but with this trust always to have it exercised only for the public weal, as the occurrences of times and change of affairs might require. Whether settled periods of their convening, or a liberty left to the prince for convoking the legislative, or perhaps a mixture of both, hath the least inconvenience attending it, it is not my business here to inquire, but only to show that, though the executive

power may have the prerogative of convoking and dissolving such conventions of the legislative, yet it is not thereby superior to it.

157   Things of this world are in so constant a flux that nothing remains long in the same state. Thus people, riches, trade, power, change their stations; flourishing mighty cities come to ruin, and prove in time neglected desolate corners, whilst other unfrequented places grow into populous countries filled with wealth and inhabitants. But things not always changing equally, and private interest often keeping up customs and privileges when the reasons of them are ceased, it often comes to pass that in governments where part of the legislative consists of representatives chosen by the people, that in tract of time this representation becomes very unequal and disproportionate to the reasons it was at first established upon. To what gross absurdities the following of custom when reason has left it may lead, we may be satisfied when we see the bare name of a town, of which there remains not so much as the ruins, where scarce so much housing as a sheepcote, or more inhabitants than a shepherd is to be found, send as many representatives to the grand assembly of law-makers as a whole county numerous in people and powerful in riches.[44] This strangers stand amazed at, and every one must confess needs a remedy; though most think it hard to find one, because the constitution of the legislative being the original and supreme act of the society, antecedent to all positive laws in it, and depending wholly on the people, no inferior power can alter it. And, therefore, the people when the legislative is once constituted, having in such a government as we have been speaking of no power to act as long as the government stands, this inconvenience is thought incapable of a remedy.

158   *Salus populi suprema lex*[45] is certainly so just and fundamental a rule, that he who sincerely follows it cannot dangerously err. If, therefore, the executive who has the power of convoking the legislative, observing rather the true proportion than fashion of representation, regulates not by old custom, but true reason, the number of members in all places, that have a right to be distinctly represented, which no part of the people, however incorporated, can pretend to, but in proportion to the assistance which it affords to the public, it cannot be judged to have set up a new legislative, but to have restored the old and true one, and to have rectified the disorders which succession of time had insensibly as well as inevitably introduced; for it being the interest as well as intention of the people to have a fair and equal representative, whoever brings it nearest to that is an undoubted friend to and establisher of the government, and cannot miss the consent and approbation of the community; prerogative being nothing but a power in the hands of the prince to provide for the public good in such cases which, depending upon unforeseen and uncertain occurrences, certain and unalterable laws could not safely direct. Whatsoever shall be done manifestly for the good of the people, and establishing the government upon its true foundations is, and always will be, just prerogative. The power of erecting new corporations,[46] and therewith new representatives, carries with it a supposition that in time the measures of representation might vary, and those have a just right to be represented which before had none; and by the same reason, those cease to have a right, and be too inconsiderable for such a privilege, which before had it. It is not a change from the present state which, perhaps, corruption or decay has introduced, that makes an inroad upon the government, but the tendency of it to injure or oppress the people, and to set up one part or party with a distinction from, and an unequal subjection of, the rest. Whatsoever cannot but be acknowledged to be of advantage to the society and people in general, upon just and lasting measures, will always, when done, justify itself; and whenever the people shall choose their representatives upon just and undeniably equal measures, suitable to the original frame of the government, it cannot be doubted to be the will

---

44   A reference to what came in the nineteenth-century to be called "rotten boroughs," i.e., places which centuries earlier had gained the right to send representatives to the House of Commons in parliament, had since become largely deserted, yet continued to exercise the right of selecting members of parliament.

45   Latin: "The welfare of the people is the highest law."

46   Local communities with rights to send representatives to the legislature.

and act of the society, whoever permitted or proposed to them so to do.

## CHAPTER 14
### OF PREROGATIVE

159 Where the legislative and executive power are in distinct hands, as they are in all moderated monarchies and well-framed governments, there the good of the society requires that several things should be left to the discretion of him that has the executive power. For the legislators not being able to foresee and provide by laws for all that may be useful to the community, the executor of the laws, having the power in his hands, has by the common law of Nature a right to make use of it for the good of the society, in many cases where the municipal law has given no direction, till the legislative can conveniently be assembled to provide for it; nay, many things there are which the law can by no means provide for, and those must necessarily be left to the discretion of him that has the executive power in his hands, to be ordered by him as the public good and advantage shall require; nay, it is fit that the laws themselves should in some cases give way to the executive power, or rather to this fundamental law of Nature and government—viz., that as much as may be all the members of the society are to be preserved. For since many accidents may happen wherein a strict and rigid observation of the laws may do harm, as not to pull down an innocent man's house to stop the fire when the next to it is burning; and a man may come sometimes within the reach of the law, which makes no distinction of persons, by an action that may deserve reward and pardon; it is fit the ruler should have a power in many cases to mitigate the severity of the law, and pardon some offenders, since the end of government being the preservation of all as much as may be, even the guilty are to be spared where it can prove no prejudice to the innocent.

160 This power to act according to discretion for the public good, without the prescription of the law and sometimes even against it, is that which is called prerogative; for since in some governments the law-making power is not always in being and is usually too numerous, and so too slow for the dispatch requisite to execution, and because, also, it is impossible to foresee and so by laws to provide for all accidents and necessities that may concern the public or make such laws as will do no harm, if they are executed with an inflexible rigor on all occasions and upon all persons that may come in their way, therefore there is a latitude left to the executive power to do many things of choice which the laws do not prescribe.

161 This power, whilst employed for the benefit of the community and suitably to the trust and ends of the government, is undoubted prerogative, and never is questioned. For the people are very seldom or never scrupulous or nice in the point or questioning of prerogative whilst it is in any tolerable degree employed for the use it was meant—that is, the good of the people, and not manifestly against it. But if there comes to be a question between the executive power and the people about a thing claimed as a prerogative, the tendency of the exercise of such prerogative, to the good or hurt of the people, will easily decide that question.

162 It is easy to conceive that in the infancy of governments, when commonwealths differed little from families in number of people, they differed from them too but little in number of laws; and the governors being as the fathers of them, watching over them for their good, the government was almost all prerogative. A few established laws served the turn, and the discretion and care of the ruler supplied the rest. But when mistake or flattery prevailed with weak princes, to make use of this power for private ends of their own and not for the public good, the people were fain,[47] by express laws, to get prerogative determined in those points wherein they found disadvantage from it, and declared limitations of prerogative in those cases which they and their ancestors had left in the utmost latitude to the wisdom of those princes who made no other but a right use of it—that is, for the good of their people.

163 And therefore they have a very wrong notion of government who say that the people have encroached upon the prerogative when they have got any part of

---

47 I.e., desirous.

it to be defined by positive laws. For in so doing they have not pulled from the prince anything that of right belonged to him, but only declared that that power which they indefinitely left in his or his ancestors' hands, to be exercised for their good, was not a thing they intended [for] him, when he used it otherwise. For the end of government being the good of the community, whatsoever alterations are made in it tending to that end cannot be an encroachment upon anybody, since nobody in government can have a right tending to any other end; and those only are encroachments which prejudice or hinder the public good. Those who say otherwise speak as if the prince had a distinct and separate interest from the good of the community, and was not made for it—the root and source from which spring almost all those evils and disorders which happen in kingly governments. And, indeed, if that be so, the people under his government are not a society of rational creatures, entered into a community for their mutual good, such as have set rulers over themselves, to guard and promote that good; but are to be looked on as a herd of inferior creatures under the dominion of a master, who keeps them and works them for his own pleasure or profit. If men were so void of reason and brutish as to enter into society upon such terms, prerogative might indeed be what some men would have it, an arbitrary power to do things hurtful to the people.

164   But since a rational creature cannot be supposed, when free, to put himself into subjection to another for his own harm (though where he finds a good and a wise ruler he may not, perhaps, think it either necessary or useful to set precise bounds to his power in all things), prerogative can be nothing but the people's permitting their rulers to do several things of their own free choice where the law was silent, and sometimes too against the direct letter of the law, for the public good and their acquiescing in it when so done. For as a good prince, who is mindful of the trust put into his hands and careful of the good of his people, cannot have too much prerogative, that is, power to do good, so a weak and ill prince, who would claim that power his predecessors exercised, without the direc-

tion of the law, as a prerogative belonging to him by right of his office, which he may exercise at his pleasure to make or promote an interest distinct from that of the public, gives the people an occasion to claim their right and limit that power, which, whilst it was exercised for their good, they were content should be tacitly allowed.

165   And therefore he that will look into the history of England will find that prerogative was always largest in the hands of our wisest and best princes, because the people observing the whole tendency of their actions to be the public good, or if any human frailty or mistake (for princes are but men, made as others) appeared in some small declinations[48] from that end, yet it was visible the main of their conduct tended to nothing but the care of the public. The people, therefore, finding reason to be satisfied with these princes, whenever they acted without, or contrary to the letter of the law, acquiesced in what they did, and without the least complaint, let them enlarge their prerogative as they pleased, judging rightly that they did nothing herein to the prejudice of their laws, since they acted conformably to the foundation and end of all laws—the public good.

166   Such God-like princes, indeed, had some title to arbitrary power by that argument that would prove absolute monarchy the best government, as that which God Himself governs the universe by, because such kings partake of his wisdom and goodness. Upon this is founded that saying, "That the reigns of good princes have been always most dangerous to the liberties of their people." For when their successors, managing the government with different thoughts, would draw the actions of those good rulers into precedent and make them the standard of their prerogative—as if what had been done only for the good of the people was a right in them to do for the harm of the people, if they so pleased—it has often occasioned contest, and sometimes public disorders, before the people could recover their original right and get that to be declared not to be prerogative which truly was never so; since it is impossible anybody in the society should ever have

48   I.e., deviations.

a right to do the people harm, though it be very possible and reasonable that the people should not go about to set any bounds to the prerogative of those kings or rulers who themselves transgressed not the bounds of the public good. For "prerogative is nothing but the power of doing public good without a rule."

167 The power of calling parliaments in England, as to precise time, place, and duration, is certainly a prerogative of the king, but still with this trust, that it shall be made use of for the good of the nation as the exigencies of the times and variety of occasion shall require. For it being impossible to foresee which should always be the fittest place for them to assemble in, and what the best season, the choice of these was left with the executive power, as might be best subservient to the public good and best suit the ends of parliament.

168 The old question will be asked in this matter of prerogative, "But who shall be judge when this power is made a right use of?" I answer: between an executive power in being, with such a prerogative, and a legislative that depends upon his will for their convening, there can be no judge on earth. As there can be none between the legislative and the people, should either the executive or the legislative, when they have got the power in their hands, design, or go about to enslave or destroy them, the people have no other remedy in this, as in all other cases where they have no judge on earth, but to appeal to Heaven; for the rulers in such attempts, exercising a power the people never put into their hands, who can never be supposed to consent that anybody should rule over them for their harm, do that which they have not a right to do. And where the body of the people, or any single man, are deprived of their right, or are under the exercise of a power without right, having no appeal on earth they have a liberty to appeal to Heaven whenever they judge the cause of sufficient moment. And therefore, though the people cannot be judge, so as to have, by the constitution of that society, any superior power to determine and give effective sentence in the case, yet they have reserved that ultimate determination to themselves which belongs to all mankind, where there lies no appeal on earth, by a law antecedent and paramount to all positive laws of men,

whether they have just cause to make their appeal to Heaven. And this judgment they cannot part with, it being out of a man's power so to submit himself to another as to give him a liberty to destroy him, God and Nature never allowing a man so to abandon himself as to neglect his own preservation. And since he cannot take away his own life, neither can he give another power to take it. Nor let any one think this lays a perpetual foundation for disorder; for this operates not till the inconvenience is so great that the majority feel it, and are weary of it, and find a necessity to have it amended. And this the executive power, or wise princes, never need come in the danger of; and it is the thing of all others they have most need to avoid, as, of all others, the most perilous.

## CHAPTER 16
### OF CONQUEST

175 Though governments can originally have no other rise than that before mentioned, nor polities be founded on anything but the consent of the people, yet such have been the disorders ambition has filled the world with, that in the noise of war, which makes so great a part of the history of mankind, this consent is little taken notice of; and, therefore, many have mistaken the force of arms for the consent of the people, and reckon conquest as one of the originals of government. But conquest is as far from setting up any government as demolishing a house is from building a new one in the place. Indeed, it often makes way for a new frame of a commonwealth by destroying the former, but, without the consent of the people, can never erect a new one.

176 That the aggressor, who puts himself into the state of war with another, and unjustly invades another man's right, can, by such an unjust war, never come to have a right over the conquered, will be easily agreed by all men, who will not think that robbers and pirates have a right of empire over whomsoever they have force enough to master, or that men are bound by promises which unlawful force extorts from them. Should a robber break into my house, and, with a dagger at my throat, make me seal deeds to convey my estate to him, would this give him any title? Just such a title by his sword has

an unjust conqueror who forces me into submission. The injury and the crime is equal, whether committed by the wearer of a crown or some petty villain. The title of the offender and the number of his followers make no difference in the offense, unless it be to aggravate it. The only difference is, great robbers punish little ones to keep them in their obedience; but the great ones are rewarded with laurels and triumphs, because they are too big for the weak hands of justice in this world, and have the power in their own possession which should punish offenders. What is my remedy against a robber that so broke into my house? Appeal to the law for justice. But perhaps justice is denied, or I am crippled and cannot stir; robbed, and have not the means to do it. If God has taken away all means of seeking remedy, there is nothing left but patience. But my son, when able, may seek the relief of the law, which I am denied; he or his son may renew his appeal till he recover his right. But the conquered, or their children, have no court—no arbitrator on earth to appeal to. Then they may appeal, as Jephtha[49] did, to Heaven, and repeat their appeal till they have recovered the native right of their ancestors, which was to have such a legislative over them as the majority should approve and freely acquiesce in. If it be objected this would cause endless trouble, I answer, no more than justice does, where she lies open to all that appeal to her. He that troubles his neighbor without a cause is punished for it by the justice of the court he appeals to. And he that appeals to heaven must be sure he has right on his side, and a right, too, that is worth the trouble and cost of the appeal, as he will answer at a tribunal that cannot be deceived, and will be sure to retribute to every one according to the mischiefs he hath created to his fellow-subjects, that is, any part of mankind. From whence it is plain that he that conquers in an unjust war can thereby have no title to the subjection and obedience of the conquered.

177   But supposing victory favors the right side, let us consider a conqueror in a lawful war, and see what power he gets, and over whom.

First, it is plain he gets no power by his conquest over those that conquered with him. They that fought on his side cannot suffer by the conquest, but must, at least, be as much free men as they were before. And most commonly they serve upon terms, and on condition to share with their leader, and enjoy a part of the spoil and other advantages that attend the conquering sword, or, at least, have a part of the subdued country bestowed upon them. And the conquering people are not, I hope, to be slaves by conquest, and wear their laurels only to show they are sacrifices to their leader's triumph. They that found absolute monarchy upon the title of the sword make their heroes, who are the founders of such monarchies, arrant "draw-can-sirs," and forget they had any officers and soldiers that fought on their side in the battles they won, or assisted them in the subduing, or shared in possessing the countries they mastered. We are told by some that the English monarchy is founded in the Norman Conquest,[50] and that our princes have thereby a title to absolute dominion, which, if it were true (as by the history it appears otherwise), and that William had a right to make war on this island, yet his dominion by conquest could reach no farther than to the Saxons and Britons that were then inhabitants of this country. The Normans that came with him and helped to conquer, and all descended from them, are free men and no subjects by conquest, let that give what dominion it will. And if I or anybody else shall claim freedom as derived from them, it will be very hard to prove the contrary; and it is plain, the law that has made no distinction between the one and the other intends not there should be any difference in their freedom or privileges.

178   But supposing, which seldom happens, that the conquerors and conquered never incorporate into one people under the same laws and freedom; let us see next what power a lawful conqueror has over the subdued, and that I say is purely despotical. He has an absolute power over the lives of those who, by an unjust war, have forfeited them, but not over the lives or fortunes of those who engaged not in the war, nor

---

49   A reference to the Old Testament, Judges 11.
50   I.e., the conquest of England by William, duke of Normandy, in 1066.

over the possessions even of those who were actually engaged in it.

179 Secondly, I say, then, the conqueror gets no power but only over those who have actually assisted, concurred, or consented to that unjust force that is used against him. For the people having given to their governors no power to do an unjust thing, such as is to make an unjust war (for they never had such a power in themselves), they ought not to be charged as guilty of the violence and injustice that is committed in an unjust war any farther than they actually abet it, no more than they are to be thought guilty of any violence or oppression their governors should use upon the people themselves or any part of their fellow-subjects, they having empowered them no more to the one than to the other. Conquerors, it is true, seldom trouble themselves to make the distinction, but they willingly permit the confusion of war to sweep all together; but yet this alters not the right; for the conqueror's power over the lives of the conquered being only because they have used force to do or maintain an injustice, he can have that power only over those who have concurred in that force; all the rest are innocent, and he has no more title over the people of that country who have done him no injury, and so have made no forfeiture of their lives, than he has over any other who, without any injuries or provocations, have lived upon fair terms with him.

180 Thirdly, the power a conqueror gets over those he overcomes in a just war is perfectly despotical; he has an absolute power over the lives of those who, by putting themselves in a state of war, have forfeited them, but he has not thereby a right and title to their possessions. This I doubt not but at first sight will seem a strange doctrine, it being so quite contrary to the practice of the world; there being nothing more familiar in speaking of the dominion of countries than to say such an one conquered it, as if conquest, without any more ado, conveyed a right of possession. But when we consider that the practice of the strong and powerful, how universal soever it may be, is seldom the rule of right, however it be one part of the subjection of the conquered not to argue against the conditions cut out to them by the conquering swords.

181 Though in all war there be usually a complication of force and damage, and the aggressor seldom fails to harm the estate when he uses force against the persons of those he makes war upon, yet it is the use of force only that puts a man into the state of war. For whether by force he begins the injury, or else having quietly and by fraud done the injury, he refuses to make reparation, and by force maintains it, which is the same thing as at first to have done it by force; it is the unjust use of force that makes the war. For he that breaks open my house and violently turns me out of doors, or having peaceably got in, by force keeps me out, does, in effect, the same thing; supposing we are in such a state that we have no common judge on earth whom I may appeal to, and to whom we are both obliged to submit, for of such I am now speaking. It is the unjust use of force, then, that puts a man into the state of war with another, and thereby he that is guilty of it makes a forfeiture of his life. For quitting reason, which is the rule given between man and man, and using force, the way of beasts, he becomes liable to be destroyed by him he uses force against, as any savage ravenous beast that is dangerous to his being.

182 But because the miscarriages of the father are no faults of the children, who may be rational and peaceable, notwithstanding the brutishness and injustice of the father, the father, by his miscarriages and violence, can forfeit but his own life, and involves not his children in his guilt or destruction. His goods which Nature, that willeth the preservation of all mankind as much as is possible, hath made to belong to the children to keep them from perishing, do still continue to belong to his children. For supposing them not to have joined in the war either through infancy or choice, they have done nothing to forfeit them, nor has the conqueror any right to take them away by the bare right of having subdued him that by force attempted his destruction, though, perhaps, he may have some right to them to repair the damages he has sustained by the war, and the defense of his own right, which how far it reaches to the possessions of the conquered we shall see by-and-by; so that he that by conquest has a right over a man's person, to destroy him if he pleases, has not thereby a right over his estate to possess and enjoy it. For it is the brutal force the aggressor has used that gives his adversary a right to take away his life and destroy him, if he pleases, as a noxious creature; but it is damage sus-

tained that alone gives him title to another man's goods; for though I may kill a thief that sets on me in the highway, yet I may not (which seems less) take away his money and let him go; this would be robbery on my side. His force, and the state of war he put himself in, made him forfeit his life, but gave me no title to his goods. The right, then, of conquest extends only to the lives of those who joined in the war, but not to their estates, but only in order to make reparation for the damages received and the charges of the war, and that, too, with reservation of the right of the innocent wife and children.

183   Let the conqueror have as much justice on his side as could be supposed, he has no right to seize more than the vanquished could forfeit; his life is at the victor's mercy, and his service and goods he may appropriate to make himself reparation; but he cannot take the goods of his wife and children; they too had a title to the goods he enjoyed, and their shares in the estate he possessed. For example, I in the state of Nature (and all commonwealths are in the state of Nature one with another) have injured another man, and refusing to give satisfaction, it is come to a state of war wherein my defending by force what I had gotten unjustly makes me the aggressor. I am conquered; my life, it is true, as forfeit, is at mercy, but not my wife's and children's. They made not the war, nor assisted in it. I could not forfeit their lives, they were not mine to forfeit. My wife had a share in my estate, that neither could I forfeit. And my children also, being born of me, had a right to be maintained out of my labor or substance. Here then is the case: the conqueror has a title to reparation for damages received, and the children have a title to their father's estate for their subsistence. For as to the wife's share, whether her own labor or compact gave her a title to it, it is plain her husband could not forfeit what was hers. What must be done in the case? I answer: the fundamental law of Nature being that all, as much as may be, should be preserved, it follows that if there be not enough fully to satisfy both—viz., for the conqueror's losses and children's maintenance, he that hath, and to spare, must remit something of his full satisfaction, and give way to the pressing and preferable title of those who are in danger to perish without it.

184   But supposing the charge and damages of the war are to be made up to the conqueror to the utmost farthing, and that the children of the vanquished, spoiled of all their father's goods, are to be left to starve and perish, yet the satisfying of what shall, on this score, be due to the conqueror will scarce give him a title to any country he shall conquer. For the damages of war can scarce amount to the value of any considerable tract of land in any part of the world, where all the land is possessed, and none lies waste. And if I have not taken away the conqueror's land which, being vanquished, it is impossible I should, scarce any other spoil I have done him can amount to the value of mine, supposing it of an extent any way coming near what I had overrun of his, and equally cultivated too. The destruction of a year's product or two (for it seldom reaches four or five) is the utmost spoil that usually can be done. For as to money, and such riches and treasure taken away, these are none of Nature's goods, they have but a fantastical imaginary value; Nature has put no such upon them. They are of no more account by her standard than the Wampompeke[51] of the Americans to an European prince, or the silver money of Europe would have been formerly to an American. And five years' product is not worth the perpetual inheritance of land, where all is possessed and none remains waste, to be taken up by him that is disseised,[52] which will be easily granted, if one do but take away the imaginary value of money, the disproportion being more than between five and five thousand; though, at the same time, half a year's product is more worth than the inheritance where, there being more land than the inhabitants possess and make use of, any one has liberty to make use of the waste. But their conquerors take little care to possess themselves of the lands of the vanquished. No damage therefore that men in the state of Nature (as all princes and governments are in reference to one another) suffer from one another can give a conqueror power to dispossess

51   Shells used as money by some Native Americans.
52   I.e., dispossessed.

the posterity of the vanquished, and turn them out of that inheritance which ought to be the possession of them and their descendants to all generations. The conqueror indeed will be apt to think himself master; and it is the very condition of the subdued not to be able to dispute their right. But, if that be all, it gives no other title than what bare force gives to the stronger over the weaker; and, by this reason, he that is strongest will have a right to whatever he pleases to seize on.

185  Over those, then, that joined with him in the war, and over those of the subdued country that opposed him not, and the posterity even of those that did, the conqueror, even in a just war, hath, by his conquest, no right of dominion. They are free from any subjection to him, and if their former government be dissolved, they are at liberty to begin and erect another to themselves.

186  The conqueror, it is true, usually by the force he has over them, compels them, with a sword at their breasts, to stoop to his conditions, and submit to such a government as he pleases to afford them; but the inquiry is, what right he has to do so? If it be said they submit by their own consent, then this allows their own consent to be necessary to give the conqueror a title to rule over them. It remains only to be considered whether promises, extorted by force, without right, can be thought consent, and how far they bind. To which I shall say, they bind not at all because whatsoever another gets from me by force, I still retain the right of, and he is obliged presently to restore. He that forces my horse from me ought presently to restore him, and I have still a right to retake him. By the same reason, he that forced a promise from me ought presently to restore it—i.e., quit me of the obligation of it; or I may resume it myself—i.e., choose whether I will perform it. For the law of Nature laying an obligation on me, only by the rules she prescribes, cannot oblige me by the violation of her rules; such is the extorting anything from me by force. Nor does it at all alter the case to say I gave my promise, no more than it excuses the force, and passes the right, when I put my hand in my pocket and deliver my purse myself to a thief who demands it with a pistol at my breast.

## CHAPTER 19
### OF THE DISSOLUTION OF GOVERNMENT

211  He that will, with any clearness, speak of the dissolution of government, ought in the first place to distinguish between the dissolution of the society and the dissolution of the government. That which makes the community, and brings men out of the loose state of Nature into one politic society, is the agreement which every one has with the rest to incorporate and act as one body, and so be one distinct commonwealth. The usual, and almost only way whereby this union is dissolved, is the inroad of foreign force making a conquest upon them. For in that case (not being able to maintain and support themselves as one entire and independent body) the union belonging to that body, which consisted therein, must necessarily cease, and so every one return to the state he was in before, with a liberty to shift for himself and provide for his own safety, as he thinks fit, in some other society. Whenever the society is dissolved, it is certain the government of that society cannot remain. Thus conquerors' swords often cut up governments by the roots, and mangle societies to pieces, separating the subdued or scattered multitude from the protection of and dependence on that society which ought to have preserved them from violence. The world is too well instructed in, and too forward to allow of this way of dissolving of governments, to need any more to be said of it; and there wants not much argument to prove that where the society is dissolved, the government cannot remain; that being as impossible as for the frame of a house to subsist when the materials of it are scattered and displaced by a whirlwind, or jumbled into a confused heap by an earthquake.

212  Besides this overturning from without, governments are dissolved from within:

First. When the legislative is altered, civil society being a state of peace amongst those who are of it, from whom the state of war is excluded by the umpirage which they have provided in their legislative for the ending all differences that may arise amongst any of them; it is in their legislative that the members of a commonwealth are united and combined together into one coherent living body. This is the soul that gives form, life, and unity to the commonwealth; from hence the several members have their mutual influence, sympathy, and connection; and therefore when the legislative is broken, or dissolved, dissolution and death follows. For the essence and union of the society consisting in having one will, the legislative, when once established by the majority, has the declaring and, as it were, keeping of that will. The constitution of the legislative is the first and fundamental act of society, whereby provision is made for the continuation of their union under the direction of persons and bonds of laws, made by persons authorized thereunto, by the consent and appointment of the people, without which no one man, or number of men, amongst them can have authority of making laws that shall be binding to the rest. When any one, or more, shall take upon them to make laws whom the people have not appointed so to do, they make laws without authority, which the people are not therefore bound to obey; by which means they come again to be out of subjection, and may constitute to themselves a new legislative, as they think best, being in full liberty to resist the force of those who, without authority, would impose anything upon them. Every one is at the disposure of his own will, when those who had, by the delegation of the society, the declaring of the public will, are excluded from it, and others usurp the place who have no such authority or delegation.

213   This being usually brought about by such in the commonwealth, who misuse the power they have, it is hard to consider it aright, and know at whose door to lay it, without knowing the form of government in which it happens. Let us suppose, then, the legislative placed in the concurrence of three distinct persons: First, a single hereditary person having the constant, supreme, executive power, and with it the power of convoking and dissolving the other two within certain periods of time. Secondly, an assembly of hereditary nobility. Thirdly, an assembly of representatives chosen, *pro tempore*,[53] by the people. Such a form of government supposed, it is evident:

214   First, that when such a single person or prince sets up his own arbitrary will in place of the laws

which are the will of the society declared by the legislative, then the legislative is changed. For that being, in effect, the legislative whose rules and laws are put in execution, and required to be obeyed, when other laws are set up, and other rules pretended and enforced than what the legislative, constituted by the society, have enacted, it is plain that the legislative is changed. Whoever introduces new laws, not being thereunto authorized, by the fundamental appointment of the society, or subverts the old, disowns and overturns the power by which they were made, and so sets up a new legislative.

215   Secondly, when the prince hinders the legislative from assembling in its due time, or from acting freely, pursuant to those ends for which it was constituted, the legislative is altered. For it is not a certain number of men—no, nor their meeting, unless they have also freedom of debating and leisure of perfecting what is for the good of the society, wherein the legislative consists; when these are taken away, or altered, so as to deprive the society of the due exercise of their power, the legislative is truly altered. For it is not names that constitute governments, but the use and exercise of those powers that were intended to accompany them; so that he who takes away the freedom, or hinders the acting of the legislative in its due seasons, in effect takes away the legislative, and puts an end to the government.

216   Thirdly, when, by the arbitrary power of the prince, the electors or ways of election are altered without the consent and contrary to the common interest of the people, there also the legislative is altered. For if others than those whom the society hath authorized thereunto do choose, or in another way than what the society hath prescribed, those chosen are not the legislative appointed by the people.

217   Fourthly, the delivery also of the people into the subjection of a foreign power, either by the prince or by the legislative, is certainly a change of the legislative, and so a dissolution of the government. For the end why people entered into society being to be preserved one entire, free, independent society, to be governed by its own laws, this is lost whenever they are given up into the power of another.

---

53   Latin: for a period of time.

218  Why, in such a constitution as this, the dissolution of the government in these cases is to be imputed to the prince is evident, because he, having the force, treasure, and offices of the state to employ, and often persuading himself or being flattered by others, that, as supreme magistrate, he is incapable of control—he alone is in a condition to make great advances towards such changes under pretense of lawful authority, and has it in his hands to terrify or suppress opposers as factious, seditious, and enemies to the government; whereas no other part of the legislative, or people, is capable by themselves to attempt any alteration of the legislative without open and visible rebellion, apt enough to be taken notice of, which, when it prevails, produces effects very little different from foreign conquest. Besides, the prince, in such a form of government, having the power of dissolving the other parts of the legislative, and thereby rendering them private persons, they can never, in opposition to him, or without his concurrence, alter the legislative by a law, his consent being necessary to give any of their decrees that sanction. But yet so far as the other parts of the legislative any way contribute to any attempt upon the government, and do either promote, or not, what lies in them, hinder such designs, they are guilty, and partake in this, which is certainly the greatest crime men can be guilty of one towards another.

219  There is one way more whereby such a government may be dissolved, and that is: when he who has the supreme executive power neglects and abandons that charge, so that the laws already made can no longer be put in execution; this is demonstratively to reduce all to anarchy, and so effectively to dissolve the government; for laws not being made for themselves, but to be, by their execution, the bonds of the society to keep every part of the body politic in its due place and function. When that totally ceases, the government visibly ceases, and the people become a confused multitude without order or connection. Where there is no longer the administration of justice for the securing of men's rights, nor any remaining power within the community to direct the force, or provide for the necessities of the public, there certainly is no government left. Where the laws cannot be executed it is all one as if there were no laws, and a government without laws is, I suppose, a mystery in politics inconceivable to human capacity, and inconsistent with human society.

220  In these, and the like cases, when the government is dissolved, the people are at liberty to provide for themselves by erecting a new legislative differing from the other by the change of persons, or form, or both, as they shall find it most for their safety and good. For the society can never, by the fault of another, lose the native and original right it has to preserve itself, which can only be done by a settled legislative and a fair and impartial execution of the laws made by it. But the state of mankind is not so miserable that they are not capable of using this remedy till it be too late to look for any. To tell people they may provide for themselves by erecting a new legislative, when, by oppression, artifice, or being delivered over to a foreign power, their old one is gone, is only to tell them they may expect relief when it is too late, and the evil is past cure. This is, in effect, no more than to bid them first be slaves, and then to take care of their liberty, and, when their chains are on, tell them they may act like free men. This, if barely so, is rather mockery than relief, and men can never be secure from tyranny if there be no means to escape it till they are perfectly under it; and, therefore, it is that they have not only a right to get out of it, but to prevent it.

221  There is, therefore, secondly, another way whereby governments are dissolved, and that is, when the legislative, or the prince, either of them act contrary to their trust.

For the legislative acts against the trust reposed in them when they endeavor to invade the property of the subject, and to make themselves, or any part of the community, masters or arbitrary disposers of the lives, liberties, or fortunes of the people.

222  The reason why men enter into society is the preservation of their property; and the end why they choose and authorize a legislative is that there may be laws made, and rules set, as guards and fences to the properties of all the society, to limit the power and moderate the dominion of every part and member of the society. For since it can never be supposed to be the will of the society that the legislative should have a power to destroy that which every one designs to secure by entering into society, and for which the people submitted themselves to legislators of their own

making, whenever the legislators endeavor to take away and destroy the property of the people, or to reduce them to slavery under arbitrary power, they put themselves into a state of war with the people, who are thereupon absolved from any farther obedience, and are left to the common refuge which God hath provided for all men against force and violence. Whensoever, therefore, the legislative shall transgress this fundamental rule of society, and either by ambition, fear, folly, or corruption, endeavor to grasp themselves, or put into the hands of any other, an absolute power over the lives, liberties, and estates of the people, by this breach of trust they forfeit the power the people had put into their hands for quite contrary ends, and it devolves to the people, who have a right to resume their original liberty, and by the establishment of a new legislative (such as they shall think fit), provide for their own safety and security, which is the end for which they are in society. What I have said here concerning the legislative in general holds true also concerning the supreme executor, who having a double trust put in him, both to have a part in the legislative and the supreme execution of the law, acts against both, when he goes about to set up his own arbitrary will as the law of the society. He acts also contrary to his trust when he employs the force, treasure, and offices of the society to corrupt the representatives and gain them to his purposes, when he openly pre-engages the electors, and prescribes, to their choice, such whom he has, by solicitation, threats, promises, or otherwise, won to his designs, and employs them to bring in such who have promised beforehand what to vote and what to enact. Thus to regulate candidates and electors, and new model the ways of election, what is it but to cut up the government by the roots, and poison the very fountain of public security? For the people having reserved to themselves the choice of their representatives as the fence to their properties, could do it for no other end but that they might always be freely chosen, and so chosen, freely act and advise as the necessity of the commonwealth and the public good should, upon examination and mature debate, be judged to require. This, those who give their votes before they hear the debate, and have weighed the reasons on all sides, are not capable of doing. To

prepare such an assembly as this, and endeavor to set up the declared abettors of his own will, for the true representatives of the people, and the law-makers of the society, is certainly as great a breach of trust, and as perfect a declaration of a design to subvert the government, as is possible to be met with. To which, if one shall add rewards and punishments visibly employed to the same end, and all the arts of perverted law made use of to take off and destroy all that stand in the way of such a design, and will not comply and consent to betray the liberties of their country, it will be past doubt what is doing. What power they ought to have in the society who thus employ it contrary to the trust went along with it in its first institution, is easy to determine; and one cannot but see that he who has once attempted any such thing as this cannot any longer be trusted.

223   To this, perhaps, it will be said that the people being ignorant and always discontented, to lay the foundation of government in the unsteady opinion and uncertain humor of the people, is to expose it to certain ruin; and no government will be able long to subsist if the people may set up a new legislative whenever they take offense at the old one. To this I answer, quite the contrary. People are not so easily got out of their old forms as some are apt to suggest. They are hardly to be prevailed with to amend the acknowledged faults in the frame they have been accustomed to. And if there be any original defects, or adventitious ones introduced by time or corruption, it is not an easy thing to get them changed, even when all the world sees there is an opportunity for it. This slowness and aversion in the people to quit their old constitutions has in the many revolutions which have been seen in this kingdom, in this and former ages, still kept us to, or after some interval of fruitless attempts, still brought us back again to our old legislative of king, lords and commons; and whatever provocations have made the crown be taken from some of our princes' heads, they never carried the people so far as to place it in another line.

224 But it will be said this hypothesis lays a ferment for frequent rebellion. To which I answer: first, no more than any other hypothesis. For when the people are made miserable, and find themselves exposed to the ill usage of arbitrary power, cry up their gover-

nors as much as you will for sons of Jupiter,[54] let them be sacred and divine, descended or authorized from Heaven; give them out for whom or what you please, the same will happen. The people generally ill treated, and contrary to right, will be ready upon any occasion to ease themselves of a burden that sits heavy upon them. They will wish and seek for the opportunity, which in the change, weakness, and accidents of human affairs, seldom delays long to offer itself. He must have lived but a little while in the world, who has not seen examples of this in his time; and he must have read very little who cannot produce examples of it in all sorts of governments in the world.

225   Secondly: I answer, such revolutions happen not upon every little mismanagement in public affairs. Great mistakes in the ruling part, many wrong and inconvenient laws, and all the slips of human frailty will be borne by the people without mutiny or murmur. But if a long train of abuses, prevarications, and artifices, all tending the same way, make the design visible to the people, and they cannot but feel what they lie under, and see whither they are going, it is not to be wondered that they should then rouse themselves, and endeavor to put the rule into such hands which may secure to them the ends for which government was at first erected, and without which, ancient names and specious forms are so far from being better, that they are much worse than the state of Nature or pure anarchy; the inconveniencies being all as great and as near, but the remedy farther off and more difficult.

226   Thirdly: I answer, that this power in the people of providing for their safety anew by a new legislative when their legislators have acted contrary to their trust by invading their property, is the best fence against rebellion, and the probablest means to hinder it. For rebellion being an opposition, not to persons, but authority, which is founded only in the constitutions and laws of the government, those, whoever they be, who, by force, break through, and, by force, justify their violation of them, are truly and properly rebels. For when men, by entering into society and civil government, have excluded force, and introduced laws for the preservation of property, peace, and unity amongst themselves, those who set up force again in opposition to the laws, do *rebellare*,[55] that is, bring back again the state of war, and are properly rebels, which they who are in power, by the pretense they have to authority, the temptation of force they have in their hands, and the flattery of those about them being likeliest to do, the properest way to prevent the evil is to show them the danger and injustice of it who are under the greatest temptation to run into it.

227   In both the forementioned cases, when either the legislative is changed, or the legislators act contrary to the end for which they were constituted, those who are guilty are guilty of rebellion. For if any one by force takes away the established legislative of any society, and the laws by them made, pursuant to their trust, he thereby takes away the umpirage which every one had consented to for a peaceable decision of all their controversies, and a bar to the state of war amongst them. They who remove or change the legislative take away this decisive power, which nobody can have but by the appointment and consent of the people, and so destroying the authority which the people did, and nobody else can set up, and introducing a power which the people hath not authorized, actually introduce a state of war, which is that of force without authority; and thus by removing the legislative established by the society, in whose decisions the people acquiesced and united as to that of their own will, they untie the knot, and expose the people anew to the state of war. And if those, who by force take away the legislative, are rebels, the legislators themselves, as has been shown, can be no less esteemed so, when they who were set up for the protection and preservation of the people, their liberties and properties shall by force invade and endeavor to take them away; and so they putting themselves into a state of war with those who made them the protectors and guardians of their peace, are properly, and with the greatest aggravation, *rebellantes*, rebels.

---

54   The chief god of the Romans.
55   Latin: to renew war; the Latin root of the English "rebel."

228   But if they who say it lays a foundation for rebellion mean that it may occasion civil wars or intestine broils to tell the people they are absolved from obedience when illegal attempts are made upon their liberties or properties, and may oppose the unlawful violence of those who were their magistrates when they invade their properties, contrary to the trust put in them, and that, therefore, this doctrine is not to be allowed, being so destructive to the peace of the world; they may as well say, upon the same ground, that honest men may not oppose robbers or pirates, because this may occasion disorder or bloodshed. If any mischief come in such cases, it is not to be charged upon him who defends his own right, but on him that invades his neighbor's. If the innocent honest man must quietly quit all he has for peace's sake to him who will lay violent hands upon it, I desire it may be considered what a kind of peace there will be in the world which consists only in violence and rapine, and which is to be maintained only for the benefit of robbers and oppressors. Who would not think it an admirable peace betwixt the mighty and the mean, when the lamb, without resistance, yielded his throat to be torn by the imperious wolf? Polyphemus's den gives us a perfect pattern of such a peace.[56] Such a government wherein Ulysses and his companions had nothing to do but quietly to suffer themselves to be devoured. And no doubt Ulysses, who was a prudent man, preached up passive obedience, and exhorted them to a quiet submission by representing to them of what concernment peace was to mankind, and by showing the inconveniencies might happen if they should offer to resist Polyphemus, who had now the power over them.

229   The end of government is the good of mankind; and which is best for mankind, that the people should be always exposed to the boundless will of tyranny, or that the rulers should be sometimes liable to be opposed when they grow exorbitant in the use of their power, and employ it for the destruction, and not the preservation, of the properties of their people?

230   Nor let any one say that mischief can arise from hence as often as it shall please a busy head or turbulent spirit to desire the alteration of the government. It is true such men may stir whenever they please, but it will be only to their own just ruin and perdition. For till the mischief be grown general, and the ill designs of the rulers become visible, or their attempts sensible to the greater part, the people, who are more disposed to suffer than right themselves by resistance, are not apt to stir. The examples of particular injustice or oppression of here and there an unfortunate man moves them not. But if they universally have a persuasion grounded upon manifest evidence that designs are carrying on against their liberties, and the general course and tendency of things cannot but give them strong suspicions of the evil intention of their governors, who is to be blamed for it? Who can help it if they, who might avoid it, bring themselves into this suspicion? Are the people to be blamed if they have the sense of rational creatures, and can think of things no otherwise than as they find and feel them? And is it not rather their fault who put things in such a posture that they would not have them thought as they are? I grant that the pride, ambition, and turbulency of private men have sometimes caused great disorders in commonwealths, and factions have been fatal to states and kingdoms. But whether the mischief hath oftener begun in the people's wantonness, and a desire to cast off the lawful authority of their rulers, or in the rulers' insolence and endeavors to get and exercise an arbitrary power over their people, whether oppression or disobedience gave the first rise to the disorder, I leave it to impartial history to determine. This I am sure, whoever, either ruler or subject, by force goes about to invade the rights of either prince or people, and lays the foundation for overturning the constitution and frame of any just government, he is guilty of the greatest crime I think a man is capable of, being to answer for all those mischiefs of blood, rapine, and desolation, which the breaking to pieces of governments bring on a country; and he who does it is justly to be esteemed

---

56   In Homer's *Odyssey*, Odysseus, whom the Romans called Ulysses, was trapped along with his men in the cave of the one-eyed giant Polyphemus, who ate some of Odysseus's men, and promised that his gift to Odysseus would be to eat Odysseus last. Odysseus and his remaining men escaped by blinding Polyphemus.

the common enemy and pest of mankind, and is to be treated accordingly.

231   That subjects or foreigners attempting by force on the properties of any people may be resisted with force is agreed on all hands; but that magistrates doing the same thing may be resisted, hath of late been denied; as if those who had the greatest privileges and advantages by the law had thereby a power to break those laws by which alone they were set in a better place than their brethren; whereas their offense is thereby the greater, both as being ungrateful for the greater share they have by the law, and breaking also that trust which is put into their hands by their brethren.

232   Whosoever uses force without right—as every one does in society who does it without law—puts himself into a state of war with those against whom he so uses it, and in that state all former ties are cancelled, all other rights cease, and every one has a right to defend himself, and to resist the aggressor. This is so evident that Barclay[57] himself—that great assertor of the power and sacredness of kings—is forced to confess that it is lawful for the people, in some cases, to resist their king, and that, too, in a chapter wherein he pretends to show that the Divine law shuts up the people from all manner of rebellion. Whereby it is evident, even by his own doctrine, that since they may, in some cases, resist, all resisting of princes is not rebellion. His words are these: ... [a long quotation in Latin follows]. In English thus:

233   "But if any one should ask: must the people, then, always lay themselves open to the cruelty and rage of tyranny—must they see their cities pillaged and laid in ashes, their wives and children exposed to the tyrant's lust and fury, and themselves and families reduced by their king to ruin and all the miseries of want and oppression, and yet sit still—must men alone be debarred the common privilege of opposing force with force, which Nature allows so freely to all other creatures for their preservation from injury? I answer: self-defense is a part of the law of Nature; nor

can it be denied the community, even against the king himself; but to revenge themselves upon him must, by no means, be allowed them, it being not agreeable to that law. Wherefore, if the king shall show an hatred, not only to some particular persons, but sets himself against the body of the commonwealth, whereof he is the head, and shall, with intolerable ill-usage, cruelly tyrannize over the whole, or a considerable part of the people; in this case the people have a right to resist and defend themselves from injury; but it must be with this caution, that they only defend themselves, but do not attack their prince. They may repair the damages received, but must not, for any provocation, exceed the bounds of due reverence and respect. They may repulse the present attempt, but must not revenge past violences. For it is natural for us to defend life and limb, but that an inferior should punish a superior is against nature. The mischief which is designed them the people may prevent before it be done, but, when it is done, they must not revenge it on the king, though author of the villainy. This, therefore, is the privilege of the people in general above what any private person hath: That particular men are allowed, by our adversaries themselves (Buchanan[58] only excepted), to have no other remedy but patience; but the body of the people may, with respect, resist intolerable tyranny, for when it is but moderate they ought to endure it."

234   Thus far that great advocate of monarchical power allows of resistance.

235   It is true, he has annexed two limitations to it, to no purpose:

First. He says it must be with reverence.

Secondly. It must be without retribution or punishment; and the reason he gives is, "because an inferior cannot punish a superior."

First. How to resist force without striking again, or how to strike with reverence, will need some skill to make intelligible. He that shall oppose an assault only with a shield to receive the blows, or in any more respectful posture, without a sword in his hand to

---

57   William Barclay (1546-1608), writer on law and political theory.
58   George Buchanan (sixteenth century), who argued that monarchy existed by the will of the people, and argued against absolutism.

abate the confidence and force of the assailant, will quickly be at an end of his resistance, and will find such a defense serve only to draw on himself the worse usage. This is as ridiculous a way of resisting as Juvenal thought it of fighting: "Ubi tu pulsas, ego vapulo tantum."[59] And the success of the combat will be unavoidably the same [as] he there describes it:

> Libertas pauperis haec est;
> Pulsatus rogat, et pugnis concisus, adorat,
> Ut liceat paucis cum dentibus inde reverti.[60]

This will always be the event of such an imaginary resistance, where men may not strike again. He, therefore, who may resist must be allowed to strike. And then let our author, or anybody else, join a knock on the head or a cut on the face with as much reverence and respect as he thinks fit. He that can reconcile blows and reverence may, for aught I know, deserve for his pains a civil, respectful cudgelling wherever he can meet with it.

Secondly. As to his second—"an inferior cannot punish a superior"—that is true, generally speaking, whilst he is his superior. But to resist force with force, being the state of war that levels the parties, cancels all former relation of reverence, respect, and superiority; and then the odds that remains is—that he who opposes the unjust aggressor has this superiority over him, that he has a right, when he prevails, to punish the offender, both for the breach of the peace and all the evils that followed upon it. Barclay, therefore, in another place, more coherently to himself, denies it to be lawful to resist a king in any case. But he there assigns two cases whereby a king may unking himself. His words are: ... [a long Latin passage follows].

Which may be thus Englished :

237    "What, then, can there no case happen wherein the people may of right, and by their own authority, help themselves, take arms, and set upon their king, imperiously domineering over them? None at all whilst he remains a king. 'Honor the king,'[61] and 'he that resists the power, resists the ordinance of God,'[62] are Divine oracles that will never permit it. The people, therefore, can never come by a power over him unless he does something that makes him cease to be a king; for then he divests himself of his crown and dignity, and returns to the state of a private man, and the people become free and superior; the power which they had in the interregnum, before they crowned him king, devolving to them again. But there are but few miscarriages which bring the matter to this state. After considering it well on all sides, I can find but two. Two cases there are, I say, whereby a king, *ipso facto*,[63] becomes no king, and loses all power and regal authority over his people, which are also taken notice of by Winzerus.[64] The first is, if he endeavor to overturn the government—that is, if he have a purpose and design to ruin the kingdom and commonwealth, as it is recorded of Nero[65] that he resolved to cut off the senate and people of Rome, lay the city waste with fire and sword, and then remove to some other place; and of Caligula,[66] that he openly declared that he would be no longer a head to the people or senate, and that he had it in his thoughts to cut off the worthiest men of both ranks, and then retire to Alexandria; and he wished that the people had but one neck that he might dispatch them all at a blow. Such designs as these, when any king harbors in his thoughts, and seriously promotes, he immediately gives up all care and thought of the commonwealth, and, consequent-

---

59    A quotation from the satires of Juvenal (first century); Latin: "Where are you during the bruising, and I only am being beaten?"

60    A second quotation from Juvenal's satires: "This is the freedom of a poor person: being beaten up, to ask—and being cut up with fists, to pay—to be allowed to leave with a few teeth."

61    New Testament, 1 Peter 2.17.

62    New Testament, Romans 13.2.

63    Latin: By the same deed.

64    Apparently an error for Ninian Winzet (also known as Winget or Wingate), a sixteenth-century writer and defender of Catholicism in Scotland.

65    Roman emperor (first century).

66    Roman emperor (first century).

ly, forfeits the power of governing his subjects, as a master does the dominion over his slaves whom he hath abandoned.

238  "The other case is, when a king makes himself the dependent of another, and subjects his kingdom, which his ancestors left him, and the people put free into his hands, to the dominion of another. For however, perhaps, it may not be his intention to prejudice the people, yet because he has hereby lost the principal part of regal dignity—viz., to be next and immediately under God, supreme in his kingdom; and also because he betrayed or forced his people, whose liberty he ought to have carefully preserved, into the power and dominion of a foreign nation. By this, as it were, alienation of his kingdom, he himself loses the power he had in it before, without transferring any the least right to those on whom he would have bestowed it; and so by this act sets the people free, and leaves them at their own disposal. One example of this is to be found in the Scotch annals."

239  In these cases Barclay, the great champion of absolute monarchy, is forced to allow that a king may be resisted, and ceases to be a king. That is in short— not to multiply cases—in whatsoever he has no authority, there he is no king, and may be resisted; for wheresoever the authority ceases, the king ceases too, and becomes like other men who have no authority. And these two cases that he instances differ little from those above mentioned, to be destructive to governments, only that he has omitted the principle from which his doctrine flows, and that is the breach of trust in not preserving the form of government agreed on, and in not intending the end of government itself, which is the public good and preservation of property. When a king has dethroned himself, and put himself in a state of war with his people, what shall hinder

them from prosecuting him who is no king, as they would any other man, who has put himself into a state of war with them, Barclay, and those of his opinion, would do well to tell us. Bilson,[67] a bishop of our Church, and a great stickler for the power and prerogative of princes, does, if I mistake not, in his treatise of "Christian Subjection," acknowledge that princes may forfeit their power and their title to the obedience of their subjects; and if there needed authority in a case where reason is so plain, I could send my reader to Bracton,[68] Fortescue,[69] and the author of the "Mirror,"[70] and others, writers that cannot be suspected to be ignorant of our government, or enemies to it. But I thought Hooker alone might be enough to satisfy those men who, relying on him for their ecclesiastical polity, are by a strange fate carried to deny those principles upon which he builds it. Whether they are herein made the tools of cunninger[71] workmen, to pull down their own fabric, they were best look. This I am sure, their civil policy is so new, so dangerous, and so destructive to both rulers and people, that as former ages never could hear the broaching of it, so it may be hoped those to come, redeemed from the impositions of these Egyptian under-taskmasters,[72] will abhor the memory of such servile flatterers, who, whilst it seemed to serve their turn, resolved all government into absolute tyranny, and would have all men born to what their mean souls fitted them [for: ] slavery.

240  Here it is like[ly] the common question will be made: who shall be judge whether the prince or legislative act contrary to their trust? This, perhaps, ill-affected and factious men may spread amongst the people, when the prince only makes use of his due prerogative. To this I reply, the people shall be judge; for who shall be judge whether his trustee or deputy acts well and according to the trust reposed in him,

---

67  Thomas Bilson (*c.* 1546-1616) who argued that religion requires obedience to royal authority.

68  Henry de Bracton (thirteenth-century) was an English lawyer; the thirteenth-century work on the Common Law which Locke attributes to him here asserts that the king is subject to the law. Recent scholarship asserts that Bracton at most only finished an already largely completed treatise.

69  Sir John Fortescue (fifteenth century) was an English lawyer who argued that law in England could not be made except by both king and parliament.

70  Presumably the *Mirror for Magistrates* (sixteenth century), which recounts how a number of English rulers were overthrown because of their misuse of their position.

71  I.e., more cunning.

72  A reference to the slavery of the Hebrews in Egypt according to the Old Testament.

but he who deputes him and must, by having deputed him, have still a power to discard him when he fails in his trust? If this be reasonable in particular cases of private men, why should it be otherwise in that of the greatest moment, where the welfare of millions is concerned and also where the evil, if not prevented, is greater, and the redress very difficult, dear, and dangerous?

241   But, farther, this question, who shall be judge? cannot mean that there is no judge at all. For where there is no judicature on earth to decide controversies amongst men, God in heaven is judge. He alone, it is true, is judge of the right. But every man is judge for himself, as in all other cases so in this, whether another hath put himself into a state of war with him, and whether he should appeal to the supreme Judge, as Jephtha did.

242   If a controversy arise betwixt a prince and some of the people in a matter where the law is silent or doubtful, and the thing be of great consequence, I should think the proper umpire in such a case should be the body of the people. For in such cases where the prince hath a trust reposed in him, and is dispensed from the common, ordinary rules of the law, there, if any men find themselves aggrieved, and think the prince acts contrary to, or beyond that trust, who so proper to judge as the body of the people (who at first lodged that trust in him) how far they meant it should extend? But if the prince, or whoever they be in the administration, decline that way of determination, the appeal then lies nowhere but to Heaven. Force between either persons who have no known superior on earth, or which permits no appeal to a judge on earth, being properly a state of war, wherein the appeal lies only to Heaven; and in that state the injured party must judge for himself when he will think fit to make use of that appeal and put himself upon it.

243   To conclude. The power that every individual gave the society when he entered into it can never revert to the individuals again, as long as the society lasts, but will always remain in the community because without this there can be no community—no commonwealth, which is contrary to the original agreement; so also when the society hath placed the legislative in any assembly of men, to continue in them and their successors, with direction and authority for providing such successors, the legislative can never revert to the people whilst that government lasts; because, having provided a legislative with power to continue for ever, they have given up their political power to the legislative, and cannot resume it. But if they have set limits to the duration of their legislative, and made this supreme power in any person or assembly only temporary; or else when, by the miscarriages of those in authority, it is forfeited, upon the forfeiture of their rulers, or at the determination of the time set, it reverts to the society, and the people have a right to act as supreme, and continue the legislative in themselves or place it in a new form, or new hands, as they think good.

# 56

# ISAAC NEWTON, THE *PRINCIPIA*

Sir Isaac Newton (1642-1727) first published his Latin work the *Principia* (the longer title of which in English is *Mathematical Principles of Natural Philosophy*) in 1687. He was also a discoverer of the branch of mathematics known as the calculus. Although the calculus would have simplified some of the calculations of the *Principia*, Newton chose to present the book in the traditional mathematics then current. He served as president of the Royal Society, the leading scientific society of his time, from 1703 until his death.

---

### 1 THE MOTION OF BODIES

*Proposition 1 Theorem 1*

*That the areas, which bodies, when moving in curves, cut off by radii drawn to a fixed center of force, are in one fixed plane and are proportional to the times.*

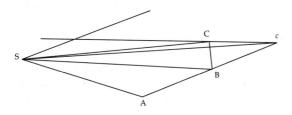

Let the time be divided into equal parts, and in the first period of time let the body driven by one force describe the line AB. In the second period, it would, if nothing hindered it, go on to $c$,[1] describing the line B$c$ equal to AB. Then by the radii AS, BS, $c$S to the center S would be cut off the equal areas ASB, BS$c$ [the bases being equal and the altitude the same]. Now when the body comes to B, a centripetal force [in the direction BS] acts upon it with uniform impulse, and makes it leave the line of direction B$c$ and pass along the line BC. Let C$c$ be drawn parallel to the direction of the force BS, meeting BC in C. Then at the end of the second (equal) period the body will be found at C, in the same plane with the triangle ASB. Draw SC. Then the triangle SBC, on account of the parallels SB and $c$C, will be equal to the triangle SB$c$ and therefore to the triangle SAB, etc. Therefore in equal times equal areas will be described in the same plane. Let the number of the triangles be increased and their altitude diminished to infinity; their ultimate perimeter will be a curve (Corollary 4; Lemma 3[2]). And therefore a centripetal force, by which a body is continually drawn from a course tangent to this curve, will act along this radius and whatever areas have been described proportional to the times will remain proportional to the same times when curvilinear. Q.E.D....[3]

---

1  Newton relies here on his first law of motion, that a body at rest remains at rest or, if in motion, continues to move at the same speed and in the same direction until or unless some other force acts upon it.
2  Corollaries and Lemmae have been largely deleted in this excerpt.
3  Q.E.D.: i.e., Latin, "Quod erat demonstrandum": "which was to be proved."

*Proposition 2 Theorem 2*

*Every body, which is moved in any curve described in a plane, and cuts off, by radii drawn to a center that is stationary or moving in a straight line with uniform motion, areas about the center proportional to the times, is drawn by a centripetal force urging it toward the center.*

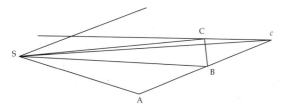

For every body that is moved in a curved line is turned from its course by some force acting upon it. And that force by which a body is turned from a straight line, and is made to describe the supposed equal triangles SAB, SBC, etc., about the fixed center S in equal times must act at the point B in a line parallel to C*c*.

[For extend AB to *c* making AB=B*c*. Then *c* is where the body would have been had it not been drawn by the new force at B. Hence at B the force acts in the direction C*c*.]

But C*c* is parallel to BS. [For since the triangle SCB= triangle SAB by hypothesis, and triangle SAB=SB*c* (equal altitude and bases), then triangles SBC and SB*c* must be equal and C*c* and SB must be parallel, in order to have the altitude equal.] Therefore at B the force acts along the line BS toward the center S. Therefore the force always acts toward the immovable center S. Q.E.D....

### 3 THE SYSTEM OF THE WORLD IN MATHEMATICAL TREATMENT

*Proposition 4 Theorem 4*

*That the moon is drawn by gravity toward the earth, and is deflected by the force of gravity from a straight line, and thus held in its orbit.*

The mean distance of the moon from the earth in terms of semi-diameters of the earth is, according to Ptolemy and many astronomers, 59; according to Vendelius and Huyghens, 60; according to Copernicus, 60 1/3; according to Streetus, 60 2/5, and according to Tycho, 56 1/2. (But Tycho has erred....) Let us assume that the mean distance is 60 semi-diameters of the earth. The moon completes its full periodic times (goes around the earth) in 27 days, 7 hours, 43 minutes, as is determined by astronomers. The circumference of the earth is 123,249,600 Paris feet, as has been calculated by French measurements. If the moon should be deprived of every other motion, and drawn by that one alone by which it is held in her orbit, it would fall to the earth. The distance it would fall in the first minute would be 15 1/12 Paris feet. This follows from calculation or from Proposition 26, Book 1, or (what amounts to the same thing) from Corollary 9, Proposition 4, the same Book.... For the versed sine (distance along the radius from the chord to the circumference) of that arc which the moon describes in one minute at her mean motion and at a distance of 60 semi-diameters of the earth from the earth is about 15 1/12 Paris feet, or, more accurately, 15 feet, 1 inch, and 1 4/9 lines.

Heavy bodies do actually fall at this rate on the earth. For the length of a pendulum, oscillating each second in the latitude of Lutetia, Paris, is 3 Paris feet and 8 1/2 lines, as Huyghens has observed, and the distance which a body falls in a second when pulled by gravity is to the length of such a pendulum as the square of the circumference of a circle to its diameter, as Huyghens has also observed; and this is 15 Paris feet, 1 inch, 1 4/9 lines. Hence the force by which the moon is held in its orbit, if it were brought down upon earth, would be equal to the force of gravity among us, and hence is that very force which we are wont to call weight or gravity....

*Proposition 5 Theorem 5 Scholium*[4]

The force which retains the celestial bodies in their orbits has been hitherto called centripetal force; but it being now made plain that it can be no other than a gravitating force, we shall hereafter call it gravity. For

---

4   I.e., a discussion to show the manner of a proof's application or its limitations.

the cause of that centripetal force which retains the moon in its orbit will extend itself to all the planets.

### Proposition 6 Theorem 6

*That all bodies gravitate towards every planet; and that the weights of bodies towards any one planet, at equal distances from the center of the planet, are proportional to the quantities of matter which they severally contain.*

It has been for a long time now observed by others that all sorts of heavy bodies (allowance being made for the inequality of retardation which they suffer from a small power of resistance in the air) descend to the earth *from equal heights* in equal times, and that equality of times we may distinguish to a great accuracy, by the help of pendulums. I tried the thing in gold, silver, lead, glass, sand, common salt, wood, water, and wheat. I provided two wooden boxes, round and equal; I filled the one with wood, and suspended an equal weight of gold (as exactly as I could) in the center of oscillation of the other. The boxes hanging by equal threads of 11 feet made a couple of pendulums perfectly equal in weight and figure, and equally receiving the resistance of the air. And, placing the one by the other, I observed them to play together forwards and backwards, for a long time, with equal vibrations... and the like happened in the other bodies. By these experiments, in bodies of the same weight, I could manifestly have discovered a difference of matter less than the thousandth part of the whole, had there been any such. But, without all doubt, the nature of gravity towards the planets is the same as towards the earth.... Moreover, since the satellites of Jupiter perform their revolutions in times which observe the 3/2th power of the proportion of their distances from Jupiter's center, their accelerating gravities towards Jupiter will be inversely proportional to the squares of their distances to Jupiter's center—that is, equal at equal distances. And, therefore, these satellites, if supposed to fall *towards Jupiter* from equal heights, would describe equal spaces in equal times, in like manner as heavy bodies do on our earth....

### Corollary 1

Hence the weights of bodies do not depend upon their forms and textures; for if the weights could be altered with the forms, they would be greater or less, according to the variety of forms, in equal matter, altogether against experience.

### Corollary 2

Universally, all bodies about the earth gravitate towards the earth; and the weights of all, at equal distances from the earth's center, are as the quantities of matter which they individually contain. This is the quality of all bodies within the reach of our experiments; and therefore (by rule 3[5]) to be affirmed of all bodies whatsoever.

### Corollary 5

The power of gravity is of a different nature from the power of magnetism; for the magnetic attraction is not as the matter attracted. Some bodies are attracted more by the magnet; others less; most bodies not at all. The power of magnetism in one and the same body may be increased and diminished; and is sometimes far stronger, for the quantity of matter, than the power of gravity; and in receding from the magnet decreases not by the square but almost by the cube of the distance, as nearly as I could judge from some rude observations.

### Proposition 7 Theorem 7

*That there is a power of gravity tending to all bodies, proportional to the several quantities of matter which they contain.*

That all the planets mutually gravitate one towards another, we have proved before, as well as that the force of gravity towards every one of them, considered apart, is reciprocally as the square of the distance of places from the center of the planet. And thence (by proposition 69, book 1, and its corollaries) it follows, that the gravity tending towards all the planets is proportional to the matter which they contain.

---

5  Newton's rule that qualities found in all bodies within reach of experimentation are to be considered the qualities of all bodies that exist.

Moreover, since all the parts of any planet A gravitate towards any other planet B; and the gravity of every part is to the gravity of the whole as the matter of the part to the matter of the whole; and (by law 3) to every action corresponds an equal reaction; therefore the planet B will, on the other hand, gravitate towards all the parts of the planet A; and its gravity towards any one part will be to the gravity towards the whole as the matter of the part to the matter of the whole. Q.E.D....

# CREDITS

Translated material in the public domain revised by M. Burger, R. Hinton, or H. Séailles.

*The Descent of Ishtar*: from *The Civilization of Babylonia and Assyria*, ed. Morris Jastrow (Philadelphia, 1915), pp. 453-59.

*The Code of Hammurabi*: from *The Code of Hammurabi and Moses*, trans. William Walter Davies (New York, 1905), prologue, epilogue, and nos. 1-9, 14-23, 26-39, 45-48, 53-57, 102-04, 108-11, 117-19, 128-82, 195-225, 268-70.

*The Enuma Elish*: from *The Civilization of Babylonia and Assyria*, ed. Morris Jastrow (Philadelphia, 1915), pp. 428-43.

Inscription of Uni: from *Ancient Records of Egypt*, trans. James Henry Breasted (Chicago, 1906), 1, § 293-94, 307-15, 320-24.

Stele of Neferhotep: from *Ancient Records of Egypt*, trans. James Henry Breasted (Chicago, 1906), 1, § 755-72.

*Hymn to Aton*: from *The Ancient Near East: An Anthology of Text and Pictures*, trans. John A. Wilson, ed. James P. Pritchard (Princeton, 1958), pp. 226-30.

*First Book of Kings* 15-19: from *The Modern Reader's Bible*, ed. Richard G. Moulton (New York, 1895).

*Book of Job* 1-14, 21-24, 38-42: from *The Modern Reader's Bible*, ed. Richard G. Moulton (New York, 1895).

Homer, The *Iliad*: from *The Iliad of Homer*, trans. Samuel Butler (London, 1898).

Plutarch, *Life of Solon*: from *Plutarch's Lives*, trans. John Dryden, revised A.H. Clough (New York, 1910).

Aristophanes, *Lysistrata*: from Aristophanes, *Comedies*, trans. anon. (privately printed for the Athenian Society), (New York, 1912) 1.

Plato, *The Symposium*: from *The Dialogues of Plato*, trans. Benjamin Jowett (third edition, Oxford, 1920), 1.

Plutarch, *Life of Alexander the Great*: from *Plutarch's Lives* (New York, 1910), trans. John Dryden, revised A.H. Clough (New York, 1910).

Marcus Tullius Cicero, *Letters*: from *The Letters of Cicero*, trans. Evelyn Shirley Shuckburgh (London, 1899-1912) 1, pp. 272; 2, pp. 55-56, 245-46, 248-49; 4, pp. 206-08, 404.

Quintus Cicero, *Letter to His Brother*: from *The Letters of Cicero*, trans. Evelyn Shirley Shuckburgh (London, 1899-1912), 1, pp. 367-81.

Vergil, The *Aeneid*: from *Virgil*, trans. H. Rushton Fairclough. 2 vols (London, 1916-18).

Augustus, *The Deeds of the Divine Augustus*: from *Monumentum Ancryanum*, ed. William Fairley, in *Transcripts and Reprints of the Original Sources of European History V* (Philadelphia, 1898).

Pliny the Younger, *Letters*: from *The Letters of Gaius Plinius Caecilius Secundus*, trans. William Melmoth, revised Frederick Charles Tindal Bosanquet, in *Harvard Classics* (New York, 1910), 10, pp. 200-02, 218-19, 240-42, 358-60, 404-07

Papyri from Oxyrhynchus: from *The Oxyrhynchus Papyri*, ed. and trans. Bernard P. Grenfell and Arthur S. Hunt (London, 1898), nos. 37-38, 56, 71-72, 91, 95, 99, 101, 125, 244, 263, 281-82.

Inscription from Mactar, trans. M.A. Claussen from *Corpus Inscriptionum Latinarum* (Berlin, 1863), 8. 11824.

*Book of Matthew* 3-9.32: from *The Modern Reader's Bible*, ed. Richard G. Moulton (New York, 1895).

John, *Book of Revelation* 15-20: from *The Modern Reader's Bible*, ed. Richard G. Moulton (New York, 1895).

Perpetua and Others, *The Martyrdom of Saint Perpetua*: from "The Passion of the Holy Martyrs Perpetua and Felicitas" in *The Ante Nicene Fathers*, ed. Alexander Roberts and James Donaldson, revised A. Cleveland Cox (Buffalo, New York, 1885-96), 3, pp. 699-706.

Augustine, *Confessions*: from *The Select Library of the Nicene and Post-Nicene Fathers of the Christian Church*, ed. Philip Schaff (New York, 1886), 1.

Tacitus, *De Germania*: from Tacitus, *Dialogus, Agricola, Germania*, trans. Maurice Hutton (London, 1914), revised D. LePan in Patrick Geary (ed.), *Readings in Medieval History* (Peterborough: Broadview Press, 1989).

Sidonius Apollinaris, *Letters*: from *Letters of Sidonius*, trans. Ormonde Maddock Dalton (Oxford, 1915), letters 2.9; 3.3-4; 6.4.

Benedict of Nursia, *The Rule*: from *The Rule of Saint Benedict*, trans. Cardinal Gasquet (London, 1909).

*Life of Balthild*: from "The Life of Saint Baltild," *Sainted Women of the Dark Ages*, ed. and trans. Jo Ann McNamara and John E. Halborg, with E. Gordon Whatley (Durham: Duke UP, 1992). Copyright 1992, Duke University Press. All rights reserved. Reprinted with permission.

Einhard, *Life of Charlemagne*: from *Life of Charlemagne by Einhard*, trans. Samuel Epes Turner (New York, 1880).

The *Dooms of King Alfred*: from Benjamin Thorpe, *Ancient Laws and Institutions of England* (London, 1840).

Gregory VII, Henry IV, and the German Bishops: from *Select Historical Documents of the Middle Ages*, trans. Ernest Flagg Henderson (London, 1905), pp. 135-48.

Marie de France, *Eliduc*: from *Marie de France: Seven of her Lays Done in English*, trans. D. Nutt (London, 1901).

*Magna Carta*: from *Select Historical Documents of the Middle Ages*, trans. Ernest Flagg Henderson (London, 1905) pp. 135-48.

Canons of the Fourth Lateran Council: from *Disciplinary Decrees of the Councils*, trans. Henry Joseph Schroeder (St. Louis, 1937).

Court Rolls of the Abbots of Ramsey and Battle: from *Select Pleas in Manorial and other Seignorial Courts, Reigns Henry III and Edward I*, ed. F. W. Maitland. Publications of the Selden Society 2 (London, 1889 for 1888), 1, pp. 90-95, 165-72.

Thomas Aquinas, *Summa Contra Gentiles*: from *The Summa Contra Gentiles of Saint Thomas Aquinas*, trans. The Dominican Fathers (London, 1924), 4 vols.

Ralph of Shrewsbury, *Letter*: trans. M. Burger from *The Register of Ralph of Shrewsbury, Bishop of Bath and Wells 1329-1363*, ed. Thomas Scott Holmes (London, 1889), Somerset Record Society Publications 10, 1, pp. 555-56.

City Officials of Cologne, *Letter*: from *The Black Death*, ed. and trans. Rosemary Horrox (New York: Manchester UP, 1994) pp. 219-220. Reprinted by permission of Manchester UP; with additional material trans. M. Burger from *Urkundenbuch der Stadt Strassburg*, 5: *Politische Urkunden von 1332 bis 1380*, ed. Hans Witte and Georg Wolfram (Strassburg, 1896), pp. 178-79.

Statute of Laborers: from *Select Historical Documents of the Middle Ages*, trans. Ernest Flagg Henderson (London, 1905), pp. 165-68.

English Statute of 1363 on Food and Clothing: trans. M. Burger from *Statutes of the Realm*, ed. A. Luders et al. (London, 1810-28), 1, pp. 378-83.

Catherine of Siena, *Dialogue*: from *The Dialogue of the Seraphic Virgin Catherine of Siena*, ed. Algar Thorold (London, 1925), pp. 120-28, 131-35, 137-42, 186-88, 209-21, 227-32.

Barducio di Piero Canigiani, *Letter*: from *The Dialogue of the Seraphic Virgin, Catherine of Siena*, ed. Algar Thorold (London, 1925).

Petrarch, *Letters of Familiar Intercourse*: from James Harvey Robinson, *Petrarch: The First Modern Scholar and Man of Letters* (New York, 1914), pp. 130-50, 217-23, 249-52.

Niccolò Machiavelli, *The Prince*: from *The Prince*, trans. N.H. Thomson, *Harvard Classics* (New York, 1910), 21.

Desiderius Erasmus, *Letters*: from the *Epistles of Erasmus from his Earliest Letters to his Fifty-First Year*, trans. F.M. Nichols (London, 1901-1918), 1, pp. 294-307; 2, pp. 315-17, 324-32, 339-70; 3, pp. 378-87.

Martin Luther, *Letters*: from *Luther's Correspondence and Other Contemporary Letters*, trans. Preserved Smith and Charles Michael Jacobs (Philadelphia, 1913-18), 2, nos. 506, 550, 583, 667, 809.

John Calvin, *Letters*: from *The Letters of John Calvin*, trans. D. Constable and M. R. Gilchrist, ed. J. Bonnet (Philadelphia, 1858), 1, pp. 295-305, 364-73, 442-47, 466-68; 2, pp. 113-14, 122-25, 129-32, 182-98, 225-28, 375-81.

*Articles of the Catholic League*: from the Department of History, University of Pennsylvania, *Translations and Reprints from the Original Sources of European History III* (1893), pp. 26-28.

Montaigne, *Essays*: from *The Essays of Michel de Montaigne*, trans. Charles Cotton, ed. William Carew Hazlitt (London, 1913), 1, pp. 186-91, 214-30.

Marie de l'Incarnation, *Letters*: from *A Few Acres of Snow*: Letters of Marie de l'Incarnation (1640-1668; i-viii, pp. 45-57) Joyce Marshall (ed., and trans.), *Word From New France: The Selected Letters of Marie L'Incarnation* (Toronto: Oxford UP, 1967).

The Grand Remonstrance and Petition from Parliament to King Charles I (December 1, 1641) and Charles's Reply (December 23, 1641).

The Author of this book and the Publisher have made every attempt to locate the authors of copyrighted material or their heirs or assigns, and would be very grateful for information that would allow them to correct any errors or omissions in a subsequent edition of the work.

# Index of Topics

To some extent the decision as to which selections are to fall under which headings has been necessarily arbitrary, especially regarding "The History of Ideas." The list of topics itself is not intended to be exhaustive. Numbers refer to selections rather than pages.

Black Death, 40, 41, 43, 46

Class/order/status, 2, 4, 10, 19, 21, 27, 28, 31, 36, 37, 43, 50, 51, 54, 55

Crusades, 33, 34, 36, 37

Cultural conflict/interaction, 1, 4, 7, 10, 13, 14, 15, 16, 17, 20, 21, 23, 24, 25, 26, 27, 30, 31, 33, 34, 51, 52, 53, 56

Disease and society, 40, 41, 43, 46, 53

Economy, 2, 8, 20, 21, 23, 25, 31, 32, 36, 43

Fall of Rome, 22, 23, 24, 25, 26, 27, 28, 29, 30, 31

Family, 9, 15, 17, 19, 25, 26, 29, 30, 31, 35, 36, 37, 39, 49, 55

Government/politics, 2, 4, 5, 7, 10, 11, 13, 15, 16, 17, 18, 19, 20, 21, 26, 27, 29, 30, 31, 32, 33, 34, 36, 37, 41, 43, 47, 50, 51, 54, 55

Heresy, 4, 25, 37, 39, 48, 49, 50, 51, 53, 54

Historiography, construction of the past, 5, 7, 9, 10, 13, 18, 22, 46, 47, 48, 49, 50, 52, 54

History of ideas, 1, 3, 6, 8, 12, 22, 28, 32, 39, 46, 47, 48, 50, 52, 55, 56

Homoeroticism, 9, 10, 12, 14, 39

Humanity and the divine, 2, 3, 6, 7, 8, 9, 17, 22, 23, 24, 25, 28, 39, 44, 45, 48, 49, 50, 53

Law, 2, 10, 31, 35, 36, 37, 38, 54, 55

Lay and clerical society, 32, 33, 35, 37, 44, 45, 47, 48, 49, 50

Literary/oral culture, 2, 4, 8, 19, 24, 28, 49

Material culture, 1, 2, 14, 26, 30, 43, 50

Natural world/science, 1, 3, 12, 37, 39, 40, 41, 44, 56

Psychology, 12, 25, 35, 37, 44, 46, 47, 48, 49, 50, 53, 55

Public/private life, 9, 10, 11, 12, 13, 14, 15, 29

Race, 4

Renaissance, 46, 47, 48, 49, 50, 52

Spirituality, 24, 25, 28, 29, 37, 44, 45, 48, 49, 50, 53

State power, 36, 37, 54, 55

Ties of dependency/slavery/serfdom, 2, 9, 10, 14, 15, 16, 18, 20, 24, 26, 27, 30, 31, 38, 48

War and society, 9, 10, 17, 18, 26, 31, 33, 34, 51, 52, 54

Women and men, 2, 3, 7, 9, 10, 11, 12, 13, 15, 16, 17, 19, 20, 24, 25, 26, 27, 29, 31, 32, 34, 35, 38, 39, 43, 44, 45, 47, 48, 49, 53, 55